W9-BSF-104

Rick Steves'®

NORTHERN EUROPEAN CRUISE PORTS

By Rick Steves with Cameron Hewitt

CONTENTS

Northern Europe

SWEDEN

FINLAND

Savonlinna

Lake Ladoga

Gulf of Bothnia

St. Petersburg

Turku

Helsinki

Peterhof

Gulf of Finland

Uppsala

Tallinn

RUSSIA

Stockholm

ESTONIA

Saaremaa

Visby

Gotland

Riga

LATVIA

Göteborg

Kalmar

Växjö

Öland

Baltic Sea

LITHUANIA

Klaipeda

Copenhagen

Malmö

Rønne

Bornholm

Vilnius

Minsk

Gdynia

RUSSIA

Warnemünde

Gdańsk

Malbork

BELARUS

Rostock

Poznań

Toruń

Berlin

Warsaw

Wittenberg

POLAND

UKRAINE

e R.

Leipzig

Dresden

Oder R.

Vistula R.

Auschwitz

Kraków

L'viv

Prague

CZECH REPUBLIC

TATRA MTNS.

rnberg

Český Krumlov

Brno

Levoča

SLOVAKIA

Munich

Melk

Bratislava

Eger

ROMANIA

Salzburg

Hallstatt

Vienna

Budapest

Innsbruck

VARIA

AUSTRIA

Lake Balaton

HUNGARY

Sighişoara

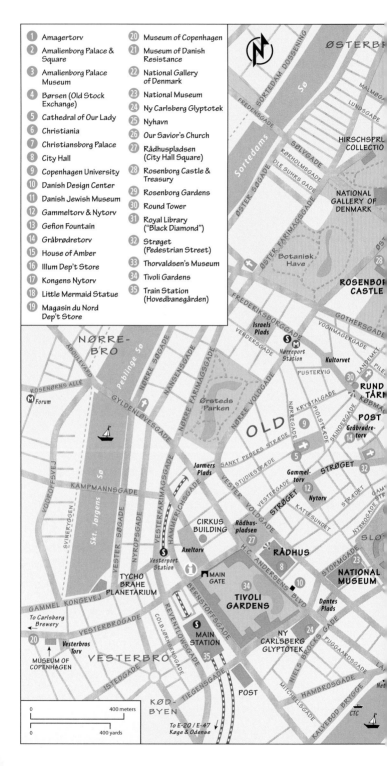

1. Amagertorv
2. Amalienborg Palace & Square
3. Amalienborg Palace Museum
4. Børsen (Old Stock Exchange)
5. Cathedral of Our Lady
6. Christiania
7. Christiansborg Palace
8. City Hall
9. Copenhagen University
10. Danish Design Center
11. Danish Jewish Museum
12. Gammeltorv & Nytorv
13. Gefion Fountain
14. Gråbrødretorv
15. House of Amber
16. Illum Dep't Store
17. Kongens Nytorv
18. Little Mermaid Statue
19. Magasin du Nord Dep't Store

20. Museum of Copenhagen
21. Museum of Danish Resistance
22. National Gallery of Denmark
23. National Museum
24. Ny Carlsberg Glyptotek
25. Nyhavn
26. Our Savior's Church
27. Rådhuspladsen (City Hall Square)
28. Rosenborg Castle & Treasury
29. Rosenborg Gardens
30. Round Tower
31. Royal Library ("Black Diamond")
32. Strøget (Pedestrian Street)
33. Thorvaldsen's Museum
34. Tivoli Gardens
35. Train Station (Hovedbanegården)

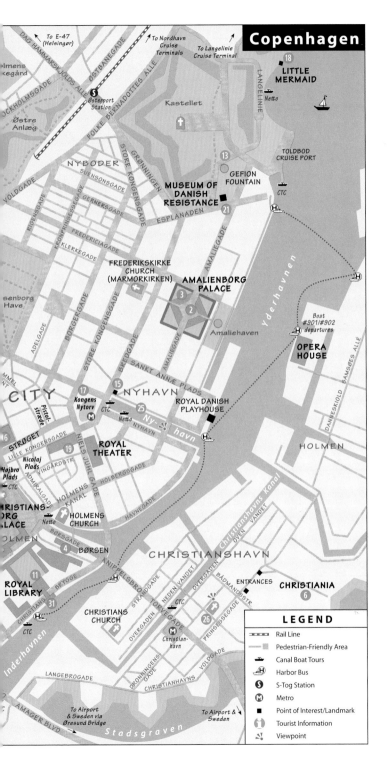

Copenhagen

LITTLE MERMAID 18

Netto

Kastellet

TOLDBOD CRUISE PORT

To E-47 (Helsingør)

To Nordhavn Cruise Terminals

To Langelinie Cruise Terminal

DAG HAMMARSKJÖLDS ALLÉ

ØSTBANEGADE

FOLKE BERNADOTTES ALLÉ

LANGELINIE

Østerport Station

Imens kegård

OCKHOLMSGADE

Østre Anlæg

NYBODER

STORE KONGENSGADE

GRØNNINGEN

SUENSONSGADE

GERNERSGADE

KRONPRINSESSEGADE

RIGENSGADE

FREDERICIAGADE

KLERKEGADE

BORGERGADE

VOLGADE

MUSEUM OF DANISH RESISTANCE 21

GEFION FOUNTAIN 13

ESPLANADEN

Yderhavnen

FREDERIKSKIRKE CHURCH (MARMORKIRKEN)

AMALIENBORG PALACE 3 2

AMALIEGADE

senborg Have

ADELGADE

STORE KONGENSGADE

BREDGADE

SANKT ANNÆ PLADS

Amaliehaven

Boat #901/#902 departures

OPERA HOUSE

DANNESKIOLD

SAMBØES ALLÉ

MMEL NT

CITY

Pistol stræde

NYHAVN 15

17 Kongens Nytorv

CTC

Netto

NY havn

NYHAVN 25

ROYAL DANISH PLAYHOUSE

STRØGET 6

LILLE KONGENSGADE

NIELS JUHLSGADE

19

Nicolaj Plads

Højbro Plads

CTC

VINGÅRDSTR

ADMIRALGADE

HOLMENS KANAL

ROYAL THEATER

HOLBERGSGADE

HOLMEN

HRISTIANS- ORG ALACE

BORGGADE

Netto

HOLMENS CHURCH

HAVNEGADE

BØRSEN 4

KNIPPELSBROGADE

STRANDGADE

OVEN VANDET

NEDEN VANDET

Christianshavns Kanal

CHRISTIANSHAVN

OVERGADEN

BÅDMANDSSTR.

ENTRANCES

CHRISTIANIA 6

ROYAL LIBRARY 11

31

CTC

CHRISTIANS CHURCH

TORVEGADE

PRINSESSEGADE

26

Christian- shavn

Inderhavnen

LANGEBROGADE

DRONNINGENS GADE

CHRISTIANSHAVNS

VOLDGADE

AMAGER BLVD

To Airport & Sweden via Øresund Bridge

To Airport & Sweden

Stadsgraven

LEGEND

- ▪▪▪▪ Rail Line
- ▬ Pedestrian-Friendly Area
- ⚓ Canal Boat Tours
- Ⓗ Harbor Bus
- ⑤ S-Tog Station
- Ⓜ Metro
- ■ Point of Interest/Landmark
- 🛈 Tourist Information
- ⌄! Viewpoint

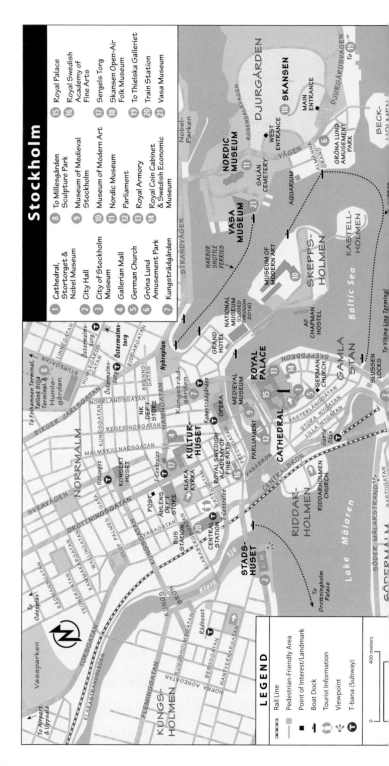

Stockholm

1. Cathedral, Stortorget & Nobel Museum
2. City Hall
3. City of Stockholm Museum
4. Gallerian Mall
5. German Church
6. Gröna Lund Amusement Park
7. Kungsträdgården
8. To Millesgården Sculpture Park
9. Museum of Medieval Stockholm
10. Museum of Modern Art
11. Nordic Museum
12. Parliament
13. Royal Armory
14. Royal Coin Cabinet & Swedish Economic Museum
15. Royal Palace
16. Royal Swedish Academy of Fine Arts
17. Sergels Torg
18. Skansen Open-Air Folk Museum
19. To Thielska Galleriet
20. Train Station
21. Vasa Museum

LEGEND

- Rail Line
- Pedestrian-Friendly Area
- Point of Interest/Landmark
- Boat Dock
- Tourist Information
- Viewpoint
- T-bana (Subway)

0   400 meters

OSLO

LEGEND

- Pedestrian-Friendly Area
- **T** T-bane (subway)
- **12** Tram #12
- **B** Bus #30
- **1** Tourist Information
- Viewpoint

```
0        1000 meters
0        1000 yards
```

1. City Hall
2. Fram Museum
3. Karl Johans Gate
4. Kon-Tiki Museum
5. To Munch Museum
6. National Gallery
7. National Historical Museum
8. Nobel Peace Center
9. Norwegian Folk Mus.
10. To Norwegian Holocaust Center
11. To Norwegian Maritime Museum
12. Oslo Cathedral
13. Oslo City Museum
14. Parliament
15. Royal Palace
16. Viking Ship Museum

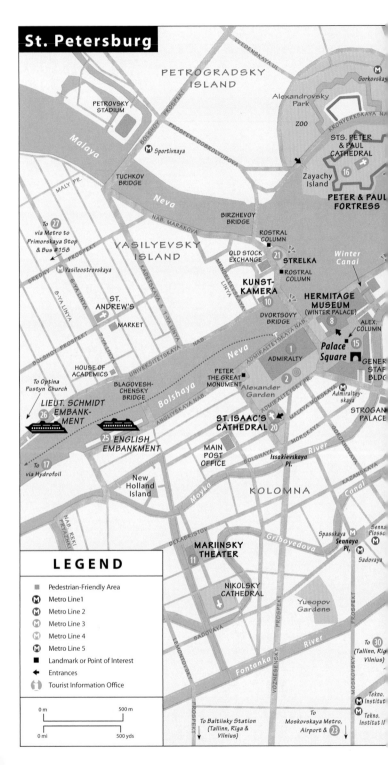

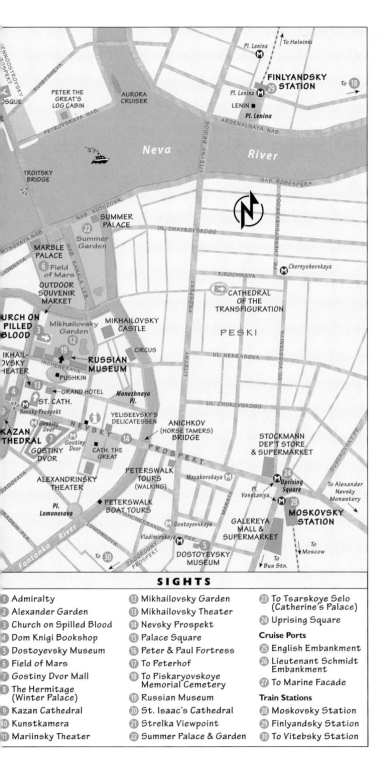

SIGHTS

1. Admiralty
2. Alexander Garden
3. Church on Spilled Blood
4. Dom Knigi Bookshop
5. Dostoyevsky Museum
6. Field of Mars
7. Gostiny Dvor Mall
8. The Hermitage (Winter Palace)
9. Kazan Cathedral
10. Kunstkamera
11. Mariinsky Theater

12. Mikhailovsky Garden
13. Mikhailovsky Theater
14. Nevsky Prospekt
15. Palace Square
16. Peter & Paul Fortress
17. To Peterhof
18. To Piskaryovskoye Memorial Cemetery
19. Russian Museum
20. St. Isaac's Cathedral
21. Strelka Viewpoint
22. Summer Palace & Garden

23. To Tsarskoye Selo (Catherine's Palace)
24. Uprising Square

Cruise Ports

25. English Embankment
26. Lieutenant Schmidt Embankment
27. To Marine Facade

Train Stations

28. Moskovsky Station
29. Finlyandsky Station
30. To Vitebsky Station

SIGHTS

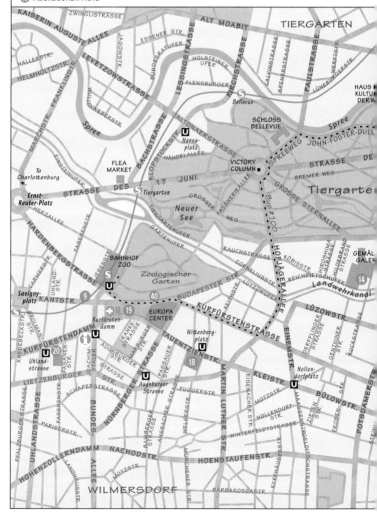

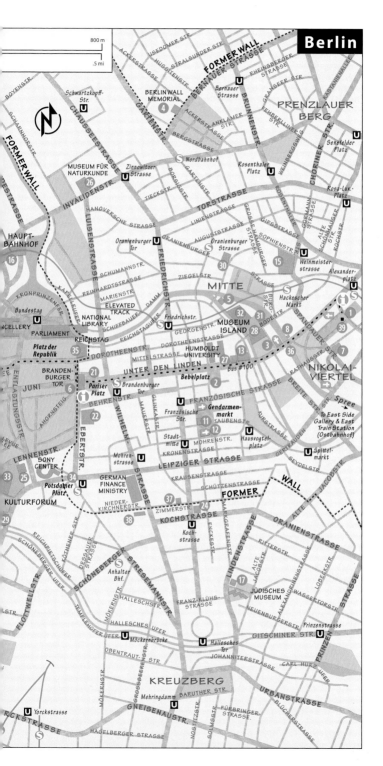

Berlin

800 m
.5 mi

FORMER WALL

USEDOMER STR.
ACKERSTRASSE
HUSSITENSTR.
STRALSUNDER STR.
RHEINSBERGER STRASSE
GRANSEER STR.
KASTANIENALLEE

BERLIN WALL MEMORIAL **4**
Bernauer Strasse
FEHRBELLINER STR.
CHORINER STR.

PRENZLAUER BERG

Schwartzkopff-Str. **U**
CHAUSSEESTRASSE
GARTENSTR.
BERNAUER STRASSE
ACKERSTR.
ANKLAMER STR.
BRUNNENSTR.
WEINBERGSWEG
Senefelder Platz **U**

FORMER WALL

MUSEUM FÜR NATURKUNDE **26**
Zinnowitzer Strasse **U**
Nordbahnhof **S**
Rosenthaler Platz **U**
Rosa-Lux.-Platz **U**

INVALIDENSTR.
HANOVERSCHE STRASSE
LUISENSTRASSE
BORSIGSTR.
GARTENSTR.
TIECKSTR.
TORSTRASSE
GORMANN-STRASSE
ALTE SCHÖNHAUSER STR.
KOCHSTR.

HAUPT-BAHNHOF

16
KRONPRINZENUFER
KAPELLE UFER
REINHARDTSTRASSE
SCHUMANNSTR.
MARIENSTR.
ELEVATED TRACK
NATIONAL LIBRARY
SCHIFFBAUER-DAMM
Oranienburger Tor **U**
FRIEDRICHSTRASSE
ORANIENBURGER STR.
Oranienburger Strasse **S**
LINIENSTRASSE
AUGUSTSTRASSE
GROSSE HAMBURGER STR.
SOPHIENSTR.
GIPSSTRASSE
ZIEGELSTR.
30
15
Weinmeister-strasse **U**
Alexanderplatz **U S**

MITTE
5
Hackescher Markt **S**
32
31
BURGSTR.
BODESTR.
28
8
1
39

Bundestag **U**
CHANCELLERY
PARLIAMENT
NATIONAL LIBRARY
REICHSTAGUFER
Friedrichstr. **U S**
GEORGENSTR.
DOROTHEENSTRASSE
MUSEUM ISLAND
13
3
36
7
NIKOLAI-VIERTEL

REICHSTAG
Platz der Republik **35**
DOROTHEENSTR.
MITTELSTRASSE
HUMBOLDT UNIVERSITY
27
Bus #100
RATHAUSSTR.
SPANDAUER STR.

JUNI
ENTLASTUNGSTR.
BRANDENBURGER TOR **6**
21
Pariser Platz
Brandenburger Tor **S**
UNTER DEN LINDEN
Bebelplatz
2
FRANZÖSISCHE STRASSE
BREITE STR.
Spree

AHORNSTEIG
Behrenstr.
WILHELMSTR.
GLINKASTR.
MAUERSTR.
Französische Str. **U**
Gendarmenmarkt
11
12
TAUBENSTR.
Hausvogtelplatz **U**
To East Side Gallery & East Train Station (Ostbahnhof)

EBERTSTR.
22
Stadtmitte **U**
MOHRENSTR.
Mohren-strasse **U**
KRONENSTRASSE
LEIPZIGER STRASSE
GERTRAUDENSTR.
SEYDELSTR.
Spittelmarkt **U**

LEVUE
LENNESTR.
SONY CENTER
33 **25**
34
Potsdamer Platz **S**
GERMAN FINANCE MINISTRY
KRAUSENSTRASSE
JACOBSTR.

KULTURFORUM
29
NIEDER-KIRCHNERSTR.
37
24
SCHÜTZENSTRASSE
WALL
FORMER
ALTE JACOBSTR.
ORANIENSTRASSE
RITTERSTR.

REICHPIETSCHUFER
SCHÖNEBERGER UFER
KÖTHENER STR.
DESSAUER STR.
STRESEMANNSTR.
SCHÖNEBERGER STRASSE
ZIMMERSTR.
38
KOCHSTRASSE
Koch-strasse **U**
ENCKESTR.
MARKGRAFENSTR.
LINDENSTRASSE
ALEXANDRINENSTR.
NEUENBURGERSTR.
JÜDISCHES MUSEUM
17
Prinzenstrasse **U**

FLOTTWELLSTR.
REICHPIETSCHUFER
SCHÖNEBERGER STR.
MÖCKERNSTR.
Anhalter Bhf.
HALLESCHESTR.
FRANZ-KLÜHS-STRASSE
WASSERTORSTR.
GITSCHINER STR.
PRINZENSTR. **U**

STR.
HALLESCHES UFER
TEMPELHOFER UFER
Möckernbrücke **U**
Hallesches Tor **U**
JOHANNITERSTRASSE
CARL-HERZ-UFER
URBANSTRASSE

OBENTRAUT-STR.
KREUZBERG
Mehringdamm **U**
BARUTHER STR.
FÜRBRINGER-STRASSE
BLÜCHERSTR.

Yorckstrasse **U**
ÖCKSTRASSE
GNEISENAUSTR.
NOSTIZSTR.
ZOSSENER STR.
SOLMSSTR.
HAGELBERGER STRASSE

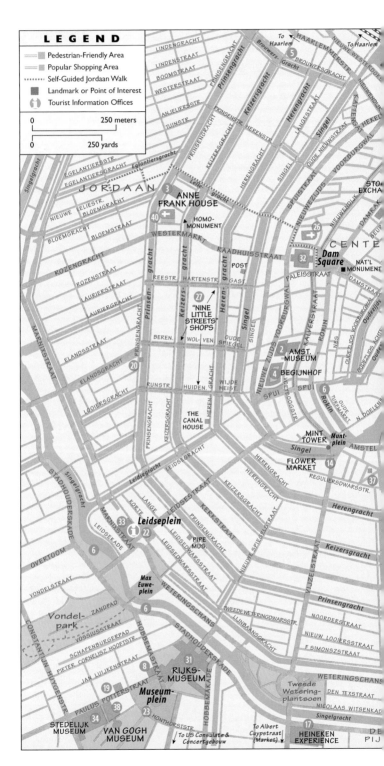

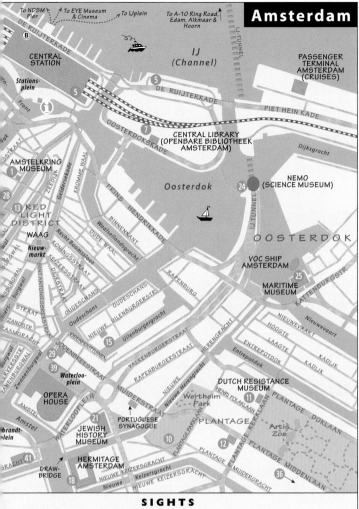

Amsterdam

To NDSM Pier   *To EYE MUSEUM & Cinema*   *To IJplein*   *To A-10 Ring Road, Edam, Alkmaar & Hoorn*

B

CENTRAL STATION

Stationsplein

IJ (Channel)

PASSENGER TERMINAL AMSTERDAM (CRUISES)

DE RUIJTERKADE

DE RUIJTERKADE

PIET HEIN KADE

OOSTERDOKSKADE

CENTRAL LIBRARY (OPENBARE BIBLIOTHEEK AMSTERDAM)

Dijksgracht

AMSTELKRING MUSEUM ❶

Oosterdok

NEMO (SCIENCE MUSEUM) ㉔

❷⑧

⑬ **RED LIGHT DISTRICT**

KROMME WAAL

PRINS HENDRIKKADE

OOSTERDOK

WAAG

Nieuwmarkt

BINNENKANT

VOC SHIP AMSTERDAM ㉕

Recht Boomssloot

OUDE WAAL

RAPENBURG

MARITIME MUSEUM

KONINGSSTRAAT

OUDESCHANS

Oudeschans

NIEUWE UILENBURGERSTR.

KATTENBURGSTR.

Nieuwevaart

HOOGTE

Uilenburgergracht

NIEUWEVAART

ST.ANTONIESBREESTRAAT

DIJKSTRAAT

KOPENHOUTTUINEN ⑮

VALKENBURGERSTRAAT

LAAGTE

KADIJK

ENTREPOTDOK

KADIJK

JODENBREESTRAAT ㉙

HERENGRACHT

Entrepotdok

Entrepotdok

ZWANENBURGWAL

RAPENBURGERSTRAAT

NIEUWE HERENGRACHT

DUTCH RESISTANCE MUSEUM ⑪

HENRI POLAKLAAN

PLANTAGE DOKLAAN

Waterlooplein

OPERA HOUSE

㊴

MUIDERSTRAAT

NIEUWE

Wertheim Park

PLANTAGE

PLANTAGE KERKLAAN

Artis Zoo

Amstel

PORTUGUESE SYNAGOGUE ⑩

PLANTAGE PARKLAAN

PLANTAGE MIDDENLAAN

JEWISH HISTORY MUSEUM ㉑

㉝

PLANTAGE MUIDERGRACHT ⑫

Rembrandtplein

㊶

HERMITAGE AMSTERDAM

NIEUWE KEIZERSGRACHT

DRAWBRIDGE

⑱

Nieuwe KEIZERSGRACHT

NIEUWE KEIZERSGRACHT

SIGHTS

Amstelkring Museum	⑮ Gassan Diamonds
Amsterdam Museum	⑯ Hash, Marijuana & Hemp Museum
Anne Frank House	
Begijnhof	⑰ Heineken Experience
Bike Rentals (3)	⑱ Hermitage Amsterdam
Canal-Boat Tours (4)	⑲ House of Bols
Central Library	⑳ Houseboat Museum
Coster Diamonds & Mus.	㉑ Jewish Hist. Museum
Damrak Sex Museum	㉒ Leidseplein
De Hortus Botanical Garden	㉓ Museumplein
	㉔ NEMO (Science Museum)
Dutch Resistance Museum	㉕ Netherlands Maritime Museum
Dutch Theater Memorial	㉖ New Church
Erotic Museum	㉗ "Nine Little Streets" Shopping District
Flower Market	

㉘ Old Church
㉙ Rembrandt's House
㉚ Rembrandtplein
㉛ Rijksmuseum
㉜ Royal Palace
㉝ Stadsschouwburg Theater
㉞ Stedelijk Museum
㉟ Tassen Museum
㊱ To Tropical Museum
㊲ Tuschinski Theater
㊳ Van Gogh Museum
㊴ Waterlooplein Flea Market
㊵ Westerkerk
㊶ Willet-Holthuysen Mus.

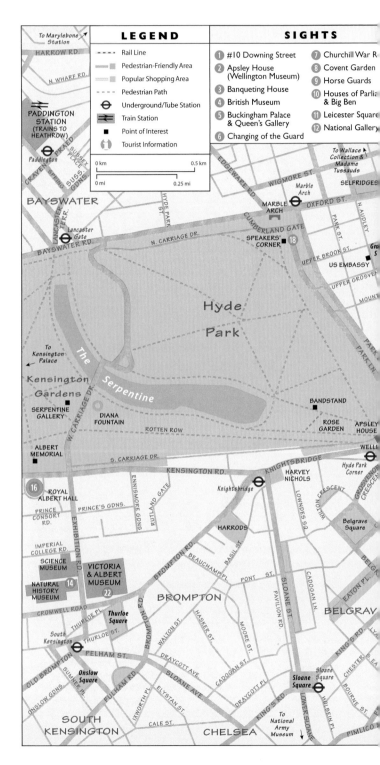

To Marylebone
Station

LEGEND

- - - - Rail Line
    Pedestrian-Friendly Area
    Popular Shopping Area
- - - - Pedestrian Path
⊖ Underground/Tube Station
⚏ Train Station
■ Point of Interest
🛈 Tourist Information

0 km	0.5 km
0 mi	0.25 mi

SIGHTS

1. #10 Downing Street
2. Apsley House (Wellington Museum)
3. Banqueting House
4. British Museum
5. Buckingham Palace & Queen's Gallery
6. Changing of the Guard
7. Churchill War R
8. Covent Garden
9. Horse Guards
10. Houses of Parlia & Big Ben
11. Leicester Square
12. National Gallery

HARROW RD.

N. WHARF RD.

PADDINGTON STATION (TRAINS TO HEATHROW)

Paddington

CRAVEN RD.

SUSSEX GDNS.

SPRING ST.

SUSSEX PLACE

LANCASTER TERR.

BAYSWATER

Lancaster Gate

BAYSWATER RD.

N. CARRIAGE DR.

EDGWARE RD.

WIGMORE ST.

Marble Arch

MARBLE ARCH

OXFORD ST.

N. AUDLEY ST.

To Wallace
Collection &
Madame
Tussauds

SELFRIDGES

HYDE PARK ST.

CUMBERLAND GATE

SPEAKERS' CORNER ■ 18

PARK ST.

UPPER BROOK ST.

US EMBASSY

UPPER GROSVEN

MOUNT

Gro S

To
Kensington
Palace

Kensington Gardens

SERPENTINE GALLERY ■

DIANA FOUNTAIN

The Serpentine

W. CARRIAGE DR.

Hyde Park

PARK LN.

PARK LN.

ROTTEN ROW

BANDSTAND ■

ROSE GARDEN

APSLEY HOUSE

ALBERT MEMORIAL ■

S. CARRIAGE DR.

KENSINGTON RD.

KNIGHTSBRIDGE

WELLI

Hyde Park Corner ⊖

16 ROYAL ALBERT HALL

PRINCE CONSORT RD.

PRINCE'S GDNS.

EXHIBITION RD.

RUTLAND GATE

ENNISMORE GDNS.

HARVEY NICHOLS

Knightsbridge ⊖

LOWNDES SQ.

CRESCENT

WILTON

GROSVENOR CRESCENT

Belgrave Square

IMPERIAL COLLEGE RD.

SCIENCE MUSEUM

NATURAL HISTORY MUSEUM

14

VICTORIA & VICTORIA MUSEUM

22

HARRODS

BROMPTON RD.

BEAUCHAMP PL.

BASIL ST.

PONT ST.

SLOANE ST.

CADOGAN LN.

PAVILION RD.

BELGRAV

EATON PL.

BELGR

CROMWELL ROAD

THURLOE PL.

Thurloe Square

WALTON ST.

HASKER ST.

MOORE ST.

BROMPTON

CADOGAN SQ.

KING'S RD.

CHESTER S EA

YA

South Kensington ⊖

THURLOE ST.

PELHAM ST.

DRAYCOTT AVE.

BROMPTON RD.

SLOANE AVE.

DRAYCOTT PL.

Sloane Square

Sloane Square ⊖

BOURNE ST.

OLD BROMPTON RD.

Onslow Square

FULHAM RD.

IXWORTH ST.

ELYSTAN ST.

ELYSTAN PL.

LOWER SLOANE

HOLBEIN PL.

PIMLICO R

ONSLOW GDNS.

SUMNER PL.

Onslow Square

SOUTH KENSINGTON

CALE ST.

CHELSEA

To
National
Army
Museum ↓

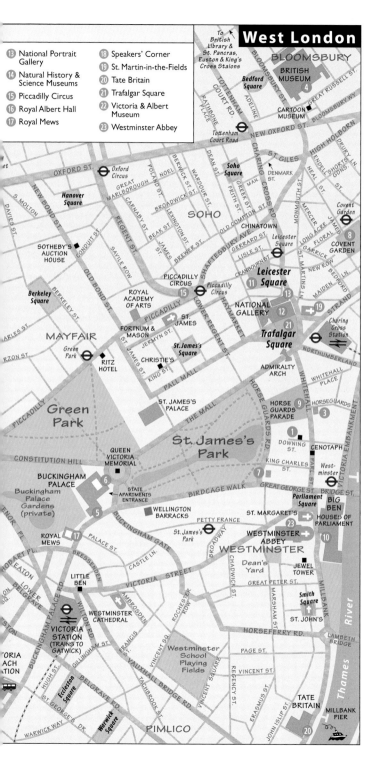

West London

13 National Portrait Gallery
14 Natural History & Science Museums
15 Piccadilly Circus
16 Royal Albert Hall
17 Royal Mews
18 Speakers' Corner
19 St. Martin-in-the-Fields
20 Tate Britain
21 Trafalgar Square
22 Victoria & Albert Museum
23 Westminster Abbey

To British Library & St. Pancras, Euston & King's Cross Stations

BLOOMSBURY
BRITISH MUSEUM
Bedford Square
CARTOON MUSEUM

OXFORD ST.
Oxford Circus
Hanover Square
SOHO
Soho Square
CHINATOWN
Leicester Square
Covent Garden
COVENT GARDEN

SOTHEBY'S AUCTION HOUSE
Berkeley Square
PICCADILLY CIRCUS
Piccadilly Circus
Leicester Square
NATIONAL GALLERY

MAYFAIR
ROYAL ACADEMY OF ARTS
FORTNUM & MASON
ST. JAMES
Trafalgar Square
Charing Cross Station

Green Park
RITZ HOTEL
CHRISTIE'S
St. James's Square
ADMIRALTY ARCH

ST. JAMES'S PALACE
THE MALL
HORSE GUARDS PARADE

Green Park
QUEEN VICTORIA MEMORIAL
St. James's Park
DOWNING ST.
CENOTAPH
West-minster

CONSTITUTION HILL
BUCKINGHAM PALACE
STATE APARTMENTS ENTRANCE
BIRDCAGE WALK
KING CHARLES ST.
BRIDGE ST.
BIG BEN

Buckingham Palace Gardens (private)
WELLINGTON BARRACKS
Parliament Square
HOUSES OF PARLIAMENT

ROYAL MEWS
St. James's Park
PETTY FRANCE
ST. MARGARET'S
WESTMINSTER ABBEY

LITTLE BEN
VICTORIA STREET
WESTMINSTER
Dean's Yard
JEWEL TOWER

WESTMINSTER CATHEDRAL
GREAT PETER ST.
Smith Square
ST. JOHN'S

VICTORIA STATION (TRAINS TO GATWICK)
Westminster School Playing Fields
HORSEFERRY RD.
LAMBETH BRIDGE

Eccleston Square
Warwick Square
PAGE ST.
VINCENT ST.
TATE BRITAIN
MILLBANK PIER

PIMLICO
Thames River

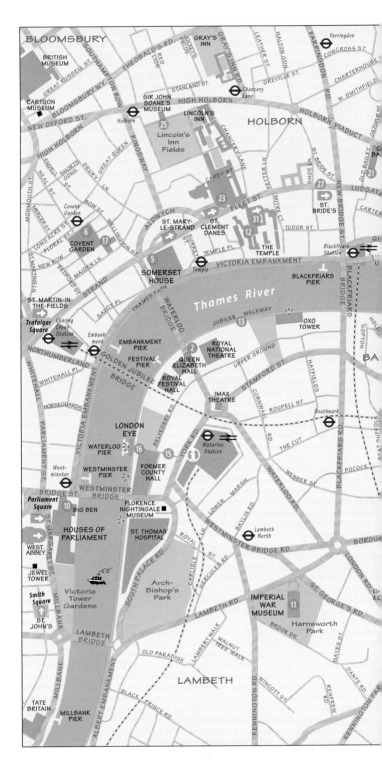

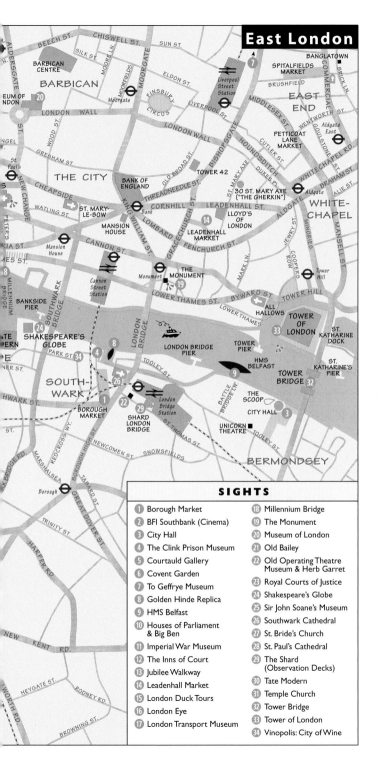

East London

SIGHTS

1. Borough Market
2. BFI Southbank (Cinema)
3. City Hall
4. The Clink Prison Museum
5. Courtauld Gallery
6. Covent Garden
7. To Geffrye Museum
8. Golden Hinde Replica
9. HMS Belfast
10. Houses of Parliament & Big Ben
11. Imperial War Museum
12. The Inns of Court
13. Jubilee Walkway
14. Leadenhall Market
15. London Duck Tours
16. London Eye
17. London Transport Museum
18. Millennium Bridge
19. The Monument
20. Museum of London
21. Old Bailey
22. Old Operating Theatre Museum & Herb Garret
23. Royal Courts of Justice
24. Shakespeare's Globe
25. Sir John Soane's Museum
26. Southwark Cathedral
27. St. Bride's Church
28. St. Paul's Cathedral
29. The Shard (Observation Decks)
30. Tate Modern
31. Temple Church
32. Tower Bridge
33. Tower of London
34. Vinopolis: City of Wine

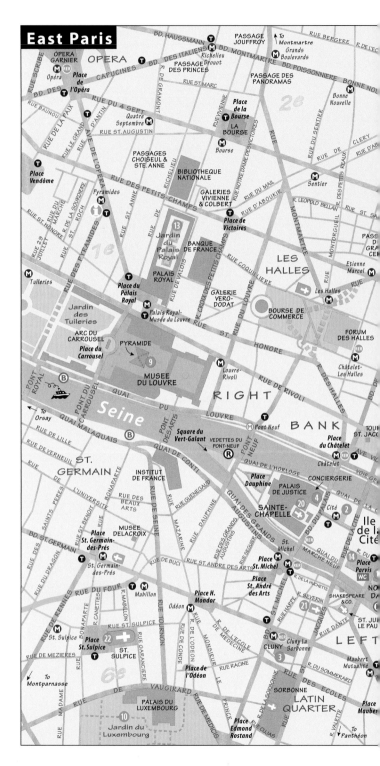

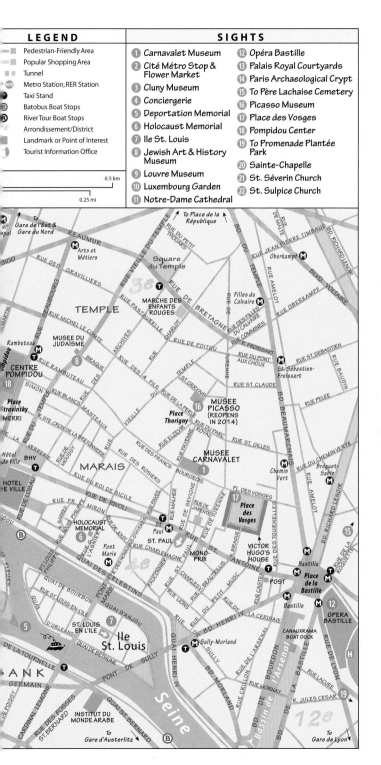

LEGEND	
▨▨▨	Pedestrian-Friendly Area
▨▨▨	Popular Shopping Area
▨▨	Tunnel
Ⓜ ⓇⒺⓇ	Metro Station, RER Station
●	Taxi Stand
Ⓑ	Batobus Boat Stops
Ⓡ	River Tour Boat Stops
	Arrondissement/District
	Landmark or Point of Interest
ⓘ	Tourist Information Office

0.5 km
0.25 mi

SIGHTS

1. Carnavalet Museum
2. Cité Métro Stop & Flower Market
3. Cluny Museum
4. Conciergerie
5. Deportation Memorial
6. Holocaust Memorial
7. Ile St. Louis
8. Jewish Art & History Museum
9. Louvre Museum
10. Luxembourg Garden
11. Notre-Dame Cathedral
12. Opéra Bastille
13. Palais Royal Courtyards
14. Paris Archaeological Crypt
15. To Père Lachaise Cemetery
16. Picasso Museum
17. Place des Vosges
18. Pompidou Center
19. To Promenade Plantée Park
20. Sainte-Chapelle
21. St. Séverin Church
22. St. Sulpice Church

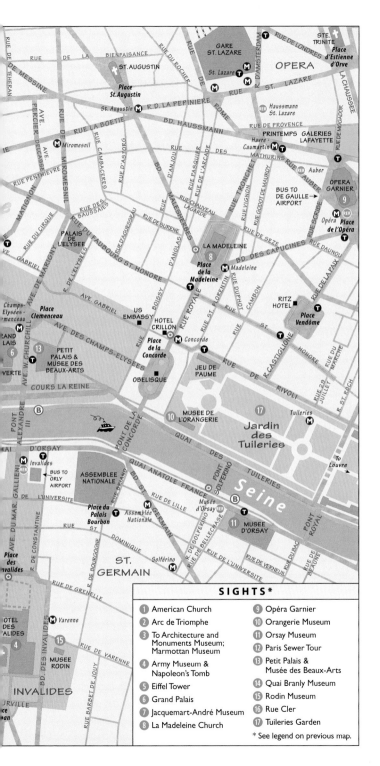

SIGHTS*

1. American Church
2. Arc de Triomphe
3. To Architecture and Monuments Museum; Marmottan Museum
4. Army Museum & Napoleon's Tomb
5. Eiffel Tower
6. Grand Palais
7. Jacquemart-André Museum
8. La Madeleine Church
9. Opéra Garnier
10. Orangerie Museum
11. Orsay Museum
12. Paris Sewer Tour
13. Petit Palais & Musée des Beaux-Arts
14. Quai Branly Museum
15. Rodin Museum
16. Rue Cler
17. Tuileries Garden

* See legend on previous map.

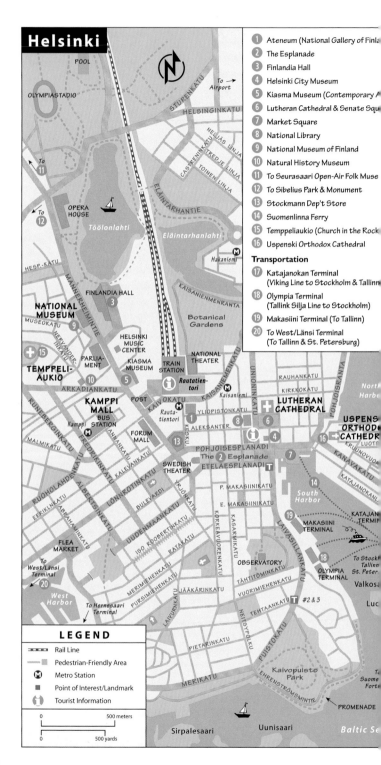

Helsinki

1. Ateneum (National Gallery of Finla...
2. The Esplanade
3. Finlandia Hall
4. Helsinki City Museum
5. Kiasma Museum (Contemporary A...
6. Lutheran Cathedral & Senate Squ...
7. Market Square
8. National Library
9. National Museum of Finland
10. Natural History Museum
11. To Seurasaari Open-Air Folk Muse...
12. To Sibelius Park & Monument
13. Stockmann Dep't Store
14. Suomenlinna Ferry
15. Temppeliaukio (Church in the Rock...
16. Uspenski Orthodox Cathedral

Transportation

17. Katajanokan Terminal
(Viking Line to Stockholm & Tallinn...
18. Olympia Terminal
(Tallink Silja Line to Stockholm)
19. Makasiini Terminal (To Tallinn)
20. To West/Länsi Terminal
(To Tallinn & St. Petersburg)

LEGEND

- Rail Line
- Pedestrian-Friendly Area
- Ⓜ Metro Station
- ■ Point of Interest/Landmark
- ℹ Tourist Information

| 0 | 500 meters |
| 0 | 500 yards |

Rick Steves'

NORTHERN EUROPEAN CRUISE PORTS

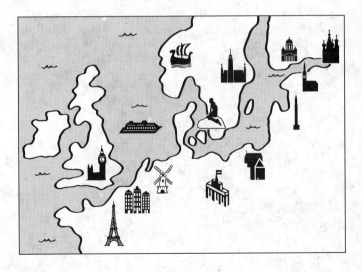

AVALON
TRAVEL

INTRODUCTION

Imagine yourself lazing on the deck of a floating city as you glide past the spiny skylines of Tallinn, Copenhagen, or St. Petersburg; the jagged fjords of Norway's west coast; or the thousands of picture-perfect islands topped by quaint red vacation cottages in the archipelago between Stockholm and Helsinki. Stepping off the gangway, you're immersed in the vivid life of a different European city each day. Tour some of the world's top museums, take a Scandinavian-style coffee break while you people-watch from a prime sidewalk café, sunbathe on a surprisingly sunny and sandy Baltic beach, and enjoy some of Europe's most expensive cities on the cheap. After a busy day in port, you can head back to the same cozy bedroom each night, without ever having to pack a suitcase or catch a train. As the sun sets and the ship pulls out of port, you have your choice of dining options—from a tuxedos-and-evening-gowns affair to a poolside burger after a swim—followed by a world of nightlife. Plying the Baltic and North Sea waters through the night, you wake up refreshed in a whole new city—ready to do it all again.

Cruising in Europe is more popular today than ever before. And for good reason. Taking a cruise can be a fun, affordable way to experience Europe—*if* you choose the right cruise, keep your extra expenses to a minimum... and use this book to make the absolute most of your time in port.

Unlike most cruising guidebooks, which dote on details about this ship's restaurants or that ship's staterooms, *Rick Steves' Northern European Cruise Ports* focuses on the main attraction:

INTRODUCTION

Map Legend

⅃ Viewpoint	🚢 Cruise Port/Dock	)(Tunnel
↑ Entrance	✈ Airport	Pedestrian Zone
ⓘ Tourist Info	ⓣ Taxi Stand	Railway
WC Restroom	Ⓣ Tram Stop	Ferry/Boat Route
Castle	Ⓑ Bus Stop	Tram
▪ Statue/Point of Interest	Ⓜ Metro Stop	Stairs
Building	Ⓣ T-Bana Stop (Oslo & Stockholm)	Walk/Tour Route
Church	Ⓢ S-Tog Station (Copenhagen)	Trail
Synagogue	Ⓗ Harbor Bus (Copenhagen)	Funicular
Fountain	Ⓟ Parking	Park

Use this legend to help you navigate the maps in this book.

some of the grandest cities in Europe. Even if you have just eight hours in port, you can still ride a red double-decker bus through London, paddle a kayak on a Norwegian fjord, stroll Berlin's Unter den Linden or Copenhagen's Strøget, and walk in Lech Wałęsa's footsteps at the Solidarity shipyards in Gdańsk.

Yes, you could spend a lifetime in Amsterdam. But you've got a few hours...and I have a plan for you. Each of this book's destination chapters is designed as a mini-vacation of its own, with advice about what to do and detailed sightseeing information for each port. And, to enable you to do it all on your own, I've included step-by-step instructions for getting into town from the cruise terminal.

For each major destination, this book offers a balanced, comfortable mix of the predictable biggies and a healthy dose of "Back Door" intimacy. Along with marveling at masterpieces in the Hermitage, the Louvre, and the Rijksmuseum, you can sip a pint in a trendy London pub and sweat with the Finns in a working-class sauna.

In each port, you'll get all the specifics and opinions necessary to wring the maximum value out of your limited time and money.

The best options in each port are, of course, only my opinion. But after spending half my adult life researching Europe, I've developed a sixth sense for what travelers enjoy.

About This Book

The book is divided into three parts: First, I'll suggest strategies for choosing which cruise to take, including a rundown of the major cruise lines, and explain the procedure for booking a cruise.

Please Tear Up This Book!

There's no point in hauling around 60 pages on Copenhagen for a day in Oslo. That's why I've designed this book to be

ripped apart. Before your cruise, attack this book with a utility knife to create an army of pocket-sized mini-guidebooks—one for each port of call.

I love the ritual of trimming down the size of guidebooks I'll be using: Fold the pages back until you break the spine, neatly slice apart the sections you want with a utility knife, then pull

them out with the gummy edge intact. If you want, finish each one off with some clear, heavy-duty packing tape to smooth and reinforce the spine, or use a heavy-duty stapler along the edge to prevent the first and last pages from coming loose.

To make things even easier, I've created a line of laminated covers with slide-on binders. Every evening, you can make a ritual of swapping out today's pages for tomorrow's. (For more on these binders, see www.ricksteves.com.)

As I travel in Europe, I meet lots of people with even more clever book treatments. This couple was proud of the

job they did in the name of packing light: cutting out only the pages they'd be using and putting them into a spiral binding.

While you may be tempted to keep this book intact as a souvenir of your travels, you'll appreciate even

more the footloose freedom of traveling light while you're in port.

Next, I'll give you a "Cruising 101"-type travel-skills briefing, with advice about what you should know before you go, and strategies for making the most of your time both on and off the ship. And finally, the vast majority of this book is dedicated to the European ports you'll visit, with complete plans for packing each day full of unforgettable experiences.

I haven't skimped on my coverage of the sights in this book—which is why it's a bricklike tome. To get the most out of the book, please don't hesitate to tear out just the pages that you need for each day in port (see sidebar).

Top Destinations

NORWEGIAN FJORDS

FLÅM

BERGEN

STAVANGER

LONDON
& PORTS OF
SOUTHAMPTON
& DOVER

AMSTERDAM

BRUGES,
BRUSSELS
& PORT OF ZEEBRUGGE

PARIS,
NORMANDY
& PORT OF LE HAVRE

Is a European Cruise Right for You?

I'm not going to try to convince you to cruise or not to cruise. If you're holding this book, I assume you've already made that decision. But if you're a cruise skeptic—or even a cruise cynic—and you're trying to decide whether cruising suits your approach to experiencing Europe, I'll let you in on my own process for weighing the pros and cons of cruising.

I believe this is the first and only cruising guidebook written by someone with a healthy skepticism about cruises. When I was

growing up, cruising was a rich person's hobby. I used to joke that for many American cruisers, the goal was not travel but hedonism: See if you can eat five meals a day and still ride a bike when you get into port.

Experiencing Europe's culture, people, and natural wonders economically and hassle-free has been my goal for three decades of traveling, tour guiding, and writing. And after all that time, I haven't found a more affordable way to see certain parts of Europe than cruising (short of sleeping on a park bench). For a weeklong European cruise that includes room, board, transportation, tips, and port fees, a couple can pay as little as $100 per night—that's as much as a budget hotel room in many cities. To link all the places on an exciting one-week European cruise on your own, the hotels, railpasses, boat tickets, taxi transfers, restaurants, and so on would add up fast. The per-day base cost for mainstream cruises beats independent travel by a mile—particularly in northern Europe, which has one of the highest costs of living in the world. (While a cruise saves money on a trip to Greece or Spain, it's an even better deal in Norway or London—where hotel costs can be more than double.) And there's no denying the efficiency of sleeping while you travel to your next destination—touring six dynamically different destinations in a single week without wasting valuable daylight hours packing, hauling your bags to the station, and sitting on a train.

And yet, I still have reservations. Just as someone trying to learn a language will do better by immersing themselves in that culture than by sitting in a classroom for a few hours, I believe that travelers in search of engaging, broadening experiences should eat, sleep, and live Europe. Good or bad, cruising insulates you from Europe. If the Russian babushkas selling nesting dolls in St. Petersburg are getting a little too pushy, you can simply retreat to the comfort of 24-hour room service, tall glasses of ice water, American sports on the TV, and a boatload of people who speak English as a first language (except, perhaps, your crew). It's fun—but is it Europe?

For many, it's "Europe enough." For travelers who prefer to tiptoe into Europe—rather than dive right in—this bite-sized approach can be a good way to get your feet wet. Cruising works well as an enticing sampler for Europe, to help you decide where you'd like to return and really get to know.

People take cruises for different reasons. Some travelers cruise as a means to an end: experiencing the ports of call. They appreciate the convenience of traveling while they sleep, waking up in an interesting new destination each morning, and making the most out of every second they're in port. This is the "first off, last on" crowd that attacks each port like a footrace. You can practically hear their mental starter's pistol go off when the gangway opens.

Other cruisers are there to enjoy the cruise experience itself. They enjoy lying by the pool, taking advantage of onboard activities, dropping some cash at the casino, ringing up a huge bar tab, napping, reading, and watching ESPN on their stateroom TVs. If the *Mona Lisa* floated past, they might crane their necks, but wouldn't strain to get out of their deck chairs.

With all due respect to the latter, I've written this book primarily for the former. But if you really want to be on vacation, aim for somewhere in the middle: Be sure to experience the ports that really tickle your wanderlust, but give yourself a "day off" every now and again in the less-enticing ports to sleep in or hit the beach.

Another advantage of cruising is that it can accommodate a family or group of people with vastly different travel philosophies. It's possible for Mom to go to the museum, Dad to lie by the pool, Sally to go for a bike ride, and Bobby to go shopping...and then all of them can have dinner together and swap stories about their perfect days. (Or, if they're really getting on each other's nerves, there's plenty of room on a big ship to spread out.)

Cruising is especially popular among retirees, particularly those with limited mobility. Cruising rescues you from packing up your bags and huffing to the train station every other day. Once on land, accessibility for wheelchairs and walkers can vary dramatically—though some cruise lines offer excursions specifically designed for those who don't walk well. A cruise aficionado who had done the math once told me that, if you know how to find the deals, it's theoretically cheaper to cruise indefinitely than to pay for a retirement home.

On the other hand, the independent, free-spirited traveler may not appreciate the constraints of cruising. For some, seven or eight hours in port is a tantalizing tease of a place where they'd

love to linger for the evening—and the obligation to return to the ship every night is frustrating. Cruisers visiting Paris will never experience the City of Light after dark. If you're antsy, energetic, and want to stroll the cobbles of Europe at all hours, cruising may not be for you. However, even some seasoned globetrotters find that cruising is a good way to travel in Europe on a shoestring budget, yet still in comfort.

One cruise-activities coordinator told me that cruisers can be divided into two groups: Those who stay in their rooms, refuse to try to enjoy the dozens of activities offered to them each day, and complain about everything; and those who get out and try to get to know their fellow passengers, make the most of being at sea, and have the time of their lives. Guess which type (according to him) enjoys the experience more?

Let's face it: Americans take the shortest vacations in the rich world. Some people choose to dedicate their valuable time off to an all-inclusive, resort-style vacation in Florida, Hawaii, or Mexico: swimming pools, song-and-dance shows, shopping, and all-you-can-eat buffets. Cruising gives you much the same hedonistic

INTRODUCTION

experience, all while you learn a lot about Europe—provided you use your time on shore constructively. It can be the best of both worlds.

Understanding the Cruise Industry

Cruising is a $30 billion-a-year business. Approximately one out of every five Americans has taken a cruise, and each year about 15 million people take one. In adjusted dollars, cruise prices haven't risen in decades. This, partly, has sparked a huge growth in the cruise industry in recent years. The aging baby boomer population has also boosted sales, as older travelers discover that a cruise is an easy way to see the world. While the biggest growth has come from the North American market, cruise lines have also started marketing more internationally.

The industry has changed dramatically over the last generation. For decades, cruise lines catered exclusively to the upper crust—people who expected top-tier luxury. But with the popularity of *The Love Boat* television series in the 1970s and 1980s, then the one-upmanship of increasingly bigger megaships in the early 1990s, cruising went mainstream. Somebody had to fill all the berths on those gargantuan vessels, and cruise lines lowered their prices to attract middle-class customers. The "newlyweds and nearly deads" stereotype about cruise clientele is now outmoded. The industry has made bold efforts to appeal to an ever-broader customer base, representing a wide spectrum of ages, interests, and income levels.

In order to compete for passengers and fill megaships, cruise lines offer fares that can be astonishingly low. In fact, they make little or no money on ticket sales—and some "loss-leader" sailings actually lose money on the ini-

tial fare. Instead, the cruise lines' main income comes from three sources: alcohol sales, gambling (onboard casinos), and excursions. So while cruise lines are in the business of creating an unforgettable vacation for you, they're also in the business of separating you from your money (once on the ship) to make up for their underpriced fares.

Just as airlines have attempted to bolster their bottom lines by "unbundling" their fares and charging more "pay as you go" fees (for food, checking a bag, extra legroom, and so on), cruise lines are now charging for things they used to include (such as "specialty restaurants"). The cruise industry is constantly experimenting with the balance between all-inclusive luxury and nickel-and-dime, à la carte, mass-market travel. (For tips on maximizing your experience while minimizing your expenses, see the sidebar on page 82.)

It's also worth noting that cruise lines are able to remain profitable largely on the backs of their low-paid crew, who mostly hail from the developing world. Working 10 to 14 hours a day, seven days a week—almost entirely for tips—the tireless crew are the gears that keep cruises spinning. (For more, see page 76.)

Understanding how the cruise industry works can help you take advantage of your cruise experience...and not the other way around. Equipped with knowledge, you can be the smart consumer who has a fantastic time on board and in port without paying a premium. That's what this book is all about.

Traveling as a Temporary Local

Most travelers tramp through Europe as if they're visiting the cultural zoo. "Ooo, that Norwegian fisherman is mending his nets! Excuse me, could you do that in the sunshine with my wife next to you so I can take a snapshot?" This is fun. It's a part of travel. But a camera bouncing on your belly tells locals you're hunting cultural peacocks. When I'm in Europe, I try to be the best Swede or Dane or Estonian I can be.

Europeans generally like Americans. But if there is a negative aspect to their image of Americans, it's that we are loud, wasteful, ethnocentric, too informal (which can seem disrespectful), and a bit naive.

Even if you believe American ways are best, your trip will go more smoothly if you don't compare. Enjoy doing things the European way, and you'll experience a more welcoming Europe.

We travel all the way to Europe to enjoy differences—to become temporary locals. You'll experience frustrations. Certain truths that we find "God-given" or "self-evident," such as cold beer, ice in drinks, bottomless cups of coffee, and bigger being better, are suddenly not so true. One of the benefits of travel is the eye-opening realization that there are logical, civil, and even better alternatives. By immersing yourself in different cultures and experiencing different people and lifestyles, you'll broaden your perspective.

While Europeans look bemusedly at some of our Yankee excesses—and worriedly at others—they nearly always afford us individual travelers all the warmth we deserve. Judging from all the happy feedback I receive from travelers who have used my books, it's safe to assume you'll enjoy a great, affordable vacation—with the finesse of an independent, experienced traveler.

Thanks, and bon voyage!

Back Door Travel Philosophy
From *Rick Steves' Europe Through the Back Door*

Travel is intensified living—maximum thrills per minute and one of the last great sources of legal adventure. Travel is freedom. It's recess, and we need it.

Experiencing the real Europe requires catching it by surprise, going casual..."through the Back Door."

In many ways, spending a lot of money on sightseeing and excursions only builds a thicker wall between you and what you came to see. Europe is a cultural carnival, and, time after time, you'll find that its best acts are free and the best seats are the cheap ones. A tight budget forces you to travel close to the ground, meeting and communicating with the people, not relying on service with a purchased smile.

Connecting with people carbonates your experience. Extroverts have more fun. If your trip is low on magic moments, kick yourself and make things happen. If you don't enjoy a place, maybe you don't know enough about it. Seek the truth. Recognize tourist traps. Give a culture the benefit of your open mind. See things as different but not better or worse. Any culture has much to share.

Of course, travel, like the world, is a series of hills and valleys. Be fanatically positive and militantly optimistic. If something's not to your liking, change your liking.

Travel can make you a happier American as well as a citizen of the world. Our Earth is home to seven billion equally precious people. It's humbling to travel and find that people don't have the "American Dream"—they have their own dreams. Europeans like us, but, with all due respect, they wouldn't trade passports.

Thoughtful travel—even from the comfortable springboard of a cruise ship—engages us with the world. In tough economic times, it reminds us what is truly important. By broadening perspectives, travel teaches new ways to measure quality of life.

Globe-trotting destroys ethnocentricity, helping you understand and appreciate different cultures. Rather than fear the diversity on this planet, celebrate it. Among your prized souvenirs will be the strands of different cultures you choose to knit into your own character. The world is a cultural yarn shop, and Back Door travelers are weaving the ultimate tapestry. Join in!

Part I
CHOOSING AND BOOKING A CRUISE

CHOOSING A CRUISE

Each cruise line has its own distinct personality, quirks, strengths, and weaknesses. Selecting a cruise that matches your travel style and philosophy can be critical for the enjoyment of your trip. On the other hand, some cruisers care only about the price, go on any line that offers a deal, and have a great time.

Still, the more your idea of "good travel" meshes with your cruise line's, the more likely you are to enjoy both your trip and your fellow passengers. For information on booking a cruise, see the next chapter.

Gathering Information

Comparison-shopping can be a fun part of the cruise experience. Read the cruise-line descriptions in this chapter, then browse the websites of the ones that interest you. Ask your friends who've cruised, and who share your interests, about the lines they've used, and what they thought of each one. Examine the cruise lines' glossy brochures (view online, request them, or get them from your local travel agent)—how the line markets itself says a lot about what sort of clientele it attracts. Tune into the ubiquitous TV commercials for cruise lines. Photos of individual ships' staterooms and amenities—which you'll also find on the cruise lines' websites—can be worth a thousand words in getting a sense of the vibe of each vessel.

Once you've narrowed down the choices, read some impartial online reviews. The most popular site, www.cruisecritic.com, has reviews of cruise lines, specific ships, tips for visiting each port, and more. Other well-respected websites are www.cruisediva.com, www.cruisemates.com, and www.avidcruiser.com. If you feel that cruising is all about the ship, check www.shipparade.com, which delves into details about each vessel.

Cruising the Internet

While there are many cruise-related websites, Cruise Critic (www.cruisecritic.com) dominates cyberspace. Not only are its forums crammed with reviews about ships, excursions, local guides, and ports of call, but it's also a nifty networking tool. By signing up on its Roll Call page for your cruise, you can introduce yourself to others on the same ship and look for partners to share taxis or local guides. Some cruise lines—such as Azamara, Celebrity, Crystal, and Royal Caribbean—even sponsor a social gathering of Cruise Critic members early in the cruise, often with complimentary food and drinks.

Many travel agencies that sell cruises have surprisingly informative websites. One of the best, www.vacationstogo.com, not only sorts different cruise options by price and destination, but also has useful facts, figures, and photos for each ship and port.

Most cruising guidebooks devotkte more coverage to detailed reviews of specific ships and their amenities than to the destinations—which make them the perfect complement to this book. Look for *The Unofficial Guide to Cruises, Frommer's European Cruises and Ports of Call, Fodor's Complete Guide to European Cruises,* and others. (For destination-specific guidebooks, see the list on page 1116.)

As you compare cruises, decide which of the factors in the following section matter the most to you, then find a cruise line that best matches what you're looking for.

Cruise Considerations

In the next few pages you'll find a wide range of issues, big and small, to take into account when selecting your cruise. Of these, the three main factors—which should be weighted about equally—are **price, itinerary** (length, destinations, and time spent in each port), and **cruise line** (personality and amenities).

If you've cruised in the Caribbean but not Europe, be aware that there are some subtle but important differences. In general, European cruises are more focused on the destinations, while Caribbean cruises tend to be more focused on the ship (passengers spend more time on the ship, and therefore the shipboard amenities are more important). People choosing among European cruises usually base their decision on the places they'll be visiting: Which cities—St. Petersburg, London, Oslo, Copenhagen—stoke your travel dreams? Would you rather max out on urban sights, or save time for the fjords and islands? In contrast, on a Caribbean cruise the priority is simply hedonistic fun in the sun.

Cruise Line

This chapter will give you a quick overview of some of the major lines to help you find a good match. For example, some cruise lines embrace cruising's nautical heritage, with decor and crew uniforms that really let you know you're on a ship. Others are more like Las Vegas casinos at sea. An armchair historian will be disappointed on a hedonistic pleasure boat, and a young person who's in a mood to party will be miserable on the *S.S. Septuagenarian.* Do you want a wide range of dining options on the ship, or do you view mealtime as a pragmatic way to fill the tank? After dinner, do you want to get to bed early, or dance in a disco until dawn?

American vs. European: While most US travelers opt for an American cruise line, doing so definitely Americanizes your travel experience. When you're on board, it feels almost as if you'd never left the good old U. S. of A.—with American shows on the TV, Heinz ketchup in the buffet line, and fellow Yanks all around you. If you'd rather leave North America behind, going with a European-flavored cruise line can be an interesting cultural experience in itself. While Europeans are likely to be among the passengers on any cruise line, they represent a larger proportion on European-owned or -operated boats. Surrounded by Germans who enthusiastically burp after a good meal, Italians who nudge ahead of you in line, and French people who enjoy sunbathing topless—and listening to every announcement translated into six different languages—you'll definitely know you're in Europe. I recently cruised for a week in Norway as one of just 13 Americans on a budget ship with more than 2,000 passengers. I never saw another Yank, spent my time on board and in port with working-class Italians and Spaniards from towns no tourist has ever heard of, and had what was quite possibly the most truly "European" experience of my life.

Environmental Impact: Most forms of travel come with a toll on the environment. And cruise ships are no exception—they gulp fuel as they ply scenic seas, struggling to find waste-disposal methods that are as convenient as possible while still being legal. Some cruise lines are more conscientious about these issues than others. If environmental impact is a major concern of yours, you can compare the record for all the major cruise lines at www.foe.org/cruise-report-card.

Length

European cruises can range in length from a few days to a few weeks. The typical cruiser sails for 7 days, but some travelers enjoy taking a 10-, 12-, or 14-day cruise, then adding a few days on land at either end to stretch their trip to two weeks or more. A cruise 7 days or shorter tends to focus on one "zone" of northern Europe

(Norwegian fjords; Baltic highlights; Western Europe); a longer cruise is more likely to provide you with a sampler of the whole area.

When to Go

Due to the chilly weather at these latitudes, the tourist season in northern Europe is extremely brief: June, July, and August. While a few straggler cruises may be offered outside that three-month window, I'd think twice before heading to Oslo, Helsinki, or St. Petersburg in other months (and if you do, be prepared for rainy and cold weather). For a month-by-month climate chart that includes various ports, see page 1120.

Fortunately, even though tourists bombard the region during those key months, northern European destinations are still typically less crowded than Mediterranean hot spots like Venice or Barcelona. (There are exceptions: Any day during cruise season, the crowds inside St. Petersburg's Hermitage museum are next to unbearable.)

Price

If you're on a tight budget and aren't fussy, look for the best deals. From the Mass-Market to the Ultra-Luxury categories, the per-person price can range from $100 to $700+ per day. Sales can lower those prices. (For more on cruise pricing, see page 18.)

While going with the cheapest option is tempting, it may be worth paying a little extra for an experience that better matches your idea of a dream cruise. If you're hoping for glitzy public spaces and sparkling nightly revues, you'll kick yourself later if you saved $40 a day—but ended up on a musty ship with stale shows. If you want to maximize time exploring European destinations, it can be worth paying an extra $20 a day for an itinerary with two more hours at each port—that translates to just 10 bucks an hour, a veritable steal compared to the extra experience it'll allow you to cram in. Don't be penny-wise and pound-foolish in this regard.

On the other hand, in my (admittedly limited) cruise experience, I've noticed a trend: The more people pay for the cruise, the higher their expectations—and, therefore, the more prone they are to disappointment. I've cruised on lines ranging from bargain-basement to top-end, and I've noticed an almost perfect correlation between how much someone pays and how much they enjoy complaining. In my experience, folks who pay less are simply more fun to cruise with. When considering the people I'll wind up dining and going on shore excursions with, price tag aside, I'd rather go with a mid-range cruise line than a top-end one.

When evaluating prices and making a budget, remember to take into account all of the "extras" you might wind up buying from the cruise line: alcoholic drinks, meals at specialty restaurants, the semi-mandatory "auto-tip" (about $10-12 per day per person), shore excursions, and your gambling tab from the casino, just to name a few. (For more details on these hidden costs, see page 81.)

Ship Size and Amenities

When it comes to cruise ships, bigger is not necessarily better... although it can be, depending on your interests.

The biggest ships offer a wide variety of restaurants, activities, entertainment, and other amenities (such as resources for kids). The main disadvantage of a big ship is the feeling that you're being herded along with thousands of other passengers—3,000 tourists piling off a ship into a small port town definitely changes the character of the place.

Smaller ships enjoy fewer crowds, access to out-of-the-way ports, and less hassle when disembarking (especially when tendering—see page 121). If you're focusing your time and energy on the destinations anyway, a smaller ship can be more relaxing to "come home" to. On the other hand, for all of the above reasons, cruises on the smallest ships are typically much more expensive. Small ships also physically can't offer the wide range of eateries and activities as the big vessels; intimate, yacht-like vessels have no room for a climbing wall or an ice rink. And finally, on a small ship, you may feel the motion of the sea more than on a big ship (though because of the stabilizers used by small ships, this difference isn't that dramatic).

Think carefully about which specific amenities are important to you, and find a cruise line that offers those things. Considerations include:

Food, both in terms of quality and variety (some cruise lines offer a wide range of specialty restaurants—explained on page 104; generally speaking, the bigger the ship, the more options are available);

Entertainment, such as a wide range of performers (musicians, dancers, and so on) in venues both big and small;

Athletic facilities, ranging from a running track around the deck, to a gym with equipment and classes, to swimming pools and hot tubs, to a simulated surf pool and bowling alley, to a spa with massage and other treatments;

Children's resources, including activities and spaces designed for teens and younger kids, and a babysitting service (for more on cruising with kids, see page 98);

Other features, including a good library, lecturers, special events, a large casino, wheelchair accessibility, and so on.

Some first-time cruisers worry they'll get bored while they're on board. Don't count on it. You'll be bombarded with entertainment options and a wide range of activities—particularly on a big ship.

Destinations

If you have a wish list of ports, use it as a starting point when shopping for a cruise. It's unlikely you'll find a cruise that visits every one of your desired destinations, but you can usually find one that comes close.

Most itineraries of a week or more include a day "at sea": no stops at ports—just you and the open sea. These are usually included for practical reasons. Most often a day at sea is needed to connect far-flung destinations where there's no worthwhile stop in between...but cruise lines also don't mind keeping passengers on board, hoping they'll spend more money. Because cruise ships generally travel at around 20 knots—that's only about 23 land miles per hour—they take a long time to cover big distances. For some cruise aficionados, days at sea are the highlight of the trip; for other passengers, they're a boring waste of time. If you enjoy time on the ship, try to maximize days at sea; if you're cruising mainly to sightsee on land, try to minimize them.

Time Spent in Port

If exploring European destinations is your priority, look carefully at how much time the ship spends in each port. Specific itinerary rundowns on cruise-line websites usually show the scheduled times of arrival and departure. Typical stops can range anywhere from 6 to 12 hours, with an average of around 8 or 9 hours. At the same port—or even on the same cruise line—the difference in port time from one cruise ship to another can vary by hours. On a recent cruise, I was on one of two ships pulling into Stavanger, Norway, at about the same time. Five hours later, I trudged back to my ship, noticing that the other ship had three more hours before embarkment...giving those passengers (unlike me) just enough time for a visit to the Lysefjord's renowned Pulpit Rock.

Most cruise lines want you on the ship as long as possible— the longer you're aboard, the more likely you are to spend money there (and for legal reasons, they can't open their lucrative casinos and duty-free shops until they're at sea).

In general, the more expensive Luxury- and Ultra-Luxury-class lines offer longer stays in port. However, even if you compare cheaper lines that are similar in price, times can vary. For example, Norwegian, Costa, and MSC tend to have shorter times in port, while Carnival and Royal Caribbean linger longer.

Repositioning Cruises

Ships that cruise in Europe are usually based in the Caribbean during the winter, so they need to cross the Atlantic Ocean each spring and fall. This journey, called a "repositioning cruise," includes a lengthy (5-7 days) stretch where the ship is entirely at sea. Also called a "crossing" or a "transatlantic crossing," these are most common in early April (to Europe), or late October and November (from Europe).

If you really want to escape from it all, and just can't get enough of all the shipboard activities, these long trips can be a dream come true; if you're a fidgety manic sightseer, they're a nightmare. Before committing to a repositioning cruise, consider taking a cruise with a day or two at sea just to be sure you really, really enjoy being on a ship that much. Several notes of warning: The seas can be rougher on transatlantic crossings than in the relatively protected waters closer to land; the weather will probably be cooler; and there are a couple of days in the middle of the voyage where most ships lose all satellite communication—no shipboard phones, Wi-Fi, or cable channels. While the officers are in touch with land in the event of emergencies, your own day-to-day contact with the outside world will disappear.

If you're considering a repositioning cruise, don't be misled by the sometimes astonishingly low sticker price. (These typically don't sell as well as the more destination-oriented cruises, so they're perennially on the push list.) You'll only need a one-way plane ticket between the US and Europe—but that may exceed the cost of a round-trip ticket (don't expect to simply pay half the round-trip price).

Cruise Lines

I don't pretend to be an expert on all the different cruise lines—the focus of this book is on the destinations rather than the ships. But this section is designed to give you an overview of options to get you started. (To dig deeper, consider some of the sources listed under "Gathering Information," at the beginning of this chapter.)

While nobody in the cruise industry formally recognizes different "classes" of companies, just about everybody acknowledges that cruise lines fall into four basic categories: **Mass-Market, Premium, Luxury** (sometimes called "**Upper Premium**"), and **Ultra-Luxury.** Of course, a few exceptions straddle these classifications and buck the trends, and some cruise lines are highly specialized—such as Disney Cruise Line (very kid-friendly and experience-focused) and Star Clippers (an authentic tall-ship experience with a mainsail that passengers can help hoist).

Most cruise lines are owned by the same handful of companies. For example, Carnival Corporation owns Carnival, Costa, Cunard, Holland America, Princess, Seabourn, and five other lines (representing about half of the worldwide cruise market). Royal Caribbean owns Celebrity and Azamara Club Cruises. Within these groups, each individual line may be, to varying degrees, operated by a different leadership, but they do fall under the same umbrella and tend to have similar philosophies and policies.

The Fine Print: In assembling the following information, I've focused exclusively on European itineraries. The average cost per day is for two people in the lowest-price, double-occupancy cabin (outside cabins have windows, inside cabins don't). Prices are based on Web-advertised rates offered during 2013; you may find even lower rates if your timing is right. Taxes, port fees, and additional expenses aren't included. The average hours in port are based on a selection of each line's sailings; your cruise could be different, so check carefully.

Mass-Market Lines

The cheapest cruise lines, these huge ships have a "resort-hotel-at-sea" ambience. Prices are enticingly low, but operators try to make up the difference with a lot of upselling on board (specialty restaurants, borderline-aggressive photographers, constant pressure to shop, and so on). The clientele is wildly diverse (including lots of families and young people) and, generally speaking, not particularly well-traveled; they tend to be more interested in being on vacation and enjoying the ship than in sightseeing. Mass-Market lines provide an affordable way to sample cruising.

Carnival

Contact Information: www.carnival.com, tel. 888-CARNIVAL

Number and Capacity of Ships: *Carnival Magic* or *Carnival Breeze* (their only ships currently sailing in Europe) each carry 3,690 passengers

Daily Cost of Cheapest Cabin: Approximately $200 for inside cabin/$230 outside cabin

Average Hours in Port: 11-12 hours

Description: Carnival has long had a reputation for a floating-frat-party "Fun Ship" ambience; the company is trying to tone down this image, though it's kept the discos and flashy decor. The line's European offerings are limited; it makes most of its money on short vacations to Alaska and the Caribbean. It tries to entice Europe-bound travelers with low prices and huge new ships—a great value, but for some, it's a "lowest common denominator" cruise experience.

Overall, expect a younger demographic with mostly Americans on board. There are plenty of youth programs, and lots of activities aimed at singles and young couples, such as a Caribbean-themed pub, an outdoor fitness area, and mini golf. The main dining room tends to serve American cuisine, but there are also plenty of specialty restaurants. Because these ships are so big, they are an attractive low-cost option, but that also means huge crowds—especially when tendering. However, the long times in port help make up for any time lost waiting in line.

Costa

Contact Information: www.costacruise.com, tel. 800-GO-COSTA

Number and Capacity of Ships: 15 ships, ranging from 800 to 3,780 passengers

Daily Cost of Cheapest Cabin: About $350 for inside cabin/$450 outside cabin

Average Hours in Port: 6-7 hours

Description: With frequent sales that can drive prices much lower than what's listed here, Costa is one of the cheapest lines for European cruises, and also has the largest fleet and the most seven-day cruises in the region. Although owned by Carnival, Costa proudly retains its Italian identity. Most of your fellow passengers will be Europeans, with large contingents of Italians,  French, Spanish, and Germans. (Only a small fraction of Costa passengers are from the US or Canada.) North American cruisers find both pros and cons about traveling with a mostly European crowd: While some relish the fact that it's truly European, others grow weary of the time-consuming multilingual announcements, and have reported "rude" behavior from some fellow passengers (some Europeans are not always polite about waiting in line). The ships' over-the-top, wildly colorful decor borders on gaudy—it can be either appealing or appalling, depending on your perspective. Onboard activities also have an Italian pizzazz, such as singing waiters or heated international bocce-ball tournaments. Outrageous ambience aside, the cruising experience itself is quite traditional (there's no open seating in the dining room, and formal nights are taken seriously). Dining options are limited to the main dining room (serving reliably well-executed, if not refined, Italian fare), huge buffets serving disappointing cafeteria fare, and sparse, overpriced, and underwhelming specialty restaurants.

Costa attracts a wide demographic—from twentysomethings to retirees—and you can expect families during the summer and school breaks. The short hours in port draw criticism—and Costa's shore excursion packages are relatively expensive.

The January 2012 *Costa Concordia* disaster took more than 30 lives and cast a pall over the cruise-ship industry. Costa's parent company, Carnival, has promised a complete investigation and increased focus on safety.

MSC Cruises

Contact Information: www.msccruises.com, tel. 877-655-4655
Number and Capacity of Ships: 11 ships, each carrying 1,000-3,275 passengers
Daily Cost of Cheapest Cabin: Roughly $300 for inside cabin/$335 outside cabin
Average Hours in Port: 6 hours
Description: "Beautiful. Passionate. Italian." MSC's slogan sums it up. Even more so than the similar Costa (described above), this low-priced, Italian-owned company caters mostly to Europeans—only about 5 percent of the passengers on their European cruises are from the US or Canada. This is a plus if you want to escape America entirely on your vacation, but can come with some language-barrier and culture-shock issues. Since children ride free, summer and school breaks tend to be dominated by families, while at other times passengers are mostly retirees.

The basic price is often a borderline-outrageous bargain (deep discounts are common), but MSC charges for amenities that are

free on many other cruise lines—such as basic drinks, room service, and snacks. In the dining room, you even have to pay for tap water. MSC has shorter hours in port than most cruise lines, and their shore excursions have a heightened emphasis on shopping. The food and entertainment are average; your choices at the breakfast and lunch buffets are same for the entire cruise. Keep your expectations low—as one passenger noted, "It's not really a cruise—just a bus tour that happens on a nice boat."

Norwegian Cruise Line (NCL)

Contact Information: www.ncl.com, tel. 866-234-7350
Number and Capacity of Ships: 11 ships, ranging from 2,000 to 4,100 passengers
Daily Cost of Cheapest Cabin: Approximately $280 for inside cabin/$320 outside cabin
Average Hours in Port: 8-9 hours

Description: Norwegian was an industry leader in the now-wide-spread trend toward flexibility, and is known for its "Freestyle Cruising" approach. "Whatever" is the big word here (as in, "You're free to do...whatever"). For example, their ships typically have no assigned seatings for meals (though reservations are encouraged), and offer the widest range of specialty restaurants, which can include French, Italian, Mexican, sushi, steakhouse, Japanese teppanyaki, and more. Norwegian also has a particularly wide range of cabin categories, from very basic inside cabins to top-of-the-line, sprawling suites that rival the Luxury lines' offerings.

Norwegian has a Las Vegas-style glitz. On the newer ships, such as the gigantic, 4,100-passenger, much-publicized *Norwegian Epic,* the entertainment is ramped up, with world-class shows—such as Blue Man Group and Cirque du Soleil—requiring advance ticket purchase. Their vessels tend to be brightly decorated—bold murals curl across the prows of their ships, and the public areas are colorful (some might say garish or even tacky). This approach, coupled with relatively low prices, draws a wide range of passengers: singles and families, young and old, American and European, middle-class and wealthy.

Onboard amenities cater to this passenger diversity; along with all of the usual services, some ships have climbing walls and bowling alleys. The crew is also demographically diverse, and the service is acceptable, but not as doting as on some cruise lines, making some passengers feel anonymous. Education and enrichment activities are a low priority—most lectures are designed to sell you something (excursions, artwork, and so on), rather than prepare you for the port.

Royal Caribbean International

Contact Information: www.royalcaribbean.com, tel. 866-562-7625

Number and Capacity of Ships: 22 ships, ranging from 1,800 to 5,400 passengers

Daily Cost of Cheapest Cabin: Around $240 for inside cabin/$300 outside cabin

Average Hours in Port: 10 hours

Description: Royal Caribbean is the world's second-largest cruise line (after Carnival). Similar to Carnival and Norwegian, but a step up in both cost and (in their mind, at least) amenities, Royal

Caribbean edges toward the Premium category.

Offering an all-around quintessential cruising experience, Royal Caribbean attracts first-time cruisers. The majority are from the US and Canada. The line likes to think of itself as catering to a more youthful demographic: couples and singles in their 30s to 50s on shorter cruises; 50 and up on cruises longer than seven nights. With longer hours in port and onboard fitness facilities (every ship has a rock-climbing wall, some have water parks and mini golf), they try to serve more active travelers.

The food on board is American cuisine, and its entertainment style matches other cruise lines in this category—expect Vegas-style shows and passenger-participation games. Even though some of its ships are positively gigantic, Royal Caribbean, which prides itself on service, delivers; most of its passengers feel well-treated.

Premium Lines

A step up from the Mass-Market lines (described earlier) both in price and in elegance, most Premium lines evoke the "luxury cruises" of yore. The ships can be nearly as big as the Mass-Market options, but are designed to feel more intimate. The upselling is still there, but it's more restrained, and the clientele tends to be generally older, better-traveled, and more interested in sightseeing. While the Mass-Market lines can sometimes feel like a cattle call, Premium lines ratchet up the focus on service, going out of their way to pamper their guests.

Celebrity

Contact Information: www.celebritycruises.com, tel. 800-647-2251

Number and Capacity of Ships: 10 ships, ranging from 1,800 to 2,850 passengers

Daily Cost of Cheapest Cabin: About $370 for inside cabin/$425 outside cabin

Average Hours in Port: 10-11 hours

Description: Originally a Greek company, Celebrity was bought by Royal Caribbean in 1997 and operates as its upscale sister cruise line. (The "X" on the smokestack is the Greek letter "chi," which stands for Chandris—the founder's family name.) Celebrity distinguishes itself from the other Premium category lines with bigger ships and a slightly younger demographic. Celebrity likes to point out that its larger ships have more activities and restaurants than the smaller Premium (or even Luxury category) ships. Most of its passengers are from the US or Canada, and it's reportedly popular with baby boomers, seniors, gay cruisers, and honeymooners. Among the Premium lines, Celebrity offers some of the best amenities for kids (aside from Disney, of course).

Celebrity's smallest stateroom is quite spacious compared with those on other lines in this category. On its European cruises, the main dining room cuisine seems more European than American (with some high-end options—a plus for many travelers), but there are plenty of specialty restaurants, ranging from Asian-fusion to a steakhouse. Most ships are decorated with a mod touch—with all the bright lights and offbeat art, you might feel like you're in Miami Beach. Adding to the whimsy, some ships even come with a real grass lawn on the top deck. Its service consistently gets high marks, and the onboard diversions include the usual spas, enrichment lectures, Broadway revues, cabarets, discos, theme parties, and casinos.

Cunard Line

Contact Information: www.cunard.com, tel. 800-728-6273
Number and Capacity of Ships: *Queen Elizabeth* carries 2,092 passengers; *Queen Victoria* carries 2,014.
Daily Cost of Cheapest Cabin: Roughly $400 for inside cabin/$540 outside cabin
Average Hours in Port: 10 hours
Description: Cunard Line plays to its long, historic tradition and caters to an old-fashioned, well-traveled, and well-to-do clientele in their 50s and older. Passengers on their European itineraries tend to be mostly British, along with some Americans and other Europeans. Although the line is suitable for families (kids' programs are staffed by trained British nannies), it's not seriously family-friendly. This line features large ships and offers a pleasantly elegant experience with a British bent—you can even have afternoon tea or enjoy bangers and mash in a pub.

About a sixth of the passengers book suites and have access to specialty restaurants—a remnant of the traditional class distinctions in jolly olde England. The entertainment and lecture programs tend to be more "distinguished"; there's a good library; and activities include ballroom dancing, croquet, tennis, fencing, and lawn bowling. Each ship has a viewable collection of historic Cunard artifacts. The famously refined Cunard dress code seems to be more of a suggestion these days, as many show up in relatively casual dress at formal dining events. Passengers report mixed reviews—some feel that the experience doesn't quite live up to the line's legacy.

Disney Cruise Line

Contact Information: www.disneycruise.com, tel. 800-951-3532
Number and Capacity of Ships: 3 ships, ranging from 2,700 to 4,000 passengers
Daily Cost of Cheapest Cabin: Approximately $385 for inside

cabin/$465 outside cabin

Average Hours in Port: 10-11 hours

Description: Although Disney doesn't run European cruises every year, it does occasionally dip into this market (check their website). Disney is the gold standard for family cruise vacations. The majority of the passengers are families and multigenerational—expect at least one-third of the passengers to be kids. There'll be plenty of Disney flicks, G-rated floor shows, and mouse ears wherever you turn. Like its amusement parks, Disney's ships have high standards for service and cleanliness. The food is kid-friendly, but the ships also have a high-end Italian restaurant for a break for parents. While your kids will never be bored, there are a few adult diversions as well (including an adults-only swimming pool)—but no casino. Disney doesn't do a lot of cruising in this region, but it may be the best option if you're taking along your kids or grandkids. Be warned: Parents who think a little Disney goes a long way might overdose on this line.

Holland America Line (HAL)

Contact Information: www.hollandamerica.com, tel. 877-932-4259

Number and Capacity of Ships: 15 ships, ranging from 835 to 2,100 passengers

Daily Cost of Cheapest Cabin: Around $290 for inside cabin/$325 outside cabin

Average Hours in Port: 9-10 hours

Description: Holland America, with a history dating back to 1873 (it once carried immigrants to the New World), prides itself on tradition. Generally, this line has one of the most elderly clienteles in the business, though they're trying to promote their cruises to a wider demographic (with some success). Cruisers appreciate the line's delicate balance between a luxury and a casual vacation—it's formal, but not *too* formal.

Ship decor emphasizes a connection to the line's nautical past, with lots of wood trim and white railings; you might feel like you're on an oversized yacht at times. That's intentional: When building their biggest ships, Holland America designers planned public spaces to create the illusion that passengers are on a smaller vessel (for example, hallways bend every so often so you can't see all the way to the far end). This line also has high service standards; they operate training academies in Indonesia and the Philippines, where virtually all of their crew hails from. These stewards are trained to be good-natured and to make their guests feel special. Dining options on board tend to be limited; there isn't a wide range of specialty restaurants.

Holland America takes seriously the task of educating their passengers about the ports; most ships have a "Travel Guide" who lectures on each destination and is available for questions, and some excursions—designated "Cruise with Purpose"—are designed to promote a more meaningful, participatory connection with the destinations (though these are relatively rare in Europe).

Princess

Contact Information: www.princess.com, tel. 800-774-6237
Number and Capacity of Ships: 17 ships, ranging from 680 to 3,080 passengers
Daily Cost of Cheapest Cabin: About $350 for inside cabin/$400 outside cabin
Average Hours in Port: 9-10 hours
Description: Princess appeals to everyone from solo travelers to families, with most passengers over 50. Because their market

reach is so huge, expect many repeat cruisers enjoying their mainstream cruise experience. While Princess has long been considered a Premium-category line, many cruise insiders suggest that the line has been lowering its prices—and, many say, its standards—so these days it effectively straddles the Premium and Mass-Market categories. Still, Princess passengers tend to be very loyal.

Princess got a big boost when the 1970s *Love Boat* TV series featured two Princess ships. Those "love boats" have now been retired, and the Princess fleet is one of the most modern in the industry—half have been launched in the last 10 years. It's known for introducing innovative features such as a giant video screen above the main swimming pool showing movies and sports all day...and into the night. Still, while the ships are new, the overall experience is traditional compared with some of the bold and brash Mass-Market lines. The line has the usual activities, such as trivia contests, galley tours, art auctions, and middle-of-the-road musical revues—though some passengers report that they found fewer activities and diversions on Princess ships than they expected for vessels of this size. While its service gets raves and the food is fine, there is some repetition in the main dining room—expect the same dessert choices each night.

Luxury Lines

While some purists (who reserve the "Luxury" label for something really top-class) prefer to call this category "Upper Premium," it's certainly a notch above the lines listed previously. Luxury lines typically use smaller ships, offer better food and service, command high prices, and have a more exclusive clientele. You get what you pay for—this is a more dignified experience, with longer days in port and less emphasis on selling you extras. In general, while Luxury ships are very comfortable, the cruise is more focused on the destinations than the ship.

Once you're in this price range, you'll find that the various lines are variations on a theme (though there are a few notable exceptions, such as the unique casual-sailboat ambience of Windstar, or the opportunity to actually rig the sails on Star Clippers). It can be hard to distinguish among the lines; within the Luxury category, passengers tend to go with a cruise line recommended to them by a friend.

Note: The Luxury and Ultra-Luxury lines (described later) generally run smaller ships, which can visit out-of-the-way ports that larger cruise ships can't. However, remember the drawbacks of smaller ships: fewer onboard activities, a narrower range of restaurants, and—for some travelers prone to seasickness—a slightly rougher ride.

Azamara Club Cruises

Contact Information: www.azamaraclubcruises.com, tel. 877-999-9553

Number and Capacity of Ships: *Journey* and *Quest* each carry 694 passengers.

Daily Cost of Cheapest Cabin: Approximately $620 for inside cabin/$700 outside cabin

Average Hours in Port: 11-12 hours

Description: Azamara Club Cruises attracts a moderately affluent, educated, and active middle-age to retirement-age traveler. This relatively new line (they were revamped and rebranded in 2010) is still finding its way in the Luxury cruise market. Some passengers call Azamara a "work in progress," but it seems to be developing a successful formula. Their stated aim is to allow their customers to immerse themselves in each destination. Azamara passengers want value and are interested in more unusual destinations and longer port stays—their itineraries include more

frequent overnight stops. The clientele is mainly American and British, along with a few Germans and other nationalities. There are no programs or facilities for children.

The atmosphere is casual, with open seating at meals and a focus on good food and wine; the cuisine is Mediterranean-influenced with other international dishes and healthy options. With a high crew-to-passenger ratio, the service is attentive. Live entertainment is more limited than on larger ships; the types of programs encourage meeting other guests, which contributes to a cozier, more social experience. Cabins and bathrooms can be small, but are well laid-out. The company's good-value, all-inclusive pricing covers many amenities you'd pay extra for on other lines, such as good house wine, specialty coffees, bottled water and sodas, basic gratuities (for cabin stewards, bar, and dining), self-service laundry, and shuttle buses in some ports.

Oceania Cruises

Contact Information: www.oceaniacruises.com, tel. 800-531-5619
Number and Capacity of Ships: *Marina* and *Riviera* each carry 1,250 passengers; *Insignia, Nautica,* and *Regatta* each carry 684.
Daily Cost of Cheapest Cabin: Roughly $750 for inside cabin/$900 outside cabin
Average Hours in Port: 9-10 hours
Description: Oceania Cruises appeals to well-traveled, well-heeled baby boomers and older retirees who want fine cuisine, excellent service, and a destination-oriented experience—toeing the fine line between upscale and snooty. The atmosphere is casually sophisticated—tastefully understated elegance. Although the line does not discourage children, kids' amenities (and young passengers) are sparse. Oceania's itineraries tend to be on the longer side; European sailings under 10 days are rare.

Staterooms are particularly well-equipped, reminiscent of stylish boutique hotels, with a cozy and intimate atmosphere. On the smaller ships, the staterooms and bathrooms are smaller than on most Luxury ships—but with great beds and fine linens. Oceania touts its cuisine; some of their menus were designed by celebrity chef Jacques Pépin, and their ships have a variety of specialty restaurants—French, Italian, steakhouse, and so on—for no extra charge (but reserve ahead). The larger ships have a culinary arts center with hands-on workshops (for a fee).

Oceania is noted for courting experienced crew members and for low crew turnover. The ships offer extensive onboard libraries, but relatively few organized activities, making these cruises best for those who can entertain themselves (or who make the most of time in port). While a few extras (such as specialty coffee drinks) are included, others are still à la carte; these, and Oceania's excursions, are a bit pricier than average.

Star Clippers

Contact Information: www.starclippers.com, tel. 800-442-0551

Number and Capacity of Ships: *Royal Clipper* carries 227 passengers; *Star Clipper* and *Star Flyer* each carry 170.

Daily Cost of Cheapest Cabin: Around $600 for inside cabin/$750 outside cabin

Average Hours in Port: 8-9 hours

Description: Star Clippers takes its sailing heritage very seriously, and its three ships are among the world's largest and tallest sailing vessels (actual "tall ships," with diesel engines for backup power). While the Windstar ships (described next) also have sails, those are mostly for show—Star Clippers' square-riggers are real sailboats. Passengers with nautical know-how are invited to pitch in when sails are hoisted or lowered. If the weather is right during the trip, you can even climb the main mast up to the crow's nest (wearing a safety harness, of course). There's a goose-bump-inducing ceremony every time you leave port: The crew raises the sails while haunting music plays over the loudspeakers.

With its sailing focus, Star Clippers draws more active, adventurous customers, ranging in age from 30s to 70s, who don't need to be pampered. Passengers are primarily Europeans (one recent sailing had passengers from 38 countries), and almost 60 percent are repeat customers. People who choose Star Clippers love the simple life on board a sailboat; enjoy a casual, easygoing cruise experience; and don't want the nightclubs and casinos offered by mainstream cruise lines. Kids are welcome, but there are no children's programs, counselors, or video-game parlors. Given the constraints of a small vessel, the cabins are not as big or luxurious as you might expect at this price range (for example, none have verandas).

The food, while adequate, comes in modest (European-size) portions. There's open seating in the dining room, the dress code is casual, and there are no rigid schedules. Activities include beach barbecues, crab races, scavenger hunts, talent nights, fashion shows, and performances by local musicians. You'll also have access to complimentary water activities, including snorkeling, kayaking, and sailing.

Windstar Cruises

Contact Information: www.windstarcruises.com, tel. 888-964-7213

Number and Capacity of Ships: *Wind Surf* carries 312 passengers; *Wind Star* and *Wind Spirit* each carry 148.

CHOOSING A CRUISE

Daily Cost of Cheapest Cabin: About $950 (all are outside cabins)
Average Hours in Port: 10 hours
Description: Windstar's gimmick is its sails—each of its ships has four big, functional sails that unfurl dramatically each time the ship leaves port. (While the sails are capable of powering the ship in strong winds, they're more decorative than practical—although they do reduce the amount of fuel used by the engines.) This line provides an enticing bridge between the more rough-around-the-edges sailboat experience of Star Clippers (described above) and the comforts of mainstream lines. For many, it's an ideal combination—the romance of sails plus the pampering of a Luxury cruise. For this price range, it has a relatively casual atmosphere, with no formal nights.

Windstar passengers are professionals and experienced independent-minded travelers who range in age from 40s to 70s. First-

time cruisers, honeymooners, and anniversary celebrants are enticed by Windstar's unique approach. The smaller ships favor more-focused itineraries and smaller ports, with generous time ashore. Passengers are more "travelers" than "cruisers"—they're here to spend as much time as possible exploring the port towns.

The small vessels also mean fewer on-ship activities. The casino and swimming pool are minuscule, the smaller ships have only one specialty restaurant, and nightlife is virtually nonexistent. However, the lounge hosts talented musicians, and each stateroom has a DVD player (there's a free DVD library). On some days when the ship is tendered, they lower a platform from the stern, allowing passengers to enjoy water-sports activities right off the back of the vessel. The food is high-quality, and there's a barbecue night on the open deck. Windstar also touts its green-ness (thanks to those sails) and its rare open-bridge policy, whereby passengers can visit the bridge during certain times to see the instruments and chat with the captain and officers.

Ultra-Luxury

You'll pay top dollar for these cruises, but get an elite experience in return. The basic features of the previously described Luxury cruises apply to this category as well: small ships (with the exception of Crystal), upscale clientele, a classier atmosphere, less emphasis on onboard activities, and a more destination-focused experience. There's less focus on selling you extras—at these prices, you can expect more and more extras to be included (ranging from alcoholic drinks to shore excursions).

Crystal Cruises

Contact Information: www.crystalcruises.com, tel. 888-722-0021
Number and Capacity of Ships: *Serenity* carries 1,070 passengers;
    Symphony carries 922 passengers.
Daily Cost of Cheapest Cabin: Approximately $1,175 (suites only)
Average Hours in Port: 10 hours
Description: While most Luxury and Ultra-Luxury lines have smaller ships, Crystal Cruises distinguishes itself by operating larger ships, closer in size to the less-expensive categories. This allows it to offer more big-ship activities and amenities, while still fostering a genteel, upper-crust ambience (which some may consider "stuffy"). Crystal attracts a retired, well-traveled, well-heeled crowd (although there are also a fair number of people under 50). Approximately 75 percent of the travelers are from the US and Canada, and the rest are mainly British. There are basic programs for children (most kids seem to come with multigenerational family groups) that are better than those on most Ultra-Luxury lines.

The food and the service are both well-regarded (and their seafood comes from sustainable and fair-trade sources). Their acclaimed enrichment programs are noted for having a wide range of minicourses in everything from foreign languages to computer skills, and excursions include opportunities for passengers to participate in a local volunteering effort.

Note: Crystal Cruises are sold exclusively through travel agents.

Regent Seven Seas Cruises (RSSC)

Contact Information: www.rssc.com, tel. 877-505-5370
Number and Capacity of Ships: *Voyager* and *Mariner* each carry
    700 passengers.
Daily Cost of Cheapest Cabin: Roughly $1,125 (suites only)
Average Hours in Port: 10-11 hours
Description: Regent Seven Seas Cruises appeal to well-educated, sophisticated, and affluent travelers—generally from mid-40s to retirees—looking for a destination-oriented experience. Their exclusive, clubby, understatedly elegant atmosphere attracts many repeat cruisers (the *Voyager* seems especially popular). Most passengers are from North America, with the rest from Great Britain, New Zealand, and Australia. The line welcomes families during summer and school breaks, when it offers a children's program; the rest of the year, there's little to occupy kids.

Their "ultra-inclusive" prices are, indeed, among the most inclusive in the industry, covering premium soft drinks, house wines, tips, ground transfers, round-trip airfare from the US, one night's pre-cruise hotel stay, and unlimited excursions. The ships are known for their spacious, elegantly appointed suites (all with verandas). This line has some of the industry's highest space-per-guest and crew member-per-guest ratios, and customers report outstanding service. The French-based cuisine has an international flair, and also attempts to mix in local fare from the ships' ports of call. Passengers tend to be independent-minded and enjoy making their own plans, rather than wanting to be entertained by the cruise line (the entertainment is low-key, and notably, there is no onboard photography service). The crew tries to incorporate the ship's destinations into the entertainment, events, and lectures. Excursions include private tours, strenuous walking tours, and some soft-adventure offerings such as kayaking.

Seabourn Cruise Line

Contact Information: www.seabourn.com, tel. 866-755-5619
Number and Capacity of Ships: *Odyssey, Sojourn,* and *Quest* each carry 450 passengers; *Pride, Spirit,* and *Legend* each carry 208.
Daily Cost of Cheapest Cabin: About $950 (suites only)
Average Hours in Port: 10 hours
Description: Seabourn Cruise Line attracts affluent, well-traveled couples in their late 40s to late 60s and older, who are not necessarily cruise aficionados but are accustomed to the "best of the best." Deep down, Seabourn passengers want to be on a yacht, but don't mind sharing it with other upper-class travelers—who, as the line brags, are "both interesting and interested." The focus is on exploring more exotic destinations rather than just relaxing on the ship. Most passengers are American, and the onboard atmosphere is classically elegant. Kids are present in summer and during school vacations, usually with multigenerational groups.

These ships feel like private clubs, with pampering as a priority. The extremely high crew member-to-guest ratio is about 1:1, and the crew addresses guests by name. Activities are designed for socializing with other passengers. Most of the ships offer a stern platform for swimming and kayaking right off the back of the ship. The line's all-inclusive pricing includes freebies like a welcome bottle of champagne, an in-suite bar (with full bottles of your preselected booze), and nearly all drinks, including decent wines at mealtime (you pay extra only for premium brands). Also included are tips, some excursions, poolside mini-massages, and activities such as exercise classes and wine-tasting seminars.

SeaDream Yacht Club

Contact Information: www.seadream.com, tel. 800-707-4911

Number and Capacity of Ships: *SeaDream I* and *SeaDream II* each carry 110 passengers.

Daily Cost of Cheapest Cabin: Around $1,210

Average Hours in Port: 12+ hours

Description: SeaDream's tiny, intimate ships—the smallest of all those described here—are essentially chic, Ultra-Luxury mega-yachts. This line appeals to active travelers who are well-heeled and well-traveled, ranging in age from 40s to 70s (the shorter itineraries appeal to those still working). Passengers are primarily from North America and Europe, the atmosphere is laid-back, and the dress code is country-club casual (with no formal nights). There are no kids' facilities or services on board.

The attentive crew anticipates guests' needs without fawning. The unstructured environment is best for independent-minded passengers, as you're pretty much on your own for entertainment. The line is perfect for those who want to relax on deck and be outdoors as much as possible. In fact, a unique—and extremely popular—activity is sleeping out under the stars on double loungers. Itineraries include overnight stays in port (allowing guests the option to experience local nightlife) and are somewhat flexible, allowing the captain to linger longer in a port or depart early. Rather than hiring local guides for all their shore excursions, some trips are led by the ship's officers or other crew members. (Note that organized excursions may be canceled if the quota isn't reached, which can happen, given the small number of passengers.) The ships have a sports platform off the stern with water-sports toys such as kayaks and water skis, and there's a fleet of mountain bikes for exploring the destinations. Prices include decent house wines, cocktails, tips, water-sports equipment, DVDs, and shore excursions.

Silversea Cruises

Contact Information: www.silversea.com, tel. 877-276-6816

Number and Capacity of Ships: *Silver Spirit* carries 540 passengers; *Silver Whisper* carries 382; *Silver Wind* and *Silver Cloud* each carry 296.

Daily Cost of Cheapest Cabin: Approximately $1,320 (suites only)

Average Hours in Port: 11 hours

Description: The Italian-owned, Monaco-based Silversea Cruises is popular with well-educated, well-traveled, upper-crust cruisers, generally ranging in age from late 40s to 80s (with many in their 70s). Most passengers are accustomed to the finest and are very discriminating. The ships' Art Deco design lends an elegant 1930s ambience, and the atmosphere on board is clubby. Half of their clientele is from North America, with the other half predominantly from the UK, Europe, and Australia. There are no organized children's programs, and you'll see few children on board.

The cuisine is considered very good, and the service excellent; the spacious suites even have an assigned butler. Partly as a function of the ships' small size and fewer passengers, the events and entertainment are low-key.

BOOKING A CRUISE

Once you've narrowed down your cruise-line options, it's time to get serious about booking. This chapter covers where, when, and how to book your cruise, including pointers on cruise pricing, cabin assignments, trip insurance, pre- and post-cruise plans, and other considerations.

Where to Book a Cruise

While plane tickets, rental cars, hotels, and most other aspects of travel have gradually migrated to do-it-yourself, cruises are the one form of travel that is still booked predominantly through a travel agent. In fact, 90 percent of cruises are booked through travel agencies.

While it's possible to book a cruise directly with the cruise line, most lines actually prefer that you go through an intermediary. That's because their customers are rarely just booking a cruise—while they're at it, they want to look into airfares, trip insurance, maybe some hotels at either end of the cruise, and so on. That's beyond the scope of what cruise lines want to sell—their booking offices mainly take orders, they don't advise—so they reduce their overhead by letting travel agents do all that hard work (and hand-holding).

It can also be cheaper to book through a travel agent. Some cruise lines discount fares that are sold through their preferred agents; because they've built up relationships with these agents over the years, they don't want to undersell them. In other cases, the travel agency reserves a block of cabins to secure the lowest possible price, and then passes the savings on to their customers.

There are, generally speaking, two different types of cruise-sales agencies: your neighborhood travel agent, where you can get in-person advice; or a giant company that sells most of its inventory online or by phone. Because cruise prices vary based on volume, a big agency can usually undersell a small one. Big agencies are also more likely to offer incentives (such as onboard credit or cabin upgrades) to sweeten the pot. However, some small agencies belong to a consortium that gives them as much collective clout as a big agency. And some travelers figure the intangible value of personal service they get at a small agency is worth the possibility of paying a little extra. (Although most travel agents don't charge a fee, their commission is built into the cruise price.)

The big cruise agencies often have websites where you can easily shop around for the best price. These include www.vacations togo.com, www.cruisecompete.com, and www.crucon.com. One site, www.cayole.com, tries to predict when prices for a particular departure may be lowest—giving you advice about how soon you should book.

I use the big websites to do some comparison-shopping. But—call me old-fashioned—when it comes time to book, I prefer to sit down with a travel agent to make my plans in person. Ideally, find a well-regarded travel agent in your community who knows cruising and will give you the personal attention you need to sort through your options. Tell them the deals you've seen online, and ask if they can match or beat them. A good travel agent knows how to look at your whole travel picture (airfare, hotels, and so on), not just the cruise component. And they can advise you about "insider" information, such as how to select the right cabin. Keep in mind that if you do solicit the advice of a travel agent, you should book the cruise through them—that's the only way they'll get their hard-earned commission. Once you've booked your cruise, you can arrange airfare through your travel agent, or you may choose to do that part on your own; for hotels, I always book direct.

When to Book a Cruise

Most cruise lines post their schedules a year or more in advance. A specific departure is called a "sailing." If you want to cruise in the summertime, and your plans are very specific (for example, you have your heart set on a certain sailing, or a particular cabin setup, such as adjoining staterooms), it's best to begin looking the preceding November. (For cruises in shoulder season—spring and fall—you may have a little more time to shop around.) Because the cruise lines want to fill up their ships as fast as possible, they typically offer early-booking discounts if you buy your cruise well in advance (at least 6-12 months, depending on the company).

Meanwhile, the most popular time of year to book a cruise is during the first few weeks of January. Dubbed "wave season" by

Sample Pretrip Timeline

While this can vary, here's a general timeline for what to do and when—but be sure to carefully confirm with your specific cruise line.

What to Do	Time Before Departure
Book cruise and pay initial deposit	8-10 months (for best selection)
Buy trip insurance, if desired	At time of booking (if through cruise line); within about 2 weeks of booking (if through a third party)
Full payment due	45-60 days
Online check-in	Between booking and full payment (check with cruise line)
Fly to meet your cruise	1-2 days ahead (remember you lose one day when flying from the US to Europe)

industry insiders, this is when a third of all cruises are booked. If you wait until this time, you'll be competing with other travelers for the deals. The sooner you book, the more likely you are to have your choice of sailing and cabin type—and potentially an even better price.

If a cruise still has several cabins available 90 days before departure, they're likely to put them on sale—but don't count on it. People tend to think the longer they wait, the more likely it is they'll find a sale. But this isn't always the case. Last-minute sales aren't as likely for Europe as they are for some other destinations, such as the Caribbean. Unlike the Caribbean market, the European market has a much shorter season and fewer ships, which means fewer beds to fill...and fewer deals to fill them. And even if you do find a last-minute deal, keep in mind that last-minute airfares to Europe can be that much more expensive.

If you're unsure of when to book, consult your travel agent.

How to Book a Cruise

Once you find the cruise you want, your travel agent may be able to hold it for you for a day or two while you think it over. When you've decided, you'll secure your passage on the cruise by paying a deposit. While this varies by cruise line, it averages about $500 per person (this becomes nonrefundable after a specified date, sometimes immediately—ask when you book). No matter how far ahead you book, you generally won't have to pay the balance until

45-60 days before departure. After this point, cancellation comes at a heftier price; as the departure date approaches, your cruise becomes effectively nonrefundable. In general, read the fine print of your cruise ticket carefully.

Cruise Pricing

Like cars or plane tickets, cruises are priced very flexibly. Some cruise lines don't even bother listing prices in their brochures—they just send customers to the Web. In general, for a Mass-Market cruise, you'll rarely pay the list price. Higher-end cruises are less likely to be discounted.

The main factor that determines the actual cost of a cruise is demand (that is, the popularity of the date, destination, and specific ship), but other factors also play a role.

Cruise lines and travel agencies use **sales and incentives** to entice new customers. With the recent proliferation of megaships, there are plenty of cabins to fill, and cruise industry insiders rigidly follow the mantra, "Empty beds are not tolerated!" The obvious approach to filling up a slow-selling cruise is to reduce prices. But they may also offer "onboard credit," which can be applied to your expenses on the ship (such as tips, alcoholic drinks, or excursions). In other cases, they may automatically upgrade your stateroom ("Pay for Category C, and get a Category B cabin for no extra charge!"). To further entice you, they might even throw in a special cocktail reception with the captain, or a night or two at a hotel at either end of your cruise. Your travel agent should be aware of these sales; you can also look online, or—if you're a fan of a particular cruise line—sign up to get their email offers.

Some cruise lines offer **discounts** for seniors (including AARP members), AAA members, firefighters, military, union workers, teachers, those in the travel industry, employees of certain corporations, and so on. It never hurts to ask.

Keep in mind that you'll pay a premium for **novelty.** It usually costs more to go on the cruise line's newest, most loudly advertised vessel. If you go on a ship that's just a few years older—with most of the same amenities—you'll likely pay less.

If you are a **repeat cruiser**—or think you may become one—sign up for the cruise line's "frequent cruiser" program. Like the airlines' mileage-rewards programs, these offer incentives, upgrades, and access to special deals.

No matter who you book your cruise through, use a **credit card** to give yourself a measure of consumer protection. A credit-card company can be a strong ally in resolving disputes.

If the **price drops after you book** your cruise, try asking for a new price. A good time to ask is just before or when you make the final payment. They don't have all your money yet and tend to be more eager to look for specials that will reduce your bottom line. You'll often be given a discount, or possibly an upgrade.

Taxes, Port Fees, and Other Hidden Charges

The advertised price for your cruise isn't all you'll pay. All the miscellaneous taxes, fees, and other expenses that the ship incurs in port are divvied up and passed on to passengers, under the category **"taxes and port fees."** While this can vary dramatically from port to port, it'll run you a few hundred dollars per person (for example, around $200 for a 7-day cruise, or around $300 for a 12-day cruise). These amounts are not locked in at the time you book; if a port increases its fees, you'll pay the difference.

Like airlines, cruise lines reserve the right to tack on a **"fuel surcharge"** in the event that the price of oil goes over a certain amount per barrel. This can be added onto your bill even after you book the cruise.

Once you're on the cruise, most lines automatically levy an **"auto-tip"** of around $10-12/day per person (which you can adjust upward or downward once on board). While this won't be included in your up-front cruise cost, you should budget for it. Many cruisers also choose to give excellent crew members an additional cash tip. For more details on tipping, see page 84.

Special Considerations

Families, singles, groups, people celebrating milestones, and those with limited mobility are all special in my book.

If you're traveling with a family, note that fares for **kids** tend to be more expensive during spring break and summertime, when they're out of school and demand is high; it can be cheaper to bring them off-season. Adjoining staterooms (also called "connecting" rooms) that share an inside door tend to book up early, particularly in the summertime. If those are sold out, consider an inside cabin across from an outside cabin. Some rooms have fold-down bunk beds (or "upper berths"), so a family of three or four can cram into one room (each passenger after the second pays a reduced fare)— but the tight quarters, already cramped for two people, can be challenging for the whole clan. Like connecting staterooms, these triple or quad cabins sell out early. Note that women who are more than six months **pregnant**—and **babies** who are younger than six months—are typically not allowed on a cruise.

Single cabins are rare on cruise ships; almost all staterooms are designed with couples in mind. Therefore, cruise rates are quoted per person, based on double occupancy. If you're traveling solo, you'll usually have to pay a "single supplement." This can range from reasonable (an additional 10 percent of the per-person double rate) to exorbitant ("100 percent" of the double rate—in other words, paying as much as two people would). On average, figure paying about 50 percent above the per-person double rate for your own single cabin. Sometimes it's possible to avoid the single supplement by volunteering to be assigned a random roommate by the cruise line, but this option is increasingly rare.

Groups taking eight or more cabins may be eligible for discounts if they're booked together—ask. The discounts often don't add up to much, but you may wrangle a shipboard credit or a private cocktail party.

If you'll be celebrating a **special occasion**—such as a birthday or anniversary—on board, mention it when you book. You may get a special bonus, such as a fancy dessert or cocktails with the captain.

If you have **limited mobility,** cruising can be a good way to go—but not all cruise lines are created equal. Some ships are wheelchair-accessible, including fully adapted cabins; others (especially small vessels) may not even have an elevator. When shopping for your cruise, ask the cruise line about the features you'll need, and be very specific. Unfortunately, once you reach port, all bets are off. While some cities are impressively accessible, others (especially smaller towns) may have fewer elevators than the ship you arrived on. The creaky and cobbled Old World doesn't accommodate wheelchairs or walkers very well. Taking a shore excursion can be a good way to see a place with minimum effort; cruise lines can typically inform you of the specific amount of walking and stairs you'll need to tackle for each excursion.

Cabin Classes

Each cruise ship has a variety of staterooms. In some cases, it can be a pretty narrow distinction ("Category A" and the marginally smaller "Category B"). On other ships, it can be the difference between a "Class 1" suite with a private balcony and a "Class 10" windowless bunk-bed closet below the waterline. On its website, each cruise line explains the specific breakdown of its various categories, along with the amenities in each one. In general, the highest demand is for the top-end and bottom-end cabins. Also, as verandas are increasingly popular, the most affordable rooms with verandas are often the first fares to sell out.

You'll see these terms:

Inside/Interior: An inside cabin has no external windows (though there's often a faux-porthole to at least create the illusion of outside light). While these terrify claustrophobes, inside cabins offer a great value that tempts budget travelers. And many cruisers figure that with a giant ship to explore—not to mention Europe at your doorstep each morning—there's not much point hanging out in your room anyway.

Outside: With a window to the sea, an outside cabin costs more—but for some travelers, it's worth the splurge to be able to see the world go by. But be aware that you're rarely able to open those windows (for that, you need a veranda—see next). If your view is blocked (by a lifeboat, for example), it should be classified as "obstructed."

Veranda: Going one better than an outside cabin, a "veranda" is cruise jargon for a small outdoor balcony attached to your

room. Because windows can't be opened, one big advantage of a veranda is that you can slide open the door to get some fresh air. The size and openness of verandas can vary wildly; for wind-shear reasons, some verandas can be almost entirely enclosed, with only a big picture window-sized opening to the sea. Sitting on the veranda while you cruise sounds appealing, but keep in mind that most of the time you're sailing, it'll be dark outside.

Suite: A multi-room suite represents the top end of cruise accommodations. These are particularly handy for families, but if you can't spring for a suite, ask about adjoining staterooms (see earlier).

Location Within Ship: In general, the upper decks (with better views, and typically bigger windows and more light) are more desirable—and more expensive—than the lower decks. Cabins in the middle of the ship (where the "motion of the ocean" is less noticeable) are considered better than those at either end. And cabins close to the engines (low and to the rear of the ship) can come with extra noise and vibrations.

Look for the **deck plan** on your cruise line's website. If you have a chance to select your own cabin (see next section), study the deck plan carefully to choose a good location. You'd want to avoid a cabin directly below a deck that has a lot of noisy foot traffic (such as the late-night disco or stewards dragging pool chairs across the deck).

Cabin Assignments and Upgrades

Cruise lines handle specific cabin assignments in different ways. While some cruise lines let you request a specific stateroom when you book, others don't offer that option; they'll assign your state-room number at a future date. In other cases, you can request a "guarantee"—you pay for a particular class and are guaranteed that class of cabin (or better), but are not yet assigned a specific state-room. As time passes and the cruise line gets a better sense of the occupancy on your sailing, there's a possibility that they will upgrade you to a better cabin for no extra charge. There's no way of predicting when you'll find out your specific cabin assignment—it can be months before departure, or days before. (Cabin assignments seem to favor repeat cruisers, rewarding customers for their loyalty.)

If you need a specific type of stateroom—for instance, you have limited mobility and need to be close to the elevator, or you're traveling with a large family and want to be as close together as possible—opt for a specific cabin assignment as early as you can.

If you don't have special needs, you might as well take your chances with a "guarantee"; you're assured of getting the class of cabin that you paid for...and you could wind up with a bonus veranda.

Assigned Dining: Traditionally, cruisers reserved not only their stateroom, but also which table and at what time they'd like to have dinner each night. Called a "seating," this tradition is fad-ing. It's still mandatory on a few lines, but most lines either make it optional or have done away with it entirely. If your cruise line requires (or you prefer) a specific seating, reserve it when you book your cruise or cabin. (For more on assigned dining, see page 101.)

Travel Insurance

Travel insurance can minimize the considerable financial risks of traveling: accidents, illness, cruise cancellations due to bad weather, missed flights, lost baggage, medical expenses, and emergency evacuation. If you anticipate any hiccups that may pre-vent you from taking your trip, travel insurance can protect your investment.

Trip-cancellation insurance lets you bail out without losing all of the money you paid for the cruise, provided you cancel for an acceptable reason, such as illness or a death in the family. This insurance also covers trip interruptions—if you begin a journey but have to cut it short for a covered reason, you'll be reimbursed for the portion of the trip that you didn't complete.

Travel insurance is also handy in the unlikely event that your ship breaks down mid-trip. Though the cruise line should reim-burse you for the cruise itself, travel insurance provides more sure-fire protection and can cover unexpected expenses, such as hotels or additional transportation you might need once you've gotten off the ship.

Travel insurance also includes basic medical coverage—-up to a certain amount. If you have an accident or come down with a case of the "cruise-ship virus," your policy will cover doctor visits, treatment, and medication (though you'll generally have to pay a deductible). This usually includes medical evacuation—in the event that you become seriously ill and need to be taken to the nearest adequate medical care (that is, a big, modern hospital).

Baggage insurance, included in most comprehensive policies (and in some homeowner or renter insurance policies), reimburses you for luggage that's lost, stolen, or damaged. However, some items aren't covered (ask for details when you buy). When you check a bag on a plane, it's covered by the airline (though, again, there are limits—ask).

Insurance prices vary dramatically, but most packages cost between 5 and 12 percent of the price of your trip. Two factors affect the price: the trip cost and your age at the time of purchase (rates go up dramatically for every decade over 50). For instance, to insure a 70-year-old traveler for a $3,000 cruise, the prices can range from about $150 to $350, depending on the level of coverage. To insure a 40-year-old for that same cruise, the cost can be about $90-215. Coverage is generally inexpensive or even free for children 17 and under. To ensure maximum coverage, it's smart to buy your insurance policy within a week of the date you make the first payment on your trip. Research policies carefully; if you wait too long to purchase insurance, you may be denied certain kinds of coverage, such as for pre-existing medical conditions.

Cruise lines offer their own travel insurance, but these policies generally aren't as comprehensive as those from third-party insurance companies. For example, a cruise-line policy only covers the cruise itself; if you book your airfare and pre- and post-cruise hotels separately, they will not be covered. And if your cruise line ceases operations, their insurance likely won't cover it. On the other hand, many cruise-line policies are not tied to age—potentially making them attractive to older passengers who find third-party policies prohibitively expensive.

Reputable independent providers include Betins (www.betins.com, tel. 866-552-8834 or 253/238-6374), Allianz (www.allianztravelinsurance.com, tel. 800-284-8300), Travelex (www.travelexinsurance.com, tel. 800-228-9792), Travel Guard (www.travelguard.com, tel. 800-826-4919), and Travel Insured International (www.travelinsured.com, tel. 800-243-3174). Insuremytrip.com allows you to compare insurance policies and costs among various providers (they also sell insurance; www.insuremytrip.com, tel. 800-487-4722).

Some credit-card companies may offer limited trip-cancellation or interruption coverage for cruises purchased with the card—it's worth checking before you buy a policy.

Airfare and Pre- and Post-Cruise Travel

When booking your airfare, think carefully about how much time you want before and after your cruise. Remember that most Europe-bound flights from the US travel overnight and arrive the following day. The nearest airport is often far from the cruise port; allow plenty of time to get to your ship. You'll need to check in at least two hours before your cruise departs (confirm with your cruise line; most passengers show up several hours earlier).

If your travel plans are flexible, consider arriving a few days before your cruise and/or departing a few days after it ends—particularly if the embarkation and disembarkation points are places you'd like to explore. Remember, if you arrive just hours before (or depart just hours after) your cruise, you won't actually have any time to see the beginning and ending ports at all. Common starting and ending points include Copenhagen, Stockholm, Amsterdam, and ports near London (Southampton and Dover)—all of which merit plenty of time (and are covered a little more thoroughly in this book for that reason).

Arriving at least a day early makes it less likely that you'll miss the start of your cruise if your flight is delayed. If you miss the ship, you're on your own to catch up with it at its next port. In talking with fellow cruisers, while I've rarely heard of people missing the boat at a port of call, I've heard many horror stories about flight delays causing passengers to miss the first day of the cruise—and often incurring a time-consuming, stressful, and costly overland trip to meet their ship at the next stop.

In the past, most cruises included what they called "free air" (or "air/sea"), but these days your airfare to and from Europe costs extra—and you're usually best off booking it yourself. (Relatively few cruise passengers book airfare through their cruise line.) If you book your airfare through the cruise line, you'll typically pay more, but in case of a flight delay, the cruise line will help you meet the cruise at a later point. However, booking your airfare this way has its disadvantages—the cruise line chooses which airline and routing to send you on. They'll select an airline they have a contract with, regardless of whether it's one you want to fly (though it's sometimes possible to pay a "deviation fee" to switch to an airline and routing of your choice).

If you decide to add some days on either end of your trip, it's best to make your own arrangements for hotels and transfers. While most cruise lines offer pre- and post-tour packages (that include the hotel, plus transfers to and from the airport and the cruise port), they tend to be overpriced. For each of the arrival and departure cities in this book, I've recommended a few hotels for you to consider.

Some embarkation ports are quite distant from town (for

example, Dover and Southampton are about 80 miles from London). For these ports, a cruise-line airport transfer—which saves you a complicated journey through a big city's downtown—may be worth considering. You can often book a transfer even if you're booking your pre- or post-tour hotel on your own—ask.

In some rare circumstances, it's convenient for a cruise passenger to leave the ship before the cruise is completed—for example, you want to get off to have some extra time in Tallinn, rather than spend a day at sea to return to your starting point in Copenhagen. Cruise lines usually permit this, but you'll pay for the full cost of the cruise (including the portion you're not using), and you'll need to get permission in advance.

Online Check-in

At some point between when you book and when your final payment is due, you'll be invited to check in online for your cruise. This takes only a few minutes. You'll register your basic information and sometimes a credit-card number (for onboard purchases—or you can do this in person when you arrive at the ship). Once registered, you'll be able to print out e-documents (such as your receipt and boarding pass), access information about shipboard life, and learn about and prebook shore excursions.

Part II
TRAVEL
SKILLS FOR
CRUISING

BEFORE YOUR CRUISE

As any sailor knows, prepare well and you'll enjoy a smoother voyage. This chapter covers what you should know before you go (including red tape, money matters, and other practicalities), as well as pointers for packing.

Know Before You Go

Red Tape

You need a **passport** to travel to the countries covered in this book. You may be denied entry into certain European countries if your passport is due to expire within three to six months of your ticketed date of return. Get it renewed if you'll be cutting it close. It can take up to six weeks to get or renew a passport (for more on passports, see www.travel.state.gov).

If your itinerary includes **St. Petersburg, Russia,** you'll have to decide if you want a visa: You'll need one to explore the city on your own—but it's pricey and must be arranged well in advance. If you pay for cruise-line excursions, you don't need a visa but must stay with your guide at all times. For all the details, see page 354.

If you're traveling with **kids,** each minor must possess a passport. Grandparents or guardians can bring kids on board sans parents only if they have a written, notarized letter of consent from the parents. Even a single parent traveling with children has to demonstrate that the other parent has given approval. Specifically, the letter should grant permission for the accompanying adult to travel internationally with the child. Include your name, the name of your child, the dates of your trip, destination countries, and the name, address, and phone number of the parent(s) at home. If you have a different last name from your child, it's smart to bring a copy of the birth certificate (with your name on it). For parents of adopted

Before-You-Go Checklist

Here are a few things to consider as you prepare for your cruise:

❑ Contact your **credit- and debit-card companies** to tell them you're going abroad and to ask about fees, limits, and more; see the next page.

❑ Ask your **health insurance** provider about overseas medical coverage, both on the ship and on shore. For more on health care, see page 85.

❑ Consider buying **trip insurance.** For details, see page 42.

❑ For cruises with **assigned dining,** request your preference for seating time and table size when you reserve. See page 101.

❑ Vegetarians, those with food allergies, or anyone with a **special diet** should notify their cruise line at least 30 days before departure. See page 100.

❑ Your US **mobile phone** may work in Europe; if you want the option to use it while traveling, contact your mobile phone service provider for details. See page 91.

❑ Be sure that you **know the PIN** for your credit and/or debit cards. You will likely encounter the chip-and-PIN payment system, which is widely used in Northern Europe. For details on this system, see page 135.

❑ If you'll be visiting **St. Petersburg,** decide whether you want to get a visa, which will enable you to sightsee independently in the city. For details, see page 354.

❑ Some major sights in **St. Petersburg, Berlin, Amsterdam,** and **Paris** allow (or require) reservations and/or advance ticket purchase options that can help you skip long lines. For a list of sights to book in advance, see page 52.

❑ If you'll be going to **Warnemünde** (Germany), check the schedules at www.bahn.com for the best connections to and from Berlin, to help you decide whether to take the train or pay for an excursion. See page 545.

❑ If you'll be going to **Flåm** (Norwegian fjords), check the schedules for the "Norway in a Nutshell" route for the day of your visit (see www.ruteinfo.no)—and compare them to your arrival and all-aboard time to be sure you can comfortably fit it in. See page 744.

❑ **Smokers,** or those determined to avoid smoke, can ask about their ship's smoking policy. See page 89.

❑ If you're prone to **seasickness,** ask your doctor for advice; certain medication requires a prescription. For a rundown of seasickness treatments, see page 85.

❑ If you're taking a **child** on a cruise without both parents, you'll need a notarized letter of permission. See facing page.

BEFORE YOUR CRUISE

children, it's a good idea to bring their adoption decree as well.

Before you leave on your trip, make two sets of **photocopies** of your passport, tickets, and other valuable documents (front and back). Pack one set of copies and leave the other set with someone at home (to fax or scan and email to you if necessary). It's easier to replace a lost or stolen passport if you have a photocopy proving that you really had what you lost. A couple of passport-type pictures brought from home can expedite the replacement process.

Money

At the start of your cruise, you must register your credit card (either at check-in or on board the ship). All purchases are made using your room number, and you'll be billed for onboard purchases when you disembark. Be aware that the cruise line may put a hold on your credit card during your trip to cover anticipated shipboard expenses; if you have a relatively low limit, you might come uncomfortably close to it. If you're concerned, ask the cruise line what the amount of the hold will be.

For your time on **land,** bring both a credit card and a debit card. You'll use the debit card at cash machines (ATMs) to withdraw local cash for most purchases, and the credit card to pay for larger items. Some travelers carry a third card as a backup, in case one gets demagnetized or eaten by a temperamental machine. As an emergency reserve, I also bring a few hundred dollars in hard cash (in easy-to-exchange $20 bills).

Cash

Most cruise ships are essentially cashless (though you may want to bring some US cash for tipping at casinos). But on land, cash is just as desirable as it is at home. Don't bother changing money before you leave home—ATMs in Europe are easy to find and use (for details, see page 134). And skip traveler's checks—they're not worth the fees or waits in line at slow banks.

Credit and Debit Cards

For maximum usability, bring cards with a Visa or MasterCard logo. You'll also need to know the PIN code for each card in numbers, as there are no letters on European keypads. Before your trip, contact the company that issued your debit or credit cards and ask them a few questions.

• Confirm your card will work overseas, and alert them that you'll be using it in Europe; otherwise, they may deny transactions if they perceive unusual spending patterns.

• Ask for the specifics on transaction **fees.** When you use your credit or debit card—either for purchases or ATM withdrawals—you'll often be charged additional "international transaction" fees of up to 3 percent (1 percent is normal) plus $5 per transaction. If your card's fees seem high, consider getting a different card just for your trip: Capital One (www.capitalone.com) and most credit unions have low-to-no international fees.

• If you plan to withdraw cash from ATMs, confirm your daily **withdrawal limit,** and if necessary, ask your bank to adjust it. Some travelers prefer a high limit that allows them to take out more cash at each ATM stop (saving on bank fees), while others prefer to set a lower limit in case their card is stolen. Note that foreign banks also set maximum withdrawal amounts for their ATMs.

• Find out your card's **credit limit.** Some cruise lines put a hold on your credit card to cover anticipated onboard expenses; if this or your on-shore spending is likely to crowd your limit, ask for a higher amount or bring a second credit card.

• Get your bank's emergency **phone number** in the US (but not its 800 number, which isn't accessible from overseas) to call collect if you have a problem.

• If you don't know it already, ask for your credit card's **PIN** in case you need to make an emergency cash withdrawal or encounter Europe's "chip-and-PIN" system (for details, see page 135). The bank won't tell you your PIN over the phone, so allow time for it to be mailed to you.

Practicalities

Time Zones: While Norwegian cruises stay within the same time zone, cruises on the Baltic are prone to crossing time zones with each sailing. Most of Western Europe—from France to Norway, Denmark, Sweden, and Poland—is in the Central European time zone, or CET (generally six/nine hours ahead of the East/West Coasts of the US). Moving farther east, the Baltic States (Estonia, Latvia, Lithuania) are in the Eastern European time zone—one hour ahead of CET. And St. Petersburg, Russia, is yet another hour ahead (i.e., two hours ahead of CET). Britain is one hour earlier than CET, so, if your cruise begins in London and stops in Tallinn on its way to St. Petersburg, before returning to Copenhagen, you'll change your watch five times. Confusing as it sounds, time changes are clearly noted in the daily program—and your cabin steward will usually leave a reminder on your bed the evening before.

The exceptions are the beginning and end of Daylight Saving Time: Europe "springs forward" the last Sunday in March (two weeks after most of North America), and "falls back" the last Sunday in October (one week before North America). For a handy online time converter, see www.timeanddate.com/worldclock.

Watt's Up? Virtually all cruise ships have American-style

Rick Steves Audio Europe

If you're bringing a mobile device, be sure to check out **Rick Steves Audio Europe,** where you can download free audio tours and hours of travel interviews (via the Rick Steves Audio Europe smartphone app, www.ricksteves.com/audioeurope, iTunes, or Google Play).

My self-guided **audio tours** are user-friendly, easy to follow, fun, and informative, covering the major sights and neighborhoods in London, Paris, and Amsterdam. Compared to live tours, my audio tours are hard to beat: Nobody will stand you up, the quality is reliable, you can take the tour exactly when you like, and they're free.

Rick Steves Audio Europe also offers a far-reaching library of intriguing **travel interviews** with experts from around the globe.

outlets, so you don't need an adapter or converter to charge your phone or blow-dry your hair. (If you're cruising with a European line, you may want to confirm the outlet type.)

But if you're staying at a hotel before or after the cruise, you'll need to adapt to Europe's electrical system, which is 220 volts, instead of North America's 110 volts. Most newer electronics or travel appliances (such as hair dryers, laptops, and battery chargers) automatically convert the voltage—if you see a range of voltages printed on the item or its plug (such as "110-220"), it'll work in Europe. But you will need an adapter plug, with three square prongs for Britain or two round prongs for the rest of Europe (sold inexpensively at travel stores in the US). Avoid bringing older appliances that don't automatically convert voltage; instead, buy a cheap replacement appliance in Europe.

Driving in Europe: If you're planning on renting a car, you'll need to bring your driver's license. An International Driving Permit—an official translation of your driver's license—is recommended in France, Germany, Britain, and Scandinavia, and required in the Netherlands (sold at your local AAA office for $15 plus the cost of two passport-type photos; see www.aaa.com). While that's the letter of the law, I've often rented cars in these countries without having this permit. If all goes well, you'll never be asked to show it—but it's a must if you end up dealing with the police.

Reservations at Major Sights: Making reservations to visit the following sights isn't mandatory, but it is smart:

In **St. Petersburg,** the famous Hermitage (palace and art museum) lets you purchase tickets on their website to avoid long ticket-buying lines (see page 387).

In **Berlin,** reservations are highly recommended for climbing the Reichstag dome (see page 581) and entering the Pergamon and Neues museums on Museum Island (see page 598).

In **Amsterdam,** several key sights—including the Rijksmuseum, the Van Gogh Museum, and the Anne Frank House—let you buy tickets online to skip long lines (see page 783).

In **Paris,** it's essential to reserve tickets for the Eiffel Tower in advance (see page 1058).

Discounts: While this book does not list discounts for sights and museums, seniors (age 60 and over), students with International Student Identification Cards, teachers with proper identification, and youths under 18 often get discounts—but you have to ask. To get a teacher or student ID card, visit www.sta travel.com or www.isic.org.

Packing

BEFORE YOUR CRUISE

One of the advantages of cruising is unpacking just once—in your stateroom. But don't underestimate the importance of packing light. Cruise-ship cabins are cramped, and large suitcases consume precious living space. Plus, you'll still need to get to the airport, on and off the plane, and between the airport and the cruise port. The lighter your luggage is, the easier your transitions will be. And when you carry your own luggage, it's less likely to get lost, broken, or stolen.

Consider packing just one carry-on-size bag (9" by 22" by 14"). I know—realistically, you'll be tempted to bring more. But cruising with one bag can be done without adversely impacting your trip (I've done it, and was happy I did). No matter how much you'd like to bring along that warm jacket or extra pair of shoes, be strong and do your best to pack just what you need.

Here's another reason to favor carry-on bags: If the airline loses your checked luggage and doesn't get it to your embarkation port by the time your ship sets sail, the bags are unlikely to catch up to you. If you booked air travel through the cruise line, the company will do what it can to reunite you with your lost bags. But if you arranged your own flights, the airline decides whether and how to help you—and rarely will it fly your bags to your next port of call. (If you purchase travel insurance, it may cover lost luggage—ask when you buy; for details on insurance, see page 42.) For this reason, even if you check a bag, be sure you pack essentials (medications, change of clothes, travel documents) in your carry-on.

If you're traveling as part of a couple, and the one-piece-per-person idea seems impossible, consider this compromise: Pack one bag each, as if traveling alone, then share a third bag for bulky cruise extras (such as formal wear). If traveling before or after the cruise, you can leave that third, nonessential bag at a friendly hotel or in a train-station luggage locker, then be footloose and fancy-free for your independent travel time.

Remember, packing light isn't just about the trip over and back—it's about your traveling lifestyle. Too much luggage marks you as a typical tourist. With only one bag, you're mobile and in control. You'll never meet a traveler who, after five trips, brags: "Every year I pack heavier."

Baggage Restrictions

Baggage restrictions provide a built-in incentive for packing light. Some cruise lines limit you to two bags up to 50 pounds apiece; others don't enforce limits (or request only that you bring "a reasonable amount" of luggage). But all airlines have restrictions on the number, size, and weight of both checked and carry-on bags. These days, except on intercontinental flights, you'll most likely pay for each piece of luggage you check—and if your bag is overweight, you'll pay even more. Check the specifics on your airline's website (or read the fine print on your airline eticket).

Knives, lighters, and other potentially dangerous items are not allowed in airplane carry-ons or on board your cruise. Large quantities of liquids or gels must be packed away in checked baggage. Because restrictions are always changing, visit the Transportation Security Administration's website (www.tsa.gov/traveler-information) for an up-to-date list of what's allowed on the plane.

If you plan to check your bag for your flight, mark it inside and out with your name, address, and emergency phone number. If you have a lock on your bag, you may be asked to remove it to accommodate increased security checks, or it may be cut off so the bag can be inspected (to avoid this, consider a TSA-approved lock). I've never locked my bag, and I haven't had a problem. Still, just in case, I wouldn't pack anything valuable (such as cash or a camera) in my checked luggage.

As baggage fees increase, more people are carrying on their luggage. Arrive early for aircraft boarding to increase the odds that you'll snare coveted storage space in the passenger cabin.

What to Bring

How do you fit a whole trip's worth of luggage into one bag? The answer is simple: Bring very little. You don't need to pack for the worst-case scenario. Pack for the best-case scenario and simply buy yourself out of any jams. Bring layers rather than pack a heavy coat. Think in terms of what you can do without—not what might be handy on your trip. When in doubt, leave it out. The shops on your cruise ship (or on shore) are sure to have any personal items you forgot or have run out of.

Use the "Packing Checklist" on page 60 to organize and make your packing decisions.

Clothing

Most cruisers will want two to three changes of clothes each day: comfortable, casual clothes for sightseeing in port; more formal evening wear for dinners on the ship; and sportswear, whether it's a swimsuit for basking by the pool or athletic gear for hitting the gym or running track. But that doesn't mean you have to bring along 21 separate outfits for a seven-day cruise. Think versatile. Some port wear can double as evening wear. Two pairs of dressy dinner slacks can be worn on alternating nights, indefinitely. As you choose clothes for your trip, a good rule of thumb is: If you're not going to wear an item more than three times, don't pack it. Every piece of clothing you bring should complement every other item or have at least two uses (for example, a scarf doubles as a shoulder wrap; a sweater provides warmth and dresses up a short-sleeve shirt). Accessories, such as a tie or scarf, can break the monotony and make you look snazzy.

First-time cruisers may worry about "formal nights." While most cruises do have a few formal nights with a dress code, they're not as stuffy as you might think. And those formal nights are optional—you can always eat somewhere other than the formal dining room. So dress up only as much as you want to (but keep in mind that if you plan to eat every meal in the dining room, you must adhere to its dress code—most cruise lines forbid shorts or jeans there at dinnertime). For a general idea of what people typically wear on board, read the sidebar on the next page, then find out what your ship's dress code is.

When choosing clothes for days in port, keep a couple of factors in mind: Most Northern European cruises set sail during the best-weather months of June, July, and August. While you shouldn't expect scorching Mediterranean temperatures, summer heat waves can hit Oslo and Berlin. But at these northern latitudes, things can get quite chilly—especially after the sun goes down. The key here is versatility: Wear layers, and always carry a light-weight sweater or raincoat in case clouds roll in and temperatures (or rain drops) drop. Also, a few Northern European churches (particularly Orthodox ones, such as those in St. Petersburg) enforce a strict "no shorts or bare shoulders" dress code. Pants with zip-off/zip-on legs can be handy in these situations.

Laundry options vary from ship to ship. Most provide 24-hour laundry service (at per-piece prices), enabling those without a lot of clothing to manage fine. But self-service launderettes are rare on board—ask your cruise line in advance about available

BEFORE YOUR CRUISE

Cruise Ship Dress Code

First-time cruisers sometimes worry about the need to dress up on their vacation. Relax. Cruise ships aren't as dressy as they used to be. And, while on certain nights you may see your fellow cruisers in tuxes and formal gowns, there's usually a place to go casual as well. (In general, the more upscale a cruise is, the more formal the overall vibe—though some luxury lines, such as Windstar, have a reputation for relaxed dress codes.)

During the day, the dress code is casual. People wear shorts, T-shirts, swimsuits with cover-ups, flip-flops, or whatever they're most comfortable in. (On pricier cruises, you may see more passengers in khakis or dressy shorts and polo shirts.)

But in the evenings, a stricter dress code emerges. On most nights, dinner is usually **"smart casual"** in the main dining room and at some (or all) specialty restaurants. People are on vacation, so they generally aren't too dressed up—though jeans, shorts, and T-shirts are no-nos. For men, slacks and a button-down or polo shirt is the norm; most women wear dresses, or pants or skirts with a nice top. Plan to wear something a little nicer on the first evening; after you get the lay of the land, you can adjust your wardrobe for the rest of the meals.

Most cruises host one or two **"formal"** nights per week. On these evenings, men are expected to put on jackets (and sometimes ties), while women generally wear cocktail dresses—or pair a dressy skirt or pants with something silky or sparkly on top. Basically, dress as you would for a nice church wedding or a night at the theater. A few overachievers show up wearing tuxedos or floor-length dresses. Note that formal nights will sometimes extend beyond the dining room into the ship's main theater venue.

Some cruises also have **"semiformal"** nights, which fall between the standard "smart casual" dress code and the for-

options. Remember that you can still bring fewer clothes and wash as needed in your stateroom sink. It helps to pack items that don't wrinkle, or look good wrinkled. You should have no trouble drying clothing overnight in your cabin (though it might take longer in humid climates).

It can be worth splurging a little to get just the right clothes for your trip. For durable, lightweight travel clothes, consider ExOfficio (www.exofficio.com), TravelSmith (www.travelsmith .com), Tilley Endurables (www.tilley.com), Eddie Bauer (www .eddiebauer.com), and REI (www.rei.com).

Ultimately—as long as you don't wear something that's outrageous or offensive—it's important to dress in a way that makes you comfortable. No matter how carefully you dress, your clothes probably will mark you as an American. And so what? To fit in

mal nights—for example, men might wear slacks and a jacket, but no tie.

Cruise passengers are evenly split on the "formal night" phenomenon: Some look forward to dressing up and do so with gusto; others just want to be as casual as possible while on vacation. For those who don't want to dress up at all, most cruise ships have dining venues that are completely informal—the buffet, the poolside grill, and so on. Here you'll see people wearing shorts, swimsuits, cover-ups, and flip-flops. If you never want to put on a collared shirt, you can simply eat at these restaurants for the entire cruise. But be aware that you'll be passing gussied-up passengers in the hallways on formal nights—so you might feel a bit out of place if you go totally casual. Bring along a presentable top and pair of pants or skirt for the nights you want to spiff up a bit.

To pack light for your cruise, bring multifunctional clothing that allows you to go minimally formal and also feel chic in port. Men can get by with slacks and a sports coat—which are more versatile than a suit. (I got a lot of good use out of my summery sports coat.) Women can wear a casual dress and jazz it up with accessories, such as nice jewelry or a wrap. A scarf, wrap, or jacket makes a regular outfit (such as black pants and a tank top) more formal.

If you want to get decked out without lugging excess clothing on board, ask if your cruise line has a tuxedo-rental program (some cruise lines also offer a rental program for women's formal wear). You may be able to borrow a loaner jacket or rent a tux on the spot, but selection can be limited—so it's better to order in advance. Simply provide your measurements beforehand, and a tux will be waiting in your cabin when you board.

and be culturally sensitive, I watch my manners, not the cut of my clothes.

Here are a few specific considerations:

Shirts/blouses. Bring short-sleeved or long-sleeved shirts or blouses in a cotton/polyester blend. A sweater or lightweight fleece is good for layering (handy for chilly evenings). Dark colors don't show wrinkles or stains, though light colors can be more comfortable on sunny days in port. Indoor areas on the cruise ship can be heavily air-conditioned, so you may need a long-sleeved top, a sweater, or a wrap even in the height of summer.

Pants/skirts and shorts. Lightweight pants or skirts work well, particularly if you hit a hot spell (these are also handy for Orthodox churches with modest dress codes). Jeans typically work well in Northern Europe—but they can get hot in muggy weather, and many cruise lines don't consider them appropriate "smart casual" wear. Button-down wallet pockets are safest (though still not as thief-proof as a money belt, described later). Shorts are perfectly acceptable aboard your ship, but on land in Europe they're considered beachwear, mostly worn in coastal or lakeside resort towns. No one will be offended if you wear shorts, but you may be on the receiving end of some second glances.

Shoes. Bring one pair of comfortable walking shoes with good traction. Comfort is essential even on board, where you'll sometimes be walking considerable distances just to get to dinner. And getting on and off tenders can involve a short hop to a pier—practical shoes are a must for port days. Sandals or flip-flops are good for poolside use or in case your shoes get wet. And don't forget appropriate footwear to go with your dinner clothes (though again, think versatile—for women, a nice, stylish pair of sandals is nearly as good as heels).

Jacket. Bring a light and water-resistant windbreaker with a hood. Or—more versatile—bring a lightweight Gore-Tex raincoat; rain and chilly weather are not uncommon, even in the peak of summer.

Swimsuit and cover-up. If you plan on doing a lot of swimming, consider bringing a second swimsuit so that you always have a dry one to put on. Most cruise lines forbid swimsuits anywhere beyond the pool area, so cover-ups are a necessity.

Packing Essentials

Money belt. This flat, hidden, zippered pouch—strapped around your waist and tucked under your clothes—is smart for the peace of mind it brings. You could lose everything except your money belt, and the trip could still go on. Lightweight and low-profile beige is best. Whenever you're in port, keep your **cash, credit cards, driver's license,** and **passport** secure in your money belt, and carry only a day's spending money in your front pocket.

Toiletries kit. Sinks in staterooms come with meager countertop space. You'll have an easier time if you bring a toiletries kit that can hang on a hook or a towel bar. Cruise ships provide small bottles of shampoo and itsy-bitsy bars of soap, so you may prefer to bring along your own supplies. Put all squeeze bottles in sealable plastic baggies, since pressure changes in flight can cause even good bottles to leak.

Bring any **medication** and vitamins you need (keep medicine in original containers, if possible, with legible prescriptions), along with a basic **first-aid kit.** If you're prone to motion sickness, consider some sort of **seasickness remedy.** For various options, see page 85. There are different schools of thought on **hand sanitizers** in preventing the spread of germs. Some cruise lines embrace them, others shun them (see page 87)—but they can come in handy when soap and water aren't readily available.

If you wear **eyeglasses** or **contact lenses,** bring a photocopy of your prescription—just in case. A strap for your glasses/sunglasses is handy for water activities or for peering over the edge of the ship in a strong breeze.

Sunscreen and sunglasses. Bring protection for your skin and your eyes. While you may think of Northern Europe as a chilly place, it can be bright and sunny in the summer—especially with the sun reflecting off all that water.

Laundry supplies (soap and clothesline). If you plan to wash your own clothes, bring a small squeeze bottle of detergent. Some cruise-ship bathrooms have built-in clotheslines, but you can bring your own just in case (the twisted-rubber type needs no clothespins).

Packing aides. Packing cubes, clothes-compressor bags, and shirt-folding boards can help keep your clothes tightly packed and looking good.

Sealable plastic baggies. Bring a variety of sizes. In addition to holding your carry-on liquids, they're ideal for packing a picnic lunch, storing damp items, and bagging potential leaks before they happen. Some cruisers use baggies to organize their materials (cruise-line handouts, maps, ripped-out guidebook chapters, receipts) for each port of call. If you bring them, you'll use them.

Small daypack. A lightweight pack is great for carrying your sweater, camera, literature, and picnic goodies when you visit sights on shore. Fanny packs (small bags with thief-friendly zippers on a belt) are an alternative, but they're magnets for pickpockets (never use one as a money belt).

Small extra bag. A collapsible tote bag can come in handy for bringing purchases home from your trip. It's also useful for the first and last days of your cruise, if you check your larger bags to be carried on or off the ship for you. During these times, you'll want to keep a change of clothes, any medications, and valuables with you.

Water bottle. If you bring one from home, make sure it's empty before you go through airport security (fill it at a fountain once you're through). The plastic half-liter mineral water bottles sold throughout Europe are reusable and work great.

Travel information. This book will likely be all you need. But if you want more in-depth coverage of the destinations or

BEFORE YOUR CRUISE

Packing Checklist

*Indicates items you can purchase online at www.ricksteves
.com.

- ❏ Shirts/blouses: long- and short-sleeve
- ❏ Sweater or lightweight fleece
- ❏ Pants/skirts
- ❏ Formal night clothes: Dress pants/skirt with nice shirt/top or cocktail dress
- ❏ Formal wear (optional): Sports coat or tux for men, evening gown for women
- ❏ Shorts
- ❏ Swimsuit and cover-up
- ❏ Underwear and socks
- ❏ Shoes: walking/sandals/dress-up
- ❏ Rainproof jacket with hood
- ❏ Tie or scarf
- ❏ Pajamas/nightgown
- ❏ *Money belt
- ❏ Money—your mix of:
    - ❏ Debit card (for ATM withdrawals)
    - ❏ Credit card
    - ❏ Hard cash (in easy-to-exchange $20 bills)
- ❏ Documents plus photocopies:
    - ❏ Passport
    - ❏ Printout of airline and cruise e-tickets
    - ❏ Driver's license
    - ❏ Student or teacher ID card
    - ❏ Insurance details
- ❏ *Daypack
- ❏ *Extra, collapsible tote bag
- ❏ Sealable plastic baggies
- ❏ Electronics—your choice of:
    - ❏ Camera (and related gear)

information on a place not covered in this book, consider collecting some other sources. (For suggestions, see page 1116.) I like to rip out appropriate chapters from guidebooks and staple them together. When I'm done, I give them away.

Address list. If you plan to send postcards, consider printing your mailing list onto a sheet of adhesive address labels before you leave.

Postcards from home and photos of your family. A small collection of show-and-tell pictures (either printed or digital) is a fun, colorful conversation piece with fellow cruisers, your crew, and Europeans you meet.

Small notepad and pen. A tiny notepad in your back pocket or daypack is a great organizer, reminder, and communication aid.

❑   Mobile phone or smartphone
❑   iPod/MP3 player/portable DVD player
❑   laptop/netbook/tablet
❑   Ebook reader
❑   chargers for each of the above
❑ Leisure reading
❑ *Empty water bottle
❑ Wristwatch and *alarm clock
❑ *Toiletries kit
    ❑ Toiletries (soap, shampoo, toothbrush, toothpaste, floss, deodorant)
    ❑ Medicines (including seasickness remedies if needed)
    ❑ First-aid kit
    ❑ Hand sanitizer
    ❑ Glasses/contacts (with prescriptions)
❑ Sunscreen and sunglasses
❑ *Laundry soap and *clothesline
❑ *Earplugs/*neck pillow
❑ *Travel information (guidebooks and maps)
❑ Address list (for sending postcards)
❑ Postcards and photos from home
❑ *Notepad/journal and pen
❑ Miscellaneous supplies (list on following page)

If you plan to carry on your luggage, note that all liquids must be in 3.4-ounce or smaller containers and fit within a single quart-size sealable baggie. For details, see www.tsa.gov/travelers.

BEFORE YOUR CRUISE

Journal. An empty book to be filled with the experiences of your trip will be your most treasured souvenir. Attach a photocopied calendar page of your itinerary. Use a hardbound type designed to last a lifetime, rather than a spiral notebook.

Electronics and Entertainment

Go light with your electronic gear: You want to experience Europe, not interface with it. Of course, some mobile devices are great tools for making your trip easier or better. Note that many of these things are big-ticket items; guard them carefully or consider insuring them (see page 42). Note that Wi-Fi aboard cruise ships can be slow and expensive—see page 90.

Consider bringing the following gadgets: **digital camera** (and associated gear); **mobile phone/smartphone** (for details on using a US phone in Europe—or on a cruise ship—see page 91); **other mobile devices** (laptop, tablet, portable media player, ereader); and **headphones/earbuds** (travel partners can bring a Y-jack for two sets of earphones). A small **auxiliary speaker** for your mobile device turns it into a better entertainment center. For each item, remember to bring the **charger** and/or extra **batteries** (you can buy batteries on cruise ships and in Europe, but at a higher price).

Most cruises have limited TV offerings and charge a premium for pay-per-view movies (though you'll find DVD players in some staterooms). If you crave digital distraction, preload your mobile device with a selection of movies or TV shows. Cruise lines generally disable your stateroom TV's input jack, so you can't run a movie from your device on the TV.

For long days at sea, bring some leisure reading, whether on an ereader or just a good old paperback. Most ships also have free lending libraries and sell US paperbacks at reasonable prices.

Some travelers use **digital recorders** to capture pipe organs, tours, or journal entries. Having a portable **radio** can be fun if you want to tune in to European stations as you travel.

Note: Most ships use North American electrical outlets, but if you're staying at a European hotel, you'll need an **adapter** to plug in electronics (for details, see "Watt's Up?" on page 51). Many staterooms have a limited number of outlets, so a lightweight **power strip** can be helpful if you have a lot of gadgets to charge at one time.

Miscellaneous Supplies

The following items are not necessities, but they generally take up little room and can come in handy in a pinch.

Basic **picnic supplies,** such as a Swiss Army-type knife and plastic cutlery, enable you to shop for a very European lunch at a market or neighborhood grocery store. Munch in port or in your stateroom (but remember not to pack a knife in your carry-on bag when flying).

Sticky notes (such as Post-Its) are great for keeping your place in your guidebook. **Duct tape** cures a thousand problems. A **tiny lock** will keep the zippers on your checked baggage shut.

A small **flashlight** is handy for reading under the sheets while your partner snoozes, or for finding your way through an unlit passage (tiny-but-powerful LED flashlights—about the size of your little finger—are extremely bright and compact).

Not every stateroom comes with an **alarm clock,** so bring a small portable one just in case (or you can use the alarm on your mobile phone). A **wristwatch** is handy for keeping track of important sailing and dinner times.

If night noises bother you, you'll love a good set of expandable foam **earplugs;** if you're sensitive to light, bring an **eye mask.** For snoozing on planes, trains, and automobiles, consider an inflatable **neck pillow.**

Spot remover (such as Shout wipes) or a dab of Goop grease remover in a small plastic container can rescue stained clothes. A small **sewing kit** can help you mend tears and restore lost buttons. Because European restrooms are often not fully equipped, carry some toilet paper or **tissue packets** (sold at all newsstands in Europe).

What Not to Pack

Don't bother packing **beach towels,** as these are provided by the cruise line.

Candles, incense, or anything else that burns is prohibited on a cruise ship—leave them at home. The same goes for clothes irons, coffee makers, and hot plates.

Virtually every cruise-ship bathroom comes equipped with a **hair dryer** (though if you need one for before or after your cruise, you may want to check with your hotels). The use of **flat irons, curlers,** or other hair-care appliances that heat up (and present a potential fire hazard) are discouraged, though most cruise lines tolerate their use.

Walkie-talkies can be handy for families who want to keep in touch when they split up to explore a giant ship, but because they transmit on European emergency channels, US models are illegal in Europe. Texting between mobile phones can be an affordable alternative, depending on your plan.

ON THE SHIP

Now that you've booked your cruise and packed your bags, it's time to set sail. This chapter focuses on helping you get to know your ship and adjust to the seafaring lifestyle.

Initial Embarkation

You've flown across the Atlantic, made your way to the port, and now finally you see your cruise ship along the pier, looming like a skyscraper turned on its side. The anticipation is palpable. But unfortunately, getting checked in and boarding the ship can be the most taxing and tiring part of the entire cruise experience. Instead of waltzing up a gangway, you'll spend hours waiting around as hundreds or even thousands of your fellow passengers are also processed. Add the fact that ports are generally in ugly and complicated, expensive-to-reach parts of town (not to mention that you're probably jet-lagged), and your trip can begin on a stressful note. Just go with the flow and be patient; once you're on the ship, you're in the clear.

Arrival at the Airport

Cruise lines offer hassle-free airport transfers directly to the ship. While expensive, these are convenient and much appreciated if you're jet-lagged or packing heavy. Taxis are always an option for easy door-to-door service but can be needlessly expensive (in many cities, taxis levy additional surcharges for both the airport and the cruise port). Public transportation can be a bit more complicated, and may be a drag with bags, but usually saves you plenty of money. For cities where cruises are likely to begin or end, I've included details on connecting to the airport on your own—either by taxi or by public transit—so you can easily compare the cost and hassle with the transfer options offered by your cruise line. I've also included hotel recommendations.

Don't schedule your arrival in Europe too close to the departure of your cruise, as flights are prone to delays. Arriving on the same day your cruise departs—even with hours to spare—can be risky. And keep in mind that flights departing from the US to Europe generally get in the next calendar day. For more on these topics, see page 44.

Remember: Arriving in Europe a day or more before your cruise gives you the chance to get over jet lag, see your departure city, and avoid the potential stress of missing your cruise.

Checking in at the Port

Before you leave home, be clear on the exact location of the port for your ship (some cities have more than one port, and large embarkation ports typically have multiple terminals), as well as the schedule for checking in and setting sail. On their initial sailing, most ships depart around 17:00, but cruise lines usually request that passengers be checked in and on board by 15:30 or 16:00. (Like Europe, this book uses the 24-hour clock.) Better yet, arrive at the port at least an hour or two before that to allow ample time to find your way to the ship and get settled in. Most ships are open for check-in around 13:00. You might be able to drop off your bags even several hours before that—allowing you to explore your embarkation port (or your ship) baggage-free until your stateroom is available. Early check-in also helps you avoid the longest check-in lines of the day, which are typically in the midafternoon.

When you arrive at the terminal, cruise-line representatives will direct you to the right place. There are basically three steps to getting on the ship, each of which might involve some waiting: 1) dropping off bags; 2) check-in; and 3) embarkation (security checkpoint, boarding the ship, and finding your stateroom).

First, you have the option to **drop off your bags**—usually at a separate location from check-in. From here, your bags will be transported to your stateroom. If you're packing light, I recommend skipping the drop-off and carrying your own bags to the cabin, which allows you to dispense with all the formalities and potential delays here (waiting to check the bags, and later, waiting for them to arrive in your cabin). But if you're packing heavy—or just want to be rid of your bags to do a little last-minute sightseeing before boarding—checking your bags typically works fine. Your cruise materials (mailed to you prior to your trip) likely included luggage tags marked with your cabin number; to save time, affix these to your bags before dropping them off (if you don't have these tags, baggage stewards can give you some on the spot). From here, the crew will deliver your bags to your stateroom. On a big

Cruising Terms Glossary

To avoid sounding like a naive landlubber, learn a few nautical terms: It's a "line," not a "rope." It's a "ship," not a "boat."

aft/stern: back of ship

all aboard: time that all passengers must be on board the ship (typically 30 minutes before departure)

astern: ahead of the stern (that is, in front of the ship)

beam: width of the ship at its widest point

bearing/course: direction the ship is heading (on a compass, usually presented as a degree)

berth: bed (in a cabin) or dock (at a port)

bridge: command center, where the ship is steered from

bulkhead: wall between cabins or compartments

colors: ship's flag (usually the country of registration)

deck: level or "floor" of the ship

deck plan: map of the ship

disembark: leave the ship

draft: distance from the waterline to the deepest point of the ship's keel

embark: board the ship

even keel: the ship is level (keel/mast at 90 degrees)

fathom: unit of nautical depth; 1 fathom = 6 feet

flag: ensign of the country in which a ship is officially registered (and whose laws apply on board)

fore/bow: front of the ship

funnel/stack: ship's smokestack

galley: kitchen

gangway: stairway between the ship and shore

gross registered tonnage: unit of a ship's volume; 1 gross registered ton = 100 cubic feet of enclosed space

hatch: covering for a hold

helm: steering device for the ship; place where steering device is located

HMS: His/Her Majesty's Ship (before the vessel name); British-flagged ships only

hold: storage area below decks

hotel manager: officer in charge of accommodations and food operations

hull: the body of the ship

keel: the "fin" of the ship that extends below the hull

knot: unit of nautical speed; 1 knot = 1 nautical mile/ hour = 1.15 land miles/hour

league: unit of nautical distance; 1 league = 3 nautical miles = 3.45 land miles

leeward: direction against the wind (that is, into the wind); downwind

lido (lido deck): deck with outdoor swimming pools, athletic area, and other amenities

line: rope

list/listing: tilt to one side

maître d': host who seats diners and manages dining room

manifest: list of the ship's passengers, crew, and cargo

midship/amidships: a spot halfway between the bow and the stern

MS/MSY: motor ship/motorized sailing yacht (used before the vessel name)

muster station: where you go if there's an emergency and you have to board the lifeboats

nautical mile: unit of nautical distance; 1 nautical mile = 1.15 land miles

pilot: local captain who advises the ship's captain, or even steers the ship, on approach to a port

pitch/pitching: rise and fall of the ship's bow as it maneuvers through waves

port: left side of the ship (here's a mnemonic device: both "left" and "port" have four letters)

prow: angled front part of the ship

purser/bursar: officer in charge of finances, sometimes also with managerial responsibilities

quay: dock or pier (pron. "key")

rigging: cables, chains, and lines

roll/rolling: side-to-side movement of a ship

seating: assigned seat and time for dinner in the dining room (often optional)

stabilizer: fin that extends at an angle from the hull of the ship into the water to create a smoother ride

staff (or **"cruise staff"**): crew members who work in the entertainment and activities division

starboard: right side of the ship

stateroom/cabin: "hotel room" on the ship

stem: very front of the prow

steward: serving crew, including the cabin steward (housekeeping), dining steward (waiter), or wine steward (sommelier)

superstructure: parts of the ship above the main deck

swell: wave in the open sea

technical call: when the ship docks or anchors, but passengers are not allowed off (except, in some cases, when those passengers have bought an excursion)

tender: small boat that carries passengers between an anchored ship and the shore

tendered: when a ship is anchored (in the open water) rather than docked (at a pier); passengers reach land by riding tender boats

upper berth: fold-down bed located above another bed

veranda: private balcony off a stateroom

wake: trail of disturbed water that a ship leaves behind it

weigh: raise (for example, "weigh anchor")

windward: in the direction the wind is blowing (with the wind); upwind

ON THE SHIP

ship, this can take hours; if you'll need anything from your luggage soon after departure—such as a swimsuit, a jacket for dinner, or medication—keep it with you. Don't leave anything fragile in your bags. And be aware that your bags might be sitting in the hallway outside your room for quite some time, where passersby have access to them; while theft is rare, you shouldn't leave irreplaceable documents or other valuables in them. Pack as you would for bags being checked on an airline.

At **check-in,** you'll be photographed (for security purposes) and given a credit-card-like room key that you'll need to show whenever you leave and reboard the ship. Crew members will inspect your passport. They also may ask for your credit-card number to cover any onboard expenses (though some cruise lines ask you to do this after boarding, at the front desk). Remember that they may place a hold on your credit card to cover anticipated charges. If you're accompanying a child on board, see page 48 for the documentation you may need.

As part of check-in, you'll fill out a form asking whether you've had any flu-like symptoms (gastrointestinal or nose/throat) over the last several days. If you have, the ship's doctor will evaluate you free of charge before you are allowed to board. This is a necessary public-health measure, considering that contagious diseases spread like wildfire on a cruise ship (see page 86).

After check-in, you'll be issued a boarding number and asked to wait in a large holding area until your number is called. It could take minutes...or hours.

When your number comes up, you'll have to clear immigration control/customs (usually just a formality—you may not even have to flash your passport) and go through a **security check** to make sure you have no forbidden items, ranging from firearms to alcohol (many cruise lines won't let you BYOB on board, and others limit how much you can bring; for details, see page 106).

Your First Few Hours on Board

Once you're on the ship, head to your **stateroom** and unpack. (For more on your stateroom, see "Settling In," later.) During this time, your cabin steward will likely stop by to greet you. The cabin steward—who is invariably jolly and super-personable—is responsible for cleaning your room (generally twice a day, after breakfast and during dinner) and taking care of any needs you might have.

As soon as you step on board, you'll be very aware that you're on a seaborne vessel. You'll quickly remember the old truism about landlubbers having to find their **"sea legs."** At first, you may stagger around like you've had one too many. Hang onto handrails (on stairways and, if it's really rough, in the hallways) and step carefully. You'll eventually get used to it, and you might even discover when you return to shore that you'll need to find your "land legs" all over again. While you may worry that the motion of the ocean will interfere with sleep, many cruisers report exactly the opposite. There's just something soothing about being rocked gently to sleep at night, with the white noise of the engines as your lullaby.

Just before departure, the crew holds an **emergency drill** (or **muster drill**) to brief you on the location of your lifejacket, how to put it on, and where to assemble in the event that the ship is evacuated (called a "muster station"). After being given a lifeboat number, you must gather at your muster station, along with others assigned to the same lifeboat (though sometimes this drill is held elsewhere on the ship). This is serious business, and all are required to participate. For more on safety on board—and how to prepare for the worst-case scenario—see the "Cruise-Ship Safety Concerns" sidebar.

It's traditional—and fun—for passengers to assemble on the deck while the ship **sets sail,** waving to people on shore and on other ships. On some lines, the ship's loudspeakers play melodramatic music as the ship glides away from land. Sometimes the initial departure comes with live musicians, costumed crew members, and a festive cocktail-party atmosphere.

You'll also get acquainted with the ship's **dining room** or other restaurants. If your ship has traditional "seatings"—an assigned time and seat for dinner each night—this first evening is an important opportunity to get to know the people you'll be dining with. If you have any special requests, you can drop by the dining room a bit before dinnertime to chat with the maître d'.

Memorize your **stateroom number**—you'll be asked for it constantly (when arriving at meals, disembarking, making onboard purchases, and so on). And be aware of not only your cruise line, but the name of your specific ship (e.g., Norwegian *Gem*, Royal Caribbean *Splendour of the Seas*, Celebrity *Constellation*, Holland America *Noordam*)—people in the cruise industry (including those in port) refer to the ship name, not the company.

Various **orientation activities** are scheduled for your first evening; these may include a ship tour or a presentation about the various shore excursions that will be offered during the cruise. While this presentation is shamelessly promotional, it can be a good use of time to find out your options.

ON THE SHIP

Life on Board

Your cruise ship is your home away from home for the duration of your trip. This section provides an overview of your ship and covers many of the services and amenities that are offered on board.

Settling In

From tiny staterooms to confusing corridors, it might take a couple of days to adjust to life on board a ship. But before long, you will be an expert at everything from getting to the dining room in the shortest amount of time to showering in tight spaces.

Your Stateroom

While smaller than most hotel rooms, your cabin is plenty big enough if you use it primarily as a place to sleep, spending the majority of your time in port and in the ship's public areas. As you unpack, you'll discover that storage space can be minimal. But—as sailors have done for centuries—cruise-ship designers are experts at cramming little pockets of storage into every nook and cranny. Remember where you tuck things so you can find them when it's time to pack up at the end of your trip.

Unpack thoroughly and thoughtfully right away. Clutter makes a small cabin even smaller. I pack heavier when cruising than when traveling on land, so I make a point to unpack completely, establishing a smart system for keeping my tight little cabin shipshape. Deep-store items you won't need in your suitcase, which you can stow under your bed (or ask your steward to show you any hidden storage areas). Survey all storage areas and make a plan to use them smartly. For example, use one drawer for all things electronic, establish a pantry for all food items, and use the safe for some things even if you don't bother locking it. Unclutter the room by clearing out items the cruise line leaves for you (such as promotional materials). I have a ritual of toggling from shore mode to ship mode by putting my pocket change and money belt (neither of which are of any value on board) in a drawer or the safe when I return to the ship.

Staterooms usually have a safe, coffee maker, minifridge, phone for calling the front desk or other cabins, and television. TV channels include information about the ship, sales pitches for shore excursions and other cruises, various American programming (such as ESPN or CNN), and pay-per-view movies. Some lines even broadcast my TV shows. The beds are usually convertible—if you've got a double bed but prefer twins, your cabin steward can pull them apart and remake them for you (or vice versa). Inside the cabin is a lifejacket for each passenger. Make note of where these are stored, and the best route to your muster station, just as you would the locations of emergency exits on an airplane.

Cabin **bathrooms** are generally tight but big enough to take

care of business. Bathrooms come equipped with hair dryers. First-time cruisers are sometimes surprised at the high water pressure and dramatic suction that powers each flush. Read and heed the warnings not to put any foreign objects down the toilet: Clogged toilets are not uncommon, and on a cruise ship, this can jam up the system for your whole hallway... not a good way to make friends.

Getting to Know Your Ship

After you're settled in your stateroom, start exploring. As you wander, begin to fill in your mental map of the ship with the things you may want to find later: front desk, restaurants, theater, and so on. Many cruises offer a tour of the ship early on, which can help you get your bearings on a huge, mazelike vessel. Deck plans (maps of the ship) are posted throughout the hallways, and you can pick up a pocket-size plan to carry with you. If your ship has touchscreen activity schedules and deck plans on each floor, use them.

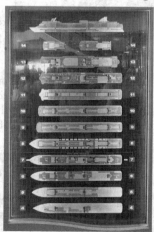

On my first day, I physically hike the entire ship, deck by deck, inside and out, to see what's where. Ships have peaceful outdoor decks that are rarely visited (perfect for sunsets). They have plenty of bars, cafés, and lounges, some of which may fit your style to a T. Crew members know about their ship's special little places, but many passengers never find them. Discover these on your first day rather than your last. Pop into each of the specialty restaurants for a chat with the maître d' and to survey the menu, cover charge, and seating.

As you walk down long hallways, it's easy to get turned around and lose track of whether you're headed for the front (fore)

or the back (aft) of the ship. For the first couple of days, I carry around my ship deck plan and try to learn landmarks: For example, the restaurants (and my cabin) are near the back of the ship, while entertainment venues (casino, big theater) are at the front. Several banks of elevators are usually spread evenly throughout the ship. Before long, you'll figure out the most direct way between your stateroom and the places you want to go. It can also be tricky to find your room in a very long, anonymous hall

with identical doors. Consider marking yours in a low-profile way (for example, tape a small picture below your room number) to help you find it in a hurry.

The double-decker main artery running through the middle of the ship, often called the **promenade deck,** connects several key amenities: theater, main dining room and other eateries, shopping area, library, Internet café, art gallery, photography sales point, and so on. Wrapping around the outside of the promenade deck is the namesake outdoor (but covered) deck, where you can go for a stroll.

At the center of the promenade deck is the main **lobby** (often called the atrium). This area, usually done up with over-the-top decor, has bars, a big screen for occasional presentations, tables of stuff to buy, and not enough seating. If you

get lost exploring the ship, just find your way to the lobby and reorient yourself.

The lobby is also where the **guest services desk** is located. Like the reception desk of a hotel, this is your point of contact if you have concerns about your stateroom or other questions. Nearby you'll usually find the excursions desk (where you can get information about and book seats on shore excursions), a "cruise consultant" (selling seats on the line's future sailings), and the financial services desk (which handles any monetary issues that the guest services desk can't).

If the lobby is the hub of information, then the **lido deck** is the hub of recreation. Generally the ship's sunny top deck, the lido

has swimming areas, other outdoor activities, and usually the buffet restaurant. With a variety of swimming pools (some adults-only, others for kids) and hot tubs; a casual poolside "grill" serving up burgers and hot dogs; ice-cream machines; long rows of sunbathing chairs; and "Margaritaville"-type live music at all hours, the lido deck screams, "Be on vacation!"

Information

Each evening, the **daily program** for the next day is placed inside your cabin or tucked under your door. These information-packed leaflets offer an hour-by-hour schedule for the day's events, from arrival and all-aboard times to dinner seatings, bingo games, and AA meetings. (They're also peppered with ads touting various spa specials, duty-free sales, and drink discounts.) With a staggering number of options each day, this list is crucial for keeping track of where you want to be and when. I tuck this in my back pocket and refer to it constantly. Bring it with you in port to avoid that moment of terror when you suddenly realize you don't remember what time you have to be back on the ship.

Most cruise lines also give you an **information sheet** about each port of call. These usually include a map and some basic historical and sightseeing information. But the dominant feature is a list of the cruise line's "recommended" shops in that port and discounts offered at each one. Essentially, these are the shops that pay the cruise line a commission. These stores can be good places to shop, but they aren't necessarily the best options. (For more details on shopping in port, see page 138.)

The daily program and/or information sheet usually lists your vessel's **port agent** for that day's stop. This is where you'd turn in the unlikely event that you miss your departing ship (for details, see page 144).

Most cruise lines offer **"port talks"**—lectures about upcoming destinations. The quality of these can vary dramatically, from educational seminars that will immeasurably deepen your

Cruise-Ship Safety Concerns

The tragic grounding of the *Costa Concordia* in January of 2012 off the coast of Italy has some cruisers asking, "How safe is my cruise ship?"

Things went wrong on the *Concordia* when the ship's captain diverged from the prescribed route to pass close by the island of Giglio for a "salute." The *Concordia* struck an underwater reef, ripping a 160-foot gash in the hull. The captain steered the listing ship into shallow waters and ran it aground. Power outages and conflicting orders from crew members added to the chaos, leaving frightened passengers in the dark (in every sense) as the ship took on water. While most of the 3,206 passengers and 1,023 crew members were eventually evacuated safely, more than 30 people lost their lives at sea.

Understandably, the shocking images of a sinking megaship and the horrifying testimonials of cruise passengers inflamed worries about the safety of cruising. Like any form of travel, cruising comes with risks. But statistically, even taking into account the *Concordia* disaster, cruising remains remarkably safe. Since 2005, more than 100 million people have taken cruises worldwide; during that time, there have been an estimated 50 deaths—nearly two-thirds of them occurring on the *Concordia*. In the US, your odds of being killed in a given year in a car accident are one in 7,000; the odds of dying in a cruise ship-related accident are one in 6 million.

Since the *Titanic* sank a century ago, a set of laws called Safety of Life at Sea (SOLAS) has regulated maritime safety. Before the *Concordia* accident, cruise ships were required to present a safety briefing immediately before or after departure, and to conduct a muster drill (physically assembling passengers to demonstrate lifejackets and explain lifeboat procedures) within 24 hours. The *Concordia* had already done its safety briefing, but the muster drill was scheduled for the following day. In the wake of that disaster, cruise lines must now combine the safety briefing and the muster drill into a single presentation *before* departure.

As ships have gotten larger, increasingly, cruise lines con-

ON THE SHIP

appreciation for the destination, to thinly veiled sales pitches for shore excursions.

Better cruises have a **destination expert** standing by when you get off the ship to answer your questions about that port (usually near the gangway or in the lobby). Again, beware: While some are legitimate experts, and others work for the local tourist board, most are employees of local shops. They can give you some good sightseeing advice, but any shopping pointers they offer should be taken with a grain of salt.

English is generally the first **language** on the ship, though—

duct their muster drills in large public spaces such as the ship-board theater—so passengers may never actually go to their designated muster station. The *Concordia* disaster underscores that cruisers should take responsibility for their own safety: Know where lifejackets are stowed, be completely clear on the location of your muster station, and know how to get there—not only from your stateroom, but from other parts of the ship. Pack a small flashlight, and keep it handy.

Generally, lifejackets are stored in your stateroom and at other strategic points around the ship. (On a few very large ships, your lifejacket may be kept at your muster station only.) Traditionally the muster drill has included actually putting on life-jackets, but these days some cruise lines skip this step. If you don't try out your lifejacket en masse, consider doing it on your own. If you are traveling with kids, ask the cruise line for child-size lifejackets to have on hand.

In the event of an evacuation, crew members are responsible for providing instructions and for loading and operating the life-boats—though, as the *Concordia* tragedy illustrated, some crews may be better-trained than others. Legally, ships are required to have one lifeboat seat per person on board, plus an additional 25 percent. Aside from the primary lifeboats, large white canis-ters on the ship's deck contain smaller inflatable lifeboats, which can be launched if the normal lifeboats are disabled. In theory, a cruise ship's evacuation procedure is designed to safely remove everyone on board within 30 minutes. However, actual full-ship evacuation is almost never practiced. The "women and children first" rule is nautical tradition, but not legally binding. The cap-tain, however, is legally obligated to stay with the ship to oversee the evacuation.

Ultimately, the *Costa Concordia* disaster is a glaring excep-tion to the otherwise sterling safety record of the cruise industry. But it is a cautionary tale that should encourage cruisers to take the initiative to protect themselves, in case the worst-case sce-nario becomes a reality.

ON THE SHIP

especially on bigger ships—announcements are repeated in other languages as well (often French, German, Italian, and/or Spanish, depending on the clientele). Most crew members who interact with passengers speak English well—though usually it's their sec-ond language.

When passing important landmarks, especially on days at sea, the **captain** may periodically come over the loudspeaker to offer commentary. Or, if the seas are rough, the captain may try to soothe rattled nerves (and stomachs) with an explanation of the weather that's causing the turbulence.

Speaking of **announcements,** cruise lines have varying philosophies about these: Some lines barrage you with announcements every hour or so. On other lines, they're rare. On most ships, in-cabin speakers are only used for emergency announcements. If you can't make out a routine announcement from inside your cabin, crack the door to hear the hallway loudspeakers, or tune your TV to the ship-information channel, which also broadcasts announcements.

Your Crew

Your hardworking crew toils for long hours and low pay to make sure you have a great vacation. Whether it's the head waiter who remembers how you like your coffee; the cabin steward who cleans your room with a smile and shows you pictures of his kids back in Indonesia; or the unseen but equally conscientious workers who prepare your meals, wash your laundry, scrub the deck, or drive the tender boats, the crew is an essential and often unheralded part of your cruise experience.

The all-purpose term for crew members is "steward"—cabin steward (housekeeping), wine steward (sommelier), dining steward (waiter), and so on. Your cabin  steward can be very helpful if you have a basic question or request; for something more complicated, ask the front-desk staff or the concierge. In the dining room, the maître d' assigns tables and manages the dining room, the head waiter takes your order, and the assistant waiters bring your food and bus your dishes.

The ship's cruise director (sometimes called a host or hostess) is a tireless cheerleader, keeping you informed about the various activities and other happenings on board, usually via perky announcements over the ship's loudspeaker several times a day. The cruise director manages a (mostly American) "cruise staff" that leads activities throughout the ship. I have a lot of sympathy for these folks, partly because of my own background as a tour guide—I can't imagine the responsibility of keeping thousands of people informed and entertained 24/7. Experienced cruisers report that the more enthusiastic and energetic the cruise director and staff are, the more likely you are to enjoy your cruise. Gradually you'll come to feel respect, appreciation, and even affection for these people who really, really want you to have a great time on your vacation.

A great bonus for me is to make friends with members of the crew. They are generally hardworking, industrious, young, and fun-loving people from the developing world who, in spite of their required smiles, genuinely enjoy people. Many are avid travelers, and you'll see them enjoying time on shore (when they are given a break) just like you. While there are strict limits to how crew members can mingle with passengers, you are more than welcome to have real and instructive conversations with them about cruise life, their world back home, or whatever.

Befriending a crew member can also come with a bonus drink. If you see a crew member nursing a drink on their own at a shipboard bar, strike up a conversation. There's a good chance they'll offer to buy you a drink. That's because when drinking alone, they have to pay for their own drinks; but if they're "entertaining" a passenger, both their drink and yours are on the cruise line. It's a win-win.

Crew Wages

Other than the officers and cruise staff, a ship's crew is primarily composed of people from the developing world. With rare exceptions, these crew members are efficient, patient, and friendly (or, at least, always smiling).

It's clear that crew members work hard. But most passengers would be surprised to learn just how long they work—and for how little. Because US labor laws don't apply to sailing vessels, cruise

lines can pay astonishingly low wages for very long hours of work. Crew members who receive tips are paid an average base salary (before tips) of about $1 each day. This makes tips an essential part of the crew's income (see "Tipping" on page 84). After tips, the English-speaking service crew who interact with passengers make about $2,000-3,000 per month, while the anonymous workers toiling at entry-level jobs below decks can make less than $1,000 per month. While clear industry-wide numbers are hard to come by, the following monthly wages (after tips) are typical:

Cabin steward	$2,000
Waiter	$3,000
Bartender	$1,800
Cook	$1,500-2,100
Dishwasher	$600
Seaman (maintenance)	$1,500
Cruise staff	$2,000
Cruise director	$5,800
Captain	$10,000

Running a Cruise Ship

The business of running a ship is divided into three branches, which work together to create a smooth experience: the engine room; the hotel (rooms and food service); and the deck. This last branch includes the physical decks and railings as well as the bridge (the area from which the ship is navigated) and tendering (shore transport). Each department has its leader (chief engineer, hotel manager, and chief officer, respectively), with the captain overseeing the entire operation.

Of course, these days the captain doesn't actually steer the ship while standing at a big wooden wheel. Modern cruise ships are mostly computerized. The "watch"—responsibility for guiding the ship and dealing with any emergencies—rotates among the officers, who usually work four hours on, then eight hours off. The watch continues when the ship

ON THE SHIP

These earnings don't seem unreasonable...until you factor in the long hours. Most crew members sign a nine- to ten-month contract, then get two or three months off. While they are under contract, they work seven days a week, at least 10 hours a day; the international legal maximum is 14 hours a day, but according to insiders, some crew members put in up to 16 hours. The hours worked are rarely consecutive—for example, a crew member might work 6 hours, have 2 or 3 hours off, then work 7 more hours. They rarely if ever get a full day off during their entire months-long contract, though they get enough sporadic time off during the day to be able to rest and occasionally enjoy the ports of call. Do the math: If most crew members work an average of 12 hours a day, 30 days a month, that's 360 hours a month—more than double the 160 hours of a 9-to-5 worker.

Cruise lines do cover their crew's accommodations, food, medical care, and transportation (including a flight home once their contract is completed). This means the crew can pocket or send home most of their earnings. While income-tax laws do not

is at anchor or docked, when officers must keep an eye on moorings, make sure the ship is in the correct position, and so on.

The ship is dry-docked (taken out of the water) every two years or so to clean algae, barnacles, and other buildup from the hull and to polish the propeller. A very smooth propeller is crucial for a fluid ride—a dented or porous one can lead to lots of noise and bubbles. Sometimes a crew engineer will put on a wetsuit and dive down to polish the rudder underwater.

As you approach a port (or a challenging-to-navigate passage), a little boat zips out to your cruise ship, and a "pilot"—a

local captain who's knowledgeable about that port—hops off. The pilot advises your ship's captain about the best approach to the dock and sometimes even takes the helm. Once the job is done, another boat might zip out to pick up the pilot.

If you're intrigued by the inner workings of your ship, ask about a behind-the-scenes tour. Many ships offer the opportunity to see the galley (kitchen), food stores, crew areas, and other normally off-limits parts of the ship (usually for a fee).

ON THE SHIP

apply on the ship, crew members are required to pay taxes in their home country.

The Secret Lives of Crew Members

Most cruise lines have somewhere between 1.5 and 2 passengers per crew member. So a 3,000-passenger ship has around 2,000 crew members, who need to be housed and fed—in some ways, they are a vast second set of passengers. The crew's staterooms—

the lowest (below the waterline, close to the rumbling engine noise) and smallest on the ship—are far more humble than your own, and usually shared by two to six people. Some cruise staff may have nicer cabins in the passenger areas, but only officers get outside cabins.

While you may see officers

eating in the passenger dining room or buffet, most of the crew dines in mess halls with menus that reflect the cuisine of their native lands. Working long hours and far from home, the crew expects to eat familiar comfort food—Southeast Asians want fish and rice; Italians get pasta; and so on. A well-fed crew is a happy crew, which leads to happy passengers—so substantial effort and resources go toward feeding the crew.

The more diverse the crew, the more complicated and expensive it can be to keep everyone satisfied. On some ships, each nationality has its own mess hall and menu that changes day to day. Some cruise lines have found it more efficient to hire employees predominantly from one or two countries. For example, on Holland America, the cabin crew is entirely Indonesian, while the kitchen and dining room crew is Filipino (to recruit employees, the cruise line operates training academies in those two countries).

Many crew members have spouses back home who are raising their children; in port, they buy cheap phone cards or use Skype to keep in touch. In fact, most portside Internet cafés and calling shops target the crew rather than the passengers ("Cheap rates to the Philippines!"). If a café near the port offers free Wi-Fi for customers, you'll invariably see a dozen of your crew huddled over their laptops, deep in conversation.

While many crew members have families to feed, others are living the single life. The crew tends to party together (the crew bar is even more rollicking than the passenger bars), and inter-crew romances are commonplace—though fraternization between crew members and passengers is strictly forbidden.

Is It Exploitation?

The national and racial stratification of the entire crew evokes the exploitation and indentured servitude of colonial times: The officers and cruise staff are often Americans, Brits, or Europeans, while those in menial roles (kitchen, waitstaff, cleaning crew, engineers) are Indonesian, Filipino, or another developing-world nationality. It's a mark of a socially conscious company when Southeast Asian employees are given opportunities to rise through the ranks and take on roles with greater responsibility.

The cruise lines argue that their employees are making far more money at sea in glamorous locations—where they get occasional time off to leave the ship and explore the ports—than they would at menial jobs back home. What some see as exploitation, others see as empowerment. Another way to look at it is as "insourcing"—importing cheap labor from the lowest bidder. For better or worse, the natural gregariousness of the crew gives cruisers the impression that they can't be so terribly unhappy with their lives. And the remarkable loyalty of many crew members (working many, many years for the same cruise line)—especially on certain lines—is a testament to the success of the arrangement.

Is it wrong to employ Third World people at low wages to wait on First World, mostly white, generally wealthy vacationers? I don't know. But I do know that your crew members are some of the friendliest people on board. Get to know them. Ask about their families back home. And make sure they know how much you appreciate everything they're doing to make your trip more meaningful.

Money Matters

Most cruise ships are essentially cashless. Your stateroom key card doubles as a credit card. When buying anything on board, you'll simply provide your cabin number, then sign a receipt for the expense. You'll likely need cash on board only for tipping (explained later), paying a crew member to babysit, or playing the casino (most slot machines and table games take cash; you can use your onboard account to finance your gambling, but you'll pay a fee for the privilege). To avoid exorbitant cash-advance fees at the front desk, bring along some US cash for these purposes.

Most cruise lines price everything on board (from drinks to tips to souvenirs) in US dollars, regardless of the countries visited during the trip.

Onboard Expenses

First-time cruisers thinking they've paid up front for an "all-inclusive" trip are sometimes surprised by how many add-ons they are offered on board. Your cruise ticket covers accommodations, all the meals you can eat in the ship's main dining room and buffet (with some beverages included), and transportation from port to port. You can have an enjoyable voyage and not spend a penny more (except for expenses in port). But the cruise industry is adept at enticing you with extras that add up quickly. These include shore excursions, casino games, premium drinks (alcohol, name-brand soft drinks, and lattes), specialty restaurant surcharges (explained later, under "Eating"), duty-free shopping, fitness classes, spa treatments, photos, and many other goods and services.

It's very easy to get carried away—a round of drinks here, a night of blackjack there, a scuba dive, a castle tour, and more. First-timers—even those who think they're keeping a close eye on their bottom line—can be astonished when they get their final onboard bill, which can easily exceed the original cost of the trip (or so hope the cruise lines).

With a little self-control, you can easily limit your extra expenditures, making your seemingly "cheap" cruise actually cheap. It's a good idea to occasionally check your current

Money-Saving Tips

Many people choose cruising because it's extremely affordable. When you consider that you're getting accommodations, food, and transportation for one low price, it's simply a steal. But reckless spending on a cruise can rip through a tight budget like a grenade in a dollhouse. If you're really watching your money, consider these strategies:

Buy as little on board as possible. Everything—drinks, Internet access, knickknacks—is priced at a premium for a captive audience. For most items, you're paying far more than you would off the ship. If you're shopping for jewelry, find a local boutique in port rather than patronize your ship's shop. On the other hand, be aware that northern Europe can be very expensive. You may find it's cheaper to buy a Coke from your stateroom minibar than at a Norwegian minimart.

Skip the excursions. While cruise-line excursions are easy and efficient, you may be charged $80-100/person for a transfer into town and a walking tour of the old center. But for the cost of a $2 bus ticket, you can get downtown yourself and join a $15 walking tour that covers most of the same sights. This book's destination chapters are designed to help you understand your options.

Stick with the main dining room. If your ship has specialty restaurants that levy a surcharge, skip them in favor of the "free" (included) meals in the main dining room—which are typically good quality.

Save some breakfast for lunch. If you're heading out for a long day in port, help yourself to a big breakfast and bag up the leftovers to keep you going until dinnertime. Some cruise lines

ON THE SHIP

balance (and look for mistaken charges) at the front desk or via your cabin TV. You don't have to avoid extras entirely. After all, you're on vacation—go ahead and have that "daily special" cocktail to unwind after a busy day of sightseeing, or stick a $20 bill into a slot machine. But you always have the right to say, "No, thanks." As long as you're aware of these additional expenses and keep your spending under control, a cruise can still be a great value.

Getting Local Cash on Board

While you don't need much cash on board the ship, you will need local money for your time in port, as many European vendors will not accept credit cards or dollars. It's possible to get local cash on board the ship—but it's expensive. At the front desk, you can exchange cash or traveler's checks into the local currency (at bad rates and often with high commissions), or you can get a cash

will sell you a packed lunch for about $10.

Minimize premium beverage purchases. Because alcohol, soda, and specialty coffee drinks all cost extra, drink tabs can add up fast. Since many cruise lines prohibit or limit bringing your own alcohol on board, you'll pay dearly for wetting your whistle.

Stay out of the casino. With a casino and slots on board, it's easy to fall into a gambling habit. Most cruise lines allow you to use your key card to get cash from your room account for gambling. But read the fine print carefully—you're paying a percentage for this convenience. Also, keep in mind that your odds of winning may be even less than at land-based casinos (see page 96).

Don't buy onboard photos. Come to think of it, don't even let them take your photo—so you won't be tempted to buy it later.

Turn off your smartphone. Shipboard Internet access and phone rates are very high. To check your email, visit an Internet café in port rather than on board. For phone options, see page 91.

Take advantage of free services on board. Rather than buy a book, check one out from the ship's library. Instead of ordering a pricey pay-per-view movie in your cabin, enjoy the cruise's free musical performances, classes, and activities. Read your daily program: There's something free going on, somewhere on the ship, virtually every minute of every day.

Don't cheap out at the expense of fun. If you're having a nice dinner, spring for a glass of wine—but keep a mental tally of all these little charges so you're not shocked by the final bill.

advance on your credit card (at a decent exchange rate but typically with exorbitant fees).

You'll save money if you plan ahead and make use of ATMs near the cruise port. For each destination, I've noted the location of the nearest ATM, which can often be found inside the cruise terminal or close to it (for more on withdrawing money in port, see page 134).

Among the destinations in this book, the euro is used in Belgium, Estonia, Finland, France, Germany, and the Netherlands. The other destinations have retained their traditional currencies—the Russian ruble, the Latvian lats, the Norwegian krone, the British pound, and so on. In certain places (as noted in each chapter), it can be tricky to get local funds near your ship. In these cases, it may be worth the added expense to change a small amount of cash on board the ship to finance your trip into town.

Tipping

Tipping procedures aboard cruise ships have changed dramatically over the last two decades. Through the late 1980s, cruising was a pastime of the wealthy, and passengers enjoyed tipping the crew royally as part of the experience. Each crew member—cabin steward, maître d', head waiter, assistant waiter, and so on—expected to be tipped a specific amount per day. After the final passenger disembarked, the crew would meet and dump all their tip money into a communal pot, to be divided equally among themselves. But as cruising went mass-market, more frugal middle-class passengers began signing up. Having already paid for their trip, many resented the expectation to tip...so they simply didn't. The crew's take-home pay plummeted, and many workers quit, leaving the cruise lines in dire straits.

These days, cruise lines use a standard "auto-tip" system, in which a set gratuity (generally about $10-12/person per day) is automatically billed to each passenger's account and then divided among the crew (this system, started around 2000, effectively formalizes the process that had been going on for decades). About a third of this tip goes to your cabin steward, a third to the restaurant stewards, and a third to others, including people who worked for you behind the scenes (such as the laundry crew). While overall tips are still not what they were 20 years ago, auto-tipping has proven to be a suitable compromise for both passengers and crew.

Cruise lines explain that, with auto-tipping, additional tipping is "not expected." But it is still most certainly appreciated by the crew. This can cause stress for passengers who are unsure whom, how much, and when to tip; conscientious tippers miss the "good old days" when there was a clearly prescribed amount earmarked for each crew member. Even more confusing, with all the new alternative dining options, you likely won't be served by the same waiter every night—in fact, you might never eat at the same restaurant twice. In general, the rule of thumb is to give a cash tip at the end of the cruise to those crew members who have provided exceptional service (for specific guidelines, see page 84).

At any point, you can increase or decrease your auto-tip amount to reflect your satisfaction with the service you've received. So, if you don't have cash for your final tip, you can simply go to the front desk and increase the auto-tip amount instead (but try to do so before the final night, when accounts are being finalized).

Some passengers prefer to zero out their auto-tip, then pay their favorite crew members in cash to make sure the money winds up with the "right" person. But this can backfire in two ways: First, many crew members adhere to the old system of pooling and dividing tips, including those received in cash—so your cash tip might be split after all. Second, your preferred crew member may choose not to split the cash tip at all—so somebody who worked hard for you, unseen, misses out on much-needed income. The fairest option is to let the auto-tip do what it's designed to do, and then add a cash bonus for the people you wish to reward.

In addition to a monetary tip, crew members appreciate it when you pass along positive feedback. Most cruise lines provide guests with comment cards for this purpose, and they can be taken very seriously when determining promotions. If someone has really gone above and beyond for you, fill out a comment card on their behalf.

Health

Health problems can strike anywhere—even when you're relaxing on a cruise ship in the middle of the Mediterranean. Every ship has an onboard doctor (though he or she may not be licensed in the US). If you have to visit the shipboard physician, you will be charged. Before you leave home, ask your health insurance company if the cost is covered or reimbursable; if you buy travel insurance, investigate how it covers onboard medical care.

Fortunately, some of the most common health concerns on cruise ships, while miserable, are temporary and relatively easy to treat.

Seasickness

Naturally, one concern novice cruisers have is whether the motion of the ship will cause them to spend their time at sea with their head in the toilet. And, in fact, a small percentage of people discover (quickly and violently) that they have zero tolerance for life at sea. But the vast majority of cruisers do just fine.

The Baltic is a mostly enclosed sea with very little tide or turbulence; the North Sea can be rougher, but is still calmer than the open ocean. Remember that you're on a gigantic floating city—it takes a lot of agitation to really get the ship moving. Cruise ships are also equipped with stabilizers—wing-like panels that extend below the water's surface and automatically tilt to counteract rolling (side-to-side movement) caused by big swells.

But rough seas can occur, and when they do, waves and winds may toss your ship around quite noticeably. (As one captain told me, "If you're in a storm in the middle of the Atlantic, no ship is big enough.") When this happens, chandeliers and other fixtures begin to jiggle and clink, motion sickness bags discreetly appear in the hallways, and the captain comes over the loudspeaker to comfortingly explain what's being done to smooth out the ride. Lying in bed, being rocked to sleep like a baby, you hear the hangers banging the sides of your closet. Some cruisers actually enjoy this experience; for others, it's pure misery.

If you're prone to motion sickness, visit your doctor before your cruise, and be prepared with a remedy (or several) in case you're laid low. Below are several options that veteran cruisers swear by.

Dramamine (generic name: Dimenhydrinate) is easy to get over the counter but is highly sedating—not ideal unless you are desperate. Some cruisers prefer the less-drowsy formula, which is actually a different drug (called Meclozine, sometimes marketed as **Bonine**). **Marezine** (generic name: Cyclizine) has similar properties and side effects to Dramamine.

Scopolamine patches (sometimes called by the brand name Transderm) are small (dime-sized) and self-adhesive; just stick one on a hairless area behind your ear. They work well for many travelers (the only major side effect is dry mouth), but require a prescription and are expensive (figure $15 for a three-day dose). Some cruisers apply them prophylactically just before first boarding the ship (especially if rough weather is forecast). After removing one of these patches, wash your hands carefully—getting the residue in your eyes can cause dilated pupils and blurry vision.

Elasticized **Sea-Bands** have little buds that press on the pressure points on your wrist associated with nausea. You can buy them in any drugstore. They are easy to wear (if a bit goofy-looking—they look like exercise wristbands), and many people prefer them as a cheap and nonmedicinal remedy.

The similar but more sophisticated **Reletex** resembles (and is worn like) a wristwatch. It operates on the same principle as Sea-Bands but is designed to be less constricting (direct pressure delivered to exactly the right spot). But it's quite expensive ($100-200) and best for those who have a big problem with seasickness.

Every cruise aficionado has a favorite homegrown seasickness remedy. Some say that eating green apples or candied ginger can help settle a queasy stomach. Others suggest holding a peeled orange under the nose. Old sea dogs say that if you stay above deck, as close to the middle of the ship as possible, and keep your eyes on the horizon, it will reduce the effects of the motion.

Illness

Like a college dorm or a day-care center, a cruise ship is a veritable incubator for communicable disease. Think about everything that you (and several thousand other passengers) are touching: elevator buttons, railings, serving spoons in the buffet, and on and on. If one person gets sick, it's just a matter of time before others do, too.

The common cold is a risk. But perhaps even more likely are basic gastrointestinal upsets, most often caused by the norovirus (a.k.a. the Norwalk virus)—tellingly nicknamed the "cruise-ship virus." Most often spread through fecally contaminated food or person-to-person contact, the norovirus is your basic nasty stomach bug, resulting in nausea, diarrhea, vomiting, and sometimes fever or cramps. It usually goes away on its own after a day or two.

Because contagious maladies are a huge concern aboard a ship, the cruise industry is compulsive about keeping things clean. Between cruises, ships are thoroughly disinfected with a powerful cleaning agent. When you check in, you'll be quizzed about recent symptoms to be sure you aren't bringing any nasty bugs on board. Some cruise lines won't allow passengers to handle the serving spoons at the buffet for the first two days—the crew serves instead. And, if you develop certain symptoms, the cruise line reserves the right to expel you from the ship at the next port of call (though, in practice, this is rare—more likely, they'll ask you to stay in your stateroom until you're no longer contagious).

Many cruise lines douse their passengers with waterless hand sanitizers at every opportunity. Dispensers are stationed around the ship, and smiling stewards might squirt your hands from a spray bottle at the entrance to restaurants or as you reboard the ship after a day in port. Whether this works is up for debate. Several studies have demonstrated that using these sanitizers can actually be counterproductive. The US Centers for Disease Control (CDC) recommend them only as an adjunct to, rather than a replacement for, hand washing with soap and warm water. The gels work great against bacteria, but not viruses

(such as the norovirus). Following the CDC's lead, some cruise lines have discontinued the use of waterless sanitizers—and have seen an immediate *decrease* in their rate of outbreaks. The logic is that hand sanitizers actually discourage proper hand-washing behavior. When people apply sanitizers, they assume their hands are clean—and don't bother to wash with soap and water. All the while, that spunky norovirus survives on their hands, gets transferred to the serving spoon at the buffet, and winds up on other people's hands while they're eating dinner.

On your stateroom TV, you might find a channel with instructions on how to wash your hands. Patronizing, yes. But not undeservedly. In a recent international study, Americans were found to be less diligent than other nationalities when it comes to washing their hands after using the bathroom. They then go straight to the buffet, and...you know the rest. It's disgusting but true. If you're a total germophobe, you have two options: Avoid the buffet entirely—or just get over it.

Water, Trash, and Poo: The Inside Scoop

Wondering how cruise ships deal with passengers' basic functions? Here are the answers to some often-asked questions:

Is the water clean and drinkable? Drinking water is usually pumped into the ship at the point of embarkation. Throughout the duration of the cruise, this supply is what comes out of your bathroom tap and is used in restaurant drinks.

Larger ships also have the capacity to desalinize (remove salt from) seawater for use aboard. While perfectly safe to drink, this water doesn't taste good, so it's reserved primarily for cleaning. The water in your stateroom's toilet or shower might be desalinated.

Waste water from the ship is purified on board. While theoretically safe to drink, it's usually deposited into the sea.

Where does the trash go? Trash from shipboard restaurants is carefully sorted into garbage, recyclables, and food waste. Garbage is removed along with other solid waste in port. Cruise lines pay recycling companies to take the recyclables (interestingly, in the US it's the other way around; the companies pay the ship for their recyclables). Food waste is put through a powerful grinder that turns it into a biodegradable puree. This "fish food" is quietly piped out the end of the ship as it sails through the night.

What happens to poo? You may wonder whether shipboard waste is deposited into the sea as you cruise. These things are dictated by local and international law as well as by the policies of individual cruise lines. Most mainstream cruise lines do not dump solid waste into the sea. Instead it is collected, stored, and removed from the ship for proper disposal in port.

Staying Fit on Board

While it's tempting to head back to the buffet for a second dessert (or even a second dinner) at 11:00 p.m., file away this factoid: A typical cruise passenger gains about a pound a day. After two weeks at sea, you've put on the "Seafaring 15."

Whether you're a fitness buff or simply want to stave off weight gain, cruise ships offer plenty of opportunities to get your body moving. Most ships have fitness centers with exercise equipment, such as bikes, treadmills, elliptical trainers, and weight machines. Some offer the services

of personal trainers, plus classes like boot camp, spinning, Pilates, and yoga (newbies and yoga-heads alike will find it an interesting challenge to hold tree pose on a moving ship). These services usually cost extra, though some classes can be free (usually things like stretching or ab work).

If you're not the gym type, there are other ways to burn calories. Besides swimming pools, many ships have outdoor running tracks that wrap around the deck, complete with fresh air and views. And some ships have more extreme-type sports, such as rock-climbing walls and surfing simulators.

Even if you don't take advantage of sports-related amenities, simply staying active throughout your cruise will help keep those multicourse dinners from going straight to your hips. With multiple levels, your cruise ship is one giant StairMaster. Take the stairs instead of the elevator (which often saves time, too), or run down to the bottom floor and hike back up to the top a couple of times a day. Opt for a walking tour instead of a bus tour when you're in port. Hit the dance floor at night. But just in case, bring along your roomy "Thanksgiving pants."

Smoking

Smoking presents both a public health issue and a fire hazard for cruise lines. While policies are evolving, these days most cruise lines prohibit smoking in nearly all enclosed public spaces as well as in many outdoor areas. You may be able to smoke in certain bars or lounges and in dedicated outdoor spots. Most cruise lines allow passengers to light up in their staterooms or on their verandas but do not have designated "smoking" cabins—they simply clean the cabin thoroughly after a smoker has stayed there (generally with impressive success). If you're a dedicated smoker or an adamant nonsmoker, research the various cruise lines' policies when choosing your vacation.

Communicating

Because phoning and Internet access are prohibitively expensive on board—and because the times you'll be in port are likely to coincide with late-night or early-morning hours back home (8:00-17:00 in most of Europe is 2:00-11:00 a.m. on the East Coast and 23:00-8:00 a.m. on the West Coast)—keeping in touch affordably can be tricky. Let the folks back home know not to expect too many calls, or figure out if there are any late evenings in ports when it might be convenient to call home.

Consider asking any crew members you befriend about the cheapest, easiest places in each port to get online or to make cheap phone calls. They spend many months away from home and are experts at staying in touch. (But keep in mind some of the options at the ports are "seamen's clubs"—open only to crew members, not the general public.)

Getting Online

It's useful to get online periodically as you travel—to confirm trip plans, get weather forecasts, catch up on email, or blog or post photos from your trip. But with high prices and slow speeds, shipboard Internet is not the best option.

Most cruise ships have an Internet café with computer terminals, and many also have Wi-Fi (some offer it in select areas of the ship, others provide it in staterooms). Either way, onboard

Internet access is very expensive—figure $0.50-1/minute (the more minutes you buy, the cheaper they are, and special deals can lower the cost substantially). Before you pay for access, be warned that— since it's satellite-based rather than hard-wired—onboard Internet is tortoise-slow compared to high-speed broadband (remember dial-up?). And while using VoIP (Skype or Google Talk) to make voice or video calls over a Wi-Fi connection is an excellent budget option on land, it's impractical on the ship. Onboard Internet access has such limited bandwidth that these services often don't work well, or at all.

In short, shipboard Internet access is practical only for a quick download of your emails. Limit the time you need to spend online by reading and composing emails offline, then going online periodically just to download/upload. You can also set up certain smartphone apps to do this; for example, some news apps let you download all of the day's top stories at once, rather than clicking to read them one at a time. When you're done, be sure that you properly log out of the shipboard network to avoid unwittingly running up Internet fees.

If you can, wait until you're in port to get online. If you have a wireless-capable mobile device, find a café on shore where you can sit and download your email over Wi-Fi while enjoying a cup of coffee—at a fraction of the shipboard cost. Or hop on a computer at an Internet café to quickly check your email. For more pointers on getting online in port, see page 131.

Phoning

If you want to make calls during your trip, you can do it either from land or at sea. It's much cheaper to call home from a pay phone on shore (explained on page 131) or from a mobile phone on a land-based network (explained later). Calling from the middle of the sea is pricey, but if you're in a pinch, you can dial direct from your stateroom telephone or use a mobile phone while roaming on the costly onboard network. For details on how to dial European phone numbers, see page 1110.

Stateroom Telephones: Calling **within the ship** (such as to the front desk or another cabin) is free on your stateroom telephone, or from phones hanging at strategic locations around the ship. Some ships provide certain crew members with an on-ship mobile phone and a four-digit phone number. If there's a crew member or service desk you want to contact, just remember their number and dial it toll-free.

Calling **to shore** (over a satellite connection) is usually possible, but expensive—anywhere from $6 to $15 a minute (if you prepay for a large block of calling time, it can be cheaper—for example, $25 for 12 minutes; ask for specifics at the front desk). Note: Similar charges apply if someone calls your stateroom from shore.

Mobile Phones: Using a mobile phone while traveling is convenient. Even if you don't expect to make many voice calls, texting (either to the US or to another mobile phone in Europe) can be particularly handy for people cruising together who want to split up occasionally and still be in touch. Before you go too far, though, read the "Mobile Phone Options" sidebar on the next page to understand what types of mobile phones can be used in Europe, and how to use them cost-effectively.

For me, the most economical way to enjoy phone service is to buy a cheap, unlocked European phone and SIM card at a phone shop in the city where your cruise starts. Since SIM cards generally can't be topped up in other countries, be sure your SIM card has an adequate amount of credit for your entire trip (if you run out, you'll need to buy another SIM card in the new country). Buy however much credit you think you'll need, and use it sparingly all along the coast. Because it's much more expensive to make calls outside of the SIM card's home country, limit yourself to extremely fast calls and text messages. If you buy your SIM card within the European Union (such as in Denmark or Sweden), roaming fees in other EU countries are capped, allowing you to make affordable calls for most destinations in this book—but be careful when crossing into non-EU territories, such as Russia, where rates can skyrocket.

ON THE SHIP

Mobile Phone Options

To use a mobile phone as you travel—whether on a cruise ship or in port—you can bring your own or buy a cheap phone once you're in Europe.

Your **US mobile phone** works in Europe if it's GSM-enabled, tri-band or quad-band, and on a calling plan that allows international calls. Phones from T-Mobile and AT&T, which use the same GSM technology that Europe does, are more likely to work overseas than Verizon or Sprint phones (if you're not sure, ask your service provider). In most European countries, your US provider will charge you $1.29-1.99 per minute to make or receive calls while roaming internationally, and 20-50 cents to send or receive text messages. (Rates in Russia can be much higher.) Signing up for an international calling plan with your provider can save a few dimes per minute. Roaming on your own phone is easy but can be pricey; it's most cost-effective if you're on a short trip or won't be making many calls.

Many **smartphones** (such as iPhone, Android, or BlackBerry) work like any other mobile phone in Europe for voice calls and text messaging. But roaming rates for using data (checking email, browsing the Internet, streaming videos, and running certain apps) are sky-high. If you don't proactively adjust your settings, the charges can *really* mount up, because the phone is constantly "roaming" to update your email and such. The best solution: Disable data roaming entirely, and only use your device when you find free Wi-Fi (which also lets you use Skype, Google Talk, or FaceTime to make calls). You can manually turn off data roaming on your phone's menu (check under the "Network" settings). For added security, call and ask your service provider to temporarily suspend your data account entirely for the length of your trip.

For calls within Europe, you'll pay much cheaper rates if you put a **European SIM card** in your mobile phone. Inserting the SIM card (usually in a slot behind the battery or on the side of your phone) will give you a European phone number, but for it

ON THE SHIP

Important: If you are using a mobile phone, it's essential to distinguish between land and sea networks. Because many European cruise itineraries stay fairly close to land, you can often roam on the cheaper **land-based networks,** even when you're at sea. Your phone will automatically find land-based networks if you're within several miles of shore. The **onboard network,** which doesn't even turn on until the ship is about 10 miles out, is far more expensive—about $2.50-5/minute (ask your mobile service provider for details about your ship).

Before placing a call from your ship, carefully note which network you're on (this is displayed on your phone's readout, generally next to the signal bars). You might not recognize the various land-

to work, your phone must be electronically "unlocked" (ask your provider about this, buy an unlocked phone before you leave, or get one in Europe—see page 91). SIM cards are sold at mobile-phone stores, post offices, and some newsstand kiosks for $5-10, and often include at least that much prepaid domestic calling time (making the card itself essentially free). When buying a SIM card, you may need to show ID, such as your passport.

Before purchasing a SIM card, always ask about fees for domestic and international calls, roaming charges, and how to check your credit balance and buy more time. When you're in the SIM card's home country, domestic calls average 10-20 cents per minute, and incoming calls are free. (Some companies offer remarkably cheap rates—5 cents per minute or less—for calls to the US.) Rates are higher if you're roaming in another country, and you may pay more to call a toll number than if dialing from a landline.

Some travelers like to carry two phones: their own US mobile phone (to stay reachable on their own phone number) and a second unlocked phone with a European SIM card (to make local calls at far cheaper rates). You could either bring two phones from home, or get one in Europe—they're sold at mobile phone stores, at hole-in-the-wall vendors at many airports and train stations, and at phone desks within larger department stores. Regardless of how you get your phone, remember that you'll need a SIM card to make it work.

For more on phoning in Europe, see www.ricksteves.com/phoning.

ON THE SHIP

based network names; to be safe, learn the name of the cruise-line network (it's usually something obvious, such as "Phone at Sea")—then avoid making any calls if that name pops up. To prevent accidentally roaming on the sea-based network, simply turn off your phone (or disable roaming, if your phone has that feature) as soon as you board the ship. And be warned that receiving a call—even if you don't answer it—costs the same as making a call.

Here's a case study: On a recent one-week cruise to Norway, at my first stop I paid $10 for a SIM card that allowed affordable calls within Europe—and cheap calls to the US. Because that cruise's itinerary rarely ventured far from land-based networks, I was able (with only a few, brief exceptions) to call home for pennies a minute, without ever needing to resort to the pricey onboard network.

Satellite Phones: If you want the freedom to make calls anywhere, anytime, at a fixed rate, consider renting a satellite phone. For example, www.bluecosmo.com rents phones for $40/week, with calling rates of $1.35-1.89/minute (depending on how many minutes you purchase), plus $10-55 for shipping. Once you add up all those costs, this option isn't cheap—but it's versatile.

Onboard Activities

Large cruise ships are like resorts at sea. In the hours spent cruising between ports, there's no shortage of diversions: swimming pools, hot tubs, and water slides; sports courts, exercise rooms, shuffleboard courts, giant chessboards, and rock-climbing walls; casinos with slots and table games; shopping malls; art galleries with works for sale; children's areas with playground equipment and babysitting services; and spas  where you can get a facial, massage, or other treatments. Many activities have an extra charge associated—always ask before you participate.

To avoid crowds, take advantage of shipboard activities and amenities at off times. The gym is quieter late in the evenings, when many cruisers are already in bed. Onboard restaurants are typically less crowded for the later seatings. If you're dying to try out that rock-climbing wall, drop by as soon as you get back on the ship in the afternoon; if you wait an hour or two, the line could get longer.

Days at sea are a good time to try all the things you haven't gotten around to on busy port days, but be warned that everyone else on the ship has the same idea. Services such as massages are particularly popular on sea days—book ahead and be prepared to pay full price (if you get a massage on a port day, you might get a discount). Premium restaurants and other activities also tend to fill up far earlier for days at sea, so don't wait around too long to book anything you have your heart set on.

Remember, the schedule and locations for all of these options—classes, social activities, entertainment, and more—are listed in your daily program.

Social Activities

Many ships offer a wide array of activities, ranging from seminars on art history to wine- and beer-tastings to classes on how to

fold towels in the shape of animals (a skill, you'll soon learn, that your cabin steward has mastered). Quite a few of these are sales pitches in disguise, but others are just for fun and a great way to make friends. Bingo, trivia contests, dancing lessons, cooking classes, goofy poolside games, newlywed games, talent shows, nightly mixers for singles, scrapbooking sessions, high tea—there's something for everyone. Note that a few offerings might use code words or abbreviations: "Friends of Bill W" refers to a meeting of Alcoholics Anonymous; "Friends of Dorothy" or "LGBT" refers to a meeting of gay people. Ships have a community bulletin board where these and other meetings are posted. You can even post your own.

Entertainment and Nightlife

Most cruise ships have big (up to 1,000-seat) theaters with nightly shows. An in-house troupe of singers and dancers generally puts on

two or three schmaltzy revue-type shows a week (belting out crowd-pleasing hits). On other nights, the stage is taken up by guest performers (comedy acts, Beatles tribute bands, jugglers, hypnotists, and so on). While not necessarily Broadway-quality, these performances are a fun diversion; since they're typically free and have open seating, it's easy to drop by for just a few minutes (or even stand in the back) to see if you like the show before you commit. On some of the biggest new megaships, the cruise lines are experimenting with charging a fee and assigning seats for more elaborate shows.

Smaller lounges scattered around the ship offer more inti-

mate entertainment with just-as-talented performers—pianists, singers, duos, or groups who attract a faithful following night after night. Some cruisers enjoy relaxing in their favorite lounge to cap their day.

Cruises often screen second-run or classic movies for

passengers to watch. Sometimes there's a dedicated cinema room; otherwise, films play in the main theater at off times.

Eating, always a popular pastime, is encouraged all hours of the day and night. While the main shipboard eateries tend to close by about midnight, large ships have one or two places that remain open 24 hours a day.

And if you enjoy dancing, you have plenty of options ranging from classy ballroom-dance venues to hopping nightclubs that pump dance music until the wee hours.

Shopping

In addition to touting shopping opportunities in port, cruise ships have their own shops on board, selling T-shirts, jewelry, trinkets, and all manner of gear embla-zoned with their logo. At busy times, they might even set up tables in the lobby to lure in even more shoppers. In accordance with international maritime law, the ship's casino and duty-free shops can open only once the ship is seven miles offshore.

While shopping on board is convenient and saves on taxes, most of the items sold on the ship can be found at home or online—for less. If you like to shop, have fun doing it in port, seeking out locally made mementos in European shops. (If you enjoy both sightseeing and shopping, balancing your port time can be a challenge; I'd suggest doing a quick surgical shopping strike in destinations where you have something in particular you'd like to buy, so you won't miss out on the great sights.) You'll find more information on shopping in port on page 138. In the destination chapters, I've given some suggestions about specific local goods to shop for.

Casino

Cruise ships offer Vegas-style casinos with all the classic games, including slots, blackjack, poker, roulette, and craps. But unlike

Vegas—where casinos clamor for your business with promises of the "loosest slots in town"—cruise ships know they have a captive audience. And that means your odds of winning are even worse than they are in Vegas. Onboard

casinos also offer various trumped-up activities to drum up excitement. Sure, a poker tournament can be exciting and competitive—but I can't for the life of me figure out the appeal of a slot tournament (no joking). If you want to test your luck—but you're not clear on the rules of blackjack, craps, or other casino games—take advantage of the free gambling classes that many cruise lines offer early in the trip.

Art Gallery

Many ships have an art gallery, and some even display a few genuinely impressive pieces from their own collection (minor works by major artists). But more often the focus is on selling new works by lesser-known artists. Your ship might offer lectures about the art, but beware: These often turn out to be sales pitches for "up-and-coming" artists whose works are being auctioned on board. While the artists may be talented, the "valuation" prices are dramatically inflated. Art auctions ply bidders with free champagne to drive up the prices...but no serious art collector buys paintings on a cruise ship.

Photography

Once upon a time, photographers snapped a free commemorative portrait of you and your travel partner as you boarded the ship. But when the cruise lines figured out that people were willing to shell out $8-15 for one of these pictures, they turned it into big business. Roving photographers snap photos of you at dinner, and makeshift

studies with gauzy backgrounds suddenly appear in the lobby on formal night. As you disembark at each port, photographers ask you to pose with models in tacky costumes. Later that day, all those photos appear along one of the ship's hallways for everyone to see (perusing my fellow passengers' deer-in-the-headlights mug shots is one of my favorite onboard activities). While it's hard to justify spending 10 bucks on a cheesy snapshot, you might be able to bargain the price down toward the end of the trip. Repeat cruisers have reported that if you swing by the photography area on the last evening, the sales-people—eager to unload their inventory—may cut a deal if you pay cash.

Spa/Beauty Salon

Most cruise ships have spa facilities, where you can get a massage, facial, manicure, pedicure, and so on. There may also be a beauty salon where you can get your hair done. While convenient, obviously these services are priced at a premium—though specials are often available. These treatments often come with a sales pitch for related products. Tip as you would back home (either in cash or by adding a tip when you sign the receipt).

Library

The onboard library has an assortment of free loaner books, ranging from nautical topics to travel guidebooks to beach reading.

Usually outfitted with comfortable chairs and tables, this can also be a good place to stretch out and relax while you read. If the ship's staterooms are equipped with DVD players, the library may have DVDs for loan or rent.

Chapel

Many ships have a nondenominational chapel for prayer or silent reflection. If you're cruising during a religious holiday, the cruise line may invite a clergy member on board to lead a service.

Cruising with Kids

Cruises can be a great way to vacation with a family. But do your homework: Cruise lines cater to kids to varying degrees. For example, Disney, Celebrity, and Royal Caribbean are extremely kid-friendly, while other lines (especially the higher-end luxury ones) offer virtually nothing extra for children—a hint that they prefer you to leave the kiddos at home.

Kids' Programs and Activities

Family-friendly cruise lines have "kids clubs" that are open for most of the day. It's a win-win situation for both parents and

ON THE SHIP

children. Kids get to hang out with their peers and fill their time with games, story time, arts and crafts, and other fun stuff, while parents get to relax and enjoy the amenities of the ship.

Most kids clubs are for children ages three and older, and require your tots to be potty-trained (Norwegian's program is for two and up). Kids are separated by age so that tweens don't have to be subjected to younger children. For older kids, there are teen-only hangouts. If you have kids under three, options are limited: You might find parent/baby classes (no drop-and-go) and, in rare cases, onboard day care (Disney offers this on some ships).

Rules for kids clubs differ across cruise lines. Some charge for it, others include it. While kids clubs are generally open through-out the day (about 9:00-22:00), some close at mealtimes, so you'll have to collect your kids for lunch and dinner. Port-day policies vary—some kids clubs require a parent or guardian to stay on board (in case they need to reach you); others are fine with letting you off your parental leash.

There are also plenty of activities outside the kids club. All ships have pools, and some take it to the next level with rock-

climbing walls, bowling alleys, and in-line skating. Arcades and movies provide hours of entertainment, and shows are almost always appropriate for all ages. Many scheduled activities are fun for the whole family, such as art classes, ice-carving contests, or afternoon tea.

ON THE SHIP

Babysitting

Because cruise lines want you to explore the ship and have fun (and, of course, spend money at bars and the casino), many have babysitting services. On some ships, you can arrange for a babysitter to come to your stateroom, while others offer late-night group babysitting for a small fee.

To line up babysitting, ask at the front desk or the kids club. Or, if your child takes a shine to one of the youth counselors at the kids club, hit him or her up for some private babysitting. Oftentimes, crew members have flexible hours and are looking to earn extra money. Some have been separated from their families and even relish the opportunity to play with your kids—let them!

When hiring a babysitter, ask up front about rates; otherwise, offer the standard amount you pay at home. And remember to have cash on hand so you can compensate the babysitter at the end of the evening.

Food

Pizza parlors, hamburger grills, ice cream stands...thanks to the diverse dining options on ships, even the pickiest of eaters should be satisfied. Here are some tips for dining with children:

If you prefer to eat with your kids each night, choose the first dinner seating, which has more families and suits kids' earlier eating schedules. If your kids are too squirmy to sit through a five-course formal dinner every night, choose the buffet or a casual poolside restaurant (described later, under "Eating").

Don't forget about room service. This can be a nice option for breakfast, so you don't have to rush around in the morning. It's also an easy solution if you're cabin-bound with a napping child in the afternoon.

If your kids have convinced you to let them drink soda (which costs extra on a cruise), buy a soft drink card for the week to save over ordering à la carte.

In Port

If you plan to take your kids off the ship and into town, remember that a lot of Europe's streets and sidewalks are old, cobbled, and uneven—not ideal for a stroller. If your kids can't walk the whole way themselves, consider bringing a backpack carrier rather than a stroller for more mobility.

While excursions are often not worth the expense, they make sense for some ports and activities, especially when you have kids in tow. You don't have to deal with transportation, nor do you have to worry about missing the boat. (For more on excursions, see page 110).

If you do take your kids into port, consider draping a lanyard around their necks with emergency contact information in case you get separated. Include your name and mobile phone number, your ship's name, the cruise line, the itinerary, a copy of the child's passport, and some emergency cash. Hopefully your kids won't blow it on junk food or some tacky souvenir—though perhaps that's the price you'll have to pay for peace of mind.

Eating

While shipboard dining used to be open-and-shut (one restaurant, same table, same companions, same waitstaff, same time every night), these days you have choices ranging from self-service buffets to truly inspired specialty restaurants. On bigger ships, you could spend a week on board and never eat at the same place twice.

Note that if you have food allergies or a special diet—such as vegetarian, vegan, or kosher—most cruise lines will do their best to accommodate you. Notify them as far ahead as possible (when you book your cruise or 30 days before you depart).

Types of Dining

Most cruise ships have a main dining room, a more casual buffet, a variety of specialty restaurants, and room service.

Main Dining Room

The main restaurant venue on your ship is the old-fashioned dining room. With genteel decor, formal waiters, and a rotating menu of upscale cuisine, dining here is an integral part of the classic cruise experience.

Traditionally, each passenger was assigned a particular seating time and table for all dinners in the dining room. But over the last decade or so, this **"assigned dining"** policy has been in flux, with various cruise lines taking different approaches. Some lines (including Royal Caribbean, Costa, MSC, Celebrity, and Disney) still have assigned dining. Others (such as Holland America, Princess, and

Cunard) make it optional: You can choose whether you want an assigned seating (if you don't, just show up, and you'll be seated at whichever table is available next). Norwegian Cruise Line, along with several of the smaller luxury lines (Oceania, Silversea, Azamara, Windstar, Star Clippers, Seabourn, Regent Seven Seas), have no assigned dining—it's first-come, first-served, in any dining venue.

If you choose assigned dining, you'll eat with the same people every night (unless you opt to dine elsewhere on some evenings). Tables for two are rare, so couples will likely wind up seated with others. You'll really get to know your tablemates...whether you like it or not. Some cruisers prefer to be at a table that's as large as possible—if you are seated with just one other couple, you risk running out of conversation topics sooner than at a table with 10 or 12 people.

Diners are assigned either to an early seating (typically around 18:30) or a late seating (around 20:45). Avid sightseers might prefer the second seating, so they can fully enjoy the port without rushing back to the ship in time to change for dinner (on the other hand, the first seating lets you turn in early to rest up for the next day's port). In general, families and older passengers seem to opt for the first seating, while younger passengers tend to prefer the later one.

Formal Nights

Many cruises have one or two designated formal nights each week in the main dining room, when passengers get decked out for dinner in suits and cocktail dresses—or even tuxes and floor-length gowns (for tips on how to pack for formal night, see the sidebar on page 56). In general, on formal nights the whole ambience of the ship is upscale, with people hanging out in the bars, casinos, and other public areas dressed to the nines. And cruises like formal nights because passengers behave better and spend more money (for example, ordering a nicer bottle of wine or buying the posed photos).

Ships may also have semiformal nights (also one or two per week), which are scaled-down versions of the formal nights—for example, men wear slacks and a tie, but no jacket.

Some passengers relish the opportunity to dress up on formal nights. But if you don't feel like it, it's fine to dress however you like—as long as you stay out of the dining room. Skip the formal dinners and eat at another restaurant or the buffet, or order room service.

If your cruise line has assigned dining (whether mandatory or optional), you can request your seating preferences (time and table size) when you book your cruise. These assignments are first-come, first-served, so the earlier you book and make your request, the better. If you don't get your choice, you can ask to be put on a waiting list.

If you're not happy with your assignment, try dropping by the dining room early on the first night to see if the maître d', who's in charge of assigning tables, can help you. He'll do his best to accommodate you (you won't be the only person requesting a change—there's always some shuffling around). If the maître d' is able to make a switch, it's appropriate to thank him with a tip.

Some people really enjoy assigned dining. It encourages you to socialize with fellow passengers and make friends. Tablemates sometimes team up and hang out in port together as well. And some cruisers form lasting friendships with people they were, once upon a time, randomly assigned to dine with. If, on the other hand, you're miserable with your dinner companions, ask the maître d' to reseat you. Be aware that the longer you wait to request a change, the more difficult (and potentially awkward) it becomes.

If you get tired of assigned dining, you can always find variety by eating at the buffet or a specialty restaurant, or by ordering room service. And if you have an early seating but decide to skip dinner one night to stay late in port, you can still dine at the other onboard restaurants. Since the various onboard eateries are all included (except for specialty-restaurant surcharges), money is no object. While I enjoy the range of people at my assigned dinner table, I usually end up dining there only about half the nights on a given cruise.

Note that the main dining room is typically also open for breakfast and lunch. At these times, it's generally open seating (no preassigned tables), but you'll likely be seated with others. The majority of travelers prefer to have a quick breakfast and lunch at the buffet (or in port). But some cruisers enjoy eating these meals in the dining room (especially on leisurely sea days) as a more civilized alternative to the mob scene at the buffet; it's also an opportunity to meet fellow passengers who normally sit elsewhere at dinner.

Dress Code: In the main dining room, most cruise lines institute a "smart casual" dress code. This means no jeans, shorts, or T-shirts. Men wear slacks and button-down or polo shirts; women wear dresses or nice separates. "Formal night" dress codes apply in the dining room (see sidebar, opposite).

Casual Dining: Buffet and Poolside Restaurants

Besides the main dining room, most ships have at least one additional restaurant, generally a casual buffet. This has much longer

hours than the dining room, and the food is not necessarily a big step down: The buffet often has some of the same options as in the dining room, and it may even have some more unusual items, often themed (Greek, Indian, sushi, and so on). Most ships also have an even more casual "grill" restaurant, usually near the pool, where you can grab a quick burger or hot dog and other snacks. These options are handy if you're in a hurry, or just want a break from the dining room.

When eating at the buffet, keep in mind that this situation—with hundreds of people handling the same serving spoons and tongs, licking their fingers, then handling more spoons and tongs—is nirvana for communicable diseases. Compound that with the fact that some diners don't wash their hands (incorrectly believing that hand sanitizer is protecting them from all illness), and you've got a perfect storm. At the risk of sounding like a germophobe, wash your hands before, during, and after your meal. For more on this cheerful topic, see page 86.

Dress Code: The buffet and "grill" restaurants have a casual dress code all the time. You'll see plenty of swimsuits and flip-flops, though most cruise lines require a shirt or cover-up in the buffet.

Specialty Restaurants

Most ships (even small ones) have at least one specialty eatery, but some have a dozen or more. If there's just one specialty restau-

rant on board, it serves food (such as steak or seafood) that's a notch above what's available in the dining room. If there are several, they specialize in different foods or cuisines: steakhouse, French, sushi, Italian, Mexican, and so on.

Because specialty restaurants are more in demand than the traditional dining room, it's smart to make reservations if you have your heart set on a particular one. At the beginning of your cruise, scope

out the dining room's menu for the week; if one night seems less enticing to you, consider booking a specialty restaurant for that evening. Days at sea are also popular nights in specialty restaurants. I enjoy using the specialty restaurants when I want to dine with people I've met on the ship outside of my usual tablemates. Remember that if you want a window seat with a view, eat early. When darkness settles, the window becomes a pitch-black pane of glass, and that romantic view is entirely gone.

Occasionally these restaurants are included in your cruise price, but more often they require a special cover charge (typically $10-30). In addition to the cover charge, certain entrées incur a supplement ($10-20). A couple ordering specialty items and a bottle of wine can quickly ring up a $100 dinner bill. If you're on a tight budget, remember: Specialty restaurants are optional. You can eat every meal at the included dining room and buffet if you'd rather not spend the extra money. (By the way, if you order a bottle of wine and don't finish it, they can put your name on it and bring it to you in the main dining hall the next night.)

Some routine cruisers allege that the cruise lines are making the food in their dining room intentionally worse in order to steer passengers to the specialty restaurants that charge a cover. But from a dollars-and-cents perspective, this simply doesn't add up. The generally higher-quality ingredients used in specialty restaurants typically cost far more than the cover charge; for example, you might pay $20 to eat a steak that's worth $30. The cover charge is designed not to be a moneymaker, but to limit the number of people who try to dine at the specialty restaurants. It's just expensive enough to keep the place busy every night, but not cheap enough that it's swamped. So if cruise food is getting worse, it's not on purpose.

Dress Code: Specialty restaurants usually follow the same dress code as the main dining room (including on formal nights), though it depends on how upscale the menu is. The steakhouse might be more formal than the main dining room; the sushi bar could be less formal. If you're unsure, ask.

Room Service

Room service is temptingly easy and is generally included in the cruise price (no extra charge). Its menu appears to be much more limited than what you'd get in any of the restaurants, but you can often request items from the dining room menu as well. (If you don't want to dress up on formal night—but still want to enjoy the generally fancier fare on those evenings—ask in advance whether you can get those same meals as room service.) Either way, it's very convenient, especially on mornings when the ship arrives in port early. By eating breakfast in your room (place your order the night before), you can get ready at a more leisurely pace and avoid the crowd at the buffet. You can also arrange for room service to be waiting when you get back on the ship from exploring a port.

It's polite to thank the person who delivers your food with about a $2 tip; sometimes you can put this on your tab and sign for it, but not always, so it's smart to have cash ready.

Dress Code: From tuxes and gowns to your birthday suit, when you order room service, it's up to you.

Cruise Cuisine

Reviews of the food on cruise ships range wildly, from raves to pans. It's all relative: While food snobs who love locally sourced bistros may turn up their noses at cruise cuisine, fans of chain restaurants are perfectly satisfied on board. True foodies should lower their expectations. High-seas cuisine is not exactly high cuisine.

Cruise food is as good as it can be, considering that thousands of people are fed at each meal. Most cruise lines replenish their food stores about every two weeks, so everything you eat—including meat, seafood, and produce—may be less than fresh. Except on some of the top-end lines, the shipboard chefs are afforded virtually no room for creativity: The head office creates the recipes, then trains all kitchen crews to prepare each dish. To ensure cooks get it just right, cruise lines hang a photo in the galley (kitchen) of what each dish should look like. This is especially important since most of the cooks and servers come from countries where the cuisine is quite different.

Cruise-ship food is not local cuisine. Today's menu, dreamed up months ago by some executive chef in Miami, bears no resemblance to the food you saw this afternoon in port. It can be frustrating to wander through a Norwegian fjordside market, offering freshly grilled salmon and herb-roasted potatoes, only to go back to your ship and be served Caesar salad and prime rib.

On the other hand, cruise menus often feature famous but unusual dishes that would cost a pretty penny in a top-end restaurant back home. It can be fun to sample a variety of odd-ball items (such as frog legs, escargot, or foie gras) and higher-end meats (filet mignon, guinea fowl, lobster, crab)...with no expense and no commitment. (If you don't like it, don't finish it. Waiters are happy to bring you something else.)

Whether cruise food is good or bad, one thing's for sure: There's plenty of it. A ship with 2,500 passengers and 1,500 crew members might brag that they prepare "17,000 meals a day." Do the math: Someone's going back for seconds. A lot of someones, in fact. (If you're one of them, see "Staying Fit on Board" on page 88.)

All things considered, cruise lines do an impressive job of providing variety and quality. But cruise food still pales in comparison to the meals you can get in port, lovingly prepared with fresh ingredients and local recipes. Some travelers figure there's no point paying for food in port when you can just eat for free on the ship. But after a few days of cruise cuisine, I can't wait to sit down at a real European restaurant or grab some authentic street food... and I can really taste the difference.

Drinks

In general, tap water, milk, iced tea, coffee and tea, and fruit juices are included. Other drinks cost extra: alcohol of any kind, name-brand soft drinks, fresh-squeezed fruit juices, and premium espresso drinks (lattes and cappuccinos). You'll also pay for any drinks you take from your stateroom's minibar (generally the same price as in the restaurants). Beverages are priced approximately the same as in a restaurant on land (though in the most expensive Scandinavian countries—such as Norway—drink prices in port can exceed what you'll pay on board).

Early in your cruise, ask about special offers for reduced drink prices, such as discount cards or six-for-the-price-of-five beer offers. This also goes for soft drinks—if you guzzle Diet Coke, you can buy an "unlimited drink card" at the start of the cruise and order as many soft drinks as you want without paying more.

Cruise lines want to encourage alcohol sales on board, but without alienating customers. Before you set sail, find out your cruise line's policy on taking alcohol aboard so you can BYOB to save money. Some cruise lines ban it outright; others prohibit only hard liquor but allow wine and sometimes beer. On some ships, you may be able to bring one or two bottles of wine when you first board the ship. Keep in mind that if you bring aboard your own bottle of wine to enjoy with dinner on the ship, you'll most likely face a corkage fee (around $10-20).

To monitor the alcohol situation, cruise lines require you to go through a security checkpoint every time you board the ship. It's OK to purchase a souvenir bottle of booze in port, but you may have to check it for the duration of the cruise. Your purchases will be returned to you on the final night or the morning of your last disembarkation.

If you're a scofflaw who enjoys a nip every now and again, note that various cruising websites abound with strategies for getting around the "no alcohol" rules.

ON THE SHIP

Eating on Port Days

For some travelers, port days present a tasty opportunity to sample the local cuisine. Others prioritize their port time for sightseeing or shopping rather than sitting at a restaurant waiting for their food to arrive. And still others economize by returning to the ship for lunch (which, to me, seems like a waste of valuable port time). For more tips on eating while in port, see page 141.

To save money, some cruise passengers suggest tucking a few items from the breakfast buffet into a day bag for a light lunch on the go. While this is, to varying degrees, frowned upon by cruise lines, they recognize that many people do it—and, after all, you are paying for the food. If you do this, do so discreetly. Some experienced cruisers suggest ordering room service for breakfast, with enough extra for lunch. Or you can get a room-service sandwich the evening before and tuck it into your minifridge until morning. To make it easier to pack your lunch, bring along sealable plastic baggies from home.

Final Disembarkation

When your cruise comes to an end, you'll need to jump through a few hoops before you actually get off the ship. The crew will give you written instructions, and you'll often be able to watch a pre-sentation about the process on your stateroom TV. Many ships even have a "disembarkation talk" on the final day to explain the procedure. I keep it very simple: I review my bill for extra charges, accept the auto-tip, and carry my own bags off the ship any time after breakfast. While the specifics vary from cruise to cruise, most include the following considerations.

On your last full day on the ship, you'll receive an itemized copy of your **bill.** This includes the auto-tip for the crew (explained on page 84), drinks, excursions, shopping, restaurant surcharges, and any other expenses you've incurred. This amount will automatically be charged to the credit card you registered with the cruise line. If there are any mistaken charges, contest them as soon as you discover them (to avoid long lines just as everyone is disembarking).

If you'd like to give an additional cash **tip** to any crew members (especially those with whom you've personally interacted or who have given you exceptional service), it's best to do so on the final night in case you can't find the tippee in the morning. It's most common to tip cabin stewards and maybe a favorite waiter or two, particularly if you dined with them several times over the course of your cruise. There is no conventional amount or way to calculate tips; simply give what you like, but keep in mind that the crew has extremely low base wages (about $1/day). Traditionally, the cruise lines provide envelopes (either at the front desk or some-times left in your stateroom on the final evening) for you to tuck a cash tip inside and hand it to the crew member.

The night before disembarking, leave any **bags** you don't want to carry off the ship (with luggage tags attached) in the hall outside your room. The stewards will collect these bags during the night, and they'll be waiting for you when you step off the ship. Be sure *not* to pack any items you may need before disembarking the next morning (such as medications, a jacket, or a change of clothes). I prefer to carry off my own bags—that way, I don't have to pack the night before and go without my personal items the last morning. Also, I can leave anytime I want, and I don't have to spend time claiming my bags after I've disembarked.

Before leaving your cabin, check all the drawers, other hidden stowage areas, and the safe—after a week or more at sea, it's easy to forget where you tucked away items when you first unpacked.

In the morning, you'll be assigned a **disembarkation time.** At that time, you'll need to vacate your cabin (so the crew can clean it for the passengers arriving in a few hours) and gather in a designated public area for further instructions on where to leave the ship and claim your luggage.

It's possible to get an **early disembarkation time**—particularly if you're in a hurry to catch a plane or train, or if you just want to get started on your sightseeing. Request early disembarkation near the start of your cruise, as there is a set number of slots, and they can fill up. Another option is to walk off with all your luggage (rather than leaving it in the hall overnight and reclaiming it once off the ship)—as this opportunity may be limited to a designated number of passengers, ask about it near the start of your cruise.

If you're hungry, you can have breakfast—your last "free" meal before re-entering the real world. Once you do leave the ship at the appointed time, the bags you left outside your room the night before will be waiting for you in the terminal building.

If you're sightseeing around town and need to **store your bags,** there is often a bag-storage service at or near the cruise terminal (I've listed specifics for certain ports in this book). If you're staying at a hotel after the cruise, you can take your bags straight there when you leave the ship; even if your room is not ready, the hotelier is usually happy to hold your bags until check-in time.

Most cruise lines offer a **transfer** service to take you to your hotel or the airport. Typically you'll do better arranging this on your own (taxis wait at the cruise terminal, and this book's destination chapters include detailed instructions for getting into town or the airport). But if you book it through the cruise line, they may offer the option to let you pay a little extra to keep your stateroom and enjoy the pool until catching the airport shuttle for your afternoon flight. Some cruise lines also offer excursions at the end of the journey that swing by the city's top sights before ending at your hotel or the airport. This can be a good way to combine a sightseeing excursion with a transfer.

For **customs** regulations on returning to the US, see page 140.

IN PORT

While some people care more about shipboard amenities than the destinations, most travelers who take a European cruise see it mainly as a fun way to get to the ports. This is your chance to explore some of Europe's most fascinating cities, characteristic seaside villages, and engaging regions.

Prior to reaching each destination, you'll need to decide whether you want to go on an excursion (booked on board through your cruise line) or see it on your own. This chapter explains the pros and cons of excursions and provides a rundown of which destinations are best by excursion—and which are easy to do independently (see the sidebar on page 114). It also fills you in on the procedure for getting off and back on the ship, and provides tips on how to make the most of your time on land.

Excursions

In each port, your cruise line offers a variety of shore excursions. In Europe, these are mostly sightseeing tours on a bus, with some walking tours, led by a freelance local guide who is hired for the day by the cruise line. While the majority of excursions involve bus tours, town walks, and guided visits to museums and archaeological sites, others are more active (biking, kayaking, hiking), and some are more passive (a trip to a beach, spa, or even a luxury-hotel swimming pool for the day). Most also include a shopping component (such as a visit to a Fabergé egg shop in St. Petersburg, a diamond-cutting demonstration in Amsterdam, or a glassblowing demonstration in Sweden). When shopping is involved, kickbacks are common. Local merchants may pay the cruise line or guide to bring the group to their shops, give them a cut of whatever's bought, or both. In extreme cases, shops even provide buses and drivers for excursions, so there's no risk the shopping stop will be missed. The prices you're charged are likely inflated to cover these payouts.

Excursions aren't cheap. On European cruises, a basic two- to three-hour town walking tour runs about $40-60/person; a half-

day bus tour to a nearby sight can be $70-100; and a full-day bus-plus-walking-tour itinerary can be $100-150 or more. Extras (such as a boat ride or a lunch) add to the cost. There seems to be little difference in excursion costs or quality between a Mass-Market and a Luxury line (in fact, excursions can be more expensive on a cheap cruise than on a pricey one).

On the day of your excursion, you'll gather in a large space (often the ship's theater, sometimes with hundreds of others), waiting for your excursion group to be called. You're given a sticker to wear with a number that corresponds to your specific group/bus number. Popular excursion itineraries can have several different busloads. Once called, head down the gangway—or to the tenders—to meet your awaiting tour bus and local guide.

Excursion Options

The types of excursions you can book vary greatly, depending on the port. In a typical mid-sized port city, there might be two different themed walking tours of the city itself (for example, one focusing on the Old Town and art museum, and another on the New Town and architecture); a panoramic drive into the countryside for scenery, sometimes with stops (such as a wine-tasting, a restaurant lunch, or a folk-dancing show); and trips to outlying destinations, such as a neighboring village or an archaeological site.

Some ports have an even wider range of options. For example, if you dock at France's port of Le Havre, you'll be offered various trips into Paris, as well as guided visits to D-Day beaches and Impressionist sights closer to your ship. In these regions, excursions feature destinations bundled in different ways—look for an itinerary that covers just what you're interested in (see the "Excursions" sidebars in each destination chapter to help you sort through your options).

In some cases, there's only one worthy destination, but it takes some effort to reach it. For example, from the German port of Warnemünde, it's a three-hour bus or train ride into Berlin. It's possible—using this book—to get to these places by public transportation. But the cruise line hopes you'll pay them to take you instead.

Most excursions include a guided tour of town, but for those who want more freedom, cruise lines also offer "On Your Own" (a.k.a. "transfer-only" or "transportation-only") excursions: A bus will meet you as you disembark, and you might have a guide who narrates your ride into town. But once you reach the main destination, you're set free and given a time to report back to the bus. While more expensive than public transportation, these transfers cost less than fully guided excursions and are generally cheaper than hiring a taxi to take you into town (although you can split the cost of a taxi with other travelers).

Most cruise lines can also arrange a private driver or guide for you. While this is billed as an "excursion," you're simply paying the cruise line to act as a middleman. It's much more cost-effective to make these arrangements yourself (you can use one of the guides or drivers I recommend in this book).

Booking an Excursion

The cruise lines make it easy to sign up for excursions. There's generally a presentation on excursions in the theater sometime during the first few days of your cruise (or during a day at sea), and a commercial for the different itineraries runs 24/7 on your stateroom TV. You can sign up at the excursions desk, through the concierge, or (on some ships) through the interactive menu on your TV. You can generally cancel from 24 to 48 hours before the excursion leaves (ask when you book); if you cancel with less notice—for any reason—you will probably have to pay for it.

You can also book shore excursion on the cruise line's website prior to your trip. But be warned: It's common to sign up in advance, then realize once on board that your interests have changed. Some cruise lines levy a cancellation fee; most waive that fee if you cancel the first day you're on board, while others will waive it if you upgrade to a more expensive excursion.

If you have to cancel because of illness, some cruise lines' excursions desks may be willing to try to sell your tickets to another passenger (and refund your money); if not, they can write you a note to help you recoup the money from your travel insurance.

Cruise lines use the words "limited space" to prod passengers to hurry up and book various extra services—especially excursions. (They're technically correct—if there's not room for every single passenger on board to join the excursion, space is, strictly speaking, "limited," even if the excursion never sells out.) Sometimes excursions truly do fill up quickly; other times, you can sign up moments before departure. This creates a Chicken Little situation: Since they *always* claim "limited space," it's hard to know whether a particular excursion truly is filling up fast. If you have your heart set on a particular excursion, book it as far ahead as you can. But if you're on the fence, ask at the excursions desk how many seats are left and how soon they anticipate filling up. If your choice is already booked when you ask, request to be added to the wait list—it's not unusual for the cruise line to have last-minute cancellations or to add more departures for popular excursions.

Take an Excursion, or Do It on My Own?

Excursions are (along with alcohol sales and gambling) the cruise lines' bread and butter. To sell you on them, they like to convey the

"insurance" aspect of joining their excursion. They'll tell you that you can rest easy, knowing that you're getting a vetted local tour guide on a tried-and-true itinerary that will pack the best experience into your limited time—and you'll be guaranteed not to miss your ship when it leaves that evening.

Some excursions are a great value, whisking you to top-tier and otherwise-hard-to-reach sights with an eloquent guide on a well-planned itinerary. But others can be disappointing time- and money-wasters, carting passengers to meager "sights" that are actually shopping experiences in disguise.

This book is designed not necessarily to discourage you from taking the cruise lines' excursions, but to help you make an informed decision, on a case-by-case basis, whether a particular excursion is a good value for your interests and budget. In some situations (such as touring the D-Day beaches from Le Havre), I would happily pay a premium for a no-sweat transfer with a hand-picked, top-notch local guide. In other cases (such as the easy walk from Tallinn's cruise port to its atmospheric Old Town), the information in this book will allow you to have at least as good an experience, with more flexibility and freedom for a fraction of the price.

Pros and Cons of Excursions

Here are some of the benefits of taking an excursion, as touted by the cruise lines. Evaluate how these selling points fit the way you travel—and whether they are actually perks, or might cramp your style.

Returning to the Ship on Time: Cruise lines try to intimidate you into signing up for excursions by gravely reminding you that if you're on your own and fail to make it back to the ship on time, it could leave without you. If, however, a cruise-line excursion runs late for some reason, the ship will wait. In most places, provided that you budget your time conservatively (and barring an unforeseen strike or other crisis), there's no reason you can't have a

Excursion Cheat Sheet

This simplified roundup shows which major ports are best by excursion and which are doable on your own (with this book in hand). How to get into town is summarized here; for the full story, read the arrival information in each chapter.

Destination (Port)	Excursion?

COPENHAGEN — **No**

Bus #26 conveniently connects both ports to downtown, but only on weekdays. At other times, train, taxi, or walk.

From Langelinie Pier: It's an easy 10-minute walk to see the *Little Mermaid;* from there, stroll all the way into town. For a faster trip, catch bus #26 from right in front of the ship or walk 15 minutes to Østerport train station.

From Frihavnen: On weekends, when the bus doesn't run, walk 15 minutes from your ship to the Nordhavn station to ride the train into town.

STOCKHOLM — **No**

From Stadsgården: From some berths, you can walk to the Old Town in about 20 minutes; from others, it's easier to catch the hop-on, hop-off boat to points around town.

From Frihamnen: Walk 5-10 minutes to the bus stop, and ride the public bus into town.

HELSINKI — **No**

From West Harbor: Ride public transportation downtown (bus #14 from Hernesaari terminal, tram #9 from West/Länsi terminal).

From South Harbor: You can walk into town from the Katajanokan and Olympia terminals in about 15 minutes (or hop on a tram).

ST. PETERSBURG — **Maybe**

Important: If you don't want to get a visa (must be arranged in advance—see page 354), you'll be allowed off the ship only with an excursion. If you are on your own...

From Marine Facade: Ride a public bus-plus-metro connection downtown.

From Lieutenant Schmidt Embankment or English Embankment: Walk or catch a public bus or tram into downtown.

TALLINN — **No**

It's an easy 15-minute walk from the cruise port into town.

RĪGA — **No**

It's an easy 10-20-minute walk from the cruise port into town.

GDAŃSK (Gdynia) — **No**

From the port at Gydnia, make your way downtown to ride the train for 35 minutes to Gdańsk; once at Gdańsk's train station, it's a 15-minute walk to the scenic heart of town.

BERLIN (Warnemünde) — **Maybe**

Warnemünde's train station, a 5- to 10-minute walk from the cruise terminals, has frequent connections to nearby Rostock (22 minutes) and sparse connections to Berlin (3 hours, often with change in Rostock). If the Berlin train schedule doesn't work well with your cruise schedule (check www.bahn.com)—and maybe even if it does—a transportation-only "On Your Own" excursion from your cruise line can be the best way to get maximum time in Berlin.

Destination (Port)	Excursion?

OSLO — **No**

From Akershus or Revierkai: It's an easy walk downtown.
From Filipstad or Sørenge: These ports are farther out and still walkable, but are more convenient by cruise-line shuttle bus (worth paying for). Avoid expensive taxis.

STAVANGER — **Maybe**

It's an easy 5- to 15-minute walk into downtown. Consider an excursion only if you want to side-trip to Pulpit Rock and the Lysefjord.

BERGEN — **No**

From Skolten: You can walk into town from the port in about 10 minutes.
From Jekteviken/Dokken: Ride the free shuttle bus into downtown.

SOGNEFJORD (Flåm) — **No**

It's possible to do the best part of the "Norway in a Nutshell" loop trip on your own (boat ride, twisty mountain bus, train ride, and another train steeply back down into the fjord). But this requires being organized, double-checking schedules (see page 756), and getting off the ship quickly.

GEIRANGERFJORD (Geiranger) — **Yes**

There's little to see in Geiranger town itself, and public transportation doesn't help much; it's smart to book a tour to local viewpoints and scenic roads—either though your cruise line or a local tour operator.

AMSTERDAM — **No**

The cruise terminal is a 3-minute tram ride or 15-minute walk from the central train station, with connections to anywhere in the city.

BRUGES AND BRUSSELS (Zeebrugge) — **No**

Ride a shuttle bus to the port gate, then walk 10 minutes to a tram stop. Ride the tram 10-15 minutes to the Blankenberge train station, where hourly trains zip to Bruges (15 minutes), Ghent (50 minutes), and Brussels (1.5 hours).

LONDON (Southampton or Dover) — **Maybe**

From Southampton: From the Ocean or City Cruise Terminals, you can walk into town, where a free bus goes to the train station; from the QEII or Mayflower Cruise Terminals, spring for a taxi. Trains go to London (1.25 hours, 2/hour) and Portsmouth (50 minutes, hourly).
From Dover: Ride a shuttle bus or taxi to the train station, where trains depart for London (1.25 hours, hourly) or Canterbury (20-30 minutes, 2/hour).

PARIS AND NORMANDY (Le Havre) — **Maybe**

Ride a cruise-line shuttle bus or walk about 35 minutes from the port to the train/bus station; from there, connect to Paris (2.25-hour train), Rouen (1-hour train), or Honfleur (30-minute bus). To see the D-Day beaches (about an hour's drive west), an excursion works best.

great day in port and easily make it back on board in time. But if you don't feel confident about your ability to navigate back to the ship on time, or you have a chronic issue with lateness, an excursion may be a good option.

Getting Off First: Those going on excursions have priority for getting off the ship. This is especially useful when tendering, as tender lines can be long soon after arrival. But if you're organized and get a tender ticket as early as possible, you can make it off the ship almost as fast as the excursion passengers. (For more on tendering, see page 121.)

Optimizing Time in Port: Most excursions are well-planned by the cruise line to efficiently use your limited time in port.

Rather than waiting around for a bus or train to your destination, you're whisked dockside-to-destination by the excursion bus. However, when weighing the "time savings" of an excursion, remember to account for how long it takes 50 people (compared to two people) to do everyday tasks: boarding a bus, walking through a castle, even making bathroom stops. If you're on your own and want to check out a particular shop, you can stay as long as you like—or just dip in and out; with a cruise excursion, you're committed to a half-hour, an hour, or however long the shopkeeper is paying your guide to keep you there. Every time your group moves somewhere, you're moving with dozens of other people, which always takes time. In many ports, you may actually reach the city center faster on your own than with an excursion, provided you are ready to hop off the ship as soon as you can, don't waste time getting to the terminal building, and know how, when, and where to grab public transport.

Many cruise lines schedule both morning and afternoon excursions. If you're a 30-minute bus ride from a major destination and select a morning excursion, your guide is instructed to bring you back to the ship (hoping that you'll join an afternoon excursion as well). If you prefer to spend your afternoon in town, it's perfectly acceptable to skip the return bus trip and make your way back to the ship, later, on your own (just be sure your guide knows you're splitting off).

Accessing Out-of-the-Way Sights: In most destinations, there's a relatively straightforward, affordable public-transportation option for getting from the cruise port to the major city or sight. But in a few cases, minor sights (or even the occasional major sight) are challenging, if not impossible, to reach without paying for a pricey taxi or rental car. For example, if your cruise is coming to Le Havre, and you've always wanted to see the D-Day beaches, you'll find it next to impossible to get there by public transportation—so the most reasonable choice is an excursion. This book is designed to help you determine how easy—or difficult—it is to reach the places you're interested in seeing.

Touring with Quality Guides: Most excursions are led by

local guides contracted through the cruise line. While all guides have been vetted by the cruise line and are generally high-quality, a few oddball exceptions occasionally sneak through. The guide is the biggest wildcard in the success of your tour, but it's also something you have very little control over. You won't know which guide is leading your excursion until he or she shows up to collect you.

An alternative can be to hire a good local guide to show you around on a private tour. For two people, this can cost about as much as buying the excursion, but you get a much more personalized experience, tailored to your interests. And if you can enlist other passengers to join you to split the cost, it's even more of a bargain. I've recommended my favorite guides for most destinations; many of them are the same ones who are hired by the cruise lines to lead their excursions. Because local guides tend to book up when a big cruise ship is in town, it's smart to plan ahead and email these guides well before your trip.

Cruise lines keep track of which guides get good reviews, and do their best to use those guides in the future. If you do go on an excursion, take the time to give the cruise line feedback, good or bad, about the quality of your guide. They really want to know.

Beware of Crew Members' Advice

While most cruise lines understand that their passengers won't book an excursion at every port, there is some pressure to get you to take them. And if you ask crew members for advice on sight-seeing (independent of an excursion), they may be less than forthcoming. Take crew members' destination advice with a grain of salt.

Philosophically, most cruise lines don't consider it their responsibility to help you enjoy your port experience—unless you pay them for an excursion. The longer you spend on the ship, the more likely you are to spend more money on board, so there's actually a financial disincentive for crew members to help you get off the ship and find your own way in the port. You're lucky if the best they offer is, "Take a taxi. I have no idea what it costs."

I have actually overheard excursion staff dispense misinformation about the time, expense, and difficulty involved in reaching downtown from a port ("The taxi takes 25-30 minutes, and I've never seen a bus at the terminal"—when in fact, the taxi takes 10 minutes and there's an easy bus connection from the terminal). Was the crew being deceptive, or just ignorant? Either way, it was still misinformation.

Friendly as they are, the crew members on your cruise don't work for a tourist information office. You're on your own for information. That's why detailed instructions for getting into town from the port are a major feature of this book. The local tourist office often sets up a desk or info tent right on the pier, in the terminal, or where shuttle buses drop you. Otherwise, you can always find a tourist information office (abbreviated **TI** in this book) in the town center.

The Bottom Line on Excursions

Some passengers are on a cruise because they simply don't want to invest the time and energy needed to be independent...they want to be on vacation. Time is money, and you spend 50 weeks a year figuring things out back home; on vacation, you want someone else to do the thinking for you. If that's you, excursions can be a good way to see a place.

But in many destinations, it honestly doesn't take that much additional effort or preparation to have a good experience without paying a premium for an excursion. And cost savings aside, if you have even a middling spirit of adventure, doing it on your own can be a fun experience in itself.

Planning Your Time

Whether you're taking an excursion, sightseeing on your own, or doing a combination of the two, it's important to plan your day on land carefully. Be sure to read this book's sightseeing information and walking tours the night before to make the most of your time in a destination, even if you're taking an excursion—many include free time at a sight or neighborhood, or leave you with extra time in port.

First, keep in mind that the advertised amount of time in port can be deceptive. If the itinerary says that the ship is in town from 8:00 to 17:00, mentally subtract an hour or two from that time. It can take a good half-hour to get off a big ship and to the terminal building (or even longer, if you're tendering), and from the terminal, you still have to reach the town center. At the end of the day, the all-aboard time is generally a half-hour before the ship departs. Not only do you have to be back on board by 16:30, but you must also build in the time it takes to get from downtown to the ship. Your nine-hour visit in port just shrank to seven hours... still plenty of time to really enjoy a place, but not quite as much as you expected.

It's essential to realize that if you are late returning to the ship, you cannot expect them to wait for you (unless you're on one of the cruise line's excursions, and it's running late). The cruise line has the right to depart without you...and they will. While this seems harsh, cruise lines must pay port fees for every *minute* they are docked, so your half-hour delay could cost them more than your cruise ticket. Also, they have a tight schedule to keep and can't be waiting around for stragglers (for tips on what to do if this happens to you, see the end of this chapter).

To avoid missing the boat, work backwards from the time you have to be back on board. Be very conservative, especially if you're going far—for example, riding a train or bus to a neighboring town. Public transportation can be delayed, and traffic can be snarled at rush hour—just when you're heading back to the ship. One strategy is to do the farthest-flung sights first, then gradually work your way back to the ship. Once you know you're within walking distance of the ship, you can dawdle to your heart's content, confident you can make it back on time.

If you're extremely concerned about missing the ship, just pretend it departs an hour earlier than it actually does. You'll still have several hours to enjoy that destination and be left with an hour to kill back at the cruise port (or on board).

Note that transportation strikes can be a problem in Europe (particularly in France). These can hit at any time, although they are usually publicized in advance. If you're going beyond the immediate area of the port, ask the local TI, "Are there any strikes planned for today that could make it difficult for me to return to my ship?" Even when there is a planned strike, a few trains and buses will still run—ask for the schedule.

If you're an early riser, you'll notice that your ship typically arrives at the port some time before the official disembarkation time. That's because local officials need an hour or more to "clear" the ship (process paperwork, passports, and so on) before passengers are allowed off. Even if you wake up and find the ship docked, you'll most likely have to wait for the official disembarkation time to get off.

While you have to plan your time smartly, don't let anxiety paralyze you: Some travelers—even adventurous ones—get so nervous about missing the boat that they spend all day within view of the cruise port, just in case. Anyone who does that is missing out: In very few cities is the best sightseeing actually concentrated near the port. Cruise excursion directors have told me that entire months go by when they don't leave anyone behind. You have to be pretty sloppy—or incredibly unlucky—to miss your ship.

Managing Crowds

Unless you're on a luxury line, you can't go on a cruise and expect to avoid crowds. It's simply a fact of life. So be prepared to visit

sights at the busiest possible time—just as your cruise ship funnels a few thousand time-pressed tourists into town (or, worse, when three or four ships simultaneously disgorge).

Keep in mind that my instructions for getting into town might sound easy—but when you're jostling with several hundred others to cram onto a public bus that comes once every 20 minutes, the reality check can be brutal. Be patient...and most important, be prepared. You'll be amazed at how many of your fellow cruisers will step off the ship knowing nothing about their options for seeing the place. By buying and reading this book, and doing just a bit of homework before each destination, you're already way ahead of the game.

Make it a point to be the first person down the gangway (or in line for tender tickets) each day, and make a beeline for what you most want to see. While your fellow passengers are lingering over that second cup of coffee or puzzling over the bus schedule, you can be the first person on top of the city wall or on the early train to your destination. Yes, you're on vacation, so if you want to take it easy, that's your prerogative. But you can't be lazy and also avoid the crowds. Choose one.

Getting Off the Ship

Your ship has arrived at its destination, and it's time to disembark and enjoy Europe. This section explains the procedure for getting off the ship and also provides a rundown of the services you'll find at the port.

Docking Versus Tendering

There are two basic ways to disembark from the ship: docking or tendering. On most European cruise itineraries, docking is far more common than tendering. (Of the ports covered in this book, the only ones where you may need to tender are on the Norwegian fjords.)

Docking

When your ship docks, it means that the vessel actually ties up to a

pier, and you can simply walk off onto dry land. However, cruise piers (like cruise ships) can be massive, so you may have to walk 10-15 minutes from the ship to the terminal building. Sometimes the port area is so vast, the cruise line will offer a shuttle bus between the ship and the terminal building.

Tendering

If your ship is too big or there's not enough room at the pier, the ship will anchor offshore and send passengers ashore using small boats called tenders. Passengers who have paid for excursions usually go first; then it goes in order of tender ticket (or tender number).

Tender tickets are generally distributed the night before or on the morning of arrival. Show up as early as you can to get your tender ticket (you may have to wait in line even before the official start time); the sooner you get your ticket, the earlier you can board your tender. Even then, you'll likely have to wait. (Sometimes passengers in more expensive staterooms are given a "VIP tender ticket," allowing them to skip the line whenever they want.)

The tenders themselves are usually the ship's lifeboats, but in some destinations, the port authority requires the cruise line to hire local tenders. Because

tenders are small vessels prone to turbulence, transferring from the ship to the tender and from the tender to shore can be rough. Take your time, be sure of your footing, and let the tender attendants give you a hand—it's their job to prevent you from going for an unplanned swim.

Tendering is, to many passengers, the scourge of cruising, as it can waste a lot of time. Obviously, not everyone on your big ship can fit on those little tenders all at once. Do the math: Your ship carries some 2,000 passengers. There are three or four tenders, which can carry anywhere from 30 to 150 people apiece, and it takes at least 20 minutes round-trip. This can all translate into a lot of waiting around.

What Should I Bring to Shore?

- Your room **key card.** No matter how you leave the ship—tendering or docking, with an excursion or on your own—the crew must account for your absence. Any time you come or go, a security guard will swipe your room key. Your photo will flash onscreen to ensure it's really you. With this punch-in-and-out system, the crew knows exactly who's on board and who's on shore at all times.
- **Local cash.** After living on a cashless cruise ship, this is easy to forget. If you plan to withdraw local currency at an ATM, be sure to bring your debit card (and a credit card if you plan to make purchases).
- **Passport.** It's smart to carry your passport at all times (safely tucked away in a money belt—explained on page 58). While you typically won't have to show a passport when embarking or disembarking at each port (except the first and possibly the last), you may need it as a deposit for renting something (such as an audioguide or a scooter), or as ID when making a credit-card purchase or requesting a VAT refund. And you'll certainly want it in case you miss the boat and have to make your way to the next port. Some ships actually keep your passport until the end of the cruise. In that case, you'll go on shore without it; if you're one of the rare few who misses the ship, you'll find your passport with the port agent at the terminal office.
- **Weather-appropriate gear.** If it's hot out, that means sunscreen, a hat for shade, sunglasses, lightweight and light-colored clothing, and a water bottle (or buy one in port). In (more likely) chilly or rainy weather, bring a lightweight sweater or raincoat.
- **Long pants.** If you plan to visit any Orthodox churches (such as those in St. Petersburg, Helsinki, or Tallinn), you'll encounter a strict "no shorts, no bare shoulders" dress code.
- Your cruise's **destination information sheet** (daily program). At a minimum, jot down the all-aboard time and—if applicable—the time of the last tender or shuttle bus to the ship, along with contact details for the port agent (see page 124).
- This **guidebook,** or—better yet—tear out just the pages you need for today's port (see sidebar on page 3).

IN PORT

There are various strategies for navigating the tender line: Some cruisers report that if you show up at the gangway, ready to go, before your tender ticket number is called, you might be able to slip on early. A crush of people will often jam the main stairwells and elevators to the gangway. Some of these folks might block your passage despite having later tender tickets than yours. If you use a different set of stairs or elevators, then walk through an alternate hallway, you might be able to pop out near the gangway rather than get stuck in the logjam on the main stairwell. If you anticipate crowd issues while tendering, scope out the ship's layout in advance, when it's not busy.

Another strategy to avoid the crush of people trying to get off the ship upon arrival is to simply wait an hour or two, when you can waltz onto a tender at will. While you'll miss out on some valuable sightseeing time on shore, some cruisers figure that's a fair trade-off for avoiding the stress of tendering at a prime time.

If there's an advantage to tendering, it's that you're more likely to be taken to an arrival point that's close to the town's main points of interest. When you figure in the time it would take to get from the main cruise port to the city center, tendering might actually save you some time—provided you get an early tender ticket. In fact, on smaller ships, it can even be an advantage to tender—there's little to no waiting, and you're deposited in the heart of town.

Strangely, crowds are rare on tenders returning to the ship; apparently passengers trickle back all through the day, so even the last tenders of the day are rarely jam-packed. (And if they are, the ship won't leave without you, provided you're waiting in the tender line.)

The Port Area

In most destinations, the port is not in the city center; in some cases (such as Zeebrugge for Bruges/Brussels, Le Havre for Paris, or Warnemünde for Berlin), the port is actually in a separate town or city a lengthy train or bus ride away. In this book's destination chapters, I describe how near (or far) the port is from the town center. Be warned that the port area is, almost as a rule, the ugliest part of town—often an industrial and/or maritime area that had its historic charm bombed to bits in World War II. But once you're in the heart of town, none of that will matter.

Many ports have a terminal building, where you'll find passport check/customs control, and usually also ATMs, some duty-

free shops, sometimes a travel agency and/or car-rental office, and (out front) a taxi stand and bus stop into town. Better terminals also have a TI that's staffed at times when cruise ships arrive.

Most ports have lines painted on the pavement (often blue) that lead you from where you step off the ship or exit the port gate to services (such as TIs or terminal buildings) or transportation options (such as bus stops).

Note: Your passport will rarely be checked on a European cruise. Most of the destinations covered in this book belong to the open-borders Schengen Agreement, so you don't need to show a passport when crossing the border. Even in other countries, it likely won't be checked—they know you're on a cruise ship, that you'll be returning to the ship that evening, and that you're likely to spend a lot of money in port, so they want to make things easy for you. Of the destination countries in this book, only Russia requires a visa for those going ashore without an excursion (explained on page 354). So, while it's wise to carry your passport for identification purposes, don't be surprised if you never actually need it.

Port Agents

In every port, your cruise line has an official port agent—a local representative who's designated to watch out for their passengers while they're in port. This person's name and contact information is listed on the port-of-call information sheet distributed by your cruise line and usually also in the daily program. Be sure to have this information with you when you go on shore; if you have an emergency and can't contact anyone from your ship, call the port agent for help. Likewise, if you're running late and realize that you won't make it back to the ship by the departure time, get in touch with your port agent, who will relay the information to the ship so they know you aren't coming. If you do miss the ship, sometimes the port agent can point you in the right direction for making your way to the next port of call on your own (for details, see "What If I Miss My Boat?" at the end of this chapter).

Sightseeing on Your Own

If you're planning to strike out on your own, you need to figure out in advance where you're going, how to get there, and what you want to do once you're there.

Getting into Town

When it's a long distance from the ship to the cruise terminal, cruise lines usually offer a free shuttle bus to the terminal; if it's a short distance, you can walk. Either way, once you're at the terminal, you'll need to find your own way into town.

By Taxi

Exiting the terminal, you'll usually run into a busy taxi stand, with gregarious, English-speaking cabbies offering to take you for a tour around the area's main sights. While taxis are efficient, be aware that most cabbies' rates are ridiculously inflated to take advantage of cruisers. You may be able to persuade them to just take you into town (generally at a hiked-up rate), though they usually prefer to find passengers willing to hire them for several hours. Sometimes just walking a block or two and hailing a cab on the street can save you half the rate.

To keep the fare reasonable, consider taking the taxi only as far as you need to (for example, to the nearest subway station to hop a speedy train into the city, rather than pay to drive all the way across town in congested traffic). Also keep in mind that there must be somebody on your ship who's going to the same place you are—strike up a conversation at breakfast or on the gangway to find someone to team up with and split the fare.

Remember: Taxis aren't just for getting from the port to town; they can also be wonderful time-savers for connecting sights within a big city. For more taxi tips, see the sidebar on page 126.

By Bus

Near the terminal, often just beyond the taxi stand, you'll usually find a **public bus** stop for getting into town. This is significantly cheaper than a taxi, and often not much slower. Even with an entire cruise ship emptying all at once, waiting in a long line for the bus is relatively rare. These buses usually take local cash only and sometimes require exact change. If you see a kiosk or ticket vending machine near the bus stop, try to purchase a bus ticket there, or at least buy something small to break big bills and get the correct change.

Occasionally, there's a **shuttle bus** into town; while handy, this is rare and reserved mostly for ports that lack a good public-transit

Taxi Tips

There's no denying that taxis are the fastest way to get from your ship to what you want to see. But you'll pay for that convenience. Regular fares tend to be high, and many cabbies are adept at overcharging tourists—especially cruise passengers—in shameless and creative ways. Here are some tips to avoid getting ripped off by a cabbie.

Finding a Cab: In most cruise-port towns, it's generally easy to flag down a cab. A taxi stand is usually right at the cruise terminal. If not (or if you're already in town), ask a local to direct you to the nearest taxi stand. Taxi stands are often listed prominently on city maps; look for the little Ts.

Fly-by-night cabbies with a makeshift "Taxi" sign on the rooftop and no company logo or phone number on the door are less likely to be honest.

Establishing a Price: To figure the fare, you can either use the taxi meter or agree on a set price up front. In either case, it's important to know the going rate (the destination chapters include the prevailing rates for the most likely journeys from each port). Even if I'm using the taxi meter, I still ask for a rough estimate up front, so I know generally what to expect.

In most cities, it's best to use the **taxi meter**—and cabbies are legally required to do so if the passenger requests it. So insist. Cabbies who get feisty and refuse are probably up to no good. If you don't feel comfortable about a situation, just get out and find another taxi.

Even with the meter, cabbies can still find ways to scam you. For instance, they may try to set it to the pricier weekend tariff, even if it's a weekday (since trips on nights and weekends gener-

connection (such as Zeebrugge or Dover). If there is a shuttle, it's often your best option. The shuttle bus typically costs about

$4-10 round-trip (buses run frequently when the ship arrives, then about every 15-20 minutes; pay attention to where the bus leaves you downtown, as you'll need to find that stop later to return to the ship).

The shuttle bus can get

ally cost more). Check the list of different meter rates (posted somewhere in the cab, often in English) to make sure your driver has set the meter to the correct tariff. If you're confused about the tariff your cabbie has selected, ask for an explanation.

It's also possible (though obviously illegal) for cabbies to tinker with a taxi meter to make it spin like a pinwheel. If you glance away from the meter, then look back and see that it's mysteriously doubled, you've likely been duped. However, some extra fees are on the level (for instance, in most cities, there's a legitimate surcharge for picking you up at the cruise port). Again, these should be listed clearly on the tariff sheet. If you suspect foul play, following the route on your map or conspicuously writing down the cabbie's license information can shame him into being honest.

Agreeing to a **set price** for the ride is another option. While this is usually higher than the fair metered rate would be, sometimes it's the easiest way to go. Just be sure that the rate you agree to is more or less in the ballpark of the rate I've listed in this book. Consider asking a couple of cabbies within a block or two of each other for estimates. You may be surprised at the variation.

Many cabbies hire out for an hourly rate; if you want the taxi to take you to a variety of outlying sights and wait for you, this can be a good value. You can also arrange in advance to hire a driver for a few hours or the whole day (for some destinations, I've listed my favorite local drivers).

Settling Up: It's best to pay in small bills. If you use a large bill, state the denomination out loud as you hand it to the cabbie. They can be experts at dropping a €50 note and picking up a €20. Count your change. To tip a good cabbie, round up about 5-10 percent (to pay a €4.50 fare, give €5; for a €28 fare, give €30). But if you feel like you're being driven in circles or otherwise ripped off, skip the tip.

IN PORT

very crowded when the ship first unloads—do your best to get off the ship and onto the bus quickly. At slower times, you might have to wait a little while for the bus to fill up before it departs. Note that the port shuttle sometimes doesn't start running until sometime after your ship actually docks (for example, you disembark at 7:00, but the bus doesn't start running until 8:30). This is a case when it can be worth springing for a taxi to avoid waiting around.

By Excursion

Cruise lines sometimes offer "On Your Own" excursions that include unguided transportation into town, then free time on your own. This may be worthwhile in places where the port is far from the main point of interest (such as the ports of Dover or Southampton for London, the port of Warnemünde for Berlin, or the port of Le Havre for Paris). While more expensive than public transportation—and sometimes even more expensive than a shared cab—this is a low-stress option that still allows you freedom to see the sights at your own pace. For details, see page 110.

Seeing the Town

If you're touring a port on your own, you have several options for getting around town and visiting the sights (see the destination chapters for specifics).

On a Tour

It's easy to get a guided tour without having to pay excessively for an excursion. And there are plenty of choices, from walking to bus tours. Cruise Critic (www.cruisecritic.com) is a great resource for exploring these options.

At or near the terminal, you'll generally find travel agencies offering **package tours.** These tours are similar to the cruise-ship excursions but usually cost far less (half or even a third as much). However, what's offered can change from day to day, so they're not as reliable as the cruise line's offerings. It's possible to reserve these in advance, typically through a third party (such as a travel agency).

A great budget alternative is to join a regularly scheduled **local walking tour** (in English, departing at a specified time every day). Again, these are very similar to the cruise lines' walking tours and often use the same guides. Look for my walking tour listings in the destination chapters or ask at the local TI.

In a large city where sights are spread out, it can be convenient to join a **hop-on, hop-off bus tour.** These buses make a circle through town every 30 minutes or so, stopping at key points where passengers can hop on or off at will. While relatively expensive (figure around €25-30 for an all-day ticket), these tours are easier than figuring out public transportation, come with commentary (either recorded or from a live guide), and generally have a stop at or near the cruise port.

Some cruisers hire a **private guide** to meet them at the ship and take them around town (see page 117). Book them direct, using the contact information in this book; if you arrange the guide through a third party—such as a local travel agent or the cruise line—you'll pay a premium.

On Your Own

If you prefer to sightsee independently and are going to London, Paris, or Amsterdam, take advantage of my free **audio tours,** which guide you through the most interesting neighborhoods and most famous sights in each of those cities. Audio tours allow your eyes to enjoy the wonders of the place while your ears learn its story. Before your trip, download the tours to your mobile device via www.ricksteves.com/audioeurope, iTunes, Google Play, or the Rick Steves' Audio Europe smartphone app. These give all the information you'll want, while saving you lots of time and money—perfect for the thoughtful, independent cruiser.

It's possible to **rent a car** to see the sights. While this makes sense for covering a wide rural area (such as the D-Day beaches or the English countryside), I would never rent a car to tour a big city—public transportation is not only vastly cheaper, but it avoids the headaches of parking, unfamiliar traffic patterns, and other problems. In general, given the relatively short time you'll have in port and the high expense of renting a car for the day (figure €40-100/day, depending on the port), this option doesn't make much sense. However, if you're interested, you'll often find car-rental offices or travel agencies at or near the terminal that are accustomed to renting cars for short time periods to cruisers. You can also look for deals online (on rental companies' websites or travel-booking sites) in advance.

In some cities, renting a **bicycle** can be a good option. Northern European cities—especially Copenhagen and Amsterdam—are flat, laced with bike lanes, and very bike-friendly. In these cities, you'll see locals using bikes more routinely than cars...join them.

With Fellow Passengers

The upside of traveling with so many other people is that you have ample opportunities to make friends. On a ship with thousands of people, I guarantee you'll find someone who shares your style of travel. If you and your traveling companion hit it off with others, consider teaming up for your shore time. This "double-dating" can save both money (splitting the cost of an expensive taxi ride) and stress (working together to figure out the best way into town). But be sure you're all interested in the same things before you head ashore—you don't want to end up on the corner in front of the Louvre, bickering about whether to tour Notre-Dame or saunter up the Champs-Elysées.

IN PORT

In-Port Travel Skills

Whether you're taking an excursion or tackling a port on your own, this practical advice will come in handy. This section includes tips on useful services, avoiding theft, using money, sightseeing, shopping, eating, and in general, making the most of your time in port.

Travel Smart

Europe is like a complex play—easier to follow and really appreciate on a second viewing. While no one does the same trip twice to gain that advantage, reading about the places you'll visit before you reach each destination accomplishes much the same thing.

Though you're bound to your ship's schedule, note the best times to visit various sights, and try to hit them as best as you can. Pay attention to holidays, festivals, and days when sights are closed. For example, many museums are closed on Mondays. Big sights and museums often stop admitting people 30-60 minutes before closing time.

Sundays have the same pros and cons as they do for travelers in the US (special events, limited hours, banks and many shops closed, limited public transportation, no rush hour). Saturdays are virtually weekdays with earlier closing times and no rush hour (though transportation connections can be less frequent than on weekdays).

When in port, visit the TI. Find a place to get online to research sights, make reservations (maybe book a guide or tour for your next destination), keep in touch with home, and so on. Then head for the sights you came so far to see.

Most important, connect with the culture. Set up your own quest to find the tastiest *kringle* in Denmark or the best *smörgåsbord* in Sweden. Slow down and be open to unexpected experiences. Enjoy the hospitality of the European people. Ask questions—most locals are eager to point you in their idea of the right direction. Wear your money belt, learn the currency, and figure out how to estimate prices in dollars. Those who expect to travel smart, do.

Services

Tourist Information: No matter how well I know a town, my first stop is always the TI. TIs are usually located on the main square, in the city hall, or at the train station (just look for signs). Many cruise ports also have a temporary TI desk, which hands out maps and answers questions for arriving cruisers. Their job is to make sure your few hours in town are enjoyable, so you'll come back on your own later. At TIs, you can get information on sights and public transit, and pick up a city map and a local entertainment guide. Ask if guided walks, self-guided walking-tour brochures, or audioguides are available. If you need a quick place to eat, ask the TI staff where they go for lunch.

Medical Help: If you get sick or injured while in port—assuming you're not in need of urgent care—do as the Europeans do and go to a pharmacist for advice. European pharmacists diagnose and prescribe remedies for most simple problems. They are usually friendly and speak English, and some medications that are only available by prescription in the US are available over the counter (surprisingly cheaply) in Europe. If necessary, the pharmacist will send you to a doctor or the health clinic. For most destinations, I've listed pharmacies close to the cruise port.

Theft or Loss: To replace a **passport,** you'll need to go in person to a US embassy or consulate during their business hours, which are generally limited and restricted to weekdays. This can take a day or two. If you lose your passport, contact the port agent or the ship's guest services desk immediately—and be aware that you may not be able to continue your cruise if a replacement passport is not available before the ship sails. Having a photocopy of your passport and a backup form of ID such as your driver's license, as well as an extra passport photo, can speed up getting a replacement.

If your **credit and debit cards** disappear, cancel and replace them (see "Damage Control for Lost or Stolen Cards" on page 135). File a **police report** on the spot for any loss (you'll need it to submit an insurance claim). For more info, see www.ricksteves .com/help.

Internet Cafés: Finding an Internet café in Europe is a breeze. While these places don't always serve food or drinks—

sometimes they're just big, functional, sweaty rooms filled with computers—they are an easy and affordable way to get online. It's even easier if you have a Wi-Fi-enabled smartphone, tablet, or netbook. There are hotspots at cafés and at other businesses. Sometimes Wi-Fi is free; other times you may have to pay by the minute or buy something in exchange for the network password.

Public Phones: Because calling from the ship or a mobile phone can be costly (see page 91), you may want to seek out a pay phone in port to make calls. Coin-op phones are rare in Europe, so you'll need to purchase one of two types of prepaid phone cards. An **insertable phone card,** which you physically slide into the telephone, can be used only at pay phones. It offers reasonable rates for domestic calls, and steeper but still acceptable rates for international calls (rarely exceeding $1/minute). You use an **international phone card** by dialing a toll-free number, then punching in a scratch-to-reveal PIN. Though designed for international calls, which can cost less than a nickel a minute, they also work for domestic calls. Both types of cards are sold in various denominations at tobacco shops, newsstands, and hole-in-the-wall long-distance shops. Generally these work best—and sometimes only—in the country where you buy them.

Outsmarting Thieves

In Europe, it's rare to encounter violent crime, but petty purse-snatching and pickpocketing are quite common. Thieves target Americans, especially cruise passengers—not because the thieves are mean, but because they're smart. Loaded down with valuables in a strange new environment, we stick out like jeweled thumbs. But being savvy and knowing what to look out for can dramatically reduce your risk of being targeted.

Pickpockets are your primary concern. To avoid them, be aware of your surroundings, don't keep anything valuable in your pockets, and wear a money belt (explained on page 58). In your money belt, carry your passport, credit and debit cards, and large cash bills. Keep just a day's spending money in your pocket—if you lose that, it's no big deal.

Many cruise lines hand out cloth bags emblazoned with their logo. Carrying these around town is like an advertisement for pickpockets and con artists (not to mention aggressive salesmen). Save them for supermarket runs back home.

Thieves thrive on tourist-packed public-transportation routes—especially buses that cover major sights. When riding the subway or bus, be alert at stops, when thieves can dash on and off with your day bag. Criminals—often dressed as successful professionals or even as tourists—will often block a bus or subway entry, causing the person behind you to "bump" into you.

Be wary of any unusual contact or commotion in crowded public places (especially touristy spots). For example, while being jostled at a crowded market, you might end up with ketchup or fake pigeon poop on your shirt. The perpetrator then offers profuse apologies while dabbing it up—and pawing your pockets. Treat

any disturbance (a scuffle breaking out, a beggar in your face,
someone falling down an escalator) as a smokescreen for theft—
designed to distract unknowing
victims.

Europe also has its share
of scam artists, from scruffy
babushkas offering you sprigs of
rosemary (and expecting money
in return) to con artists running
street scams, such as the shell game, in which players pay to guess
which of the moving shells hides the ball (don't try it—you'll lose
every time). Or somebody sells you an item, and turns around to
put it in a box while you're getting out your money. Later on the
ship, when you open the box, you find only...rocks. Always look
inside the box before walking away.

The most rampant scams are more subtle, such as being
overcharged by a taxi driver (see the "Taxi Tips" sidebar, earlier). Another common scam is the "slow count": A cashier counts
change back with odd pauses, in hopes the rushed tourist will
gather up the money quickly without checking that it's all there.
Waiters may pad the bill with mysterious charges—carefully scan
the itemized bill and account for each item. If paying a small total
with a large bill, clearly state the amount you're handing over, and
be sure you get the correct change back. Don't be upset about these
little scams—treat them as sport.

Nearly all crimes suffered by tourists are nonviolent and
avoidable. Be aware of the pitfalls of traveling, but relax and have
fun.

Money

Whenever you leave the ship, you must use local currency. Many
of the countries in this book (Belgium, Estonia, Finland, France,
Germany, and the Netherlands) use the euro; stock up on euros
early in your trip, and use them throughout the region.

The other destinations in this book don't officially use the
euro. I've occasionally heard cruise-line employees tell their passengers, "We're only in the country for a day, and everyone takes
euros, so you don't need to change money." That's true in many
cases: Many merchants in non-euro countries do accept euros. But
exchange rates are bad, and some vendors might flat-out refuse
euros. Plus, euros often aren't accepted on public transportation
or at major sights and museums. That's why it's better to get local
cash, even if you're in town just for a few hours. In most port cities,
ATMs are easy to find (I've listed the nearest locations for each

destination). But in some of the more out-of-way ports, exchanging a small amount of money for local currency at the cruise ship's front desk can save you time looking for an ATM.

Because Scandinavian and some Baltic countries have individual currencies, you'll likely wind up with leftover cash. Coins can't be exchanged once you leave the country, so try to spend them while you're in port. But bills are easy to convert to the "new" country's currency. When changing cash, use exchange bureaus rather than banks. The Forex desks (easy to find at major train stations) are considered reliable and fair.

Cash

Cash is just as desirable in Europe as it is at home. Small businesses (restaurants, shops, etc.) may prefer that you pay with cash.

While most Northern European vendors take credit cards, American cards may not work properly, making cash a smart backup. Cash is the best—and sometimes only—way to pay for bus fare, taxis, and local guides.

Throughout Europe, cash machines (ATMs) are the standard way for travelers to get cash. In every instance, I've tried to give directions for getting you (cash-free) to the nearest ATM. Stay away from "independent" ATMs such as Travelex or Euronet, which charge huge commissions and have terrible exchange rates. Note that in many Scandinavian and Baltic countries, ATMs are relatively rare; in some ports, there may not be one right where you'll step off the ship. Fortunately, credit cards are widely accepted in this part of the world, even for small transactions.

When using an ATM, try to withdraw large sums of money to reduce the number of per-transaction bank fees you'll pay. Although you can use a credit card for ATM transactions, it only makes sense in an emergency because it's considered a cash advance (with a high fee) rather than a withdrawal. To safeguard your cash, wear a money belt (described on page 58).

Credit and Debit Cards

For purchases, Visa and MasterCard are more commonly accepted than American Express. Just like at home, credit or debit cards work easily at larger restaurants, shops, and hotels. I typically use my debit card to withdraw cash to pay for most purchases. I use my credit card only in a few specific situations: to book hotel reservations by phone (when staying in Europe before or after a cruise),

Damage Control for Lost or Stolen Cards

If you lose your credit, debit, or ATM card, report the loss immediately to a customer-assistance center. Call these 24-hour US numbers collect: Visa (tel. 303/967-1096), MasterCard (tel. 636/722-7111), and American Express (tel. 336/393-1111). European toll-free numbers (listed by country) can be found at the websites for Visa and MasterCard.

At a minimum, you'll need to know the name of the financial institution that issued you the card, along with the type of card (classic, platinum, or whatever). Providing the following information will allow for a quicker cancellation of your missing card: full card number, whether you are the primary or secondary cardholder, the cardholder's name exactly as printed on the card, billing address, home phone number, circumstances of the loss or theft, and identification verification (your birth date, your mother's maiden name, or your Social Security number—memorize this, don't carry a copy). If you are the secondary cardholder, you'll also need to provide the primary cardholder's identification-verification details (see www.ricksteves.com/help for more).

If you report your loss within two days, you typically won't be responsible for any unauthorized transactions on your account, although many banks charge a liability fee of $50.

to cover major purchases, and to pay for things near the end of my trip (to avoid another visit to the ATM).

While you can use either a credit or a debit card for most purchases, using a credit card offers a greater degree of fraud protection (since debit cards draw funds directly from your bank account).

Note that in most of Scandinavia, credit cards are widely accepted even for small purchases. Danes, Swedes, and Norwegians rarely use cash. This can be a relief for cruisers in town who don't want to hassle with ATMs. But there's a catch: In these countries, most people use the potentially problematic chip-and-PIN system, described next.

Chip and PIN: If your card is declined for a purchase in Europe, it may be because Europeans are increasingly using chip-and-PIN cards, which are embedded with an electronic chip (rather than the magnetic stripe used on our American-style cards). Much of Europe—particularly in the north—is adopting this system, and some merchants rely on it exclusively. You're most likely to encounter chip-and-PIN problems at automated payment machines, such as luggage lockers and ticket machines at train and

Making Your Card Work

If you're using an American credit or debit card at a chip-and-PIN point of sale, there's no predicting whether—and how—your card might work. To be prepared, know your PIN for both your debit card and your credit card. Most Americans don't use their credit-card PIN regularly, but your card has one: Ask your bank before you leave, and memorize it.

Here's how to make your card work:

1. Swipe your credit card in the chip-and-PIN terminal.
2. When prompted for the PIN, ask the clerk (if there is one) to print out a receipt for you to sign instead.
3. If it's not possible to print out a receipt, try punching in your credit card's PIN.
4. If the PIN isn't accepted (or if you don't remember it), try swiping your debit card and entering its PIN. Some chip-and-PIN machines accept debit cards but not credit cards.

If none of the above works, find an ATM nearby to get cash; ask if the vendor will take euros or dollars (if you have any); or...simply skip the purchase.

subway stations.

Many travelers who are carrying only magnetic-stripe cards never encounter any problems. But as this system is widespread in several countries in this book (particularly Denmark, Norway, Sweden, and the Netherlands), there's a good chance you'll run into it. Don't panic. If your first attempt to use your card doesn't work, there are several alternate strategies (outlined in the sidebar above). Carrying some cash, just in case, can help avoid awkward situations where your card won't work (though some automated machines don't accept cash either).

If you're still concerned, you can apply for a chip card in the US (though I think that's overkill). While big US banks offer these cards with high annual fees, a better option is the no-fee GlobeTrek Visa, offered by Andrews Federal Credit Union in Maryland (open to all US residents; see www.andrewsfcu.org).

Dynamic Currency Conversion: If merchants offer to convert your purchase price into dollars (called dynamic currency conversion, or DCC), refuse this "service." You'll pay even more in fees for the expensive convenience of seeing your charge in dollars.

At Sights

Most cruise passengers are faced with far more to see and do than they have time for. That's why it's helpful to know what you can typically expect when visiting sights:

Perhaps the biggest challenge (and frustration) is **long lines.**

At sights such as the Hermitage in St. Petersburg, the Eiffel Tower in Paris, the Pergamon in Berlin, and the Anne Frank House in Amsterdam, lines can be a real frustration. Study up, plan ahead, and use the information in this book to minimize time spent in line. For details on making **reservations** or **buying advance tickets** at major sights, see page 52.

Some important sights require you to **check daypacks and coats.** To avoid checking a small backpack, carry it under your arm like a purse as you enter. From a guard's point of view, a backpack is generally a problem, while a purse is not.

A modest **dress code** (no bare shoulders, shorts, or above-the-knee skirts) is enforced at Orthodox churches you may want to enter in St. Petersburg, Tallinn, and Helsinki. If you are caught by surprise, you can improvise, using maps to cover your shoulders and a jacket tied around your waist to hide your legs.

Flash **photography** is often banned, but taking photos without a flash is usually allowed. Flashes damage oil paintings and distract others in the room. Even without a flash, a handheld camera will take a decent picture (or buy postcards or posters at the museum bookstore).

Museums may have **special exhibits** in addition to their permanent collection. Some exhibits are included in the entry price, while others come at an extra cost (which you may have to pay even if you don't want to see that exhibit).

Expect changes—artwork can be on tour, on loan, out sick, or shifted at the whim of the curator. To adapt, pick up any available free floor plans as you enter. Ask museum staff if you can't find a particular item.

Many sights rent **audioguides,** which generally offer excellent recorded descriptions in English. If you bring your own earbuds, you can enjoy better sound and avoid holding the device to your ear. To save money, bring a Y-jack and share one audioguide with your travel partner. I've produced free downloadable **audio tours** of the major sights in Amsterdam, Paris, and London; see page 52.

IN PORT

Important sights may have an **on-site café** or **cafeteria** (usually a handy place to rejuvenate during a long visit). The WCs at sights are free and generally clean.

Many places sell **postcards** that highlight their attractions. Before you leave a sight, scan the postcards and thumb through the biggest guidebook (or skim its index) to be sure you haven't overlooked something at that sight that you'd like to see.

Most sights **stop admitting people** 30-60 minutes before closing time, and some rooms may close early (often about 45 minutes before the actual closing time). Guards will usher people out, so don't save the best for last.

Every sight or museum offers more than what's covered in this book. Use the information in this book as an introduction—not the final word.

Shopping

Shopping can be a fun part of any traveler's European trip. To have a good experience when you go ashore, be aware of the ins and outs of shopping in port.

At every stop, your cruise line will give you an information sheet that highlights local shopping specialties and where to buy them. Remember that these shops commonly give kickbacks to cruise lines and guides. This doesn't mean that the shop (or what it sells) isn't good quality; it just means you're probably paying top dollar.

Regardless of whether a store is working with the cruise line or not, many places jack up their rates when ships arrive, knowing they're about to get hit with a tidal wave of rushed and desperate shoppers. Remember: Northern Europe's cruise season lasts approximately three months, and many people who live and work in that town must extract a year's worth of earnings from visitors during that period.

Finding Deals

So how can you avoid paying over-the-top, inflated prices for your treasured souvenirs? Go ahead and patronize the obvious tourist shops, but be sure to check out local shopping venues, too. Large department stores often have a souvenir section with standard knickknacks and postcards at prices way below those at cruise-recommended shops. These large stores generally work just like ours, and in big cities, most department-store staff are accustomed to wide-eyed foreign shoppers and can speak some English.

If you're adept at bargaining, head over to some of Europe's vibrant outdoor flea markets, where you can find local specialties and soft prices. In Russia and at street markets in some other countries, haggling is the accepted (and expected) method of finding a compromise between the wishful thinking of both the merchant and the tourist.

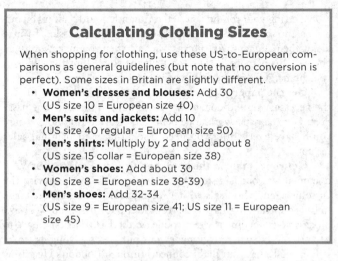

Calculating Clothing Sizes

When shopping for clothing, use these US-to-European comparisons as general guidelines (but note that no conversion is perfect). Some sizes in Britain are slightly different.

- **Women's dresses and blouses:** Add 30
  (US size 10 = European size 40)
- **Men's suits and jackets:** Add 10
  (US size 40 regular = European size 50)
- **Men's shirts:** Multiply by 2 and add about 8
  (US size 15 collar = European size 38)
- **Women's shoes:** Add about 30
  (US size 8 = European size 38-39)
- **Men's shoes:** Add 32-34
  (US size 9 = European size 41; US size 11 = European size 45)

Bargaining Tips: To be a successful haggler-shopper, first determine the item's value to you. Many tourists think that if they can cut the price by 50 percent they are doing great. So merchants quadruple their prices and the tourist happily pays double the fair value. The best way to deal with crazy prices is to ignore them. Show some interest in an item but say, "It's just too much money." You've put the merchant in a position to make the first offer.

Many merchants will settle for a nickel profit rather than lose a sale entirely. Work the cost down to rock bottom. When it seems to have fallen to a record low, walk away. That last price hollered out as you turn the corner is often the best price you'll get. If the price is right, go back and buy. And don't forget that prices often drop at the end of the day, when flea-market merchants have to think about packing up.

Getting a VAT Refund

Every year, tourists visiting Europe leave behind millions of dollars of refundable sales taxes. While for some, the headache of collecting the refund is not worth the few dollars at stake, if you do any serious shopping, it's hard cash—free and easy.

Wrapped into the purchase price of your souvenirs is a Value-Added Tax (VAT) of between 18 and 25 percent, depending on the country (for a list, see www.ricksteves.com/plan/tips). Almost all European countries require a minimum purchase for a refund, ranging from about $30 to several hundred dollars. If you spend that minimum at a store that participates in the VAT-refund scheme, you're entitled to get most of that tax back. Typically, you must ring up the minimum at a single retailer—you can't add up your purchases from various shops to reach the required amount.

Getting your refund is usually straightforward and, if you buy a substantial amount of souvenirs, well worth the hassle. If you're lucky, the merchant will subtract the tax when you make your purchase. (This is more likely to occur if the store ships the goods to your home.) Otherwise, you'll need to:

Get the paperwork. Have the merchant completely fill out the necessary refund document. You'll have to present your passport. Get the paperwork done before you leave the store to ensure you'll have everything you need (including your original sales receipt).

Get your stamp at the border or airport. Process your VAT document at your last stop (for example, at the airport) with the customs agent who deals with VAT refunds. For purchases made in EU countries (in this book, everywhere but Russia and Norway), process your document when you leave the EU. It doesn't have to be the country where you made your purchases as long as you're still in the EU; if your flight connects through London's Heathrow airport, you can do it there. For non-EU countries such as Russia and Norway, process your VAT document at your last stop in that country (VAT refunds for tourists are a recent innovation in Russia; don't be surprised if the system still has a few kinks—or disappears). Before checking in for your flight, find the local customs office, and be prepared to stand in line. Keep your purchases readily available for viewing by the customs agent (ideally in your carry-on bag—don't make the mistake of checking the bag with your purchases before you've seen the agent). You're not supposed to use your purchased goods before you leave. If you show up at customs wearing your Norwegian sweater, officials might look the other way—or deny you a refund.

Collect your refund. You'll need to return your stamped document to the retailer or its representative. Many merchants work with a service, such as Global Blue or Premier Tax Free, that has offices at major airports, ports, or border crossings (either before or after security, probably strategically located near a duty-free shop). These services, which extract a 4 percent fee, can refund your money immediately in cash or credit your card (within two billing cycles). If the retailer handles VAT refunds directly, it's up to you to contact the merchant for your refund. You can mail the documents from home, or more quickly, from your point of departure (using an envelope you've prepared in advance or one that's been provided by the merchant). You'll then have to wait—it can take months.

Customs for American Shoppers

You are allowed to take home $800 worth of items per person duty-free, once every 30 days. You can also bring in a liter of alcohol duty-free. As for food, you can take home many processed and packaged foods: vacuum-packed cheeses, dried herbs, jams, baked goods, candy, chocolate, oil, vinegar, mustard, and honey. Fresh fruits and vegetables and most meats are not allowed. Any liquid-containing foods must be packed in checked luggage, a potential recipe for disaster. To check customs rules and duty rates, visit www.cbp.gov.

Eating in Port

Eating in Europe is sightseeing for your taste buds. The memories of good meals can satisfy you for years. Even though most of

your meals will be on the ship, you can still experience Europe's amazing cuisine when you're in port. Your options range from grabbing a lunch on the run to lingering over a leisurely meal at a sit-down restaurant. When deciding where to eat, be aware

that table service in Europe is slow—sometimes painfully so—by American standards. Don't expect to dine and dash, but you can try explaining to the waitstaff that you're in a hurry.

Lunch on the Go

You can eat quickly and still have a local experience. Every country has its own equivalent of the hot-dog stand, where you can grab a filling bite on the go: Danish *pølse* (sausage) carts and *smørrebrød* (open-face sandwich) shops, Berlin's Currywurst stands, Russian *bliny* (potato pancake) shops, and French *crêperies*. Or stop in a heavenly smelling bakery and buy a pastry or sandwich.

Ethnic eateries are usually cheap; eat in, or get your meal to go. Cafeterias, delis, and fast-food chains with salad bars are tourist-friendly and good for a quick meal.

Like businesspeople, cruise travelers have a lot on their daytime agendas and want to eat well but quickly. A good bet is to eat lunch at a place that caters to the local business clientele. You'll find many fine little restaurants advertising fast, two-course business lunches. These are inexpensive and served quickly. Each neighborhood is also likely to have a favorite deli/sandwich place where you'll see a thriving crowd of office workers spilling out onto the curb, eating fine, small meals or gourmet sandwiches—and often sipping a glass of top-end wine with their food.

Picnicking takes a little more time and planning but can be an even more exciting cultural experience: It's fun to dive into a marketplace and actually get a chance to do business there. Europe's colorful markets overflow with varied cheeses, meats, fresh fruits, vegetables, and still-warm-out-of-the-oven bread. Most markets are not self-service: You point to what you want and let the merchant weigh and bag it for you. The unit of measure throughout the Continent is a kilo, or 2.2 pounds. A kilo has 1,000 grams. One hundred grams is a common unit of sale for cheese or meat—and just the right amount to tuck into a chunk of French bread for a satisfying sandwich.

Keep an eye out for some of my favorite picnic treats: *Wasa* cracker bread (Sport is my favorite; *flatbrød* is ideal for munchies), packaged meat and cheese, brown "goat cheese" *(geitost),* drinkable yogurt, freshly cooked or smoked fish from markets, fresh fruit and vegetables, lingonberries, and squeeze tubes of mustard and sandwich spreads (shrimp, caviar), which are perfect on rye bread.

Sit-Down Restaurants

For some cruisers, it's unimaginable to waste valuable port time

lingering at a sit-down restaurant when they could be cramming their day with sightseeing. For others, a good European restaurant experience beats a cathedral or a museum by a mile.

To find a good restaurant, head away from the tourist center and stroll around until you find a place with a happy crowd of locals. Look for menus handwritten in the native language (usually posted outside) and offering a small selection. This

means they're cooking what was fresh in the market that morning for loyal return customers.

Restaurants in Europe usually do not serve meals throughout the day, so don't wait too long to find a place for lunch. Typically restaurants close from the late afternoon (about 14:00) until the dinner hour.

When entering a restaurant, feel free to seat yourself at any table that isn't marked "reserved." Catch a server's eye and signal to be sure it's OK to sit there. If the place is full, you're likely to simply be turned away: There's no "hostess" standing by to add your name to a carefully managed waiting list.

If no English **menu** is posted, ask to see one. And be aware that the word "menu" can mean a fixed-price meal. Particularly in Scandinavian countries, many restaurants offer cheap daily lunch specials *(dagens rett)* and buffets for office workers.

In restaurants, Europeans generally drink bottled **water** (for taste, not health), served with or without carbonation. You can normally get free tap water, but you may need to be polite, patient, inventive, and know the correct phrase. There's nothing wrong with ordering tap water, and it is safe to drink in all the countries in this book, except for Russia.

One of the biggest surprises for Americans at Europe's restaurants is the service, which can seem excruciatingly slow when you're eager to get out and sightsee (or in a hurry to get back to your cruise ship). Europeans will spend at least two hours enjoying a good meal, and fast service is considered rude service. If you need to eat and run, make it very clear when you order.

To get the **bill,** you'll have to ask for it. Don't wait until you are in a hurry to leave. Catch the waiter's eye and, with raised hands, scribble with an imaginary pencil on your palm. Before it comes, make a mental tally of roughly how much your meal should cost. If the total is a surprise, ask to have it itemized and explained.

Tipping: At European restaurants, a base gratuity is already included in your bill. Virtually anywhere in Europe, if you're pleased with the service, you can round up a euro or more. In most restaurants, 5 percent is adequate and 10 percent is considered a big tip. Please believe me—tipping 15-20 percent in Europe is unnecessary, if not culturally insensitive. Tip only at restaurants with waitstaff; skip the tip if you order food at a counter. Servers prefer to be tipped in cash even if you pay with your credit card; otherwise the tip may never reach them (specifics on tipping are also provided in each country's introduction chapter).

Returning to the Ship

When it's time to head back to your ship, remember that the posted departure time is a bit misleading: The all-aboard time (when you absolutely, positively must be on your ship) is usually a half-hour before departure. And the last shuttle bus or tender back to the ship might leave an hour before departure...trimming your port time even more. If you want to max out on time ashore, research alternative options—such as a taxi or a public bus—that get you back to the ship even closer to the all-aboard time (but, of course, be cautious not to cut it *too* close). Before leaving the ship,

make sure you understand when you need to be back on board, and (if applicable) when the last shuttle bus or tender departs.

All of that said, feel free to take every minute of the time you've got. If the last tender leaves at 16:30, don't feel you need to get back to the dock at 16:00.

I make it a point to be the last person back on the ship at every port...usually five minutes or so before all-aboard time. I sometimes get dirty looks from early birds who've been waiting for a few minutes on that last tender, but I didn't waste their time... they did.

What If I Miss My Boat?

You can't count on the ship to wait for you if you get back late. If you're cutting it close, call ahead to the port agent (the phone number is on your ship's port-of-call information sheet and/or daily program) and let them know you're coming. They will notify the ship's crew, so at least they know they didn't miscount the returning passengers. And there's a possibility (though a very slim one) that the ship could wait for you. But if it sets sail, and you're not on it, you're on your own to reach the next port. The cruise line will not cover any of your transportation or accommodations expenses, and you will not be reimbursed for any unused portion of your cruise.

You have approximately 24 hours to reach the ship before it departs from its next destination. Be clear on where the next stop is. If you're lucky, it's an easy two-hour train ride away, giving you bonus time in both destinations. If you're unlucky, it's a 20-hour overland odyssey or an expensive last-minute flight—or worse, the ship is spending the day at sea, meaning you'll miss out on two full cruising days.

First, ask the **port agent** for advice. The agent can typically give you a little help or at least point you in the right direction. Be aware that you'll be steered to the easiest, but not necessarily the most affordable, solution. For example, the agent might suggest hiring a private driver for hundreds of dollars, rather than taking a $50 bus ride. If your ship's policy is to hold passenger passports during the cruise, he'll have it waiting for you.

You can also ask for help from the **TI,** if it's still open. Local **travel agencies** should know most or all of your connection options and can book tickets for you (they'll charge you a small commission). Or—to do it yourself—find an **Internet café** and get online to research your train, flight, and bus options. German Rail's handy, all-Europe train timetables are a good place to start: www.bahn.com. Check the website of the nearest airport; these usually show the schedule of upcoming flights in the next day or two. To compare inexpensive flights within Europe, try www.sky scanner.com.

Don't delay in making your plans. The sooner you begin investigating your options, the more choices you may have. If you realize you've missed your ship at 20:00, there may be an affordable night train to the next stop departing from the train station across town at 21:00...and if you're not on it, you could pay through the nose for a last-minute flight instead.

Remember, most ships never leave anyone behind over the course of the entire cruise. While the prospect of missing your ship is daunting, don't let it scare you into not enjoying your shore time. As long as you keep a close eye on the time and are conservative in estimating how long it'll take you to get back to the ship, it's easy to enjoy a very full day in port and be the last tired but happy tourist sauntering back onto the ship.

Overnighting in Port
At some major destinations (most often in St. Petersburg), the cruise ship might spend two days and an overnight in port. This allows you to linger in the evening and really feel like you've been to a place—treating your cruise ship like a hotel.

IN PORT

Part III
NORTHERN EUROPEAN CRUISE PORTS

NORTHERN EUROPEAN CRUISE PORTS

The rest of this book focuses on the specific cruise ports where you'll be spending your days. For each one, I've provided detailed instructions for getting from the port into town, and included my suggested self-guided tours and walks for the best one-day plan in that town.

Rick Steves' Northern European Cruise Ports is a personal tour guide in your pocket, organized by destination. Each major destination is a mini-vacation on its own, filled with exciting sights, strollable neighborhoods, and memorable places to eat. You'll find the following sections in most of the destination chapters (although, because cruise port details can vary from place to place, not every destination will include all of these elements):

Planning Your Time suggests a schedule for how to best use your limited time in port. These plans are what I'd do with my time if I had only a few hours to spend in a particular destination, and assume that you're ambitious about spending the maximum amount of time in port sightseeing, rather than relaxing, shopping, or dining. For each option, I've suggested the minimum amount of time you can reasonably expect to spend to get a good look at the highlights. If you find that my plan packs too much in, or shortchanges something you'd like to focus on, modify the plan by skipping one or two time-consuming options (read the descriptions in the chapters to decide which items interest you).

The **Excursions** sidebars help you make informed, strategic decisions about which cruise-line excursions to outlying destinations best match your interests.

Arrival at the Port sections provide detailed, step-by-step instructions for getting from your cruise ship to wherever you're going (whether it's to the city center, or, in some cases, to a nearby town). Each one begins with a brief "Arrival at a Glance" section to help you get oriented to your options. I've also tracked down helpful services (such as ATMs, Internet access, and pharmacies) at or near each port.

Orientation includes specifics on public transportation, helpful hints, local tour options, easy-to-read maps, and tourist information.

Self-Guided Walks and Tours take you through interesting neighborhoods and museums.

Sights describes the top attractions and includes their cost and hours. The "At a Glance" sections offer a quick overview of the sightseeing options in town (though I've provided additional coverage only of the sights you're most likely to see during your limited time).

Eating serves up a range of options, from inexpensive eateries to fancy restaurants.

Shopping offers advice on the most authentic local souvenirs and where to buy them.

The **What If I Miss My Boat?** sections give you a quick list of options for reaching your next port, in case you get stranded.

The **Starting or Ending Your Cruise** sections in the most common embarkation/disembarkation points (Copenhagen, Stockholm, Amsterdam, and London) give advice about how to get from the airport to the cruise port, and list a few of my favorite hotels.

I've also included **practicalities** sections for each of the 13 countries with ports in this book, providing basic facts and figures, along with useful notes (such as the local currency, time zone, phone system, and tipping customs).

Key to This Book
Updates
This book is updated regularly, but things change. For the latest, visit www.ricksteves.com/update. For a valuable list of reports and experiences—good and bad—from fellow travelers, check www.ricksteves.com/feedback.

Abbreviations and Times
I use the following symbols and abbreviations in this book:

Sights are rated:

▲▲▲	**Don't miss**
▲▲	**Try hard to see**
▲	**Worthwhile if you can make it**
No rating	**Worth knowing about**

Tourist information offices are abbreviated as **TI,** and bathrooms are **WCs.**

CRUISE PORTS

Like Europe, this book uses the **24-hour clock** for schedules. It's the same through 12:00 noon, then keep going: 13:00, 14:00, and so on. For anything over 12, subtract 12 and add p.m. (14:00 is 2:00 p.m.).

When giving **opening times,** I include both peak season and off-season hours if they differ. So, if a museum is listed as "May-Oct daily 9:00-16:00," it should be open from 9:00 a.m. until 4:00 p.m. from the first day of May until the last day of October (but expect exceptions).

For **transit** or **tour departures,** I first list the frequency, then the duration. So, a train connection listed as "2/hour, 1.5 hours" departs twice each hour, and the journey lasts an hour and a half.

Sleep Code

In each of the cities where you're likely to begin or end your trip, I list a few of my favorite accommodations. To help you easily sort through these listings, I've divided the accommodations into three categories, based on the price for a double room with bath:

$$$ Higher Priced
  $$ Moderately Priced
    $ Lower Priced

To give maximum information in a minimum of space, I use the following code to describe accommodations. Prices in this book are listed per room, not per person.

S = Single room, or price for one person in a double.
D = Double or twin room.
T = Three-person room.
Q = Four-person room.
b = Private bathroom with toilet and shower or tub.
s = Private shower or tub only. (The toilet is down the hall.)

COPENHAGEN
Denmark

Denmark Practicalities

Denmark (Danmark), between the Baltic and the North Sea, is the smallest of the Scandinavian countries (16,600 square miles—roughly double the size of Massachusetts). But in the 16th century, it was the largest; at one time, Denmark ruled all of Norway and the three southern provinces of Sweden. Today's population is about 5.5 million, 10 percent immigrant, and 90 percent Protestant (mostly Evangelical Lutheran). The country consists of the largely flat, extensively cultivated Jutland peninsula, as well as 400 islands (78 of which are inhabited, including Sjælland/Zealand, where Copenhagen is located).

Money: 6 Danish kroner (kr, officially DKK) = about $1. An ATM is called a *pengeautomat*. The local VAT (value-added sales tax) rate is 25 percent; the minimum purchase eligible for a VAT refund is 300 kr (for details on refunds, see page 139).

Language: The native language is Danish. For useful phrases, see page 236.

Emergencies: Dial 112 for police, medical, or other emergencies. In case of theft or loss, see page 131.

Time Zone: Denmark is on Central European Time (the same as most of the Continent, one hour ahead of Great Britain, and six/nine hours ahead of the East/West Coasts of the US).

Embassies in Copenhagen: The **US embassy** is at Dag Hammarskjölds Allé 24 (tel. 33 41 71 00, after-hours emergency tel. 33 41 74 00, http://denmark.usembassy.gov). The **Canadian embassy** is at Kristen Bernikowsgade 1 (tel. 33 48 32 00, www.denmark.gc.ca). Call ahead for passport services.

Phoning: Denmark's country code is 45; to call from another country to Denmark, dial the international access code (011 from the US/Canada, 00 from Europe, or + from a mobile phone), then 45, followed by the local number. For local calls within Denmark, just dial the number as it appears in this book—whether you're calling from across the street or across the country. To place an international call from Denmark, dial 00, the code of the country you're calling (1 for US and Canada), and the phone number. For more help, see page 1110.

Tipping: Gratuity is included in the price of sit-down meals, so you don't need to tip further, though it's nice to round up your bill about 5-10 percent for great service. Tip a taxi driver by rounding up the fare a bit (pay 90 kr on an 85-kr fare). For more tips on tipping, see page 143.

Tourist Information: www.visitdenmark.com

COPENHAGEN

København

Copenhagen, Denmark's capital, is the gateway to Scandinavia. It's an improbable combination of corny Danish clichés, well-dressed executives having a business lunch amid cutting-edge contemporary architecture, and some of the funkiest counterculture in Europe. And yet, it all just works so tidily together. With the Øresund Bridge connecting Sweden and Denmark (creating the region's largest metropolitan area), Copenhagen is energized and ready to dethrone Stockholm as Scandinavia's powerhouse city. Live it up in Scandinavia's cheapest and most fun-loving capital.

Planning Your Time

Copenhagen is a spread-out city with lots of sightseeing options. You can't squeeze everything into one day, so be selective. Here are your most likely choices; I'd suggest starting with the first two, then choosing from the remaining list with whatever time you have left. If several of the later items appeal to you (or if the weather is dreary and you prefer indoor options), feel free to skip the walk and harbor cruise.

• **Self-Guided Walk:** This stroll through town gives you your bearings in about 1.5 hours (not counting stops).

• **Harbor Cruise:** Getting you out on the water and showing you corners of the city hard to see otherwise, this is well worth the hour it takes—on a sunny day. But if it's cold or rainy, I'd skip it.

• **Rosenborg Castle:** For a classic Renaissance castle experience right in the city center, plus a peek at the crown jewels, tour this palace. Allow 1.5 hours.

• **National Museum:** Offering an illuminating look at Danish history, this deserves at least 1.5 hours for the quickest visit (ideally longer).

• **Thorvaldsen's Museum** or **Ny Carlsberg Glyptothek:** For fans of Neoclassical sculpture or antiquities and paintings (respectively), each of these museums deserves an hour or more.

• **Christiana:** You can stroll through this unique hippie squatters' commune in about an hour, though it takes some time to get here.

• **Tivoli Gardens:** This quintessentially Danish amusement park is a delightful way to burn up whatever time you have remaining at the end of your busy Copenhagen day (allow at least an hour for strolling and Dane-watching). Conveniently located across the street from the main train station, Tivoli lets you hop right on bus #26 or an S-tog (suburban train) to hightail it back to your ship.

Arrival at the Port of Copenhagen

As one of the primary cruise ports on the Baltic—and one of the most common places to begin or end a cruise—Copenhagen handles a vast volume of cruise traffic. Ships generally use one of three port areas:

• **Langelinie Pier,** within long walking distance of downtown, is used by larger ships—though, since it lacks space for processing luggage, is typically not used as a beginning or ending point for cruises.

• **Frihavnen ("Freeport"),** about three miles north of downtown, is a sprawling port area used by both industrial and cruise vessels. Many cruises start or finish at this port, which is divided into several separate piers.

• **Toldbod,** the scenic quay running between Kastellet Park and Amalienborg Palace, is where a fortunate few smaller cruise ships tie up. It's an easy walk straight into town from here.

I've included detailed arrival instructions for both Langelinie and Frihavnen later in this section. Each one is conveniently served by bus #26 into downtown (though this bus does not run on weekends), and each one is also within a 15-minute walk of a train station with fast connections to downtown. Because getting into town from Toldbod is so simple—step off the ship and you're already there—no additional directions are necessary.

Tourist Information: There is no TI at any of Copenhagen's cruise ports, though signs help you find your way to the nearest bus stop or train station. You'll also likely find free city maps at displays around the port area. Once in town, you can visit

Excursions from Copenhagen

Most cruise lines offer a variety of bus and/or walking tours of **Copenhagen.** These often include guided tours of sights such as Tivoli Gardens, Rosenborg Castle, Amalienborg Palace, Christiansborg Palace, and Christianshavn. But all of these sights—and my self-guided walk through downtown Copenhagen—are easy to visit on your own and thoroughly covered in this book. Similarly, I wouldn't pay your cruise line for a harbor or canal tour, as these are much easier and cheaper to book directly once you arrive.

Excursions to a few out-of-town sights may be worth considering. Many cruise lines offer a tour combining two of the best castles just outside the city: **Frederiksborg** (with sumptuous rooms and an outstanding museum of Danish history) and **Kronborg** (less engaging inside, but very picturesque and with tentative ties to Hamlet). If you're not interested in Copenhagen itself, an excursion combining these two castles (tricky by public transit) could be a good choice. However, I'd skip the side-trip to the pretty but very touristy fishing village of **Dragør** (the much-touted view of Øresund Bridge from here is only a bit closer than what you'll see from the deck of your ship).

Copenhagen's official TI, near the main train station (see page 163 for more on the TI).

Services: There are not many services—such as ATMs or Internet access—directly at the piers. You'll need to head into town to take care of those chores. Fortunately, credit cards are widely accepted (but you'll likely need to know your PIN—see next), and you can buy bus #26 tickets on board with euros or dollars.

Credit Card Problems: The lack of ATMs at Copenhagen's port areas is potentially stressful for arriving cruisers, particularly given Denmark's use of chip-and-PIN credit cards. These have an embedded microchip, and require that you punch in a PIN (rather than sign a receipt) to authorize a purchase. Your American credit card may not work when buying public transit tickets at an automated machine (such as a train ticket from the unstaffed Østerport station to downtown). The trick is to **know your PIN**; if you don't know your credit-card PIN, try using your debit card with its PIN. As long as you can enter a PIN, the card should work.

Tour Options

Hop-on, hop-off bus tour routes include stops at the various cruise ports, where they hustle to attract customers. These are worth considering to get your bearings in this spread-out city. The two dominant outfits, City Sightseeing Copenhagen (red buses) and Open Top Tours (green buses), are owned by the same company; a competitor is called Step On Step Off.

For other tour options—including the highly recommended harbor cruises and Richard Karpen's excellent group walking tours—see "Tours in Copenhagen" on page 170.

Arrival at Langelinie Pier

Arrival at a Glance: It's an easy 10-minute walk to see the *Little Mermaid*; from there, you can stroll all the way into town. For a faster trip, catch bus #26 from right in front of the ship, or (on weekends, when the bus doesn't run) walk 15 minutes to Østerport train station.

Port Overview

Straightforward Langelinie Pier, jutting out from the north end of Kastellet Park, has two berths for big ships, a pier-front road with bus stops (for both public bus #26 and hop-on, hop-off tour buses), and a row of cruise-oriented shops (duty-free, outlet stores).

As this pier is ideal for quickly reaching *The Little Mermaid*, a good option could be to do my self-guided walk in reverse, starting at the *Mermaid* and ending at Rådhuspladsen (City Hall Square; see page 173). Or ride bus #26 into the town center, do my walk in the suggested order, then keep on walking right to your ship.

Services: There's little at the port, although the Crew Bar (among the row of shops, at #26), offers free Wi-Fi with the purchase of a drink. There are no ATMs at or near the port.

Getting into Town

By Taxi
Taxis cluster near the pier, offering a ride into downtown for about 160 kr. But given the ease of walking or public transportation, I'd skip the taxi.

By Foot or Public Transportation
Your basic options are to walk all the way into town (10 minutes to *The Little Mermaid*, another 15 minutes to Amalienborg Palace, then another 10 minutes to Nyhavn); to take bus #26 (stops right in front of the ship, but does not run on Sat-Sun); or to walk 15 minutes to the Østerport suburban (S-tog) train station, then ride a train to Copenhagen's main station, the Hovedbanegården (on signs as *København H*).

Bus #26

Public bus #26—described in detail on page 160—stops at three points along Langelinie Pier (from the base to the tip, the stops are called Langeliniekaj; Langelinie Mole midt; and Langeliniekaj Østmolen). Leaving your ship, find the nearest stop and catch a bus going toward Ålholm Plads. Get off at whichever stop suits your sightseeing plans (the Rådshuspladsen stop is ideal if you want to start with my self-guided walk). Note: On Saturdays or Sundays, this bus doesn't run.

Walking to Town (or to the Østerport Train Station)

It's an easy stroll: Turn left from your ship and walk the length of the pier, passing a row of shops on your right. At the end of the pier, continue straight beyond the overpass (on your right) and the statue of the decidedly *not*-little mermaid, and cross the footbridge. Keep going straight, bearing slightly to your right, to walk with the sailboat harbor on your left.

Pass through the park with the angel monument, then decide: *Little Mermaid* or train station?

To *The Little Mermaid* and by Foot to Downtown: From the park, turn left and head along the water to the commotion of tourists at the *Mermaid*. From the *Mermaid*, you can keep walking along the waterfront past Kastellet Park and the Museum of Danish Resistance all the way to Amalienborg Palace (about 15 minutes beyond the *Little Mermaid*). From the palace, it's about another 10-minute walk to the colorful Nyhavn canal, at the edge of the town center.

To the Østerport Train Station: For this option, after you pass through the park with the angel monument, turn right at the next street, crossing the bridge. At the next crosswalk, cross over, go down the stairs, then turn right to circle around the moat of Kastellet Park (curving around the park's western edge). Enjoy this walk through the park for a few minutes, passing the windmill across the canal. Just after the windmill, you'll see a monument on your right; walk up the hill just behind the monument, bear right, then go down the stairs and over the bridge. Turning right, you'll pop out at busy Folke Bernadottes Allé; the Østerport train station is directly across the street ahead of you.

By Train from Østerport Station

The unstaffed Østerport station has automated ticket machines (credit cards accepted but PIN required). Trains leave frequently for the town center—take trains A or E in direction: Køge; trains C or H in direction: Frederikssund or direction: Ballerup; or train B in direction: Høje Taastrup. The first stop for any of these trains, Nørreport, is near Rosenborg Castle. The third stop, København

H, is the main train station, near Tivoli, Rådhuspladsen (City Hall Square), and the start of my self-guided walk. For details on the main train station, see page 164.

Returning to Your Ship

You can ride bus #26 back to the pier from various points down-town (including the train station, Holmenskirke near Slottsholmen island, or Kongens Nytorv near Nyhavn). Note: Because this bus line splits to go to the two different cruise ports, be sure you take one going to Langeliniekaj. Get off at whichever of the three stops along the pier is closest to your ship. Be aware that bus #26 runs only on weekdays (see page 160).

You can also take the S-tog (suburban train) from the main train station or Nørreport to Østerport train station. Arriving at Østerport, exit the station, turn left, and cross the busy street. Head down into the park, turn left, and walk around the moat of Kastellet Park. Exiting from the north end of the park, you're a short walk from Langelinie.

See page 229 for help if you miss your boat.

Arrival at Frihavnen

Arrival at a Glance: On weekdays, the best choice is to take bus #26 into town. On Saturdays and Sundays (when the bus doesn't run), walk 15 minutes from your ship to the Nordhavn station to ride the train into town.

Port Overview

The sprawling Frihavnen port area consists of multiple long piers shared by industry and cruise traffic. Most cruises use the piers closest to town: **Sundkaj, Orientkaj,** and **Fortkaj.** From these, it's an easy 5- to 10-minute walk to the port gate. Some cruises put in at the farther-out **Levantkaj,** to the north; as this is a much longer walk, the port provides a free shuttle bus to the port gate.

New Terminal: The Frihavnen area is under development. A new cruise terminal is being built at the northern edge of the port; when completed, this will likely be connected to the port gate by a free shuttle bus (as Levantkaj is now). The area just south of Fortkaj is being developed into a residential housing neighborhood.

Services at the Port: There's no ATM at the port, but you will find a small money-exchange office (Ria Money Transfer, huddled next to a red-brick building at the base of Sundkaj) that also sells cheap phone cards, SIM cards, and Internet access. The port's terminal buildings are equipped with free Wi-Fi; look for posters with instructions on how to log on.

Getting into Town

Your first step is getting to the port gate; from there, you can either take bus #26 (on weekdays) or walk to the Nordhavn station to take a train (your best option on weekends, when the bus doesn't run).

By Taxi
Taxis charge about 200 kr for the ride into town. I'd skip this pricey option in favor of one of the fairly easy public transportation choices explained below—though on weekends (when there's no bus #26) or with bags (i.e., if going to a hotel at the end of a tour), a taxi may be worth the splurge.

By Cruise-Line Shuttle Bus
Most cruise lines run shuttle buses between the port and town, usually stopping at Kongens Nytorv (near Nyhavn) and/or Rådhuspladsen (City Hall Square). This can be pricey (varies by cruise line, but figure €12 round-trip)—though in this expensive city, that's not much more than the cost of round-trip public transit tickets. I'd consider the shuttle for the convenience—especially on weekends, when the best public transit option (bus #26) isn't running.

By Public Transportation
Your two options are either public bus #26 (weekdays only) or the speedy train from Nordhavn station (runs daily, about a 15-minute walk from the ship). Both options are outlined below.

From Your Ship to the Port Gate: Whichever option you choose, your first step will be making your way from your ship to the port gate. If your ship is at Sundkaj, Orientkaj, or Fortkaj, when you exit the terminal area, just look for the thick blue line painted in the sidewalk. Follow this directly to the port gate (a 5- to 10-minute stroll). If you're arriving at the farther-flung Levantkaj (or, possibly, at the new terminal farther to the north), a free shuttle bus will meet your ship for the quick ride to the port gate.

Bus #26
If you're arriving on a weekday, this bus—described in detail in the sidebar—is your best bet, as it leaves from right near the port gate and takes you past several key locations downtown. (On weekends, when the bus doesn't run, the train described next is your

Public Bus #26

This made-for-cruisers bus is a handy way to connect either cruise port to various points in downtown Copenhagen. The catch is that the bus runs **only on weekdays;** on Saturday and Sunday, you'll need to consider other options (from either port, the train is speedy but requires a longer walk).

Bus #26 runs about every 20 minutes from stops near either port, and the ride downtown takes about 20 minutes. Stops are marked by a dark-blue post with a yellow top and the number 26. Coming from the port into the city, be sure to take a bus going in the direction of Ålholm Plads.

The bus costs 24 kr, but if you don't have cash yet, drivers (on this bus route only) also take dollars or euros (figure about $4.25 or €3.25). They'll give you change in Danish kroner.

After it leaves either cruise port and heads south, bus #26 makes several stops handy to downtown sightseeing, including:

• **Østerport Stn:** Østerport train station, for fast trains downtown

• **Kongens Nytorv:** Big square near the colorful Nyhavn sailor's quarter

• **Holmenskirke:** Church facing Slotsholmen island and starting point for harbor cruises

• **Christiansborg:** Palace on Slotsholmen island

• **Stormboren, Nationalmuseet:** National Museum

• **Rådhuspladsen:** City Hall Square, at the start of my self-guided walk

• **Hoevdbanegården:** Main train station, across the street from Tivoli amusement park

Returning to the Port: North of downtown Copenhagen, bus #26 splits into two different routes, reaching each of the city's cruise ports. If you're riding the bus from downtown back to your ship, be sure to get on one going to the right place: Buses marked *Langeliniekaj* return to Langelinie Pier (get off at the stop next to the ship), while those marked *Færgehavn Nord* head toward Frihavnen (you'll get off at the Færgehavn Nord stop, a short walk from the port gate).

best option.)

To find the stop for bus #26, exit straight from the port gate, and walk about 50 yards to the end of the street. You'll hit a T-intersection with a wide road (Sundkrogsgade). Turn right, walk along this road for about a half-block (passing the stop for bus #26 going *away* from town), then cross the street at the low-profile crosswalk (look for the blue-and-white arrow in the middle of the street). Once across, you'll find the stop for bus #26 (dark-blue post with yellow top) going into downtown Copenhagen (direction: Ålholm Plads). Hop on the bus (3/hour) and ride it into town; the

Rådshuspladsen (City Hall Square) stop is handiest if you want to begin with my self-guided walk.

By Train from Nordhavn Station

The train from Nordhavn suburban train (S-tog) station is fast and convenient, zipping you in just minutes to the main train station. Nordhavn is a 10-minute (boring) walk from the port gate.

Here's how to do it: Exit straight from the port gate, and continue to the big T-intersection with the wide road (Sundkrogsgade). Turn left, following the faded, sporadic blue dotted line in the sidewalk. You'll soon hit an intersection with the highway called Kalkbrænderihavnsgade. Turn left and walk along this busy road until the first traffic light; here, use the crosswalk to cross the street, proceed directly under the railway underpass, then immediately turn left. Walk along this residential street, with the elevated train tracks on your left, until you reach the station for the S-tog (marked with a big *S*). Go upstairs and use the automated ticket machines to buy a ticket (24 kr; credit cards accepted but PIN required). You can take any train on the track facing away from the cruise port area (on the left as you come up the stairs); these include trains A or E in direction: Køge; trains C or H in direction: Frederikssund or direction: Ballerup; or train B in direction: Høje Taastrup. Ride two stops to Nørreport (near Rosenborg Palace), or stay on four stops to København H—the main train station, near Tivoli, Rådhuspladsen (City Hall Square), and the start of my self-guided walk. For details on the main train station, see page 164.

Returning to Your Ship

From downtown, bus #26 (weekdays only) will get you close to the port. The train (to Nordhavn station, runs daily) gets you within a 10-minute walk. For details, see "Getting from Downtown to the Cruise Port" on page 231.

See page 229 for help if you miss your boat.

Orientation to Copenhagen

Copenhagen is huge (with a million people), but for most visitors, the walkable core is the diagonal axis formed by the train station, Tivoli Gardens, Rådhuspladsen (City Hall Square), and the Strøget pedestrian street, ending at the colorful old Nyhavn sailors' harbor. Bubbling with street life, colorful pedestrian zones, and most of the city's sightseeing, the Strøget is fun (and most of it is covered by this chapter's self-guided walk). But also be sure to

The Story of Copenhagen

If you study your map carefully, you can read the history of Copenhagen in today's street plan. København (literally, "Merchants' Harbor") was born on the little island of Slotsholmen—today home of Christiansborg Palace—in 1167. What was Copenhagen's medieval moat is now a string of pleasant lakes and parks, including Tivoli Gardens. You can still make out some of the zigzag pattern of the moats and ramparts in the city's greenbelt.

Many of these fortifications—and several other landmarks—were built by Denmark's most memorable king. You need to remember only one character in Copenhagen's history: Christian IV. Ruling from 1588 to 1648, he was Denmark's Renaissance king and a royal party animal (see the "King Christian IV" sidebar, later). The personal energy of this "Builder King" sparked a Golden Age when Copenhagen prospered and many of the city's grandest buildings were erected. In the 17th century, Christian IV extended the city fortifications to the north, doubling the size of the city, while adding a grid plan of streets and his Rosenborg Castle. This old "new town" has the Amalienborg Palace and *The Little Mermaid* site.

In 1850, Copenhagen's 140,000 residents all lived within this defensive system. Building in the no-man's-land outside the walls was only allowed with the understanding that in the event of an attack, you'd burn your dwellings to clear the way for a good defense.

Most of the city's historic buildings still in existence were built within the medieval walls, but conditions became too crowded, and outbreaks of disease forced Copenhagen to spread outside the walls. Ultimately those walls were torn down and replaced with "rampart streets" that define today's city center: Vestervoldgade (literally, "West Rampart Street"), Nørrevoldgade ("North Rampart Street"), and Østervoldgade ("East Rampart Street"). The fourth side is the harbor and the island of Slotsholmen, where København was born.

COPENHAGEN

get off the main drag and explore. By doing things by bike or on foot, you'll stumble onto some charming bits of Copenhagen that many miss.

Outside of the old city center are three areas of interest to tourists:

1. To the north are Rosenborg Castle and *The Little Mermaid* area (Amalienborg Palace and Museum of Danish Resistance).

2. To the east, across the harbor, are Christianshavn (Copenhagen's "Little Amsterdam" district) and the alternative enclave of Christiania.

3. To the west (behind the train station) is Vesterbro, a young and trendy part of town with lots of cafés, bars, and boutiques (including the hip Meatpacking District called Kødbyen).

All of these sights are walkable from the Strøget, but taking a bike, bus, or taxi is more efficient. I rent a bike for my entire visit (for about the cost of a single cab ride per day) and get anywhere in the town center faster than by taxi—nearly anything is within a 10-minute pedal. In good weather, the city is an absolute delight by bike (for more on biking in Copenhagen, see "Getting Around Copenhagen: By Bike," later).

Tourist Information

Copenhagen's questionable excuse for a TI, which bills itself as "Wonderful Copenhagen," is actually a blatantly for-profit company. As in a (sadly) increasing number of big European cities, it provides information only about businesses that pay a hefty display fee of thousands of dollars each year. This colors the advice and information the office provides. While they can answer basic questions, the office is worthwhile mostly as a big rack of advertising brochures—you can pick up the free map at many other places in town (May-June Mon-Sat 9:00-18:00, closed Sun; July-Aug Mon-Sat 9:00-20:00, Sun 10:00-18:00; Sept-April Mon-Fri 9:00-16:00, Sat 9:00-14:00, closed Sun; just up the street from train station—to the left as you exit the station—at Vesterbrogade 4A, good Lagkagehuset bakery in building, tel. 70 22 24 42, www.visit copenhagen.com).

The **Copenhagen Card,** which includes free entry to many of the city's sights (including expensive ones, like Tivoli and Rosenborg Castle) and all local transportation throughout the greater Copenhagen area, can save busy sightseers some money; if you're planning on visiting a lot of attractions with steep entry prices, do the arithmetic to see if buying this pass adds up (249 kr/24 hours, 479 kr/72 hours, 699 kr/120 hours; sold at the TI and some hotels).

Alternative Sources of Tourist Information: Because the TI's bottom line competes with its mission to help tourists, you may want to seek out other ways to inform yourself. The local English-language newspaper, *The Copenhagen Post,* has good articles about what's going on in town (comes out each Thursday, often available free at TI, or buy it at a newsstand, www.cphpost.dk). The witty alternative website **www.aok.dk** has several articles in English (and many more in Danish—readable and very insightful if you translate them in Google Translate).

Arrival in Copenhagen

The **main train station** is linked by train to the aiport (see page 230), to Langelinie Pier via Nordhavn station (see page 231), and to Frihavnen via Østerport station (see page 231).

The main train station is a hive of travel-related activity (and 24-hour thievery). Locals call it Hovedbanegården (HOETH-bahn-gorn; look for *København H* on signs and schedules). Kiosks and fast-food eateries cluster in the middle of the main arrivals hall; other services include a train information office, baggage storage, pay WCs, a post office, and ATMs. The tracks at the back of the station (tracks 9-10 and 11-12) are for the suburban train (S-tog).

Just walk out the front door and you'll run into one of the entrances for Tivoli amusement park; if you go around its left side and up a couple of blocks, you'll be at Rådhuspladsen (City Hall Square), where my self-guided walk begins.

Helpful Hints

Pharmacy: Steno Apotek is across from the train station (open 24 hours, Vesterbrogade 6C, tel. 33 14 82 66).

Blue Monday: As you plan, remember that most sights close on Monday, but these attractions remain open: Amalienborg Palace Museum (closed Mon Nov-April), Christiansborg Palace (closed Mon Oct-April), City Hall, Danish Design Center, Museum of Copenhagen, Rosenborg Castle (closed Mon Nov-April), Round Tower, Royal Library, Our Savior's Church, Tivoli Gardens (generally closed late Sept-mid-April), canal tours, and walking or bike tours. You can explore Christiania, but Monday is its rest day ("resting" from what, I'm not sure), so it's unusually quiet and some restaurants are closed.

Internet Access: Wi-Fi is easy to find in Copenhagen (available free at many cafés). **Telestation,** tucked behind the train station kitty-corner from the TI, is a call shop with several Internet terminals (10 kr/15 minutes, 15 kr/30 minutes, 25 kr/1 hour; Mon-Sat 10:00-21:00—until 19:00 in winter, Sun 11:00-20:00—until 18:00 in winter, Banegårdspladsen 1, tel. 33 93 00 02). Additionally, several places offer free Internet access (designed for quick info and email checks): **Copenhagen Central Library** (most terminals, least wait, midway between Nørreport and the Strøget at Krystalgade 15, Mon-Fri 10:00-19:00, Sat 10:00-14:00, closed Sun); **"Black Diamond" library** (2 stand-up terminals on the skyway over the street nearest the harbor, see page 199); and the main **university building** (corner of Nørregade and Sankt Peders Stræde, 2 terminals just inside the door).

Laundry: Pams Møntvask is a good coin-op laundry near Nørreport (31 kr/load wash, 6 kr for soap, 2 kr/minute to dry, daily
6:00-21:00, 50 yards from Ibsens Hotel at 86 Nansensgade).
Tre Stjernet Møntvask ("Three Star Laundry") is a few
blocks behind the train station at Istedgade 45, near the
Meatpacking District (wash-27 kr/load, soap-5 kr, dry-1
kr/1.5 minutes, daily 6:00-21:00). *Vaskel* is wash, *torring* is dry,
and *sæbe* is soap.

Updates to This Book: For news about changes to this book's coverage since it was published, see www.ricksteves.com/update.

Getting Around Copenhagen

By Public Transit: It's easy to navigate Copenhagen, with its fine
buses, Metro, and S-tog (a suburban train system with stops in
the city; Eurail valid on S-tog). For a helpful website that covers
public-transport options (nationwide) in English, consult www
.rejseplanen.dk.

The same **tickets** are used throughout the system. A 24-kr,
two-zone ticket gets you an hour's travel within the center—pay
as you board buses, or buy from station ticket offices or vending machines for the Metro. Remember that automated ticket
machines may not work with all American credit cards; for strategies, see page 155. Assume you'll be within the middle two zones
unless traveling to or from the airport, which requires a three-
zone ticket (36 kr).

One handy option is the blue, two-zone *klippekort*, which can
be shared—for example, two people can take five rides each (145 kr
for 10 rides, insert it in the validation box each time you board a
train and it'll snip off one of your rides).

If you're traveling exclusively in central Copenhagen, the **City
Pass** is a good value (75 kr/24 hours, 190 kr/72 hours, covers travel
within zones 1-4, including the airport). All passes are sold at stations, the TI, 7-Elevens, and other kiosks. Validate any all-day or
multi-day ticket by stamping it in the
yellow machine on the bus or at the
station.

While the train system is slick
(Metro and S-tog, described later),
its usefulness is limited for the typical tourist—but **buses** serve all of
the major sights in town every five to
eight minutes during daytime hours. If
you're not riding a bike everywhere, get
comfortable with the buses. Bus drivers are patient, have change, and speak
English. City maps list bus routes.

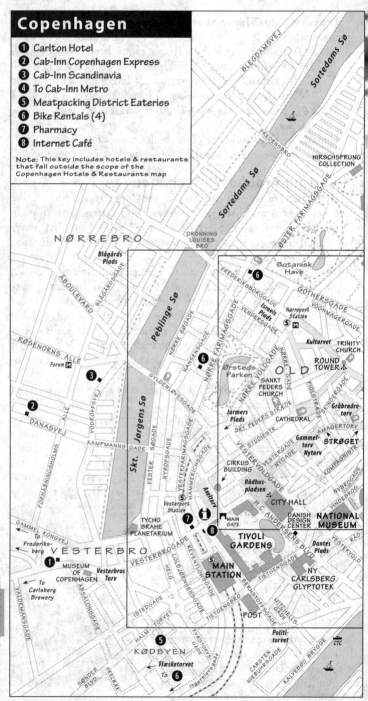

Copenhagen

1. Carlton Hotel
2. Cab-Inn Copenhagen Express
3. Cab-Inn Scandinavia
4. To Cab-Inn Metro
5. Meatpacking District Eateries
6. Bike Rentals (4)
7. Pharmacy
8. Internet Café

Note: This key includes hotels & restaurants that fall outside the scope of the Copenhagen Hotels & Restaurants map

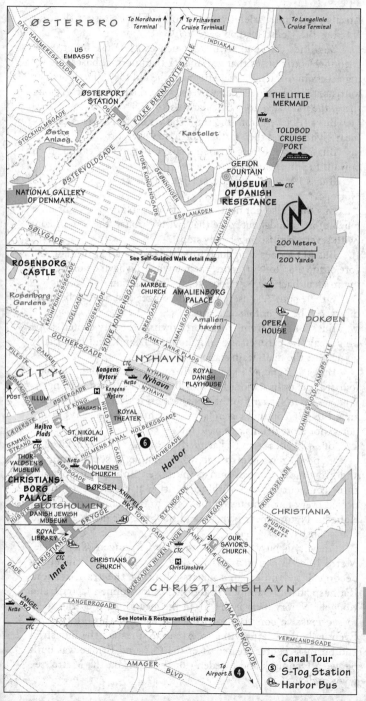

ØSTERBRO

To Nordhavn Terminal

To Frihavnen Cruise Terminal

To Langelinie Cruise Terminal

US EMBASSY

DAG HAMMERESKJOLDS ALLE

INDIAKAJ

ØSTERPORT STATION

Oslo Plads

FOLKE BERNADOTTES ALLE

STOCKHOLMSGADE

Østre Anlaeg

STORE KONGENSGADE

GRØNNINGEN

ØSTERVOLDGADE

Kastellet

THE LITTLE MERMAID

Netto

TOLDBOD CRUISE PORT

GEFION FOUNTAIN

MUSEUM OF DANISH RESISTANCE

CTC

NATIONAL GALLERY OF DENMARK

ESPLANADEN

AMALIEGADE

SØLVGADE

200 Meters

200 Yards

ROSENBORG CASTLE

See Self-Guided Walk detail map

Rosenborg Gardens

KRONPRINSESSEGADE

ADELGADE

BORGERGADE

STORE KONGENSGADE

MARBLE CHURCH

BREDGADE

AMALIENBORG PALACE

Amalien-haven

OPERA HOUSE

DOKØEN

GÖTHERSGADE

SANKT ANNAE PLADS

AMALIEGADE

DANNESKIOLD-SAMSØS ALLE

PILESTR.

GAMMEL MØNT

NYHAVN

CITY

KØBMAGERGADE

Kongens Nytorv

CTC

NYHAVN

Netto

Nyhavn

ROYAL DANISH PLAYHOUSE

POST

ILLUM

ØSTERGADE

LILLE KONG.

Kongens Nytorv

NYHAVN

LADERSTR.

Magasin

NIELS JUUL GADE

ROYAL THEATER

Hojbro Plads

ST. NIKOLAJ CHURCH

HOLMENS KANAL

HOLBERGSGADE

GAMMEL STRAND

CTC

6

THOR-VALDSEN'S MUSEUM

Netto

BORSGADE

HOLMENS CHURCH

HAVNEGADE

Harbor

CHRISTIANS-BORG PALACE

SLOTSHOLMEN

BØRSEN

KNIPPELS-BRO

BRO TORV

STRANDGADE

OVERGADEN

PRINSESSEGADE

CHRISTIANIA

DANISH JEWISH MUSEUM

BRYGGE

"PUSHER STREET"

ROYAL LIBRARY

CTC

CHRISTIANS GADE

Inner

CHRISTIANS CHURCH

OVERGADEN NEDEN VANDET

SANKT ANNAE GADE

CTC

OUR SAVIOR'S CHURCH

M

Christianshavn

LANGE-BRO

Netto

C H R I S T I A N S H A V N

CTC

LANGEBROGADE

See Hotels & Restaurants detail map

AMAGERBROGADE

VERMLANDSGADE

AMAGER BLVD.

To Airport & 4

Canal Tour

S S-Tog Station

Harbor Bus

COPENHAGEN

Locals are usually friendly and helpful. There's also a floating "Harbor Bus" (described on page 169).

Bus lines that end with "A" (such as #1A) use quiet, eco-friendly electric buses that are smaller than normal buses, allowing access into the narrower streets of the old town. Designed for tourists, these provide an easy overview to the city center. Among these, the following are particularly useful:

Bus **#1A** loops from the train station up to Kongens Nytorv (near Nyhavn) and then farther north, to Østerport.

Bus **#2A** goes from Christianshavn to the city center, then onward to points west.

Bus **#5A** connects the station more or less directly to Nørreport.

Bus **#6A** also connects the station to Nørreport, but on a much more roundabout route that twists through the central core (with several sightseeing-handy stops).

Bus **#11A** does a big loop from the train station through the core of town up to Nørreport, then down to Nyhavn before retracing its steps back via Nørreport to the train station.

Other, non-"A" buses, which are bigger and tend to be more direct, can be faster for some trips:

Bus **#14** runs from Nørreport down to the city center, stopping near the Strøget and Slotsholmen Island, and eventually going near the main train station.

Buses **#15** and **#26** run a handy route right through the main tourist zone: train station/Tivoli to Slotsholmen Island to Kongens Nytorv (near Nyhavn) to the Amalienborg Palace/*Little Mermaid* area. Bus #26 continues even farther northward to the city's cruise ports (for more details, see page 160).

Bus **#29** goes from Nyhavn to Slotsholmen Island to Tivoli.

Copenhagen's **Metro** line, while simple, is super-futuristic and growing. For most tourists' purposes, only the airport and three consecutive stops within the city matter: Nørreport (connected every few minutes by the S-tog to the main train station), Kongens Nytorv (near Nyhavn and the Strøget's north end), and Christianshavn.

The city is busy at work on the new Cityringen (City Circle) Metro line. When it opens in 2018, the Metro will instantly become far handier for tourists—linking the train station, Rådhuspladsen, Gammel Strand (near Slotsholmen Island), and Kongens Nytorv (near Nyhavn). In the meantime, you can expect to see massive construction zones at each of those locations. Eventually the Metro will also extend to Ørestad, the industrial and business center created after the Øresund Bridge was built between Denmark and Sweden (for the latest on the Metro, see www.m.dk).

COPENHAGEN

The **S-tog** is basically a commuter line that links stations on the main train line through Copenhagen; for those visiting the city, the most important stops are the main train station and Nørreport (where it ties into the Metro system).

By Boat: The hop-on, hop-off "Harbor Bus" (Havnebus) boat stops at the "Black Diamond" library, Christianshavn (near Knippels Bridge), Nyhavn, the Opera House, and Nordre Tolbod, which is a short walk from *The Little Mermaid* site (and a slightly longer walk from the Langelinie cruise pier). The boat is actually part of the city bus system (lines #901 and #902) and covered by the tickets described earlier. Taking a long ride on this boat—from the library to the end of the line—is the "poor man's cruise," without commentary (runs 6:00-19:00). Or, for a true sightseeing trip, consider a guided harbor cruise (described later, under "Tours in Copenhagen").

By Taxi: Taxis are plentiful, easy to call or flag down, and pricey (26-kr pickup charge and then 13 kr/kilometer). For a short ride, four people spend about the same by taxi as by bus. Calling 35 35 35 35 will get you a taxi within minutes...with the meter already running.

By Bike: Cyclists see more, save time and money, and really feel like locals. With a bike, you have Copenhagen at your command. I'd rather have a bike than a car and driver at my disposal. Virtually every street has a dedicated bike lane (complete with bike signal lights). Police issue 500-kr tickets to anyone riding on sidewalks or through pedestrian zones. Note also that bikes can't be parked just anywhere. Observe others and park your bike among other bikes. The simple built-in lock that binds the back tire is adequate.

Consider one of these rental outfits in or near the city center:

• **Baisikeli Bike Rental,** behind Ørsteds Park just south of Nørreport (budget bike: 50 kr/6 hours, 80 kr/24 hours, 35 kr/extra day; better "standard" bike: 80 kr/6 hours, 110 kr/24 hours, 50 kr/extra day; daily 10:00-18:00; Turesensgade 10—see map on page 166, tel. 53 71 02 29, this location closed in winter; second location tucked behind the Kødbyen district and train station at Ingerslevsgade 80; www.cph-bike-rental.dk). *Baisikeli* means "bike" in Swahili, and this company donates their refurbished used bikes to Africa.

• **Københavns Cyklebørs,** also near Nørreport (75 kr/1 day, 140 kr/2 days, 200 kr/3 days, 350 kr/week, Mon-Fri 9:00-17:30, Sat 10:00-13:30-but you can return bike until 21:00, closed Sun, Gothersgade 157—see map on page 166, tel. 33 14 07 17, www.cykelborsen.dk).

• **Gammel Holm Cykler,** near Nyhavn (Holbergsgade 12—see map on page 224, tel. 33 33 83 84).

From May through November, 2,400 clunky but practical little **free bikes** are scattered around the old town center (basi-  cally the terrain covered in the Copenhagen map in this chapter). Simply locate one of the hundred-some racks, unlock a bike by popping a 20-kr coin into the handlebar, and pedal away. When you're done, plug your bike back into any other rack, and your deposit coin will pop back out; if you can't find a rack, just abandon your bike and someone will take it back and pocket your coin. These simple bikes come with theft-proof parts (unusable on reg-ular bikes) and—they claim—embedded computer chips so that bike patrols can trace and retrieve strays. The bikes are funded by advertisements painted on the wheels and by a progressive elec-torate. Copenhagen's radical city-bike program is a clever idea, but in practice, it doesn't work very well for sightseers. It's hard to find bikes in working order, and when you get to the sight and park your bike, it'll gone by the time you're ready to pedal on. (The 20-kr deposit coin acts as an incentive for any kid or home-less person to pick up city bikes not plugged back into their special racks.) Use the free bikes for a one-way pedal here and there. For efficiency, pay to rent one.

Tours in Copenhagen

By Foot

Copenhagen is an ideal city to get to know by foot. You have two good options:

▲▲Hans Christian Andersen Tours by Richard Karpen—Once upon a time, American Richard Karpen visited Copenhagen and fell in love with the city. Now, dressed as Hans Christian Andersen in a 19th-century top hat and long coat, he leads one-hour tours that wander in and out of buildings, court-yards, back streets, and unusual parts of the old town. Along the way, he gives insight-ful and humorous background on the his-tory, culture, and contemporary life of Denmark, Copenhagen, and the Danes.

Richard offers three entertaining and informative walks: "Castles and Kings,"

"Royal Copenhagen," and "Romantic Copenhagen." Each walk includes a stroll of a little more than a mile (with breaks) and covers different parts of the historic center (100 kr apiece, kids under 12 free; departs from the TI, up the street from the main train station at Vesterbrogade 4A—at the corner with Bernstorffsgade and directly across from Hard Rock Café; mid-May-mid-Sept Mon-Sat at 10:30, none on Sun; departs promptly—if you miss him try to catch up with the tour at the next stop on Rådhuspladsen). Richard's tours, while all different, complement each other and are equally valuable introductions to the city.

Richard also does excellent tours of Rosenborg Castle (80 kr, doesn't include castle entry, mid-May-mid-Sept Mon and Thu at 13:30, one hour, led by dapper Renaissance "Sir Richard," meet outside castle ticket office). You can also hire him for a private tour of the city or of Rosenborg Castle (1,000 kr, or save a bit by paying $165 in US dollars, May-Sept, advance notice required, mobile 60 43 48 26, copenhagenwalks@yahoo.com).

For details, see www.copenhagenwalks.com. No reservations are needed for Richard's scheduled tours—just show up.

▲▲**Copenhagen History Tours**—Christian Donatzky, a charming young Dane with a master's degree in history, runs a walking tour on Saturday mornings. Themes vary by month: In April and May, Christian offers "Reformed Copenhagen" (covering the period from 1400-1600); in June and July, he runs the "King's Copenhagen" (1600-1800); and in August and September, he leads special themed tours—in 2013, he will focus on Danish philosopher Søren Kierkegaard (in honor of the thinker's 200th birthday), while in 2014 and beyond, the tour will feature "Hans Christian Andersen's Copenhagen" (1800-present). The tours are thoughtfully designed, and those with a serious interest in Danish history find them time well spent. Strolling with Christian is like walking with your own private Danish encyclopedia (80 kr, Sat at 10:00, approximately 1.5 hours, small groups of 5-15 people, tours depart from statue of Bishop Absalon on Højbro Plads between the Strøget and Christiansborg Palace, English only, no reservations necessary—just show up, tel. 28 49 44 35, www.history tours.dk, info@historytours.dk).

By Boat

For many, the best way to experience the city's canals and harbor is by canal boat. Two companies offer essentially the same live, three-language, one-hour cruises. Both boats leave at least twice an hour from Nyhavn and Christiansborg Palace, cruise around the palace and Christianshavn area, and then proceed into the wide-open harbor. Best on a sunny day, it's a relaxing way to see *The Little Mermaid* and munch on a lazy picnic during the slow-moving narration.

▲**Netto-Bådene**—These inexpensive cruises cost about half the price of their rival, Canal Tours Copenhagen. Go with Netto; there's no reason to pay double (45 kr, mid-March-mid-Oct daily 10:00-17:00, runs later in summer, sign at dock shows next departure, generally every 20 minutes, dress warmly—boats are open-top until Sept, tel. 32 54 41 02, www.havnerundfart.dk). Netto boats often make two stops where passengers can get off, then hop back on a later boat—at the bridge near *The Little Mermaid*, and at the Langebro bridge near Danhostel. Not every boat makes these stops; check the clock on the bridges for the next departure time.

Don't confuse the cheaper Netto and pricier Canal Tours Copenhagen boats: At Nyhavn, the Netto dock is midway down the canal (on the city side), while the Canal Tours Copenhagen dock is at the head of the canal. Near Christiansborg Palace, the Netto boats leave from Holmen's Bridge in front of the palace, while Canal Tours Copenhagen boats depart from Gammel Strand, 200 yards away. Boats leaving from Christiansborg are generally less crowded than those leaving from Nyhavn.

Canal Tours Copenhagen—This more expensive option does the same cruise as Netto for 70 kr (daily March-late Oct 9:30-17:00, until 20:00 late June-late Aug; late-Oct-Dec 10:00-15:00, no tours Jan-Feb, boats are sometimes covered if it's raining, tel. 32 96 30 00, www.stromma.dk).

In summer, Canal Tours Copenhagen also runs unguided hop-on, hop-off **"water bus"** tours (40 kr/single trip, 70 kr/24 hours, daily late May-early Sept 10:15-18:45).

By Bus

Hop-on, Hop-off Bus Tours—These offer a basic 1.25- to 1.5-hour circle of the city sights, allowing you to get on and off as you like: Tivoli Gardens, Gammel Strand near Christiansborg Palace, *The Little Mermaid* site, Rosenborg Castle, Nyhavn sailors' quarter, and more, with recorded narration. The options include **City Sightseeing** (red buses, 155 kr, 185 kr includes Carlsberg and Christiania routes, ticket good for 24 hours, 2/hour, May-Aug daily 10:00-16:30, shorter hours off-season, bus departs City Hall below the *Lur Blowers* statue—to the left of City Hall—or at many other stops throughout city, pay driver, tel. 25 55 66 88, www.city-sightseeing.dk) and **Open Top Tours** (green buses, 175 kr, 35 kr more to add cruise on Canal Tours Copenhagen, ticket good for 24 hours, 2/hour, departures 10:00-16:00, www.stromma

.dk/en/opentoptours). Another operation—called **Step On Step Off**—does a similar route with slightly lower frequency (every 45 minutes in summer, hourly in winter; 170 kr/1 day, 200 kr/2 days, www.steponstepoff.dk).

By Bike

▲**Bike Copenhagen with Mike**—Mike Sommerville offers a good three-hour guided tour of the city daily at 10:30 (with a second departure at 14:30 Tue-Wed, Fri, and Sat in June-Aug, and on Sat in Sept; 290 kr including bike rental, cash only). A Copenhagen native, Mike enjoys showing off his city to visitors by biking at a leisurely pace, "along the high roads, low roads, in-roads, and off-roads of Copenhagen." All tours are in English, and depart from the Bike Copenhagen with Mike tour base at Sankt Peders Straede 47, in the Latin Quarter (see the map on page 224). Mike also offers private tours; see the details at www.bike copenhagenwithmike.dk.

Self-Guided Walk in Copenhagen

The Strøget: Copenhagen's Heart and Soul

Start from Rådhuspladsen (City Hall Square), the bustling heart of Copenhagen, dominated by the tower of the City Hall. Today this square always seems to be hosting some lively community event, but it was once Copenhagen's fortified west end. For 700 years, Copenhagen was contained within its city walls. By the mid-1800s, 140,000 people were packed inside. The overcrowding led to hygiene problems. (A cholera outbreak killed 5,000.) It was clear: The walls needed to come down...and they did. Those formidable town walls survive today only in echoes—a circular series of roads and the remnants of moats, now people-friendly city lakes (see "The Story of Copenhagen" sidebar, earlier).

• *Stand 50 yards in front of City Hall and turn clockwise for a...*

Rådhuspladsen Spin-Tour

The **City Hall,** or Rådhus, is worth a visit (described on page 190). Old **Hans Christian Andersen** sits to the right of City Hall, almost begging to be in another photo (as he used to in real life). Climb onto his well-worn knee. (While up there, you might take off your shirt for a racy photo, as many Danes enjoy doing.)

The wooded area behind Andersen is **Tivoli Gardens.** In 1843, magazine publisher Georg Carstensen convinced the king to let him build a pleasure garden outside the walls of crowded Copenhagen. The king quickly agreed, knowing that happy people care less about fighting for democracy. Tivoli became Europe's first

Hans Christian Andersen
(1805-1875)

The author of such classic fairy tales as *The Ugly Duckling* was an ugly duckling himself—a misfit who blossomed. Hans Christian

Andersen (called H. C., pronounced "hoe see" by the Danes) was born to a poor shoemaker in Odense. As a child he was gangly, high-strung, and effeminate. He avoided school because the kids laughed at him, so he spent his time in a fantasy world of books and plays. When his father died, the 11-year-old was on his own, forced into manual labor. He loved playing with a marionette theater that his father had made for him, sparking a lifelong love affair with the theater. In 1819, at the age of 14, he moved to Copenhagen to pursue an acting career and worked as a boy soprano for the Royal Theater. When his voice changed, the director encouraged him to return to school. He dutifully attended—a teenager among boys—and eventually went on to the university. As rejections piled up for his acting aspirations, Andersen began to shift his theatrical ambitions to playwriting.

After graduation, Andersen won a two-year scholarship to travel around Europe, the first of many trips he'd make and write about. His experiences abroad were highly formative, providing inspiration for many of his tales. Still in his 20s, he published an (obviously autobiographical) novel, *The Improvisatore,* about a poor young man who comes into his own while traveling in Italy. The novel launched his writing career, and soon he was hobnobbing with the international crowd—Charles Dickens, Victor Hugo, Franz Liszt, Richard Wagner, Henrik Ibsen, and Edvard Grieg.

Despite his many famous friends, Andersen remained a

great public amusement park. When the train lines came, the station was placed just beyond Tivoli.

The big, broad boulevard is **Vesterbrogade** ("Western Way"), which led to the western gate of the medieval city (behind you, where the pedestrian boulevard begins). Here, in the traffic hub of this huge city, you'll notice...not many cars. Denmark's 180 percent tax on car purchases makes the bus, Metro, or bike a sweeter option.

Down Vesterbrogade towers the **SAS building,** Copenhagen's only skyscraper. Locals say it seems so tall because the clouds hang so low. When it was built in 1960, Copenhageners took one look

lonely soul who never married. Of uncertain sexuality, he had very close male friendships and journaled about unrequited love affairs with several women, including the famous opera star of the day, Jenny Lind, the "Swedish Nightingale." (For more on this aspect of his life, see the sidebar on page 186.) Without a family of his own, he became very close with the children of his friends—and, through his fairy tales, with a vast extended family of kids around the world.

Though he wrote novels, plays, and travel literature, it was his fairy tales, including *The Ugly Duckling*, *The Emperor's New Clothes*, *The Princess and the Pea*, *The Little Mermaid*, and *The Red Shoes*, that made him famous in Denmark and abroad. They made him Denmark's best-known author, the "Danish Charles Dickens." Some stories are based on earlier folk tales, and others came straight from his inventive mind, all written in an informal, conversational style that was considered unusual and even surprising at the time.

Andersen's compelling tales appeal to children and adults alike. They're full of magic and touch on strong, universal emotions—the pain of being different, the joy of self-discovery, and the struggle to fit in. The ugly duckling, for example, is teased by his fellow ducks before he finally discovers his true identity as a beautiful swan. In *The Emperor's New Clothes*, a boy is derided by everyone for speaking the simple, self-evident truth that the emperor is fooling himself. Harry Potter author J. K. Rowling recently said, "The indelible characters he created are so deeply implanted in our subconscious that we sometimes forget that we were not born with the stories." (For more on Andersen's famous story *The Little Mermaid*—and what it might tell us about his life—see page 186.)

By the time of his death, the poor shoemaker's son was wealthy, cultured, and had been knighted. His rise through traditional class barriers mirrors the social progress of the 19th century.

and decided—that's enough of a skyline.

The golden **weather girls** (on the corner, high above Vesterbrogade) indicate the weather: on a bike (fair weather) or with an umbrella. These two have been called the only women in Copenhagen you can trust, but for years they've been stuck in almost-sunny mode...with the bike just peeking out. Notice that the red temperature dots max out at 28° Celsius (that's 82° Fahrenheit).

To the right, just down the street, is the Tiger Store (a popular local dime store...everything is priced at 10 or 20 kr). The next street (once the local Fleet Street, with the big newspapers) still has the offices for *Politiken* (the leading Danish newspaper) and the best bookstore in town, Boghallen.

As you spin farther right, three fast-food joints stand at the entry to the Strøget (STROY-et), Copenhagen's grand pedestrian boulevard—where we're heading next. Just beyond that and the Art Deco-style Palace Hotel (with a tower to serve as a sister to

the City Hall) is the ***Lur Blowers sculpture,*** which honors the earliest warrior Danes. The *lur* is a curvy, trombone-sounding horn that was used to call soldiers to battle or to accompany pagan religious processions. The earliest bronze *lurs* date as far back as 3,500 years ago. Later, the Vikings used a wood version of the *lur.* The ancient originals, which still play, are displayed in the National Museum. (City tour buses leave from below these Vikings.)

• *Now head down the pedestrian boulevard.*

The Strøget

The American trio of Burger King, 7-Eleven, and KFC marks the start of this otherwise charming pedestrian street. Finished in 1962, Copenhagen's experimental, tremendously successful, and much-copied pedestrian shopping mall is a string of lively (and individually named) streets and lovely squares that bunny-hop through the old town from City Hall to the Nyhavn quarter, a 20-minute stroll away.

As you wander down this street, remember that the commercial focus of a historic street like the Strøget drives up the land value, which generally trashes the charm and tears down the old buildings. Look above the modern window displays and street-level advertising to discover bits of 19th-century character that still survive. Though the Strøget has become hamburgerized, historic bits and attractive pieces of old Copenhagen are just off this commercial cancan.

After one block (at Kattesundet), make a side-trip three blocks left into Copenhagen's colorful **university district.** Formerly the old brothel neighborhood, later the heart of Copenhagen's hippie community in the 1960s, today this "Latin Quarter" is Soho chic. At Sankt Peders Stræde, turn right and walk to the end of the street.

Along the way, look for large mansions that once circled expansive **courtyards.** As the population grew, the city walls constricted Copenhagen's physical size. The courtyards were gradually filled with higgledy-piggledy secondary buildings. Today, throughout the old center you can step off a busy pedestrian mall and back in time into these characteristic half-timbered time-warps. Replace the parked car with a tired horse and the bikes with a line of outhouses, and you're in 19th-century Copenhagen. If you see an open courtyard door, you're welcome to discreetly wander in and look around.

You'll also pass funky shops, and the big brick **Sankt Peders Church**—the old German merchant community's church, which still holds services in German. Its crypt (filling a ground-floor building out back due to the boggy nature of the soil) is filled with fancy German tombs (fee to enter).

• *When Sankt Peders Stræde intersects with Nørregade, look right to find the big, Neoclassical...*

Cathedral of Our Lady (Vor Frue Kirche)

The obelisk-like **Reformation Memorial** across the street from the cathedral celebrates Denmark's break from the Roman

Catholic Church to become Lutheran in 1536. Walk around and study the reliefs of great Danish reformers protesting from their pulpits. The relief facing the church shows King Christian III presiding over the pivotal town council meeting when they decided to break away from Rome. As a young man, Prince Christian had traveled to Germany, where he was influenced by Martin Luther. He returned to take the Danish throne by force, despite Catholic opposition. Realizing the advantages of being the head of his own state church, Christian confiscated church property and established the state Lutheran Church. King Christian was crowned inside this cathedral. Because of the reforms of 1536, there's no Mary in the Cathedral of Our Lady.

The cathedral's **facade** looks like a Greek temple. (Two blocks to the right, in the distance, notice more Neoclassicism—the law courts.) You can see why Golden Age Copenhagen (early 1800s) fancied itself a Nordic Athens. Old Testament figures (King David and Moses) flank the cathedral's entryway. Above, John the Baptist stands where you'd expect to see Greek gods. He invites you in...to the New Testament.

The **interior** is a world of Neoclassical serenity. Go inside (free, open daily 8:00-17:00). This pagan temple now houses Christianity. The nave is lined by the 12 apostles, clad in classical robes—masterpieces by the great Danish sculptor Bertel

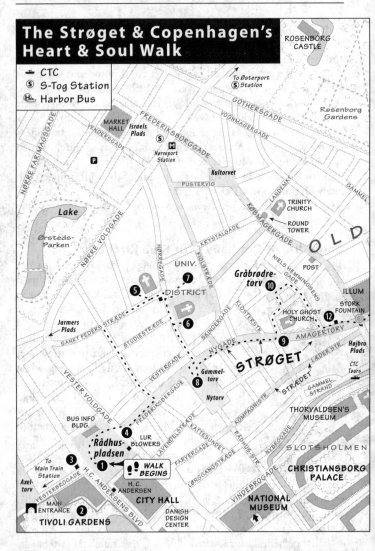

The Strøget & Copenhagen's Heart & Soul Walk

- ↔ CTC
- Ⓢ S-Tog Station
- ⒣ Harbor Bus

Thorvaldsen (see sidebar, page 197). Each strikes a meditative pose, carrying his identifying symbol: Peter with keys, Andrew with the X-shaped cross of his execution, Matthew and John writing their books, and so on. They lead to a statue of the *Risen Christ*, standing where the statue of Zeus would have been: inside a temple-like niche, flanked by col-

COPENHAGEN

1. Rådhuspladsen
2. Tivoli Gardens
3. Weather Girls
4. Start of the Strøget
5. Sankt Peders Church
6. Cathedral of Our Lady
7. Copenhagen University
8. Gammeltorv & Nytorv
9. Amagertorv
10. Gråbrødretorv
11. Bishop Absalon Statue
12. Royal Copenhagen Store & Illums Bolighus
13. Pistolstræde
14. Kongens Nytorv
15. Nyhavn
16. Cheap Beer Kiosk
17. Royal Danish Theatre Playhouse
18. Amalienborg Palace
19. To Little Mermaid & End of Walk

umns, and topped with a pediment. Rather than wearing a royal robe, Jesus wears his burial shroud, opens his arms wide, and says, "Come to me." (Mormons will recognize this statue—a replica stands in the visitors center at Salt Lake City's Temple Square and is often reproduced in church publications.) The marvelous acoustics are demonstrated in free organ concerts on Saturdays at noon in July and August. Notice how, in good Protestant style, only the front half of the pews are "reversible," allowing the congregation to flip around and face the pulpit (in the middle of the church) to better hear the sermon.

• *Head back outside. If you face the facade and look to the left (across the square called Frue Plads), you'll see...*

Copenhagen University

Now home to 30,000 students, this university was founded by the king in the 15th century to stop the Danish brain drain to Paris.

Today tuition is free (but room, board, and beer are not). Locals say it's easy to get in, but, given the wonderful lifestyle, very hard to get out.

Go up the middle steps of the university's big building and enter a colorful lobby, starring Athena and Apollo. The frescoes celebrate high thinking, with themes such as the triumph of wisdom over barbarism. Notice how harmoniously the architecture, sculpture, and painting work together. (Just inside the door are two stand-up terminals offering free Internet access.)

Outside, busts honor great minds from the faculty, including (at the end) Niels Bohr, a professor who won the 1922 Nobel Prize for theoretical physics. He evaded the clutches of the Nazi science labs by fleeing to America in 1943, where he helped develop the atomic bomb.

• *Rejoin the Strøget (down where you saw the law courts) at the twin squares called...*

Gammeltorv and Nytorv

This was the old town center. In Gammeltorv ("Old Square"), the Fountain of Charity (Caritas) is named for the figure of Charity on top. It has provided drinking water to locals since the early 1600s. Featuring a pregnant woman squirting water from her breasts next to a boy urinating, this was just too much for people of the Victorian Age. They corked both figures and raised the statue to what they hoped would be out of view. The Asian-looking kiosk was one of the city's first commu-nity telephone centers from the days before phones were privately owned. Look at the reliefs ring-ing its top: an airplane with bird wings (c. 1900) and two women talking on the newfangled phone. (It was thought business would popularize the telephone, but actually it was women.)

While Gammeltorv was a place of happiness and merriment, Nytorv ("New Square") was a place of severity and judgment. Walk to the small raised area in front of the old ancient-Greek-style former City Hall. Do a 360. The square is Neoclassical (built mostly around 1800). Read the old Danish on the City Hall facade: "With Law Shall Man Build the Land." Look down at the pavement and read the plaque: "Here stood the town's *Kag* (whipping post) until 1780."

• *Now walk down the next stretch of the Strøget to reach…*

Amagertorv

This is prime real estate for talented street entertainers and pickpockets. Walk to the stately brick Holy Ghost church (Helligåndskirken). The fine spire is typical of old Danish churches. Under the stepped gable was a medieval hospital run by monks (one of the oldest buildings in town, dating from the 12th century).

A block behind the church (walk down Valkendorfsgade—the street just before the church—and through a passage under the rust-colored building at #32) is the leafy and caffeine-stained **Gråbrødretorv.** This "Grey Friars' Square," surrounded by fine old buildings, is a popular place for an outdoor meal or drink in the summer. At the end of the

square, the street Niels Hemmingsens Gade returns to the Strøget.

Once at the Strøget, turn left and continue down Amagertorv, with its fine inlaid Italian granite stonework, to the next square with the "stork" fountain (actually three herons). From the fountain, you can see the imposing Parliament building, Christiansborg Palace (with its "three crowns" spire) and an equestrian statue of Bishop Absalon, the city's founder (canal boat tours depart nearby). The Victorian WCs here (steps down from fountain, 2 kr, free urinals) are a delight.

Amagertorv is a highlight for shoppers, with the Royal Copenhagen store—stacked with three floors of porcelain—and Illums Bolighus' three floors of modern Danish design (see "Shopping in Copenhagen," later). A block toward the canal—running parallel to the Strøget—starts Strædet, which is a "second Strøget" featuring cafés, antique shops, and no fast food.

North of Amagertorv, a broad pedestrian mall called **Købmagergade** leads past a fine modern bakery (Illum Bager, next to McDonald's; salads, sandwiches, and traditional pastries) to Christian IV's Round Tower and the Latin Quarter (university

Copenhagen at a Glance

▲▲▲**Tivoli Gardens** Copenhagen's classic amusement park, with rides, music, food, and other fun. **Hours:** Mid-April–late Sept daily 11:00–22:00, later Fri-Sat and mid-June–late Aug, also open daily 11:00–22:00 for a week in mid-Oct and mid-Nov–late Dec. See page 188.

▲▲▲**National Museum** History of Danish civilization with tourable 19th-century Victorian Apartment. **Hours:** Museum—Tue-Sun 10:00–17:00, closed Mon; Victorian Apartment—tours June-Sept Sat at 14:00. See page 192.

▲▲▲**Rosenborg Castle and Treasury** Renaissance castle of larger-than-life "warrior king" Christian IV. **Hours:** June-Aug daily 10:00–17:00; May and Sept-Oct daily 10:00–16:00; Nov-Dec Tue-Sun 11:00–14:00 (treasury until 16:00), closed Mon; Jan-April Tue-Sun 11:00–16:00, closed Mon. See page 202.

▲▲▲**Christiania** Colorful counterculture squatters' colony. **Hours:** Always open. See page 212.

▲▲**Christiansborg Palace** Royal reception rooms with dazzling tapestries. **Hours:** Palace—daily 10:00–17:00 except closed Mon Oct-April; stables—daily 13:30–16:00 except closed Mon Oct-April. See page 195.

▲▲**Museum of Danish Resistance** Chronicle of Denmark's struggle against the Nazis. **Hours:** May-Sept Tue-Sun 10:00–16:00, Oct-April Tue-Sun 10:00–15:00, closed Mon year-round. See page 201.

▲▲**Thorvaldsen's Museum** Works of the Danish Neoclassical sculptor. **Hours:** Tue-Sun 10:00–17:00, closed Mon. See page 196.

district). The recommended Café Norden overlooks the fountain—a good place for a meal or coffee with a view. The second floor offers the best vantage point.

The final stretch of the Strøget leads to **Pistolstræde** (leading off the Strøget to the left from Østergade at #24, just after crossing the busy street), a cute lane of shops in restored 18th-century buildings. Wander back into the half-timbered section.

• *Continuing along the Strøget, passing major department stores (see "Shopping in Copenhagen," later), you'll come to the biggest square in town...*

▲**City Hall** Copenhagen's landmark, packed with Danish history and symbolism and topped with a tower. **Hours:** Mon-Fri 8:30-16:30, some Sat 10:00-13:00, closed Sun. See page 190.

▲**Ny Carlsberg Glyptotek** Scandinavia's top art gallery, featuring Egyptians, Greeks, Etruscans, French, and Danes. **Hours:** Tue-Sun 11:00-17:00, closed Mon. See page 191.

▲**Museum of Copenhagen** The story of Copenhagen, displayed in an old house. **Hours:** Daily 10:00-17:00. See page 195.

▲**Danish Jewish Museum** Exhibit tracing the 400-year history of Danish Jews, in a unique building by American architect Daniel Libeskind. **Hours:** June-Aug Tue-Sun 10:00-17:00; Sept-May Tue-Fri 13:00-16:00, Sat-Sun 12:00-17:00; closed Mon year-round. See page 199.

▲**Amalienborg Palace Museum** Quick and intimate look at Denmark's royal family. **Hours:** May-Oct daily 10:00-16:00; Nov-April Tue-Sun 11:00-16:00, closed Mon. See page 200.

▲**Rosenborg Gardens** Park surrounding Rosenborg Castle, filled with statues and statuesque Danes. **Hours:** Always open. See page 209.

▲**National Gallery of Denmark** Good Danish and Modernist collections. **Hours:** Tue-Sun 10:00-17:00, Wed until 20:00, closed Mon. See page 209.

▲**Our Savior's Church** Spiral-spired church with bright Baroque interior. **Hours:** Church—daily 11:00-15:30 but may close for special services; tower—July-mid-Sept Mon-Sat 10:00-19:00, Sun 10:30-19:00; April-June and mid-Sept-Nov daily until 16:00, closed Dec-March and in bad weather. See page 211.

Kongens Nytorv

The "King's New Square" is home to the National Theater, French embassy, and venerable Hotel d'Angleterre. In the mid-1600s the city expanded, pushing its wall farther east. The equestrian statue in the middle of the square celebrates Christian V, who made this square the city's geographical and cultural center. In 1676, King Christian rode off to re-conquer

the southern tip of Sweden and reclaim Denmark's dominance. He returned empty-handed and broke. Denmark became a second-rate power, but Copenhagen prospered. In the winter this square becomes a popular ice-skating rink.

Before entering the square, walk to the right, toward the small glass pyramids (marking the Metro). Wander into **Hviids Vinstue**, the town's oldest wine cellar (from 1723, before the Metro station, at #19, under the Bali Restaurant) to check out its characteristic interior and fascinating old Copenhagen photos. It's a colorful spot for an open-face sandwich and a beer (three sandwiches and a beer for 65 kr at lunchtime). Their wintertime *gløgg* (hot spiced wine) is legendary. Across the street, towering above the Metro station, is Magasin du Nord, the grandest old department store in town.

The **Metro** that runs underground here features state-of-the-art technology (automated cars, no driver...sit in front to watch the tracks coming at you). As the cars come and go without drivers, compare this system to the public transit in your town.

• *Back up at ground level, walk across the square to the trendy harbor of...*

Nyhavn

Established in the 1670s along with Kongens Nytorv, Nyhavn ("New Harbor") is a recently gentrified sailors' quarter. (Hong Kong is the last of the nasty bars from the rough old days.) With its trendy cafés, jazz clubs, and tattoo shops (pop into Tattoo Ole at #17—fun photos, very traditional), Nyhavn is a wonderful place to hang out. The canal is filled with glamorous old sailboats of all sizes. Historic sloops are welcome to moor here in Copenhagen's ever-changing boat museum. Hans Christian Andersen lived and wrote his first stories here (in the red double-gabled building on the right at #20). A minuscule amber museum is above the House of Amber at the head of the canal (see "Shopping in Copenhagen," page 217).

Wander the quay, enjoying the frat-party parade of tattoos (hotter weather reveals more tattoos). Celtic and Nordic mythological designs are in (as is bodybuilding, by the looks of things). The place thrives—with the cheap-beer drinkers dockside and the richer and older ones looking on from comfier cafés.

A note about all this public beer-drinking: There's no more beer consumption here than in the US; it's just out in public. Many young Danes can't afford to drink in a bar, so they "picnic drink" their beers in squares and along canals, spending a quarter of the bar price for a bottle from a nearby kiosk. Consider grabbing a cold 10-kr beer yourself and joining the scene (the kiosk is on Holbergsgade, just over the bridge and on the left, open daily until 24:00).

From the end of Nyhavn canal, turn left around the **Royal Danish Theatre's Playhouse.** Continuing north along the harbor,

you'll stroll a delightful waterfront promenade to the modern fountain of Amaliehaven Park, immediately across the harbor from Copenhagen's slick Opera House. The **Opera House** is bigger than it looks because much of it is underground. Its striking design is controversial. Completed in 2005 by Henning Larsen, it was a $400 million gift to the nation from an oil-shipping magnate.

• *A block inland (behind the fountain) is the orderly...*

Amalienborg Palace and Square

Queen Margrethe II and her husband.live in the mansion to your immediate left as you enter the square from the harborside. (If the flag's flying, she's home.) Her son and heir to the throne, Crown Prince Frederik, recently moved into the mansion across the street with his wife, Australian businesswoman Mary Donaldson, and their four children.

Though the guards change with royal fanfare at noon only when the queen is in residence, they shower every morning. The royal guard often has a police escort when it marches through town on special occasions—leading locals to joke that theirs is "the only army in the world that needs police protection."

The small **Amalienborg Palace Museum** offers an intimate look at royal living (far side of square, described on page 200).

The equestrian statue of Frederick V is a reminder that this square was the centerpiece of a planned town he envisioned in 1750. It was named for him—Frederikstaden. During the 18th century, Denmark's population grew and the country thrived (as trade flourished and its neutrality kept it out of the costly wars impoverishing much of Europe). Frederikstaden, with its strong Neoclassical harmony, was designed as a luxury neighborhood for the city's business elite. Nobility and other big shots moved in, but

The Little Mermaid and Hans Christian Andersen

"Far out in the ocean, where the water is as blue as a cornflower, as clear as crystal, and very, very deep..." there lived a young mermaid. So begins one of Hans Christian Andersen's (1805-1875) best-known stories. The plot line starts much like the Disney children's movie, but it's spiced with poetic description and philosophical dialogue about the immortal soul.

The mermaid's story goes like this: One day, a young mermaid spies a passing ship and falls in love with a handsome human prince. The ship is wrecked in a storm, and she saves the prince's life. To be with the prince, the mermaid asks a sea witch to give her human legs. In exchange, she agrees to give up her voice and the chance of ever returning to the sea. And, the witch tells her, if the prince doesn't marry her, she will immediately die heartbroken and without an immortal soul. The mermaid agrees, and her fish tail becomes a pair of beautiful but painful legs. She woos the prince—who loves her in return—but he eventually marries another. Heartbroken, the mermaid prepares to die. She's given one last chance to save herself: She must kill the prince on his wedding night. She sneaks into the bedchamber with a knife...but can't bear to kill the man she loves. The mermaid throws herself into the sea to die. Suddenly, she's miraculously carried up by the mermaids of the air, who give her an immortal soul as a reward for her long-suffering love.

The tale of unrequited love mirrors Andersen's own sad love life. He had two major crushes—one of them for the famous opera singer, Jenny Lind—but he was turned down both times, and he never married. Scholars with access to Andersen's diary believe he was bisexual and died a virgin. The great author is said to have feared he'd lose his artistic drive if he ever actually made love to another person. His dearest male friend, Edvard Collin, inherited Andersen's entire estate (which was not unusual in the Romantic 19th century, when men tended to have more emotional and intimate friendships than today).

the king came here only after his other palace burned down in a 1794 fire.

Just inland, the striking Frederikskirke—better known as the **Marble Church**—was designed to fit this ritzy new quarter. If it's open, step inside to bask in its vast, serene, Pantheon-esque atmosphere (free, Mon-Thu 10:00-17:00, Fri-Sun 12:00-17:00).
• *From the square, Amaliegade leads two blocks north to...*

Kastellet Park
In this park, you'll find some worthwhile sightseeing. Just before the park's entrance, look for Denmark's fascinating (and free)

WWII-era **Museum of Danish Resistance** (see page 201). Beyond that is the 1908 **Gefion Fountain,** which illustrates the myth of the goddess who was given a single night to carve a hunk out of Sweden to make into Denmark's main island, Sjælland (or "Zealand" in English), which you're on. Gefion transformed her four sons into oxen to do the job, and the chunk she removed from Sweden is supposedly Vänern, Sweden's largest lake. If you look at a map showing Sweden and Denmark, the island and the lake are, in fact, roughly the same shape.

Next to the fountain is an Anglican church built of flint. Climb up the stairs by the fountain and continue along the top of the rampart about five minutes to reach the harborfront site of the overrated, overfondled, and overphotographed symbol of Copenhagen, ***Den Lille Havfrue—The Little Mermaid.*** *The Little Mermaid* statue was a gift to the city of Copenhagen in 1909 from brewing magnate Carl Jacobsen (whose art collection forms the basis of the Ny Carlsberg Glyptotek). Inspired by a ballet performance of Andersen's story, Jacobsen hired the young sculptor Edvard Eriksen to immortalize the mermaid as a statue. Eriksen used his wife Eline as the model.

For the non-Disneyfied *Little Mermaid* story—and insights into Hans Christian Andersen—see the sidebar.
• *Our walking tour is finished. You can get back downtown on foot, by taxi, or on bus #1A or #15 from Store Kongensgade on the other side of Kastellet Park, or bus #26 from farther north, along Folke Bernadottes Allé. Or, if your cruise ship is at the Langelinie Pier and you're ready to head back, you're just a short walk away.*

COPENHAGEN

Sights in Copenhagen

Near the Train Station

Copenhagen's great train station, the Hovedbanegården, is a fascinating mesh of Scandinavian culture and transportation efficiency. From the station, delightful sights fan out into the old city. The following attractions are listed roughly in order from the train station to Slotsholmen Island.

▲▲▲**Tivoli Gardens**—The world's grand old amusement park—

since 1843—is 20 acres, 110,000 lanterns, and countless ice cream cones of fun. You pay one admission price and find yourself lost in a Hans Christian Andersen wonderland of rides, restaurants, games, marching bands, roulette wheels, and funny mirrors. A roller coaster screams through the middle of a tranquil Asian food court, the Small-World-inspired Den Flyvende Kuffert ride floats through Hans Christian Andersen fairy tales, and a fancy pavilion hides one of the most respected restaurants in Copenhagen. It's a children's fantasyland midday, but it becomes more adult-oriented later on. With or without kids, this place is a true magic kingdom. Tivoli doesn't try to be Disney. It's wonderfully and happily Danish. I find it worth the price of admission just to see Danes—young and old—at play.

Cost: 95 kr, free for kids under 8. To go on rides, you'll buy

ride tickets from the automated machines (25 kr, color-coded rides cost 1, 2, or 3 tickets apiece); or you can buy an all-day ride pass for 199 kr. If you'll be using at least eight tickets, buy the ride pass instead. To leave and come back later, you'll have to buy a 15-kr re-entry ticket before you exit. Tel. 33 15 10 01, www.tivoli.dk.

Hours: Mid-April-late Sept daily 11:00-22:00, later Fri-Sat and mid-June-late Aug. Dress warm for chilly evenings any time of year. There are lockers by each entrance.

Getting There: Tivoli is across Bernstoffsgade from the train station. If you're catching an overnight train, this is *the* place to spend your last Copenhagen hours.

Entertainment at Tivoli: If you're overnighting in Copenhagen before or after your cruise, Tivoli is a festive place to spend the evening. Upon arrival (through main entrance, on left in the service center), pick up a map and look for the events schedule. Take a moment to sit down and plan your entertainment for the evening. Events are spread between 15:00 and 23:00; the 19:30 concert in the concert hall can be as little as 50 kr or as much as 1,200 kr, depending on the performer (box office tel. 33 15 10 12). If the Tivoli Symphony is playing, it's worth paying for. The ticket box office is outside, just to the left of the main entrance (daily 10:00-20:00; if you buy a concert ticket you get into Tivoli for free).

Free concerts, pantomime theater, ballet, acrobats, puppets, and other shows pop up all over the park, and a well-organized visitor can enjoy an exciting evening of entertainment without spending a single krone beyond the entry fee. Friday evenings feature a (usually free) rock or pop show at 22:00. People gather around the lake 45 minutes before closing time for the "Tivoli Illuminations" (except on Fri, when there's no show). Fireworks blast a few nights each summer. The park is particularly romantic at dusk, when the lights go on.

Eating at Tivoli: Inside the park, expect to pay amusement-park prices for amusement-park-quality food. Still, a meal here is part of the fun. **Søcafeen** serves only traditional open-face sandwiches in a fun beer garden with lakeside ambience. They allow picnics if you buy a drink (and will rent you plates and silverware for 10 kr per person). The *pølse* (sausage) stands are cheap, and there's a bagel sandwich place in the amusements corner. **Færgekroen** offers a quiet, classy lakeside escape from the amusement-park intensity, with traditional dishes washed down by its own microbrew (190-265-kr hearty pub grub). **Wagamama,** a modern pan-Asian slurpathon from the UK, serves healthy noodle dishes (at the far back side of the park, also possible to enter from outside, 100-130-kr meals). **Nimb's Terrasse** has dignified French food in a garden setting (175-225-kr dishes). **Café Georg,** to the left of the concert hall, has tasty 75-kr sandwiches and a lake view (also 100-kr salads and omelets). The kid-pleasing **Piratiriet** lets you dine on a pirate ship (140-170-kr main dishes).

For something more upscale, consider the complex of Nimb restaurants, in the big Taj Mahal-like pavilion near the entrance facing the train station. **Nimb's Louise** is Tivoli's big splurge, with seasonal menus that are well-regarded even by non-parkgoers (lunch: three courses-495 kr; dinner: four courses-750 kr, eight courses-1125 kr). **Nimb's Brasserie,** sharing the same lobby, has more affordable prices (175-235-kr main dishes).

If it's chilly, you'll find plenty of **Mamma Mokka** coffee takeaway stands. If you get a drink "to go," you'll pay an extra 5-kr deposit for the cup, which you can recoup by inserting the empty cup into an automated machine (marked on maps).

▲**City Hall (Rådhus)**—This city landmark, between the train station/Tivoli and the Strøget, is free and open to the public; you can wander throughout the building and into the peaceful garden out back. It also offers private tours and trips up its 345-foot-tall tower.

Cost and Hours: Free, Mon-Fri 8:30-16:30; you can usually slip in Sat 10:00-13:00 when weddings are going on, or join the Sat tour; closed Sun. Guided English-language tours-30 kr, 45 minutes, gets you into more private, official rooms; Mon-Fri at 15:00, Sat at 10:00. Tower-20 kr, 300 steps for the best aerial view of Copenhagen, June-Sept Mon-Fri at 11:00 and 14:00, Sat at 12:00, closed Sun and Oct-May. Tel. 33 66 33 66.

Visiting City Hall: It's draped, inside and out, in Danish symbolism. The city's founder, Bishop Absalon, stands over the door. Absalon (c. 1128-1201)—bishop, soldier, and foreign-policy wonk—was King Valdemar I's right-hand man. In Copenhagen, he drove out pirates and built a fort to guard the harbor, turning a miserable fishing village into a humming Baltic seaport. The polar bears climbing on the rooftop symbolize the giant Danish protectorate of Greenland. Six night watchmen flank the city's gold-and-green seal under the Danish flag.

Step inside. The info desk (on the left as you enter) has racks of tourist information (city maps and other brochures). The building and its huge tower were inspired by the city hall in Siena, Italy (with the necessary bad-weather addition of a glass roof). Enormous functions fill this grand hall (the iron grate in the center of the floor is an elevator  for bringing up 1,200 chairs), while the busts of four illustrious local boys—fairy-tale writer Hans Christian Andersen, sculptor Bertel Thorvaldsen, physicist Niels Bohr, and the building's architect, Martin Nyrop—look on. Underneath the floor are national archives dating back to 1275, popular with Danes researching their family roots.

Danish Design Center—This center shows off the best in Danish design as well as top examples from around the world, including architecture, fashion, and graphic arts. A visit to this low-key display for sleek Scandinavian objects offers an interesting glimpse into a culture that takes pride in functionalism and minimalism. The ground and upper floors are filled with changing exhibits; the basement houses the "semipermanent" Denmark by Design exhibit (likely through sometime in 2013), with samples of Danish design from 1950 to 2000. The boutique next to the ticket counter features three themes: travel light (chic travel accessories and gadgets), modern Danish classics, and books and posters. Sometimes it feels a bit like an Ikea showroom—suggesting the prevalence of Scandinavian design in our everyday lives. But perusing the exhibits here, you'll come to see design not just as something pleasing to the eye, but as an invaluable tool that can improve lives and solve problems.

Cost and Hours: 55 kr, Mon-Fri 10:00-17:00, Wed until 21:00, Sat-Sun 11:00-16:00—July-Aug until 17:00, across from Tivoli Gardens and down the street from City Hall at H. C. Andersen Boulevard 27, tel. 33 69 33 69, www.ddc.dk.

Eating: The café on the main level, under the atrium, serves light lunches (55-65-kr sandwiches and salads, three *smørrebrød* for 125 kr).

▲**Ny Carlsberg Glyptotek**—Scandinavia's top art gallery is

an impressive example of what beer money can do. Brewer Carl Jacobsen (son of J. C. Jacobsen, who funded the Museum of National History at Frederiksborg Castle) was an avid collector and patron of the arts. (Carl also donated *The Little Mermaid* statue to the city.) His namesake museum has intoxicating artifacts from the ancient world, along with some fine art from our own times. The next time you sip a Carlsberg beer, drink a toast to Carl Jacobsen and his marvelous collection. *Skål!*

Cost and Hours: 75 kr, free Sun; open Tue-Sun 11:00-17:00, closed Mon, classy cafeteria under palms, behind Tivoli at Dantes Plads 7, tel. 33 41 81 41, www.glypto teket.com.

Visiting the Museum: Pick up a floor plan as you enter to help navigate the confusing layout. For a chronological swing, start with Egypt (mummy coffins and sarcophagi, a 5,000-year-old hippo statue), Greece (red-and-black painted vases, statues), the Etruscan world (Greek-looking vases), and Rome (grittily realistic statues and portrait busts). The sober realism of 19th-century Danish Golden Age painting reflects the introspection of

COPENHAGEN

a once-powerful nation reduced to second-class status—and ultimately embracing what made them unique. The "French Wing" (just inside the front door) has Rodin statues. A heady, if small, exhibit of 19th-century French paintings (in a modern building within the back courtyard) shows how Realism morphed into Impressionism and Post-Impressionism, and includes a couple of canvases apiece by Géricault, Delacroix, Monet, Manet, Millet, Courbet, Degas, Pissarro, Cézanne, Van Gogh, Picasso, Renoir, and Toulouse-Lautrec. Look for art by Gauguin—from before Tahiti (when he lived in Copenhagen with his Danish wife and their five children) and after Tahiti. There's also a fine collection of modern (post-Thorvaldsen) Danish sculpture.

Linger with marble gods under the palm leaves and glass dome of the very soothing winter garden. Designers, figuring Danes would be more interested in a lush garden than in classical art, used this wonderful space as leafy bait to cleverly introduce locals to a few Greek and Roman statues. (It works for tourists, too.) One of the original *Thinker* sculptures by Rodin (wondering how to scale the Tivoli fence?) is in the museum's backyard.

▲▲▲**National Museum**—Focus on this museum's excellent and curiously enjoyable Danish collection, which traces this civilization from its ancient beginnings. Its prehistoric collection is the best of its kind in Scandinavia. Exhibits are laid out chronologically and eloquently described in English.

Cost and Hours: Free, Tue-Sun 10:00-17:00, closed Mon, mandatory lockers take a 10-kr coin that will be returned, enter at Ny Vestergade 10, tel. 33 13 44 11, www.natmus.dk. The café overlooking the entry hall serves coffee, pastries, and lunch (90-145 kr).

❍ **Self-Guided Tour:** Pick up the museum map as you enter, and head for the Danish history exhibit. It fills three floors, from the bottom up: prehistory, the Middle Ages and Renaissance, and modern times (1660-2000).

Start before history did, in the **Danish Prehistory** exhibit (on the right side of the main entrance hall). Recently updated, this collection is slick and extremely well-presented.

In the Stone Age section, you'll see primitive tools and still-clothed skeletons of Scandinavia's reindeer-hunters. The oak coffins were originally covered by burial mounds (called "barrows"). People put valuable items into the coffins with the dead, such as a folding chair (which, back then, was a real status symbol). In the farming section, ogle the ceremonial axes and amber necklaces.

The Bronze Age brought the sword (several are on display). The

"Chariot of the Sun"—a small statue of a horse pulling the sun across the sky—likely had religious significance for early Scandinavians (whose descendants continue to celebrate the solstice with fervor). In the same room are those iconic horned helmets. Contrary to popular belief (and countless tourist shops), these helmets were not worn by the Vikings, but by their predecessors—for ceremonial purposes, centuries earlier. In the next room are huge cases filled with still-playable *lur* horns (see page 176). Another room shows off a bitchin' collection of well-translated rune stones proclaiming heroic deeds.

This leads to the Iron Age and an object that's neither Iron

nor Danish: the 2,000-year-old Gundestrup Cauldron of art-textbook fame. This 20-pound, soup-kitchen-size bowl made of silver was found in a Danish bog, but its symbolism suggests it was originally from Thrace (in northeast Greece) or Celtic Ireland. On the sides, hunters slay bulls, and gods cavort with stags, horses, dogs, and dragons. It's both mysterious and fascinating.

Prehistoric Danes were fascinated by bogs. To make iron, you need ore—and Denmark's many bogs provided that critical material in abundance, leading people to believe that the gods dwelled there. These Danes appeased the gods by sacrificing valuable items (and even people) into bogs. Fortunately for modern archaeologists, bogs happen to be an ideal environment for preserving fragile objects. One bog alone—the Nydam bog—has yielded thousands of items, including three whole ships.

No longer bogged down in prehistory, the people of Scandinavia came into contact with Roman civilization. At about this time, the Viking culture rose; you'll see the remains of an old warship. The Vikings, so feared in most of Europe, are still thought of fondly here in their homeland. You'll notice the descriptions straining to defend them: Sure, they'd pillage, rape, and plunder. But they also founded thriving, wealthy, and cultured trade towns. Love the Vikings or hate them, it's impossible to deny their massive reach—Norse Vikings even carved runes into the walls of the Hagia Sophia church (in today's Istanbul).

Next, go upstairs. You'll enter (awkwardly) right between the **Middle Ages and Renaissance** sections; to go in chronological order, go left, cover your eyes, and walk through the exhibits to the start of the Middle Ages and the coming of Christianity. Then retrace your steps through the Middle Ages (eyes open this time). Here you'll find lots of bits and pieces of old churches, such

as golden altars and *aquamaniles*, pitchers used for ritual hand-washing. The Dagmar Cross is the prototype for a popular form of crucifix worn by many Danes (Room 102, small glass display case, smallest of the three crosses in this case—with colorful enamel paintings). Another cross in this case (the Roskilde Cross, studded with gemstones) was found inside the wooden head of Christ that's displayed high on the opposite wall. There are also exhibits on tools and trade, weapons, drinking horns, and fine, wood-carved winged altarpieces. Carry on to find fascinating material on the Reformation, an exhibit on everyday town life in the 16th and 17th centuries, and, in Room 126, a unique "cylinder perspective" of the noble family (from 1656) and two peep shows. (Don't get too excited—they're just church interiors.)

The next floor takes you into **modern times,** with historic toys and a slice-of-Danish-life (1600-2000) gallery where you'll see

everything from rifles and old bras to early jukeboxes. You'll learn that the Danish Golden Age (which dominates most art museums in Denmark) captured the everyday pastoral beauty of the countryside, celebrated Denmark's smallness and peace-loving nature, and mixed in some Nordic mythology. With industrialization came the

labor movement and trade unions. After delving into the World Wars, Baby Boomers, creation of the postwar welfare state, and the "Depressed Decade" of the 1980s (when Denmark suffered high unemployment), the collection is capped off by a stall that, until recently, was used for selling marijuana in the squatters' community of Christiania.

The Rest of the Museum: If you're eager for more, there's plenty left to see. The National Museum also has exhibits on the history of this building (the Prince's Palace), a large ethnology collection, antiquities, coins and medallions, temporary exhibits, and a good children's museum. The floor plan will lead you to what you want to see.

▲**National Museum's Victorian Apartment**—The National Museum (listed above) inherited an incredible Victorian apartment just around the corner. The wealthy Christensen family managed to keep its plush living quarters a 19th-century time capsule until the granddaughters passed away in 1963. Since then, it's been part of the National Museum, with all but two of its rooms look-ing just as they did around 1890.

Cost and Hours: 50 kr, required one-hour tours in English leave from museum reception desk, June-Sept Sat only at 14:00.

▲**Museum of Copenhagen (Københavns Museum)**—This fine old house is filled with an entertaining and creative exhibit telling the story of Copenhagen. The ground floor covers the city's origins, the upper floor is dedicated to the 19th century, and the top floor includes a fun year-by-year walk through Copenhagen's 20th century, with lots of entertaining insights into contemporary culture.

Cost and Hours: 20 kr, daily 10:00-17:00, behind the train station at Vesterbrogade 59, tel. 33 21 07 72, www.copenhagen.dk.

On Slotsholmen Island

This island, where Copenhagen began in the 12th century, is a short walk from the train station and Tivoli, just across the bridge from the National Museum. It's dominated by Christiansborg Palace and several other royal and governmental buildings.

▲▲**Christiansborg Palace**—A complex of government buildings

 stands on the ruins of Copen-hagen's original 12th-century fortress: the Parliament, Supreme Court, prime minister's office, royal reception rooms, royal library, several museums, and royal stables. Although the cur-rent palace dates only from 1928 and the royal family moved out 200 years ago, this building—the sixth to stand here in 800 years— is rich with tradition.

Three palace sights (the reception rooms, old castle ruins, and stables) are open to the public, giving us commoners a glimpse of the royal life.

Cost and Hours: Reception rooms-80 kr, ruins-40 kr, sta-bles-40 kr, combo-ticket for all three-110 kr; reception rooms and ruins open daily 10:00-17:00 except closed Mon Oct-April, recep-tion rooms may close at any time for royal events; stables and car-riage museum daily 13:30-16:00 except closed Mon Oct-April; tel. 33 92 64 92, www.christiansborgslot.dk.

Visiting the Palace: From the equestrian statue in front, go through the wooden door; the entrance to the ruins is in the cor-ridor on the right, and the door to the reception rooms is out in the next courtyard, also on the right.

Royal Reception Rooms: While these don't quite rank among Europe's best palace rooms, they're worth a look. This is still the place where Queen Margrethe II impresses visiting dignitaries. The information-packed 50-minute English tours of the rooms are excellent (included in ticket, daily at 15:00). At other times, you'll wander the rooms on your own, reading the sparse English descriptions. As you slip-slide on protect-the-floor slippers through 22 rooms, you'll gain a good feel for Danish history, royalty, and politics. For instance, the family portrait of King Christian IX illustrates why he's called the "father-in-law of Europe"—his children eventually became or married royalty in Denmark, Russia, Greece, Britain, France, Germany, and Norway. You'll see the Throne Room; the balcony where new monarchs are proclaimed (most recently in 1972); the Velvet Room, where royals privately greet VIP guests before big functions; and the grand Main Hall lined with boldly colorful (almost gaudy) tapestries. The palace highlight is this dazzling set of modern tapestries—Danish-designed but Gobelin-made in Paris. This gift, given to the queen on her 60th birthday in 2000, celebrates 1,000 years of Danish history, from the Viking age to our chaotic times...and into the future. Borrow the laminated descriptions for blow-by-blow explanations of the whole epic saga.

Castle Ruins: An exhibit in the scant remains of the first fortress built by Bishop Absalon, the 12th-century founder of Copenhagen, lies under the palace. A long passage connects to another set of ruins, from the 14th-century Copenhagen Castle. There's precious little to see, but it is, um, old and well-described. A video covers more recent palace history.

Royal Stables and Carriages Museum: This facility is still home to the horses that pull the Queen's carriage on festive days, as well as a collection of historic carriages.

Old Stock Exchange (Børsen)—The eye-catching red-brick stock exchange was inspired by the Dutch Renaissance, like much of 17th-century Copenhagen. Built to promote the mercantile ambitions of Denmark in the 1600s, it was the "World Trade Center" of Scandinavia. The facade reads, "For the profitable use of buyer and seller." The dragon-tail spire with three crowns represents the Danish aspiration to rule a united Scandinavia—or at least be its commercial capital. The Børsen (which is not open to tourists) symbolically connected Christianshavn (the harbor, also inspired by the Dutch) with the rest of the city, in an age when trade was a very big deal.

▲▲Thorvaldsen's Museum—This museum, which has some of the best swoon-worthy art you'll see anywhere, tells the story

Bertel Thorvaldsen
(1770-1844)

Bertel Thorvaldsen was born, raised, educated, and buried in Copenhagen, but his most productive years were spent in Rome. There he soaked up the prevailing style of the time: Neoclassical. He studied ancient Greek and Roman statues, copying their balance, grace, and impassive beauty. The simple-but-noble style suited the patriotism of the era, and Thorvaldsen got rich off it. Public squares throughout Europe are dotted with his works, celebrating local rulers, patriots, and historical figures looking like Greek heroes or Roman conquerors.

In 1819, at the height of his fame and power, Thorvaldsen returned to Copenhagen. He was asked to decorate the most important parts of the recently bombed, newly rebuilt Cathedral of Our Lady: the main altar and nave. His *Risen Christ* on the altar (along with the 12 apostles lining the nave) became his most famous and reproduced work—without even realizing it, most people imagine the caring features of Thorvaldsen's Christ when picturing what Jesus looked like.

The prolific Thorvaldsen depicted a range of subjects. His grand statues of historical figures (Copernicus in Warsaw, Maximilian I in Munich) were intended for public squares. Portrait busts of his contemporaries were usually done in the style of Roman emperors. Thorvaldsen carved the *Lion Monument,* depicting a weeping lion, into a cliff in Luzern, Switzerland. He did religious statues, like the *Risen Christ*. Thorvaldsen's most accessible works are from Greek mythology—*The Three Graces,* naked *Jason with the Golden Fleece,* or Ganymede crouching down to feed the eagle Jupiter.

Though many of his statues are of gleaming white marble, Thorvaldsen was not a chiseler of stone. Like Rodin and Canova, Thorvaldsen left the grunt work to others. He fashioned a life-sized model in plaster, which could then be reproduced in marble or bronze by his assistants. Multiple copies were often made, even in his lifetime.

Thorvaldsen epitomized the Neoclassical style. His statues assume perfectly balanced poses—maybe even a bit stiff, say critics. They don't flail their arms dramatically or emote passionately. As you look into their faces, they seem lost in thought, as though contemplating deep spiritual truths.

In Copenhagen, catch Thorvaldsen's *Risen Christ* at the Cathedral of Our Lady, his portrait bust at City Hall, and the full range of his long career at the Thorvaldsen Museum.

and shows the monumental work of the great Danish Neoclassical sculptor Bertel Thorvaldsen (see sidebar). Considered Canova's equal among Neoclassical sculptors, Thorvaldsen spent 40 years in Rome. He was lured home to Copenhagen with the promise to showcase his work in a fine museum, which opened in the revolutionary year of 1848 as Denmark's first public art gallery. Of the 500 or so sculptures Thorvaldsen completed in his life—including 90 major statues—this museum has most of them, in one form or another (the plaster model used to make the original, the original marble, or a copy done in marble or bronze).

Cost and Hours: 40 kr, free Wed, includes excellent audioguide on request, Tue-Sun 10:00-17:00, closed Mon, located in Neoclassical building with colorful walls next to Christiansborg Palace, tel. 33 32 15 32, www.thorvaldsensmuseum.dk.

Visiting the Museum: The ground floor showcases his statues. After buying your ticket, go straight in and ask to borrow a free iPod audioguide at the desk. This provides a wonderful statue-by-statue narration of the museum's key works.

Just past the audioguide desk, turn left into the Great Hall, which was the original entryway of the museum. It's filled with

replicas of some of Thorvaldsen's biggest and grandest statues—national heroes who still stand in the prominent squares of their major cities (Munich, Warsaw, the Vatican, and others). Two great equestrian statues stare each other down from across the hall; while they both take the classic, self-assured pose of looking one way while pointing another (think Babe Ruth calling his home run), one of them (Jozef Poniatowski) is modeled after the ancient Roman general Marcus Aurelius, while the other (Bavaria's Maximilian I) wears modern garb.

Then take a spin through the smaller rooms that ring the central courtyard. Each of these is dominated by one big work—mostly classical subjects drawn from mythology. At the far end of the building stand the plaster models for the iconic *Risen Christ* and the 12 apostles (the final marble versions stand in the Cathedral of Our Lady—

see page 177). Peek into the central courtyard to see the tomb of Thorvaldsen himself. Speaking of which, continuing into the next row of rooms, look for Thorvaldsen's (very flattering) self-portrait, leaning buffly against a partially finished sculpture.

Upstairs, get into the mind of the artist by perusing his personal possessions and the private collection of paintings from which he drew inspiration.

Royal Library—Copenhagen's "Black Diamond" (Den Sorte Diamant) library is a striking, supermodern building made of shiny black granite, leaning over the harbor at the edge of the palace complex. From the inviting lounge chairs, you can ponder this stretch of harborfront, which serves as a showcase for architects. Inside, wander through the old and new sections, catch the fine view from the "G" level, read a magazine, surf the Internet (free terminals in the skyway lobby over the street nearest the harbor), and enjoy a classy—and pricey—lunch.

Cost and Hours: Free, special exhibitions generally 30 kr; reading room open generally Mon-Fri 9:00-21:00, Sat 10:00-17:00, closed Sun; different parts of the library have varying hours, tel. 33 47 47 47, www.kb.dk.

▲Danish Jewish Museum (Dansk Jødisk Museum)—This museum, which opened in 2004 in a striking building by American architect Daniel Libeskind, offers a very small but well-exhibited display of 400 years of the life and impact of Jews in Denmark.

Cost and Hours: 50 kr; June-Aug Tue-Sun 10:00-17:00; Sept-May Tue-Fri 13:00-16:00, Sat-Sun 12:00-17:00; closed Mon year-round; behind the Royal Library's "Black Diamond" branch at Proviantpassagen 6—enter from the courtyard behind the red-brick, ivy-covered building; tel. 33 11 22 18, www.jewmus.dk.

Visiting the Museum: Frankly, the architecture overshadows the humble exhibits. Libeskind—who created the equally conceptual Jewish Museum in Berlin, and whose design is the basis for redeveloping the World Trade Center site in New York City—has literally written Jewish culture into this building. The floor plan, a seemingly random squiggle, is actually in the shape of the Hebrew characters for *Mitzvah*, which loosely translated means "act of kindness."

Be sure to watch the two introductory films about the Jews' migration to Denmark, and about the architect Libeskind (12-minute loop total, English subtitles, plays continuously). As you tour the collection, the uneven floors and asymmetrical walls give you the feeling that what lies around the corner is completely unknown...much like the life and history of Danish Jews. Another interpretation might be that the uneven floors give you the sense of motion, like waves on the sea—a reminder that despite Nazi occupation in 1943, nearly 7,000 Danish Jews were ferried across the waves by fishermen to safety in neutral Sweden.

Near the Strøget

Round Tower—Built in 1642 by Christian IV, the tower con-

nects a church, library, and observatory (the oldest functioning observatory in Europe) with a ramp that spirals up to a fine view of Copenhagen (though the view from atop Our Savior's Church is far better—see page 211).

Cost and Hours: 25 kr, nothing to see inside but the ramp and the view; tower—daily June-Sept 10:00-20:00, Oct-May 10:00-17:00; observatory—summer Sun 13:00-16:00 and mid-Oct-mid-March Tue-Wed 19:00-22:00; just off the Strøget on Købmagergade.

Amalienborg Palace and Nearby

For more information on this palace and nearby attractions, including the famous *Little Mermaid* statue, see the end of my self-guided walk (page 173).

▲**Amalienborg Palace Museum (Amalienborgmuseet)**—While Queen Margrethe II and her husband live quite privately in one of the four mansions that make up the palace complex, another mansion has been open to the public since 1994. It displays the private studies of four kings of the House of Glucksborg, who ruled from 1863-1972 (the immediate predecessors of today's Queen). Your visit is short—six or eight rooms on one floor—but it affords an intimate and unique peek into Denmark's royal family. You'll see the private study of each of the last four kings of Denmark. They feel particularly lived-in—with cluttered pipe collections and bookcases jammed with family pictures—because they were. It's easy to imagine these blue-blooded folks just hanging out here, even today. The earliest study, Frederik VIII's (c. 1869), feels much older and more "royal"—with Renaissance gilded walls, heavy drapes, and a polar bear rug. Temporary exhibits fill the larger halls.

Cost and Hours: 80 kr, or 110-kr combo-ticket with Rosenborg Palace; May-Oct daily 10:00-16:00; Nov-April Tue-Sun 11:00-16:00, closed Mon; with your back to the harbor, the entrance is at the far end of the square on the right; tel. 33 15 32 86, www.dkks.dk.

Amalienborg Palace Changing of the Guard—This noon-time event is boring in the summer, when the queen is not in residence—the guards just change places. (This goes on for quite a long time—no need to rush here at the stroke of noon, or to crowd in during the first few minutes; you'll have plenty of good photo ops.) If the queen's at home (indicated by a flag flying above her home), the changing of the guard is accompanied by a military band.

▲▲Museum of Danish Resistance (Frihedsmuseet)—On April 9, 1940, Hitler's Nazis violated a peace treaty and invaded Denmark, overrunning the tiny nation in mere hours. This museum tells what happened next—the compelling story of Denmark's heroic Nazi-resistance struggle (1940-1945). While relatively small, the museum rewards those who take the time to read the English explanations and understand the fascinating artifacts. Video touchscreens let you hear interviews with the participants of history (dubbed into English).

Cost and Hours: Free; May-Sept Tue-Sun 10:00-16:00, Oct-April Tue-Sun 10:00-15:00, closed Mon year-round; hours likely to be reduced—call or check website to confirm; guided tours June-Aug Tue, Thu, and Sun at 14:00; on Churchillparken between Amalienborg Palace and *The Little Mermaid* site; bus #1A or #15 from downtown/Tivoli/train station stops right in front, a 10-minute walk from Østerport train station, or bus #26 from Langelinie cruise port or downtown; tel. 41 20 62 91, www.friheds museet.dk.

◉ Self-Guided Tour: From the main hall, you'll take a counterclockwise spin through the collection. The first section, **Adaptation to Avoid Nazification,** examines the unenviable situation the Danes found themselves in in 1940: Cooperate with the Nazis (at least symbolically) to preserve some measure of self-determination, or stand up to them and surely be crushed

by their military might. Denmark opted for the first option, but kept a fierce resistance always at a rolling boil. Be sure to carefully examine the odd, sometimes macabre items from this period: A delicate, miniature rose made of chewed bread, given as a gift to an inmate at Ravensbrück Concentration Camp; Himmler's eye patch, worn as a disguise; actual human skin tattooed with the SS symbol, removed from a reformed Nazi after the war (at his own request); the pistol of the Danish Nazi leader, Fritz Clausen; RAF (British Royal Air Force) caps and stars-and-stripes bowties, worn as a symbol of resistance and rebellion by young people in the early days of Nazi occupation; cheaply made aluminum Nazi coins, crudely imprinted with messages of Danish resistance; and an old printing press used to produce anti-Nazi leaflets.

Moving down the hallway, you pass into the next section, **Resistance and Sabotage.** You'll learn how the Danish resistance, supported by the SOE (Special Operations Executive, a British governmental agency tasked with subverting Nazi control), bravely stood up to the Nazis, with occasional supplies airlifted in by the Allies. On display are many items used during the resistance, including slugs and bullet casings from a shootout between the resistance and Nazi-friendly forces, and a clandestine radio and telegraph. You'll also learn about everyday life (shortages and rationings for the Nazi war effort), and see a Nazi plate and cutlery emblazoned with a swastika.

The next section, **German Terror,** explains the Nazis' campaign of extermination against Jewish people, and details the valiant Danish effort to rescue some 7,000 Jews by ferrying them across the sea to neutral Sweden; only 481 were murdered by the Nazis (a tiny fraction of the toll in most countries). You'll see articles of the Jewish faith left behind by a refugee (who didn't want to risk being discovered with them), and some identification armbands from a concentration camp. You'll also see exhibits on industrial sabotage, and the growth of the underground army in the waning days of the war.

Finally we end at **The Liberation** (May 5, 1945). A giant stained-glass window in the lobby honors the victims of the Nazis. The moving, handwritten letters in the display cases in front (translated into English) are the final messages of Danes who had been sentenced to death by the Nazis.

Rosenborg Castle and Nearby

▲▲▲**Rosenborg Castle (Rosenborg Slot) and Treasury**—This finely furnished Dutch Renaissance-style castle was built by King Christian IV in the early 1600s as a summer residence. Rosenborg was his favorite residence and where he chose to die. Open to the public since 1838, it houses the Danish crown jewels and 500 years of royal knickknacks. While the old palace interior is a bit dark and not as immediately impressive as many of Europe's later Baroque masterpieces, it has a certain lived-in charm. It oozes the personality of the

King Christian IV:
A Lover and a Fighter

King Christian IV (1577-1648) inherited Denmark at the peak of its power, lived his life with the exuberance of the age,

and went to his grave with the country in decline. His legacy is obvious to every tourist—Rosenborg Castle, Frederiksborg Palace, the Round Tower, Christianshavn, and on and on. Look for his logo adorning many buildings: the letter "C" with a "4" inside it and a crown on top. Thanks to both his place in history and his passionate personality, Danes today regard Christian IV as one of their greatest monarchs.

During his 60-year reign, Christian IV reformed the government, rebuilt the army, established a trading post in India, and tried to expand Denmark's territory. He took Kalmar from Sweden and cap-

tured strategic points in northern Germany. The king was a large man who also lived large. A skilled horseman and avid hunter, he could drink his companions under the table. He spoke several languages and gained a reputation as outgoing and humorous. His lavish banquets were legendary, and his romantic affairs were numerous.

But Christian's appetite for war proved destructive. In 1626, Denmark again attacked northern Germany, but was beaten back. In 1643, Sweden launched a sneak attack, and despite Christian's personal bravery (he lost an eye), the war went badly. By the end of his life, Christian was tired and bitter, and Denmark was drained.

The heroics of Christian and his sailors live on in the Danish national anthem, "King Christian Stood by the Lofty Mast."

fascinating Christian IV and has one of the finest treasury collections in Europe. Notice that this is one of the only major sights in town open on Mondays (in summer only). For more on Christian, read the sidebar.

Cost and Hours: 80 kr, 110-kr ticket also includes Amalienborg Palace Museum, 20 kr for permission to take photos; June-Aug daily 10:00-17:00; May and Sept-Oct daily 10:00-16:00; Nov-Dec Tue-Sun 11:00-14:00 (treasury until 16:00), closed Mon; Jan-April Tue-Sun 11:00-16:00, closed Mon; mandatory lockers take 20-kr coin, which will be returned; Metro or S-tog: Nørreport, then 5-minute walk on Østervoldgade and through park; tel. 33 15 32 86, www.dkks.dk.

Tours: Richard Karpen leads fascinating one-hour tours in princely garb (mid-May–mid-Sept Mon and Thu at 13:30, 80 kr plus entry fee, see "Tours in Copenhagen," earlier). Or take the following self-guided tour that I've woven together from the highlights of Richard's walk. If you have a mobile device, you can take advantage of the palace's free Wi-Fi signal, which is intended to let you follow the "Konge Connect" step-by-step tour through the palace highlights (with text explanations on your phone; for instructions, pick up the brochure at the ticket desk).

● **Self-Guided Tour:** Buy your ticket, then head back out and look for the *castle* sign. You'll tour the ground floor room by room, then climb to the third floor for the big throne room. After a quick sweep of the middle floor, finish in the basement (enter from outside) for the jewels. Begin the tour on the palace's ground floor (turn right as you enter), in the Winter Room.

Ground Floor: Here in the wood-paneled **Winter Room,** all eyes were on King Christian IV. Today, your eyes should be on him, too. Take a close look at his bust by the fireplace (if it's not here, look for it out in the corridor by the ticket-taker). Check this guy out—earring and fashionable braid, hard drinker, hard lover, energetic statesman, and warrior king. Christian IV was dynamism in the flesh, wearing a toga: a true Renaissance guy. During his reign, Copenhagen doubled in size. You're surrounded by Dutch paintings (the Dutch had a huge influence on 17th-century Denmark). Note the smaller statue of the 19-year-old king, showing him jousting jauntily on his coronation day. In another case, the golden astronomical clock—with musical works and moving figures—did everything you can imagine. Flanking the fireplace (opposite where you entered), beneath the windows, look for the panels in the tile floor that could be removed to let the music performed by the band in the basement waft in. (Who wants the actual musicians in the dining room?) The audio holes were also used to call servants.

The **study** (or "writing closet," nearest where you entered) was small (and easy to heat). Kings did a lot of corresponding. We know a lot about Christian because 3,000 of his handwritten letters survive. The painting on the right wall shows Christian at age eight. Three years later, his father died, and little Christian technically ascended the throne, though Denmark was actually ruled by a regency until Christian was 19. A portrait of his mother hangs above the boy, and opposite is a portrait of Christian in his prime—having just conquered

Sweden—standing alongside the incredible coronation crown you'll see later.

Going back through the Winter Room, head for the door to Christian's **bedroom.** Before entering, notice the little peephole

in the door (used by the king to spy on those in this room—well-camouflaged by the painting, and more easily seen from the other side), and the big cabinet doors for Christian's clothes and accessories, flanking the bedroom door (notice the hinges and keyholes). Heading into the bedroom, you'll

see paintings showing the king as an old man...and as a dead man. (Christian died in this room.) In the case are the clothes he wore at his finest hour. During a naval battle against Sweden (1644), Christian stood directing the action when an explosion ripped across the deck, sending him sprawling and riddling him with shrapnel. Unfazed, the 67-year-old monarch bounced right back up and kept going, inspiring his men to carry on the fight. Christian's stubborn determination during this battle is commemorated in Denmark's national anthem. Shrapnel put out Christian's eye. No problem: The warrior king with a knack for heroic publicity stunts had the shrapnel bits removed from his eye and forehead and made into earrings as a gift for his mistress. The earrings hang in the case with his blood-stained clothes (easy to miss, right side). Christian lived to be 70 and fathered 25 children (with two wives and three mistresses). Before moving on, you can peek into Christian's private bathroom—elegantly tiled with Delft porcelain.

Proceed into the **Dark Room.** Here you'll see wax casts of royal figures. This was the way famous and important people were portrayed back then. (If the wax casts aren't here, they're likely out in the corridor.) The chair (possibly gone for restoration) is a forerunner of the whoopee cushion. When you sat on it, metal cuffs pinned your arms down, allowing the prankster to pour water down the back of the chair (see hole)—making you "wet your pants." When you stood up, the chair made embarrassing tooting sounds.

The **Marble Room** (which may be closed for restoration) has a particularly impressive inlaid marble floor. Imagine the king meeting emissaries here in the center, with the emblems of Norway (right), Denmark (center), and Sweden (left) behind him.

The end room, called the **King's Chamber,** was used by Christian's first mistress. You might want to shield children from the sexually explicit art in the case next to the door you just passed. Notice the tamer ceiling painting, with an orchestra looking down on you as they play.

The long **stone passage** leading to the staircase exhibits an intriguing painting (by the door to the King's Chamber) showing

the crowds at the coronation of Christian's son, Frederick III. After Christian's death, a weakened Denmark was invaded, occupied, and humiliated by Sweden (Treaty of Roskilde, 1658). Copenhagen alone held out through the long winter of 1658-1659 (the Siege of Copenhagen), and Sweden eventually had to withdraw from the country. During the siege, Frederick III distinguished himself with his bravery. He seized upon the resulting surge of popularity as his chance to be anointed an absolute, divinely ordained monarch (1660). This painting marks that event—study it closely for slice-of-life details. Next, near the ticket-taker, a sprawling family tree makes it perfectly clear that Christian IV comes from good stock. Notice the tree is labeled in German—the second language of the realm.

The queen had a hand-pulled elevator, but you'll need to hike up two flights of stairs to the throne room.

Throne Room (Third Floor): The **Long Hall**—considered one of the best-preserved Baroque rooms in Europe—was great

for banquets. The decor trumpets the accomplishments of Denmark's great kings. The four corners of the ceiling feature the four continents known at the time. (America—at the far-right end of the hall as you enter—was still con-sidered pretty untamed; notice the decapitated head with the arrow sticking out of it.) In the center, of course, is the proud seal of the Danish Royal Family. The tapestries, designed for this room, are from the late 1600s. Effective propaganda, they show the Danes defeating their Swedish rivals on land and at sea. The king's throne—still more propaganda for two centuries of "absolute" monarchs—was made of "unicorn horn" (actually narwhal tusk from Greenland). Believed to bring protection from evil and poison, the horn was the most precious material in its day. The queen's throne is of hammered silver. The 150-pound lions are 300 years old.

The small room to the left holds a delightful **royal porcelain** display with Chinese, French, German, and Danish examples of the "white gold." For five centuries, Europeans couldn't figure out how the Chinese made this stuff. The difficulty in just getting it back to Europe in one piece made it precious. The Danish pieces, called "Flora Danica" (on the left as you enter), are from a huge royal set showing off the herbs and vegetables of the realm.

On your way back down, the middle floor is worth a look.

Middle Floor: Circling counterclockwise, you'll see more fine clocks, fancy furniture, and royal portraits. The queen enjoyed her royal lathe (with candleholders for lighting and pedals to spin it hidden away below; in the Christian IV Room). The small mirror room (up the stairs from the main hall) was where the king played Hugh Hefner—using mirrors on the floor to see what was under those hoop skirts. In hidden cupboards, he had a fold-out bed and a handy escape staircase.

Back outside, turn right and find the stairs leading down to the...

Royal Danish Treasury (Castle Basement): The palace was a royal residence for a century and has been the royal vault right up until today. As you enter, first head to the right, into the **wine cellar,** with thousand-liter barrels and some fine treasury items. The first room has a vast army of tiny golden soldiers, and a wall lined with fancy rifles. Heading into the next room, you'll see fine items of amber (petrified tree resin, 30-50 million years old) and ivory. Study the large box made of amber (in a freestanding case, just to the right as you enter)—the tiny figures show a healthy interest in sex.

Now head back past the ticket-taker and into the main part of the treasury, where you can browse through exquisite royal knickknacks.

The diamond- and pearl-studded **saddles** were Christian IV's—the first for his coronation, the second for his son's wedding. When his kingdom was nearly bankrupt, Christian had these constructed lavishly—complete with solid-gold spurs—to impress visiting dignitaries and bolster Denmark's credit rating.

The next case displays **tankards.** Danes were always big drinkers, and to drink in the top style, a king had narwhal steins (#4030). Note the fancy Greenland Inuit (Eskimo) on the lid (#4023). The case is filled with exquisitely carved ivory. On the other side of that case, what's with the mooning snuffbox (#4063)? Also, check out the amorous whistle (#4064).

Drop by the case on the wall in the back-left of the room: The 17th century was the age of **brooches.** Many of these are made of freshwater pearls. Find the fancy combination toothpick and ear spoon (#4140). Look for #4146: A queen was caught having an affair after 22 years of royal marriage. Her king gave her a special present: a golden ring—showing the hand of his promiscuous queen shaking hands with a penis.

Step downstairs, away from all this silliness. Passing through the serious vault door, you come face-to-face with a big, jeweled **sword.** The tall, two-handed, 16th-century coronation sword was drawn by the new king, who cut crosses in the air in four directions, symbolically promising to defend the realm from all attacks. The cases surrounding the sword contain everyday items used by the king (all solid gold, of course). What looks like a trophy case of gold records is actually a collection of dinner plates with amber centers (#5032).

Go down the steps. In the center case is Christian IV's **coronation crown** (from 1596, seven pounds of gold and precious stones, #5124), which some con-

sider to be the finest Renaissance crown in Europe. Its six tallest gables radiate symbolism. Find the symbols of justice (sword and scales), fortitude (a woman on a lion with a sword), and charity (a nursing woman—meaning the king will love God and his people as a mother loves her child).

The pelican, which according to medieval legend pecks its own flesh to feed its young, symbolizes God sacrificing his son, just as the king would make great sacrifices for his people. Climb the footstool to look inside—it's as exquisite as the outside. The shields of various Danish provinces remind the king that he's surrounded by his realms.

Circling the cases along the wall (right to left), notice the fine enameled lady's goblet with traits of a good woman spelled out in Latin (#5128) and above that, an exquisite prayer book (with handwritten favorite prayers, #5134). In the fifth window, the big solid-gold baptismal basin (#5262) hangs above tiny oval silver boxes that contained the royal children's umbilical cords (handy for protection later in life, #5272); two cases over are royal writing sets with wax, seals, pens, and ink (#5320).

Go down a few more steps into the lowest level of the treasury and last room. The two **crowns** in the center cases are more modern (from 1670), lighter, and more practical—just gold and diamonds without all the symbolism. The king's crown is only four pounds, the queen's a mere two.

The cases along the walls show off the **crown jewels.** These were made in 1840 of diamonds, emeralds, rubies, and pearls from earlier royal jewelry. The saber (#5540) shows emblems of the realm's 19 provinces. The sumptuous pendant features a 19-carat diamond cut (like its neighbors) in the 58-facet "brilliant" style for maximum reflection (far-left case, #5560). Imagine these on the dance floor. The painting shows the coronation of Christian VIII at Frederiksborg Chapel in 1840. The crown jewels are still worn by the queen on special occasions several times a year.

▲**Rosenborg Gardens**—Rosenborg Castle is surrounded by the royal pleasure gardens and, on sunny days, a minefield of sunbathing Danish beauties and picnickers. While "ethnic Danes" grab the shade, the rest of the Danes worship the sun. When the royal family is in residence, there's a daily changing-of-the-guard miniparade from the Royal Guard's barracks adjoining Rosenborg Castle (at 11:30) to Amalienborg Castle (at 12:00). The Queen's Rose Garden (across the moat from the palace) is a royal place for a picnic. The fine statue of Hans Christian Andersen in the park—erected while he was still alive (and approved by him)—is meant to symbolize how his stories had a message even for adults.

▲**National Gallery of Denmark (Statens Museum for Kunst)**—The museum fills a stately building with Danish and

European paintings from the 14th century through today. This is particularly worthwhile for the chance to be immersed in great art by the Danes, and to see its good collection of French Modernists.

Cost and Hours: Permanent collection-free, special exhibits-95 kr, Tue-Sun 10:00-17:00, Wed until 20:00, closed Mon, Sølvgade 48, tel. 33 74 84 94, www.smk.dk.

Visiting the Museum: The ground floor holds special exhibits; the second floor has collections of Danish and Nordic artists from 1750 to 1900, and European art from 1300 to 1800; and the Danish and International Art after 1900 is spread between the second and third floors.

Head first to the Danish and Nordic artists section, and pick up the excellent floor plan that suggests a twisting route through the collection. Take the time to read the descriptions in each room, which put the paintings into historical context. In addition to Romantic works by well-known, non-Danish artists (such as the Norwegian J. C. Dahl and the German Caspar David Friedrich), this is a chance to learn about some very talented Danish painters not well known outside their native land. Make a point to meet the "Skagen Painters," including Anna Ancher, Michael Ancher, Peder Severin Krøyer, and others (find them in the section called "The Modern Breakthrough I-II"). This group, with echoes of the French Impressionists, gathered in the fishing village of Skagen on the northern tip of Denmark, surrounded by the sea and strong light, and painted heroic folk fishermen themes in the late 1800s. Also worth seeking out are the canvases of Laurits Andersen Ring, who portrayed traditional peasant scenes with modern style; and Jens Ferdinand Willumsen, who pioneered "Vitalism" (celebrating man in nature). Other exhibits are cleverly organized by theme, such as gender or the body.

In the 20th-century section, the collection of early French Modernism is particularly impressive (with works by Matisse, Picasso, Braque, and more). This is complemented with works by Danish artists, who, inspired by the French avant-garde, introduced new, radical forms and colors to Scandinavian art.

Christianshavn

Across the harbor from the old town, Christianshavn is one of the most delightful districts in town to explore. A little background helps explain what you'll see.

Copenhagen's planned port, Christianshavn, was vital to Danish power in the 17th and 18th centuries. Denmark had always been second to Sweden when it came to possession of natural resources, so the Danes tried to make up for it by acquiring resource-rich overseas colonies. They built Christianshavn (with Amsterdam's engineering help) to run the resulting trade business—giving this neighborhood a "little Amsterdam" vibe today.

Since Denmark's economy was so dependent on trade, the port town was the natural target of enemies. When the Danes didn't support Britain against Napoleon in 1807, the Brits bombarded Christianshavn. In this "blackest year in Danish history," Christianshavn burned down. That's why today there's hardly a building here that dates from before 1807.

Christianshavn remained Copenhagen's commercial center until the 1920s, when a modern harbor was built. Suddenly, Christianshavn's economy collapsed and it became a slum. Cheap prices attracted artsy types, giving it a bohemian flavor.

In 1971, several hundred squatters took over an unused military camp and created the Christiania commune (described below). City officials looked the other way because back then, no one cared about the land. But by the 1980s, the neighborhood had become gentrified, and today it's some of priciest real estate in town. (A small apartment costs around $300,000.) Suddenly developers are pushing to take back the land from the squatters, and the very existence of Christiania is threatened.

Christianshavn

- ① Ravelinen Restaurant
- ② Bastionen & Løven Restaurant
- ③ Lagkagehuset Bakery
- ④ Spicy Kitchen Indian
- ⑤ Spiseloppen Restaurant

Christianshavn prices are driven up by wealthy locals (who pay about 60 percent of their income in taxes) paying too much for apartments, renting them cheaply to their kids, and writing off the loss. Demand for property is huge. Prices have skyrocketed. Today the neighborhood is inhabited mostly by rich students and young professionals. Apart from pleasant canalside walks and trendy restaurants to enjoy, there are two things to see in Christianshavn: Our Savior's Church (with its fanciful tower) and Christiania (before it's gone).

▲Our Savior's Church (Vor Frelsers Kirke)

The church recently reopened after a restoration, which has left it gleaming inside and out. Its bright Baroque interior (1696) is shaped like a giant cube. The magnificent pipe organ is supported by elephants (a royal symbol of the prestigious Order of the Elephant). Looking up to the ceiling, notice elephants also sculpted into the stucco of the dome, and a little one hanging from the main

chandelier. Best of all, you can climb the unique spiral spire (with an outdoor staircase winding up to its top—398 stairs in all) for great views of the city and of the Christiania commune below.

Cost and Hours: Church interior-free, open daily 11:00-15:30 but may close for special services; church tower-35 kr; July-mid-Sept Mon-Sat 10:00-19:00, Sun 10:30-19:00; April-June and mid-Sept-Nov daily until 16:00; closed Dec-March and in bad weather; bus #2A, #19, or Metro: Christianshavn, Sankt Annægade 29, tel. 41 66 63 57, www.vorfrelserskirke.dk.

⊙ Spin-Tour from the Top of Our Savior's Church: Climb up until you run out of stairs. As you wind back down, look for these landmarks:

The modern windmills are a reminder that Denmark generates 20 percent of its power from wind. Below the windmills is a great aerial view of the Christiania commune. Beyond the windmills, across Øresund (the strait that separates Denmark and Sweden), stands a shuttered Swedish nuclear power plant. The lone skyscraper in the distance—the first and tallest skyscraper in Scandinavia—is in Malmö, Sweden. The Øresund Bridge made Malmö an easy 35-minute bus or train ride from Copenhagen (it's become a bedroom community, with much cheaper apartments making the commute worthwhile).

Farther to the right, the big red-roof zone is Amager Island. Five hundred years as the city's dumping grounds earned Amager the nickname "Crap Island." Circling on, you come to the towering Radisson Blu hotel. The area beyond it is slated to become a forest of skyscrapers—the center of Europe's biomedical industry.

Downtown Copenhagen is decorated with several striking towers and spires. The tower capped by the golden ball is a ride in Tivoli Gardens. Next is City Hall's pointy brick tower. The biggest building, with the three-crown tower, is Christiansborg Palace. The Børsen (old stock exchange) is just beyond, with its unique dragon-tail tower. Behind that is Nyhavn. Just across from that and the new Playhouse is the dramatic new Opera House (with the flat roof and big, grassy front yard).

Christiania

If you're interested in visiting a freewheeling community of alternative living, Christiania is a ▲▲▲ sight.

In 1971, the original 700 Christianians established squatters' rights in an abandoned military barracks just a 10-minute walk from the Danish parliament building. A generation later, this "free city" still stands—an ultra-human mishmash of idealists, hippies, potheads, non-materialists, and happy children (600 adults, 200 kids, 200 cats, 200 dogs, 2 parrots, and 17 horses). There are even a handful of Willie Nelson-type seniors among the 180 remaining

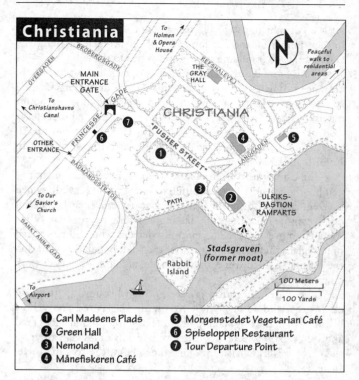

1 Carl Madsens Plads		**5** Morgenstedet Vegetarian Café	
2 Green Hall		**6** Spiseloppen Restaurant	
3 Nemoland		**7** Tour Departure Point	
4 Månefiskeren Café			

here from the original takeover. And an amazing thing has happened: The place has become the third-most-visited sight among tourists in Copenhagen. Move over, *Little Mermaid*.

"Pusher Street" (named for the sale of soft drugs here) is Christiania's main drag. Get beyond this touristy side of Christiania, and you'll find a fascinating, ramshackle world of moats and earthen ramparts, alternative housing, cozy tea houses, carpenter shops, hippie villas, children's playgrounds, peaceful lanes, and people who believe that "to be normal is to be in a straitjacket." (A local slogan claims, *"Kun døde fisk flyder med strømmen"*—"Only dead fish swim with the current.") Be careful to distinguish between real Christianians and Christiania's motley

guests—drunks (mostly from other countries) who hang out here in the summer for the freedom. Part of the original charter guaranteed that the community would stay open to the public.

Hours and Tours: Christiania is open all the time (main entrance is down Prinsessegade behind the Our Savior's Church spiral tower in Christianshavn). You're welcome to snap photos, but ask residents before you photograph them. Guided tours leave from the front entrance of Christiania at 15:00 (just show up, 30 kr, 1.5 hours, daily late June-Aug, only Sat-Sun rest of year, in English and Danish, tel. 32 57 96 70).

The Community: Christiania is broken into 14 administrative neighborhoods on a former military base. The land is still owned by Denmark's Ministry of Defense. Locals build their homes but don't own the land; there's no buying or selling of property. When someone moves out, the community decides who will be invited in to replace that person. A third of the adult population works on the outside, a third works on the inside, and a third doesn't work much at all.

There are nine rules: no cars, no hard drugs, no guns, no explosives, and so on. The Christiania flag is red and yellow because when the original hippies took over, they found a lot of red and yellow paint onsite. The three yellow dots in the flag are from the three "i"s in Christiania (or, some claim, the "o"s in "Love, Love, Love").

The community pays the city about $1 million a year for utilities and has about $1 million a year more to run its local affairs. A few "luxury hippies" have oil heat, but most use wood or gas. The ground here was poisoned by its days as a military base, so nothing is grown in Christiania. There's little industry within the commune (Christiania Cykler, which builds fine bikes, is an exception—www.pedersen-bike.dk). The community has one mailing address (for 25 kr/month, you can receive mail here). A phone chain provides a system of communal security (they have had bad experiences calling the police). Each September 26, the day those first squatters took over the barracks in 1971, Christiania has a big birthday bash.

Tourists are entirely welcome here, because they've become a major part of the economy. Visitors react in very different ways to the place. Some see dogs, dirt, and dazed people. Others see a haven of peace, freedom, and no taboos. Locals will remind judgmental Americans (whose country incarcerates more than a quarter of the world's prison inmates) that a society must make the choice: Allow for alternative lifestyles...or build more prisons.

Even since its inception, Christiania has been a political hot potato. No one in the Danish establishment wanted it. And no one had the nerve to mash it. In the last decade, Christiania has

connected better with the rest of society—such as paying for its utilities and taxes. But when Denmark's conservative government took over in 2001, they vowed to "normalize" Christiania (with pressure from the US), and in recent years police have regularly conducted raids on pot sellers. There's talk about opening the commune to market forces and developing posh apartments to replace existing residences, according to one government plan. But Christiania has a legal team, and litigation will likely drag on for many years.

Many predict that Christiania will withstand the government's challenge, as it has in years past. The community, which also calls itself Freetown, fended off a similar attempt in 1976 with the help of fervent supporters from around Europe. *Bevar Christiania*—"Save Christiania"—banners fly everywhere, and locals are confident that their free way of life will survive. As history has shown, the challenge may just make this hippie haven a bit stronger.

Orientation Tour: Passing under the gate, take Pusher Street directly into the community. The first square—a kind of market square (souvenirs and marijuana-related stuff)—is named Carl Madsens Plads, honoring the lawyer who took the squatters' case to the Danish supreme court in 1976 and won. Beyond that is Nemoland (a food circus, on the right). A huge warehouse called the Green Hall (Den Gronne Hal) is a recycling center and hardware store (where people get most of their building materials) that does double duty at night as a concert hall and as a place where children work on crafts. If you go up the stairs between Nemoland and the Green Hall, you'll climb up to the ramparts that overlook the canal.

On the left beyond the Green Hall, a lane leads to the Månefiskeren café, and beyond that, to the Morgenstedet vegetarian restaurant. Beyond these recommended restaurants, you'll find yourself lost in the totally untouristy, truly local residential parts of Christiania, where kids play in the street and the old folks sit out on the front stoop—just like any other neighborhood. Just as St. Mark's Square isn't the "real Venice," the hippie-druggie scene on Pusher Street isn't the "real Christiania"—you can't say you've experienced Christiania until you've strolled these back streets.

A walk or bike ride through Christiania is a great way to see how this community lives. When you leave, look up—the sign above the gate says, "You are entering the EU."

Smoking Marijuana: Pusher Street was once lined with stalls selling marijuana, joints, and hash. Residents intentionally destroyed the stalls in 2004 to reduce the risk of Christiania being disbanded by the government. (One stall was spared and is on display at the National Museum.) Walking along Pusher Street today, you may witness policemen or deals being made—but never at the same time. You may also notice wafts of marijuana smoke and whispered offers of "hash" during your visit. And, in fact, on my last visit there was a small stretch of Pusher Street dubbed the "Green Light District" where pot was being openly sold (signs acknowledged that this activity was still illegal, and announced three rules here: 1. Have fun; 2. No photos; and 3. No running—"because it makes people nervous"). However, purchasing and smoking may buy you more time in Denmark than you'd planned—possession of marijuana is illegal. With the recent police crackdown on marijuana sales, the street price has skyrocketed, crime has crept into the scene, and someone was actually murdered in a drug scuffle near Christiania—problems unthinkable in mellower times.

About hard drugs: For the first few years, junkies were tolerated. But that led to violence and polluted the mellow ambience residents envisioned. In 1979, the junkies were expelled—an epic confrontation in the community's folk history now—and since then the symbol of a fist breaking a syringe is as prevalent as the leafy marijuana icon. Hard drugs are emphatically forbidden in Christiania.

Eating in Christiania: The people of Christiania appreciate good food and count on tourism as a big part of their economy. Consequently, there are plenty of decent eateries. Most of the restaurants are closed on Monday (the community's weekly holiday). **Pusher Street** has a few grungy but tasty falafel stands, as well as a popular burger bar. **Nemoland** is the hangout zone—a fun collection of stands peddling Thai food, burgers, *shawarma*, and other fast hippie food with great, tented outdoor seating (30-110-kr meals). Its stay-a-while atmosphere comes with backgammon, foosball, bakery goods, and fine views from the ramparts. **Månefiskeren** ("Moonfisher Bar") looks like a modern-day Brueghel painting, with billiards, chess, snacks, and drinks (Tue-Sun 10:00-23:00, closed Mon). **Morgenstedet** ("Morning Place") is a good, cheap vegetarian café with a mellow, woody interior and a rustic patio outside (75-100-kr meals, Tue-Sun 12:00-21:00, closed Mon, left after Pusher Street). **Spiseloppen** is *the* classy, good-enough-for-Republicans restaurant in the community (closed Mon, described on page 226).

Shopping in Copenhagen

Shops are generally open Monday through Friday from 10:00 to 19:00 and Saturday from 9:00 to 16:00 (closed Sun). While big department stores dominate the scene, many locals favor the characteristic, smaller artisan shops and boutiques.

Uniquely Danish souvenirs to look for include intricate paper cuttings with idyllic motifs of swans, flowers, or Christmas themes; mobiles with everything from bicycles to Viking ships (look for the quality Flensted brand); and the colorful artwork (posters, postcards, T-shirts, and more) by Danish artist Bo Bendixen.

For a street's worth of shops selling **"Scantiques,"** wander down Ravnsborggade from Nørrebrogade.

Copenhagen's colorful **flea markets** are small but feisty and surprisingly cheap (May-Nov Sat 8:00-14:00 at Israels Plads; May-Sept Fri and Sat 8:00-17:00 along Gammel Strand and on Kongens Nytorv). For other street markets, ask at the TI.

The city's top **department stores** (Illum at Østergade 52, and Magasin du Nord at Kongens Nytorv 13) offer a good, if expensive, look at today's Denmark. Both are on the Strøget and have fine cafeterias on their top floors. The department stores and the Politiken Bookstore on Rådhuspladsen have a good selection of maps and English travel guides.

The section of the Strøget called **Amagertorv** is a highlight for shoppers. The Royal Copenhagen store here sells porcelain on three floors (Mon-Fri 10:00-19:00, Sat 10:00-17:00, Sun 12:00-17:00). The first floor up features figurines and collectibles. The second floor has a free museum with demonstrations and a great video (10 minutes, plays continuously, English only). In the basement, proving that "even the best painter can miss a stroke," you'll find the discounted seconds. Next door, Illums Bolighus shows off three floors of modern Danish design (Mon-Fri 10:00-19:00, Sat

9:00-17:00, Sun 10:00-17:00, shorter hours off-season).

Shoppers who like jewelry look for amber, known as "gold of the North." Globs of this petrified sap wash up on the shores of all the Baltic countries. **House of Amber** has a shop and a tiny two-room museum with about 50 examples of prehistoric insects trapped in the amber (remember *Jurassic Park*?) under magnifying glasses. You'll also see remarkable items made of amber, from necklaces and chests to Viking ships and chess sets (25 kr, daily May-Aug 10:00-19:00, Sept-April 10:00-18:00, museum closes 30 minutes earlier, at the top of Nyhavn at Kongens Nytorv 2; 4 other locations sell amber, but only the Nyhavn location houses a museum as well). If you're visiting Rosenborg Castle, you'll see even better examples of amber craftsmanship in its treasury.

For stylish and practical items of Danish design, check out the boutique in the **Danish Design Center** (see page 190).

Eating in Copenhagen

While most of the restaurants listed here are lunch places, I've also included a few dinner options in case you spend a night here before or after your cruise.

Cheap Meals

For a quick lunch, try a *smørrebrød*, a *pølse*, or a picnic. Finish it off with a pastry.

Smørrebrød

Denmark's 300-year-old tradition of open-face sandwiches survives. Find a *smørrebrød* take-out shop and choose two or three that look good (about 20 kr each). You'll get them wrapped and ready for a park bench. Add a cold drink, and you have a fine, quick, and very Danish lunch. Tradition calls for three sandwich courses: herring first, then meat, and then cheese. Downtown, you'll find these handy local alternatives to Yankee fast-food chains. They range from splurges to quick stop-offs.

Between Copenhagen University and Rosenborg Castle

My three favorite *smørrebrød* places are particularly handy when connecting your sightseeing between the downtown Strøget core and Rosenborg Castle.

Restaurant Schønnemann is the foodies' choice—it has been written up in international magazines and frequently wins awards for "Best Lunch in Copenhagen." It's a cozy cellar restaurant crammed with small tables—according to the history on the menu, people "gather here in intense togetherness." The sand on the floor evokes a bygone era when passing traders would leave their horses out on the square while they lunched here. You'll need to reserve to get a table, and you'll pay a premium for their *smørrebrød* (50-130 kr). At these prices, the sandwiches had better be a cut above...fortunately, they deliver (two lunch seatings Mon-Sat: 11:30-14:00 and 14:14-17:00, closed Sun, no dinner, Hauser Plads 16, tel. 33 12 07 85).

Café Halvvejen is a small mom-and-pop place serving traditional lunches and open-face sandwiches in a woody and smoke-stained café, lined with portraits of Danish royalty. You can eat inside or at an outside table in good weather (50-70 kr *smørrebrød*, 80-100-kr main dishes, food served Mon-Sat 12:00-15:00, closed Sun, next to public library at Krystalgade 11, tel. 33 11 91 12).

Slagteren ved Kultorvet, a few blocks northwest of the university, is a small butcher shop with bowler-hatted clerks selling good, inexpensive sandwiches to go for about 35 kr. Choose from ham, beef, or pork (sorry—no vegetarian options, Mon-Thu 8:00-17:30, Fri 8:00-19:00, Sat 8:00-14:00, closed Sun, just off Kultorvet square at #4 Frederiksborggade, look for gold bull's head hanging outside).

Near Gammeltorv/Nytorv

Restaurant and Café Nytorv has pleasant outdoor seating on Nytorv (with cozy indoor tables available nearby) and a great deal on a *smørrebrød* sampler for about 179 kr—perfect for two people to share. This "Copenhagen City Plate" gives you a selection of the traditional sandwiches and extra bread on request (daily 9:00-22:00, Nytorv 15, tel. 33 11 77 06). **Sorgenfri** offers a local experience in a dark, woody spot just off the Strøget (80-100 kr, Mon-Sat 11:00-20:45, Sun 12:00-18:00, Brolæggerstræde 8, tel. 33 11 58 80). Or consider **Domhusets Smørrebrød** (Mon-Fri 8:00-15:00, closed Sat-Sun, off the City Hall end of the Strøget at Kattesundet 18, tel. 33 15 98 98).

The *Pølse*

The famous Danish hot dog, sold in *pølsevogne* (sausage wagons)

throughout the country, is another typically Danish institution that has resisted the onslaught of our global, prepackaged, fast-food culture. Study the photo menu for variations. These are fast, cheap, tasty, and, like their American cousins, almost worthless nutritionally. Even so, what the locals call the "dead man's finger" is the dog Danish kids love to bite.

There's more to getting a *pølse* than simply ordering a "hot dog" (which in Copenhagen simply means a sausage with a bun on the side, generally the worst bread possible). The best is a *ristet* (or grilled) hot dog *med det hele* (with the works). Employ these other handy phrases: *rød* (red, the basic boiled weenie), *medister* (spicy, better quality), *knæk* (short, stubby, tastier than *rød*), *brød* (a bun, usually smaller than the sausage), *svøb* ("swaddled" in bacon), *Fransk* (French style, buried in a long skinny hole in the bun with sauce). *Sennep* is mustard and *ristet løg* are crispy, fried onions. Wash everything down with a *sodavand* (soda pop).

By hanging around a *pølsevogn*, you can study this institution. Denmark's "cold feet cafés" are a form of social care: People who have difficulty finding jobs are licensed to run these wiener-mobiles. As they gain seniority, they are promoted to work at more central locations. Danes like to gather here for munchies and *pølsesnak*—the local slang for empty chatter (literally, "sausage talk"). And traditionally, after getting drunk, guys stop here for a hot dog and chocolate milk on the way home—that's why the stands stay open until the wee hours.

For sausages a cut above (and from a storefront—not a cart), stop by the little grill restaurant **Andersen Bakery,** directly across the street from the train station (next to the Tivoli entrance). The menu is limited—either pork or veal/beef—but the ingredients are high-quality and the weenies are tasty (50-kr gourmet dogs, daily 7:00-19:00, Bernstorffsgade 5, tel. 33 75 07 35).

Picnics

Throughout Copenhagen, small delis *(viktualiehandler)* sell fresh bread, tasty pastries, juice, milk, cheese, and yogurt (drinkable, in tall liter boxes). Two of the largest supermarket chains are **Irma** (in arcade on Vesterbrogade next to Tivoli) and **Super Brugsen.** **Netto** is a cut-rate outfit with the cheapest prices. And, of course, there's the ever-present **7-Eleven** chain, with branches seemingly on every corner; while you'll pay a bit more here, there's a reason they're called "convenience" stores—and they also serve pastries and hot dogs.

Pastry

The golden pretzel sign hanging over the door or windows is the Danes' age-old symbol for a bakery. Danish pastries, called *wienerbrød* ("Vienna bread") in Denmark, are named for the Viennese bakers who brought the art of pastry-making to this country, where the Danes say they perfected it. Try these bakeries: **Lagkagehuset** (multiple locations around town; the handiest options include one right in the train station, another nearby inside the TI, one along the Strøget at Frederiksborggade 21, and another on Torvegade just across from the Metro station in Christianshavn) and **Nansens** (on corner of Nansensgade and Ahlefeldtsgade, near Ibsens Hotel). For a genteel bit of high-class 1870s Copenhagen, pay a lot for a coffee and a fresh Danish at **Konditori La Glace,** just off the Strøget at Skoubogade 3.

Restaurants

I've listed restaurants in three areas: the downtown core, the funky Christianshavn neighborhood across the harbor, and the trendy "Meatpacking District" behind the train station. Most of my suggestions in the high-rent downtown are tired but reliable Danish classics. For a broader range of Copenhagen's culinary scene of today, it's worth the short walk to the Meatpacking District.

Due to the high cost of water in Denmark, it's common to be charged for tap water with your meal if you do not order any other beverage. You'll often save money by paying with cash; many Danish restaurants charge a fee for credit-card transactions (about 2-5 percent).

In the Downtown Core

Det Lille Apotek ("The Little Pharmacy") is a reasonable, candlelit place. It's been popular with locals for 200 years, and now it's also quite touristy. Their specialty is "Stone Beef," a big slab of tender, raw steak plopped down and cooked in front of you on a scalding-hot soapstone. Cut it into smaller pieces and it's cooked within minutes (sandwich lunches, traditional dinners for 125-190 kr, nightly from 17:30, just off the Strøget, between Frue Church and Round Tower at Store Kannikestræde 15, tel. 33 12 56 06).

Riz-Raz Vegetarian Buffet has two locations in Copenhagen: around the corner from the canal boat rides at Kompagnistræde 20 (tel. 33 15 05 75) and across from Det Lille Apotek at Store Kannikestræde 19 (tel. 33 32 33 45). At both places, you'll find a healthy all-you-can-eat Middle Eastern/Mediterranean/vegetarian buffet lunch for 79 kr (cheese but no meat, great falafel, daily 11:30-16:00) and an even bigger dinner buffet for 99 kr (16:00-24:00). Use lots of plates and return to the buffet as many times as you like. They also offer à la carte and meat options for 65-95 kr. Tap water is 8 kr per jug.

Tight resembles a trendy gastropub, serving an eclectic international array of cuisine in a split-level maze of hip rooms that mix old timbers and brick with bright colors. You can only order a fixed-price meal here, unless you want their prizewinning burger (two courses-225 kr, three courses-275 kr, burger-140 kr; Mon-Thu 17:00-22:00, Fri 17:00-23:00, Sat 12:00-23:00, Sun 12:00-22:00, just off the Strøget at Hyskenstræde 10, tel. 33 11 09 00).

Café Norden, very Danish with modern "world cuisine" and fine pastries, is a big, venerable institution overlooking Amagertorv by the heron fountain. They have good light meals and salads, and great people-watching from window seats on the second floor (120-160-kr sandwiches and salads, 150-160-kr main dishes, huge splittable portions, daily 9:00-24:00, order at bar, Østergade 61, tel. 33 11 77 91).

Holberg No. 19, a cozy American-run café with classic ambience, sits just a block off the tourist crush of the Nyhavn canal. With a loose, friendly, low-key vibe, it offers more personality and lower prices than the tourist traps along Nyhavn (60-95-kr salads and sandwiches, order at the bar, Mon-Fri 10:00-22:00, Sat 10:00-20:00, Sun 10:00-18:00, sometimes opens at 8:00, Holberg 19, tel. 33 14 01 90).

Københavner Caféen, cozy and a bit tired, feels like a ship captain's dining room. The staff is enthusiastically traditional, serving local dishes and elegant open-face sandwiches for a good value. Lunch specials (80-100 kr) are served until 17:00, when the more expensive dinner menu kicks in (plates for 120-200 kr, daily, kitchen closes at 22:00, at Badstuestræde 10, tel. 33 32 80 81).

The Ricemarket, an unpretentious Asian fusion bistro, is buried in a modern cellar between the Strøget and Rosenborg Castle. It's the more affordable (and more casual) side-eatery of a popular local restaurant, and offers a break from Danish food (65-95-kr small dishes, 115-185-kr big dishes, 95-kr lunch special includes drink, Mon-Sat 11:00-22:00, Sun 11:00-21:00, Hausergade 38 near Kultorvet, tel. 35 35 75 30).

Illum and **Magasin du Nord** department stores serve cheery, reasonable meals in their cafeterias. At Illum, eat outside at tables along the Strøget, or head to the elegant glass-domed top floor (Østergade 52). Magasin du Nord (Kongens Nytorv 13) also has a great grocery and deli in the basement.

Also try **Restaurant and Café Nytorv** at Nytorv 15 or **Sorgenfri** at Brolæggerstræde 8 (both are described under "*Smørrebrød,*" earlier).

In Christianshavn

This neighborhood is a 10-minute walk across the bridge from the old center, or a 3-minute ride on the Metro. Choose one of my listings (for locations, see map on page 211), or simply wander the blocks between Christianshavntorv, the main square, and the Christianshavn Canal—you'll find a number of lively neighborhood pubs and cafés.

Ravelinen Restaurant, on a tiny island on the big road 100 yards south of Christianshavn, serves traditional Danish food at reasonable prices to happy local crowds. Dine indoors or on the

The Latest Culinary Phe-noma-non

Foodies visiting Denmark probably already know that Copenhagen is home to the planet's top-rated restaurant. In 2010 and 2011, San Pellegrino and *Restaurant* magazine named noma the "Best Restaurant in the World." With the closure of El Bulli near Barcelona in 2011, noma has emerged as *the* reservation to get in the foodie universe. Chef René Redzepi is a pioneer in the burgeoning "New Nordic" school of cooking, which combines modern nouvelle cuisine and molecular gastronomy techniques with locally sourced (and, in some cases, foraged) ingredients from Denmark and other Nordic lands. So, while they use sophisticated cooking methods, they replace the predictable French and Mediterranean ingredients with Nordic ones. The restaurant's name comes from the phrase *nordisk mad* (Nordic food).

But noma, which is located at the northern edge of the trendy Christianshavn district (Strandgade 93, tel. 32 96 32 97), is not cheap. The seven-course *menu* runs 1,500 kr; accompanying wines add 950 kr to the bill. A couple going for the whole shebang is looking at spending close to $800. And even if you're willing to take the plunge, you have to plan ahead—noma is booked up around three months ahead. Check their website (www.noma.dk) for the latest procedure; you'll likely need to call on a specific date, at 10:00 in the morning Copenhagen time, about three months before your desired reservation...and hope you get through. You can also put your name on their waiting list, using their online form.

If you can't commit that far out (or don't want to spend that much), many of the top restaurants in Copenhagen (including Kødbyens Fiskebar, listed on page 227) are run by former chefs from noma—giving you at least a taste of culinary greatness.

lovely lakeside terrace (which is tented and heated, so it's comfortable even on blustery evenings). This is like Tivoli without the kitsch and tourists (70-130-kr lunch dishes, 180-280-kr dinners, mid-April-late Dec daily 11:30-21:00, closed off-season, Torvegade 79, tel. 32 96 20 45).

Bastionen & Løven, at the little windmill (Lille Mølle), serves gourmet Danish nouveau cuisine with a French inspiration from a small but fresh menu, on a Renoir terrace or in its Rembrandt interior. The classiest, dressiest, and most gourmet of all my listings, this restaurant fills a classic old mansion. Reservations for indoor dining are required; they don't take reservations for outdoor seating, as the weather is unpredictable (65-165-kr lunches, 170-185-kr dinners, 325-kr three-course meal, daily 11:30-24:00, walk to end of Torvegade and follow ramparts

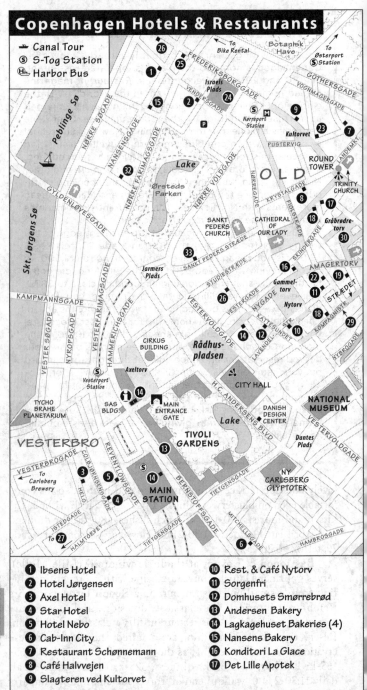

Copenhagen Hotels & Restaurants

- 🚤 Canal Tour
- Ⓢ S-Tog Station
- Ⓗ Harbor Bus

OLD

VESTERBRO

NATIONAL MUSEUM

TIVOLI GARDENS

1. Ibsens Hotel
2. Hotel Jørgensen
3. Axel Hotel
4. Star Hotel
5. Hotel Nebo
6. Cab-Inn City
7. Restaurant Schønnemann
8. Café Halvvejen
9. Slagteren ved Kultorvet
10. Rest. & Café Nytorv
11. Sorgenfri
12. Domhusets Smørrebrød
13. Andersen Bakery
14. Lagkagehuset Bakeries (4)
15. Nansens Bakery
16. Konditori La Glace
17. Det Lille Apotek

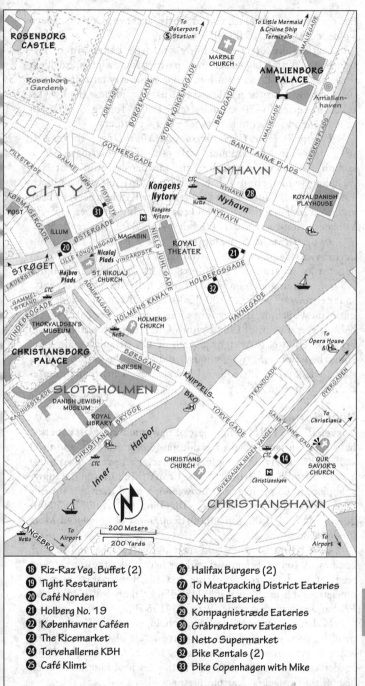

18 Riz-Raz Veg. Buffet (2)
19 Tight Restaurant
20 Café Norden
21 Holberg No. 19
22 Københavner Caféen
23 The Ricemarket
24 Torvehallerne KBH
25 Café Klimt

26 Halifax Burgers (2)
27 To Meatpacking District Eateries
28 Nyhavn Eateries
29 Kompagnistræde Eateries
30 Gråbrødretorv Eateries
31 Netto Supermarket
32 Bike Rentals (2)
33 Bike Copenhagen with Mike

up to restaurant, at south end of Christianshavn, Christianshavn Voldgade 50, tel. 32 95 09 40).

Lagkagehuset is everybody's favorite bakery in Christianshavn. With a big selection of pastries, sandwiches, excellent fresh-baked bread, and award-winning strawberry tarts, it's a great place for breakfast or picnic fixings (pastries for less than 20 kr, take-out coffee for 30 kr, daily 6:00-19:00, Torvegade 45). For other locations closer to the town center, see earlier.

Ethnic Strip on Christianshavn's Main Drag: Torvegade, which is within a few minutes' walk of the Christianshavn Metro station, is lined with appealing and inexpensive ethnic eateries, including Italian, cheap kebabs, Mexican (thriving with a nightly 109-kr buffet), Chinese, and more. **Spicy Kitchen** serves cheap and good Indian food—tight and cozy, it's a hit with locals (55-70-kr plates, Mon-Sat 17:00-23:00, Sun 14:00-23:00, Torvegade 56).

In Christiania: **Spiseloppen** ("The Flea Eats") is a wonderfully classy place in Christiania. It serves great 135-165-kr vegetarian meals and 175-260-kr meaty ones by candlelight. It's gourmet anarchy—a good fit for Christiania, the free city/squatter town (Tue-Sun 17:00-22:00, closed Mon, occasional live music on weekends, reservations often necessary Fri-Sat; 3 blocks behind spiral spire of Our Savior's Church, on top floor of old brick warehouse, turn right just inside Christiania's main gate, enter the wildly empty warehouse, and climb the graffiti-riddled stairs; tel. 32 57 95 58). Other, less-expensive Christiania eateries are listed on page 216.

Near Nørreport

Torvehallerne KBH is in a pair of new, modern, glassy market halls right on Israel Plads. In addition to produce, fish, and meat stalls, it has several inviting food counters where you can sit to eat a meal, or grab something to go. I can't think of a more enjoyable place in Copenhagen to browse for a meal than this upscale food court (prices vary per place, Tue-Thu 10:00-19:00, Fri 10:00-20:00, Sat 9:00-17:00, Sun 10:00-15:00, most places closed Mon, Frederiksborggade 21).

Café Klimt is a tight and thriving place, noisy and lit with candles. A young, hip crowd gathers here under the funky palm tree for modern world cuisine—salads, big pastas, burgers, omelets, and brunch until 16:00 (80-150 kr, daily 9:30-24:00, later Fri-Sat, Frederiksborggade 29, tel. 33 11 76 70).

Halifax, part of a small local chain, serves up "build-your-own" burgers, where you select a patty, a side dish, and a dipping sauce for your fries (100-125 kr, daily 12:00-22:00, Sun until 21:00, Frederiksborggade 35, tel. 33 32 77 11). They have another location just off the Strøget (at Larsbjørnsstræde 9).

In the Meatpacking District (Kødbyen)

Literally "Meat Town," Kødbyen is an old warehouse zone huddled up against the train tracks behind the main station. There are three color-coded sectors—brown, gray, and white—each one a cluster of old industrial buildings. The brown zone, closest to the station, is a row of former slaughterhouses that has been converted into gallery space. At the far end is the white zone (Den Hvide Kødby), which has been overtaken by some of the city's most trendy and enjoyable eateries, mingling with surviving offices and warehouses for the local meatpacking industry. All of the places I list here are within a few steps of each other (except for the Mother pizzeria, a block away).

The curb appeal of this area is zilch (it looks like, well, a meatpacking district), but inside, these restaurants are bursting with life and flavor. While youthful and trendy, this scene is also very accessible—as much yuppie as it is avant-garde. Most of these eateries are in buildings with old white tile; this, combined with the considerable popularity of this area, can make the dining rooms quite loud. These places can fill up, especially on weekends (when it's virtually impossible to get a table if you just show up)—be sure to reserve ahead.

It's a very close stroll from the station: If you go south on the bridge called Tietgens Bro, which crosses the tracks just south of the station, and carry on for about 10 minutes, you'll run right into the area. Or you can ride the S-tog to the Dybbølsbro stop, which is also just on the edge of this area.

Kødbyens Fiskebar ("Fish Bar"), one of the first and still the most acclaimed restaurant in the Meatpacking District, is run by a former chef from the famous noma restaurant (see sidebar). Focusing on small, thoughtfully composed plates of modern Nordic seafood, the Fiskebar has a stripped-down white interior with a big fish tank and a long cocktail bar surrounded by smaller tables. It's extremely popular (reservations are essential), and feels a bit too trendy for its own good. While the prices are high, so is the quality; diners are paying for a taste of the "New Nordic" style of cooking that's so in vogue here (100-145-kr small plates, 200-245-kr main dishes; Tue-Thu 17:30-24:00, Fri 15:30-24:00, Sat 12:00-2:00 in the morning, Sun 12:00-15:30, closed Mon; Flæsketorvet 100, tel. 32 15 56 56).

BioMio, in the old Bosch building, is a fresh take on an old cafeteria: First, claim a table (don't be afraid to share—Danes don't bite—and make a note of your table number). Then pick up a plastic card from the front desk to keep track of your purchases. Select your meal from the 100 percent organic, eclectic menu (with "world fusion" food—curries, wok dishes, Moroccan meatballs, and so on). Survey the line of chefs working in the open kitchen, choose which one you want to cook your meal, and place your order directly with him or her. Buy your drinks at the bar, and return to your seat to wait for your food to be delivered. When you're finished, just bring your card to the cashier to settle up. While prices are high for a self-

service model, it's a unique experience, with fun ambience and good, healthy food (55-kr small plates, 105-185-kr dinners with big portions, 100-kr two-course lunch available Mon-Fri, open daily 12:00-23:00, Halmtorvet 19, tel. 33 31 20 00).

Paté Paté, next door to BioMio, is a tight, rollicking bistro in a former pâté factory. While a wine bar at heart, it also has a full menu of pricey, carefully prepared modern cuisine and a cozy atmosphere rare in the Meatpacking District (85-115-kr starters, 165-195-kr main dishes, Mon-Sat 9:00-24:00, closed Sun, Slagterboderne 1, tel. 39 69 55 57).

Mother is a pizzeria named for the way the sourdough for their crust must be "fed" and cared for to flourish. You can taste that care in the pizza, with a delicious tangy crust. Out front are comfortable picnic benches, while the interior curls around the busy pizza oven and chefs pulling globs of dough that will become the basis for your pizza (30-kr bruschetta, 75-140-kr pizzas, a block beyond the other restaurants listed here at Høkerboderne 9, tel. 22 27 58 98).

Nose2Tail Madbodega (*mad* means "food") prides itself on locally sourced, sustainable cooking, using the entire animal for your meal (hence the name). You'll climb down some stairs into an unpretentious white-tiled cellar (50-kr small plates, 70-180-kr large plates, Mon-Sat 18:00-24:00, closed Sun, Flæsketorvet 13A, tel. 33 93 50 45).

Other Central Neighborhoods to Explore

To find a good restaurant, try simply window-shopping in one of these inviting districts.

Nyhavn's harbor canal is lined with a touristy strip of restaurants set alongside its classic sailboats. Here thriving crowds are served mediocre, overpriced food in a great setting. On any sunny day, if you want steak and fries (120 kr) and a 50-kr beer, this can be fun. On Friday and Saturday, the strip becomes the longest bar in the world.

Kompagnistræde is home to a changing cast of great little eateries. Running parallel to the Strøget, this street has fewer tourists and lower rent, and encourages places to compete creatively for

What If I Miss My Boat?

Remember that you can get help from the cruise line's port agent (listed on the destination information sheet distributed on the ship) or the local TI (see page 163). If the port agent suggests a costly solution (such as a private car with a driver), you may want to consider public transit.

To reach **Oslo,** you could hop on the night boat (DFDS, tel. 33 42 30 10, www.dfdsseaways.us). Otherwise, you can take the train; in addition to Oslo, trains run regularly to **Stockholm, Berlin** (a 3-hour connection to **Warnemünde**), **Amsterdam,** and **Brussels** (a 1.5-hour connection to **Zeebrugge**). For other points in **Norway,** connect through Oslo; for **Gdańsk,** you'll connect through Berlin. To look up specific connections, use www.bahn.com.

Some destinations may be most easily reached by **plane.** Kastrup, Copenhagen's international airport, is easily reached by train from downtown. For airport details, see "Starting or Ending Your Cruise in Copenhagen," later.

Local **travel agents** in Copenhagen can help you sort through your options. For more advice on what to do if you miss the boat, see page 144.

the patronage of local diners.

Gråbrødretorv ("Grey Friars' Square") is perhaps the most popular square in the old center for a meal. It's like a food court, especially in good weather. Choose from Italian, French, or Danish. Two respected steakhouses are **Jensen's Bøfhus** (100-kr burgers, 120-220-kr main dishes) and the pricier **Bøf & Ost** (170-250-kr main dishes). **Skildpadden** ("The Turtle") is a student hit, with make-it-yourself sandwiches (69 kr, choose the type of bread, salami, and cheese you want) and a 49-kr salad bar, plus draft beer (30 kr, or 22 kr after 16:00—sort of a reverse happy hour). It's in a cozy cellar with three little tables on the lively square (Mon-Fri 11:30-22:30, Sat-Sun 11:30-20:30, Gråbrødretorv 9, tel. 33 13 05 06).

Istedgade and the surrounding streets behind the train station (just above the Meatpacking District) are home to an assortment of inexpensive ethnic restaurants. You will find numerous kebab, Chinese, Thai, and pizza places. The area can be a bit seedy, especially right behind the station, but walk a few blocks away to take your pick of inexpensive, ethnic eateries frequented by locals.

Starting or Ending Your Cruise in Copenhagen

If your cruise begins or ends in Copenhagen, you'll want some extra time here; for most travelers, at least a full day is a minimum for seeing the city's highlights. For a longer visit here, pick up my *Rick Steves' Snapshot Copenhagen & The Best of Denmark* guidebook; for other nearby destinations, see my *Rick Steves' Scandinavia* book.

Of Copenhagen's two main port areas, only Frihavnen can accommodate cruises that begin or end here.

Airport Connections

Copenhagen Airport

Kastrup, Copenhagen's international airport, is a traveler's dream, with a TI, baggage check, bank, ATMs, post office, shopping mall, grocery store, bakery, and more. There are three check-in terminals, within walking distance of each other (departures screens tell you which terminal to go to). But on arrival, all flights feed into one big arrivals lobby in Terminal 3. When you pop out here, there's a TI kiosk on your left, taxis out the door on your right, trains straight ahead, and shops and eateries filling the atrium above you. You can use dollars or euros at the airport, but you'll get change back in kroner (airport code: CPH, airport info tel. 32 31 32 31, www.cph.dk).

Getting from Copenhagen Airport to Downtown

If you're spending the night in central Copenhagen before meeting your ship, your options for reaching your hotel include the Metro, trains, and taxis. There are also buses into town, but the train/Metro is generally better.

The **Metro** runs directly from the airport to Christianshavn, Kongens Nytorv (near Nyhavn), and Nørreport, making it the best choice for getting into town if you're staying in any of these areas (36-kr three-zone ticket, yellow M2 line, direction: Vanløse, 4-10/hour, 11 minutes to Christianshavn). The Metro station is located at the end of Terminal 3 and is covered by the roof of the terminal.

Convenient **trains** also connect the airport with downtown (36-kr three-zone ticket, covered by railpass, 4/hour, 12 minutes). Buy your ticket from the ground-level ticket booth (look for *DSB: Tickets for Train, Metro & Bus* signs) before riding the escalator down to the tracks. Track 2 has trains going into the city (track 1 is for trains going east, to Sweden). Trains into town stop at the main train station (signed *København H;* handy if you're sleeping at my recommended hotels behind the station), as well as the Nørreport and Østerport stations. At Nørreport, you can connect to the Metro for Kongens Nytorv (near Nyhavn) and Christianshavn. At Østerport, you can switch to another train that goes one more stop to Nordhavn, near the cruise port.

With the train/Metro trip being so quick, frequent, and cheap, I see no reason to take a taxi here. But if you do, **taxis** are fast, civil, accept credit cards, and charge about 250 kr for a ride to the town center (or 325 kr to Frihavnen cruise port).

Getting from Copenhagen Airport to the Cruise Port

If you want to head from the airport directly to Frihavnen, the easiest choice is to spring for a taxi (figure around 325 kr). But the public-transportation alternative is workable and much less expensive.

Trains from the airport don't directly reach the Nordhavn train station, which is a 10-minute walk from the Frihavnen port gate. But they do reach the Østerport station, just one stop to the south. Getting off at Østerport, you have two choices: Switch to a train that goes the one additional stop to Nordhavn (these include trains B and E in direction: Hillerød, trains A and H in direction: Farum, and train C in direction: Klampenborg); or take bus #26, which brings you closer to the cruise port itself, but runs only on weekdays (see details on page 160). To find bus #26, exit the train station, turn left, and walk to the corner. The bus stop across the busy street is where you can catch bus #26 to the Frihavnen port area.

Getting from Downtown to the Cruise Port

If you're coming from downtown, the bus gets you closer to Frihavnen itself, but it runs only weekdays; the train is a bit faster but leaves you about a 10-minute walk farther from the cruise port (no fun with luggage). The easiest option is a taxi (about 200 kr from downtown).

Bus #26: You can catch this bus (described in detail on page 160) at various points downtown, including in front of the train station, near Rådhuspladsen (City Hall Square), and at Kongens Nytorv (near Nyhavn). Be aware that this bus does not run on Saturdays or Sundays, and that the bus route splits to reach the two different cruise ports; be sure you're on one that's headed for Færgehavn Nord (not Langeliniekaj). Get off when you see the cruise ships, at the Færgehaven Nord stop; you'll see the port gate just down the little side street from the bus stop.

Train: From the main train station (look for the big red S, which stands for S-tog or suburban train, at tracks 9-10 and 11-12) or the Nørreport station (near some recommended hotels), you can ride the train to the Nordhavn station. Take any S-tog train in direction: Hillerød (trains B and E), direction: Hotle (train B), direction: Farum (trains A and H), or direction: Klampenborg (train C). These come frequently and take you to Nordhavn in just minutes. Note: Don't confuse Nordhavn (the stop you want, with the cruise ships) with Nørreport (two stops before it).

Arriving at the Nordhavn station, go down the stairs and exit the station to the right. Walk along the residential street (with the elevated tracks on your right) until you reach the railway underpass. Go through it, then proceed straight across the street at the crosswalk, and turn left along the busy highway—walking with the port on your right. At the next intersection, turn right; at the intersection after that, the port gate is just to your right.

Arriving at Frihavnen

Follow the instructions above to reach the port gate. From there, you should be able to see your ship—cruise liners are spread out before you, and signs direct you to individual ships. The Fortkaj pier is straight ahead; Sundkaj and Orientkaj are to your left. Thick blue lines painted in the sidewalk lead you to each pier; it's a 5- to 10-minute walk. If your ship is at the farther-out Levantkaj pier (or the new terminal being built beyond it), a free shuttle just inside the port gate will take you right to your ship.

Departing from Copenhagen Airport

To get from the cruise port to the airport, you can pay about 325 kr for a taxi, or you can take a train-plus-bus or train-plus-train connection. Follow the directions on page 159 to reach either bus #26 or Nordhavn train station. If you choose the bus (which doesn't run on Sat-Sun), you'll have to change to the airport train either at Østerport train station or at the main train station. The train-plus-train option runs daily and involves an easier change (either at Østerport station—the next stop after leaving Nordhavn—or at the main train station), but the train station is a 10-minute walk farther than the bus stop. Either way, make your way to the train that zips you quickly and smoothly right to the airport.

For more information on the airport itself, and details on the airport train, see the beginning of this section.

Hotels in Copenhagen

If you need a hotel in Copenhagen before or after your cruise, here are a few to consider (see the map on pages 224-225 for their locations). Big Copenhagen hotels have an exasperating pricing policy. Their high rack rates are actually charged only about 20 or 30 days a year—the rest of the time you'll probably pay less. Check hotel websites for deals. Prices include breakfast unless noted otherwise. All of these hotels are big and modern, with elevators and non-smoking rooms upon request, and all accept credit cards. Beware: Many hotels have rip-off phone rates even for local calls.

Nightlife Neighborhoods: If you're sleeping in Copenhagen before or after your cruise, be sure to explore some of its interesting neighborhoods. The Meatpacking District, which I've listed for its restaurants (see page 227), is also one of the city's most up-and-coming destinations for bars and nightlife. On warm evenings, Nyhavn canal becomes a virtual nightclub, with packs of young people hanging out along the water, sipping beers. Christiania always seems to have something musical going on after dark. Tivoli has evening entertainment daily from mid-April through late September (see page 188).

Near Nørreport

To reach these hotels from the main train station, ride the S-tog from the station two stops to Nørreport, within about a 10-minute walk of the hotels. Check your train schedule carefully; many local trains (including ones from the airport) continue through the main train station to the Nørreport station, saving you an extra step.

$$$ Ibsens Hotel is a stylish 118-room hotel in a charming neighborhood away from the main train station commotion and a short walk from the old center (on average Sb-1,000-1,200 kr, Db-1,100-1,400 kr, very slushy rates flex with demand—ask about discounts when booking or check website; higher prices are for larger rooms, third bed-300 kr, great bikes-150 kr/24 hours, entirely non-smoking, free Internet access and Wi-Fi, parking-185 kr/day, Vendersgade 23, S-tog: Nørreport, tel. 33 13 19 13, fax 33 13 19 16, www.ibsenshotel.dk, hotel@ibsenshotel.dk).

$$ Hotel Jørgensen is a friendly little 30-room hotel in a great location just off Nørreport with some cheap, grungy rooms and some good-value, nicer rooms. A good budget option, it's a bit worn around the edges. While the lounge is welcoming, the halls are a narrow, tangled maze (basic S-575 kr, Sb-675 kr, very basic D-675 kr, nicer Db-850 kr, cheaper off-season, extra bed-200 kr, free Wi-Fi, Rømersgade 11, tel. 33 13 81 86, fax 33 15 51 05, www.hoteljoergensen.dk, hoteljoergensen@mail.dk). They also rent 175-kr dorm beds to those under 35 (4-12 beds per room, sheets-30 kr).

Behind the Train Station

The area behind the train station mingles elegant old buildings, trendy nightspots, and a hint of modern sleaze. The main drag running away from the station, Iseldgade, has long been Copenhagen's red-light district; but increasingly, this area is gentrified and feels safe (in spite of the few remaining, harmless sex shops). These hotels are also extremely handy to the up-and-coming Meatpacking District restaurant zone.

To reach these hotels from the main train station, slip out the back door—just go down the stairs marked *Reventlowsgade* at the back of the station.

$$$ Axel Hotel and **$$$ Carlton Hotel,** operated by the Guldsmeden ("Dragonfly") company, have more character than most—a restful spa-like ambience decorated with imported Balinese furniture, and an emphasis on sustainability and organic materials. I've listed average prices, but rates can change dramatically, depending on when you book—check their website for the best deals (Axel: Sb-845-975 kr, Db-985-1,145 kr, breakfast-165 kr, 129 rooms, request a quieter back room overlooking the pleasant garden, free Internet access and Wi-Fi, restful spa area with sauna and Jacuzzi-295 kr/person per stay, a block behind the train station at Helgolandsgade 7, tel. 33 31 32 66, fax 33 31 69 70, booking @hotelguldsmeden.com; Carlton: a bit cheaper than Axel, 64 rooms, Vesterbrogade 66, see map on page 166, tel. 33 22 15 00, fax 33 22 15 55, carlton@hotelguldsmeden.com). They share a website: www.hotelguldsmeden.com.

$$ Star Hotel has 134 charmless, cookie-cutter rooms at reasonable prices. Rates vary with the season and online specials (Sb-555-1,100 kr, Db-800-1,555 kr but usually around 950-1,000 kr, breakfast included in some rates—otherwise 65 kr, elevator, free Internet access and Wi-Fi, Colbjørnsensgade 13, tel. 33 22 11 00, star@copenhagenstar.dk).

$$ Hotel Nebo, a secure-feeling refuge with a friendly welcome and 84 comfy rooms, is a half-block from the station (S-420 kr, Sb-650-700 kr, D-650-845 kr, Db-950 kr, most rates include breakfast—otherwise 60 kr, cheaper Oct-April, periodic online deals, extra bed-150 kr, elevator, free Internet access, pay Wi-Fi, Istedgade 6, tel. 33 21 12 17, fax 33 23 47 74, www.nebo.dk, nebo @nebo.dk).

A Danish Motel 6

$$ Cab-Inn is a radical innovation and a great value, with several locations in Copenhagen (as well as Odense, Aarhus, and elsewhere): identical, mostly collapsible, tiny but comfy, cruise-ship-type staterooms, all bright, molded, and shiny, with TV, coffeepot, shower, and toilet. Each room has a single bed that expands into a twin-bedded room with one or two fold-down bunks on the walls. It's tough to argue with this kind of efficiency (general rates: teensy "economy" Sb-485 kr, Db-615 kr; still small "standard" Sb-545 kr, Db-675 kr, flip-down bunk Tb-805 kr; larger "commodore" Sb-645 kr, Db-775 kr; relatively gigantic "captain's" Sb-745 kr,

Db-875; larger family rooms also available, breakfast-60 kr, easy parking-60 kr, free Internet access and Wi-Fi, www.cabinn.com). The best of the bunch is **Cab-Inn City,** with 350 rooms and a great central location (no economy rooms here; a short walk south of the main train station and Tivoli at Mitchellsgade 14, tel. 33 46 16 16, fax 33 46 17 17, city@cabinn.com). Two more, nearly identical Cab-Inns are a 15-minute walk northwest of the station (for locations, see map on page 166): **Cab-Inn Copenhagen Express** (86 rooms, Danasvej 32-34, tel. 33 21 04 00, fax 33 21 74 09, express @cabinn.com) and **Cab-Inn Scandinavia** (201 rooms, some quads, Vodroffsvej 55, tel. 35 36 11 11, fax 35 36 11 14, scandinavia@cab inn.com). The newest and largest is **Cab-Inn Metro,** near the Ørestad Metro station (710 rooms, some quads, on the airport side of town at Arne Jakobsens Allé 2, tel. 32 46 57 00, fax 32 46 57 01, metro@cabinn.com).

COPENHAGEN

Danish Survival Phrases

The Danes tend to say words quickly and clipped. In fact, many short vowels end in a "glottal stop"—a very brief vocal break immediately following the vowel. While I haven't tried to indicate these in the phonetics, you can listen for them in Denmark...and (try to) imitate.

Three unique Danish vowels are æ (sounds like the *e* in "egg"), ø (sounds like the German *ö*—purse your lips and say "oh"), and å (sounds like the *o* in "bowl"). The letter *r* is not rolled—it's pronounced farther back in the throat, almost like a *w*. A *d* at the end of a word sounds almost like our *th;* for example, *mad* (food) sounds like "math." In the phonetics, ī sounds like the long *i* sound in "light," and bolded syllables are stressed.

English	Danish	Pronunciation
Hello. (formal)	Goddag.	goh-**day**
Hi. / Bye. (informal)	Hej. / Hej-hej.	hī / hī-hī
Do you speak English?	Taler du engelsk?	**tay**-lehr doo **eng**-elsk
Yes. / No.	Ja. / Nej.	yeah / nī
Please. (May I?)*	Kan jeg?	kan yī
Please. (Can you?)*	Kan du?	kan doo
Please. (Would you?)*	Vil du?	veel doo
Thank you (very much).	(Tusind) tak.	(**too**-sin) tack
You're welcome.	Selv tak.	sehl tack
Can I help (you)?	Kan jeg hjælpe (dig)?	kan yī **yehl**-peh (dī)
Excuse me. (to pass)	Undskyld mig.	**oon**-skewl mī
Excuse me. (Can you help me?)	Kan du hjælpe mig?	kan doo **yehl**-peh mī
(Very) good.	(Meget) godt.	(**mī**-ehl) goht
Goodbye.	Farvel.	fah-**vehl**
one / two	en / to	een / toh
three / four	tre / fire	tray / feer
five / six	fem / seks	fehm / sehks
seven / eight	syv / otte	syew / **oh**-deh
nine / ten	ni / ti	nee / tee
hundred	hundrede	**hoon**-reh
thousand	tusind	**too**-sin
How much?	Hvor meget?	vor **mī**-ehl
local currency: (Danish) crown	(Danske) kroner	(**dahn**-skeh) **kroh**-nah
Where is...?	Hvor er...?	vor ehr
...the toilet	...toilettet	toh-ee-**leh**-teht
men	herrer	**hehr**-ah
women	damer	**day**-mah
water / coffee	vand / kaffe	vehn / **kah**-feh
beer / wine	øl / vin	uhl / veen
Cheers!	Skål!	skohl
Can I have the bill?	Kan jeg få regningen?	kan yī foh **rī**-ning-ehn

*Because Danish has no single word for "please," they approximate that sentiment by asking "May I?", "Can you?", or "Would you?", depending on the context.

STOCKHOLM
Sweden

Sweden Practicalities

Scandinavia's heartland, Sweden (Sverige) is far bigger than Denmark (174,000 square miles—just larger than California) and far flatter than Norway. This family-friendly land is home to Ikea, Volvo, ABBA, and long summer vacations at red-painted, white-trimmed summer cottages. Today's population numbers 9.5 million people. Once the capital of blond, Sweden is now home to a huge mix of immigrants. The majority of ethnic Swedes are nominally Lutheran. A mountain range and several islands separate Sweden's heavily forested landscape from Norway.

Money: 7 Swedish kroner (kr, officially SEK) = about $1. An ATM is called a *bankomat*. The local VAT (value-added sales tax) rate is 25 percent; the minimum purchase eligible for a VAT refund is 200 kr (for details on refunds, see page 139).

Language: The native language is Swedish. For useful phrases, see page 304.

Emergencies: Dial 112 for police, medical, or other emergencies. In case of theft or loss, see page 131.

Time Zone: Sweden is on Central European Time (the same as most of the Continent, and six/nine hours ahead of the East/West Coasts of the US). That puts Stockholm one hour behind Helsinki, Tallinn, and Rīga; and two hours behind St. Petersburg.

Embassies in Stockholm: The **US embassy** is at Dag Hammarskjölds Väg 31 (tel. 08/783-4375, http://stockholm.us embassy.gov). The **Canadian embassy** is at Klarabergsgatan 23 (tel. 08/453-3000, www.sweden.gc.ca). Call ahead for passport services.

Phoning: Sweden's country code is 46; to call from another country to Sweden, dial the international access code (011 from the US/Canada, 00 from Europe, or + from a mobile phone), then 46, followed by the area code (without initial zero) and the local number. For calls within Sweden, dial just the number if you are calling locally, and add the area code if calling long distance. To place an international call from Sweden, dial 00, the code of the country you're calling (1 for US and Canada), and the phone number. For more help, see page 1110.

Tipping: A gratuity is included in the price of sit-down meals, so you don't need to tip further. But for great service, round up your bill—no more than 10 percent. Tip a taxi driver by rounding up the fare a bit (pay 90 kr on an 85-kr fare). For more tips on tipping, see page 143.

Tourist Information: www.visitsweden.com

STOCKHOLM

If I had to call one European city home, it might be Stockholm. One-third water, one-third parks, one-third city, on the sea, surrounded by woods, bubbling with energy and history, Sweden's stunning capital is green, clean, and underrated.

The city is built on an archipelago of islands connected by bridges. Its location midway along the Baltic Sea made it a natural port, vital to the economy and security of the Swedish peninsula. In the 1500s, Stockholm became a political center when Gustav Vasa established the monarchy (1523). A century later, the expansionist King Gustavus Adolphus made it an influential European capital. The Industrial Revolution brought factories and a flood of farmers from the countryside. In the 20th century, the fuming smokestacks were replaced with steel-and-glass Modernist buildings housing high-tech workers and an expanding service sector.

Today, with more than two million people in the greater metropolitan area (one in five Swedes), Stockholm is Sweden's largest city, as well as its cultural, educational, and media center. It's also the country's most ethnically diverse city. Despite its size, Stockholm is committed to limiting its environmental footprint. Development is strictly monitored, and pollution-belching cars must pay a toll to enter the city.

For the visitor, Stockholm offers both old and new. Explore Europe's best-preserved old warship and relax on a scenic harbor boat tour. Browse the cobbles and antique shops of the lantern-lit Old Town. Take a trip back in time at Skansen, Europe's first and best open-air folk museum. Marvel at Stockholm's glittering City Hall, slick shopping malls, and art museums.

While progressive and sleek, Stockholm respects its heritage. In summer, military bands parade daily through the heart of town to the Royal Palace, announcing the Changing of the Guard and turning even the most dignified tourist into a scampering kid.

Planning Your Time

Stockholm is a spread-out city with a diverse array of sightseeing choices scattered across several islands. On a short, one-day cruise visit, you'll have to be selective. Here are your basic options:

• **Gamla Stan (Old Town):** Follow my self-guided stroll through the historic (if touristy) core of town, allowing about an hour. Add an hour to also tour the Nobel Museum, or 1-2 hours for the sights at the Royal Palace (depending on which sights you see, and how long you stay). If your timing is right, you can catch the Changing of the Guard—or even just the parade through town (begins summer Mon-Sat at 11:45, reaches palace at 12:15, one hour later on Sun; not every day off-season).

• **Djurgården:** Stockholm's lush park island has three great sights that could easily gobble up a day: The Vasa Museum, Sweden's single most-visited sight, is tops for the chance to see an astonishingly well-preserved 17th-century warship (allow 1.5-2 hours). The Nordic Museum traces local history (allow 1-2 hours). And Skansen is Europe's original open-air folk museum (allow 2 hours). These time estimates are minimum for a brief but meaningful visit; if you delve into details, any of these could consume hours. On a nice day, you could also rent a bike for a 1.5-hour spin around the island.

• **Modern City:** My self-guided walk leads you through the hardworking, but not particularly charming, urban core of town in about 1.5 hours.

• **City Hall:** Touring Stockholm's City Hall is worthwhile, but its location (on a different island beyond the train station, about a 15-minute walk from either the station or Gamla Stan) makes it tougher to squeeze into a tightly scheduled day in port. Once there, allow an hour for the required tour, plus another hour (including the walk up and down, plus possible waiting time) if you want to climb the tower.

• **Outlying Sights:** If you've already seen Stockholm's biggies, are in town for more than a short port visit (i.e., your cruise begins or ends here), or just want to get out of town, you could visit Drottningholm Palace. You'll need to allow about an hour of travel time each way, plus an hour for the guided tour, and at least another hour to explore the grounds—a total of four hours minimum. Another option is the sculpture park at Millesgården (allow about 1.5 hours round-trip travel time, plus at least an hour to see the sculptures—a total of 2.5 hours minimum). Taking a boat trip

Excursions from Stockholm

Stockholm, a large and spread-out city, can be challenging to see in a hurry. If your sightseeing is focused, you can do it on your own—but a cruise-line excursion can help you get a good overview. Excursions within Stockholm may include bus or canal-boat trips in town, a walking tour of Gamla Stan (the Old Town), a panoramic visit to Fjällgatan (a scenic viewpoint in Södermalm, just above the cruise port), and/or tours of the Vasa Museum, City Hall, or Royal Palace. Less appealing are the visits to the Ice Bar (one of many such touristy ventures in Scandinavia) and the Ericsson Globe Arena (a gigantic, spherical sports arena with "SkyView" observation pods offering distant views of Stockholm). Jewish-themed tours of the city generally include stops in Gamla Stan, the Great Synagogue, and the Holocaust Monument. There's also a "rooftop walk" along the ridgeline of a building on the downtown island of Riddarholmen. If you have a special interest, either of these may be worth considering (and less convenient to do on your own). Bike tours around Djurgården may entice you, but it's easy to rent your own bike, pick up a free map, and tour the island on your own.

Out of town, options include the grand **Drottningholm Palace** and its gardens (impressive and described on page 284, but time-consuming to reach—Copenhagen has similar palaces that are easier to see), **Sigtuna** (a historic and touristy small town with traditional architecture, described on page 286), **Lake Mälaren** (the huge lake just west of Stockholm— less beautiful and far less convenient than the archipelago your cruise ship will sail through in the opposite direction), and **Haga Park** (another garden-and-palace ensemble, but second-rate after Drottningholm). While some of these—particularly Drottningholm—could be well worth your while on a longer visit, with a short day in port I'd stick to Stockholm proper.

through Stockholm's archipelago makes little sense, since you'll see much the same scenery as you sail into and/or out of the city.

The Best Plan: Choose either the Djurgården sights or Gamla Stan, or squeeze in a few items from each.

When planning your day, think carefully through your transportation options. Public transit is expensive, and taxis are even more so (especially if you get ripped off—for tips on avoiding this, see page 255). But there are several different ways to connect any two points: Consider the Metro (T-bana), buses, trams, and the often-overlooked boats that shuttle passengers strategically between visit-worthy points (such as the one that connects Djurgården and Gamla Stan). The hop-on, hop-off harbor boat tours are also handy, but more expensive; still, especially for those arriving at certain cruise docks, this can be a very efficient way to get around.

Arrival at the Port of Stockholm

Stockholm has two main port areas: **Stadsgården** (on Södermalm, facing Gamla Stan) and **Frihamnen** (about three miles northeast of the city center). Stadsgården is used mainly for ships that are just stopping for the day, while cruises that begin or end in Stockholm typically use Frihamnen. A few small ships (or tenders) may occasionally dock right along the embankment of **Gamla Stan;** as this is right in the center of the city (and arrivals here are both easy and rare), I haven't described it in detail.

Tourist Information: TI kiosks (with bus tickets, city guides, and maps) open at both cruise ports when ships arrive, and remain open for about three hours.

Cruise-Line Shuttle Buses

From both ports, many cruise lines offer shuttle buses into Stockholm. While these can be pricey (varies by line, but likely around €12/$15 round-trip), they can be a handy way to avoid the complicated port areas. And, given the expense of public transit in Stockholm (where even a basic one-way bus or subway ride costs about $5), the shuttle is not necessarily a bad value.

Cruise-line shuttles generally drop off along the waterfront side of the Opera House, facing the Royal Palace and Gamla Stan across the harbor. From this point, here are your options:

• To reach **Gamla Stan,** simply cross the bridge, and you'll find yourself directly below the Royal Palace.

• To reach **Djurgården** (and the Vasa Museum), first walk up the big, long park (called Kungsträdgården) that runs alongside the Opera House. At the top end of the square, cross one lane of traffic behind the TGI Friday's to reach the tram stop. Take tram #7 going to the right (direction: Djurgården/Waldemarsudde), which takes you straight to Djurgården. Get off after crossing the bridge, at the Nordiska museet/Vasamuseet stop.

• My **"Stockholm's Modern City"** self-guided walk begins from Kungsträdgården, the big park right around the corner from where the bus drops off.

Tour Options

At either cruise port, you'll be met by **hop-on, hop-off tour buses;** from Stadsgården, you'll also see **hop-on, hop-off boats.** Some tickets let you use both. Both types of tours are operated by two different companies, which offer similar trips (for details, see page 256). Note: While the hop-on, hop-off boat tours are an excellent choice for those arriving at Stadsgården, these boats don't go all the way out to Frihamnen. If you arrive at Frihamnen and want to do the boat trip, you'll first need to make your way downtown (by bus or taxi) to join the tour there.

For information on local tour options in Stockholm—including local guides for hire, walking tours, and bus tours—see "Tours in Stockholm" on page 256.

Arrival at Stadsgården

Arrival at a Glance: Your plan depends on which particular dock you arrive at and where in town you'd like to head first (the tips below assume you'll want to visit either Gamla Stan or Djurgården/Vasa Museum). If your cruise line offers a shuttle bus (described earlier), consider taking it to downtown.

Arriving at **Stadsgården, berth 165/167:** From here, the hop-on, hop-off boat is a handy way to reach both Djurgården and Gamla Stan; or you can walk to Gamla Stan in about 30 minutes (a hard-to-find public bus can trim some time off the walk).

Arriving at **Stadsgården, berth 160:** It's an easy 15-minute walk into Slussen; from there, walk across the bridge to Gamla Stan, where you can start exploring or hop a harbor ferry to Djurgården.

Port Overview

Stadsgården stretches along the northern edge of the island called Södermalm, which faces the city center of Stockholm across the harbor. Arriving at Stadsgården, all of Stockholm spreads out scenically before you. Everything here is within walking distance of town; however, from the more distant berth 165/167, it's a long walk, making other transit options worth considering. The best plan also depends on where you'd like to go in town. In general, if you're heading for Djurgården (with the Vasa Museum), the hop-on, hop-off harbor boat may be your best option. To reach Gamla Stan, walking is simple. And if you want to head for the modern city center (Kungsträdgården park), consider the cruise-line shuttle bus.

Services at the Port of Stadsgården

A TI kiosk, near berth 165/167, opens during ship arrivals. The nearest hub for other services is the Viking Line Terminal building, next to berth 165/167; inside you'll find free WCs, ATMs, lockers, Internet access, and an automated pharmacy vending machine labeled *Mini Apotek*. For a real pharmacy, you'll have to head into the city (see "Medical Help" on page 252).

Getting into Town

The Stadsgården embankment is dominated by the Viking Line Terminal, a hub for overnight boats to Helsinki. Cruise-ship ports flank the Viking Line Terminal. If you arrive at **berth 165/167**, at the far tip of Stadsgården (beyond the Viking Line Terminal), it's a long 30-minute walk into Gamla Stan. From **Berth 160** at the near side of the Viking Line Terminal, close to the red-brick Stockholm Cruise Center, it's a short 15-minute walk to the Old Town/Gamla Stan.

By Hop-On, Hop-Off Sightseeing Boat

Particularly if you're arriving at the far end of Stadsgården (berth 165/167), these boats are likely the easiest, most affordable, and all-around best solution for getting around town. Departing from the dock right near where you exit your cruise ship, the boats make a handy circle to stops you'll likely want to visit: Slussen/Old Town, the Royal Palace, Nybro harbor, the Vasa Museum, the modern art museum of Skeppsholmen Island, and Gröna Lund amusement park (on Djurgården). Two companies run virtually the same route for the same price, 100 kr or €10 for the entire day (notice it's substantially cheaper if you pay in euros): Stockholm Sightseeing (better frequency at 3/hour, adds a couple of additional minor stops, www.stromma.se) and Royal Sightseeing (2/hour, www.royalsightseeing.com). Both run from May to mid-September, with departures roughly from 10:00 to 17:00. Considering that the all-day ticket costs less than three one-way public transit tickets, this is a great value if it connects the places you want to visit. For example, you could ride it from the cruise dock to Djurgården; then from Djurgården to Gamla Stan; then from Gamla Stan back to your awaiting ship.

By Foot and/or Public Transportation

To get just about anywhere you'll want to go in the city, your first goal is Slussen, an underground hub for Metro and bus lines that's at the west end of the Stadsgården embankment. From Slussen, it's just a five-minute walk across the bridge to Gamla Stan. Once in Gamla Stan, many sights in downtown Stockholm are within walking distance. Boats leave from Gamla Stan for Djurgården (Vasa Museum, Nordic Museum, and Skansen).

Stadsgården is not well set up for using public buses. There is a bus stop (called "Londonviadukten"), connecting it to Slussen and points beyond; unfortunately, it's inconveniently located on a busy road above the port area.

Here are the instructions for walking into town, including how to reach the bus stop (if you want to use it). This is narrated from the farthest cruise terminal (berth 165/167), passing the nearer one (berth 160) en route:

Step 1: From the Port to Slussen

As you exit **berth 165/167,** you'll see three color-coded lines painted on the pavement. The red line leads left, to the dock for convenient hop-on, hop-off sightseeing boats. The blue and yellow lines lead right, to the exit from the port area, a taxi stand, the stop for the hop-on, hop-off bus tour, and (eventually) into town.

To head toward town, turn right and follow the blue line to the port gate. Exiting the gate, continue along the blue line past the small TI kiosk, taxi stands, and the stops for the hop-on, hop-off bus tours. On your right is the huge Viking Line Terminal. Out front is the Viking Line shuttle to the train station; though it runs infrequently (timed to Viking ship arrivals and departures—see posted schedule), it can be handy if one happens to be departing soon (40 kr).

Continue past the terminal and up the slight incline. At the first traffic light, if you want to take a public bus, you could make a sharp left turn and walk along the viaduct (with the port area and parking garage just below you on the left) to reach the Londonviadukten bus stop (see "Bus Options," later). Otherwise, continue straight through the traffic light, between the port and the busy road. After a few minutes, you'll pass the second cruise dock—**berth 160**—next to the red-brick Stockholm Cruises Center. The far end of this terminal (closest to the Old Town) houses the Museum of Photography (Fotografiska), with excellent rotating exhibits of prominent photographers (110 kr, daily 7:00-21:00, Stora Tullhuset 22, tel. 08 50 90 50 00, www.fotografiska .eu). At the small boat dock just past the Museum of Photography, you can catch the hop-on, hop-off sightseeing boat (handy for reaching various points in town). From this point, it's about another 10 minutes—past the Birka Cruises terminal—along the waterfront to Slussen (see next).

Bus Options: From the Londonviadukten bus stop (described above), here are your options: **Any bus starting with #4** (such as #401) zips directly to the Slussen stop, under the bridge to the Old Town (just find the stairs up to Gamla Stan) and the Slussen metro/T-bana stop, with connections throughout the city.

Bus #53 (5-8/hour Mon-Fri, 3-4/hour Sat-Sun) loops up through the fun Södermalm area, then goes past Slussen and along the west side of Gamla Stan to the train station, and finally up to Odenplan.

Bus #71 (2/hour) begins the same way, then goes along the eastern edge of Gamla Stan and ends near Kungsträdgården (the starting point of my self-guided walk through the modern city).

Step 2: From Slussen to Other Points in Stockholm

Slussen, the gloomy, under-the-bridge transportation hub for this area, is not Stockholm's prettiest corner—but it will get you where you're going.

Approaching Slussen on foot from the cruise ports, you'll see the subway and bus lines beneath the huge underpass. But due to heavy traffic, the easiest way to reach them is from above: First, bear right and uphill along the ramp to the bridge. Once at the bridge, turn left and walk up to the base of the big elevator; here you'll find stairs down to the Slussen subway (T-bana) and bus station, with connections around the city (including the train station, T-Centralen). Or turn right on the bridge, to reach Gamla Stan and the embankment with ferries across the harbor to Djurgården.

By Taxi

Taxis wait in the big parking lot outside the Viking Line Terminal (to reach them, follow the blue line painted on the pavement). The port authority recommends the following one-way rates for taxis:

To the Old Town: 115 kr

To City Hall: 150 kr

To the Vasa Museum (across the harbor, at Djurgården): 190 kr

Be warned that taxis can charge whatever rates they want; one taxi can literally charge triple what the next one does. Check the rates (posted in the back window) and carefully read my advice on page 255.

Returning to Your Ship

Stadsgården is **walkable** from Gamla Stan—you can see your ship in the distance—though leave yourself plenty of time for the relatively long distance (figure about 15 minutes to berth 160, and 30 minutes to berth 165/167).

To ride back to berth 165/167 by **public bus,** your stop is called Londonviadukten. Buses serving this stop include #53 (from the train station, or from the embankment on the west side of Gamla Stan); or bus #71 (from the Opera House or Gamla Stan's eastern embankment). Both buses circle high above the port on Södermalm, then loop down to your stop, Londonviadukten. From here, you'll have to walk along the busy road back toward town to reach the ramp leading back down to the port area. (Note: Do not take buses starting with #4 from Slussen; while these work going *from* the port *to* Slussen, they go back along a different route.) There's no point taking a bus to return to berth 160, as the Londonviadukten bus stop is a 15-minute walk away—you're better off returning to Slussen and walking from there.

See page 297 for help if you miss your boat.

Arrival at Frihamnen

Arrival at a Glance: The best plan is to walk to the bus stop and take bus #76 to Djurgården or to Gamla Stan. If your cruise line offers a shuttle bus (described earlier), consider taking it to downtown.

Port Overview

Frihamnen is a sprawling port just over a wooded hill (with the big TV tower) from downtown Stockholm. It's used by cruise ships as

well as industrial ships and overnight ferries to Helsinki, Tallinn, St. Petersburg, Rīga, and other places. That means it's a large and potentially confusing area at first glance. Fortunately, most cruises use one section of the port, and connections into town are fairly straightforward.

At Frihamnen, cruise ships use one of three berths: **berth 638,** at the end of a gigantic pier, is the main berth (and the only one with a dedicated terminal building); **berth 650,** on the pier across the water from berth 638; or **berth 634,** sharing the same pier as berth 638, but situated closer to land.

Getting into Town

Here are your directions from each of Frihamnen's three berths. In every case, your goal is to get to the public bus stop that sits where the piers meet the mainland. As a general rule of thumb, just follow the blue line painted on the ground.

Services at the Port of Frihamnen

The only real terminal building is at berth 638, marked **Stockholm Cruise Center** (a.k.a. Kryssningsterminal). Inside you'll find a user-friendly TI (offers maps and bus tickets), WCs, and a gift shop, but no ATMs or Internet access. Otherwise, here are your options:

ATMs: The handiest one is inside the Frihamnsterminalen building, at the base of the pier. Just ride up the escalator.

Tourist Information: You'll find a TI window, dispensing maps and selling bus tickets, in the little red shed with white trim next to the bus stop.

Internet Access and Other Services: The **Seafarers Service** (Sjömanskyrkan) is intended for crew members (you'll see dozens of them huddled over their laptops, Skyping home), but also welcomes passengers. They offer free Wi-Fi, sell bus tickets, and can answer basic questions (but try the TI first). To find it from the main pier and Frihamnsterminalen, continue straight out and bear right with the road; across the street, it's the smallest of the three cute red houses with white trim (open anytime ships are in port, Södra Hamn 15, tel. 08/5569-4330, www.sjomanskyrkan.nu).

Supermarket: While not particularly handy for the port, if you have some time to kill and need to stock up on groceries, there's an **ICA Kvantum** supermarket a dreary 10-minute walk from the bus stop. Head toward the Seafarers Service, then continue past it as the road goes up and crosses an overpass; as you crest the hill, look over the parking lot on your right to see the supermarket.

From Berth 638

This is the only cruise berth at Frihamnen with a dedicated terminal building, marked *Stockholm Cruise Center* (a.k.a. Kryssningsterminal). Among other services (see the sidebar), it houses a TI (which hands out town maps and brochures, and sells bus tickets—buy one now if you're planning on bussing into town). As you exit the terminal buildings, hop-on, hop-off buses await (see page 256 for details), as well as taxis (see "By Taxi," later). (If you're desperate for Wi-Fi, you could mill around outside the hop-on, hop-off buses, which offer free access.)

From here, follow the blue line on the pavement for the 10-minute walk down the long, wide pier. At the base of the pier, you'll pass (on the right) the Frihamnsterminalen—the terminal building for Tallink Silja and St. Peter Line ships. Inside and up the escalator, you'll find an ATM (labeled *Uttagsautomat*) and WCs. From this terminal building, cross the street and turn left to reach the TI window, and just beyond it, the bus stop (see "Public Buses into Town," later); along this street, you'll also find more stops for hop-on, hop-off buses. If you need to get online, from the Frihamnsterminalen intersection, you could continue straight ahead and bear right with the road to find the Seafarers Service (across the street; see sidebar).

From Berth 650

You'll exit the port gate at a red-and-white souvenir stand (but no TI). Just follow the blue line out of the parking lot, and turn right at the road. Ahead on the left, you'll pass the bus stop for buses #76 and #1 (see "Public Buses into Town," later), and just beyond it, a TI kiosk (where you can buy a bus ticket). If you kept going on this road, you'd pass the Frihamnsterminalen (described above; ATM upstairs) on the right, then the Seafarers Service (with Internet access and bus tickets; see sidebar) on the left.

From Berth 634

This one's simple: Just head straight down the pier, and you'll run right into the bus stop and TI, across the street.

Public Buses into Town

Regardless of which Frihamnen berth you arrive at, you'll use the same stop for the public bus into town. It's along the road that skirts the port, near the red-and-white TI booth (see specific directions from each berth earlier). You have two options for getting to town:

Bus #76 is the most convenient, passing several major sights in town (4-7/hour Mon-Fri, 2-3/hour Sat, none Sun). Stops include Djurgårdsbron (at the bridge a short walk from the Vasa Museum and other Djurgården sights), Nybroplan, Kungsträdgården (near the Opera House and the start of my self-guided walk through the modern city), Slottsbacken (by the palace in Gamla Stan), Räntmästartrappan (at the southern end of Gamla Stan), Slussen, then through Södermalm and back the way it came. The only catch is the limited frequency on weekends—especially on Sunday—when you may be better off on bus #1.

Bus #1 is less convenient, cutting across the top of Östermalm and Norrmalm to the train station (every 5-8 minutes daily).

You can't buy tickets on board, so be sure to get them before you reach the stop. You can buy a ticket at either TI (inside the terminal or at the booth near the bus stop), or at the Seafarers Service (see sidebar). There's also an automated machine at the bus stop. It takes credit cards, but getting the correct ticket can be tricky: First, select English. Then choose "Purchase and Load Tickets," then "All Tickets." Now you'll have to arrow down (past several choices you don't want) to either "Zone A Ticket Full" (for a single ride, 36 kr) or "24 Hours Ticket Full" (for an all-day ticket, 115 kr).

By Taxi

Taxis meet arriving cruise ships, but many overcharge. Before hopping in a cab, carefully read the tips on page 255 about how to be sure you get a fair fare. Here are the suggested rates for likely journeys:

To the Vasa Museum (at Djurgården): 150 kr

To the Old Town or City Hall: 235 kr

Returning to Your Ship

From several points in town (see list of stops earlier), you can take public bus #76 or #1. Get off at the Frihamnen stop (closer to berth 650) or—on bus #76—stay on one more stop to "Magasin 3," directly in front of the red-brick Frihamnsterminalen building. Then walk up the pier to the right of that building to reach berths 634 and 638, both on the right-hand side of the pier.

See page 297 for help if you miss your boat.

Orientation to Stockholm

Greater Stockholm's two million residents live on 14 islands woven together by 54 bridges. Visitors need only concern themselves with these districts, most of which are islands:

• **Norrmalm** is downtown, with many hotels and shopping areas, and the combined train and bus station. Östermalm, to the east, is more residential.

• **Kungsholmen,** the island across from Norrmalm, is home to City Hall and several inviting lakefront eateries.

• **Gamla Stan** is the Old Town island of winding, lantern-lit streets, antiques shops, and classy cafés clustered around the Royal Palace.

• **Skeppsholmen** is the small, central, traffic-free park/island with the Museum of Modern Art.

• **Djurgården** is the park island—Stockholm's wonderful green playground, with many of the city's top sights (bike rentals just over bridge as you enter island).

• **Södermalm,** just south of the other districts, is sometimes called "Stockholm's Brooklyn" and is the primary setting for Stieg Larsson's Millennium novels (see sidebar on page 277). Its "SoFo" quarter (south of Folkungagatan) is young, creative, and trendy. Apart from its fine views and some good eateries, this residential island may be of less interest to those on a quick visit.

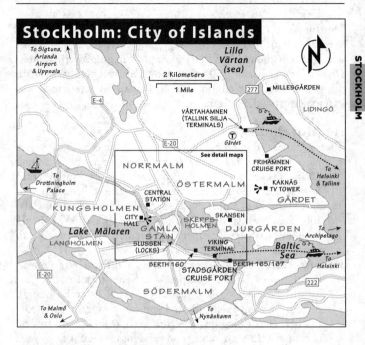

Stockholm: City of Islands

(map showing) To Sigtuna, Arlanda Airport & Uppsala · Lilla Värtan (sea) · 2 Kilometers · 1 Mile · E-4 · 277 · MILLESGÅRDEN · LIDINGÖ · VÅRTAHAMNEN (TALLINK SILJA TERMINALS) · E-20 · Gärdet · See detail maps · NORRMALM · FRIHAMNEN CRUISE PORT · To Helsinki & Tallinn · ÖSTERMALM · KAKNÄS TV TOWER · To Drottningholm Palace · CENTRAL STATION · GÄRDET · KUNGSHOLMEN · CITY HALL · SKANSEN · Lake Mälaren · GAMLA STAN · SKEPPS-HOLMEN · DJURGÅRDEN · To Archipelago · LÅNGHOLMEN · SLUSSEN (LOCKS) · VIKING TERMINAL · Baltic Sea · To Helsinki · E-20 · BERTH 160 · BERTH 165/167 · STADSGÅRDEN CRUISE PORT · To Malmö & Oslo · SÖDERMALM · To Nynäshamn · 222

Tourist Information

While small info kiosks pop up near the cruise berths when ships arrive, the main branch of Stockholm's official **TI** is across the street from the main entrance to the train station. The efficient staff provides free city maps, pamphlets on everything, Stockholm Cards (see below), transportation passes, and day-trip and bus-tour information and tickets. Avoid lines at the counter by looking up sightseeing details on one of the 10 user-friendly computer terminals (some with Internet access, 1 kr/minute; free Wi-Fi also available). Check out their helpful "today's events" board and grab a copy of *What's On Stockholm*, a free monthly magazine with hours and directions for most sights, special event listings, and details on public transportation (Mon-Fri 9:00-19:00—until 18:00 in winter, Sat 9:00-16:00, Sun 10:00-16:00, Vasagatan 14, T-bana: T-Centralen, tel. 08/5082-8508, www.visitstockholm .com). The tourist booth in the Gallerian shopping mall is not an official TI.

The Stockholm Card, a 24-hour pass for 450 kr, includes all public transit, free entry to almost every sight (75 attractions), some free or discounted tours, and a handy sightseeing handbook. An added bonus is the substantial pleasure of doing everything without considering the cost (many of Stockholm's sights are worth the time but not the money). The card pays for itself if you use public transportation and see Skansen, the Vasa Museum, and

Drottningholm Palace. You can stretch it by entering Skansen on your 24th hour. A child's pass (age 7-17) costs about 60 percent less. The Stockholm Card also comes in 48-hour (625 kr), 72-hour (750 kr), and 120-hour (950 kr) versions. Cards are sold at the main TI, airport TI, larger subway stations, Pressbyrån newsstands, and at www.visitstockholm.com.

Helpful Hints

Theft Alert: Even in Stockholm, when there are crowds, there are pickpockets (such as at the Royal Palace during the Changing of the Guard). Too-young-to-arrest teens—many from Eastern Europe—are hard for local police to control.

Medical Help: For around-the-clock medical advice, call 08/320-100, then press 2 to get into the queue. The **C. W. Scheele** 24-hour pharmacy is near the train station at Klarabergsgatan 64 (tel. 08/454-8130).

Internet Access: Some **7-Eleven** stores and **Pressbyrån** newsstands host "Sidewalk Express" Internet terminals. These are the best deal going. Just buy a card (29 kr/1.5 hours), remember your password, and you can pop into participating branches to log on. The card is shareable (but only one person at a time can use it) and valid for three days from your first log-in (branches open daily until late). There's a Sidewalk Express nook at the T-Centralen subway station and at the airport departure lounge (good if you have time to kill and an unexpired card).

English Bookstore: The aptly named **English Bookshop,** in Gamla Stan, sells a variety of reading materials (including Swedish-interest books) in English (Mon-Fri 10:00-18:30, Sat 10:00-16:00, Sun 12:00-15:00, Lilla Nygatan 11, tel. 08/790-5510).

Laundry: Tvättomaten is a rare find—the only independent launderette in Stockholm (self-service-100-120 kr/load, Mon-Fri 8:30-18:30, Sat 9:30-15:00, closed Sun, across from Gustav Vasa church, Västmannagatan 61 on Odenplan, T-bana: Odenplan, tel. 08/346-480, www.tvattomaten.com).

Bike Rental: You can rent bikes and boats at **Djurgårdsbrons Sjöcafe,** next to Djurgårdsbron bridge near the Vasa Museum (bikes-80 kr/hour, 275 kr/day; canoes-150 kr/hour, kayaks-125 kr/hour, handy city cycle maps, May-Oct daily 8:00-21:00, closed off-season and in bad weather, tel. 08/660-5757). It's ideally situated as a springboard for a pleasant bike ride around the park-like Djurgården island.

Stockholm's **City Bikes** program, similar to those in several other European cities, is another option for seeing this bike-friendly town. Purchase a 165-kr, three-day City Bike card at the TI or at the SL Center (Stockholm Transport) office at Sergels Torg. The card allows you to grab a bike from one of the more than 90 City Bike racks around the city. You must return it within three hours (to any rack), but if you want to keep riding, just check out another bike. You can do this over and over for three days (available April-Oct only, www.citybikes.se).

Updates to This Book: For news about changes to this book's coverage since it was published, see www.ricksteves.com/update.

Getting Around Stockholm

By Subway, Bus, and Tram: Stockholm's fine public transport network (officially Storstockholms Lokaltrafik—but signed as *SL*) includes subway (Tunnelbana—universally called "T-bana") and

bus systems, and a tram to the sights at Djurgården. Special passes take the bite out of the cost. It's a spread-out city, so most visitors will need public transport at some point (transit info tel. 08/600-1000, press * for English, www.sl.se/english). The subway is easy to figure out, but many sights are better served by

bus. The main lines are listed on the map in *What's On Stockholm*. A more detailed system map is posted around town and available free from subway ticket windows and SL info desks in main stations. Check out the modern public art in the subway (such as at Kungsträdgården station). Because of rail construction near the main train station, some T-bana stops in the vicinity may be temporarily closed: Look for orange information signs or ask the helpful staff.

The subway and buses are covered by three different tickets: simple **paper tickets** (36 kr for a single ride); **travelcards** good for 24 hours (115 kr) or 72 hours (250 kr)—these are issued as reloadable smartcards, so you'll pay an additional 20 kr for the card itself; and presold **strip tickets** called *Förköpsremsa* (you pay 200 kr for a strip of 16 "coupons"; each ride costs 2 coupons, so the per-ride cost is 25 kr—but if you don't use all the rides, you're out of luck). Buy tickets from machines (US credit cards OK if you know your

STOCKHOLM

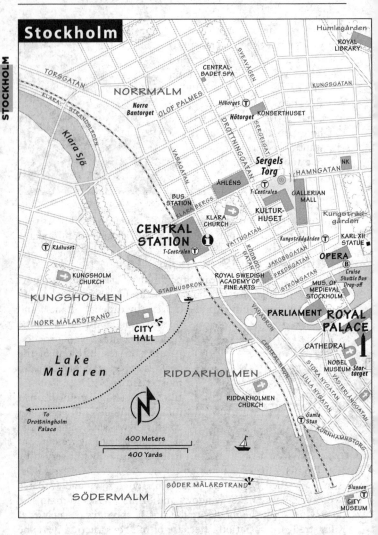

Stockholm

Humlegården

ROYAL LIBRARY

TORSGATAN

KLARA STRANDLEDEN

NORRMALM

CENTRAL-BADET SPA

SVEAVÄGEN

KUNGSGATAN

Klara Sjö

Norra Bantorget

OLOF PALMES

DROTTNINGGATAN

Hötorget T

Hötorget

KONSERTHUSET

Sergels Torg

HAMNGATAN

NK

VASAGATAN

KLARABERGS

ÅHLÉNS

SERGELGATAN

T-Centralen

GALLERIAN MALL

Kungsträdgården

T Rådhuset

BUS STATION

KLARA CHURCH

KULTUR-HUSET

KARL XII STATUE

CENTRAL STATION

T-Centralen T

VATTUGATAN

Kungsträdgården T

JAKOBSGATAN

KLARABERGS GATAN

KUNGSHOLM CHURCH

ROYAL SWEDISH ACADEMY OF FINE ARTS

FREDSGATAN

OPERA

STRÖMGATAN

MUS. OF MEDIEVAL STOCKHOLM

Cruise Shuttle Bus Drop-off

KUNGSHOLMEN

NORR MÄLARSTRAND

STADHUSBRON

VASABRON

PARLIAMENT

ROYAL PALACE

CITY HALL

CENTRALBRON

CATHEDRAL

Lake Mälaren

RIDDARHOLMEN

NOBEL MUSEUM

Stortorget

STORA NYGATAN

LILLA NYGATAN

VÄSTERLÅNGGATAN

To Drottningholm Palace

RIDDARHOLMEN CHURCH

Gamla Stan T

KORNHAMNSTORG

400 Meters

400 Yards

SÖDER MÄLARSTRAND

Slussen

CITY MUSEUM

SÖDERMALM

PIN; strip tickets may not be available) or ticket booths (cash only) in underground stations, or at the Pressbyrån newsstands scattered throughout the city and inside almost every T-bana station. All SL ticket-sellers are clearly marked with a blue flag with the SL logo. Tickets are not sold on buses—buy one before you board.

By Harbor Shuttle Ferry: In summer, ferries let you make a fun, practical, and scenic shortcut across the harbor to Djurgården island. Boats leave from Slussen (at the south end of Gamla Stan) every 10-20 minutes, docking near the Gröna Lund amusement park on Djurgården (May-mid-Sept only, 10-minute trip, 45 kr, tel. 08/679-5830, www.waxholmsbolaget.se). There's also a ferry

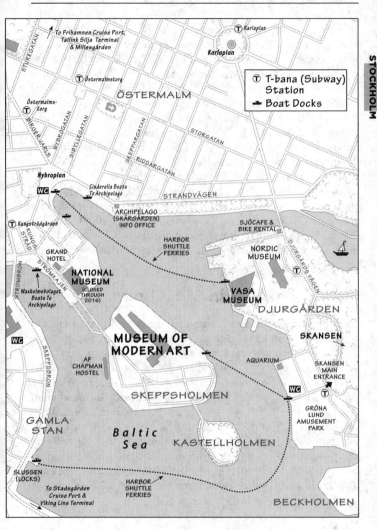

that stops near the Museum of Modern Art on Skeppsholmen Island. The Nybro ferry makes the five-minute journey from Nybroplan to Djurgården, landing next to the Vasa Museum (3/hour, June-Aug daily 10:00-20:00, check with TI for off-season schedule, 45 kr, tel. 08/1200-4000, www.stromma.se). The hop-on, hop-off boat tour (described later) also connects many of these stops. While buses and trams run between the same points more frequently, the ferry option gets you out onto the water and can be faster than overland connections.

By Taxi: Stockholm is a good taxi town—provided you find a reputable cab that charges fair rates. Taxis are unregulated, so companies can charge whatever they like. Before hopping in a taxi, look carefully at the big yellow label in the back window, which lists various fares. On the left, you'll see the per-kilometer fares for weekdays, evenings and weekends, and holidays. The largest number, on the right, shows their "highest comparison price" *(högsta järnförpriset)* for a specified ride; this number should be between 290 and 390—if it's higher, move on. (Legally, you're not obligated to take the first cab in line—feel free to compare fares.) Most cabs charge a drop fee of about 45 kr. Taxis with inflated rates tend to congregate at touristy places like the Vasa Museum or in Gamla Stan. I've been ripped off enough by cabs here to take only Taxi Stockholm cabs with the phone number (08/150-000) printed on the door. (Other companies that are reportedly honest include Taxi Kurir, tel. 08/300-000, and Taxi 020, tel. 08/850-400 or 020-20-20-20.) Your restaurant or museum can call a cab, which will generally arrive within minutes (you'll pay no extra charge—the meter starts when you hop in).

Tours in Stockholm

Stockholm Sightseeing and its parent company Strömma seem to have a lock on all city sightseeing tours, whether by bus, by boat, or on foot. Their website (www.stockholmsightseeing.com) covers the entire program; many of the options are listed below. For more information on their tours, call 08/1200-4000. Tours can be paid for in advance online, or simply as you board. The Stockholm Card provides the following discounts on Strömma's tours: hop-on, hop-off bus—60 kr off the 260-kr price; 1.25-hour quickie bus tour—50 percent discount on late afternoon departures; Royal Canal Tour—40 kr off the 150-kr price; 50-minute Historic Canal boat tour—free; hop-on, hop-off boat—free in May and Sept only. The Stockholm Card does not cover the Under the Bridges boat tour or Old Town walk.

By Bus

Hop-On, Hop-Off Bus Tour—Strömma/Open Top Tours' topless double-decker buses make a 1.5-hour circuit of the city, linking all the essential places (the combo-ticket covers a total of 25 stops). The bus provides a convenient connection to sights from Skansen to City Hall, and the recorded commentary is good. The blue line tours the north part of town (and serves the Frihamnen cruise port); the yellow line covers the south end (and stops at the Stadsgården cruise port). A combo-ticket allows you to switch between lines (260 kr/24-hour combo-ticket; May-Sept 2/hour daily 10:00-16:00, fewer in off-season, none mid-Jan-mid-Feb, www.stromma.se). **Stockholm Red Buses** offers a similar hop-on, hop-off itinerary for the same price (only one route, 19 stops, also serves both cruise ports, 3/hour, www.redbuses.se).

Quickie Orientation Bus Tour—Several different city bus tours leave from the Royal Opera House on Gustav Adolfs Torg. Strömma/Stockholm Sightseeing's Stockholm Panorama tour provides a good overview (260 kr, 1.25 hours; daily at 10:00, 12:00, and 14:00; more frequent in summer).

By Boat

▲**City Boat Tours**—For a good floating look at Stockholm and a pleasant break, consider a sightseeing cruise. The handiest are

the Strömma/Stockholm Sightseeing boats, which leave from Strömkajen, in front of the Grand Hotel, and from Nybroplan (each with recorded commentary). The **Royal Canal Tour** is short and informative (160 kr, 50 minutes, departs at :30 past each hour, generally daily May-Aug 10:30-18:30 but often as late as 19:30, April and Sept 10:30-16:30, Oct-Dec 10:30-13:30, none Jan-March). The nearly two-hour **Under the Bridges Tour** goes through two locks and under 15 bridges (210 kr, May-mid-Sept daily 10:00-16:00, June-Aug until 19:00, departures on the hour). A third option, the **Historic Canal Tour,** leaves from the Stadshusbron dock at City Hall (160 kr, 50 minutes, daily June-Aug 10:30-16:30, departs at :30 past each hour). You'll circle Kungsholmen island while learning about Stockholm's history from the early Industrial Age to modern times.

Hop-On, Hop-Off Boat Tour—Stockholm is a city surrounded by water, making this boat option enjoyable and practical. Two companies (Strömma/Stockholm Sightseeing and Royal Sightseeing) offer the same small loop, stopping at key spots such as Djurgården (Skansen and Vasa Museum), Gamla Stan (near Slussen and again near the Royal Palace), the Viking Line dock next to the cruise terminal at Stadsgården, and Nybroplan. Use the boat strictly as transport from Point A to Point B, or make the whole 50-minute, eight-stop loop and enjoy the recorded commentary (100-kr or €10 ticket good 24 hours, runs May-mid-Sept daily 2-3/hour roughly 10:00-17:00, pick up map for locations of boat stops, www.stromma.se or www.royalsightseeing.com).

By Foot

Old Town Walk—Strömma/Stockholm Sightseeing offers a 1.25-hour Old Town walk (150 kr; daily July-Aug at 11:30, 13:30, and 15:30; leaves from Gustav Adolfs Torg, near the Royal Opera House).

Local Guides—**Marita Bergman** is a teacher and a licensed guide who enjoys showing visitors around during her school breaks (1,500 kr/half-day tour, mobile 073-511-9154, maritabergman @bredband.net). **Håkan Frändén** is another excellent guide who brings Stockholm to life (mobile 070-531-3379, hakan .franden@hotmail.com). You can also hire a private guide by calling 08/5082-8508 (Mon-Fri 9:00-17:00, closed Sat-Sun) or visiting www.guidestockholm.com. The standard rate is about 1,500 kr for up to a three-hour tour.

Self-Guided Walks in Stockholm

This section includes two different walks to introduce you to Stockholm, both old (Gamla Stan) and new (the modern city).

▲▲Stockholm's Old Town (Gamla Stan)

Stockholm's historic island core is charming, photogenic, and full of antiques shops, street lanterns, painted ceilings, and surprises. Until the 1600s, all of Stockholm fit on Gamla Stan. Stockholm traded with other northern ports such as Amsterdam, Lübeck, and Tallinn. German culture influenced art, building styles, and even the language, turning Old Norse into modern Swedish. With its narrow alleys and stairways, Gamla Stan mixes poorly with cars and modern economies. Today, it's been given over to the Royal Palace and to the tourists—sometimes seemingly unaware that most of Stockholm's best attractions are elsewhere—who throng Gamla Stan's main drag, Västerlånggatan. While you could just happily wander, this quick walk gives meaning to Stockholm's Old Town.

• *Start at the base of Slottsbacken (the Palace Hill esplanade) leading up to the...*

Royal Palace: Check out the ❶ **statue of King Gustav III** gazing at the palace, which was built on the site of Stockholm's first castle (described later, under "Sights in Stockholm"). Gustav turned Stockholm from a dowdy Scandinavian port into a sophisticated European capital, modeled on buildings he'd seen in Paris, Vienna, and Berlin. Gustav loved the arts, and he founded the Royal Dramatic Theater and the Royal Opera in Stockholm. Ironically, he was assassinated at a masquerade ball at the Royal Opera House in 1792, inspiring Verdi's opera *Un Ballo in Maschera*.

Walk up the broad, cobbled boulevard. Partway up the hill, stop and scan the harbor. The grand building across the water is the National Museum, which is often mistaken for the palace. Beyond

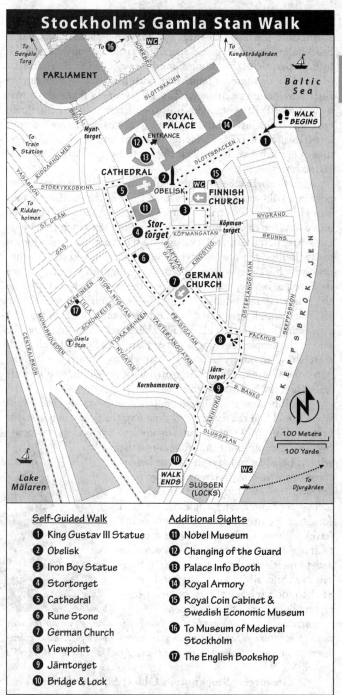

Stockholm's Gamla Stan Walk

To Sergels Torg
To 16
HÖGBRO
WC
To Kungsträdgården

PARLIAMENT

Baltic Sea

SLOTTSKAJEN

To Train Station

ROYAL PALACE

14

👣 WALK BEGINS
1

RIDDARHOLMEN
Mynt-torget
12 ENTRANCE
13

SLOTTSBACKEN

VASABRON

STORKYRKOBRINK

CATHEDRAL

2
5
OBELISK
15
WC
FINNISH CHURCH

To Riddar-holmen

ST. GRAM

11
3
NYGRÄND

4
Stor-torget
KÖPMANGATAN
Köpman-torget

BRUNNS

GAS

6
SVARTMAN-GATAN
KINDSTUG

GERMAN CHURCH

7

ÖSTERLÅNGGATAN

SKEPPSBRON

KÅKBRINKEN
17
STORA NYGATAN

PRÄSTGATAN

LILLA
SCHÖNFELTS

8
PACKHUS

Gamla Stan

YSKA BRINKEN
VÄSTERLÅNGGATAN

MUNKBROLEDEN

NYGATAN

Järn-torget
9
S. BANKO

CENTRALBRON

Kornhamnstorg

JÄRNTORG

N

100 Meters
100 Yards

SLUSSPLAN

10

⚓
Lake Mälaren

WALK ENDS

WC

SLUSSEN (LOCKS)

To Djurgården

Self-Guided Walk

❶ King Gustav III Statue
❷ Obelisk
❸ Iron Boy Statue
❹ Stortorget
❺ Cathedral
❻ Rune Stone
❼ German Church
❽ Viewpoint
❾ Järntorget
❿ Bridge & Lock

Additional Sights

⓫ Nobel Museum
⓬ Changing of the Guard
⓭ Palace Info Booth
⓮ Royal Armory
⓯ Royal Coin Cabinet & Swedish Economic Museum
⓰ To Museum of Medieval Stockholm
⓱ The English Bookshop

that, in the distance, is the fine row of buildings on Strandvägen street. Until the 1850s, this area was home to peasant shacks, but as Stockholm entered its grand stage, it was cleaned up and replaced by fine apartments, including some of the city's smartest addresses. (Tiger Woods shared a home here with his Swedish wife during their now-defunct marriage.) The TV tower—a major attraction back in the 1970s—stands tall in the distance. (The Frihamnen cruise port sits just behind it.) Turn to the palace facade on your left (finished in 1754, replacing one that burned in 1697). The niches are filled with Swedish bigwigs (literally) from the mid-18th century.

The ❷ **obelisk** honors Stockholm's merchant class for its support in a 1788 war against Russia. In front of the obelisk are tour buses (their drivers worried about parking cops) and a sand pit used for *boules*. The royal family took a liking to the French game during a Mediterranean vacation, and it's quite popular around town today. Behind the obelisk stands Storkyrkan, Stockholm's cathedral (which we'll visit later in this walk). From this angle, you see its Baroque facade, added to fit with the newer palace. Opposite the palace (orange building on left) is the Finnish church (Finska Kyrkan), which originated as the royal tennis hall. When the Protestant Reformation hit in 1527, church services could at last be said in the peoples' languages rather than in Latin. Suddenly, each merchant community needed its own church. Finns worshiped here, the Germans built their own church (coming up on this walk), and the Swedes got the cathedral.

Stroll behind the Finnish church into the shady churchyard where you'll find the fist-sized ❸ *Iron Boy,* the tiniest public statue (out of about 600 statues) in Stockholm.

Swedish grannies knit caps for him in the winter. Local legend says the statue honors the orphans who had to transfer cargo from sea ships to lake ships before Stockholm's locks were built. Some people rub his head for good luck (which the orphans didn't have). Others, likely needy when it comes to this gift, rub his head for wisdom. The artist says it's simply a self-portrait of himself as a child, sitting on his bed and gazing at the moon (notice the moonbeam-projecting light on the top of a pipe).

• *Continue through the yard, cross Trädgårdsgatan, go down the tiny lane to Köpmangatan (the medieval merchants' street, now popular with antiques dealers), turn right, and head for Stortorget, the old square.*

❹ **Stortorget, Stockholm's Oldest Square:** Colorful old

buildings topped with gables line this square, which was the heart of medieval Stockholm (pop. 6,000 in 1400). This was where the many tangled lanes intersected, becoming the natural center for shopping and the town well. Today Stortorget is home to tourists, concerts, occasional demonstrators, and—in winter—Christmas shoppers at an outdoor market.

The grand building on the right is the **Stock Exchange.** It now houses the noble Nobel Museum (described later, under "Sights in Stockholm"). On the immediate left is the social-services agency **Stockholms Stadsmission** (offering the cheapest and best lunch around at the recommended Grillska Huset). If you peek into one wing of the café, you'll get a fine look at the richly decorated ceilings characteristic of Gamla Stan in the 17th century. The exotic flowers and animals implied that the people who lived or worked here were worldly. Stockholms Stadsmission's trendy secondhand shop is just across the square at Trångsund 8. The town well is still a popular meeting point. Scan the fine old facades.

The site of the **Stockholm Bloodbath** of 1520, this square has a notorious history. During a Danish power grab, many of Stockholm's movers and shakers who had challenged Danish rule—Swedish aristocracy, leading merchants, and priests—were rounded up, brought here, and beheaded. Rivers of blood were said to have flowed through the streets. Legend holds that the 80 or so white stones in the fine red facade across the square symbolize the victims. (One victim's son escaped, went into hiding, and resurfaced to lead a Swedish revolt against the Danish rulers. Three years later, the Swedes elected that rebel, Gustav Vasa, as their first king. He went on to usher in a great period in Swedish history—the Swedish Renaissance.) This square long held the town's pillory.

• *At the far end of the square (under the finest gables), turn right and follow Trångsund toward the cathedral.*

❺ Cathedral (Storkyrkan): Just before the church, you'll see my personal phone booth (Rikstelefon) and the gate to

the churchyard—guarded by statues of Caution and Hope. Enter the yellow-brick church—Stockholm's oldest, from the 13th century (40 kr, free on Sun; open daily mid-May-mid-Sept 9:00-18:00, until 16:00 off-season; worthwhile included English-language flier describes the interior). Signs explain events (busy with tours and services in summer).

The interior is cobbled with centuries-old **tombstones.** At one time, more than a thousand people were buried under the church. The tombstone of the Swedish reformer Olaus Petri is appropriately simple and appropriately located—under the pulpit. A witness to the Stockholm Bloodbath, Petri was nearly executed himself. He went on to befriend Gustav Vasa and guide him in Lutheranizing Sweden (and turning this cathedral from Catholic to Protestant).

Opposite the pulpit, find the **bronze plaque.** It recalls the 1925 Swedish-led ecumenical meeting of all Christian leaders—except the pope—that encouraged the Church to speak out against the type of evil that resulted in World War I's horrific death toll.

The **royal boxes** (between the pulpit and the altar) date from 1684. In front (on the left), *Saint George and the Dragon* (1489) is carved of oak and elk horn. To some, this symbolizes the Swedes' overcoming the evil Danes. In a broader sense, it's an inspiration to take up the struggle against even non-Danish evil. Regardless, it must be the gnarliest dragon's head in all of Europe.

Near the exit, a **painting** depicts Stockholm in the early 1500s, showing a walled city (today's Gamla Stan). It's a 1630 copy of the 1535 original. The strange sun and sky predicted big changes in Sweden—and as a matter of fact, that's what happened. Gustav Vasa brought on huge reforms in religion and beyond. (The copies show you the same painting, minus the glare.)

In June of 2010, this church hosted a royal wedding (Crown Princess Victoria, heir to the throne, married Daniel Westling, her personal trainer.) Imagine the pomp and circumstance as the nation's attention was drawn to this spot.

The plain door on the right leads to a free WC. The exit door next to the painting takes you into the kid-friendly churchyard (which was once the cemetery).

• *With your back to the church's front door, turn right and continue down Trångsund. At the next corner, go downhill on Storkyrkobrinken and take the first left on...*

Prästgatan Lane: Enjoy a quiet wander down this peaceful "Priests' Lane." (Västerlånggatan, the touristy drag, parallels this lane one block over—you can walk back up on it later.) As you stroll this 15th-century lane, look for hoists (merchants used these to lift goods into their attics), tie bolts (iron bars necessary to bind the timber beams of tall buildings together), small coal or wood hatches (for fuel delivery back in the good old days), and flaming gold phoenixes under red-crown medallions (telling firefighters which houses paid insurance and could be saved in case of fire—for example, #46). Like

other Scandinavian cities, Stockholm was plagued by fires until it was finally decreed that only stone, stucco, and brick construction (like you see here) would be allowed in the town center.

After a few blocks (at Kåkbrinken), a cannon barrel on the corner (look down) guards a Viking-age ❻ **rune stone.** In case you can't read the old Nordic script, it says: "Torsten and Frogun erected this stone in memory of their son."

Continue farther down Prästgatan to Tyska Brinken and turn left. You will see the powerful brick steeple of the ❼ **German Church** (Tyska Kyrkan, free, Mon-Sat 11:00-17:00, closed Sun except for services). Its carillon has played four times a day since 1666. Think of the days when German merchants worked here. Today, Germans come to Sweden not to run the economy, but to enjoy its pristine nature (which is progressively harder to find in their own crowded homeland). Sweden formally became a Lutheran country even before the northern part of Germany— making this the first German Lutheran church.

• *Wander through the churchyard and out the back. Exit right onto Svartmangatan and follow it to the right, ending at an iron railing overlooking Österlånggatan.*

❽ **Viewpoint:** From this perch, survey the street below to the left and right. Notice how it curves. This marks the old shoreline. In medieval times, piers stretched out like fingers into the harbor. Gradually, as land was reclaimed and developed, these piers were extended, becoming lanes leading to piers farther away. Behind you is a cute shop where elves can actually be seen making elves.

Walk right along Österlånggatan to ❾ **Järntorget**—a customs square in medieval times, and home of Sweden's first bank back in 1680 (the yellow building with the bars on the windows). A nearby Co-op Nära supermarket offers picnic fixings. From here, Västerlånggatan—the eating, shopping, and commercial pedestrian mall of Gamla Stan—leads back across the island. You'll be there in a minute, but first finish this walk by continuing out of the square (opposite where you entered) down Järntorgsgatan.

Walk out into the traffic hell and stop on the ❿ **bridge** above the canal. This area is called Slussen, named for the locks between the salt water of the Baltic Sea (to your left) and the fresh water of the huge Lake Mälaren (to your right). In fact, Stockholm exists because this is where Lake Mälaren meets the sea. Traders would sail their goods from far inland to this point, where they'd meet merchants who would ship the goods south to Europe. In the 13th century, the new Kingdom of Sweden needed revenue, and began levying duty taxes on all the iron, copper, and furs shipped through here. From the bridge, you may notice a current in the water, indicating that the weir has been lowered and water is spilling from Lake Mälaren (about two feet above sea level) into the sea. Today, the locks are nicknamed "the divorce lock" because this is where captains and first mates learn to communicate, under pressure and in the public eye.

Survey the view. Opposite Gamla Stan is the island of **Södermalm**—bohemian, youthful, artsy, and casual—with its popular Katarina viewing platform (see "Orientation Views," page 275). Moored on the saltwater side are the cruise ships, which bring thousands of visitors into town each day during the season. Many of these boats are bound for Finland. The old steamer *Patricia* (see its two white masts, 200 or so yards toward Södermalm) is a local favorite for raucous dining and dancing. The towering white syringe is the Gröna Lund amusement park's free-fall ride. The revolving *Djurgården Färjan* sign marks the ferry that zips from here directly to Gröna Lund and Djurgården. The equestrian statue is Jean-Baptiste Bernadotte, the French nobleman invited to establish the current Swedish royal dynasty in the early 1800s.

You could catch bus #2, which heads back downtown (the stop is just beyond Bernadotte, next to the waterfront). But better yet, linger longer in Gamla Stan—day or night, it's a lively place to enjoy. Västerlånggatan, Gamla Stan's main commercial drag, is a festival of distractions that keeps most visitors from seeing the historic charms of Old Town—which you just did. Now you can window-shop and eat (see "Eating in Stockholm"). Or, if it's late, find some live music (see "Nightlife in Stockholm").

• *For more sightseeing, consider the other sights in Gamla Stan or at the Royal Palace (all described later, under "Sights in Stockholm"). If you continue back up Västerlånggatan (always going straight), you'll reach the Parliament building and cross the water back over onto Norrmalm (where the street becomes Drottninggatan). This pedestrian street leads back into Stockholm's modern, vibrant new town.*

From here it's also a 10-minute walk to Kungsträdgården, the starting point of my Modern City self-guided walk (described below). On the way there, you'll walk past the Royal Opera House and Gustav Adolfs Torg, with its imposing statue of Gustavus Adolphus. He was the king who established the Swedish empire. Considered by many the father of modern warfare for his innovative tactics, he was a Protestant hero of the Thirty Years' War.

Stockholm's Modern City

On this walk, we'll use the park called Kungsträdgården as a springboard to explore the modern center of Stockholm—a commercial zone designed to put the focus not on old kings and mementos of superpower days, but on shopping.

• *Find the statue of King Karl XII at the harbor end of the park.*

Kungsträdgården: Centuries ago, this "King's Garden" was the private kitchen garden of the king, where he grew his cabbage salad. Today, this downtown people-watching center, worth ▲, is considered Stockholm's living room, symbolizing the Swedes' freedom-loving spirit. While the English info board (near the harbor, 20 yards to the statue king's immediate right) describes the garden as a private royal domain, the nearby giant clump of elm trees reminds locals that it's the people who rule now. In the 1970s, demonstrators chained themselves to these trees to stop the building of an underground train station here. They prevailed, and today, locals enjoy the peaceful, breezy ambience of a teahouse instead. Watch the life-size game of chess and enjoy a summer concert at the bandstand. There's always something going on.

Kungsträdgården—surrounded by the harborfront and tour boats, the Royal Opera House, and, on the far side, a welcoming Volvo showroom (showing off the latest in Swedish car design), and the NK department store—is *the* place to feel Stockholm's pulse (but always ask first: *"Kan jag kanna på din puls?"*).

Kungsträdgården also throws huge parties. The Taste of Stockholm festival runs for a week in early June, when restaurateurs show off and bands entertain all day. Beer flows liberally—a rare public spectacle in Sweden.

The nearby Kungsträdgården T-bana station (on the side street called Arsenalsgatan) is famous for having the best art of any station in town. The man at the turnstile is generally friendly to tourists who ask *snälla rara* (snel-lah rar-rah; pretty please) for permission to nip down the escalator to see the far-out design, proving to the gullible that Stockholm sits upon a grand, ancient civilization.

• *Walk back to the park and stroll through Kungsträdgården up to Hamngatan street. Go left, and look for the...*

Gallerian Mall: Among this two-story world of shops, you'll find plenty of affordable little lunch bars, classy cafés for your *fika* (traditional Swedish coffee-and-bun break), and even a spa providing an oasis of relaxation for stressed-out shoppers.

• *Just beyond this huge mall, Hamngatan street leads to...*

Sergels Torg: This square, worth ▲, dominates the heart of

modern Stockholm with its stark 1960s-era functionalist architecture. The glassy tower in the middle of the fountain plaza is ugly in daylight but glows at night, symbolic of Sweden's haunting northern lights. The big, boxy, and glassy building overlooking the square is Stockholm's "culture center," the **Kulturhuset.** Inside, just past the welcoming info desk, you'll find a big model of the city. There's a library, Internet café, chessboards, fun shops, fine art cinema, art exhibits, a venue for new bands, and a rooftop café with foreign newspapers and a grand view (Tue-Fri 9:00-19:00, Sat-Sun 11:00-17:00, closed Mon but retail shops stay open; tel. 08/5083-1508, www.kulturhuset.stockholm.se).

Stand in front of the Kulturhuset (across from the fountain) and survey the expansive square nicknamed "Plattan" (the platter). Everything around you dates from the 1960s and 1970s, when this formerly run-down area was reinvented as an urban "space of the future." In the 1970s, with no nearby residences, the desolate Plattan became the domain of junkies. Now the city is actively revitalizing it, and the Plattan is becoming the people-friendly heart of the commercial town. Designtorget (on the lower level) is a place for independent Swedish designers to market and sell their clever products. Perhaps you need a banana case?

Nearby are the major boutiques and department stores: Nordiska Kompaniet (NK), H&M, and Åhléns. The thriving pedestrian street **Sergelgatan** leads past the five uniform white towers you see beyond the fountain. These office towers, so modern in the 1960s, have gone from seeming hopelessly out-of-date to being considered "retro," and are now quite popular with young professionals.

• *Walk up Sergelgatan past the towers, enjoying the public art and people-watching, to the market at Hötorget.*

Hötorget: "Hötorget" means "Hay Market," but today its stalls feed people rather than horses. The adjacent indoor market, Hötorgshallen, is fun and fragrant. It dates from 1914 when, for hygienic reasons, the city forbade selling fish and meat outdoors. Carl Milles' statue of *Orpheus Emerging from the Underworld* (with seven sad muses) stands in front of the city concert hall (which hosts the annual Nobel Prize award ceremony). The concert house, from 1926, is Swedish Art Deco (a.k.a. "Swedish Grace"). The

lobby (open through most of summer, 70-kr tours) still evokes Stockholm's Roaring Twenties.

Popping into the Hötorget T-bana station provides a fun glimpse at local urban design. Stockholm's subway system was inaugurated in the 1950s, and many stations are modern art installations in themselves.

• *Our walk ends here. For more shopping and an enjoyable pedestrian boulevard leading back into the Old Town, cut down a block to Drottninggatan and turn left. This busy drag leads straight out of the commercial district, passes the Parliament, then becomes the main street of Gamla Stan.*

Sights in Stockholm

Gamla Stan

The best of Gamla Stan is covered in my self-guided walk, earlier. But here are a few ways to extend your time in the Old Town.

▲**Nobel Museum (Nobelmuseet)**—Opened in 2001 for the 100-year anniversary of the Nobel Prize, this wonderful little

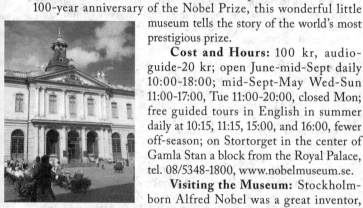

museum tells the story of the world's most prestigious prize.

Cost and Hours: 100 kr, audio-guide-20 kr; open June-mid-Sept daily 10:00-18:00; mid-Sept-May Wed-Sun 11:00-17:00, Tue 11:00-20:00, closed Mon; free guided tours in English in summer daily at 10:15, 11:15, 15:00, and 16:00, fewer off-season; on Stortorget in the center of Gamla Stan a block from the Royal Palace, tel. 08/5348-1800, www.nobelmuseum.se.

Visiting the Museum: Stockholm-born Alfred Nobel was a great inventor, with more than 300 patents. His most famous invention: dynamite. Living in the late 1800s, Nobel was a man of his age. It was a time of great optimism, wild ideas, and grand projects. His dynamite enabled entire nations to blast their way into the modern age with canals, railroads, and tunnels. It made warfare much more destructive. And it also made Alfred Nobel a very wealthy man. Wanting to leave a legacy that celebrated and supported people with great ideas, Alfred used his fortune to fund the Nobel Prize. Every year since 1901, laureates have been honored in the fields of physics, chemistry, medicine, literature, and peacemaking.

Inside, portraits of all 700-plus prizewinners hang from the ceiling—shuffling around the room like shirts at the dry cleaner's (miss your favorite, and he or she will come around again in three hours). Two video rooms run a continuous montage of quick programs (three-minute bios of various winners in one program, five-minute films celebrating various intellectual environments—from Cambridge to Parisian cafés—in the other). The Viennese-style Bistro Nobel is the place to get creative with your coffee...and sample the famous Nobel ice cream. All Nobel laureates who visit the museum are asked to sign the bottom of a chair in the café. Turn yours over and see who warmed your chair. And don't miss the lockable hangers, to protect your fancy, furry winter coat. The

Stockholm at a Glance

▲▲▲**Skansen** Europe's first and best open-air folk museum, with more than 150 old homes, churches, shops, and schools. **Hours:** Park—daily May-mid-June 10:00-19:00, mid-June-Aug 10:00-22:00, Sept 10:00-18:00, Oct and March-April 10:00-16:00, Nov-Feb 10:00-15:00; historical buildings—generally 11:00-15:00, June-Aug some until 19:00, most closed in winter. See page 278.

▲▲▲**Vasa Museum** Ill-fated 17th-century warship dredged from the sea floor, now the showpiece of an interesting museum. **Hours:** June-Aug daily 8:30-18:00; Sept-May daily 10:00-17:00, Wed until 20:00. See page 280.

▲▲**Military Parade and Changing of the Guard** Punchy daily pomp starting near Nybroplan and finishing at Royal Palace outer courtyard. **Hours:** Mid-May-mid-Sept Mon-Sat parade begins at 11:45 (reaches palace at 12:15), Sun at 12:45 (palace at 13:15); April-mid-May and mid-Sept-Oct Wed and Sat at 11:45 (palace at 12:15), Sun at 12:45 (palace at 13:15); Nov-March starts at palace Wed and Sat at 12:15, Sun at 13:15. See page 271.

▲▲**Royal Armory** A fine collection of ceremonial medieval royal armor, historic and modern royal garments, and carriages, in the Royal Palace. **Hours:** May-June daily 11:00-17:00; July-Aug daily 10:00-18:00; Sept-April Tue-Sun 11:00-17:00, Thu until 20:00, closed Mon. See page 271.

▲▲**City Hall** Gilt mosaic architectural jewel of Stockholm and site of Nobel Prize banquet, with tower offering the city's best views. **Hours:** Required tours daily generally June-Aug every 30 minutes 9:30-16:00, off-season hourly 10:00-15:00. See page 273.

▲▲**Nordic Museum** Danish Renaissance palace design and five fascinating centuries of traditional Swedish lifestyles. **Hours:** Daily 10:00-17:00, Wed until 20:00 Sept-May. See page 282.

▲▲**Drottningholm Palace** Resplendent 17th-century royal residence with a Baroque theater. **Hours:** May-Aug daily 10:00-16:30, Sept daily 11:00-15:30, Oct and April Fri-Sun only 11:00-15:30, Nov-Dec and mid-Jan-March Sat-Sun only 12:00-15:30, closed last two weeks of Dec. See page 284.

▲**Nobel Museum** Star-studded tribute to some of the world's most accomplished scientists, artists, economists, and politicians. **Hours:** June-mid-Sept daily 10:00-18:00; mid-Sept-May Wed-Sun 11:00-17:00, Tue 11:00-20:00, closed Mon. See page 267.

▲**Royal Palace Museums** Complex of Swedish royal museums, the two best of which are the Royal Apartments and Royal Treasury. **Hours:** Mid-May-mid-Sept daily 10:00-17:00; mid-Sept-mid-May Tue-Sun 12:00-16:00, closed Mon. See page 272.

▲**Royal Coin Cabinet and Swedish Economic Museum** Europe's best look at the history of money, with a sweep through the evolution of the Swedish economy to boot. **Hours:** Daily 10:00-16:00. See page 273.

▲**Kungsträdgården** Stockholm's lively central square, with life-size chess games, concerts, and perpetual action. **Hours:** Always open. See page 264.

▲**Sergels Torg** Modern square with underground mall. **Hours:** Always open. See page 265.

▲**National Museum of Fine Arts** Closes for renovation in mid-2013, but part of the collection—which features works by locals Larsson and Zorn, along with Rembrandt, Rubens, and Impressionists—will be on display at the Royal Swedish Academy of Fine Arts. **Hours:** Inquire locally. See page 275.

▲**Thielska Galleriet** Enchanting waterside mansion with works of local artists Larsson and Zorn, and Norwegian artist Munch. **Hours:** Tue-Sun 12:00-17:00, Thu until 20:00, closed Mon. See page 283.

▲**Millesgården** Dramatic cliffside museum and grounds featuring works of Sweden's greatest sculptor, Carl Milles. **Hours:** May-Sept daily 11:00-17:00; Oct-April Tue-Sun 11:00-17:00, closed Mon. See page 283.

Swedish Academy, which awards the Nobel Prize for literature each year, is upstairs.

Parliament (Riksdaghuset)—For a firsthand look at Sweden's government, tour the Parliament buildings. It's also possible to watch the Parliament in session.

Cost and Hours: Free one-hour tours in English late June-Aug; usually Mon-Fri at 12:00, 13:00, 14:00, and 15:00; enter at Riksgatan 3a, call 08/786-4862 to confirm times, www.riks dagen.se.

Museum of Medieval Stockholm (Medeltidsmuseet)—This museum, recently renovated, provides a good look at medieval Stockholm. When the government was digging a parking garage near the Parliament building in the 1970s, workers uncovered a major archaeological find: parts of the town wall that King Gustav Vasa built in the 1530s, as well as a churchyard. This underground museum preserves these discoveries and explains how Stockholm grew from a medieval village to a major city.

Cost and Hours: 100 kr; July-Aug daily 12:00-17:00, Wed until 19:00; Sept-June Tue-Sun 12:00-17:00, Wed until 19:00, closed Mon; English audioguide, enter museum from park in front of Parliament, tel. 08/5083-1790, www.medeltidsmuseet .stockholm.se.

Nearby: The museum sits in **Strömparterren** park. With its café and Carl Milles statue of the *Sun Singer* greeting the day, it's a pleasant place for a sightseeing break (pay WC in park, free WC in museum).

Royal Palace (Kungliga Slottet)

Although the royal family beds down at Drottningholm, this complex in Gamla Stan is still the official royal residence. The palace, designed in Italian Baroque style, was completed in 1754 after a fire wiped out the previous palace. Today its exterior is undergoing a 20-year renovation—don't be surprised if parts are covered in scaffolding.

The Changing of the Guard and the awesome, can't-miss Royal Armory are the palace's highlights. The Royal Treasury is worth a look; the chapel is nice but no big deal; the Apartments of State are not much as far as palace rooms go; and you can skip Gustav III's Museum of Antiquities and the Museum of Three Crowns. The information booth in the semicircular courtyard (at the top, where the guard changes) gives out an explanatory brochure with a map marking the different entrances (main entrance is on the west side—away from the water—but the Royal Armory has a separate entrance). They also have a list of today's guided tours. In peak season, there are up to three different English tours a day (included in the admission)—allowing you to systematically cover nearly the entire complex. Since the palace is used for state functions, it is sometimes closed to tourists.

▲▲Military Parade and Changing of the Guard—Starting two blocks from Nybroplan (in front of the Army Museum at Riddargatan 13), Stockholm's daily military parade marches over Norrbro bridge and up to the Royal Palace's outer courtyard, where the band plays and the guard changes.

The performance is fresh and spirited, because the soldiers are visiting Stockholm just like you—and it's a chance for young soldiers from all over Sweden, in every branch of the service, to show their stuff in the big city. Pick your place at the palace courtyard, where the band arrives at about 12:15 (13:15 on Sun). The best spot to stand is along the wall in the inner courtyard, near the palace information and ticket office. There are columns with wide

pedestals for easy perching, as well as benches that people stand on to view the ceremony (arrive early). Generally, after the barking and goose-stepping formalities, the band shows off for an impressive 30-minute marching concert. Though the royal family lives out of town at Drottningholm, the palace guards are for real. If the guard by the cannon in the semicircular courtyard looks a little lax, try wandering discreetly behind him.

Cost and Hours: Free; mid-May-mid-Sept Mon-Sat parade begins at 11:45 (reaches palace at 12:15), Sun at 12:45 (palace at 13:15); April-mid-May and mid-Sept-Oct Wed and Sat at 11:45 (palace at 12:15), Sun at 12:45 (palace at 13:15); Nov-March starts at palace Wed and Sat at 12:15, Sun at 13:15. Royal appointments can disrupt the schedule; confirm times at TI. In summer, you might also catch the mounted guards (but they do not appear on a regular schedule).

▲▲Royal Armory (Livrustkammaren)—The oldest museum in Sweden is more than an armory and less than an armory. It displays impressive ceremonial royal armor (never used in battle), but there's a lot more to see. Everything is beautifully lit and displayed, and well-described in English and by the museum's evocative audioguide.

Cost and Hours: 90 kr; May-June daily 11:00-17:00; July-Aug daily 10:00-18:00; Sept-April Tue-Sun 11:00-17:00, Thu until 20:00, closed Mon; 20-kr audioguide is excellent—romantic couples can share it if they crank up the volume, information sheets in English available in most rooms; entrance at bottom of Slottsbacken at base of palace, tel. 08/5195-5546, www.livrust kammaren.se.

Visiting the Museum: The first room is almost a shrine for Swedish visitors. It contains the clothes Gustavus Adolphus wore, and even the horse he was riding, when he was killed in the Thirty Years' War. The exquisite workmanship on the **ceremonial armor** in this room is a fine example of weaponry as an art form. The next room shows royal suits and gowns through the ages. The 1766 wedding dress of Queen Sofia is designed to cleverly show off its fabulously rich fabric (the dress seems even wider when compared to her 20-inch corseted waist). There are some modern royal dresses here as well. The royal children get a section for themselves, featuring a cradle that has rocked heirs to the throne since the 1650s; eventually it will leave the armory to rock the next royal offspring as well. It's fun to imagine little princes romping around their 600-room home with these toys. A century ago, one prince treasured his boxcar and loved playing cowboys and Indians.

The basement is a royal garage filled with **lavish coaches.** The highlight: a plush coronation coach made in France in about 1700 and shipped to Stockholm, ready to be assembled Ikea-style. It last rolled a king to his big day—with its eight fine horses and what was then the latest in suspension gear—in the mid-1800s. A display of royal luggage over the centuries makes it obvious that Swedish royalty didn't know how to pack light.

▲**Other Royal Palace Museums**—The four museums below can be accessed through the main entrance. Stockholm Card-holders can go straight into each museum, bypassing the ticket office.

Cost and Hours: 150-kr combo-ticket, generally includes guided tour; mid-May-mid-Sept daily 10:00-17:00; mid-Sept-mid-May Tue-Sun 12:00-16:00, closed Mon; tel. 08/402-6130, www.royalcourt.se.

Royal Apartments: The stately palace exterior encloses 608 rooms (one more than Britain's Buckingham Palace) of glittering 18th-century Baroque and Rococo decor. Clearly the palace of Scandinavia's superpower, it's steeped in royal history. You'll walk the long halls through four sections: the Hall of State (with an exhibit of fancy state awards), the lavish Bernadotte Apartments (some fine Rococo interiors and portraits of the Bernadotte dynasty), the State Apartments (with rooms dating to the 1690s), and the Guest Apartments, where visiting heads of state still crash. Guided tours in English run daily in summer at 11:00 and 14:00

(45 minutes, off-season at 14:00 and 15:00).

Royal Treasury (Skattkammaren): Climbing down into the super-secure vault, you'll see 12 cases filled with fancy crowns, scepters, jeweled robes, and plenty of glittering gold. Nothing is explained, so pay for the flier or take the guided tour in English (May-Sept daily at 13:00, Oct-April Tue-Sun at 13:00).

Gustav III's Museum of Antiquities (Gustav III's Antik-museum): In the 1700s, Gustav III traveled through Italy and brought home an impressive gallery of classical Roman statues. These are displayed exactly as they were in the 1790s. This was a huge deal for those who had never been out of Sweden (closed mid-Sept-mid-May).

Museum of Three Crowns (Museum Tre Kronor): This museum shows off bits of the palace from before a devastating 1697 fire. It's basically just more old stuff, interesting only to real history buffs (guided tours in English at 15:00 in summer).

▲**Royal Coin Cabinet and Swedish Economic Museum (Kungliga Myntkabinettet/Sveriges Ekonomiska Museum)**— More than your typical royal coin collection, this is the best money museum I've seen in Europe. A fine exhibit tells the story of money from crude wampum to credit cards, and traces the development of the modern Swedish economy. Unfortunately, there aren't many English translations, which makes the included audio-guide critical.

Cost and Hours: 70 kr, free on Mon, open daily 10:00-16:00, Slottsbacken 6, tel. 08/5195-5304, www.myntkabinettet.se.

Downtown Stockholm

Waterside Walk—Enjoy Stockholm's ever-expanding shoreline promenades. Tracing the downtown shoreline while dodging in-line skaters and ice-cream trolleys (rather than cars and buses), you can walk from Slussen across Gamla Stan, all the way to the good ship *Vasa* in Djurgården. Perhaps the best stretch is along waterfront Strandvägen street (from Nybroplan past weather-beaten old boats and fancy facades to Djur-gården). As you stroll, keep in mind that there's free fishing in central Stockholm, and the harbor waters are restocked every spring with thousands of new fish. Locals tell of one lucky lad who pulled in an 80-pound salmon.

▲▲**City Hall (Stadshuset)**—The Stadshuset is an impressive mix of eight million red bricks, 19 million chips of gilt mosaic, and lots of

Stockholm pride. While churches dominate cities in southern Europe, in Scandinavian capitals, city halls seem to be the most impressive buildings, celebrating humanism and the ideal of people working together in community. Built in 1923, this is still a functioning city hall. The members of the city council—101 people (mostly women) representing the 850,000 people of Stockholm— are hobby legislators with regular day jobs. That's why they meet in the evening. One of Europe's finest public buildings, the site of the annual Nobel Prize banquet, and a favorite spot for weddings (they do two per hour on Saturday afternoons), City Hall is particularly enjoyable and worthwhile for its entertaining and required 50-minute tour.

Cost and Hours: 100 kr; English-only tours offered daily, generally June-Aug every 30 minutes 9:30-16:00, off-season hourly 10:00-15:00; call to confirm, 300 yards behind the central train station—about a 15-minute walk from either the station or Gamla Stan, bus #3 or #62, tel. 08/5082-9059, www.stockholm.se/city hall). City Hall's cafeteria, which you enter from the courtyard, serves complete lunches for 95 kr (Mon-Fri 11:00-14:00, closed Sat-Sun).

Visiting City Hall: On the tour, you'll see the building's sumptuous National Romantic-style interior (similar to Britain's

Arts and Crafts style), celebrating Swedish architecture and craftwork, and created almost entirely with Swedish materials. Highlights include the so-called Blue Hall (the Italian piazza-inspired, loggia-lined courtyard that was originally intended to be open air—hence the name—where the 1,300-plate Nobel banquet takes place); the City Council Chamber (with a gorgeously painted wood-beamed ceiling that resembles a Viking longhouse—or maybe an overturned Viking boat); the Gallery of the Prince (lined with frescoes executed by Prince Eugene of Sweden); and the glittering, gilded, Neo-Byzantine-style, and aptly named Golden Hall, where the Nobel recipients cut a rug after the banquet. In this over-the-top space, a glimmering mosaic Queen of Lake Mälaren oversees the proceedings with a welcoming but watchful eye, as East (see Istanbul's Hagia Sophia and the elephant, on the right) and West (notice the skyscrapers with the American flag, on the left) meet here in Stockholm. Above the door across the hall is Sweden's patron saint, Erik, who seems to have lost his head (due to some sloppy mosaic planning). On the tour, you'll find out exactly how many centimeters each Nobel banquet attendee gets at the table, why the building's plans were altered at the last minute to make the tower exactly one meter taller, where the prince got the inspiration for his scenic frescoes, and how the Swedes reacted when they first saw that Golden Hall (hint: they weren't pleased).

▲**City Hall Tower**—This 348-foot-tall tower (an elevator takes you halfway up, leaving you 350 steps to mount) rewards those who

make the climb with a grand city view. As you huff your way up, you'll come upon models of busts and statues that adorn City Hall and a huge, 25-foot-tall statue of St. Erik. Erik, the patron saint of Stockholm, was supposed to be hoisted by cranes up through the middle of the tower to stand at its top. But plans changed, big Erik is forever parked halfway up the structure, and the tower's top is open for visitors to gather and enjoy the view. At the roof terrace, you'll find smaller statues of Erik, Klara, Maria Magdalena, and Nikolaus: patron saints facing their respective parishes. Finally, you'll find yourself in the company of the tower's nine bells, with Stockholm spreading out all around you.

Cost and Hours: 40 kr, daily June-Aug 9:15-17:15, May and Sept 9:15-16:00, closed Oct-April. As only 30 people at a time are allowed up into the tower, there's often a very long wait. If there's a long line, I'd skip it.

▲**Orientation Views**—For a bird's-eye perspective on this wonderful urban mix of water, parks, concrete, and people, consider these three viewpoints: **City Hall Tower** (described above; view from tower pictured above); **Kaknäs Tower** (at 500 feet, once the tallest building in Scandinavia—45 kr; June-Aug daily 9:00-22:00; Sept-May Mon-Sat 10:00-21:00, Sun 10:00-18:00; restaurant on 28th floor, east of downtown—bus #69 from Nybroplan or Sergels Torg, tel. 08/667-2105); and the **Katarina** viewing platform in Södermalm, near the Slussen T-bana stop. (The Katarina elevator is no longer working, but you can get to the platform via a pedestrian bridge from Mosebacke Torg, to the south.)

▲**National Museum of Fine Arts (Nationalmuseum) at the Royal Swedish Academy of Fine Arts (Kungliga Akademien för de Fria Konsterna)**—Stockholm's 200-year-old art museum (on the Blasieholmen peninsula) is finally getting a facelift, as its home closes from mid-2013 through 2016 for an extensive renovation. Beginning in the fall of 2013, part of the collection will be on display at the Royal Swedish Academy of Fine Arts.

Cost and Hours: Inquire locally about cost, hours, and

STOCKHOLM

other specifics of the National Museum's exhibition at the Royal Swedish Academy of Fine Arts; the academy is between the train station and the palace at Fredsgatan 12, tel. 08/232-925, www.konstakademien.se.

Visiting the Collection: Though mediocre by European standards, the National Museum owns a few good pieces. Highlights include several canvases by Rembrandt and Rubens, a fine group of Impressionist works, and a sizeable collection of Russian icons. Seek out the exquisite paintings by the Swedish artists Anders Zorn and Carl Larsson. It's unclear exactly which items will be on display at the Royal Swedish Academy of Fine Arts; if you visit, look for the following:

The Stockholm-born **Carl Larsson** (1853-1919) became very popular as the Swedish Norman Rockwell, chronicling the everyday family life of his own wife and brood of kids. If his two vast, 900-square-foot murals celebrating Swedish history are on display, they're worth a close look. *The Return of the King* shows Gustav Vasa astride a white horse. After escaping the Stockholm Bloodbath and leading Sweden's revolt, he drove out the Danes and was elected Sweden's first king (1523). Now he marches his victorious troops across a drawbridge, as Stockholm's burghers bow and welcome him home. In *The Midwinter Sacrifice*, it's solstice eve, and Vikings are gathered at the pagan temple at Gamla Uppsala. Musicians blow the *lur* horns, a priest in white raises the ceremonial hammer of Thor, and another priest in red (with his back to us) holds a sacrificial knife. The Viking king arrives on his golden sled, rises from his throne, strips naked, gazes to the heavens, and prepares to sacrifice himself to the gods of winter, so that spring will return to feed his starving people.

The museum also has an excellent collection that walks you through the evolution of modern Swedish design: gracefully engraved glass from the 1920s, works from the Stockholm Exhibition of 1930, industrial design of the 1940s, Scandinavian Design movement of the 1950s, plastic chairs from the 1960s, modern furniture from the 1980s, and the Swedish new simplicity from the 1990s.

Museum of Modern Art (Moderna Museet)—This bright, cheery gallery on Skeppsholmen island is as far out as can be, with Picasso, Braque, Dalí, Matisse, and lots of goofy Dada art (such as *Urinal*), as well as more contemporary stuff. Don't miss the beloved *Goat with Tire*. The excellent and included audioguide makes modern art meaningful to visitors who wouldn't

Once in a Millennium:
Stieg Larsson's Stockholm

With more than 65 million copies of Stieg Larsson's Millennium trilogy of novels in circulation—and both Swedish and Hollywood film adaptations—Stockholm has a new breed of tourist. Fans of Larsson's punked-out computer hacker heroine Lisbeth Salander and jaded journalist hero Mikael Blomkvist are stalking the city's neighborhoods, particularly Södermalm, just south of the Old Town.

Stockholm's geography is key to Larsson's crime thrillers: Most of the good guys live and work in the formerly working-class Södermalm, while many of the villains hail from tony neighborhoods near Parliament and City Hall, across the water.

If you come looking for Lisbeth or Mikael, the best place to start is the **City of Stockholm Museum** in Södermalm, near the Slussen T-bana stop (70 kr, Tue-Sun 11:00-17:00, Thu until 20:00, closed Mon, Ryssgården, tel. 08/5083-1620, www.stadsmuseum.stockholm.se). The museum hosts a display of Larsson artifacts, including a reconstruction of Mikael Blomkvist's office at *Millennium* magazine, and offers Millennium walking tours in English (120 kr, Wed at 18:00, Sat at 11:30) and a Millennium sights map (40 kr).

A few blocks from the museum is the site of the fictional *Millennium* offices, above the Greenpeace headquarters at the corner of Götgatan and Hökens Gata (really it's just apartments). Two real businesses in Södermalm figure prominently in the trilogy: **Kvarnen,** an old-style pub where Lisbeth hangs out with an all-girl punk band (Tjärhovsgatan 4, near the Medborgarplasten T-bana stop; see "Eating in Stockholm," later); and the **Mellqvist café** (Hornsgatan 78, near the Hornstull T-bana stop), where the love-struck Lisbeth sees Mikael kiss his mistress.

otherwise appreciate it.

Cost and Hours: 120 kr, Tue and Fri 10:00-20:00, Wed-Thu and Sat-Sun 10:00-18:00, closed Mon, fine bookstore, harborview café, T-bana: Kungsträdgården plus 10-minute walk, or take bus #65, tel. 08/5195-5200, www.modernamuseet.se.

▲**Swedish Massage, Spa, and Sauna**—To treat yourself to a Swedish spa experience—maybe with an authentic "Swedish massage"—head for the elegant circa-1900 **CentralBadet Spa.** Admission includes entry to an extensive gym, "bubblepool," sauna, steam room, and an elegant Art Nouveau pool. A classic massage (50 minutes) costs 650 kr—you don't have to pay the entry fee if that's all you want. Reservations are smart. If you won't make it to Finland, enjoy a sauna here. There are two saunas—one coed, one not. Bring your towel into the sauna—not for modesty, but for hygiene (to separate your body from the bench). The steam room is mixed; bring two towels (one for modesty and the other to sit on). The pool is more for floating than for jumping and splashing. The leafy courtyard restaurant is a relaxing place to enjoy affordable, healthy, and light meals.

Cost and Hours: 220 kr, increases to 320 kr on Sat, towels and robes available for rent; open Mon-Fri 7:00-21:00, Sat 9:00-21:00, Sun 9:00-18:00, last entry one hour before closing, ages 18 and up, Drottninggatan 88, 10 minutes up from Sergels Torg, tel. 08/5452-1300, tel. 08/5452-1313, www.centralbadet.se.

Djurgården

Four hundred years ago, Djurgården was the king's hunting ground. Now this entire lush island is Stockholm's fun center, protected as a national park. It still has a smattering of animal life among its biking paths, picnicking local families, art galleries, and various amusements. Of the three great sights on the island, the Vasa and Nordic museums are neighbors, and Skansen is a 10-minute walk away (or hop on any bus—they come every couple of minutes). To get around more easily, consider renting a bike as you enter the island (see page 252).

Getting There: Take tram #7 from Sergels Torg (the stop is right under the highway overpass) and get off at the Nordic Museum (also for the Vasa Museum), or continue on to the Skansen stop. In summer, you can take a ferry from Nybroplan or Slussen (see "Getting Around Stockholm," earlier). Walkers can enjoy the harborside Strandvägen promenade, which leads from Nybroplan directly to the island.

▲▲▲Skansen

This is Europe's original open-air folk museum, founded in 1891. It's a huge park that encompasses more than 150 historic buildings (homes, churches, shops, and schoolhouses) transplanted from all corners of Sweden.

Cost and Hours: 160 kr, kids-60 kr, less off-season; park open daily May-mid-June 10:00-19:00, mid-June-Aug 10:00-22:00, Sept 10:00-18:00, Oct and March-April 10:00-16:00, Nov-Feb 10:00-15:00; historical buildings generally open 11:00-15:00, June-Aug some until 19:00, most closed in winter. Check their excellent website for "What's Happening at Skansen" during your visit (www.skansen.se) or call 08/442-8000 (press 1

Stockholm's Djurgården

for a live operator). Gröna Lund, Stockholm's amusement park, is across the street (described later).

Music: Skansen does great music in summer, but mostly in the evenings (if you're here for an evening visit before or after your cruise, ask about the schedule as you enter).

Aquarium: Admission to the aquarium is the only thing not covered on your Skansen ticket, but it is covered by the Stockholm Card (100 kr; June-

Aug daily 10:00-20:00; Sept-May Tue-Sun 10:00-16:30, closed Mon; tel. 08/660-1082, www.skansen-akvariet.se).

Visiting Skansen: Skansen was the first in what became a Europe-wide movement to preserve traditional architecture in open-air museums. Other languages have even borrowed the Swedish term "Skansen" (which originally meant "the Fort") to describe an "open-air museum." Today, tourists still explore this Swedish-culture-on-a-lazy-Susan, seeing folk crafts in action and wonderfully furnished old interiors. While it's lively June through August before about 17:00, at other times of the year it can seem pretty dead; consider skipping it if you're here off-season.

In "Old Stockholm" (top of the escalator), shoemakers, potters, and glassblowers are busy doing their traditional thing (daily 10:00-17:00) in a re-created Old World Stockholm. The rest of Sweden spreads out from Old Stockholm. Northern Swedish culture and architecture is in the north (top of park map), and southern Sweden's in the south (bottom of map).

Take advantage of the free map, and consider the 50-kr museum guidebook. With the book, you'll understand each building you duck into and even learn about the Nordic animals awaiting you in the zoo. Check the live crafts schedule at the information stand by the main entrance beneath the escalator to make a smart Skansen plan. Guides throughout the park are happy to answer your questions—but only if you ask them. The old houses come alive when you take the initiative to get information.

Kids love Skansen, where they can ride a life-size wooden *Dala*-horse and stare down a hedgehog, visit Lill' Skansen (a children's zoo), and take a mini-train or pony ride.

Eating at Skansen: The most memorable meals are at the small folk food court on the main square, **Bollnastorget.** Here, among the duck-filled lakes, frolicking families, and peacenik local toddlers who don't bump on the bumper cars, kiosks dish up "Sami slow food" (smoked reindeer), waffles, hot dogs, and more. There are lots of picnic benches—Skansen encourages **picnicking.** (A small grocery store is tucked away across the street and a bit to the left of the main entrance.) For a sit-down meal, three eateries share a building just up the hill inside the main entrance: Skansen's primary restaurant, **Solliden,** serves a big *smörgåsbord* lunch in a grand blue-and-white room (310 kr, June-Aug daily 12:00-16:00); **Tre Byttor Taverne** captures 18th-century pub ambience with an à la carte menu (June-Aug daily 12:00-21:00, shorter hours off-season); and the **Skansen Terrassen** cafeteria offers less-expensive self-service lunches with a view (90-kr daily specials; mid-June-mid-Aug daily 11:00-19:00, shorter hours off-season). Nearby, the old-time **Stora Gungan Krog,** right at the top of the escalator, is a cozy inn; their freshly baked cakes will tempt you (80-160-kr indoor or outdoor lunches—meat, fish, or veggie—with a salad-and-cracker bar, daily 10:00-22:00, until 15:00 in winter).

▲▲▲Vasa Museum (Vasamuseet)

Stockholm turned a titanic flop into one of Europe's great sightseeing attractions. The glamorous but unseaworthy warship *Vasa*—

top-heavy with an extra cannon deck—sank 40 minutes into her 1628 maiden voyage when a breeze caught the sails and blew her over. After 333 years at the bottom of Stockholm's harbor, she rose again from the deep with the help of marine archaeologists. Rediscovered in 1956 and raised in 1961, this Edsel of the sea is today the best-preserved ship of its age anywhere—housed since 1990 in a brilliant museum. The masts perched atop the roof—best seen from a distance—show the actual height of the ship.

Cost and Hours: 130 kr, includes video and tour; June-Aug daily 8:30-18:00; Sept-May daily 10:00-17:00, Wed until 20:00; Galärvarvet, Djurgården, tel. 08/5195-4800, www.vasamuseet.se.

Getting There: The *Vasa* is on the waterfront immediately behind the stately brick Nordic Museum (described below), a 10-minute walk from Skansen. Or you can take tram #7 from downtown. The museum also has a good café inside. To get from the Nordic Museum to the Vasa Museum, face the Nordic Museum and walk around to the right (going left takes you into a big dead-end parking lot).

Crowd-Beating Tips: The museum can have very long lines. But don't panic, as the lines generally move quickly. You likely won't wait more than 15-20 minutes, but extremely busy times can cause 30-minute delays (if it hits capacity, they have to stop admitting people for a while).

Planning Your Time: For a thorough visit, plan on spending at least an hour and a half: Watch the 17-minute video (which explains the modern-day excavation and preservation of the ship), take the free 25-minute tour (which generally focuses on the *Vasa*'s history)—in either order—then explore the boat and wander through the various exhibits. The **video** generally runs three times per hour; almost all showings are either in English or with English subtitles (check at the info desk). In summer, English **tours** run on the hour and at :30 past the hour; listen for the loudspeaker announcement, or check at the info desk; off-season (Sept-May), tours go only at :30 past each hour beginning at 9:30 (last tour departs at 16:30). Because each guide is given license to cover whatever he or she likes, no two tours are alike—if you're fascinated by the place, consider taking two different tours to pick up new details.

Background: The *Vasa*, while not quite the biggest ship in the world, had the most firepower, with two fearsome decks of cannons. The 500 carved wooden statues draping the ship—once painted in bright colors—are all symbolic of the king's power. The 10-foot lion on the magnificent prow is a reminder that Europe considered the Swedish King Gustavus Adolphus the "Lion from the North." With this great ship, Sweden was preparing to establish its empire and become more engaged in European power politics. Specifically, the Swedes (who already controlled much of today's Finland and Estonia) wanted to push south to dominate the whole of the Baltic Sea, in order to challenge their powerful rival, Poland.

Designed by a Dutch shipbuilder, the *Vasa* had 72 guns of the same size and type (a rarity on mix-and-match warships of the age), allowing maximum efficiency in reloading—since there was no need to keep track of different ammunition. Unfortunately, the king's unbending demands to build it high (172 feet tall) but skinny (less than 16 feet wide) made it extremely unstable; no amount of ballast could weigh the ship down enough to prevent it from tipping.

Visiting the Museum: Exhibits are situated on six levels around the grand hall, circling the ship itself. Most exhibits are on the entrance level (4). The lowest level (2) has displays about the shipyards where the *Vasa* was built; upstairs on level 5, you can walk through replicas of ship interiors (handy, since you can't enter the actual ship). All displays are well described in English. You'll learn about the ship's rules (bread can't be older than eight years), why it sank (heavy bread?), how it's preserved (the ship, not the bread), and so on. Best of all is the chance to do slow laps around the magnificent vessel at different levels. Now painstakingly restored, 95 percent of the *Vasa*'s wood is original (modern bits are the brighter and smoother planks).

▲▲Nordic Museum (Nordiska Museet)

Built to look like a Danish Renaissance palace, this museum offers a fascinating peek at 500 years of traditional Swedish lifestyles. It's arguably more informative than Skansen. Take time to let the excellent, included audioguide enliven the exhibits. Carl Milles' huge painted-wood statue of Gustav Vasa, father of modern Sweden, overlooks the main gallery.

Highlights are on the top two floors. The middle floor (level 3) holds the *Traditions* exhibit (showing and describing each old-time celebration of the Swedish year) and a section of exquisite table settings, and fancy fashions from the 18th through the 20th centuries. The top floor (level 4) has an extensive Sami (Lapp) collection, old furniture, and an exhibit showing Swedish living rooms over the last century; it provides an insightful look at today's Swedes, including an intimate peek at modern bedrooms (match photos of the owners with the various rooms).

Cost and Hours: 100 kr, free Wed after 17:00 Sept-May; daily 10:00-17:00, Wed until 20:00 Sept-May; Djurgårdsvägen 6-16, at Djurgårdsbron, tram #7 from downtown, tel. 08/5195-6000, www .nordiskamuseet.se.

Other Djurgården Sights

The long-rumored ABBA museum, backed by a former band member, is expected to open in 2013 on Djurgården. For the latest details, check www.abbathemuseum.com.

Gröna Lund—Stockholm's venerable and lowbrow Tivoli-type amusement park still packs in the local families and teens on cheap dates. It's a busy venue for local pop concerts.

Cost and Hours: 100 kr, May-Sept daily 12:00-23:00, closed off-season, www.gronalund.com.

▲Thielska Galleriet—If you liked the Larsson and Zorn art in the National Gallery, and/or if you're a fan of Norwegian artist Edvard Munch, this charming mansion on the water at the far end of the Djurgården park is worth the trip.

Cost and Hours: 100 kr, Tue-Sun 12:00-17:00, Thu until 20:00, closed Mon, bus #69—not #69K—from downtown, tel. 08/662-5884, www.thielska-galleriet.se.

▲Biking the Garden Island—In all of Stockholm, Djurgården is the natural place to enjoy a bike ride. There's a good and reasonably priced bike-rental place just over the bridge as you enter the island (see "Bike Rental" on page 252), and a world of park-like paths and lanes with harbor vistas to enjoy. Ask for a free map and route tips when you rent your bike. Figure about an hour to pedal around Djurgården's waterfront perimeter; it's mostly flat, though the stretches that take you up and over the middle of the island can be temporarily steep. A garden café at the eastern tip of the island offers a scenic break midway through your pedal. For a longer ride, you can cross the canal to the Ladugårdsgärdet peninsula ("Gärdet" for short), a swanky, wooded residential district just to the north.

Outer Stockholm

▲Millesgården—The villa and garden of Carl Milles is a veritable forest of statues by Sweden's greatest sculptor. Millesgården is dramatically situated on a bluff overlooking the harbor in Stockholm's upper-class suburb of Lidingö. While the art is engaging and enjoyable, even the curators have little to say about it from an interpretation point of

view—so your visit is basically without guidance. But in Milles' house, which dates from the 1920s, you can see his north-lit studio and get a sense of his creative genius.

Carl Milles spent much of his career living in Michigan. But he's buried here at his villa, where he lived and worked for 20 years, lovingly designing this sculpture garden for the public. Milles wanted his art to be displayed on pedestals...to be seen "as if silhouettes against the sky." His subjects—often Greek mythological figures such as Pegasus or Poseidon—stand out as if the sky was a blank paper. Yet unlike silhouettes, Milles' images can be enjoyed from many angles. And Milles liked to enliven his sculptures by incorporating water features into his figures. *Hand of God*, perhaps his most famous work, gives insight into Milles' belief that when the artist created, he was—in a way—divinely inspired.

Cost and Hours: 100 kr, 30-kr or 75-kr English booklet explains the art; May-Sept daily 11:00-17:00; Oct-April Tue-Sun 11:00-17:00, closed Mon; restaurant and café, tel. 08/446-7590, www.millesgarden.se.

Getting There: Catch the T-bana to Ropsten, then take bus #207 to within a five-minute walk of the museum (allow about 45 minutes total each way).

▲▲**Drottningholm Palace (Drottningholms Slott)**—The queen's 17th-century summer castle and current royal residence has been called "Sweden's Versailles." Touring the palace, you'll see art that makes the point that Sweden's royalty is divine and belongs with the gods. You can walk the two floors on your own, but with no explanations or audioguides, it makes sense to take the included guided tour.

Cost and Hours: 100 kr, May-Aug daily 10:00-16:30, Sept daily 11:00-15:30, Oct and April Fri-Sun only 11:00-15:30, Nov-Dec and mid-Jan-March Sat-Sun only 12:00-15:30, closed last two weeks of Dec; free-with-admission palace tours in English are offered June-Aug usually at 10:00, 12:00, 14:00, and 16:00; fewer tours off-season; tel. 08/402-6280, www.royalcourt.se.

Services: There is no WC in the palace. The closest WC is a three-minute walk from the entrance, near the café and boat dock. The café serves light meals, and taxis usually wait nearby.

Getting There: Reach the palace via a relaxing one-hour boat ride (120 kr one-way, 175 kr round-trip, 130 kr round-trip with Stockholm Card, departs from Stadhusbron across from City Hall on the hour through the day, tel. 08/1200-4000), or take the T-bana to Brommaplan, where you can catch any #300-series bus

to Drottningholm (54 kr one-way, allow 30-45 minutes from city center). Consider approaching by water (as the royals traditionally did) and then returning by bus and T-bana (as a commoner).

Visiting the Palace: You'll see two floors of lavish rooms, where Sweden's royalty did their best to live in the style of Europe's divine monarchs. While rarely absolute rulers, Sweden's royals long struggled with stubborn parliaments. Perhaps this made the propaganda value of the palace decor even more important. Portraits and busts legitimize the royal family by connecting the Swedish blue bloods with Roman emperors, medieval kings, and Europe's great royal families. The portraits you'll see of France's Louis XVI and Russia's Catherine the Great are reminders that Sweden's royalty was related to or tightly networked with the European dynasties.

The king's bedroom looks like (and was) more of a theater than a place for sleeping. In the style of the French monarchs, this is where the ceremonial tucking-in and dressing of the king would take place. The Room of War—with kings, generals, battle scenes, and bugle-like candleholders—is from the time when Sweden was a superpower (1600-1750). The murals commemorate a victory over the Danes: It's said Swedish kings enjoyed taking the Danish ambassador here.

Of course, today's monarchs are figureheads ruled by a constitution. The royal family makes a point to be accessible and as "normal" as royalty can be. King Carl XVI Gustaf (b. 1946)—whose main job is handing out Nobel Prizes once a year—is a car nut who talks openly about his dyslexia. He was the first Swedish king not to be crowned "by the grace of God." The popular Queen Silvia is a businessman's daughter. At their 1976 wedding festivities, she was serenaded by ABBA singing "Dancing Queen." Their daughter and heir to the throne, Crown Princess Victoria, studied political science at Yale and interned with Sweden's European Union delegation. In 2010 she married gym owner Daniel Westling—the first royal wedding in Sweden since her parents' marriage. Victoria and Daniel's first child, Princess Estelle, was born on February 23, 2012—and instantly became the next heir to the throne.

Drottningholm Court Theater (Drottningholms Slotts-teater): This 18th-century theater somehow survived the ages—complete with its instruments, sound-effects machines, and stage sets. It's one of two such theaters remaining in Europe (the other is in Český Krumlov, Czech Republic). Visit it on a 30-minute guided tour, offered at the top of the hour (90 kr, May-Aug 10:00-17:00, Sept 11:00-15:30, no tours off-season, tel. 08/759-0406), or check their schedule for the rare opportunity to see perfectly authentic operas (about 25 performances each summer). Tickets for this popular time-travel musical and theatrical experience cost 275-895 kr and go on sale each March; purchase online or by phone or fax (see www.dtm.se).

Sigtuna—This town, an old-time lakeside jumble of wooden houses and waffle shops, presents a fluffy, stereotyped version of Sweden in the olden days. You'll see a medieval lane lined with colorful tourist boutiques, cafés, a romantic park, waterfront promenade, old town hall, and rune stones. The TI can help you get oriented (tel. 08/5948-0650, http://sal.sigtuna.se/turism). It's probably not worth the tedious one-hour trip out (take the *pendeltåg* suburban train from Stockholm to Märsta and then change to bus #570).

▲▲▲Archipelago (Skärgården)—Some of Europe's most scenic islands (thousands of them) stretch 80 miles from Stockholm out to the open Baltic Sea. Best of all, you'll automatically get a good dose of this island beauty as you cruise into and out of Stockholm.

Shopping in Stockholm

Sweden offers a world of shopping temptations. **Nordiska Kompaniet** (NK, short for "no kronor left"), Stockholm's top-end department store, is located in an elegant early 20th-century building that dominates the far end of Kungsträdgården. If it feels like an old-time American department store, that's because its architect was inspired by grand stores he'd seen in the US (circa 1910). The Swedish design section (downstairs) and the kitchenware section are particularly impressive.

The classy **Gallerian** mall is just up the street from NK and stretches seductively nearly to Sergels Torg. The Åhléns store, nearby at Sergels Torg, is less expensive than NK and has two cafeterias and a supermarket. Fashion-forward **H&M** is right across the street. Drottninggatan is a long pedestrian boulevard lined with shops.

Designtorget, a store dedicated to contemporary Swedish design, receives a commission for selling the unique works of local designers (Mon-Fri 10:00-19:00, Sat 10:00-18:00, Sun 11:00-

17:00, underneath Sergels Torg—enter from basement level of Kulturhuset, tel. 08/219-150, www.designtorget.se).

For more on Swedish design, pick up the *Design Guide* flier at the TI (listing smaller stores throughout town with a flair for design). The trendy and exclusive shops (including Orrefors and Kosta) line Biblioteksgatan just off Stureplan.

Traditionally, stores are open weekdays 10:00-18:00, Saturdays until 17:00, and Sundays 11:00-16:00. Some of the bigger stores (such as NK, H&M, and Åhléns) are open later on Saturdays and Sundays.

When Swedes want the latest fashions by local designers, they skip the downtown malls and head for funky Södermalm. The main drag that leads from Slussen up to this neighborhood, **Götgatan,** is a particularly good choice, with shop after shop of Swedish (not international) designers. Local boutiques along here include Weekday jeans, Filippa K, J.Lindeberg, Tiogruppen, and others. For more on this area, see page 293 in "Eating in Stockholm."

For a *smörgåsbord* of Scanjunk, visit the **Loppmarknaden,** northern Europe's biggest flea market, at the planned suburb of Skärholmen (free entry weekdays and Sat-Sun after 15:00, 15 kr on weekends—when it's busiest; open Mon-Fri 11:00-18:00, Sat 10:00-16:00, Sun 11:00-16:00; T-bana: Varberg—on line #13—is just steps from the shopping action, tel. 08/710-0060, www.lopp marknaden.se). Hötorget, the produce market, also hosts a Sunday flea market in summer (see page 266).

Stockholms Stadsmission's secondhand shop in Gamla Stan is a great place to pick up an unusual gift and contribute to this worthwhile charity (near Stortorget at Trångsund 8, Mon-Fri 10:00-18:00, Sat 11:00-16:00, Sun 12:00-16:00, tel. 08/787-8682, www.stadsmissionen.se/secondhand).

Systembolaget is Sweden's state-run liquor store chain. A sample of each bottle of wine or liquor sits in a display case. A card in front explains how it tastes and suggests menu pairings. Look for the item number and order at the counter. There's a branch in Gamla Stan at Lilla Nygatan 18, in Hötorget underneath the movie theater complex, and in Norrmalm at Vasagatan 21 (Mon-Wed 10:00-18:00, Thu-Fri 10:00-19:00, Sat 10:00-15:00, closed Sun, www.systembolaget.se).

Eating in Stockholm

While most of the restaurants listed here are lunch places, I've also included a few dinner options in case you're spending a night here before or after your cruise.

Swedish Cuisine

Most people don't travel to Sweden for the food—I used to call it Wonder Bready. Though potatoes and heavy sauces are a focus of Sweden's cuisine, its variety of meat and fish dishes can be surprisingly satisfying. If you don't think you'll like Swedish or Scandinavian food, be sure to splurge at a good-quality place before you pass final judgment.

Every region of Sweden serves different specialties, but you'll always find *svenska köttbullar* on the menu (Swedish meatballs made from beef and pork in a creamy sauce). This Swedish favorite is topped with lingonberry jam, which is served with many meat dishes across Scandinavia. Potatoes, seemingly the only vegetable known to Sweden, make for hearty *kroppkakor* dumplings filled with onions and minced meat. The northern variation, *pitepalt,* is filled with pork. Southern Sweden takes credit for *pytt i panna,* a medley of leftover meat and diced potatoes that's fried and served with an egg yolk on top. And it seems that virtually every meal you'll eat here includes a side of boiled, small new potatoes.

Though your meals will never be short on starch, be sure to try Sweden's most popular baked good, *kanelbulle,* for a not-so-light snack during the day. This pastry resembles a cinnamon roll, but it's made with cardamom and topped with pearl sugar. Enjoy one during *fika,* the daily Swedish coffee break so institutionalized that many locals use the term as a verb (see page 292).

Like those of its Nordic neighbors, Sweden's extensive coastline produces some of the best seafood in the world. A light, tasty appetizer is *gravad lax,* a dill-cured salmon on brown bread or crackers. You'll also likely encounter *Toast Skagen.* This appetizer-spread is made from shrimp, dill, mayonnaise, and Dijon mustard, and eaten on buttered toast.

For a main course, the most popular seafood dish is crayfish. Though only eaten by the aristocracy in the 16th century, these shellfish have since become a nationwide delicacy; they're cooked in brine with dill and eaten cold as a finger food. Traditional crayfish parties take place outdoors on summer evenings, particularly in August. Friends and family gather around to indulge in this specialty with rye bread and a strong cheese. The Swedes also love Baltic herring; try *stekt strömming,* a specialty of the east coast, which is herring fried with butter and parsley. As usual, it's served with potatoes and lingonberry jam. Adventurous diners can have their herring pickled or fermented—or order more unusual dishes like reindeer.

As for beer, the Swedes classify theirs by alcohol content. The higher the number, the higher the alcohol content—and the higher the price. *Klass 1* is light beer—very low-alcohol. *Klass 2* is stronger, but still mild. And *Klass 3* has the most body, the most alcohol, and the highest price.

Budget Tips: At lunch, cafés and restaurants have 95-kr daily special plates called *dagens rätt* (generally Mon-Fri only). Most museums have handy cafés (with lots of turnover and therefore fresh food, 100-kr lunch deals, and often with fine views). Convenience stores serve gas station-style food (and often have seats). As anywhere, department stores and malls are eager to feed shoppers and can be a good, efficient choice. If you want culturally appropriate fast food, stop by a local hot dog stand. Picnics are a great option. There are plenty of park-like, harborside spots to give your cheap picnic some class.

In Gamla Stan

Most restaurants in Gamla Stan serve the 95-kr weekday lunch special mentioned above, which comes with a main dish, small

salad, bread, and free tap water. Choose from Swedish, Asian, or Italian cuisine. Several popular places are right on the main square (Stortorget) and near the cathedral. Järntorget, at the far end, is another fun tables-in-the-square scene and has a small Co-op Nära supermarket for picnic shopping. The Munkbrohallen supermarket downstairs in the Gamla Stan T-bana station is very picnic-friendly (daily 7:00-22:00). Touristy places line Västerlånggatan. You'll find more romantic spots hiding on side lanes. I've listed my favorites below (for locations, see the map on following page).

Grillska Huset is a cheap and handy cafeteria run by Stockholms Stadsmission, a charitable organization helping the poor. It's grandly situated right on the old square, with indoor and outdoor seating (tranquil garden up the stairs and out back), fine daily specials, a hearty salad bar, and a staff committed to helping others. You can feed the hungry (that's you) and help house the homeless at the same time. The 85-kr daily special gets you a hot plate, salad, and coffee, or choose the 85-kr salad bar—both available Mon-Fri 11:00-14:00 (café serves sandwiches and salads daily 10:00-18:00, Stortorget 3, tel. 08/787-8605). They also have a fine little bakery.

Vapiano Pasta Pizza Bar, a mod, high-energy Italian place, issues you an electronic card as you enter. Circulate, ordering up whatever you like as they swipe your card. It's fun to oversee the construction of your 100-kr pasta, pizza, or salad. Portions are huge and easily splittable. As you leave, your card indicates the bill. Season things by picking a leaf of basil or rosemary from the potted plant on your table. Because tables are often shared, this a great

STOCKHOLM

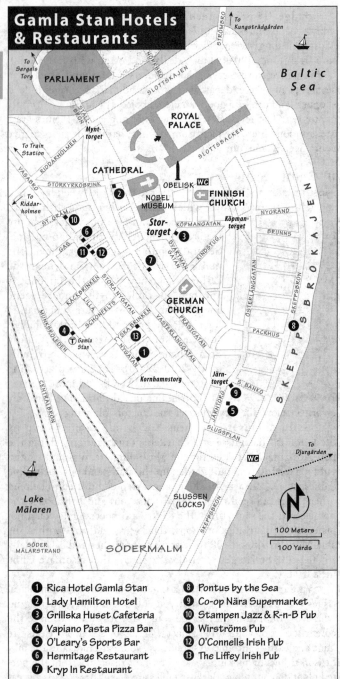

Gamla Stan Hotels & Restaurants

To Kungsträdgården

To Sergels Torg

PARLIAMENT

Baltic Sea

ROYAL PALACE

Mynt-torget

To Train Station

RIDDARHOLMEN

CATHEDRAL

STORKYRKOBRINK

To Riddar-holmen

ST. GRÅM.

NOBEL MUSEUM

OBELISK

WC

FINNISH CHURCH

Stor-torget

KÖPMANGATAN

Köpman-torget

NYGRÄND

BRUNNS

GAS.

Stora Nygatan

SVARTMAN GATAN

KINDSTUG.

GERMAN CHURCH

ÖSTERLÅNGGATAN

SKEPPSBRON

KÄCKBRINKEN

LILLA NYGATAN

SCHÖNFELTS

PRÄSTGATAN

VÄSTERLÅNGGATAN

PACKHUS

MUNKBROLEDEN

T Gamla Stan

TYSKABRINKEN

NYGATAN

Kornhamnstorg

Järn-torget

S. BANKO

JÄRNTORG.

SLUSSPLAN

CENTRALBRON

WC

To Djurgården

Lake Mälaren

SLUSSEN (LOCKS)

SKEPPSBRON

N

100 Meters
100 Yards

SÖDER MÄLARSTRAND

SÖDERMALM

❶ Rica Hotel Gamla Stan
❷ Lady Hamilton Hotel
❸ Grillska Huset Cafeteria
❹ Vapiano Pasta Pizza Bar
❺ O'Leary's Sports Bar
❻ Hermitage Restaurant
❼ Kryp In Restaurant
❽ Pontus by the Sea
❾ Co-op Nära Supermarket
❿ Stampen Jazz & R-n-B Pub
⓫ Wirströms Pub
⓬ O'Connells Irish Pub
⓭ The Liffey Irish Pub

place for solo travelers. They have Pilsner Urquell on tap but watch out—my glass of Chianti cost more than my pizza (daily 11:00-24:00, Fri-Sat until 1:00 in the morning, right next to entrance to Gamla Stan T-bana station, Munkbrogatan 8, tel. 08/222-940). They also have locations on Östermalm (facing Humlegården park at Sturegatan 12) and Norrmalm (between the train station and Kungsholmen at Kungsbron 15)—for these locations, see the map on page 295.

O'Leary's Sports Bar is a sudsy place that transports you to Ireland. While sloppy, it's good for basic pub grub and beer. And if a game is on, this is the place to be—their motto is, "Better than live" (120-kr meals, Järntorgsgatan 3, tel. 08/239-923).

Hermitage Restaurant serves tasty vegetarian food in a warm communal dining setting. Their daily special (100-kr lunch, 110-kr dinner after 15:00) buys a hot plate, salad, bread, and coffee (Mon-Fri 11:00-20:00, Sat-Sun 12:00-20:00, Stora Nygatan 11, tel. 08/411-9500).

Kryp In, a small, cozy restaurant (the name means "hide away") tucked into a peaceful lane, has a stylish hardwood and candlelit interior, great sidewalk seating, and an open kitchen letting you in on Vladimir's artistry. If you dine well in Stockholm once (or twice), I'd do it here. It's gourmet without pretense. They serve delicious, modern Swedish cuisine with a 445-kr three-course dinner. From June to August, they have weekend lunch specials starting at 120 kr (200-250-kr plates, Mon-Fri 17:00-23:00, Sat 12:30-23:00, open Sun in summer only 12:30-22:00, a block off Stortorget at Prästgatan 17, tel. 08/208-841).

Harborview Dining in Gamla Stan and Östermalm

Pontus by the Sea is a classy restaurant with a long, covered, and heated veranda offering grand harbor views. Pontus is well-respected for its modern mix of French and Swedish cuisine. Half the place is a sofas-on-the-harbor cocktail lounge. Though the restaurant is pricey, their bar menu offers some deals. Call to reserve a harborside table (daily 12:00-24:00, off-season closed Sun, Tullhus 2, tel. 08/202-095).

Djurgårdsbrons Sjöcafe, beautifully situated and greedily soaking up the afternoon sun, fills a woody terrace stretching along the harbor just over the Djurgårdsbron bridge. In summer, this is a fine place for a meal or just a drink before or after your Skansen or *Vasa* visit. They have cheap lunch plates (90 kr, Mon-Fri 11:00-13:00 only); at other times, you'll pay 130-180 kr per plate (order at the bar, daily 11:00-22:00, closed off-season, behind the bike-rental hut, tel. 08/661-4488). For the location, see the map on page 279.

Fika: Sweden's Coffee Break

Swedes drink more coffee per capita than just about any other country in the world. The Swedish coffee break—or *fika*—is a ritual. *Fika* is to Sweden what teatime is to Britain. The typical *fika* is a morning or afternoon break in the workday, but can happen any time, any day. It's the perfect opportunity (and excuse) for tourists to take a break as well.

Fika-fare is coffee with a snack—something sweet or savory. Your best bet is a *kanel-bulle*, a Swedish cinnamon bun, although some prefer *pariser-bulle*, a bun filled with vanilla cream. These can be found nearly everywhere coffee is sold, including just about any café or *konditori* (bakery) in Stockholm. A coffee and a cinnamon bun in a café will cost you about 40 kr. (Most cafés will give you a coffee refill for free.) But at Pressbyrån, the Swedish convenience stores found all over town, you can satisfy your *fika*-fix for 25 kr by getting a coffee and bun to go. Grab a park bench or waterside perch, relax, and enjoy.

In Kungsholmen: Lakefront Behind City Hall

On a balmy summer's eve, **Mälarpaviljongen** is a dreamy spot with hundreds of locals enjoying the perfect lakefront scene, as trendy glasses of rosé shine like convivial lanterns. From City Hall, walk 15 minutes along Lake Mälaren (a treat in itself) and you'll find a hundred casual outdoor tables on a floating restaurant and among the trees on shore. Line up at the cafeteria to order a drink, snack, or complete meal. If it's cool, they have heaters and blankets. The walk along the lake back into town caps the experience beautifully (56-kr beer, 125-kr cocktails, 100-kr lunch plates, 150-200-kr evening plates, open in good weather April-Sept daily 11:00-late, easy lakeside walk or T-bana to Freedomsplace plus a 5-minute walk to Nörr Mälarstrand 63, no reservations, tel. 08/650-8701).

In Södermalm

Just south of Gamla Stan, the Södermalm district is the gritty, funky, proud-to-be-working-class part of town. It's the downscale antidote to the upscale, ritzy areas where most tourists spend their time (Norrmalm, Östermalm, Djurgården, and Gamla Stan). And it's recently in vogue, thanks to the Stieg Larsson's Millennium trilogy of novels, in which Lisbeth Salander and her cohorts represent the "real," hardscrabble Stockholm (all the villains come from the posh north side). While often referred to as "Stockholm's Brooklyn," this relatively sterile area lacks the loosey-goosey hipster charm of many such neighborhoods in the US and other parts of Europe, but it does have a nice variety of restaurants where locals outnumber tourists. Combine a meal here with a stroll through a side of Stockholm many visitors miss. The best areas are along Götgatan (described next) and the zone south of Folkungagatan street—nicknamed "SoFo."

Götgatan: This main drag, leading from Slussen (where Södermalm meets Gamla Stan) steeply up into the heart of Södermalm, is the neighborhood's liveliest artery. Here, mixed between the boutiques, you'll find cafés tempting you to join the Swedish coffee break called *fika*, plus plenty of other eateries. Even if you don't dine in Södermalm, it's worth a stroll here just for the window-shopping fun. At the top you'll pop out into the big square called Medborgarplasten, filled with outdoor restaurant and café tables and fronted by a big food hall. (There's also a T-bana stop here.) The recommended Kvarnen beer hall (see next) is just around the corner to the left. The big white sphere on the horizon is the Ericsson Globe, a hockey arena.

Classic Swedish Beer Halls: Two different but equally traditional Södermalm beer halls serve well-executed, hearty Swedish grub in big, high-ceilinged, orange-tiled spaces with rustic wooden tables. While both could use a bit more personality, the food is good and the ambience is lively. **Kvarnen** ("The Mill") is a reliable choice that recently enjoyed its 15 minutes of fame as a setting for the Millennium novels (90-120-kr starters, 125-165-kr main dishes, Mon-Fri 11:00-24:00, Sat 12:00-24:00, Sun 12:00-23:00, 87-kr lunch special available Mon-Fri 11:00-14:00, Tjärhovsgatan 4, tel. 08/643-0380). **Pelikan** is an old-school beer hall in a trendy neighborhood a bit deeper into Södermalm (90-125-kr starters, 190-260-kr main dishes, Mon-Thu 16:00-23:00, Fri-Sun 13:00-23:00, Blekingegatan 40, tel. 08/5560-9092).

Nytorget Urban Deli is the epitome of Södermalm's trendy-hipster vibe. It's half fancy artisanal delicatessen—with all manner of ingredients—and half eatery, with indoor and outdoor tables filled with Stockholm yuppies eating well (90-170-kr light meals, 190-225-kr bigger meals, Sun-Tue 8:00-23:00, Wed-Thu 8:00-24:00, Fri-Sat 8:00-1:00 in the morning, Nytorget 4, tel. 08/5990-9180).

On Norrmalm

Royal *Smörgåsbord* at the Grand Hotel

To stuff yourself with all the traditional Swedish specialties (a dozen kinds of herring, salmon, reindeer, meatballs, lingonberries,

STOCKHOLM

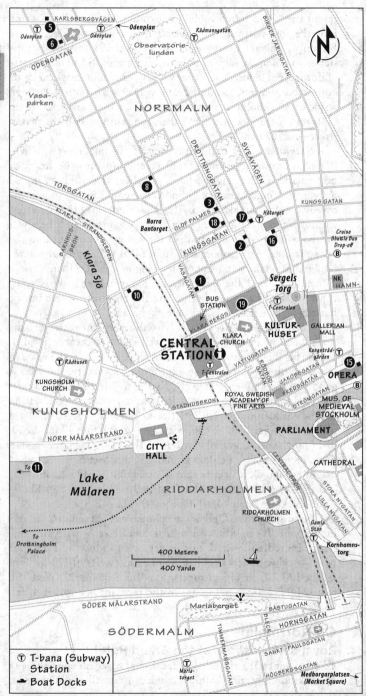

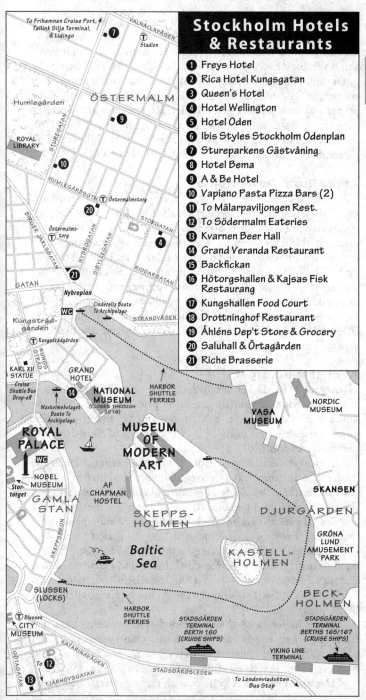

Stockholm Hotels & Restaurants

1. Freys Hotel
2. Rica Hotel Kungsgatan
3. Queen's Hotel
4. Hotel Wellington
5. Hotel Oden
6. Ibis Styles Stockholm Odenplan
7. Stureparkens Gästvåning
8. Hotel Bema
9. A & Be Hotel
10. Vapiano Pasta Pizza Bars (2)
11. To Mälarpaviljongen Rest.
12. To Södermalm Eateries
13. Kvarnen Beer Hall
14. Grand Veranda Restaurant
15. Backfickan
16. Hötorgshallen & Kajsas Fisk Restaurang
17. Kungshallen Food Court
18. Drottninghof Restaurant
19. Åhléns Dep't Store & Grocery
20. Saluhall & Örtagården
21. Riche Brasserie

and shrimp, followed by a fine table of cheeses and desserts) with a super harbor view, consider splurging at the Grand Hotel's dressy **Grand Veranda Restaurant.** While very touristy and a bit tired, this is the finest *smörgåsbord* in town. The Grand Hotel, where royal guests and Nobel Prize winners stay, faces the harbor across from the palace. Pick up their English flier for a good explanation of the proper way to enjoy this grand buffet. Reservations are necessary (425 kr, tap water is free, other drinks extra, nightly 18:00-22:00, Sat-Sun also 13:00-16:00, May-Sept also Mon-Fri 12:00-15:00, no shorts, Södra Blasieholmshamnen 8, tel. 08/679-3586).

At the Royal Opera House

The Operakällaren, one of Stockholm's most exclusive restaurants, runs a little "hip pocket" restaurant called **Backfickan** on the side, specializing in traditional Swedish quality cooking at reasonable prices. It's ideal for someone eating out alone, or for anyone wanting an early dinner (they serve daily specials from 12:00 all the way up to 20:00). Sit inside—at tiny private side tables or at the big counter with the locals—or, in good weather, grab a table on the sidewalk. Choose from two different daily specials (about 150-200 kr), or pay 200-250 kr for main dishes from their regular menu (Mon-Sat 12:00-22:00, closed Sun, on the inland side of Royal Opera House, tel. 08/676-5809).

At or near Hötorget

Hötorget ("Hay Market"), a vibrant outdoor produce market just two blocks from Sergels Torg, is a fun place to picnic-shop. The outdoor market closes at 18:00, and many merchants put their unsold produce on the push list (earlier closing and more desperate merchants on Sat).

Hötorgshallen, next to Hötorget (in the basement under the modern cinema complex), is a colorful indoor food market with an old-fashioned bustle, plenty of exotic and ethnic edibles, and—in the tradition of food markets all over Europe—some great little eateries. The best is **Kajsas Fisk Restaurang,** hiding behind the fish stalls. They serve delicious fish soup to little Olivers who can hardly believe they're getting...more. For 85 kr, you get a big bowl of hearty soup, a simple salad, bread and crackers, butter, and water—plus one soup refill (100-kr daily fish specials, Mon-Fri 11:00-18:00, Sat 11:00-16:00, closed Sun, Hötorgshallen 3, tel. 08/207-262).

Kungshallen, an 800-seat indoor food court across the street from Hötorget, has 14 eateries—mostly chain restaurants and fast-food counters, including Chinese, sushi, pizza, Greek, and Mexican (Mon-Fri 9:00-23:00, Sat-Sun 12:00-23:00).

Drottninghof is a busy place with tables perfectly positioned

What If I Miss My Boat?

Remember that you can get help from the cruise line's port agent (listed on the destination information sheet distributed on the ship) and the local TI (see page 251). If the port agent suggests a costly solution (such as a private car with a driver), you may want to consider public transit.

Many cruise port cities are accessible by train from Stockholm, including **Oslo** and **Copenhagen** (via Malmö; buses also connect to Oslo and Copenhagen); for points south (such as **Warnemünde/Berlin, Amsterdam,** and **Gdańsk**), you'll probably have to go via Copenhagen. For points in Norway (such as **Bergen, Stavanger,** or **Flåm**), you'll take the train to Oslo and connect from there.

Stockholm is a hub for overnight boats on the Baltic. From here, you can sail overnight to **Helsinki** (two companies: Viking Line, tel. 08/452-4000, www.vikingline.fi; or Tallink Silja, tel. 08/222-140, www.tallinksilja.com), to **Tallinn** (Tallink Sijla), to **Rīga** (Tallink Sijla), and—in two nights—to **St. Petersburg** (St. Peter Line, www.stpeterline.com). It's faster to reach St. Petersburg by taking the night boat first to Helsinki, then hopping on the express train (www.vr.fi). But remember that you'll need a visa to enter Russia (arranged well in advance of your trip, not possible at the last minute); if you don't have one, you'll likely need to meet your ship at a later port of call.

You may find it's faster to **fly** to many places. Stockholm's Arlanda Airport is an easy train ride from downtown (tel. 08/797-6000, www.arlanda.se); for more on the airport, see "Starting or Ending Your Cruise in Stockholm" on page 298.

For more advice on what to do if you miss the boat, see page 144.

for people-watching on the busy pedestrian boulevard (good-value 159-kr dinner specials, hearty 150-250-kr plates, Mon-Thu 11:00-24:00, Fri-Sat 11:00-1:00 in the morning, Sun 12:00-23:00, Drottninggatan 67, tel. 08/227-522).

Near Sergels Torg

The many modern shopping malls and department stores around Sergels Torg all have appealing, if pricey, eateries catering to the needs of hungry local shoppers. Åhléns department store has a Hemköp supermarket in the basement (Mon-Fri 8:00-21:00, Sat-Sun 10:00-21:00) and two restaurants upstairs with 80-110-kr daily lunch specials (Mon-Fri 11:00-19:30, Sat 11:00-18:30, Sun 11:00-17:30).

In Östermalm

Saluhall, on Östermalmstorg square (near recommended Hotel Wellington), is a great old-time indoor market with top-quality artisanal producers and a variety of sit-down and take-out eateries. While it's nowhere near "cheap," it's one of the most pleasant market halls I've seen, oozing with upscale yet traditional Swedish  class (Mon-Thu 9:30-18:00, Fri until 17:30, Sat until 16:00, closed Sun).

Örtagården, upstairs from the Saluhall, is primarily a vegetarian restaurant and serves a 99-kr buffet weekdays until 17:00 and a larger 129-kr buffet evenings and weekends (Mon-Fri 10:30-22:00, Sat-Sun 11:00-21:00, entrance on side of market building at Nybrogatan 31, tel. 08/662-1728).

Riche, a Parisian-style brasserie just a few steps off Nybroplan at Östermalm's waterfront, serves up pricey but elegantly executed Swedish and international dishes. The seating is tight—either in the winter garden, the bright dining room, or the white-tile-and-wine-glass-chandeliered bar—and it's a high-energy environment (125-225-kr starters, 200-300-kr main dishes, Mon-Fri 7:30-24:00, Sat-Sun 12:00-24:00, Birger Jarlsgatan 4, tel. 08/5450-3560).

Starting or Ending Your Cruise in Stockholm

If your cruise begins and/or ends in Stockholm, you'll want some extra time here. While you can squeeze the city into a day, two days will let you see more. For a longer visit, pick up my *Rick Steves' Snapshot Stockholm* or *Rick Steves' Scandinavia* guidebooks.

Of Stockholm's two cruise ports, **Frihamnen** is primarily used by cruises that are beginning or ending in the city.

Airport Connections

Stockholm's Arlanda Airport

Stockholm's Arlanda Airport is 28 miles north of town (airport code: ARN, tel. 08/797-6000, www.arlanda.se). The airport TI (in Terminal 5, where most international flights arrive, staffed daily 6:00-24:00) can advise you on getting into Stockholm and on your sightseeing plans.

Getting Downtown from Arlanda Airport

The **airport shuttle train**, the Arlanda Express, is the fastest way to zip between the airport and the central train station—but it's not cheap (260 kr one-way, 490 kr round-trip, kids under 17 free with adult, covered by railpass; generally 4/hour—departing at :05, :20, :35, and :50 past the hour in each direction; even more frequent midday, 20-minute trip, has its own dedicated train station platform—follow signs to *Arlanda*, toll-free tel. 020-222-224, www.arlandaexpress.com). Buy your ticket either at the window near the track or from a ticket-vending machine, or pay an extra 50 kr to buy it on board. In summer and on weekends, a special fare lets two people travel for nearly half-price (two for 280 kr one-way, available daily mid-June-Aug, Sat-Sun year-round).

Airport shuttle buses (Flygbussarna) run between the airport and Stockholm's train/bus stations (99 kr, 6/hour, 40 minutes, may take longer at rush hour, buy tickets from station kiosks or at airport TI, www.flygbussarna.se).

Taxis between the airport and the city center or cruise port take about 30-40 minutes (about 520 kr, depends on company, look for price posted in back window). On weekdays outside of summer, two people pay about the same for a taxi as for the train. Establish the price first. Reputable taxis accept credit cards.

The **cheapest airport connection** is to take bus #583 from the airport to Märsta, then switch to the *pendeltåg* (suburban train, 4/hour), which goes to Stockholm's central train station (72 kr, 1 hour total journey time, covered by Stockholm Card).

Arriving in Downtown Stockholm: Stockholm's adjacent train (Centralstation) and bus (Cityterminalen) stations, at the southwestern edge of Norrmalm, are a hive of services, shops, exchange desks, and people on the move. Underground is the T-Centralen subway (T-bana) station, and taxi stands are outside. Stockholm is building a new commuter rail line right beneath the T-Centralen station—expect lots of construction until at least 2014.

Getting from the Airport or Downtown to Frihamnen Cruise Port

When meeting your cruise, it helps to know which berth your ship leaves from—berth 650, 634, or 638. As Frihamnen is a sprawling area, knowing this will help you find your ship faster.

The easiest but most expensive way to reach your cruise ship is by **taxi**—figure about 520 kr from the airport to Frihamnen, or around 200-250 kr from downtown.

Public transportation is workable (and often cheaper), but there's no direct connection from the airport. First make your way downtown using one of the methods outlined above; then catch the bus to the port: Ride bus #1 from the train station (handy if you're catching the airport train) or bus #76 from various points downtown (including some close to my recommended hotels—see the list later). On weekends (when bus #76 runs infrequently or not at all), you'll likely need to take bus #1 regardless. For more on these buses, see page 249.

Arriving at Frihamnen: Near the cruise terminals, there are two stops: Both buses stop at "Frihamnen" (near berth 650), while bus #76 continues one more stop to "Magasin 3" (closer to berths 634 and 638).

If getting off at the "Frihamnen" stop, continue straight ahead along the street to the first intersection, where you'll bear right to reach berth 650 and left to reach berth 634 or 638 (walking along this road, you'll soon pass the "Magasin 3" stop mentioned next).

If you get off the bus at "Magasin 3," proceed straight until you reach the Frihamnsterminalen; turn right just before it and head out the long, wide pier—first passing berth 634, then berth 638. (Berth 638 and the cruise terminal is near warehouse, or *magasin*, #6 and #8.)

A blue line painted in the sidewalk leads to the ships—but confusingly, it leads to each of the three berths, so don't just march off—you may accidentally follow the wrong line.

Departing from Stockholm's Arlanda Airport

If your cruise ends in Stockholm, you can either take a taxi to the airport (figure about 520 kr), or make a roundabout connection via public transit: First take bus #1 to the train station (explained on page 249), then transfer to the airport shuttle train or bus explained earlier (under "Getting Downtown from Arlanda Airport").

Alternate Airport

Some discount airlines use Skavsta Airport, about 60 miles south of Stockholm (airport code: NYO, www.skavsta.se). Flygbussarna shuttle buses connect to the city (149 kr, timed to meet arriving flights, 80 minutes, www.flygbussarna.se).

Hotels in Stockholm

If you need a hotel in Stockholm before or after your cruise, here are a few to consider (see the maps on pages 290 and 294-295 for locations).

Peak season for Stockholm's hotels—weeknights outside of summer vacation time—is dictated by business travelers. Rates drop by 30-50 percent in the summer (mid-June-mid-Aug) and on Friday and Saturday nights year-round. Because many hotels set prices based on demand, rates listed in this section can have a wide range. If you ask for discounts and comparison-shop, you're likely to save plenty.

A program called **Destination Stockholm** is, for many (especially families), the best way to book a big hotel on weekends or during the summer. When you reserve a hotel room through this service, a Stockholm à la Carte card is thrown in for free. It covers public transportation, most major sights, and lots of tours—and is even better than the Stockholm Card. Kids sleep and get cards for free, too. The card is valid every day of your stay, including arrival and departure days. Reserve by phone or online; be sure to review the cancellation policy before you commit (tel. 08/663-0080, www.destination-stockholm.com).

Nightlife in Stockholm: The easiest choices are the bars and other live-music venues in Gamla Stan. The street called Stora Nygatan, with several lively bars, has perhaps the most accessible and reliable place for good jazz in town—**Stampen Jazz & Rhythm n' Blues Pub.** It has two venues: a stone-vaulted cellar below and a fun-loving saloon-like bar upstairs (check out the old instruments and antiques hanging from the ceiling). From Monday through Thursday, there's live music only in the saloon. On Friday and Saturday, bands alternate sets in both the saloon and the cellar (160-kr cover Fri-Sat only, 58-kr beers, open Mon-Sat 20:00-1:00 in the morning, even later Fri-Sat, free blues Mon-Thu, special free jam session Sat 14:00-18:00, closed Sun, Stora Nygatan 5, tel. 08/205-793, www.stampen.se). For the location, see the map on page 290. Several other lively spots are within a couple of blocks of Stampen on Stora Nygatan, including **Wirströms Pub** (live blues bands play in crowded cellar Tue-Sat 21:00-24:00, no cover, 62-kr beers, open daily 11:00-1:00 in the morning, Stora Nygatan 13, www.wirstromspub.se), **O'Connells Irish Pub** (a lively expat sports bar with music downstairs, daily 12:00-1:00 in the morning, Stora Nygatan 21, www.oconnells.se), and **The Liffey** (classic Irish pub with 160-200-kr pub grub, live music nightly at 21:30, daily in summer 11:00-late, off-season 16:00-late, Stora Nygatan 40-42, www.theliffey.se).

In Downtown Norrmalm, near the Train Station

$$$ Freys Hotel is a Scan-mod, four-star place, with 124 compact, smartly designed rooms on a quiet pedestrian street. While big, it works hard to be friendly and welcoming. It's well-situated, located on a dead-end street across from the central train station. Its cool, candlelit breakfast room becomes a bar in the evening, popular for its selection of Belgian microbrews (Sb-1,050-1,750 kr, Db-1,550-2,050 kr, Internet access, Bryggargatan 12, tel. 08/5062-1300, fax 08/5062-1313, www.freyshotels.com, freys@freyshotels.com).

Check their website for summer specials.

$$ Rica Hotel Kungsgatan, central but characterless, fills the top floors of a downsized department store with 270 rooms. If the Starship *Enterprise* had a low-end hotel, this would be it. Save 150-400 kr by taking a room with no windows—the same size as other rooms, extremely quiet, and well-ventilated. This is the rare hotel where you'll get the best price by booking online with a travel website—calling direct will get you a more expensive rate (Db-1,195-1,895 kr, Kungsgatan 47, tel. 08/723-7220, fax 08/723-7299, www.rica.se, rica@rica.no).

$$ Queen's Hotel enjoys a great location at the quiet top end of Stockholm's main pedestrian shopping street (about a 10-minute walk from the train station or Gamla Stan). The 52 well-priced rooms feel old-fashioned but have been renovated, and the plush Old World lounge is inviting. Three types of double rooms vary only in size (Sb-1,020-1,220 kr, "small standard" Db-1,120-1,320 kr, "large standard" Db-1,220-1,520 kr, "superior" Db with pull-out sofa bed-1,320-1,620 kr, 10 percent discount for readers who book direct—be sure to ask for it, extra bed-250 kr, elevator, free Internet access and Wi-Fi, Drottninggatan 71A, tel. 08/249-460, fax 08/217-620, www.queenshotel.se, info@queenshotel.se).

In Norrmalm and Östermalm, in Quieter Residential Areas

These options are in stately, elegant neighborhoods of five- and six-story turn-of-the-century apartment buildings. All are too long of a walk from the station with luggage, but still in easy reach of downtown sights and close to T-bana stops.

$$$ Hotel Wellington, two blocks off Östermalmstorg square, is in a less handy but charming part of town. It's modern and bright, with hardwood floors, 60 rooms, and a friendly welcome. While it may seem pricey, it's a cut above in comfort and its great amenities—such as a very generous buffet breakfast, free coffee all day long, and free buffet dinner in the evening—add up to a good value (prices range widely, but in summer generally Sb-1,220 kr, Db-1,420-1,620 kr, smaller Db for 200 kr less, fill out their Choice Card and save 5 percent, mention this book when reserving and you might save a little more, free Internet access and Wi-Fi, free sauna, old-fashioned English bar, garden terrace bar, T-bana: Östermalmstorg, exit to Storgatan and walk toward big church to Storgatan 6; tel. 08/667-0910, fax 08/667-1254, www.wellington.se, cc.wellington@choice.se).

$$ Hotel Oden, a recently renovated 140-room place with all the comforts, is three T-bana stops from the train station (Sb-960-1,410 kr, Db-1,240-1,750 kr, extra bed-160-190 kr, sauna, free Internet access and Wi-Fi, free coffee and tea in the evening; T-bana: Odenplan, exit in direction of Västmannagatan, Karlbergsvägen 24; tel. 08/457-9700, fax 08/457-9710, www .hoteloden.se). Some rooms come with a kitchenette for the same price (just request one).

$$ Ibis Styles Stockholm Odenplan, a half-block from Hotel Oden, rents 76 rooms on several floors of a late-19th-century apartment building (S-from 950 kr, Db-from 1,150 kr, lower in summer if you book two months in advance, T-bana: Odenplan, Västmannagatan 61, tel. 08/1209-0000, fax 08/307-372, www.ibis styles.se, odenplan@uniquehotels.se).

$$ Stureparkens Gästvåning, carefully run by Challe, an Iraqi-Swede, is one floor of an apartment building converted into nine bright, clean, quiet, and thoughtfully appointed rooms. Only two rooms have private bathrooms (S-850 kr, D-895-990 kr, Tb-1,495 kr, sprawling Db apartment-2,250 kr, kitchen, guest laundry facility, free Internet access; T-bana: Stadion, across from Stureparken at Sturegatan 58, take elevator to fourth floor; tel. 08/662-7230, fax 08/661-5713, www.hotelstureparken.se, info @hotelstureparken.se).

$$ Hotel Bema is a humble place that rents out 12 fine rooms for some of the best prices in town (S-550-900 kr, Db-800-1,100 kr, extra person-250 kr, breakfast served in room, bus #65 from station to Upplandsgatan 13, tel. 08/232-675, www.hotelbema.se, hotell.bema@stockholm.mail.telia.com).

$$ A & Be Hotel, with 12 homey rooms, fills the first floor of a grand old building in a residential area (S-540 kr, Sb-840 kr, D-690 kr, Db-990 kr, breakfast-50 kr, free Wi-Fi, T-bana: Stadion, Grev Turegatan 50, tel. 08/660-2100, fax 08/660-5987, www.abehotel.com, info@abehotel.com).

On Gamla Stan

These options are in the midst of sightseeing, a short bus or taxi ride from the train station. For locations, see the map on page 290.

$$$ Rica Hotel Gamla Stan offers Old World elegance in the heart of Gamla Stan (a 5-minute walk from Gamla Stan T-bana station). Its 51 small rooms are filled with chandeliers and hardwood floors (Sb-900-1,800 kr, Db-1,200-2,200 kr, 200 kr extra for larger room, Lilla Nygatan 25, tel. 08/723-7250, fax 08/723-7259, www.rica.se, info.gamlastan@rica.se).

$$$ Lady Hamilton Hotel, expensive and lavishly furnished, is shoehorned into Gamla Stan on a quiet street a block below the cathedral and Royal Palace. The centuries-old building has 34 small, plush rooms and is filled with antiques and thoughtful touches (Db-1,450-3,200 kr, free Internet access, Storkyrkobrinken 5, tel. 08/5064-0100, fax 08/5064-0110, www .ladyhamiltonhotel.se, info@ladyhamiltonhotel.se).

Swedish Survival Phrases

Swedish pronunciation (especially the vowel sounds) can be tricky for Americans to say, and there's quite a bit of variation across the country; listen closely to locals and imitate, or ask for help. The most difficult Swedish sound is *sj*, which sounds roughly like a guttural "*h*w" (made in your throat); however, like many sounds, this is pronounced differently in various regions—for example, Stockholmers might say it more like "shw."

English	Swedish	Pronunciation
Hello. (formal)	*Goddag!*	goh-**dah**
Hi. / Bye. (informal)	*Hej. / Hej då*	hey / hey doh
Do you speak English?	*Talar du engelska?*	**tah**-lahr doo eng-ehl-skah
Yes. / No.	*Ja. / Nej.*	yaw / nay
Please.	*Snälla. / Tack.**	**snehl**-lah / tack
Thank you (very much).	*Tack (så mycket).*	tack (soh **mee**-keh)
You're welcome.	*Ingen orsak.*	**eeng**-ehn **oor**-sahk
Can I help you?	*Kan jag hjälpa dig?*	kahn yaw **jehl**-pah day
Excuse me.	*Ursäkta.*	**oor**-sehk-tah
(Very) good.	*(Mycket) bra.*	(**mee**-keh) brah
Goodbye.	*Adjö.*	ah-**yew**
one / two	*en / två*	ehn / tvoh
three / four	*tre / fyra*	treh / **fee**-rah
five / six	*fem / sex*	fehm / sehks
seven / eight	*sju / åtta*	hwoo / **oh**-tah
nine / ten	*nio / tio*	**nee**-oh / **tee**-oh
hundred	*hundra*	**hoon**-drah
thousand	*tusen*	**tew**-sehn
How much?	*Hur mycket?*	hewr **mee**-keh
local currency: (Swedish) kronor	*(Svenske) kronor*	(svehn-**skeh**) **kroh**-nor
Where is...?	*Var finns...?*	vahr feens
...the toilet	*...toaletten*	toh-ah-**leh**-tehn
men	*man*	mahn
women	*kvinna*	**kvee**-nah
water / coffee	*vatten / kaffe*	**vah**-tehn / **kah**-feh
beer / wine	*öl / vin*	url / veen
Cheers!	*Skål!*	skohl
The bill, please.	*Kan jag få notan, tack.*	kahn yaw foh **noh**-tahn tack

*Swedish has various ways to say "please," depending on the context. The simplest is *snälla*, but Swedes sometimes use the word *tack* (thank you) in the way we use "please."

HELSINKI
Finland

Finland Practicalities

We think of Finland (Suomi) as Scandinavian, but it's better to call it "Nordic" (along with Iceland and Estonia). Finland is bordered by Russia to the east, Sweden and Norway to the north, the Baltic Sea to the west, and Estonia to the south. After gaining independence from Russia in 1917, Finland resisted invasion during World War II—and a low-key but pervasive Finnish pride has percolated here ever since. A mostly flat, forested, lake-filled country of 130,500 square miles (almost twice the size of Washington state), Finland is home to 5.2 million people. Finland's population is over 80 percent Lutheran, and the vast majority (93 percent) is of Finnish descent.

Money: €1 (euro) = about $1.30. An ATM is called a *pankkiautomaatti*; these are often marked *Otto*. The local VAT (value-added sales tax) rate is 25 percent; the minimum purchase eligible for a VAT refund is €40 (for details on refunds, see page 139).

Language: The native language is Finnish. For useful phrases, see page 346.

Emergencies: Dial 112 for police, medical, or other emergencies. In case of theft or loss, see page 131.

Time Zone: Finland is one hour ahead of Central European Time (seven/ ten hours ahead of the East/West Coasts of the US). That puts Helsinki in the same time zone as Tallinn and Rīga; one hour ahead of Stockholm, the rest of Scandinavia, and most other continental cruise ports (including Gdańsk and Warnemünde); and one hour behind St. Petersburg.

Embassies in Helsinki: The **US embassy** is at Itäinen Puistotie 14B (tel. 40/140-5957, emergency tel. 09/616-250, http://finland.usembassy.gov). The **Canadian embassy** is at Pohjoisesplanadi 25B (tel. 09/228-530, www.finland.gc.ca). Call ahead for passport services.

Phoning: Finland's country code is 358; to call from another country to Finland, dial the international access code (011 from the US/Canada, 00 from Europe, or + from a mobile phone), then 358, followed by the area code (without initial zero) and the local number. For calls within Finland, dial just the number if you are calling locally, and add the area code if calling long distance. To place an international call from Finland, dial 999 or another 900 number (depending on the phone service you're using), the code of the country you're calling (1 for US and Canada), and the phone number. For more help, see page 1110.

Tipping: The bill for a sit-down meal already includes gratuity, so you don't need to add more, though it's nice to round up about 5-10 percent for good service. Round up taxi fares a bit (pay €3 on an €2.85 fare). For more tips on tipping, see page 143.

Tourist Information: www.visitfinland.com

HELSINKI

Helsinki is the only European capital with no medieval past. Although it was founded in the 16th century by the Swedes in hopes of countering Tallinn as a strategic Baltic port, it never amounted to more than a village until the 18th century. Then, in 1746, Sweden built a huge fortress on an island outside Helsinki's harbor, and the village boomed as it supplied the fortress. After taking over Finland in 1809, the Russians decided to move Finland's capital and university closer to St. Petersburg—from Turku to Helsinki. They hired a young German architect, Carl Ludvig Engel, to design new public buildings for Helsinki and told him to use St. Petersburg as a model. This is why the oldest parts of Helsinki (around Market Square and Senate Square) feel so Russian—stone buildings in yellow and blue pastels with white trim and columns. Hollywood used Helsinki for the films *Gorky Park* and *Dr. Zhivago,* because filming in Russia was not possible during the Cold War.

Though the city was part of the Russian Empire in the 19th century, most of its residents still spoke Swedish, which was the language of business and culture. In the mid-1800s, Finland began to industrialize. The Swedish upper class in Helsinki expanded the city, bringing in the railroad and surrounding the old Russian-inspired core with neighborhoods of four- and five-story apartment buildings, including some Art Nouveau masterpieces. Meanwhile, Finns moved from the countryside to Helsinki to take jobs as industrial laborers. The Finnish language slowly acquired equal status with Swedish, and eventually Finnish speakers became the majority in Helsinki (though Swedish remains a co-official language).

Since downtown Helsinki didn't exist until the 1800s, it was more conscientiously designed and laid out than other European capitals. With its many architectural overleafs and fine Neoclassical and Art Nouveau buildings, Helsinki often turns guests into students of urban design and planning. Good neighborhoods for architecture buffs to explore are Katajanokka, Kruununhaka, and Eira. If you're intrigued by what you see, look for the English-language guide to Helsinki architecture (by Arvi Ilonen) in bookstores.

All of this makes Helsinki sound like a very dry place. It's not. Despite its sometimes severe cityscape and chilly northern latitude, the city bursts with vibrant street life and a joyful creative spirit. In 2012, Helsinki celebrated its stint as a "World Design Capital," seizing the opportunity to spiff up the city with exciting new projects—including the new Helsinki Music Center concert hall, an extensive underground bike tunnel that cuts efficiently beneath congested downtown streets, and an all-around rededication to its already impressive design. While parts of the city may seem dark and drab, splashes of creativity and color hide around every corner—but you'll only discover them if you take the time to look.

Planning Your Time

Helsinki will keep you busy on your day in port. While the downtown core, with most of the big sights, is compact and walkable, several worth-a-detour attractions require a longer walk or bus/tram/taxi ride. Below I've listed the most important sights in town, starting from Market Square and moving outward; while this order makes sense for those arriving at the South Harbor, if you're arriving at the West Harbor, it may be more logical to link these sights differently. To best manage your time, start at the farthest-flung sights, then work your way back toward the town center (and your ship).

• **Market Square:** This delightful harborfront zone is worth at least a 30-minute browse—more for shoppers or if you grab lunch here.

• **"Welcome to Helsinki" Self-Guided Walk:** Starting at Market Square, this approximately one-hour walk (without stops) introduces you to the city's sightseeing spine.

• **Senate Square and Churches:** Near Market Square and the start of my self-guided walk, be sure to stroll through Senate Square, visit the **Lutheran Cathedral** (allow 30 minutes or less), and tour the **Uspenski Orthodox Cathedral** (allow 30 minutes). This part of town won't take you much more than an hour.

• **Orientation Bus Tour:** Early in your visit, consider a 1.75-hour bus tour (or one of the one-hour hop-on, hop-off loops) to

Excursions from Helsinki

Helsinki itself has plenty to fill a day, but many of its sights—including its architectural highlights, the remarkable Church in the Rock, and the Sibelius Monument—are spread far and wide. This, plus the fact that Helsinki is unusually car-friendly (and less pedestrian-oriented), makes an orientation **bus tour** a good way to get your bearings. While your cruise line likely offers an excursion for this, you'll have a similar experience and pay far less if you join a local bus tour when you arrive (see options on page 319). Various cruise lines also offer **walking tours** of downtown Helsinki, including Senate Square and the Esplanade, but you'll do just as well following my self-guided walk. Finally, you might combine either a bus ride or a walking tour with a Helsinki **harbor tour,** offering a closer look at the Suomenlinna islands (described on page 320) or, far beyond that, the Archipelago Sea (studded with thousands of little islands, but less scenic than the Stockholm Archipelago).

While gimmicky Ice Bar experiences in other cities are skippable, excursions to Helsinki's **"Winter World"** facility offers something extra—a complete, snowy indoor world where you can ride a sled, toss a snowball, and hike on a snowy hill. While undoubtedly a tourist trap, this may be worth it on a hot day if you have a limited appetite for Helsinki and prefer snowballs and vodka to sightseeing.

Out-of-town excursions can include the excellent **Seurasaari Open-Air Museum,** offering a look at traditional Finnish culture (and described on page 337); **Porvoo,** the second-oldest town in Finland, with fine wooden architecture; **Sipoo,** a very old and traditional farming area with the stone St. Sigfrid's Church; and **Hvittträsk,** a landmark of Finnish architecture in a pleasant forests-and-lake countryside setting. While any of these might be interesting on a longer visit, with just one day I'd rather explore Helsinki proper (or, if you have a special interest, choose an excursion combining one of these outlying sights with places in town).

conveniently link the outlying areas of Helsinki (including the **Sibelius Monument**—which is worth seeing, but not worth the long trip to see on your own).

• **National Museum:** For those curious about Finland's story, this newly enhanced exhibit tells it well; allow at least an hour (likely more). The landmark Finlandia Hall is across the street and also worth a peek (10 minutes).

• **Temppeliaukio:** The dramatic "Church in the Rock" is one of Helsinki's best sights—but also one of its least convenient, burrowed into a residential zone a 10-minute walk behind the National Museum. Allow 30 minutes (plus the time it takes to get there).

• **Out of Town:** Two out-of-town sights are worth the trek for those with a special interest, but either one will eat up the better part of your time in port. **Suomenlinna Fortress,** the fortified island defending Helsinki's harbor, is reached by a 15-minute boat trip; once there, you'll want at least an hour to explore, plus 30 minutes for the museum and 30 minutes for the "multi-vision" show. **Seurasaari Open-Air Folk Museum** requires a 30-minute bus ride each way from downtown, plus at least 1.5 hours to see the dozens of historic structures.

If you move fast on a longish day in port, you can probably squeeze in all the in-town sights; if you're tight on time, skip the National Museum.

Arrival at the Port of Helsinki

Arrival at a Glance: If arriving at the West Harbor, your best bet for getting downtown is public transportation (bus #14 from Hernesaari terminal, tram #9 from West/Länsi terminal). From the South Harbor (Katajanokan and Olympia terminals), you can walk into town in about 15 minutes (or hop on a tram—#4T from Katajanokan, #2 from Olympia).

Port Overview

Cruises arrive at several ports in Helsinki. These circle two large harbors: West Harbor or South Harbor. Each individual cruise berth is designated by a two- or three-letter code (noted below, along with each terminal's name in both Finnish and Swedish). The setup can be confusing—but you need to pay attention only to the port you're arriving at. For a detailed map, see www.portof helsinki.fi.

The **West Harbor** (Länsistama/Västra Hamnen), an ugly industrial port, is about 1.5 miles west of downtown. This harbor has two cruise ports:

• **Hernesaari Terminaali** (Ärtholmen in Swedish), the primary cruise port for Helsinki, sits on the eastern side of West Harbor. It has two berths (Quay B, code: LHB; and Quay C, code: LHC), a handy TI kiosk, and a nearby stop for public bus #14, which heads into town.

• **West Terminal** (Länsiterminaali/Västra Terminalen), on the western side of West Harbor, has a cruise berth at Melkki Quay (code: LMA), a 10-minute walk from tram #9 into town.

The **South Harbor** (Eteläsatama/Södra Hamnen) is conveniently and scenically located within walking distance of downtown. Ringing this harbor are several terminals for both cruises

---

Services in Downtown Helsinki

Most of the port areas lack services (though a few have terminal buildings with ATMs or Internet access, and the TI at Hernesaari terminal is helpful). For most services, you'll do best if you wait to get into town. I've noted the options handiest to Market Square, right on the South Harbor.

ATMs: Cash machines (usually marked *Otto*) are abundant in downtown Helsinki, especially along the Esplanade.

Internet Access: The most convenient place to get online is inside the City Hall, facing Market Square (see page 318 for details).

Pharmacy: The handiest pharmacy is facing City Hall and the TI (see page 317).

---

and overnight ferries; two of these are most commonly used by cruise ships:

• **Katajanokan Terminaali** (Skatudden in Swedish), along the harbor's northern embankment, is near two cruise berths (codes: ERA and ERB). A third berth (code: EKL), used more by overnight ferries than cruise ships, is closer to town. From any of these, it's an easy walk or quick ride on tram #4T into town.

• **Olympiaterminaali** (code: EO), along the southern embankment, is used mostly by smaller cruise ships, and is also an easy walking distance into town (or hop on tram #2).

• The South Harbor berths that are closest to downtown (**Kanavaterminaali** and **Makasiiniterminaali**) are used mostly by overnight ferries, though occasionally overflow cruise ships may end up here.

Tourist Information: Among the cruise ports, the only one with a dedicated TI is the Hernesaari terminal. Otherwise, head into town and visit the helpful TI right on Market Square.

Getting into Town

Below, I cover arrival details for each of Helsinki's four ports. From any harbor, your cruise line may offer a **shuttle bus,** dropping you off near Stockmann department store downtown—so I've also included arrival instructions for that option. In addition, I've listed some **tour** options.

West Harbor

While you can walk downtown from the West Harbor (about 2 miles/40-50 minutes), I don't recommend it—it's partly through an ugly industrial port zone, and partly through a nondescript residential neighborhood.

HELSINKI

Arriving at Hernesaari Terminaali

As you exit the port gate, you'll run right into a small outdoor mall of souvenir vendors, and a handy kiosk housing a branch TI. This is a good place to pick up a map, get questions answered, buy an all-day transit pass, and get online (free Wi-Fi, but no terminals). There is no ATM here, but the TI (like other vendors here) accepts credit cards. Just beyond the TI and shops is a parking lot with cruise excursion buses, taxis (figure €15-20 to downtown), and hop-on, hop-off tour buses (for details, see later). There are plans for a typical Finnish sauna in this area—a nice way to relax, Helsinki-style, if you have time to kill before re-boarding your ship.

If you want to ride **public bus #14** into town, buy a €7 all-day transit pass at the TI kiosk (no individual tickets sold), or wait to buy a €2.70 single-ride ticket from the driver. The bus stop is about a five-minute walk: From the TI, head through the parking lot (passing all the buses) to the far end. When you reach the street, turn left and follow it for a short block, then turn right at the first intersection; the bus stop is halfway down this street on the left (marked *Pajamäki/Smedjebacka*). From here, bus #14 takes you downtown (runs every 10-20 minutes). Two stops are most useful: First, after about 10 minutes, the bus stops at Kamppi—a 10-minute walk from the train station area, Stockmann department store, and the Esplanade (you can also join my self-guided tram tour here—just hop on tram #2 and turn to page 327). If you'd like to see Temppeliaukio ("Church in the Rock"), stay on to the Kauppakorkeakoulut/Handelshögskolorna stop. Stepping off the bus here, continue straight ahead one block (in the direction the bus was headed) and turn right up Luthernikatu to reach the back of Temppeliaukio; circle around the right side to find the entrance.

Another option in summer is to take a **ferry** from Hernesaari directly to Market Square. While it's pricey (€7 one-way, €10 all day), infrequent (3/day in each direction, starting at 9:30), and slow (30 minutes, with stops at various waterfront cafés en route), it offers a romantic approach to Helsinki's scenic front door (daily late June-early Aug, Sat-Sun only early-late June and early-late Aug, no boats Sept-May, buy tickets on board, mobile 040-736-2329, www.seahelsinki.fi). To find the ferry, head straight out past the warehouses to the seashore on the opposite side of the pier, then turn left.

Arriving at West Terminal (Länsiterminaali)

If you arrive here, your ship puts in at the most desolate part of the port. Exiting, you'll pass through the deserted-feeling **Ristelly**

Terminal building, with a few souvenir shops and no real services. Once outside, you'll see taxis (figure about €15-20 downtown) and bus stops for cruise excursions. To head into town on your own, proceed straight out the port gate, then follow the green line painted on the pavement for about 10 minutes, bearing right slightly, through dull shipyards to the **Länsiterminaali** building (which is used primarily by Tallink and St. Peter Line boats). Inside the terminal are ATMs, WCs, lockers, a newsstand, and a rack of TI brochures. A taxi stand is just outside the terminal's side door. Across the wide street is the big Verkkokauppa.com shopping complex; its lobby (open 24/7) has free Internet terminals, and upstairs is a sprawling Best Buy-like electronics store (Mon-Fri 9:00-21:00, Sat 9:00-18:00, Sun 12:00-18:00).

Directly in front of the Länsiterminaali building is the stop for **tram #9**, which takes you downtown. You can buy tickets at the newsstand inside the terminal, or at the automated machine by the tram stop (cash or credit card, €2.20 for a single ticket, €7 for an all-day ticket). This is the start of the line, so you can't go in the wrong direction—just hop on any tram that shows up (runs every 10 minutes). Get off at the train station (Rautatieasema/Järnvägsstationen stop), right in the middle of my self-guided walk, and an easy walking distance to many top sights.

South Harbor

From any of the South Harbor berths, you can see the green dome marking the Lutheran Cathedral and Helsinki's city center. If the weather's nice and you're up for a walk, just stroll toward the dome. I've noted your other options below. (If you happen to arrive at **Kanavaterminaali** or **Makasiiniterminaali**—which few cruises do—walking is certainly the easiest option, as both are within a five-minute walk of Market Square.)

While it makes little sense to hire a taxi for the short ride into town, figure about €10-15 for a trip from any of these terminals to any sights in the downtown area.

Arriving at Katajanokan Terminaali

As you exit the port area, turn left and walk until you see the Viking Line terminal building. Inside, you'll find an ATM, WCs, lockers, and a newsstand; out front are hop-on, hop-off buses and (at 10:30) Helsinki Expert orientation tour buses (see page 319). Directly across the street from the terminal building is the start-of-the-line stop for **tram #4T**. You can ride it straight into town (4-8/hour): the fourth stop, Ritarihuone/Riddarhuset, is the City Hall (near Market Square and TI); the next stop is Senate Square (Senaatintori/Senatstorget); and from there, the tram continues along Aleksanterinkatu, parallel to the Esplanade, to the train station area (Lasipalatsi/Glaspalatset stop), then the National Museum (Kansallismuseo/Nationalmuseet stop).

Alternatively, you can **walk** into town in about 10 minutes: simply proceed past the Viking Line terminal and continue straight ahead (with the harbor on your left, passing a gas station, then several brick warehouses) to Market Square.

Arriving at Olympiaterminaali

Ships put in near the Olympiaterminaali building (used primarily by Tallink Silja overnight boats to Stockholm), which has ATMs, WCs, lockers, and a newsstand. Out front are hop-on, hop-off buses and (at 10:30) Helsinki Expert orientation tour buses. It's an easy 15-minute **walk** around the harbor to Market Square (just walk toward the green dome). To shave some time off the trip, hop on **tram #2**, which departs from the street in front of the terminal and zips you into town (ride it to the right, direction: Eläintarha). The third stop is Senate Square (Senaatintori/Senatstorget); the sixth stop is the train station (Rautatieasema/Järnvägsstationen); and the tenth stop (Sammonkatu) is near Temppeliaukio, the Church in the Rock. You can also simply stay on tram #2 all the way around for the full one-hour loop, and follow my self-guided tram tour on page 327.

Other Options

If you'd rather not navigate your way into town yourself, consider your cruise line's shuttle bus or a Helsinki-based guided tour.

Cruise-Line Shuttle Buses

Regardless of which port they use, many cruise lines offer a shuttle bus into downtown (price varies, but usually around €8 one-way, €12 round-trip). This is especially worth considering if you're arriving at the far-flung ports of the West Harbor (Hernesaari terminal or West/Länsi terminal).

Arrival in Downtown Helsinki: Most cruise shuttles drop off across the street from Stockmann department store (near the corner of Mannerheimintie and Lönnrotinkatu, right by the Ylioppilastalo stop for tram #3—see my self-guided tram tour on page 327). While this is a handy entry point that lets you walk to many sights, it can be hard to get your bearings in this bustling shopping zone. From the bus stop, cross the busy boulevard with the tram tracks and proceed straight down the street between the huge, red-brick Stockmann and the white, round Swedish Theater (Svenska Teatern). This is the start of the Esplanade, which leads regally down to Market Square and the beginning of my self-guided walk.

Tours

Bus tours can be an excellent way to get your bearings in this somewhat spread-out city; after getting oriented, you can choose where to spend the rest of your time.

You have two options: **orientation bus tours** that do a 1.75-hour circuit around the big sights; or **hop-on, hop-off bus tours** that allow you to get off wherever you like and catch another bus later. Neither type of tour serves all of the cruise ports (though hop-on, hop-off buses do meet arriving cruisers at the primary Hernesaari terminal, and orientation tours leave from near the Katajanokan and Olympia terminals at times when overnight boats from Stockholm arrive); in most cases, you'll need to make your way downtown to catch the bus. If considering the hop-on, hop-off tour, carefully note the frequency of buses (which can be sparse), and make sure you understand the schedule and departure point for the bus back to your port.

Other tour options in Helsinki include harbor boat tours, a "pub tram," an architectural walk, and local guides for hire.

For more on all of these, see "Tours in Helsinki" on page 319.

Returning to Your Ship

By Shuttle Bus

If your cruise line offers a shuttle bus, you'll find it across the street from the Stockmann department store, along the busy and wide Mannerheimintie boulevard. The easiest way to get there from Market Square is to head straight up the Esplanade, curl around the right side of the big, white Swedish Theater, then cross the busy street straight ahead.

On Your Own

West Harbor: If returning to West Harbor terminals, leave plenty of time for public transportation. To get to **Hernesaari,** hop on bus #14 (direction: Hernesaaren laituri) and get off at the last stop (you'll see your ship). The only catch is finding a handy bus stop for the #14 downtown; the most convenient is probably Kamppi, a 10-minute walk down Salomonkatu from the train station/Finlandia Hall area. To get to the **West/Länsi** terminal, ride tram #9 (direction: Länsiterminaali); the easiest place to catch it downtown is in front of the train station. Remember to leave yourself at least 10 minutes for the walk from the tram stop to your ship.

South Harbor: Returning to South Harbor ports, it's probably easiest just to walk—you should be able to see your ship from Market Square, and it won't take longer than 15 minutes. (If you have time to kill before heading back, it's a delight to spend it on

HELSINKI

Market Square or the adjacent Senate Square.) But if you want to get there faster—or are coming from another part of town—you can take the tram: To reach the **Katajanokan** terminal, catch tram #4T (not #4) from various points in town—including the National Museum, Lasipalatsi (near the train station), Senate Square, and the Ritarihuone stop by City Hall—and ride it to its end point at the Katajanokan terminaali stop. To reach the **Olympia** terminal, take tram #2 from various points in town—including Sammonkatu (near Temppeliaukio), the train station, Senate Square, and City Hall—to its end station, Olympialaituri.

See page 344 for help if you miss your boat.

Orientation to Helsinki

Like most big European cities, Helsinki (pop. 602,000) has a compact core. The city's natural gateway is its main harbor, where

many cruise ships and ferries dock. At the top of the harbor is Market Square (Kauppatori), an outdoor food and souvenir bazaar. Nearby are two towering, can't-miss-them landmarks: the white Lutheran Cathedral and the red-brick Orthodox Cathedral.

Helsinki's grand pedestrian boulevard, the Esplanade, begins right at Market Square, heads up past the TI, and ends after a few blocks in the central shopping district. The broad, traffic-filled Mannerheimintie, a bustling avenue that veers north through town past the train and bus stations, begins at the far end of the Esplanade. For a do-it-yourself orientation to town along this route, follow my "Welcome to Helsinki" self-guided walk on page 322. The "Tram #2/#3 Tour" (see page 327) also provides a good drive-by introduction to the main sights.

Tourist Information

The friendly, energetic **main TI,** just off the harbor, offers great service, and its brochure racks are fun to graze through. It's located a half-block inland from Market Square, on the right just past the fountain, at the corner of the Esplanade and Unioninkatu (May-Sept Mon-Fri 9:00-20:00, Sat-Sun 9:00-18:00, Oct-April closes two hours earlier, free Internet access, tel. 09/3101-3301, www .visithelsinki.fi). Pick up a city map, a public-transit map, and the free *Helsinki This Week* magazine (lists sights, hours, concerts, and events). Also consider these free brochures: the scenic #2 tram route/map, *Helsinki on Foot* (which maps out five well-described walking tours), and *Finnish Design*. If interested, ask about concerts; popular venues are Kallio Church and the Lutheran Cathedral.

The tiny **train station TI,** which consists of a one-person desk inside the Helsinki Expert office, provides many of the same services and publications.

Helsinki Expert: This private service sells the Helsinki Card (described next) and sightseeing tours. They have one branch in the train station hall, with another occupying the front desks in the main TI on Market Square (both have similar hours: June-Aug Mon-Fri 9:00-18:30, Sat-Sun 9:00-17:00; Sept-May Mon-Fri 9:00-16:30, Sat 10:00-16:00, closed Sun; tel. 09/2288-1500, www .helsinkiexpert.com), plus a small sightseeing kiosk out on the Esplanade (summer only, not all services).

Helsinki Card: If you're planning to visit a lot of museums in Helsinki, this card can be a good deal (€36/24 hours, €46/48 hours, €56/72 hours, €3 less if bought online and picked up on arrival at the downtown TI's Helsinki Expert desk; includes free entry to over 50 museums, fortresses, and other major sights; free use of buses, trams, and the ferry to Suomenlinna; free city bus tour; and a 72-page booklet; sold at all Helsinki Expert locations and both Viking Line and Tallink Silja ferry terminals, www .helsinkicard.com).

For a cheaper alternative, you could buy a public-transit day ticket (see "Getting Around Helsinki," later), take my self-guided tours (the "Welcome to Helsinki" walk and "Tram #2/#3 Tour"), visit the free churches (Temppeliaukio Church, Lutheran Cathedral, and Uspenski Orthodox Cathedral), and stop by the free Helsinki City Museum.

Helpful Hints

Bilingual Confusion: Because Finland is officially bilingual, you'll often see both Finnish and Swedish spellings for everything from street names to tram stops and map labels. This can be confusing, especially since the two names often look completely different. For example, the South Harbor—where many overnight boats arrive—is called Eteläsatama in Finnish and Södra Hamnen in Swedish; the train station is Rautatieasema in Finnish, Järnvägsstationen in Swedish.

Pharmacy: The central **Apteekki Palvelee** faces the TI and City Hall just off Market Square (Mon-Fri 8:00-19:00, Sat 9:00-17:00, Sun 11:00-16:00, Eteläesplanadi 2). A **24-hour pharmacy**—*apteekki*—is located at Mannerheimintie 96 (at Kansaneläkelaitos stop for tram #2, #4/4T, or #10, tel. 020-320-200).

Laundry: PesuNet, primarily a dry-cleaning shop, welcomes travelers to use its half-dozen self-service machines. It's around the corner from the Iso Roobertinkatu stop for tram #3 (€9.30/load, not coin-op—pay staff who will help, Mon-Thu 8:00-20:00, Fri 8:00-18:00, Sat 10:00-15:00, closed Sun, Punavuorenkatu 3, tel. 09/622-1146).

Internet Access: The **City Hall,** facing Market Square and the harbor, has six free, fast terminals and speedy Wi-Fi in its inviting lobby (get code from desk, Mon-Fri 9:00-19:00, Sat-Sun 10:00-16:00). At the **train station,** go down the escalators from the main hall and you'll see a bank of red terminals on your right (€2/hour).

Bike Rental: Try **Greenbike** (one-speed bike-€20/4 hours, €30/24 hours; three-speed bike-€5 more; May-mid-Sept daily 10:00-18:00, until 20:00 in Aug, usually no rentals off-season; Narinkka 3 in front of Kamppi shopping center; mobile 050-404-0400, www.greenbike.fi).

Best View: The **Torni Tower's Ateljee Bar** offers a free panoramic view. Ride the elevator from the lobby of the venerable Torni Hotel (built in 1931) to the 12th floor, where you can browse around the perch or sit down for a drink (Sun-Thu 14:00-24:00, Fri-Sat 12:00-24:00, Yrjönkatu 26, tel. 020-123-4604).

What's With the Slot Machines? Finns just have a love affair with lotteries and petty gambling. You'll see coin-operated games of chance everywhere, including restaurants, supermarkets, and the train station.

Updates to This Book: For news about changes to this book's coverage since it was published, see www.ricksteves.com/update.

Getting Around Helsinki

In compact Helsinki, you won't need to use public transportation as much as in big cities like Stockholm.

By Bus and Tram: With the public-transit route map (available at the TI, also viewable on the Helsinki Region Transport website—www.hsl.fi) and a little mental elbow grease, the buses and trams are easy, giving you Helsinki by the tail. The single Metro line is also part of the system, but is not useful unless you're traveling to my recommended sauna (described later).

Single tickets are good for an hour of travel (€2.70 from driver, €2.20 at automated ticket machines at a few larger bus and tram stops). A day ticket (€7/24 hours of unlimited travel) pays

Helsinki Transit

500 Meters
500 Yards

NATIONAL MUSEUM · Kansallismuseo
Sammonkatu
TEMPPELIAUKIO CHURCH #14
ARKADIANKATU
Tram #3T
Kamppi Tram, Metro & Bus Stn.
Tram #9
#14
Tram #9 & #2
Lasipalatsi
TRAIN STATION
Rautatieasema
Tram #2, #4 & #4T
Tram #5B
Tram #4 & #2
LUTHERAN CATHEDRAL
Senaatintori
ESPLANADE
Cruise Line Shuttle Bus Stop
Ylioppilastalo
Kauppatori (Market Square) BOATS TO SUOMENLINNA
North Harbor
USPENSKI ORTHODOX CATHEDRAL
Tram #4/4T
Tram #4
KANAVA
Tram #4T
Katajan-okka
South Harbor
Eteläranta
ERA/ERB
KATAJA-NOKAN
CRUISES, VIKING LINE TO STOCKHOLM & TALLINN
Tram #5
MAKASIINI LINDA LINE TO TALLINN
Iso Roobertinkatu
#14 B
NOTE: TRAM CHANGES NUMBER HERE
Olympia-laituri
EO
Luoto
West Harbor
Tram #3
OLYMPIA TALLINK SILJA LINE TO STOCKHOLM
WEST/LÄNSI TALLINK SILJA LINE & ECKERÖ LINE TO TALLINN; ST. PETER LINE TO ST. PETERSBURG
To West Cruise Terminal (LMA)
To Suomenlinna Fortress
LHB/LHC HERNESAARI (SOME CRUISE SHIPS)
Munkkisaari #14 B
Sirpalesaari
Harakka
Not all Tram & Bus Stops are shown

Tram
Bus
Boat

N

HELSINKI

for itself if you take four or more rides; longer versions are also available (€3.50 per extra 24 hours, 7-day maximum). Day tickets can be bought at the ubiquitous yellow-and-blue R-Kiosks (convenience stores), as well as at TIs, the train station, Metro stations, and automated ticket machines at a handful of stops, but not from drivers. The Helsinki Card also covers public transportation. All of these tickets and cards are valid only within the city of Helsinki, not the suburbs.

Tours in Helsinki

For a fun, cheap tour, take public tram #2—it makes the rounds of most of the town's major sights in an hour. Use my self-guided "Tram #2/#3 Tour" (described later and rated ▲▲) to follow along with what you see, and also pick up the helpful tram #2 explanatory brochure—free at TIs and often on board the tram.

▲▲▲**Orientation Bus Tours**—These 1.75-hour bus tours, run by Helsinki Expert, give an ideal city overview with a look at all of the important buildings, from the recently remodeled Olympic Stadium to Embassy Row. You stay on the bus the entire time, except for a short stop or two (e.g., for 10 minutes at the Sibelius Monument, and when possible, Temppeliaukio Church). You'll learn strange facts, such as how Finns took down the highest steeple in town during World War II so that the Soviet bombers flying in from Estonia couldn't see their target. The tour leaves from the corner of Fabianinkatu and the Esplanade (mid-June-mid-Aug daily at 11:00, 12:00, 13:30, and 15:00; fewer tours off-season, but 11:00 departure runs year-round). Additional departures are timed to meet arriving overnight (non-cruise) ferries from Stockholm (these depart from the Viking Line and Tallink Silja boat docks at 10:30), which could be convenient if your ship puts in near one of those terminals at South Harbor. Tours cost €28, but are free with the Helsinki Card, and are €3 cheaper if you book on the Helsinki Expert website (www.helsinkiexpert.com). Tours get booked up, so it's wise to reserve in advance online (or call 09/2288-1600, email sightseeing@helsinkiexpert.fi).

Hop-On, Hop-Off Bus Tours—If you'd enjoy the tour described above, but want the chance to hop on and off at will, consider **Open Top Tours** (owned by Strömma/Helsinki Sightseeing). Their two one-hour, complementary routes—yellow around the southern part of town and to the Hernesaari cruise terminal, and green to points north, including the Sibelius Monument and Olympic Stadium—depart every 30-45 minutes (€25 for either route or €30 for both, €35 combo-ticket also includes harbor cruise—see next, all tickets good for 24 hours, May-Sept daily 10:00-16:00, tel. 020-741-8210, www.stromma.fi). A different company, **Sightseeing City Tour,** offers a similar combination of routes for similar prices, but has fewer departures (www.citytour.fi). The buses depart from various points around town, including some cruise terminals.

Harbor Tours—Three boat companies compete for your attention along Market Square, offering snoozy cruises around the harbor and its islands roughly hourly from 10:00 to 18:00 in summer (typically 1.5 hours for €17-20; www.royalline.net, www.ihalines.fi, www.stromma.fi). The narration is slow-moving—often recorded and in as many as four languages. I'd call it an expensive nap. Taking the ferry out to Suomenlinna and back gets you onto the water for much less money (€5 round-trip, covered by day ticket or Helsinki Card).

Pub Tram—In summer, this antique red tram makes a 50-minute circle through the city while its passengers get looped on the beer for sale on board (€8 to ride, €5.50 beer, mid-May-Aug Tue-Sat 14:00-20:00, no trams Sun-Mon, leaves at the top of each hour from in front of the Fennia building, Mikonkatu 17, across from train-station tower, www.koff.net).

Helsinki at a Glance

▲▲▲**Temppeliaukio Church** Awe-inspiring, copper-topped 1969 "Church in the Rock." **Hours:** June-Sept Mon-Sat 10:00-17:45, Sun 11:45-17:45; closes one hour earlier off-season. See page 333.

▲▲**Uspenski Orthodox Cathedral** Orthodoxy's most prodigious display outside of Eastern Europe. **Hours:** Mon-Fri 9:30-16:00, Sat 9:30-14:00, Sun 12:00-15:00. See page 331.

▲▲**Lutheran Cathedral** Green-domed, 19th-century Neoclassical masterpiece. **Hours:** June-Aug Mon-Sat 9:00-24:00, Sun 12:00-24:00; Sept-May Mon-Sat 9:00-18:00, Sun 12:00-18:00. See page 332.

▲▲**National Museum of Finland** The scoop on Finland, featuring folk costumes, an armory, czars, and thrones; the prehistory exhibit is best. **Hours:** Tue-Sun 11:00-18:00, closed Mon. See page 334.

▲▲**Seurasaari Open-Air Folk Museum** Island museum with 100 historic buildings from Finland's farthest corners. **Hours:** June-Aug daily 11:00-17:00; late May and early Sept Mon-Fri 9:00-15:00, Sat-Sun 11:00-17:00, buildings closed mid-Sept-mid-May. See page 337.

▲▲**Suomenlinna Fortress** Helsinki's harbor island, sprinkled with picnic spots, museums, and military history. **Hours:** Daily May-Sept 10:00-18:00, Oct-April 10:30-16:30. See page 337.

▲**Senate Square** Consummate Neoclassical square, with Lutheran Cathedral. **Hours:** Always open. See page 332.

▲ **Helsinki City Museum** Tells the city's history well and in English. **Hours:** Mon-Fri 9:00-17:00, Thu until 19:00, Sat-Sun 11:00-17:00. See page 333.

▲**Ateneum, The National Gallery of Finland** Largest collection of art in Finland, including local favorites plus works by Cézanne, Chagall, Gauguin, and Van Gogh. **Hours:** Tue and Fri 10:00-18:00, Wed-Thu 10:00-20:00, Sat-Sun 11:00-17:00, closed Mon. See page 334.

▲**Sibelius Monument** Stainless-steel sculptural tribute to Finland's greatest composer. **Hours:** Always open. See page 336.

HELSINKI

Architectural Walk—Archtour's two-hour guided walk shows you a few of Helsinki's late-19th-century architectural highlights, including the university's library and the stock exchange building (€20, mid-June-Aug Mon-Fri at 14:00, no tours on weekends, leaves from middle of Senate Square, tel. 09/477-7300, www.arch tours.com).

Local Guides—**Helsinki Expert** can arrange a private guide (book at least three days in advance, €220/3 hours, tel. 09/2288-1222). **Christina Snellman** is a good, licensed guide (mobile 050-527-4741, chrisder@pp.inet.fi).

Self-Guided Walk in Helsinki

▲▲Welcome to Helsinki

This walk offers a convenient spine for your Helsinki sightseeing. Several points of interest on this walk are described in more detail later, under "Sights in Helsinki."

❶ **Market Square:** Start at the obelisk in the center of the harborfront market. This is the Czarina's Stone, with its double-headed eagle of imperial Russia. It was the first public monument in Helsinki, designed by Carl Ludvig Engel and erected in 1835 to celebrate the visit by Czar Nicholas I and Czarina Alexandra. Step over the chain and climb to the top step for a clockwise spin-tour:

The big, red Viking ship and white Tallink Silja ship are each floating hotels for those making the 40-hour Stockholm-Helsinki round-trip. The brown-and-tan brick building is the old market hall. A number of harbor cruise boats vie for your business. The trees mark the beginning of Helsinki's grand promenade, the Esplanade (where we're heading). Hiding in the leaves is the venerable iron-and-glass Café Kappeli. The yellow building across from the trees is the TI. From there, a string of Neoclassical buildings face the harbor. The blue-and-white City Hall building was designed by Engel in 1833 as the town's first hotel, built to house the czar and czarina. Now it houses a public Internet point, free WCs, and free exhibits on Helsinki history (often photography). The Lutheran Cathedral is hidden from view behind this building. Next is the Swedish Embassy (flying the blue-and-yellow Swedish flag and designed to look like Stockholm's Royal Palace). Then comes the Supreme Court and, in the far corner, Finland's Presidential Palace. Standing proud, and reminding Helsinki of the Russian behemoth to its east, is the Uspenski Orthodox Cathedral.

Explore the colorful outdoor market—part souvenirs and crafts, part fruit and veggies, part fish and snacks (Mon-Fri roughly 6:30-17:00, Sat 6:30-16:00, only tourist stalls on Sun

10:00-16:00). Then, with your back to the water, walk left to the fountain, *Havis Amanda*, designed by Ville Vallgren and unveiled here in 1908. The fountain has become the symbol of Helsinki, the city known as the "Daughter of the Baltic"—graduating students decorate her with a school cap. The voluptuous figure, modeled after the artist's Parisian mistress, was a bit too racy for the conservative town, and Vallgren had trouble getting paid. But as artists often do, Vallgren had the last laugh: For more than a hundred years now, the city budget office (next to the Sasso restaurant across the street) has seen only her backside.

A one-block detour up Unioninkatu (noteworthy shops listed in "Shopping in Helsinki," later) takes you to the Neoclassical Senate Square and Lutheran Cathedral.

To continue with this walk, backtrack to the TI. In the park across the street is the delightful...

❷ **Café Kappeli:** If you've got some time, dip into this old-fashioned, gazebo-like oasis of coffee, pastry, and relaxation (get what you like at the bar inside and sit anywhere). In the 19th century, this was a popular hangout for local intellectuals and artists. Today the café offers romantic tourists waiting for their ship a great €3-cup-of-coffee memory. The bandstand in front hosts music nearly daily and dance performances in summer.

❸ **The Esplanade:** Behind Café Kappeli stretches the Esplanade, Helsinki's top shopping boulevard, sandwiching a park in the middle (another Engel design from the 1830s). The grandiose street names Esplanadi and Bulevardi, while fitting today, must have been bombastic and almost comical in rustic little 1830s Helsinki. To help you imagine this elegant promenade in the 19th century, informative signs (in English) explain Esplanade Park's background and its many statues.

The north side (with the TI) is interesting for window-shopping, people-watching, and sun-worshiping. You'll pass several stores specializing in Finnish design. At #35, Gamla Passage leads to a courtyard hopping with bars and live music at night. Farther up on the right, at #39, is the huge Academic Bookstore (Akateeminen Kirjakauppa), designed by Alvar Aalto, with an extensive map and travel section, periodicals, English books, and Café Aalto (bookstore and café open Mon-Fri 9:00-21:00, Sat 9:00-18:00, also usually open Sun 12:00-18:00).

❹ **Stockmann Department Store:** Finally, you'll come to the prestigious Stockmann department store—Finland's answer

HELSINKI

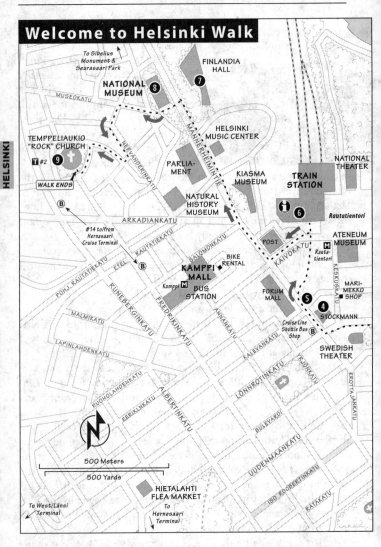

Welcome to Helsinki Walk

to Harrods or Macy's. Stockmann is the biggest, best, and oldest department store in town, with a great gourmet supermarket in the basement (see listing under "Shopping in Helsinki," later). Just beyond is Helsinki's main intersection, where Esplanade and Mannerheimintie meet. (Mannerheimintie is named for Carl Gustaf Mannerheim, the Finnish war hero who frustrated the Soviets in World War II.)

❺ **The *Three Blacksmiths* Statue:** Turn right on Mannerheimintie and, at the far side of Stockmann, you'll see the famous *Three Blacksmiths* (from 1932). While there's no universally

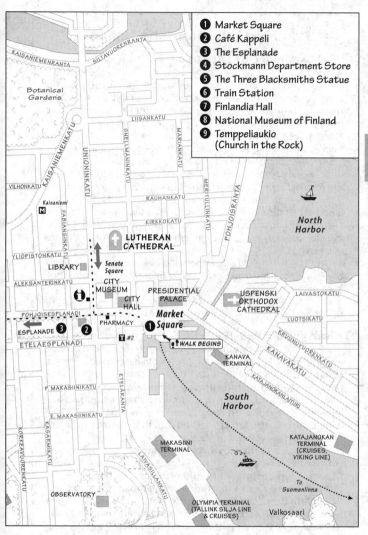

① Market Square
② Café Kappeli
③ The Esplanade
④ Stockmann Department Store
⑤ The Three Blacksmiths Statue
⑥ Train Station
⑦ Finlandia Hall
⑧ National Museum of Finland
⑨ Temppeliaukio (Church in the Rock)

accepted meaning, most say it celebrates human labor and cooperation and shows the solid character of the Finnish people. Note the rare, surviving bullet damage from World War II on the base. The most serious Russian shelling came in February of 1944. Overall, Helsinki emerged from the war with little damage.

Two Men Who Remade Helsinki

Eliel Saarinen (1873-1950)

At the turn of the 20th century, architect Eliel Saarinen burst on the scene by pioneering the Finnish National Romantic style. Inspired by peasant and medieval architectural traditions, his work was fundamental in creating a distinct—and modern—Finnish identity. The château-esque National Museum of Finland, designed by Saarinen and his two partners after winning a 1902 architectural competition, was his first major success (see page 334).

Two years later, Saarinen won the contract to construct the Helsinki train station (completed in 1919). Its design marks a transition into the Art Nouveau style of the early 1900s. The landmark station—characterized by massive male sculptures flanking its entrance, ornate glass and metalwork, and a soaring clock tower—currently welcomes over 300,000 travelers each day.

In the early 1920s, Saarinen and his family emigrated to the US, where his son, Eero, would become the architect of such iconic projects as the Gateway Arch in St. Louis and the main terminal at Dulles International Airport near Washington, DC.

Alvar Aalto (1898-1976)

Alvar Aalto was a celebrated Finnish architect and designer working in the Modernist tradition; his buildings used abstract forms and innovative materials without sacrificing functionality. Finlandia Hall in Helsinki, undoubtedly Aalto's most famous structure, employs geometric shapes and sweeping lines to create a striking concert hall, seating up to 1,700 guests. Aalto designed an inclined roof to try to maximize the hall's acoustics, with marginal success.

A Finnish Frank Lloyd Wright, Aalto concerned himself with nearly every aspect of design, from furniture to light fixtures. Perhaps most notable of these creations was his sinuous Savoy Vase, a masterpiece of simplicity and sophistication that is emblematic of the Aalto style. His designs became so popular that in 1935 he and his wife opened Artek, a company that manufactures and sells his furniture, lamps, and textiles to this day (see page 340).

Stockmann's entrance on Aleksanterinkatu, facing the *Three Blacksmiths*, is one of the city's most popular meeting points. Everyone in Finland knows exactly what it means when you say: "Let's meet under the Stockmann's clock." Tram #2 also makes a stop right at the clock (see "Tram #2/#3 Tour," opposite page). Across the street from the clock, the Old Student Hall is decorated with mythic Finnish heroes.

❻ **Train Station:** Just past the *Three Blacksmiths*, look for a passageway to your right through a shopping arcade. Walking through it, you'll emerge in front of the harsh (but serene) architecture of the train station (by Eliel Saarinen; see sidebar). The four people on the facade symbolize peasant farmers with lamps coming into the Finnish capital. Duck into the main hall and the Eliel Restaurant inside to catch the building's ambience.

Continuing past the post office and the equestrian statue of Mannerheim, return to Mannerheimintie, which passes the Kiasma Museum, Parliament, and Helsinki Music Center on the way to the large, white ❼ **Finlandia Hall,** another Aalto masterpiece. Across the street is the excellent little ❽ **National Museum of Finland** (looks like a château with a steeple), and a few blocks behind that is the sit-down-and-wipe-a-tear beautiful "Church in the Rock," ❾ **Temppeliaukio.** Sit. Enjoy the music. It's a wonderful place to end this walk.

If you want to continue on to the Sibelius Monument, located in a lovely park setting, take bus #24 (direction: Seurasaari) from nearby Arkadiankatu street. The same ticket is good for your return trip (within one hour), or continue to the end of the line for the bridge to Seurasaari Island and Finland's open-air folk museum. From there, bus #24 returns to the top of the Esplanade.

Self-Guided Tram Tour

▲▲Tram #2/#3 Tour

Of Helsinki's many tram routes, #2 seems made-to-order for a tourist's joyride. In fact, the TI hands out a free little map with the described route, making this tour easier to follow. (Helsinki revised the numbering of some tram routes in summer 2013; old tram line #3T is now #2, and #3B is #3. Signs should be changed over by the time of your visit.)

If you buy a single ticket, just stay on the tram for the entire circuit (€2.70 from driver, €2.20 from ticket machines at a few major stops, good for one hour). Using a day ticket (see "Getting Around Helsinki," earlier) or a Helsinki Card allows you to hop off to tour a sight, then catch a later tram (runs every 10 minutes).

You can't get lost because the route makes a figure-eight, and an hour after you start, you end up back at the beginning. The only confusing thing is that the tram has a different route number at different parts of the figure-eight; the top-left and bottom-right lobes are #2, the other lobes are #3—the number on the tram's sign changes at the north and south ends of the route. A few departures circle only the top or bottom loop, so confirm with the driver before boarding that your tram will make the entire figure-eight.

HELSINKI

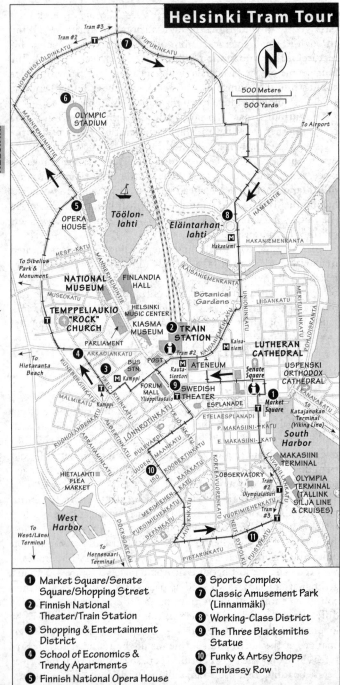

Helsinki Tram Tour

Tram #2
Tram #3
Tram #2

OLYMPIC STADIUM

To Airport

500 Meters
500 Yards

OPERA HOUSE

Töölön-lahti

Eläintarhan-lahti

Hakaniemi

HAKANIEMENRANTA

To Sibelius Park & Monument

NATIONAL MUSEUM

FINLANDIA HALL

KAISANIEMENRANTA

Botanical Gardens

TEMPPELIAUKIO "ROCK" CHURCH

Helsinki Music Center

KIASMA MUSEUM

TRAIN STATION

Tram #2

LUTHERAN CATHEDRAL

To Hietaranta Beach

PARLIAMENT

ARKADIANKATU

BUS STN.

POST

Kamppi

Rauta-tientori

ATENEUM

Kaisa-niemi

USPENSKI ORTHODOX CATHEDRAL

FORUM MALL
Ylioppilastalo

SWEDISH THEATER

Senate Square

Market Square

ESPLANADE

To Katajanokan Terminal (Viking Line)

MALMIKATU

ETELAESPLANADI

P. MAKASIINI-KATU

E. MAKASIINI-KATU

HIETALAHTI FLEA MARKET

BULEVARDI

UUDEN MAANKATU

MAKASIINI TERMINAL

OBSERVATORY

Tram #2
Olympialaituri

OLYMPIA TERMINAL (TALLINK SILJA LINE & CRUISES)

West Harbor

To West/Länsi Terminal

To Hernesaari Terminal

PIETARINKATU

Tram #3

1. **Market Square/Senate Square/Shopping Street**
2. **Finnish National Theater/Train Station**
3. **Shopping & Entertainment District**
4. **School of Economics & Trendy Apartments**
5. **Finnish National Opera House**
6. **Sports Complex**
7. **Classic Amusement Park (Linnanmäki)**
8. **Working-Class District**
9. **The Three Blacksmiths Statue**
10. **Funky & Artsy Shops**
11. **Embassy Row**

While you can hop on anywhere, it's most convenient to start—and end—at Market Square by the TI. However, depending on where your cruise arrives, it may be easier to join at a different point along this route—the Kamppi stop is convenient by bus from Hernesaari (see stop #3, below); the Ylioppilastalo stop is reachable by shuttle bus from any cruise port (see #9, below); and the Olympialaituri stop is right in front of the Olympia terminal (just before stop #1, below).

❶ **Market Square:** Stand at the tram stop that is between the fountain and the market and wait for one of the frequent #2 trams. Since the tracks split here briefly, it's hard to get on in the wrong direction; still, confirm that the destination listed on the front of the tram is *Eläintarha,* not *Kaivopuisto.* From Market Square, you'll first pass **Senate Square** (with the gleaming white Lutheran Cathedral, a statue of Alexander II—Finland's favorite czar, and many of the oldest buildings in town) and then head up Aleksanterinkatu street. It's Helsinki's Fifth Avenue-type shopping drag (tram stop: Aleksanterinkatu).

❷ **Finnish National Theater/Train Station:** After the Mikonkatu stop, you'll pass a big square. Fronting it is Finland's granite National Theater in Art Nouveau style. The statue in the square honors Aleksis Kivi, the father of Finnish literature, who in 1870 wrote *The Seven Brothers,* the first great novel in Finnish. The mid-19th century was a period of national awakening. By elevating the language to high culture, Kivi helped inspire his countrymen to stand strong and proud during a period of attempted "Russification." On the left is the **Ateneum,** Finland's national art gallery. From there (on the right), you'll pass the striking train station—with its iconic countrymen stoically holding their lamps—designed by the great Finnish architect, Eliel Saarinen.

❸ **Shopping and Entertainment District:** Crossing the busy Mannerheimintie boulevard, you'll pass the Kamppi mall (tram and Metro stop: Kamppi, with bus station in basement). The adjacent Tennis Palace is a cultural zone with galleries and movie theaters.

❹ **School of Economics and Trendy Apartments:** After passing the yellow brick buildings of the School of Economics (on your left, note facade—Kauppakorkeakoulut stop), you'll enter a neighborhood with lots of desirable 1920s-era apartments. Young couples start out here, move to the suburbs when they have their kids, and return as empty-nesters. The Temppeliaukio Church (a.k.a. "Church in the Rock"), while out of sight, is just a block uphill from the next stop (Sammonkatu).

❺ **Finnish National Opera House:** Built in 1993, the National Opera House is the white, sterile, shower-tile building on the right (tram stop: Ooppera). The next stop (Töölön halli) is a short walk from the Sibelius Monument and its pretty park (detour along a street called Sibeliuksenkatu).

❻ **Sports Complex:** A statue honors long-distance runner Paavo Nurmi (early-20th-century Finn who won a slew of Olympic gold medals, on left). The white building with the skinny tower (in the distance on the right) marks the Olympic Stadium, used for the summer games in 1952. After the Aurorankatu stop, you'll see skateboarders enjoying a park of their own (on the right). At the next stop, Eläintarha, the tram may pause as it changes to become #3 (stay seated).

❼ **Classic Amusement Park: Linnanmäki,** Helsinki's low-end, Tivoli-like amusement park is by far the most-visited sight in town (on the right, free admission to park but rides cost €4-6, open daily until late, tram stop: Alppila, www.linnanmaki.fi). Roller-coaster nuts enjoy its classics from the 1950s.

❽ **Working-Class District:** Next you'll enter an old working-class neighborhood. Its soccer fields (on your left) are frozen into ice rinks for hockey in the winter. You'll pass the striking granite **Kallio Church** (Art Nouveau, on your right) and **Hakaniemi** square, with a big indoor/outdoor market (on your left). Crossing a saltwater inlet, you'll pass Helsinki's **Botanical Gardens** (on the right), and then head back toward the town center. As you return to the train station with its buff lamp-holders, you've completed the larger, top loop of the figure-eight.

❾ **The *Three Blacksmiths* Statue:** After turning left on big, busy Mannerheimintie, you'll pass the most famous statue in town, the *Three Blacksmiths* (on your left), which honors hard work and cooperation. Towering above the smiths is the Stockmann department store. Then (at the Ylioppilastalo stop), the round, white Swedish Theater marks the top of the town's graceful park—the Esplanade—which leads back down to the harbor. From here, you'll loop through a colorful and artsy district.

❿ **Funky and Artsy Shops:** The cemetery of the church (which dates from 1827) on the right was cleaned out to make a park. It's called the "Plague Park," recalling a circa-1700 plague that killed more than half the population. Coming up, funky small boutiques, cafés, and fun shops line the streets (stops: Fredrikinkatu, Iso Roobertinkatu, and Viiskulma). After the Art Deco brick church (on your right), the tram makes a hard left (at the Eiran Sairaala stop, for a hospital) and enters a district with Art Nouveau buildings. Look down streets on the right for facades and decorative turrets leading to the Baltic Sea.

⓫ **Embassy Row and Back to Market Square:** After the Neitsytpolku stop, spy the Russian Embassy (on left), still sporting its hammer and sickle; it was built to look like London's Buckingham Palace. Across the street is the Roman Catholic church, and beyond that (on the right), a street marked "no entry" leads to an embattled US Embassy. Returning to the harbor, you'll likely see the huge Tallink Silja ship that leaves at 17:00 each evening for Stockholm. Its terminal (the appropriately named Olympiaterminaali) was built for the 1952 Olympics, which inundated Helsinki with visitors. Across the harbor stands the Uspenski Orthodox Cathedral. Then, after passing the cute brick market hall (with several great little eateries), you'll arrive at Market Square.

Sights in Helsinki

Near the South Harbor

▲▲**Uspenski Orthodox Cathedral**—This house of worship was built in 1868 for the Russian military back when Finland belonged to Russia. *Uspenski* is Russian for the Assumption of Mary. It hovers above Market Square and faces the Lutheran Cathedral as Russian culture faces Europe.

Cost and Hours: Free; Mon-Fri 9:30-16:00, Sat 9:30-14:00, Sun 12:00-15:00, Kanavakatu 1.

Visiting the Cathedral: The uppermost "onion dome" represents the "sacred heart of Jesus," while the smaller ones represent the hearts of the 12 apostles. The cathedral's interior is a potentially emotional icon experience. Its rich images are a stark contrast to the sober Lutheran Cathedral. While commonly called the "Russian church," the cathedral is actually Finnish Orthodox, answering to the patriarch in Constantinople (Istanbul). Much of eastern Finland (parts of the Karelia region) is Finnish Orthodox.

The cathedral's Orthodox Mass is beautiful, with a standing congregation, candles, incense, icons in action, priests behind the iconostasis (screen), and timeless music (human voices only—no instruments). In the front left corner, find the icon featuring the Madonna and child, surrounded by rings and jewelry (under glass), given in thanks for prayers answered. Across from the icon is a white marble table with candle holes and a dish of wheat seeds, representing recent deaths. Wheat seeds symbolize that death is not the end, but just a change.

Though the cathedral is worthwhile, the one in Tallinn is even nicer, so skip this one if you're visiting both cities and short on time. Better yet, several St. Petersburg churches put both cities' efforts to shame.

▲▲Lutheran Cathedral—With its prominent green dome, gleaming white facade, and the 12 apostles overlooking the city and harbor, this church is Carl Ludvig Engel's masterpiece.

Cost and Hours: Free; June-Aug Mon-Sat 9:00-24:00, Sun 12:00-24:00; Sept-May Mon-Sat 9:00-18:00, Sun 12:00-18:00; sometimes closes for events; on Senate Square, www.helsingi nseurakunnat.fi.

Visiting the Cathedral: Finished in 1852, the interior is pure architectural truth. Open a pew gate and sit, surrounded by the saints of Protestantism, to savor Neoclassical nirvana. Physically, this church is perfectly Protestant—austere and unadorned—with the emphasis on preaching (prominent pulpit) and music (huge organ). Statuary is limited to the local Reformation big shots: Martin Luther, Philipp Melanchthon (Luther's Reformation sidekick), and the leading Finnish reformer, Mikael Agricola. A follower of Luther at Wittenberg, Agricola brought the Reformation to Finland. He also translated the Bible into Finnish and is considered the father of the modern Finnish language. Agricola's Bible is to Finland what the Luther Bible is to Germany and the King James Bible is to the English-speaking world.

▲Senate Square—Once a town square with a church and City Hall, this square's original buildings were burned in 1808. Later, after Finland became a grand duchy of the Russian Empire, the czar sent in architect Carl Ludvig Engel (a German who had lived and worked in St. Petersburg) to give the place some Neo-class. The result: the finest Neoclassical square in Europe.

Survey Senate Square from the top of the Lutheran Cathedral steps. The Senate building (now the prime minister's office) is on your left. The small, blue, stone building with the slanted mansard roof in the far-left corner, from 1757, is one of just two pre-Russian-conquest buildings remaining in Helsinki. On the right, the line of once-grand Russian administration buildings now houses the **university** (36,000 students, 60 percent female). Symbolically (and physically), the university and government buildings are connected via the cathedral, and both use it as a starting point for grand ceremonies.

The **statue** in the center of the square honors Russian Czar Alexander II. While he wasn't popular in Russia (he was assassinated), he was well-liked by the Finns. That's because he gave Finland more autonomy in 1863 and never pushed the "Russification" of Finland. The statue shows him holding the Finnish constitution, which he supported. It defined internal independence and affirmed autonomy.

The huge staircase leading up to the cathedral is a popular meeting (and tanning) spot in Helsinki. This is where students from the nearby university gather...and romances are born. Café Engel (opposite the cathedral at Aleksanterinkatu 26) is a fine place for a light lunch or cake and coffee. The café's winter lighting seems especially designed to boost the spirits of glum, daylight-deprived Northerners.

National Library—This fine, purpose-built Neoclassical building is open to the public and worth a look (on Senate Square, immediately to the left as you face the cathedral). In czarist times, the National Library received a copy of every book printed in the Russian Empire. With all the chaos Russia suffered throughout the 20th century, a good percentage of its Slavic texts were destroyed. But Helsinki, which enjoyed relative stability, claims to have the finest collection of Slavic books in the world.

Cost and Hours: Free, July-Aug Mon-Thu 9:00-18:00, Fri 9:00-16:00, closed Sat-Sun; Sept-June Mon-Thu 9:00-20:00, Fri-Sat 9:00-16:00, closed Sun; www.nationallibrary.fi.

▲**Helsinki City Museum**—This interesting museum, a half-block south of Senate Square, gives an excellent, accessible overview of the city's history in English. Unfortunately, it may close or relocate in the future—inquire locally.

Cost and Hours: Free, Mon-Fri 9:00-17:00, Thu until 19:00, Sat-Sun 11:00-17:00, Sofiankatu 4, www.helsinkicitymuseum.fi.

Elsewhere in Central Helsinki

▲▲▲**Temppeliaukio Church**—A more modern example of great church architecture (from 1969), this "Church in the Rock" was

blasted out of solid granite. It was designed by architect brothers, Timo and Tuomo Suomalainen, and built within a year's time. Barren of decor except for a couple of simple crosses, the church is capped with a copper-and-skylight dome; it's normally filled with live or recorded music and awestruck visitors. Grab a pew. Gawk upward at a 13-mile-long coil of copper ribbon. Look at the bull's-eye and ponder God. Forget your camera. Just sit in the middle, ignore the crowds, and be thankful for peace...under your feet is an air-raid shelter that can accommodate 6,000 people.

Cost and Hours: Free, June-Sept Mon-Sat 10:00-17:45, Sun 11:45-17:45, closes one hour earlier off-season and for special events and concerts, Lutherinkatu 3, tel. 09/2340-6320, www.helsingin seurakunnat.fi.

Getting There: The church is at the top of a hill in a residential neighborhood, about a 15-minute walk north of the bus station or a 10-minute walk behind the National Museum (or take tram #2 to Sammonkatu stop).

▲▲**National Museum of Finland (Kansallismuseo)**—This pleasant, easy-to-handle collection (covering Finland's story from A to Z, with good English descriptions) is in a grand building designed by three of Finland's greatest architects—including Eliel Saarinen—in the early 1900s. The Neoclassical furniture, folk costumes, armory, and portraits of Russia's last czars around an impressive throne are interesting, but the highlight is Finland's largest permanent archaeological collection, covering the prehistory of the country. The fine, new 20th-century exhibit bookends your visit by bringing the story up to the present day. The interactive top-floor workshop is worth a look for its creative teaching.

Cost and Hours: €8, free on Fri 16:00-18:00; open Tue-Sun 11:00-18:00, closed Mon; Mannerheimintie 34, tel. 09/4050-9544 or mobile 040-128-6469, www.nba.fi. The museum café, with a tranquil outdoor courtyard, has light meals and Finnish treats such as lingonberry juice and reindeer quiche (open until 17:00). It's just a five-minute walk from Temppeliaukio Church.

Visiting the Museum: Following the clear English-language descriptions, visit each of the museum's four parts, in chronological order. First, straight ahead from the ticket desk is the **Prehistory of Finland,** where you'll learn how the Stone, Bronze, and Iron Age tribes of Finland lived. Back out in the main entrance hall, proceed into **The Realm** (to the left from the ticket desk), which continues upstairs and sends you directly into **A Land and Its People.** Finally, head back down to the ground floor for Finland in **The 20th Century,** starting with the birth of modern Finland in 1917 and its 1918 civil war. Touchscreen tables help tell the story of the fledgling nation, as do plenty of well-presented artifacts (including clothing, household items, vehicles, a typical 1970s living room, and a traditional outhouse). A 15-minute film presents archive newsreel footage from throughout the 20th century.

▲**Ateneum, The National Gallery of Finland**—This museum showcases Finnish artists on the top floor (mid-18th to 20th century), hosts exhibits, and has a fine international collection including works by Cézanne, Chagall, Gauguin, and Van Gogh.

Cost and Hours: €12, Tue and Fri 10:00-18:00, Wed-Thu 10:00-20:00, Sat-Sun 11:00-17:00, closed Mon, near train station at Kaivokatu 2, tel. 09/173-361, www.ateneum.fi.

HELSINKI

Sauna

Finland's vaporized fountain of youth is the sauna—Scandinavia's answer to support hose and facelifts. A tradi-

tional sauna is a wood-paneled room with wooden benches and a wood-fired stove topped with rocks. The stove is heated blistering hot. Undress entirely before going in. Lay your towel on the bench, and sit or lie on it (for hygienic reasons). Ladle water from the bucket onto the rocks to make steam. Choose a higher bench for hotter temperatures.

The famous birch branches are always available for slapping. Finns claim this enhances circulation and say the chlorophyll released with the slapping opens your sinuses while emitting a refreshing birch aroma. (Follow the lead of the locals around you—tourists merrily flagellating themselves can be really annoying.) Let yourself work up a sweat, then, just before bursting, go outside to the shower for a Niagara of liquid ice. Suddenly your shower stall becomes a Cape Canaveral launch pad, as your body scatters to every corner of the universe. A moment later you're back together and can re-enter the steam room and repeat as necessary. Only rarely will you feel so good. The Finnish Sauna Society's informative website details the history of saunas and sweat baths (www.sauna.fi).

Public saunas are a dying breed these days, because most Finns have private saunas in their homes or cabins. But some public saunas survive in rougher, poorer neighborhoods. For a good, traditional wood-heated sauna with a coarse and local crowd, try the **Kotiharjun Sauna.** There are no tourists and no English signs, but the guy at the desk speaks English and can help: Pay €12 plus €3 for a towel (cash only), find a locker, strip (keep the key on your wrist), and head for the steam. Cooling off is nothing fancy, just a bank of cold showers. A woman in a fish-cleaner's apron will give you a wonderful scrub with Brillo pad-like mitts (€9, only on Tue and Fri-Sat 16:00-19:00). Regulars relax with beers on the sidewalk just outside (open Tue-Sat 14:00-21:30, closed Sun-Mon, last entry 2 hours before closing; men—ground floor, women—upstairs; 200 yards from Sörnäinen Metro stop, Harjutorinkatu 1, tel. 09/753-1535, www.kotiharjunsauna.fi).

▲Sibelius Monument—Six hundred stainless-steel pipes called "Love of Music"—built on solid rock, as is so much of Finland—

shimmer in a park to honor Finland's greatest composer, Jean Sibelius. It's a forest of pipe-organ pipes in a forest of trees. The artist, Eila Hiltunen, was forced to add a bust of the composer's face to silence critics of her otherwise abstract work. City orientation bus tours stop here for 10 minutes—long enough. Bus #24 stops here (30 minutes until the next bus, or catch a quick glimpse on the left from the bus) on its way to the Seurasaari Open-Air Folk Museum. The #2 tram, which runs more frequently, stops a few blocks away.

Finlandia Hall (Finlandia-Talo)—Alvar Aalto's most famous building in his native Finland means little to the non-architect

without a tour. To see the building from its best angle, view it from the seaside parking lot, not the street—where nearly everyone who looks at the building thinks, "So what?"

Cost and Hours: €11, tours in summer held often at 14:00, call ahead or visit website to check times; hall information shop open Mon-Fri 7:30-17:00, closed Sat-Sun; Mannerheimintie 13e, tel. 09/40241, www.finlandiatalo.fi.

Kiasma Museum—Finland's museum of contemporary art, designed by American architect Steven Holl, hosts temporary exhibitions and doesn't have a permanent collection. Ask at the TI or check online to find out what's showing.

Cost and Hours: €10, Tue 10:00-17:00, Wed-Thu 10:00-20:30, Fri 10:00-22:00, Sat-Sun 10:00-17:00, closed Mon, Mannerheiminaukio 2, near train station, tel. 09/1733-6501, www.kiasma.fi.

Natural History Museum—Recently renovated and run by the University of Helsinki, this museum has about eight million animal specimens, the largest collection of its kind in Finland. Displays range from spiders to dinosaurs, all with English descriptions.

Cost and Hours: €6, free on Thu 16:00-18:00; open Tue-Fri 9:00-16:00 except Thu until 18:00, Sat-Sun 10:00-16:00, closed Mon, Pohjoinen Rautatiekatu 13, www.luomus.fi.

Outer Helsinki

A weeklong car trip up through the Finnish lakes and forests to Mikkeli and Savonlinna would be relaxing, but you can actually enjoy Finland's green-trees-and-blue-water scenery without leaving Helsinki. Here are three great ways to get out and go for a walk on a sunny summer day. If you have time, do at least one of them during your stay.

▲▲Seurasaari Open-Air Folk Museum

Inspired by Stockholm's Skansen, also on a lovely island on the edge of town, this is a collection of 100 historic buildings from

every corner of Finland. It's wonderfully furnished and gives rushed visitors an opportunity to sample the far reaches of Finland without leaving the capital city. If you're not taking a tour, get the €1.20 map or the helpful €6 guidebook. You're welcome to bring a picnic, or you can have a light lunch (snacks and cakes) in the Antti farmstead at the center of the park. Off-season, when the buildings are closed, the place is empty and not worth the trouble.

Cost and Hours: Free park entry, €8 to enter buildings; June-Aug daily 11:00-17:00; late May and early Sept Mon-Fri 9:00-15:00, Sat-Sun 11:00-17:00; closed mid-Sept-mid-May; tel. 09/4050-9660, www.seurasaari.fi.

Tours: English tours are free with €8 entry ticket, offered mid-June-mid-Aug generally at 15:00, and take one hour (confirm times on their website).

Getting There: To reach the museum, ride bus #24 (from the top of the Esplanade, 2/hour) to the end (note departure times for your return) and walk across the quaint footbridge.

▲▲Suomenlinna Fortress

The island guarding Helsinki's harbor served as a strategic fortress for three countries: Finland, Sweden, and Russia. It's now a popular park with several museums and a visitors center located about five minutes from the boat dock. The free Suomenlinna guidebook (stocked at the Helsinki TI, ferry terminal, and the visitors center) covers the island thoroughly.

Suomenlinna Timeline

1748—Construction began.

1788—The fort was used as a base for a Swedish war against Russia.

1808—It was surrendered by Sweden to Russia.

1809—Finland became part of the Russian Empire and the fort was used as a Russian garrison for 108 years.

1855—French and British navies bombarded the fort during the Crimean War, inflicting heavy damage.

1917—Finland declared independence.

1918—The fort was annexed by Finland and renamed Suomenlinna.

1939—The fort served as a base for the Finnish navy.

1973—The Finnish garrison moved out, the fort's administration was transferred to the Ministry of Education, and the fort was opened to the public.

Cost and Hours: Visitors center-free, Suomenlinna Museum-€6.50, both open daily May-Sept 10:00-18:00, Oct-April 10:30-16:30, tel. 09/684-1850, www.suomenlinna.fi. The island has several skippable smaller museums, including a toy museum and several military museums (€3-4 each, open summer only).

Tours: The museum's film on the island's history runs twice hourly (last showing 30 minutes before closing; pick up English translation of exhibits by entrance). The English-language island tour, which runs daily in summer (otherwise only on weekends), departs from the visitors center (€8, free with Helsinki Card, June-Aug daily at 11:00 and 14:00, Sept-May Sat-Sun only at 13:30).

Getting There: Catch a ferry to Suomenlinna from Market Square. Walk past the high-priced excursion boats to the public HKL ferry (€5 round-trip, covered by day ticket and Helsinki Card, 15-minute trip, May-Aug 2-3/hour—generally at :00, :20, and :40 past the hour, but pick up schedule to confirm; Sept-April every 40-60 minutes). If you'll be taking at least two tram rides within 24 hours of visiting Suomenlinna, it pays to get a day ticket instead of a round-trip ticket. A private ferry, JT Line, also runs to Suomenlinna from Market Square in summer (at least hourly, €6.50 round-trip, tel. 09/534-806, www.jt-line.fi).

Background: The fortress was built by the Swedes with French financial support in the mid-1700s to counter Russia's rise to power. (Peter the Great had built his new capital, St. Petersburg, on the Baltic and was eyeing the West.) Named Sveaborg ("Fortress of Sweden"), the fortress was Sweden's military pride and joy. With five miles of walls and hundreds of cannons, it was the second strongest fort of its kind in Europe after Gibraltar. Helsinki, a small community of 1,500 people before 1750, soon became a boomtown supporting this grand "Gibraltar of the North."

The fort, built by more than 10,000 workers, was a huge investment and stimulated lots of innovation. In the 1760s, it had the world's biggest and most modern dry dock. It served as a key naval base during a brief Russo-Swedish war in 1788-1790. But in 1808, the Russians took the "invincible" fort without a fight—by siege—as a huge and cheap military gift.

Visiting Suomenlinna: Today, Suomenlinna has 1,000 permanent residents, is home to Finland's Naval Academy, and is most appreciated by locals for its fine scenic strolls. The island is large—actually, it's four islands connected by bridges—and you and your imagination get free run of the fortifications and dungeon-like chambers. When it's time to eat, you'll find a half-dozen cafés and plenty of picnic opportunities.

Across from the ferry landing are the Jetty Barracks, housing a convenient WC, free modern art exhibit, and the pricey Panimo Brewery restaurant. From here, start your stroll of the island. The garrison church, which was Orthodox until its 20th-century conversion to Lutheranism, doubled as a lighthouse. A five-minute walk from the ferry brings you to the visitors center, which houses the worthwhile Suomenlinna Museum, where the island's complete history is presented in a fascinating 25-minute "multi-vision" show.

From the visitors center, climb uphill to the right into Piper Park, past its elegant 19th-century café, up and over the ramparts to a surreal swimming area. See the King's Gate on the far side of the island before heading back to the ferry.

Shopping in Helsinki

The Esplanade: The Esplanade is capped by the enormous, eight-floor **Stockmann** department store, arguably Scandinavia's most impressive (Mon-Fri 9:00-21:00, Sat 9:00-18:00, open most Sundays 12:00-18:00, great basement supermarket, Aleksanterinkatu 52B, www.stockmann.fi).

The rest of the Esplanade is lined with smaller stores ideal for window-shopping. Keep an eye out for sleek Scan-design gifts. Consider the purses, scarves, clothes, and fabrics from **Marimekko,** the well-known Finnish fashion company famous for striped designs (at #33, plus a new larger branch nearby at the corner of Aleksanterinkatu and Keskuskatu; www.marimekko.com).

The **Artek** store (#18), founded by designers Alvar and Elissa Aalto, showcases expensive, high-end housewares in the modern, practical style that IKEA commercialized successfully for the mass market (www.artek.fi). **Aarikka** (#25) and **Iittala** (#27) also have Finnish housewares and ceramics. Bookworms enjoy the impressive **Academic Bookstore** just before Stockmann (#39, same hours as Stockmann).

Fans of Tove Jansson's Moomin children's stories will enjoy the **Moomin Shop,** on the second floor of the Forum shopping mall at Mannerheimintie 20, across from Stockmann (Mon-Fri 9:00-21:00, Sat 9:00-18:00, Sun 12:00-18:00, www.moomin.fi).

Bus Station: For less glamorous shopping needs, the **Kamppi** mall above and around the bus station is good.

Market Square: This harborfront square is packed not only

with fishmongers and producers, but also with stands selling Finnish souvenirs and more refined crafts (roughly Mon-Fri 6:30-17:00, Sat 6:30-16:00, only tourist stalls open on Sun 10:00-16:00). Sniff the stacks of trivets, made from cross-sections of juniper twigs—an ideal, fragrant, easy-to-pack gift for the folks back home (they smell even nicer when you set something hot on them).

Flea Market: If you brake for garage sales, Finland's biggest flea market, the outdoor **Hietalahti Market,** is worth the 15-minute walk from the harbor or a short ride on tram #6 from Mannerheimintie to the Hietalahdentori stop (June-Aug Mon-Fri 9:00-19:00, Sat 8:00-16:00, Sun 10:00-16:00; less action, shorter hours, and closed Sun off-season). The stalls in the adjacent red-brick indoor market specialize in antiques (Mon-Fri 10:00-17:00, Sat 10:00-15:00, closed Sun).

Unioninkatu: This short street (connecting the harbor with the Lutheran Cathedral) has a few fun shops. **Kalevala Jewelry,** at #25, sells quality made-in-Finland jewelry. Some pieces look modern, while others are inspired by old Scandinavian, Finnish, and Sami themes (VAT refunds available, Mon-Fri 10:00-18:00, Sat 10:00-16:00, closed Sun, tel. 020-761-1380, www.kalevalakoru .com).

Fishermen head next door to #23, where the **Schröder** sporting goods store shows off its famous selection of popular Finnish-made Rapala fishing lures—ideal for the fisherfolk on your gift list.

Eating in Helsinki

Helsinki's many restaurants are smoke-free and a good value for lunch on weekdays. Finnish companies get a tax break if they distribute lunch coupons (worth €9) to their employees. It's no surprise that most downtown Helsinki restaurants offer weekday lunch specials that cost exactly the value of the coupon. These low prices evaporate on Saturday and Sunday, when picnics and Middle Eastern kebab restaurants are the only budget options.

HELSINKI

Fun Harborfront Eateries

Stalls on Market Square: Helsinki's delightful and vibrant square is magnetic any time of day...but especially at lunchtime. This really is the most memorable, casual, quick-and-cheap lunch place in town. A half-dozen orange tents (erected to shield diners from bird bombs) serve fun food on paper plates until 18:00. It's not unusual for the Finnish president to stop by here with visiting dignitaries. There's a crêpe place, and at the far end—my favorites—several salmon grills (€8-9 for a good meal). The only real harborside dining in this part of town is picnicking. While these places provide picnic tables, you can also have your food foil-wrapped to go and grab benches right on the water down near Uspenski Orthodox Cathedral.

Market Hall: Just beyond the harborside market is a cute, red-brick, indoor market hall (Mon-Fri 8:00-18:00, Sat 8:00-16:00, closed Sun). Today, along with produce stalls, it's a hit for its fun, inexpensive eateries. The tiny, four-table **Soppakeittiö** ("Soup Kitchen") serves big bowls of filling, tasty seafood soup for €8.50, including bread and water (Mon-Fri 11:00-16:00, Sat 11:00-15:00—except closed Sat in summer, closed Sun year-round). A sushi place is across the lane. In the middle of the hall, the only slightly larger **Snellman** café is popular for its €3.50 meat pies *(lihapirakka)* and €2.70 pastries called "apple pigs" *(munkkipossu)*.

Sundmans Krog Bistro is sedate and Old World but not folkloric, filling an old merchant's mansion facing the harbor. As it's the less fussy and more affordable (yet still super-romantic) little sister of an adjacent, posh, Michelin-rated restaurant, quality is assured. A rare and memorable extra is their Baltic fish buffet—featuring salmon, Baltic sprat, and herring with potatoes and all the toppings—€14 as a starter, €19 as a main course. The €18 lunch special (Mon-Fri 11:00-15:00) includes the buffet plus the main dish of the week—often more fish (€21-25 main courses, €42-49 three-course dinners, Mon-Fri 11:00-22:00, Sat 12:00-22:00, Sun 13:00-22:00, Eteläranta 16, tel. 09/6128-5450).

Central Helsinki Restaurants

Finnish-Themed Dining: Tractors and Lapp Cuisine

Zetor, the self-proclaimed *traktor* restaurant, mercilessly lampoons Finnish rural culture and cuisine (while celebrating it deep down). Sit next to a cow-crossing sign at a tractor-turned-into-a-table, in a "Finnish Western" atmosphere reminiscent of director Aki Kaurismäki's movies. Main courses run €14-20 and include reindeer, vendace (small freshwater fish), and less exotic fare. This place, while touristy and tacky, can be fun (daily 12:00-24:00, 200 yards north of Stockmann department store, across street from McDonald's at Mannerheimintie 3-5, tel. 010-766-4450).

Lappi Restaurant is a fine place for Lapp cuisine, with an entertaining menu (they smoke their own fish) and creative decor that has you thinking you've traveled north and lashed your reindeer to the hitchin' post. The friendly staff serves tasty Sami dishes in a snug and very woody atmosphere (€23-39 main courses, Mon-Fri 12:00-24:00, Sat 13:00-24:00, closed Sun, off Bulevardi at Annankatu 22, tel. 09/645-550).

1. Market Hall Eateries
2. Sundmans Krog Bistro
3. Zetor Restaurant
4. Lappi Restaurant
5. Teatterin Grilli
6. Strindberg Restaurant
7. Lasipalatsi Café
8. Stockmann Dep't Store
9. Café Kappeli
10. Café Aalto (in Academic Bookstore)
11. Ateljee Bar (in Torni Tower)

HELSINKI

Venerable Esplanade Cafés

Highly competitive restaurants line the sunny north side of the Esplanade—offering enticing and creative lunch salads and light meals in their cafés (with fine sidewalk seating), plush sofas for cocktails in their bars, and fancy restaurant dining upstairs.

Teatterin Grilli, next to the landmark Swedish Theater, has fine, park-side seating indoors and out. Order a salad from the café counter (€9 with bread, choose two meats or extras to add to crispy base, Caesar salad option). The long cocktail bar is popular with office workers yet comfortable for baby-boomer tourists; there's also a dressy restaurant (café counter open Mon-Sat 11:00-20:00, June-mid-Aug Sun 11:00-20:00, closed Sun off-season, at the top of the Esplanade, Pohjoisesplanadi 2, tel. 09/6128-5000).

Strindberg is also popular (at the corner of the Esplanade and Mikonkatu). Downstairs is an elegant café with outdoor and indoor tables great for people-watching (€8-9 sandwiches and salads). The upstairs cocktail lounge—with big sofas and bookshelves giving it a den-like coziness—attracts the after-work office crowd. Also upstairs, the inviting restaurant has huge main dishes for

What If I Miss My Boat?

Remember that you can get help from the cruise line's port agent (listed on the destination information sheet distributed on the ship) and the local TI (see page 316). If the port agent suggests a costly solution (such as a private car with a driver), you may want to consider public transit.

Two fine and fiercely competitive lines—Viking Line (tel. 0600-15700, www.vikingline.fi) and Tallink Silja (tel. 0600-41577, www.tallinksilja.com)—connect Helsinki to **Stockholm.** Several companies run fast boats to **Tallinn,** including Tallink Silja, Viking Line, Linda Line (www.lindaline.ee), and Eckerö Line (www.eckeroline.fi). To reach points farther west, you could take the night boat to Stockholm, then the train from there to **Copenhagen** or **Oslo** (or take the overnight boat from Stockholm to **Rīga**). To research train schedules, see www.bahn.com. But for many of these places, you're probably better off flying.

St. **Petersburg** is well connected to Helsinki, but your options depend on whether you have a Russian visa (impossible to get last-minute if you don't already have one). With a visa, you can take a speedy train (www.vr.fi) or a slower bus. But if you don't have a visa, you're likely better off waiting and meeting your ship at the next stop.

If you need to catch a **plane** to your next destination, you can take a bus to Helsinki's airport, about 10 miles north of the city (www.helsinki-vantaa.fi).

Local **travel agents** in Helsinki can help you; I'd check first with the user-friendly Helsinki Expert desk inside the main TI (see page 316). For more advice on what to do if you miss the boat, see page 144.

€18-26, with fish, meat, pasta, and vegetarian options; reserve in advance to try to get a window seat overlooking the Esplanade (restaurant open Mon 11:00-23:00, Tue-Sat 11:00-24:00, closed Sun; café open Mon 9:00-23:00, Tue-Sat 9:00-24:00, Sun 10:00-22:00, Pohjoisesplanadi 33, tel. 09/681-2030).

Functional Eating

Lasipalatsi, the renovated, rejuvenated 1930s Glass Palace, is on Mannerheimintie between the train and bus stations. The café (with a youthful terrace on the square out back) offers a self-service lunch buffet for €12 on weekdays and a €15 brunch on weekends; there are always €5 sandwiches and €4 cakes (lunch/brunch served 11:00-15:00, café open Mon-Fri 7:30-22:00, Sat 9:00-23:00, Sun 11:00-22:00, more expensive restaurant upstairs—closed Sun, across from post office at Mannerheimintie 22-24, tel. 09/612-6700).

Picnics

In supermarkets, buy the semi-flat bread (available dark or light) that Finns love—every slice is a heel. Finnish liquid yogurt is also a treat (sold in liter cartons). Karelian pasties, filled with rice or mashed potatoes, make a good snack. A beautiful, upscale supermarket is in the basement of the **Stockmann** department store—follow the *Delikatessen* signs downstairs (Mon-Fri 9:00-21:00, Sat 9:00-18:00, open most Sun 12:00-18:00, Aleksanterinkatu 52B). Two blocks north, a more workaday, inexpensive supermarket is **S Market,** under the Sokos department store next to the train station (Mon-Sat 7:00-22:00, Sun 10:00-22:00).

Finnish Survival Phrases

In Finnish, the emphasis always goes on the first syllable. Double vowels (e.g., *ää* or *ii*) sound similar to single vowels, but are held a bit longer. The letter *y* sounds like the German *ü* (purse your lips and say "oo"). In the phonetics, ī sounds like the long *i* in "light," and bolded syllables are stressed.

English	Finnish	Pronunciation
Good morning. (formal)	Hyvää huomenta.	**hew**-vaah **hwoh**-mehn-tah
Good day. (formal)	Hyvää päivää.	**hew**-vaah **pī**-vaah
Good evening. (formal)	Hyvää iltaa.	**hew**-vaah **eel**-taah
Hi. / Bye. (informal)	Hei. / Hei, hei.	hey / hey hey
Do you speak English?	Puhutko englantia?	**poo**-hoot-koh **en**-glahn-tee-yah
Yes. / No.	Kyllä. / Ei.	**kewl**-lah / ay
Please.	Ole hyvä.	oh-leh **hew**-vah
Thank you (very much).	Kiitos (paljon).	**kee**-tohs (**pahl**-yohn)
You're welcome.	Kiitos. Or: Ei kestä.	**kee**-tohs / ay **kehs**-tah
Can I help you?	Voinko auttaa?	**voin**-koh **owt**-taah
Excuse me.	Anteeksi.	**ahn**-teek-see
(Very) good.	(Oikein) hyvä.	(**oy**-kayn) **hew**-vah
Goodbye.	Näkemiin.	**nah**-keh-meen
one / two	yksi / kaksi	**ewk**-see / **kahk**-see
three / four	kolme / neljä	**kohl**-meh / **nehl**-yah
five / six	viisi / kuusi	**vee**-see / **koo**-see
seven / eight	seitsemän / kahdeksan	**sayt**-seh-mahn / **kah**-dehk-sahn
nine / ten	yhdeksän / kymmenen	**ew**-dehk-sahn / **kewm**-meh-nehn
hundred	sata	**sah**-tah
thousand	tuhat	**too**-haht
How much?	Paljonko?	**pahl**-yohn-koh
local currency: euro	euro	**ay**-oo-roh
Where is...?	Missä on...?	**mee**-sah ohn
...the toilet	...WC	**vay**-say
men	miehet	**mee**-ay-heht
women	naiset	**nī**-seht
water / coffee	vesi / kahvi	**veh**-see / **kahkh**-vee
beer / wine	olut / viini	**oh**-luht / **vee**-nee
Cheers!	Kippis!	**kihp**-pihs
The bill, please.	Saisinko laskun, kiitos.	**sī**-seen-koh **lahs**-kuhn **kee**-tohs

ST.
PETERSBURG
Russia

Russia Practicalities

Russia (Россия) is a vast, multiethnic country of more than 140 million people. The world's biggest country by area (6.6 million square miles), it is nearly double the size of the US. Though no longer the great military and political power that it was during the Cold War, Russia remains a country of substantial natural resources, including oil. St. Petersburg—Russia's "window on the West"—is the country's northwestern outpost, peering across the Baltic Sea to Europe.

Money: 33 Russian rubles (R, official RUB) = about $1. (To roughly convert Russian prices, divide by three and drop a zero.) An ATM is called a bankomat (банкомат). The local value-added sales tax (called НДС/NDS) is 18 percent; the minimum purchase eligible for a VAT refund is 10,000 R (for details on refunds, see page 139). At many sights, you'll see higher "foreigner prices" for non-Russians.

Language: The native language is Russian, which uses the Cyrillic alphabet. For details, see page 368.

Emergencies: Dial 112 for police or other emergencies. Pickpockets and petty theft are a problem in St. Petersburg; for tips, see page 367. In case of theft or loss, see page 131.

Time Zone: St. Petersburg is on Moscow Time (one hour ahead of Helsinki, Tallinn, and Rīga; two hours ahead of Scandinavia and most of the Continent, including Stockholm and Copenhagen; and eight/eleven hours ahead of the East/West Coasts of the US).

Consulate in St. Petersburg: The **US consulate** is at Furshtadtskaya 15 (tel. 331-2600, http://stpetersburg.usconsulate.gov). There is no **Canadian embassy** in St. Petersburg; instead, contact the Moscow branch (23 Starokonyushenny Pereulok, tel. 495/925-6000, www.russia.gc.ca). Call ahead for passport services.

Phoning: Russia's country code is 7, and St. Petersburg's area code is 812. To call from another country to Russia, dial the international access code (011 from the US/Canada, 00 from Europe, or + from a mobile phone), then 7, followed by the area code and local number. For calls within Russia, dial just the number if you are calling locally; if you're calling long distance, dial 8, then the area code and the number. To call the US or Canada from Russia, dial 8, then dial 10, then 1, then your area code and phone number. For more tips, see page 1110.

Tipping: As service is included at sit-down meals, you don't need to tip further. Tip a taxi driver by rounding up the fare a bit (pay 300 R on an 280-R fare). For more tips on tipping, see page 143.

Dress Code: In Orthodox churches, modest dress is expected (no shorts or bare shoulders; women are encouraged to cover their heads with a scarf).

ST. PETERSBURG

Санкт-Петербург

 Once a swamp, then an imperial capital, and now a showpiece of vanished aristocratic opulence shot through with the dingy ruins of communism, St. Petersburg is Russia's most accessible and most tourist-worthy city. (It's also, arguably, European Russia's least "Russian" city.) Palaces, gardens, statues, and arched bridges over graceful waterways bring back the time of the czars. Two of the world's greatest art museums and some sumptuous Orthodox churches top it off.

But the city also challenges its visitors, most of whom have to jump through hoops to get a visa. Cruise-ship travelers have the option of seeing the city without a visa, but to do so must join a sanitized package excursion. Those who tackle the city independently struggle with not enough time, little or no English, and few Western standards of service and predictability.

Challenges aside, most visitors leave St. Petersburg with vivid memories of a magnificent city that lives according to its own rules. While this place can be exasperating, it is worth grappling with. Beyond its brick-and-mortar sights, St. Petersburg gives first-timers a perfect peek into the enigmatic Russian culture.

Russia was poor and remote for centuries, with a good part of the population bound in serfdom until the 1860s. In the late 19th century, Russia began to industrialize, built closer ties to Europe, and fostered writers such as Tolstoy, Dostoyevsky, and Chekhov. One of the new ideas that came to Russia from the West was communism. Led by Lenin and Stalin, the communist experiment lasted almost 75 years before it collapsed in 1991. Since then, despite widespread corruption, Russia has managed to build up something akin to a market economy. In St. Petersburg's shopping

ST. PETERSBURG

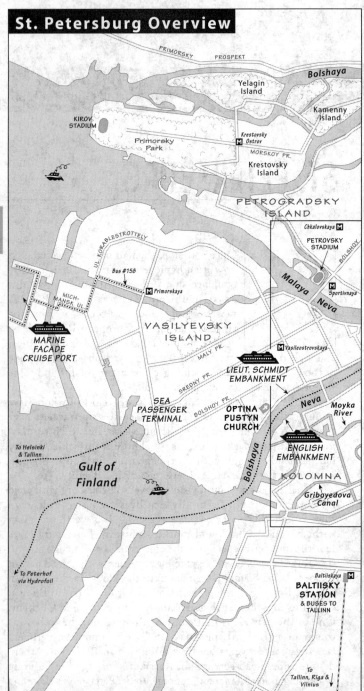

St. Petersburg Overview

PRIMORSKY PROSPEKT

Bolshaya

Yelagin Island

KIROV STADIUM

Primorsky Park

Kamenny Island

Krestovsky Ostrov Ⓜ

MORSKOY PR.

Krestovsky Island

PETROGRADSKY ISLAND

Chkalovskaya Ⓜ

PETROVSKY STADIUM

BOLSHOY

UL. KORABLESTROITELY

Bus #158

Primorskaya Ⓜ

MICH-MANSK UL.

Malaya Neva

Sportivnaya Ⓜ

MARINE FACADE CRUISE PORT

VASILYEVSKY ISLAND

MALY PR.

Vasileostrovskaya Ⓜ

SREDNY PR.

LIEUT. SCHMIDT EMBANKMENT

BOLSHOY PR.

SEA PASSENGER TERMINAL

OPTINA PUSTYN CHURCH

Neva

Moyka River

Bolshaya

ENGLISH EMBANKMENT

To Helsinki & Tallinn

Gulf of Finland

KOLOMNA

Griboyedova Canal

To Peterhof via Hydrofoil

Baltiiskaya Ⓜ

BALTIISKY STATION & BUSES TO TALLINN

To Tallinn, Riga & Vilnius

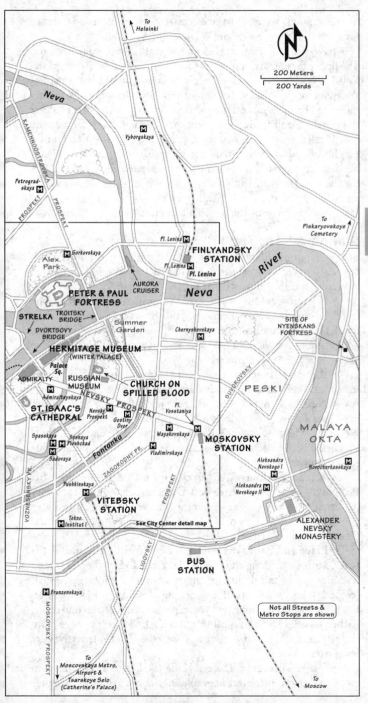

districts, you'll watch Russians release decades of pent-up desire for once-forbidden goods and services.

Save time on a sunny day just to walk. Keep your head up: The upper facades are sun-warmed and untouched by street grime. While Nevsky Prospekt—the city's famous main boulevard—encapsulates all that's wonderful and discouraging about this quixotic burg, it's essential to also explore the back streets along the canals. Stroll through the Summer Garden. Shop for a picnic at a local market hall. Go for a canal-boat cruise. Step into a neighborhood church, inhale the incense, and watch the devout bend at the waist to kiss an icon. Take a Metro ride anywhere, just for the experience. Climb St. Isaac's Cathedral for the view. The next day, when the Baltic Sea brings clouds and drizzle, plunge into the Hermitage or the Russian Museum.

Planning Your Time

St. Petersburg is fantastic and gigantic, with much to see. With two days here, your priorities should include the following (see later for a specific hour-by-hour plan).

• **Hermitage:** One of the world's finest palaces, housing one of the world's best art collections. Four hours is just enough for a quick taste (one hour for the staterooms, one hour for Old Masters art, one hour for Modern Masters, and an extra hour just to move around the huge and crowded complex).

• **Russian Museum:** Excellent, manageable, and relatively uncrowded collection of Russian art. Allow two hours.

• **Nevsky Prospekt:** St. Petersburg's bustling main drag, explained by my self-guided walk from Palace Square (behind the Hermitage) to the Fontanka River, and passing several of the biggies listed here. Allow two hours for the walk, not counting sightseeing stops.

• **Kazan Cathedral, Church on Spilled Blood, and St. Isaac's:** St. Petersburg's three best Orthodox churches—each very different (so they're complementary). Allow about 30 minutes apiece for a quick visit, plus another 30 minutes to climb to the viewpoint atop St. Isaac's.

• **Peter and Paul Fortress:** The city's fortified-island birthplace, with stout ramparts, the burial cathedral of the czars, and a smattering of mildly interesting museums. For a targeted visit (cathedral and quick stroll around the grounds), allow about an hour; an additional hour lets you dip into some of the museums. Either way, budget about 30 minutes each way to get here from the city center (by foot over the Neva, or by Metro from Nevsky Prospekt).

• **Other Museums:** These include the Dostoyevsky Museum and the Kunstkamera (ethnography museum). Allow 30 minutes for each one—potentially much more if you're especially interested in their subjects.

   • **Out-of-Town Sights:** Those who love opulent palaces can make a pilgrimage to two over-the-top Romanov residences on the city outskirts: **Peterhof** (with gorgeous gardens) or **Tsarskoye Selo** (with Catherine's Palace and its sumptuous Amber Room). Either place can be seen in a half-day targeted tour if you go by taxi or with a hired driver; otherwise, allow a full day. Given the relative complexity of reaching either palace, most cruisers skip these to focus on the abundant sights in the city center.

Best One-, Two-, and Three-Day Plans
Two- or Three-Day Plans

Most cruises stop in St. Petersburg for two days. I've also provided suggestions for a third day, in case you have it. To maximize your daytime sightseeing, see if your cruise line offers an evening visit to the Hermitage (for details, and pros and cons, see page 358).

Day 1

9:00	Follow my self-guided walk along Nevsky Prospekt to acquaint yourself with the city.
11:00	Visit the Kazan Cathedral and Church on Spilled Blood, and grab a quick lunch.
13:00	Tour the Russian Museum.
15:00	Take a canal-boat cruise or visit the Dostoyevsky Museum.
16:30	Ride the bus to St. Isaac's Cathedral.
18:30	Dinner.
Evening	Ballet (seasonal), a concert, or the circus—or possibly an evening Hermitage visit (through your cruise line).

Day 2

10:30	Plunge into the Hermitage.
13:30	Grab a quick lunch, then walk across the Neva River to the Strelka viewpoint, continuing to Peter and Paul Fortress.
15:30	If you're not pooped yet, tour the Kunstkamera; for a break, stroll through the Summer Garden.
18:30	Return to the city center for dinner (if your ship's departure time allows it).

Day 3

Add more time in the Hermitage or the Russian Museum; visit Piskaryovskoye Memorial Cemetery; or go to Peterhof or Tsarskoye Selo for the day.

ST. PETERSBURG

To Visa or Not to Visa?

Note: *The following information was accurate as of early 2013, but Russian visa regulations are notoriously changeable. Confirm everything stated here before you make your plans. For the latest requirements, see www.ricksteves.com/russianvisa.*

Residents of most countries, including the US and Canada, are required to obtain a visa in advance to enter Russia. An exception is made for travelers arriving by cruise ship, who are allowed to be in the country for up to 72 hours without a visa. However, there's a catch: You must be accompanied by a local tour operator. You are required to remain with your guide or escort the entire time you are on land—which means you'll have virtually no free time to explore. (A loophole in St. Petersburg allows some tour operators to provide a downtown "shuttle service" to passengers arriving on the St. Peter Line ferries from Helsinki, Tallinn, and Stockholm, but this service isn't extended to those arriving on a cruise ship.)

Cruisers in St. Petersburg have a choice to make: You can either 1) obtain a visa to explore the city on your own, or 2) see the city with a guide (on an excursion offered by your cruise line, or on an excursion arranged through a private operator). The visa route buys you independence, but you must hassle with the visa application process well in advance. An excursion is more expensive and completely scripted, but virtually effortless (you can typically wait to book excursions until you're on board, unless St. Petersburg is your first stop).

Obtaining a visa is an expensive headache. But it's still cheaper than paying for cruise-line excursions, and frees you up to see and do much more than you otherwise could. If you're an adventurous traveler and want to experience the real Russia, at least consider going the visa route.

How to Get a Visa

Getting a Russian visa is not exactly difficult, but it does take several steps and a few weeks to accomplish. Don't expect any help whatsoever from your cruise line (they'd rather see you buy their visa-free but pricey excursions). If the steps outlined below make your head spin, skip down to "Third-Party Visa Agencies."

1. Before applying for a visa, you must first get an official document called a **"visa invitation"** (*priglashenie*; sometimes called a **"letter of invitation," "visa sponsor,"** or **"visa support letter"**) from a Russian organization recognized by the Russian Foreign Ministry. Visa invitations are typically issued either by a hotel or by a tour operator; if you're arriving by cruise, you'll need to arrange an invitation through a third-party agency (see below). Don't expect the invitation process to make sense; it feels (and is) bureaucratic and possibly corrupt. The organization that issues your invitation is legally responsible for you during

your stay in Russia, but in practice, you will never have any contact with them.

2. Fill out the **Electronic Visa Application Form** (available online at http://visa.kdmid.ru). You'll need to choose between a multiple-entry visa (valid for three years, $180) or a double-/single-entry visa ($140). If your cruise will be in Russia for just two days (as most are), the cheaper double-/single-entry visa is fine. But if there's any chance that you'll be returning to Russia soon, choose the multiple-entry version to save the trouble of applying again later. Also note that your passport must be valid for at least six months beyond the date of your departure from Russia, and must have two adjacent blank pages to accommodate the visa.

3. Submit the invitation, the form, your passport, a passport photograph, and the processing fee (money order or cashier's check only) to the Russian Embassy. Applications are accepted anywhere from **30 to 90 days before departure** (the specific timeframe changes constantly, but you'll certainly need at least a month for the full process). It's important to note that Russia's embassies and consulates in the US do not accept visa applications by mail. If you live near one of the Russian consulates in Washington, D.C., New York, San Francisco, Seattle, or Houston, you can deliver your documents in person. (For specific locations and more details, see www.russianembassy.org.) Otherwise, you must submit your application through a third-party service, which can be a smart idea anyway.

Third-Party Visa Agencies: Various agencies specialize in steering your visa application through the process. They can also help you arrange visa invitations and navigate the confusing application. I've had a good experience with Passport Visa Express.com (www.passportvisasexpress.com).

In addition to the $140/$180 visa price, visa agencies charge a service fee of about $50-85 (including the invitation fee). To ship your passport securely to and from the visa agency costs another $50 or so. Figure at least $250 total per person.

Entering Russia with a Visa: When you enter Russia, the immigration officer will ask you to fill out a **"migration card"** in duplicate, listing your name, passport number, and other details. The officer will stamp both parts of the card and keep one. Don't lose the other half—it must be presented when you leave the country. (A digital version of this card is being phased in, but you'll still need to carry the hard copy.) When entering the country, you may also be asked to show your visa invitation—keep it handy.

While in Russia, you are required to carry your original passport (not just a copy) with you at all times. Police in Russia can stop you at any time for any reason and ask to see your documents, though this seldom happens to tourists.

One-Day Plan

A few cruises are in town for only one day. In this case, devout art lovers should tour the Hermitage, then follow my self-guided Nevsky Prospekt walk. But for a wider-ranging experience, skip the Hermitage and follow this ambitious plan (if you're not up for it all, omit the Russian Museum):

9:00   Follow my self-guided Nevsky Prospekt walk (about 2 hours), stopping in the Kazan Cathedral (30 minutes), Church on Spilled Blood (30 minutes), and Russian Museum (2 hours). Along the way, grab a quick lunch (30 minutes) and take some time to shop and linger (30 minutes).

15:00   Take a canal-boat cruise.

16:00   Ride the Metro to the Peter and Paul Fortress, and tour the Romanov tombs at the cathedral.

18:00   Walk back across the Neva, pausing at Strelka for a panoramic view.

19:00   Dinner, ballet, or...back to your ship (depending on departure time).

Arrival at the Port of St. Petersburg

Arrival at a Glance: From the **Marine Facade port,** either take a taxi or brave the fun and cheap bus-plus-Metro option to reach Nevsky Prospekt. If your ship puts in along the river in the city, at the **Lieutenant Schmidt** or **English embankments,** it's a longish walk or quick taxi ride to major sights.

Port Overview

St. Petersburg has constructed an enormous, U-shaped cruise port called the **Marine (Morskoy) Facade.** Built on reclaimed land at the western tip of the giant Vasilyevsky Island (facing the Gulf of Finland), it can accommodate a staggering seven ships at once, feeding into four separate terminal buildings. The land around the cruise port is slated to be redeveloped into an upscale residential complex (for more information, see www.ppspbmf.ru).

A lucky few ships—generally smaller, luxury vessels—dock along the Neva River embankment (either the **Lieutenant Schmidt Embankment** or the **English Embankment**) closer to the city center, within a (long) walk of the Hermitage and other sights.

Tourist Information: There are small TI kiosks at the Marine Facade terminals, but they're not particularly helpful (and often closed). If you happen to see an open one, pick up a map.

Otherwise, make your way downtown to find the TI on Nevsky Prospekt (see page 366).

Tour Options in St. Petersburg

Tour opportunities for cruisers in St. Petersburg—including local guides for hire, walking tours, and bus tours—are not as robust as in other European port cities. For choices, see "Tours in St. Petersburg" on page 374.

Arrival at the Marine Facade

As your ship sails in from the Gulf of Finland, it runs right into the Marine Facade cruise port. You'll feel like you're out on the edge of town, because you are. Each of the four Marine Facade terminals has roughly the same services. In muggy weather, keep your veranda door closed; St. Petersburg was built on a swamp, and bugs swarm here when conditions are right.

Leaving your ship, you'll go through the **immigration** checkpoint (regardless of whether you have a visa or are with an excursion, you'll go through the same process). If you do have a visa, keep your letter of invitation handy, as you may be asked for it.

After the immigration checkpoint, you'll enter a sleek terminal building with a crowd of prearranged drivers and tour guides (holding signs with the names of their clients), an **ATM** dispensing rubles, a desk for booking a taxi, and several souvenir stands perfectly positioned to help departing cruisers burn through whatever rubles remain in their pockets.

Getting into Town

By Taxi

Taxis line up out front, charging 600-800 R for a ride downtown (figure 1,400 R one-way to Peterhof, or 1,200 R to Tsarskoye Selo). If no taxis are standing by, look for someone with a *TAXI* clipboard (they may be at a small desk inside the terminal).

By Public Transportation

It's easy, cheap (less than $2), and very local to ride public transportation from the Marine Facade into downtown. The basic plan: Ride a bus to the nearest Metro station, then either whoosh under the city by subway all the way downtown, or get off at the first stop and walk through interesting neighborhoods the rest of the way into the city.

At the curb in front of the terminal, look for the stop for **bus #158.** This bus passes through about twice hourly, looping around

Excursions from St. Petersburg

The majority of cruisers in St. Petersburg don't want to go through the hassle of getting a visa (see page 354), so they see the city exclusively with excursions. While this can be a great experience, it pays to be an informed consumer. Keep in mind that you'll likely be in town for two full days and, without a visa, you are allowed to leave the ship *only* with an excursion.

To make the most of your time, you'll need to book multiple itineraries, and the cost can add up. For example, on a mid-range cruise line, an all-day bus-and-walking tour (including a Hermitage tour, evening ballet performance, and trip to the countryside palaces the next day) costs about $500 per person.

Also be aware that a small cabal of tour operators controls all of the cruise tourism business in St. Petersburg. They employ their own stable of guides (whose quality varies widely), and generally take you only to shops and restaurants that they own. (This means that virtually all of the money you spend "in St. Petersburg" actually goes into the pockets of a few super-wealthy local magnates, rather than supporting the broader community.) It's my preference to secure a visa in advance, then arrange an independent shore tour through a well-regarded third-party company (read online reviews to select one; for more, see page 374). That said, the reality is that the majority of cruisers landing in St. Petersburg will opt for the simplicity of packaged excursions. Here's a rundown of the typical choices:

The basic St. Petersburg visit includes a narrated **bus ride** around town, with brief photo-op stops at pretty buildings (such as the Peter and Paul Fortress and Cathedral, Strelka viewpoint, Church on Spilled Blood, and St. Isaac's Cathedral). Many also include a shopping stop and a meal. To add more substance, you can book a tour that includes in-depth tours of individual sights. The most popular choice is the **Hermitage/Winter Palace,** the grand Romanov residence jammed with great artwork. Excursions to this impossibly vast and crowded sight usually consist of a once-over-lightly surgical strike of the main historical rooms and a few select masterpiece paintings. Don't expect "free time" to linger at your favorites or to explore rooms not on the tour. (For example, lovers of Impressionism should be sure to book a tour that explicitly includes this collection—some don't.) If your cruise line offers an after-hours **evening visit of the Hermitage** (which may include a concert in one of the grand halls), it's worth considering simply because it spares you from the crowds and saves valuable daylight time for other priorities. (This may be worthwhile even for those touring on their own with a visa, as it's the only way to get into the Hermitage after hours.)

Other popular stops are the two sprawling countryside palaces outside of town: **Peterhof** (sometimes called the **Summer Palace**) to the west; and **Tsarskoye Selo** (usually billed as **Catherine's Palace** for its grandest structure, sometimes called by its old communist name, Pushkin), to the south. A tour to both is overkill (especially with so much to see in the city itself)—choose just one. Peterhof has more impressive grounds, while Tsarskoye Selo has more opulent interiors (especially the famous Amber Room in Catherine's Palace). Some tours to Catherine's Palace tack on a quick stop at yet another nearby palace, **Pavlovsk.**

You may also see excursions that include a **river cruise,** which is well worthwhile for the excellent orientation it provides—but skip those that include a pointless stop at **Yusupov Palace,** notable only as the site of Rasputin's assassination. Other excursions specialize either in **cathedrals and churches** (of which St. Petersburg has many fascinating and lavish examples) or the **Grand Choral Synagogue** (worthwhile only if you have a special interest). Some excursions include a ride on the **Metro,** just for kicks—an enlightening and local-feeling peek at an impressive people-mover.

Evening entertainment includes **folklore shows** and **ballet.** While ballet is a Russian forte, note that great venues such as the Mariinsky and Mikhailovsky Theaters are on hiatus between mid-July and mid-September; carefully read the fine print of any ballet excursion you're offered. Often, it's a crowd-pleasing, made-for-tourists show put on by lower-tier performers in a tired old ballroom.

And, believe it or not, some cruise lines offer one-day excursions all the way to **Moscow** (round-trip by plane). While there's no shortage of things to see in St. Petersburg, if this is the closest you'll ever be to the Russian capital, for some it's worth the trip.

Unfortunately, cruise-line excursions rarely go to a few excellent sights—including the outstanding Russian Museum, the powerful WWII-era Piskaryovskoye Memorial Cemetery, Peter the Great's quirky Kunstkamera, and the Dostoyevsky Museum; to see those, you'll need a visa.

the Marine Facade, with stops at
each terminal. Hop on and pay
the conductor (25 R). You'll get
off the bus at the Primorskaya
Metro station. Watch closely
for your stop: After leaving the
port and driving past apartment
blocks, the bus turns left onto a
big boulevard with tram tracks,
with several shops on the right.

This is where you hop off (if you're not sure, you can ask fellow
passengers: "Metro?"). Exiting the bus, walk straight ahead, and
proceed alongside the big shopping center. Look for the Metro
sign—it looks like an "M" that's bulging on the sides.

Head into the Metro station, turn right to find the ticket window, and buy a token (28 R). Use the token to pass through the
turnstile, and head down the long escalator. This is the terminus
of the green line, so trains run only in the direction of downtown
(toward Rybatskoye). Hop on a train. (For more on St. Petersburg's
Metro system, see page 370.)

Option 1: Metro to Downtown

The easiest plan on a tight schedule is to ride the Metro two stops
to the **Gostiny Dvor** station. This pops you out onto the busiest
stretch of the city's main avenue, Nevsky Prospekt. From here, it's
a 10-minute walk to several major sights, including the Russian
Museum, Church on Spilled Blood, and Kazan Cathedral. If you
want to reach the start of Nevsky Prospekt (near Palace Square,
behind the Hermitage), ride bus #3, #7, #22, #24, #27, or #191;
or take trolley bus #1, #5, #7, #10, #11, or #22. Of these, trolley
buses #5 and #22 continue to St. Isaac's Cathedral. Alternatively,
to get to Peter and Paul Fortress, ride the Metro to Gostiny Dvor,
then switch to the other Metro line (blue, Nevsky Prospekt stop);
ride this line in the direction of Parnas, and get off at the first
stop, Gorkovskaya—about a 10-minute walk from the fortress (see
directions on page 420).

Option 2: Back Street and
Riverfront Walk to Downtown

If you're interested in exploring some back streets where few
tourists venture, here's another option: From the Primorskaya
Metro station near the port, ride the subway to the first stop,
Vasileostrovskaya. From this stop, it's a 15-minute walk (passing a
local market) to the riverfront, another 15 scenic minutes along the
riverfront to the Strelka viewpoint, and 10 more minutes to either
the Peter and Paul Fortress or the Hermitage and Nevsky Prospekt

(in opposite directions).

Exiting the Metro station, you're in the heart of **Vasilyevsky Island,** a residential zone stretching from the city center all the way to the Marine Facade. Turn right, then right again, to head down the pedestrian street called "**Ulitsa 7-ya Liniya / Ulitsa 6-ya Liniya**" (улица 7-я Линия / улица 6-я Линия). Carefully planned Vasilyevsky Island has 30 numbered north/west streets (called "lines") that cross its three big east/west thoroughfares (named "big"/*bolshoy,* "medium"/*sredny,* and "small"/*maly*). Each side of the street has a different number—in this case, 6 on the left, 7 on the right.

Enjoy strolling down this lively, colorful, traffic-free street— one of the oldest in the city. After one very long block, on the left you'll see **St. Andrew's Cathedral.** Step inside for a totally untouristy Russian Orthodox experience (women can borrow a head scarf; for more on the faith and the features of its churches, see page 412). Like most of St. Petersburg, this church echoes European styles—its Baroque exterior would be at home in Bavaria. But the interior is filled with Orthodox icons.

Continuing past the church, you'll reach a big intersection (Bolshoy Prospekt, "Big Avenue"). Cross the street, then detour a block to the left (past the little park) to reach the **farmer's market** (yellow building with big green sign). Poke through the gateway into the inner courtyard to find some open-air stalls (including a tasty tandoor bakery), then head inside. Survey the variety of offerings at the stands: pickled items, smoked and salted fish, honey, cheeses, fresh cream, dried fruits, and lots of produce. (For tips on browsing a farmer's market, see page 432.)

Backtrack to the street you were on (Ulitsa 6-ya Liniya), and continue in the direction you were headed, following the arcade of the long building. At the end of the street, just before the river, look for the **House of Academics,** the yellow building on the right (with the heads over the windows). Each of the black plaques honors a great Russian scientist. The blue plaque by the door identifies the former apartment of Ivan Pavlov. If that name rings a bell, it's because he famously studied conditioned responses (and was the first Russian to win a Nobel Prize).

Just past the House of Academics, you'll pop out at the Annunciation (Blagoveshchensky) Bridge over the **Neva River.** Just to your right, notice the many cargo ships stacked up along the embankment. St. Petersburg is at the mouth of the Neva River, but its 342 bridges impede the progress of ships wanting to head upstream. The solution: Each night, from about 1:30 to 5:00 in the morning, drawbridges throughout the city center open, allowing cargo boats to proceed. Boats arriving during the day tie up here to wait their turn.

From here (before crossing the bridge), you can turn left and walk about 15 minutes (with the water on your right) to the Strelka viewpoint (described on page 416) to get your bearings. From that point, you can easily walk to the Hermitage or the Peter and Paul Fortress.

For a detour to another church—this one particularly beautiful—turn right at the river and walk (with the river on your left) for about 10 minutes, to the gold-domed **Optina Pustyn**. This is one of the many branch churches of the Eastern Orthodox Optina monastery (the main center is about 150 miles south of Moscow). Impressive as the structure is from the outside, be sure to check out the interior with its spectacular frescoes (daily 8:00-20:00; tourists welcome but be discreet). Repurposed by the communists (like many churches), this house of worship spent time as a hockey rink; restorers found hockey pucks embedded in the walls. Now the building has reclaimed its sacred purpose, and its male choir is one of Russia's most beloved.

Returning to Your Ship

To return to the Marine Facade, reverse the directions above: From Gostiny Dvor downtown (right on the busiest stretch of Nevsky Prospekt), hop on the green Metro line and ride two stops to the end of the line, Primorskaya. Head out front and take bus #158 back to your ship at the Marine Facade.

Arrival at the Neva Embankment

Smaller ships sometimes put in along either embankment of the Neva River, closer to the city center. Consider yourself lucky if your ship docks here, as it's within (fairly long) walking distance of the big sights.

Getting into Town

Lieutenant Schmidt Embankment (North Bank)

Named for a naval officer who fought in the 1917 Russian Revolution, the Lieutenant Schmidt (Leytenanta Shmidta) embankment is a scenic 30-minute walk (1.5 miles) from the heart of town. It's right in front of the beautiful, golden-domed Optina Pustyn church (described earlier—be sure to drop in for a peek).

To **walk** into town, simply stroll with the river on your right. Cross at the second bridge, Dvortsovy Most, to reach the Hermitage, Palace Square, and Nevsky Prospekt; or turn left just after that bridge to find the Strelka viewpoint and the bridge to Peter and Paul Fortress.

To reach handy **buses, trolley buses, and trams** from the north embankment, walk to the Optina Pustyn church and turn up the street called "Ulitsa 14-ya Liniya / Ulitsa 15-ya Liniya" (улица 14-я Линия / улица 15-я Линия). After one long block, you'll hit a main thoroughfare, Bolshoy Prospekt. Turn left and walk a half-block to the stop for trolley bus #10 or #11 or bus #7, all of which cross Dvortsovy Most to reach Palace Square, then continue up Nevsky Prospekt to Uprising Square.

If you're heading to Peter and Paul Fortress, walk one very long block beyond the busy Bolshoy Prospekt to Sredny Prospekt; once there, turn right a half-block to the stop for tram #6 or #40. Ride this going to the right; you'll hop out at the first stop after crossing the river—at Zverinskaya street; you can also stay on for three more stops and get off right next to the Gorkovskaya Metro station (it looks like a flying saucer), and walk through the park to the fortress. For either option, once you've boarded the tram, wait for the conductor to come to you to pay the fare (35 R).

English Embankment (South Bank)

The nearest berth to the town center, the English (Angliyskaya) embankment is a 20-minute walk from the Hermitage (about a mile away)—head out with the river on your left until you reach the second bridge (Dvortsovy Most). There's no easy, direct public-transit connection.

Returning to Your Ship

Both embankment terminals are walkable (and visible) from the city center. If you get turned around, just make your way to the Neva and look downriver for your ship. But leave yourself plenty of time to walk back—it's farther than it looks, and may take as long as 30 minutes from the Hermitage to either terminal. Or consider the tram, bus, and trolley bus connections noted above.

Orientation to St. Petersburg

Get to know Nevsky Prospekt (Невский Проспект), St. Petersburg's main street. Almost everything you'll want to see is either along Nevsky or a few blocks to either side. A few spots—including the Peter and Paul Fortress, Kunstkamera, and Strelka viewpoint—are just across the river.

Nevsky starts at the slender-spired Admiralty building, next to the river, Hermitage, and Palace Square. Running outward

ST. PETERSBURG

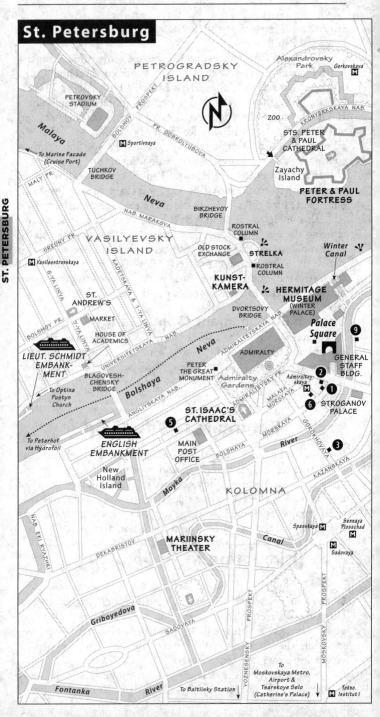

St. Petersburg

PETROGRADSKY ISLAND

Alexandrovsky Park

Gorkovskaya M

PETROVSKY STADIUM

Malaya

Sportivnaya M

BOLSHOY PROSPEKT

PR. DOBROLYUBOVA

To Marine Facade (Cruise Port)

MALY PR.

TUCHKOV BRIDGE

Neva

NAB. MARAKOVA

BIRZHEVOY BRIDGE

ZOO

KRONVERKSKAYA NAB.

STS. PETER & PAUL CATHEDRAL

Zayachy Island

PETER & PAUL FORTRESS

SKEDNY PR.

VASILYEVSKY ISLAND

Vasileostrovskaya M

6-YA LINYA

KADETSKAYA & 1-YA LINYA

ROSTRAL COLUMN

OLD STOCK EXCHANGE

STRELKA

ROSTRAL COLUMN

Winter Canal

ST. ANDREW'S

MARKET

HOUSE OF ACADEMICS

BOLSHOY PR.

7-YA LINYA

KUNST-KAMERA

HERMITAGE MUSEUM (WINTER PALACE)

DVORTSOVY BRIDGE

DVORTSOVAYA NAB.

Palace Square

GENERAL STAFF BLDG.

9

LIEUT. SCHMIDT EMBANK-MENT

BLAGOVESH-CHENSKY BRIDGE

UNIVERSITETSKAYA NAB.

Bolshaya

ANGLIYSKAYA NAB.

Neva

PETER THE GREAT MONUMENT

ADMIRALTEYSKAYA NAB.

ADMIRALTY

Admiralty Gardens

ADMIRALTEYSKY PR.

Admiraltey-skaya M

MALAYA MORSKAYA

2

1

STROGANOV PALACE

6

GOROKHOVAYA

To Optina Pustyn Church

To Peterhof via Hydrofoil

ENGLISH EMBANKMENT

New Holland Island

ST. ISAAC'S CATHEDRAL

5

MAIN POST OFFICE

Moyka

BOLSHAYA

MORSKAYA

KAZANSKAYA

River

3

KOLOMNA

NAB. EKI KYAZHKI

DEKABRISTOV

MARIINSKY THEATER

Canal

Spasskaya M

Sennaya Plosschad M

Sadovaya M

Griboyedova

SADOVAYA

VOZNESENSKY PROSPEKT

MOSKOVSKY PROSPEKT

To Moskovskaya Metro, Airport & Tsarskoye Selo (Catherine's Palace)

Tekno. Institut I M

Fontanka

River

To Baltilsky Station

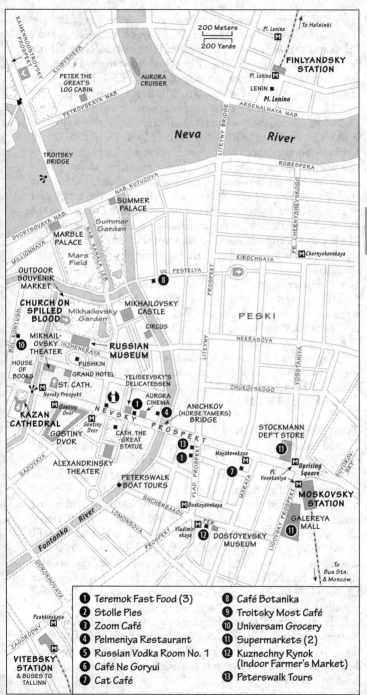

1. Teremok Fast Food (3)
2. Stolle Pies
3. Zoom Café
4. Pelmeniya Restaurant
5. Russian Vodka Room No. 1
6. Café Ne Goryui
7. Cat Café
8. Café Botanika
9. Troitsky Most Café
10. Universam Grocery
11. Supermarkets (2)
12. Kuznechny Rynok (Indoor Farmer's Market)
13. Peterswalk Tours

from the center, it crosses three concentric waterways: first the Moyka (Мойка) River, then the Griboyedova Canal (Канал Грибоедова), and finally the Fontanka (Фонтанка) River. A little farther out, Uprising Square (Ploshchad Vosstaniya, Площадь Восстания)—home to a tall obelisk and the Moskovsky train station—marks the end of the zone of interest to most tourists.

Maps make St. Petersburg appear smaller than it is. What looks like just a few blocks can easily translate into a half-hour walk. The two-mile walk along Nevsky from the Admiralty to Uprising Square takes about 45 minutes at a brisk pace. To cross the river or go to more distant sites, you'll need to use public transport. Getting between any two points in different parts of the center, whether by foot or Metro, can easily eat up the better part of an hour. Even crossing from one side of Nevsky Prospekt to the other is no small task (look for sporadic underground walkways, like the one in front of the Gostiny Dvor shopping mall). The bus system is quick and handy, but isn't user-friendly for non-Russian speakers.

A few terms you'll see on maps: *ulitsa* is "street," *ploshchad* is "square," *prospekt* is "avenue," and *most* is "bridge." Many street signs are conveniently bilingual. They usually list the house number of the building they're on, as well as of the buildings to either side (this is convenient, as buildings can be very large).

You may see free maps around town, but if you'll be navigating on your own, buy a good map at one of the bookstores listed later, under "Helpful Hints." I like the *Saint Petersburg for Visitors* map by Karta (about 120 R).

Tourist Information

Tourist information is hard to come by in St. Petersburg. The city does run an official TI at Sadovaya Ulitsa 14, a few yards off Nevsky Prospekt, across from Gostiny Dvor (you'll need to go up one flight of stairs). When I visited, the staff was friendly, but it's small and they only have a few brochures—I wouldn't make a special trip (Mon-Fri 10:00-19:00, Sat 12:00-18:00, closed Sun, www.visit-petersburg.ru or www.ispb.info). You may see TI kiosks in high-tourist areas such as Palace Square and St. Isaac's Cathedral—but hours and services are unpredictable. The city also runs a 24-hour "Tourist Help Line," with English operators, at tel. 300-3333 (or 0333 if your mobile phone is using the Megafon network).

The weekly, English-language *St. Petersburg Times* (www .sptimes.ru), which comes out on Wednesdays, will keep you up-to-date on events in the city. The bimonthly *St. Petersburg In Your Pocket* guidebook is good; you can browse it online at www .inyourpocket.com.

Helpful Hints

Closed Day: The Hermitage and Peterhof are closed on Mondays, the Russian Museum and Tsarskoye Selo on Tuesdays, and many religious sites (St. Isaac's, Church on Spilled Blood) are closed on Wednesdays.

Don't Drink the Water: While new water treatment plants have improved quality in recent years, and most locals wash fruit and brush their teeth with tap water, they still don't drink it—and neither should you. Buy bottled water cheaply in grocery stores.

Theft Alert: Russia has hardworking, often unusually aggressive pickpockets who target tourists. Be particularly aware anywhere along Nevsky Prospekt, in crowded shopping areas (such as Gostiny Dvor), and on public transport. Assume that any scuffle is a distraction by a team of thieves, and that anyone who approaches you on the street is trying to pull off a scam. Some thieves are well-dressed and even carry guidebooks to fool you.

Pedestrian Safety: *Always* use crosswalks and look both ways before crossing, as traffic laws are loosely obeyed and drivers often go much too fast, even on small city-center streets. Nevsky Prospekt has eight lanes of traffic moving at terrifying speeds; *don't* jaywalk.

Language Barrier: St. Petersburg is awash in tourists, but most of them are Russian. Don't expect anybody you interact with to speak English. (And, when they realize you don't speak Russian, locals will often simply ignore you.) Fortunately, Metro signs and some street signs are bilingual.

Online Translation Tip: If a website you want is available only in Russian, try using the Chrome browser (available free at www .google.com/chrome), which automatically senses a foreign language and offers to (roughly) translate the page for you.

Business Hours: Many shops and services are open the same hours seven days a week (the legacy of communism, which tried to do away with weekends). Offices are more likely to close or have shorter hours on Saturday and particularly Sunday.

"Sightseeing Tax" for Foreigners: You may notice that the admission price for Russians to various sights can be much less—often less than half—the cost for foreigners. I've listed only the "foreigner" price, but if you happen to have a Russian passport, be sure to pay the lower price.

Pharmacy: Look for **366,** with branches at Gorokhovaya 16, near the Admiralteyskaya Metro stop (Mon-Fri 9:00-23:00, Sat-Sun 10:00-22:00, tel. 314-3457) and Nevsky Prospekt 98, near the Mayakovskaya Metro stop (Mon-Fri 24 hours, Sat-Sun 10:00-21:00, tel. 275-8189).

ST. PETERSBURG

The Russian Language

Most Russians in the tourist industry speak English well, but out on the street you'll encounter a language barrier. In general, young Russians usually know at least a little halting schoolroom English, while older people speak none at all. A few Russian phrases go a long way:

English	Russian (Cyrillic/ Roman)	Pronounced
Hello. (formal)	Здравствуйте. / Zdravstvuytye.	ZDRAH-stvooy-tyeh
Hi. (informal)	Привет. / Privyet.	pree-VYEHT
Yes.	Да. / Da.	dah
No.	Нет. / Nyet.	nyeht
Please.	Пожалуйста. / Pozhaluysta.	pah-ZHAHL-stah
Thank you.	Спасибо. / Spasibo.	spah-SEE-bah
Excuse me.	Извините. / Izvinitye.	eez-vee-NEE-tyeh
Where is?	Где? / Gdye?	guh-DYEH
How much?	Сколько стоит? / Skolko stoit?	SKOHL-kah STOH-yeet
Do you speak English?	Вы говорите по-английски? / Vy govoritye po angliyski?	vih gah-vah-REE-tyeh pah ahn-GLEE-skee
I (don't) understand.	Я (не) понимаю. / Ya (nye) ponimayu.	yah (nyeh) poh-nyih-MAH-yoo
Goodbye.	До свидания. / Do svidaniya.	dah svee-DAHN-yah

Medical/Dental Services: The (entirely Russian-staffed) **American Medical Clinic** is near St. Isaac's Cathedral on the Moyka Embankment (Nab. reki Moyki 78, tel. 740-2090, www.amclinic.com, info@amclinic.ru).

Bridge Openings: Between about 1:30 and 5:00 in the morning, many of St. Petersburg's bridges are lifted for river traffic, making it impossible to get between the city's different islands. Make sure not to get stranded if out late.

Internet Access: You can get online in an Internet café at the back of the Subway restaurant at Nevsky Prospekt 11 (enter on side

It pays to take the time to learn the Cyrillic alphabet; there's a quick learning curve if you just practice reading signs around town. The table below shows the Cyrillic alphabet (both capital and lowercase), and in the second column, the Roman equivalent. The letters A, E, K, M, O, and T stand for basically the same sound in Cyrillic and Roman; B, C, H, P, X, and У are "false friends" that have a different sound than the Roman letter they look like. For some letters, think Greek: Г (gamma), Д (delta with a flat top), П (pi), Ф (phi), and X (chi).

The letter Ы, which stands for a sound somewhat similar to the *i* in English "bit," looks like two letters but is treated as one. The letter Ш is pronounced like *sh*; the similar-looking letter Щ (*shch*), with the little hook, is pronounced as in "fresh cheese." The "hard sign" and "soft sign" are silent letters that affect the pronunciation of the preceding consonant in ways you need not worry about.

Cyrillic	Roman	Cyrillic	Roman	Cyrillic	Roman
Аа	a	Кк	k	Хх	kh
Бб	b	Лл	l	Цц	ts
Вв	v	Мм	m	Чч	ch
Гг	g	Нн	n	Шш	sh
Дд	d	Оо	o	Щщ	shch
Ее	ye, e	Пп	p	Ъъ	hard sign
Ёё	yō	Рр	r	Ыы	y
Жж	zh	Сс	s	ьь	soft sign
Зз	z	Тт	t	Ээ	e
Ии	i	Уу	u	Юю	yu
Йй	y	Фф	f	Яя	ya

Two important words that you'll see often but are easy to confuse (they differ by only one letter) are вход (vkhod), which means entrance, and выход (vykhod)—exit.

street and take stairs up to second floor; 120 R/hour, Skype installed, open 24 hours, tel. 314-6705, www.5.3ghz.ru). Some cafés, such as the ubiquitous Coffee House (Кофе Хауз) chain, offer free Wi-Fi.

Bookstore: The city's best-known bookstore, **Dom Knigi** ("House of Books," Дом Книги), is in the old Singer sewing machine building at Nevsky Prospekt 28 (by the Griboyedova Canal, across from Kazan Cathedral). It sells English novels and locally produced guidebooks and has a pretty second-floor café with a view over the Kazan Cathedral (daily 9:00-24:00).

Anglia Bookshop (Англия), just off Nevsky Prospekt facing the Fontanka River (next to the horse statues on the Anichkov Bridge, at the end of my self-guided walk), has a fine selection of English-language books by Russian authors and about Russian history (Mon-Sat 11:00-20:00, Sun 12:00-19:00, Fontanka 38, tel. 579-8284). You'll also see the **Bukvoyed** (Буквоед) bookstore chain around town, with a handy branch at Nevsky Prospekt 13 (daily 10:00-23:00).

ATMs: The word for ATM is банкомат *(bankomat)*. They are most commonly *inside* banks, hotels, restaurants, and other establishments, though you will find a few out on the street.

Telephones: There are no pay phones in St. Petersburg. For international calls, your best bet is to use Skype or another computer-based service from an Internet café. For local calls, if you have an unlocked mobile phone that works in Europe, you can pick up a prepaid Russian SIM card easily for 150-200 R (including that much credit); local calls cost about 1 R a minute. You'll need to show your passport and visa (so this isn't an option for those on visa-free cruises). The three main operators—Megafon (Мегафон), MTS (МТС), and Beeline (Билайн)—have offices all over town.

Mail: Mailboxes are blue, with "Почта России" in white lettering. The central post office, open 24 hours, is in a historic building a couple of blocks beyond St. Isaac's Cathedral at Pochtamtskaya Ulitsa 9 (look for the archway that crosses the street). A postcard stamp costs 25 R and can be bought from the shop in the center of the atrium. The Russian mail service has a reputation for delivering things extremely slowly, if at all, but just for postcards—well, you can take the risk.

What's With All the Weddings? It's a Russian tradition for bride and groom to visit about 10 different parks and monuments around town on their wedding day and have their photo taken.

Getting Around St. Petersburg

By Metro: St. Petersburg has one of the most impressive people-movers on the planet—at rush hour, it's astonishing to simply stand on the platform and watch the hundreds upon hundreds of commuters pile in and out of each train. For a tourist, the Metro's usefulness for getting around the city center is limited—but it's essential for longer trips. And it's worth taking at least once just for the experience.

You enter with a metal token (*zheton*, жетон), which you can buy for 28 R—either at the ticket windows, or from automated machines in station entrances (in Russian only, but easy to figure out: push button labeled Купить жетоны—"buy tokens," select the number of tokens you want, then insert money). A 10-journey pass is sold at ticket windows only (265 R, valid 7 days, cannot be shared). There are no day passes.

Signs in the Metro are fully bilingual and easy to follow, and maps of the system are posted widely. Each of the five lines is numbered and color-coded. It also helps to know the end station in the direction you're traveling. Unlike most European subway systems, transfer stations (where two lines meet) have two names, one for each line. Some stations in the center have flood doors along the boarding area that open only when trains arrive. Trains run from about 6:00 in the morning to a little after midnight. The official website (www.metro.spb.ru) is in Russian only.

Though St. Petersburg's Metro is not as ornate as Moscow's, some stations are works of art, often with themes from the communist era (work on the system started in the 1940s). Pushkinskaya (which celebrates the writer Pushkin) and Ploshchad Vosstaniya (which celebrates the 1917 revolution) are the most interesting stations in the center. Farther out, Avtovo (celebrating auto workers) is generally considered the most beautiful station. It's OK to take pictures in the Metro, but you can't use a flash.

Because bedrock is far beneath the city surface, the Metro is very deep. The Admiralteyskaya station is nearly 350 feet below ground. The escalator ride alone takes a good three minutes, long enough that you'll see people pull out ebook readers, play smartphone solitaire, or kiss.

By Bus and Tram: Trolley buses (with overhead wires) and regular buses are very quick, cheap, and convenient for getting around the center of town—and let you see the city instead of burying you underground like the Metro.

Along the street, stops are marked by an A (for buses), a T (for trams), a flat-topped *M* for trolley buses, and a K for *marshrutki* minibuses (explained below). Bus information at stops—when it exists—is in Russian only, listing the route number, frequency at different times of day, and sometimes the names of the stops en route. Trams run only in the city's outer districts.

All surface transport costs 25 R per ride; board, find a seat, and pay the conductor, who wears a reflective vest and will give you a thin paper-slip ticket. There are no transfers, so you pay again if you switch buses.

The buses and trolley buses that run along Nevsky Prospekt

A Timeline of Russian History

800s	Spurred by Viking trade along Russia's rivers, states form around the cities of Novgorod and Kiev. ("Russia" comes from a Viking word.)
988	Kiev converts to Christianity and becomes part of the Eastern Orthodox world.
1224-1242	Tatar (Mongol) hordes conquer Russia and exact tribute. Russia, however, succeeds where the Baltics failed: at keeping the Germans out.
1465-1557	The Russian czars consolidate power in Moscow, drive away the Tatars, and form a unified Russian state.
1613	Foundation of the Romanov dynasty, which lasts until 1917.
1703	Czar Peter the Great founds St. Petersburg as Russia's "window on the West." Russia expands southward and eastward under Peter and his successor, Catherine.
1812	Napoleon burns Moscow, but loses an army on the way home.
1855-1861	Russia loses Crimean War and decides to modernize, including freeing the serfs.
1905	Russia loses a war with the Japanese, contributing to a failed revolution later glorified by the communists as a manifestation of the workers' consciousness.
1917	In March, the Romanov czar is ousted by a provisional government led by Aleksandr Kerensky; in the October Revolution (which actually took place in November on the modern calendar), the provisional government is ousted by the Bolsheviks (communists), led by Vladimir Lenin. A few months later, the entire Romanov family is executed.
1924-1939	Josef Stalin purges the government and the army. Forced collectivization causes famine and tens of millions of deaths in Ukraine.

(between its start, at Malaya Morskaya Ulitsa, and Uprising Square/Ploshchad Vosstaniya) are useful for almost all visitors: buses #3, #7, #22, #24, #27, and #191, and trolley buses #1, #5, #7, #10, #11, and #22. Don't be afraid to make mistakes; if you take the wrong bus and it turns off Nevsky, just hop out at the next stop. Trolley buses #5 and #22 conveniently veer off from the lower end of Nevsky down Malaya Morskaya Ulitsa to St. Isaac's Cathedral

1939-1945	In World War II, Russia loses 20 million people to the Germans, but winds up with control over a sizable chunk of Eastern Europe.
1945-1962	At the peak of the Cold War, Russia acquires the atom bomb, and launches the first satellite and the first manned space mission.
1970s	During a "time of stagnation" under Leonid Brezhnev, the communist system slowly fails.
1985	Mikhail Gorbachev comes to power and declares the beginning of glasnost (openness) and perestroika (restructuring).
1991	Reactionaries try to topple Gorbachev. They fail to keep power, but so does Gorbachev. Boris Yeltsin takes control of the government and starts reforms.
1993	Reactionaries fail to topple Yeltsin. Weakened, Yeltsin manages to hang on to power until 1999, despite grumbling from the ultra-nationalist right and the communist left.
1999	On New Year's Eve, Yeltsin suddenly and inexplicably resigns, handing the country over to Vladimir Putin.
2000-2008	Putin rules as president.
2008-2012	The term-limited Putin becomes prime minster, keeping a close watch on the presidency of his handpicked successor, Dmitry Medvedev. (Cynical onlookers dub the arrangement a "tandemocracy.")
2012	Surprise! A conveniently timed change in the law allows Putin to return as president, while Medvedev swaps roles to become prime minster. Russian protesters and international observers alike grumble about "reforms" that shore up Putin's power.
2014	The Russian city of Sochi, on the Black Sea, hosts the Winter Olympics.
2016	Russia hosts the World Cup.

and the Mariinsky Theater.

The best available English-language **journey planner** for St. Petersburg is www.spb.rusavtobus.ru/en. Though it's not very user-friendly, it covers both the Metro and surface transport.

By Taxi: Locals tend to avoid cabs, and you should use them only with caution. You won't see taxi stands in St. Petersburg, and you should walk away from cabbies who hail *you* down ("Taxi?").

But you can always call and order an **official taxi** by phone (you'll probably need a Russian speaker to help, as few dispatchers or cabbies speak English). Official taxis are a little more expensive and safer than those hailed on the street. Pay the fare on the meter, rounding up a little.

Two reliable companies are **068** (tel. 068, 350-R minimum, www.en.taxi068.ru) and **Novoye Zhyoltoye** (New Yellow Taxis, Новое Жёлтое; tel. 600-8888, 310-R minimum, www.peterburg .nyt.ru/en). You can send in a form from the English-language section of either website to order a taxi, but you'll need to give a local phone number. The **Ladybird** taxi service (tel. 900-0504, 300-R minimum, www.ladybird-taxi.ru) has only women drivers and provides car seats for kids.

Most Russians in need of a ride just hail any passing private car and negotiate a price with the driver. This custom demands some common-sense caution (never get into a car with passengers), not to mention hurdling the language barrier. If you're a decent negotiator and can speak Russian, an average trip within the center will run about 200 R.

Marshrutki (**Minibuses**): These "share taxis" travel along fixed, numbered routes, prefixed with the letter K. You can wave them down anywhere along the way and ask to be dropped off at any point along the route. They're designed more for residents than for tourists, but can be useful for going to Peterhof, Tsarskoye Selo, or the airport.

Tours in St. Petersburg

Walking Tours—**Peterswalk** has been doing excellent, English-language walking tours of the city since 1996. Their original, four-hour tour is a great way to get your bearings here (650 R/person, mobile +7-921-943-1229, www.peterswalk.com, info@peterswalk .com). This tour begins every day in summer (April-Oct) at 10:30 at Hostel Life, at Nevsky Prospekt 47 (near the Fontanka River—enter around the corner at Vladimirsky Prospekt 1 by ringing the bell and going up to the fourth floor; tour may run sporadically off-season—check website).

You can also hire a **private guide** through Peterswalk (1,200 R/hour for up to 8 people, 4-hour minimum; this price assumes you already have visas, but for an extra fee they can also arrange a visa-free private excursion—email the owner Peter to arrange details).

Other Local Guides and Agencies—Various local agencies offer private guides for custom tours around the city. This is an expensive option; for a two-day visit with 6-8 hours of sightseeing each day, plus red tape expenses, a couple will likely pay at least

$1,200. (On the other hand, two all-day cruise-line excursions for two people will likely approach this price; arranging your own buys you a more individualized, less crowded experience.) If you make your plans well in advance, the local agency can typically arrange for a visa exception, meaning you don't have to go through the cumbersome visa application process before your trip. The trade-off is that the guide is officially responsible for you while you're on land, and you'll likely have no "free time" on your own. As there are many options and it's an ever-changing scene, read some online reviews (cruisecritic.com is a good resource) to find and contact a reputable company.

Bike Tours—Peterswalk (listed above) offers 3.5-hour weekend and late-night bike tours (mid-May-Sept Sat-Sun at 11:00, also mid-May-Aug Tue and Thu at 22:30, 1,200 R/person, starts at SkatProkat bike shop at Goncharnaya Ulitsa 7, near Moskovsky train station and Ploschad Vosstaniya).

Boat Tours—St. Petersburg is a delight to see from the water. Low-slung canal boats ply their way through the city, offering a handy orientation to major landmarks. After curling through

narrow, urban waterways, your boat pops out onto the wide Neva River, offering a grand panorama of the Hermitage, Admiralty, Peter and Paul Fortress, and beyond. Various companies offer essentially the same one-hour, 500-R cruise, advertising at touristy points near canals; most cater to Russian tourists and have zero English information. (Before booking, specifically ask whether there's any English commentary.) Better yet, hold out for the one-hour cruise from **Peterswalk,** whose guides not only speak English, but tailor the commentary to passengers' interests. While it costs a bit more, it's worth it (600 R/person, 3-4/day in peak season—but check website for specifics as schedule and offerings are subject to change, departs from Fontanka 53—along the Fontanka River a long block south of Nevsky Prospekt; same contact details as for walking tours, earlier).

Bus Tours—CityTour runs red, double-decker, hop-on, hop-off buses that make a circuit of major sights in the center, with recorded commentary. The full circle takes two hours, but the frequency is sparse (once per hour)—potentially leaving you with more time than you want at a particular stop. The first buses start around 9:00 and the last one finishes its route just before 21:00. A ticket good for the whole day costs 500 R; buy it on the bus (tel. 718-4769, mobile tel. +7-961-800-0755, www.citytourspb.ru).

St. Petersburg's History

The Neva River delta around St. Petersburg has been strategically important for centuries. Scandinavians, who had important trade routes running down to the Black Sea, settled throughout the area and were influential in Russia's early history. At the height of its world power in the 1600s, Sweden controlled both shores of the Baltic and built a fort and settlement called Nyenskans where St. Petersburg is today (Nyen is the Swedish name for the Neva River).

By and by, the Slavic-speaking Russians organized their own state around Kiev and Moscow. Seeing the advantage of having a Baltic seaport, in 1700, Russia (under Peter the Great) went to war against Sweden with the aim of gaining easier access to the North Atlantic (Great Northern War, 1700-1721). Sweden held on to Finland, but Russia captured part of Estonia (including Tallinn), and much of modern-day Latvia (with Rīga). Then, in the spring of 1703, Nyenskans fell to Russia; later that year, the Russians began to build what is now called the Peter and Paul Fortress.

Peter the Great had studied shipbuilding in Holland and wanted to make St. Petersburg a great naval base—and the new capital of Russia. He also envisioned the city as a "window on the West"—a gateway for Europeans coming to Russia, and a mirror of Peter's concept of a European metropolis. Across the river from the Peter and Paul Fortress, top Italian architects laid out the city, with the Admiralty at its center (symbolizing the importance of naval power) and three avenues radiating from it. Of these, Nevsky Prospekt wound up becoming the city's main thoroughfare. The city was named Petersburg—after Peter—but the German ending (-burg) hints at the enduring importance of German settlers and the German language in the Baltic. The island of Kronshtadt, which guards St. Petersburg out in the Gulf of Finland, was also fortified (arriving cruise ships and passenger

Self-Guided Walk in St. Petersburg

▲▲▲Nevsky Prospekt (Невский Проспект)

Nevsky Prospekt—St. Petersburg's famous main thoroughfare—represents the best and the worst of this beguiling metropolis. Along its two-mile length from the Neva River to Uprising Square, this superlative boulevard passes some of the city's most opulent palaces

ferries still pass this island today).

Sweden responded by building a huge naval base and fort a few hours' sail to the west—today's Helsinki. But during the Napoleonic wars, Russia took over Finland as well, extending its empire even farther west at Sweden's expense. This would be the pinnacle of Russia's push to the west. The first setback came when French and British forces reduced Bomarsund—Russia's huge fortress in the Åland Islands (west of Finland)—to rubble during the Crimean War in 1854. At the end of World War I, with the Bolshevik Revolution underway, Finland, Estonia, and Latvia broke away, leaving St. Petersburg as Russia's northwestern outpost.

Meanwhile, St. Petersburg grew into a cosmopolitan and intellectual city, with a multiethnic population, beautiful architecture, and the country's governing and economic elite. It was the setting for much great Russian literature (think Dostoyevsky's *Crime and Punishment* and Tolstoy's *Anna Karenina*). The railway to Moscow was completed in 1851, to Warsaw in 1862, and to Helsinki in 1870.

After the communist takeover, the city was renamed Petrograd and the seat of government moved back to Moscow. After Lenin's death in 1924, the city was renamed in his honor: Leningrad. During World War II, Germany held Finland and Estonia and thought it would be short work to crush Leningrad, as if between the pincers of a crab. At great cost, the city held out for nearly 900 days in what came to be called the Siege of Leningrad (see Piskaryovskoye Memorial Cemetery on page 424). By the end of the communist era, Leningrad had become a huge city of five million people, larger than Berlin and comparable in size to the San Francisco Bay Area. In 1991, the name was changed back to St. Petersburg.

(such as the Hermitage), top museums (the Hermitage and Russian Museum), most important churches (Kazan Cathedral, Church on Spilled Blood), finest urban architecture, liveliest shopping zones, lushest parks, and slices upon slices of Russian life. Taking about two hours (not counting sightseeing stops), this walk offers a fascinating glimpse of the heart of the city.

It also gives you a taste of the smog, congestion, and general chaos with which the city perennially grapples. Pickpockets are brazen here (blurring the line between petty theft and mugging), as are drivers—it's essential to be watchful, remain calm, and cross the street only at designated crosswalks (and even then, use caution).

As Nevsky Prospekt cuts diagonally through town from the Admiralty building (the bull's eye of this city's urban layout), it crosses three waterways. We'll focus on the first mile-and-a-quarter stretch to the Fontanka River—though you could carry on all the way to Uprising Square and beyond.

• *Begin your walk on the vast square behind the Hermitage.*

Palace Square to the Admiralty

The impressively monumental **Palace Square** (Dvortsovaya Ploshchad)—with the arcing, Neoclassical General Staff Building facing the bubbly, Baroque Hermitage—lets you know you're in an imperial capital. It oozes blue-blood class. The Alexander Column honors Czar Alexander I, who built the square in the early 18th century to celebrate Russia's military victory over Napoleon. Along with Moscow's

Red Square, this is the stage upon which much of modern Russian history has played out. On January 22, 1905, the czar's imperial guard opened fire on peaceful protesters here, massacring hundreds (or possibly thousands). Soon after, in 1917, the czar was ousted. The provisional government that replaced him was in turn dislodged by the Bolsheviks' October Revolution—kicking off 75 years of communist rule.

• *As you face the Hermitage, turn 90 degrees to your left and cross the busy street at the crosswalk.*

The **Alexander Gardens** (Alexandrovsky Sad), with benches and jungle gyms, are a favorite place for families. It's the backyard of the **Admiralty** building—the stately structure with the golden spire. When Peter the Great was laying out his new capital, he made the Admiralty its centerpiece—indicating the importance he placed on his imperial navy. From here, three great avenues *(prospekts)* fan out through the city; of these, Nevsky Prospekt is *the* main drag.

Before we head up the street, notice that **St. Isaac's Cathedral** is a 10-minute walk away (to the right, with your back to the Admiralty, at the far end of this park)—you can see its glittering golden dome from here. (For more on this church, see page 414.)

• *Turn your back to the Admiralty, head out to the corner of the park, and cross over the busy Admiralteyskaya street to reach Nevsky Prospekt. For now, stay on the right side of the street.*

Admiralty to the Moyka River

Halfway down this first block, watch on the right for the shop marked КОФЕ ХАУЗ. Visitors are intimidated by the Cyrillic alphabet, but with a little practice (and the alphabet tips on page

369), you can decode signs easily—often surprising yourself when they turn out to be familiar words. In this case, Кофе Хауз is Kofe Haus...coffeehouse. This Moscow-based Starbucks clone is popular, but very expensive. Russia's deeply stratified society has an enormous lower class, a tiny upper class, and virtually no middle class. Trendy shops like this (where a latte costs more than at your hometown Starbucks) are filled with upwardly mobile urbanites, but the poorer locals around you could never dream of affording a drink here.

In the next block, halfway down on the right, is **Stolle** (Штолле), a good chain restaurant to grab a snack or light lunch. They specialize in savory and sweet pies (see "Eating in St. Petersburg," later).

Look across the street at the building with *1939* above the door. On the pillar just to the right of the door, notice the small

length of barbed wire and blue plaque. This is a monument to the **Siege of Leningrad** (one of St. Petersburg's former names). During World War II, Nazi forces encircled the city and bombarded its mostly civilian population for 872 days (from September 1941 through January 1944). Claiming more lives than any other siege in world history (some estimates say over 600,000 people died), the siege devastated St. Petersburg's buildings, if not the spirit of those who refused to surrender. The north side of the street was in the direct line of fire from Nazi shells, lobbed in from the Germans' position southwest of the city. The blue sign reads, roughly, "Citizens: During artillery bombardment, this side is more dangerous."

About 30 yards down, on the right, the Буквоед sign marks an outlet of the **Bukvoyed** bookstore chain—a handy place to pick up a St. Petersburg map if you need one. (The looong Cyrillic words over the door look intimidating. But sound it out: книжный супермаркет = knizhniy supermarket = "book supermarket.")

At the next intersection, look left down Bolshaya Morskaya street to see the magnificent **yellow arch** of the General Staff Building. The archway opens to Palace Square—where we started this walk. To the right, the street leads to a handy branch of the **Teremok** (Теремок) Russian fast-food chain (see page 429) and, beyond that, to the square in front of St. Isaac's Cathedral.

• *Continuing one more block on Nevsky Prospekt brings you to the first of St. Petersburg's concentric waterways, the Moyka River. As you proceed straight across the bridge, stick to the right side of the street.*

ST. PETERSBURG

Moyka River to Kazan Cathedral

Crossing the Moyka, you'll likely see many touts selling tickets for **canal cruises.** While this is an excellent way to get your bearings in St. Petersburg, most operations have commentary only in Russian. Confirm the language before you hop aboard—and consider taking the English-language Peterswalk cruise that leaves from near the end of our walk (see page 374).

The elaborate pink building with white columns (on your right as you cross the water) is the **Stroganov Palace.** The

aristocratic family that resided here left their mark all over Russia—commissioning opulent churches, financing the czars' military agendas, and fostering the arts—but their lasting legacy is the beef dish, likely named for them, that has made "Stroganoff" a household name around the world.

Continue another long block, and watch across the street (on the left) for another chance to practice your Russian—though the distinctive logo may give it away: САБВЭЙ ("SABVAY" = Subway).

Farther along, looking left (across the street), notice the pretty, parklike street (Bolshaya Konyushennaya) flanked by beautiful buildings. On the left side of this street is a sort of community center for **Dutch** transplants, while the building on the right is for **Germans.** Catherine the Great (r. 1762-1796), who loved to promote the multiethnic nature of her empire, encouraged various cultural enclaves to settle in community buildings like these. Each enclave consisted of several apartment houses clustered around a church. You'll see an example as you proceed up Nevsky Prospekt,

where the German **Lutheran Church of St. Peter and St. Paul** is set back between two yellow buildings (across the street). This is only one of the many houses of worship built along this avenue under the auspices of the czars. Later, the aggressively atheistic communist regime repurposed churches all over the city; in this case, the church was turned into a swimming pool.

• *Coming up on the right is the Kazan Cathedral, with its stately semicircular colonnade and grand dome.*

Kazan Cathedral to Griboyedova Canal

Built in the early 1800s and named for a revered Russian icon, the church was later converted into a "Museum of Atheism" under the communists. It's since been restored to its former glory, and is free to enter. To find the main entrance, go down Kazanskaya street (which runs perpendicular to Nevsky, just before the church). Go in through what looks like a "side" door, and soak in the mystical Orthodox ambience. Inside you'll find a dim Neo-Romanesque interior, a much-venerated replica of the icon of Our Lady of Kazan, a monument to the commander who fended off Napoleon's 1812 invasion, and lots of candles and solemn worshippers (for details, see page 410). You'll exit through the left transept, which pops you out into a delightful little **grassy park** facing Nevsky Prospekt. This is a good spot to sit, relax, and maybe buy a drink from a vendor.

It's appropriate that Nevsky Prospekt is lined with so many important churches. It's named for Alexander Nevsky (1220-1263), an esteemed Russian saint who, as an influential prince, fought off encroaching German and Swedish foes—including in a pivotal 1240 battle on the Neva River, near what would later become St. Petersburg.

• *Leaving the park, head to the intersection and cross over Nevsky Prospekt.*

Scrutinize the distinctive oxidized-copper tower of the Art Nouveau building on the corner (at #28). At the base of the

globe-topped turret is an unlikely symbol—an American bald eagle, wings spread wide, grasping a laurel wreath in its talon and wearing a stars-and-stripes shield on its breast. Architecture fans know this building as the Singer House (yes, the Russian headquarters of the American sewing machine company). Today it's home to **Dom Knigi** ("House of Books"). Up close, take a minute to examine the building's fine decorative details. Inside, the inviting bookshop has a delightfully atmospheric—if pricey ($8 lattes)—turn-of-the-century café on the second floor (daily 9:00-1:00 in the morning).

• *The Singer building sits next to the Griboyedova Canal. Walk to the midsection of the intersection/bridge over the water (watch out for pickpockets in this high-tourist-concentration zone).*

Griboyedova Canal to Gostiny Dvor

Looking down the length of the river, you can't miss one of Russia's most distinctive buildings: the **Church on Spilled Blood.**

Dramatically scenic from here, it gets even better as you get closer. If you want to snap some classic photos, work your way to the small bridge partway down the river. If you plan to visit this church, now's a good time; the **Russian Museum** is also nearby (the yellow building fronting the canal just before the church is a side-wing of that museum; we'll have an opportunity to reach the museum's main entrance later on this walk). The church and museum are both described in more detail later, under "Sights in St. Petersburg." If you want to do some souvenir shopping, there's a handy (if touristy and overpriced) **crafts market** just behind the church. I'll wait right here.

Back already? Let's continue down Nevsky Prospekt (for now, stay on the left side). Just after the river is the **Small Philharmonic** (Малый филармония)—one of the "big four" cultural institutions in St. Petersburg (the others are the Great Philharmonic, the Mariinsky Theater, and the Mikhailovsky Theater). Consider taking in a performance while you're in town; on a short visit, the ballet is a popular choice (for details, see "Entertainment in St. Petersburg," later).

A half-block farther along, tucked between buildings on the left, you'll see the pale yellow facade of the Roman Catholic **St. Catherine's Church.** This is one of many "St. Catherines" that line Nevsky Prospekt—many congregations named their churches for the empress who encouraged their construction. This one has an endearing starving artists' market out front.

At the next corner, on the left, is the **Grand Hotel Europe**— an ultra-fancy (if dated) five-star hotel that opened in 1875. Its opulence attracted guests like Tchaikovsky, Stravinsky, Debussy, and H. G. Wells.

The hotel sits at the corner of Mikhailovskaya street. If you detour one long block down this street, you'll find the main entrance of the **Russian Museum,** which houses a fantastic collection of works by exclusively Russian artists. (While the Hermitage's art collection is world-class, there's nothing "local" about it.) For a self-guided tour of the highlights of the Russian Museum, see page 405. Presiding over the park in front of the museum (Ploshchad Iskusstv, "Square of the Arts") is a statue of **Alexander Pushkin** (1799-1837)—Russia's leading poet, considered by many to have raised modern Russian literature to an art form.

• *Back along Nevsky, continue from the hotel to the middle of the next block.*

In a gap in the buildings on the left, you'll see yet another church—the beautiful robin-egg-blue home of the local Armenian community. **St. Catherine's Gregorian Church** belongs to the Armenian Apostolic faith, one of the oldest branches of Christianity— founded in A.D. 301, when St. Gregory the Illuminator baptized the Armenian king. Approaching the front door, look for the little shop on the right, which sells items imported from Armenia to comfort transplants here.

ST. PETERSBURG

Now face across the street to confront the gigantic, yellow Gostiny Dvor shopping complex. We'll cross over later to take a look, but for now, continue past the church. Keep an eye out on the left for #48 (look for the Пассажъ sign above the door; it's before the ramp leading to a pedestrian underpass). Step inside

and climb the stairs into the gorgeously restored, glass-roofed **"Passazh" arcade,** an elite haven for high-class shoppers since 1846 (daily 10:00-21:00), making it one of the first shopping malls in the world. The communists converted the Passazh into a supermarket and, later, into a "model store," intended to leave foreigners with a (misleadingly) positive impression of the availability of goods in the USSR. These days it feels a bit low-rent, but the space itself retains a genteel air, with mellow music playing in the background.

• *At the end of the block, use the pedestrian underpass (which also leads to a pair of very convenient downtown Metro stops—Nevsky Prospekt on the blue line, and Gostiny Dvor on the green line) to cross beneath Nevsky Prospekt: Take the ramp down, turn right, then turn right again up the next ramp.*

Gostiny Dvor to Fontanka River

You'll pop out of the underpass at **Gostiny Dvor** (which means, basically, "guest courtyard"—like a Turkish caravanserai). Built in the 1760s, this marketplace is a giant but hollow structure, with two stories of shops (more than 100 in all) wrapping around a central courtyard. To see an undiscovered corner of Nevsky that most tourists miss, head upstairs: At the corner of the building nearest the underpass, go through the door and up the stairs, then find your way back outside to reach the tranquil, beautifully symmetrical arcades. Standing at the corner, the arches seem to recede in both directions nearly as far as the eye can see.

Take note of the open plaza area in front of Gostiny Dvor. This is a popular place for **political protests**—which, in Putin's Russia, are barely tolerated. Article 31 of the Russian constitution guarantees the freedom of assembly—a right whose legitimacy seems always to be in question. To push the boundaries, on the 31st of every month, peaceful demonstrators routinely seek government permission to stage a protest here, are denied, then stage the protest anyway—only to be dutifully arrested by riot gear-clad cops. This so-called Strategy-31 movement tries to keep the issue of free speech in the consciousness of a Russia that increasingly seems willing to let that freedom lapse.

• *Continue heading up the right side of Nevsky Prospekt for one more block.*

You'll soon reach **Ostrovsky Square** (Ploshchad Ostrovskogo), a gorgeous park anchored by a statue of **Catherine the Great** (1729-1796). While Peter the Great founded this city (and gave it his name), Catherine is arguably the one who truly made it great. A Prussian blue-blood (born in today's Poland), Catherine married Russia's Czar Peter III, then quickly overthrew him in a palace coup. Throughout her 30-year reign, Catherine never remarried, but she is believed to have cleverly parlayed sexual politics to consolidate her power.

On the pillar below Catherine is **Prince Grigory Potemkin,** one of the statesmen and military leaders with whom Catherine collaborated and consorted. Potemkin is the namesake of a fascinating story about how even a great ruler can be fooled. After Potemkin conquered the Crimean peninsula during the

Russo-Turkish War, Catherine visited to survey her new domain. To convince her that "Russification" of the Crimea had been a success, Potemkin supposedly created artificially perfect villages, with stage-set houses peopled by "Russian villagers" custom-ordered from Centralsky Casting. To this day the term "Potemkin village" describes something artificial used to hoodwink a gullible target—a term as applicable to modern Russian and American politics as it was to Catherine's nation-building. In 1972, when President Nixon visited St. Petersburg (then dubbed Leningrad), Nevsky Prospekt itself was similarly spruced up to disguise Russia's economic hardships. (Because Nixon would view the street from a limo, the Soviets only fixed up the bottom two floors of each facade.)

• *From the square, use the crosswalk to head back over Nevsky Prospekt.*

Just across from the park is the pleasantly pedestrianized street called Malaya Sadovaya. On the corner, **Yeliseevsky's**

delicatessen occupies a sumptuously decorated Art Nouveau building (at #56). Once the purveyor of fine food to the Russian aristocracy (like Dallmayr's in Munich), Yeliseevsky's was bumped down several pegs when the communists symbolically turned it into "Grocery Store #1." Now, in another sign of the times, it's been remodeled into an almost laughably over-the-top delicatessen with a small, expensive café—drop in to browse the selection of cheese and chocolates (daily 10:00-22:00). You'll be required to take a shopping basket at the door (whether you're browsing or not), and photography is strictly prohibited.

A few steps beyond Yeliseevsky's, find the passage (at #60, just past the Teremok fast-food joint) leading to the historic **Aurora (Аврора) Cinema.** Step inside to appreciate the elegant lobby of what was one of the first movie houses in St. Petersburg. Peruse the movie posters to see how American blockbusters are marketed in Russia (and spelled in Cyrillic). A few are shown in their original language ("originale kopie").

• *Continue along Nevsky Prospekt for another block and a half, until you hit the Fontanka River.*

Fontanka River to Uprising Square

Of St. Petersburg's many beautiful and interesting bridges, the **Anichkov Bridge** is one of the finest. On pillars anchoring each end are statues of a man with a horse. The ensemble, sculpted in 1841 and known collectively as *The Horse Tamers*, expresses humanity's ongoing desire to corral nature. Watch the relationship between horse and man evolve from a struggle, with the man overwhelmed by the wild beast's power, to a cooperative arrangement, with the man leading the bridled and saddled horse. Looking over the Fontanka River, it's easy to think of this as a metaphor for St. Petersburg's relationship to the water. To survive and prosper, the city has had to tame the inhospitable, swampy delta on which it is built.

• *The Peterswalk* **canal-boat tour** *in English departs from the Fontanka Embankment; just turn right and walk along the canal (with the water on your left) for about five minutes. To sightsee at the* **Russian Museum,** **Church on Spilled Blood, Kazan Cathedral,** *or* **Hermitage,** *walk back along Nevsky the way you came, or hop on a bus (see page 371 for buses that make the trip; note that a few trolley buses veer off from the end of Nevsky for* **St. Isaac's Cathedral,** *saving an extra 10-minute walk).*

To easily reach the **Peter and Paul Fortress,** *take the Metro: Backtrack to the underpass in front of Gostiny Dvor, find the Nevsky Prospekt station on the blue line, and ride one stop to Gorkovskaya—a short walk from the fortress.*

You've walked the most interesting stretch of Nevsky Prospekt, but if you'd like to see more of the city center, continue (by foot or by bus) down Nevsky for a half-mile until you reach...

Uprising Square (Ploshchad Vosstaniya): This intimidatingly gigantic transit hub is a showcase of Russia's bigger-is-better city planning aesthetic. Admire the round subway station entryway—classically Soviet in design—and the Moskovsky train station across the square. On top of the big building facing the station, a sign still reads *Hero City Leningrad* (Город-Герой Ленинград, using the Soviet name for the city)—a tribute to the city's resistance during the Nazis' WWII siege. The star-topped obelisk in the center of the traffic circle also commemorates the "Hero City." Nearby are two large shopping malls and supermarkets (see "Picnic Shopping" on page 431).

• *The Ploshchad Vosstaniya Metro station (green line) zips from here back to the Gostiny Dvor stop in the middle of Nevsky Prospekt (one stop), or all the way back to Primorskaya (three stops) for the cruise port.*

Sights in St. Petersburg

▲▲▲The Hermitage (Эрмитаж)

Built by Peter the Great's daughter, Elizabeth, the Hermitage was later filled with the art collection of Catherine the Great. The Hermitage's vast collections of just about everything—but especially its European masterworks—make it one of the world's top art museums, ranking with the Louvre and the Prado. Housed in the Romanovs' Winter Palace, the Hermitage (EHR-mee-tazh,

officially the State Hermitage, Государственный Эрмитаж), is actually two top-notch sight-seeing experiences in one: an art gallery of European works and an imperial residence. Enjoy the Leonardos, Rembrandts, and Matisses while imagining the ostentatious lifestyles of the czars who collected them. Between the canvases, you glide through some of the most opulent ballrooms and throne rooms ever built.

Cost: 400 R at the door (students free); $17.95/1 day, $25.95/2 days if you buy online in advance (details below).

Hours: Tue-Sat 10:30-18:00, Sun 10:30-17:00, closed Mon. Some cruise lines offer after-hour visits (explained later). Tel. 710-9625 (recorded info) or 710-9079; www.hermitagemuseum.org.

Advance Tickets: If visiting on your own, paying for your ticket in advance by credit card on the Hermitage web store (www.hermitageshop.org) is a *must*. Prepaid tickets are a little more expensive than those bought at the door, but it's money well spent. You're not tied to a particular entry time, and you can skip the often hour-long line to get into the entry hall. You'll receive an email confirmation when you pre-book—print it out and bring it on the day you visit the museum. Find the little booth for prepaid ticket pickup (under the archway as you enter the Hermitage courtyard from Palace Square), and exchange your confirmation for your ticket. If you want extras, such as a guided tour or photo permit, you'll need to buy them at the ticket windows inside (short line).

Getting In: The Hermitage has several doors. Individual visitors enter through the courtyard that faces the grand Palace Square with the Alexander Column (the opposite side from the Neva River). From the column and square, you'll go through a passageway (if you've bought advance tickets, stop at the kiosk here to pick them up), then emerge into a large courtyard with the long ticket-buying queue. Advance-ticketholders can skip the line and head right into the entry hall. There, line up at the security checkpoint to scan your ticket at the turnstile and enter the museum.

Tours: Immediately beyond the security checkpoint is a desk where you can rent an English **audioguide** (350 R, leave ID as deposit; less-crowded audioguide stand at top of main stairway). It has handy, digestible descriptions of the palace's historical rooms and of major paintings, but isn't worth the high price for a single traveler on a short visit. **Guided tours** (300 R) are offered in the entry hall.

Services: Pick up a free **map** at the information desk. Down the stairs from the entry hall is an **ATM,** a **cloakroom** (remember which of the 14 sections you use), a tiny **bookstore** (there are better ones later, inside the museum), and a crowded **WC** (there are more later). In the hall to the right, before you reach the stairway, are more **WCs,** a mediocre and crowded **café,** an inexpensive **Internet** access point (50 R/hour), several large gift shops, and a large **bookstore.**

Photography: You'll need a photo permit (200 R, sold in entry hall).

Planning Your Time: Some people come to St. Petersburg just to see this place, especially because some of its riches (including a cache of Impressionist masterpieces) were for decades hidden away by the communist regime. Others don't want to spend time on painters whose work can more easily be admired in New York, Paris, or Madrid. The first sort of person could spend days inside without exhausting the Hermitage's treasures; the second might bypass the place entirely in favor of the Russian Museum (described on page 404) or no museums at all. For many visitors, though, a middle strategy works well: Plan a brief visit (3-4 hours) to the museum, focusing on one or two artistic periods as well as a few museum rooms important to Russian history. My self-guided tour (see below) fits this bill. If you're a serious museumgoer and want more than a half-day here, buy the two-day pass, which lets you spread out your time over subsequent days.

Cruise-Line Evening Visits: Some cruise lines offer an evening visit to the Hermitage, which generally includes a brief guided tour of the highlights (royal rooms and a few Old Masters), often followed by a chamber music concert in an opulent hall. While this can be pricey, and is very selective (you'll see only part of what's on my self-guided tour), it frees up lots of daylight for other sightseeing. If you have a visa and will be exploring the city during the day, ask your excursion director if, where, and when you can meet the group at the Hermitage (groups often use the main door facing the river); afterwards, you can just hop on your excursion bus back to the ship.

Length of this Tour: It should take about four hours—including one full hour just to fight the crowds and connect the dots. When weighing your strategy, keep in mind that the Hermitage can be miserably crowded, with dozens of tour groups blocking every room; it's wise to have a backup plan for your targeted visit.

Self-Guided Tour

This tour will take you quickly through the Hermitage's highlights, divided into three parts: 1) historical rooms; 2) Old Masters (Leonardo, Raphael, Rembrandt, etc.), and 3) Modern Masters

(Matisse, Chagall, Picasso, etc.). Very roughly, the first (ground) floor, where you enter, shows ancient art; the second floor has the historical rooms plus galleries covering the medieval, Renaissance, and Baroque eras (Old Masters); and the third floor is devoted to the 19th and 20th centuries (Modern Masters).

Part 1: Historical Rooms

• *At the end of the entry area (the hall with the metal detectors and audioguide stand), head up the...*

Stairway to the Second Floor: The stairway gives you a good feeling for the building's architecture. You are in the Winter

Palace, the czar's official city residence, which was built by Italian architects (notably Francesco Rastrelli) between 1754 and 1762, in high Baroque style. (At this time, all of St. Petersburg—like this staircase—drew on the talents of artists and artisans imported from Western Europe.)

The gilded ceiling shows the Greek gods relaxing in the clouds. A serious fire damaged the palace in 1837, but it was quickly restored. The museum occupies the Winter Palace plus two connected buildings, the Small Hermitage and the Large Hermitage, which were built next to the Winter Palace in the late 18th century. The museum takes its name from these buildings, where the royal art collections were originally housed.

• *Go through the door at the top of the stairs and pass through the large rooms 192, 191, and 190 (notice the room numbers posted over doorways) to reach room 189.*

The Malachite Room: This drawing room, which dates from just after the 1837 fire, is decorated with malachite, a green copper-based mineral found in Russia's Ural Mountains. After the first

stage of the Russian Revolution in spring 1917, in which the czar was ousted, a provisional government led by Alexander Kerensky declared Russia a republic. This government took over the Winter Palace (which had been little used under the czars) and met in the Malachite Room, overlooking the Neva River. Their last meeting was on November 7, 1917. That evening, communist forces loyal to Lenin and the Bolshevik Party seized power of the city

ST. PETERSBURG

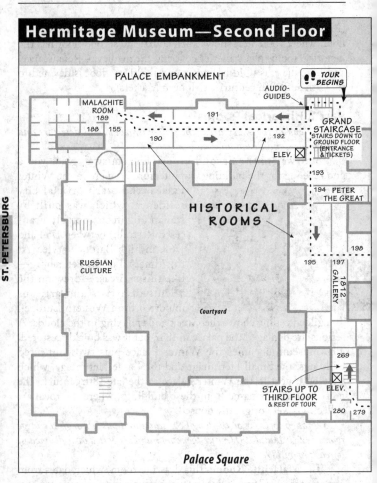

Hermitage Museum—Second Floor

PALACE EMBANKMENT

TOUR BEGINS

AUDIO-GUIDES

MALACHITE ROOM 189

188   155

191

190

192

ELEV.

GRAND STAIRCASE
STAIRS DOWN TO GROUND FLOOR (ENTRANCE & TICKETS)

193

194   PETER THE GREAT

HISTORICAL ROOMS

198

RUSSIAN CULTURE

195   197   1812 GALLERY

Courtyard

269

ELEV.

STAIRS UP TO THIRD FLOOR & REST OF TOUR

280   279

ST. PETERSBURG

Palace Square

in a largely bloodless coup. (Although the Bolsheviks took over in November, back then Russia still used the old Julian calendar—so technically it was an "October" Revolution.)

• Backtrack to the stairway, and take the doorway into room 193, the...

Field Marshals' Hall: This hall was for portraits of Russia's military generals—perhaps it helped the ruling family keep names and faces straight! After 1917, the paintings were taken down and moved to other museums. In recent years, though, the original portraits from the 1830s have been returned to their places here.

• The next room (194) is the...

Memorial Hall of Peter the Great: This hall pays homage to Peter the Great, who died in 1725, a generation before the Winter Palace's construction. You see his portrait (with Minerva, the goddess of wisdom) and a copy of his throne. Above, on the wall to

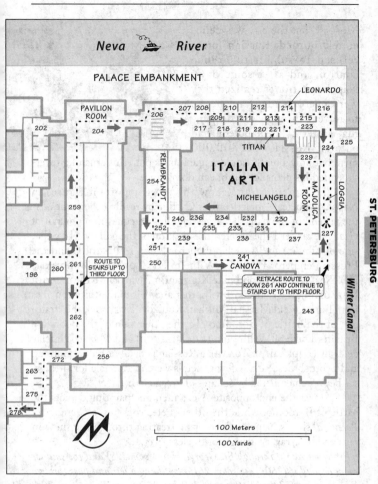

Neva River
PALACE EMBANKMENT
PAVILION ROOM
LEONARDO
ITALIAN ART
REMBRANDT
TITIAN
MICHELANGELO
MAJOLICA ROOM
LOGGIA
CANOVA
ROUTE TO STAIRS UP TO THIRD FLOOR
RETRACE ROUTE TO ROOM 261 AND CONTINUE TO STAIRS UP TO THIRD FLOOR
Winter Canal
100 Meters
100 Yards

ST. PETERSBURG

either side, are paintings commemorating his decisive victories over Sweden, at Lesnaya in 1708 and Poltava in 1709.

• *Continue into the **Armorial Hall** (room 195), a banquet hall with golden columns and sculptures of knights with spears in each corner, and take a left into the long, skinny room 197, known as the...*

War Gallery of 1812: Opened in 1826, this hall displays over 300 portraits of the generals who helped to expel Napoleon from Russia in 1812 and pursue him back to France. The Russian and French armies fought to a draw at the battle of Borodino, just west of Moscow, in September. The French troops were lured into

Moscow, but the city was deliberately burned, Russian forces refused to submit to French control, and after some days, Napoleon's troops realized they were overextended and began to retreat through the deepening winter cold. Napoleon had entered Russia with 400,000 men, but only a tenth would make it back out. This crushing reversal ended his plans for European dominance.

The large portraits show the most important figures in Napoleon's defeat—practice your Cyrillic by reading the names. At the far end of the hall, the largest of all is an equestrian portrait of Czar Alexander I (he ordered the creation of the gallery). To either side of him are the Austrian emperor Franz I (Франц I) and the Prussian emperor Friedrich Wilhelm III (Фридрих-Вильхельм III). Next comes Grand Duke Konstantin Pavlovich (Константин Павлович), the czar's unruly brother and heir to the throne; across from him is Field Marshal Mikhail Kutuzov (Кутузов), the strategist of the battle of Borodino. To the other side of the doors are Britain's Duke of Wellington (Веллингтон) and Michael Barclay de Tolly (Барклай де Толли), a Russian general of Baltic-German and Scottish descent. (A few generals weren't available for sittings, so they're remembered by squares of green cloth.)

At the end opposite Alexander, one painting depicts the battle of Borodino, while the other (Peter von Hess's *Crossing the Berezina*) shows Napoleon's troops retreating through the snow in rags and disarray, crossing a bridgeless river.

• *Proceed straight through St. George Hall (room 198) and the smaller room beyond it (260) into room 261; here, hang a left and pass through looong room 259 and little room 203 before stepping into room 204, the...*

Pavilion Room: You're in the Small Hermitage, the nearer of the two buildings connected to the Winter Palace. Admire the fine view of the interior courtyard. The room was decorated in the 1850s by architect Andrei Stakenschneider, and contains the fun

Peacock Clock, a timepiece made by British goldsmith James Cox and purchased by Catherine the Great. (The controls are in the large mushroom.) Across the hall, scrutinize the remarkably detailed inlaid floor.

• *You've seen the most important historical rooms in the Hermitage. At this point, most people do best to focus on one or two artistic periods from among the Hermitage's vast collections. The basic options are to proceed directly into the **Old Masters** collection—with an emphasis on Italian Renaissance, plus an excellent Rembrandt collection—in the adjoining rooms (for details, see the next section); or to skip forward several centuries and head upstairs to the fine **Modern Masters** collection (for directions on walking there, see page 399).*

Part 2: Old Masters

• *The Italian Renaissance works we'll see are on the same floor as the historic rooms. Just beyond the Pavilion Room and the Peacock Clock, proceed straight through the top of the stairwell (with the huge, green malachite-and-bronze vase) and enter the long hallway. Here begins the Old Hermitage's collection of Italian art. While there's a lot to see, for now pass through several rooms—209 (pause at the Fra Angelico fresco of Mary and Baby Jesus with Thomas Aquinas and St. Dominic), 210 (with some fine majolica), 211, 212, and 213—until you emerge in the grand room 214.*

Leonardo da Vinci

Considering that there are only about 20 paintings in existence by the great Renaissance Man, the two humble Madonnas in the Hermitage are world-class treasures. Leonardo da Vinci (1452-1519) reinvented the art of painting and influenced generations of artists. These two small works were landmarks in technique, composition, and the portrayal of natural human emotion.

Paintings of mother Mary with Baby Jesus had always been popular in Renaissance Italy. But before Leonardo, large altarpieces typically showed the Madonna and Child seated formally on a throne, surrounded by saints, angels, elaborate architecture, and complex symbolism. Leonardo reinvented the theme in intimate, small-scale works for private worship. He deleted extraneous characters and focused on the heart of the story—a mother and her child alone in a dark room, sharing a private moment.

Benois Madonna (1475-1478): Mary shows Jesus a flower. Jesus (with his Casper-the-Friendly-Ghost-like head) inspects this wondrous thing with a curiosity and concentration that's wise beyond his years. Mary practically giggles with delight. It's a tender, intimate moment, but with a serious psychological undertow. The mustard flower—with four petals—symbolizes the cross of

Jesus' eventual Crucifixion. Jesus and Mary play with it innocently, oblivious to the baby's tragic destiny.

This is one of Leonardo's earliest known works. In fact, it may be the first painting he did after quitting the workshop of his teacher, Verrocchio, to strike out on his own. The painting, which was often copied (including by Raphael), was revolutionary. The painstaking detail astonished his contemporaries—the folds in Mary's clothes, Jesus' dimpled flesh, the tiniest wisps of haloes, Mary's brooch. How did he do it? The secret was a new technological advance—oil-based paints. Unlike the more common tempera (egg-based) paint, oils could be made nearly transparent. This allowed Leonardo to apply layer after layer to make the subtlest transitions of color, mimicking real life.

Also, Leonardo used different shades of color—light and dark (*chiaroscuro*)—to create his figures. For example, Mary's "blue" dress ranges from almost black navy-blue (the folds) to nearly white powder-blue (the raised areas). These create the illusion of a three-dimensional body rising cameo-like from the dark background. Leonardo accentuates the contrast between the shadowy "valleys" of the folds and the brightly lit "hills" to make the folds seem unnaturally deep.

Litta Madonna (1490-1491): Mary nurses Baby Jesus, gazing down proudly. Jesus keeps locked onto Mary's breast but turns outward absentmindedly—dreamy-eyed with milk—to face the viewer, drawing us into the scene. The highlight of the painting is clearly Mary's radiant face, gracefully tilted down and beaming with tenderness.

Having left Florence, Leonardo settled in Milan (c. 1482-1499). At the same time he was creating the *Litta Madonna*, he was also painting his famous *Last Supper*, creating the largest bronze equestrian statue of the Renaissance, inventing a hang-glider, and filling notebooks with sketches like the Vitruvian Man. Leonardo managed his own workshop, and this Madonna may have been done in collaboration with his prize student, Boltraffio. As was his practice, Leonardo made preliminary sketches to work out the various details of Mary's face and the baby's legs and position on his mother's lap (a surviving sketch of Mary's head is in the Louvre).

Compare the *Litta Madonna* and *Benois Madonna*—each is a slight variation on a popular theme. Both are set in dark interiors lit by windows looking out on a distant landscape (though the *Benois* landscape remains unfinished). Subconsciously, this accentuates the intimacy and tranquility of the setting. Both paintings were originally done on wood panels before being transferred to canvas (and retouched) a century ago. Both paintings are named for the family that at one point owned them. One difference is in the style. The *Litta Madonna* has crisper outlines—either because it was done in (less subtle) tempera or by a (less subtle) apprentice.

What they have in common is realistic emotion, and this sets all of Leonardo's Madonnas apart from those of his contemporaries. With a tilt of the head, a shining face, a downturned mouth, the interplay of touching hands and gazes, Leonardo captured an intimacy never before seen in painting. He draws aside a curtain to reveal an unguarded moment, showing mother and child interacting as only they can. These holy people don't need haloes (or only the wispiest) to show that sacred bond.

• *The door across from the* Benois Madonna *leads to room 221, where we'll find...*

Titian

Danae (1553-1554): One of art history's most blatantly sexual paintings, this nude has fascinated people for centuries—both

for its subject matter and for Titian's bravura technique. The Hermitage's canvas is the second (or third) of five nearly identical paintings Titian painted of the popular legend.

It shows Danae from Greek mythology, lying naked in her bedchamber. Her father has locked her up to prevent a dreadful prophecy from coming true—that Danae will bear a son who will grow up to kill him. As Danae daydreams, suddenly a storm cloud gathers overhead. In the lightning, a divine face emerges—it's Zeus. He transforms himself into a shower of gold coins. Danae tilts her head and gazes up, transfixed. She goes weak-kneed with desire, and her left leg flops outward. Zeus rains down between Danae's legs, impregnating her. Meanwhile, Danae's maid tries to catch the divine spurt with her apron.

This legend has been depicted since ancient times. Symbolically, it represented how money can buy sexual favors. In medieval times, Danae was portrayed as being as money-hungry as the maid. But Titian clearly wants to contrast Danae and the maid. He divides the canvas, with Danae's warm, golden body on one side and the frigid-gray old maid on the other. Zeus rains straight down, enriching them both, and uniting the composition.

ST. PETERSBURG

Danae is a celebration of giving yourself to love.

• *Backtrack through the Leonardo room (214), continue through rooms 215 and 216 (at the corner), and hook right. Pass straight through room 224 to reach room 227 and an homage to...*

Raphael

Loggia: This long, narrow hallway—more than 200 feet long, only 13 feet wide, and decorated with colorful paintings—is a rep-lica of one of the painter Raphael's crowning achievements, the Vatican Loggia in Rome. (The original loggia, in the Vatican Palace, was designed by the architect Bramante—who also authored St. Peter's Basilica in Rome; Raphael and his assistants completed the log-gia's fresco decorations in 1518-19.)

In the 1780s, after admiring color engrav-ings of the Vatican Loggia, Catherine the Great had this exact replica built of Raphael's famous hallway. It's virtually identical to the original, though the paintings here are tempera on canvas. They were copied from the frescoes in Rome (under the direction of Austrian painter Christoph Unterberger) and sent to St. Petersburg along with a scale model of the entire ensemble.

The Loggia exudes the spirit of the Renaissance, melding the Christian world (52 biblical scenes on the ceiling) and the Classical world (fanciful designs on the walls and arches). The ceiling tells Christian history chronologically, starting with Adam and Eve and ending with Christ's Last Supper. For the walls, Raphael used the "grotesque" style found in ancient archaeological sites, or "grottos." This ancient style—lacy designs, garlands, flowers, vases, and mythological animals—was resurrected by Raphael and became extremely popular with European nobility. The complex symbolism, mixing the Christian and pagan, also intrigued the educated elite, and the Loggia has come to be called "Raphael's Bible."

• *When you're done in the Loggia, go back to the start of the hallway and turn left into room 229, known as the **Majolica Room**. Here you'll find two authentic masterpieces by Raphael.*

Conestabile Madonna (c. 1504): The dinner-plate-size painting just opposite the entrance is one of Raphael's first known works, painted when he was still a teenager. Mother Mary multitasks, cradling baby Jesus while trying to read. Precocious Jesus seems to be reading, too. Though realistic enough, the work shows a geometrically perfect world: Mary's oval face, Jesus' round face, and the perfect oval frame. The influence of Leonardo is clear: in

the tilt of Mary's head and position of Jesus' pudgy legs (similar to the *Litta Madonna*) and in the child's beyond-his-years focus on an object (from the *Benois Madonna*). The picture is remarkable for its color harmonies and its perfected forms—characteristics that Raphael would beautifully develop in his later works. While you're in this room, look also for Raphael's somber *Holy Family* (c. 1507), another rare early work. It's also known as *Madonna with Beardless Joseph,* for obvious reasons.

• *At the far end of the Raphael room, hook right into room 230. In the center of this gallery is a sculpture by...*

Michelangelo

Crouching Boy (c. 1530): The nude figure crouches down within the tight "frame" of the block of marble he came from. The statue was likely intended to pose forlornly at the base of a tomb in the Medici Chapel in Florence, possibly to symbolize the vanquished spirit of the deceased's grieving relatives. Though the project (and this statue) were never fully finished, the work possesses Michelangelo's trademark pent-up energy.

• *We'll leave the Italian Renaissance now. Proceed straight through the next series of rooms (231-236 and 240), eventually popping out in room 252. Turn right into room 254, a treasure trove of works by...*

Rembrandt

The great Dutch painter is beautifully represented at the Hermitage. We'll tune into two works in particular.

• *As you enter the room, look to the left to find...*

Danae (1636): Compare this large-scale nude of the Greek demi-goddess to Titian's version, which we saw earlier. The scene is similar—a nude woman reclines diagonally on a canopied bed, awaiting her lover (the randy god Zeus), accompanied by her maid (in the dim background). But Rembrandt depicts a more practical, less ecstatic tryst. Where Titian's Danae was helpless with rapture, Rembrandt's is more in control. She's propped upright and focused, and her legs aren't splayed open. Danae motions to her offstage lover—either welcoming him into her boudoir or warning him to be cautious. Historians note that Danae has the body of Rembrandt's first wife (the original model) and the face of his mistress (painted over a decade later).

Catherine the Great—herself no stranger to bedroom visitors—bought this painting in 1772 as one of the works that grew into the Hermitage collection. In 1985, a crazed visitor to the museum slashed the canvas with a knife and threw acid on Danae's face, causing significant damage to the painting. A heroic restoration project repaired the canvas and retouched the melted paint.

• *At the far end of the room, look for...*

The Prodigal Son (c. 1669): In the Bible, Jesus tells this story of the young man who wastes his inheritance on wine, women, and song. He returns home, drops to his knees before his father, and begs forgiveness. Rembrandt recounts the whole story—past, present, and future— in this single moment, frozen in time. The Prodigal Son's tattered clothes and missing shoe hint at the past—how he was once rich and wearing fine clothes, but ended up penniless, alone, bald, and living in a pigsty. His older brother (standing to the right) is the present: He looks down in judgment, ready to remind their dad what a bad son the

Prodigal is. But the father's face and gestures foretell the story's outcome, as he bends down to embrace his son with a tenderness that says all will be forgiven. The father's bright-red cloak wraps around the poor Prodigal like loving arms.

Many artists have depicted this story. Most play up the drama and big emotions: the Prodigal's wild life of pleasure, the abject misery of his poverty, or the joyous celebration after he returns. Rembrandt is more subtle. He uses the tilt of the Prodigal's head against his father's lap to show his regret for all those wasted years. The father's lined face telegraphs the pain of loss, relief, love, and acceptance. He oh-so-gently places his hands on his son's shoulders, giving a blessing. The bystanders look on in total silence. Rembrandt's rough, messy brushstrokes and dark brooding atmosphere suggest the strong emotions going on below the surface.

The Prodigal Son is one of Rembrandt's last paintings. Some read Rembrandt's own life story into the painting: Rembrandt had been a young prodigy whose God-given talent brought him wealth, fame, and the love of a beautiful woman. Then he lost it all, and was even forced to sell off his possessions to pay his debts. His last years were spent in relative poverty and obscurity.

On a more universal level, Jesus' parable was about how God, like a loving father, forgives even the worst of sinners. The painting resonates with anyone who's found themselves feeling lost, not living up to expectations, or estranged from a parent, family, or god. Note that Rembrandt shows us the scene from the Prodigal's point of view. That could be you or I rushing into the painting, to be received, forgiven, and enfolded in the warmth of a loving embrace.

• *We'll make one more stop on our way up to the modern collection. From the Rembrandt room, head back the way you came, going through rooms 252 and 251. Turn left into room 239, then turn right into long, pastel-hazy, light-filled room 241. Slow your pace and stroll through this gorgeous array of Neoclassical sculpture. Just after the doors, look for...*

Canova

The Three Graces (1813-1816): The great Venetian sculptor shows the three mythological ladies who entertained the Greek gods at dinnertime. They huddle up, hugging and exchanging glances, their heads leaning together. Each pose is different, and the statue is interesting from every angle. But the group is united by their common origin—having come from the same, single block of marble—and by the sash that joins them. The ladies' velvety soft skin is Canova's signature element. Antonio Canova (1757-1822) combines the cool, minimal lines of Neoclassicism with the warm sentiment of Romanticism.

• *From here, it's a long haul up to the Impressionists on the third floor. First find your way back to the Pavilion Room (204, with the Peacock Clock): From the Canova, continue to the end of the Neoclassical gallery, then hook left, then right, to find Raphael's Loggia; head all the way back up the Loggia and turn left at the corner, passing back through the string of Italian Renaissance rooms you started in.*

*Once back in the **Pavilion Room** (or if you're skipping the Old Masters and heading directly up to the modern section), find your way down the long and skinny rooms 259 and 262, then turn right and loop through smaller rooms 272-280 to find the stairs up to the third floor.*

Part 3: Modern Masters

The Hermitage has an impressive collection of paintings by Impressionist and Post-Impressionist masters. It's perfect for seeing how these artists—living in France in the late 19th century—influenced one another. Many of these works became public museum pieces when the Soviet Union nationalized the collections of rich businessmen so the proletariat could enjoy them.

Overview: So many canvases are crammed into these small rooms, it's hard to keep track of who's who. Here's a primer on just a few of the many famous names represented here: **Edouard Manet** (1832-1883) bucked the strict academic system to paint realistic scenes of everyday life, rather than prettified goddesses. Manet inspired his friend **Edgar Degas** (1834-1917) to sketch candid snapshots of the modern Parisian lifestyle—café scenes, workers, and well-dressed families bustling through Parisian streets. **Claude Monet** (1840-1926) and his close friend **Auguste Renoir** (1841-1919) took things another step, setting their canvases up outdoors and painting quickly to capture shimmering landscapes using a mosaic of bright colors. **Vincent van Gogh** (1853-1890), a moody Dutchman, learned this Impressionist technique from the bohemians in Paris, but infused his landscapes with swirling brushwork and an emotional expressiveness. Van Gogh's Post-Impressionist style was adopted by his painting partner, **Paul Gauguin** (1848-1903), who used bright patches of colors and simplified forms to re-create the primitive look of tribal art. **Henri Matisse** (1869-1954) went further, creating the art of "wild beasts" (Fauves), using even brighter colors and simpler forms than Gauguin. Gauguin had greatly admired a brilliant-but-struggling artist named **Paul Cézanne** (1839-1906), who also rejected traditional three-dimensionality to compose paintings as geometrical blocks of color. As the 20th century dawned, **Pablo Picasso** (1881-1973) broke Cezanne's blocks of colors into shards and "cubes" of color, all jumbled up, anticipating purely abstract art.

The Hermitage offers a unique chance to see this evolution—if you're inclined to look for it. If not, just switch off your cerebral cortex and simply browse, enjoying room after room of pretty, colorful, pleasant paintings by these modern masters. I've highlighted a few paintings that always catch my eye.

• *This floor's rooms are smaller—which means they're easier to navigate but more crowded. Sharpen your elbows and, from the top of the stairs, head straight into room 314, turn left, and do a loop through rooms 332, 331, 330, 323, and 322. Then turn right into room 321, where you'll find…*

Renoir

Later in life, Renoir—who, along with Monet, was one of the founding fathers of Impressionism—changed his style. He veered from the Impressionist credo of creating objective studies in color and light to begin painting things that were unabashedly "pretty." He populated his canvases with rosy-cheeked, middle-class girls performing happy domestic activities, rendered in a warm, inviting style. As Renoir himself said, "There are enough ugly things in life."

Young Girls at a Piano (1892): The painting is as uncompli-cated as its title—it shows two girls playing the piano. It's one of six slightly different versions Renoir made of the same subject. This one is done in oil, but the artist's light touch gives it the soft blush of watercolor or pastel. It looks unfinished, but it must have been the "look" Renoir was aiming for, because he signed it.

In the Garden (1885): Renoir's sentimental streak is on display here, too. Renoir became the chronicler of France's blissful era of peace and prosperity, known as the Belle Époque (from the late 19th century until World War I). The leafy garden is captured as a straightforward Impressionist mosaic of colorful brushstrokes. Then Renoir adds a happy couple in love. The woman appears to have the features of Renoir's future wife. The man—a stand-in for Renoir—gazes ardently at the woman's creamy face, limpid eyes, and plump rosy lips. Their arms intertwine like vines in the garden.

• *Now head into room 320, with paintings by **Degas** (his* Place de la Concorde *is a classic example of an Impressionistic everyday street scene) and **Manet**. Then continue into room 319, dominated by **Monet**. Next up, room 318 features lots of **Cézanne** (including* Lady in Blue). *And room 317 is packed with works by...*

Vincent van Gogh

A self-taught phenom who absorbed the Impressionist technique before developing his own unique style, Vincent van Gogh struck out on his own in Arles, in the south of France, in 1888. For the next two years of his brief life, he cranked out a canvas nearly every other day. He loved painting the rural landscape and the colorful life of the locals.

The Arena at Arles (1888): Like a spontaneous photograph, this painting captures the bustle of spectators at the town's bullfighting ring. The scene is slightly off-kilter, focusing on the crowds rather than on the action in the ring. Van Gogh typically painted in a hurry, and you can see it in the hurried lines and sketchy faces.

Memories of the Garden at Etten (*Ladies of Arles*, 1888): In the fall of 1888, Gauguin came to visit Van Gogh. The two friends  roomed together and painted side by side. It was Gauguin who suggested that Vincent change things up and paint something besides Impressionist scenes of everyday life. The result was this startling canvas, in which Vincent portrayed a garden he remembered from his childhood. The vivid colors had special meaning to him, representing the personalities of his mother and sister. The style shows the influence of Gauguin—big swaths of bright colors, divided by thick black outlines.

The Lilac Bush (1889): On December 23, 1888, a drunk and angry Van Gogh turned on Gauguin, threatening him with a knife. Then he cut off a piece of his own ear and sent it to a prostitute. Judged insane, Van Gogh checked into a mental hospital for treatment. There he painted this simple subject that bristles with life, a forest of thick brushstrokes charged with Van Gogh's strong emotions.

The Cottages (1890): Van Gogh moved north of Paris in 1890 to be under a doctor's care. The wavy brushstrokes and surreal colors of this work suggest an uncertain frame of mind. This was one of Vincent's last paintings. A few weeks later, he wandered into a field near these homes and shot himself, having spent his life in poverty and artistic obscurity. No sooner had he died than his work took wings.

• *The next room (316), has a wonderful collection of...*

Paul Gauguin

The Hermitage typically displays about a dozen paintings of the French Post-Impressionist Paul Gauguin, who famously left his stockbroker job and family to paint full-time. Eventually he fulfilled his lifelong dream to live and work in the South Seas, especially Tahiti. He spent much of his later life there, painting island life in all its bright color and simplicity.

Tahitian Pastorals (1892): This work, from Gauguin's first stay in Tahiti, captures the paradise he had always envisioned. He paints an island-dotted landscape peopled by exotic women doing simple tasks and making music. A lounging dog dominates the foreground. The style is intentionally "primitive," collapsing 3-D landscapes into a two-dimensional pattern of bright colors. In *Woman Holding a Fruit* (1893) a native girl enjoys the simple pleasures of life in all her naked innocence.

• *Continue straight across the bridge, peering down into a pastel-blue hall decorated with a whipped-cream can. Don't miss the wonderful view over Palace Square from the windows on your left. You'll head straight into rooms 343 and 344; the largest, most famous, and most important canvas here is by...*

Matisse

The Dance (1909-1910): Five dancers strip naked, join hands, and go ring-around-the-rosy, creating an infectious air of abandon.

This large, joyous work was one of Matisse's personal favorites. It features his Fauvist colors—bright red dancers on a blue-and-green background. Meanwhile, the undulating lines that join the dancers create a pleasing design that anticipates modern, abstract art.

Other Matisse works in this room (and the previous one) trace his evolution from a realistic painter of still lifes to Impressionism to bright Fauvist colors to his semi-abstract works that pioneered modern abstract art.

• *Pass through rooms 346 and 347 to reach rooms 348 and 349, focusing on the works of...*

Pablo Picasso

In the year 1900, the 19-year-old Spaniard Pablo Picasso arrived in Paris, the world art capital. Poor, lonely, and depressed by the suicide of his close friend, he painted other outcasts of society.

The Absinthe Drinker (1901): A woman sits alone in a grimy café, contemplating her fate, soothed by a glass of that highly potent and destructive form of alcohol. She leans on a table, deep in thought, with her distorted right arm wrapped protectively around herself. All of the lines of sight—her unnaturally vertical forearm and the lines on the wall behind her—converge on her face, boxing her into a corner. The painting shows Picasso's facile mastery of the techniques of the earlier generation of Impressionists and Post-Impressionists. It's a snapshot café scene reminiscent of Degas, with the flat two-dimensional feel of Gauguin and the emotional expressiveness of Van Gogh. Notice the signature at top. Though his full Spanish name was Pablo Ruiz Picasso, by this time he has dropped his father's surname (Ruiz) and kept his Mom's to create the one-name brand that would become world-famous—Picasso.

Two Sisters (1902): From Picasso's Blue Period, painted with a gloomy palette, this canvas looks sympathetically at people who, like Picasso, felt sad and alienated. The painting started with a sketch Picasso had made of two sisters—one a prostitute and one a nun. From that specific source, he developed a work of universal character.

Three Women (1908): This work (and the studies near it) shows how Picasso was rethinking how artists look at the world. He shattered reality into shards and cubes of color, then reassembled the pieces like a collage on canvas—the style called Cubism.

• *While there's much more to be seen, our tour is finished. If you're still craving more, the private apartments of Maria Alexandronovna (wife of Czar Alexander II; rooms 289 and 304-307) are impressive, especially room 304, with its gold decor and view.*

Otherwise, make your way back down to the ground floor and plot your escape. Just follow signs with your new favorite word in the Russian language: ВЫХОД…"exit."

▲▲▲Russian Museum (Русский Музей)

Here's a fascinating collection of Russian art, particularly 18th- and 19th-century painting and portraiture. People who are disappointed that the Hermitage is mostly Western European art love the Russian Museum, since the artists shown here are largely unknown in the West. Much of the work reveals Russians exploring their own culture and landscape: marshes, birch stands, muddy village streets, the conquest of Siberia, firelit scenes

in family huts, and Repin's portrait of Tolstoy standing barefoot in the woods.

The museum is comparatively uncrowded, and it is especially meaningful as it adds depth to the experience you have as a visitor to St. Petersburg—these artists saw the same rooftops, churches, and street scenes as you. The artworks bring you in touch with the country's turbulent political history and capture the small-town wooden architecture and forest landscapes that you won't see on a visit to this big city.

The museum occupies the Mikhailovsky Palace, built for Grand Duke Mikhail Pavlovich (a grandson of Catherine the Great) in the 1820s. Though the interiors aren't as impressive as those at the Hermitage, original decorations in a few rooms give you a taste of how the Russian nobility lived.

Cost and Hours: 350 R, photo permit-250 R, English audio-guide-350 R, Wed-Sun 10:00-18:00, Mon 10:00-17:00, closed Tue, last entry one hour before closing. The museum is at Inzhenernaya Ulitsa 4, two blocks north of Nevsky Prospekt along Griboyedova Canal, close to the Church on Spilled Blood. Tel. 595-4248, www .rusmuseum.ru.

Entering the Museum: The entrance is at basement level in the right-hand corner as you enter the main courtyard. Purchase your tickets (and a photo permit, if you want), pick up a photocopied map (listing room numbers), and go through the security checkpoint. Staying on the basement level, you'll find cloakrooms, a bookstore, toilets, a small café (Wed-Sun 10:00-17:00, Mon 10:00-16:00, closed Tue). For later, notice the back exit, which gives you the option of leaving through the gardens on the north side of the museum (from here, you can bear left through the park to reach the Church on Spilled Blood). To reach the exhibits, take the stairs up one flight and show your ticket; here, at the base of the grand staircase, you can rent the good audioguide, which interprets three hundred of the museum's best works; or, for a quick visit, just use the self-guided tour, below.

Layout: The museum has 109 numbered rooms (find numbers over doorways), which lend themselves to a route in more or less numerical order. When this book went to press, rooms 23-29 were closed for renovation; when they reopen, some painting locations may change.

Self-Guided Tour

The museum's most exciting works cover the period from roughly 1870 to 1940. Russia was in ferment during these years—first with the end of serfdom and agitation for social change and equality; later with World War I, industrialization, and the beginnings of communism; and throughout with artistic currents such as Impressionism, Art Nouveau, and Modernism coming in from the West. After you see these highlights, consider spending some time on the museum's earlier collections and special exhibits.

• *Start in the late 19th century, near the audioguide desks and the bottom of the grand staircase. Reaching the top of the stairs, turn right and pass through room 38 into room 37.*

19th- and Early 20th-Century Painting

Vasily Surikov: One of Russia's foremost historical painters, Surikov grew up in Siberia but later moved to European Russia. In room 37, the painting with the rowboat commemorates Stepan Razin, who led an uprising against the czar in 1670. In room 36, the gigantic *Yermak's Conquest of Siberia* (1895) is a reminder that Russia (like the US) has an uneasy relationship with its native peoples. Here, Caucasian-featured soldiers armed with guns cross a river by boat, meeting Siberian forces on the other shore who are armed with bow and arrow.

• *Peek into the room down the stairs from here (room 54), where Ilya Repin's large canvas shows the aristocracy at work in a Russian State Council meeting from 1901. For more by Repin, head back up the stairs and turn left, passing through room 35 to reach room 34.*

Ilya Repin: Repin came from a modest background and often explored the rural life of common people—he could be called an early Socialist Realist. His painting met approval during the Soviet period for its focus on the working class. Repin famously painted Leo Tolstoy in peasant's clothing, standing barefoot in the woods (1901). Also in this room, in *Seeing Off a Recruit* (1879), a young man hugs his mother as he prepares to let the army take him far away—showing the pathos of military service in a way that is still relevant today.

• *Turn into room 33.*

With *Barge Haulers on the Volga* (1870-1873), Repin polished his local celebrity and gained renown in the West. Eleven wretched

workers (called *burlaks*)—bodies groaning, pain etched on each face—are yoked like livestock for the Sisyphean task of pulling a ship against the current. The youngest *burlak* in the center, with inexplicable optimism, strikes a classically heroic pose. A steamship on the horizon emphasizes how cruelly outdated this form of labor is in the modern age. It's no wonder the Soviets embraced this painting as a perfect metaphor for the timeless struggle of the working class.

• *Now backtrack to room 35 and turn right, down the stairs, to room 39.*

Vasily Vereshchagin: Vereshchagin specialized in photo-realistic paintings emphasizing two subjects: military scenes and exotic views of Eastern cultures (which he explored in his travels to the Balkans, Central Asia, and British India). Many of his warfare paintings were deemed too graphic or unsettling to be exhibited during his lifetime. Vereshchagin takes a warts-and-all approach to combat—trying to show it realistically rather than glorify it. *Shipka-Shaynovo* shows Russia's 1877 victory over the Ottoman Empire at the battle of Shipka Pass, in what's now Bulgaria (see photo at top of next page). The victorious Russian general rides past cheering troops, but the composition is dominated by

the grotesque corpses of soldiers scattered in the snow-covered foreground. Vereshchagin's evocatively detailed *At the Entrance to the Mosque* makes evident the artist's fascination with the very Eastern cultures whose decline is documented on his other canvases.

• *Go straight through rooms 40–43 to reach room 44.*

Leon Bakst: With its free brushstrokes and nonchalant air, *Portrait of Sergei Diaghilev and His Nanny* (1906) shows a move toward Modernism. Diaghilev, an editor, impresario, ballet entrepreneur, and one of the main figures in the turn-of-the-century St. Petersburg art world, stands off-center, his gaze fixed on the viewer. Somewhat improbably, the painting includes his elderly nanny sitting in the background.

• *Head into the next room, #45.*

Pre-Modern Russia: *Moscow Street of the 17th Century on a Festive Day* (1895), by **Andrei Ryabushkin,** shows a semi-romanticized view of pre-modern Russian village life: wooden houses, unpaved streets, women in headscarves and men in long beards, beggars, and a colorful, onion-domed village church. On the opposite wall is **Nikolai Roerich**'s *Battle In Heaven* (1912). Roerich, of aristocratic Baltic German descent, spent many years traveling in Central Asia and painted startling, imaginary, Himalayan landscapes in icy blue colors. He turned himself into a sort of spiritual guru and still has a cult following in Russia and elsewhere—some people even claim to be his reincarnation. Roerich's best works are not on display, but you can see four more large canvases by him in the stairway off room 74.

• *Continue through rooms 46 and 47, then traverse the stairwell to reach room 48.*

Folk Art Detour: Here, get a glimpse of small-town Russia with a peek into the small folk art wing, worth perusal if only for its collection of village woodcarvings.

• *After touring the folk-art collection, head back out to room 48 and go down the long corridor to reach a flight of stairs. Take this up to the top floor of the museum's Benois Wing, housing most of the museum's 20th-century art. You'll begin in room 66.*

More 20th-Century Art

Mikhail Vrubel: The modern art wing kicks off with Vrubel's *Bogatyr* (1898), painted on the cusp of the new century. A massive, ogre-like knight errant sits on a fantastically fat horse. The decorative style borrows from the Art Nouveau movement, the theme echoes Russian myths and stories, and the surrealistic presentation anticipates expressionist painting.

• *Go through the door to the right of the ogre, and proceed straight through rooms 67-69 to reach room 70.*

Valentin Serov: Serov made his name as the best Russian portrait painter of his day. Many Russian celebrities sat for him, eager for one of his freely brushed, technically adept portraits. He departed from his usual approach for his 1910 nude portrait of Ida Rubinstein, a famous Russian ballerina. Daring in its simplicity and starkness, the painting has the

flatness and sharp outlines of Art Nouveau. This was one of the last paintings Serov completed before his death.

• *Continue into room 71.*

Boris Kustodiev: Although his bread and butter was book illustration, Kustodiev was also known for his colorful paintings, such as *Shrovetide* (1916). Here you see the inescapably recurrent theme of winter in Russian painting: sleigh rides, snow-covered roofs, festivals, and fairy-tale churches, all under an achingly beautiful winter sky of swirling pink-and-blue pastels.

• *Continue around this wing, passing through rooms 72-79, to reach rooms 80-85 and...*

Socialist Art: The Bolshevik revolution threw artistic trends in Russia onto a new track. Art from the early Soviet period (rooms 80-83) glorified workers and the "dictatorship of the proletariat."

In room 80, Alexander Samokhvalov's *Militarized Komsomol* (1932-1933) conveys the Socialist Realist aesthetic: "realistically" showing everyday people who are, in an idealized way, eagerly participating in the socialist society. In this case, we see scouts learning how to scout—and, potentially, do more than that, should the need arise.

By the door in room 81, Vyacheslav Pakulin's Impressionistic *Nevsky on 9 July 1945* shows St. Petersburg's main drag at the end of the devastating World War II—looking much like it does today.

The canvases in room 82 depict idyllic nature and peasant scenes, extolling the simple life held central in the Soviet worldview. Arkady Plastov's *Midday* and Alexei and Sergei

Tkachev's *Children* make you want to sign up for a Russian-countryside summer vacation.

But in rooms 84-85, you can feel change in the air. Rather than idealizing everyday Russian life, these works—from the later

Soviet years—are clearly critical of it. In room 85, Alexei Sundukov's *Queue* (1986) is a perhaps too-on-the-nose depiction of the trials of a communist consumer. In the center of this room, Dmitry Kaminker's *The Oarsman* (1987), sculpted under perestroika, communicates the hopeless feeling of the last years of communism.

• *Our tour of the core collection is finished. If you'd like, detour downstairs to rooms 101-109, which are reserved for special exhibitions.*

To see the palatial rooms on the top floor, return to the main wing of the palace (go back downstairs and down the long hall, then continue down the even longer hall—marked To Mikhailovsky Palace*) and head up the grand staircase to the second floor.*

Early Russian Art
• *Once upstairs, turn left, making a quick circle through rooms 1-17.*

Rooms 1-4: These rooms house Russian icons, the earliest dating back to the 1100s. Icons are a key part of Orthodox traditions of worship, and have roots in medieval Greek and Byzantine artistic styles.

Rooms 5-12: You'll find the grandest architecture in the museum in these rooms overlooking the gardens out back, along with mostly 18th-century portraits.

Rooms 13-17: These rooms cover the Romantic era of the early 19th century. In Room 16, tucked in among more exotic Mediterranean destinations, are some small, easily missed views of St. Petersburg by Sylvester Shchedrin.

• *Your tour is over. Descend the grand staircase like a 19th-century Russian aristocrat, walk down the smaller stairs to the coatroom and café area, and find the exit.*

Gardens Behind the Russian Museum
The zone behind the Russian Museum is filled with delightful parks and gardens. Directly behind the building, the inviting, tree-filled **Mikhailovsky Garden** (Михайловский сад) leads (across the canal) into the geometrically regimented **Field of Mars** (Марсово поле) park, designed to showcase military parades.

Just to its east (across another canal) is one of St. Petersburg's most enjoyable public spaces, the **Summer Garden** (Летний сад,

Letny Sad). This park—laced with walking trails, studded with fountains and statues, and generously tree-shaded—was created by Peter the Great himself, where the Fontanka River meets the Neva. Like St. Petersburg itself, it's the gorgeous result of a collaboration between the most talented artistic minds of the time: Dutch and French garden engineers helped to plot and populate the space with beautiful trees and hedges, and Venetian artists lined its walkways with stony sculptures. Along the Fontanka is Peter's own **Summer Palace** (Летний дворец)—a strikingly modest mansion where it's easy to imagine Peter sitting back, relaxing, and gazing out over the waterways of his namesake city. On a sunny day with some time to spare, there are few more enjoyable activities in St. Petersburg than strolling through the Summer Garden (garden open in summer daily 10:00-21:00; off-season Wed-Mon 10:00-19:30, closed Tue).

Churches

Russian Orthodoxy has revived since the end of communism. Duck into any neighborhood church, full of incense, candles,

and liturgical chants. It's usually OK to visit discreetly during services, when the priest opens the doors of the iconostasis, faces the altar, and leads the standing congregation in chant. Dress conservatively (no shorts or bare shoulders) and try to remain standing (though churches have a few seats for the truly pooped). Women are encouraged, though not normally required, to cover their heads with a scarf or bandanna, sometimes available at the entrance. Smaller churches are full of Russians morning, noon, and night, and will give you more of a feeling for Russian religion than will church-museums such as St. Isaac's or the Church on Spilled Blood. Plus, entrance is free, though you can leave a small donation toward renovations, or buy and light a candle. Alongside the religious revival in Russia, many fault the church for promoting nationalism and isolationist politics, and for its strenuously anti-gay stance.

▲▲**Kazan Cathedral (Казанский Собор)**—This huge, functioning house of worship, right along Nevsky Prospekt next to the Griboyedova Canal, offers an accessible Orthodox experience (although its interior is not very typical). Reopened as a church after years as a "Museum of Atheism," this can't-miss-it sight has a sweeping exterior portico modeled after St. Peter's in Rome.

Cost and Hours: Free, daily 9:00-20:00, services generally at 10:00 and 18:00, Kazanskaya 2, www.kazansky-spb.ru.

Visiting the Church: Although the church seems to be facing Nevsky Prospekt, you'll enter (per Christian tradition) through the west-facing main door, which is down a side street (Ulitsa Kazanskaya).

Entering, let your eyes adjust to the low light. Appreciate the brilliant silver-arched **iconostasis.** Notice the rounded arches of the Neo-Romanesque-style interior.

Worshippers wait in a long line to kiss the church's namesake, the **Icon of Our Lady of Kazan.** Considered the single most important icon of the Russian Orthodox faith, the icon was discovered by a young girl (directed by a vision of the Virgin Mary) in a tunnel beneath the city of Kazan in 1579. A monastery was erected on that site, and replicas of the icon were sent to other Russian cities—including St. Petersburg—to be venerated by the faithful. The original icon was stolen from Kazan in 1904 and went missing for nearly 100 years (it resurfaced in the Vatican and was returned to Kazan in 2005, although its authenticity has been questioned). Either way, this is a replica, but still considered holy.

The icon is important partly because it was invoked in many successful military campaigns, including the successful defense of Russia during Napoleon's 1812 invasion. In the left transept, find the statue and tomb of **Field Marshal Mikhail Kutuzov** (1745-1813), who led Russian troops during that conflict. Up above, notice the original Napoleonic banners seized in the invasion. On the left are the symbolic keys to the Russian cities that Kutuzov's forces retook from Napoleon.

▲▲▲**Church on Spilled Blood (Спас на крови)**—This exuberantly decorative church, with its gilded carrot top of onion domes, is a must-see photo op just a short walk off Nevsky Prospekt.

It's built on the place where a suicide bomber assassinated Czar Alexander II in 1881—explaining both the evocative name and the structure's out-of-kilter relationship to the surrounding street plan. Ticket windows are on the north side of the church, facing away from Nevsky

The Russian Orthodox Church

In the fourth century A.D., the Roman Empire split in half, dividing Eastern Europe and the Balkan Peninsula down the middle. Seven centuries later, with the Great Schism, the Christian faith diverged along similar lines, into two separate branches: Roman Catholicism in the west (based in Rome and including most of Western and Central Europe), and Eastern or Byzantine Orthodoxy in the east (based in Constantinople—today's Istanbul—and prevalent in Russia, far-eastern Europe, the eastern half of the Balkan Peninsula, and Greece). The root word *orthos* is Greek for "right belief"—and it's logical that if you're sure you're right, you're more conservative and resistant to change.

Over the centuries, the Catholic Church shed old traditions and developed new ones. Meanwhile, the Eastern Orthodox Church—which remained consolidated under the stable and wealthy Byzantine Empire—stayed true to the earliest traditions of the Christian faith. In the mid-15th century, Russia's branch of Orthodoxy officially split from Constantinople, moving its religious capital to Moscow. And today, rather than having one centralized headquarters (such as the Vatican for Catholicism), the Eastern Orthodox Church is divided into about a dozen regional, autocephalous ("self-headed") branches that remain administratively independent even as they share many of the same rituals. The largest of these (with about half of the world's 300 million Orthodox Christians) is the Russian Orthodox Church.

The doctrines of Catholic and Orthodox churches remain very similar, but many of the rituals and customs are different. For example, in Orthodox churches that are active houses of worship, women are expected to cover their heads (many can loan you a scarf if you don't have one); churches that are tourist attractions may be more flexible. Women and men both must have their knees covered.

As you enter any Russian Orthodox church, you can join in the standard routine: Drop a coin in the wooden box, pick up a candle, say a prayer, light the candle, and place it in the candelabra. Make the sign of the cross and kiss the icon.

Where's the altar? Orthodox churches come with an altar screen covered with curtains and icons (the "iconostasis"). The standard iconostasis design calls for four icons flanking the central door, with John the Baptist and Jesus to the right, Mary and the Baby Jesus on the left, and an icon featuring the saint or event that the church is dedicated to on the far left.

The iconostasis divides the lay community from the priests—the material world from the spiritual one. The spiritual heavy lifting takes place behind the iconostasis, where the priests symbolically turn bread and wine into the body and blood of Jesus. Then they open the doors or curtains and serve the Eucharist to their faithful flock—spooning the wine from a chalice while holding a cloth under each chin so as not to drop any on the floor.

Notice that there are few (if any) pews. Worshippers stand during the service as a sign of respect (though some older parishioners sit on the seats along the walls). Traditionally, women stand on the left side, men on the right (equal distance from the altar—to represent that all are equal before God).

The Orthodox faith tends to use a Greek cross, with four equal arms (like a plus sign, sometimes inside a circle), which focuses on God's perfection. The longer Latin cross, typically used by Catholics, more literally evokes the Crucifixion, emphasizing Jesus' death and sacrifice. Many Orthodox churches have Greek-cross floor plans rather than the elongated nave-and-transept designs that are common in Western Europe.

Unlike many Catholic church decorations, Orthodox icons (paintings of saints) are not intended to be lifelike. Packed with intricate symbolism and cast against a shimmering golden background, they're meant to remind viewers of the metaphysical nature of Jesus and the saints rather than their physical form. You'll almost never see statues, which, to Orthodox people, feel a little too close to the forbidden worship of graven images.

Most Eastern Orthodox churches have at least one mosaic or painting of Christ in a standard pose—as *Pantocrator,* a Greek word meaning "Ruler of All." The image, so familiar to Orthodox Christians, shows Christ as King of the Universe, facing directly out, with penetrating eyes. Behind him is a halo divided by a cross, with only three visible arms—an Orthodox symbol for the Trinity (the fourth arm is hidden behind Christ).

Orthodox services generally involve chanting (a dialogue that goes back and forth between the priest and the congregation), and the church is filled with the evocative aroma of incense, combining to heighten the experience for worshippers. While many Catholic and Protestant services tend to be more of a theoretical and rote covering of basic religious tenets (come on—don't tell me you understand every phrase in the Nicene Creed), Orthodox services are about creating a religious experience. Each of these elements does its part to help the worshipper transcend the physical world and enter communion with the spiritual one.

Under communism, the state religion—atheism—trumped the faith professed by the majority of Russians. The Russian Orthodox Church survived, but many church buildings were seized by the government and repurposed (as ice-hockey rinks, swimming pools, and so on). Many more were destroyed. Soviet citizens who openly belonged to the Church sacrificed any hope of advancement within the communist system. But since the fall of communism, Russians have flocked back to their church. (Even Vladimir Putin, a former KGB agent and avowed atheist, revealed that he had secretly been an Orthodox Christian all along.) These days, new churches are being built, and destroyed ones are being rebuilt or renovated...and all of them, it seems, are filled with worshippers. Today, three out of every four Russian citizens follows this faith—high numbers for a country whose government was aggressively atheistic just a generation ago.

Prospekt. Go inside to appreciate the mysteriously dim interior, slathered with vivid mosaics.

Cost and Hours: 250 R, audioguide-100 R; May-mid-Sept daily 10:00-19:00, may stay open until 23:00 for extra charge; mid-Sept-April daily 11:00-19:00; last entry one hour before closing, Kanał Griboyedova 2b, tel. 315-1636, http://eng.cathedral.ru.

Visiting the Church: Begun just after Alexander's assassination but not finished until 1907, the church is built in a neo-Russian, Historicist style. That means that its designers created a building that was a romantic, self-conscious, fairy-tale image of their own national history and traditions—similar to Neuschwanstein Castle in Bavaria or the Matthias Church in Budapest. Looted during the 1917 Russian Revolution, the church was used for storage during the communist era, then restored in the 1990s. It is still not used for services, though.

Enter the church and look up; Christ gazes down at you from the top of the dome, bathed in light from the windows and ringed

by the gold balcony railing. The walls are covered with exquisite mosaics (nothing is painted) that show how Orthodoxy continues the artistic traditions of early Christianity. Walk up to the iconostasis (the partition dividing the altar from the main part of the church). Typically made of wood, this one is of marble, with inlaid doors. In the back of the church, the canopy shows the spot where Czar Alexander II was mortally wounded.

Nearby: Just behind the church is a good outdoor souvenir market (see "Shopping in St. Petersburg," later). And the church's apse points to the tranquil, beautiful Mikhailovsky Garden, which runs behind the Russian Museum (for more on nearby gardens, see page 409).

▲▲St. Isaac's Cathedral (Исаакиевский Собор)— The gold dome of St. Isaac's glitters at the end of Malaya Morskaya Ulitsa, not far from the Admiralty. St. Isaac's was built between 1818 and 1858, and its Neoclassical exterior reminds Americans of the US Capitol building. While

the lavish interior is very impressive, if you're short on time I'd skip this in favor of the more typical (and arguably more opulent) Church on Spilled Blood.

The **interior** has a few exhibits, but ultimately it's all about the grand space. It feels like a big European Catholic church. To many, it's reminiscent of St. Peter's in Rome, but with a few typically Orthodox elements (iconostasis, no pews). Aside from a small side chapel (at the left end of the iconostasis), this is not a functioning house of worship—it's technically a museum.

It's worthwhile to climb the colonnade stairway to the **roof**

(262 steps) for the view. Every tenth step (heading up and down) is numbered in a countdown to your goal.

Cost and Hours: Interior/"museum"-250 R, Thu-Tue 10:00-19:00, closed Wed year-round; roof-150 R, daily 10:00-18:00 except closed second Wed of each month; entire complex opens at 11:00 mid-Sept-April; last entry one hour before closing, Isaakievskaya pl. 4, tel. 315-9732, http://eng.cathedral.ru.

Getting Tickets: The ticket windows take a break from 13:00-13:30 and 15:45-16:15, but the church and roof remain open. You can bypass the line at the ticket window, or buy tickets when the window is closed, by using the automatic machines (in English, bills only—no coins).

Evening Visits: In summer (May-Sept), to squeeze more sightseeing into your busy St. Petersburg days, consider saving this church for an after-hours but higher-cost visit (interior-350 R, Thu-Tue 18:15-22:30, closed Wed; roof-300 R, Thu-Tue 18:15-23:00, closed Wed; last entry for both 30 minutes earlier).

Neighborhood Churches—Two convenient neighborhood churches are at Vladimirskaya Metro stop, by the Dostoyevsky Museum and the indoor market (at the south end of Mokhovaya Ulitsa, by the first bridge across the Fontanka going north from Nevsky). For a serious Orthodox experience, take the Metro to Ploshchad Aleksandra Nevskogo and visit the church in the *lavra* (monastery) across the street from the Metro exit, where Dostoyevsky is also buried.

Near Nevsky Prospekt

▲**Dostoyevsky Museum (Музей Ф. М. Достоевского)**—
Although many of the furnishings are gone, a visit to this six-
room apartment gives you a feel for how the famous writer lived.

Dostoyevsky, his second wife, and
their three children lived here for
the last two and a half years of his
life, while he wrote *The Brothers
Karamazov*. Visiting is quick and
simple. You could rent the audioguide or buy the English guidebook,
but I found that the multilingual
laminated cards in each room were
enough explanation. The *babushki*
who run the place put a new half-cup
of tea on Dostoyevsky's desk every
morning. An extra exhibition room
shows photos of Dostoyevsky, his family, and the St. Petersburg
of his times.

Dostoyevsky chain-smoked, wrote all night, slept until noon,
edited his work in the afternoon, and then had dinner with his
family, whom he adored. Unlike Pushkin, an aristocrat who lived
in the wealthy part of town near the czar's palace, Dostoyevsky
came from a middle-class background and wrote about the lives of
the poor. He favored this grittier section of St. Petersburg, which
kept him in touch with the world of his subjects. Dostoyevsky had
recovered from a gambling addiction and was gaining recognition
as a writer when he moved here, but he suffered badly from
epilepsy and emphysema, and died at the age of 60.

Cost and Hours: 160 R, audioguide-170 R, English
guidebook-200 R, photo permit-70 R; Tue-Sun 11:00-18:00, last
entry 30 minutes before closing, www.md.spb.ru. The museum is
at Kuznechny Pereulok 5, across the street from the Kuznechny
Rynok market and a block from Metro: Dostoevskaya or
Vladimirskaya.

Across the Neva River

From the riverfront side of the Hermitage, you can spot several
sights across the river that are worth visiting. But you'll have to
allow plenty of time; while these places appear close, it takes a
while to reach them by foot.

▲▲**Strelka Spin-Tour**—On your way between the Hermitage
area and the Peter and Paul Fortress, you'll cross the Dvortsovy
Bridge and then pass a strategic viewpoint, called Strelka, that
offers a sweeping 360-degree view of St. Petersburg's core. Head
down to the park that fills the knob of land at water level (between

the two pink columns) and survey the scene.

You're standing on a corner of the large **Vasilyevsky Island**—one of the many islands that make up St. Petersburg. (A nickname for the town is "City on 101 Islands," although an official count is elusive.) The Marine Facade cruise ship terminal is at the opposite end of this same island, four miles due west.

Literally meaning "Little Arrowhead," **Strelka** sticks out into the very heart of the Neva River and St. Petersburg. The park filling the point—and especially the promenade along the water—is one of about 10 different sites around town where newlyweds are practically obligated to come for wedding pictures. They toast with champagne, then break their glasses against the big marble ball (watch your step).

Begin by facing the can't-miss-it **Hermitage,** just across the Neva—the Winter Palace of the czars and today a world-class art museum. Notice that this sprawling complex has several wings: it's not just the main green-and-white structure, but also the yellow one next to that, as well as the mint-green one (separated by a canal and a walkway) after that. No wonder it could take days to fully see the place (though my self-guided tour narrows it down to the highlights).

Now begin spinning to the left. The Art Nouveau **Trinity Bridge** (Troitsky Most)—one of St. Petersburg's longest and most beautiful—was built in 1903, its design having beat out a submission by Gustav Eiffel. Before the 1750s, no permanent bridges spanned the Neva; one crossed only on pontoon bridges (in the summer) or a frozen river (in winter). Some years, St. Petersburgers got stranded where they were and had to simply wait for the river either to freeze enough to walk on or to thaw enough for the bridges. Just beyond the bridge, you can faintly see trees marking the delightful **Summer Garden**—once the private garden for Peter the Great's cute little Summer Palace, and now a public park and a wonderful place for a warm-weather stroll (for details, see page 409).

A bit farther upriver, on the other side of the river (not quite visible from here), are two more sights you may see if you venture farther afield on a bus or boat tour. The cruiser *Aurora* (moored along the Petrogradskaya embankment, around the corner from the Peter and Paul Fortress) fired the shot that signaled the start of Vladimir Lenin's first assault in the October Revolution of 1917. Halfway between the fortress and the *Aurora*, along the Petrovskaya embankment, is **Peter the Great's log cabin,** entombed in a small 19th-century brick house in a tiny park. Peter lived here briefly in 1703.

Closer to you, on the left side of the river, you'll see the stoutly walled **Peter and Paul Fortress,** with its slender golden spire (for details, see page 419). St. Petersburg was born here in 1703, when Peter the Great began building this fortress to secure territory he had won in battle against the Swedes. Think for a moment about how strategic this location is, at the mouth of the Neva River. The Neva is very short (only 46 miles), but it's an essential link in a vital series of shipping waterways. The Neva flows from Lake Ladoga, which itself feeds (via a network of canals) into Russia's "mother river," the Volga—Europe's longest river, which cuts north-to-south through the Russian heartland all the way to the Caspian Sea. The Volga also connects to the Moskva River, the Black Sea, and the Danube. That makes the Neva the outlet for all Russian waterways to the Baltic Sea, and from there, to all of Europe and beyond. In other words, you could sail from Iran to Volgograd (formerly Stalingrad) to Istanbul to Budapest to Moscow to Lisbon—but you would have to go through St. Petersburg.

Turning farther left, you'll spot the first of the two giant, pink **rostral columns** that flank Strelka. Inspired by similar towers built by ancient Greeks and Romans to celebrate naval victories, these columns are decorated with anchors and studded with the prows of ships. Once topped by gaslights (now electric), the pillars trumpet St. Petersburg's nautical heritage. (A similar column stands in the middle of New York City's Columbus Circle.) Facing Strelka is the **Old Stock Exchange** (Beurs), flanked by yellow warehouses.

Just to the left, the turreted pastel-blue building is Peter the Great's **Kunstkamera,** a sort of ethnographical museum built around the czar's original collection (described next). "Kunstkamera" and "Hermitage" are both European words and concepts that Peter the Great imported to class up his new, European-style capital.

Circling a bit farther to the left, the yellow buildings at the end of the bridge (just right of the Hermitage) are the **Admiralty,** the geographical center of St. Petersburg and the headquarters of Peter the Great's imperial navy.

▲**Kunstkamera (Кунсткамера)**—Peter the Great, who fancied himself a scientist, founded this—the first state public museum in Russia—in 1714. He filled it with his personal collections, consisting of "fish, reptiles, and insects in bottles," scientific instruments, and books from his library. The expanded museum now fills this grand building with its many anthropological and ethnographic collections (including, for example, the best exhibit on northern Native Americans that you'll find on this side of the Atlantic).

Cost and Hours: 250 R, Tue-Sun 11:00-19:00, closed Mon, also closed last Tue of each month, last entry at 18:00, Universitetskaya Nab. 3, tel. 328-0812, www.kunstkamera.ru.

Visiting the Museum: While the displays are quite old-fashioned, there's ample English information. You can explore the two floors (plus the tower) of mostly geographically arranged exhibits, but most tourists are drawn to the "First Scientific Collections of the Kunstkamera"—especially Peter's stomach-turning exhibit on teratology, the study of deformities: a grand hall packed with jars of two-headed human fetuses pickled in formaldehyde, a double-headed calf, skeletons of a human giant and conjoined twins, and Peter the Great's own death mask. Not for the faint of heart, this might be Europe's most offbeat—and nauseating—sight. As strange and titillating as it seems, this collection is based in sound science: Peter wanted to understand the scientific underpinnings of deformity to dispel the small-minded superstitions of his subjects. While many tourists dismiss the Kunstkamera as a "museum of curiosities," locals are proud of its scientific tradition and its impressive collections.

▲▲**Peter and Paul Fortress (Петропавловская Крепость)**—Founded by Peter the Great in 1703 during the Great Northern War with Sweden, this fortress on an island in the Neva was

the birthplace of St. Petersburg. Its gold steeple catches the sunlight, and its blank walls face the Winter Palace across the river. While it'd be easy to spend all day here, the best visit for those on a tight schedule is to simply wander the grounds, dip into the cathedral to see the tombs of the Romanovs (Russia's czars), and maybe do a little sunbathing on the beach. For those wanting to delve into history, the grounds also have museums about city history, space exploration, and the famous-to-Russians prison that once occupied this space.

Cost and Hours: It's free to enter and explore the grounds (open daily 6:00-22:00). The sights inside are covered by individual tickets (cathedral-200 R, prison-130 R, St. Petersburg history museum-100 R, fortress history museum-100 R, space/rocketry museum-50 R) and a variety of combo-tickets (cathedral and prison-300 R, everything-370 R). Climbing up onto the "Neva

Curtain Wall" is included in the comprehensive combo-ticket; the "Neva Panorama" has a separate 150-R ticket. The cathedral and prison are open daily 10:00-19:00, last entry 30 minutes before closing. The smaller museums are open Thu-Mon 11:00-19:00, Tue 11:00-18:00, closed Wed. The 250-R audioguide provides more information. Info: www.spbmuseum.ru.

Getting There: Two footbridges connect Hare Island (Zayachy Ostrov, with the fortress) to the rest of St. Petersburg. The main entrance is through the park from the flying saucer-shaped Gorkovskaya Metro station (go through the park to the busy road with the gas station, then head for the pointy golden steeple and cross the footbridge). The other entrance is at the west end, easily walkable from Palace Square and the Hermitage. Like a lot of things in this city, it looks close but takes a while—give yourself at least 20 minutes for the scenic walk: Cross the bridge (Dvortsovy Most) by the Hermitage, angle right past the Strelka viewpoint (worth a quick stop to enjoy the view—described earlier), then cross the second bridge (Birzhevoy Most), turn right, and follow the waterline to a footbridge leading to the fortress' side entrance.

Background: There's been a fortress here as long as there's been a St. Petersburg. When he founded the city, in 1703, this was the first thing Peter the Great built to defend this strategic meeting point of the waterways of Russia and the Baltic (and, therefore, the rest of Europe). Originally the center of town was just east of here (near the preserved log cabin where Peter the Great briefly resided). Eventually it became too challenging to connect between the fortress and the mainland across the river (especially when the river froze or thawed), so the city center was transplanted there.

Visiting the Fortress: Pick up a map when you buy your ticket to navigate the sprawling complex. You can't miss the cathedral, with its skinny golden spire shooting up from the middle of the island.

Strolling the **grounds**, you'll get an up-close look at the stout brick wall surrounding the island. From the cathedral, head straight out to the water through the gateway to get a look outside the wall. You can also circle around the fortress exterior to find the delightful sandy beach huddled alongside the wall—an understandably popular place for St. Petersburgers to sunbathe on balmy days.

The **Sts. Peter and Paul Cathedral** is the centerpiece of the fortress. Still the tallest building in the city, it's mostly famous as the final resting place of the Romanov czars, who ruled Russia from 1613 through 1917. People are understandably caught up in the romance of this glamorous dynasty, which met a tragic end with Lenin's October Revolution; if you've been bitten by Romanov mania, this is a good place to stoke your imperial daydreams. You can pick up a floor plan identifying each member of the dynasty (starting in the front-right corner with Peter the Great and working chronologically counterclockwise), but we'll skip to a few highlights.

Entering, watch on the left (under the stairs) for **Alexei Petrovich** (1690-1718), the son of Peter the Great, who was tortured to death by his own father—Alexei was in cahoots with a group that planned to overthrow Peter and reverse his many reforms. (To this day, a similar tension dominates contemporary Russian politics: between conservative forces who—like Alexei—turn their back on Europe, and liberal forces—like Peter—pushing to reform and integrate with Europe.) At the front of the church, to the right of the iconostasis, is a bombastic bust of **Peter the Great** (1672-1725; for more on him, see page 423).

About a third of the way from the main door to the iconostasis, on the left, find **Maria Fedorovna** (1847-1928). This Danish princess (known as Dagmar in her native land) moved from Copenhagen to St. Petersburg, married the second-to-the-last czar (Alexander III), gave birth to the last czar (Nicholas II), and fled the October Revolution to live in exile in Denmark. After her death, she was buried with her fellow Danish royals at Roskilde Cathedral; in 2006, her remains were brought back here with great fanfare to join her adopted clan. Hers is one of the most popular graves in the church.

Next, head to the small chapel (sealed off with a barrier, to the left of the main door as you face it). Here lies the much-romanticized family of the final Romanov czar: **Nicholas II** (1868-1918), his wife, Alexandra, and their four daughters and one son. The czar abdicated in March of 1917, and was imprisoned with the rest of his family. The Bolsheviks murdered them all on the night of July 16, 1918. The details are gruesome. The children were shot at point-blank range with handguns; because the daughters had diamonds sewn into their dresses, some of the bullets were deflected at crazy angles, making the execution far from surgical. Originally buried in an unmarked grave, the remains of most of the family members were only rediscovered in 1991, and reburied here in 1998.

Persistent legends surround the fate of the Romanov daughter **Anastasia,** who was rumored to have escaped the execution. In the decades since the massacre, different women emerged claiming to be the long-lost Anastasia—most famously Anna Anderson, who turned up in Berlin in the 1920s. But very recent DNA testing has positively identified the remains of the real Anastasia (found only in 2007 and now interred here), while similar tests disproved Anderson's claim.

Exit the cathedral through the chapel to the left of the iconostasis. This hallway features the graves of the siblings of the czars—**Grand Dukes and Grand Duchesses.** The quite recent dates on some of these graves are a reminder that many of these Romanov cousins long outlived their ancestors' reign.

The czars incarcerated political prisoners in **Trubetskoy Bastion Prison** in the late 19th and early 20th centuries. While famous among Russians as the place  that held many of its revolutionaries, it's difficult for Americans to appreciate. You'll wind your way through long, somber hallways past cells marked with plaques (in Russian and English) identifying former inmates. American visitors may recognize the names of Fyodor Dostoyevsky, Leon Trotsky, Maxim Gorky, and Lenin's brother, Alexander Ulyanov. The Soviets closed the prison, disdaining it as a symbol of czarist oppression, but it's now a popular attraction.

Three museums are worth considering for those fascinated by St. Petersburg's past. The **History of St. Petersburg, 1703-1918** exhibit, in the Commandant's House, fills two floors with an excellent, chronological survey of the relatively short history of this grand city, displaying artifacts, maps, models, paintings, and costumes—but with minimal English. It's engaging if you already know a bit of local history, but otherwise challenging to appreciate. The **History of the Peter and Paul Fortress** exhibit features old architectural drawings and maps, a replica of the angel weathervane that tops the cathedral spire, and some English descriptions. And the forgotten **Museum of Space Exploration and Rocket Technology** is a surprisingly extensive collection honoring the ingenuity that allowed this nation to kick off the space race with the 1957 launch of Sputnik (a replica of which you'll see here). There are old photos of scientists, newspaper headlines, desks and lab equipment, rocket bases, and space capsules—but virtually no English information.

Outer St. Petersburg

While each of these sights is well worth a visit, they're out on the edge of town and time-consuming to reach. On a one- or two-day visit, focus on sights in the city center instead. But with a third day or a special interest, the trek to any of these is rewarding.

If choosing between the two grand palaces, consider this: Peterhof has a fine interior but particularly grand gardens, with canals, waterfalls, and fountains populated by gilded statues.

Peter the Great

During the four decades he ruled Russia (1682-1725), Czar Peter I transformed his country into a major European power.

Even more egotistical and self-assured than your average monarch, Peter gave himself the nickname "Peter the Great"—and it stuck. He stood well over six feet tall, and his height was a sign of how he would rule Russia: with towering power and determination. Full of confidence and charm, Peter mixed easily with all classes of people and at times even dressed cheaply and spoke crudely.

Although Peter is revered by many Russians today, his reign was not without scandal. A heavy drinker with a short temper, Peter was known to lash out against even his closest advisors. Even those closest to Peter suffered. He had his own son killed and exiled his first wife to a convent.

After coming to the throne, Peter grew bored with courtly life in Moscow. He soon began planning a trip to Western Europe—a remarkable undertaking, given that no Russian czar had set foot in Europe during peacetime in more than 100 years. He focused his travels on Holland and England, great maritime powers from whom Peter wanted to learn everything he could about shipbuilding, technology, navigation, and seamanship (he even went undercover for a stint in an Amsterdam shipyard).

Upon his return, Peter began implementing the reforms that would give his Russia a fresh start. He refashioned Russia's army to resemble Western models, and he founded the Russian navy. He started the Great Northern War with Sweden to ensure that Russia would have access to the Baltic Sea for trade and strategic purposes. He built an entirely new capital in St. Petersburg and established a shipbuilding industry there. He reorganized the government and introduced new taxes to support his foreign policy.

Despite his cruelties, Peter left a large imprint on Russian history. When Peter took the throne, Russia was a backwater, stuck in the Middle Ages. When he died, his country had become a European powerhouse.

ST. PETERSBURG

Tsarskoye Selo's claim to fame is Catherine's Palace, with a peerless interior that includes the famously sumptuous Amber Room.

▲Piskaryovskoye Memorial Cemetery
(Пискарёвское Мемориальное Кладбище)

This is a memorial to the hundreds of thousands who died in the city during the Nazi Siege of Leningrad in World War II. The cemetery, with its eternal flame, acres of mass grave bunkers (marked only with the year of death), moving statue of Mother Russia, and many pilgrims bringing flowers to remember lost loved ones, is an awe-inspiring experience even for an American tourist to whom the Siege of Leningrad is just another page from the history books.

Cost and Hours: Free, daily 9:00-21:00, until 18:00 in winter, www.pmemorial.ru.

Getting There: The memorial is northeast of the city at Nepokorennykh Prospekt 72. From downtown, take the red Metro line (catch it at Uprising Square, near the end of Nevsky Prospekt) and ride it toward Devyatkino, getting off at the Ploshchad Muzhestva stop. Exit to the street, cross to the eastbound bus stop, and take bus #123 to the sixth stop—you'll see the cemetery buildings on your left.

▲▲Peterhof (Петергоф)

Peter the Great's lavish palace at Peterhof (sometimes still called by its communist name, Petrodvorets/Петродворец) sits along the Gulf of Finland west of the city. This is Russia's Versailles and the target of many tour groups and travel poster photographers. Promenade along the grand canal, which runs through landscaped grounds from the boat dock up to the terraced fountains in front of the palace. There are ice cream stands aplenty. You can visit the museum inside the palace if you want, but it's more fun to stay outdoors here. Children love to run past the so-called trick fountains—sometimes they splash you, sometimes they don't.

Cost and Hours: Park—400 R, open daily in summer 9:00-20:00; Grand Palace museum—500 R, audioguide-500 R, Tue-Sun 10:30-18:00, closed Monday; www.peterhofmuseum.ru.

Getting There: In summer, "Meteor" **hydrofoils,** run by at least three competing companies, leave for Peterhof from docks to either side of the busy bridge by the Hermitage (first boat leaves around 10:00 and every 30 minutes thereafter, last boat returns from Peterhof at 18:00, 30-40-minute trip, 500-600 R one way or 900-1000 R roundtrip, plus 400 R entry to the palace grounds; hydrofoils stop running in even mildly strong winds). Of the hydrofoil companies, only one has a good English website (www .peterhof-express.com, tel. 647-0017).

Outside hydrofoil hours, if it's windy, or in winter, the best way to reach Peterhof is by going to the Avtovo Metro station and boarding one of the *marshrutka* minibuses that run to the palace. You can also take a suburban train from the Baltiisky Vokzal to Novy Peterhof (Новый Петергоф) station, but this leaves you with a 40-minute walk to the palace itself. A taxi from the Marine Facade cruise port should run about 1,400 R one-way.

▲▲Tsarskoye Selo (Царское Село)

In the town of Pushkin, about 15 miles south of St. Petersburg, sits a cluster of over-the-top-opulent Romanov palaces—the "Czars' Village" (Tsarskoye Selo). This gorgeous ensemble of residences, pavilions, and gardens was born shortly after St. Petersburg, when Peter the Great's wife Catherine founded a church and began erecting palaces here. During the second half of the 18th century, Peter's heirs built the most impressive building at the site: the grand **Catherine's Palace,** a sumptuous, sprawling palace most famous for its breathtaking Amber Room—a riot of gilded panels, embedded with amber and slathered with mirrors. Like the rest of the palace, the Amber Room had to be restored (mostly using funds donated by Germany) after Tsarskoye Selo was badly damaged during the WWII Siege of Leningrad. The adjacent **Catherine Park,** studded with various pavilions and other decorative flourishes (each with its own entry ticket) surrounds a sprawling pond. And to the north, the "modest" (relative only to the other sights here) **Alexander Palace** has a lived-in feel; it was a favorite residence of the last Russian czar, Nicholas II. **Alexander Garden** provides even more regal places to stroll.

Cost and Hours: Catherine's Palace—320 R, Wed-Mon 10:00-18:00 (during peak months, individuals can enter only at certain times—see later), closed Tue and last Mon of each month; Catherine Park—100-R admission fee collected 9:00-18:00—free at other times, open daily 7:00-21:00; Alexander Palace—250 R, Wed-Mon 10:00-18:00, closed Tue and last Wed of each month; last entry for all sights one hour before closing; tel. 466-6669, http://eng.tzar.ru.

Crowd-Beating Tips: Be aware that in peak season (May-Sept), individuals may enter the biggest attractions (such as Catherine's Palace) only from 12:00-14:00 & 16:00-18:00—and tickets can sell out, so line up as early as possible. During busy times, you'll be required to join a (likely Russian-only) guided tour.

Getting There: Tsarskoye Selo is most easily reached on an

excursion, which provides door-to-door service and an efficient, highly focused tour of just the highlights. If you prefer to linger at your own pace (you could easily spend the day here), it's also possible by **public transportation** (figure about an hour each way from downtown): From the Nevsky Prospekt stop downtown, ride the blue Metro line toward Kupchino, and get off at Moskovskaya (the third-to-last stop). Exit the platform at the back end of the train. Surface onto the large square—with a huge, iconic statue of Lenin, with his jacket flapping behind him. There's a bus stop directly behind Lenin's back, where minibuses go constantly to Pushkin (ask around for "Pushkin?"). You'll ride the bus for about 30 minutes, and get off at the palaces (50-70 R one-way). Otherwise, figure 1,200 R for a one-way **taxi** ride from the Marine Facade cruise port.

Nearby: Just four miles southeast, **Pavlovsk** is a popular side-trip that's often combined with an excursion to Tsarskoye Selo. Another sprawling complex of gardens and opulent palaces, the highlight here is Pavlovsk Palace, a grandly domed hall with semicircular wings defining an oval courtyard—also built by Catherine the Great.

Shopping in St. Petersburg

With a variety of vivid cultural artifacts for sale and relatively low prices, St. Petersburg is a favorite shopping stop for many tourists.

The famous Russian nesting dolls called *matryoshka* are one of the most popular items. The classic design shows a ruby-cheeked Russian peasant woman, wearing a babushka and traditional dress, but don't miss the entertaining modern interpretations. You'll see Russian heads of state (Peter the Great inside Lenin inside Stalin inside Gorby inside Putin), as well as every American professional and college sports team you can imagine—each individual player wearing his actual number.

One good bet for *matryoshka* and other trinkets is the outdoor souvenir market across the street on the north side of the Church on Spilled Blood. There are no marked prices, so you can and should haggle. There are also stalls in the pedestrian underpass in front of Gostiny Dvor, the city's historic shopping arcade. For marked prices, try inside Gostiny Dvor—the section on the ground floor right along Nevsky has some decent souvenir stalls (daily 10:00-22:00; beyond this, Gostiny Dvor's shopping is mostly local-oriented).

Although the prices are inflated and the variety isn't as engaging, souvenir stands strategically located inside the cruise terminals at the Marine Facade allow passengers to blow through their remaining rubles before boarding their ship and leaving the country.

Entertainment in St. Petersburg

▲▲**Ballet**—The two best theaters in St. Petersburg for ballet are the Mariinsky (formerly Kirov) Theater and the Mikhailovsky Theater. Both have storied histories, classic opera-house interiors (the Mariinsky's is a bit more opulent), and well-designed websites that allow you to buy tickets online in advance, in English. The ballet season at both theaters runs from mid-September to mid-July (so there are no shows in the summer—exactly when many cruises are in town). The **Mikhailovsky Theater** is more convenient, at Ploshchad Isskustv 1, by the Russian Museum, a block off Nevsky (box office open daily 10:00-21:00, tel. 595-4305, www.mikhailovsky.ru). The **Mariinsky Theater** is at Teatralnaya Ploshchad, on the edge of downtown and at least a half-hour's walk southwest from Nevsky Prospekt (box office open 11:00-19:00, tel. 326-4141, www.mariinsky.ru). Buses take you right there; you can also take the Metro to Sadovaya and walk about 20 minutes. There are other ballet companies in town as well as performances in summer staged especially for tourists. Same-day tickets are often available (though not for the most popular ballets).

Opera and Music—Besides ballet, the Mariinsky and Mikhailovsky Theaters (listed above) host world-class opera and musical performances (the Mariinsky also stages some performances in its new concert hall—a few blocks beyond the theater at Dekabristov 37). Your best bet is to peruse their websites to see what's on; unfortunately, the theaters go dark in August.

▲**Circus**—The St. Petersburg circus is a revelation: Performed in one intimate ring, it has the typical tigers and lions but also a zany assortment of other irresistible animal acts (ostriches, poodles) as well as aerial acrobats (no nets), impossibly silly clowns, and more. Its performers have been staging their shows since 1877 in the stone "big top" on the edge of the Fontanka River. It's just east of the Russian Museum; some maps label it "Ciniselli Circus" after the Italian circus family that first built the place (tickets 500-2,000 R, box office open daily 11:00-19:00, tel. 570-5390 or 570-5411, www.circus.spb.ru).

ST. PETERSBURG

Eating in St. Petersburg

St. Petersburg has a huge selection of eating options, and it's easy to find attractive cafés and restaurants—but hard to find ones that are value-priced. The listings below are all standouts in location or value for money, and all have English-language menus. Many cafés offer speedy, convenient light meals. Russians are big on soups and appetizers, and it's perfectly reasonable to order two or three of these at a meal and skip the main dishes. Some restaurants have "business lunch" specials, served until 15:30 or 16:00.

Russian Food

You'll find many cafés serving sandwiches, light meals, salads, and crepes *(bliny)* with both sweet and savory fillings. A restaurant usually has higher prices and a more formal atmosphere.

Russians love soup—popular kinds are borscht (made with beet-based broth), *ukha* (with fish), *shchi* (cabbage-based), and *solyanka* (meat soup). Russian cuisine is also heavy on small dishes that we might think of as appetizers or sides, such as *pelmeni* and *vareniki* (types of dumplings), *kasha* (buckwheat groats) prepared in various ways, *bliny,* and high-calorie salads. As in Italy, the main dishes tend to be the least exciting part of the meal. You'll see beef stroganoff and chicken Kiev on menus at touristy restaurants, but these dishes are rarely served in Russian homes—they were both introduced to Russia in the late 19th century and are really more European than Russian. Berries, mushrooms, various kinds of sour cream and yogurt, fresh garden vegetables, and herbs like dill and coriander are common in home cooking. Bread (a staple of the Russian diet under communism) is often served as an automatic side order in restaurants.

In recent years, franchise restaurants (both locally based and Western) have sprouted up all over Russia. You'll see Subway, Pizza Hut, KFC, McDonald's, and more. Russian chains such as Teremok and Chainaya Lozhka are very popular with locals, serve authentic food, and can be very convenient time-savers during a day of sightseeing.

Russian beer is good. It goes without saying that there are many vodkas to choose from. Russians like to drink inexpensive sparkling wine that's still called *Sovyetskoye shampanskoye* (Soviet champagne). Try *kvas*, a fizzy, fairly sweet, grain-based beverage that is marketed as non-alcoholic (but often has a very small, almost negligible alcohol content) and *mors* (berry juice). In Russia, always drink bottled water, which is available widely in shops.

Speedy Chain Restaurants

Teremok (Теремок) is a chain with branches literally all over town. It's is quick and convenient for those who don't speak

Russian, handy for families, and lets you share and try lots of different dishes. Though sometimes derided as "Russian fast food," it actually serves a perfectly healthy array of Russian standards at very affordable prices. Choose borscht, *ukha* (fish soup), *pelmeni* (dumplings), sweet or savory *bliny* (crepes), or *kasha* (buckwheat groats) prepared in various ways. *Kvas* and *mors* (berry juice) are on the drinks menu. It's the setting that's fast-foody, complete with orange uniforms for the staff, plastic trays filled at the sales counter, and trash bins for your paper plates and napkins. Expect somewhat brisk service, and if you don't see the English menu brochure, ask for it (75-150-R main courses; Bolshaya Morskaya Ulitsa 11, Nevsky Prospekt 60, and Vladimirsky Prospekt 3 are three of many locations; all open daily at least 10:00-23:00).

Stolle (Штолле), another Russia-wide chain, specializes in crispy pies, both savory and sweet. Their handiest location, near the start of Nevsky Prospekt (at #11), combines order-at-the-counter, point-to-what-you-want efficiency with a refined drawing-room atmosphere. This makes it popular with local tour guides...and with pickpockets (pies sold by weight—figure about 200-250 R for a large portion, daily 8:00-22:00).

Sit-Down Restaurants

Zoom Café (Zoom Кафе) serves solid Russian cuisine at good prices in a pleasant basement-level dining area. Popular and a good choice for a sit-down Russian meal, it's just off Griboyedova Canal, a bit south of Nevsky Prospekt (130-200-R soups, 180-330-R main courses, by the corner of Gorokhovaya and Kazanskaya at Gorokhovaya Ulitsa 22, Mon-Fri 9:00-24:00, Sat 11:00-24:00, Sun 13:00-24:00, tel. 448-5001).

Pelmeniya (Пельмения) is a great place to sample the food for which it's named: delicious filled dumplings—both Russian-style and from other cuisines. Besides Russian *pelmeni*, choices include *khinkali* (from Georgia, with a thick dough "handle"), *varenyky* (from Ukraine, like Polish pierogi), *manti* (from Turkey and the Caucasus), *gyoza* (from Asia), and even ravioli. The modern interior overlooks the Fontanka River next to the Anichkov Bridge (100-150-R small portion, 150-400-R large portion, well-described English menu, daily 11:00-23:00, Fontanka 25, tel. 571-8082).

Russian Vodka Room No. 1, connected with St. Petersburg's vodka museum, is a fancier, more expensive restaurant with classy food and service (and yes, 200 types of vodka) that caters to tourists. It's a little beyond St. Isaac's Cathedral—trolleybuses #5 and #22 stop conveniently on the same street. The huge building has multiple restaurants—look for the Vodka Room between entrances (подъезд) 5 and 6 (400-800-R main courses, Konnogvardeisky Bulvar 4, tel. 570-6420).

Georgian Food

Although it's not strictly "Russian," Georgian cuisine is a much appreciated, arguably more flavorful alternative that's popular with Russians and visitors alike. If you've never tried Georgian food before, grab your chance. As with Russian food, the secret is to order appetizers. Some of the classic Georgian dishes are *khachapuri* (хачапури)—hot bread filled with cheese, somewhat like a calzone; *pkhali* (пхали)—chopped greens; chicken *satsivi* (сациви)—diced chicken in a spicy yellow sauce; *baklazhan* (баклажан)—eggplant; *lobio* (лобио)—beans, served hot or cold; and plenty of *lavash* (лаваш)—bread. If you want soup, try *kharcho* (харчо), a spicy broth with lots of meat and onions. Main dishes are less special (often grilled meat). Georgian cuisine fills the same niche in Russian life as Italian cuisine does in Germany and northern Europe—raven-haired immigrants from the south run neighborhood restaurants serving hot cheese-bread.

Café Ne Goryui (Кафе Не Горюй), a couple of doors down from the Admiralteyskaya Metro station entrance, is a reasonably priced Georgian restaurant close to main sights that serves all the Georgian standards (300-400-R main courses, *khachapuri* starts at 220 R for a single-person size, daily 12:00-24:00, Kirpichny Pereulok 3, tel. 571-6950).

Cat Café has a cute interior with only eight tables (reservations recommended) and a friendly vibe (250-350-R *khachapuri*, 200-300-R soups, 300-400-R main courses, Stremyannaya Ulitsa 22, daily 12:00-23:00, tel. 571-3377).

Vegetarian Fare

Café Botanika (Кафе Ботаника) is a few blocks beyond the Russian Museum, past the Summer Garden and just over the Fontanka River. It's fresh and attractive, with seating both indoors and streetside (180-220-R soups, 350-450-R main courses, daily 11:00-24:00, Ulitsa Pestelya 7, tel. 272-7091).

Troitsky Most (Троицкий Мост) is a tiny, inexpensive vegetarian café just north of Nevsky along the Moyka River. Order at the counter and then find a seat—a board, partly translated into

What If I Miss My Boat?

Remember that you can get help from the cruise line's port agent (listed on the destination information sheet distributed on the ship) and the local TI (see page 366). If the port agent suggests a costly solution (such as a private car with a driver), you may want to consider public transit.

Your biggest concern is a visa. If you've entered St. Petersburg with an excursion (meaning without a visa), chances are your ship won't leave without you, since they are responsible for your presence in Russia. On the off chance that you're left behind, head for the US embassy to navigate the red tape—your lack of a visa will make leaving the country next to impossible without eliciting help.

If do you have a visa and missed your ship, you can reach **Helsinki** on the fast train (trains leave from Finland Station/ Finlyandsky Vokzal/Финляндский Вокзал, Metro: Ploshchad Lenina; train info: www.vr.fi) or a much slower bus. To **Tallinn,** ride the slow bus or the occasional St. Peter Line overnight boat (www.stpeterline.com). To reach **Stockholm** or **Rīga,** you'll probably do best to connect through Tallinn.

If you need to catch a **plane** to your next destination, St. Petersburg's Pulkovo airport is reachable by a Metro-plus-bus combination (via the Moskovskaya Metro stop; www.pulkovo airport.ru).

Local **travel agents** in St. Petersburg can help you. For more advice on what to do if you miss the boat, see page 144.

English, lists the day's specials (130-150-R main courses, daily 9:00-23:00, Naberezhnaya Reki Moyki 30).

Picnic Shopping

There are small stores in every neighborhood (often down a few steps from street level and open late or even 24 hours) where you can pick up basic necessities. Look for signs saying Продукты ("products") or Универсам (Universam, meaning "self-service store"). In the very center, the 24-hour *universam* at Bolshaya Konyushennaya Ulitsa 4 (at the corner of Shvedsky Pereulok) is convenient and decent-sized. For a larger shopping trip, try either of two modern **supermarkets** at Uprising Square (Ploshchad Vosstaniya; both open daily 10:00-23:00): the basement supermarket in the Finnish-owned Stockmann (Стокманн) department store at Nevsky 112, by the round entrance building to the Ploshchad Vosstaniya Metro stop, or the Okei Express (Окей Экспресс) supermarket in the Galereya (Галерея) shopping mall at Ligovsky Prospekt 30A, around the right side of the Moskovsky train station (enter the mall and follow the left corridor to the end).

Farmer's Markets: Any Russian farmer's market (*rynok*, рынок) is worth a visit even if you're not shopping. Twenty years ago, these markets were the only way to buy fresh vegetables on the open market. St. Petersburg's best and most central farmer's market is at Kuznechy Pereulok 3, next to the Vladimirskaya Metro entrance and right across the street from the Dostoyevsky Museum (look for the big Рынок sign). In the honey (*myod*, мёд)

section, a chorus line of white-aproned *babushki* stands ready to let you dip and test each kind. Fruit sellers shout *"Molodoi chelovyek!"* (young man) and *"Devushka!"* (young lady) as they try to entice you toward their piles of oranges, tomatoes, cucumbers, and pears. In the herbs section, you can sniff massive bunches of fresh coriander (*kinza*, кинза) and wade through a lifetime supply of horseradish (*khren*, хрен). You may see some lamb. While traditional Russian cuisine doesn't make use of lamb, many of the market workers are Muslim—"internal immigrants" from Central Asia and the Caucasus (Mon-Sat 8:00-20:00, Sun 8:00-19:00.)

TALLINN

Estonia

SAMPO

Estonia Practicalities

Wedged between Latvia and Russia, Estonia (Eesti) borders the Baltic Sea and Gulf of Finland (at 17,500 square miles, it's roughly the size of New Hampshire and Vermont combined). The country also encompasses more than 1,500 islands and islets. Like Finland, Estonia struggled against Swedish and Russian domination throughout its history. After World War I, Estonia achieved independence, but with the next world war, it fell victim to a 50-year communist twilight, from which it's still emerging. Joining the European Union in 2004 has helped bring the country forward. Estonia is home to 1.3 million people, a quarter of whom are of Russian descent (Russian is still Estonia's second language). Even two decades after independence, tension still simmers between the ethnic-Estonian and ethnic-Russian populations.

Money: €1 (euro) = about $1.30. An ATM is called a *pangaautomaat*, and is sometimes marked *Otto*. The local VAT (value-added sales tax) rate is 25 percent; the minimum purchase eligible for a VAT refund is €38 (for details on refunds, see page 139).

Language: The native language is Estonian. For useful phrases, see page 471.

Emergencies: In case of emergency, dial 112. For police, dial 110. In case of theft or loss, see page 131.

Time Zone: Estonia is one hour ahead of Central European Time (seven/ten hours ahead of the East/ West Coasts of the US. That puts Tallinn in the same time zone as Helsinki and Rīga; one hour ahead of Stockholm, the rest of Scandinavia, and most other continental cruise ports (including Gdańsk and Warnemünde); and one hour behind St. Petersburg.

Embassies in Tallinn: The **US embassy** is at Kentmanni 20 (tel. 668-8128, emergency tel. 509-2129, http://estonia.usembassy.gov). The **Canadian embassy** is at Toomkooli 13 (tel. 627-3311, www.canada.ee). Call ahead for passport services.

Phoning: Estonia's country code is 372; to call from another country to Estonia, dial the international access code (011 from the US/Canada, 00 from Europe, or + from a mobile phone), then 372, followed by the local number. For local calls within Estonia, just dial the number as it appears in this book—whether you're calling from across the street or across the country. To place an international call from Estonia, dial 00, the code of the country you're calling (1 for US and Canada), and the phone number. For more tips, see page 1110.

Tipping: The bill for a sit-down meal includes gratuity so you don't need to tip further, though it's nice to round up 5-10 percent for good service. For taxis, round up the fare a bit (pay €3 on an €2.85 fare) For more on tipping, see page 143.

Tourist Information: www.visitestonia.com

TALLINN

Tallinn is a rising star in the tourism world, thanks to its strategic location (an easy boat ride from Stockholm, Helsinki, and St. Petersburg); its perfectly preserved, atmospheric Old Town, bursting with quaint sightseeing options; and its remarkable economic boom since throwing off Soviet shackles just over two decades ago. Easily the most accessible part of the former USSR, Estonia was only the third post-communist country to adopt the euro (in 2011) and has weathered recent Europe-wide economic crises like a champ. While the city still struggles to more effectively incorporate its large Russian minority, Tallinn feels ages away from its Soviet past—having eagerly reclaimed its unique Nordic identity. Estonian pride is in the air...and it's catching.

Among Nordic medieval cities, there's none nearly as well-preserved as Tallinn. Its mostly intact city wall includes 26 watchtowers, each topped by a pointy red roof. Baroque and choral music ring out from its old Lutheran churches. I'd guess that Tallinn (with 400,000 people) has more restaurants, cafés, and surprises per capita and square inch than any city in this book—and the fun is comparatively cheap.

Though it's connected by boat to Helsinki and Stockholm, Tallinn is very different from those cities. Yes, Tallinn's Nordic Lutheran culture and language connect it with Scandinavia, but two centuries of tsarist Russian rule and 45 years as part of the Soviet Union have blended in a distinctly Russian flavor.

As a member of the Hanseatic League, the city was a medieval stronghold of the Baltic trading world. In the 19th and early 20th centuries, Tallinn industrialized and expanded beyond its walls. Architects encircled the Old Town, putting up broad streets of public buildings, low Scandinavian-style apartment buildings, and single-family wooden houses. After 1945, Soviet planners ringed the city with stands of now-crumbling concrete high-rises where many of Tallinn's Russian immigrants settled. Like Prague and Kraków, Tallinn has westernized at an astounding rate since the fall of the Soviet Union in 1991. Yet the Old World ambience within its walled town center has been beautifully preserved.

Tallinn is still busy cleaning up the mess left by the com-munist experiment. New shops, restaurants, and hotels are burst-ing out of old buildings. The city changes so fast, even locals can't keep up. The Old Town is get-ting a lot of tourist traffic now, so smart shopping is wise. You'll eat better for half the price by seeking out places that cater to locals.

Tallinn's Old Town is a fasci-nating package of pleasing towers, ramparts, facades, *striptiis* bars, churches, shops, and people-watching. It's a rewarding detour for those who want to spice their Scandinavian travels with a Baltic twist.

Planning Your Time

Tallinn is a snap for cruisers: The port is within walking distance of the Old Town, which contains most of what you'll want to see. On a busy day in port, I'd do the following, in this order:

• To hit the ground running, walk 15 minutes to the Fat Margaret Tower and launch into my **self-guided walk,** which leads you past virtually all of the best sights (allow 2-3 hours, more if you want to linger).

• Spend the afternoon shopping and browsing—or, to get out of the cruiser rut, tram or taxi to **Kadriorg Park** for a stroll through the palace gardens and to tour the delightful Estonian art collection at Kumu (allow about an hour, including transit time, to see the park, and add another hour for Kumu).

• With more time, you could visit the Song Festival Grounds (beyond Kadriorg Park; allow at least an extra hour for a quick visit) or the Estonian Open-Air Museum (allow 30 minutes each way to get there, plus a couple of hours to tour the grounds).

While Tallinn's Old Town is understandably popular, some-times it feels *too* popular; when several cruises are in town, the cobbles can be uncomfortably crammed. If crowds bother you, consider keeping your Old Town visit brief and instead focus on

Excursions from Tallinn

Tallinn is so walkable, and its Old Town sights so easy to appreciate, that there's no reason to take an excursion here. Most cruise lines offer a walking tour through the **Old Town** with a few brief sightseeing stops (often including quick visits to Town Hall Square, Palace Square, the Russian Orthodox Cathedral, Dome Church, and various viewpoints)—but the self-guided walk in this chapter covers the same ground at your own pace. Other excursions may include a bus tour around the city, sometimes with stops at outlying sights such as the manicured, palatial **Kadriorg Park** and the stirring **Song Festival Grounds**—but these are also doable on your own (and even affordable by taxi).

A few places farther out of town are a bit more challenging to reach on your own on a short port visit. These include the **Estonian Open-Air Museum** at Rocca al Mare (described on page 463); the communist-planned apartment district of **Lasnamäe** (sometimes billed as "Pirita"); the town of **Rakvere**, about 60 miles east (with its 13th-century castle and "town citizen's museum" of 19th-century life); and the beaches and forests of the **Kakumäe** district, on the western edge of Tallin. But Tallinn itself is so appealing that these excursions don't merit consideration on a brief visit. Just stick around the city and enjoy the Old World ambience.

the sights just out of town, such as Kadriorg Park. You'll see a side of Tallinn that most cruisers miss entirely.

Remember to bring a jacket—Tallinn can be chilly even on sunny summer days. And, given that locals call their cobbled streets "a free foot massage," sturdy shoes are smart, too.

Arrival at the Port of Tallinn

Arrival at a Glance: It's a quick 15-minute walk from Tallinn's cruise port into town; the fair taxi rate is less than €5.

Port Overview

All cruises come into Tallinn's Old Town Port, which is less than a mile northeast of the Old Town. Within this sprawling area, the primary cruise dock consists of a long, skinny pier at the northern edge; overflow cruise ships might dock near one of the port area's other terminals (which are mainly used for ferries and catamarans to Helsinki, Stockholm, and St. Petersburg). In this case, you'll

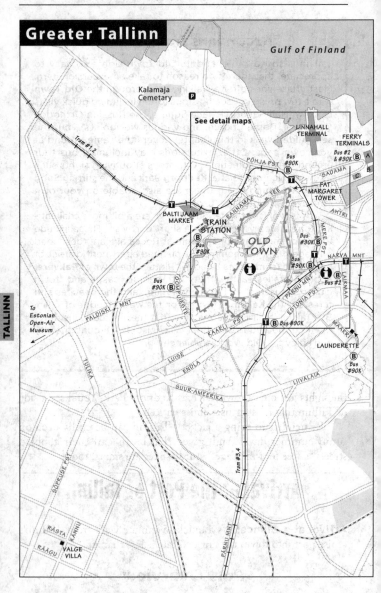

arrive near A-Terminal/B-Terminal/C-Terminal (all three are clustered in the same area, between the main cruise port and the sailboat marina), D-Terminal (south of the marina), or occasionally at the Linnahall terminal (west of the cruise port). Regardless of where you arrive, it's easy to walk into town.

Tourist Information: There's no TI at the port, though the main cruise terminal does have a privately run desk that hands

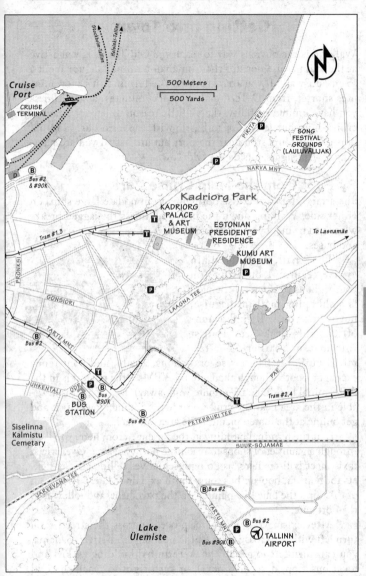

out town maps, answers basic questions, and rents a 16-stop town audioguide for €10 (skip it—my self-guided walk in this chapter is better). The public terminal buildings (at A-Terminal and D-Terminal) have racks of basic tourist brochures; if you're desperate, the free *Baltic Guide* tabloid has a Tallinn map inside. Otherwise, head into the Old Town Square and visit the TI and/or the nearby Travellers' Tent (see "Tourist Information," later).

Getting into Town

Walking is the obvious way to reach the Old Town. If you arrive at the main cruise port (or the Linnahall terminal), figure about a 15-minute walk. If you arrive at A-/B-/C-Terminal, it's a few minutes shorter; from D-Terminal, it's a few minutes longer. Unless you have limited mobility, there's little reason to pay for a taxi or cruise-line shuttle bus, or to hassle with the local bus. Hop-on, hop-off bus tours stop near the port but are best if you are planning to visit sights outside the Old Town.

By Foot from the Main Cruise Port

The straightforward cruise port can accommodate large ships on either side. Walking down the pier, you'll pass the jagged break-water and be met by a row of taxis and buses.

The small, metallic, **main cruise terminal** building (on your right as you step off the pier) is a shopping mall in disguise, but inside you will find a non-official info desk (see "Tourist Information," earlier). The terminal building also has several shops, a café, and a currency exchange booth (though there are no ATMs—the nearest is in the A-Terminal building, a 5-minute walk away). Free Wi-Fi is available in the area near the cruise terminal building; you can sit and get online at the tented picnic-table area out back.

Exit the terminal building at the far end. From here, you'll go through a gauntlet of shops to reach the port gate area. Overpriced taxis meet cruisers here, as do representatives selling all-day tickets for hop-on, hop-off bus tours (both explained later). Bypass all of this, find the blue line painted on the pavement, and follow it to the port gate.

After exiting the port gate, proceed across the street, then turn left with the crosswalks. At the next big cross street, Sadama, you can turn left to get to the A-Terminal building (ATM and local bus stop, described next), or turn right to reach the Old Town: Walk a couple of long blocks on Sadama (passing the erotic nudes that mark the entrance to a surely classy hotel). Then, at the gas station, you'll approach a confusing intersection; turn left across two lanes, then right, and head straight toward the pointy steeple. Soon after, angle right across the street, then straight, and climb the steps to the stout, round, stone Fat Margaret Tower; on the way up, you'll pass the ferry memorial mentioned at the start of my self-guided walk.

By Foot from the Other Terminals

If you arrive at any of the other terminals, look for a blue line painted on the pavement; this leads you out of the port area. The best strategy is to walk toward the tallest pointy tower and the round, fat stone gate at its base (visible from most of the port area), which mark the start of my self-guided walk.

From the pier beyond **D-Terminal,** walk five minutes (follow the blue line) to the D-Terminal building. Inside is an ATM, WCs, lockers, and stands with sparse tourist brochures. From the D-Terminal, you can see the spire marking the Old Town, about a 15-minute walk away.

If you arrive near **A-/B-/C-Terminals,** walk to the **A-Terminal building.** While primarily for ferry passengers, it has various services also useful to cruisers. Just outside the door are two ATMs, and inside are WCs, lockers, a café, and a newsstand selling bus tickets. The parking lot in front of the terminal is a good place to look for a taxi that charges fair rates. Both public bus #2 and private bus #90K leave from the shelter at the edge of the parking lot in front of A-Terminal (for details on both buses, see "Getting into Town," later). To reach the Old Town on foot, walk straight out of A-Terminal, following the walking instructions up Sadama street outlined earlier.

By Taxi

Taxis meet arriving cruise ships near the main cruise port, happy to overcharge arriving passengers for the laughably brief ride into town. A legitimate taxi using the meter should charge €5 or less to anywhere in the Old Town—though when I asked cabbies at the port, they shamelessly told me, "€10 to lower town, €15 to upper town." It can be worth the walk to the area in front of A-Terminal, where you may find a taxi with more reasonable posted rates. Before choosing a taxi, read my tips on page 446.

By Cruise-Line Shuttle Bus or Local Bus

Some cruise lines offer **shuttles** into town. Unless it's free, it's often not worth it: The bus takes you to a point at the edge of the Old Town that's only slightly more convenient than the port itself. Cruise shuttles drop off along the busy ring road, at the pleasant park next to the Russian Cultural Center (Vene Kultuurikeskus). Get off here, walk straight ahead in the same direction (with the busy street on your left), and pass the charming local-style Viru Turg market to reach Viru street (with a big taxi stand, flower vendors, and an archway from the old city wall). Walk straight up Viru street into town.

The **local bus** is affordable (€1-2). But by the time you walk to the bus stop (in front of either A-Terminal or D-Terminal), wait

Services near the Port

You'll find a few services at the port areas; for others, wait until you're downtown.

ATMs: There's no ATM at the cruise port itself, but there are two just outside the front door of the nearby A-Terminal building. There's also an ATM inside D-Terminal (useful only if your ship arrives there). Once in the Old Town, ATMs are easy to find.

Internet Access: The area near the main cruise terminal has free Wi-Fi. For Internet access in the city center, see "Helpful Hints," later.

Pharmacy: The best (and most memorable) choice is in the Old Town—the historic (and still-functioning) pharmacy on Old Town Square (described on page 453).

for a bus, and walk into town from the stop, you could have walked all the way to town. There are two buses, using the same stops at the terminals: Public bus #2 (€1 ticket sold at newsstands inside either terminal, €1.60 on board) is cheaper and goes more directly to a stop handy to the Old Town: Hop off at A. Laikmaa, and walk into town through the Viru Gate. Private bus #90K (€2, sold on board only) does a long loop past the train station and around the west end of town before stopping near the Viru Gate. Even if bus #90K shows up first, you may be better off (time-wise) waiting for #2. For more on both buses, see page 446.

By Tour

Two fiercely competitive companies (Tallinn City Tours and CitySightseeing Tallinn) run three different **hop-on, hop-off bus tour routes** for the same price (all day–€16) and meet each arriving ship to drum up business (sometimes offering discounts, such as €10 for the day). Aside from a stop near Toompea Castle, the routes are entirely outside the Old Town, and the frequency is low, which could leave you stranded if you want to hop on again soon. And realistically, on a short day in port, you'll likely spend most or all of your day in the walkable Old Town—making a bus trip unnecessary. However, if you're planning to get to outlying sights, these can be a good way to do it.

For information on other local tour options in Tallinn—including local guides for hire, good Tallinn Traveller Tours offered by a youthful walking-tour company, bike tours, and more—see "Tours in Tallinn" on page 447.

Returning to Your Ship

The easiest choice is to simply walk back; it takes about 15 minutes to reach the main cruise terminal from the Old Town (a bit less to the A-/B-/C-Terminals, a bit longer to D-Terminal). Walk through town on Pikk street, popping out at Fat Margaret Tower; look right, and you'll see the ships.

If you catch a taxi, insist on the meter. It should be no more than €5 from the Old Town area (possibly a euro more from Kadriorg Park). From Old Town Square, walk down Viru street (see the last section of my self-guided walk) and go through Viru Gate, where you'll usually find several reputable taxis.

See page 469 for help if you miss your boat.

Orientation to Tallinn

Tallinn's walled Old Town is an easy walk from the ferry and cruise terminals. The Old Town is divided into two parts (historically, two separate towns): the upper town (Toompea), and the lower town, with Town Hall Square. A remarkably intact medieval wall surrounds the two towns, which are themselves separated by another wall.

Town Hall Square (Raekoja Plats) marks the heart of the medieval lower town. The main TI is nearby, as are many sights and eateries. Pickpockets have become a problem in the more touristy parts of the Old Town, so keep valuables carefully stowed. The area around the Viru Keskus mall and Hotel Viru, just east of the Old Town, is useful for everyday shopping (bookstores and supermarkets), practical services (laundry and Internet café), and public transport.

Tourist Information

The hardworking, English-speaking **TI** has maps, concert listings, and free brochures. It also sells *Tallinn in Your Pocket* and the Tallinn Card, both described later (May-Aug Mon-Fri 9:00-19:00—until 20:00 mid-June-Aug, Sat-Sun 9:00-17:00—until 18:00 mid-June-Aug; Sept-April Mon-Fri 9:00-18:00, Sat-Sun 9:00-15:00; a block off Town Hall Square at Kullassepa 4, tel. 645-7777, www.tourism.tallinn.ee, turismiinfo@tallinnlv.ee).

Travellers' Tent isn't an official information center, but a creative service offered by young people for young visitors. Working from a tent in the park immediately in front of the TI, the friendly staff is a great source for backpacker info, youthful tours, and bike rental (daily June-Aug 10:00-18:00, mobile 5837-4800). Their free

map is packed with fun tips to enjoy
Tallinn down, dirty, and on the
cheap. While their map and information services are free, they appreciate
donations. Consider their inexpensive and spirited tours (see "Tours in
Tallinn," later).

Tallinn in Your Pocket is the best
city guidebook on Tallinn (€2.20 at
TIs and all over town). It's worth
buying for its complete restaurant and sight listings that go far
beyond what's in this book (for pre-trip planning, use the online
edition at www.inyourpocket.com).

Tallinn Card: This card—sold at the TIs, travel agencies,
and ferry ports—gives you free use of public transport and entry
to more than 40 museums and major sights (€12/6 hours, €24/24
hours, €32/48 hours, €40/72 hours, comes with good info booklet,
www.tallinncard.ee). From the 24-hour level up, it includes one
tour of your choice, plus a 50 percent discount on any others—by
bus, by bike, or on foot (see "Tours in Tallinn," later, for specifics).
If you're planning to take one of these tours (otherwise €13-20)
and to visit several sights (otherwise €3-6), this card will likely
save you money. Add up the cost of your intended sightseeing to
confirm. But don't buy the card primarily for its public transport
benefits, as transit passes are much cheaper.

Helpful Hints

Internet Access: Metro 24 is on the lower level of the Viru Keskus
mall, where city buses depart (across from platform 6; €2.60/
hour, Mon-Fri 7:00-23:00, Sat-Sun 10:00-23:00, tel. 610-
1519). The **main TI** has one terminal where you can briefly
check your email for free. There are open Wi-Fi networks literally all over town; look for the orange-and-black "wifi.ee"
logo in shop windows.

Laundry: Pesumaja Sol is just walkable from the Old Town,
beyond the Viru Keskus mall and Kaubamaja department
store (or take tram #2 or #4 to the Paberi stop, a few blocks
away—see map on page 438). Choose between self-serve
(€5/load, ask staff to interpret Estonian-only instructions) or
full-service (€9.50/load, Mon-Fri 7:00-20:00, Sat 8:00-16:00,
closed Sun, Maakri 23, tel. 677-1551).

Travel Agency: Estravel, at the corner of Suur-Karja and
Müürivähe, is as good as any. It's handy and sells boat tickets
for no extra fee (Mon-Fri 9:00-18:00, closed Sat-Sun, Suur-
Karja 15, tel. 626-6233).

Bike Rental: Head for **City Bike,** at the north end of the Old

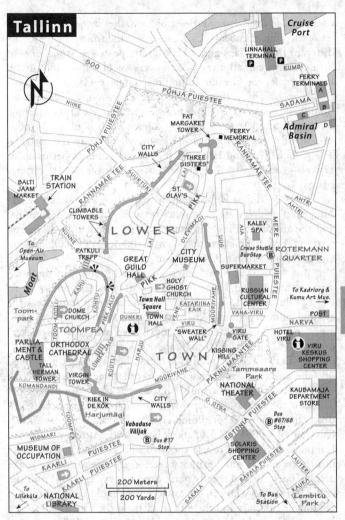

Town near the ferry terminals (one-speeds–€7.50/6 hours, €10/24 hours; better bikes–€10/6 hours, €13/24 hours; includes helmet and reflective vest; daily May-Sept 9:00-19:00, Oct-April 9:00-17:00, Uus 33, mobile 511-1819, www.citybike.ee). They also do bike tours (see "Tours in Tallinn," later).

Getting Around Tallinn

By Public Transportation: The Old Town and surrounding areas can be explored on foot, but use public transit to reach outlying sights (such as Kadriorg Park, Kumu Art Museum, or Estonian Open-Air Museum). Tallinn has buses, trams, and trolleys (buses connected to overhead wires)—avoid mistakes by noting that they reuse the same numbers (bus #2, tram #2, and trolley #2 are totally different lines). Maps and schedules are posted at stops, or visit http://soiduplaan.tallinn.ee (for an overview of transit stops useful to visitors, see the Greater Tallinn map on page 438).

Stop by any yellow-and-blue R Kiosk convenience store (found all over town) to buy a ticket, then stamp it in the machine on board. Single tickets cost €1; a pack of 10 is €8. A 24-hour pass (valid from the moment it's stamped) is handy and costs €4. The 72-hour (€6) and 120-hour (€7) passes are even better deals. Drivers grudgingly sell single tickets on board for €1.60, but not passes.

Bus #2 (Moigu-Reisisadam) is helpful on arrival and departure, running every 20-30 minutes between the port's A-Terminal and the airport. En route it stops at D-Terminal; at A. Laikmaa, next to the Viru Keskus mall (a short walk south of the Old Town); and at the long-distance bus station.

Bus #90K is also convenient, connecting many of the same stops—and additional ones—in a different order (airport, southern end of Old Town, D-Terminal, A-Terminal, train station, northern and western ends of Old Town, then back to the airport); however, since it's privately run, it is not covered by regular bus tickets or passes (€2, 3/hour, www.hansabuss.ee).

By Taxi: Taxis in Tallinn are handy, but it's easy to get ripped off. The safest way to catch a cab is to order one by phone (or ask a trusted local to call for you)—this is what Estonians usually do. Tulika is the largest company, with predictable, fair prices (€3.10 drop charge plus €0.65/kilometer, €0.77/kilometer from 23:00-6:00, tel. 612-0001 or 1200, check latest prices at www.tulika.ee). Cabbies are required to use the meter and to give you a meter-printed receipt. If you don't get a receipt, it's safe to assume you're being ripped off and legally don't need to pay. The trip from the cruise port to anywhere in the town center should be no more than €5; longer rides around the city (e.g., from the Old Town to the Estonian Open-Air Museum) should run around €8-10.

If you must catch a taxi off the street, go to a busy taxi stand where lots of cabs are lined up. It's also OK to use the stands at the ferry terminals near the cruise ports. Before doing *anything* else, take a close look at the yellow price list on the rear passenger-side door; the base fare should be around €3.10 and the per-kilometer charge under €1. If it's not, keep looking. Glance inside—a photo ID license should be attached to the middle of the dashboard. Don't negotiate or ask for a price estimate; let the driver use the meter. Rates must be posted by law, but are not capped or regulated, so the most common scam—unfortunately widespread, and legal—is to list an inflated price on the yellow price sticker (as much as €3/

kilometer), and simply wait for a tourist to hop in without noticing. Singleton cabs lurking in tourist areas are usually fishing for suckers, as are cabbies who flag you down ("Taxi?")—give them a miss. It's fun to play spot-the-scam as you walk around town.

Tours in Tallinn

Bus and Walking Tour—This thoroughly enjoyable, narrated 2.5-hour tour of Tallinn comes in two parts: first by bus for an overview of sights outside the Old Town, such as the Song Festival Grounds and Kadriorg Park, then on foot to sights within the Old Town (€20, pay driver; covered by 24-hour or longer Tallinn Card—not the 6-hour version; in English and Finnish; daily morning and early afternoon departures from A-Terminal, D-Terminal, and major hotels in city center, later afternoon trip added in summer, tel. 610-8634—to see the schedule, go to www .tourism.tallinn.ee and type "official sightseeing tour"—without quotes—in search box).

Local Guides—**Mati Rumessen** is a top-notch guide, especially for car tours inside or outside town (€32/hour for driving or walking tours, mobile 509-4661, www.tourservice.ee, mati700@hot.ee). Other fine guides are **Antonio Villacis** (mobile 5662-9306, antonio .villacis@gmail.com) and **Miina Puusepp** (€20/hour, mobile 551-7028, miinap@hot.ee).

Tallinn Traveller Tours—These student-run tours show you the real city without the political and corporate correctness of official tourist agencies. All tours start from the Travellers' Tent, across from the main TI; reserve by dropping by the tent, by calling (mobile 5837-4800), or online (www.traveller.ee). Their **City Introductory Walking Tour** is free, but tips are encouraged (around €5/person if you enjoy yourself, daily at 12:00, 2 hours, English only, runs year-round; off-season, this tour meets at the corner just outside the TI). On the **Funky Bike Tour,** you'll pedal through industrial zones and offbeat residential districts, learn about the divide between Estonian and Russian speakers, and visit an old prison (€13, June-Aug daily at 12:00, 3.5 hours). The **Beautiful Bike Tour** takes you to the Song Festival Grounds, Kadriorg, and more (€13, June-Aug daily at 16:00, 3.5 hours). They also offer a minibus excursion to the **Western Coast** and the Soviet military town of Paldiski (€39, daily at 10:00, 7 hours), and one to **Lahemaa National Park** east of town (€49, daily at 10:00, 9 hours). Both excursions go year-round but require at least two people to run. You can also book any one of these tours for your own small group for the same per-person price (4-person minimum).

City Bike Tours—City Bike offers a two-hour, nine-mile **Welcome to Tallinn** bike tour that takes you outside the city walls

Tallinn at a Glance

▲▲▲**Tallinn's Old Town** Well-preserved medieval center with cobblestoned lanes, gabled houses, historic churches, and turreted city walls. **Hours:** Always open. See page 458.

▲▲**Kumu Art Museum** The best of contemporary Estonian art displayed in a strikingly modern building. **Hours:** May-Sept Tue-Sun 11:00-18:00, closed Mon; Oct-April Wed-Sun 11:00-18:00, closed Mon-Tue; open Wed until 20:00 year-round. See page 460.

▲**Museum of Occupation** Estonia's tumultuous, sometimes secret history under Soviet and Nazi occupiers from 1940 to 1991. **Hours:** June-Aug Tue-Sun 10:00-18:00, Sept-May Tue-Sun 11:00-18:00, closed Mon year-round. See page 458.

▲**Kadriorg Park** Vast, strollable oasis with the palace gardens, Kumu Art Museum, and a palace built by Tsar Peter the Great. **Hours:** Park always open. See page 459.

▲**Song Festival Grounds** National monument and open-air theater where Estonians sang for freedom. **Hours:** Open long hours. See page 462.

▲**Estonian Open-Air Museum** Authentic farm and village buildings preserved in a forested parkland. **Hours:** Late April-Sept—park open daily 10:00-20:00, buildings open until 18:00; Oct-late April—park open daily 10:00-17:00 but buildings closed. See page 463.

Town Hall and Tower Gothic building with history museum and climbable tower on the Old Town's main square. **Hours:** Museum—July-Aug Mon-Sat 10:00-16:00, closed Sun and rest of year; tower—May-mid-Sept daily 11:00-18:00, closed rest of year. See page 458.

to Tallinn's more distant sights: Kadriorg, Song Festival Grounds, the beach at Pirita, and more (€16, free with Tallinn Card valid 24 hours or more; includes helmet and reflective vest, daily at 11:00 year-round—weather permitting, departs from their office at Uus 33 in the Old Town). They also do €49 day trips (car and bike) to Lahemaa National Park (mobile 511-1819, www.citybike.ee).

Toomas the Tourist Train—This red choo-choo train, mostly for kids and their parents, leaves (when full) from the top of Town Hall Square (€5, June-Aug daily 12:00-17:00, May and Sept Sat-Sun only, doesn't run Oct-April, look for *Rong Toomas* sign).

Self-Guided Walk in Tallinn

▲▲▲Welcome to Tallinn

This walk explores the "two towns" of Tallinn. The city once consisted of two feuding medieval towns separated by a wall. The upper town—on the hill, called Toompea—was the seat of Estonia's government. The lower town was an autonomous Hanseatic trading center filled with German, Danish, and Swedish merchants who hired Estonians to do their menial labor. Many of the Old Town's buildings are truly old, dating from the boom times of the 15th and 16th centuries. Decrepit before the 1991 fall of the Soviet Union, the Old Town has been slowly revitalized, though there's still plenty of work to be done.

Two steep, narrow streets—the "Long Leg" and the "Short Leg"—connect Toompea and the lower town. This walk winds through both towns, going up the short leg and down the long leg. The walk starts near the cruise and ferry terminals. If you're coming from elsewhere in Tallinn, take tram #1 or #2 to the Linnahall stop, or just walk out to the Fat Margaret Tower from anywhere in the Old Town.

❶ To Fat Margaret Tower and Start of Walk: From the cruise and ferry terminals, hike toward the tall tapering spire, go

through a small park, and enter the Old Town through the archway by the squat Fat Margaret Tower (Paks Margareeta). Just outside the tower on a bluff overlooking the harbor is a broken black arch, a memorial to 852 people who perished in September of 1994 when the *Estonia* passenger-and-car ferry sank in stormy conditions during its Tallinn-Stockholm run. The ship's bow visor came off, and water flooded into the car deck, throwing the boat off-balance. Only 137 people survived. The crew's maneuvering of the ship after it began taking on water is thought to have caused its fatal list and capsizing.

Fat Margaret Tower (so-called for its thick walls) guarded the entry gate of the town in medieval times (the sea once came much closer to this point than it does today). The relief above the gate dates from the 16th century, during Hanseatic times, when Sweden took Estonia from Germany. The Estonian Maritime Museum in the tower is paltry (€4, Wed-Sun 10:00-18:00, closed Mon-Tue, tel. 641-1408).

Just inside the gate, you'll feel the economic power of those early German trading days. The buildings nicknamed "Three Sisters" (on the right), now a hotel, are textbook examples of a merchant home/warehouse/office from the 15th-century Hanseatic Golden Age. The charmingly carved door near the corner evokes the wealth of Tallinn's merchant class.

• *Head up Pikk (which means "long") street.*

❷ **Pikk Street:** The medieval merchants' main drag, leading from the harbor up into town, is lined with interesting buildings—many were warehouses complete with cranes on the gables. After a block, you'll pass St. Olav's Church (Oleviste Kirik, a Baptist church today), notable for what was once the tallest spire in the land. Its plain, whitewashed interior is skippable, though climbing 234 stairs up the tower rewards you with a great view (church—free entry, daily 10:00-18:00, July-Aug until 20:00; tower—€2, open April-Oct only; www.oleviste.ee).

While tourists see only a peaceful scene today, locals strolling this street are reminded of dark times under Moscow's rule. The

KGB used the tower at St. Olav's Church to block Finnish TV signals. The once-handsome building nearby at Pikk 59 (the second house after the church, on the right) was, before 1991, the sinister local headquarters of the KGB. "Creative interrogation methods" were used here. Locals well knew that the road of suffering started here, as Tallinn's troublemakers were sent to Siberian gulags. The ministry building was called the "tallest" building in town (because "when you're in the basement, you can already see Siberia"). Notice the bricked-up windows at foot level and the plaque (in Estonian only).

A few short blocks farther up Pikk (after the small park), the fine house of the **Brotherhood of the Blackheads** (on the left, at #26, with the extremely ornate doorway) dates from 1440. For 500 years, until Hitler invited Estonian Germans back to their historical fatherland in the 1930s, this was a German merchants' club.

Until the 19th century, many Estonians lived as serfs on the rural estates of the German nobles who dominated the economy. In Tallinn, the German big shots were part of the Great

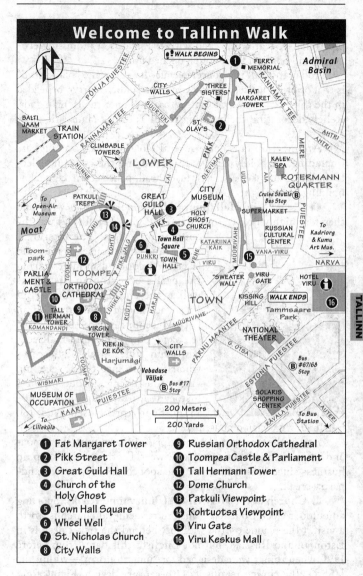

Welcome to Tallinn Walk

1 Fat Margaret Tower
2 Pikk Street
3 Great Guild Hall
4 Church of the Holy Ghost
5 Town Hall Square
6 Wheel Well
7 St. Nicholas Church
8 City Walls
9 Russian Orthodox Cathedral
10 Toompea Castle & Parliament
11 Tall Hermann Tower
12 Dome Church
13 Patkuli Viewpoint
14 Kohtuotsa Viewpoint
15 Viru Gate
16 Viru Keskus Mall

Guild, while the German little shots had to make do with the Brotherhood of the Blackheads. This guild or business fraternity was limited to single German men. In Hanseatic towns, when a fire or battle had to be fought, single men were deployed first, because they had no family. Because single men were considered unattached to the community, they had no opportunity for power in the Hanseatic social structure. When a Blackhead member married a local woman, he automatically gained a vested interest in the town's economy and well-being. He could then join the more prestigious Great Guild, and with that status, a promising economic and political future often opened up.

Today the hall is a concert venue. Its namesake "black head" is that of St. Maurice, an early Christian soldier-martyr, beheaded in the third century A.D. for his refusal to honor the Roman gods. Reliefs decorating the building recall Tallinn's Hanseatic glory days.

Architecture fans enjoy several fanciful facades along here (including the boldly Art Nouveau #18 and the colorful, eclectic building across the street). Just ahead, pause at the big yellow building on the right.

❸ **Great Guild Hall (Suurgildi Hoone):** With its wide (and therefore highly taxed) front, the Great Guild Hall (#17) was the

epitome of wealth. The interior is less grand and houses a museum (Eesti Ajaloomuuseum) covering the basics of Estonian history as well as the Guild Hall's past. (But I'd spend time in the nearby Tallinn City Museum instead—closed Tue; see page 458.) The Guild Hall does have a fun "time capsule" in the cellar where you can insert your face into videos illustrating episodes in local history (€5, May-Aug daily 10:00-18:00, Sept-April closed Wed, tel. 641-1630, www.ajaloomuuseum.ee).

Across the street, at #16 (look for *Kalev* awnings), the famous and recommended Maiasmokk ("Sweet Tooth") coffee shop, in business since 1864, remains a fine spot for a cheap coffee-and-pastry break.

❹ **Church of the Holy Ghost (Pühavaimu Kirik):** Sporting an outdoor clock from 1633, this pretty medieval church is worth a visit. (The plaque on the wall just behind the ticket desk is in Estonian and Russian, but not English; this dates from before 1991, when things were designed for "inner tourism"—within the USSR). The church retains its 14th-century design. Flying from the back pillar, the old flag of Tallinn—the same as today's red and white Danish flag—recalls 13th-century Danish rule. (The name "Tallinn" means "Danish Town.") The Danes sold Tallinn to the German Teutonic Knights, who lost it to the Swedes, who lost it to the Russians. The windows are mostly from the 1990s (€1, Mon-Sat 9:00-17:00, closed Sun to non-worshippers, Pühavaimu 2, tel. 646-4430, www.eelk.ee). The church hosts English-language Lutheran services Sundays at 15:00.

• *Leading alongside the church, tiny Saiakang lane (meaning "White Bread"—bread, cakes, and pies have been sold here since medieval times) takes you to...*

❺ **Town Hall Square (Raekoja Plats):** A marketplace through the centuries, with a cancan of fine old buildings, this is

the focal point of the Old Town. The square was the center of the autonomous lower town, a merchant city of Hanseatic traders. Once, it held criminals chained to pillories for public humiliation and knights showing off in chivalrous tournaments; today it's full of Scandinavians savoring cheap beer, children singing on the bandstand, and cruise-ship groups following the numbered paddles carried high by their well-scrubbed local guides.

The 15th-century Town Hall (Raekoda) dominates the square; it's now a museum, and climbing its tower earns a commanding view (for details see page 458). On the opposite side of the square, across from #12 in the corner, the pharmacy (Raeapteek) dates from 1422 and claims—as do many—to be Europe's oldest. With decor that goes back to medieval times, the still-functioning pharmacy welcomes visitors with painted ceiling beams, English descriptions, and long-expired aspirin (Tue-Sat 10:00-18:00, closed Sun-Mon). Town Hall Square is ringed by inviting but

touristy eateries, a few of which are still affordable, such as Troika and the Kehrwieder cafés. The TI is a block away (behind Town Hall).

• *Facing the Town Hall, head right up Dunkri street one block to the...*

❻ **Wheel Well:** The well is named for the "high-tech" wheel, a marvel that made fetching water easier.

• *Turn left on Rataskaevu street (which soon becomes Rüütli) and walk two blocks to...*

❼ **St. Nicholas (Niguliste) Church:** This 13th-century Gothic church-turned-art-museum served the German merchants and knights who lived in this neighborhood 500 years ago. On March 9, 1944, while Tallinn was in German hands, Soviet forces bombed the city, and the church and surrounding area—once a charming district, dense with medieval buildings—were burned out; only the church was rebuilt (€3.50, Wed-Sun 10:00-17:00, closed Mon-Tue; organ concerts Sat and Sun at 16:00 are included in admission).

• At the corner opposite the church, climb uphill along the steep, cobbled, Lühike Jalg ("Short Leg Lane"), home to a few quality craft shops. Pass through the giant stone tower, noticing the original oak door—one of two gates through the wall separating the two cities. This passage is still the ritual meeting point of the mayor and prime minister whenever there is an important agreement between town and country.

Climb up through the gate and pop out on the street above. Turn left up the street, then hook left for a good view of the fortifications around the city.

❽ City Walls: The imposing city wall once had 46 towers— the stout, round tower is nicknamed "Kiek in de Kök." (While fun

to say, it means "Peek in the Kitchen" in Low German.) It was situated so that "peek" is exactly what guards could do. It's now a small museum with cannons and other relics from the 16th-century Livonian wars.

Above you is the so-called "Danish King's Garden." Tallinn is famous among Danes as the birthplace of their flag. According to legend, the Danes were losing a battle here. Suddenly, a white cross fell from heaven and landed in a pool of blood. The Danes were inspired and went on to win. To this day, their flag is a white cross on a red background.

• You're standing at the back of Tallinn's onion-domed Russian cathedral. Circle around to the far side (facing the pink palace) to enjoy a great view of the church, and to find the entrance.

❾ Russian Orthodox Cathedral: The Alexander Nevsky Cathedral was built here in 1900, smack in Tallinn's political power center and over the supposed grave of a legendary Estonian hero, Kalevipoeg; a statue of Martin Luther was also taken down to make room.

While it's a beautiful building, its placement was a crass attempt to flex Russian cultural muscle during a period of Estonian (and German) national revival, and there were plans (later shelved) to remove it in the 1920s after Estonia became independent. The church has been exquisitely renovated inside and out. Step inside for a sample of Russian Orthodoxy. It's OK to visit discreetly during services (daily at 10:00 and 18:00), when you'll hear priests singing the liturgy in a side chapel. About 40 percent of Tallinn's population is ethnic Russian (church free and open daily 8:00-19:00, icon art in gift shop).

• *Across the street is the...*

❿ Toompea Castle (Toompea Loss): The pink palace is an 18th-century Russian addition onto the medieval Toompea Castle. Today, it's the Estonian Parliament (Riigigoku) building, flying the Estonian flag—the flag of both the first (1918-1940) and second (1991-present) Estonian republics. Notice the Estonian seal: three lions for three great battles in Estonian history, and oak leaves for strength and stubbornness. Ancient pagan Estonians, who believed spirits lived in oak trees, would walk through forests of oak to toughen up. (To this day, Estonian cemeteries are in forests. Keeping some of their pagan sensibilities, they believe the spirits of the departed live on in the trees.)

• *Facing the palace, go left through the gate into the park to see the...*

⓫ Tall Hermann Tower (Pikk Hermann): This tallest tower of the castle wall is a powerful symbol here. For 50 years, while Estonian flags were hidden in cellars, the Soviet flag flew from Tall Hermann. As the USSR was unraveling, Estonians proudly and defiantly replaced the red Soviet flag here with their own black, white, and blue flag.

• *Backtrack and go uphill, passing the Russian church on your right. Climb Toom-Kooli street to the...*

⓬ Dome Church (Toomkirik): Estonia is ostensibly Lutheran, but few Tallinners go to church. A recent Gallup Poll showed Estonia to be the least religious country in the European Union—only 14 percent of respondents identified religion as an important part of their daily lives. Most churches double as concert venues or museums, but this one is still used for worship. Officially St. Mary's Church but popularly called the Dome Church, it's a perfect example of simple Northern European Gothic, built in the 13th century during Danish rule, then rebuilt after a 1684 fire. Once the church of Tallinn's wealthy German-speaking

aristocracy, it's littered with more than a hundred coats of arms, carved by local masters as memorials to the deceased and inscribed with German tributes. The earliest dates from the 1600s, the latest from around 1900. For €5, you can climb 140 steps up the tower to enjoy the view (church entry free, daily 9:00-18:00, www.eelk.ee/tallinna.toom).

• *Leaving the church, turn left and hook around the back of the building. You'll pass the slanted tree and the big, green, former noblemen's clubhouse on your right (vacated when Germans left Estonia in the 1930s), then go down cobbled Rahukohtu lane. Government offices and embassies have moved into the buildings and spruced up the neighborhood. But as you pass under the yellow Patkuli Vaateplats arch, notice a surviving ramshackle bit of the 1980s. Just a few years ago, the entire city looked like this.*

Belly up to the grand...

⓭ **Patkuli Viewpoint:** Survey the scene. On the far left, the Neoclassical facade of the executive branch of Estonia's govern-

ment enjoys the view. Below you, a bit of the old moat remains. The *Group* sign marks Tallinn's tiny train station, and the clutter of stalls behind that is the rustic market. Out on the water, ferries shuttle to and from Helsinki (just 50 miles away). Beyond the lower town's medieval wall and

towers stands the green spire of St. Olav's Church, once 98 feet taller and, locals claim, the world's tallest tower in 1492. Far in the distance is the 985-foot-tall TV tower (much appreciated by Estonians for heroically keeping the people's airwaves open during the harrowing days when they won independence from the USSR). During Soviet domination, though, Finnish TV was even more important, as it gave Estonians their only look at Western lifestyles. Imagine: In the 1980s, many locals had never seen a banana or pineapple—except on TV. People still talk of the day that Finland broadcast the soft-porn movie *Emmanuelle*. A historic migration of Estonians purportedly flocked from the countryside to Tallinn to get within rabbit-ear's distance of Helsinki and see all that flesh on-screen. The TV tower was recently refurbished and opened to visitors.

• *Go back through the arch, turn immediately left down the narrow lane, turn right (onto Toom-Rüütli), take the first left, and pass through the trees to...*

⓮ **Kohtuotsa Viewpoint:** On the far left is St. Olav's Church, then the busy cruise port and the skinny white spire of the Church

of the Holy Ghost. The narrow gray spire farther to the right is the 16th-century Town Hall tower. On the far right is the tower of St. Nicholas Church. Below you, visually trace Pikk street, Tallinn's historic main drag, which winds through the Old Town, leading from Toompea down the hill (from right to left),

through the gate tower, past the Church of the Holy Ghost, behind St. Olav's, and out to the harbor. Less picturesque is the clutter of Soviet-era apartment blocks on the distant horizon. The nearest skyscraper (white) is Hotel Viru, in Soviet times the biggest hotel in the Baltics, and infamous as a clunky, dingy slumbermill. Locals joke that Hotel Viru was built from a new Soviet wonder material called "micro-concrete" (60 percent concrete, 40 percent microphones). Underneath the hotel is the modern Viru Keskus, a huge shopping mall and local transit center, where this walk will end. To the left of Hotel Viru, between it and the ferry terminals, is the Rotermann Quarter, where old industrial build-

ings are being revamped into a new commercial zone.

• *From the viewpoint, descend to the lower town. Go out and left down Kohtu, past the Finnish Embassy (on your left). Back at the Dome Church, the slanted tree points the way, left down Piiskopi ("Bishop's Street"). At the onion domes, turn left again and follow the old wall down Pikk Jalg ("Long Leg Lane") into the lower town. Go under the tower, then straight on Pikk street, and after two doors turn right on Voorimehe, which leads into Town Hall Square.*

⓯ **Through Viru Gate:** Cross through the square (left of the Town Hall's tower) and go downhill (passing the kitschy medieval Olde Hansa Restaurant, with its bonneted waitresses and merry men). Continue straight down Viru street toward Hotel Viru, the blocky white skyscraper in the distance. Viru street is old Tallinn's busiest and kitschiest shopping street. Just past the strange and modern wood/glass/stone mall, Müürivahe street leads left along the old wall, called the "Sweater Wall." This is a colorful and tempting gauntlet of women selling knitwear (anything with images and bright colors is likely machine-made). Beyond the sweaters, Katariina Käik, a lane with glassblowing shops, leads left. Back on Viru street, pass the golden arches and walk through the medieval arches—Viru Gate—that mark the end of old Tallinn. Outside the gates, opposite Viru 23, above the flower stalls, is a small park on a piece of old bastion known as the Kissing Hill (come up here after dark and you'll find out why).

• *Use the crosswalk to your right to reach the...*

🕙 **Viru Keskus Mall:** Here, behind Hotel Viru, at the end of this walk, you'll find the real world: branch TI, Internet café, basement supermarket, ticket service, bookstore, and many bus and tram stops. If you still have energy, you can cross the busy street by the complex and explore the nearby Rotermann Quarter (see page 459).

Sights in Tallinn

TALLINN

In or near the Old Town

Central Tallinn has dozens of small museums, most suitable only for specialized tastes (complete listings in *Tallinn in Your Pocket*). The following sights are the ones I'd visit first.

Town Hall (Raekoda) and Tower—This museum, facing Town Hall Square, has exhibits on the town's administration and history, along with an interesting bit on the story of limestone. The tower, the place to see all of Tallinn, rewards those who climb its 155 steps with a wonderful city view.

Cost and Hours: Museum—€4, entrance through cellar, July-Aug Mon-Sat 10:00-16:00, closed Sun and Sept-June; tower—€3, May-mid-Sept daily 11:00-18:00, closed rest of year; tel. 645-7900, www.tallinn.ee/raekoda.

Tallinn City Museum (Tallinna Linnamuuseum)—This humble museum features Tallinn history from 1200 to the 1950s. Well-described in English, it offers some intimate looks at local lifestyles and a few exhibits on the communist days.

Cost and Hours: €3.20, March-Oct Wed-Mon 10:30-18:00, Nov-Feb Wed-Mon 10:00-17:30, closed Tue year-round, last entry 30 minutes before closing, Vene 17, at corner of Pühavaimu, tel. 615-5183, www.linnamuuseum.ee.

▲**Museum of Occupation (Okupatsioonide Muuseum)**—It's said that Estonia didn't formally lose its independence from 1940 to 1991, but was just "occupied"—first by the Soviets, then by the Nazis, and then again by the USSR. Built with funding from a wealthy Estonian-American, this compact museum tells the history of Estonia during those years.

Cost and Hours: €4, skip the amateurish €3 audioguide, June-Aug Tue-Sun 10:00-18:00, Sept-May Tue-Sun 11:00-18:00, closed Mon year-round, Toompea 8, at corner of Kaarli Puiestee, tel. 668-0250, www.okupatsioon.ee.

Visiting the Museum: It's organized around seven TV monitors screening documentary films in English and Estonian, each focusing on a different time period. Among the artifacts displayed are suitcases, a reminder of people who fled the country. Exhibits and videos tell how the Soviets kept the Estonians in line. Surveillance was a part of daily life, as Estonians were tough to bring into the Soviet fold. Prison doors evoke the countless lives lost to detention and deportation. In the basement by the WCs is a collection of Soviet-era statues of communist leaders—once they lorded over the people, now they're in the cellar guarding the toilets. The ticket desk sells a well-chosen range of English-language books on the occupation years.

Rotermann Quarter—Sprawling between Hotel Viru and the port, this 19th-century industrial zone is being redeveloped into shopping, office, and living space. To see the first completed section, start at Hotel Viru, cross busy Narva Maantee and walk down Roseni street. At #7 you'll find the hard-to-resist Kalev chocolate shop, selling Estonia's best-known sweets (Mon-Sat 10:00-20:00, Sun 11:00-18:00).

Kadriorg Park and the Kumu Museum

▲**Kadriorg Park**—This expansive seaside park, home to a summer royal residence and the Kumu Art Museum, is just a five-minute tram ride or a 25-minute walk from Hotel Viru. After Russia took over Tallinn in 1710, Peter the Great built the cute, pint-sized Kadriorg Palace for Tsarina Catherine (the palace's name means "Catherine's Valley"). Stately, peaceful, and crisscrossed by leafy paths, the park has a rose garden, duck-filled pond, playground and benches, and old tsarist guardhouses harkening back to the days of Russian rule. It's a delightful place for a stroll or

a picnic. If it's rainy, duck into one of the cafés in the park's art museums (described below).

Getting There: Reach the park on tram #1 or #3 (direction: Kadriorg; catch at any tram stop around the Old Town). Get off at the Kadriorg stop (the end of the line, where trams turn and head back into town), and walk 200 yards straight ahead and up Weizenbergi, the park's main avenue. Peter's summer palace is on the left; behind it, visit the formal garden (free). At the end of the avenue is the Kumu Art Museum, the park's most important sight. A taxi from Hotel Viru to this area should cost €5 or less.

Visiting Kadriorg Park: The palace's manicured **gardens** (free to enter) are a pure delight; on weekends, you'll likely see a steady parade of brides and grooms here, posing for wedding pictures. The summer palace itself is home to the **Kadriorg Art Museum** (Kadrioru Kunstimuuseum), with very modest Russian and Western European galleries (€4.50; May-Sept Tue-Sun 10:00-17:00, Wed until 20:00; Oct-April Wed-Sun 10:00-17:00, closed Tue; closed Mon year-round; tel. 606-6400, www.kadrioru muuseum.ee/en).

The fenced-off yard directly behind the garden is where you'll spot the local "White House" (although it's pink)—home of **Estonia's president.** Walk around to the far side to find its main entrance, with the seal of Estonia above the door, flagpoles flying both the Estonian and the EU flags, and stone-faced guards.

A five-minute walk beyond the presidential palace takes you to the Kumu Art Museum, described next. For a longer walk from here, the rugged park rolls down toward the sea.

▲▲Kumu Art Museum (Kumu Kunstimuuseum)—This main branch of the Art Museum of Estonia brings the nation's best art together in a striking modern building designed by an international (well, at least Finnish) architect, Pekka Vapaavuori. The entire collection is accessible, well-presented, and engaging, with a particularly thought-pro-voking section on art from the Soviet period. The museum is well worth the trip for art lovers,

or for anyone intrigued by the unique spirit of this tiny nation—particularly when combined with a stroll through the nearby palace gardens (described earlier) on a sunny day.

Cost and Hours: €5.50, or €4.20 for just the permanent collection, audioguide-€3.20; May-Sept Tue-Sun 11:00-18:00, closed Mon; Oct-April Wed-Sun 11:00-18:00, closed Mon-Tue; Wed until 20:00 year-round; trendy café, tel. 602-6000, www.kumu.ee.

TALLINN

Getting There: To reach the museum, follow the instructions for Kadriorg Park, earlier; Kumu is at the far end of the park. To get from the Old Town to Kumu directly, without walking through the park, take bus #67 or #68 (each runs every 10-15 minutes, #68 does not run on Sun); both leave from Teatri Väljak, on the far side of the pastel yellow theater, across from the Solaris shopping mall. Get off at the Kumu stop, then walk up the stairs and across the bridge.

❯ Self-Guided Tour: Just off the ticket lobby, the **great hall** has temporary exhibits; however, the permanent collection on the third and fourth floors is Kumu's main draw. While you can rent an audioguide, I found the free laminated sheets in most rooms enough to enjoy the collection. The maze-like layout on each floor presents the art chronologically.

The **third floor,** which focuses on classics of Estonian art, starts with 18th-century portraits of local aristocrats, moves through 19th-century Romanticism (including some nice views of Tallinn and idealized images of Estonian peasant women in folk costumes), winds through several rooms of local Expressionists and other Modernist painters, and ends with art produced during World War II. One very high-ceilinged room has a wall lined with dozens of expressive busts by sculptor Villu Jaanisoo.

The **fourth-floor exhibit,** called "Difficult Choices," is an interesting survey of Estonian art from the end of World War II until "re-independence" in 1991. Some of the works are mainstream, while others are by dissident artists.

Estonian art parted ways with Western Europe with the Soviet takeover in 1945. The Soviets insisted that artworks actively promote the communist struggle, and to that end, Estonian artists were forced to adopt the Stalinist formula, making paintings that were national in style but socialist in content—in the style now called **Socialist Realism.**

Socialist Realism had its roots in the early 20th-century Realist movement, whose artists wanted to depict the actual conditions of life rather than just glamour and wealth—in America, think of John Steinbeck's novels or Walker Evans' photographs of the rural poor. In the Soviet Union, this artistic curiosity about the working class was perverted into an ideology: Art was supposed to glorify labor and the state's role in distributing its fruits. In a system where there was ultimately little incentive to work hard, art was seen as a tool to motivate the masses, and to support the Communist Party's hold on power.

In the collection's first room, called "A Tale of Happiness," you'll see syrupy images of what Soviet leadership imagined to be the ideal of communist Estonia. In *Agitator Amongst the Voters* (1952), a stern portrait of Stalin in the hazy background keeps an eye on a young hotshot articulating some questionable ideas; his listeners' reactions range from shudders of horror to smirks of superiority. *The Young Aviators* (1951) shows an eager youngster wearing a bright-red neckerchief (indicating his membership in the Pioneers, the propaganda-laden communist version of Scouts) telling his enraptured schoolmates stories about a model airplane.

The next room shows canvases of miners, protesters, speech-ifiers, metalworkers, and more, all doing their utmost for the communist society. You'll also see paintings of industrial achievements (like bridges), party meetings, and, of course, the great leader Stalin himself. Because mining was big in Estonia, miners were portrayed as local heroes, marching like soldiers to their glorious labor. Women were depicted toiling side by side with men, as equal partners. (Though they're not always on display here, posters were a natural fit, with slogans exhorting laborers to work hard on behalf of the regime.)

While supposedly a reflection of "real" life, Socialist Realism art was formulaic and showed little creative spirit. Though some Estonian artists flirted with social commentary and the avant-garde, a few ended up in Siberia as a result.

Later, in the Brezhnev years, Estonian artists managed to slip Surrealist, Pop, and Photorealist themes into their work (for example, Rein Tammik's large painting *1945-1975*). Estonia was the only part of the USSR that recognized Pop Art. As the Soviets would eventually learn, change was unstoppable.

The rest of the museum is devoted to temporary exhibits, with contemporary art always on the **fifth floor** (where there's a nice view back to the Old Town from the far gallery). It's also worth admiring the mostly successful architecture—the building is partly dug into the limestone hill, and the facade is limestone, too.

Outer Tallinn

▲**Song Festival Grounds (Lauluväljak)**—At this open-air theater, built in 1959 and resembling an oversized Hollywood Bowl, the Estonian nation gathers to sing. Every five years, these grounds host a huge national song festival with 25,000 singers and 100,000 spectators. While it hosts big pop-music acts, too, it's a national monument for the compelling role it played in Estonia's fight for independence.

Since 1988, when locals sang patriotic songs here in defiance of Soviet rule, these grounds have taken on a symbolic importance to the nation. Locals vividly recall putting on folk costumes knit-

Estonia's Singing Revolution

When you are just a million people in a humble country lodged between Russia and Germany (and tyrants such as Stalin and Hitler), simply surviving as a nation is a challenge. Estonia was free from 1920 to 1939. Then they had a 50-year Nazi/Soviet nightmare. Estonians say, "We were so few in numbers that we had to emphasize that we exist. We had no weapons. Being together and singing together was our power." Singing has long been a national form of expression in this country; the first Estonian Song Festival occurred in 1869, and has been held every five years since then.

Estonian culture was under siege during the Soviet era. Moscow wouldn't allow locals to wave their flag or sing patriotic songs. Russians and Ukrainians were moved in, and Estonians were shipped out in an attempt to dilute the country's identity. But as cracks began to appear in the USSR, the Estonians mobilized—by singing.

In 1988, 300,000 Estonians—imagine...a third of the population—gathered at the Song Festival Grounds outside Tallinn to sing patriotic songs. On August 23, 1989—the 50th anniversary of a notorious pact between Hitler and Stalin—the people of Latvia, Lithuania, and Estonia held hands to make "the Baltic Chain," a human chain that stretched 360 miles from Tallinn to Vilnius in Lithuania. Some feared a Tiananmen Square-type bloodbath, but Estonians kept singing.

In February of 1990, the first free parliamentary elections took place in all three Baltic states, and pro-independence candidates won majorities. In 1991, hard-line communists staged a coup against Soviet leader Mikhail Gorbachev, and Estonians feared a violent crackdown. The makeshift Estonian Parliament declared independence. Then, the coup in Moscow failed. Suddenly, the USSR was gone, and Estonia was free.

Watch the documentary film *The Singing Revolution* before your visit (www.singingrevolution.com) to tune into this stirring bit of modern history and to draw inspiration from Estonia's valiant struggle for freedom.

TALLINN

ted by their grandmothers (some of whom later died in Siberia) and coming here with masses of Estonians to sing. Overlooking the grounds from the cheap seats is a statue of Gustav Ernesaks, who directed the Estonian National Male Choir for 50 years, through the darkest times of Soviet rule. He was a power in the drive for independence, and lived to see it happen.

Cost and Hours: Free, open long hours, bus #1A, #5, #8, #34A, or #38 to Lauluväljak stop.

▲**Estonian Open-Air Museum (Vabaõhumuuseum)**— Influenced by their ties with Nordic countries, Estonians are enthusiastic advocates of open-air museums. For this one, they salvaged farm buildings, wind-mills, and an old church from rural areas and transported them to a park-like setting just outside town (4 miles west of the Old Town). The goal: to both save and share their heri-tage. Attendants are posted in  many houses, but to really visu-alize life in the old houses, rent the audioguide (€7/3 hours). The park's Kolu Tavern serves traditional dishes. You can rent a bike (€3/hour) for a breezy roll to quiet, faraway spaces in the park.

Cost and Hours: Late April-Sept: €6, park open daily 10:00-20:00, historic buildings until 18:00; Oct-late April: €3, park open daily 10:00-17:00 but historic buildings closed. Tel. 654-9100, www.evm.ee.

Getting There: Take bus #21 from the train station to Rocca al Mare stop—because buses back to Tallinn run infrequently, check the departure schedule as soon as you arrive, or ask staff how to find the Zoo stop, with more frequent service, a 15-minute walk away.

Shopping in Tallinn

With so many cruise-ship tourists inundating Tallinn, the Old Town is full of trinkets, but it is possible to find good-quality stuff. Wooden goods, like butter knives and juniper-wood trivets, are a good value. Marvel at the variety on sale in Tallinn's liquor stores, popular with visiting Scandinavians. Tucked into the Old Town are many craft and artisan shops where prices are lower than in Nordic countries.

The **"Sweater Wall"** is a fun place to browse sweaters and woolens, though few are hand-knitted by grandmoth-ers these days. Find the stalls under the wall on Müüri-vahe street (daily 10:00-17:00, near the corner of Viru street, described on page 457). From there, explore **Katariina Käik,** a small alley between Müürivahe and Vene streets, which has several handicraft stores and workshops selling pieces that make nice souvenirs.

The cheery **Navitrolla Gallerii** is filled with work by the well-known Estonian artist who goes just by the name Navitrolla. His whimsical, animal-themed prints are vaguely reminiscent of *Where the Wild Things Are* (Mon-Fri 10:00-18:00, Sat 10:00-17:00, Sun 10:00-16:00, Sulevimägi 1, near Tallinn Backpackers, tel. 631-3716, www.navitrolla.ee).

The **Rahva Raamat** bookstore in the Viru Keskus mall (floors 3-4) has plenty of English books mixed throughout its shelves (daily 9:00-21:00).

Balti Jaam Market, Tallinn's bustling traditional market, is behind the train station and has little of touristic interest besides

wonderful photo ops. That's why I like it. It's a great time-warp scene, fragrant with dill, berries, onions, and mushrooms. You'll hear lots of Russian. The indoor sections sell meat, clothing, and gadgets (look for the Jaama Turg gate beyond track 9, Mon-Fri 8:00-18:00, Sat-Sun 8:00-17:00, better early).

For something tamer, the **Viru Turg outdoor market,** a block outside the Old Town's Viru Gate, has a lively, tourist-oriented collection of stalls selling mostly clothing and textiles (daily May-Sept 9:00-17:00, Oct-April 10:00-16:00, north of Viru street at Mere Puiestee 1).

Eating in Tallinn

The Old Town's thriving restaurant culture serves not just tourists but also locals, who like to meet downtown after work. In the

obvious, high-traffic locations, such as Town Hall Square and Viru street, prices have risen to Western European levels, and average main dishes can cost €15-20. Instead, roam at least a block or two off the main drags, where you can find great food at what seems like fire-sale prices. Some restaurants have good-value lunch specials on weekdays (look for the words *päeva praad*). Tipping is not required, but if you like the service, round your bill up by 5-10 percent when paying.

A few years ago it was hard to find authentic local cuisine, but

TALLINN

Tallinn Restaurants

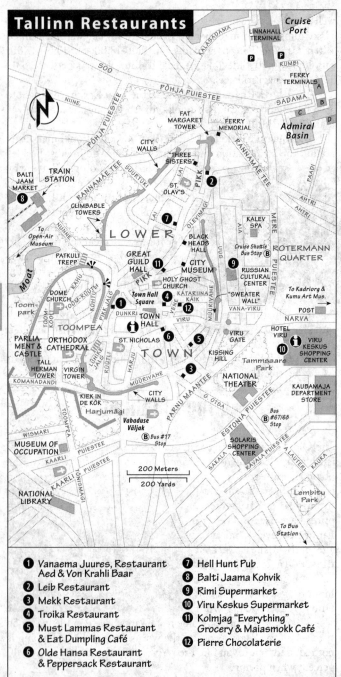

1. Vanaema Juures, Restaurant Aed & Von Krahli Baar
2. Leib Restaurant
3. Mekk Restaurant
4. Troika Restaurant
5. Must Lammas Restaurant & Eat Dumpling Café
6. Olde Hansa Restaurant & Peppersack Restaurant
7. Hell Hunt Pub
8. Balti Jaama Kohvik
9. Rimi Supermarket
10. Viru Keskus Supermarket
11. Kolmjag "Everything" Grocery & Maiasmokk Café
12. Pierre Chocolaterie

now Estonian food is trendy—a hearty Northern mixture of meat, potatoes, root vegetables, mushrooms, dill, garlic, bread, and soup. Pea soup is a local specialty. You usually get a few slices of bread as a free, automatic side (as in the rest of the ex-USSR). A typical pub snack is Estonian garlic bread *(küüslauguleivad)*—deep-fried strips of dark rye bread smothered in garlic and served with a dipping sauce. Estonia's Saku beer is good, cheap, and on tap at most eateries. Try the nutty, full-bodied Tume variety.

Dining in the Old Town
Estonian Restaurants

Vanaema Juures ("Grandma's Place"), an eight-table cellar restaurant, serves homey, traditional Estonian meals, such as pork roast with sauerkraut and horseradish. This is a fine bet for local cuisine. No tacky medieval stuff here—just good food at fair prices in a pleasant ambience, where you expect your waitress to show up with her hair in a bun and wearing granny glasses (€8-17 main dishes, Mon-Sat 12:00-22:00, Sun 12:00-18:00, Rataskaevu 10/12, tel. 626-9080, Ava mothers you).

Restorant Aed is an elegant, almost gourmet, health-food eatery calling itself "the embassy of pure food." While not vegetarian, it is passionate about serving modern, organic Estonian cuisine in a woody, romantic setting (€7-14 main dishes, Mon-Sat 12:00-22:00, Sun 12:00-18:00, Rataskaevu 8, tel. 626-9088).

At **Leib,** at the seaside end of the Old Town, you enter up steps into a fun garden under the medieval walls, and can sit indoors or out. As at other reasonably priced places, a great three-course meal costs no more than €20: Try pea soup (€4.50), followed by free-range chicken (€10) and a €4 dessert (daily 12:00-23:00, Uus 31, tel. 611-9026).

Mekk is a small, fresh, more upscale place whose name stands for "modern Estonian cuisine." They offer two great deals: artful weekday lunch specials for just €5, and a €30 four-course set-price menu for serious eaters. Young, elegant locals take their lunch breaks here (€16-25 main dishes, Mon-Sat 12:00-23:00, closed Sun, Suur-Karja 17/19, tel. 680-6688).

Russian and Caucasian Food

As about a third of the local population is enthusiastically Russian, there are plenty of places serving Russian cuisine (see also under "Budget Eateries," next page).

Troika is my choice for Russian food. Right on Town Hall Square, with a folkloric-costumed waitstaff, they serve €6-9 *bliny* (pancakes) and *pelmeni* (dumplings), and €12-20 main dishes. Sit out on the square; down in the trippy, trendy cellar; or in the more casual tavern—at ground level out back, prices 15 percent lower (daily 12:00-23:00, Raekoja Plats 15, tel. 627-6245).

Must Lammas is straightforward and elegant, focusing on just plain tasty Caucasian food from Georgia, Armenia, and Azerbaijan (€9 lunch specials, €10-18 main dishes, Mon-Sat 12:00-23:00, Sun 12:00-18:00, Sauna 2, tel. 644-2031).

Medieval Cuisine

Two well-run restaurants just below Town Hall Square specialize in re-creating medieval food (from the days before the arrival of the potato and tomato from the New World). They are each grotesquely touristy, complete with gift shops where you can buy your souvenir goblet. Both have street seating, but you'll get all the tourists and none of the atmosphere.

Olde Hansa, filling three creaky old floors and outdoor tables with tourists, candle wax, and scurrying medieval waitresses, can be quite expensive (€13-35 main dishes, daily 10:00-24:00, musicians circulate nightly after 18:00, a belch below Town Hall Square at Vana Turg 1, reserve in advance, tel. 627-9020). **Peppersack,** across the street, tries to compete (Vana Turg 6, tel. 646-6800).

Pubs in the Old Town

Young Estonians eat well and affordably at pubs. In some pubs, you go to the bar to look at the menu, order, and pay. Then find a table, and they'll bring your food out when it's ready.

Hell Hunt Pub ("The Gentle Wolf") was the first Western-style pub to open after 1991, and it's still going strong, attracting a mixed expat and local crowd with its tasty food. Consider making a meal from the great pub snacks (€2.50-€4.50) plus a salad (€5-6). Choose a table in its convivial interior or in the rustic courtyard across the street (€4.50 soups, €6-10 main dishes, daily 12:00-1:00 in the morning, Pikk 39, tel. 681-8333).

Von Krahli Baar serves cheap, substantial Estonian grub—such as potato pancakes *(torud)* stuffed with mushrooms or shrimp (€5)—in a big, dark space that doubles as a center for Estonia's alternative theater scene; there's also seating in the tiny courtyard where you enter. It started as the bar of the theater upstairs, then expanded to become a restaurant, so it has a young, avant-garde vibe. You'll feel like you're eating backstage with the stagehands (€4-7 main dishes, Mon-Sat 12:00-22:00, Sun 12:00-18:00, Rataskaevu 10/12, a block uphill from Town Hall Square, near Wheel Well, tel. 626-9090).

Budget Eateries

Eat, a laid-back, cellar-level student hangout with a big foosball table and a book exchange, serves the best-value lunch in town. Its menu is very simple: three varieties of *pelmeenid* (dumplings),

What If I Miss My Boat?

Remember that you can get help from the cruise line's port agent (listed on the destination information sheet distributed on the ship) and the local TI (see page 443). If the port agent suggests a costly solution (such as a private car with a driver), you may want to consider public transit.

Frequent fast boats connect Tallinn to **Helsinki;** these are operated by Tallink Silja (tel. 640-9808, www.tallinksilja .com), Linda Line (tel. 699-9333, www.lindaline.ee), Eckerö Line (tel. 664-6000, www.eckeroline.fi), and Viking Line (tel. 666-3966, www.vikingline.fi). Tallink Silja boats also go to **Stockholm** overnight. St. Peter Line boats connect to **St. Petersburg,** but you can do this only if you've arranged a visa long in advance (www.stpeterline.com). To reach **Rīga,** the bus is easy. For many other destinations—such as **Copenhagen** or **Oslo**—you can take an overnight boat to Stockholm, then connect by train. (To research train schedules, see www.bahn.com.) But for these and other destinations, it may be even better to fly.

If you need to catch a **plane,** you can ride the bus to the convenient Tallinn airport (Tallinna Lennujaam), just three miles southeast of downtown (www.tallinn-airport.ee).

Local **travel agents** in Tallinn, such as Estravel, can help you (see page 444). For more advice on what to do if you miss the boat, see page 144.

plus sauces, beet salad, and pickles. You dish up what you like and pay by weight (€2-3/big bowl). Ask for an education in the various dumplings and sauces and then go for the complete experience. Enjoy with abandon—you can't spend much money here, and you'll feel good stoking their business (Mon-Sat 11:00-21:00, closed Sun, Sauna 2, tel. 644-0029).

Balti Jaama Kohvik, at the end of the train station near the Balti Jaam Market, is an unimpressive-looking 24-hour diner with no real sign (look for a red awning and *Kohvik avatud 24 tundi*— "café open 24 hours"—on the door). The bustling stainless-steel kitchen cranks out traditional Russian/Estonian dishes—the cheapest hot food in town. While you won't see or hear a word of English here, the glass case displays the various offerings and prices (€3 meals, €1.60 soups, dirt-cheap-yet-wonderful savory pancakes, and tasty *beljaš*—a kind of pierogi). Unfortunately, the area feels dangerous after dark.

Supermarkets: For picnic supplies, try the **Rimi** supermarket just outside the Old Town at Aia 7, near the Viru Gate (daily 8:00-22:00). A larger, more upscale supermarket in the basement of the **Viru Keskus** mall (directly behind Hotel Viru) has convenient, inexpensive take-away meals (daily 9:00-22:00). The handy little **Kolmjag "Everything"** grocery is a block off Town Hall Square (daily 24 hours, Pikk 11, tel. 631-1511).

Pastries

The **Maiasmokk** ("Sweet Tooth") café and pastry shop, founded in 1864, is the grande dame of Tallinn cafés—ideal for dessert. Even through the Soviet days, this was *the* place for a good pastry or a glass of herby Tallinn schnapps ("Vana Tallinn"). Point to what you want from the selection of classic local pastries at the counter, and sit down for coffee on the other side of the shop. Everything's reasonable (Mon-Fri 8:00-22:00, Sat 9:00-22:00, Sun 9:00-21:00, Pikk 16, across from church with old clock, tel. 646-4079). They also have a marzipan shop (separate entrance).

Pierre Chocolaterie at Vene 6 has scrumptious fresh pralines, sandwiches, and coffee in a courtyard filled with craft shops (daily 8:30-late, tel. 641-8061).

Estonian Survival Phrases

Estonian has a few unusual vowel sounds. The letter *ä* is pronounced "ah" as in "hat," but *a* without the umlaut sounds more like "aw" as in "hot." To make the sound *ö,* say "oh" and purse your lips; the letter *õ* is similar, but with the lips less pursed. Listen to locals and imitate. In the phonetics, ī sounds like the long *i* in "light," and bolded syllables are stressed.

English	Estonian	Pronunciation
Hello. (formal)	*Tervist.*	**tehr**-veest
Hi. / Bye. (informal)	*Tere. / Nägemist.*	**teh**-reh / **nah**-geh-meest
Do you speak English?	*Kas te räägite inglise keelt?*	kahs teh **raah**-gee-the **een**-glee-seh kehlt
Yes. / No.	*Jah. / Ei.*	yah / ay
Please. / You're welcome.	*Palun.*	**pah**-luhn
Thank you (very much).	*Tänan (väga).*	**tah**-nahn (**vah**-gaw)
Can I help you?	*Saan ma teid aidata?*	saahn mah tayd ī-dah-tah
Excuse me.	*Vabandust.*	**vaw**-bahn-doost
(Very) good.	*(Väga) hea.*	(**vah**-gaw) **hey**-ah
Goodbye.	*Hüvasti.*	**hew**-vaw-stee
one / two	*üks / kaks*	ewks / kawks
three / four	*kolm / neli*	kohlm / **nay**-lee
five / six	*viis / kuus*	vees / koos
seven / eight	*seitse / kaheksa*	**sayt**-seh / **kaw**-hehk-sah
nine / ten	*üheksa / kümme*	**ew**-hehk-sah / **kew**-meh
hundred	*sada*	**saw**-daw
thousand	*tuhat*	**too**-hawt
How much?	*Kui palju?*	quee **pawl**-yoo
local currency: (Estonian) crown	*(Eesti) krooni*	(**eh**-stee) **kroo**-nee
Where is...?	*Kus asub...?*	koos ah-**soob**
...the toilet	*...tualett*	**too**-ah-leht
men	*mees*	mehs
women	*naine*	**nī**-neh
water / coffee	*vesi / kohvi*	**vay**-see / **kohkh**-vee
beer / wine	*õlu / vein*	**oh**-loo / vayn
Cheers!	*Terviseks!*	**tehr**-vee-sehks
The bill, please.	*Arve, palun.*	**ahr**-veh **pah**-luhn

RĪGA
Latvia

Latvia Practicalities

Latvia (Latvija) borders the Baltic Sea, sitting between the other Baltic states: Estonia (to the north) and Lithuania (to the south). The country's population (2.2 million) is made up largely of native Latvians (very roughly two-thirds of the population) and Russians (about a third). Latvia's terrain (generally low plains) covers 25,000 square miles, about the size of West Virginia. Latvia's major city and capital is Rīga (at 700,000 residents, the Baltic states' largest city). Like its Baltic neighbors, Latvia spent most of its history occupied by foreign powers—Sweden, Russia, Germany, the USSR—but became independent in 1991 (following the breakup of the Soviet Union) and joined both NATO and the European Union in the spring of 2004.

Money: About 0.50 Latvian lat (Ls, officially LVL) = $1 (to figure US prices, divide the lat price in half). An ATM is called a *bankomāti*. The local VAT (value-added sales tax) rate is 22 percent; the minimum purchase eligible for a VAT refund is 30.25 Ls (for details on refunds, see page 139).

Language: The native language is Latvian.

Emergencies: Dial 112 for police, medical, or other emergencies. (You can also dial 02 for police and 03 for an ambulance.) In case of theft or loss, see page 131.

Time Zone: Latvia is one hour ahead of Central European Time (seven/ten hours ahead of the East/West Coasts of the US). That puts Rīga in the same time zone as Helsinki and Tallinn; one hour ahead of Stockholm, the rest of Scandinavia, and most other continental cruise ports (including Gdańsk and Warnemünde); and one hour behind St. Petersburg.

Embassies in Riga: The **US embassy** is at 1 Samnera Velsa Iela (tel. 6710-7000, http://riga.usembassy.gov/). The **Canadian embassy** is at 20/22 Baznicas Iela (tel. 6781-3945, www .canada.ee). Call ahead for passport services.

Phoning: Latvia's country code is 371; to call from another country to Latvia, dial the international access code (011 from the US/Canada, 00 from Europe, or + from a mobile phone), then 371, followed by the local number. For local calls within Latvia, just dial the number as it appears in this book—whether you're calling from across the street or across the country. To place an international call from Latvia, dial 0, the code of the country you're calling (1 for US and Canada), and the phone number. For more help, see page 1110.

Tipping: If a gratuity is included in the price of your sit-down meal, you don't need to tip further; otherwise, a tip of roughly 10 percent is customary. Tip a taxi driver by rounding up the fare a bit (pay 4 Ls on a 3.5-Ls fare). For more tips on tipping, see page 143.

Tourist Information: www.latvia.travel

RĪGA

The biggest city of the Baltics is an under-rated gem, with a charming but not cutesy Old Town, a sprawling real-world market, a smattering of good museums, the finest collection of fanciful Art Nouveau buildings in Europe, a palpable civic pride expressed in its luscious parks and stately facades, and fewer cruise passengers clogging its cobbles than most other towns in this book. From a cruiser's perspective, Rīga (pronounced REE-gah) is the sleepy antidote to its Baltic rival, the tourist-crazed Tallinn. Rīga has a bit less Scandinavian-mod style and sugary Old World charm, but it enjoys more big-city realness. And, while Tallinn's ties to the former USSR feel like ancient history, Rīga's Russian connection is more palpable, giving visitors a glimpse into a "half-Russian" society without plunging into the full monty of St. Petersburg.

Centuries before it was Russian (or even Latvian), Rīga was a prominent trading city. Bishop Albert of Bremen, German merchants, and the Teutonic Knights made it the center of Baltic Christianization, commercialization, and colonization when they founded the city in the early 1200s. Rīga came under Polish control for a while during the 16th century; later, in the 17th century, the czars made it the Russian Empire's busiest commercial port. Latvia gained its independence for the first time following World War I in 1918, but that lasted just over two decades; with World War II, it was folded into the USSR's holdings.

Under Soviet rule, Rīga became first an important military center and later, because of its high standard of living, one of the favored places for high-ranking military officers to retire to (to keep them at arm's length from power, they were given a choice of

Excursions from Rīga

Rīga can easily be enjoyed without an excursion. Getting into town is simple, the sights are pleasant but don't require a lot of explanation to enjoy, and the basics are covered in this chapter. Even the outlying sights (such as the Central Market, and the Art Nouveau quarter and museum) are an easy and pleasant walk from downtown. And joining a tour or hiring your own guide in Rīga is easy and affordable (see "Tours in Rīga," later).

Most cruise lines offer walking tours of Rīga's **Old Town,** or a bus-plus-walking-tour option. You can't really see the Old Town core by bus, so if you'd like to get all the stories and legends, a walking tour is best. If you're interested in Rīga's **Art Nouveau** facades, choose a tour that includes some walking, not just a bus ride. A bus tour zips you past several fine examples, but doesn't allow you to linger over the stunning details.

Those with an interest in **Jewish history** may find worthwhile a tour that includes several sites related to Rīga's difficult Holocaust experience: the memorial at the site of the Grand Choral Synagogue (burned down by Nazis), the site of the Old Jewish Cemetery (defiled by Nazis), the monument at Rumbula (the site of a mass execution in a forest), and the memorial at Salaspils (the largest Nazi concentration camp in the Baltics).

Cruise lines offer a wide range of excursions to outlying attractions. These include **Jurmala** (Rīga's seaside resort, sometimes combined with a spa visit); **"Middle Ages Rīga"** (including the Gauja River northeast of town, the evocative ruins of Sigulda Medieval Castle, the reconstructed Turaida Castle and nearby church, and the legend-packed Gutmanis cave); and the **Latvian Open-Air Ethnographic Museum** (with 118 traditional buildings relocated here from around the country). Again, as Rīga itself is so easy to enjoy in a relaxed day, I'd skip all of these options.

RĪGA

anywhere in the USSR *except* Moscow, Kiev, and St. Petersburg). The Soviets encouraged Russian immigration, and by the time the USSR fell, Latvians were in the minority in their own capital city. Perceptive travelers will notice that Russian is still widely spoken here. Though Russian-Estonian tensions in neighboring Estonia grab more headlines, Latvia has its own tricky mix to negotiate.

But for visitors, Rīga is a purely enjoyable city, regardless of what language is spoken by the people you'll meet. Even just a few hours are enough for you to get a satisfying taste. Stroll the Old Town, browsing the shops and dipping into a museum or two; the excellent Museum of the Occupation of Latvia is tops for those intrigued by the Baltics' tumultuous 20th century. For a revealing look at an extremely local-feeling market, linger in the Central Market, which trudges on seemingly oblivious to the cruise passengers just over the berm. (As one of the cheapest destinations in this book, Rīga is a fine place to do a little shopping—or just buy a picnic.) Save some time to stroll through some of Rīga's delightful parks, following the meandering river (once a moat) that runs right in front of the towering Freedom Monument. And make a pilgrimage to some of the city's gorgeous Art Nouveau facades, which scream out with fanciful, entertaining details. Making things even better, Rīga has been hard at work gearing up for its stint as a European Capital of Culture in 2014; several long-neglected buildings and museums are receiving facelifts and should soon be ready for prime time.

Planning Your Time

Get your bearings with a stroll through the Old Town. Midmorning, walk to the Central Market for some people-watching and to harvest ingredients for a picnic lunch or snack. Then head back to town to see the Museum of the Occupation of Latvia (opens at 11:00) and/or the Art Museum Rīga Bourse. For a good picnic alternative, consider lunch at one of the many al fresco cafés downtown. In early afternoon, wander out of the Old Town core to see the Freedom Monument, Orthodox Cathedral, and (a few blocks north) the best of Rīga's many Art Nouveau facades, plus the wonderful little Art Nouveau Museum. From the Art Nouveau sights, it's a fairly short walk (mostly through parklands) to the cruise dock.

RĪGA

Arrival at the Port of Rīga

Arrival at a Glance: It's an easy 10- to 20-minute stroll into town—no taxis or buses needed.

Port Overview

One of the simplest, most manageable cruise ports in northern

Europe, Rīga is made-to-order for cruise passengers. Ships dock along a river embankment just a 10-minute walk from the edge of the Old Town, or a 20-minute walk from the very heart of town.

To reach Rīga, your ship will pick up a pilot for the journey up the Daugava River. The sailing from the Baltic up the river gives you a revealing glimpse of the grimy, hardworking industry that makes Rīga the Baltics' no-non-sense muscleman. Don't fret—the core of town (where you'll be spending time) is far more pleasant.

Tourist Information: There's no tourist information what-soever at the port; just walk into town to find TIs on Town Hall Square and just north, along the main drag (see "Tourist Information," later).

Getting into Town

Step off the ship, turn right, and walk toward the spires. It's really that simple, but for more details, see below.

Taxis may meet arriving ships, attempting to drastically over-charge cruisers 10-20 Ls (or even more) for the laughably short ride into town. (The fair, metered rate would be closer to 2-3 Ls.) As you'll have trouble getting a fair price, and the walk is so easy, I see little reason to consider a taxi.

For a fun ride into and around town, consider the **golf-cart tours** that meet arriving ships. They charge 7 Ls per person for a one-hour tour either through the Old Town or to the Art Nouveau area (2-person minimum; other options also listed).

Walking into Town

After going ashore and turning right to walk along the embank-ment (with the river on your right), proceed straight and pass under the bridge. At the first crosswalk, turn left and cross the busy highway. Once across, continue straight up Poļu Gāte, along-side the pastel-blue church. At the intersection, turn right onto Pils Iela, which takes you right to Cathedral Square in the heart of town. If you'd like to visit the TI, you can continue straight all the way to the far end of Cathedral Square (past all the al fresco tables), and turn right down the narrow, café-lined Tirgoņu Iela. The next small square has even more café tables, plus a fun outdoor souvenir market. As you walk through it, watch on your right for a big gap leading to an ugly modern building—this is the Museum of the Occupation of Latvia, which shares Town Hall Square with the TI (in the ornate building in the foreground).

Returning to Your Ship

Just head north along the river (with the river on your left-hand side); you'll run right into your ship. If you're coming from the Art Nouveau district, use a map to navigate your way diagonally through the big Kronvalda Park. When you pop out at the other end, you're just a quick walk from the dock. To cross the highway,

Services near the Port

Because the cruise port is so close to town, there's very little at the port itself. Stepping off the ship, turn left to find Rīga's passenger port terminal building (marked *Rīga Pasazieru Osta*), with **ATMs,** lockers, WCs, a newsstand, and a café. But you might as well turn right and walk into the Old Town, where ATMs abound. The Old Town also has several **pharmacies.**

it's easiest and safest to use the busy bridge that crosses over both highway and the river (you can find steps up to the bridge level near the Statoil gas station). Cross partway over, but before reaching the river, look for the stairs down (on your right) to the port gate area.

See page 491 for help if you miss your boat.

Orientation to Rīga

With about 700,000 people, Rīga is the biggest city in the Baltics. But the town core feels small and manageable, even on a brief visit. Rīga's Old Town (called Vecrīga) is on the right bank of the wide Daugava River. The cruise port is next to the northernmost of Rīga's bridges. From the river, the main drag—Kaļķu Iela—leads through the Old Town to the Freedom Monument, where it becomes Brīvības Bulvāris and continues out of town. You'll find plenty to keep you busy within the Old Town or a short walk from it.

The Old Town is hemmed in on the east side by a chain of relaxing parks, with the once-genteel urban residential zone stretching beyond. One of Rīga's most worthwhile areas is the cluster of Art Nouveau facades about a 20-minute walk (or 2- to 3-Ls taxi ride) northeast of the city center. There's no reason to cross the river.

A couple of terms you'll see around town: *Iela* is "street," while *Bulvāris* is "boulevard."

Tourist Information

The tourist office is in the ornate brick building attached to the House of Blackheads, right on Town Hall Square. The helpful staff hands out a free map and a variety of brochures (daily May-Sept 9:00-19:00, Oct-April 10:00-18:00, Rātslaukums 6, tel. 6703-7900, www.liveriga.com). A second branch is just a few short blocks away along the main drag, Kaļķu Iela (at #16, tel. 6722-7444).

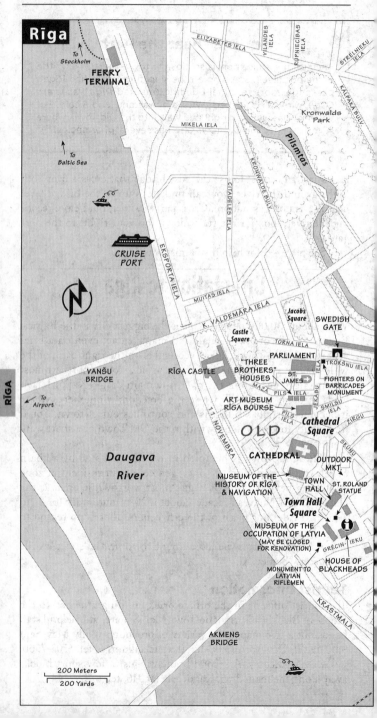

RĪGA

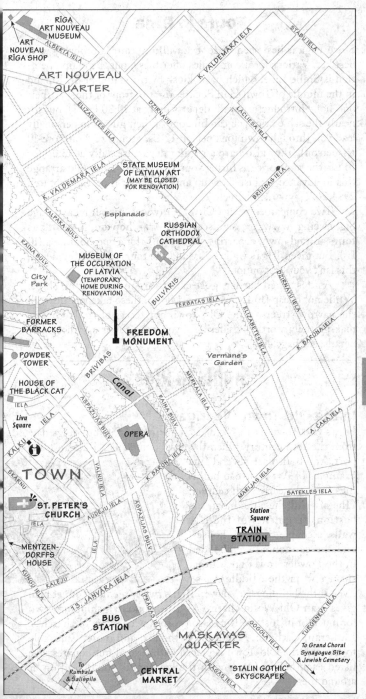

Tours in Rīga

Since Rīga is best seen by foot, a **walking tour** is probably your best bet. Various local companies offer these, but the main operation is Smile Line, which has a kiosk by the statue of St. Roland in the middle of Town Hall Square, right in front of the TI. Their one-hour introductory walk departs daily at 10:30 (7 Ls), but for nearly the same price you can hire one of their guides to personally lead you through town (one person-12 Ls, groups of 2 or more-10 Ls/person). They also have a regular departure daily at 13:00 for 10 Ls (the same price as hiring your own guide). You could arrange this in advance, or just show up and ask about it on the spot (tel. 2954-2626, www.smileline.lv).

Two companies—Rīga City Tour (www.citytour.lv) and Rīga Sightseeing (www.riga-sightseeing.lv)—run **hop-on, hop-off bus tours** around town, departing about hourly for a one-hour loop (10 Ls). But given Rīga's walkability and the tours' measly frequency, this isn't your best option.

As described earlier, **golf-cart tours** meet arriving ships. While not cheap (10 Ls/person for 1 hour), these take you through the narrow streets of the Old Town not accessible to big buses, making them worth considering if you want a tour on wheels (for details, see page 478).

Sights in Rīga

In the Old Town (Vecrīga)

Rīga's Old Town isn't as "old" as some; most of its buildings date from the 18th century, when the city boomed as a Russian trade port. You'll also see several fine examples of Art Nouveau buildings from the early 20th century. (The big churches, the moat, the bastion, fragments of the city walls, a couple of dozen houses, and the cannonballs embedded in the Powder Tower are all that survive from the Middle Ages.)  Even if the buildings are newer, Rīga's twisty medieval street plan gives it an Old World charm. As a cosmopolitan shipping town for much of its history, Rīga also boasts a wide range of churches: Lutheran, Catholic, Anglican, Orthodox, and more. Enjoyable to explore, the Old Town is graced with several fine squares; I've listed each below, along with the landmarks you'll find on or around them.

RĪGA

Town Hall Square (Rātslaukums)—Though not as big or as inviting as Cathedral Square, this space—closer to the river—is arguably Rīga's "main square." After World War II, when this area was devastated, Soviets rebuilt in an ugly, blocky style (some of which remains). But after independence, the Latvians set about restoring the square to its former glory. Here you'll find the TI, one of the city's top museums (outlining the Soviet occupation of Latvia—described later), and

its finest non-Art Nouveau building: the **House of Blackheads.** Made of vibrant red brick liberally sprinkled with gilded decorations, this was originally the guildhall of a merchant society that chose as its patron St. Mauritius, a third-century North African. The nickname came from the guild seal with disembodied black heads. (Racial sensitivity was clearly not a medieval forte—and, judging by the fact that the guild seal is still here, it's not quite a priority these days, either.) See the dates at the top: Although the guildhall was originally built in 1334, it was destroyed in World War II and only rebuilt in 1999. The left half of the building (containing the TI) looks as if it's part of the House of Blackheads, but was built centuries later.

Facing the House of Blackheads is Rīga's stately Town Hall. On the square between them stands a statue of **St. Roland,** Rīga's patron saint. Back then, the tip of Roland's sword was considered the geographical center of the city—the point from which all distances were measured.

A block above Town Hall Square is the towering, almost-onion steeple of **St. Peter's Church** (Petera Baznica), with an austere Lutheran interior and an elevator to an observation deck (4 Ls, closed Mon).

Along the bottom of Town Hall Square is the Soviet-era building that now (with a flourish of poetic justice) houses the Museum of the Occupation of Latvia (described next). Around the far side of the building, facing the river, stands the proud **Monument to the Latvian Riflemen.** These soldiers fought on the side of the czar during World War I, but then defected to join Lenin's Bolshevik Revolution. During communist times, the Soviets strategically chose local heroes to venerate in each of its satellites (the heroes conveniently also echoed Soviet ideals).

▲Museum of the Occupation of Latvia (Latvijas Okupācijas Muzejs)—This spunky, thorough exhibit tells Latvia's story during the tumultuous five decades between 1940 and 1991. Located next to the House of Blackheads, it fills the large upstairs hall of the dreary, communist-style, corroded-copper building that mars the otherwise architecturally quaint Town Hall Square. Opened soon after the fall of the Soviet Union, the ragtag exhibits (with lots of reading and few actual artifacts) are undergoing a much-needed overhaul. During the 2013 cruise season, you'll find the exhibit at either the main building or at its temporary home in the former US embassy, just outside the Old Town at Raiņa Bulvāris 7 (double-check with the TI for the current location).

Starting in 2014, the new collection promises to include more interactive features, but will keep the focus on the period of Soviet oppression—particularly the deportations of Latvians to Siberia. (You can step into a replica of a gulag barrack and see prisoners' letters home written on strips of birch bark.) To get the full story, try to time your visit to join one of the guided tours. Don't expect a balanced and self-critical presentation; this is a pro-Latvian place.

Cost and Hours: Note that all of these details may change due to ongoing renovations. Free, but donations suggested, 2 Ls to take photos, May-Sept Tue-Sun 11:00-18:00, Oct-April Tue-Sun 11:00-17:00, closed Mon year-round, Strelnieku Laukums 1 or Raiņa Bulvāris 7 (temporary location), tel. 6721-2715, www.okupacijasmuzejs.lv.

Tours: Guided tours are generally offered in English at 12:00 and 16:00, but confirm times; 2 Ls per person with an 8-Ls minimum.

▲▲**Cathedral Square (Doma Laukums)**—In old Rīga's biggest square, three things jockey for attention: The enormous cathedral, the Art Nouveau facade of the old stock exchange museum (now an art museum—described next), and café tables spilling out over the cobbles in every direction.

The **cathedral** (Doma Baznica), with its distinctive copper roof, dates from 1211. Dwarfing everything around it, it's positively huge for the Baltics, where big churches are rare. With additions built over the generations, it's a hodgepodge of architectural styles. During Soviet times, the altars and other religious decorations were taken out and the cathedral was converted into a concert hall. Finally, after decades of neglect, the cathedral has been undergoing a huge restoration project, due to be completed by 2014. Inside, the inscriptions recall Latvia's German Lutheran heritage, and the crypt holds what's left of Bishop Albert of Bremen, who started it all. It also has a particularly fine and gigantic organ (with more than 6,700 pipes), which is played for brief noontime concerts during the tourist season (generally Mon-Sat at 12:00, www.doms.lv).

Facing the cathedral from across the square is the ornately decorated former stock exchange building, or **Bourse,** which houses the Art Museum Rīga Bourse (described next). The second-story grille hides a carillon, which sweetly chimes the hour.

The far end of the square is the terrain of outdoor café and restaurant tables—a tempting place to sit, nurse a coffee or Latvian beer, and watch the parade of tourists and locals.

From here, you can tour the art museum, wander a couple of streets with fine Art Nouveau houses, or walk along Pils Iela to Rīga Castle (all described later).

Art Museum Rīga Bourse—Rīga's stately old stock exchange building has been meticulously restored to its original diarrhea-brown color, which glistens in the sun.

Its interior (also gorgeously restored, and also diarrhea brown) houses temporary exhibits and a modest collection of "foreign art." While the changing collections are generally good, the permanent exhibits (fourth floor—Western European art and painting gallery, third floor—Oriental art) take a backseat to the finely restored rooms that house them. The highlights are the airy atrium with beautiful tile floors (viewable for free) and the fourth floor, with gilded chandeliers and other details whose sumptuousness outshines the art.

Cost and Hours: permanent exhibit-2 Ls, temporary exhibit in ground-floor "Great Hall"-3 Ls, temporary exhibit in small hall-1 Ls, 4.50-Ls combo-ticket for all exhibits; Tue-Sun 10:00-18:00, Fri until 20:00, closed Mon, Doma Laukums 6, tel. 6722-3434, www.rigasbirza.lv.

Rīga Castle—Leave Cathedral Square and walk down Pils Iela to this relatively unimpressive, blocky fortress (a "palace" it ain't) that was the no-nonsense headquarters of the Teutonic Knights who ruled Rīga. Built in the 14th century, the castle stoutly anchored the northern tip of the Old Town as it kept careful watch downriver for potential invaders. The door on the landward side of the castle, with a guard out front, is the office of the Latvian president; nearby is the entrance to the skippable Latvian National History Museum. During Soviet times, the castle was converted into the "Children's Palace"—many older Latvians recall visiting here as youngsters.

Walk to Swedish Gate and Former Barracks—From Rīga Castle, take a stroll through the most historic quarter of the Old

Town. With your back to the big, round tower, walk straight ahead up Mazā Pils Iela a block and a half to find (on the right) the **"Three Brothers"**—a trio of the oldest surviving houses in Rīga. The oldest, white house (#17) has minuscule windows—dating from the 15th century, when taxa-

tion was based on window size. Yellow #19 is newer, from 1646, while green and narrow #21 is the baby of the bunch, from the turn of the 18th century.

Continue past the Brothers and turn left up Jēkaba Iela. On the left, you'll pass the corner of Latvia's **parliament.** This is the building where—back when it was the seat of the Latvian Supreme Soviet—independence from the USSR was declared on May 4, 1990. On the nearby corner, look for the little pyramid-shaped monument to the **Fighters on the Barricades,** a brave group of about 15,000 Latvians who, at great personal risk, protected stra-tegic Latvian areas when skirmishes with pro-Soviet forces broke out in January of 1991; seven were killed. The Latvians were unsure of whether Soviet leader Mikhail Gorbachev would send the full force of the Red Army to reclaim the Baltics. Although that never happened, Latvians still honor those who were willing to make the ultimate sacrifice for sovereignty.

Near the top of Jēkaba Iela, turn right down the tiny, rocky lane called **Trokšņu Iela.** Watch your step on this ankle-twisting

alley, paved with rocks originally car-ried as ballast on big ships. After a block on this street, you'll pop out at the so-called **Swedish Gate** (built in the 17th century by Swedish soldiers stationed here). Going through it, you'll discover a long row of yellow **barracks** filled with shops and cafés, facing a recon-structed stretch of the former town wall (along Torņa Iela). At the far end is the **Powder Tower,** which once housed the town's supply of gunpowder. The tower defended that cache well over the cen-turies, as nine Russian cannonballs (from the 17th and 18th centu-ries) are supposedly embedded in the walls. The Museum of War inside is skippable.

From the Powder Tower, you could turn right and head down Smilšu, for some fun Art Nouveau facades on the way back down to Cathedral Square.

RĪGA

Old Town Art Nouveau—While arguably the best Art Nouveau in Rīga is just outside the historic core (described later), several fine examples from that age line the Old Town streets. The best examples are on or near two streets leading off from Cathedral Square: Smilšu (especially #2 and #8), to the east; and Šķūņu, to the south. Just off of Smilšu, at Meistaru 10, is the famous **House of the Black Cat;** while the building itself is relatively tame, its corner turret is topped with a cat with its back arched defiantly, supposedly placed there as an offensive gesture toward a guild that denied its creator membership.

Other Museums—Rīga's Old Town is packed with small, modest museums that are worth perusing if you have a special interest or a rainy day. The **Museum of the History of Rīga and Navigation** (Rīgas Vestures un Kugniecibas Muzejs) gives a fairly good idea of Rīga's early history as a center on the Baltic-Black Sea trade route, explains the Old Town's street plan in terms of a now-silted-up river that used to flow through the center, and shows you everything you wanted to see on inter-war Rīga (daily, behind the cathedral at Palasta Iela 4, www.rigamuz.lv). The **Mentzendorffs House** is a meticulously restored 17th-century aristocrat's town-house (daily, Grēcinieku Iela 18, enter on Kungu Iela, www.mencendorfanams.com).

Outside of the Old Town

While many cruisers stick to the cobbles, some of Rīga's most appealing (and certainly its most local-feeling) attractions are just a short walk beyond the former city walls. The Central Market, mentioned first, is just south of the Old Town, while the other places noted here are to the east. I've listed these roughly in order, from nearest to farthest from the Old Town.

▲▲Central Market (Centralais Tirgus)—What do you do when you have five perfectly good zeppelin airship hangars left

behind by the Germans after World War I? Latvia's answer: Move them to the center of the capital city and turn them into extremely spacious market halls. Just beyond the southern edge of the Old Town—only a 15-minute walk from the quaint cobbled squares—is this vast, sprawl-

ing market that feels like the outskirts of Moscow. This is not a touristy souvenir market (though you may find a stall or two), but a real, thriving market where locals buy whatever they need at reasonable prices. If you've been cruising through Scandinavia's more expensive cities, you'll find basic foodstuffs here to be almost

RĪGA

scandalously cheap. It's open and bustling every day, though some sections close on certain Mondays (www.centraltirgus.lv).

To get to the market, walk to the south end of the Old Town, cross the tram tracks, and find the underpass that runs beneath the big berm. Then explore to your heart's content, wishing you had a full kitchen in your stateroom to cook up all the tempting ingredients. Just past the one hangar that runs sideways, find the colorful and fragrant flower market, which seems to go on and on. Then poke through all five of the zeppelin hangars, each one with a different variety of meats, cheeses, bakery items, dry goods, and (in the final, smelly hall) fish. While nothing here is exactly gourmet—this is not an artisan, organic market—it makes it easy to imagine life for an everyday Rīgan. The old brick warehouses just toward the river from the market zone have recently been refurbished and now house finer shops.

The Central Market also marks the Maskavas, or **"Little Moscow"** neighborhood, which contains a huge Russian population. While all of the Baltic states have large Russian populations, Rīga became especially Russified during the Soviet period, leaving an awkward tension between its Latvian and Russian groups. As if to mark this territory, looming overhead is a classic "Stalin Gothic" tower (virtually identical in style to similar towers in Warsaw, Moscow, and elsewhere). Originally designed to be a hotel and conference center for collective farmers (who had little use for either hotels or a conference center), it later became, and remains, the Academy of Science.

▲▲Freedom Monument (Brivibas Piemniekelis)— Dedicated in 1935, located on a traffic island in the middle of

Brīvības Bulvāris, this monument features Lady Liberty (here nicknamed "Milda"), holding high three stars representing the three regions of Latvia. At the base of the tower, strong and defiant Latvians break free from their chains and march to the future. The Soviets must have decided that removing the monument was either too difficult or too likely to spur protests among Latvians, because they left it standing— but reassigned its major characters: The woman became Mother Russia, and the three stars, the Baltic states. (KGB agents apprehended anyone who tried to come near it.) Now it is again the symbol of independent Latvia, and locals lay flowers between the two soldiers who stand stoically at the monument's base. The grand building nearby is the Opera House. The bridge near the monument offers beautiful views over Rīga's great parks.

Parks—Rīga's Old Town is hemmed in on its eastern edge by delightful, manicured parks that line up along a picturesque stream that was once the fortified city's moat.

Russian Orthodox Cathedral—Just past the Freedom Monument on Rīga's main drag (Brīvības Bulvāris), sitting at the edge of a park, this striking house of worship dates from the 19th century. During the Soviet period, when the atheistic regime notoriously repurposed houses of worship, the building was used as a planetarium and "house of knowledge." While the interior is far from original—it was gutted by the Soviets—it's serene and otherworldly. Especially if you won't be visiting the Orthodox churches in Tallinn or St. Petersburg, it's worth the short walk out of the Old Town to take a peek.

State Museum of Latvian Art (Latvijas Valsts Mākslas Muzejs)—Housed in a stately old building in the parklands just east of the town center, this fine museum collects works by Latvian and Russian artists. A long-planned but often-delayed renovation may close the museum at some point—confirm with the TI that it's open before making the trip. The collection, almost entirely from 1910 to 1940, concentrates all the artistic and political influences that stirred Latvia then: French impressionism, German design, and Russian propaganda-poster style on the one hand; European internationalism, Latvian nationalism, rural romanticism, and Communism on the other. The Russian art section is particularly worthwhile if you won't be going to St. Petersburg's superb Russian Museum.

Cost and Hours: 3 Ls, Wed-Mon 11:00-18:00, Fri until 20:00, closed Tue, Kr. Valdemara Iela 10, www.lnmm.lv.

▲▲Art Nouveau Rīga—Worth ▲▲▲ for architecture fans, but interesting even to those who don't know Art Nouveau from Art

Garfunkel, Rīga's more than 800 exuberantly decorated facades from the late 19th and early 20th centuries make it Europe's single best city for the distinctive, eye-pleasing style of Art Nouveau. These are not the flowing, organic curves of Barcelona's Modernista style, but geometrically precise patterns adorned with fanciful details, including an army of highly expressive, gargoyle-like heads.

Art Nouveau Walk: While easy-to-love facades are scattered throughout the city center (including some wonderful examples in the Old Town—see page 482), it's worth the 20-minute walk northeast of the center to find a particularly impressive batch. It's

RĪGA

a pleasant stroll—you can follow the parks most of the way there, and you can tie in visits to the Orthodox Church and (if it's open) the State Museum of Latvian Art.

For the best short stretch of houses, begin at the corner of the park nearest Elizabets Iela, Strēlnieku Iela, and Kaplaka Bulvāris. Head up **Strēlnieku;** on the right, at #4, is a magnificent blue-and-white facade almost *too* cluttered with adornments: stripes, rings, slinky women holding wreaths of victory, and stylized helmeted heads over the windows. (This, like most buildings in this area, was decorated by Mikhail Eisenstein—whose director son Sergei earned a place in every "Intro to Film" college class with his seminal 1925 film, *The Battleship Potemkin*.) At the corner, you'll see the yellow turreted building that houses the Art Nouveau Museum, and the fine shop across the street (both described later). If you turn right just before this house, on **Alberta Iela,** you'll find several more grandiose examples: #13 (pale pink, on right; notice the moaning heads at the bases of the turrets), #8 (blue and white, on the left; tree-trunk supports grow and leaf into a lion's head), #4 (beige, on the left; with griffins flanking the ornately framed doorway, three Medusa heads up top, and lions guarding the towers), and (shabby but still impressive, the next two on the left) #2 and #2a. At the end of Alberta, jog right for a block, then head left down **Elizabets Iela** to find a couple more examples at #10a and #10b (blue and gray, with hoot-owls over the doors). It's strange to think that all of these glorious buildings were turned into communal apartments under the communist regime.

Rīga Art Nouveau Museum: When you're done ogling the facades, head back the way you came, to the corner of Alberta and Strēlnieku. Head a few steps up Strēlnieku (to the right) to find the excellent little Rīga Art Nouveau Museum, in the bottom of the yellow castle-like building with the pointy red turret (3.50 Ls, audioguide-1.50 Ls, guided tour-10 Ls/group—call or email ahead to arrange, Tue-Sun 10:00-18:00, closed Mon, Alberta 12, enter on Strēlnieku, tel. 6718-1465, www.jugendstils.riga.lv, jugendstils @riga.lv).

This museum shows what life was like behind those slinky facades back in the early 20th century. Buzz the doorbell to get inside, then peer up the stairwell. Inside the museum, you're greeted by docents dressed in period costumes, who invite you to don a fancy, feathery hat for your stroll through a finely decorated, circa-1903 apartment, with furniture, clothes, decorative items, rugs, and lots of other

What If I Miss My Boat?

Remember that you can get help from the cruise line's port agent (listed on the destination information sheet distributed on the ship) and the local TI (see page 479). If the port agent suggests a costly solution (such as a private car with a driver), you may want to consider public transit.

Buses connect Rīga to **Tallinn** (about 3/day, 4.5 hours, www.businessline.ee). For **Stockholm,** Tallink Silja offers overnight ferry trips (www.tallinksilja.com). To get to **St. Petersburg** or **Helsinki,** it's probably easier to go to Tallinn or Stockholm and connect from there (but remember that you'll need a visa—arranged weeks in advance—to enter Russia). **Gdańsk** requires a long overland journey; because the route from Latvia to Poland is flanked by Kaliningrad (part of Russia) and Belarus, both of which require transit visas, you'll need to determine a route via the relatively short Lithuanian-Polish border instead—ask the TI for help.

If you need to catch a **plane** to your next destination, you can ride a public bus to Rīga's international airport (www .riga-airport.com).

Local **travel agents** in Rīga can help you. For more advice on what to do if you miss the boat, see page 144.

details dating from the age.

This was the personal apartment of architect Konstantīns Pēkšēns, whose photo you'll see in the first room. You'll go through several rooms, including a dining room, bedroom, kitchen (with tiny maid's chamber on the side), bathroom (the apartment had hot water and even central heating—cutting-edge at the time), and more. Take your time and savor all the details—the gently seductive curve of the plant stand, the ribbons delicately tied to flower vases on the dining table, the old-school icebox and coffee grinder in the kitchen, and the natural motifs painted high on the walls in each room (based on items found in the Latvian country-side). Very few barriers or cordons separate you from the world of a century ago, making this a particularly appealing and immersive little museum.

Nearby: If you'd like to take some of this Art Nouveau home with you, directly across the street from the museum is the **Art Nouveau Rīga shop,** with piles of souvenirs inspired by this distinctive style (daily 10:00-19:00, Strēlnieku 9, tel. 6733-3030, www.artnouveauriga.lv).

More Art Nouveau: The tiny area described above is just the beginning of Rīga's Art Nouveau neighborhood. A couple of blocks to the west, just north of the parklands, **Vīlandes Iela** and the parallel **Rūpniecības Iela** have several fine facades. The area

RĪGA

just south and east of the Brīvības Bulvāris main drag (such as **Tērbatas Iela** and **A.Čaka Iela**) also has several examples.

Shopping in Rīga

The souvenirs you'll see most often here are linens (tablecloths, placemats, and scarves) and carved-wood items (such as spoons and trivets). There are a few sparse souvenir stands at the **Central Market,** but that's really designed more for the natives. Souvenir shops are peppered through the Old Town, and an entertaining open-air **souvenir market** pops up in summer in the small square just north of Town Hall Square.

If you're turned on by Rīga's Art Nouveau bounty, another good option is "faux Nouveau"—replica items such as tiles, cards, textiles, jewelry, and so on. The best choices are at the **Art Nouveau Rīga shop,** across the street from the Art Nouveau Museum (described earlier).

Eating in Rīga

Central Rīga—particularly the area between Cathedral Square and Town Hall Square—is full of tempting open-air cafés and restaurants. Rather than seek out a particular place, I'd simply window-shop to find an appealing cuisine and people-watching vantage point.

GDAŃSK
Poland

Poland Practicalities

Poland (Polska), arguably Europe's most devoutly Catholic country, is sandwiched between Protestant Germany and Eastern Orthodox Russia. Nearly all of the 38.5 million people living in Poland are ethnic Poles. The country is 122,000 square miles (the same as New Mexico) and extremely flat, making it the chosen path of least resistance for many invading countries since its infancy. Poland was dominated by foreigners for the majority of the last two centuries, finally gaining true independence (from the Soviet Union) in 1989. While parts of the country are still cleaning up the industrial mess left by the Soviets, Poland also has some breathtaking medieval cities—such as Gdańsk—that show off its kindhearted people, dynamic history, and unique cultural fabric.

Money: 1 złoty (zł, or PLN) = 100 groszy (gr) = about 30 cents; 3 zł = about $1. An ATM is called a *bankomat*. The local VAT (value-added sales tax) rate is 23 percent; the minimum purchase eligible for a VAT refund is 200 zł (for details on refunds, see page 139).

Language: The native language is Polish. For useful phrases, see page 541.

Emergencies: Dial 112 for police, medical, or other emergencies. In case of theft or loss, see page 131.

Time Zone: Poland is on Central European Time (the same as most of the Continent, one hour ahead of Great Britain, and six/nine hours ahead of the East/West Coasts of the US). That puts Gdańsk one hour behind Rīga, Tallinn, and Helsinki, and two hours behind St. Petersburg.

Embassies in Warsaw: The **US embassy** is at Ulica Piękna 12 (tel. 022-625-1401, http://poland.usembassy.gov). The **Canadian embassy** is at Ulica Jana Matejki 1-5 (tel. 022-584-3100, toll-free emergency tel. 800-111-4319, www.poland .gc.ca). Call ahead for passport services.

Phoning: Poland's country code is 48; to call from another country to Poland, dial the international access code (011 from the US/Canada, 00 from Europe, or + from a mobile phone), then 48, followed by the local number. For local calls within Poland, just dial the number as it appears in this book— whether you're calling from across the street or across the country. To place an international call from Poland, dial 00, the code of the country you're calling (1 for US and Canada), and the phone number. For more tips, see page 1110.

Tipping: A gratuity is included at sit-down meals, so you don't need to tip further, though it's nice to round up your bill about 5-10 percent for great service. Tip a taxi driver by rounding up the fare a bit (pay 30 zł on an 27-zł fare). For more tips on tipping, see page 143.

Tourist Information: www.poland.travel

GDAŃSK
and the PORT of GDYNIA

Gdańsk (guh-DAYNSK) is a true find on the Baltic Coast of Poland. You may associate Gdańsk with dreary images of striking dockworkers from the nightly news in the 1980s—but there's so much more to this city than shipyards, Solidarity, and smog. It's surprisingly easy to look past the urban sprawl to find one of northern Europe's most historic and picturesque cities.

Gdańsk is second only to Kraków as Poland's most appealing destination. The gem of a Main Town boasts block after block of red-brick churches and narrow, colorful, ornately decorated Hanseatic burghers' mansions. The riverfront embankment, with its trademark medieval Crane, oozes salty maritime charm. Gdańsk's history is also fascinating—from its medieval Golden Age to the headlines of our own generation, big things happen here. You might even see old Lech Wałęsa still wandering the streets.

And yet, Gdańsk is also looking to its future, finally repairing some of its WWII damage after a long communist hibernation. Things have picked up even more in recent years, as the city hosted matches for the Euro Cup 2012 soccer tournament. The flurry of construction included a futuristic new stadium, shaped like a translucent glob of amber, and high-speed train lines that have more efficiently linked the city to the rest of Poland. Gdańsk is poised to reclaim its former greatness as a top European city.

Gdańsk is the anchor of the three cities that make up the metropolitan region known as the Tri-City (Trójmiasto). The other two parts are as different as night and day: a once-swanky resort town (Sopot) and a practical, nose-to-the-grindstone business center and cruise port (Gdynia). Although your ship arrives at Gdynia

Excursions from Gdynia

Gdańsk is clearly the best choice. Most cruise-line excursions include a walking tour through the Main Town; some may include guided visits to the giant, red-brick **St. Mary's Cathedral** or the "**Roads to Freedom**" exhibit at the Solidarity shipyard. You'll want to explore the town after your tour, so look for an itinerary that includes some free time—or skip the return bus ride to your ship and head back later on your own (by train, using this book's instructions).

I'd prefer to spend a full day in Gdańsk, but excursions often tack on visits to other locations outside town. These may include (in order of worthiness):

Sopot: A relaxing beach resort, this town's location halfway between Gdynia and Gdańsk makes it an easy add-on.

Malbork Castle: The fearsome Teutonic Knights built this sprawling castle as their headquarters. Though impressive, it's farther from town than other sights, and the expansive complex takes time to fully see.

Stutthof Concentration Camp: This Nazi concentration camp memorial offers a poignant look at this region's troubled 20th century.

Oliwa Cathedral: This red-brick church is far from unique in this region, but its impressive organ (with animated figures that move when it plays) is a crowd-pleaser.

Gdynia: The workaday port city where you dock offers little of sightseeing interest.

(guh-DIN-yah), don't waste your time there—make a beeline to the main attraction, Gdańsk (and with extra time, consider a quick visit to Sopot).

Planning Your Time

Minimize your time in Gdynia and max out in Gdańsk. The best plan is to spend the morning in Gdańsk's Main Town and along the embankment, and the afternoon at the Solidarity shipyard. (From the shipyard, it's easy to get to the train station; for efficiency, wrap up your Main Town activities before heading to Solidarity.)

• **Gdańsk Main Town:** Follow my self-guided walking tour of the picturesque old core and embankment (allow 30 minutes without stops, or 1.5 hours to linger and enjoy).

• **Main Town Sights:** Peruse this book's listings and choose the sights that appeal to you most; these include **St. Mary's Church, Amber Museum, Uphagen House, Main Town Hall, Artus Court,** and **Central Maritime Museum** (allow about 30 minutes apiece for a quick stop, more for an in-depth visit).

• **Walking to the Solidarity Shipyard:** My self-guided walk brings meaning to this 20-minute stroll.

• **Touring the Solidarity Shipyard and "Roads to Freedom" exhibit:** Allow about 1.5-2 hours for this entire area.

In addition to the sights in Gdańsk, if you have time to kill on your way back to Gdynia, you could hop off the train in **Sopot** and stroll down the manicured main drag to the pleasure pier and beach. Allow at least 15 minutes to walk between Sopot's station and its beachfront, plus up to 15 minutes waiting for the train to Gdynia, plus however much time you want to linger at the beach.

When planning your day, be sure to allow plenty of time to make it from your ship in Gdynia to your point of interest in Gdańsk. For example: 5-10 minutes for the shuttle from your ship into Gdynia, then 15 minutes walking to the Gdynia train station, then 35 minutes for the train ride into Gdańsk (plus whatever time you need to wait for your train—up to 15 minutes), then 15-20 minutes walking from Gdańsk's main train station to the Main Town. Rounding up, plan roughly 1.5 hours each way.

Arrival at the Port of Gdynia

Arrival at a Glance: Ride the shuttle bus into Gdynia's town center (to avoid the dreary walk through industrial ports), then walk 15 minutes to the train station for the 35-minute ride into Gdańsk; from Gdańsk's train station, it's about a 15-minute walk into the heart of the Main Town.

Port Overview

Because Gdańsk's port is relatively shallow, the biggest cruise ships must put in at Gdynia...leaving confused tourists to poke around town looking for some medieval quaintness, before coming to their senses and heading for Gdańsk.

Gdynia is less historic (and less attractive) than Gdańsk or Sopot, as it was mostly built in the 1920s to be Poland's main harbor after Gdańsk became a "free city" (see "Gdańsk History" sidebar, later). Today, Gdynia is a major business center, and—thanks to its youthful, progressive city government—has edged ahead of the rest of Poland in transitioning from communism.

Like an Eastern Bloc bodybuilder, Gdynia's port area is muscular and hairy. Cruise ships are shuffled among hardworking industrial piers that make the area feel uninviting. Among northern European cruise ports, Gdynia is the least user-friendly for arriving passengers, with few amenities (such as ATMs) available in the immediate port area. Each of the sprawling port's many

GDAŃSK

Gdynia/Gdańsk Area

To Karlskrona, Sweden

Władysławowo

Jastarnia

To Szczecin & Berlin Jurata

Hel Peninsula

Hel

Gdynia

Sopot

Oliwa

TRI-CITY

WESTERPLATTE

Gdańsk

Pruszcz Gdański

Motława River

Vistula River

E-75

Tczew

E-77

Malbork

To Poznań & Berlin

Starogard Gdański

To Toruń & Warsaw

Baltic Sea

Baltijsk RUSSIA (Kaliningrad)

A-194

Wiślany Lagoon

To Kaliningrad & Vilnius, Lithuania

Braniewo

POLAND

Elbląg

Orneta

Pasłęk

E-77

To Warsaw

20 Kilometers

20 Miles

piers is named for a country or region. Three are used for cruises: **Nabrzeże Francuskie** (French Quay), where most large ships dock; **Nabrzeże Stanów Zjednoczonych** (United States Quay), farther out, a secondary option for large ships; and convenient **Nabrzeże Pomorskie** (Pomeranian Quay, part of the Southern Pier), used by small ships and located alongside Gdynia's one "fun" pier, with museums and pleasure craft. Port information: www .port.gdynia.pl.

Money Matters: Gdynia has the only cruise port area I've seen with no ATMs or money-exchange options at or near the cruise-ship berths. This makes the public-transportation options (which generally don't accept euros or dollars) unworkable, unless you happen to have złotys handy when you step off the ship. If your ship offers on-board currency conversion, consider it. But if you're riding the shuttle into downtown Gdynia (the easiest option), you'll find that ATMs are plentiful there, so you might as well wait. Taxi drivers generally take euros, though their off-the-cuff exchange rate may not be favorable.

The best place to find an **ATM** is along Skwer Kościuski, where the shuttle drops you off. Several banks line this square.

Tourist Information: There's no TI directly at the port, but TI representatives meet arriving cruise ships to hand out maps and answer questions. As you disembark, look for helpers sporting orange shirts, blue jackets, and backpacks. In Gdynia, the TI is on the main drag between the shuttle-bus drop-off and the train station (Mon-Fri 9:00-18:00, Sat-Sun 9:00-16:00, closes one hour earlier and closed Sun off-season, on the right at 24 ulica 10 Lutego, tel. 58-622-3766). In Gdańsk, the TI has handy offices at the train station and in the Main Town (see page 504).

Sights in Gdynia: Most of the city's sightseeing is along its waterfront. Directly toward the water from the shuttle-bus drop-off (through the park) is the **Southern Pier** (Molo Południowe). This concrete slab—nowhere near as charming as Sopot's wooden-boardwalk version—features a modern shopping mall and a smattering of sights, including an aquarium and a pair of permanently moored museum boats. If you have time to kill in Gdynia before returning to your ship, spend it here. Plans are afoot to convert the big warehouse at the Nabrzeże Francuskie pier into an **emigration museum,** possibly as early as 2014; if and when this opens, it will offer a handy sightseeing opportunity for cruisers arriving here.

Alternate Port Near Gdańsk: A few small ships may dock at **Nabrzeże Oliwskie** (Oliwa Quay) at Gdańsk's New Port (Nowy Port), about four miles north of downtown. Used infrequently, this port has few services for cruisers, although TI representatives do meet arriving ships. Trams and buses connect this port to downtown Gdańsk, but because the port area has no ATM, these do you little good. If your cruise line offers a shuttle bus, take it; from the drop-off point, just walk over the two bridges to reach the center of the Main Town. An honest taxi should charge about 40-50 zł for the ride into town.

Getting to Gdańsk

These instructions assume that you're arriving in Gdynia and plan to head directly to Gdańsk (which you should). While taxis are fast, they're pricey, and the public-transportation option is cheap and doable.

By Taxi

Taxi drivers line up to meet arriving cruise ships. While I've listed the legitimate fare estimates below, many cabbies try to charge far more. Try asking several drivers until you get a quote that resembles my figures, and be sure they use the meter. Remember, taxi drivers generally accept (and give quotes in) euros—though if you have Polish złotys, they'll take those too.

To Gdynia's train station (*Dworzec*, DVOH-zhets): 20 zł (about €5)

To Gdańsk's Main Town: 125 zł (about €30)

To Sopot (beach resort between Gdynia and Gdańsk): 60-80 zł (about €15-20)

Many of the taxis that line up at the ship are looking for the long fare into Gdańsk and may not be willing to take you on the shorter trip to the Gdynia train station. If that's the case, walk out the port gate and look for a taxi there—but be warned that the outside-the-port cabbies are probably unregulated and more likely to overcharge.

By Public Transportation

The basic plan: From the **Nabrzeże Francuskie** or **Nabrzeże Stanów Zjednoczonych** piers, ride the shuttle bus (or public bus) into downtown Gdynia, walk up to the train station, ride the train to Gdańsk, then walk into Gdańsk's historic Main Town. The step-by-step details are outlined below (it sounds more complicated than it is).

If you're fortunate enough to arrive at the **Nabrzeże Pomorskie** pier, you can simply walk straight up (away from the waterfront) about 10 minutes to reach Skwer Kościuski, then skip to step 2.

From anywhere in town, you can take a **taxi** to Gdynia's main train station (Dworzec Główna), and skip to step 3.

Step 1. From the Port to Downtown Gdynia (Skwer Kościuski)

The easiest option is to take your cruise line's **shuttle bus** into downtown (5-minute trip; given the size, gloominess, and user-unfriendliness of Gdynia's port, I'd skip walking and take the shuttle bus, even if you have to pay). The shuttle drops you off at Skwer Kościuski, in the heart of downtown Gdynia. (From here, look toward the waterfront, at the far end of the long park. You'll see a broad pier lined with museums and other attractions, with a beach next to it—a handy place to kill a little time on the way back to your ship.)

If you don't want to spring for your cruise line's shuttle bus, you could take a **public bus** to the train station (skipping step 2, next page). Unfortunately, drivers only accept złotys, and there's no ATM at the port—so this option works only if you change money on board your ship or happen to have złotys. From just outside the Nabrzeże Francuskie port gate, catch bus #119 (2-3/hour), #137 (2-3/hour), or #147 (sparse frequency). Bus #119 and bus #147 also stop just outside the Nabrzeże Stanów Zjednoczonych port gate.

The very long, dull **walk**—though not advisable—is possible in a pinch. From the nearer Nabrzeże Francuskie, it takes about 20-30 minutes at a fast pace: Walk straight out of the port gate, bear left (past the bus stop), and continue with the industrial cranes on your right (following sporadic *City* arrow signs). At the round-about, turn right and work your way straight into town; the road passes through industrial zones, wooded areas, residential neigh-borhoods, and over train tracks. (When the main road veers to the left to climb onto an overpass, continue straight on the low road.) You'll suddenly pop out in a downtown-feeling area on the street called Portowa; after a few blocks, this becomes Świętojańska, the city's main drag. Soon you'll hit the tree-lined boulevard called Skwer Kościuski (near the cruise-line shuttle bus stop—see next); turn right and head up ulica 10 Lutego to the train station, as described in step 2.

If you arrive at the even more distant Nabrzeże Stanów Zjednoczonych pier, the walk downtown will take up to 45 min-utes. From the port gate, walk straight ahead to the roundabout, and continue straight along the same road as it bends left along the train tracks. Continue to the next big roundabout, where you'll cross the street, bear left, and walk along the road with the train tracks on your right. This will take you (after a long walk) to the roundabout described above. Turn right and continue into town to reach Skwer Kościuski.

Step 2. From Skwer Kościuski to Gdynia Main Train Station

From the shuttle-bus stop at Skwer Kościuski, it's about a 15-minute **walk** to the train station: Head up the broad, parklike boulevard, going away from the water (if you need cash, you'll spot several ATMs in this part of town). At the top of the square, the street becomes ulica 10 Lutego and continues straight (very grad-ually uphill)—follow it. A few short blocks later, watch for the Gdynia TI on the right (see "Tourist Information" on page 504). Just beyond that, the street curves to the right; once you're around the corner, use the crosswalk to reach the train station (marked *Dworzec Podmiejski*).

Step 3. From Gdynia Main Train Station to Gdańsk Main Train Station

Gdynia's main train station (Gdynia Główna) has an ATM just outside the station's front door; inside are lockers, WCs, and snack stands.

The station is best connected to Gdańsk, Sopot, and other towns by yellow-and-blue regional commuter trains (*kolejka*, oper-ated by SKM). These **SKM trains** go in each direction about every 10-15 minutes (less often after 19:30), and make several stops en route to Gdańsk (35 minutes, 5.40 zł), including the resort town of Sopot (15 minutes, 3.60 zł).

As you enter the Gdynia train station, look to the right to

see the **ticket office** *(kasa biletowa)*, where you can buy a ticket for Gdańsk. These tickets must be stamped in the easy-to-miss yellow slots at the bottom of the stairs leading up to the tracks (you're likely to be fined if you don't validate your ticket). You can also buy tickets at the **automated ticket machine** marked *SKM Bilety* (near the head of platform 4, with English instructions); these tickets do not need to be validated. Climb the stairs to platform 1; Gdańsk-bound trains leave from the side of the platform facing away from the city center and sea (labeled *tor 502*; look for *Gdańsk* on the list of stops).

Know Your Stop: Each city has multiple stops. In Gdańsk, use Gdańsk Główny (the main station)—don't just hop off at the first stop with "Gdańsk" in the name. To visit Sopot, use the stop called simply Sopot (only one word). When returning to Gdynia, your stop is Gdynia Główna (the main station).

PKP Trains: Gdynia's main train station is also served by long-distance PKP trains, operated by the national railway. These are faster but less frequent than SKM commuter trains—unless one is leaving at a convenient time, stick with the easy SKM trains. Tickets for one system can't be used on the other. Trains for the two systems chug along on the same tracks, but use different (but nearby) platforms/stations (at Gdańsk's main train station, national PKP trains use platforms 1-3, while regional SKM trains use platforms 3-5; in Sopot, the SKM station is a few hundred feet before the PKP station).

Step 4. From Gdańsk Main Train Station to the Main Town

Gdańsk's main train station (Gdańsk Główny) is a pretty brick palace on the western edge of the old center. SKM trains arriving from Gdynia use the shorter tracks 3-5.

Inside the terminal building, you'll find lockers, ATMs, and ticket windows. Outside, the pedestrian underpass by the McDonald's has a helpful TI, and leads you beneath the busy road (go down the stairs and turn right; first set of exits: tram stop; end of corridor: Old Town). To reach the heart of the Main Town, it's easiest to take a **taxi** (which shouldn't cost more than 15 zł to any point in the city center). Or you can ride the **tram** (buy tickets—*bilety*—at the *RUCH* kiosk by track 4 or at any window marked *Bilety ZKM* in the pedestrian underpass; access tram stop via underpass, then board tram #2, #3, #6, #8, or #11 going to the right with your back to the station; go just one stop to Brama Wyżynna, in front of the LOT airlines office). For more on trams, see page 505. But by the time you buy your ticket and wait for the tram, you might as well **walk** the 15 minutes to the same place (go through underpass, exit to the right, circle around the right side of Cinema City, and follow the busy road until you reach the LOT airlines office, then head left toward the brick towers).

Once in town, follow my first self-guided walk (on page 505).

By Tour

Few good tour options exist in Gdynia. I'd hightail it into Gdańsk, where you'll find the options described under "Tours in Gdańsk," page 505.

Returning to Your Ship

Taxis run passengers back to the ship for similar rates as those listed on page 505.

To take the train back to Gdynia, return to the Gdańsk main train station (figure about 15-20 minutes from the Main Town, or a little less from the shipyard area). Before boarding the train, buy tickets at any ticket window or automated machine marked *SKM*. If you buy the ticket from a kiosk (rather than a machine), be sure to stamp it in the yellow box for validation. Then take any blue-and-yellow SKM train heading for Gdynia. If you have lots of time to spare before your ship leaves, consider hopping out at Sopot for a stroll down to the waterfront. In Gdynia, get off at the stop called **Gdynia Główna** (the main station). Exiting the station, simply head down toward the water on ulica 10 Lutego, and find your cruise shuttle-bus stop in the middle of Skwer Kościuski.

See page 540 for help if you miss your boat.

GDAŃSK

Orientation to Gdańsk

Gdańsk, with 460,000 residents, is part of the larger urban area known as the Tri-City (Trójmiasto, total population of 1 million). But the tourist's Gdańsk is compact, welcoming, and walkable—virtually anything you'll want to see is within a 20-minute stroll of everything else.

Focus on the Main Town (Główne Miasto), home to most of the sights described, including the spectacular Royal Way main drag, ulica Długa. The Old Town (Stare Miasto) has a handful of old brick buildings and faded, tall, skinny houses—but the area is mostly drab and residential, and not worth much time. Just beyond the northern end of the Old Town (about a 20-minute walk from

the heart of the Main Town) is the entrance to the Gdańsk Shipyard, with the excellent Solidarity museum. From here, shipyards sprawl for miles.

The second language in this part of Poland is German, not English. As this was a predominantly German city until the end of World War II, German tourists flock here in droves. But you'll win no Polish friends if you call the city by its more familiar German name, Danzig.

Tourist Information

Gdańsk has two different TIs. The far better, local TI has three locations: at the bottom (river) end of the main drag, at **Długi Targ 28/29** (just to the left as you face the gate; April-Sept daily 9:00-19:00; Oct-March Mon-Sat 9:00-17:00, Sun 9:00-16:00; tel. 58-301-4355, www.gdansk4u.pl); in the underpass at the **main train station** (Mon-Sat 9:00-17:00, Sun 9:00-16:00, tel. 58-721-3277); and at the **airport** (same hours as train station TI, tel. 58-348-1368). Pick up the free map and brochure, and browse through the other brochures and guidebooks. In a pinch, you can also grab some brochures at the other TI, which is sloppily run by the national government and owns a prominent location in a red, high-gabled building across **ulica Długa** from the Town Hall (May-Sept Mon-Fri 9:00-18:00, Sat-Sun 10:00-18:00, until 20:00 during busy times; Oct-April Mon-Fri 9:00-18:00, Sat-Sun 9:00-16:30; ulica Długa 45, tel. 58-301-9151, www.pttk-gdansk.pl).

Sightseeing Card: Busy sightseers should consider the **Tourist Card,** which includes entry to 24 sights in Gdańsk, Gdynia, and Sopot, and discounts at others. Check the list of what's covered (most of the biggies in town are free with the card, while the Solidarity museum is 50 percent off), and do the arithmetic. If you'll be seeing several included museums, this card could save you some money ("standard" card: 22 zł/24 hours, 35 zł/72 hours; "max" card also includes local public transit: 45 zł/24 hours, 75 zł/72 hours; sold at TIs).

Helpful Hints

Blue Monday: Off-season, most of Gdańsk's museums are closed Monday. In the busy summertime, the Gdańsk Historical Museum branches are open—and free—for limited hours on Monday. If museums are closed, Monday is a good day to visit churches or take a side-trip to Sopot.

Internet Access: You'll find several free Wi-Fi hotspots in major tourist zones around central Gdańsk.

Getting Around Gdańsk

Most of the recommended sights are within easy walking distance. Public transportation is generally unnecessary for sightseers spending their time in town.

By Public Transportation: Gdańsk's trams and buses work on the same tickets: Choose between a single-ride ticket (3 zł), one-hour ticket (3.60 zł), and 24-hour ticket (12 zł). Buy tickets *(bilety)* at kiosks marked *RUCH* or *Bilety ZKM,* or on board (1-hour and 24-hour tickets only sold on board). In the city center, the stops worth knowing about are Plac Solidarnośći (near the shipyards), Gdańsk Główny (in front of the main train station), and Brama Wyżynna (near the heart of the tourist zone, in front of the LOT airlines office). When buying tickets, don't confuse *ZKM* (the company that runs Gdańsk city transit) with *SKM* (the company that runs regional commuter trains to outlying destinations).

By Taxi: Taxis cost about 7 zł to start, then 2 zł per kilometer (or 3 zł at night). Find a taxi stand, or call a cab (try Super Hallo Taxi, tel. 191-91).

Tours in Gdańsk

Walking Tours—In peak season, the TI sometimes offers a pricey 2.5-hour English walking tour (80 zł/person, offered with demand in July-Aug only, no set schedule—ask at TI).

Private Guide—Hiring your own local guide is an exceptional value. **Agnieszka Syroka** is bubbly and personable (400 zł for up to 4 hours, more for all day, mobile 502-554-584, www.tourguide gdansk.com, asyroka@interia.pl or syroka.agnieszka@gmail.com).

Self-Guided Walks in Gdańsk

These two tours show you complementary sides of Gdansk: its sumptuously decorated, time-capsule main drag, and a more modern zone leading from the tourist core to the shipyard where the Solidarity protests took place.

▲▲▲Gdańsk's Royal Way

In the 16th and 17th centuries, Gdańsk was Poland's wealthiest city, with gorgeous architecture (much of it in the Flemish Mannerist style) rivaling that found in the two historic capitals, Kraków and Warsaw. During this Golden Age, Polish kings would visit this city of well-to-do Hanseatic League merchants,

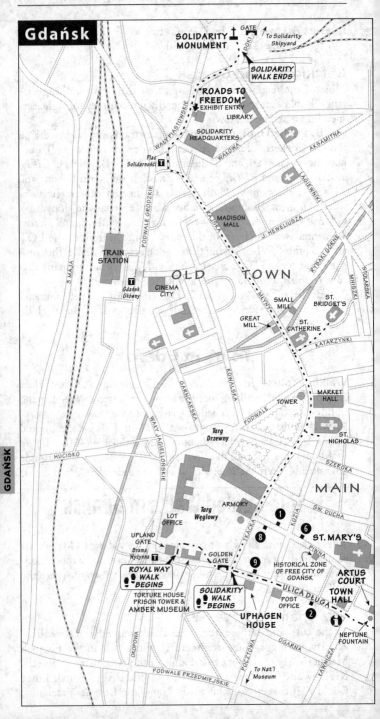

Gdańsk

SOLIDARITY MONUMENT
↑ To Solidarity Shipyard
GATE

SOLIDARITY WALK ENDS

"ROADS TO FREEDOM"
EXHIBIT ENTRY
LIBRARY

SOLIDARITY HEADQUARTERS

WAŁY PIASTOWSKIE
WAŁOWA
AKSAMITNA

Plac Solidarności ⊤

PODWALE GRODZKIE

MADISON MALL

RAJSKA
ŁAGIEWNIKI
J. HEWELIUSZA
RYBAKI GÓRNE
STOLARSKA
MNISZKI

TRAIN STATION

OLD   TOWN

Gdańsk Główny ⊤

CINEMA CITY

SMALL MILL

ST. BRIDGET'S

GREAT MILL

ST. CATHERINE

KATARZYNKI

5 MAJA

GARNCARSKA

KOWALSKA

MŁYNY

MARKET HALL

WAŁY JAGIELLOŃSKIE

PODWALE

TOWER

Targ Drzewny

ST. NICHOLAS

HUCISKO

SZEROKA

MAIN

ARMORY

Targ Węglowy

LOT OFFICE

1

KUŹNIA

SW. DUCHA

8

6

ST. MARY'S

UPLAND GATE
Brama Wyżyna ⊤

GOLDEN GATE

9

PIWNA

HISTORICAL ZONE OF FREE CITY OF GDAŃSK

ARTUS COURT

TOWN HALL

ROYAL WAY WALK BEGINS

TORTURE HOUSE, PRISON TOWER & AMBER MUSEUM

SOLIDARITY WALK BEGINS

UPHAGEN HOUSE

ULICA DŁUGA

POST OFFICE

2

i

NEPTUNE FOUNTAIN

OKOPOWA

POCZTOWA

OGARNA

ŁAWNICZA

PODWALE PRZEDMIEJSKIE

To Nat'l Museum

TKACKA

GDAŃSK

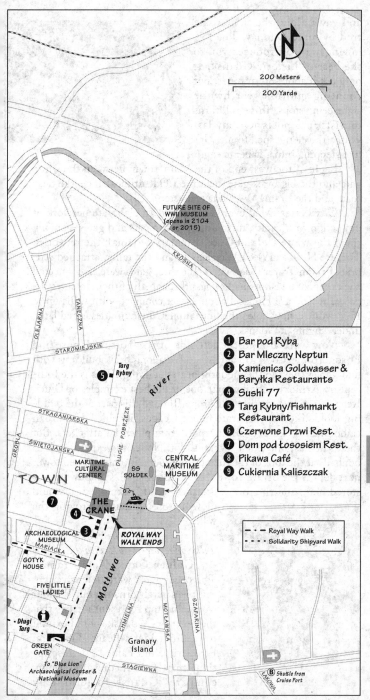

N

200 Meters

200 Yards

FUTURE SITE OF
WWII MUSEUM
(opens in 2104
or 2015)

KROSNA

STAROMIEJSKIE

OLEJARNA

TANECZNA

River

Targ
Rybny

STRAGANIARSKA

DLUGIE POBRZEZE

GROBLA

ŚWIĘTOJAŃSKA

MARITIME
CULTURAL
CENTER

SS
SOLDEK

CENTRAL
MARITIME
MUSEUM

T O W N

THE
CRANE

ROYAL WAY
WALK ENDS

ARCHAEOLOGICAL
MUSEUM

MARIACKA

GOTYK
HOUSE

FIVE LITTLE
LADIES

Długi
Targ

GREEN
GATE

To "Blue Lion"
Archaeological Center &
National Museum

Motlawa

Granary Island

CHMIELNA

MOTLAWSKA

SZAFARINA

STAGIEWNA

ŁAKOWA

B Shuttle from
Cruise Port

1. Bar pod Rybą
2. Bar Mleczny Neptun
3. Kamienica Goldwasser &
   Baryłka Restaurants
4. Sushi 77
5. Targ Rybny/Fishmarkt
   Restaurant
6. Czerwone Drzwi Rest.
7. Dom pod Łososiem Rest.
8. Pikawa Café
9. Cukiernia Kaliszczak

—・—・— Royal Way Walk
・・・・・・・ Solidarity Shipyard Walk

GDAŃSK

and gawk along the same route trod by tourists today. The following walk introduces you to the best of historic Gdańsk. It only takes about 30 minutes, not counting multiple worthwhile sightseeing stops. This stroll turns tourists into poets. On my last visit, a traveler gasped to me, "It's like stepping into a Fabergé egg."

Begin at the west end of the Main Town, between the white gate and the big brick gate (near the LOT airlines office, the busy road, and the Brama Wyżynna tram stop).

City Gates: Medieval Gdańsk had an elaborate network of protection for the city, including several moats and gates—among them the white **Upland Gate** (Brama Wyżynna); the red-brick **Torture House** (Wieża Więzienna); and the taller, attached red-brick **Prison Tower** (Katownia). The three gates were all connected back then, and visitors had to pass through all of them to enter the city. The Torture House/Prison Tower complex, with walls up to 15 feet thick, now holds the fine **Amber Museum** (described later, under "Sights in Gdańsk").

Now walk around the left side of the Torture House and Prison Tower. Look to your left to see a long brick building with four gables (next to the modern theater building). This is the 16th-century **Armory** (Zbrojownia), one of the best examples of Dutch Renaissance architecture in Europe. Though this part of the building looks like four separate house facades, it's a kind of urban camouflage to hide its real purpose from potential attackers. But there's at least one clue to what it's for: Notice the exploding cannonballs at the tops of the turrets. The round, pointy-topped tower next door is the **Straw Tower** (Baszta Słomiana). Gunpowder was stored here, and the roof was straw—so if it exploded, it would blow its top without destroying the walls.

• *Continue around the brick buildings until you're face-to-face with the...*

Golden Gate (Złota Brama): The other gates were defensive, but this one's purely ornamental. The four women up top represent virtues that the people of Gdańsk should exhibit toward outsiders: Peace, Freedom, Prosperity, and Fame. The inscription, a psalm in medieval German, compares Gdańsk to Jerusalem:

famous and important. In the middle is one of the coats of arms of Gdańsk—two white crosses under a crown on a red shield. We'll see this symbol many times today.

• Now go through the gate, entering the "Long Street"...

Ulica Długa: Look back at the gate you just came through. The women on top of this side represent virtues the people of Gdańsk should cultivate in themselves: Wisdom, Piety, Justice, and Concord (if an arrow's broken, let's take it out of the quiver and fix it).

Wander this intoxicating promenade. Gdańsk was cosmopolitan and exceptionally tolerant in the Middle Ages, attracting a wide range of people, including many who were persecuted elsewhere: Jews, Scots, Dutch, Flemish, Italians, Germans, and more. Members of each group brought with them strands of their culture, which they wove into the tapestry of this city—demonstrated by the eclectic homes along this street.

This lovely street wasn't always so lively and carefree. At the end of World War II, ulica Długa was in ruins. The city was badly damaged when the Nazis first invaded, but the worst devastation came when the Soviets arrived. This was the first traditionally German city that the Red Army reached on their march toward Berlin—and the soldiers were set loose to level the place in retaliation for all the pain the Nazis had caused. (Soviets didn't destroy nearby Gdynia—which they considered Polish, not German.) Soviet officers turned a blind eye as their soldiers raped and brutalized residents. An entire order of horrified nuns committed suicide by throwing themselves into the river. Upwards of 80 percent of this area was destroyed. It was only thanks to detailed drawings and photographs that these buildings could be so carefully reconstructed, mostly using the original brick.

During Gdańsk's Golden Age, these houses were taxed based on frontage (like the homes lining Amsterdam's canals)—so they were built skinny and deep. The widest houses belonged to the super-elite. Different as they are from the outside, every house had the same general plan inside. Each had three parts, starting with the front and moving back: First was a fancy drawing room, to show off for visitors. Then came a narrow corridor to the back rooms—often along the side of an inner courtyard. Because the houses had only a few windows facing the outer street, this courtyard provided much-needed sunlight to the rest of the house. The residential quarters were in the back, where the family actually lived: bedroom, kitchen, office. To see the interior of one of these homes, pay a visit to the very interesting **Uphagen House** (#12, on the right, a block and a half in front of the Golden Gate; described later, under "Sights in Gdańsk").

Across the street and a little farther down are some of the

GDAŃSK

Gdańsk History

Visitors to Gdańsk are surprised at how "un-Polish" the city's history is. In this cultural melting pot of German, Dutch, and Flemish merchants (with a smattering of Italians and Scots), Poles were only a small part of the picture until the city became exclusively Polish after World War II. However, in Gdańsk, cultural backgrounds traditionally took a back seat to the bottom line. Wealthy Gdańsk was always known for its economic pragmatism—no matter who was in charge, merchants here made money.

Gdańsk is Poland's gateway to the waters of Europe—where its main river (the Vistula) meets the Baltic Sea. The town was first mentioned in the 10th century, and was seized in 1308 by the Teutonic Knights (who called it "Danzig"). The Knights encouraged other Germans to settle on the Baltic coast, and gradually turned Gdańsk into a wealthy city. In 1361, Gdańsk joined the Hanseatic League, a trade federation of mostly Germanic merchant towns that provided mutual security. By the 15th century, Gdańsk was a leading member of this mighty network, which virtually dominated trade in northern Europe (and also included Toruń, Kraków, Lübeck, Hamburg, Bremen, Bruges, Bergen, Tallinn, Novgorod, and nearly a hundred other cities).

In 1454, the people of Gdańsk rose up against the Teutonic Knights, burning down their castle and forcing them out of the city. Three years later, the Polish king borrowed money from wealthy Gdańsk families to hire Czech mercenaries to take the Teutonic Knights' main castle, Malbork. In exchange, the Gdańsk merchants were granted special privileges, including exclusive export rights. Gdańsk now acted as a middleman for much of the trade passing through Polish lands, but paid only a modest annual tribute to the Polish king.

The 16th and 17th centuries were Gdańsk's Golden Age. Now a part of the Polish kingdom, the city had access to an enormous hinterland of natural resources to export—yet it maintained a privileged, semi-independent status. Like Amsterdam, Gdańsk became a tolerant, progressive, and booming merchant

most striking **facades** along ulica Długa. The blue-and-white house with the three giant heads is from the 19th century, when the hot style was eclecticism—borrowing bits and pieces from various architectural eras. This was one of the few houses on the street that survived World War II.

At the next corner on the right is the huge, blocky, red **post office,** which doesn't quite

city. Its mostly Germanic and Dutch burghers imported Dutch, Flemish, and Italian architects to give their homes an appropriately Hanseatic flourish. At a time of religious upheaval in the rest of Europe, Gdańsk became known for its tolerance—a place that opened its doors to all visitors (many Mennonites and Scottish religious refugees emigrated here). It was also a haven for great thinkers, including philosopher Arthur Schopenhauer and scientist Daniel Fahrenheit (who invented the mercury thermometer).

Gdańsk declined, along with the rest of Poland, in the late 18th century, and became a part of Prussia (today's northern Germany) during the Partitions. But the people of Gdańsk—even those of German heritage—had always taken pride in their independence, and weren't enthusiastic about being ruled from Berlin. After World War I, in a unique compromise to appease its complex ethnic makeup, Gdańsk did not fall under German or Polish control, but once again became an independent city-state: the Free City of Danzig (populated by 400,000 ethnic Germans and only 15,000 Poles). The city, along with the so-called Polish Corridor connecting it to Polish lands, effectively cut off Germany from its northeastern territory. On September 1, 1939, Adolf Hitler started World War II when he invaded Gdańsk in order to bring it back into the German fold. Nearly 80 percent of the city was destroyed in the war.

After World War II, Gdańsk officially became part of Poland, and was painstakingly reconstructed (mostly replicating the buildings of its Golden Age). In 1970, and again in 1980, the shipyard of Gdańsk witnessed strikes and demonstrations that would lead to the fall of European communism. Poland's great anti-communist hero and first post-communist president—Lech Wałęsa—is Gdańsk's most famous resident, and still lives here.

A city with a recent past that's both tragic and uplifting, Gdańsk celebrated its 1,000th birthday in 1997. This occasion, and preparations for the Euro Cup 2012 soccer matches, kicked off a wave of renovation and refurbishment that has the gables of the atmospheric Hanseatic quarter gleaming once again.

GDAŃSK

fit with the skinny facades lining the rest of the street. But step inside. With doves fluttering under an airy glass atrium, the interior's a class act. (To mail postcards, take a number—category C—from the machine on the left.)

Across the street and a few doors down from the post office, notice the colorful **scenes** just overhead on the facade of the cocktail bar. These are slices of life from 17th-century Gdańsk: drinking, talking, buying, fighting, playing music. The ship is a *koga*, a typical symbol of Gdańsk.

A couple of doors down from the cocktail bar is **Neptun Cinema** (marked *KINO*). In the 1980s, this was the only movie theater in the city, and locals lined up all the way down the street to get in. Adults remember coming here with their grandparents to see a full day of cartoons. Now, as with traditional main-street cinemas in the US, this one is threatened by the rising popularity of multiplexes outside the town center.

Across the street from the theater are three houses belonging to the very influential medieval **Ferber family,** which produced many burghers, mayors, and even a bishop. On the house with the little dog over the door (#29), look for the heads in the circles. These are Caesars of Rome. At the top of the building is Mr. Ferber's answer to the constant question, "Why build such an elaborate house?"—*PRO INVIDIA,* "For the sake of envy."

A few doors down, notice the outdoor tables for Gdańsk's most popular milk bar, the recommended **Bar Mleczny Neptun.** Now you're just a few steps from the **Main Town Hall** (Ratusz Głównego Miasta). Consider climbing its observation tower and visiting its superb interior, which features ornately decorated meeting rooms for the city council (described later, under "Sights in Gdańsk"). The **TI** is across the street, on the right.

• *Just beyond the Main Town Hall, ulica Długa widens and becomes...*

Długi Targ (Long Square): The centerpiece of this square is one of Gdańsk's most important landmarks, the statue of **Neptune**—god of the sea. He's a fitting symbol for a city that dominates the maritime life of Poland. Behind him is another fine museum, the **Artus Court** (described later, under "Sights in Gdańsk"). This meeting hall for various Gdańsk brotherhoods is home to the most impressive stove you've ever seen.

As you continue down Długi targ, notice the **balconies** extending out into the square, with access to cellars underneath. These were a common feature on ulica Długa in Gdańsk's Golden Age, but were removed in the 19th century to make way for a new tram system. You can find more balconies like these on Mariacka street, which runs parallel to this one (2 blocks to the left).

• *At the end of Długi targ is the...*

Green Gate (Zielona Brama): This huge gate was actually built as a residence for visiting kings...who usually preferred to stay back by Neptune instead (maybe because the river, just on the other side of this gate, stank). It might not have been good enough for kings and queens, but it's plenty fine for a former president—Lech Wałęsa's office is upstairs (see the plaque, *Biuro Lecha Wałęsy*).

Other parts of the building are used for temporary exhibitions.

Notice that these bricks are much smaller than the ones we've seen earlier on this walk, which were locally made. These, however, are Dutch: Boats from Holland would come here empty of cargo but with a load of bricks for ballast. Traders filled their ships with goods for the return trip, leaving the bricks behind to be turned into this gate.

• *Now go through the gate, and turn left along the...*

Riverfront Embankment: The Motława River—actually a side channel of the mighty Vistula—was the source of Gdańsk's phenomenal Golden Age wealth. This embankment was jam-packed in its heyday, the 14th and 15th centuries. It was so crowded with boats that you would hardly have been able to see the water, and boats had to pay a time-based tax for tying up to a post. Instead of an actual embankment (which was built later), a series of wooden piers connected the boats directly to the gates of the city. Now it's a popular place to stroll and to buy amber. Keep an eye out for old-fashioned **galleons** plying the waters here—these boats depart hourly for a fun cruise to Westerplatte and back. While kitschy, the galleons are a fun way to get out on the water.

Across the river is **Granary Island** (Spichrze), where grain was stored until it could be taken away by ships. Before World War II, there were some 400 granaries here; today the island is still in ruins. Three granaries that have been reconstructed on the next island up house exhibits for the Central Maritime Museum (described later, under "Sights in Gdańsk"); two others are now hotels. A big international company has bought this island, and plans to develop the prime real estate into a new city-center zone of shops, restaurants, houses, and hotels.

Continue along the embankment until you see the five big, round stones on your left. These are the **five little ladies**—mysterious ancient sculptures. If you look closely, you can make out their features, especially the chubby one on the end.

In the next block, the huge red-brick fort houses the **Archaeological Museum** and a tower you can climb for a good view (described later, under "Sights in Gdańsk"). The gate in the middle of the building leads to **Mariacka street,** a calm, atmospheric drag lined with old balconies, amber shops, and imaginative gargoyles (which locals call "pukers" when it rains).

Consider taking a few minutes to window-shop your way up Mariacka street, comparison-pricing amber souvenirs. At the end of the street on the left (at #1), the **Gotyk House** hotel has a characteristic little shop in the cellar that sells heavenly ginger-bread from the town of Toruń. As that city was the hometown of Nicholas Copernicus—and Copernicus' former lover supposedly once lived in this very house—the shop also has a fondly presented mini-museum dedicated to the couple. Just after Gotyk House and the gingerbread shop, you're face-to-face with **St. Mary's Church** (enter around the far side; described later, under "Sights in Gdańsk").

• *Back on the embankment, head past a few tempting eateries (including the recommended Kamienica Goldwasser and Sushi 77) before running right into Gdańsk's number-one symbol, and our last stop...*

The Crane (Żuraw): This monstrous 15th-century crane was once used for loading ships, picking up small crafts for repairs,

 and hoisting masts...beginning a ship-building tradition that continued to the days of Lech Wałęsa. The crane mechanism was operated by several hardworking sailors scrambling around in giant hamster wheels up top (you can see the wheels if you look up). The Crane belongs to the Central Maritime Museum, as does the modern building just beyond it (museum described under "Sights in Gdańsk," later). And along here, you might see a stand selling smoked fish.

• *Our orientation tour is over. Now get out there and enjoy Gdańsk... do it for Lech!*

From the Main Town to the Solidarity Shipyard

This lightly guided walk links Gdańsk's two most important sight-seeing areas. Along the way, we'll see some historic landmarks, tour two of Gdańsk's more interesting red-brick churches, and wander through the city's best shopping district. The stroll takes about 20 minutes, not counting stops for sightseeing and shopping.

Begin at the top of ulica Długa, with your back to the Golden Gate. Head a few steps down the street and take a left on Tkacka. After one long block, on the left, you can see the back of the **Armory** building (described earlier). This pearl of Renaissance architecture recently had a striking facelift—examine the exquisite decorations.

After three short blocks, detour to the right down Świętojańska and use the side door to enter the brick **St. Nicholas Church** (Kościół Św. Mikołaja, with the ornate towers on the ends). Archaeologists have found the bodies of 3,000 Napoleonic soldiers buried here. Near the end of World War II, when the Soviet army reached Gdańsk on its march westward, they were given the order to burn all the churches. Only this one—dedicated to Russia's patron saint—was spared. As the best-preserved church in town, it has a more impressive interior than the others, with lavish black-and-gold Baroque altars.

Backtrack out to the main street and continue north. Immediately after the church (on the right) is Gdańsk's renovated **Market Hall.** Look for the coat of arms of Gdańsk over each of its four doors (two white crosses on a red shield). Inside you'll find mostly local shoppers—browsing through produce, other foods, and clothing—as well as the graves of medieval Dominican monks, which were discovered in the basement when the building was refurbished. Look up to appreciate the delicate steel-and-glass canopy.

Across the street from the Market Hall is a round, red-brick **tower,** once part of the city's protective wall. This marks the end of the Main Town and the beginning of the Old Town.

Another long block up the street is the huge **St. Catherine's Church** (Kościół Św. Katarzyny, on the right). "Katy," as locals call it, is the oldest church in Gdańsk. In May of 2006, a carelessly discarded cigarette caused the church roof to burst into flames. Local people ran into the church and pulled everything outside, so nothing valuable was damaged; even the carillon bells were saved. However, the roof and wooden frame were totally destroyed. The people of Gdańsk were determined to rebuild this important symbol of the city. Within days of the fire, fund-raising concerts were held to scrape together most of the money needed to raise the roof once more.

The church hiding behind Katy—named for Catherine's daughter Bridget—has important ties to Solidarity, and is worth a quick detour. To get there, walk up ulica Katarzynki, along the side of St. Catherine's Church, and past the monument to Pope John Paul II.

St. Bridget's Church (Kościół Św. Brygidy) was the home church of Lech Wałęsa during the tense days of the 1980s. This church and its priest, Henryk Jankowski, were particularly aggressive in supporting the ideals of Solidarity. Jankowski became a mouthpiece for the movement, and Wałęsa named his youngest daughter Brygida in gratitude for the church's support. In the back corner, under the wall of wooden crosses, find the memorial to Solidarity martyr Jerzy Popiełuszko, a famously outspoken Warsaw priest who in 1984 was kidnapped, beaten, and murdered by the communist secret police. Notice that the figure's hands and feet are tied. At the front of the church, check out the enormous, unfinished altar made entirely of amber, featuring the Black Madonna of Częstochowa and a royal Polish eagle. If and when it's finished, it'll be 36 feet high, 20 feet wide, and 10 feet deep. But some locals criticize this ambitious project as an example of Father Jankowski's missteps. Despite his fame and contributions

Gdańsk at a Gdlance

▲▲▲**Ulica Długa** Gdańsk's colorful showpiece main drag, cutting a picturesque swath through the heart of the wealthy burghers' neighborhood. **Hours:** Always open. See page 509.

▲▲▲**Solidarity Sights and Gdańsk Shipyard** Home to the beginning of the end of European communism, housing a towering monument and an excellent museum. **Hours:** Memorial and shipyard gate—always open. "Roads to Freedom" exhibit—May-Sept Tue-Sun 10:00-18:00, Oct-April Tue-Sun 10:00-17:00, closed Mon year-round. See page 528.

▲▲**Main Town Hall** Ornately decorated meeting rooms, exhibits of town artifacts, and climbable tower with sweeping views. **Hours:** Mid-June-late Sept Mon 10:00-15:00, Tue-Sat 10:00-18:00, Sun 11:00-18:00; late Sept-mid-June Tue 10:00-15:00, Wed-Sat 10:00-16:00, Sun 11:00-16:00, closed Mon. See page 520.

▲▲**Artus Court** Grand meeting hall for guilds of Golden Age Gdańsk, boasting an over-the-top tiled stove. **Hours:** Mid-June-late Sept Mon 10:00-15:00, Tue-Sat 10:00-18:00, Sun 11:00-18:00; late Sept-mid-June Tue 10:00-15:00, Wed-Sat 10:00-16:00, Sun 11:00-16:00, closed Mon. See page 521.

▲▲**St. Mary's Church** Giant red-brick church crammed full of Gdańsk history. **Hours:** June-Sept Mon-Sat 9:00-18:30, Sun 13:00-18:30; closes progressively earlier off-season. See page 522.

to Solidarity, Jankowski's public standing took a nosedive near the end of his life—thanks to ego-driven projects like this, as well as accusations of anti-Semitism and implications of pedophilia and corruption. Forced to retire in 2007, Jankowski died in 2010.

Backtrack out past St. Catherine's Church to the main street. Just across from the church is a red-brick building with a lot of little windows in the roof. This is the **Great Mill** (Wielki Młyn), which has been converted into a shopping mall (daily 10:00-19:00). As you continue north and cross the stream, you'll also see the picturesque **Small Mill** (Mały Młyn) straddling the stream on your right.

After another block, on your right, is the modern **Madison shopping mall** (Mon-Sat 9:00-21:00, Sun 10:00-20:00). Two blocks to your left (up Heweliusza) are more shopping malls and the main train station.

▲**Amber Museum** High-tech new exhibit of valuable golden globs of petrified tree sap. **Hours:** Mid-June-late Sept Mon 10:00-15:00, Tue-Sat 10:00-18:00, Sun 11:00-18:00; late Sept-mid-June Tue 10:00-15:00, Wed-Sat 10:00-16:00, Sun 11:00-16:00, closed Mon. See page 518.

▲**Uphagen House** Tourable 18th-century interior, typical of the pretty houses that line ulica Długa. **Hours:** Mid-June-late Sept Mon 10:00-15:00, Tue-Sat 10:00-18:00, Sun 11:00-18:00; late Sept-mid-June Tue 10:00-15:00, Wed-Sat 10:00-16:00, Sun 11:00-16:00, closed Mon. See page 520.

▲**Central Maritime Museum** Sprawling exhibit on all aspects of the nautical life, housed in several venues (including the land-mark medieval Crane and a permanently moored steamship) connected by a ferry boat. **Hours:** July-Aug daily 10:00-18:00; Sept-Oct and March-June Tue-Sun 10:00-16:00, closed Mon; Nov-Feb Tue-Sun 10:00-15:00, closed Mon. See page 525.

Historical Zone of the Free City of Gdańsk Tiny museum examining Gdańsk's unique status as a "Free City" between the World Wars. **Hours:** May-Nov Tue-Sun 11:00-18:00, Dec-April Tue-Sun 13:00-17:00, closed Mon year-round. See page 524.

Archaeological Museum Decent collection of artifacts from this region's past. **Hours:** July-Aug Tue-Fri 9:00-17:00, Sat-Sun 10:00-17:00, closed Mon; Sept-June Tue and Thu-Fri 8:00-16:00, Wed 9:00-17:00, Sat-Sun 10:00-16:00, closed Mon. See page 524.

GDAŃSK

But to get to the **shipyard,** keep heading straight up Rajska. After another long block, jog right (between the big, green-glass skyscraper and today's Solidarity headquarters) and head for the three tall crosses.

On the way, you'll see signs leading to the **"Roads to Freedom" exhibit** (the entrance to this underground museum is actually a freestanding kiosk by the side of the road).

But before you visit this museum, head to the shipyard to begin my self-guided tour there (see page 531). Near the entrance to the museum are two artifacts from communist times. First, parked in front of the museum is an **armored personnel carrier,** just like the ones used by the ZOMO (riot police) to terrorize Polish citizens after martial law was declared in 1981. Nearby, watch for the two big chunks of **wall:** on the left, a piece of the Berlin Wall; and on the right, a chunk of the shipyard wall Lech

Wałęsa scaled to get inside and lead the strike. The message: What happened behind one wall eventually led to the fall of the other Wall.

For the whole story, continue to the monument with the three tall crosses, and turn to page 528.

Sights in Gdańsk

Main Town (Główne Miasto)

The following sights are all in the Main Town, listed roughly in the order you'll see them on the self-guided walk of the Royal Way.

Gdańsk Historical Museum

The Gdańsk Historical Museum has four excellent branches: the Amber Museum, Uphagen House, Main Town Hall, and Artus Court. All have the same cost and hours, but you must buy a separate ticket for each.

Cost and Hours: 10 zł apiece, free Mon in summer and Tue off-season; open mid-June-late Sept Mon 10:00-15:00, Tue-Sat 10:00-18:00, Sun 11:00-18:00; late Sept-mid-June Tue 10:00-15:00, Wed-Sat 10:00-16:00, Sun 11:00-16:00, closed Mon; last entry 30 minutes before closing.

Information: The museums share a phone number and website (central tel. 58-767-9100, www.mhmg.gda.pl).

▲**Amber Museum (Muzeum Bursztynu)**—Housed in a pair of connected brick towers just outside the Main Town's Golden Gate, this museum has two oddly contradictory parts. One shows off Gdańsk's favorite local resource, amber, while the other focuses on implements of torture (cost and hours above, overpriced 1.5-hour audioguide—25 zł, enter at end facing Golden Gate).

Visiting the Museum: Partially explained in English, the Amber Museum offers a good introduction to the globby yellow stuff, but you'll have to walk up several flights of stairs to see it all. For a primer before you go, check out the "All About Amber" sidebar.

Climb up one flight of stairs, buy your ticket, then head up to the second floor for a scientific look at amber. View inclusions (items trapped in the resin) through a magnifying glass and microscope, and see dozens of samples showing the full rainbow of amber shades. Interactive video screens explain the creation of amber. The third-floor exhibit explains the "Amber Route" (the ancient Celtic trade road connecting Gdańsk to Italy), outlines medicinal uses of the stuff, and displays a wide range of functional items made from amber—clocks, pipe stems, candle-

All About Amber

Poland's Baltic seaside is known as the Amber Coast. You can see amber *(bursztyn)* in Gdańsk's Amber Museum and in shop windows everywhere. This fossilized tree resin originated here on the north coast of Poland 40 million years ago. It comes in as many different colors as Eskimos have words for snow: 300 distinct shades, from yellowish white to yellowish black, from opaque to transparent. (I didn't believe it either, until I toured Gdańsk's museum.) Darker-colored amber is generally mixed with ash and sand—making it more fragile, and generally less desirable. Lighter amber is mixed with gases and air bubbles.

Amber has been popular since long before there were souvenir stands. Archaeologists have found Roman citizens (and their coins) buried with crosses made of amber. Almost 75 percent of the world's amber is mined in northern Poland, and it often simply washes up on the beaches after a winter storm. Some of the elaborate amber sculptures displayed at the museum are joined with "amber glue"—melted-down amber mixed with an adhesive agent. More recently, amber craftsmen are combining amber with silver to create artwork—a method dubbed the "Polish School."

In addition to being good for the economy, some Poles believe amber is good for their health. A traditional cure for arthritis pain is to pour strong vodka over amber, let it set, and then rub it on sore joints. Other remedies call for mixing amber dust with honey or rose oil. It sounds superstitious, but users claim that it works.

sticks, chandeliers, jewelry boxes, and much more. The fourth floor shows off more artistic items made of amber—sculptures, candelabras, beer steins, chessboards, and a model ship with delicate sails made of amber. At the top floor, you'll find a modern gallery showing more recent amber craftsmanship, and displays about amber's role in fashion today.

On your way back down, detour along the upper level of the courtyard to find the museum's dark side (the Torture Museum). First is a brief exhibit about the building's history, including its chapter as a prison tower. The rest of the exhibit—with sound effects, scant artifacts, and mannequins helpfully demonstrating the grisly equipment—tries hard to make medieval torture and imprisonment interesting.

GDAŃSK

▲**Uphagen House (Dom Uphagena)**—This interesting place at ulica Długa 12 is your chance to glimpse what's behind the colorful facades lining this street (see cost and hours earlier).

Visiting the Museum: Check out the cutaway model just inside the entry to see the three parts you'll visit: dolled-up visitors' rooms in front, a corridor along the courtyard, and private rooms in the back. As you enter, the costumed staffers will likely usher you to the top floor, which houses temporary exhibits. Back down on the middle floor, ogle the finely decorated salon, which was used to show off for guests. Most of this furniture is original (saved from WWII bombs by locals who hid it in the countryside). Passing into the dining room, note the knee-high paintings of hunting and celebrations. Along the passage to the back, each room has a theme: butterflies in the smoking room, then flowers in the next room, then birds in the music room. In the private rooms at the back, notice how much simpler the decor is. Downstairs, you'll pass through the kitchen, the pantry, and a room with photos of the house before the war, which were used to reconstruct what you see today.

▲▲**Main Town Hall (Ratusz Głównego Miasta)**—This landmark building contains remarkable decorations from Gdańsk's

Golden Age (see cost and hours on page 518). You can also climb to the top of the **tower** for commanding views (5 zł extra, mid-June-mid-Sept only).

Visiting the Museum: Buy your ticket down below (good gift shop), then head up the stairs and inside.

In the entry room, examine the photo showing this building at the end of World War II (you'll see more upstairs). The ornately carved wooden **door,** which we'll pass through in a minute, also deserves a close look. Above the door are two crosses under a crown. This seal of Gdańsk is being held—as it's often depicted—by a pair of lions. The felines are stubborn and independent, just like the citizens of Gdańsk. Close the door partway to look at the carvings of crops. Around the frame of the door are mermen, reminding us that this agricultural bounty, like so many of Poland's resources, is transported on the Vistula and out through Gdańsk.

Go through the door into the **Red Hall,** where the Gdańsk city council met in the summertime. (The lavish fireplace—with another pair of lions holding the coat of arms of Gdańsk—was just for show.) City council members would sit in the seats around the room, debating city policy. The shin-level paintings depict the earth; the exquisitely detailed inlaid wood just over the seats are animals; the paintings on the wall above represent the seven virtues the burghers meeting in this room should have; and the ceiling is all about theology. Examine that ceiling. It has 25 paintings in total, with both Christian and pagan themes—meant to inspire the decision-makers in this room to make good choices. The smaller ones around the edges are scenes from mythology and the Bible. The one in the middle (from 1607) shows God's relationship to Gdańsk. In the foreground, the citizens of Gdańsk go about their daily lives. Above them, high atop the arch, God's hand reaches down (from within clouds of Hebrew characters) and grasps the city's steeple. The rainbow arching above also symbolizes God's connection to Gdańsk. Mirroring that is the Vistula River, which begins in the mountains of southern Poland (on the right), runs through the country, and exits at the sea in Gdańsk (on the left, where the rainbow ends).

Continue into the not-so-impressive Winter Hall, with another fireplace and coat of arms held by lions. Keep going through the next room, into a room with before-and-after photos of **WWII damage.** At the foot of the destroyed crucifix is a book with a bullet hole in it. The twist of wood is all that's left of the main support for the spiral staircase (today reconstructed in the room where you entered). Ponder the inspiring ability of a city to be reborn after the tragedy of war.

Upstairs are some temporary exhibits and several examples of **Gdańsk-style furniture.** These pieces are characterized by three big, round feet along the front, lots of ornamentation, and usually a virtually impossible-to-find lock (sometimes hidden behind a movable decoration). You can also see a coin collection, from the days when Gdańsk had the elite privilege of minting its own currency.

▲▲Artus Court (Dwór Artusa)—In the Middle Ages, Gdańsk was home to many brotherhoods and guilds (like businessmen's clubs). For their meetings, the city provided this elaborately

decorated hall, named for King Arthur—a medieval symbol for prestige and power. Just as in King Arthur's Court, this was a place where powerful and important people came together. Such halls were once common in Baltic Europe, but this is the only original one that survives (cost and hours on page 518, dry and too-thorough audioguide-5 zł; in tall, white, triple-arched building behind Neptune statue at Długi targ 43-44).

Visiting the Museum: In the grand hall, various **cupboards** line the walls. Each organization that met here had a place to keep its important documents and office supplies. Suspended from the ceiling are seven giant **model ships** that depict Baltic vessels, symbolic of the city's connection to the sea.

In the far-back corner is the museum's highlight: a gigantic **stove** decorated with 520 colorful tiles featuring the faces of kings, queens, nobles, mayors, and burghers. Half of these people were Protestant, and half were Catholic, mixed together in no particular order—a reminder of Gdańsk's religious tolerance. Virtually all the tiles are original, having survived WWII bombs. But not all of the original tiles are here: Three of them were recently discovered by a bargain-hunter wandering through a flea market in the southern part of the country, who returned them to their rightful home.

Notice the huge **paintings** on the walls above, with 3-D animals emerging from flat frames. Hunting is a popular theme in local artwork. Like minting coins, hunting was a privilege usually reserved for royalty, but extended in special circumstances to the burghers of special towns...like Gdańsk. If you look closely, it's obvious that these "paintings" are new, digitally generated reproductions of the originals, which were damaged in World War II.

The next room—actually in the next-door building—is a typical front room of the burghers' homes lining ulica Długa. Ogle the gorgeously carved wooden staircase. Upstairs (through the door to the right of the stairs) is a hall of knights—once again evoking Arthurian legend. If you've rented an audioguide, take it back up front to return it; otherwise, exit through the back, just down the street from St. Mary's Church; to get back to the main drag, go back around the block, to the left.

Other Museums and Churches in the Main Town

▲▲**St. Mary's Church (Kościół Mariacki)**—Gdańsk has so many striking red-brick churches, it's hard to keep track of them. But if you visit only one, make it St. Mary's. This is the biggest brick church in the world—with a footprint larger than a football field (350 feet long and 210 feet wide), it can accommodate up to 25,000 standing worshippers. Built over 159 years in the 14th and 15th centuries, the church is an important symbol of Gdańsk.

Cost and Hours: 4 zł, June-Sept Mon-Sat 9:00-18:30, Sun 13:00-18:30, closes progressively earlier off-season, tel. 58-301-3982, www.bazylikamariacka.pl.

Visiting the Church: As you enter the church, notice all

the white, empty space—unusual in a
Catholic country, where frilly Baroque
churches are the norm. In the Middle
Ages, Gdańsk's tolerance attracted
people who were suffering religious
persecution. As the Protestant population grew, they needed a place to
worship. St. Mary's, like most other
Gdańsk churches, eventually became
Protestant—leaving these churches with
the blank walls you see now. Today you'll
find only one Baroque church in central
Gdańsk (the domed pink-and-green chapel behind St. Mary's).

Most Gothic stone churches are built in the basilica style—
with a high nave in the middle, shorter aisles on the side, and
flying buttresses to support the weight. (Think of Paris' Notre-
Dame.) But that design doesn't work with brick. So, like all
Gdańsk churches, St. Mary's is a "hall church"—with three naves
the same height, and no exterior buttresses.

Also like other Gdańsk churches, St. Mary's gave refuge to
the Polish people after the communist government declared martial law in 1981. When a riot broke out and violence seemed imminent, people would flood into churches for protection. The ZOMO
riot police wouldn't follow them inside.

Most of the church decorations are original. A few days
before World War II broke out in Gdańsk, locals hid precious
items in the countryside. Take some time now to see a few of the
highlights.

Head up the right nave and find the opulent family marker to
the right of the main altar, high on the pillar. Look for the falling
baby (under the crown). This is Constantine Ferber. As a precocious child, Constantine leaned out his window on ulica Długa
to see the king's processional come through town. He slipped and
fell, but landed in a salesman's barrel of fish. Constantine grew up
to become the mayor of Gdańsk.

Look on the side of the same pillar for a coat of arms with
three pigs' heads. It relates to another member of the illustrious
Ferber clan. An enemy army that was laying siege to the town
tried to starve its people out. A clever Ferber decided to load the
cannons with pigs' heads to show the enemy that they had plenty
of food—it worked, and the enemy left.

Circle around, past the front of the beautifully carved main
altar. Behind it is the biggest stained-glass window in Poland.
Below the window (behind the main altar) is a huge, empty

glass case. The case was designed to hold Hans Memling's *Last Judgment* painting, which used to be on display here, but is currently being held hostage by the skippable National Museum, south of town. To counter the museum's claim that the church wasn't a good environment for such a precious work, the priest had this display case built—but that still wasn't enough to convince the museum to give the painting back. You can see a smaller replica up by the main door of the church (in the little chapel on the right just before you exit).

Before you head back out to the mini-Memling (and the exit), venture to the far side of the altar and check out the elaborate **astronomical clock**—supposedly the biggest wooden clock in the world. Below is the circular calendar showing the saint's day, and above are zodiac signs and the time (only one hand).

Tower Climb: If you've got the energy, climb the 408 steps up the church's 270-foot-tall tower. You'll be rewarded with sweeping views of the entire city (tower climb-5 zł; July-Aug Mon-Sat 9:00-18:00, Sun 13:00-18:00; April-June and Sept-Oct Mon-Sat 9:00-17:00, Sun 13:00-17:00; closed Nov-March; entrance in back corner).

Historical Zone of the Free City of Gdańsk (Strefa Historyczna Wolne Miasto Gdańsk)

—In a city so obsessed with its Golden Age and Solidarity history, this charming little collection illuminates a unique but often-overlooked chapter in the story of Gdańsk: The years between World Wars I and II, when—in an effort to find a workable compromise in this ethnically mixed city—Gdańsk was not part of Germany nor of Poland, but a self-governing "free city" *(wolne miasto)*. Like a holdover from medieval fiefdoms in modern times, the city-state of Gdańsk even issued its own currency and stamps. This modest museum earnestly shows off artifacts from the time—photos, stamps, maps, flags, promotional tourist leaflets, and other items from the free city, all marked with the Gdańsk symbol of two white crosses under a crown on a red shield. The brochure explains that four out of five people living in the free city identified themselves not as German or Poles, but as "Danzigers." While some might find the subject obscure, this endearing collection is a treat for WWII history buffs.

Cost and Hours: 5 zł, May-Nov Tue-Sun 11:00-18:00, Dec-April Tue-Sun 13:00-17:00, closed Mon year-round, a few steps in front of St. Mary's at ulica Piwna 19-21, tel. 58-320-2828, www.tpg.info.pl.

Archaeological Museum (Muzeum Archeologiczne)

—This simple museum is worth a quick peek for those interested in archaeology. The ground floor has exhibits on excavated finds from Sudan, where the museum has a branch program. Upstairs, look for the distinctive urns with cute faces, which date from the Hallstatt Period and were discovered in slate graves around Gdańsk. Also upstairs are some Bronze and Iron Age tools; before-and-after photos of WWII Gdańsk; and a reconstructed 12th-century Viking-like Slavonic longboat. You can also climb the building's tower, with good views up Mariacka street toward St. Mary's Church.

Cost and Hours: Museum-8 zł, tower-3 zł; July-Aug Tue-Fri 9:00-17:00, Sat-Sun 10:00-17:00, closed Mon; Sept-June Tue and Thu-Fri 8:00-16:00, Wed 9:00-17:00, Sat-Sun 10:00-16:00, closed Mon; ulica Mariacka 25-26, tel. 58-322-2100, www.archeologia.pl.

▲**Central Maritime Museum (Centralne Muzeum Morskie)**— Gdańsk's history and livelihood are tied to the sea. This collection, spread among several buildings on either side of the river, examines all aspects of this connection. While nautical types may get a thrill out of the creaky, sprawling museum, most visitors find it little more than a convenient way to pass some time and enjoy a cruise across the river. The museum's lack of English information is frustrating; fortunately, some exhibits have descriptions you can borrow.

Cost and Hours: Each part of the museum has its own admission (5-8 zł); a ticket for the whole shebang (including the ferry across the river) costs 28 zł. (If you skip the Maritime Cultural Center—which is less worthwhile if you don't have kids—a ticket to everything *else* is just 18 zł.) It's open July-Aug daily 10:00-18:00; Sept-Oct and March-June Tue-Sun 10:00-16:00, closed Mon; Nov-Feb Tue-Sun 10:00-15:00, closed Mon; ulica Ołowianka 9-13, tel. 58-301-8611, www.cmm.pl.

Visiting the Museum: The exhibit has four parts. The first two are on the Main Town side of the river: The landmark medieval **Crane** (Żuraw)—Gdańsk's most important symbol—houses an exhibit on living in the city during its Golden Age (16th-17th centuries). You can see models of Baltic buildings (including the Crane you're inside), plus traditional tools and costumes. For more on the Crane itself, see page 514. The new **Maritime Cultural Center,** next door to the Crane, is a beautiful facility with sparse exhibits. For adults, the most interesting areas are on the third floor ("Working Boats," with examples of vessels from around the world and English explanations) and the fourth floor (temporary exhibits). The second floor has a lively, kid-oriented interactive exhibition called "People-Ships-Ports," with lots of hands-on activities to get youngsters excited about seafaring. Tickets covering the interactive exhibit cost extra, and you can enter that area only at the top of each hour; it's not worth the expense or hassle for adults traveling sans kids.

The rest of the museum is across the river on Ołowianka Island, which you can reach via the little **ferry** (*prom*, 1 zł one-way,

GDAŃSK

Lech Wałęsa

In 1980, the world was turned on its ear by a walrus-mustachioed shipyard electrician. Within three years, this seemingly run-of-the-mill Pole had precipitated the collapse of communism, led a massive 10-million-member trade union with enormous political impact, was named *Time* magazine's Man of the Year, and won a Nobel Peace Prize.

Lech Wałęsa was born in Popowo, Poland, in 1943. After working as a car mechanic and serving two years in the army, he became an electrician at the Gdańsk Shipyard in 1967. Like many Poles, Wałęsa felt stifled by the communist government, and was infuriated that a system that was supposed to be for the workers clearly wasn't serving them.

When the shipyard massacre took place in December of 1970 (see page 528), Wałęsa was at the forefront of the protests. He was marked as a dissident, and in 1976, he was fired. Wałęsa hopped from job to job and was occasionally unemployed—under communism, a rock-bottom status reserved for only the most despicable derelicts. But he soldiered on, fighting for the creation of a trade union and building up quite a file with the secret police.

In August of 1980, Wałęsa heard news of the beginnings of the Gdańsk strike and raced to the shipyard. In an act that has since become the stuff of legend, Wałęsa scaled the shipyard wall to get inside.

Before long, Wałęsa's dynamic personality won him the unofficial role of the workers' leader and spokesman. He negotiated with the regime to hash out the August Agreements, becoming a rock star-type hero during the so-called 16 Months of Hope...until martial law came crashing down in December of 1981. Wałęsa was arrested and interned for 11 months in a coun-

included in 28-zł museum ticket). The ferry runs about every 15 minutes in peak season (during museum hours only), but frequency declines sharply in the off-season (and it doesn't run if the river freezes). This also gives fine views back on the Crane.

Once on the island, visit the three rebuilt **Old Granaries** (Spichlerze). These make up the heart of the exhibit, tracing the history of Gdańsk—particularly as it relates to the sea—from prehistoric days to the present. Models of the town and region help put things into perspective. Other exhibits cover underwater exploration, navigational aids, artifacts of the Polish seafaring tradition, peek-a-boo cross-sections of multilevel ships, and models of the

try house. After being released, he continued to struggle underground, becoming a symbol of anti-communist sentiment.

Finally, the dedication of Wałęsa and Solidarity paid off, and Polish communism dissolved—with Wałęsa rising from the ashes as the country's first post-communist president. But the skills that made Wałęsa a rousing success at leading an uprising didn't translate to the president's office. Wałęsa proved to be a stubborn, headstrong politician, frequently clashing with the parliament. He squabbled with his own party, declaring a "war at the top" of Solidarity and rotating higher-ups to prevent corruption and keep the party fresh. He also didn't choose his advisors well, enlisting several staffers who wound up immersed in scandal. His overconfidence was his Achilles' heel, and his governing style verged on authoritarian.

Unrefined and none too interested in scripted speeches, Wałęsa was a simple man who preferred playing Ping-Pong with his buddies to attending formal state functions. Though lacking a formal education, Wałęsa had unsurpassed drive and charisma... but that's not enough to lead a country—especially during an impossibly complicated, fast-changing time, when even the savviest politician would certainly have stumbled.

Wałęsa was defeated at the polls, by the Poles, in 1995, and when he ran again in 2000, he received a humiliating 1 percent of the vote. Since leaving office, Wałęsa has kept a lower profile, but still delivers speeches worldwide. Many poor Poles grumble that Lech, who started life simple like them, has forgotten the little people. But his fans point out that he gives much of his income to charity. And on his lapel, he still always wears a pin featuring the Black Madonna of Częstochowa—the symbol of Polish Catholicism.

Poles say there are at least two Lech Wałęsas: the young, working-class idealist Lech, at the forefront of the Solidarity strikes, who will always have a special place in their hearts; and the failed President Wałęsa, who got in over his head and tarnished his legacy.

modern-day shipyard where Solidarity was born. This place is home to more miniature ships than you ever thought you'd see, and the Nautical Gallery upstairs features endless rooms with paintings of boats.

Finally, crawl through the holds and scramble across the deck of a decommissioned steamship docked permanently across from the Crane, called the *Sołdek* (ship generally closed in winter). This was the first postwar vessel built at the Gdańsk shipyard. Below decks, you can see where they shoveled the coal; wander through a maze of pipes, gears, valves, gauges, and ladders; and visit the rooms where the sailors lived, slept, and ate. You can even play captain in the bridge.

▲▲▲Solidarity (Solidarność) and the Gdańsk Shipyard (Stocznia Gdańska)

Gdańsk's single best experience is exploring the shipyard that witnessed the beginning of the end of communism's stranglehold on Eastern Europe. Here in the former industrial wasteland that Lech Wałęsa called the "cradle of freedom," this evocative site tells the story of the brave Polish shipyard workers who took on—and ultimately defeated—an Evil Empire.

A visit to the Solidarity sights has two main parts: the memorial and gate out in front of the shipyard, and the excellent "Roads to Freedom" exhibit nearby. Begin at the towering monument—with three anchor-adorned crosses—near the entrance gate to the shipyard, and allow two hours for the whole visit.

Getting to the Shipyard: The Solidarity monument and shipyard are at the north end of the Old Town, about a 20-minute walk from ulica Długa. For the most interesting approach, follow my self-guided "From the Main Town to the Solidarity Shipyard" walk on page 514.

Background: After the communists took over Eastern Europe at the end of World War II, oppressed peoples throughout the Soviet Bloc rose up in different ways. The most dramatic uprisings—Hungary's 1956 Uprising and Czechoslovakia's 1968 "Prague Spring"—were brutally crushed under the treads of Soviet tanks. The formula for freedom that finally succeeded was a patient, decade-long series of strikes spearheaded by Lech Wałęsa and his trade union, called Solidarność—"Solidarity." (The movement also benefited from good timing, as it coincided with the *perestroika* and *glasnost* policies of the Soviet premier Mikhail Gorbachev.) While some American politicians might like to take credit for defeating communism, Wałęsa and his fellow workers were the ones fighting on the front lines, armed with nothing more than guts.

Monument of the Fallen Shipyard Workers

The seeds of August 1980 were sown a decade before. Since becoming part of the Soviet Bloc, the Poles staged frequent strikes, protests, and uprisings to secure their rights, all of which were put down by the regime. But the bloodiest of these took place in December of 1970—a tragic event memorialized by this monument.

The 1970 strike was prompted by price hikes. The communist government set the prices for all products. As Poland endured drastic food shortages in the 1960s and 1970s, the regime frequently announced what it called "regulation of prices." Invariably, this meant an increase in the cost of essential foodstuffs. (To be able to claim "regulation" rather than "increase," the regime would symbolically lower prices for a few select items—but these were always nonessential luxuries, such as elevators and TV sets, which nobody could afford anyway.)

The regime was usually smart enough to raise prices on January 1—when the people were fat and happy after Christmas, and too hung-over to complain. But on December 12, 1970, bolstered by an ego-stoking visit by West German Chancellor Willy Brandt, Polish premier Władysław Gomułka increased prices. The people of Poland—who cared more about the price of Christmas dinner than relations with Germany—struck back.

A wave of strikes and sit-ins spread along the heavily industrialized north coast of Poland, most notably in Gdańsk, Gdynia, and Szczecin. Thousands of angry demonstrators poured through the gate of this shipyard, marched into town, and set fire to the Communist Party Committee building. In an attempt to quell the riots, the government-run radio implored the people to go back to work. On the morning of December 17, workers showed up at shipyard gates across northern Poland—and were greeted by the army and police. Without provocation, the Polish army opened fire on the workers. While the official death toll for the massacre stands at 44, others say the true number is much higher. This monument, with a trio of 140-foot-tall crosses, honors those lost to the regime that December.

Go to the middle of the wall behind the crosses, to the monument of the worker wearing a flimsy plastic work helmet, attempting to shield himself from bullets. Behind him is a list—pockmarked with symbolic bullet holes—of workers murdered on that day. *Lat* means "years old"—many teenagers were among the dead. The quote at the top of the wall is from Pope John Paul II, who was elected eight years after this tragedy. The Pope was known for his clever way with words, and this very carefully phrased quote—which served as an inspiration to the Poles during their darkest hours—skewers the regime in a way subtle enough to still be tolerated: "Let thy spirit descend, and renew the face of the earth—*this* earth" (that is, Poland). Below that is the dedication:

"They gave their lives so you can live decently."

Stretching to the left of this center wall are plaques representing labor unions from around Poland—and around the world (look for the Chinese characters)—expressing solidarity with these workers. To the right is an enormous Bible verse: "May the Lord give strength to his people. May the Lord bless his people with the gift of peace" (Psalms 29:11).

More than a decade after the massacre, this monument was finally constructed. It marked the first time a communist regime ever allowed a monument to be built to honor its own victims. Wałęsa called it a harpoon in the heart of the communists. Inspired by the brave sacrifice of their true comrades, the shipyard workers rose up here in August of 1980, formulating the "21 Points" of a new union called Solidarity. The demands included the right to strike and form unions, the freeing of political prisoners, and an increase in wages. These 21 Points are listed in Polish on the panel at the far end of the right wall, marked *21 X TAK Solidarność* ("21 times yes Solidarity").

• *Now continue to the gate and peer through into the birthplace of Eastern European freedom.*

Gdańsk Shipyard (Stocznia Gdańska) Gate #2

When a Pole named Karol Wojtyła was elected Pope in 1978—and visited his homeland in 1979—he inspired his 40 million coun-

trymen to believe that impossible dreams can come true. Prices continued to go up, and the workers continued to rise up. By the summer of 1980, it was clear that the dam was about to break.

In August, Anna Walenty- nowicz—a Gdańsk crane opera- tor and known dissident—was fired unceremoniously just short of her retirement. This sparked a strike in the Gdańsk Shipyard (then called the Lenin Shipyard) on August 14, 1980. An electrician named Lech Wałęsa had been fired as an agitator years before and wasn't allowed into the yard. But on hearing news of the strike, Wałęsa went to the shipyard and climbed over the wall to get inside. The strike now had a leader.

Imagine being one of the 16,000 workers who stayed here for 18 days during the strike—hungry, cold, sleeping on sheets of Styrofoam, inspired by the new Polish pope, excited about finally standing up to the regime...and terrified that at any moment you might be gunned down, like your friends had been a decade before. Workers, afraid to leave the shipyard, communicated with the outside world through this gate—wives and brothers showed up here and asked for a loved one, and those inside spread the word until the striker came forward. Occasionally, a truck pulled up inside the gate, with Lech Wałęsa standing atop its cab with a megaphone. Facing the thousands of people assembled outside the gate, Wałęsa gave progress reports on the negotiations and pleaded for supplies. The people of Gdańsk responded, bringing armfuls of bread and other food to keep the workers going. This truly was Solidarity.

During the strike, two items hung on the fence. One of them (which still hangs there today) was a picture of Pope John Paul II—a reminder to believe in your dreams and have faith in God. The other item was a makeshift list of the strikers' 21 Points—demands scrawled in red paint and black pencil on pieces of plywood.

· *You'll likely see construction in the area beyond the gate.*

Today's Shipyard

This part of the shipyard, long abandoned, is gradually being redeveloped into a **"Young City"** (Młode Miasto)—envisioned as a new city center for Gdańsk, with shopping, restaurants, and homes. Rusting shipbuilding equipment will be torn down, and old brick buildings will be converted into gentrified flats. Just behind the monument will be the new European Center of Solidarity (still an active union in some countries). The shipyard gate, monument, and other important sites from the Solidarity strikes will stay put. Work will likely wrap up in 2013.

· *Walk to the right and go through the gate.*

The path leading into the shipyard passes through two huge **symbolic gateways.** The first resembles the rusted hull of a ship, representing the protest of the shipbuilders. The next gateway—a futuristic, colorful tower—is a small-scale contemporary reinterpretation of a 1,000-foot-tall monument planned in 1919 by the prominent Russian constructivist artist Vladimir Tatlin. Tatlin's unrealized design represented the optimism of the communist "utopia" before it was fatally perverted by totalitarianism.

The path leads to a low-profile, red-brick building—the **BHP Conference Hall,** where the communists sat down across the table from Lech Wałęsa and worked out a compromise. Today it houses an interesting exhibition called "There Is One Solidarity," celebrating the trade union that got its start here (free, Tue-Sun 10:00-17:00, closed Mon, www.salabhp.pl). Less historical and impartial than the excellent "Roads to Freedom" museum (described next), this exhibition trumpets the accomplishments of the still-active Solidarity organization, which is straining to remain relevant in today's world.

Speaking of which, nearby you may notice the construction of a brand-new **headquarters for Solidarity,** which may be opening in late 2013.

• *The museum where we'll learn the rest of the story is about 100 yards back toward the Main Town. With the main shipyard gate to your back, walk straight ahead, passing the green-and-yellow building on your right. Cross the street and walk toward the green skyscraper. After about a block, note the stairs leading underground, into the...*

"Roads to Freedom" Exhibit

This small but outstanding museum captures (better than any other sight in the country) the Polish reality under communism, and traces the step-by-step evolution of the Solidarity movement.

Cost and Hours: 6 zł, 2 zł on Wed; open May-Sept Tue-Sun 10:00-18:00, Oct-April Tue-Sun 10:00-17:00, closed Mon year-round; Wały Piastowskie 24, tel. 58-308-4428, museum: www.ecs .gda.pl, organization: www.fcs.org.pl.

Possible Move: When the new Solidarity headquarters inside the shipyard is completed, this exhibit will likely move there. Confirm locally. If the exhibit does move, it's also possible that the details described below may change.

⊙ Self-Guided Tour: Walk downstairs—startled by angry shouts from the ZOMO—and buy your ticket, which is designed to look like the communist ration coupons that all Poles had to carry and present before they could buy certain goods. Cashiers would stand with scissors at the ready, prepared to snip off a corner of your coupon after making the sale. Consider picking up a Solidarity book or other souvenir at the excellent gift shop here before moving on.

To the right of the ticket desk are some depressing reminders of the communist days. The phone booth is marked *Automat Nieczynny*—"Out of Order"—as virtually all phone booths were back then. In the humble, authentic commie WC, notice that instead of toilet paper, there's a wad of old newspapers. Actual toilet paper was cause for celebration. Notice the mannequin with several rolls on a string around her neck—time to party!

Across from the ticket desk is a typical **Polish shop** (marked *spożyw*, a truncated version of *spożywczy*, "grocery store") from the 1970s, at the worst of the food shortages. Great selection, eh? Often the only things in stock were vinegar and mustard. Milk and bread were generally available, but they were low quality—it wasn't unusual to find a cigarette butt in your loaf. The few blocks of cheese and other items in the case weren't real—they were props, placed there so the shop wouldn't look completely empty. Sometimes they'd hang a few pitiful, phony salamis from the hooks—otherwise, people might think it was a tile shop. The only real meat in here were the flies on the flypaper. Despite the meager supplies, shoppers (mostly women) would sometimes have to wait in line literally all day long just to pick over these scant choices. People didn't necessarily buy what they needed; instead, they'd buy anything that could be bartered on the black market. On the counter, notice the little jar holding clipped-off ration coupons.

Continue into the exhibit. The first room explains the **roots** of the shipyard strikes, including the famous uprisings in Hungary and Czechoslovakia, and the December 1970 riots in Poland. (Interactive computer screens tell you more about these events.) The prison cell is a reminder of Stalin's strong-arm tactics for getting the people of Eastern Europe to sign on to his new system.

Then head into the heart of the exhibit, **August 1980.** Near the plaster statue of Lenin are several tables. These were the actual tables used (in the red-brick building back in the shipyard) when the communist authorities finally agreed to negotiate after 18 days of protests. On the afternoon of August 31, 1980, the Governmental Commission and the Inter-Factory Strike Committee (MKS) came together and signed the August Agreements, which legalized Solidarity—the first time any communist government permitted a workers' union. Photos and a video show the giddy day, as the Polish Bob Dylan laments the evils of the regime. Lech Wałęsa—sitting at the big table, with his characteristic walrus moustache—signed the agreement with a big, red, souvenir-type pen adorned with a picture of Pope John Paul II (displayed across the room). Other union reps, sitting at smaller tables, tape-recorded the proceedings, and played them later at their own factories to prove that the unthinkable had happened. Near the end of this room are replicas of the plywood boards featuring the 21 Points, which hung on the front gate we just saw.

While the government didn't take the agreements very seriously, the Poles did...and before long, 10 million of them—one out of every four—joined Solidarity. So began the **16 Months of Hope**—the theme of the next room. Newly legal, Solidarity continued to stage strikes and make its opposition known. Slick Solidarity posters and children's art convey the childlike enthusiasm with which the Poles seized their hard-won kernels of freedom. The poster with a baby in a Solidarity T-shirt—one year old, just like the union itself—captures the sense of hope. The communist authorities' hold on the Polish people began to slip. The rest of the Soviet Bloc looked on nervously, and the Warsaw Pact army assembled at the Polish border and glared at the uprisers. The threat of invasion hung heavy in the air.

Turn the corner to see Solidarity's progress come crashing down. On Sunday morning, December 13, 1981, the Polish head of state, General Wojciech Jaruzelski, appeared on national TV and announced the introduction of **martial law.** Solidarity was outlawed, and its leaders were arrested. Frightened Poles heard the announcement and looked out their windows to see Polish Army tanks rumbling through the snowy streets. Jaruzelski claimed that he imposed martial law to prevent the Soviets from invading. Today, many historians question whether martial law was really necessary—though Jaruzelski remains unremorseful. Martial law was a tragic, terrifying, and bleak time for the Polish people. It didn't, however, kill the Solidarity movement, which continued its fight after going underground. Notice that the movement's martial-law-era propaganda was produced with far more primitive printing equipment than their earlier posters.

In the next room, you see a clandestine print shop like those used to create that illegal propaganda. Surrounding the room are sobering displays of **ZOMO riot gear.** A film reveals the ugliness of martial law. Watch the footage of General Jaruzelski—wearing his trademark dark glasses—reading the announcement of martial law. Chilling scenes show riots, demonstrations, and crackdowns by the ZOMO police—including one in which a demonstrator is run over by a truck. An old woman is stampeded by a pack of fleeing demonstrators.

The next room shows a film tracing the whole history of **communism in Poland** (with a copy of Lech Wałęsa's Nobel Peace Prize).

For a happy ending, head into the final room, with an uplifting film about the **fall of the Iron Curtain** across Eastern Europe—right up through the 2004 "Orange Revolution" in Ukraine.

Here's how it happened in Poland: By the time the Pope visited his homeland again in 1983, martial law had finally been lifted, and Solidarity—still technically illegal—was gaining momentum, gradually pecking away at the communists. With the moral support of the Pope and the entire Western world, the brave Poles were the first European country to throw off the shackles of communism when, in the spring of 1989, the "Round Table Talks" led to the opening up of elections. The government arrogantly called for parliamentary elections, reserving 65 percent of seats for themselves. The plan backfired, as virtually every open seat went to Solidarity. This success inspired people all over Eastern Europe, and by that winter, the Berlin Wall had crumbled and the Czechs and Slovaks had staged their Velvet Revolution. Lech Wałęsa—the shipyard electrician who started it all by jumping over a wall—became the first president of post-communist Poland. And a year later, in Poland's first true elections since World War II, 29 different parties won seats in the parliament. This celebration of democracy was brought to the Polish people by the workers of Gdańsk.

North of the Main Town, near the Gdańsk Shipyard

World War II Museum—As if to emphasize its pivotal role in 20th-century history, Gdańsk is building this large, state-of-the-art museum just east of the Solidarity shipyard, along the river. It promises high-tech interactive exhibits about Gdańsk's experience during the war that began on its doorstep. The museum is likely to open in 2014 or 2015; ask the TI for the latest details (or check www.muzeum1939.pl).

Shopping in Gdańsk

The big story in Gdańsk is amber *(bursztyn)*, a fossil resin available in all shades, shapes, and sizes (see the "All About Amber" sidebar, earlier). While you'll see amber sold all over town, the best place to browse and buy is along the atmospheric ulica Mariacka (between the Motława River and St. Mary's Church). This pretty street, with old-fashioned balconies and dozens of display cases, is fun to wander even if you're not a shopper. Other good places to buy amber are along the riverfront embankment and on ulica Długa. To avoid rip-offs—such as amber that's been melted and reshaped—always buy it from a shop, not from someone standing on the street. (But note that most shops also have a display case and salesperson out front, which are perfectly legit.) Prices everywhere are about the same, so rather than seeking out a specific place, just window-shop until you see what you want. Styles range from gaudy necklaces with huge globs of amber, to tasteful smaller pendants in silver settings, to cheap trinkets. All shades of amber—from near-white to dark brown—cost about the same, but you'll pay more for inclusions (bugs or other objects stuck in the amber).

Gdańsk also has several modern shopping malls, most of them in the Old Town or near the main train station. The walk between the Main Town and the Solidarity shipyard goes past some of the best malls (see page 514).

Eating in Gdańsk

In addition to traditional Polish fare, Gdańsk has some fine Baltic seafood. Herring *(śledź)* is popular here, as is cod *(dorsz)*. Natives brag that their salmon *(łosoś)* is better than Norway's. For a stiff drink, sample *Goldwasser* (similar to Goldschlager). This sweet and strong liqueur, flecked with gold, was supposedly invented here in Gdańsk. The following options are all in the Main Town, within three blocks of ulica Długa.

GDAŃSK

Budget Restaurants in the City Center

These two places are remarkably cheap, tasty, quick, and wonderfully convenient—on or very near ulica Długa. They're worth considering even if you're not on a tight budget.

Bar pod Rybą ("Under the Fish") is nirvana for fans of baked potatoes *(pieczony ziemniak)*. They offer more than 20 varieties, piled high with a wide variety of toppings and sauces, from Mexican beef to herring to Polish cheeses. They also serve fish dishes with salad and potatoes, making this a cheap place to sample local seafood. The tasteful decor—walls lined with old bottles, antique wooden hangers, and paintings by the owner—is squeezed into a single cozy room packed with happy eaters. In the summer, order inside, and they'll bring your food to you at an outdoor table (potatoes and fish dishes are each about 15-25 zł, daily 10:00-22:00, ulica Piwna 61/63, tel. 58-305-1307).

Bar Mleczny Neptun is your best milk-bar (communist-style budget cafeteria) option in the Main Town. A hearty meal of traditional Polish fare, including a drink, runs about 15-20 zł. This popular place has more charm than your typical institutional milk bar, including outdoor seating along the most scenic stretch of the main drag, and an upstairs dining room overlooking it all. Most of the items on the counter are for display—rather than take what's there, point to what you want and they'll dish it up fresh (Mon-Fri 7:30-18:00, until 20:00 in summer, Sat-Sun 10:00-17:00, free Wi-Fi, ulica Długa 33-34, tel. 58-301-4988).

On the Riverfront Embankment

Perhaps the most appealing dining zone in Gdańsk stretches along the riverfront embankment near the Crane. While you have several good options along here, the following are particularly well-regarded.

Kamienica Goldwasser offers high-quality Polish and international cuisine at fair prices. Choose between cozy, romantic indoor seating on several levels, or scenic outdoor seating (most main dishes 40-75 zł, daily 10:00-24:00, occasional live music, Długie Pobrzeże 22, tel. 58-301-8878).

Baryłka ("Barrel"), next door to Goldwasser, has a similar menu and outdoor seating. The elegant upstairs dining room, with windows overlooking the river, is appealing (40-65-zł main dishes, daily 9:00-24:00, Długie Pobrzeże 24, tel. 58-301-4938).

Sushi 77, serving up a wide selection of surprisingly good sushi right next to the Crane, is a refreshing break from ye olde

Polish food. Choose between the outdoor tables bathed in red light, or the mod interior (30-50-zł sushi sets, daily 12:00-23:00, Długie Pobrzeże 30, tel. 58-682-1823).

Targ Rybny/Fishmarkt ("The Fish Market")—run by the Goldwasser people (see listing earlier)—is farther up the embankment, overlooking a park and parking lot. The outdoor seating isn't too scenic, but the warm, mellow-yellow nautical ambience inside is pleasant, making this a good bad-weather option. It features classy but not stuffy service, and an emphasis on fish (most main dishes 30-50 zł, plus pricier seafood splurges, daily 10:00-23:00, ulica Targ Rybny 6C, tel. 58-320-9011).

Other Restaurants in Central Gdańsk

Czerwone Drzwi ("The Red Door") serves up tasty Polish and international cuisine in a single-room, six-table restaurant. The decor is artsy, and there's live piano music nightly at 19:00; at other times, recorded jazz sets the mood (22-28-zł pierogi, big 20-25-zł salads, 30-45-zł main dishes, daily 10:00-22:00, ulica Piwna 52/53, tel. 58-301-5764).

Dom pod Łososiem ("House Under the Salmon") is a venerable old standby with over-the-top formality. This place will make you feel like a rich burgher's family invited you over (right down to the greeting by a stiff, bow-tied maître d'). This elegant splurge restaurant has been serving guests for more than 400 years, racking up an impressive guest list (some pictured in the lobby)—and, somewhere in there, inventing *Goldwasser* (most main dishes 50-80 zł, emphasis on fish, small portions, daily 12:00-23:00, ulica Szeroka 52-54, tel. 58-301-7652).

Coffee and Sweets

Gdańsk's Main Town is full of hip cafés that lure in young people with long menus of exotic coffee drinks and tasty cakes. Here are two good options—one new, one old.

Pikawa (as in "3.14 Coffee," pronounced "pee-kah-vah") is a trendy, atmospheric café with a wide variety of coffee drinks and herbal teas, best accompanied by the delicious *szarlotka* (Polish apple cake). The decor is cozy Old World, the outdoor seating is pleasant, and the café is packed with socializing locals (8-16-zł cakes, daily 10:00-22:00, until 24:00 in summer, ulica Piwna 5-6, tel. 58-309-1444).

Cukiernia Kaliszczak, a bakery right on ulica Długa, is a no-frills throwback to the communist days. It's cheap but not cheery, with delicious 3-zł cakes and ice cream and no-nonsense service—just line up and place your order, comrade. If you want ice cream, order first at the register rather than at the display case (daily 9:00-22:00, ulica Długa 74, tel. 58-301-0895).

Between Gdynia and Gdańsk: Sopot

Sopot (SOH-poht), dubbed the "Nice of the North," was a celebrated haunt of beautiful people during the 1920s and 1930s, and remains a popular beach getaway to this day. Cruisers see Sopot as a handy place to kill time on their way back to their cruise ship in Gdynia. As it's halfway between Gdynia and Gdańsk, right on the train line, this is an easy stopover.

Sopot was created in the late 19th century by Napoleon's doctor, Jean Georges Haffner, who believed Baltic Sea water to be therapeutic. By the 1890s, it had become a fashionable seaside resort. This gambling center boasted enough high-roller casinos to garner comparisons to Monte Carlo.

The casinos are gone, but the health resorts remain, and you'll still see more well-dressed people here per capita than just about anywhere in the country. While it's not quite Cannes, Sopot feels relatively high class, which is unusual in otherwise unpretentious Poland. But even so, a childlike spirit of summer-vacation fun pervades this St-Tropez-on-the-Baltic, making it an all-around enjoyable place.

Orientation to Sopot

The main pedestrian drag, Monte Cassino Heroes street (ulica Bohaterów Monte Cassino), leads to the Molo, the longest pleasure pier in Europe. From the Molo, a broad, sandy beach stretches in each direction. Running parallel to the surf is a tree-lined, people-filled path made for strolling.

Tourist Information: Sopot's helpful TI is directly in front of the PKP train station (look for blue *it* sign). Pick up the free map, info booklet, and events schedule (daily June-mid-Sept 9:00-20:00, mid-Sept-May 10:00-18:00, ulica Dworcowa 4, tel. 58-550-3783, www.sopot.pl).

Arrival in Sopot: From the SKM station, exit to the left and walk down the street. After a block, you'll see the PKP train station on your left—detour here to find the TI (described above). Then continue on to the can't-miss-it main drag, ulica Bohaterów

Monte Cassino (marked by the big red-brick church steeple).
Follow it to the right, down to the seaside.

Sights in Sopot

▲**Monte Cassino Heroes Street (Ulica Bohaterów Monte
Cassino)**—Nicknamed "Monciak" (MOHN-chak) by locals, this
in-love-with-life promenade may well be Poland's most manicured
street. Especially after all the suburban and industrial dreck you
passed through to get here, it's easy to be charmed by this pretty
drag. The street is lined with happy tourists, trendy cafés, al fresco
restaurants, movie theaters, and late-19th-century facades (known
for their wooden balconies).

The most popular building along here (on the left, about halfway down) is the so-called **Crooked House** (Krzywy Domek), a
trippy, Gaudí-inspired building that looks like it's melting. Hard-
partying Poles prefer to call it the "Drunken House," and say that
when it looks straight, it's time to stop drinking.

At the bottom of the boulevard, just before the Molo, pay 4 zł
to climb to the top of the Art Nouveau lighthouse for a waterfront
panorama.

Molo (Pier)—At more than 1,600 feet long, this is Europe's longest wooden entertainment pier. While you won't find any amusement-park rides, you will be surrounded by vendors, artists, and
Poles having the time of their lives. Buy a *gofry* (Belgian waffle
topped with whipped cream and fruit) or an oversized cloud of
wata cukrowa (cotton candy), grab your partner's hand, and stroll
with gusto (5 zł, free Oct-April, open long hours daily).

Scan the horizon for sailboats and tankers. Any pirate ships?
For a jarring reality check, look over to Gdańsk. Barely visible from the Molo are two of the most important sites in 20th-
century history: the towering monument at Westerplatte, where
World War II started, and the cranes rising up from the Gdańsk
Shipyard, where Solidarity was born and European communism
began its long goodbye.

In spring and fall, the Molo is a favorite venue for pole
vaulting—or is that Pole vaulting?

The Beach—Yes, Poland has beaches. Nice ones. When I heard
Sopot compared to places like Nice, I'll admit that I scoffed. But
when I saw those stretches of inviting sand as far as my eye could
see, I wished I'd packed my swim trunks. (You could walk from
Gdańsk to Gdynia on beaches like this.) The sand is finer than
anything I've seen in Croatia...though the water's not exactly
crystal-clear. Most of the beach is public, except for a small private stretch in front of the Grand Hotel Sopot. Year-round, it's

What If I Miss My Boat?

Remember that you can get help from the cruise line's port agent (listed on the destination information sheet distributed on the ship) and the local TI (see page 504). If the port agent suggests a costly solution (such as a private car with a driver), you may want to consider public transit.

Most train connections—including **Warnemünde, Copenhagen, Amsterdam,** and beyond—are via Berlin (4/day, 7-7.5 hours, transfer in Szczecin or Poznań). To research train schedules, see www.bahn.com. Overland connections to **Rīga** and **Tallinn** are time-consuming; for these and other points north and east, flying may be your best choice. Gdańsk's **Lech Wałęsa Airport** is well-connected to downtown by public bus #210, shuttle van, or taxi (tel. 58-348-1163, www.airport .gdansk.pl).

Local **travel agents** in Gdańsk can help you. For more advice on what to do if you miss the boat, see page 144.

crammed with locals. At these northern latitudes, the season for bathing is brief and crowded.

Overlooking the beach next to the Molo is the **Grand Hotel Sopot.** It was renovated to top-class status just recently, but its history goes way back. They could charge admission for room #226, a multiroom suite that has hosted the likes of Adolf Hitler, Marlene Dietrich, and Fidel Castro (but not all at the same time). With all the trappings of Sopot's belle époque—dark wood, plush upholstery, antique furniture—this room had me imagining Hitler sitting at the desk, looking out to sea, and plotting the course of World War II.

Polish Survival Phrases

Keep in mind a few Polish pronunciation tips: **w** sounds like "v," **ł** sounds like "w," **ch** is a back-of-your-throat "kh" sound (as in the Scottish "loch"), and **rz** sounds like the "zh" sound in "pleasure." The vowels with a tail (**ą** and **ę**) have a slight nasal "n" sound at the end, similar to French.

English	Polish	Pronunciation
Hello. (formal)	Dzień dobry.	jehn **doh**-brih
Hi. / Bye. (informal)	Cześć.	cheshch
Do you speak English? (asked of a man)	Czy Pan mówi po angielsku?	chih pahn **moo**-vee poh ahn-**gyehl**-skoo
Do you speak English? (asked of a woman)	Czy Pani mówi po angielsku?	chih **pah**-nee **moo**-vee poh ahn-**gyehl**-skoo
Yes. / No.	Tak. / Nie.	tahk / nyeh
I (don't) understand.	(Nie) rozumiem.	(nyeh) roh-**zoo**-myehm
Please. / You're welcome. / Can I help you?	Proszę.	**proh**-sheh
Thank you (very much).	Dziękuję (bardzo).	jehn-**koo**-yeh (**bard**-zoh)
Excuse me. / I'm sorry.	Przepraszam.	psheh-**prah**-shahm
(No) problem.	(Żaden) problem.	(**zhah**-dehn) **proh**-blehm
Good.	Dobrze.	**dohb**-zheh
Goodbye.	Do widzenia.	doh veed-**zay**-nyah
one / two	jeden / dwa	**yeh**-dehn / dvah
three / four	trzy / cztery	tzhih / **chteh**-rih
five / six	pięć / sześć	pyench / sheshch
seven / eight	siedem / osiem	**shyeh**-dehm / **oh**-shehm
nine / ten	dziewięć / dziesięć	**jeh**-vyench / **jeh**-shench
hundred / thousand	sto / tysiąc	stoh / **tih**-shants
How much?	Ile?	**ee**-leh
local currency	złoty (zł)	**zwoh**-tih
Write it.	Napisz to.	**nah**-peesh toh
Is it free?	Czy to jest za darmo?	chih toh yehst zah **dar**-moh
Is it included?	Czy jest to wliczone?	chih yehst toh vlee-**choh**-neh
Where can I find / buy...?	Gdzie mogę dostać / kupić...?	guh-**dyeh** moh-geh **doh**-statch / **koo**-peech
I'd like...(said by a man)	Chciałbym...	**khchaw**-beem
I'd like...(said by a woman)	Chciałabym...	**khchah**-wah-beem
We'd like...	Chcielibyśmy...	**khchehl**-ee-bish-mih
...a room.	...pokój.	**poh**-kooey
...a ticket to ___.	...bilet do ___.	**bee**-leht doh ___
Is it possible?	Czy jest to możliwe?	chih yehst toh mohzh-**lee**-veh
Where is...?	Gdzie jest...?	guh-**dyeh** yehst
...the train station	...dworzec kolejowy	**dvoh**-zhehts koh-leh-**yoh**-vih
...the bus station	...dworzec autobusowy	**dvoh**-zhehts ow-toh-boos-**oh**-vih
...the tourist information office	...informacja turystyczna	een-for-**maht**-syah too-ris-**titch**-nah
...the toilet	...toaleta	toh-ah-**leh**-tah
men / women	męska / damska	**mehn**-skah / **dahm**-skah
left / right	lewo / prawo	**leh**-voh / **prah**-voh
straight	prosto	**proh**-stoh
At what time...	O której godzinie...	oh kuh-**too**-ray gohd-**zhee**-nyeh
...does this open / close?	...będzie otwarte / zamknięte?	**bend**-zheh oht-**vahr**-teh / zahm-**knyehn**-teh
Just a moment.	Chwileczkę.	khvee-**letch**-keh
now / soon / later	eraz / niedługo / później	**teh**-rahz / nyed-**woo**-goh / **poozh**-nyey
today / tomorrow	dzisiaj / jutro	**jee**-shigh / **yoo**-troh

In the Restaurant

English	Polish	Pronunciation
I'd like to reserve... (said by a man)	Chciałbym zarezerwować...	**khchaw**-beem zah-reh-zehr-**voh**-vahch
I'd like to reserve... (said by a woman)	Chciałabym zarezerwować...	**khchah**-wah-beem zah-reh-zehr-**voh**-vahch
We'd like to reserve...	Chcielibyśmy zarezerwować...	**khchehl**-ee-bish-mih zah-reh-zehr-**voh**-vahch
...a table for one person / two people.	...stolik na jedną osobę / dwie osoby.	**stoh**-leek nah **yehd**-now oh-**soh**-beh /dvyeh oh-**soh**-bih
Non-smoking.	Niepalący	nyeh-pah-**lohnt**-sih
Is this table free?	Czy ten stolik jest wolny?	chih tehn **stoh**-leek yehst **vohl**-nih
Can I help you?	W czym mogę pomóc?	vchim **moh**-geh **poh**-moots
The menu (in English), please.	Menu (po angielsku), proszę.	**meh**-noo (poh ahn-**gyehl**-skoo) **proh**-sheh
service (not) included	usługa (nie) wliczona	oos-**woo**-gah (nyeh) **vlee**-choh-nah
cover charge	wstęp	vstenp
"to go"	na wynos	nah **vih**-nohs
with / without	z / bez	z / behz
and / or	i / lub	ee / loob
milk bar (cheap cafeteria)	bar mleczny	bar **mletch**-nih
fixed-price meal (of the day)	zestaw (dnia)	**zehs**-tahv (dih-**nyah**)
specialty of the house	specjalność zakładu	speht-**syahl**-nohshch zah-**kwah**-doo
half portion	pół porcji	poow **ports**-yee
daily special	danie dnia	**dah**-nyeh dih-**nyah**
appetizers	przystawki	pshih-**stahv**-kee
bread	chleb	khlehb
cheese	ser	sehr
sandwich	kanapka	kah-**nahp**-kah
soup	zupa	**zoo**-pah
salad	sałatka	sah-**waht**-kah
meat	mięso	**myehn**-soh
poultry	drób	droob
fish	ryba	**rih**-bah
seafood	owoce morza	oh-**voht**-seh **moh**-zhah
fruit	owoce	oh-**voht**-seh
vegetables	warzywa	vah-**zhih**-vah
dessert	deser	**deh**-sehr
(tap) water	woda (z kranu)	**voh**-dah (**skrah**-noo)
mineral water	woda mineralna	**voh**-dah mee-neh-**rahl**-nah
carbonated / not carbonated	gazowana / niegazowana	gah-zoh-**vah**-nah / **nyeh**-gah-zoh-vah-nah
milk	mleko	**mleh**-koh
(orange) juice	sok (pomarańczowy)	sohk (poh-mah-rayn-**choh**-vih)
coffee	kawa	**kah**-vah
tea	herbata	hehr-**bah**-tah
wine	wino	**vee**-noh
red / white	czerwone / białe	chehr-**voh**-neh / bee-**ah**-weh
sweet / dry / semi-dry	słodkie / wytrawne / półwytrawne	**swoht**-kyeh / vih-**trahv**-neh / poow-vih-**trahv**-neh
glass / bottle	szklanka / butelka	**shklahn**-kah / boo-**tehl**-kah
beer	piwo	**pee**-voh
vodka	wódka	**vood**-kah
Cheers!	Na zdrowie!	nah **zdroh**-vyeh
Enjoy your meal.	Smacznego.	smatch-**neh**-goh
More. / Another.	Więcej. / Inny.	**vyehnt**-say / **ee**-nih-nih
The same.	Taki sam.	**tah**-kee sahm
the bill	rachunek	rah-**khoo**-nehk
I'll pay.	Ja płacę.	yah **pwaht**-seh
tip	napiwek	nah-**pee**-vehk
Delicious!	Pyszne!	**pish**-neh

BERLIN
Germany

Germany Practicalities

Germany (Deutschland) is energetic, efficient, and organized. It's Europe's muscleman, both economically and wherever people line up (Germans have a reputation for pushing ahead). At 138,000 square miles (about half the size of Texas), Germany is bordered by nine countries. The terrain gradually rises—from the flat lands of the north to the rugged Alps in the south. The European Union's most populous country and biggest economy, Germany is home to 82 million people—one-third Catholic and one-third Protestant. Germany is young compared to most of its European neighbors ("born" in 1871) but was a founding member of the EU. While it's easy to fixate on the eerie Nazi remnants and chilling reminders of the Cold War, don't overlook Germany's lively squares, fine people zones, and many high-powered sights.

Money: 1 euro (€) = about $1.30. An ATM is called a *Geldautomat*. The local VAT (value-added sales tax) rate is 19 percent; the minimum purchase eligible for a VAT refund is €25 (for details on refunds, see page 139).

Language: The native language is German. For useful phrases, see page 625.

Emergencies: Dial 112 for police, medical, or other emergencies. In case of theft or loss, see page 131.

Time Zone: Germany is on Central European Time (the same as most of the Continent, one hour ahead of Great Britain, and six/nine hours ahead of the East/West Coasts of the US).

Embassies in Berlin: The **US embassy** is at Pariser Platz 2, tel. 030/83050; consular services at Clayallee 170 (tel. 030/8305-1200—consular calls answered Mon-Thu 14:00-16:00 only, www.usembassy.de). The **Canadian embassy** is at Leipziger Platz 17 (tel. 030/203-120, www.germany.gc.ca). Call ahead for passport services.

Phoning: Germany's country code is 49; to call from another country to Germany, dial the international access code (011 from the US/Canada, 00 from Europe, or + from a mobile phone), then 49, followed by the area code (without initial zero) and the local number. For calls within Germany, dial just the number if you are calling locally, and add the area code if calling long distance. To place an international call from Germany, dial 00, the code of the country you're calling (1 for US and Canada), and the phone number. For more tips, see page 1110.

Tipping: A gratuity is included in your bill at sit-down meals, so you don't need to tip further, but it's nice to round up your bill about 5-10 percent for great service. Tip a taxi driver by rounding up the fare a bit (pay €3 on an €2.85 fare). For more tips on tipping, see page 143.

Tourist Information: www.germany.travel

BERLIN
and the PORT of WARNEMÜNDE

Warnemünde • Rostock • Berlin

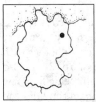

Berlin—Germany's historic and reunited capital—is one of Europe's great cities, and certainly deserves a place on any itinerary. But cruise ships visiting landlocked Berlin actually put in at the port town of Warnemünde (VAHR-neh-mewn-deh), three hours by train or bus to the north. At 150 miles from downtown Berlin, Warnemünde decisively wins the prize for "longest journey time in port." Even if you have a generous 12 to 14 hours in port (as many cruises do here), a visit to Berlin means you'll spend almost as much time in transit as you will in Berlin itself. This leads cruisers to the unavoidable question: To Berlin or not to Berlin?

This chapter covers detailed directions for getting from Warnemünde's cruise port to Berlin, and tips on how to spend your limited time in the city. But for those who don't want to make the trek, I've also suggested ideas for how to spend a day in Warnemünde and the neighboring city of Rostock.

To Berlin or Not to Berlin?

Your first decision is whether to make the long trip to the German capital. Make no mistake: By train, by tour bus, or by Porsche on the Autobahn, plan on at least three hours of travel time each way between your cruise ship at Warnemünde and Berlin—plus time spent sightseeing in Berlin and waiting for train connections.

Fortunately, Warnemünde's train station, which has some direct connections to Berlin, is a simple 5- to 10-minute walk from your ship. (Most trains from Warnemünde require an easy change in Rostock.) I've noted likely departure times on page 553. Better yet, put this book down and go online to www.bahn.com.

Check the times for trains from Warnemünde to "Berlin Hbf" (Hauptbahnhof, the city's main station) on the date you'll arrive, and look for return trains that will give you plenty of time to make the all-aboard. This will give you a realistic sense of how much time you would have in Berlin. A "Berlin On Your Own" cruise excursion, while more expensive than the train, may suit your schedule better and help you avoid the stress of train connections.

If you'd rather not make the trip, you can stick around the Warnemünde/Rostock area. Both towns were part of the communist former East Germany (DDR), which has left them with some less-than-charming architecture. But today **Warnemünde** is a fun, borderline-tacky seafront resort, with a vast sandy beach and a pretty harbor lined with low-impact diversions. And parts of the nearby city of **Rostock** (a 22-minute train ride away) verge on quaint—it has a fine old church, some museums, and a pedestrian core lined with shops and eateries that cater more to locals than to tourists.

Neither Warnemünde nor Rostock would be worth a special trip if you were putting together a "best of Germany" itinerary by train or car. But for a cruiser who doesn't want to bother with Berlin, I can think of worse places to spend a day. You could also treat this as a "half-day at sea"—enjoy nearby sightseeing for a few hours, then retreat to your ship for whatever onboard activities you haven't gotten around to yet.

Planning Your Time

In Berlin

Remember, it takes at least six hours round-trip to go to and from Berlin. That likely leaves you with five or six hours in the city. Arriving by train at the Hauptbahnhof (Berlin's main train station), here's what I'd do:

• **Reichstag, Brandenburg Gate, and Unter den Linden Walk:** From the Hauptbahnhof, ride the U-Bahn or walk about 15 minutes (past grand governmental buildings) to the Reichstag. Ogle the exterior (or, if you've made reservations, ascend the dome—see page 581), then see the Brandenburg Gate, pause at the Memorial to the Murdered Jews of Europe, and follow my self-guided walk up Unter den Linden (considering a detour partway along to the Checkpoint Charlie Museum—see next). Allow 1.5 hours without stops, or—better—up to 3 hours if you fit in a few sights en route. The pleasant square called Gendarmenmarkt is worth the easy five-minute detour south of Unter den Linden (and is on the way to the 20th-century sights mentioned next).

From this sightseeing spine, you'll have to be selective. These are your top options:

• **Museum of the Wall at Checkpoint Charlie, Stretch of Wall, and Topography of Terror:** If you're interested in Berlin's turbulent 20th-century history, consider detouring a few blocks south of Unter den Linden to this little pocket of sights. Allow an hour for the Checkpoint Charlie Museum, and another hour or so for the surviving stretch of the Berlin Wall and Topography of Terror—history buffs should budget even more time.

• **Art Museums:** If you're primarily interested in art, consider spending some of your day at Museum Island (especially the Pergamon Museum, for ancient items—allow 1-2 hours—and the Neues Museum, to see the bust of Nefertiti—allow 1 hour), or at the Kulturforum (the top museum here is the Gemäldegalerie, with Old Masters—allow 2 hours). These two museum zones are in different parts of town—ideally, choose one or the other.

• **Other Museums on Unter den Linden:** If you're staying on the Reichstag/Brandenburg Gate/Unter den Linden sightseeing spine outlined on the previous page, you may want to choose additional museums that are right on the way. These include Museum Island (several branches, described earlier); the excellent German History Museum (allow at least 1 hour, likely more); or the quirky DDR Museum, for a look at communist-era East Germany (allow 1 hour).

• **Additional Sights in Berlin:** If you have a special interest, consider the Jewish Museum Berlin (allow 1-2 hours) or the Berlin Wall Memorial (allow 1.5 hours). Be aware that because they're not right along the Unter den Linden, they'll eat up more transit time. If you're more interested in Berlin's thriving hipster street scene than in museums and history, you could stroll through Prenzlauer Berg (wander north from the Hackescher Markt S-Bahn station). On a very short visit, I'd skip Charlottenburg Palace and other western Berlin sights.

Remember, don't be too ambitious. You'll have time for the Reichstag/Brandenburg Gate/Unter den Linden walk and possibly one of the items listed above (two if you're quick). The key in Berlin is being selective—read my descriptions on the train ride in, make your choices, then hit the ground running.

In Warnemünde and Rostock

If the weather is nice, you could head to the beach in Warnemünde right away; otherwise, take the train to Rostock, see that town, then return to Warnemünde for an afternoon at the beach.

For a quick, targeted visit to Rostock, ride the tram to the Neuer Markt in the Old Town (allow 15 minutes or less), tour St. Mary's Church (allow 30 minutes), walk to University Square and poke around (allow 30 minutes), and consider visiting various museums and churches (none takes more than 30 minutes). On the way back to the station, history buffs will want to visit the Stasi Documentation Center and Memorial (allow about an hour). All told, three or four hours is plenty to get a good taste of Rostock.

Arrival at the Port of Warnemünde

Arrival at a Glance: Walk (5-10 minutes) to the train station to catch a train to Berlin (3 hours one-way, usually requires change in Rostock, infrequent—check schedules) or to Rostock (22 minutes, departures every 15 minutes). To stay in Warnemünde, you can walk to the beach and town center in 15-20 minutes. Consider a train to Berlin only if the schedule works for your cruise arrival and departure—otherwise spring for an "On Your Own" shuttle-bus excursion through your cruise line (more direct and reliable than the train, and generally only a bit more expensive).

Port Overview

Warnemünde is a pleasant former fishing town/seaside resort, situated at the mouth of the Warnow River. Though its port sprawls over a wide area, cruise ships put in at the most convenient location possible—a long pier immediately next to the train station and a short walk from the heart of town. Two main piers feed into empty-feeling terminal buildings.

Tourist Information: There is no TI at the port, but the main branch is about a 10-minute walk away—just past the train station and Alter Strom canal (walking directions later). They hand out free maps and brochures about Warnemünde and Rostock, and try to convince cruisers to remain in the area instead of making the long trip into Berlin (TI open May-Oct Mon-Fri 9:00-18:00, Sat-Sun 10:00-15:00; Nov-April Mon-Fri 10:00-17:00, Sat 10:00-15:00, closed Sun; Am Strom 59, enter around the corner on Kirchenstrasse, tel. 0381/548-000, www.rostock.de).

Alternate Port: On the relatively rare occasions that Warnemünde's main cruise port is full, cruise ships put in across the river and harbor area, at the **passenger ferry terminal (Fährterminal).** From here, there's no direct connection into Warnemünde, but you're about halfway to Rostock; walk about 10 minutes to the suburban railway (S-Bahn) station called Seehafen, and ride the train into Rostock. Some cruise lines also provide a shuttle bus from this terminal into Rostock. From Rostock, you can connect to Berlin or to Warnemünde.

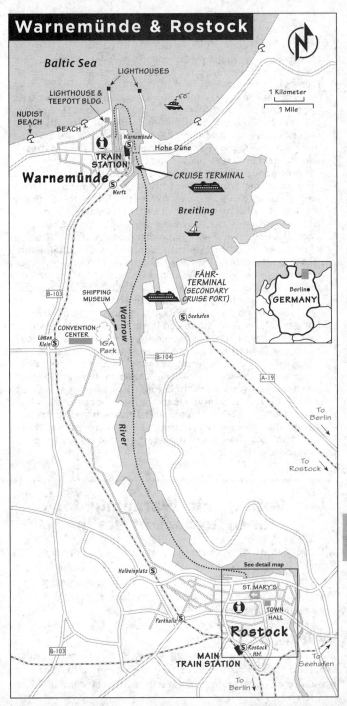

Warnemünde & Rostock

Baltic Sea

LIGHTHOUSES

LIGHTHOUSE &
TEEPOTT BLDG.

NUDIST
BEACH

BEACH

Warnemünde

Ⓢ *Warnemünde*

Hohe Düne

TRAIN
STATION

Warnemünde

Ⓢ

CRUISE TERMINAL

Ⓢ *Werft*

Breitling

B-103

SHIPPING
MUSEUM

FÄHR-
TERMINAL
(SECONDARY
CRUISE PORT)

Warnow

Ⓢ *Seehafen*

CONVENTION
CENTER

Ⓢ
*Lütten
Klein*

IGA
Park

B-104

A-19

To
Berlin

To
Rostock

River

1 Kilometer

1 Mile

Berlin●
GERMANY

Holbeinplatz Ⓢ

See detail map

ST. MARY'S

Parkhalle Ⓢ

TOWN
HALL

Rostock

Ⓢ *Rostock
Hbf.*

MAIN
TRAIN STATION

To
Seehafen

To
Berlin

BERLIN

Excursions from Warnemünde

Most cruisers arriving in Warnemünde head into **Berlin** (3 hours each way by tour bus; some cruise lines charter a train for the journey).

For maximum freedom, consider a **Berlin On Your Own**-type excursion, which is simply a round-trip bus transfer to a central point in the city (often Gendarmenmarkt, just south of Unter den Linden). At around $150-175, this costs 10-35 percent more than the round-trip train fare, but it saves you the stress of coordinating train schedules to get there and back in time.

For about double the price ($300-350), most cruise lines offer an **all-day trip** that includes transportation to Berlin and back, a narrated bus ride around the city, and photo-op stops at major landmarks (these may include the Reichstag, Brandenburg Gate, Memorial to the Murdered Jews of Europe, Checkpoint Charlie, Gendarmenmarkt, Babelplatz, or Potsdamer Platz—all of which are well worth seeing). Some tours also include more in-depth sightseeing stops at a sight or two and/or time on your own before returning to the ship. After transit time, if you have roughly six hours in Berlin, a two- to three-hour bus tour combined with about three hours of free time is a good day.

Carefully note which sights are included in your excursion. For example, cruisers interested in antiquities may appreciate a tour of the **Pergamon,** one of Europe's best museums for ancient sculpture. A **boat trip** on the Spree River through downtown Berlin provides a fine orientation to the city center. Some sights, however, are a waste of your time. **Charlottenburg Palace,** while pretty, ranks low on the list of European castles; it may be worth a drive-by, but its interior does not merit your precious time. And, while the distantly located **Allied Museum** tells the fascinating story of the early days of the Cold War here, I'd much rather spend an hour walking the streets where that history happened than reading about it in a museum.

Getting into Warnemünde, or to Rostock or Berlin

It's a very short stroll to the train station (with connections to Rostock or Berlin), and just a bit farther to Warnemünde's town center, TI, lone museum, and beach. Taxis aren't necessary in Warnemünde unless you're in a hurry to reach Rostock or want to pay a premium to reach Berlin.

By Taxi

Only a few taxis meet arriving ships. While they'll highball estimates for various trips, the fair one-way price to downtown Rostock is €15-20. A ride all the way to Berlin costs around €250.

A themed excursion is worth considering if you're interested in the topic. Most cruise lines offer a guided tour to several actual sites of important **Nazi/WWII/Cold War** history. **Jewish heritage** excursions may visit the outstanding Jewish Museum, the sumptuous New Synagogue, and the poignant Memorial to the Murdered Jews of Europe.

For those who want to stay closer to the ship, there are several options—but be aware that cruise lines push these more for their proximity to the ship than for their sightseeing worthiness. Most common are guided visits of **Warnemünde** (walking tour, sometimes organ concert at the church) and **Rostock** (churches, Old Town, and city wall)—either separately or combined. Sometimes, Warnemünde and Rostock tours throw in a shopping stop in the village of Rövershagen, or a visit to a local microbrewery. Nearby are **Bad Doberan** (with a red-brick Cistercian convent-turned-minster)—a visit here is often combined with a ride on the Molli narrow-gauge steam train to the seaside resorts of Heiligendamm and/or Kühlungsborn; **Wismar** (colorful Hanseatic port town oozing with red-brick buildings), sometimes combined with the even more striking town of **Lübeck; Güstrow Castle** (housing an art museum); and **Schwerin Castle** (a pretty Loire-style palace overlooking an idyllic lake). The Worst Possible Value award goes to the **Rostock On Your Own** "excursion," providing a round-trip bus ride to downtown Rostock and back for $60—more than 10 times the price of the easy train connection.

If you have a special interest, you might consider the palaces of Prussian royalty at **Potsdam** (opulent, but not uniquely so) and **Sachsenhausen Concentration Camp** (with a compelling documentation center of Nazi atrocities). However, both of these are quite close to Berlin (in other words, far from Warnemünde)—and won't save you much more bus time than simply going all the way to the capital.

By Foot to the Train Station or into Downtown Warnemünde

Regardless of which cruise pier you arrive at, go through the terminal building, exit to the right, and walk with the train tracks on your left and the river on your right. Just watch for bull's-eye and *City* signs. You'll pass a hokey gift shop/restaurant (Pier 7 by Karl's), then a small car ferry across the river, and excursion boats to Rostock (€10 one-way, €14 round-trip, departs about hourly, 45 minutes each way). About 50 yards beyond the car-ferry dock, look for signs on the left *(Tourist Information / Historischer Ortkern)* and follow them through the trees and into an underpass that goes beneath the train tracks. On the other side is the **train station** plaza. A departures board is overhead, and red-and-white automated ticket machines are to your left. To your right, you can follow signs for *DB Reiseagentur / Travelcenter* to enter the building with the ticket office (marked *Reiseagentur*). In the same building is the Crew Corner, offering Wi-Fi and Internet access. For more on choosing and buying tickets to Rostock or Berlin, see the next section.

To continue into **town,** proceed through the station area from where you popped out at the underpass, and walk straight ahead across the little bridge, which gives you a good look at the Alter Strom (old harbor). Once over the bridge, continue straight to find the TI, Heimatmuseum (both on the left after one block), and—one block farther—the big Kirchplatz (Church Square, with ATMs and a pharmacy). To reach Warnemünde's beach, turn right just after the bridge and walk up the waterfront street called Am Strom. Stroll along here for about 10 minutes, with pleasure craft on your right and cheesy seaside-resort shops on your left. When the buildings end and you start to see sand dunes, look left to find Warnemünde's trademark old lighthouse and Teepott building (with the wavy roof). Going up the stairs past the lighthouse, you'll come to Warnemünde's boardwalk-like beachfront promenade, with several beach access points on your right.

If you'd like to explore a bit on the way back to the port, consider taking the lane that runs parallel to the old harbor a block inland, Alexandrinenstrasse; while sleepy, it's lined by picturesque cottages.

BERLIN

By Train to Rostock or Berlin

From Warnemünde's little station, trains depart for both Rostock and Berlin.

To reach **Rostock,** suburban trains (called S-Bahn, with the green *S* symbol) depart every 15 minutes. A one-way ticket costs just €1.80. There's also a €4.80 all-day ticket that includes the round-trip journey between Warnemünde and Rostock, plus trams within Rostock (so, if you take the tram from Rostock's station into its town center and back again, this ticket definitely saves you some money). There are multiple stops named Rostock on this line; you'll get off at Rostock Hbf (Hauptbahnhof, the main station). For tips on getting into the town center once you arrive in Rostock, see page 559.

For **Berlin,** train departures are sparse and can vary depending on the day of the week. The times below were accurate as of the 2013 cruise season; note that for most, you need to change trains in Rostock:

Departs Warnemünde	Departs Rostock	Arrives Berlin Hbf.	Type of Train	One-Way Ticket
7:28 (Sat only)	7:42	10:30	ICE (InterCity Express)	€53
8:02 (must transfer in Rostock)	8:34	11:17	RE (regional express)	€45
10:02 (must transfer in Rostock)	10:34	13:17	RE (regional express)	€45
12:02 (must transfer in Rostock)	12:34	15:17	RE (regional express)	€45

Warning: Times change. Double-check the schedule carefully at www.bahn.com (or, when you arrive at Warnemünde, ask at the train station ticket office or use the automated machines). Be aware that delays can occur. You'll need to decide for yourself how close you're willing to cut it getting back to Warnemünde before your all-aboard time.

Schedule Notes: You may see more trains on the schedule; these require a second change, in the town of Schwerin and take about 30-40 minutes longer.

The trains noted above are operated by the German Railway, DeutscheBahn. A different company, called InterConnex (noted by "X" instead of "DB" on schedules), runs private trains along this same route. While these usually don't work well for arriving cruisers, you could check their schedule to see if a handy connection has been added (see www.interconnex.com).

BERLIN

Notice that departures are infrequent—if you're heading to Berlin, don't dawdle getting off the ship. The 8:02 train works best. If you miss it (and it's any day but Sat), you'll have two hours to kill in Warnemünde or Rostock.

The ICE trains are a bit faster and more comfortable—and also more expensive—than the regional trains. But it's not worth waiting around for an ICE departure. Just take whichever train suits your schedule.

For a list of return trains, see the opposite page.

Buying and Validating Tickets: You can buy tickets for either type of train at the red-and-white automated ticket machines at the platform. These have English instructions and take both cash (euros only) and credit cards. (If you happen to be taking an InterConnex train—which is unlikely—you can't buy tickets at these machines.) You can buy any type of ticket at the desk inside the station.

If you buy your ticket at the machine, be sure to validate it in the orange box at the platform before boarding your train.

Arrival in Berlin: Your train will arrive at **Berlin's Hauptbahnhof** (main train station). For more on arriving at this station—and how to get into town from there—turn to page 567.

By Cruise-Line Excursion

In addition to fully guided excursions to Berlin, many cruise lines offer a transportation-only "On Your Own" option: An unguided bus ride from the pier in Warnemünde to Berlin and back at an appointed time, generally leaving you five or six hours in the capital. Some cruise lines even charter a train to make this trip. Although this is pricey (around $150-200 or more, compared to around $115-135 for a round-trip train ticket), it's worth thinking about for the peace of mind it buys. Remember, if you're on a cruise-line trip and there's a traffic jam coming back, the ship will wait for you—but not so if you're returning on your own and your train is late. If one of the public train departures works perfectly for your trip, I'd opt for the train. But if the train times don't sync with your schedule, the "On Your Own" excursion could be well worth the extra $50-75 to buy a couple of extra hours in Berlin.

Your shuttle will likely drop you off at the delightful square called **Gendarmenmarkt**, just south of Unter den Linden in the very center of the Berlin (for a description of this square, see page 604). If you wind up here, you can walk two blocks up Charlottenstrasse and turn left on Unter den Linden to reach Brandenburg Gate and the Reichstag. Then, backtrack down Unter den Linden and continue all the way to Museum Island, following my self-guided walk.

By Tour

Several Berlin tour companies pick up groups at the dock in Warnemünde for all-day tours of the city. Although a tour can be quite expensive on your own, when you divide the cost with fellow cruisers, it becomes affordable. **Ship2shore,** with top-quality guides and a dedication to personal service, offers Berlin day trips tailored to your interests starting at €99 per person (based on a minimum of 12 people; smaller groups also possible: €799/2 people, €880/3-4 people, €975/5-6 people, €1,099/6-11 people; tel. 030/243-58058, www.ship2shore.de, info@ship2shore.de). The **Original Berlin Walks** walking-tour company also runs excursions from Warnemünde into Berlin (€760 for up to 3 people in a minibus, €60/additional person up to a maximum of 7—team up with others on your cruise to reduce the per-person cost; see contact information on page 578).

If you want to stick closer to your ship, consider the **Friends of Dave Tours,** with itineraries focusing on Warnemünde and Rostock, Hanseatic history, or the royal Mecklenburg family (€120-135/person, various tours run every day a cruise is in town, mobile 0174-302-1499, www.friendsofdavetours.com).

Once you reach Berlin, there's a world of great walking tours, hop-on, hop-off bus tours, private guides for hire, and other sightseeing options. For details, see page 574.

Returning to Your Ship

In planning your return from Berlin, be very clear on your ship's all-aboard time and work backward—factoring in the possibility of delays. (For other details, see "Returning to Warnemünde" on page 623.)

Below are some trains that may work for you. The times given here were accurate as of the 2013 cruise season—confirm these locally or at www.bahn.com.

Departs Berlin Hbf.	Arrives Rostock Hbf.	Arrives Warnemünde	Type of Train	One-Way Ticket
14:43	17:24	17:51 (requires change in Rostock)	RE (regional express)	€45
16:43	19:24	19:51 (requires change in Rostock)	RE (regional express)	€45
17:26	19:54	20:10	ICE (InterCity Express)	€53
18:44	21:24	21:51 (requires change in Rostock)	RE (regional express)	€45

BERLIN

Remember, you'll likely need to change trains in Rostock: Local suburban trains (S-Bahn) make this trip every 15 minutes, and the journey to Warnemünde takes 22 minutes. Also figure in the walk from the Warnemünde train station to the cruise port (5-10 minutes, depending on where your ship is docked).

Arriving at the Warnemünde station, go down the stairs between tracks 3 and 4 (labeled *Passaßgierkai*); walk through the trees, turn right, and follow the water to your awaiting ship.

If you get back to Warnemünde with time to spare, explore the town a bit. Walk along the old harbor (Alter Strom—just a 10- to 15-minute walk from your ship), poke around the cottages of the old center, or—with more time—head out to the beach.

See page 623 for help if you miss your boat.

Sights in Warnemünde

A pleasant old fishing town that managed to escape much of the ugliness of the DDR, Warnemünde feels like a tacky, unabashedly fun beachfront resort—like New Jersey's Atlantic City or England's Brighton or Blackpool...although on a much smaller scale. This town has more than its share of bars, fast-food joints, divey hotels, beachwear boutiques, and Euro-vacationers. Those who find Rostock dull and  dreary believe Warnemünde (which is practically its suburb) the city's saving grace. While Warnemünde offers little in the way of culturally broadening sightseeing, it's a fun spot for a beachy break.

See "Arrival at the Port of Warnemünde," earlier, for walking directions from the cruise port into town and its attractions. I've listed items here in the order you'll reach them as you approach from your ship.

Old Harbor (Alter Strom)—Lined with colorful boats and fronted by bars, restaurants, hotels, and shops, this historic canal runs through the middle of Warnemünde. A boat-spotting stroll here is an entertaining way to while away some of your vacation time. From the seaward end of the canal, excursion boats try to lure you in for a one-hour cruise around the harbor and back (generally around €9, catering mostly to German tourists).

Warnemünde History Museum (Heimatmuseum)—This modest museum, tucked in a cute 18th-century house near the TI, traces the history of this modest burg from fishing village to seaside resort, and lets visitors walk through preserved historic rooms.

Cost and Hours: €3; April-Oct Tue-Sun 10:00-18:00, closed Mon; Nov-March Wed-Sun 10:00-17:00, closed Mon-Tue; Alexandrinenstrasse 31, tel. 0381/52667, www.heimatmuseum-warnemuende.de.

Lighthouse (Leuchtturm)—Strategically situated to watch over both the Old Harbor and the beach, Warnemünde's symbol is its 105-foot-tall, tile-clad lighthouse. Completed in 1898, the lighthouse sits next to the distinctively shaped (and aptly named) Teepott building. In the summer, you can climb to the tower's top for a view over Warnemünde and its beach.

Cost and Hours: €2, May-Oct daily 10:00-19:00, closed off-season.

The Beach (Badestrand)—Those who don't associate Germany with beaches haven't laid eyes on its Baltic seafront. Warnemünde

has an incredibly broad, long stretch of white sand. While access to the beach is free, German holiday makers enjoy renting charming, almost whimsical, wicker cabana chairs called *Strandkörbe* for some shade and comfort (you'll find a big swathe of these at the lighthouse end of the beach; €3/hour, €11/day, €13/day for the front row facing the sea, €8 after 14:00). Eyeing this broad expanse of beach, it's easy to see how German imaginations could so easily be seized by David Hasselhof's *Baywatch*. At the far end of the beach, you may see the letters "FKK"—German code for "nude beach."

Near Warnemünde: Rostock

Rostock, a regional capital with sprawling industrial ports and a tidy Old Town, clusters along the Warnow River about nine miles inland from the sea (and Warnemünde). Dating back to Hanseatic times, Rostock was an important shipping and shipbuilding town. Unfortunately, the mid-20th century dealt the town a devastating one-two punch: First, because it had several important aircraft factories, it was leveled by WWII bombs. Second, in the postwar era, it fell on the eastern side of the Iron Curtain, and—although it was the DDR's primary industrial port—Rostock's communist caretakers did an architecturally questionable job of rebuilding. A few historic buildings are scattered around town, and it all feels quite well-kept, but on the whole it lacks the appeal of many German cities of its size. You get the feeling that if Rostock weren't next to a major cruise port, it would get virtually no

BERLIN

tourism...and that would be just fine with everyone.

That said, the city does have a smattering of attractions for cruisers who'd like to do some real sightseeing during their day at the port of Warnemünde.
The hulking St. Mary's Church anchors an Old Town that's not quite old, but is where you'll find most of what there is to see: fragments of the old city walls (including an intact tower), a few museums and churches, and, above all, a workaday urban core

where locals seem to go about their business oblivious to the big glitzy cruise ships that put in just down the river. The nondescript zone between the Old Town and train station hides a fascinating site for those interested in the Cold War: a former Stasi (communist secret police) prison block that's been converted into a museum and documentation center of that dark time.

Orientation to Rostock

With about 200,000 inhabitants, Rostock sprawls along the Warnow River. But nearly everything worth seeing on a quick visit is in the compact Old Town (Altstadt), which is about a mile due north of the Hauptbahnhof. There's little to see in the tidy residential area between the station and the Old Town, with one big exception: the Stasi Museum, which is a five-minute walk south of the Old Town and ring road.

Rostock's waterfront, severed from the Old Town by a busy highway, is dreary and dull—don't go there hoping for a charming, salty stroll.

Tourist Information

Rostock's helpful TI is on University Square in the heart of the Old Town (May-Oct Mon-Fri 9:00-18:00, Sat-Sun 10:00-15:00; Nov-April Mon-Fri 10:00-17:00, Sat 10:00-15:00, closed Sun; Universitätsplatz 6, tel. 0381/381-222, www.rostock.de).

Tours: The historical society based at the Kröpelin Gate leads one-hour walking tours of Rostock in English (€5, every day that a cruise is in town, departs from the gate at 11:00).

Arrival in Rostock

Rostock is a 22-minute suburban train ride from Warnemünde (for specifics on taking the train here, see page 553). Get off the train at the Rostock Hauptbahnhof (main train station, abbreviated Hbf). From here, it's a 15-minute walk or five-minute tram ride to the

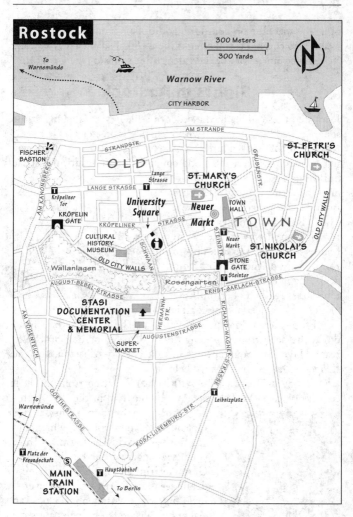

main square and Old Town.

To **walk,** head out the main door to the plaza in front of the station, and proceed straight ahead through the roundabout and up the big street called Rosa-Luxemburg-Strasse; bear left when this becomes Richard-Wagner-Strasse (just follow the tram tracks). You'll cross the ring road, pass the Steintor (Stone Gate of the old city fortifications), and carry on one long block to Neuer Markt and St. Mary's Church.

Taking the **tram** is simple: From the concourse connecting the tracks inside the station, follow the tram icon signs to find the stairs leading down to the tram stop (marked *A*). Buy a €1.80 ticket either at the machine near the tram stop (then stamp it on board)

BERLIN

or at the machine on board (no additional stamp necessary). The ride is also covered if you bought the €4.80 all-day ticket (see page 553). Take tram #5 or #6, and ride it three stops to Neuer Markt.

Sights in Rostock

I've listed these sights in the order of a likely visit, starting at the square called Neuer Markt (with its handy tram stop).

Neuer Markt (New Market Square)—The city's central gathering point, this square is an odd combination of beautiful historic buildings and blah communist-era construction. Highlights include the pretty, pink Town Hall (Rathaus) and the nicely reconstructed row of merchant houses facing it. The fountain in the middle of the square, from 2001, depicts Neptune and his four sons. And the big, hulking brick building overlooking it all is St. Mary's Church.

From Neuer Markt, you can tour the church, then head down the pedestrian shopping drag called Kröpeliner Strasse to reach University Square, the Cultural History Museum, and the Kröpelin Gate—all described below.

▲St. Mary's Church (Marienkirche)—Dating from the 14th century (with WWII damage finally repaired in the 1990s), this is Rostock's main church. Inside, this Gothic brick church is tall, white, and spacious—classic Lutheran. While you'll see bigger and better churches in Germany, this one has a few charming details that are worth lingering over—including a fine astronomical clock, an elaborately decorated bronze baptismal font, and a sumptuous organ loft.

Cost and Hours: €1.50 suggested donation, Mon-Sat 10:00-18:00, Sun 11:15-17:00.

Visiting the Church: Entering through the right transept (facing Neuer Markt), drop your donation in the box, and head into the nave. Turn right and walk up the aisle, circling back behind the main altar to find (in the apse) the intricately detailed **astronomical clock**. Built in 1472, it supposedly still has all of its original working parts. The upper dial tells the time and the sign of the zodiac, while the bottom dial lists the saint's day and pinpoints the date Easter will fall on each year

(I rely on Wikipedia). At noon, the little door next to Jesus at the very top of the clock opens so that the apostles can shuffle around their Savior.

Continue circling around to the other side of the nave, and keep an eye out for the **baptismal font.** Dating from 1290, it's loaded with symbolic details—from the four figures supporting it (representing the four elements) to the bird perched proudly on top (the Holy Spirit, which appeared in the form of a bird at Jesus' own baptism). The base of the font features scenes from Jesus' life. The pointy lid tells the story of Jesus' baptism and his Ascension to heaven; above those panels are female figures depicting the story of the wise virgins who conserved their oil (see the flames in their cups), and the foolish virgins who squandered theirs (notice the empty cups and sad expressions).

Circle back around to the transept. On one of the pillars is an elaborately decorated Renaissance **pulpit.** The prominence of the pulpit, and the fact that the pews are oriented toward the center of the church (and the pulpit) rather than the main altar, are clear indicators that this is a Protestant church—which emphasizes the sermon over the rituals at the altar.

And finally, the pièce de resistance: the gorgeously decorated Baroque **organ** at the back of the church. At the bottom of the altar (and actually predating it) is the Rococo prince's gallery, designed to give a prince who had donated generously to the church a suitable seat for the service.

Organ Performance: Mondays through Saturdays, a brief prayer service from 12:00 to 12:10 includes organ music. Music lovers who show up a few minutes early can meet the organist and go up into the loft to watch him play. In return, they ask that you make a donation and consider buying a CD.

University Square (Universitätsplatz)—From Neuer Markt, the lively, shop-lined Kröpeliner Strasse leads to this square. The TI is in the pretty yellow building on the left as you enter the square. The centerpiece *Fountain of Joy*, a communist-era creation (displaying a lightheartedness unusual for that time), sits in front of the university headquarters. Along the right side (as you face the fountain) are the so-called Five Gables—brick buildings with modern flourishes that were designed to echo the shape and style of the historic houses at these same addresses that were blown apart by WWII bombs. Around the left side of the fountain, past the mustard-yellow building with columns and through the brick gate, is a charming lane leading to the Cultural History Museum (described next).

When you're done exploring here, you can continue two more short blocks on Kröpeliner Strasse (out the far end of the square) to reach the Kröpelin Gate.

BERLIN

Cultural History Museum (Kulturhistorisches Museum)—This fine collection of historical items relating to Rostock is situated around a pleasant former cloister. Unfortunately, its near-total lack of English information makes the eclectic collection challenging to appreciate. The ground floor has local artifacts, a town model, grave markers, historic portraits of important Rostockers, and old wooden chests. Up on the first floor you'll find a particularly nice collection of old toys, porcelain and glassware, clocks, and coins. A small top-floor room shows off early 20th-century art. The museum also often has special exhibits. I consider this a free way to pass some time or get in out of the rain, though true historians or fans of dusty bric-a-brac may find something to get excited about.

Cost and Hours: Free, Tue-Sun 10:00-18:00, closed Mon, Klosterhof 7, tel. 0381/203-5901.

Kröpelin Gate (Kröpeliner Tor)—One of two surviving watchtowers from the old city wall, this picturesque gate (which strikes a medieval pose at the end of Kröpeliner Strasse) contains an exhibit about the town walls and the history of Rostock. You can pay to climb the 109 steps, pausing along the way to see various historical exhibits.

Cost and Hours: €2, daily 10:00-18:00, until 17:00 Nov-Jan, tel. 0381/121-6415.

Nearby: Next to the gate is a surviving stretch of the original town wall. This also marks the course of an inviting park that hems in the southern end of the Old Town.

More Churches—Two other historic churches, interesting for very different reasons, are on the eastern edge of the Old Town.

St. Nikolai's Church (Nikolaikirche), a few blocks east of Neuer Markt, is generally closed to the public, but it's worth taking a close look at its roofline from down below. Are those windows and balconies? During the communist period, the atheistic regime converted part of this church into an apartment complex. Although much of the building has been reclaimed for religious services, if you go to the church's front door, you'll still find a panel of doorbells for people who live here.

St. Petri's Church (Petrikirche), in the northeastern corner of town, overlooks the Alte Markt (Old Market Square). The empty-feeling, white, oh-so-Lutheran interior has little to distinguish it, but you can pay €3 to ride the elevator up to the tower for an okay view over town (which is blocked by fine mesh—making it impossible to get a good photo).

Between the Old Town and the Train Station

▲**Stasi Documentation Center and Memorial**—Hiding in a humdrum residential area, incongruously sharing a parking lot

The Stasi (East German Secret Police)

To keep their subjects in line, the DDR government formed the Ministerium für Staatssicherheit (MfS, "Ministry for State Security")—nicknamed the Stasi. Modeled after the Soviet Union's secret police, the Stasi actively recruited informants from every walk of life, often intimidating them into cooperating by threatening their employment, their children's education, or worse. The Stasi eventually gathered an army of some 600,000 "unofficial employees" (inoffizielle Mitarbeiter), nearly 200,000 of whom were still active when communism fell in 1989. These "employees" were coerced into reporting on the activities of their coworkers, friends, neighbors, and even their own immediate family members.

Preoccupied with keeping track of "nonconformist" behavior, the Stasi collected whatever bits of evidence they could about suspects—including saliva, handwriting, odors, and voice recordings—and wound up with vast amounts of files. In late 1989, when it was becoming clear that communism was in its waning days, Stasi officials attempted to destroy their files—but barely had time to make a dent before government officials decreed that all documentation be preserved as evidence of their crimes. These days, German citizens can read the files that were once kept on them. (Locals struggle with the agonizing decision: Request a full view of their record—and see which friends and loved ones were reporting on them—or avoid the likely painful truth.) For a film that brilliantly captures the paranoid Stasi culture, see the 2006 Oscar-winner The Lives of Others.

with a Penny supermarket, is a building that once held prisoners of the communist state. Today this former prison block has been con-

verted into a museum and documentation center about the crimes of the former regime—specifically, its secret police, known as the Stasi (see sidebar). Worth at least ▲▲ for those interested in the Cold War period in this part of Germany, the museum provides an opportunity to better understand some of Rostock's darkest days.

From 1960 to 1989, this prison held a total of 4,800 people (110 at a time) who were accused of crimes against the state—ranging from participating in protests to attempting to flee the country to simply telling a joke about the regime. Though this was thought to be a "pre-trial prison," some individuals were held here for up to a year and a half. With the help of English explanations and a free

BERLIN

audioguide, you'll walk through the actual prison, peering into cells; some contain exhibits about the Stasi, while others are preserved as they were when they held prisoners. Artifacts illustrate the crimes and methods of the Stasi. For example, the jars with yellow cloths are impregnated with a suspect's scent (they sweat on a chair while being interrogated)—one bizarre example of the many ways the Stasi kept tabs on those they were investigating.

Cost and Hours: Free; March-Oct Tue-Fri 10:00-18:00, Sat 10:00-17:00, closed Sun-Mon; Nov-Feb Tue-Fri 9:00-17:00, Sat 10:00-17:00, closed Sun-Mon; Hermannstrasse 34b, tel. 0381/498-5651, www.bstu.de.

Getting There: The prison, buried in a residential zone, is a bit tricky to find, but it's marked with brown signs when you get nearby—ideally, get a map locally (at the TI). The easiest way to find it is to begin on University Square and head south on Schwaansche Strasse. Passing through the park just south of the Old Town, cross the ring road and continue straight as the street becomes Hermannstrasse. Watch on the right for the Penny supermarket; the prison block is directly across from the entrance.

Between Rostock and Warnemünde

IGA Park and Ship Building and Shipping Museum (Schiffbau- und Schifffahrtmuseum)—If you have ample time and are intrigued by all things maritime, consider hopping off the S-Bahn on your way between Rostock and Warnemünde to see this fine park loaded with kid-friendly attractions (including mini-golf, Chinese and Japanese gardens, flower gardens, a "miniature world," and more). You'll also find the Shipping Museum—which fills five decks of a retired ship—and a boat-building workshop that uses historical techniques.

Cost and Hours: Park-€1, park and museum-€4, daily April-Oct 9:00-18:00 except museum closed Mon in July, Nov-March 10:00-16:00, get off the S-Bahn at the Rostock Lütten Klein stop and walk 15 minutes past the convention center toward the river, www.iga-park-rostock.de.

Berlin

While it takes some effort to reach Berlin from Warnemünde, that effort is warranted. Berlin has emerged as one of Europe's top destinations: captivating, lively, fun-loving, all-around enjoyable—and easy on the budget. For the last two decades, Berlin has been a construction zone. Standing on ripped-up tracks and under a canopy of cranes, visitors witnessed the rebirth of a great European capital. Although construction continues, today the once-divided city is thoroughly woven back together.

As you enjoy the thrill of walking over what was the Wall and through the well-patched Brandenburg Gate, it's clear that history is not contained in some book, but is an exciting story of which we are a part. In Berlin, the fine line between history and current events is excitingly blurry. But even for non-historians, Berlin is a city of fine experiences. Explore the fun and funky neighborhoods emerging in the former East, packed with creative hipster eateries and boutiques trying to one-up each other. Go for a cruise along the delightful Spree riverfront. In the city's world-class museums, stroll up the steps of a classical Greek temple amid rough-and-tumble ancient statuary, and peruse canvases by Dürer, Rembrandt, and Vermeer. Nurse a stein of brew in a rollicking beer hall, or dive into a cheap *Currywurst* (arguably the most beloved food ever to come out of Berlin).

Of course, Berlin is still largely defined by its tumultuous 20th century. The city was Hitler's capital during World War II, and in the postwar years, Berlin became the front line of a new global war—one between Soviet-style communism and American-style capitalism. The East-West division was set in stone in 1961, when the East German government boxed in West Berlin with the Berlin Wall. The Wall stood for 28 years. In 1990, less than a year after the Wall fell, the two Germanys—and the two Berlins—officially became one. When the dust settled, Berliners from both sides of the once-divided city faced the monumental challenge of reunification.

Berliners joke that they don't need to travel anywhere because their city's always changing. Spin a postcard rack to see what's new. A 10-year-old guidebook on Berlin covers a different city. City planners have seized on the city's reunification and the return of the national government to make Berlin a great capital once again. When the Wall fell, the East was a decrepit wasteland and the West was a paragon of commerce and materialism. More than 20 years later, the roles are reversed: It's eastern Berlin where you feel the vibrant pulse of the city, while western Berlin seems like yesterday's news.

BERLIN

Today, Berlin is like the nuclear fuel rod of a great nation. It's vibrant with youth, energy, and an anything-goes-and-anything's-possible buzz. As a booming tourist attraction, Berlin now welcomes more visitors than Rome.

Orientation to Berlin

Berlin is huge, with 3.4 million people. Your time in the city will be short, so you'll need to prioritize.

Most visitors focus on **Eastern Berlin,** with the highest concentration of notable sights and colorful neighborhoods. Near the landmark Brandenburg Gate, you'll find the Reichstag building, Pariser Platz, and the Memorial to the Murdered Jews of Europe. From Brandenburg Gate, the famous Unter den Linden boulevard runs eastward through former East Berlin, passing the German History Museum and Museum Island (Pergamon Museum, Neues Museum, and Berlin Cathedral) on the way to Alexanderplatz (TV Tower). South of Unter den Linden are the delightful Gendarmenmarkt square, most Nazi sites (including the Topography of Terror), some good Wall-related sights (Museum of the Wall at Checkpoint Charlie and East Side Gallery), the Jewish Museum, and the colorful Turkish neighborhood of Kreuzberg. North of Unter den Linden are these worth-a-wander neighborhoods: Oranienburger Strasse (Jewish Quarter and New Synagogue), Hackescher Markt, and Prenzlauer Berg. Eastern Berlin's pedestrian-friendly Spree riverbank is also worth a stroll (or a river cruise).

With so much to see in eastern Berlin, and so little time, it's unlikely you'll venture into the city's other zones. But in case you do, here's the scoop:

Central Berlin is dominated by the giant Tiergarten park. South of the park are Potsdamer Platz and the Kulturforum museum cluster (including the Gemäldegalerie). To the north, the huge Hauptbahnhof (main train station) straddles the former Wall in what was central Berlin's no-man's-land.

Western Berlin centers on the Bahnhof Zoo (Zoo train station, often marked "Zoologischer Garten" on transit maps) and the grand Kurfürstendamm boulevard, nicknamed "Ku'damm" (transportation hub, tours, information, and shopping). On a short visit, I'd skip this part of town—it's long since lost its Cold War-era "downtown" cachet.

Tourist Information

With any luck, you won't have to use Berlin's TIs—they're for-profit agencies working for the city's big hotels, which colors the information they provide. TI branches, appropriately called

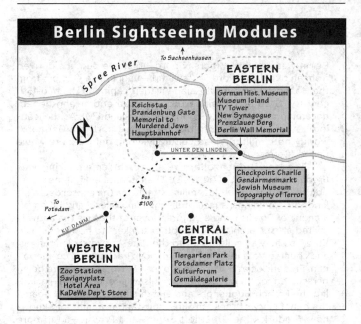

Berlin Sightseeing Modules

Spree River

To Sachsenhausen

EASTERN BERLIN

German Hist. Museum
Museum Island
TV Tower
New Synagogue
Prenzlauer Berg
Berlin Wall Memorial

Reichstag
Brandenburg Gate
Memorial to Murdered Jews
Hauptbahnhof

UNTER DEN LINDEN

Checkpoint Charlie
Gendarmenmarkt
Jewish Museum
Topography of Terror

To Potsdam

Bus #100

KU'DAMM

WESTERN BERLIN

Zoo Station
Savignyplatz
Hotel Area
KaDeWe Dep't Store

CENTRAL BERLIN

Tiergarten Park
Potsdamer Platz
Kulturforum
Gemäldegalerie

"info-stores," are unlikely to have the information you need (tel. 030/250-025, www.visitberlin.de). You'll find them at the **Hauptbahnhof** train station (daily 8:00-22:00, by main entrance on Europaplatz), **Ku'damm** (Kurfürstendamm 22, in the glass-and-steel Neues Kranzler Eck building, Mon-Sat 9:30-20:00, Sun 9:30-18:00), and the **Brandenburg Gate** (daily 9:30-19:00).

Skip the TI's €1 map, and instead pick up any of the walking tour companies' brochures—they include nearly-as-good maps for free. If you take a walking tour, your guide is likely a better source of shopping and restaurant tips than the TI.

Museum Passes: The three-day, €19 **Museumspass** gets you into more than 50 museums, including the national museums and most of the recommended biggies, on three consecutive days (sold at the TI and participating museums). As you'll routinely spend €6-10 per admission, this pays for itself if you'll be visiting multiple museums. However, you'd have to be a very busy sightseer to make the pass pay for itself on a brief visit. The €14 **Museum Island Pass** (Bereichskarte Museumsinsel, price can change with special exhibits) covers all the museums on Museum Island (otherwise €8-13 each) and is a good value if you're spending the day museum-hopping on the island.

Arrival by Train at Berlin Hauptbahnhof

Trains from Warnemünde and Rostock arrive at Berlin's newest and grandest train station, Berlin Hauptbahnhof (main train

The History of Berlin

Berlin was a humble, marshy burg—its name perhaps derived from an old Slavic word for "swamp"—until prince electors from the Hohenzollern dynasty made it their capital in the mid-15th century. Gradually their territory spread and strengthened, becoming the powerful Kingdom of Prussia in 1701. As the leading city of Prussia, Berlin dominated the northern Germanic world—both militarily and culturally—long before there was a united "Germany."

The only Hohenzollern ruler worth remembering was Frederick the Great (1712-1786). The ultimate enlightened despot, he was both a ruthless military tactician (he consolidated his kingdom's holdings, successfully invading Silesia and biting off a chunk of Poland) and a cultured lover of the arts (he actively invited artists, architects, and other thinkers to his lands). "Old Fritz," as he was called, played the flute, spoke six languages, and counted Voltaire among his friends. Practical and cosmopolitan, Frederick cleverly invited groups to Prussia who were being persecuted for their Protestantism elsewhere in Europe—including the French Huguenots and Dutch traders. Prussia became the beneficiary of these groups' substantial wealth and know-how. Frederick the Great left Berlin—and Prussia—a far more modern and enlightened place than he found it. Thanks largely to Frederick, Prussia was well-positioned to become a magnet of sorts for the German unification movement in the 19th century.

When Germany first unified, in 1871, Berlin (as the main city of its most powerful constituent state, Prussia) was its natural capital. After Germany lost World War I, although the country was in disarray, Berlin thrived as an anything-goes, cabaret-crazy cultural capital of the Roaring '20s. The city was Hitler's headquarters—and the place where the Führer drew his final breath—during World War II. When the Soviet Army reached Berlin, the protracted fighting (and vengeful postwar destruc-

station, a.k.a. simply "der Bahnhof," abbreviated Hbf). Europe's biggest, mostly underground train station is unique for its major lines coming in at right angles; this is where the national train system meets the city's train system (S-Bahn).

The gigantic station can be intimidating on arrival, but it's laid out logically on five floors (which, confusingly, can be marked in different ways). Escalators and elevators connect the **main floor** (*Erdgeschoss*, EG, a.k.a level 0); the two **lower levels** (*Untergeschoss*, UG1 and UG2, a.k.a. levels

tion) left the city in ruins.

In the years following World War II, Berlin was divided by the victorious Allied powers: The American, British, and French sectors became West Berlin, and the Soviet sector, East Berlin. In 1948 and 1949, the Soviet Union tried to starve the Western half (with approximately 2.2 million people) into submission in an almost medieval-style siege, blockading all roads into and out. But the siege was foiled by the Western Allies' Berlin Airlift, which flew in supplies from Frankfurt 24 hours a day for 10 months. With the overnight construction of the Berlin Wall—which completely surrounded West Berlin—in 1961, an Iron (or, at least, concrete) Curtain literally cut through the middle of the city. For details, see "The Berlin Wall (and Its Fall)" on page 608.

While the wild night when the Wall came down was inspiring, Berlin still faced a long and fitful transition to reunification. Two cities—and countries—became one at a staggering pace. Reunification had its negative side, and locals say, "The Wall survives in the minds of some people." Some "Ossies" (impolite slang for Easterners) miss their security. Some "Wessies" miss their easy ride (military deferrals, subsidized rent, and tax breaks offered to West Germans willing to live in an isolated city surrounded by the communist world). For free spirits, walled-in West Berlin was a citadel of freedom within the East.

But in recent years, the old East-West division has faded more and more into the background. Ossi-Wessi conflicts no longer dominate the city's political discourse. The city government has been eager to charge forward, with little nostalgia for anything that was associated with the East. Big corporations and the national government have moved in, and the dreary swath of land that was the Wall and its notorious "death strip" has been transformed. Berlin is a whole new city—ready to welcome visitors.

-1 and -2); and the two **upper levels** (*Obergeschoss*, OG1 and OG2, a.k.a. levels +1 and +2). Tracks 1-8—most often used by trains to and from Rostock/Warnemünde—are in the lowest underground level (UG2), while tracks 11-16 (along with the S-Bahn, for connecting to other points in town) are on the top floor (OG2). Shops and services are concentrated on the three middle levels (EG, OG1, and UG1). The south entrance (toward the Reichstag and downtown, with a taxi stand) is marked *Washingtonplatz*, while the north entrance is marked *Europaplatz*.

Services: The **TI** is on the main floor (EG)—facing the north/*Europaplatz* entrance, look left; a 24-hour **pharmacy** is across the hall on the right (one floor above you, on OG1). The **"Rail & Fresh WC"** facility (public pay toilets) is on the main

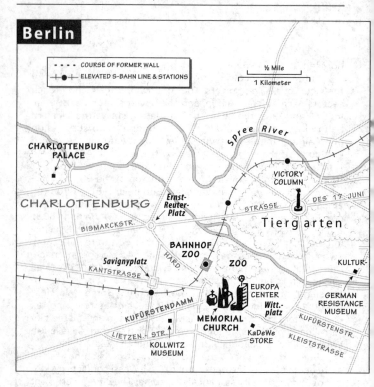

Berlin

- - - COURSE OF FORMER WALL
+•+•+•+• ELEVATED S-BAHN LINE & STATIONS

½ Mile
1 Kilometer

CHARLOTTENBURG PALACE

Spree River

VICTORY COLUMN

CHARLOTTENBURG

Ernst-Reuter-Platz

STRASSE   DES 17 JUNI

Tiergarten

BISMARCKSTR.

BAHNHOF ZOO

Savignyplatz

HARD.

KANTSTRASSE

ZOO

KULTUR-

EUROPA CENTER

Witt.-platz

GERMAN RESISTANCE MUSEUM

KUFÜRSTENDAMM

MEMORIAL CHURCH

LIETZEN.- STR.

KOLLWITZ MUSEUM

KaDeWe STORE

KUFÜRSTENSTR.

KLEISTSTRASSE

floor (EG) near the Burger King and food court.

Train Information and Tickets: Before leaving the station, it's smart to reconfirm the schedule for trains back to Warnemünde—and, while you're at it, buy your ticket. The station has two DeutscheBahn *Reisezentrum* information counters: one on the upper level (OG1/+1, daily 6:00-22:00), and the other on the lower level (UG1/-1, Mon-Fri 8:00-22:00, Sat-Sun 10:00-20:00; this branch also has the EurAide counter described next). **EurAide** is an English-speaking information desk with answers to your questions about train travel around Europe. It operates from a single counter in the underground shopping level *Reisezentrum* (follow signs to tracks 5-6 and *Reisezentrum -1*). It's American-run, so communication is simple (www.euraide.com).

Shopping: In addition to all those trains, the Hauptbahnhof is also the home of 80 shops with long hours—some locals call the station a "shopping mall with trains" (daily 8:00-22:00, only stores selling travel provisions are open Sun). The Kaisers supermarket (on underground shopping level UG1, follow signs for tracks 1-2) is handy for assembling a picnic for your train ride.

Getting into Town: If you're in town for just a few hours, you'll likely want to head straight for the Brandenburg Gate,

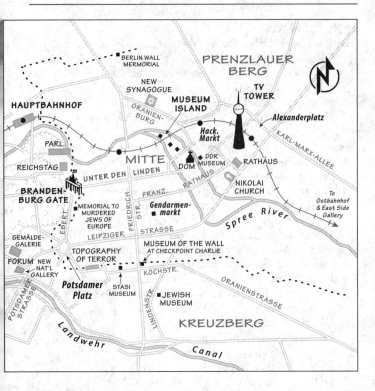

next to the Reichstag and at the start of Unter den Linden. You can **walk** (past big, governmental buildings) from the station to the Brandenburg Gate in about 15 minutes (use the exit marked *Washingtonplatz*, cut through the plaza to the footbridge, cross the river, and bear left past the boxy Bundestag building toward the glass dome—the Reichstag). To save time, ride the **subway:** The station's sole U-Bahn line—U55—goes only two stops, to the Brandenburger Tor station. The U-Bahn isn't covered by your train ticket, so you'll have to buy a ticket before hopping on; it's covered by the cheap €1.40 *Kurzstrecke* short-ride ticket (for details, see page 573).

To reach other points in town (or for a quick return to the station), consider the handy cross-town express **S-Bahn** train line. All S-Bahn trains are on tracks 15 and 16 at the top of the station (level OG2/+2). All trains on track 15 go east, stopping at Friedrichstrasse, Hackescher Markt (with connections to Prenzlauer Berg), Alexanderplatz, and Ostbahnhof; trains on track 16 go west, toward Bahnhof Zoo and Savignyplatz. Your train ticket or railpass to the station covers your connecting S-Bahn ride into town (and your ticket out includes the transfer via S-Bahn to the Hauptbahnhof).

Helpful Hints

Medical Help: "**Call a doc**" is a nonprofit referral service designed for tourists (tel. 01805-321-303, phone answered 24 hours a day, www.calladoc.com). Payment is arranged between you and the doctor, and is likely far more affordable than similar care in the US. The US Embassy also has a list of local English-speaking doctors (tel. 030/83050, www.usembassy.de).

Museum Tips: Some major Berlin museums are closed on Monday—if you're in town on that day, review hours carefully before making plans.

Addresses: Many Berlin streets are numbered with odd and even numbers on the same side of the street, often with no connection to the other side (for example, Ku'damm #212 can be across the street from #14). To save steps, check the white street signs on curb corners; many list the street numbers covered on that side of the block.

Cold War Terminology: Cold War history is important here, so it's helpful to learn a few key terms. What Americans called "East Germany" was technically the German Democratic Republic—known here by its German name, the Deutsche Demokratische Republik. The initials **DDR** (day-day-AIR) are the shorthand you'll still see around what was once East Germany. The formal name for "West Germany" was the Federal Republic of Germany—the Bundesrepublik Deutschland (BRD)—and is the name now shared by all of reunited Germany.

Internet Access: You'll find Internet access at small Internet cafés all over the city. Near Savignyplatz, **Internet-Terminal** is at Kantstrasse 38. In eastern Berlin, try **Hotdog World** in Prenzlauer Berg (Weinbergsweg 4, just a few steps from U8: Rosenthaler Platz toward Kastanienallee), or **Surf Inn** at Alexanderplatz 9. Bahnhof Zoo, Friedrichstrasse, and Hauptbahnhof train stations have coin-operated Internet terminals (though these unmanned machines can come with greater security risks).

Bookstore: Berlin Story, a big, cluttered, fun bookshop, has a knowledgeable staff and the best selection anywhere in town of English-language books on Berlin. They also stock an amusing mix of knickknacks and East Berlin nostalgia souvenirs (Mon-Sat 10:00-19:00, Sun 10:00-18:00, Unter den Linden 40, tel. 030/2045-3842, www.berlinstory.de). I'd skip the overpriced little museum in the back.

Other Berlin Souvenirs: If you're taken with the city's unofficial mascot, the *Ampelmännchen* (traffic-light man), you'll find a world of souvenirs slathered with his iconic red and green image at **Ampelmann Shops** (various locations, including near Gendarmenmarkt at Markgrafenstrasse 37, near Museum Island inside the DomAquarée mall, in the Hackeschen Höfe, and at Potsdamer Platz).

Updates to this Book: For news about changes to this book's coverage since it was published, see www.ricksteves.com/update.

Getting Around Berlin

Berlin's sights spread far and wide. Right from the start, commit yourself to the city's fine public-transit system.

By Public Transit: Subway, Train, Tram, and Bus

Berlin's many modes of transportation are consolidated into one system that uses the same tickets: U-Bahn (*Untergrund-Bahn*, Berlin's subway), S-Bahn (*Stadtschnellbahn*, or "fast urban train," mostly aboveground and with fewer stops), *Strassenbahn* (streetcars, called "trams" by locals), and buses. For all types of transit, there are three lettered zones (A, B, and C). Most of your sightseeing will be in zones A and B (the city proper). Get and use the excellent *Discover Berlin by Train and Bus* map-guide published by the public transit operator BVG (at subway ticket windows).

Ticket Options: You have several options for tickets.

• The €2.30 **basic** ticket *(Einzelfahrschein)* covers two hours of travel in one direction on buses or subways. It's easy to make this ticket stretch to cover several rides...as long as they're all in the same direction.

• The €1.40 **short-ride** ticket *(Kurzstrecke)* covers a single ride of six bus stops or three subway stations (one transfer allowed).

• The €8.20 **four-trip** ticket *(4-Fahrten-Karte)* is the same as four basic tickets at a small discount.

• The **day pass** *(Tageskarte)* is good until 3:00 the morning after it expires (€6.30 for zones AB, €6.80 for zones ABC). The *Kleingruppenkarte* lets groups of up to five travel all day (€15 for zones AB, €15.50 for zones ABC).

Buying Tickets: You can buy U- and S-Bahn tickets from machines at stations. (They are also sold at BVG pavilions at train stations and the TI, and on board trams and buses—drivers give change.) *Erwachsener* means "adult"—anyone 14 or older. Don't be afraid of the automated machines: First select the type of ticket you want, then load the coins or paper bills. As you board the bus or tram, or enter the subway system, punch your ticket in a red or yellow clock machine to validate it (or risk a €40 fine—which may increase to €200 in 2013; for an all-day or multiday pass, stamp it only the first time you ride). Be sure to travel with a valid ticket. Tickets are checked frequently, often by plainclothes inspectors. Within Berlin, train tickets or railpasses are good only on S-Bahn connections from the train station when you arrive and to the station when you depart.

Transit Tips: The S-Bahn crosstown express is a river of public transit through the heart of the city, in which many lines converge on one basic highway. Get used to this, and you'll leap within a few minutes between key locations: Savignyplatz (in western Berlin), Bahnhof Zoo (Ku'damm), Hauptbahnhof (all major trains in and out of Berlin), Friedrichstrasse (a short walk north of the heart of Unter den Linden), Hackescher Markt (Museum Island, restaurants, near Prenzlauer Berg), and Alexanderplatz (eastern end of Unter den Linden).

Sections of the U- or S-Bahn sometimes close temporarily for repairs. In this situation, a bus route often replaces the train (*Ersatzverkehr,* or "replacement transportation"; *zwischen* means "between").

Berlin's public transit is operated by BVG (except the S-Bahn, run by the DeutscheBahn). Schedules, including bus timetables, are available on the helpful BVG website (www.bvg.de).

By Taxi

Taxis are easy to flag down, and taxi stands are common. A typical ride within town costs €8-10, and a crosstown trip (for example, Bahnhof Zoo to Alexanderplatz) will run about €15. Tariff 1 is for a *Kurzstrecke* (see below). All other rides are tariff 2 (€3.20 drop plus €1.65/kilometer). If possible, use cash—paying with a credit card comes with a hefty surcharge (about €4, regardless of the fare).

Money-Saving Taxi Tip: For any ride of less than two kilometers (about a mile), you can save several euros if you take advantage of the *Kurzstrecke* (short-stretch) rate. To get this rate, it's important that you flag the cab down on the street—not at or even near a taxi stand. Also, you must ask for the *Kurzstrecke* rate as soon as you hop in: Confidently say *"Kurzstrecke, bitte"* (KOORTS-shtreh-keh, BIT-teh), and your driver will grumble and flip the meter to a fixed €4 rate (for a ride that would otherwise cost €7).

Tours in Berlin

▲▲▲Hop-on, Hop-off Bus Tours

Several companies offer the same routine: a €15 circuit of the city with unlimited hop-on, hop-off privileges all day (about 14 stops at the city's major sights) on buses with cursory narration in English and German by a live (but tired) guide or a boring recorded commentary in whatever language you want to dial up. In season, each company has buses running four times per hour. They are cheap and great for photography—and Berlin really lends itself to this kind of bus-tour orientation. You can hop off at any major tourist spot (Potsdamer Platz, Museum Island, Brandenburg Gate, and so on). If possible, go with a live guide rather than the recorded spiel. When choosing seats, check the sun/shade situation—some buses are entirely topless, and others are entirely covered. My favorites are topless with a shaded covered section in the back (April-Oct daily 10:00-18:00, last bus leaves all stops at 16:00, 2-hour loop; for specifics, look for brochures at the TI). Keep your ticket so you can hop off and on (with the same company) all day. In winter (Nov-March), buses come only twice an hour, and the last departure is at 15:00. Brochures explain extras offered by each company.

▲▲▲Walking Tours

Berlin, with a fascinating recent history that can be challenging to appreciate on your own, is an ideal place to explore with a walking tour. The city is a battle zone of extremely competitive and creative walking-tour companies. Unlike many other European countries, Germany has no regulations controlling who can give city tours. This can make guide quality hit-or-miss, ranging from brilliant history buffs who've lived in Berlin for years while pursuing their PhDs, to new arrivals who memorize a script and start leading tours after being in town for just a couple of weeks. A good Berlin tour guide is equal parts historian and entertainer; the best tours make the city's dynamic story come to life. While upstart companies abound, in general you have the best odds of landing a great guide by using one of the more established companies I recommend in this section.

Most outfits offer walks that are variations on the same themes: general **introductory** walk, **Third Reich** (Hitler and Nazi sites), and day trips to Potsdam and the Sachsenhausen Concentration Camp Memorial (which you won't have time for on a quick port visit). Most in-town tours cost about €12-15 and last about three to four hours; public-transit tickets and entrances to sights are extra. I've included some basic descriptions for each company, but for details—including prices and specific schedules—see the various websites or look for brochures in town (widely available at TIs, hotel reception desks, and many cafés and shops).

Vive Berlin—Formed by some of the city's most experienced guides, this "guiding collective" offers an introductory walk (Essential Berlin, Mon-Tue at 10:00), Third Reich and Cold War itineraries, and a Kreuzberg bike tour. Each tour is woven around the experiences of a real-life Berliner. Meet at Potsdamer Platz 10,

BERLIN

Berlin at a Glance

▲▲▲German History Museum The ultimate swing through Germany's tumultuous story. **Hours:** Daily 10:00-18:00. See page 596.

▲▲▲Pergamon Museum World-class museum of classical antiquities on Museum Island, featuring the fantastic second-century B.C. Greek Pergamon Altar and frieze. **Hours:** Daily 10:00-18:00, Thu until 21:00. See page 599.

▲▲Reichstag Germany's historic parliament building, topped with a striking modern dome you can climb (reservations required). **Hours:** Daily 8:00-24:00, last entry at 23:00. See page 580.

▲▲Brandenburg Gate One of Berlin's most famous landmarks, a massive columned gateway, at the former border of East and West. **Hours:** Always open. See page 586.

▲▲Memorial to the Murdered Jews of Europe Holocaust memorial with almost 3,000 symbolic pillars, plus an exhibition about Hitler's Jewish victims. **Hours:** Memorial always open; information center open Tue-Sun 10:00-20:00, Oct-March until 19:00, closed Mon. See page 587.

▲▲Unter den Linden Leafy boulevard through the heart of former East Berlin, lined with some of the city's top sights. **Hours:** Always open. See page 590.

▲▲Neues Museum and Egyptian Collection Proud home (on Museum Island) of the exquisite 3,000-year-old bust of Queen Nefertiti. **Hours:** Daily 10:00-18:00, Thu-Sat until 20:00. See page 599.

▲▲Gendarmenmarkt Inviting square bounded by twin churches (one with a fine German history exhibit), a chocolate shop, and a concert hall. **Hours:** Always open. See page 604.

▲▲Topography of Terror Chilling exhibit documenting the Nazi perpetrators, built on the site of the former Gestapo/SS headquarters. **Hours:** Daily 10:00-20:00. See page 606.

▲▲**Museum of the Wall at Checkpoint Charlie** Kitschy but moving museum with stories of brave Cold War escapes, near the former site of the famous East-West border checkpoint; the surrounding street scene is almost as interesting. **Hours:** Daily 9:00-22:00. See page 607.

▲▲**Jewish Museum Berlin** Engaging, accessible museum celebrating Jewish culture, in a highly conceptual building. **Hours:** Daily 10:00-20:00, Mon until 22:00. See page 610.

▲▲**Gemäldegalerie** Germany's top collection of 13th- through 18th-century European paintings, featuring Holbein, Dürer, Cranach, Van der Weyden, Rubens, Hals, Rembrandt, Vermeer, Velázquez, Raphael, and more. **Hours:** Tue-Sun 10:00-18:00, Thu until 22:00, closed Mon. See page 616.

▲**Old National Gallery** German paintings, mostly from the Romantic Age. **Hours:** Tue-Sun 10:00-18:00, Thu until 22:00, closed Mon. See page 600.

▲**DDR Museum** Quirky collection of communist-era artifacts. **Hours:** Daily 10:00-20:00, Sat until 22:00. See page 602.

▲**New Synagogue** Largest prewar synagogue in Berlin, damaged in World War II, with a rebuilt facade and modest museum. **Hours:** March-Oct Sun-Mon 10:00-20:00, Tue-Thu 10:00-18:00, Fri 10:00-17:00—until 14:00 Oct and March-May, closed Sat; Nov-Feb Sun-Thu 10:00-18:00, Fri 10:00-14:00, closed Sat. See page 612.

▲**Berlin Wall Memorial** A "docu-center" with videos and displays, several outdoor exhibits, and lone surviving stretch of an intact Wall section. **Hours:** Visitor Center April-Oct Tue-Sun 9:30-19:00, Nov-March until 18:00, closed Mon; outdoor areas accessible 24 hours daily. See page 614.

▲**Potsdamer Platz** The "Times Square" of old Berlin, long a postwar wasteland, now rebuilt with huge glass skyscrapers, an underground train station, and—covered with a huge canopy—the Sony Center mall. **Hours:** Always open. See page 615.

BERLIN

in front of Balzac Coffee (U2/S-Bahn: Potsdamer Platz, use Stresemannstrasse exit; tel. 0157/845-46696, www.viveberlintours.de).

Insider Tour—This well-regarded company runs the full gamut of itineraries: introductory walk (daily), Third Reich, Cold War, Jewish Berlin, and bike tours. Their tours have two meeting points (some tours convene at both, others at just one—check the schedule): in the West at the McDonald's across from Bahnhof Zoo, and in the East at AMT Coffee at the Hackescher Markt S-Bahn station (tel. 030/692-3149, www.insidertour.com).

Brewer's Berlin Tours—Specializing in longer, more in-depth walks, this company was started by Terry Brewer, who retired from the British diplomatic service in East Berlin. Today Terry's guides lead exhaustive—or, for some, exhausting—tours through the city (their Best of Berlin introductory tour, billed at 6 hours, can last 8 hours or more; daily at 10:30). Terry himself (who can be a bit gruff) leads a "six-hour" tour to some off-the-beaten-path hidden gems of Berlin twice weekly. They also do all-day Potsdam tours. Their tours depart from Bandy Brooks ice cream shop at the Friedrichstrasse S-Bahn station (tel. 030/2248-7435, mobile 0177-388-1537, www.brewersberlintours.com).

Original Berlin Walks—Aiming at a clientele that's curious about the city's history, their flagship introductory walk, Discover Berlin, offers a good overview in four hours (daily year-round, meet at 10:00 at Bahnhof Zoo, April-Oct also daily at 13:30). They offer a Third Reich walking tour (4/week in summer) and themed Jewish Life in Berlin and Nest of Spies walks (both 1/week April-Oct only). Readers of this book get a €1 discount per tour in 2013. You can buy tickets in advance at any S-Bahn service center, or just show up and buy a ticket from the guide. All tours meet at the taxi stand in front of the Bahnhof Zoo train station; the Discover Berlin and Jewish Life tours also have a second departure point opposite East Berlin's Hackescher Markt S-Bahn station, outside the Weihenstephaner restaurant (tour info: tel. 030/301-9194, www.berlinwalks.de).

Sandeman's New Europe Berlin "Free" Tours—You'll see this company advertising supposedly "free" introductory tours, plus paid itineraries similar to those offered by competitors. But Sandeman's tours aren't really free—just misleading. Guides for the "free" tours pay the company a cut of €3 per person, so they hustle for tips. They expect to be "tipped in paper" (i.e., €5 minimum tip per person). This business model leads to high guide turnover, meaning that the guides are, overall, less experienced (though some are quite entertaining). They offer the standard Berlin itineraries, but target a younger crowd. Basic introductory city walks leave daily at 9:00, 11:00, 13:00, and 16:00 from outside the Starbucks on Pariser Platz, near the Brandenburg Gate (tel.

030/5105-0030, www.newberlintours.com).

Local Guides—**Nick Jackson** (mobile 0171-537-8768, nick.jackson @berlin.de) and **Lee Evans** (mobile 0177-423-5307, lee.evans @berlin.de) enjoy sharing the story of their adopted hometown with visitors. If they're busy, try **Jennifer DeShirley** at Berlin and Beyond—this company has a crew of excellent, professional guides with an academic bent (tel. 030/8733-0584, mobile 0176-633-55565, info@berlinandbeyond.de). **Bernhard Wagner** is a young, enthusiastic historian with a particular passion for Germany's 20th-century history (mobile 0176-6422-9119, schlegelmilch @gmx.net).

Bike Tours

Fat Tire Bike Tours—Choose among five different tours (each €24, 4-6 hours, 6-10 miles): **City Tour** (March-Nov daily at 11:00, May-Sept also daily at 16:00, Dec-Feb Wed and Sat at 11:00), **Berlin Wall Tour** (April-Oct Mon, Thu, and Sat at 10:30), **Third Reich Tour** (April-Oct Wed, Fri, and Sun at 10:30), **"Raw" Tour** (covers countercultural, creative aspects of contemporary Berlin, April-Oct Tue, Fri, and Sun at 10:30), and **Gardens and Palaces of Potsdam Tour** (April-Oct Wed, Sat, and Sun at 10:00). For any tour, meet at the TV Tower at Alexanderplatz—but don't get distracted by the Russians pretending to be Fat Tire (reserve ahead for the Wall, Third Reich, Raw, and Potsdam tours, no reservations necessary for City Tour, tel. 030/2404-7991, www.fattire biketours.com).

Finding Berlin Tours—This small, easygoing company offers tours that take you away from the mainstream sights and focus on Berlin's neighborhoods, people, and street art (€20-25/person, max 8 people, 3-5 hours, meet at Revaler Strasse 99, near intersection with Warschauer Strasse—look for gate with *RAW* sign and walk into courtyard to their shipping-container kiosk, S-Bahn: Warschauer Strasse, mobile 0176-9933-3913, see schedule at www .findingberlin-tours.com).

Boat Tours

Spree River Cruises—Several boat companies offer one-hour,

€10 trips up and down the river. A relaxing hour on one of these boats can be time and money well-spent. You'll listen to excellent English audioguides, see lots of wonderful new government-commissioned architecture, and enjoy the lively park action fronting the river. Boats leave from

various docks that cluster near the bridge at the Berlin Cathedral (just off Unter den Linden). I enjoyed the Historical Sightseeing Cruise from **Stern und Kreisschiffahrt** (mid-March-Nov daily 10:30-18:30, leaves from Nikolaiviertel Dock—cross bridge from Berlin Cathedral toward Alexanderplatz and look right, tel. 030/536-3600, www.sternundkreis.de). Confirm that the boat you choose comes with English commentary.

Sights in Eastern Berlin

The following sights are arranged roughly west to east, from the Reichstag down Unter den Linden to Alexanderplatz. It's possible to link these sights as a convenient self-guided orientation walk (I've included walking directions for this purpose)—allow about 1.5 hours without stops for sightseeing. Adding tours of several sights can easily fill a whole day. Remember that reservations are required for the Reichstag dome, and you'll need timed-entry tickets for the Pergamon and Neues Museums.

Also described here are sights to the south and north of Unter den Linden.

▲▲Reichstag

The parliament building—the heart of German democracy—has a short but complicated and emotional history. When it was

inaugurated in the 1890s, the last emperor, Kaiser Wilhelm II, disdainfully called it the "chatting home for monkeys" *(Reichsaffenhaus)*. It was placed outside of the city's old walls—far from the center of real power, the imperial palace. But it was from the Reichstag that the German Republic was proclaimed in 1918.

In 1933, this symbol of democracy nearly burned down. The Nazis—whose influence on the German political scene was on the rise—blamed a communist plot. A Dutch communist, Marinus van der Lubbe, was eventually convicted and guillotined for the crime. Others believed that Hitler himself planned the fire, using it as a handy excuse to frame the communists and grab power. Even though Van der Lubbe was posthumously pardoned by the German government in 2008, most modern historians concede that he likely was indeed guilty, and had acted alone—the Nazis were just incredibly lucky to have his deed advance their cause.

The Reichstag was hardly used from 1933 to 1999. Despite the fact that the building had lost its symbolic value, Stalin ordered his troops to take the Reichstag from the Nazis by May 1, 1945 (the date of the workers' May Day parade in Moscow). More than 1,500 Nazi soldiers made their last stand here—extending World War II by two days. On April 30, after fierce fighting on this roof-top, the Reichstag fell to the Red Army.

For the building's 101st birthday in 1995, the Bulgarian-American artist Christo wrapped it in silvery gold cloth. It was then wrapped again—in scaffolding—and rebuilt by British archi-tect Lord Norman Foster into the new parliamentary home of the Bundestag (Germany's lower house, similar to the US House of Representatives). To many Germans, the proud resurrection of the Reichstag symbolizes the end of a terrible chapter in their coun-try's history.

The **glass cupola** rises 155 feet above the ground. Its two sloped ramps spiral 755 feet to the top for a grand view. Inside the dome, a cone of 360 mirrors reflects natural light into the legisla-tive chamber below. Lit from inside at night, this gives Berlin a memorable nightlight. The environmentally friendly cone—with an opening at the top—also helps with air circulation, drawing stale air out of the legislative chamber (no joke) and pulling in cool air from below.

Because of recent concerns about terrorist threats, the entry procedure has been in flux in recent years; a reservation is techni-cally required and strongly encouraged, but you may be able to get in without one.

Cost and Hours: Free but reservations highly recom-mended—see below, daily 8:00-24:00, last entry at 23:00, metal detectors, no big luggage allowed, Platz der Republik 1; S- or U-Bahn: Friedrichstrasse, Brandenburger Tor, or Bundestag; tel. 030/2273-2152, www.bundestag.de.

Reservations: To visit the dome, it's best to make a reser-vation (free); spots book up several days in advance. If you're in Berlin without a reservation, try dropping by the visitors center (on the Tiergarten side of Scheidemannstrasse, across from Platz der Republik) to ask if they have open slots (whole party must be pres-ent, ID required, slots available no less than 2 hours and no more than 2 days out).

Your only way to guarantee a spot is to reserve further ahead **online.** The website is user-friendly, if (not surprisingly) a bit bureaucratic. Go to www.bundestag.de, click "English" at the top of the screen, and—under the "Visit the Bundestag" menu—select "Online registration." On this page, select "Visit the dome." Fill in the number of people in your party, ignore the "Comments" field, and click "Next." After entering the scrambled captcha code, you can select your preferred visit date and time (you can request

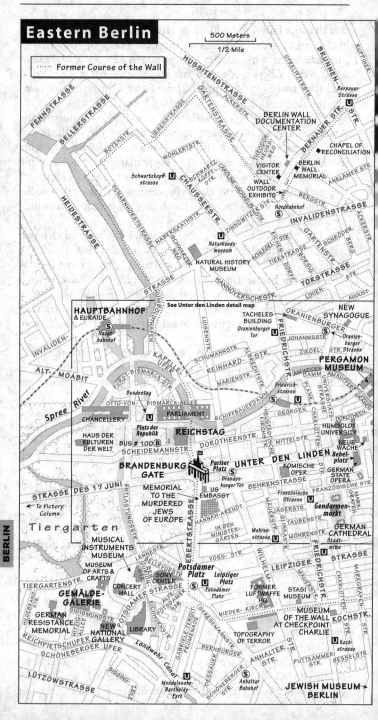

Eastern Berlin

500 Meters
1/2 Mile

········ Former Course of the Wall

FENNSTRASSE
SELLERSTRASSE
HEIDESTRASSE
BRUNNEN-STR. U-STR.
RUPPINER
STRELITZER STR.
HUSSITENSTRASSE
BOYENSTR.
GARTENSTRASSE
LIESENSTR.
ACKERSTR.
Bernauer Strasse
BERNAUER STR.
WÖHLERTSTR.
THEODOR-HEUSS-WEG
BERLIN WALL DOCUMENTATION CENTER
CHAPEL OF RECONCILIATION
VISITOR CENTER
BERLIN WALL MEMORIAL
Schwartzkopff-strasse U
SCHWARTZ-KOPFF-STR.
CAROLINE-MICHAELIS-STR.
WALL OUTDOOR EXHIBITS
ANKLAMER STR.
SCHARNHORSTSTRASSE
HABERSAATHSTR.
CHAUSSEESTR
ZINNOWITZER STR.
BERGSTR.
S Nordbahnhof
GARTENSTR.
SCHRÖDER
BERG
INVALIDENSTRASSE
SCHWARZ-WEG
SCHLEGELSTR.
EICHEN-STR.
TIECKSTR.
DÖFFL.
ALT-MOABIT
INVALIDEN-STRASSE
Naturkunde-museum U
NATURAL HISTORY MUSEUM
HANNOVERSCHESTR.
LINIEN-STR.
TORSTRASSE
STR.
AUGUST
See Unter den Linden detail map
HAUPTBAHNHOF & EURAIDE
Haupt-bahnhof
SCHUMANNSTR.
LUISENSTR.
ALBRECHTSTR.
REINHARD-STR.
MARIENSTR.
TACHELES BUILDING
Oranienburger Tor
ORANIENBURGER
FRIEDRICHSTR.
JOHANNISSTR.
ZIEGEL
NEW SYNAGOGUE
Oranien-burger STR. Strasse
Spree River
KÄPELLE-UFER
FÜRST-BISMARCK-STR.
Bundestag
OTTO-VON-BISMARCK-ALLEE
CHANCELLERY U
PARLIAMENT
Platz der Republik
HAUS DER KULTUREN DER WELT
BUS # 100 B
SCHEIDEMANNSTR.
REICHSTAG
DOROTHEENSTR.
SCHIFFBAUERDAMM
Friedrich-strasse U
AM WEIDEN-DAMM
NEUSTÄDTISCHE
KIRCHSTR.
GEORGEN-STR.
AM KUPFER-GRABEN
UNIVERSITÄTS-STR.
CHARLOTTEN-STR.
DOROTHEEN-STR.
PERGAMON MUSEUM
HUMBOLDT UNIVERSITY
MITTELSTR.
NEUE WACHE
STRASSE DES 17 JUNI
← To Victory Column
Tiergarten
ENTLASTUNGSSTR.
EBERTSTRASSE
BRANDENBURG GATE
Brandenburger Tor
Pariser Platz
US EMBASSY
BEHRENSTR.
MEMORIAL TO THE MURDERED JEWS OF EUROPE
HANNAH-ARENDT-STR.
IN DEN MINISTER-GÄRTEN
Mohren-strasse U
UNTER DEN LINDEN
Bebel-platz
KOMISCHE OPER
GERMAN STATE OPERA
FRANZÖSISCHE STR.
Französische Strasse U
JÄGERSTR.
TAUBENSTR.
MOHRENSTR.
GLINKA-STR.
MARK-
Gendarmen-markt
GERMAN CATHEDRAL
Stadt-mitte U
FRIEDRICHSTR.
CHARLOTTEN-STR.
MUSICAL INSTRUMENTS MUSEUM
MUSEUM OF ARTS & CRAFTS
TIERGARTENSTR.
GEMÄLDE-GALERIE
GERMAN RESISTANCE MEMORIAL
LENNÉSTR.
BELLEVUE-STR.
CONCERT HALL
SONY CENTER
POTSDAMER STRASSE
ALTE POTSDAMER
Potsdamer Platz S
Leipziger Platz
Potsdamer Platz S
VOSS- STR.
WILHELM-STR.
FORMER LUFTWAFFE HQ
LEIPZIGER STR.
STASI MUSEUM
MUSEUM OF THE WALL AT CHECKPOINT CHARLIE
Koch-strasse U
KOCHSTR.
NEW NATIONAL GALLERY
SIGISMUNDSTR.
HITZIGALLEE
HILDEBRAND-STR.
REICHPIETSCHUFER
SCHÖNEBERGER UFER
EICHHORNSTR.
LIBRARY
GABRIELE-TERGIT-PROMENADE
STRESEMANNSTR.
LINK-STR.
NIEDER-KIRCH-
TOPOGRAPHY OF TERROR
BERNBURGER STR.
ANHALTER STR.
CHARLOTTEN-STR.
MAGREFEN-STR.
STRASSE
BESSELSTR.
PUTTKAMER-STR.
LÜTZOWSTRASSE
Landwehr Canal
PISSING-ZEILE
Mendelssohn-Bartholdy-Park U
SCHÖNEBERGER STR.
DESSAUER STR.
Anhalter Bahnhof S
JEWISH MUSEUM BERLIN →

BERLIN

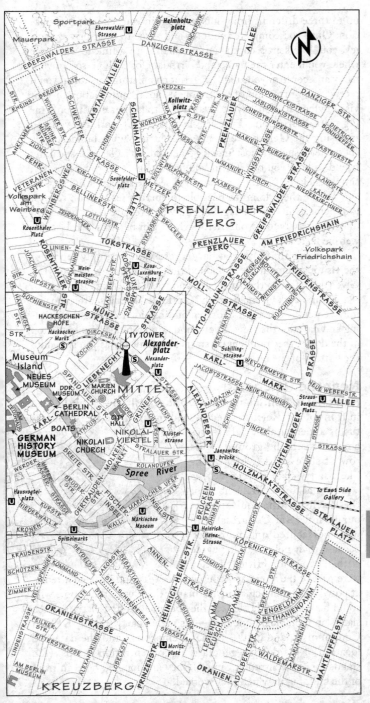

up to three different time slots) and fill in your contact information. Once you complete the form and agree to their privacy policy, you'll be sent a confirmation email with a link to a website where you'll enter the name and birthdate for each person in your party and confirm your request. After completing this form, you'll receive a confirmation of your request (not a confirmation of your visit) by email. You have to wait for yet another email confirming your reservation. If the English page isn't working, you can try using the German version: Go to https://www.bundestag.de/besuche/besucherdienst/index.jsp and call up a German-speaking friend to help you out. Or, if you use Google's Chrome browser, simply click the "Translate" button to see the steps in English.

While they claim it's possible to **email** a reservation request (kuppelbesuch@bundestag.de), you won't receive a confirmation until the day before your visit—which can be stressful. Use the website instead.

Getting In: Once you have a reservation, simply report to the visitors center at the appointed time, and be ready to show ID. Give your name to the attendant, and you'll be let right in.

Tours: Pick up the English **"Outlooks" flier** just after the visitors center. The free GPS-driven **audioguide** explains the building and narrates the view as you wind up the spiral ramp to the top of the dome; the commentary starts automatically as you step onto the bottom of the ramp.

Near the Reichstag

Memorial to Politicians Who Opposed Hitler—Near the road in front of the Reichstag, enmeshed in all the security apparatus, is a memorial of slate stones embedded in the ground. This row of slate slabs (which looks like a fancy slate bicycle rack) is a memorial to the 96 members of the Reichstag (the equivalent of our members of Congress) who were persecuted and murdered because their politics didn't agree with Chancellor Hitler's. They

were part of the Weimar Republic, the weak and ill-fated attempt at post-WWI democracy in Germany. These were the people who could have stopped Hitler...so they became his first victims. Each slate slab remembers one man—his name, party (mostly KPD—Communists, and SPD—Social Democrats), and the date and location of his death—generally in concentration camps. (*KZ* stands for "concentration camp.") They are honored here, in front of the building in which they worked.

• *Facing the Reichstag, you can take a short side-trip to the river by circling around to the left of the building.*

Spree Riverfront—Admire the wonderful architecture incorporating the Spree River into the people's world. It's a poignant

spot because this river was once a symbol of division—the East German regime put nets underwater to stymie those desperate enough for freedom to swim to the West. When kings ruled Prussia, government buildings went right up to the water. But today, the city is incorporating the river thoughtfully into a people-friendly cityscape. From the Reichstag, a delightful riverside path leads around the curve, past "beach cafés," to the Chancellery. For a slow, low-impact glide past this zone, consider a river cruise (see page 579; we'll pass the starting point—on Museum Island—later on this walk). The fine bridges symbolize the connection of East and West.

• *Leaving the Reichstag, return to the busy road, and cross the street at your first opportunity, to the big park. Walk (with the park on your right) to the corner. Along the railing at the corner of Scheidemannstrasse and Ebertstrasse is a small memorial of white crosses. This is the...*

Berlin Wall Victims Memorial—This monument—now largely usurped by business promos and impromptu, wacko book stalls—

commemorates some of the East Berliners who died trying to cross the Wall. Of these people, many perished within months of the Wall's construction on August 13, 1961. Most died trying to swim the river to freedom. The monument used to

stand right on the Berlin Wall behind the Reichstag. Notice that the last person killed while trying to escape was 20-year-old Chris Gueffroy, who died nine months before the Wall fell. (He was shot through the heart in no-man's-land.) For more on the Wall, see "The Berlin Wall (and Its Fall)" sidebar on page 608.

Nearby: In the park just behind the memorial is the **Monument to the Murdered Sinti and Roma (Gypsies) of Europe.** The Sinti and Roma, as persecuted by the Nazis as the Jews were, lost the same percentage of their population to Hitler. Unveiled in 2012 after years of delays, the monument consists of a circular pool and an information wall.

• *From here, head to the Brandenburg Gate. Stay on the park side of the street for a better view of the gate ahead. As you cross at the light, notice the double row of* **cobblestones**—*it goes around the city, marking where the Wall used to stand.*

Brandenburg Gate and Nearby

▲▲**Brandenburg Gate (Brandenburger Tor)**—The historic Brandenburg Gate (1791) was the grandest—and is the last survi-

vor—of 14 gates in Berlin's old city wall (this one led to the neighboring city of Brandenburg). The gate was the symbol of Prussian Berlin—and later the symbol of a divided Berlin. It's crowned by a majestic four-horse chariot, with the Goddess of Peace at the reins. Napoleon took this statue to the Louvre in Paris in 1806. After the Prussians defeated Napoleon and got it back (1813), she was renamed the Goddess of Victory.

The gate sat unused, part of a sad circle dance called the Wall, for more than 25 years. Now postcards all over town show the ecstatic day—November 9, 1989—when the world enjoyed the sight of happy Berliners jamming the gate like flowers on a parade float. Pause a minute and think about struggles for freedom—past and present. (There's actually a special room built into the gate for this purpose.) Around the gate, look at the information boards with pictures of how this area changed throughout the 20th century. There's a TI within the gate (daily 9:30-19:00, S-Bahn: Brandenburger Tor).

The Brandenburg Gate, the center of old Berlin, sits on a major boulevard running east to west through Berlin. The western segment, called Strasse des 17 Juni (named for a workers' uprising against the DDR government on June 17, 1953), stretches for four miles from the Brandenburg Gate and Victory Column to the Olympic Stadium. But we'll follow this city axis in the opposite direction, east, walking along a stretch called Unter den Linden—into the core of old imperial Berlin and past what was once the palace of the Hohenzollern family who ruled Prussia and then Germany. The palace—the reason for just about all you'll see—is a phantom sight, long gone. Alexanderplatz, which marks the end of this walk, is near the base of the giant TV Tower hovering in the distance.

• *Cross through the gate into...*

▲**Pariser Platz**—"Parisian Square," so named after the Prussians defeated Napoleon in 1813, was once filled with important government buildings—all bombed to smithereens in World War II. For decades, it was an unrecognizable, deserted no-man's-land—cut off from both East and West by the Wall. But now it's rebuilt, and the banks, hotels, and embassies that were here before the bombing have reclaimed their original places—with a few additions: a palace of coffee (Starbucks) and the small Kennedys Museum (described later). The winners of World War II enjoy this prime real estate: The American, French, British, and Soviet (now Russian) embassies are all on or near this square.

Face the gate and look to your left. The **US Embassy** reopened in its historic location in 2008. The building has been controversial: For safety's sake, Uncle Sam wanted more of a security zone around the building, but the Germans wanted to keep Pariser Platz a welcoming people zone. (Throughout the world, American embassies are the most fortified buildings in town.) The compromise: The extra security the US wanted is built into the structure. Easy-on-the-eyes barriers keep potential car bombs at a distance, and its front door is on the side farthest from the Brandenburg Gate.

Just to the left, the **DZ Bank building** is by Frank Gehry, famous for designing Bilbao's organic Guggenheim Museum, Prague's Dancing House, Seattle's Experience Music Project, Chicago's Millennium Park, and Los Angeles' Walt Disney Concert Hall. Gehry fans might be surprised at the DZ Bank building's low profile. Structures on Pariser Platz are designed to be bland so as not to draw attention away from the Brandenburg Gate. (The glassy facade of the Academy of Arts, next to Gehry's building, is controversial for drawing attention to itself.) For your fix of the good old Gehry, step into the lobby and check out its undulating interior. It's a fish—and you feel like you're both inside and outside of it. The architect's vision is explained on a nearby plaque. The best view of the roof of Gehry's creation is from the Reichstag dome.

• *Enter the Academy of Arts (Akademie der Kunst), next door to Gehry's building. Its doors lead to a lobby (with a small food counter, daily 10:00-20:00), which leads directly to the vast...*

▲▲Memorial to the Murdered Jews of Europe (Denkmal für die Ermordeten Juden Europas)

—This Holocaust memorial, consisting of 2,711 gravestone-like pillars (called "stelae") and completed in 2005, is an essential stop for any visit to Berlin. It was the first formal, German government-sponsored Holocaust memorial. Jewish American architect Peter Eisenman won the competition for the commission (and built it on time and on budget—€27

million). It's been criticized for focusing on just one of the groups targeted by the Nazis, but the German government has promised to erect memorials to other victims.

Cost and Hours: Free, memorial always open; information center open Tue-Sun 10:00-20:00, Oct-March until 19:00, closed Mon year-round; last entry 45 minutes before closing, S-Bahn: Brandenburger Tor or Potsdamer Platz, tel. 030/2639-4336, www .stiftung-denkmal.de. The €4 audioguide augments the experience.

Visiting the Memorial: The pillars are made of hollow concrete, each chemically coated for easy removal of graffiti. (Notably, the chemical coating was developed by a subsidiary of the former IG Farben group—the company infamous for supplying the Zyklon B gas used in Nazi death camps.) The number of pillars isn't symbolic of anything; it's simply how many fit on the provided land.

Once you enter the memorial, notice that people seem to appear and disappear between the columns, and that no matter where you are, the exit always seems to be up. Is it a labyrinth...a symbolic cemetery...and intentionally disorienting? It's entirely up to the visitor to derive the meaning, while pondering this horrible chapter in human history.

The pondering takes place under the sky. For the learning, go under the field of concrete pillars to the state-of-the-art **infor-**

mation center (there may be a short line because of the mandatory security check). Inside, a thought-provoking exhibit (well-explained in English) studies the Nazi system of extermination and humanizes the victims, while also providing space for silent reflection. In the Starting Hall, exhibits trace the historical context of the Nazi and WWII era, while six portraits—representing the six million Jewish victims—look out on the visitors. The Room of Dimensions has glowing boxes in the floor containing diaries, letters, and final farewells penned by Holocaust victims. The Room of Families presents case-studies of 15 Jewish families from around Europe, to more fully convey the European Jewish experience. Remember: Behind these 15 stories are millions more tales of despair, tragedy, and survival. In the Room of Names, a continually running soundtrack lists the names and brief biographical sketches of Holocaust victims; reading the names of all those murdered would take more than six and a half years. The Room of Sites documents some 220 different places of genocide. You'll also find exhibits about other

Imagining Hitler in the 21st Century

More than six decades after the end of World War II, the bunker where Hitler killed himself lies hidden underneath a Berlin parking lot. While the Churchill War Rooms are a major sight in London, no one wants to turn Hitler's final stronghold into a tourist attraction.

Germans tread lightly on their past. It took 65 years for the Germany History Museum to organize its first exhibit on the life of Hitler. Even then, the exhibit was careful not to give neo-Nazis any excuse to celebrate—even the size of the Hitler portraits was kept to a minimum.

The image of Hitler has been changing in Germany. No longer is he exclusively an evil mass murderer—sometimes he is portrayed as a nervous wreck, such as in the 2004 film *Downfall*, or as an object of derision. He's even a wax figure in the Berlin branch of Madame Tussauds.

But 21st-century Germans still treat the subject with extraordinary sensitivity. The Bavarian state government holds the copyright to Hitler's political manifesto—*Mein Kampf*—and won't allow any version to be published in German, even one annotated by historians (although it is readily available on the Internet and in the US). Any visit to Hitler's mountain retreat in Berchtesgaden includes a stop at the Nazi Documentation Center, where visitors see Nazi artifacts carefully placed in their historical context.

Many visitors to Berlin are curious about Hitler sites, but few artifacts of that dark period survive. The German Resistance Memorial is presented in German only and difficult for the tourist to appreciate. Hitler's bunker is completely gone (near Potsdamer Platz). The best way to learn about Hitler sites is to take a Third Reich tour offered by one of the many local walking-tour companies (see "Tours in Berlin," page 574), or to visit the Topography of Terror, a fascinating exhibit located in a rebuilt hall on the same spot where the SS and Gestapo headquarters once stood (see page 606).

It's a balancing act, but when it comes to *der Führer*, Germans seem to be confronting their regrettable past.

BERLIN

Holocaust monuments and memorials, a searchable database of victims, and a video archive of interviews with survivors.

The memorial's location—where the Wall once stood—is coincidental. Nazi propagandist Joseph Goebbels' bunker was discovered during the work and left buried under the northeast corner of the memorial. Hitler's bunker is just 200 yards away, under a nondescript parking lot. Such Nazi sites are intentionally left hidden to discourage neo-Nazi elements from creating shrines.

• *Now backtrack to Pariser Platz (through the yellow building). Across the square (next to Starbucks), consider dropping into...*

The Kennedys Museum—This crisp private enterprise facing the Brandenburg Gate recalls John F. Kennedy's Germany trip in 1963, with great photos and video clips as well as a photographic shrine to the Kennedy clan in America. It's a small, overpriced, yet delightful experience with interesting mementos—such as old campaign buttons and posters, and JFK's notes with the phonetic "Ish bin ein Bearleener." Jacqueline Kennedy commented on how strange it was that this—not even in his native language—was her husband's most quotable quote. Most of the exhibit consists of photographs that, if nothing else, spark a nostalgic longing for the days of Camelot.

Cost and Hours: €7, includes special exhibits, reduced to €3.50 for a broad array of visitors—dream up a discount and ask for it, daily 10:00-18:00, Pariser Platz 4a, tel. 030/2065-3570, www.thekennedys.de.

• *Leave Pariser Platz and begin strolling...*

▲▲Unter den Linden

The street called Unter den Linden is the heart of former East Berlin. In Berlin's good old days, Unter den Linden was one of Europe's grand boulevards. In the 15th century, this carriageway led from the palace to the hunting grounds (today's big Tiergarten). In the 17th century, Hohenzollern princes and princesses moved in and built their palaces here so they could be near the Prussian king.

Named centuries ago for its thousand linden trees, this was the most elegant street of Prussian Berlin before Hitler's time, and the main drag of East Berlin after his reign. Hitler replaced the venerable trees—many 250 years old—with Nazi flags. Popular discontent actually drove him to replant the trees. Today, Unter den Linden is no longer a depressing Cold War cul-de-sac, and its pre-Hitler strolling café ambience has returned. Notice how it is divided, roughly at Friedrichstrasse, into a business section that stretches toward the Brandenburg Gate, and a culture section that spreads out toward Alexanderplatz. Frederick the Great wanted to have culture, mainly the opera and the university, closer to his palace, and to keep business (read: banks) farther away, near the city walls.

❍ Self-Guided Walk: As you walk toward the giant TV Tower, the big building you see jutting out into the street on your right is the **Hotel Adlon.** In its heyday, it hosted such notables as Charlie Chaplin, Albert Einstein, and Greta Garbo. This was the setting for Garbo's most famous line, "I vant to be alone,"

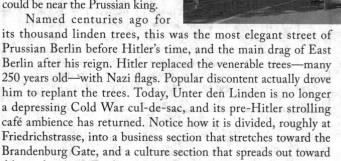

uttered in the film *Grand Hotel.* Damaged by the Russians just after World War II, the original hotel was closed with the construction of the nearby Wall in 1961 and later demolished. The grand Adlon was rebuilt in 1997. It was here that the late Michael Jackson shocked millions by dangling his baby, Blanket, over the railing (second balcony up, on the side of the hotel next to the Academy of Art). See how far you can get inside.

Descend into the Brandenburger Tor S-Bahn station ahead of you. It's one of Berlin's former **ghost subway stations.** During the Cold War, most underground train tunnels were simply blocked at the border. But a few Western lines looped through the East. To make a little hard Western cash, the Eastern government rented the use of these tracks to the West, but the stations (which happened to be in East Berlin) were strictly off-limits. For 28 years, the stations were unused, as Western trains slowly passed through and passengers saw only eerie DDR (East German) guards and lots of cobwebs. Literally within days of the

fall of the Wall, these stations were reopened, and today they are a time warp (looking essentially as they did when built in 1931, with dreary old green tiles and original signage). Walk along the track (the walls are lined with historic photos of the Reichstag through the ages) and exit on the other side, following signs to *Russische Botschaft* (the Russian Embassy).

The **Russian Embassy** was the first big postwar building project in East Berlin. It's built in the powerful, simplified Neoclassical style that Stalin liked. While not as important now as it was a few years ago, it's as immense as ever. It flies the Russian white, blue, and red. Find the hammer-and-sickle motif decorating the window frames—a reminder of the days when Russia was the USSR.

Continuing past the Aeroflot airline offices, look across Glinkastrasse to the right to see the back of the **Komische Oper** (Comic Opera; program and view of ornate interior posted in window). While the exterior is ugly, the fine old theater interior—amazingly missed by WWII bombs—survives.

BERLIN

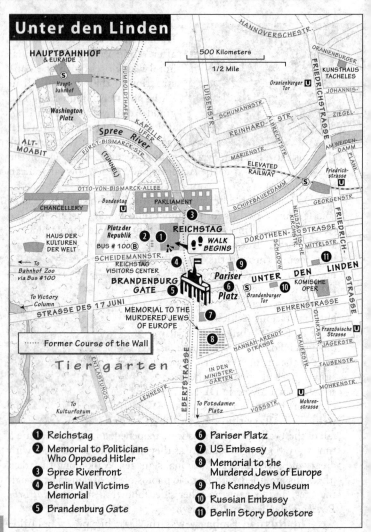

Unter den Linden

500 Kilometers

1/2 Mile

- ❶ Reichstag
- ❷ Memorial to Politicians Who Opposed Hitler
- ❸ Spree Riverfront
- ❹ Berlin Wall Victims Memorial
- ❺ Brandenburg Gate
- ❻ Pariser Platz
- ❼ US Embassy
- ❽ Memorial to the Murdered Jews of Europe
- ❾ The Kennedys Museum
- ❿ Russian Embassy
- ⓫ Berlin Story Bookstore

BERLIN

    Back on the Unter den Linden, on the left at #40 is an entertaining bookstore, Berlin Story. In addition to a wide range of English-language books, this shop has a modest (but overpriced) museum and a wide range of nostalgic knickknacks from the Cold War. The West lost no time in consuming the East; consequently, some have felt a wave of *Ost-*algia for the old days of East Berlin. At election time, a surprising number of the former East Berlin's voters still opt for the extreme left party, which has ties to the bygone Communist Party, although the East-West divide is no longer at the forefront of most voters' minds.

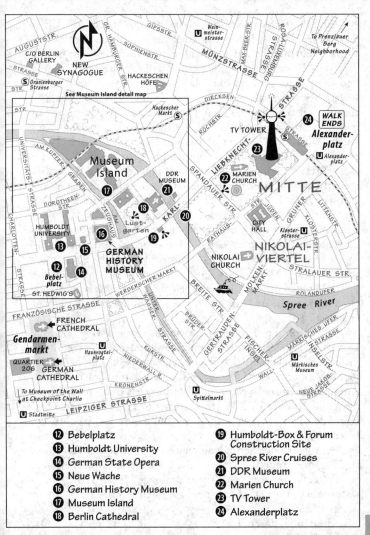

12 Bebelplatz
13 Humboldt University
14 German State Opera
15 Neue Wache
16 German History Museum
17 Museum Island
18 Berlin Cathedral

19 Humboldt-Box & Forum Construction Site
20 Spree River Cruises
21 DDR Museum
22 Marien Church
23 TV Tower
24 Alexanderplatz

One symbol of that communist era has been given a reprieve. As you continue to Friedrichstrasse, look at the DDR-style pedestrian lights, and you'll realize that someone had a sense of humor back then. The perky red and green men—*Ampelmännchen*—were recently under threat of replacement by far less jaunty Western-style signs. Fortunately, after a 10-year court battle, the DDR signals were kept after all.

At **Friedrichstrasse,** look right. Before the war, the Unter den Linden/Friedrichstrasse intersection was the heart of Berlin. In the 1920s, Berlin was famous for its unrestricted love of life. This was the cabaret drag, a springboard to stardom for young and vampy entertainers like Marlene Dietrich. (Born in 1901, Dietrich starred in one of the first German talkies—*The Blue Angel*—and then headed straight to Hollywood.) Over the last few years, this boulevard—lined with super department stores (such as Galeries Lafayette) and big-time hotels (such as the Hilton and Regent)—has been attempting to replace Ku'damm as the grand commerce-and-café boulevard of Berlin. More recently, western Berlin has retaliated with some new stores of its own. And so far, Friedrichstrasse gets little more than half the pedestrian traffic that Ku'damm gets in the West. Why? Locals complain that this area has no daily life—no supermarkets, not much ethnic street food, and so on. Consider detouring to Galeries Lafayette, with its cool marble-and-glass, waste-of-space interior (Mon-Sat 10:00-20:00, closed Sun; check out the vertical garden on its front wall, belly up to its amazing ground-floor viewpoint, or have lunch in its recommended basement cafeteria).

If you continued down Friedrichstrasse, you'd wind up at the sights listed under "South of Unter den Linden," on page 604—including Checkpoint Charlie (a 10-minute walk from here). But for now, continue along Unter den Linden. At the corner, the **VW Automobil Forum** shows off the latest models from the many car companies owned by VW (free, corner of Friedrichstrasse and Unter den Linden, VW art gallery and handy VW WC in the basement).

As you explore Berlin, you may see big, colorful **water pipes** running overground. Wherever there are big construction projects, streets are laced with these drainage pipes. Berlin's high water table means that any new basement comes with lots of pumping out.

Continue down Unter den Linden a few more blocks, past the large equestrian statue of Frederick the Great, and turn right into the square called **Bebelplatz.** Stand on the glass window set into the pavement in the center.

Frederick the Great— who ruled from 1740 to 1786—established Prussia not just as a military power, but as a cultural and intellectual heavyweight as well. This square was the center of the "new Athens" that

Frederick envisioned. His grand palace was just down the street (explained later).

Look down through the glass you're standing on: The room of empty bookshelves is a memorial repudiating the notorious Nazi **book burning.** It was on this square in 1933 that staff and students from the university threw 20,000 newly forbidden books (like Einstein's) into a huge bonfire on the orders of the Nazi propaganda minister Joseph Goebbels. A plaque nearby reminds us of the prophetic quote by the German poet Heinrich Heine. In 1820, he wrote, "Where they burn books, at the end they also burn people." The Nazis despised Heine because he was Jewish before converting to Christianity. A century later, his books were among those that went up in flames on this spot.

Great buildings front Bebelplatz. Survey the square counterclockwise:

Humboldt University, across Unter den Linden, is one of Europe's greatest. Marx and Lenin (not the brothers or the sisters) studied here, as did the Grimms (both brothers) and more than two dozen Nobel Prize winners. Einstein, who was Jewish, taught here until taking a spot at Princeton in 1932 (smart guy). Used-book merchants set up their tables in front of the university, selling books by many of the authors whose works were once condemned to Nazi flames just across the street.

The former **state library** (labeled *Juristische Fakultät,* facing Bebelplatz on the right with your back to Humboldt University) is where Vladimir Lenin studied during much of his exile from Russia. If you climb to the second floor of the library and go through the door opposite the stairs, you'll see a 1968 vintage stained-glass window depicting Lenin's life's work with almost biblical reverence. On the ground floor is Tim's Espressobar, a great little café with light food, student prices, and garden seating (€3 plates, Mon-Fri 8:00-20:00, Sat 9:00-17:00, closed Sun, handy WC).

Between the library and the church, the square is closed by one of Berlin's swankiest lodgings—**Hotel de Rome,** housed in a historic bank building with a spa and lap pool fitted into the former vault.

The round, Catholic **St. Hedwig's Church,** nicknamed the "upside-down teacup," was built by the pragmatic Frederick the Great to encourage the integration of Catholic Silesians after his empire annexed their region in 1742. (St. Hedwig is the patron saint of Silesia, a region now shared by Germany, Poland, and the Czech Republic.) When asked what the church should look like, Frederick took a Silesian teacup and slammed it upside-down on a table. Like all Catholic churches in Berlin, St. Hedwig's is not on the street, but stuck in a kind of back lot—indicating inferiority

BERLIN

to Protestant churches. You can step inside the church to see the cheesy DDR government renovation (generally daily until 17:00).

The **German State Opera** was bombed in 1941, rebuilt to bolster morale and to celebrate its centennial in 1943, and bombed again in 1945. Now it's being renovated (through 2013).

Cross Unter den Linden to the university side. The Greek-temple-like building set in the small chestnut-tree-filled park is the

Neue Wache (the emperor's "New Guardhouse," from 1816). Converted to a memorial to the victims of fascism in 1960, the structure was transformed again, after the Wall fell, into a national memorial. Look inside, where a replica of the Käthe Kollwitz statue, *Mother with Her Dead Son*, is surrounded by thought-provoking silence. This marks the tombs of Germany's unknown soldier and an unknown concentration camp victim. The inscription in front reads, "To the victims of war and tyranny." Read the entire statement in English (on wall, left of entrance). The memorial, open to the sky, incorporates the elements—sunshine, rain, snow—falling on this modern-day *pietà*.

• *After the Neue Wache, the next building you'll see is Berlin's pink-yet-formidable Zeughaus (arsenal). Dating from 1695, it's considered the oldest building on the boulevard, and now houses the...*

▲▲▲German History Museum (Deutsches Historisches Museum)

This fantastic museum is a two-part affair: the pink former Prussian arsenal building and the I. M. Pei-designed annex. The main building (fronting Unter den Linden) houses the permanent collection, offering the best look at German history under one roof, anywhere. The modern annex features good temporary exhibits surrounded by the work of a great contemporary architect. While this city has more than its share of hokey "museums" that slap together WWII and Cold War bric-a-brac, then charge too much for admission, this thoughtfully presented museum—with more than 8,000 artifacts telling not just the story of Berlin, but of all Germany—is clearly the top history museum in town.

Cost and Hours: €8, daily 10:00-18:00, Unter den Linden 2, tel. 030/2030-4751, www.dhm.de.

Audioguide: For the most informative visit, invest in the excellent €3 audioguide, with six hours of info to choose from.

• *Back on Unter den Linden, head toward the Spree River. Just before*

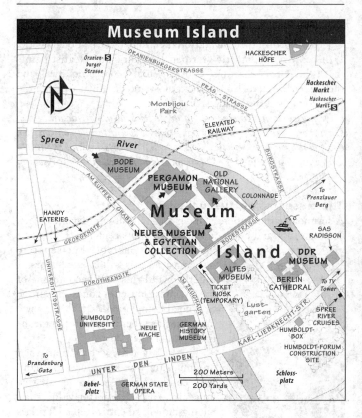

Museum Island

the bridge, wander left along the canal through a tiny but colorful arts-and-crafts market (weekends only; a larger flea market is just outside the Pergamon Museum). Continue up the riverbank two blocks and cross the footbridge over the Spree. This takes you to...

Museum Island (Museumsinsel)

This island is filled with some of Berlin's most impressive museums (all part of the Staatliche Museen zu Berlin). The first building—the Altes Museum—went up in the 1820s, and the rest of the complex began development in the 1840s under King Friedrich

Wilhelm IV, who envisioned the island as a place of culture and learning. The island's imposing Neoclassical buildings host five grand museums: the **Pergamon Museum** (classical antiquities, including the top-notch Pergamon Altar, with its temple and frieze); the **Neues Museum** ("New

BERLIN

Museum," famous for its Egyptian collection with the bust of Queen Nefertiti); the **Old National Gallery** (Alte Nationalgalerie, 19th-century art, mostly German Romantic and Realist paintings); the **Altes Museum** ("Old Museum," more antiquities); and the **Bode Museum** (European statuary and paintings through the ages, coins, and Byzantine art).

• *The museums of Museum Island are described in more detail below. On a short port visit, you may have time to sprint through one or two, but you'll have to be selective. Or, to see more of Berlin and bypass the museums, skip ahead to the "Museum Island to Alexanderplatz" section on page 602.*

The Museums of Museum Island

A formidable renovation is under way on Museum Island. When complete, a grand entry and unified visitors center will serve the

island's five venerable but separate museums; tunnels will lace the complex together; and this will become one of the grandest museum zones in Europe (intended completion date: 2015, www .museumsinsel-berlin.de). In the meantime, pardon their dust.

Cost: If you are visiting more than one museum, the €14 Museum Island Pass combo-ticket—covering all five museums—is a far better value than buying individual entries (€8-€13; prices can vary depending on special exhibits).

All five museums are also included in the city's €19 Museumspass (both passes described on page 567). Special exhibits are extra.

Hours: Pergamon—daily 10:00-18:00, Thu until 21:00. Neues Museum—daily 10:00-18:00, Thu-Sat until 20:00. Old National Gallery and Bode Museum—Tue-Sun 10:00-18:00, Thu until 22:00, closed Mon; same hours for Altes Museum except closes Thu at 20:00. Tel. 030/266-424-242, www.smb.museum.

Required Reservation for Pergamon and Neues Museums: Visiting either the Pergamon Museum or Neues Museum requires a *Zeitfensterticket* ("time-window ticket") that gives you a 30-minute time slot for entering the museum (included with admission; separate appointments required for each museum). Once inside, you can stay as long as you like. Reserve your time online (www .smb.museum) or in person at any Museum Island ticket office. (At less busy times, tickets are sometimes sold without any particular time slot.)

You can usually get a time slot within about an hour, often sooner—except at the busiest times (Sat and Sun mornings), when

BERLIN

you may have to wait longer.

Buying Tickets: The temporary kiosk on Bodestrasse functions as the ticket booth for the Neues Museum and comes with avoidable lines. Long ticket-buying lines also plague the Pergamon Museum. Avoid them by purchasing your museum pass (and getting your assigned entry time) at one of the island's three never-crowded museums: Altes, Bode, or Old National Gallery. (From Unter den Linden, Altes is most convenient; if coming from Prenzlauer Berg, try the Bode.)

Getting There: The nearest S-Bahn station is Hackescher Markt, about a 10-minute walk away.

▲▲▲Pergamon Museum (Pergamonmuseum)

The star attraction of this world-class museum, part of Berlin's

Collection of Classical Antiquities (Antikensammlung), is the fantastic and gigantic Pergamon Altar, where carved gods tumble down a grand staircase. The Babylonian Ishtar Gate (slathered with glazed blue tiles from the 6th century B.C.) and the museum's many ancient Greek, Mesopotamian, Roman, and early Islamic treasures are also impressive.

Audioguide: Make ample use of the superb audioguide (included with admission)—it will broaden your experience. Punching #10 on the audioguide gets you the "Pergamon in 30 Minutes" general tour.

▲▲Neues (New) Museum and Egyptian Collection

Oddly, Museum Island's so-called "new" museum features the oldest stuff around. There are three collections here: the Egyptian Collection (with the famous bust of Queen Nefertiti; floor 0 and parts of floors 1-2), the Museum of Prehistory and Early History (floor 3 and parts of floors 1-2), and some items from the Collection of Classical Antiquities (artifacts from ancient Troy—famously excavated by German adventurer Heinrich Schliemann—and Cyprus, just off the entrance).

The top draw here is the Egyptian art—clearly one of the world's best collections. But let's face it: The main reason to visit is to enjoy one of the great thrills in art appreciation—gazing into the still-young-and-beautiful face of Queen Nefertiti. If you're in a pinch for time, make a beeline to her (floor 2, far corner of Egyptian Collection in room 210; for more on the museum, see www.neues-museum.de).

The 3,000-year-old bust of **Queen Nefertiti** (the wife of King Akhenaton, c. 1340 B.C.) is the most famous piece of Egyptian art in Europe. Called "Berlin's most beautiful woman," Nefertiti has all the right beauty marks: long neck, symmetrical face, and the perfect amount of makeup. And yet, she's not completely idealized. Notice the fine wrinkles that show she's human (though these only enhance her beauty). Like a movie star discreetly sipping a glass of wine at a sidewalk café, Nefertiti seems somehow more dignified in person. The bust never left its studio, but served as a master model for all other portraits of the queen. (That's probably why the left eye was never inlaid.) Stare at her long enough, and you may get the sensation that she's winking at you. Hey, beautiful!

Audioguide: The fine audioguide (included with admission) celebrates new knowledge about ancient Egyptian civilization and offers fascinating insights into workaday Egyptian life as it describes the vivid papyrus collection, slice-of-life artifacts, and dreamy wax portraits decorating mummy cases.

▲Old National Gallery (Alte Nationalgalerie)

This gallery, behind the Neues Museum and Altes Museum, is designed to look like a Greek temple. Spanning three floors, it focuses on art (mostly paintings) from the 19th century: Romantic German paintings (which I find most interesting) on the top floor, and French and German Impressionists and German Realists on the first and second floors. You  likely won't recognize any specific paintings, but it's still an enjoyable stroll through German culture from the century in which that notion first came to mean something. The included audioguide explains the highlights.

Bode Museum

At the "prow" of Museum Island, the Bode Museum (designed to appear as if it's rising up from the river), is worth a brief stop. Just inside, a grand statue of Frederick William of Brandenburg on horseback, curly locks blowing in the wind, welcomes you into the lonely halls of the museum. This fine building contains a hodgepodge of collections: Byzantine art, historic coins, ecclesiastical art, sculptures, and medals commemorating the fall of the Berlin Wall and German reunification. For a free, quick look at its lavish interior, climb the grand staircase to the charming café on the first floor.

Altes (Old) Museum

The least interesting of the five museums, this building features the rest of the Collection of Classical Antiquities (the best of which is in the Pergamon Museum)—namely, Etruscan, Roman, and Greek art. I'd pass it up.

Other Sights on and near Museum Island

In addition to the five museums just described, Museum Island is home to the following sights. One more sight (the DDR Museum) sits just across the river.

Lustgarten—For 300 years, the island's big central square has flip-flopped between being a military parade ground and a people-friendly park, depending upon the political tenor of the time. During the revolutions of 1848, the Kaiser's troops dispersed a protesting crowd that had assembled here, sending demonstrators onto footpaths. Karl Marx later commented, "It is impossible to have a revolution in a country where people stay off the grass."

For decades, it was *verboten* to relax or walk on the Lustgarten's grass. But in 1999, the Lustgarten was made into a park (read the history posted in the corner opposite the church). On a sunny day, it's packed with relaxing locals and is one of Berlin's most enjoyable public spaces.

Berlin Cathedral (Berliner Dom)—This century-old church towers over Museum Island. Inside, the great reformers (Luther, Calvin, and company) stand around the brilliantly restored dome like stern saints guarding their theology. Frederick I rests in an ornate tomb (right transept, near entrance to dome). The 270-step climb to the outdoor dome gallery is tough but offers pleasant, breezy views of the city at the finish line. The crypt downstairs is not worth a look.

Cost and Hours: €7 includes access to dome gallery, €10 with audioguide, not covered by Museum Island ticket, Mon-Sat 9:00-20:00, Sun 12:00-20:00, until 19:00 Oct-March, closes early—around 17:30—on some days for concerts, interior closed but dome open during services, tel. 030/2026-9136, www.berliner-dom.de.

Humboldt-Forum Construction Site (Former Site of Hohenzollern Palace)—Across Unter den Linden from Berlin Cathedral is a big lawn that for centuries held the Baroque palace of the Hohenzollern dynasty of Brandenburg and Prussia. Much of that palace actually survived World War II but was replaced by the communists with a blocky, Soviet-style "Palace" of the Republic—East Berlin's parliament building/entertainment complex and a showy symbol of the communist days. The landmark building fell into disrepair after reunification and was eventually dismantled in 2007. After much debate about how to use this prime real estate, the German parliament decided to construct the Humboldt-Forum, a huge public venue filled with museums, shops, galleries, and concert halls behind a facade constructed in imitation of the original Hohenzollern palace. With a €1.2 billion price tag, many Berliners consider the reconstruction plan a complete waste of money.

The temporary **Humboldt-Box** has been set up to help the public follow the construction of the new Humboldt-Forum. The multiple floors of the futuristic "box" display building plans and models for the project (€4; daily 10:00-20:00—after that, free entry to terrace-café until 23:00; tel. 01805-030-707, www.humboldt-box.com). On the top floor, the terrace-café with unobstructed views over Berlin serves coffee, desserts, and light €5-15 lunch dishes until 18:00.

Spree River Cruises—The recommended Spree River boat tours depart from the riverbank near the bridge by the Berlin Cathedral. For details, see page 579.

• *Directly across the bridge from Museum Island, down along the riverbank, look for the...*

▲**DDR Museum**—Although this exhibit began as a tourist trap, it has expanded and matured into a genuinely interesting look at life in former East Germany (DDR). It's well-stocked with kitschy everyday items from the communist period, plus photos, video clips, and concise English explanations. The exhibits are interactive—you're encouraged to pick up and handle anything that isn't behind glass. You'll crawl through a Trabant car (designed by East German engineers to compete with the West's popular VW Beetle) and pick up some DDR-era jokes ("East Germany had 39 newspapers, four radio stations, two TV channels...and one opinion.") The reconstructed communist-era home lets you tour the kitchen, living room, bedrooms, and more. You'll learn about the Russian-imported *Dacha*—the simple countryside cottage (owned by one in six East Germans) used for weekend retreats from the grimy city. (Others vacationed on the Baltic Coast, where nudism was all the rage, as a very revealing display explains.) Lounge in DDR movie chairs as you view a subtitled propaganda film or clips from beloved-in-the-East TV shows (including the popular kids' show *Sandmännchen*—"Little Sandman"). Even the meals served in the attached restaurant are based on DDR-era recipes.

Cost and Hours: €6, daily 10:00-20:00, Sat until 22:00, just across the Spree from Museum Island at Karl-Liebknecht-Strasse 1, tel. 030/847-123-731, www.ddr-museum.de.

Museum Island to Alexanderplatz

• *Continue walking down Unter den Linden. Before crossing the bridge (and leaving Museum Island), look across the river. The pointy twin* *spires of the 13th-century Nikolai Church mark the center of medieval Berlin. This **Nikolaiviertel** (Viertel means "quarter") was restored by the DDR and was trendy in the last years of communism. Today, it's a lively-at-night riverside restaurant district.*

As you cross the bridge, look left in the distance to see the gilded **New Synagogue** dome, rebuilt after WWII bombing (described on page 612).

Across the river to the left of the bridge, directly below you, is the **DDR Museum** (described earlier). Just beyond that is the giant **SAS Radisson Hotel** and shopping center, with a huge aquarium in the center. The elevator goes right through the middle of a deep-sea world. (You can see it from the unforgettable Radisson hotel lobby—tuck in your shirt and walk past the guards with the confidence of a guest who's sleeping there.) Here in the center of the old communist capital, it seems that capitalism has settled in with a spirited vengeance.

In the park immediately across the street (a big jaywalk from the Radisson) are grandfatherly statues of **Marx and Engels** (nicknamed "the old pensioners"). Surrounding them are stainless-steel monoliths with evocative photos that show the struggles of the workers of the world.

Walk toward **Marien Church** (from 1270), just left of the base of the TV Tower. An artist's rendering helps you follow the interesting but very faded old "Dance of Death" mural that wraps around the narthex inside the door.

The big red-brick building past the trees on the right is the **City Hall,** built after the revolutions of 1848 and arguably the first democratic building in the city.

The 1,200-foot-tall **TV Tower** (Fernsehturm) has a fine view from halfway up (€12, daily March-Oct 9:00-24:00, Nov-Feb 10:00-24:00, www.tv-turm.de). The tower offers a handy city orientation and an interesting view of the flat, red-roofed sprawl of Berlin—including a peek inside the city's many courtyards *(Höfe)*. Consider a kitschy trip to the observation deck for the view and lunch in its revolving restaurant (mediocre food, €12 plates, horrible lounge music, tel. 030/242-3333). The retro tower is quite trendy these days, so it can be crowded (your ticket comes with an assigned entry time). Built (with Swedish know-how) in 1969 for the 20th anniversary of the communist government, the tower was meant to show the power of the atheistic state at a time when DDR leaders were having the crosses removed from church domes and spires. But when the sun shined on their tower—the greatest spire in East Berlin—a huge cross was reflected on the mirrored ball. Cynics called it "The Pope's Revenge." East Berliners dubbed the tower the "Tele-Asparagus." They joked that if it fell over, they'd have an elevator to the West.

Farther east, pass under the train tracks into **Alexanderplatz.**

This area—especially the former Kaufhof department store (now Galeria Kaufhof)—was the commercial pride and joy of East Berlin. Today, it's still a landmark, with a major U- and S-Bahn station. The once-futuristic, now-retro "World Time Clock," installed in 1969, is a nostalgic favorite and a popular meeting point. Stop in the square for a coffee and to people-watch. It's a great scene.

• *Our orientation stroll is finished. From here, you can hike back a bit to catch the riverboat tour, take in the sights south of Unter den Linden, or venture into the colorful Prenzlauer Berg neighborhood.*

South of Unter den Linden

The following sights—heavy on Nazi and Wall history—are listed roughly north to south (as you reach them from Unter den Linden).

▲▲Gendarmenmarkt

Many cruise-line shuttle buses from Warnemünde drop off and pick up at this delightful, historic square. The space is bounded by

twin churches, a tasty chocolate shop, and the Berlin Symphony's concert hall (designed by Karl Friedrich Schinkel, the man who put the Neoclassical stamp on Berlin and Dresden). In summer, it hosts a few outdoor cafés, *Biergarten*s, and sometimes concerts. Wonderfully symmetrical, the square is considered by

Berliners to be the finest in town (U6: Französische Strasse; U2 or U6: Stadtmitte).

The name of the square—part French and part German (after the *Gens d'Armes*, Frederick the Great's royal guard, who were headquartered here)—reminds us that in the 17th century, a fifth of all Berliners were French émigrés—Protestant Huguenots fleeing Catholic France. Back then, Frederick the Great's tolerant Prussia was a magnet for the persecuted (and for their money). These émigrés vitalized Berlin with new ideas and know-how...and their substantial wealth.

Of the two matching churches on Gendarmenmarkt, the one to the south (bottom end of square) is the **German Cathedral** (Deutscher Dom). This cathedral (not to be confused with the Berlin Cathedral on Museum Island) was bombed flat in the war and rebuilt only in the 1980s. It houses the thought-provoking Milestones, Setbacks, Sidetracks *(Wege, Irrwege, Umwege)* exhibit, which traces the history of the German parliamentary system—worth ▲. As the exhibit is designed for Germans rather than foreign tourists, there are no English descriptions—but you can follow the essential, excellent, and free 1.5-hour English audioguide or buy the wonderfully detailed €10 guidebook (free entry, Tue-Sun May-Sept 10:00-19:00, Oct-April 10:00-18:00, closed Mon year-round, tel. 030/2273-0431).

The **French Cathedral** (Französischer Dom), at the north end of the square, offers a humble museum on the Huguenots (€2, Tue-Sat 12:00-17:00, Sun 11:00-17:00, closed Mon, enter around the right side) and a viewpoint in the dome up top (€3, daily 10:30-19:00, last entry at 18:00, 244 steps, enter through door facing square). Fun fact: Neither of these churches is a true cathedral,

as they never contained a bishop's throne; their German title of *Dom* (cathedral) is actually a mistranslation from the French word *dôme* (cupola).

Fassbender & Rausch, on the corner near the German Cathedral, claims to be Europe's biggest chocolate store (Mon-Sat 10:00-20:00, Sun 11:00-20:00, corner of Mohrenstrasse at Charlottenstrasse 60, tel. 030/2045-8440).

Gendarmenmarkt is buried in what has recently emerged as Berlin's "Fifth Avenue" shopping district. For the ultimate in top-end shops, find the corner of Jägerstrasse and Friedrichstrasse and wander through the **Quartier 206** (Mon-Fri 11:00-20:00, Sat 10:00-18:00, closed Sun, www.quartier206.com). The adjacent, middlebrow **Quartier 205** has more affordable prices.

BERLIN

Nazi and Cold War Sites on Wilhelmstrasse

Fragment of the Wall—Surviving stretches of the Wall are virtually nonexistent in downtown Berlin. One of the most convenient places to see a bit is at the intersection of Wilhelmstrasse and Zimmerstrasse/Niederkirchnerstrasse, a few blocks southwest of Gendarmenmarkt. Many visitors make the short walk over here from the Checkpoint Charlie sights (described later), then drop into the museum listed next.

▲▲Topography of Terror (Topographie des Terrors)—Coincidentally, the patch of land behind the surviving stretch of Wall was closely associated with a different regime: It was once

the nerve center for the most despicable elements of the Nazi government, the Gestapo and the SS. This stark-gray, boxy building is one of the few memorial sites that focuses on the perpetrators rather than the victims of the Nazis.

It's chilling but thought-provoking to see just how seamlessly and bureaucratically the Nazi institutions and state structures merged to become a well-oiled terror machine. There are few actual artifacts; it's mostly written explanations and photos, like reading a good textbook standing up. And, while you could read this story anywhere, to take this in atop the Gestapo headquarters is a powerful experience. The exhibit's a bit dense, but WWII historians (even armchair ones) will find it fascinating. The complex has two parts: indoors, in the modern boxy building, and outdoors, in the trench that runs along the surviving stretch of Wall.

Cost and Hours: Free, daily 10:00-20:00, outdoor exhibit closes at sunset in winter, Niederkirchnerstrasse 8, tel. 030/254-5090, www.topographie.de.

Checkpoint Charlie

This famous Cold War checkpoint was not named for a person, but for its checkpoint number—as in Alpha (#1, at the East-West German border, a hundred miles west of here), Bravo (#2, as you enter Berlin proper), and Charlie (#3, the best known because most foreigners passed through here). While the actual checkpoint has long since been dismantled, its former location is home to a fine museum and a mock-up of the original border crossing. The area

has become a Cold War freak show and—as if celebrating the final victory of crass capitalism—is one of Berlin's worst tourist-trap zones. A McDonald's stands defiantly overlooking the former haunt of East German border guards. You can even pay an exorbitant €10 for a full set of Cold War-era stamps in your passport. (For a more sober and intellectually redeeming look at the Wall's history, head for the out-of-the-way Berlin Wall Memorial at Bernauer Strasse, north of here near the Prenzlauer Berg neighborhood and described on page 614. Local officials, likely put off by the touristy crassness of the Checkpoint Charlie scene, have steered local funding to that area.)

▲**Checkpoint Charlie Street Scene**—Where Checkpoint Charlie once stood, notice the thought-provoking post with larger-than-life **posters** of a young American soldier facing east and a young Soviet soldier facing west. The rebuilt **guard station** now hosts two actors playing American guards who pose for photos. (Across the street is Snack Point Charlie.) A **photo exhibit** stretches down the street, with great English descriptions telling the story of the Wall. While you could get this information from a book, it's moving to stand here in person and ponder the gripping history of this place.

A few yards away (on Zimmerstrasse), a **glass panel** describes the former checkpoint. From there, a double row of **cobbles** in Zimmerstrasse traces the former path of the Wall. These innocuous cobbles run throughout the city, even through some buildings.

Farther down on Zimmerstrasse, before Charlottenstrasse, find the **Memorial to Peter Fechter** (set just off the sidewalk, barely inside the Wall marker), who was shot and left for dead here in the early days of the Wall. For more on his sad story, see "The Berlin Wall (and Its Fall)" sidebar.

▲▲**Museum of the Wall at Checkpoint Charlie (Mauer-museum Haus am Checkpoint Charlie)**—While the famous border checkpoint between the American and Soviet sectors is long gone, its memory is preserved by one of Europe's most cluttered museums. During the Cold War, the House at Checkpoint Charlie stood defiantly—spitting distance from the border guards—

BERLIN

The Berlin Wall (and Its Fall)

The 96-mile-long "Anti-Fascist Protective Rampart," as it was called by the East German government, was erected almost overnight in 1961 to stop the outward flow of people from East to West (3 million had leaked out between 1949 and 1961). The Wall *(Mauer)* was actually two walls; the outer was a 12-foot-high concrete barrier whose rounded, pipe-like top (to discourage grappling hooks) was adorned with plenty of barbed wire. Sandwiched between the walls was a no-man's-land (or "death strip") between 30 and 160 feet wide. More than 100 sentry towers kept a close eye on the Wall. On their way into the death strip, would-be escapees would trip a silent alarm, which alerted sharpshooters.

During the Wall's 28 years, border guards fired 1,693 times and made 3,221 arrests, and there were 5,043 documented successful escapes (565 of these were East German guards). Officially, 136 people were killed at the Wall while trying to escape. One of the first, and most famous, was 18-year-old Peter Fechter. On August 17, 1962, East German soldiers shot and wounded Fechter as he was trying to climb over the Wall. For more than an hour, Fechter lay bleeding to death while soldiers and bystanders on both sides of the Wall did nothing. In 1997, a German court sentenced three former border guards to two years in prison for manslaughter.

As a tangible, almost too-apt symbol for the Cold War, the Berlin Wall got a lot of attention from politicians both East and West. Two of the 20th century's most repeated presidential quotes were uttered within earshot of the death strip. In 1963, US President John F. Kennedy stood in front of the walled-off Brandenburg Gate and professed American solidarity with the struggling people of Berlin: *"Ich bin ein Berliner."* A generation later in 1987, with the stiff winds of change already blowing westward from Moscow, President Ronald Reagan came here to issue an ultimatum to his Soviet counterpart: "Mr. Gorbachev, tear down this wall."

The actual fall of the Wall had less to do with presidential proclamations than with the obvious failings of the Soviet system, a general thawing in Moscow (where Gorbachev introduced *perestroika* and *glasnost*, and declared that he would no longer employ force to keep Eastern European satellite states under Soviet rule)—and a bureaucratic snafu.

By November of 1989, it was clear that change was in the air. Hungary had already opened its borders to the West that summer, making it next to impossible for East German authorities to keep people in. A series of anti-regime protests had swept nearby Leipzig a few weeks earlier, attracting hundreds of thousands of supporters. On October 7, 1989—on the 50th anniversary of the official creation of the DDR—East German premier Erich Honecker said, "The Wall will be standing in 50 and even in 100 years." He was only off by 99 years and 11 months. A similar rally in East Berlin's Alexanderplatz on November 4—with a half-million protesters chanting, "*Wir wollen raus!*" (We want out!)—persuaded the East German politburo to begin a gradual process of relaxing travel restrictions.

The DDR's intention was to slightly crack the door to the West, but an inarticulate spokesman's confusion inadvertently threw it wide open. The decision was made on Thursday, November 9, to tentatively allow a few more Easterners to cross into the West—a largely symbolic reform that was intended to take place gradually, over many weeks. Licking their wounds, politburo members left town early for a long weekend. The announcement about travel restrictions was left to a spokesman, Günter Schabowski, who knew only what was on a piece of paper handed to him moments before he went on television for a routine press conference. At 18:54, Schabowski read the statement dutifully, with little emotion, seemingly oblivious to the massive impact of his own words: "exit via border crossings...possible for every citizen." Reporters, unable to believe what they were hearing, began to prod him about when the borders would open. Schabowski looked with puzzlement at the brief statement, shrugged, and offered his best guess: "*Ab sofort, unverzüglich.*" ("Immediately, without delay.")

Schabowski's words spread like wildfire through the streets of both Berlins, the flames fanned by West German TV broadcasts (and Tom Brokaw, who had rushed to Berlin when alerted by NBC's bureau chief). East Berliners began to show up at Wall checkpoints, demanding that border guards let them pass. As the crowds grew, the border guards could not reach anyone who could issue official orders. (The politburo members were effectively hiding out.) Finally, around 23:30, a border guard named Harald Jäger at the Bornholmer Strasse crossing decided to simply open the gates. Easterners flooded into the West, embracing their long-separated cousins, unable to believe their good fortune. Once open, the Wall could never be closed again.

The carnival atmosphere of those first years after the Wall fell is gone, but hawkers still sell "authentic" pieces of the Wall, DDR flags, and military paraphernalia to gawking tourists. When it fell, the Wall was literally carried away by the euphoria. What managed to survive has been nearly devoured by decades of persistent "Wall-peckers."

Americans—the Cold War victors—have the biggest appetite for Wall-related sights, and a few bits and pieces remain for us to seek out. Berlin's best Wall-related sights are the Berlin Wall Memorial along Bernauer Strasse, with a long stretch of surviving Wall (near S-Bahn: Nordbahnhof; page 614) and the Museum of the Wall at Checkpoint Charlie (see page 607). Other stretches of the Wall still standing include the short section at Zimmerstrasse/Wilhelmstrasse (near the Topography of Terror exhibit; page 606) and the longer East Side Gallery (near the Ostbahnhof; page 611).

BERLIN

showing off all the clever escapes over, under, and through the Wall. Today, while the drama is over and hunks of the Wall stand like trophies at its door, the museum survives as a living artifact of the Cold War days. The yellowed descriptions, which have scarcely changed since that time, tinge the museum with nostalgia. It's dusty, disorganized, and overpriced, with lots of reading involved, but all that just adds to this museum's borderline-kitschy charm.

Cost and Hours: €12.50, assemble 20 tourists and get in for €8.50 each, €3.50 audioguide, not covered by Museumspass, daily 9:00-22:00, U6 to Kochstrasse or—better from Zoo—U2 to Stadtmitte, Friedrichstrasse 43-45, tel. 030/253-7250, www.mauer museum.de.

▲▲Jewish Museum Berlin (Jüdisches Museum Berlin)

This museum is one of Europe's best Jewish sights. The highly conceptual building is a sight in itself, and the museum inside—

an overview of the rich culture and history of Europe's Jewish community—is excellent, particularly if you take advantage of the informative and engaging audioguide. Rather than just reading dry texts, you'll feel this museum as fresh and alive—an exuberant celebration of the Jewish experience that's accessible to all. Even though the museum is in a nondescript residential neighborhood, it's well worth the trip.

Cost and Hours: €5, sometimes extra for special exhibits, daily 10:00-20:00, Mon until 22:00, last entry one hour before closing, closed on Jewish holidays. Tight security includes bag check and metal detectors. The excellent €3 audioguide—with four hours of commentary on 151 different items—is essential to fully appreciate the exhibits. Tel. 030/2599-3300, www.jmberlin.de.

Getting There: Take the U-Bahn to Hallesches Tor, find the exit marked *Jüdisches Museum*, exit straight ahead, then turn right on Franz-Klühs-Strasse. The museum is a five-minute walk ahead on your left, at Lindenstrasse 9.

Eating: The museum's restaurant, Liebermanns, offers good Jewish-style meals, albeit not kosher (€9 daily specials, lunch served 12:00-16:00, snacks at other times, tel. 030/2593-9760).

More Sights South of Unter den Linden

East Side Gallery—The biggest remaining stretch of the Wall is now "the world's longest outdoor art gallery." It stretches for nearly a mile and is covered with murals painted by artists from around the world. The murals got a facelift in 2009, when the city invited the original artists back to re-create their work for the 20th anniversary of the fall of the Wall. This segment of the Wall makes a poignant walk. For a quick look, take the S-Bahn to the Ostbahnhof station (follow signs to Stralauerplatz exit; once outside, TV Tower will be to your right; go left and at next corner look to your right—the Wall is across the busy street). Even though classified as protected monuments, the murals are slowly being consumed by developers. If you walk the entire length of the East Side Gallery, you'll find a small Wall souvenir shop at the end and a bridge crossing the river to a subway station at Schlesisches Tor (in Kreuzberg). The bridge, a fine example of Brandenburg Neo-Gothic brickwork, has a fun neon "rock, paper, scissors" installment poking fun at the futility of the Cold War (visible only after dark).

North of Unter den Linden

There are few major sights to the north of Unter den Linden, but this area has some of Berlin's trendiest, most interesting neighborhoods. I've listed these roughly from south to north, as you'd approach them from the city center and Unter den Linden. On a sunny day, a stroll (or tram ride) through these bursting-with-life areas can be as engaging as any museum in town.

Hackescher Markt

This area, in front of the S-Bahn station of the same name, is a great people scene day and night. The brick trestle supporting the train track is another classic example of the city's Brandenburg Neo-Gothic brickwork. Most of the brick archways are now filled with hip shops, which have official—and newly trendy—addresses such as "S-Bahn Arch #9, Hackescher Markt." Within 100 yards of the S-Bahn station, you'll find Hackeschen Höfe (described next), recommended Turkish and Bavarian restaurants, walking-tour and pub-crawl departure points, and tram #M1 to Prenzlauer Berg.

Hackeschen Höfe (a block in front of the Hackescher Markt S-Bahn station) is a series of eight courtyards bunny-hopping through a wonderfully restored 1907 *Jugendstil* (German Art

Nouveau) building. Berlin's apartments are organized like this—courtyard after courtyard leading off the main roads. This complex is full of trendy restaurants (including the recommended Turkish eatery, Hasir), theaters, and cinemas. This is a wonderful example of how to make huge city blocks livable. Two decades after the Cold War, this area has reached the final evolution of East Berlin's urban restoration. (These courtyards also serve a useful lesson for visitors: Much of Berlin's charm hides off the street front.)

Oranienburger Strasse

Oranienburger Strasse is anchored by an important and somber sight, the New Synagogue. But the rest of this zone (roughly between the synagogue and Torstrasse) is colorful and quirky. The streets behind Grosse Hamburger Strasse flicker with atmospheric cafés, *Kneipen* (pubs), and art galleries.

▲**New Synagogue (Neue Synagogue)**—A shiny gilded dome marks the New Synagogue, now a museum and cultural center.

Consecrated in 1866, this was once the biggest and finest synagogue in Germany, with seating for 3,200 worshippers and a sumptuous Moorish-style interior modeled after the Alhambra. It was desecrated by Nazis on Crystal Night (Kristallnacht) in 1938, bombed in 1943, and partially rebuilt in 1990. Only the dome and facade have been restored—a window overlooks the vacant field marking what used to be the synagogue. On its facade, a small plaque—added by East Berlin Jews in 1966—reads "Never forget" *(Vergesst es nie)*. At that time East Berlin had only a few hundred Jews, but now that the city is reunited, the Jewish community numbers about 12,000.

Cost and Hours: Main exhibit-€3.50, dome-€2, temporary exhibits-€3, €7 combo-ticket covers everything, audioguide-€3; March-Oct Sun-Mon 10:00-20:00, Tue-Thu 10:00-18:00, Fri 10:00-17:00—until 14:00 in Oct and March-May, closed Sat; Nov-Feb Sun-Thu 10:00-18:00, Fri 10:00-14:00, closed Sat; Oranienburger Strasse 28/30, enter through the low-profile door in the modern building just right of the domed synagogue facade, S-Bahn: Oranienburger Strasse, tel. 030/8802-8300 and press 1, www.cjudaicum.de.

▲Prenzlauer Berg

Young, in-the-know locals agree that Prenzlauer Berg (PRENTS-low-er behrk) is one of Berlin's most colorful neighborhoods (roughly between Helmholtzplatz and Kollwitzplatz and along

Stolpersteine (Stumbling Stones)

As you wander through the Hackeschen Höfe and Oranien-burger Strasse neighborhoods—and throughout Germany—you might stumble over small brass plaques in the sidewalk called *Stolpersteine. Stolpern* means "to stumble," which is what you are meant to do. These plaques are placed in front of former homes of residents who were killed during World War II. The *Stolpersteine* serve not only to honor the victims, but also to stimulate thought and discussion on a daily basis (rather than only during visits to memorial sites) and to put an individual's name on the mass horror.

More than 25,000 of these plaques have been installed across Germany. They're made of brass so they stay polished as you walk over them, instead of fading into the sidewalk. On each plaque is the name of the victim who lived in that spot, and how and where that person died. While some Holocaust memorials formerly used neutral terminology like "perished," now they use words like "murdered"—part of the very honest way in which today's Germans are dealing with their country's past. The city of Munich, however, has banned *Stolpersteine*, saying that the plaques were insulting and degrading to victims of persecution, who would continue to be trod on by "Nazi boots." Installation of a *Stolperstein* can be sponsored for €95 and has become popular in schools, where students research the memorialized person's life as a class project.

Kastanienallee, U2: Senefelderplatz and Eberswalder Strasse; or take the S-Bahn to Hackescher Markt and catch tram #M1 north). Tourists call it "Prenzl'berg" for short, while Berliners just call it "der Berg." This part of the city was largely untouched during World War II, but its buildings slowly rotted away under the communists. After the Wall fell, it was overrun with laid-back hipsters, energetic young families, and clever entrepreneurs who breathed life back into its classic old apartment blocks, deserted factories, and long-forgotten breweries. Ten years of rent control kept things affordable for its bohemian residents. But now landlords are free to charge what the market will bear, and the vibe is changing. This is ground zero for Berlin's baby boom: Tattooed and pierced young moms and dads, who've joined the modern rat-race without giving up their alternative flair, push their youngsters in designer strollers past trendy boutiques and restaurants. You'll count more kids here than just about anywhere else in town. Locals complain that these days the cafés and bars cater to yuppies sipping prosecco, while the working class and artistic types are being pushed out. While it has changed plenty, I still find Prenzlauer Berg a celebration of life and a joy to stroll through.

BERLIN

▲Berlin Wall Memorial (Gedenkstätte Berliner Mauer)

While tourists flock to Checkpoint Charlie, local authorities have been investing in this site to develop Berlin's most substantial attraction relating to its gone-but-not-forgotten Wall. Exhibits line up along a two-block stretch of Bernauer Strasse, stretching northeast from the Nordbahnhof S-Bahn station. You can enter two different museums (a Visitor Center and a Documentation Center, each with movies about  the Wall); see several actual fragments of the Wall, plus various open-air exhibits and memorials; and peer from an observation tower down into a preserved, complete stretch of the Wall system (as it was during the Cold War). To prepare for a visit here, read "The Berlin Wall (and Its Fall)" sidebar on page 608.

Cost and Hours: Free; Visitor Center and Documentation Center open April-Oct Tue-Sun 9:30-19:00, Nov-March until 18:00, closed Mon year-round; outdoor areas accessible 24 hours daily; Bernauer Strasse 111, tel. 030/4679-86666, www.berliner-mauer-gedenkstaette.de.

Getting There: Take the S-Bahn (line S-1, S-2, or S-25—all handy from Potsdamer Platz, Brandenburger Tor, or Friedrichstrasse) to the Nordbahnhof. The Nordbahnhof's underground hallways have history exhibits in English. Exit by following signs for *Bernauer Strasse*, and you'll pop out across the street from a long chunk of Wall and kitty-corner from the Visitor Center.

Sights in Central Berlin

Tiergarten Park and Nearby

Berlin's "Central Park" stretches two miles from Bahnhof Zoo to the Brandenburg Gate.

Victory Column (Siegessäule)—The Tiergarten's newly restored centerpiece, the Victory Column, was built to commemorate the Prussian defeat of Denmark in 1864...then reinterpreted after the defeat of France in 1870. The pointy-helmeted Germans rubbed it in, decorating the tower with French cannons and paying for it all with francs received as war reparations. The three lower rings commemorate Bismarck's victories. I imagine the statues of Moltke and other German military greats—which lurk in the trees nearby—goose-stepping around the floodlit angel at night.

Climbing its 270 steps earns you a breathtaking Berlin-wide view and a close-up of the gilded bronze statue of the goddess Victoria (go ahead, call her "the chick on a stick"—everybody here does). You might recognize Victoria from Wim Wenders' 1987 art-house classic *Wings of Desire*, or the *Stay (Faraway, So Close!)* video he directed for the rock band U2.

Cost and Hours: €2.20; April-Oct Mon-Fri 9:30-18:30, Sat-Sun 9:30-19:00; Nov-March Mon-Fri 10:00-17:00, Sat-Sun 10:00-17:30; closes in the rain, WCs for paying guests only, no elevator, bus #100, tel. 030/8639-8560. From the tower, the grand Strasse des 17 Juni leads east to the Brandenburg Gate.

Potsdamer Platz

The "Times Square of Berlin," and possibly the busiest square in Europe before World War II, Potsdamer Platz was cut in two by the Wall and left a deserted no-man's-land for 40 years. Today, this immense commercial/residential/entertainment center, sitting on a futuristic transportation hub, is home to the European corporate headquarters of several big-league companies.

The new Potsdamer Platz was a vision begun in 1991, when it was announced that Berlin would resume its position as the capital of Germany. Sony, Daimler, and other major corporations have turned the square once again into a center of Berlin. Like great Christian churches built upon pagan holy grounds, Potsdamer Platz—with its corporate logos flying high and shiny above what was the Wall—trumpets the triumph of capitalism.

Potsdamer Platz's centerpiece is the **Sony Center,** under a grand canopy (designed to evoke Mount Fuji). Office workers

and tourists eat here by the fountain, enjoying the parade of people. The modern Bavarian Lindenbräu beer hall—the Sony boss wanted a *Bräuhaus*—serves traditional food (€11-17, daily 11:00-24:30, big €8 salads, three-foot-long taster boards of eight different beers, tel. 030/2575-1280). Across the plaza, Josty Bar is built around a surviving bit of a venerable hotel that was a meeting place for Berlin's rich and famous before the bombs (€10-17 meals, daily 10:00-24:00, tel. 030/2575-9702).

BERLIN

Kulturforum

Just west of Potsdamer Platz, Kulturforum rivals Museum Island as the city's cultural heart, with several top museums and Berlin's concert hall—home of the world-famous Berlin Philharmonic orchestra (admission to all Kulturforum sights covered by a single €8 Bereichskarte Kulturforum combo-ticket—a.k.a. Quartier-Karte—and also by the Museumspass; info for all museums: tel. 030/266-424-242, www.kulturforum-berlin.de). Of its sprawling museums, only the Gemäldegalerie is a must (S- or U-Bahn to Potsdamer Platz, then walk along Potsdamer Platz).

▲▲Gemäldegalerie—Literally the "Painting Gallery," Germany's top collection of 13th- through 18th-century European paintings (more than 1,400 canvases) is beautifully displayed in a building that's a work of art in itself. The North Wing starts with German paintings of the 13th to 16th centuries, including eight by Albrecht Dürer. Then come the Dutch and Flemish—Jan van Eyck, Pieter Brueghel, Peter Paul Rubens, Anthony van Dyck, Frans Hals, and Jan Vermeer. The wing finishes with German, English, and French 18th-century artists, such as Thomas Gainsborough and Antoine Watteau. An octagonal hall at the end features an impressive stash of Rembrandts. The South Wing is saved for the Italians—Giotto, Botticelli, Titian, Raphael, and Caravaggio.

Cost and Hours: Covered by €8 Kulturforum combo-ticket, Tue-Sun 10:00-18:00, Thu until 22:00, closed Mon, audioguide included with entry, clever little loaner stools, great salad bar in cafeteria upstairs, Matthäikirchplatz 4.

New National Gallery (Neue Nationalgalerie)—This gallery features 20th-century art, with ever-changing special exhibits.

Cost and Hours: Covered by €8 Kulturforum combo-ticket, Tue-Fri 10:00-18:00, Thu until 22:00, Sat-Sun 11:00-18:00, closed Mon, café downstairs, Potsdamer Strasse 50.

Museum of Decorative Arts (Kunstgewerbemuseum)—Wander through a mazelike floor plan displaying a thousand years of applied arts—porcelain, fine *Jugendstil* (German Art Nouveau) furniture, Art Deco, and reliquaries. There are no English descriptions and no crowds.

Cost and Hours: Covered by €8 Kulturforum combo-ticket, Tue-Fri 10:00-18:00, Sat-Sun 11:00-18:00, closed Mon, Herbert-von-Karajan-Strasse 10.

▲**Musical Instruments Museum (Musikinstrumenten Museum)**—This impressive hall is filled with 600 exhibits spanning the 16th century to modern times. Wander among old keyboard instruments and funny-looking tubas. Pick up the included audioguide and free English brochure at the entry. In addition to the English commentary, the audioguide has clips of various

instruments being played (just punch in the number next to the instrument you want to hear). This place is fascinating if you're into pianos.

Cost and Hours: €4, covered by €8 Kulturforum comboticket, Tue-Fri 9:00-17:00, Thu until 22:00, Sat-Sun 10:00-17:00, closed Mon, low-profile white building east of the big yellow Philharmonic Concert Hall, tel. 030/2548-1178.

Eating in Berlin

Don't be too determined to eat "Berlin-style." The city is known only for its mildly spicy sausage and for its street food (*Currywurst* and *Döner Kebab*—see the sidebar on the next page). Germans—especially Berliners—consider their food old-school; when they go out to eat, they're not usually looking for the "traditional local fare" many travelers are after. Nouveau German is California cuisine with scant memories of wurst, kraut, and pumpernickel. If the kraut is getting the wurst of you, take a break with some international or ethnic offerings—try one of the many Turkish, Italian, pan-Asian, and Balkan restaurants.

Colorful pubs—called *Kneipen*—offer light, quick, and easy meals and the fizzy local beer, *Berliner Weiss*. Ask for it *mit Schuss* for a shot of fruity syrup in your suds.

My recommendations, below, are near the sightseeing core, in eastern Berlin.

Near Unter den Linden

Cheap Eats: **Bier's Curry und Spiesse,** under the tracks at the Friedrichstrasse S-Bahn stop, is a great, greasy, cheap, and generous place for an old-fashioned German hot dog. This is the local favorite near Unter den Linden for €2 *Currywurst*. Experiment with variations (the *Flieschspiess* is excellent) and sauces—and don't hold the fried *Zwiebeln* (onions). You'll munch standing at a counter, where the people-watching is great (daily 11:00-5:00 in the morning; from inside the station, take the Friedrichstrasse exit and turn left).

Near the Pergamon Museum: Georgenstrasse, a block behind the Pergamon Museum and under the S-Bahn tracks, is lined with fun eateries filling the arcade of the train trestle—close to the sightseeing action but in business mainly for students from nearby Humboldt University. **Deponie3** is a trendy Berlin *Kneipe* usually

Berliner Street Fare

In Berlin, it's easy to eat cheap, with a glut of *Imbiss* snack stands, bakeries (for sandwiches), and falafel/kebab counters. Train stations have grocery stores, as well as bright and modern fruit-and-sandwich bars.

Sausage stands are everywhere (I've listed a couple of local favorites). Most specialize in **Currywurst,** created in Berlin after World War II, when a fast-food cook got her hands on some curry and Worcestershire sauce from British troops stationed here. It's basically a grilled *Bockwurst*-type pork sausage smothered with curry sauce. *Currywurst* comes either *mit Darm* (with casing) or *ohne Darm* (without casing). If the casing is left on to grill, it gives

the sausage a smokier flavor. (*Berliner Art*—"Berlin-style"—means that the sausage is boiled *ohne Darm*, then grilled.) Either way, the grilled sausage is then chopped into small pieces or cut in half (East Berlin style) and topped with sauce. While some places simply use ketchup and sprinkle on some curry powder, real *Currywurst* joints use tomato paste, Worcestershire sauce, and curry. With your wurst comes either a toothpick or small wooden fork; you'll usually get a plate of fries as well, but rarely a roll. You'll see *Currywurst* on the menu at some sit-down restaurants, but local purists say that misses the whole point: You'll pay triple and get a less authentic dish than you would at a street stand under elevated S-Bahn tracks.

Other good street foods to consider are *Döner Kebab* (Turkish-style skewered meat slow-roasted and served in a sandwich) and *Frikadelle* (like a hamburger patty; often called *Bulette* in Berlin).

filled with students. Garden seating in the back is nice if you don't mind the noise of the S-Bahn passing directly above you. The interior is a cozy, wooden wonderland of a bar with several inviting spaces. They serve basic salads, traditional Berlin dishes, and hearty daily specials (€4-8 breakfasts, good €8 brunch Sun 10:00-15:00, €5-11 lunches, open daily from 9:00, sometimes live music, Georgenstrasse 5, tel. 030/2016-5740). For Italian food, **Die Zwölf Apostel** is nearby (daily until 24:00, food served until 22:00).

In the Heart of Old Berlin's Nikolai Quarter: The *Nikolaiviertel* marks the original medieval settlement of Cölln, which would eventually become Berlin. The area was destroyed during the war but was rebuilt for Berlin's 750th birthday in 1987. The whole area has a cute, cobbled, and characteristic old town feel...Middle Ages meets Socialist Realism. Today, the district is pretty soulless by day but a popular restaurant zone at night. **Bräuhaus Georgbrau** is a thriving beer hall serving homemade suds on a picturesque courtyard overlooking the Spree River. Eat in the lively and woody but mod-feeling interior, or outdoors with fun riverside seating— thriving with German tourists. It's a good place to try one of the few typical Berlin dishes: *Eisbein* (boiled ham hock) with sauer-kraut and mashed peas with bacon (€10 with a beer and schnapps). The statue of St. George once stood in the courtyard of Berlin's old castle—until the Nazis deemed it too decadent and not "German" enough, and removed it (€10-13 plates, three-foot-long sampler board with a dozen small glasses of beer, daily 10:00-24:00, 2 blocks south of Berlin Cathedral and across the river at Spreeufer 4, tel. 030/242-4244).

In City Hall: Consider lunching at one of Berlin's many *Kantine*. Located in government offices and larger corporations, *Kantine* offer fast, filling, and cheap lunches, along with a unique opportunity to see Germans at work (though the food can hardly be considered gourmet). There are thousands of *Kantine* in Berlin, but the best is **Die Kantine im Roten Rathaus,** in the basement of City Hall. For less than €4, you can get filling German dishes like *Leberkäse* (German-style baloney) or stuffed cabbage (Mon-Fri 11:00-15:00, closed Sat-Sun, Rathausstrasse 15).

Near Gendarmenmarkt, South of Unter den Linden

The twin churches of Gendarmenmarkt seem to be surrounded by people in love with food. The lunch scene is thriving with upscale restaurants serving good cuisine at highly competitive prices to local professionals (see map on page 620 for locations). If in need of a quick-yet-classy lunch, stroll around the square and along Charlottenstrasse. For a quick bite, head to the cheap *Currywurst* stand behind the German Cathedral.

Lutter & Wegner Restaurant is well-known for its Austrian cuisine (*Schnitzel* and *Sauerbraten*) and popular with businesspeople. It's dressy, with fun sidewalk seating or a dark and elegant interior (€9-18 starters, €16-22 main dishes, daily 11:00-24:00, Charlottenstrasse 56, tel. 030/202-9540). They have a second location, called **Beisl am Tacheles,** near the New Synagogue (Oranienburger Strasse 52, tel. 030/2478-1078).

Augustiner am Gendarmenmarkt, next door to Lutter & Wegner, lines its sidewalk with trademark Bavarian white-and-blue-checkerboard tablecloths; inside, you'll find a classic Bavarian beer-hall atmosphere. Less pretentious than its neighbor, it offers good beer and affordable Bavarian classics in an equally appealing

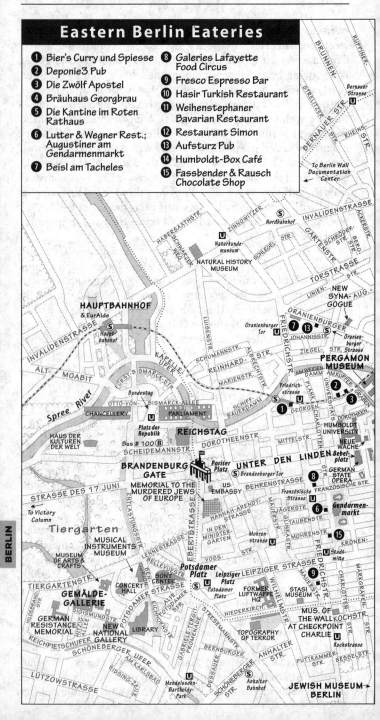

Eastern Berlin Eateries

1 Bier's Curry und Spiesse
2 Deponie3 Pub
3 Die Zwölf Apostel
4 Bräuhaus Georgbrau
5 Die Kantine im Roten Rathaus
6 Lutter & Wegner Rest.; Augustiner am Gendarmenmarkt
7 Beisl am Tacheles

8 Galeries Lafayette Food Circus
9 Fresco Espresso Bar
10 Hasir Turkish Restaurant
11 Weihenstephaner Bavarian Restaurant
12 Restaurant Simon
13 Aufsturz Pub
14 Humboldt-Box Café
15 Fassbender & Rausch Chocolate Shop

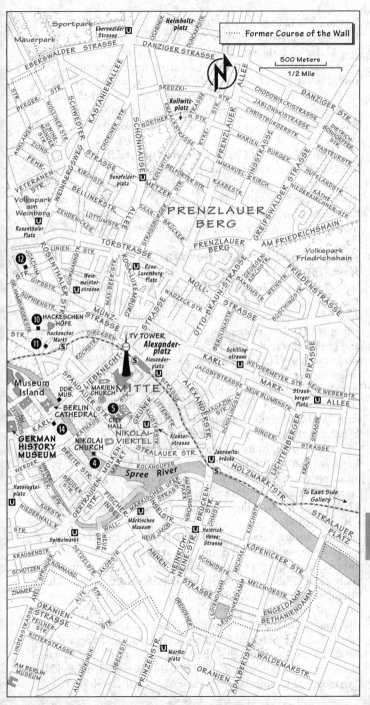

location (€6-12 light meals, €10-15 bigger meals, daily 9:00-24:00, Charlottenstrasse 55, tel. 030/2045-4020).

Galeries Lafayette Food Circus is a French festival of fun eateries in the basement of the landmark department store. You'll find a good deli and prepared-food stands, dishing up cuisine that's good-quality but not cheap (most options €10-15, cheaper €8-10 sandwiches and savory crepes, Mon-Sat 10:00-20:00, closed Sun, Friedrichstrasse 76-78, U-Bahn: Französische Strasse, tel. 030/209-480).

Near Checkpoint Charlie: **Fresco Espresso Bar** is a touristy joint, handy for made-to-order sandwiches. Israeli-born Sagi makes his own bread daily and piles on the fixin's for €4-6. This is a popular stop for walking-tour groups: If you get here when they do, expect a line (Mon-Sat 7:30-19:00, Sun 8:00-19:00, in summer until 20:30, Friedrichstrasse 200, tel. 030/2061-6693).

At and near Hackescher Markt

Hasir Turkish Restaurant is your chance to dine with candles, hardwood floors, and happy Berliners savoring meaty Anatolian specialties. As Berlin is the world's largest Turkish city outside of Asia Minor, it's no wonder you can find some good Turkish restaurants here. But while most locals think of Turkish food as fast and cheap, this is a dining experience. The restaurant, in a courtyard next to the Hackeschen Höfe shopping complex (see page 611), offers indoor and outdoor tables filled with an enthusiastic local crowd. The service can be a bit questionable, so bring some patience (€6-10 starters, €14-20 main dishes, large and splittable portions, daily 11:30-1:00 in the morning, a block from the Hackescher Markt S-Bahn station at Oranienburger Strasse 4, tel. 030/2804-1616).

Weihenstephaner Bavarian Restaurant serves upmarket Bavarian traditional food for around €10-15 a plate; offers an atmospheric cellar, an inner courtyard, and a busy people-watching street-side terrace; and, of course, has excellent beer (daily 11:00-23:00, Neue Promenade 5 at Hackescher Markt, tel. 030/8471-0760).

Restaurant Simon dishes up tasty Italian and German specialties—enjoy them either in the restaurant's simple yet atmospheric interior, or opt for streetside seating (€6-12 main dishes, daily 12:00-23:00, Auguststrasse 53, at intersection with Kleine Auguststrasse, tel. 030/2789-0358).

Aufsturz, a lively pub with live music, pours more than 100 different beers and 40 varieties of whiskey, and dishes up "traditional Berliner pub grub"—like nachos—and great potato soup for under €5. The traditional "Berlin board" for €17 can easily feed three voracious carnivores (daily 12:00-24:00, a block beyond New Synagogue at Oranienburger Strasse 67, tel. 030/2804-7407).

What If I Miss My Boat?

Remember that you can get help from the cruise line's port agent (listed on the destination information sheet distributed on the ship) and the local TI (see page 566). If the port agent suggests a costly solution (such as a private car with a driver), you may want to consider public transit.

Rostock has a few sporadic long-distance overnight ferry connections to other cities, but these are sparse and unlikely to reach where you're going. For the most part, you'll need to go by train to Berlin (3 hours) and connect from there to just about any other cruise port: to **Amsterdam** (and onward to **Zeebrugge, Paris/LeHavre,** or **London**); to **Copenhagen** (and onward to **Stockholm, Oslo,** and other Norwegian stops); to **Gdańsk;** and so on.

If you need to catch a **plane** to your next destination, you'll find an easy train connection from downtown Berlin to Willy Brandt Berlin-Brandenburg International Airport (tel. 01805-000-186).

Local **travel agents** in Warnemünde, Rostock, or Berlin can help you. For more advice on what to do if you miss the boat, see page 144.

Returning to Warnemünde

If you're meeting an "On Your Own" cruise-line **shuttle bus,** it'll pick you up wherever it left you off. Many of these stop at Gendarmenmarkt, a short walk south of Unter den Linden (down Charlottenstrasse) and within a block of two different U-Bahn stations (U6: Französische Strasse; U2 or U6: Stadtmitte).

If you're planning to ride the **train** back to Warnemünde, be very clear on the departure time. Be sure that you'll arrive in Warnemünde with plenty of time to return to your ship (about 5-10 minutes from the Warnemünde train station), and build in wiggle room for potential delays.

Trains to Warnemünde depart from Berlin Hauptbahnhof, the main train station. The main east-west **S-Bahn** line zips you there from various points in town (including the Friederichstrasse station, three blocks north of Unter den Linden; Hackescher Markt, a short walk north of Museum Island; and Alexanderplatz, at the end of Unter den Linden). From these stops, take any train going west, and hop off at Hauptbahnhof. You'll exit the S-Bahn on the top level of the station, but your Warnemünde train likely leaves from the bottom level, five stories below (confirm and ride the elevator down). This S-Bahn ride is covered by your ticket to Warnemünde. Alternatively, you could ride the **U-Bahn** line two stops from the Brandenburger Tor stop (but this ride is *not* covered by your train ticket). If you're in a rush, hail a **taxi** and say, "Hauptbahnhof."

For more on the ride back to Warnemünde, including train schedules and how to get from the station back to your ship, see "Returning to Your Ship" on page 555.

German Survival Phrases

In the phonetics, ī sounds like the long i in "light," and bolded syllables are stressed.

English	German	Pronunciation
Good day.	Guten Tag.	**goo**-tehn tahg
Do you speak English?	Sprechen Sie Englisch?	**shprehkh**-ehn zee **ehgn**-lish
Yes. / No.	Ja. / Nein.	yah / nīn
I (don't) understand.	Ich verstehe (nicht).	ikh fehr-**shtay**-heh (nikht)
Please.	Bitte.	**bit**-teh
Thank you.	Danke.	**dahng**-keh
I'm sorry.	Es tut mir leid.	ehs toot meer līt
Excuse me.	Entschuldigung.	ehnt-**shool**-dig-oong
(No) problem.	(Kein) Problem.	(kīn) proh-**blaym**
(Very) good.	(Sehr) gut.	(zehr) goot
Goodbye.	Auf Wiedersehen.	owf **vee**-der-zayn
one / two	eins / zwei	īns / tsvī
three / four	drei / vier	drī / feer
five / six	fünf / sechs	fewnf / zehkhs
seven / eight	sieben / acht	**zee**-behn / ahkht
nine / ten	neun / zehn	noyn / tsayn
How much is it?	Wieviel kostet das?	**vee**-feel **kohs**-teht dahs
Write it?	Schreiben?	**shrī**-behn
Is it free?	Ist es umsonst?	ist ehs oom-**zohnst**
Included?	Inklusive?	in-kloo-**zee**-veh
Where can I buy / find...?	Wo kann ich kaufen / finden...?	voh kahn ikh **kow**-fehn / **fin**-dehn
I'd like / We'd like...	Ich hätte gern / Wir hätten gern...	ikh **heh**-teh gehrn / veer **heh**-tehn gehrn
...a room.	...ein Zimmer.	īn **tsim**-mer
...a ticket to ____.	...eine Fahrkarte nach ____.	ī-neh **far**-kar-teh nahkh
Is it possible?	Ist es möglich?	ist ehs **mur**-glikh
Where is...?	Wo ist...?	voh ist
...the train station	...der Bahnhof	dehr **bahn**-hohf
...the bus station	...der Busbahnhof	dehr **boos**-bahn-hohf
...tourist information	...das Touristen-informations-büro	dahs too-**ris**-tehn-in-for-maht-see-**ohns**-**bew**-roh
...toilet	...die Toilette	dee toh-**leh**-teh
men	Herren	**hehr**-rehn
women	Damen	**dah**-mehn
left / right	links / rechts	links / rehkhts
straight	geradeaus	geh-**rah**-deh-**ows**
When is this...	Um wieviel Uhr ist hier...	oom **vee**-feel oor ist heer
...open / closed?	...geöffnet / geschlossen?	geh-**urf**-neht / geh-**shloh**-sehn
At what time?	Um wieviel Uhr?	oom **vee**-feel oor
Just a moment.	Moment.	moh-**mehnt**
now / soon / later	jetzt / bald / später	yehtst / bahld / **shpay**-ter
today / tomorrow	heute / morgen	**hoy**-teh / **mor**-gehn

BERLIN

In the Restaurant

English	German	Pronunciation
I'd like / We'd like...	Ich hätte gern / Wir hätten gern...	ikh **heh**-teh gehrn / veer **heh**-tehn gehrn
...a reservation for...	...eine Reservierung für...	**ī**-neh reh-zer-**feer**-oong fewr
...a table for one / two.	...einen Tisch für ein / zwei.	**ī**-nehn tish fewr īn / tsvī
Non-smoking.	Nichtraucher.	**nikht**-rowkh-er
Is this seat free?	Ist hier frei?	ist heer frī
Menu (in English), please.	Speisekarte (auf Englisch), bitte.	**shpī**-zeh-kar-teh (owf **ehng**-lish) **bit**-teh
service (not) included	Trinkgeld (nicht) inklusive	**trink**-gehlt (nikht) in-kloo-**zee**-veh
cover charge	Eintritt	**īn**-trit
to go	zum Mitnehmen	tsoom **mit**-nay-mehn
with / without	mit / ohne	mit / **oh**-neh
and / or	und / oder	oont / **oh**-der
menu (of the day)	(Tages-) Karte	(**tah**-gehs-) **kar**-teh
set meal for tourists	Touristenmenü	too-**ris**-tehn-meh-new
specialty of the house	Spezialität des Hauses	**shpayt**-see-ah-lee-**tayt** dehs **how**-zehs
appetizers	Vorspeise	**for**-shpī-zeh
bread	Brot	broht
cheese	Käse	**kay**-zeh
sandwich	Sandwich	**zahnd**-vich
soup	Suppe	**zup**-peh
salad	Salat	zah-**laht**
meat	Fleisch	flīsh
poultry	Geflügel	geh-**flew**-gehl
fish	Fisch	fish
seafood	Meeresfrüchte	**meh**-rehs-**frewkh**-teh
fruit	Obst	ohpst
vegetables	Gemüse	geh-**mew**-zeh
dessert	Nachspeise	**nahkh**-shpī-zeh
mineral water	Mineralwasser	min-eh-**rahl**-vah-ser
tap water	Leitungswasser	**lī**-toongs-vah-ser
milk	Milch	milkh
(orange) juice	(Orangen-) Saft	(oh-**rahn**-zhehn-) zahft
coffee	Kaffee	kah-**fay**
tea	Tee	tay
wine	Wein	vīn
red / white	rot / weiß	roht / vīs
glass / bottle	Glas / Flasche	glahs / **flah**-sheh
beer	Bier	beer
Cheers!	Prost!	prohst
More. / Another.	Mehr. / Noch ein.	mehr / nohkh īn
The same.	Das gleiche.	dahs **glīkh**-eh
Bill, please.	Rechnung, bitte.	**rehkh**-noong **bit**-teh
tip	Trinkgeld	**trink**-gehlt
Delicious!	Lecker!	**lehk**-er

For more user-friendly German phrases, check out *Rick Steves' German Phrase Book and Dictionary* or *Rick Steves' French, Italian & German Phrase Book.*

OSLO
Norway

Norway Practicalities

Norway (Norge) is stacked with superlatives—it's the most mountainous, most scenic, and most prosperous of all the Scandinavian countries. Perhaps above all, Norway is a land of intense natural beauty, its famously steep mountains and deep fjords carved out and shaped by an ancient ice age. Norway (148,900 square miles—just larger than Montana) is on the western side of the Scandinavian Peninsula, with most of the country sharing a border with Sweden to the east. Rich in resources like timber, oil, and fish, Norway has rejected joining the European Union, mainly to protect its fishing rights. Where the country extends north of the Arctic Circle, the sun never sets at the height of summer and never comes up in the deep of winter. The majority of Norway's 5 million people consider themselves Lutheran.

Money: 6 Norwegian kroner (kr, officially NOK) = about $1. An ATM is called a *minibank*. The local VAT (value-added sales tax) rate is 25 percent; the minimum purchase eligible for a VAT refund is 315 kr (for details on refunds, see page 139).

Language: The native language is Norwegian (the two official forms are Bokmål and Nynorsk). For useful phrases, see page 691.

Emergencies: Dial 112 for police, medical, or other emergencies. In case of theft or loss, see page 131.

Time Zone: Norway is on Central European Time (the same as most of the Continent, one hour ahead of Great Britain, and six/nine hours ahead of the East/West Coasts of the US).

Embassies in Oslo: The **US embassy** is at Henrik Ibsens Gate 48 (tel. 21 30 85 58, emergency tel. 21 30 85 40, http://norway.usembassy.gov). The **Canadian embassy** is at Wergelandsveien 7 (tel. 22 99 53 00, www.norway.gc.ca). Call ahead for passport services.

Phoning: Norway's country code is 47; to call from another country to Norway, dial the international access code (011 from the US/Canada, 00 from Europe, or + from a mobile phone), then 47, followed by the local number. For local calls within Norway, just dial the number as it appears in this book—whether you're calling from across the street or across the country. To place an international call from Norway, dial 00, the code of the country you're calling (1 for US and Canada), and the phone number. For more tips, see page 1110.

Tipping: As service is included at sit-down meals, you don't need to tip further, though for great service it's nice to round up your bill about 5-10 percent. Tip a taxi driver by rounding up the fare (pay 90 kr on an 85-kr fare). For more tips on tipping, see page 143.

Tourist Information: www.goscandinavia.com

OSLO

While Oslo is the smallest of the Scandinavian capitals, this brisk little city offers more sightseeing thrills than you might expect. As an added bonus, you'll be inspired by a city that simply has its act together.

Sights of the Viking spirit—past and present—tell an exciting story. Prowl through the remains of ancient Viking ships, and marvel at more peaceful but equally gutsy modern boats (the *Kon-Tiki*, *Ra*, and *Fram*). Dive into the traditional folk culture at the Norwegian open-air folk museum, and get stirred up by the country's heroic spirit at the Norwegian Resistance Museum.

For a look at modern Oslo, tour the striking City Hall, take a peek at sculptor Gustav Vigeland's people pillars, walk all over the Opera House, and celebrate the world's greatest peacemakers at the Nobel Peace Center.

Situated at the head of a 60-mile-long fjord, surrounded by forests, and populated by more than a half-million people, Oslo is Norway's cultural hub. For 300 years (1624-1924), the city was called Christiania, after Danish King Christian IV. With independence, it reverted to the Old Norse name of Oslo. As an important port facing the Continent, Oslo has been one of Norway's main cities for a thousand years and the de facto capital since around 1300. Still, Oslo has always been small by European standards; in 1800, Oslo had 10,000 people, while cities such as Paris and London had 50 times as many.

Today the city sprawls out from its historic core to encompass over a million people in its metropolitan area, about one in five Norwegians. Oslo's port hums with international shipping and a sizeable cruise industry. Its waterfront, once traffic-congested and slummy, has undergone a huge change: Cars and trucks now travel in underground tunnels, upscale condos and restaurants are taking over, and the neighborhood has a splashy Opera House. Though it's always been a great city, Oslo seems to be constantly improving its infrastructure and redeveloping slummy old quarters

along the waterfront into cutting-edge residential zones. Oslo feels as if it's rushing to prepare for an Olympics-like deadline. But it isn't—it just wants to be the best city it can be.

Oslo is full of rich Norwegians and is, understandably, expensive. Its streets are a mix of grand Neoclassical facades and boxy 60s-style modernism. But overall, the feel of this major capital is green and pastoral—spread out, dotted with parks and lakes, and surrounded by hills and forests. For the visitor, Oslo is an all-you-can-see *smörgåsbord* of historic sights, trees, art, and Nordic fun.

Planning Your Time

Oslo is spread out, with its sightseeing highlights concentrated in three zones (noted below). On a short port visit, I'd focus on one of these zones, and possibly squeeze in one other if time allows. If you're nervous about straying too far from your ship, all of the city-center sights listed here are reassuringly nearby, but some of Oslo's best sights are a bus, tram, or boat ride away. Logistically, it makes sense to start at the farthest-flung areas (Bygdøy or Frogner Park), then work your way back toward the ship and do the city-center sights last.

• **City Center:** To get a look at today's Oslo, take my "Welcome to Oslo" self-guided walk (allow 30 minutes to sprint or an hour to linger). The two top sights downtown—both within a few steps of the walking route—are **City Hall** (allow one hour for a guided tour), and the **National Gallery** (allow about an hour for my self-guided tour). Lesser, but still worthwhile, sights include the **Nobel Peace Center, Opera House,** and **Norwegian Resistance Museum** (choose the ones that appeal to you, and allow 30-60 minutes each).

• **Frogner Park:** This delightful people zone, populated by locals, tourists, and Gustav Vigeland's remarkable statues, is worth the 15-minute tram or bus ride west of downtown; once there, allow at least an hour to explore.

• **Bygdøy:** This "museum island" is most easily reached on a 10-minute ferry ride from Oslo's main harbor (carefully check return schedule to leave plenty of time to get back to your ship).

Once here, you could spend all day at the many fine museums, ranging from an open-air folk museum to Viking ships to other Norwegian seafaring vessels (for full descriptions, see page 670 and choose your favorites; allow at least an hour per museum—and even more time for the spread-out Norwegian Folk Museum).

• **Other Options:** Most one-day visitors will want to focus on these main sights. But to escape the tourist trail and delve into workaday Oslo, consider my walk to the **Grünerløkka district** (allow an hour or more round-trip). Olympics pilgrims may want to visit **Holmenkollen Ski Jump and Ski Museum;** for most, it's not worth the long trip (25-minute train ride plus 10-minute walk

Excursions from Oslo

Most cruise lines offer activities within **Oslo** itself. As the city is user- and pedestrian-friendly (in most areas, and public transit works fine for others), I wouldn't pay for an excursion here. But if you'd like someone else to do the planning, various walking and bus tours lead you through the city center (Karl Johans Gate and harborfront area, including City Hall, Akershus Fortress, and Norwegian Resistance Museum), while others focus on the sights at Bygdøy (open-air museum—with Gol stave church—as well as Viking ship and other nautical museums). Still others may include a trip out to the Holmenkollen Ski Jump and surrounding hills. Any or all of these can be worthwhile—skim this chapter's descriptions to see what appeals to your interests, then look for an excursion that combines the sights you want to see. One place I'd avoid is the Ice Bar, a decidedly touristy venture a half-block from the National Museum. While it's entertaining, and can be refreshing on the rare hot day in Oslo, it's hardly an authentic look at the city or Norwegian culture.

A few excursions also include some out-of-town sights, such as a boat trip on the **Oslofjord** (which doesn't seem worth it—since you'll cruise in and out of the fjord on your ship anyway—unless you opt for a trip that's on a tall ship or makes stops that appeal to you) and a visit to the charming but super-touristy fjordside village of **Drøbak**. Train enthusiasts might enjoy a trip on the steam-powered **Krøderbanen** heritage railway line, while shoppers enjoy the 250-year-old **Hadeland Glassverk.** All of these less-urban options have their fans, but Oslo has plenty to fill a day.

each way, and—on sunny days—a possible wait for the elevator to the top).

Arrival at the Port of Oslo

Arrival at a Glance: It's easy to walk downtown from the **Akershus** or **Revierkai** ports; **Filipstad** and **Sørenge** are farther out—still walkable, but more convenient by cruise-line shuttle bus. I'd avoid taxis, as the hefty $30 minimum makes even a short trip outrageously expensive.

Port Overview

Oslo has four main areas where cruise ships arrive. I've listed them more or less in order of usage. All of them are, to varying degrees, a walkable distance to and from downtown, though the farther-flung ports are easier with wheels.

• **Akershus:** Right on the harbor below Akershus Fortress, a short walk from the City Hall and town center, and the only port with a real terminal building, this is the handiest and most common entry point. There are technically two separate, adjacent berths here: **Søndre Akershuskai,** closer to town, and **Vippetangen,** a bit farther out (at the tip of the peninsula).

• **Revierkai:** Around the east side of the Akershus Fortress peninsula, this port faces Oslo's new Opera House. Sights in the center are easily walkable from here.

• **Filipstad:** Just west of downtown, next to the brand-new Tjuvholmen development (around the far side of Aker Brygge from City Hall), this farther-out port is still walkable, but more convenient by cruise-line shuttle bus.

• **Sørenge:** The farthest afield, this port is around the east side of the bay that Oslo's Opera House sits on. Equipped for the biggest ships, it hasn't been used in recent seasons because of ongoing construction in this part of town. Once that's complete, it will likely be used again. Sørenge is a long (but scenic) walk to the Opera House and train station area, but works best by shuttle bus.

Public transportation isn't really useful for getting to town from the port areas themselves, but it can help connect the dots once you're in town (I've offered tips below). From the farther-out cruise berths (Filipstad and Sørenge), the cruise line's shuttle service is worth considering, even if you have to pay for it.

Expect Changes: In general, Oslo's waterfront has been undergoing extensive development for the last few years, and work won't end anytime soon. Because much of this work also affects the cruise port areas, don't be surprised if some of the details in this section have changed.

Tourist Information: A TI kiosk opens in the terminal building along Akershuskai when ships are in town. Otherwise, the most convenient TIs are just behind City Hall (useful for those arriving at Filipstad) and in front of the train station (workable for those walking in from Revierkai or Sørenge). For more on the TIs, see page 639.

Getting into Town

First I'll cover your taxi and tour options. Then I'll offer walking instructions from each of the ports. In general, from most ports you'll wind up at the City Hall/Aker Brygge area overlooking the harbor; however, if you're coming in from Revierkai or Sørenge, it's easier to visit the Opera House first, then head to the train station to take my self-guided walk, which ends near City Hall/Aker Brygge.

By Taxi

A few taxis meet arriving ships, but they're very pricey and the city is workable without them. The 150-kr minimum (yes, that's a hefty $30) is enough to cover your trip into downtown from any of the cruise ports. A taxi to the museums at Bygdøy is also quite pricey, at around 300 kr (about $60) from downtown. I'd skip the big bill and make use of Oslo's fine public transportation. If you need a taxi but can't find one, call 02323.

By Tour

Various local tour options can be a good use of your time. Two different **hop-on, hop-off bus tours** meet arriving cruise ships and provide a good, affordable way to connect outlying sights, including Frogner Park and Bygdøy. Your options are CitySightseeing Oslo (all-day ticket-€20 or 150 kr, 16 stops, www.citysightseeing .no) and Open Top/Oslo Sightseeing (all-day ticket-€25 or 220 kr, 20 stops, www.opentopsightseeing.no). Both have buses every 30 minutes and headphone commentary in English.

For other options in Oslo—including regular bus tours, fjord tours, walking tours, and local guides for hire—see "Tours in Oslo" on page 642.

By Foot from Each Port

The walking directions from each of Oslo's ports will get you close to the City Hall area at the head of the main harbor, which is also where most cruise-line shuttle buses drop off. This area is described in detail in the next section.

Akershus

By far the easiest place in town to arrive, the Akershus berths are within pleasant strolling distance of City Hall (10 minutes or less).

From the **Søndre Akershuskai** berth, a bit closer to town, you can see the boxy twin towers of City Hall—just turn left from your ship and head straight for it. The cruise terminal in front of this pier has lots of shops and a currency exchange desk (but no ATMs—for that, see "Services near City Hall or the Train Station," later), plus a helpful TI kiosk that also handles tax refunds.

From **Vippetangen**, a bit farther out, it's still an easy walk (just 5 minutes longer). You may not be able to see City Hall from your ship—just walk with the water on your left. As you head into town, you'll pass the cruise terminal and TI described earlier.

OSLO

Revierkai

Around the far (east) side of the Akershus peninsula, this pier faces Oslo's *other* big landmark: the strikingly modern Opera House, with its sloping roof leading right to the waters of the Oslofjord. If arriving here, you have several options: A fun first activity is to go for a stroll on the **Opera House** roof—to get there, simply walk to the end of the harbor and hook around to the right.

If you want to head to the **City Hall** area, several streets leading away from your ship can take you there; the most direct shot is along Rådhusgata, which is just beyond the giant, pink building with the towers. Walk along this street for about 15 minutes, and you'll pop out at City Hall.

If you want to begin with my self-guided walk—which ends near City Hall and shows you a lot more of downtown Oslo en route—head to the **train station:** First make your way to the Opera House. Then take the pedestrian bridge over the complicated intersection at the end of the harbor, and proceed straight ahead directly into the side door of the station. Continue straight up the escalators, turn left down the station's main hall, exit out the front, and start the walk. From your ship to the station, figure about a 15-minute walk.

Filipstad

Located in an unappealing industrial port area just west of downtown, Filipstad is still walking distance to the center (figure about 20 minutes from your ship to City Hall)—but the stroll is far from interesting.

The cutting-edge Tjuvholmen harborfront residential zone, just across the little harbor from your ship, has enlivened this area. As of this writing, construction around Tjuvholmen makes it impossible to cross directly to reach the city center; I've described a roundabout approach (below). However, once work at Tjuvholmen wraps up, it may be possible to use that neighborhood as a shortcut to reach Aker Brygge, Oslo's main harbor, and City Hall. Your ship's upper deck provides the perfect high-altitude vantage point for scouting your options before disembarking.

Exiting your ship at Filipstad, find your way to the port gate (at the far-left end of the big parking-lot zone at the pier). Continue straight out to the little roundabout and turn right, following the path out of the port area. You'll pass the stop for bus #33; intended for port workers, it runs only in the mornings and afternoons, but could shave some time off your walk (check the posted schedule— in 2012, the last morning departures were at 8:23 and 8:38). There's nowhere to buy tickets nearby, so you'll have to pay extra on board (45 kr—at around $9, this is likely more expensive than your cruise line's shuttle bus). If you take the bus, get off at Frederiksgate, near

---

Services near City Hall and the Train Station

There are few services at Oslo's various cruise ports; even the terminal at Akershus lacks an ATM and Wi-Fi. But once you're in town, resources abound. Assuming you'll enter town near City Hall or the train station, here are some services in each place.

ATMs: Behind the **City Hall,** you'll find an ATM inside the 7-Eleven (basically across the street from the TI). Many ATMs are easy to find in and around the **train station.**

Internet Access: Your best bet is in the TI behind **City Hall;** they have both an Internet terminal (free, limited to 20 minutes, also free printing) and Wi-Fi (look for the password posted inside).

Pharmacy: An Apotek 1 is two blocks over from the TI, between **City Hall** and Karl Johans Gate. There's a 24-hour pharmacy directly across the street and tram tracks from the **train station's** main entrance (see page 641).

---

the National Theater.

If you keep walking past the bus stop, you'll hit a foot/bike path that runs along a busy highway; turn right and follow this path into town. (Watch for signs to *Sentrum*.) Reaching the next big roundabout, a hard right would get you to Tjuvholmen; to reach City Hall, continue straight (bearing right just slightly) along the busiest road, lined with new, modern buildings. Soon you'll see City Hall's boxy twin towers ahead. When you reach the cross-street called Dokkveien (with the tram tracks), you have a choice: To get to the harbor, turn right and take the road down to Aker Brygge and the Nobel Peace Center. If you'd rather head to the park near Karl Johans Gate in the heart of Oslo, go straight, and you'll pop out at the National Theater.

Because this walk is fairly long and not particularly pretty, your cruise line's **shuttle bus** is worth considering. The bus may be free, or your line may charge (likely about €12 or $15 round-trip). With the cost of a basic bus ticket here at about $6, this is a decent value. Most shuttles drop you off (and pick you up later) right next to the Nobel Peace Center, at the City Hall/Aker Brygge area (described later).

Sørenge

This port, far to the east, will likely not be used until ongoing development work in this part of town is complete. But in case you arrive at Sørenge, here are some details:

Given this area's distance from downtown, you'll be better

off paying for your cruise line's **shuttle bus,** which drops you conveniently downtown. However, if you don't mind a longish **walk** (figure 20 minutes to the Opera House, then another 10-15 minutes to either the train station or City Hall), it's a scenic one that takes you past some of Oslo's newest housing developments.

From the port, walk with the water on your left, getting glimpses of the City Hall's boxy towers on the next harbor over. In the foreground you'll see the gray towers of a new residential development on the adjacent pier, also called Sørenge. You could continue all the way around the harbor to the Opera House from here (you can't miss it—it's the big, angular, white building that looks like it's sliding into the fjord). But for a scenic shortcut, veer left when you reach the end of the small harbor, and cut through the Sørenge housing complex to the far side of the pier. Look for the footbridge that leads you scenically across the port area straight to the Opera House. Once at the Opera House, you can walk across the pedestrian bridge to the train station, or curl around to Rådshusgata and take it on a straight shot to the City Hall (for details on both, see arrival tips for Revierkai, earlier).

Arriving at City Hall, Aker Brygge, and the Harbor

No matter where your ship puts in, you'll probably start your Oslo exploration in the harborfront zone in front of City Hall—with the Akershus Fortress on one side, and the Nobel Peace Center and Aker Brygge mall complex on the other. In addition to those four sightseeing options (all described later, under "Sights in Oslo"), here are some other choices:

To get oriented, you can follow the last parts of my **self-guided walk,** starting with "City Hall" on page 650.

To reach the **TI,** circle around the City Hall building and go up the street directly behind it; you'll find the TI at the start of this street, on the left. If you keep going up this street two more short blocks, you'll run into the inviting park that runs alongside Oslo's main drag, **Karl Johans Gate,** a short walk from the National Gallery and other sights.

From the harborfront, a boat trundles tourists across the bay to the sights at **Bygdøy** (boat and museums described on page 670).

If you'd like to zip to the **train station** area and the start of my self-guided walk (it ends near City Hall), you can take a tram. You'll find two tram stops (serving the same trams) in the zone in front of City Hall: The Aker Brygge stop is in front of the yellow Nobel Peace Center (to the right as you face the harbor), and the Rådhusplassen stop is at the far end of the City Hall complex, near the start of the Akershus Fortress area (look for the grass strip around the tracks, to the left as you face the harbor). From either tram stop, take tram #12 (direction: Disen) and ride it three stops to Jernbanetorget, the square in front of the train station.

You can also use tram #12 to reach **Frogner Park.** Hop on at either of the stops mentioned above, going in the direction of Majorstuen, and get off at the Vigelandsparken stop.

If you'd like to do my **self-guided tram tour** (on trams #12 and #11), you don't have to go to the train station to start it—you can pick it up right here at either of the City Hall-area stops (get on tram #12, direction: Majorstuen). After turning into #11, this tram takes you to the station area (exit there to do my self-guided walk), and continues back to City Hall.

Enjoy Oslo!

Returning to Your Ship

To reach the cruise berths near **Akershus,** just head for City Hall and look for your ship (tram #12 brings you to the Rådhusplassen stop, between City Hall and your ship). To get back to **Revierkai,** make your way to the train station, exit out the side to cross the pedestrian walkway to the Opera House, and circle around the harbor to your ship (or, from the City Hall area, walk 10 minutes up Rådhusgata). Leave yourself plenty of time for the dull hike back to **Filipstad,** or—ideally—catch the cruise-line shuttle bus by the Nobel Peace Center. A cruise shuttle is also the best option for **Sørenge;** otherwise, leave plenty of time for the long walk from the Opera House.

If you have some time to kill before heading back, the lively people zone around City Hall and Aker Brygge is a fine place to spend it. Consider dropping into the Nobel Peace Center to while away any remaining time before returning to your ship.

See page 689 for help if you miss your boat.

Orientation to Oslo

Oslo is easy to manage. Its sights cluster around the main boulevard, Karl Johans Gate (with the Royal Palace at one end and the train station at the other), and in the Bygdøy (big-doy) district, a 10-minute ferry ride across the harbor. The city's other main sight, Frogner Park (with Gustav Vigeland's statues), is about a mile behind the palace.

The monumental, homogenous city center contains most of the sights, but head out of the core to see the more colorful neighborhoods. Choose from Majorstuen and Frogner (chic boutiques, trendy restaurants), Grünerløkka (bohemian cafés, hipsters), and Grønland (multiethnic immigrants' zone).

OSLO

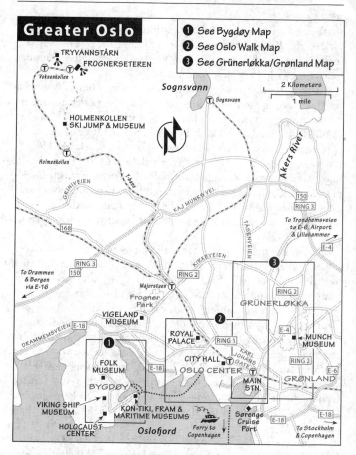

Greater Oslo

1. See Bygdøy Map
2. See Oslo Walk Map
3. See Grünerløkka/Grønland Map

Tourist Information

Oslo has two centrally located TIs: The **Oslo Tourist Information Center** faces the back of City Hall (June-Aug Mon-Fri 9:00-19:00, Sat-Sun 9:00-18:00, shorter hours and closed Sat-Sun off-season, Fridtjof Nansens Plass 5, enter from Roald Amundsens Gate, www.visitoslo.com). Another TI is in front of the **train station** (Mon-Fri 7:00-20:00; Sat-Sun 8:00-18:00). Go early or late to avoid lines; otherwise, grab a number as you enter and wait. They answer the phone only on weekdays from 9:00 to 16:00 (tel. 81 53 05 55). Also, a **TI kiosk** at the port opens when cruise ships arrive (Akershusstranda 15, tel. 81 53 05 55).

At any TI, pick up these freebies: an Oslo map, the helpful public-transit map, the annual *Oslo Guide* (with plenty of details on sightseeing, shopping, and eating), the *What's On in Oslo* monthly (for the most accurate listing of museum hours and special events), and *Streetwise* magazine (an insightful, worthwhile student guide

OSLO

that's fun to read and full of offbeat ideas). If you're traveling on, pick up the *Bergen Guide* and information for the rest of Norway, including the useful, annual *Fjord Norway Travel Guide*. Consider buying the Oslo Pass (described below).

Use It, a hardworking information center, is officially geared for those under age 26 but is generally happy to offer anyone its solid, money-saving, experience-enhancing advice (Mon-Fri 11:00-17:00, Sat 12:00-17:00, longer hours in Aug, closed Sun; Møllergata 3, look for *Ungdomsinformasjonen* sign, tel. 24 14 98 20, www.use-it.no). They offer free Internet access (30-minute limit, may have to wait for a computer). Their free *Streetwise* magazine—packed with articles on Norwegian culture, ideas on eating and sleeping cheap, good nightspots, the best beaches, and so on—is a must for young travelers and worthwhile for anyone curious about probing the Oslo scene.

Oslo Pass: This pass covers the city's public transit, ferry boats, and entry to nearly every major sight—all described in a useful handbook (270 kr/24 hours, 395 kr/48 hours, 495 kr/72 hours; big discounts for kids ages 4-15 and seniors age 67 and over, www.visitoslo.com/en/activities-and-attractions/oslo-pass/). Cruisers who show their stateroom cards get a 20 percent discount, potentially making this an even better value. Do the math before buying; add up the individual costs of the sights you want to see to determine whether an Oslo Pass will save you money. (Here are some sample charges: 8-ride transit pass-216 kr, Nobel Peace Center-80 kr, three boat museums at Bygdøy-210 kr, National Gallery-50 kr. These costs alone, which total 556 kr, more than justify buying a 48-hour pass.)

Entertainment Listings: The periodical *What's On in Oslo* has an extensive listing of happenings every day. Pick it up free at the TI, and review the busy lineup of special events, tours, and concerts. *Streetwise* magazine is also good.

Helpful Hints

Pickpocket Alert: They're a problem in Oslo, particularly in crowds on the street and in subways and buses. Always wear your money belt. To call the police, dial 112.

Street People and Drug Addicts: Oslo's street population loiters around the train station. While a bit unnerving to some travelers, locals consider this rough-looking bunch harmless. The police have pretty much corralled them to the square called Christian Frederiks Plass, south of the station.

Currency Exchange: Banks in Norway don't change money. Use ATMs or Forex exchange offices (outlets near City Hall at Fridtjof Nansens Plass 6, at train station, and at Egertorget at the crest of Karl Johans Gate; hours vary by location but generally Mon-Fri 9:00-18:00, Sat 9:00-16:00, closed Sun).

Internet Access: You have two options at the train station. **Sidewalk Express,** the budget choice, is near the Forex exchange office by the south exit—look for *South Exit* signs (29 kr/1.5 hours, open 24/7, coin-op). **@rctic Internet Café,** in the station's main hall and above track 13, is quieter but pricey (60 kr/hour, daily 8:00-23:00, sells international phone cards). The main TI (near City Hall) also has free, but limited, Internet access and Wi-Fi (see "Tourist Information," earlier).

Post Office: It's in the train station.

Pharmacy: Between City Hall and Karl Johans Gate, **Apotek 1** is two blocks over from the TI at Rosenkrantzgate (Mon-Fri 9:00-17:00, Sat 10:00-14:00, closed Sun, Stortingsgata 6, but enter around the corner on Rosenkrantzgate). **Jernbanetorgets Vitus Apotek** is open 24 hours daily (across from train station on Jernbanetorget, tel. 23 35 81 00).

Laundry: **Selva Laundromat** is on the corner of Wessels Gate and Ullevålsveien at Ullevålsveien 15, a half-mile north of the train station (daily self-serve 8:00-21:00, full-serve 10:00-19:00, walk or catch bus #37 from station, tel. 41 64 08 33).

Bike Rental: Bikes are tough to rent in Oslo. A public system lets you grab simple, one-speed city bikes out of locked racks at various points around town (80 kr/24 hours; rent card from TI that allows you to release bike from rack, leave credit-card number as deposit, and return card to TI).

Updates to This Book: For news about changes to this book's coverage since it was published, see www.ricksteves.com/update.

Getting Around Oslo

By Public Transit: Oslo's excellent transit system is made up of buses, trams, ferries, and a subway (*Tunnelbane,* or T-bane for short). Use the TI's free public transit map to navigate. The system runs like clockwork, with schedules clearly posted and followed. Many stops have handy electronic reader boards showing the time remaining before the next tram arrives (usually less than 10 minutes). **Ruter,** the public-transit information center, faces the train station under the glass tower (same building as TI; Mon-Fri 7:00-22:00, Sat-Sun 8:00-22:00, tel. 177 or 81 50 01 76, www.ruter.no).

Individual **tickets** work on buses, trams, ferries, and the T-bane for one hour (30 kr if bought at a Narvesen kiosk/convenience store, or 50 kr if bought on board). Other options include the **Reisekort** smartcard (216 kr for 8 rides within zone 1; buy at Narvesen, 7-Eleven stores, or transit offices; the cost of a ride is automatically deducted from the smartcard balance, reload at machines, not shareable with others on same ride), the 24-hour **Dagskort Tourist Ticket** (75 kr, pays for itself in 3 rides), and the **Oslo Pass** (gives free run of entire system; described earlier). Validate your ticket or smartcard by holding it next to the card reader when you board.

By Taxi: Taxis come with a 150-kr drop charge that covers you for three or four kilometers—about two miles (more on evenings and weekends). To get a taxi, wave one down, find a taxi stand, or call 02323.

Tours in Oslo

Oslo Fjord Tours—A fascinating world of idyllic islands sprinkled with charming vacation cabins is minutes away from the Oslo harborfront. For locals, the fjord is a handy vacation getaway. Tourists can get a glimpse of this island world by public ferry or tour boat. Cheap ferries regularly connect the nearby islands with downtown (covered by Oslo Pass, transit tickets, and Reisekort smartcard).

Several tour boats leave regularly from pier 3 in front of City Hall. Båtservice has a relaxing and scenic 1.5-hour hop-on, hop-off service, with a live-but-boring multilanguage commentary, which departs from the City Hall dock (175 kr, daily at 9:45, 11:15, 12:45, and 14:15; departs 30 minutes later from Opera House and one hour later from Bygdøy; tel. 23 35 68 90, www.boatsightseeing.com). They won't scream if you bring something to munch. They also offer two-hour fjord tours (250 kr, 3-4/day late March-Sept).

Bus Tours—Båtservice, which runs the harbor cruises (above), also offers four-hour **bus tours** of Oslo, with stops at the ski jump, Bygdøy museums, and Frogner Park (340 kr, 2/day late May-Aug, departs from ticket office on pier 3, longer tours also available, tel. 23 35 68 90, www.boatsightseeing.com). HMK also does daily city bus tours (200 kr/2 hours, 340 kr/4 hours, departs from TI across from City Hall, tel. 22 78 94 00, www.hmk.no). For details on **hop-on, hop-off bus tours,** see page 634.

Guided Walking Tour—The local guides' union offers 1.5-hour historic "Oslo Promenade" walks (150 kr, free with Oslo Pass; Mon, Wed, Fri at 17:30 in summer; leaves from sea side of City Hall, confirm departures at TI, tel. 22 42 70 20, www.guideservice.no).

Local Guide—To hire a private guide, call the guides' association at tel. 22 42 70 20 (1,550 kr/2 hours, www.guideservice.no). Another local guide bureau is at tel. 22 42 28 18.

OSLO

Self-Guided Tram Tour in Oslo

Tram #11/#12: A Hop-On, Hop-Off Introduction to Oslo

Tram #12, which becomes tram #11 halfway through its loop (at Majorstuen), circles the city from the train station, lacing together many of Oslo's main sights. Apart from the practical value of being

able to hop on and off as you sightsee your way around town (trams come by at least every 10 minutes), this 40-minute trip gives you a fine look at parts of the city you wouldn't otherwise see.

The route starts at the main train station, at the traffic-island tram stop located immediately in front of the transit office tower. The route makes almost a complete circle and finishes at Stortorvet (the cathedral square), dropping you off a three-minute walk from where you began the tour. You want tram #12 leaving from the second set of tracks, going toward Majorstuen. (Confirm with your driver that the particular tram #12 you're boarding becomes tram #11 and finishes at Stortorvet; some of these may turn into tram #19 instead, which takes a different route. If yours becomes #19, simply hop out at Majorstuen and wait for the next #11.) Note that you can also begin this tour at either of the harborfront tram stops in front of City Hall (see page 637).

Here's what you'll see and ideas on where you might want to hop out:

From the **station,** you'll go through the old grid streets of 16th-century Christiania, King Christian IV's planned Renaissance town. After the city's 17th fire, in 1624, the king finally got fed up. He decreed that only brick and stone buildings would be permitted in the city center, with wide streets to serve as fire breaks.

You'll turn a corner at the **fortress** (Christiana Torv stop; get off here for the fortress and Norwegian Resistance Museum), then head for **City Hall** (Rådhus stop). Next comes the harbor and upscale **Aker Brygge** waterfront neighborhood (jump off at the Aker Brygge stop for the harbor and restaurant row). Passing the harbor, you'll see on the left a few old shipyard buildings that still survive. Then the tram goes uphill, past the **House of Oslo** (a mall of 20 shops highlighting Scandinavian interior design; Vikatorvet stop) and into a district of ugly 1960s buildings (when elegance was replaced by "functionality"). The tram then heads onto the street

OSLO

Norwegians renamed **Henrik Ibsens Gate** in 2006 to commemorate the centenary of Ibsen's death, honoring the man they claim is the greatest playwright since Shakespeare.

After Henrik Ibsens Gate, the tram follows Frognerveien through the chic **Frogner neighborhood.** Behind the fine old facades are fancy shops and spendy condos. Here and there you'll see 19th-century mansions built by aristocratic families who wanted to live near the Royal Palace; today, many of these house foreign embassies. Turning the corner, you roll along the edge of **Frogner Park,** stopping at its grand gate (hop out at the Vigelandsparken stop for Frogner Park and Vigeland statues).

Ahead on the left, a statue of 1930s ice queen Sonja Henie marks the arena where she learned to skate. Turning onto Bogstadveien, the tram usually becomes #11 at the Majorstuen stop. **Bogstadveien** is lined with trendy shops, restaurants, and cafés—it's a fun place to stroll and window-shop. (You could get out here and walk along this street all the way to the Royal Palace park and the top of Karl Johans Gate.) The tram veers left before the palace, passing the **National Historical Museum** and stopping at the **National Gallery** (Tullinløkka stop). As you trundle along, you may notice that lots of roads are ripped up for construction. It's too cold to fix the streets in winter, so, when possible, the work is done in summer. Jump out at **Stortorvet** (a big square filled with flower stalls and fronted by the cathedral and the big GlasMagasinet department store). From here, you're a three-minute walk from the station, where this tour began.

Self-Guided Walk in Oslo

▲▲Welcome to Oslo

This stroll covers the heart of Oslo—the zone where most tourists find themselves walking—from the train station, up the main drag, and past City Hall to the harborfront. It takes a brisk 30 minutes if done nonstop.

Train Station: Start at the plaza just outside the main entrance of Oslo's central train station (Oslo Sentralstasjon). The statue of the tiger prowling around out front commemorates the 1,000th birthday of Oslo's founding, celebrated in the year 2000. The statue alludes to the town's nickname of Tigerstaden ("Tiger Town"). In the 1800s, Oslo was considered an urban tiger, leaving its mark on the soul of simple country folk who ventured into the wild and crazy New York City of Norway. (These days, the presence of so many beggars, or *tigger*, has prompted the nickname "Tiggerstaden.")

With your back to the train station, look for the glass Ruter tower that marks the **public transit office** (and TI); from here, trams zip to City Hall (harbor, boat to Bygdøy), and the underground subway (T-bane, or *Tunnelbane*—look for the *T* sign to your right) goes to Frogner Park (Vigeland statues) and Holmenkollen. Tram #12—featured in the self-guided tram tour described earlier—leaves from directly across the street.

The green building behind the Ruter tower is a shopping mall called **Byporten** (literally, "City Gate," see big sign on rooftop), built to greet those arriving from the airport on the shuttle train. Oslo's 37-floor pointed-glass **skyscraper,** the Radisson Blu Plaza Hotel, looms behind that. Its 34th-floor pub welcomes the public with air-conditioned views and pricey drinks (daily 16:00-24:00). The tower was built with reflective glass so that, from a distance, it almost disappears. The area behind the Radisson—the lively and colorful "Little Karachi," centered along a street called Grønland—is where most of Oslo's immigrant population settled. It's become a vibrant nightspot, offering a fun contrast to the predictable homogeneity of Norwegian cuisine and culture.

Oslo allows hard-drug addicts and prostitutes to mix and mingle in the station area. (While it's illegal to buy sex in Norway, those who sell it are not breaking the law.) Troubled young people come here from small towns in the countryside for anonymity and community. The two cameras near the top of the Ruter tower monitor drug deals. Signs warn that this is a "monitored area," but victimless crimes proceed while violence is minimized.

• *Turn your attention to Norway's main drag, called...*

Karl Johans Gate: This grand boulevard leads directly from the train station to the Royal Palace. The street is named for the French general Jean Baptiste Bernadotte, who was given a Swedish name, established the current Swedish dynasty, and ruled as a popular king (1818-1844) during the period after Sweden took Norway from Denmark.

Walk three blocks up Karl Johans Gate. This stretch is referred to as **"Desolation Row"** by locals because it has no soul, just shops greedily looking to devour tourist dollars and euros.

• *Hook right around the curved old brick structure of an old market and walk to the...*

Oslo Cathedral (Domkirke): This Lutheran church, from 1697, is where Norway commemorates its royal marriages and deaths. Seventy-seven deaths were mourned here following the tragic shootings and bombing of July 2011 (see sidebar, page 680). In the grass in front of the cathedral, you may see a semi-permanent memorial to the victims, consisting of a row of stones shaped like a heart.

Before going inside, stroll around to the right, behind the church. The **courtyard** is lined by a circa-1850 circular row of stalls

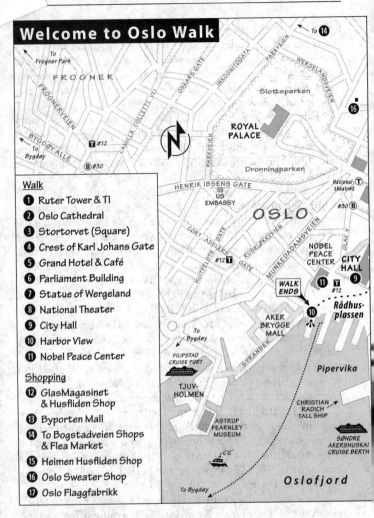

Welcome to Oslo Walk

To ⑭

To
Frogner Park

FROGNER

Slottsparken

⑯

ROYAL
PALACE

Dronningparken

HENRIK IBSENS GATE

US
EMBASSY

OSLO

National-
théatret

#30 Ⓑ

NOBEL
PEACE
CENTER

CITY
HALL
⑨

Ⓣ #12

WALK
ENDS

⑪

⑩

Rådhus-
plassen

AKER
BRYGGE
MALL

Pipervika

FILIPSTAD
CRUISE PORT

TJUV-
HOLMEN

CHRISTIAN
RADICH
TALL SHIP

ASTRUP
FEARNLEY
MUSEUM

SØNDRE
AKERSHUSKAI
CRUISE BERTH

To Bygdøy

Oslofjord

Ⓣ #12
Ⓑ #30

Walk

① Ruter Tower & TI
② Oslo Cathedral
③ Stortorvet (Square)
④ Crest of Karl Johans Gate
⑤ Grand Hotel & Café
⑥ Parliament Building
⑦ Statue of Wergeland
⑧ National Theater
⑨ City Hall
⑩ Harbor View
⑪ Nobel Peace Center

Shopping

⑫ GlasMagasinet
   & Husfliden Shop
⑬ Byporten Mall
⑭ To Bogstadveien Shops
   & Flea Market
⑮ Heimen Husfliden Shop
⑯ Oslo Sweater Shop
⑰ Oslo Flaggfabrikk

from an old market. Rusty meat hooks now decorate the lamps of a peaceful café, which has quaint tables around a fountain. The atmospheric **Café Bacchus,** at the far left end of the arcade, serves food outside and in a classy café downstairs (light 150-kr meals, Mon-Fri 11:00-22:00, Sat 12:00-21:00, closed Sun, salads, good cakes, coffee, tel. 22 33 34 30).

Now go around the other side to face the cathedral's main door (under the tall tower). Look for the cathedral's cornerstone (right of entrance), a thousand-year-old carving from Oslo's first and long-gone cathedral showing how the forces of good and evil tug at each of us. Step inside beneath the red, blue, and gold seal of Oslo and under an equally colorful ceiling. The box above on the

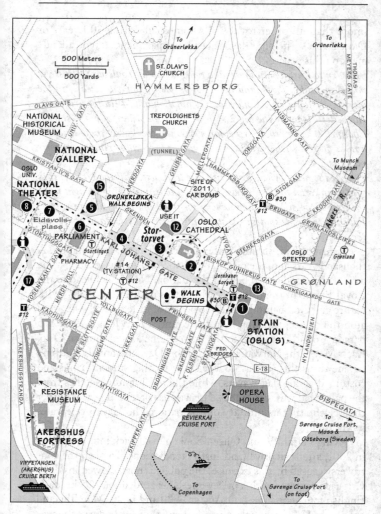

right is for the royal family. Back outside, notice the tiny square windows midway up the copper cupola—once the lookout quarters of the fire watchman.

• *The big square that faces the cathedral is called...*

Stortorvet: In the 17th century, when Oslo's wall was located about here, this was the point where farmers were allowed to enter and sell their goods. Today it's still lively as a flower and produce market (Mon-Fri). The statue shows Christian IV, the Danish king who ruled Norway around 1600, dramatically gesturing that-a-way. He named the city, rather immodestly, Christiania. (Oslo took back its old Norse name only in 1924.) Christian was serious about Norway. During his 60-year reign, he visited it 30 times (more than all other royal visits combined during 300 years of Danish rule). The big GlasMagasinet department store is a landmark on this square.

• *Return to Karl Johans Gate, and continue up the boulevard past street musicians, cafés, shops, and hordes of people. If you're here early in the morning (Mon-Fri) you may see a commotion at #14 (in the first block, on the left, look for the big 2 sign). This is the studio of a TV station (channel 2) where the Norwegian version of the* Today *show is taped, and as on Rockefeller Plaza, locals gather here, clamoring to get their mugs on TV.*

At the next corner, Kongens Gate leads left, past the 17th-century grid-plan town to the fortress. But we'll continue hiking straight up to the crest of the hill, enjoying some of the street musicians along the way. Pause at the wide spot in the street just before Akersgata to appreciate the...

Crest of Karl Johans Gate: Look back at the train station. A thousand years ago, the original (pre-1624) Oslo was located at the foot of the wooded hill behind the station. Now look ahead to the Royal Palace in the distance, which was built in the 1830s "with nature and God behind it and the people at its feet." If the flag flies atop the palace, the king is in the country. Karl Johans Gate is a parade ground from here to the palace—the axis of modern Oslo. Each May 17th, Norway's Constitution Day, an annual children's parade turns this street into a sea of marching student bands and costumed young flag-wavers, while the royal family watches from the palace balcony. Since 1814, Norway has preferred peace. Rather than celebrating its military on the national holiday, it celebrates its children.

King Harald V and Queen Sonja moved back into the palace in 2001, after extensive (and costly) renovations. To quell the controversy caused by this expense, the public is now allowed inside to visit each summer with a pricey one-hour guided tour (95 kr, daily English tours late June-mid-Aug at 14:00 and 14:20, Mon-Thu and Sat also at 12:00, buy tickets in advance at any post office or convenience store, or by calling 81 53 31 33, www.kongehuset.no).

In the middle of the small square, the *T* sign marks a stop of the T-bane (Oslo's subway). Let W. B. Samson's bakery tempt you with its pastries (and short cafeteria line; WC in back). Next to that, David Andersen's jewelry store displays traditional silver art and fine enamel work. Inside, halfway down the wall on the right (next to the free water dispenser), is a display of Norwegian folk costumes *(bunader)* with traditional jewelry—worn on big family occasions and church holidays. From here, the street called Akersgata kicks off a worthwhile stroll past the site of the July 2011 bombing, the national cemetery, and through a park-like river gorge to the trendy Grünerløkka quarter (an hour-long walk, described on page 679).

People-watching is great along Karl Johans Gate, but remember that if it's summer, half of the city's regular population is gone—vacationing in their cabins or farther away—and the city center is filled mostly with visitors.

Hike two blocks down Karl Johans Gate, past the big brick Parliament building (on the left). This section of sidewalk is heated during the frigid winter so it won't be icy. On the right, seated in the square, is a statue of the painter Christian Krohg. Farther down Karl Johans Gate, just past the Freia shop (Norway's oldest and best chocolate), the venerable **Grand Hotel** (Oslo's celebrity hotel—Nobel Peace Prize winners sleep here) overlooks the boulevard.

• *Ask the waiter at the Grand Café if you can pop inside for a little sightseeing (he'll generally let you).*

Grand Café: This historic café was for many years the meeting place of Oslo's intellectual and creative elite (the playwright Henrik Ibsen was a regular here). Notice the photos and knickknacks on the wall. At the back of the café, a mural shows Norway's literary and artistic clientele—from a century ago—enjoying this fine hangout. On the far left, find Ibsen, coming in as he did every day at 13:00. Edvard Munch is on the right, leaning against the window, looking pretty drugged. Names are on the sill beneath the mural.

• *For a cheap bite with prime boulevard seating, continue past the corner to Deli de Luca, a convenience store with a super selection of takeaway food and a great people-watching perch. Across the street, a little park faces Norway's...*

Parliament Building (Stortinget): Norway's Parliament meets here (along with anyone participating in a peaceful protest outside). Built in 1866, the building seems to counter the Royal Palace at the other end of Karl Johans Gate. If the flag's flying, Parliament's in session. Today the king is a figurehead, and Norway is run by a unicameral Parliament and a prime minister. Guided tours of the Stortinget are offered for those interested in Norwegian government (free; mid-June-Aug Mon-Fri at 10:00, 11:30, and 13:00; enter on Karl Johans Gate side, tel. 23 31 35 96, www.stortinget.no).

• *Cross over into the park and stroll toward the palace, past the fountain. Pause at the...*

Statue of Wergeland: The poet Henrik Wergeland helped inspire the movement for Norwegian autonomy. In the winter, the pool here is frozen and covered with children happily ice-skating. Across the street behind Wergeland stands the **National Theater** and statues of Norway's favorite playwrights: Ibsen and Bjørnstjerne Bjørnson. Across Karl Johans Gate, the pale yellow building is the first university building in Norway, dating from 1854. A block behind that is the National Gallery, with Norway's best collection of paintings (self-guided tour on page 658).

• *Facing the theater, follow Roald Amundsens Gate left, to the towering brick...*

City Hall (Rådhuset): Built mostly in the 1930s with contributions from Norway's leading artists, City Hall is full of great art and is worth touring (see page 654). The mayor has his office here (at the base of one of the two 200-foot towers), and every December 10, this building is where the Nobel Peace Prize is presented. For the best exterior art, circle the courtyard clockwise, studying the colorful woodcuts in the arcade.

Each shows a scene from Norwegian mythology, well-explained in English: Thor with his billy-goat chariot, Ask and Embla (a kind of Norse Adam and Eve), Odin on his eight-legged horse guided by ravens, the swan maidens shedding their swan disguises, and so on. Circle around City Hall on the right to the front. The statues (especially the six laborers on the other side of the building, facing the harbor, who seem to guard the facade) celebrate the nobility of the working class.

• *Walk to the...*

Harbor: A decade ago, you would have dodged several lanes of busy traffic to get to Oslo's harborfront. But today, most cars cross underneath the city in tunnels. In addition, the city has made its town center relatively quiet and pedestrian-friendly by levying a traffic-discouraging 27-kr toll for every car entering town. (This system, like a similar one in London, subsidizes public transit and the city's infrastructure.)

At the water's edge, find the shiny metal plaque (just left of center) listing the contents of a sealed time capsule planted in 2000 out in the harbor in the little Kavringen lighthouse straight ahead (to be opened in 1,000 years). Go to the end of the stubby pier (on the right). This is the ceremonial "enter the city" point for momentous occasions. One such instance was in 1905, when Norway gained its independence from Sweden and a Danish prince sailed in from Copenhagen to become the first modern king of Norway. Another milestone event occurred at the end of World War II, when the king returned to Norway after the country was liberated from the Nazis.

• *Stand at the harbor and give it a sweeping counterclockwise look.*

Harborfront Spin-Tour: Oslofjord is a huge playground, with 40 city-owned, park-like islands. Big white cruise ships—

OSLO

Browsing

Oslo's pulse is best felt by strolling. Three good areas are along and near the central Karl Johans Gate, which runs from the train station to the palace (follow my self-guided walk); in the trendy harborside Aker Brygge mall, a glass-and-chrome collection of sharp cafés, fine condos, and polished produce stalls (really lively at night, trams #10 and #12 from train station); and along Bogstadveien, a lively shopping street with no-nonsense modern commerce, lots of locals, and no tourists (T-bane to Majorstuen and follow this street back toward the palace and tourist zone). While most tourists never get out of the harbor/Karl Johans Gate district, the real, down-to-earth Oslo is better seen elsewhere, in places such as Bogstadveien. The bohemian, artsy Grünerløkka district, described on page 679, is good for a daytime wander.

a large part of the local tourist economy—dock just under the Akershus Fortress on the left. Just past the fort's impressive 13th-century ramparts, a statue of FDR grabs the shade. He's here in gratitude for the safe refuge the US gave to members of the royal family (including the young prince who is now Norway's king) during World War II—while the king and his government-in-exile waged Norway's fight against the Nazis from London.

Enjoy the grand view of City Hall. The yellow building farther to the left was the old West Train Station; today it houses the **Nobel Peace Center,** which celebrates the work of Nobel Peace Prize winners (see page 656). The next pier is the launchpad for harbor boat tours and the shuttle boat to the Bygdøy museums. A fisherman often moors his boat here, selling shrimp from the back.

At the other end of the harbor, shipyard buildings (this was the former heart of Norway's once-important shipbuilding industry) have been transformed into **Aker Brygge**—Oslo's thriving restaurant/shopping/nightclub zone (see "Eating in Oslo").

Just past the end of Aker Brygge is a brand-new housing development, which you may see still under construction, called **Tjuvholmen.** It's anchored by the Astrup Fearnley Museum—an international modern art museum complex designed by renowned architect Renzo Piano (most famous for Paris' Pompidou Center; www.afmuseet.no). This zone is just one more reminder of Oslo's bold march toward becoming a city that is at once futuristic and people-friendly. An ambitious urban renewal project called Fjord City (Fjordbyen)—which kicked off years ago with Aker Brygge, and led to the construction of Oslo's dramatic new Opera House (see page 656)—is making remarkable progress in turning the formerly industrial waterfront into a thriving people zone.

OSLO

Oslo at a Glance

▲▲▲**City Hall** Oslo's artsy 20th-century government building, lined with huge, vibrant, municipal-themed murals, best visited with included tour. **Hours:** Daily 9:00-18:00; tours daily at 10:00, 12:00, and 14:00, tours run Wed only in winter. See page 654.

▲▲▲**National Gallery** Norway's cultural and natural essence, captured on canvas. **Hours:** Tue-Fri 10:00-18:00, Thu until 19:00, Sat-Sun 11:00-17:00, closed Mon. See page 658.

▲▲▲**Frogner Park** Sprawling park with works by Norway's greatest sculptor, Gustav Vigeland, and the studio where he created them (now a museum). **Hours:** Park—always open; Vigeland Museum—June-Aug Tue-Sun 10:00-17:00, Sept-May Tue-Sun 12:00-16:00, closed Mon year-round. See page 666.

▲▲▲**Norwegian Folk Museum** Norway condensed into 150 historic buildings in a large open-air park. **Hours:** Daily mid-May-mid-Sept 10:00-18:00, off-season park open Mon-Fri 11:00-15:00, Sat-Sun 11:00-16:00, but most historical buildings closed. See page 672.

▲▲**Norwegian Resistance Museum** Gripping look at Norway's tumultuous WWII experience. **Hours:** June-Aug Mon-Sat 10:00-17:00, Sun 11:00-17:00; Sept-May Mon-Fri 10:00-16:00, Sat-Sun 11:00-16:00. See page 658.

▲▲**Viking Ship Museum** An impressive trio of ninth-century Viking ships, with exhibits on the people who built them. **Hours:** Daily May-Sept 9:00-18:00, Oct-April 10:00-16:00. See page 673.

▲▲**Fram Museum** Captivating exhibit on the Arctic exploration ship. **Hours:** June-Aug daily 9:00-18:00; May and Sept daily 10:00-17:00; Oct and March-April daily 10:00-16:00; Nov-Feb Mon-Fri 10:00-15:00, Sat-Sun 10:00-16:00. See page 674.

▲▲**Kon-Tiki Museum** Adventures of primitive *Kon-Tiki* and *Ra II* ships built by Thor Heyerdahl. **Hours:** Daily June-Aug 9:00-18:00, March-May and Sept-Oct 10:00-17:00, Nov-Feb 10:00-16:00. See page 675.

▲▲**Holmenkollen Ski Jump and Ski Museum** Dizzying vista and schuss through skiing history. **Hours:** Daily June-Aug 9:00-20:00, May and Sept 10:00-17:00, Oct-April 10:00-16:00. See page 676.

▲**Nobel Peace Center** Exhibit celebrating the ideals of the Nobel Peace Prize and the lives of those who have won it. **Hours:** Mid-May-Aug daily 10:00-18:00; Sept-mid-May Tue-Sun 10:00-18:00, closed Mon. See page 656.

▲**Opera House** Stunning performance center that's helping revitalize the harborfront. **Hours:** Foyer and café/restaurant open Mon-Fri 10:00-23:00, Sat 11:00-23:00, Sun 12:00-22:00. See page 656.

▲**Akershus Fortress Complex and Tours** Historic military base and fortified old center, with guided tours, a ho-hum castle interior, and a couple of museums (including the excellent Norwegian Resistance Museum, listed earlier). **Hours:** Park generally open daily 6:00-21:00; 45-minute tours of the grounds generally offered May-mid-June Sat-Sun at 13:00; late June daily at 13:00 and 16:00; July-mid-Aug daily at 11:00, 13:00, 14:00, and 16:00; late Aug Sat-Sun at 15:00, no tours off-season. See page 657.

▲**Norwegian Holocaust Center** High-tech walk through rise of anti-Semitism, the Holocaust in Norway, and racism today. **Hours:** Daily mid-June-mid-Aug 10:00-18:00, mid-Aug-mid-June 11:00-16:00. See page 674.

▲**Norwegian Maritime Museum** Dusty cruise through Norway's rich seafaring heritage. **Hours:** Mid-May-Aug daily 10:00-18:00; Sept-mid-May Tue-Fri 10:00-15:00, Sat-Sun 10:00-16:00, closed Mon. See page 675.

▲**Edvard Munch Museum** Works of Norway's famous Expressionistic painter. **Hours:** June-Aug daily 10:00-17:00; Sept-May Tue-Sat 10:00-16:00, Sun 10:00-17:00, closed Mon. See page 677.

▲**Grünerløkka** Oslo's bohemian district, with bustling cafés and pubs. **Hours:** Always open. See page 679.

• *From here, you can tour City Hall (cheap lunches Mon–Fri 12:30–13:30 only), visit the Nobel Peace Center, hike up to Akershus Fortress, take a harbor cruise (see "Tours in Oslo," earlier), or catch a boat across the harbor to the museums at Bygdøy (from pier 3). The sights just mentioned are described in detail in the following section.*

Sights in Oslo

Near the Harborfront

▲▲▲**City Hall (Rådhuset)**—In 1931, Oslo tore down a slum and began constructing its richly decorated City Hall. It was finally finished—after a WWII delay—in 1950 to celebrate the city's 900th birthday. Norway's leading artists all contributed to the building, an avant-garde thrill in its day. City halls, rather than churches, are the dominant buildings in Scandinavian capitals. The prominence of this building on the harborfront makes sense in this most humanistic, yet least churchgoing, northern end of

the Continent. Up here, people pay high taxes, have high expectations, and are generally satisfied with what their governments do with their money.

Cost and Hours: Free, daily 9:00-18:00, free 50-minute guided tours daily at 10:00, 12:00, and 14:00 in summer, tours run Wed only in winter, free WC, enter on Karl Johans Gate side, tel. 23 46 12 00.

Visiting City Hall: At Oslo's City Hall, the six statues facing the waterfront—dating from a period of Labor Party rule in Norway—celebrate the nobility of the working class. The art implies a classless society, showing everyone working together. The theme continues inside, with 20,000 square feet of bold and colorful Socialist Realist murals showing town folk, country folk, and people from all walks of life working harmoniously for a better society. The huge murals take you on a voyage through the collective psyche of Norway, from its simple rural beginnings through the scar tissue of the Nazi occupation and beyond. Filled with significance and symbolism—and well-described in English—they become even more meaningful with the excellent guided tours.

The main hall feels like a temple to good government, with its altar-like mural celebrating "work, play, and civic administration." The mural emphasizes Oslo's youth participating in community life—and rebuilding the country after Nazi occupation. Across the bottom, the slum that once cluttered up Oslo's harborfront is being cleared out to make way for this building. Above that, scenes show Norway's pride in its innovative health care and education systems. Left of center, near the top, Mother Norway rests on a church—reminding viewers that the Lutheran Church of Norway (the official state religion) provides a foundation for this society. On the right, four forms represent the arts; they illustrate how creativity springs from children. And in the center, the figure of Charity is surrounded by Culture, Philosophy, and Family.

The "Mural of the Occupation" lines the left side of the hall.

It tells the story of Norway's WWII experience. Looking left to right, you'll see the following: The German blitzkrieg overwhelms the country. Men head for the mountains to organize a resistance movement. Women huddle around the water well, traditionally where news is passed, while Quislings (traitors named after the Norwegian fascist who ruled the country as a Nazi puppet) listen in. While Germans bomb and occupy Norway, a family gathers in their living room. As a boy clenches his fist (showing determination) and a child holds the beloved Norwegian flag, the Gestapo steps in. Columns lie on the ground, symbolizing how Germans shut down the culture by closing newspapers and university. Two resistance soldiers are executed. A cell of resistance fighters (wearing masks and using nicknames so if tortured they can't reveal their compatriots' identities) plan a sabotage mission. Finally, prisoners are freed, the war is over, and Norway celebrates its happiest day: May 17, 1945—the first Constitution Day after five years under Nazi control.

While gazing at these murals, keep in mind that the Nobel Peace Prize is awarded in this central hall each December (though the general Nobel Prize ceremony occurs in Stockholm's City Hall). You can see videos of the ceremony and acceptance speeches in the adjacent Nobel Peace Center (see next).

Eating: A wonderful budget-lunch cafeteria is downstairs, offering a simple hot meal and salad bar at a nonprofit price; it's primarily for the building's workers, but the public is welcome (Mon-Fri 12:30-13:30 only). Fans of the explorer Fridtjof Nansen might enjoy a coffee or beer across the street at Fridtjof, an atmospheric bar filled with memorabilia from Nansen's Arctic explorations (Mon-Sat 12:00 until late, Sun 14:00-22:00, Nansens Plass 7, near Forex, tel. 93 25 22 30).

▲**Nobel Peace Center (Nobels Fredssenter)**—This thoughtful and thought-provoking museum, housed in the former West Train Station (Vestbanen), poses the question, "What is the opposite of conflict?" It celebrates the 800-some past and present Nobel Peace Prize winners with engaging audio and video exhibits and high-tech gadgetry (all with good English explanations). Allow time for reading about past prizewinners and listening to acceptance speeches by recipients from President Carter to Mother Theresa. Check out the astonishing interactive book detailing the life and work of Alfred Nobel, the Swedish inventor of dynamite, who initiated the prizes—perhaps to assuage his conscience.

Cost and Hours: 80 kr; mid-May-Aug daily 10:00-18:00; Sept-mid-May Tue-Sun 10:00-18:00, closed Mon; included guided tours at 12:00, 14:00, and 15:00, fewer in winter; Brynjulfs Bulls Plass 1, tel. 48 30 10 00, www.nobelpeacecenter.org.

▲**Opera House**—Opened in 2008, Oslo's striking Opera House is the talk of the town and a huge hit. The Opera House rises from the water on the city's eastern harbor, across the highway from

the train station (use the sky-bridge). Its boxy, low-slung, glass center holds a state-of-the-art, 1,400-seat main theater. The jutting white marble planes of its roof double as a public plaza. When visiting, you feel a need to walk all over it. The Opera House is part of a larger harbor-redevelopment plan that includes rerouting traffic into tunnels and turning a once-derelict industrial zone into an urban park.

Cost and Hours: Foyer and café/restaurant open Mon-Fri 10:00-23:00, Sat 11:00-23:00, Sun 12:00-22:00.

Tours: In summer, the Opera House offers guided tours of the auditorium and backstage area (100 kr, daily usually at 14:00, time can vary) and sporadic foyer concerts (50 kr, generally at 13:00). For tours, reserve by email at omvisninger@operaen.no or online at www.operaen.no (tel. 21 42 21 00).

Getting There: The easiest way to get to the Opera House is from the train station. Just follow signs for *Exit South/Utgang Syd* (standing in the main hall with the tracks to your back, it's to the left). Exiting the station, proceed straight ahead onto the pedestrian bridge (marked *Velkommen til Operaen*), which takes you effortlessly above the traffic congestion to your goal.

▲Akershus Fortress Complex

This park-like complex of sights scattered over Oslo's fortified old center is still a military base. But as you dodge patrol guards and vans filled with soldiers, you'll see the castle, a prison, war memorials, the Norwegian Resistance Museum, the Armed Forces Museum, and cannon-strewn ramparts affording fine harbor views and picnic perches. There's an unimpressive changing of the guard daily at 13:30 (at the parade ground, deep in the castle complex). The park is generally open daily 6:00-21:00, but because the military is in charge here, times can change without warning. Expect bumpy cobblestone lanes and steep hills. To get here from the harbor, follow the stairs (which lead past the FDR statue) to the park.

Fortress Visitors Center: Located immediately inside the gate, the information center has an interesting exhibit tracing the story of Oslo's fortifications from medieval times through the environmental struggles of today. Stop here to pick up a castle overview booklet, quickly browse through the museum, watch the quick video, and consider catching a tour (see next; museum entry free, mid-June-mid-Aug Mon-Fri 10:00-17:00, Sat-Sun 11:00-17:00, shorter hours off-season, tel. 23 09 39 17, www.mil.no /felles/ak).

▲Fortress Tours—The free 45-minute English walking tours of the grounds help you make sense of the most historic piece of real estate in Oslo (offered May-mid-June Sat-Sun at 13:00; late June daily at 13:00 and 16:00; July-mid-Aug daily at 11:00, 13:00, 14:00, and 16:00; late Aug Sat-Sun at 15:00; no tours off-season; depart from Fortress Visitors Center, call center at tel. 23 09 39 17 in advance to confirm times).

Akershus Castle—Although it's one of Oslo's oldest buildings (c.

1300), the castle overlooking the harbor is mediocre by European standards; the big, empty rooms recall Norway's medieval poverty. From the old kitchen, where the ticket desk and gift shop are located, you'll follow a one-way circuit of rooms open to the public. Descend through a secret passage to the dungeon, crypt, and royal tomb. Emerge behind the altar in the chapel, then walk through echoing rooms including the Daredevil's Tower, Hall of Christian IV, and Hall of Olav I. There are terrific harbor views from the rampart just outside.

Cost and Hours: 70 kr, sparse English descriptions throughout; May-Aug Mon-Sat 10:00-16:00, Sun 12:30-16:00; Sept-April Sat-Sun 12:00-17:00 only, closed Mon-Fri; tel. 22 41 25 21.

▲▲**Norwegian Resistance Museum (Norges Hjemme-frontmuseum)**—This fascinating museum tells the story of Norway's WWII experience: appeasement, Nazi invasion (they made Akershus their headquarters), resistance, liberation, and, finally, the return of the king.

Cost and Hours: 50 kr, 100-kr family ticket covers 2 adults plus up to 2 kids; June-Aug Mon-Sat 10:00-17:00, Sun 11:00-17:00; Sept-May Mon-Fri 10:00-16:00, Sat-Sun 11:00-16:00; next to castle, overlooking harbor, tel. 23 09 31 38, www.mil.no/felles/nhm.

Visiting the Museum: It's a one-way, chronological, can't-get-lost route—enter through the 1940 door.

You'll see propaganda posters attempting to get Norwegians to join the Nazi party, and the German ultimatum to which the king gave an emphatic "No." Various displays show secret radios, transmitters, underground newspapers, crude but effective home-made weapons, and the German machine that located clandestine radio stations. Exhibits explain how the country coped with 350,000 occupying troops; how airdrops equipped a home force of 40,000 ready to coordinate with the Allies when liberation was imminent; and the happy day when peace and freedom returned to Norway.

The museum is particularly poignant because many of the patriots featured inside were executed by the Germans right outside the museum's front door; a stone memorial marks the spot. (At war's end, the traitor Vidkun Quisling was also executed here.) With good English descriptions, this is an inspirational look at how the national spirit can endure total occupation by a malevolent force.

Armed Forces Museum (Forsvarsmuseet)—Across the fortress parade ground, a too-spacious museum traces Norwegian military history from Viking days to post-World War II. The early stuff is sketchy, but the WWII story is compelling.

Cost and Hours: Free, May-Aug Mon-Fri 10:00-17:00, Sat-Sun 11:00-17:00, shorter hours off-season, tel. 23 09 35 82.

▲▲▲National Gallery (Nasjonalgalleriet)

While there are many schools of painting and sculpture displayed in Norway's National Gallery, focus on what's uniquely Norwegian. Paintings come and go in this museum (pesky curators may have even removed some of the ones listed in the self-guided tour on the next page), but you're sure to see plenty that showcase the harsh beauty of Norway's landscape and people. A thoughtful visit here gives those heading into the mountains and fjord country a chance to pack along a little of Norway's cultural soul. Tuck these images carefully away with your goat cheese—they'll sweeten your explorations.

The gallery also has several Picassos, a noteworthy Impressionist collection, a Van Gogh self-portrait, and some Vigeland statues. Its many raving examples of Edvard Munch's work, including one of his famous *Scream* paintings, make a trip to the Munch Museum unnecessary for most (see page 677). It has about 50 Munch paintings in its collection, but only about a third are on display. Be prepared for changes, but don't worry—no matter what the curators decide to show, you won't have to scream for Munch's masterpieces.

Cost and Hours: 50 kr, free on Sun, Tue-Fri 10:00-18:00, Thu until 19:00, Sat-Sun 11:00-17:00, closed Mon, chewing gum prohibited, Universitets Gata 13, tel. 22 20 04 04, www.national museum.no.

The museum's 20-kr audioguide covers 15 paintings, has a poetic narrative with quotes from artists, and forces you to linger at each work of art—but doesn't have much more information than my self-guided tour below.

Self-Guided Tour

This easy-to-handle museum gives an effortless tour back in time and through Norway's most beautiful valleys, mountains, and fjords, with the help of its Romantic painters (especially Johan Christian Dahl). The paintings are organized roughly chronologically, from 1814 through 1950.

• *Go up the stairs, but before entering the first room, look to the right at the large canvas in the stairwell.*

❶ **Christian Krohg—*Albertine to See the Police Surgeon* (c. 1885-1887):** Christian Krohg (1852-1925) is known as Edvard Munch's inspiration, but to Norwegians, he's famous in his own right for his artistry and giant personality. Krohg had a sharp interest in social justice. In this painting, Albertine, a sweet girl from the countryside, has fallen into the world of prostitution in the big city. She's the new kid on the red-light block in the 1880s, as Oslo's prostitutes are pulled into the police clinic for their regular checkup. Note her traditional dress and the disdain she gets

National Gallery—Upper Floor

1 KROHG — Albertine to See the Police Surgeon

2 DAHL — View of Fortundalen

3 DAHL — Hellefossen near Hokksund

4 FEARNLEY — Labro Falls at Kongsberg

5 TIDEMAND & GUDE — The Bridal Voyage

6 TIDEMAND — Low Church Devotion

7 PETERSSEN — Christian II

8 KROHG — A Sick Girl

9 SUNDT-HANSEN — Burial at Sea

10 SOHLBERG — Winter Night in the Mountains

11 MUNCH — Self-Portrait with a Cigarette

12 MUNCH — Puberty

13 MUNCH — The Sick Child

14 MUNCH — Madonna

15 MUNCH — The Scream

16 MUNCH — Dance of Life

from the more experienced girls. Krohg has buried his subject in this scene. His technique requires the viewer to find her, and that search helps humanize the prostitute.

• *We'll look at more stark Norwegian realism later. But for now, let's head somewhere more idyllic. Walk into Room Z, turn left, and enter Room L.*

Landscape Paintings and Romanticism

Landscape painting has always played an important role in Norwegian art, perhaps because Norway provides such an awesome and varied landscape to inspire artists. The style reached its peak during the Romantic period in the mid-1800s, which stressed the beauty of unspoiled nature. (This passion for landscapes sets Norway apart from Denmark and Sweden.) After 400 years of Danish rule, the soul of the country was almost snuffed out. But with semi-independence and a constitution in the early 1800s, there was a national resurgence. Romantic paintings featuring the power of Norway's natural wonders and the toughness of its salt-of-the-earth folk came into vogue.

❷ Johan Christian Dahl—*View of Fortundalen* (1836): This painting epitomizes the Norwegian closeness to nature. It shows a view similar to the one that 21st-century travelers still enjoy on the Norwegian fjords: mountains, rivers, and a waterfall. Painted in 1836, it's textbook Romantic style. Nature rules—the background is as detailed as the foreground, and you are sucked in.

Johan Christian Dahl (1788-1857) is considered the father of Norwegian Romanticism. Romantics such as Dahl (and Turner, Beethoven, and Lord Byron) put emotion over rationality. They reveled in the power of nature—death and pessimism ripple through their work. The birch tree—standing boldly front and center—is a standard symbol for the politically downtrodden Norwegian people: hardy, cut down, but defiantly sprouting new branches. In the mid-19th century, Norwegians were awakening to their national identity. Throughout Europe, nationalism and Romanticism went hand in hand.

Find the typical Norse farm with its haystacks looking like rune stones. It reminds us that these farmers are hardworking, independent, small landowners. There was no feudalism in medieval Norway. People were poor...but they owned their own land. You can almost taste the *geitost*.

• *Look at the other works in Rooms L, and M. Dahl's paintings and those by his Norwegian contemporaries, showing heavy clouds and glaciers, repeat these same themes—drama over rationalism, nature pounding humanity. Human figures are melancholy. Norwegians, so close to nature, are fascinated by those plush, magic hours of dawn and twilight. The dusk makes us wonder: What will the future bring?*

In particular, focus on the painting to the left of the door in Room L.

❸ Dahl—*Hellefossen near Hokksund* (1838): Another typical Dahl setting: romantic nature and an idealized scene. A fisherman checks on wooden baskets designed to catch salmon migrating up the river. In the background, a water-powered sawmill slices trees into lumber. Note another Dahl birch tree at the left, a subtle celebration of the Norwegian people and their labor.

• *Now continue into Room M. At the far end is...*

❹ Thomas Fearnley—*Labro Falls at Kongsberg* (1837): Man cannot control nature or his destiny. The landscape in this painting is devoid of people—the only sign of humanity is the jumble of sawn logs in the foreground. A wary eagle perched on one log seems to be saying, "While you can cut these trees, they'll always be mine."

• *Facing this painting, turn left into Room N.*

❺ Adolph Tidemand and Hans Gude—*The Bridal Voyage*
(1848): This famous painting
shows the ultimate Norwegian
scene: a wedding party with
everyone decked out in traditional garb, heading for the
stave church on the quintessential fjord (Hardanger). It's a
studio work (not real) and a collaboration: Hans Gude painted
the landscape, and Adolph

Tidemand painted the people. Study their wedding finery. This
work trumpets the greatness of both the landscape and Norwegian
culture.

• *Also in Room N are examples of...*

The Photographic Eye

At the end of the 19th century, Norwegian painters traded the
emotions of Romanticism for more slice-of-life detail. This was the
end of the Romantic period and the beginning of Realism. With
the advent of photography, painters went beyond simple realism
and into extreme realism.

❻ Tidemand—*Low Church Devotion* (1848): This scene
shows a dissenting Lutheran church group (of which there were
many in the 19th century) worshipping in a smokehouse. The light
of God powers through the chimney, illuminating salt-of-the-
earth people with strong faiths. Rather than accept the Norwegian
king's "High Church," they worshipped in their homes in a more
ascetic style. Later, many of these people emigrated to America for
greater religious freedom.

• *On the facing wall is...*

❼ Eilif Peterssen—*Christian II* (1875): The Danish king
signs the execution order for the man who'd killed the king's
beloved mistress. With camera-like precision, the painter captures
the whole story of murder, anguish, anger, and bitter revenge in
the king's set jaw and steely eyes.

• *Go through Rooms O and P and into Room Q. Take time to browse
the paintings.*

Vulnerability

Death, disease, and suffering were themes seen again and again in
art from the late 1800s. The most serious disease during this period
was tuberculosis (which killed Munch's mother and sister).

❽ Krohg—*A Sick Girl* (1880): This extremely realistic painting shows a child dying of tuberculosis, as so many did in Norway in the 19th century. The girl looks directly at you. You can almost feel the cloth, with its many shades of white.

❾ Carl Sundt-Hansen—*Burial at Sea* (1890): While Monet and the Impressionists were busy abandoning the realistic style, Norwegian artists continued to embrace it. In this painting, you're invited to participate. A dead man's funeral is attended by an ethnically diverse group of sailors and passengers, but only one is a woman—the widow. Your presence completes the half-circle at the on-deck ceremony. Notice how each person in the painting has his or her own way of confronting death. Their faces speak volumes about the life of toil here. A common thread in Norwegian art is the cycle—the tough cycle—of life. There's also an interest in everyday experiences. *Burial at Sea* may not always be on display. If it's not here, you may instead see a similar canvas, **Erik Werenskiold's** *A Peasant Burial* (1885).

Also in this room may be another Krohg painting, *I Leden* (1892), which is notable for non-artistic reasons: It was on loan to one of the Oslo buildings that was damaged in the July 2011 car bombing (see sidebar on page 680). The painting was badly damaged, but has since been repaired. You may see the painting, along with a small exhibit about how the canvas, shredded by a madman, has been lovingly repaired.

• *Continue through Room R and into Room S.*

Atmosphere

Landscape painters were often fascinated by the phenomena of nature, and the artwork in this room takes us back to this ideal from the Romantic Age. Painters were challenged by capturing atmospheric conditions at a specific moment, since it meant mak-

ing quick sketches outdoors, before the weather changed yet again.

❿ Harald Sohlberg—*Winter Night in the Mountains* (1914): Harald Sohlberg was inspired by this image while skiing in the mountains in the winter of 1899. Over the years, he attempted to re-create the scene that inspired this remark: "The mountains in winter reduce one to silence. One is overwhelmed, as in a mighty, vaulted church, only a thousand times more so."

• *Follow the crowds into Room T, the Munch room.*

Turmoil

Room T is filled with works by Norway's single most famous painter, Edvard Munch (see sidebar). Norway's long, dark winters and social isolation have produced many gloomy artists, but none gloomier than Munch. He infused his work with emotion and expression at the expense of realism. After viewing the paintings in general, take a look at these in particular (listed in clockwise order).

⓫ Edvard Munch—*Self Portrait with a Cigarette* (1895): In this self-portrait, Munch is spooked, haunted—an artist working, immersed in an oppressive world. Indefinable shadows inhabit the background. His hand shakes as he considers his uncertain future. (Ironic, considering he created his masterpieces during this depressed period.) After eight months in a Danish clinic, he found peace—and lost his painting power. Afterward, Munch never again painted another strong example of what we love most about his art.

⓬ Munch—*Puberty* (1894-1895): One of the artist's most important non-*Scream* canvases reveals his ambivalence about women (see also his *Madonna*, below). This adolescent girl, grappling with her emerging sexuality, covers her nudity self-consciously. The looming shadow behind her—frighteningly too big and amorphous—threatens to take over the scene. The shadow's significance is open to interpretation—is it phallic, female genitalia, death, an embodiment of sexual anxiety...or Munch himself?

⓭ Munch—*The Sick Child* (1896): The death of Munch's sister in 1877 due to tuberculosis likely inspired this painting. The girl's face melts into the pillow. She's becoming two-dimensional, halfway between life and death. Everything else is peripheral, even her despairing mother saying good-bye. You can see how Munch scraped and repainted the face until he got it right.

⓮ Munch—*Madonna* (1894-1895): Munch had a tortured relationship with women. He never married. He dreaded and struggled with love, writing that he feared if he loved too much, he'd lose his painting talent. This painting is a mystery: Is she standing or lying? Is that a red halo or some devilish accessory? Munch wrote that he would strive to capture his subjects at their holiest moment. His alternative name for this work: *Woman Making Love.* What's more holy than a woman at the moment of conception?

⓯ Munch—*The Scream* (1893): Munch's most famous work shows a man screaming, capturing the fright many feel as the

Edvard Munch
(1863-1944)

Edvard Munch (pronounced "moonk") is Norway's most famous and influential painter. His life was rich, complex, and sad. His father was a doctor who had a nervous breakdown. His mother and sister both died of tuberculosis. He knew suffering. And he gave us the enduring symbol of 20th-century pain, *The Scream*.

He was also Norway's most forward-thinking painter, a man who traveled extensively through Europe, soaking up the colors of the Post-Impressionists and the curves of Art Nouveau. He helped pioneer a new style—Expressionism—using lurid colors and wavy lines to "express" inner turmoil and the angst of the modern world.

After a nervous breakdown in late 1908, followed by eight months of rehab in a clinic, Munch emerged less troubled—but a less powerful painter. His late works were as a colorist: big, bright, less tormented...and less noticed.

human "race" does just that. The figure seems isolated from the people on the bridge—locked up in himself, unable to stifle his scream. Munch made four versions of this scene, which has become *the* textbook example of Expressionism. On one, he graffitied: "This painting is the work of a madman." He explained that the painting "shows today's society, reverberating within me...making me want to scream." He's sharing his internal angst. In

fact, this Expressionist masterpiece is a breakthrough painting; it's angst personified.

🔟 **Munch—*Dance of Life* (1899-1900)**: In this scene of five dancing couples, we glimpse Munch's notion of femininity. To him, women were a complex mix of Madonna and whore. We see Munch's take on the cycle of women's lives: She's a virgin (discarding the sweet flower of youth), a whore (a jaded temptress in red), and a widow (having destroyed the man, she is finally alone, aging, in black). With the phallic moon rising on the lake, Munch demonizes women as they turn men into green-faced, lusty monsters.

• *Our tour is over, but there's more to see in this fine collection. Take a break from Nordic gloom and doom by visiting Rooms O and Y, with works by Impressionist and Post-Impressionist artists...even Munch got into the spirit with his Parisian painting, titled* Rue Lafayette. *You'll see lesser known, but still beautiful, paintings by non-Norwegian big names such as Picasso, Modigliani, Monet, Manet, Van Gogh, Gauguin, and Cézanne.*

Near the National Gallery

National Historical Museum (Historisk Museum)—Directly behind the National Gallery and just below the palace is a fine Art Nouveau building offering an easy (if underwhelming) peek at Norway's history.

Cost and Hours: 50 kr, included 45-minute Viking tours daily at noon in the summer; mid-May-mid-Sept Tue-Sun 10:00-17:00, mid-Sept-mid-May Tue-Sun 11:00-16:00, closed Mon year-round; Frederiks Gate 2, tel. 22 85 99 12, www.khm.uio.no.

Visiting the Museum: The ground floor offers a walk through the local history from prehistoric times. It includes the country's top collection of Viking artifacts, displayed in low-tech, old-school exhibits with barely a word of English to give it meaning. There's also some medieval church art. The museum's highlight is upstairs: an exhibit (well-described in English) about life in the Arctic for the Sami people (previously known to outsiders as Laplanders). In this overview of the past, a few Egyptian mummies and Norwegian coins through the ages are tossed in for good measure.

▲▲▲Frogner Park

This 75-acre park contains a lifetime of work by Norway's greatest sculptor, Gustav Vigeland (see sidebar). In 1921, he made a deal with the city. In return for a great studio and state support, he'd spend his creative life beautifying Oslo with this sculpture garden. From 1924 to 1943 he worked on-site, designing 192 bronze and granite statue groupings—600 figures in all, each nude and unique. Vigeland even planned the landscaping. Today the park is loved and respected by the people of Oslo (no police, no fences—and no graffiti). The Frognerbadet swimming pool is also at Frogner Park.

Cost and Hours: The garden is always open and free. The park is safe (cameras monitor for safety) and lit in the evening.

Getting There: Tram #12—which leaves from the central train station, Rådhusplassen in front of City Hall, Aker Brygge, and other points in town—drops you off right at the park gate (Vigelandsparken stop). Tram #19 (with stops along Karl Johans

OSLO

Gustav Vigeland
(1869-1943)

As a young man, Vigeland studied sculpture in Oslo, then supplemented his education with trips abroad to Europe's art capitals. Back home, he carved out a successful, critically acclaimed career feeding newly independent Norway's hunger for homegrown art.

During his youthful trips abroad, Vigeland had frequented the studio of Auguste Rodin, admiring Rodin's naked, restless, intertwined statues. Like Rodin, Vigeland explored the yin/yang relationship of men and women. Also like Rodin, Vigeland did not personally carve or cast his statues. Rather, he formed them in clay or plaster, to be executed by a workshop of assistants. Vigeland's sturdy humans capture universal themes of the cycle of life—birth, childhood, romance, struggle, child-rearing, growing old, and death.

Gate) takes you to Majorstuen, a 10-minute walk to the gate (or you can change at Majorstuen to tram #12 and ride it one stop to Vigelandsparken).

Visiting the Park: Vigeland's park is more than great art: It's a city at play. Appreciate its urban Norwegian ambience. The park is huge, but this visit is a snap. Here's a quick, four-stop, straight-line, gate-to-monolith tour.

1. Enter the Park from Kirkeveien: For an illustrated guide and fine souvenir, pick up the 75-kr book in the Visitors Center (Besøkssenter) on your right as you enter. The modern cafeteria has sandwiches (indoor/outdoor seating, daily 9:00-20:30, shorter hours Sun and off-season), plus books, gifts, and WCs. Look at the

statue of Gustav Vigeland (hammer and chisel in hand, drenched in pigeon poop) and consider his messed-up life. He lived with his many models. His marriages failed. His children entangled his artistic agenda. He didn't age gracefully. He didn't name his statues, and refused to explain their meanings. While those who know his life story can read it clearly in the granite and bronze, I'd forget Gustav's troubles and see his art as observations on the bittersweet cycle of life in general—from a man who must have had a passion for living.

2. Bridge: The 300-foot-long bridge is bounded by four granite columns: Three show a man fighting a lizard, the fourth shows a woman submitting to the lizard's embrace. Hmmm. (Vigeland was familiar with medieval mythology, where dragons represent man's primal—and sinful—nature.) But enough lizard love; the 58 bronze statues along the bridge are a general study of the human body. Many deal with relationships between people. In the middle, on the right, find the circular statue of a man and woman going round and round—perhaps the eternal attrac-

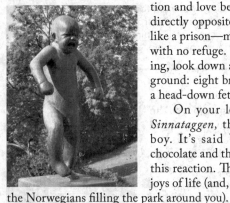

tion and love between the sexes. But directly opposite, another circle feels like a prison—man against the world, with no refuge. From the man escaping, look down at the children's playground: eight bronze infants circling a head-down fetus.

On your left, see the famous *Sinnataggen,* the hot-headed little boy. It's said Vigeland gave him chocolate and then took it away to get this reaction. The statues capture the joys of life (and, on a sunny day, so do the Norwegians filling the park around you).

3. Fountain: Continue through a rose garden to the earliest sculpture unit in the park. Six giants hold a fountain, symbolically toiling with the burden of life, as water—the source of life—cascades steadily around them. Twenty tree-of-life groups surround the fountain. Four clumps of trees (on each corner) show humanity's relationship to nature and the seasons of life: childhood, young love, adulthood, and winter.

Take a quick swing through life, starting on the right with youth. In the branches you'll see a swarm of children (Vigeland called them "geniuses"): A boy sits in a tree, boys actively climb while most girls stand by quietly, and a girl glides through the branches wide-eyed and ready for life...and love. Circle clockwise to the next stage: love scenes. In the third corner, life becomes more complicated: a sad woman in an animal-like tree, a lonely child, a couple plummeting downward (perhaps falling out of love), and finally an angry man driving

away babies. The fourth corner completes the cycle, as death melts into the branches of the tree of life and you realize new geniuses will bloom.

The 60 bronze reliefs circling the basin develop the theme further, showing man mixing with nature and geniuses giving the carousel of life yet another spin. Speaking of another spin, circle again and follow these reliefs.

The sidewalk surrounding the basin is a maze—life's long and winding road with twists, dead ends, frustrations, and, ultimately, a way out. If you have about an hour to spare, enter the labyrinth (on the side nearest the park's entrance gate, there's a single break in the black border) and follow the white granite path until (on the monolith side) you finally get out. (Tracing this path occupies older kids, affording parents a peaceful break in the park.) Or you can go straight up the steps to the monolith.

4. Monolith: The centerpiece of the park—a teeming monolith of life surrounded by 36 granite groups—continues Vigeland's cycle-of-life motif. The figures are hunched and clearly earthbound, while Vigeland explores a lifetime of human relationships. At the center, 121 figures carved out of a single block of stone rocket skyward. Three stone carvers worked daily for 14 years, cutting Vigeland's full-size plaster model into the final 180-ton, 50-foot-tall erection.

Circle the plaza, once to trace the stages of life in the 36 statue groups, and a second time to enjoy how Norwegian kids relate to the art. The statues—both young and old—seem to speak to children.

Vigeland lived barely long enough to see his monolith raised. Covered with bodies, it seems to pick up speed as it spirals skyward. Some people seem to naturally rise. Others struggle not to fall. Some help others. Although the granite groups around the monolith are easy to understand, Vigeland left the meaning of the monolith itself open. Like life, it can be interpreted many different ways.

From this summit of the park, look a hundred yards farther, where four children and three adults are intertwined and spinning in the Wheel of Life. Now, look back at the entrance. If the main gate is at 12 o'clock, the studio where Vigeland lived and worked—now the Vigeland Museum—is at 2 o'clock (see the green copper tower poking above the trees). His ashes sit in the top of the tower in clear view of the monolith. If you liked the park, visit the

Vigeland Museum (described next), a delightful five-minute walk away, for an intimate look at the art and how it was made.

▲▲Vigeland Museum—Filled with original plaster casts and well-described exhibits on his work, this palatial city-provided

studio was Vigeland's home and workplace. The high south-facing windows provided just the right light.

Vigeland, who had a deeply religious upbringing, saw his art as an expression of his soul. He once said, "The road between feeling and execution should be as short as possible." Here, immersed in his work, Vigeland supervised his craftsmen like a father, from 1924 until his death in 1943.

Cost and Hours: 50 kr; June-Aug Tue-Sun 10:00-17:00, Sept-May Tue-Sun 12:00-16:00, closed Mon year-round; bus #20 or tram #12 to Frogner Plass, Nobels Gate 32, tel. 23 49 37 00, www.vigeland.museum.no.

Oslo City Museum (Oslo Bymuseum)—This hard-to-be-thrilled-about little museum tells the story of Oslo. For a quick overview of the city, watch the 15-minute English video.

Cost and Hours: Free, Tue-Sun 11:00-17:00, closed Mon, borrow English description sheet, located in Frogner Park at Frogner Manor Farm across street from Vigeland Museum, tel. 23 28 41 70, www.oslomuseum.no.

▲▲Oslo's Bygdøy Neighborhood

This thought-provoking and exciting cluster of sights is on a park-like peninsula just across the harbor from downtown. It provides a busy and rewarding half-day (at a minimum) of sightseeing. Here, within a short walk, are six important sights (listed in order of importance):

• **Norwegian Folk Museum,** an open-air park with traditional log buildings from all corners of the country.

• **Viking Ship Museum,** showing off the best-preserved Viking longboats in existence.

• **Fram Museum,** showcasing the modern Viking spirit with the ship of arctic-exploration fame.

• **Kon-Tiki Museum,** starring the *Kon-Tiki* and the *Ra II*, in which Norwegian explorer Thor Heyerdahl proved that

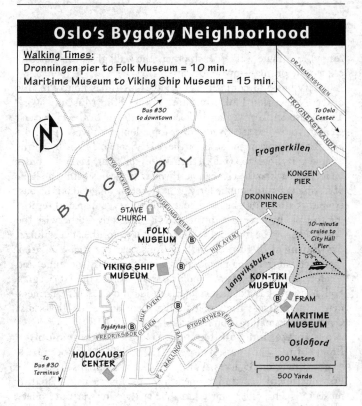

Oslo's Bygdøy Neighborhood

Walking Times:
Dronningen pier to Folk Museum = 10 min.
Maritime Museum to Viking Ship Museum = 15 min.

(Map labels: DRAMMENSVEIEN; FROGNERSTRANDA; To Oslo Center; Bus #30 to downtown; BYGDØY; BYGDØVEIEN; MUSEUMSVEIEN; Frognerkilen; KONGEN PIER; DRONNINGEN PIER; STAVE CHURCH; FOLK MUSEUM; HUK AVENY; 10-minute cruise to City Hall Pier; VIKING SHIP MUSEUM; Langviksbukta; KON-TIKI MUSEUM; HUK AVENY; FRAM; BYGDØYNESVEIEN; MARITIME MUSEUM; Bygdøyhus; FREDRIKSBORGVEIEN; Oslofjord; To Bus #30 Terminus; P.T. MALLINGS VEI; HOLOCAUST CENTER; 500 Meters; 500 Yards)

early civilizations—with their existing technologies—could have crossed the oceans.

• **Norwegian Maritime Museum,** interesting mostly to old salts, has a wonderfully scenic movie of Norway.

• **Norwegian Holocaust Center,** a high-tech look at the Holocaust in Norway and contemporary racism.

Getting There: Sailing from downtown to Bygdøy is fun, and it gets you in a seafaring mood. Ride the Bygdøy ferry—marked *Public Ferry Bygdøy Museums*—from pier 3 in front of City Hall (50 kr one-way; covered by Oslo Pass, transit tickets, and Reisekort smartcard; May-Sept daily 8:45-20:45, usually 3/hour; doesn't run Oct-April). Boats generally leave from downtown and from the museum dock at :05, :25, and :45 past each hour. In summer, avoid the nearby, and much more expensive, tour boats. For a less memorable approach, you can take bus #30 (from train station or National Theater, direction: Bygdøy).

Getting Around Bygdøy: The Norwegian Folk and Viking Ship museums are a 10-minute walk from the ferry's first stop (Dronningen). The other boating museums (*Fram, Kon-Tiki,* and Maritime) are at the second ferry stop (Bygdøynes). The Holocaust

Center is off Fredriksborgveien, about halfway between these two museum clusters. All Bygdøy sights are within a pleasant (when sunny) 15-minute walk of each other. The walk gives you a picturesque taste of small-town Norway.

City bus #30 connects the sights four times hourly in this order: Norwegian Folk Museum, Viking Ship Museum, Kon-Tiki Museum, Norwegian Holocaust Center. (For the Holocaust Center, you'll use the Bygdøyhus stop a long block away; tell the bus driver you want the stop for the "HL-Senteret.") The bus turns around at its final stop (Huk), then passes the sights in reverse order on its way back to the city center. If you take the bus within an hour of having taken the public ferry, your ticket is still good on the bus. Note that after 17:00, bus and boat departures are sparse. If returning to Oslo by ferry, get to the dock a little early—otherwise the boat is likely to be full, and you'll have to wait for the next sailing.

Eating at Bygdøy: Lunch options near the *Kon-Tiki* are a sandwich bar (relaxing picnic spots along the grassy shoreline) and a cafeteria (with tables overlooking the harbor). The Norwegian Folk Museum has a decent cafeteria inside and a fun little farmers' market stall across the street from the entrance. The Holocaust Center has a small café on its second floor.

▲▲▲Norwegian Folk Museum (Norsk Folkemuseum)— Brought from all corners of Norway, 150 buildings have been reassembled here on 35 acres. While Stockholm's Skansen was the first museum of this kind to open to the public (see page 278), this museum is a bit older, started in 1882 as the king's private collection (and the inspiration for Skansen).

Cost and Hours: 100 kr, daily mid-May-mid-Sept 10:00-18:00, off-season park open Mon-Fri 11:00-15:00, Sat-Sun 11:00-16:00 but most historical buildings closed, free lockers, Museumsveien 10, bus #30 stops immediately in front, tel. 22 12 37 00, www.norskfolkemuseum.no.

Visiting the Museum: Think of the visit in three parts: the park sprinkled with old buildings, the re-created old town, and the folk-art museum. In peak season, the park is lively, with craftspeople doing their traditional things and costumed guides all around. (They're paid to happily answer your questions—so ask many.) The evocative Gol stave church, at the top of a hill at the park's edge, is a must-see (built in 1212 in Hallingdal and painstakingly reconstructed here). Across the park, the old town comes complete with apartments from various generations (including some reconstructions of actual peoples' homes) and offers an intimate look at lifestyles here in 1905, 1930, 1950, 1979, and even a modern-day Norwegian-Pakistani apartment.

The museum beautifully presents woody, colorfully painted folk art (ground floor), exquisite-in-a-peasant-kind-of-way

OSLO

folk costumes (upstairs), and temporary exhibits. Everything is thoughtfully explained in English. Don't miss the best Sami culture exhibit I've seen in Scandinavia (across the courtyard in the green building, behind the toy exhibit).

Upon arrival, pick up the site map and review the list of activities, concerts, and guided tours on that day. In summer,

guided tours go daily at 12:00 and 14:00; the Telemark Farm hosts a small daily fiddle-and-dance show on the hour; and a folk music-and-dance show is held each Sunday at 14:00. The folk museum is lively only June through mid-August, when buildings are open and staffed. Otherwise, the indoor museum is fine, but the park is just a walk past lots of locked-up log cabins. If you don't take a tour, glean information from the 10-kr guidebook and the informative attendants stationed in buildings throughout the park.

▲▲Viking Ship Museum (Vikingskiphuset)—In this impressive museum, you'll gaze with admiration at two finely crafted, majestic oak Viking ships dating from the 9th and 10th centuries.

Along with the well-preserved ships, you'll see remarkable artifacts that may cause you to consider these notorious raiders in a different light. Over a thousand years ago, three things drove Vikings on their far-flung raids: hard economic times in their bleak homeland, the lure of prosperous and vulnerable communities to the south, and a mastery of the sea. There was a time when most frightened Europeans closed every prayer with, "And deliver us from the Vikings, Amen." Gazing up at the prow of one of these sleek, time-stained vessels, you can almost hear the screams and smell the armpits of those redheads on the rampage.

Cost and Hours: 60 kr, daily May-Sept 9:00-18:00, Oct-April 10:00-16:00, Huk Aveny 35, tel. 22 13 52 80, www.khm .uio.no.

Visiting the Museum: You'll see two ships, starting with the *Oseberg,* from A.D. 834. With its ornate carving and impressive rudder, it was likely a royal pleasure craft. It seems designed for sailing on calm inland waters during festivals, but not in the open ocean.

The *Gokstad*, from A.D. 950, is a practical working boat, capable of sailing the high seas. A ship like this brought settlers to the west of France (Normandy was named for the Norsemen). And in such a vessel, explorers such as Eric the Red hopscotched from Norway to Iceland to Greenland and on to what they called Vinland—today's Newfoundland in Canada. Imagine 30 men hauling on long oars out at sea for weeks and months at a time. In 1892, a replica of this ship sailed from Norway to America in 44 days to celebrate the 400th anniversary of Columbus *not* discovering America.

The ships tend to steal the show, but don't miss the hall displaying **jewelry and personal items** excavated along with the ships. The ships and related artifacts survived so well because they were buried in clay as part of a gravesite. Many of the finest items were not actually Viking art, but goodies they brought home after raiding more advanced (but less tough) people. Still, there are lots of actual Viking items, such as metal and leather goods, that give insight into their culture. Highlights are the cart and sleighs, ornately carved with scenes from Viking sagas.

The museum doesn't offer tours, but it's easy to eavesdrop on the many guides leading big groups through the museum. Everything is well-described in English. You probably don't need the little museum guidebook—it repeats exactly what's already posted on the exhibits.

▲**Norwegian Holocaust Center (HL-Senteret)**—Located in the stately former home of Nazi collaborator Vidkun Quisling, this museum and study center offers a high-tech look at the racist ideologies that fueled the Holocaust. To show the Holocaust in a Norwegian context, the first floor displays historical documents about the rise of anti-Semitism and personal effects from Holocaust victims. Downstairs, the names of 760 Norwegian Jews killed by the Nazis are listed in a bright, white room. The *Innocent Questions* glass-and-neon sculpture outside shows an old-fashioned punch card, reminding viewers of how the Norwegian puppet government collected seemingly innocuous information before deporting its Jews. The *Contemporary Reflections* video is a reminder that racism and genocide continue today.

Cost and Hours: 50 kr, ask for free English audioguide or catalog with translation of exhibit text, daily mid-June-mid-Aug 10:00-18:00, mid-Aug-mid-June 11:00-16:00, Huk Aveny 56—follow signs to *HL-Senteret*, tel. 22 84 21 00, www.hlsenteret.no.

▲▲**Fram Museum (Frammuseet)**—This museum holds the 125-foot, steam- and sail-powered ship that took modern-day Vikings Roald Amundsen and Fridtjof Nansen deep into the Arctic and Antarctic, farther north and south than any vessel had gone before. For three years, the *Fram*—specially designed to sur-

vive the crushing pressures of a frozen-over sea—drifted, trapped in the Arctic ice. The exhibit is engrossing and newly improved.

Cost and Hours: 80 kr; June-Aug daily 9:00-18:00; May and Sept daily 10:00-17:00; Oct and March-April daily 10:00-16:00; Nov-Feb Mon-Fri 10:00-15:00, Sat-Sun 10:00-16:00; Bygdøynesveien 36, tel. 23 28 29 50, www.frammuseum.no.

Visiting the Museum: Read the ground-floor displays, check out the videos below the bow of the ship, then climb the steps to the third-floor gangway to explore the *Fram*'s claustrophobic but fascinating interior. Also featured are a tent like the one Amundsen used, reconstructed shelves from his Artic kitchen, models of the *Fram* and the motorized sled they used to traverse the ice and snow, and a "polar simulator" plunging visitors to a 15° Fahrenheit environment.

The museum also tells the chilling tales of other Arctic and Antarctic adventures undertaken beneath the Norwegian flag. The polar sloop *Gjøa*, dry-docked outside next to the ferry dock, is the ship that Amundsen and a crew of six used from 1903 to 1906 to "discover" the Northwest Passage.

▲▲Kon-Tiki Museum (Kon-Tiki Museet)—Next to the *Fram* is a museum housing the *Kon-Tiki* and the *Ra II*, the ships built by Thor Heyerdahl (1914-2002). In 1947, Heyerdahl and five crewmates constructed the *Kon-Tiki* raft out of balsa wood, using only pre-modern tools and techniques. They set sail from Peru on the tiny craft, surviving for 101 days on fish, coconuts, and sweet potatoes (which were native to Peru). About 4,300 miles later, they arrived in Polynesia. The point was to show that early South Americans could have settled Polynesia. (While Heyerdahl proved they could have, anthropologists doubt they did.) The *Kon-Tiki* story became a best-selling book and award-winning documentary (and helped spawn the "Tiki" culture craze in the US). In 1970, Heyerdahl's *Ra II* made a similar 3,000-mile journey from Morocco to Barbados to prove that Africans could have populated America. Both ships are well-displayed and described in English. Short clips from *Kon-Tiki*, the Oscar-winning 1950 documentary film, play in a small theater at the end of the exhibit.

Cost and Hours: 70 kr, daily June-Aug 9:00-18:00, March-May and Sept-Oct 10:00-17:00, Nov-Feb 10:00-16:00, Bygdøynesveien 36, tel. 23 08 67 67, www.kon-tiki.no.

▲Norwegian Maritime Museum (Norsk Sjøfartsmuseum)—If you like the sea, this museum is a salt lick, providing a

OSLO

wide-ranging look at Norway's maritime heritage. Its dusty collection includes the charred remains of Norway's oldest boat (2,200 years old), artifacts from the immigration days, and a case devoted to World War II. Don't miss the movie *The Ocean: A Way of Life*, included with your admission. It's a breathtaking widescreen film swooping you scenically over Norway's dramatic sea and fishing townscapes from here all the way to North Cape in a comfy theater (20 minutes, shown at the top and bottom of the hour, follow *Supervideografen* signs).

Cost and Hours: 60 kr, kids under 6 free; mid-May-Aug daily 10:00-18:00; Sept-mid-May Tue-Fri 10:00-15:00, Sat-Sun 10:00-16:00, closed Mon; Bygdøynesveien 37, tel. 24 11 41 50, www.marmuseum.no.

Outer Oslo

▲▲Holmenkollen Ski Jump and Ski Museum—The site of one of the world's oldest ski jumps (from 1892), Holmenkollen has hosted many championships, including the 1952 Winter Olympics. To win the privilege of hosting the 2011 World Ski Jump Championship, Oslo built a bigger jump to match modern ones built elsewhere. This futuristic, cantilevered, Olympic-standard **ski jump** has a tilted elevator that you can ride to the top (on a sunny day, you may have to wait your turn for the elevator). Stand right at the starting gate, just like an athlete, and get a feel for this daredevil sport. The jump empties into a 50,000-seat amphitheater, and if you go when it's clear, you'll see one of the best possible views of Oslo.

The **ski museum,** a must for skiers, traces the evolution of the sport, from 4,000-year-old rock paintings to crude 1,500-year-old wooden sticks to the slick and quickly evolving skis of modern times, including a fun exhibit showing the royal family on skis. You'll see gear from Roald Amundsen's famous trek to the South Pole, including the stuffed remains of Obersten (the Colonel), one of his sled dogs.

Cost and Hours: 110-kr ticket includes museum and viewing platform at top of jump; daily June-Aug 9:00-20:00, May and Sept 10:00-17:00, Oct-April 10:00-16:00; tel. 22 92 32 64, www.holmenkollen.com or www.skiforeningen.no.

Simulator: To cap your Holmenkollen experience, step into the simulator and fly down the ski jump and ski in a virtual downhill race. My legs were exhausted after the five-minute terror. This simulator (or should I say stimulator?), at the lower level of the complex, costs 60 kr (if you pay for four tickets, try getting a fifth one free).

Getting There: T-bane line #1 gets you out of the city, through the hills, forests, and mansions that surround Oslo, and to the jump (direction: Frognerseteren; alternatively, you can take any westbound train—that's *tog mot vest*—to Majorstuen, then transfer to line #1). From the Holmenkollen station, you'll hike up the road 10 minutes to the ski jump.

For an easy downhill jaunt through the Norwegian forest, with a woodsy coffee or meal break in the middle, stay on the T-bane past Holmenkollen to the end of the line (Frognerseteren) and walk 10 minutes downhill to the recommended **Frognerseteren Hovedrestaurant,** a fine traditional eatery with a sod roof, reindeer meat on the griddle, and a city view. Continue on the same road another 20 minutes downhill to the ski jump, and then to the Holmenkollen T-bane stop.

▲**Edvard Munch Museum (Munch Museet)**—The only Norwegian painter to have had a serious impact on European art, Munch (pronounced "moonk") is a surprise to many who visit this fine museum, located one mile east of Oslo's center. The emotional, disturbing, and powerfully Expressionistic work of this strange and perplexing man is arranged chronologically. You'll see an extensive collection of paintings, drawings, lithographs, and photographs. Note that Oslo's centrally located National Gallery, which also displays many Munch works, can be a good alternative if you find the Munch Museum too time-consuming to reach.

The Munch Museum was in the news in August 2004, when two Munch paintings, *Madonna* and a version of his famous *Scream*, were brazenly stolen right off the walls in broad daylight. Two men in black hoods simply entered through the museum café, waved guns at the stunned guards and tourists, ripped the paintings off the wall, and sped off in a black Audi station wagon. Happily, in 2006, the thieves were caught and the stolen paintings recovered. Today they are on display behind glass with heightened security.

Cost and Hours: 95 kr; June-Aug daily 10:00-17:00; Sept-May Tue-Sat 10:00-16:00, Sun 10:00-17:00, closed Mon; 25-kr audioguide, guided tours daily July-Aug at 13:00, T-bane or bus #20 to Tøyen, Tøyengata 53, tel. 23 49 35 00, www.munch .museum.no. For more on Munch, see page 665.

From Akers River to the Grünerløkka District

Connect the dots by following the self-guided "Walk up the Akers River to Grünerløkka" (see page 679).

Akers River—This river, though only about five miles long, powered Oslo's early industry: flour mills in the 1300s, sawmills in the 1500s, and Norway's Industrial Revolution in the 1800s. A walk along the river not only spans Oslo's history, but also shows the contrast the city offers. The bottom of the river (where this walk doesn't go)—bordered by the high-rise Oslo Radisson Blu Plaza

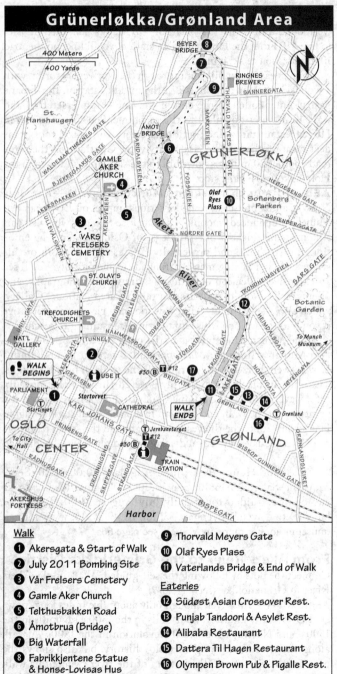

Grünerløkka/Grønland Area

Walk
1. Akersgata & Start of Walk
2. July 2011 Bombing Site
3. Vår Frelsers Cemetery
4. Gamle Aker Church
5. Telthusbakken Road
6. Åmotbrua (Bridge)
7. Big Waterfall
8. Fabrikkjentene Statue & Honse-Lovisas Hus
9. Thorvald Meyers Gate
10. Olaf Ryes Plass
11. Vaterlands Bridge & End of Walk

Eateries
12. Südøst Asian Crossover Rest.
13. Punjab Tandoori & Asylet Rest.
14. Alibaba Restaurant
15. Dattera Til Hagen Restaurant
16. Olympen Brown Pub & Pigalle Rest.
17. Café Con Bar

Hotel and the "Little Pakistan" neighborhood of Grønland—has its share of drunks and drugs, reflecting a new urban reality in Oslo. Farther up, the river valley becomes a park as it winds past decent-size waterfalls and red-brick factories. The source of the river (and Oslo's drinking water) is the pristine Lake Maridal, situated at the edge of the Nordmarka wilderness. The idyllic recreation scenes along Lake Maridal are a world apart from the rougher reality downstream.

▲Grünerløkka—The Grünerløkka district is the largest planned urban area in Oslo. It was built in the latter half of the 1800s to house the legions of workers employed at the factories powered by the Akers River. The first buildings were modeled on similar places built in Berlin. (German visitors observe that there's now more turn-of-the-20th-century Berlin here than in present-day Berlin.) While slummy in the 1980s, today it's trendy. Locals sometimes refer to it as "Oslo's Greenwich Village." Although that's way over the mark, it is a bustling area with lots of cafés, good spots for a fun meal, and few tourists.

Getting There: Grünerløkka can be reached from the center of town by a short ride on tram #11, #12, or #13, or by taking the short but interesting walk described next.

▲Walk up the Akers River to Grünerløkka—While every tourist explores the harborfront and main drag of Oslo, few venture into this neighborhood that evokes the Industrial Revolution. Once housing poor workers, it now attracts hip professionals. A hike up the Akers River, finishing in the stylish Grünerløkka district, shines a truly different light on Oslo. Allow about an hour at a brisk pace, including a fair bit of up and down. Navigate with the TI's free city map and the map in this chapter. This walk is best during daylight hours.

Begin the walk by leaving Karl Johans Gate at the top of the hill, and head up **Akersgata**—Oslo's "Fleet Street" (lined with major newspaper companies). After two blocks, at Apotekergata, you may see the side street blocked off and construction work to the right. They're cleaning up from the horrific bombing of July 2011 (see sidebar); the car bomb went off just a block to the right of here, on Grubbegata. Posters around this area identify four buildings that suffered structural damage in the bombing. Continuing up Akersgata, the street name becomes Ullevålsveien as it passes those buildings. Norwegians are planning to build a memorial here in the near future.

Continuing past this somber site, you'll approach the massive brick Trefoldighets Church and St. Olav's Church before reaching the **Vår Frelsers (Our Savior's) Cemetery.** Enter the cemetery across from the Baby Shop store (where Ullevålsveien meets Wessels Gate).

In Cold Blood

Norway likes to think of itself as a quiet, peaceful nation on the edge of Europe—after all, its legislators award the Nobel Peace Prize. So the events of July 22, 2011—when an anti-immigration fanatic named Anders Behring Breivik set off a car bomb in Oslo, killing eight, and then traveled to a Labor Party summer camp where he shot and killed 69 young people and counselors—have had a profound effect on the country's psyche.

Unlike the US, Britain, or Spain, Norway had escaped 21st-century terrorism until Breivik's attack. When the public found

out that the man behind the bombing and gunfire was a native Norwegian—dressed in a policeman's uniform—who hunted down his victims in cold blood, it became a national nightmare.

Though Norwegians are often characterized as stoic, there was a huge outpouring of grief. Bouquets flooded the square in front of Oslo Cathedral. Permanent memorials will eventually be built at the sites of the tragedies.

Breivik, who was arrested after the shootings, was described by police as a gun-loving fundamentalist obsessed with what he saw as the "threat" of multiculturalism and immigration to

Stop at the big metal map just inside the gate to chart your course through the cemetery: Go through the light-green Æreslunden section—with the biggest plots and highest eleva-tion—and out the opposite end (#13 on the metal map) onto Akersveien. En route, check out some of the tombstones of the illuminati and literati bur-ied in the honorary Æreslunden section. They include Munch, Ibsen, Bjørnson, and many of the painters whose works you can see in the National Gallery (all marked on a map posted at

the entrance). Exiting on the far side of the cemetery, walk left 100 yards up Akersveien to the church.

The Romanesque **Gamle Aker Church** (from the 1100s), the oldest building in Oslo, is worth a look inside (free, Mon-Thu 14:00-16:00, Fri 12:00-14:00). The church, which fell into ruins and has been impressively rebuilt, is pretty bare except for a pulpit

Norwegian values. His targets were the Norwegian government and politically active youths—some only 14 years old—and their counselors at an island summer camp sponsored by Norway's center-left party.

It's true that Norway has a big and growing immigrant community. More than 11 percent of today's Norwegians are not ethnic Norwegians, and a quarter of Oslo's residents are immigrants. These "new Norwegians" have provided a much-needed and generally appreciated labor force, filling jobs that wealthy Norwegians would rather not do.

But there is some resentment in a country that is disinclined to be a melting pot. There have been scuffles between Norwegian gangs and immigrant groups. Another source of friction is the tough love Norwegians feel they get from their government compared to the easy ride offered to needy immigrants: "They even get pocket money in jail!"

Horrified by Breivik's actions, many Norwegians are now going out of their way to make immigrants feel welcome. And the anti-immigrant Progress Party (which condemned the attacks) lost support in a round of local elections held shortly after the attack.

Norway seems determined not to let the July 22 massacre poison its peaceful soul. Calls for police to start carrying weapons or to reinstate the death penalty were quickly rejected. "Breivik wanted to change Norway," an Oslo resident told me. "We're determined to keep Norway the way it was."

and baptismal font from the 1700s.

From the church, backtrack 20 yards, head left at the playground, and go downhill on the steep **Telthusbakken Road** toward the huge, gray former grain silos (now student housing). The cute lane is lined with colorful old wooden houses: The people who constructed these homes were too poor to meet the no-wood fire-safety building codes within the city limits, so they built in what used to be suburbs. At the bottom of Telthusbakken, cross the busy Maridalsveien and walk directly through the park to the

Akers River. The lively Grünerløkka district is straight across the river from here, but if you have 20 minutes and a little energy, detour upstream first and hook back down. Don't cross the river yet.

Walk along the riverside bike lane upstream through the river gorge park. Just above the first waterfall, cross **Åmotbrua,** the big white springy suspension footbridge from 1852 (moved here in 1958). Keep hiking uphill along the river. At the base of the next big waterfall, cross over again to the large brick buildings, hiking up the stairs to the Beyer bridge (above the falls) with *Fabrikkjentene*, a statue of four women laborers. They're pondering the textile factory where they and 700 others like them toiled long and hard. This gorge was once lined with the water mills that powered Oslo through its 19th-century Industrial Age boom. The tiny red house next to the bridge—the **Honse-Lovisas Hus** cultural center—makes a good rest-stop (Tue-Sun 11:00-18:00, closed Mon, coffee and cake). Cross over to the red-brick Ringnes Brewery and follow **Thorvald Meyers Gate** downhill directly into the heart of Grünerløkka. The main square, called **Olaf Ryes Plass,** is a happening place to grab a meal or drink. Trams take you from here back to the center.

• *To continue exploring, you could keep going straight and continue walking until you reach a T-intersection with a busy road (Trondheimsveien). From there (passing the recommended Südøst Asian Crossover Restaurant), you can catch a tram back to the center, or drop down to the riverside path and follow it downstream to Vaterlands bridge in the Grønland district. From here the train station is a five-minute walk down Stenersgata. (The last section, around Grønland, is a bit seedy and best done in daylight.)*

Shopping in Oslo

Shops in Oslo are generally open 10:00-18:00. Many close early on Saturday and all day Sunday. Shopping centers are open Monday through Friday 10:00-21:00, Saturday 9:00-18:00, and are closed Sunday. Remember, when you make a purchase of 315 kr or more, you can get the 25 percent tax refunded when you leave the country if you hang on to the paperwork (see page 139).

Oslo's fanciest department store is **GlasMagasinet** (top end, near the cathedral on Stortorvet, good souvenir shop). The big, splashy **Byporten** mall, adjoining the central train station, is more youthful and hip (Mon-Fri 10:00-21:00, Sat 10:00-20:00, closed Sun). The trendiest boutiques and chic, high-quality shops lie along the street named **Bogstadveien** (running from behind the Royal Palace to Frogner Park). And on Saturday mornings, you can browse the **flea market** at Vestkanttorvet (March-Nov only, two blocks east of Frogner Park at the corner of Professor Dahl's Gate and Neubergsgate).

Sweaters and colorful Norwegian folk crafts are on many visitors' shopping lists. The **Husfliden shop,** in the basement of the GlasMagasinet department store, is much appreciated for its traditional yarn and Norsk folk items (Mon-Fri 10:00-18:00, Thu until

19:00, Sat 10:00-16:00, closed Sun, tel. 22 42 10 75). For a superb selection of sweaters and other Norwegian crafts (top quality at high prices), visit **Heimen Husfliden** (Mon-Fri 10:00-18:00, Sat 10:00-15:00, closed Sun, Rosenkrantz Gate 8, tel. 22 41 40 50). The **Oslo Sweater Shop** has good prices for sweaters (Mon-Fri 10:00-18:00, Sat 10:00-15:00, closed Sun, in Radisson Blu Scandinavia Hotel at Tullinsgate 5, tel. 22 11 29 22). For flags (a long, skinny *vimple* dresses up a boat or cabin wonderfully), pop into **Oslo Flaggfabrikk** (Mon-Fri 9:00-17:00, Sat 10:00-15:00, closed Sun, near City Hall at Hieronymus Heyerdahlsgate 1, tel. 22 40 50 60).

Vinmonopolet stores are the only place where you can buy wine and spirits in Norway. The most convenient location is at the central train station (Mon-Thu 10:00-18:00, Fri 9:00-18:00, Sat 9:00-15:00, closed Sun). The bottles used to be kept behind the counter, but now you can actually touch the merchandise. Locals say it went from being a "jewelry store" to a "grocery store."

Eating in Oslo

Eating Cheaply

How do the Norwegians afford their high-priced restaurants? They don't eat out much. This is one city in which you might just settle for simple or ethnic meals—you'll save a lot and miss little. Many menus list small and large plates. Because portions tend to be large, choosing a small plate or splitting a large one makes some otherwise pricey options reasonable. You'll notice many locals just drink free tap water, even in fine restaurants. For a description of Oslo's classic (and expensive) restaurants, see the TI's *Oslo Guide* booklet.

Picnic for lunch. Basements of big department stores have huge, first-class supermarkets with lots of alternatives to sandwiches. The little yogurt tubs with cereal come with collapsible spoons. Wasa crackers and meat, shrimp, or cheese spread in a tube are cheap and pack well. The central station has an ICA supermarket with long hours (Mon-Fri 6:00-21:00, Sat 8:00-19:00, Sun 10:00-18:00).

You'll save 12 percent by getting take-away food from a restaurant rather than eating inside. (The VAT on take-away food is 12 percent; restaurant food is 24 percent.) Fast-food restaurants ask if you want to take away or not before they ring up your order on the cash register. Even McDonald's has a two-tiered price list.

Oslo is awash with little budget eateries (modern, ethnic, fast food, pizza, department-store cafeterias, and so on). **Deli de Luca,** a cheery convenience store chain, notorious for having a store on every key corner in Oslo, is a step up from the similarly ubiquitous

OSLO

Norwegian Cuisine

Traditionally Norwegian cuisine doesn't rank very high in terms of excitement value. But the typical diet of meat, fish, and potatoes is now evolving to incorporate more diverse products, and the food here is steadily improving. Fresh produce, colorful markets, and efficient supermarkets abound in Europe's most expensive corner.

In this land of farmers and fishermen, you'll find raw ingredients like potatoes, salmon, or beef in traditional recipes. Norway's national dish is *Fårikål*, a lamb or mutton stew with cabbage, peppercorns, and potatoes. It's served with lingonberry jam and *lefse*—a soft flatbread made from potatoes, milk, and flour. This dish is so popular that the last Thursday in September is *Fårikål* day in Norway. Norwegian grandmothers prepare this hearty stew by throwing together the basic ingredients with whatever leftovers are lying around the kitchen. There's really no need for a recipe, so every stew turns out differently—and every grandma claims hers is the best.

Because of its long, cold winters, Norway relies heavily on the harvesting and preservation of fish. Smoked salmon, called *laks*, is prepared by salt-curing the fish and cold-smoking it, ensuring the temperature never rises above 85°F. This makes the texture smooth and almost raw. *Bacalao* is another favorite: salted and dried cod that is soaked in water before cooking. You'll often find *bacalao* served with tomatoes and olives.

Some Norwegians serve lutefisk around Christmas time, but you'll rarely see this salty, pungent dish on the menu. Instead, try the more pleasant *fiskekake*, small white fish cakes made with cream, eggs, milk, and flour. You can find these patties year-round. For a break from the abundance of seafood, try local specialties such as reindeer meatballs, or pork-and-ground-beef meat cakes called *kjøttkaker*. True to Scandinavian cuisine, *kjøttkaker* are usually slathered in a heavy cream sauce.

Dessert and coffee after a meal are essential. *Bløtkake*, a popular delight on Norway's Constitution Day (May 17), is a layered cake drizzled with strawberry juice, covered in whipped cream, and decorated with fresh strawberries. The cloudberry, which grows in the Scandinavian tundra, makes a unique jelly that tastes delicious on vanilla ice cream, or even whipped into a rich cream topping for heart-shaped waffles. Norwegians are proud of their breads and pastries, and you'll never be too far from a bakery that sells an almond-flavored *kringle* or a cone-shaped *krumkake* cookie filled with whipped cream.

7-Elevens. Most are open 24/7, selling sandwiches, pastries, sushi, and to-go boxes of warm pasta or Asian noodle dishes. You can fill your belly here for about 75 kr. Some outlets (such as the one at the corner of Karl Johans Gate and Rosenkrantz Gate) have seating on the street or upstairs. Beware: Because this is still a *convenience* store, not everything is well-priced. Convenience stores—while convenient—charge double what supermarkets do.

Eating on or near Karl Johans Gate

Consider the restaurants and eateries listed below. They're grouped by those that are from Karl Johans Gate and slightly to the north (between this main boulevard and the National Gallery) and to the south (between Karl Johans Gate and City Hall).

Strangely, **Karl Johans Gate** itself—the most Norwegian of boulevards—is lined with a strip of good-time American chain eateries where you can get ribs, burgers, and pizza, including T.G.I. Fridays and the Hard Rock Cafe. Egon Pizza offers a daily 100-kr all-you-can-eat pizza deal (available Tue-Sat 11:00-18:00, Sun-Mon all day). Each place comes with great sidewalk seating and essentially the same prices.

Grand Café is perhaps the most venerable place in town. At lunchtime, they set up a sandwich buffet (110-kr single sandwich, 310-kr all-you-like). Lunch plates are 150 kr. Reserve a window, and if you hit a time when there's no tour group, you're suddenly a posh Norwegian (daily 11:00-23:00, Karl Johans Gate 31, tel. 23 21 20 18).

Deli de Luca, just across from the Grand Café, offers good-value food and handy seats on Karl Johans Gate. For a fast meal with the best people-watching view in town, you may find yourself dropping by here repeatedly (daily 11:00-23:00, slightly shorter hours Sat-Sun, Karl Johans Gate 33, tel. 22 33 35 22).

Kaffistova is where my thrifty Norwegian grandparents always took me. After remaining unchanged for 30 years, it got a facelift in 2007. This alcohol-free cafeteria still serves simple, hearty, and typically Norwegian (read: bland) meals for a good price (Mon-Fri 10:00-21:00, Sat-Sun 11:00-19:00; Rosenkrantz Gate 8, tel. 23 21 42 10).

Brasserie 45, overlooking Stortingsgata and the National Theater from its second-floor perch, is a modern eatery offering decent Continental cuisine with energetic service. While larger entrées go for about 200 kr, their "wok chicken" goes for 140 kr. It's worth calling ahead to reserve a window seat with a view of Karl Johans Gate (Mon-Thu 15:00-23:00, Fri-Sat 14:00-24:00, Sun 14:00-22:00, always a veggie option, Stortingsgata 20, tel. 22 41 34 00).

City Hall workers' cafeteria, just steps off the harborfront,

Oslo Restaurants

1. Grand Café
2. Deli de Luca
3. Kaffistova Cafeteria
4. Brasserie 45 Restaurant
5. City Hall Workers' Cafeteria
6. Aker Brygge Eateries

OSLO

welcomes the public with the cheapest lunch I've found in Oslo. It has soup, an inexpensive salad bar measured by weight (35 kr for a meal-sized bowl), and a daily hot dish for around 50 kr (Mon-Fri 12:30-13:30 only). While City Hall workers get access to the place before 12:30 and the food can be pretty picked over, it's still a fine, handy value. From the grand harbor entrance, it's up one flight of stairs above the city info desk and WC. From the tour entrance on its inland courtyard, it's just downstairs.

Harborside Dining in Aker Brygge

The **Aker Brygge** harborfront mall is popular with businesspeople and tourists. While it isn't cheap, its inviting cafés and restaurants with outdoor, harborview tables make for a memorable waterfront

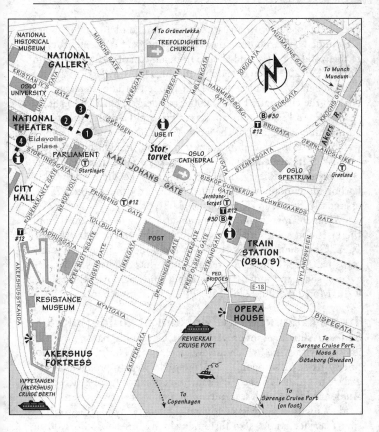

meal. Before deciding where to eat, you might want to walk the entire lane (including the back side), considering both the regular places (some with second-floor view seating) and the various floating options. Nearly all are open for lunch and dinner.

Druen, the first restaurant on the strip—while not a particularly good food value—is best for people-watching. I like the balcony seats upstairs, under outside heaters and with a harbor view. They serve international dishes—spicy Asian, French, and seafood—on small plates for 175 kr, hearty salads for 155 kr, and big meals for 220-260 kr (daily from 11:00, Stranden 1, Aker Brygge, tel. 23 11 54 60).

Lekter'n, right on the water, offers the best harbor view (rather than views of strolling people). This trendy bar has a floating dining area open only when the weather is warm. It serves hamburgers, pizza, and shrimp buckets. Budget eaters can split a 160-kr pizza (all outdoors, Stranden 3, tel. 22 83 76 46).

Rorbua, the "Fisherman's Cabin," is a lively yet cozy eatery tucked into this mostly modern stretch of restaurants. Inside, it's extremely woody with a rustic charm and candlelit picnic tables surrounded by harpoons and old B&W photos. Grab a stool at one of the wooden tables, and choose from a menu of meat-and-potato dishes (150-200 kr) and seafood offerings (200-250 kr). A hearty daily special with coffee for 145 kr is one of the best restaurant deals in the city (daily 12:30-23:00, Stranden 71, tel. 22 83 53 86).

Lofoten Fiskerestaurant serves fish amid a dressy yacht-club atmosphere at the end of the strip. While it's beyond the people-watching action, it's comfortable even in cold and blustery weather because of its heated atrium, which makes a meal here practically outdoor dining. Reservations are a must, especially if you want a harborside window table (lunch-150-225 kr, dinner from 275 kr, open daily, Stranden 75, tel. 22 83 08 08).

Budget Tips: If you're on a budget, get a take-out meal from the fast-food stands and grab a bench along the boardwalk. The **ICA "Gourmet"** grocery store—in the middle of the mall a few steps behind all the fancy restaurants—has salads, warm take-away dishes, and more (turn in about midway down the board-walk, Mon-Fri 9:00-22:00, Sat 9:00-20:00, closed Sun).

Trendy Dining at the Bottom of Grünerløkka

Südøst Asian Crossover Restaurant, once a big bank, now fills its vault with wine (which makes sense, given Norwegian alcohol prices). Today it's popular with young Norwegian professionals as a place to see and be seen. It's a fine mix of Norwegian-chic woody ambience inside with a trendy menu, and a big riverside terrace outdoors with a more casual menu. Diners enjoy its chic setting, smart service, and Asian fusion cuisine (Mon-Fri 16:00-1:00 in the morning, Sat 13:00-3:00 in the morning, Sun 13:00-22:00, also serves lunch in summer, at bottom of Grünerløkka, tram #17 to Trondheimsveien 5, tel. 23 35 30 70).

Eating Cheap and Spicy in Grønland

The street called Grønland leads through this colorful immigrant neighborhood (a short walk behind the train station or T-bane: Grønland). After the cleanliness and orderliness of the rest of the city, the rough edges and diversity of people here can feel like a breath of fresh air. Whether you eat here or not, the street is fun to explore. In Grønland, backpackers and immigrants munch street food. Cheap and tasty *börek* (feta, spinach, mushroom) is sold hot and greasy to go for 25 kr.

Punjab Tandoori is friendly and serves hearty meals (lamb and chicken curry, tandoori specials) for 70 kr. They're open late when other places aren't. I like eating outside here with a view of the street scene (daily 11:00-23:00, Grønland 24).

Alibaba Restaurant is clean, simple, and cheap for Turkish

What If I Miss My Boat?

Remember that you can get help from the cruise line's port agent (listed on the destination information sheet distributed on the ship) and the local TI (see page 639). If the port agent suggests a costly solution (such as a private car with a driver), you may want to consider public transit.

Trains connect Oslo easily to **Bergen** and **Stavanger. Flåm** is an easy bus or train ride off the main Oslo-Bergen line. Trains are also likely your best option for **Copenhagen** and **Stockholm;** for other points on the continent (such as **Amsterdam, Warnemünde/Berlin,** or **Zeebrugge/Brussels**), you'll probably connect through Copenhagen (for train connections, see www.bahn.com). To reach **Tallinn, Helsinki,** or **St. Petersburg** (only if you already have a visa), your best option is likely to train to Stockholm, then take the boat from there.

Another option for reaching **Copenhagen** is the overnight boat operated by DFDS Seaways (Danish tel. 00 45 33 42 30 10, www.dfdsseaways.us).

If you need to catch a **plane** to your next destination, you can ride an express train to Oslo's airport (lufthavn), also called Gardermoen (tel. 91 50 64 00, www.osl.no). Some discount airlines use smaller airports that are farther out: Rygge Airport (near the city of Moss, 40 miles south of Oslo, tel. 69 23 00 00, www.en.ryg.no) or Sandefjord Airport Torp (70 miles south of Oslo, tel. 33 42 70 00, www.torp.no).

Local **travel agents** in Oslo can help you. For more advice on what to do if you miss the boat, see page 144.

food. They have good indoor or outdoor seating (99-kr fixed-price meal Mon-Thu only, open daily 12:30-22:30, corner of Grønlandsleiret and Tøyengata at Tøyengata 2, tel. 22 17 22 22). The 99-kr special is much cheaper than the menu items, but isn't advertised very clearly; you may need to request it.

Asylet is more expensive and feels like it was here long before Norway ever saw a Pakistani. This big, traditional eatery—like a Norwegian beer garden—has a rustic, cozy interior and a gravelly backyard filled with picnic tables (150-200-kr plates and hearty dinner salads, daily 11:00-24:00, Grønland 28, tel. 22 17 09 39).

Dattera Til Hagen feels like a college party. It's a lively scene filling a courtyard with picnic tables and benches under strings of colored lights. If it's too cold, hang out inside. Locals like it for the tapas, burgers, and salads (150-kr plates, pricey beers, Grønland 10, tel. 22 17 18 61).

Olympen Brown Pub is a dressy dining hall that's a blast from the past. You'll eat in a spacious woody saloon with big dark furniture, faded paintings of circa-1920 Oslo lining the walls, and

OSLO

huge chandeliers. It's good for solo travelers, because sharing the long tables is standard practice. They serve hearty 200-kr plates and offer a huge selection of beers. The grill restaurant upstairs, called **Pigalle,** comes with music and can be more fun (daily 11:00-2:00 in the morning, Grønlandsleiret 15, tel. 22 17 28 08).

Café Con Bar is a trendy yuppie eatery on the downtown edge of Grønland. Locals consider it to have the best burgers in town (150 kr). While the tight interior seating is very noisy, the sidewalk tables are great for people-watching (open daily, kitchen closes at 23:00, bar closes late; where Grønland hits Brugata).

Roasted Rudolph Under a Thatched Roof High on the Mountain

Frognerseteren Hovedrestaurant, nestled high above Oslo (and 1,400 feet above sea level), is a classy, sod-roofed old restaurant. Its terrace, offering a commanding view of the city, is a popular stop for famous apple cake and coffee. The café is casual and less expensive, with indoor and outdoor seating (90-kr sandwiches and cold dishes, 125-kr entrées, Mon-Sat 11:00-22:00, Sun 11:00-21:00, reservations unnecessary). The elegant view restaurant is pricier (275-365-kr plates, Mon-Fri 12:00-22:00, Sat 13:00-22:00, Sun 13:00-21:00, reindeer specials, tel. 22 92 40 40).

You can combine a trip into the forested hills surrounding the city with lunch and get a chance to see the famous Holmenkollen Ski Jump up close (see page 676).

Norwegian Survival Phrases

Norwegian can be pronounced quite differently from region to region. These phrases and phonetics match the mainstream Oslo dialect, but you'll notice variations. Vowels can be tricky: *å* sounds like "oh," *æ* sounds like a bright "ah" (as in "apple"), and *u* sounds like the German *ü* (purse your lips and say u). Certain vowels at the ends of words (such as *d* and *t*) are sometimes barely pronounced (or not at all). In some dialects, the letters *sk* are pronounced "sh." In the phonetics, ī sounds like the long i in "light," and bolded syllables are stressed.

English	Norwegian	Pronunciation
Hello. (formal)	*God dag.*	goo dahg
Hi. / Bye. (informal)	*Hei. / Ha det.*	hī / hah deh
Do you speak English?	*Snakker du engelsk?*	**snahk**-kehr dew **eng**-ehlsk
Yes. / No.	*Ja. / Nei.*	yah / nī
Please.	*Vær så snill.*	vayr soh sneel
Thank you (very much).	*(Tusen) takk.*	(**tew**-sehn) tahk
You're welcome.	*Vær så god.*	vayr soh goo
Can I help you?	*Kan jeg hjelpe deg?*	kahn yī **yehl**-peh dī
Excuse me.	*Unnskyld.*	**ewn**-shuld
(Very) good.	*(Veldig) fint.*	(**vehl**-dee) feent
Goodbye.	*Farvel.*	fahr-**vehl**
one / two	*en / to*	ayn / toh
three / four	*tre / fire*	treh / **fee**-reh
five / six	*fem / seks*	fehm / sehks
seven / eight	*syv / åtte*	seev / **oh**-teh
nine / ten	*ni / ti*	nee / tee
hundred	*hundre*	**hewn**-dreh
thousand	*tusen*	**tew**-sehn
How much?	*Hvor mye?*	voor **mee**-yeh
local currency: (Norwegian) crown	*(Norske) kroner*	(**norsh**-keh) **kroh**-nehr
Where is...?	*Hvor er...?*	voor ehr
...the toilet	*...toalettet*	toh-ah-**leh**-teh
men	*menn* Or: *herrer*	mehn / **hehr**-rehr
women	*damer*	**dah**-mehr
water / coffee	*vann / kaffe*	vahn / **kah**-feh
beer / wine	*øl / vin*	uhl / veen
Cheers!	*Skål!*	skohl
The bill, please.	*Regningen, takk.*	**rī**-ning-ehn tahk

STAVANGER
Norway

Norway Practicalities

Norway (Norge) is stacked with super-latives—it's the most mountainous, most scenic, and most prosperous of all the Scandinavian countries. Perhaps above all, Norway is a land of intense natural beauty, its famously steep mountains and deep fjords carved out and shaped by an ancient ice age. Norway (148,900 square miles—just larger than Montana) is on the western side of the Scandinavian Peninsula, with most of the country sharing a border with Sweden to the east. Rich in resources like timber, oil, and fish, Norway has rejected joining the European Union, mainly to protect its fishing rights. Where the country extends north of the Arctic Circle, the sun never sets at the height of summer and never comes up in the deep of winter. The majority of Norway's 5 million people consider themselves Lutheran.

Money: 6 Norwegian kroner (kr, officially NOK) = about $1. An ATM is called a *minibank*. The local VAT (value-added sales tax) rate is 25 percent; the minimum purchase eligible for a VAT refund is 315 kr (for details on refunds, see page 139).

Language: The native language is Norwegian (the two official forms are Bokmål and Nynorsk). For useful phrases, see page 691.

Emergencies: Dial 112 for police, medical, or other emergencies. In case of theft or loss, see page 131.

Time Zone: Norway is on Central European Time (the same as most of the Continent, one hour ahead of Great Britain, and six/nine hours ahead of the East/West Coasts of the US).

Embassies in Oslo: The **US embassy** is at Henrik Ibsens Gate 48 (tel. 21 30 85 58, emergency tel. 21 30 85 40, http://norway.usembassy.gov). The **Canadian embassy** is at Wergelandsveien 7 (tel. 22 99 53 00, www.norway.gc.ca). Call ahead for passport services.

Phoning: Norway's country code is 47; to call from another country to Norway, dial the international access code (011 from the US/Canada, 00 from Europe, or + from a mobile phone), then 47, followed by the local number. For local calls within Norway, just dial the number as it appears in this book— whether you're calling from across the street or across the country. To place an international call from Norway, dial 00, the code of the country you're calling (1 for US and Canada), and the phone number. For more tips, see page 1110.

Tipping: As service is included at sit-down meals, you don't need to tip further, though for great service it's nice to round up your bill about 5-10 percent. Tip a taxi driver by rounding up the fare (pay 90 kr on an 85-kr fare). For more tips on tipping, see page 143.

Tourist Information: www.goscandinavia.com

STAVANGER

This burg of about 117,000 is a mildly charming (if unspectacular) waterfront city whose streets are lined with unpretentious shiplap cottages that echo its perennial ties to the sea. Stavanger feels more cosmopolitan than most small Norwegian cities, thanks in part to its oil industry—which brings multinational workers (and their money) into the city. Known as Norway's festival city, Stavanger hosts several lively events, including jazz in May (www.maijazz.no), Scandinavia's biggest food festival in July (www.gladmat.no), and chamber music in August (www.icmf.no). With all of this culture, it's no surprise that Stavanger was named a European Capital of Culture for 2008.

From a sightseeing perspective, Stavanger barely has enough to fill a day: The Norwegian Petroleum Museum is the only big-time sight in town, while the Norwegian Emigration Center thrills only those with family ties here. The city's fine cathedral is worth a peek. But for most visitors, the main reason to come to Stavanger is to use it as a launch pad for side-tripping to Lysefjord and/or the famous, iconic Pulpit Rock: an eerily flat-topped peak thrusting up from the fjord, offering perfect, point-blank views deep into the Lysefjord.

Planning Your Time

Stavanger is a small town with enjoyable ambience, but it lacks big sights; you'll probably look for ways to kill time rather than run out of it. The one big exception is a side-trip to the Lysefjord and/or Pulpit Rock, which can eat up the better part of your day in port (but may not be possible, depending on your cruise arrival and departure schedule).

Excursions from Stavanger

The one cruise-line excursion that's worth considering is to the **Lysefjord,** across the bay, and the iconic **Pulpit Rock** that overlooks it. You can do a similar trip on your own, but your options are limited, and it's tricky to coordinate schedules with your cruise's arrival and departure. If you've always wanted to see Pulpit Rock, and this is your best chance, an excursion may be the right choice.

Otherwise, various excursions cobble together sights in and around Stavanger, including the Petroleum Museum, the Sverd i Fjell (Swords in Mountain) monument honoring a historic A.D. 872 battle, an Iron Age farm, a cheese factory, the charming and well-preserved Utstein Abbey (often with a musical recital), a pile of prehistoric avalanche boulders called Gloppedalsura, and a drive to Byrkjelandsvatnet Lake. Any of these can be interesting, and—as there's little to see in Stavanger itself—they can be a nice way to get out into the countryside. The cruise around Stavanger Archipelago is pointless (little to see beyond what you'll see coming and going on your cruise ship).

If you stick around town, take your pick from these options—noting that some may open well after your ship docks.

• **Cathedral:** This is worth a quick look (easy to see in less than 30 minutes).

• **Norwegian Petroleum Museum:** The city's main museum deserves at least an hour, or double that if you want to watch all the movies (or are traveling with kids who'd enjoy the interactive features).

• **Other Museums:** Stavanger's many small museums (my favorite is the Norwegian Emigration Center) can round out your day, but none of them demands more than 30 to 60 minutes.

• **Strolling Town:** Spend whatever time you have left exploring, especially the atmospheric lanes of Gamle Stavanger and Kirkegata, the main drag through town.

With relatively little else to do in Stavanger, many visitors choose to use this day for a side-trip to the **Lysefjord** and/or **Pulpit Rock.** Handy fjord excursion boats leave from the harbor, near where the cruise ships put in. Ideally, do some homework and confirm schedules before you arrive, so you know which company (if any) has a trip that fits with your ship's arrival and departure.

Important Note: Before joining a Lysefjord or Pulpit Rock excursion run by anyone other than your cruise line, be absolutely clear on the return time—and before you book, make sure they know what time you need to be back.

Arrival at the Port of Stavanger

Arrival at a Glance: It's simple: Just walk along the harbor into the town center (5-15 minutes, depending on where you're docked).

Port Overview

Cruise ships put in on either side of Stavanger's central harbor (Vågen), an inlet between Gamle Stavanger (the old town) and the city-center peninsula. Ships dock either along the west side of the harbor, an embankment called **Strandkaien;** or along the east side, called **Skagenkaien.** When more ships are in town,

they dock farther out along these embankments; the walk to the end of the harbor and the town center can take anywhere from 5 minutes (from the nearest berths) to 15 minutes (from the farthest).

Tourist Information: There's no TI at the cruise port itself, but it's a short walk to the main branch, overlooking the plaza in front of the cathedral (see "Tourist Information" on page 700).

Getting into Town

Stavanger is extremely cruiser-friendly. From either embankment, you can just stroll along the harbor into town, following the handy directional signs you pass along the way. Specifics for each pier are below. The route's so walkable that taxis don't bother meeting cruise ships, and there's no point taking public transportation. You'll see **hop-on, hop-off buses** at the dock, but in this small and compact city, they're unlikely to be useful (150 kr/day, 10 stops, every 20 minutes).

From Strandkaien

Arriving at Strandkaien, you face rows of pointy-topped, white, wooden houses climbing the hill (Gamle Stavanger).

Exiting your ship, turn left and walk along the waterfront. On your way, you'll pass the Norwegian Emigration Center, then the Maritime Museum (with free Wi-Fi in the lobby). If you need cash, also keep an eye out for the Fokus Bank, with an ATM inside. Circling around the end of the harbor, head up through the small market plaza to reach the cathedral and, facing it, the TI.

Note that Gamle Stavanger is directly above the Strandkaien

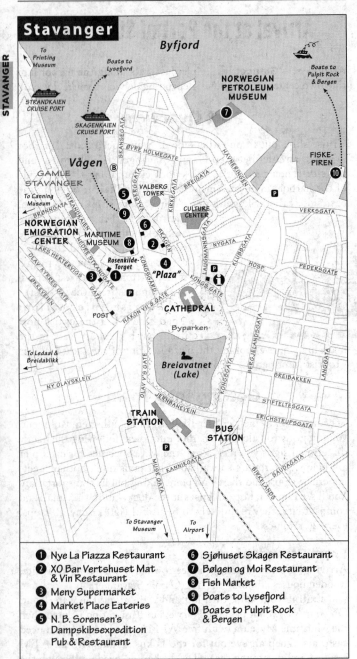

Stavanger

STAVANGER

Byfjord

To Printing Museum

Boats to Lysefjord

STRANDKAIEN CRUISE PORT

SKAGENKAIEN CRUISE PORT

Vågen

GAMLE STAVANGER

To Canning Museum

BRØNNGATA

NORWEGIAN EMIGRATION CENTER

MARITIME MUSEUM

Rosenkilde-Torget

"Plaza"

POST

NY OLAVSKLEIV

To Ledaal & Breidablikk

TRAIN STATION

BUS STATION

NORWEGIAN PETROLEUM MUSEUM

FISKE-PIREN

Boats to Pulpit Rock & Bergen

VALBERG TOWER

CULTURE CENTER

CATHEDRAL

Byparken

Breiavatnet (Lake)

To Stavanger Museum

To Airport

VERKSGATA

PEDERSGATE

To Canning Museum

ØVRE HOLMEGATE

SKANSEGATA

VALBERGATA

KIRKEGATA

BEIEGATA

HAVNERINGEN

SKAGEN

LAUGMANNSGATA

NYGATA

KONGS-GATE

KONGSGATA

KLUBBGATA

HOSP

BERGELANDSGATA

BREIBAKKEN

STIFTELTESGATA

ERICHSTRUPSGATA

SAUDAGATA

LANGGATA

BIRKELANDS

KANNIKGATA

MUSÉ GATA

OLAV V'S GATE

JERNBANEVEIEN

HAKON VII'S GATE

KONGSGATA

NEDRE STRANDGATE

LARS HERTERVIGS

OLAV KYRRES GATE

LØKKEVEIEN

STRANDKAIEN

1. Nye La Piazza Restaurant
2. XO Bar Vertshuset Mat & Vin Restaurant
3. Meny Supermarket
4. Market Place Eateries
5. N. B. Sorensen's Dampskibsexpedition Pub & Restaurant
6. Sjøhuset Skagen Restaurant
7. Bølgen og Moi Restaurant
8. Fish Market
9. Boats to Lysefjord
10. Boats to Pulpit Rock & Bergen

Services in Stavanger

Take the short walk into the heart of town, where you'll find the following:

ATMs: The closest locations to each dock are noted under "Getting into Town," earlier; the most central option is at the SpareBank overlooking the market square, facing the cathedral and TI.

Internet Access: The TI can tell you the password for their free Wi-Fi connection. There's also free Wi-Fi in the lobby of the Maritime Museum, along Strandkaien. For Internet terminals, try the library up the street from the TI.

Pharmacy: The handiest is Apotek 1, inside the Torgterrassen mall facing the market plaza just below the cathedral and TI (Mon-Fri 10:00-20:00, Sat 10:00-18:00, closed Sun).

embankment—just head up any narrow cobbled lane to find it. This makes for a handy place to kill any remaining time before boarding your ship.

From Skagenkaien

Exiting your ship, turn right and walk along the harborfront, passing the departure point for excursion boats to the Lysefjord. You'll quickly arrive at the end of the harbor; from here, you can angle up through the market square to reach the cathedral and TI. If you need cash, look for an ATM at the entrance to the 7-Eleven and another in the SpareBank at the top of the square.

Returning to Your Ship

Just walk—you can see your ship from almost anywhere in town. Remember, if you have time to kill on your way back, you could wander the pretty Gamle Stavanger zone just above Strandkaien, or use the free Wi-Fi inside the Maritime Museum (also along Strandkaien).

See page 706 for help if you miss your boat.

Orientation to Stavanger

The most scenic and interesting parts of Stavanger surround its harbor. Here you'll find the Norwegian Emigration Center, lots of shops and restaurants (particularly around the market plaza and along Kirkegata, which connects the cathedral to the Petroleum Museum), the indoor fish market, and a produce market

STAVANGER

(Mon-Fri 9:00-16:00, Sat 9:00-15:00, closed Sun). The artificial Lake Breiavatnet—bordered by Kongsgaten on the east and Olav V's Gate on the west—separates the train and bus stations from the harbor.

Tourist Information

The helpful staff at the TI can help you plan your time in Stavanger, and can also give you hiking tips and day-trip information. Pick up a free city guide and map (June-Aug daily 9:00-20:00; Sept-May Mon-Fri 9:00-16:00, Sat 9:00-14:00, closed Sun; Domkirkeplassen 3, tel. 51 85 92 00, www.regionstavanger.com).

Sights in Stavanger

▲**Stavanger Cathedral (Domkirke)**—While it's hardly the most impressive cathedral in Scandinavia, Stavanger's top church—which overlooks the town center on a small ridge—has a harmonious interior and a few intriguing details worth lingering over. Good English information throughout the church brings meaning to the place.

Cost and Hours: 30 kr, free weekdays after 16:00, open May-mid-Sept Mon-Fri 8:30-14:00 & 16:00-19:00, Sat 9:00-13:00, Sun 13:00-19:00, free and open shorter hours off-season, tel. 51 84 04 00, www.kirken.stavanger.no.

Visiting the Church: St. Swithun's Cathedral (its official name) was originally built in 1125 in a Norman style, with basket-handle Romanesque arches. After a fire badly damaged the church in the 13th century, a new chancel was added in the pointy-arched Gothic style. You can't miss where the architecture changes about three-quarters of the way up the aisle. On the left, behind the baptismal font, notice the ivy-lined railing on the stone staircase; this pattern is part of the city's coat of arms. And nearby, appreciate the colorful, richly detailed "gristle Baroque"-style pulpit (from 1658). Notice that the whole thing is resting on Samson's stoic shoulders—even as he faces down a lion.

Stroll the church, perusing its several fine "epitaphs" (tomb markers), which are paintings in ornately decorated frames. Go on a scavenger hunt for two unique features; both are on the second columns from the back of the church. On the right, at the top and facing away from the nave, notice the stone carvings of Norse mythological figures: Odin on the left, and a wolf-like beast on the right. Although the medieval Norwegians were Christians, they weren't ready to entirely abandon all of their pagan traditions. On the opposite column, circle around the base and look at ankle level, facing away from the altar. Here you see a grotesque sculpture that looks like a fish head with human hands. Notice that its head has been worn down. One interpretation is that early worshippers would ritualistically put their foot on top of it, as if to push the evil back to the underworld. Mysteriously, both of these features are one-offs—you won't find anything like them on any other column in the church.

▲▲**Norwegian Petroleum Museum (Norsk Oljemuseum)**— This entertaining, informative museum—dedicated to the discov-

ery of oil in Norway's North Sea in 1969 and the industry built up around it—offers an unapologetic look at Norway's biggest moneymaker. With half of Western Europe's oil reserves, Norway is the Arabia of the North. Since the discovery of oil here in 1969, the formerly poor agricultural nation has been transformed into a world-class player. It's ranked third among the world's top oil exporters, producing 1.6 million barrels a day.

Cost and Hours: 100 kr; June-Aug daily 10:00-19:00; Sept-May Mon-Sat 10:00-16:00, Sun 10:00-18:00; tel. 51 93 93 00, www.norskolje.museum.no. The small museum shop sells various petroleum-based products. The museum's Bølgen og Moi restaurant, which has an inviting terrace over the water, serves lunch and dinner (see listing under "Eating in Stavanger," later).

Visiting the Museum: The exhibit describes how oil is formed, how it's found and produced, and what it's used for. You'll see models of oil rigs, actual drill bits, see-through cylinders that you can rotate to investigate different types of crude, and lots of explanations (in English) about various aspects of oil. Interactive exhibits cover everything from the "History of the Earth" (4.5 billion years displayed on a large overhead globe, showing how our planet has changed—stay for the blast that killed the dinosaurs), to day-to-day life on an offshore platform, to petroleum products in our lives (though the peanut-butter-and-petroleum-jelly sandwich is a bit much). Kids enjoy climbing on the model drilling platform, trying out the emergency escape chute at the platform outside, and playing with many other hands-on exhibits.

Several included movies delve into specific aspects of oil: The kid-oriented "Petropolis" 3-D film is primitive but entertaining and informative, tracing the story of oil from creation to extraction. Other movies (in the cylindrical structures outside) highlight intrepid North Sea divers and the construction of an oil platform. Each film is 12 minutes long and runs in English at least twice hourly.

Even the museum's architecture was designed to echo the foundations of the oil industry—bedrock (the stone building), slate and chalk deposits in the sea (slate floor of the main hall), and the rigs (cylindrical platforms). While the museum has its fair share of propaganda, it also has several good exhibits on the environmental toll of drilling and consuming oil.

Norwegian Emigration Center (Det Norske Utvandrer-senteret Ble)—This fine facility, in an old warehouse near the wharf where the first boats sailed with emigrants to "Amerika" in 1825, is worth ▲▲▲ for anyone seeking his or her Norwegian roots.

Cost and Hours: Library—free, museum—20 kr, Mon-Fri 9:00-15:00, closed Sat-Sun, Strandkaien 31, enter through the door just to the left of the tacky souvenir shop, tel. 51 53 88 60, www.emigrationcenter .com.

Visiting the Center: On the first floor up, the modest but nicely presented **People on the Move exhibit** traces the Norwegian emigrant experience. It tells the story of the first emigrants who left for America—why they left, their journey, and what life was like in the New World. You'll learn how the Norwegian population boom in the early to mid-19th century (from 882,000 people in 1810, to 1.7 million in 1865) led to a critical shortage of basic resources. While only 78,000 Norwegians emigrated before 1865, the number leaped to 677,000 in the steamship era (1865-1915). Once in North America, Norwegians (unique among immigrant groups) tended to settle in rural farmlands rather than cities.

On the second floor, you'll find a **study center and library.** It's free to use the computers, microfilm viewers, and historic record books to look up your relatives. The staff can help answer questions and steer you in the right direction at no charge, or you can pay them to do a step-by-step consultation (see below).

Researching Your Roots: The Emigration Center is a great resource for those hoping to trace their ancestors' trail from the Old Country. But to get the most out of the experience, do some homework ahead of time. Many of the resources used by the center are digitized and available free online. Most helpful is the official national archive at www.arkivverket.no/digitalarkivet (free, English menus); the center also uses www.ancestry.com (fee) and www.norwayheritage.com (most useful for earlier emigrations). See what you can find on these sites, then use the center to fill in the rest. Their library has many resources not available online; it's lined with shelves of *bygdebøker*—books from farm districts all over Norway, documenting the history of landowners and local families. When looking up relatives, it helps to know at least two or three of the following: family surname, farm name, birth year, and emigration year. (If your family records show two different surnames for the same person, it's likely the one ending in -son or -sen is the surname, and the other one is the farm name.)

Or you can pay them to do all the work for you. They charge 500 kr per hour of research time, and estimate that most cases take about two hours of work. If you'd like to do this, it's smart to contact them before your trip to let them know you're coming. You can fill out the form on their website and pay by credit card. You don't need to actually be in Stavanger to use this service, but searching for your roots in the place where your ancestors likely took their last steps on Norwegian soil has a certain romantic appeal.

Gamle Stavanger—Stavanger's "old town" centers on Øvre Strandgate, on the west side of the harbor. Wander the narrow, winding, cobbled back lanes, with tidy wooden houses, oasis gardens, and flower-bedecked entranceways. Peek into a workshop or gallery to find ceramics, glass, jewelry, and more. Many shops are open roughly daily 10:00-17:00, coinciding with the arrival of cruise ships (which loom ominously right next to this otherwise tranquil zone).

Museum Stavanger (M.U.S.T.)—This "museum" is actually 10 different museums scattered around town. The various branches include the **Stavanger Museum,** featuring the history of the city and a zoological exhibit (Muségate 16); the **Maritime Museum** (Sjøfartsmuseum), right next to the cruise dock on Strandkaien (Nedre Strandgate 17-19); the **Norwegian Canning Museum** (Norsk Hermetikkmuseum; the *brisling*—herring—is smoked mid-June-mid-Aug Tue and Thu, Øvre Strandgate 88A); the **Printing Museum** (24 Sandvigå); **Ledaal,** a royal residence and manor house (Eiganesveien 45); and **Breidablikk,** a wooden villa from the late 1800s (Eiganesveien 40A).

Cost: You can buy one 100-kr ticket to cover all of them, or you can pay 60 kr for any individual museum (if doing at least two, the combo-ticket is obviously the better value). Note that a single 60-kr ticket gets you into the Maritime Museum, Canning

Museum, and Printing Museum, which are a three-for-one sight. You can get details and buy tickets at any of the museums; handiest is the Maritime Museum, right along the harbor.

Hours: Museum hours vary but generally open mid-June–mid-Aug daily 10:00 or 11:00-16:00; off-season Tue-Sun 11:00-16:00, closed Mon, except Ledaal, Breidablikk, and Printing Museum—these are open Sun only in winter; www.museum stavanger.no.

Day Trips to Lysefjord and Pulpit Rock

The nearby Lysefjord is an easy day trip. Those with more time (and strong legs) can hike to the top of the 1,800-foot-high Pulpit Rock (Preikestolen). The dramatic 270-square-foot plateau atop the rock gives you a fantastic view of the fjord and surrounding mountains. The TI has brochures for several boat tour companies and sells tickets.

Warning: Remember, timing a Pulpit Rock trip that coincides with your cruise-ship departure is risky business. Be absolutely clear on your trip's return time and your ship's all-aboard time—and don't cut it close, just in case.

Boat Tour of Lysefjord—**Rødne Clipper Fjord Sightseeing** offers three-hour round-trip excursions from Stavanger to Lysefjord (including a view of Pulpit Rock—but no stops). Conveniently, their boats depart from the main Vågen harbor in the heart of town (east side of the harbor, in front of Skansegata, along Skagenkaien; 400 kr; July-Aug daily at 10:00 and 14:00, Thu-Sat also at 12:00; June daily at 10:00 and 14:00; May and Sept daily at 12:00; Oct-April Wed-Sun only at 12:00; tel. 51 89 52 70, www.rodne.no). A different company, **Norled,** also runs similar trips, as well as slower journeys up the Lysefjord on a "tourist car ferry" (www.norled.no).

Ferry and Bus to Pulpit Rock—Hiking up to the top of Pulpit Rock is a popular outing that will take the better part of a day; plan on at least four hours of hiking (two hours up, two hours down), plus time to linger at the top for photos, plus round-trip travel from Stavanger (about an hour each way by a ferry-and-bus combination)—eight hours minimum should do it. The trailhead is easily reached in summer by public transit or tour package. Then comes the hard part: the hike to the top. The total distance is 4.5 miles, and the elevation gain is roughly 1,000 feet. Pack a lunch and plenty of water, and wear good shoes.

Two different companies sell ferry-and-bus packages to the trailhead from Stavanger. Ferries leave from the Fiskepiren boat terminal to Tau; buses meet the incoming ferries and head to Pulpit Rock cabin or to Preikestolen Fjellstue, the local youth hostel. Be sure to time your hike so that you can catch the last bus leaving Pulpit Rock cabin for the ferry (confirm time when booking your ticket). These trips generally go daily from mid-May through mid-September; weekends only in April, early May, and late September; and not at all from October to March (when the ferry stops running). As the details tend to change from year to year, confirm all schedule details with the TI or the individual companies: **Tide Reiser** (240 kr, best options for an all-day round-trip are departures at 8:00 or 9:30, last return bus from trailhead to ferry leaves at 18:15, mobile 97 04 74 19, www.tidereiser.com) and **Boreal** (140 kr for the bus plus 88 kr for the ferry—you'll buy the ferry ticket separately, best options depart at 8:30 or 9:00, last return bus from trailhead to ferry leaves at 19:55, tel. 51 74 02 40, www.pulpitrock.no).

Rødne Clipper Fjord Sightseeing (listed earlier) may run a handy trip in July and August that begins with a scenic Lysefjord cruise, then drops you off at Oanes to catch the bus to the Pulpit Rock hut trailhead; afterwards, you can catch the bus to Tau for the ferry return to Stavanger. It's similar to the options described above, but adds a scenic fjord cruise at the start. To confirm this is still going and get details, contact Rødne (650 kr plus 44 kr for return ferry to Stavanger, tel. 51 89 52 70, www.rodne.no).

Eating in Stavanger

For information on Norwegian cuisine, see page 684.

Casual Dining

Nye La Piazza, just off the harbor, has an assortment of pasta and other Italian dishes, including pizza, for 145-200 kr (100-kr lunch special, 275-320-kr meat options, Mon 13:00-24:00, Tue-Sat 12:00-24:00, Sun 12:00-22:00, Rosenkildettorget 1, tel. 51 52 02 52).

XO Bar Vertshuset Mat & Vin, in an elegant setting, serves up big portions of traditional Norwegian food and pricier contemporary fare (280-350 kr, light meals-180-190 kr, open daily 11:00-22:30, a block behind main drag along harbor at Skagen 10 ved Prostbakken, tel. 51 89 51 12).

Meny is a large supermarket with a good selection and a fine deli for super-picnic shopping (Mon-Fri 9:00-20:00, Sat until 18:00, closed Sun, in Straen Senteret shopping mall, Lars Hertervigs Gate 6, tel. 51 50 50 10).

Market Plaza Eateries: The busy square between the cathedral and the harbor is packed with reliable Norwegian chain restaurants. If you're a fan of **Deli de Luca, Peppe's Pizza,** or **Dickens Pub,** you'll find all of them within a few steps of here.

What If I Miss My Boat?

Remember that you can get help from the cruise line's port agent (listed on the destination information sheet distributed on the ship) and the local TI (see page 700). If the port agent suggests a costly solution (such as a private car with a driver), you may want to consider public transit.

You can catch the boat to **Bergen** (Flaggruten catamarans, tel. 55 23 87 00, www.tide.no) or the train to **Oslo**. For **Flåm,** it's probably best to take the boat to Bergen, then a boat or train to the Sognefjord. For any points **outside Norway,** you'll most likely connect through Oslo. To research train schedules, see www.bahn.com.

If you need to catch a **plane** to your next destination, Stavanger's Sola Airport is a nine-mile bus ride outside the city (tel. 67 03 10 00, www.avinor.no).

Local **travel agents** in Stavanger can help you. For more advice on what to do if you miss the boat, see page 144.

Dining Along the Harbor with a View

The harborside street of Skansegata is lined with lively restaurants and pubs, and most serve food. Here are a couple of options:

N. B. Sorensen's Dampskibsexpedition has a lively pub on the first floor (245-365 kr for pasta, fish, meat, and vegetarian dishes; Mon-Sat 11:00-24:00, Sun 13:00-24:00). The restaurant is named after an 1800s company that shipped from this building, among other things, Norwegians heading to the US. Passengers and cargo waited on the first floor, and the manager's office was upstairs. The place is filled with emigrant-era memorabilia.

Sjøhuset Skagen, with a woodsy interior, invites diners to its historic building for lunch or dinner. The building, from the late 1700s, housed a trading company. Today, you can choose from local seafood specialties with an ethnic flair, as well as plenty of meat options (160-180-kr lunches, 230-390-kr dinners, Mon-Sat 11:30-23:00, Sun 13:00-21:30, Skagenkaien 16, tel. 51 89 51 80).

Bølgen og Moi, the restaurant at the Petroleum Museum, has fantastic views over the harbor (lunch: 170-kr lunch special, 150-200-kr main dishes, served daily 11:00-17:00, Kjeringholmen 748, tel. 51 93 93 53).

BERGEN
Norway

Norway Practicalities

Norway (Norge) is stacked with superlatives—it's the most mountainous, most scenic, and most prosperous of all the Scandinavian countries. Perhaps above all, Norway is a land of intense natural beauty, its famously steep mountains and deep fjords carved out and shaped by an ancient ice age. Norway (148,900 square miles—just larger than Montana) is on the western side of the Scandinavian Peninsula, with most of the country sharing a border with Sweden to the east. Rich in resources like timber, oil, and fish, Norway has rejected joining the European Union, mainly to protect its fishing rights. Where the country extends north of the Arctic Circle, the sun never sets at the height of summer and never comes up in the deep of winter. The majority of Norway's 5 million people consider themselves Lutheran.

Money: 6 Norwegian kroner (kr, officially NOK) = about $1. An ATM is called a *minibank*. The local VAT (value-added sales tax) rate is 25 percent; the minimum purchase eligible for a VAT refund is 315 kr (for details on refunds, see page 139).

Language: The native language is Norwegian (the two official forms are Bokmål and Nynorsk). For useful phrases, see page 691.

Emergencies: Dial 112 for police, medical, or other emergencies. In case of theft or loss, see page 131.

Time Zone: Norway is on Central European Time (the same as most of the Continent, one hour ahead of Great Britain, and six/nine hours ahead of the East/West Coasts of the US).

Embassies in Oslo: The **US embassy** is at Henrik Ibsens Gate 48 (tel. 21 30 85 58, emergency tel. 21 30 85 40, http://norway.usembassy.gov). The **Canadian embassy** is at Wergelandsveien 7 (tel. 22 99 53 00, www.norway.gc.ca). Call ahead for passport services.

Phoning: Norway's country code is 47; to call from another country to Norway, dial the international access code (011 from the US/Canada, 00 from Europe, or + from a mobile phone), then 47, followed by the local number. For local calls within Norway, just dial the number as it appears in this book—whether you're calling from across the street or across the country. To place an international call from Norway, dial 00, the code of the country you're calling (1 for US and Canada), and the phone number. For more tips, see page 1110.

Tipping: As service is included at sit-down meals, you don't need to tip further, though for great service it's nice to round up your bill about 5-10 percent. Tip a taxi driver by rounding up the fare (pay 90 kr on an 85-kr fare). For more tips on tipping, see page 143.

Tourist Information: www.goscandinavia.com

BERGEN

Bergen is permanently salted with robust cobbles and a rich sea-trading heritage. Norway's capital in the 12th and 13th centuries, Bergen's wealth and importance came thanks to its membership in the heavyweight medieval trading club of merchant cities called the Hanseatic League. Bergen still wears her rich maritime heritage proudly—nowhere more scenically than the colorful wooden warehouses that make up the picture-perfect Bryggen district along the harbor.

Protected from the open sea by a lone sheltering island, Bergen is a place of refuge from heavy winds for the giant working boats that serve the North Sea oil rigs. (Much of Norway's current affluence is funded by the oil it drills just offshore.) Bergen is also one of the most popular cruise-ship ports in northern Europe, hosting hundreds of ships a year and up to seven ships a day in peak season. Each morning is rush hour, as cruisers hike past the fortress and into town.

Bergen gets an average of 80 inches of rain annually (compared to 30 inches in Oslo). A good year has 60 days of sunshine. The natives aren't apologetic about their famously lousy weather. In fact, they seem to wear it as a badge of pride. "Well, that's Bergen," they'll say matter-of-factly as they wring out their raincoats. When I complained about an all-day downpour, one resident cheerfully informed me, "There's no such thing as bad weather—just inappropriate clothing"...a local mantra that rhymes in Norwegian.

With 250,000 people, Bergen has big-city parking problems and high prices, but visitors sticking to the old center find it charming. Enjoy Bergen's salty market, then stroll the easy-on-foot old quarter, with cute lanes of delicate old wooden houses.

Excursions from Bergen

There's little reason to take an excursion here, as Bergen's top sights are easy to reach and appreciate on your own from the cruise ports. Most **Bergen** excursions include a walking tour around town (including Bryggen), often with tours of Håkon's Hall and Rosenkrantz Tower, and sometimes the funicular trip up Mount Fløyen. Outside town, excursions typically bundle Edvard Grieg's Home at **Troldhaugen** (at Nordås Lake) with **Fantoft Stave Church.** These sights are time-consuming to link by public transportation, so if you're dying to see them, an excursion may be worthwhile. Another excursion covers the ornately decorated, wooden **Villa Lysøen,** the former home of Ole Bull (built on its own little island). While it's interesting, it's also fairly distant (about a 30-minute bus ride each way); I'd rather save time for sights in Bergen itself.

From downtown Bergen, a funicular zips you up a little mountain for a bird's-eye view of this sailors' town. A short foray into the countryside takes you to a variety of nearby experiences: a dramatic cable-car ride to a mountaintop perch (Ulriken643); a scenic stave church (Fantoft); and the home of Norway's most beloved composer, Edvard Grieg, at Troldhaugen.

Planning Your Time

Bergen is compact, with several good sightseeing options that can be visited quickly.

• **Bryggen Walking Tour:** In summer (June-Aug), plan your day around this excellent 1.5-hour guided tour, which leads you through the historic, wooden Bryggen Hanseatic quarter and includes short visits to the top two museums, noted below (daily at 11:00 and 12:00, smart to reserve ahead in July). If the tour's not running when you're in town, you can still visit the sights on your own.

• **Bryggens Museum:** This fine archaeological museum focuses on early Bryggen history. Allow one hour.

• **Hanseatic Museum:** Explore the fascinating, still-furnished interior of one of Bryggen's historic wooden houses. Allow one hour.

• **Fløibanen Funicular:** This seven-minute trip takes you to bird's-eye views over town from atop Mount Fløyen. Allow 30-45 minutes round-trip, more if you want to hike down.

• **Other Sights in Town:** Many of Bergen's lesser attractions—including Håkon's Hall/Rosenkrantz Tower at the fortress, Fortress Museum, Theta Museum, cathedral, and Leprosy Museum—can be seen in 30 minutes each (though the hall and

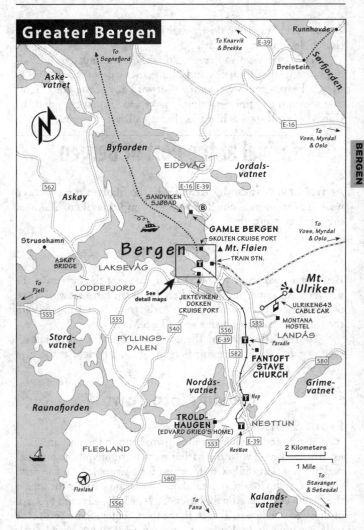

Greater Bergen

tower at the fortress are best if you have an hour to spare for the guided tour). The branches of the Bergen Art Museum (conveniently located next to where some cruise-line shuttle buses drop off) could keep an art lover busy for hours, but a brief walk through the main collection can take less than an hour. The aquarium and Gamle Bergen (Old Bergen) take longer to reach; I'd skip these unless you have a special interest.

• **Out-of-Town Sights:** If you're feeling adventurous and want to get out of town, you can head out to the **Ulriken643 Cable Car,** Edvard Grieg's Home at **Troldhaugen,** or **Fantoft Stave Church**—but each requires a bus or tram ride (figure about an hour each way from downtown Bergen to Troldhaugen or the church, less for the cable car).

For one busy day in Bergen, I'd take the walking tour (including visits to the Bryggens and Hanseatic Museums), ride up to Mount Fløyen, and wrap up my visit with any of the other sights that sound intriguing—or simply poke around Bryggen and the Fish Market. It sounds like a lot, but it's all easily doable.

Arrival at the Port of Bergen

Arrival at a Glance: It's easy: From the **Skolten** port, you can walk into town in about 10 minutes; from **Jekteviken/Dokken,** ride the free shuttle bus.

Port Overview

Bergen has two cruise ports: **Skolten,** just past the fortress at the north end of town; and **Jekteviken/Dokken,** farther away, south of downtown. If your ship gets in early, you'll be setting up with the fishermen and merchants at the Fish Market.

Tourist Information: There are no TIs at the ports, but it's easy to get downtown to visit Bergen's main TI (right at the Fish Market; see page 715).

Getting into Town

From Skolten

It's a simple and scenic **walk** into town. Exiting the port area, follow the busy road with the harbor on your right and the fortress/park on your left (follow traffic signs for *Sentrum*). Near the port, you'll see a stop for the hop-on, hop-off tour bus. Along the road is the Skuteviksторget stop for buses #3, #4, #5, #6, #39, and #83. All of these go one stop to Torget, in the town center—but because the walk is simple and takes you past some great sights, there's little point in taking a bus. If you're headed out of town, note that bus #83 goes from Skutevikstorget to stops near Fantoft Stave Church (Paradis stop) and Edvard Grieg's Home at Troldhaugen (Hop stop; 2/hour, about 30 minutes).

Passing the bus stop, continue along the harborfront road, crossing over to the fortress side at the crosswalk. Very shortly you'll pass the side entrance into the fortress complex, which is also the starting point of my self-guided walk.

If you want to skip the walk for now and head straight downtown, just keep walking, and you'll be there (at the Fish Market, with the TI nearby) in about five more minutes. If you need cash,

---

Services in Bergen

Services are virtually nonexistent at the ports. But since both ports are easily connected to downtown, you can find what you need there.

ATMs: Various ATMs are scattered around the city-center zone near the Fish Market. On your way into town from the Skolten port, the first ATM you'll pass is at the **Windfjord** souvenir shop, two blocks past the fortress on the harborside road.

Internet Access: The **TI** (near the Fish Market) has a strong, fast, free Wi-Fi connection; the password is posted on the wall. For suggested Internet cafés, see page 715.

Pharmacy: Two handy options are right downtown, near all the sightseeing: **Boots Apotek** is just a half-block in front of the funicular station to Mount Fløyen (Mon-Fri 9:00-17:00, Thu until 18:00, Sat 9:00-16:00, closed Sun, Vetrlidsallmenningen 11). **Apotek 1** is inside the Galleriet Shopping Mall, facing the Seafarers' Monument on the main square, Torgallmenningen (Mon-Fri 9:00-21:00, Sat 9:00-18:00, closed Sun).

---

look for the ATM two short blocks after the fortress—on the left, at the Windfjord souvenir shop.

From Jekteviken/Dokken

This arrival point is in a drab, sprawling industrial port just south of downtown. Although it's only a 15- to 20-minute walk to the center, the port authority (which doesn't want tourists wandering around all the big containers) provides a **free shuttle bus** to the center. This convenient service takes you to a stop along the south side of Lille Lungegårdsvann, the cute manmade lake in the city center. Stepping off the bus, you'll be on the street called Rasmus Meyers Allé, which is right in front of the four branches of the Bergen Art Museum (described on page 731). From here, it's a pleasant and easy 10-minute walk to the Fish Market, TI, harbor, and most sightseeing: First, walk with the lake on your right. At the end of the lake, you'll reach the park called Byparken (the terminus for the tram to Fantoft Stave Church and Edvard Grieg's Home at Troldhaugen is nearby). Continue through the park, straight past the pretty pavilion, and up the long square called Ole Bulls Plass. This is the finishing point of my self-guided walk (consider doing it in reverse from here; or, if you take the walk later, it'll lead you back here and to the bus). Head halfway up Ole Bulls Plass (passing the fountain of the namesake violinist) to the big, bluish stone slab. Turn right and head up another long, broad square, Torgallmenningen; at the end of this, you'll pass the blocky Seafarers' Monument. The Fish Market, TI, and Bryggen are just beyond it.

By Taxi

There's little need for a taxi from **Skolten,** thanks to its easy proximity to town. But if you must take one, plan on 50-60 kr to points downtown. Likewise, taxis aren't necessary for the **Jekteviken/ Dokken** port, since the free shuttle takes you straight downtown. But if you need to take a taxi for some reason, plan on around 100 kr between the port and downtown.

If taxis aren't waiting at the port, call 07000 or 08000 to summon one.

By Tour

Remember: If you're in town in June, July, or August, I highly recommend taking the **Bryggen Walking Tour** to get oriented (departs at 11:00 and 12:00; details on page 718).

Hop-on, hop-off bus tours meet arriving ships at Skolten; if arriving at Jekteviken/Dokken, you can ride the shuttle bus into town and catch the bus tour at Byparken (155 kr for all day, 2/hour; for more details, see page 719). But in this compact and walkable city, these bus tours don't make much sense (unless the weather is miserable and you just want a once-over-lightly look at the town).

For more information on this and other local tour options in Bergen, see "Tours in Bergen" on page 718.

Returning to Your Ship

To **Skolten,** it's an easy walk around the fortress (just walk with the harbor on your left). If you have time to kill before "all aboard," you can browse through Bryggen (which is a quick 10-minute walk from your ship) or tour the fortress sights (even closer).

To return to **Jekteviken/Dokken,** catch the shuttle bus right where it dropped you, in front of the Bergen Art Museum by the little lake along Rasmus Meyers Allé; my self-guided walk leads you there. If you've got time to kill, take a quick spin through the museum.

See page 740 for help if you miss your boat.

Orientation to Bergen

Bergen clusters around its harbor—nearly everything listed in this chapter is within a few minutes' walk. The busy Torget (the square with the Fish Market) is at the head of the harbor. As you face the sea from here, Bergen's TI is at the left end of the Fish Market. The

town's historic Hanseatic Quarter, Bryggen (BREW-gun), lines the harbor on the right. Express boats to the Sognefjord (Balestrand and Flåm) and Stavanger dock at the harbor on the left.

Charming cobbled streets surround the harbor and climb the encircling hills. Bergen's popular Fløibanen funicular climbs high above the city to the top of Mount Fløyen for the best view of the town. Surveying the surrounding islands and inlets, it's clear why this city is known as the "Gateway to the Fjords."

Tourist Information

The centrally located TI is upstairs in the long, skinny, modern, yellow-and-red-striped Torghallen market building, which runs alongside the harbor next to the Fish Market (June-Aug daily 8:30-22:00; May and Sept daily 9:00-20:00; Oct-April Mon-Sat 9:00-16:00, closed Sun; tel. 55 55 20 00, www.visitbergen.com). The TI covers Bergen and western Norway, provides information and tickets for tours, has a fjord information desk, and maintains a very handy events board listing today's slate of tours, concerts, and other events. Pick up this year's edition of the free *Bergen Guide*, which has a fine map and lists all sights, hours, and special events. This booklet can answer most of your questions. If you need assistance and there's a line, take a number. They also have free Wi-Fi: Look for the password posted on the wall.

Bergen Card: You have to work hard to make this greedy little card pay off (200 kr/24 hours, 260 kr/48 hours, sold at TI and Montana Family & Youth Hostel). It gives you free use of the city buses, half off the Mount Fløyen funicular, free admission to most museums (but not the Hanseatic Museum; aquarium included only in winter), and discounts on some events and sights—such as a discount on Edvard Grieg's Home.

Helpful Hints

Museum Tours: Many of Bergen's sights are hard to appreciate without a guide. Fortunately, several include a wonderful and intimate guided tour with admission. Make the most of the following sights by taking advantage of their included tours: Håkon's Hall and Rosenkrantz Tower, Bryggens Museum, Hanseatic Museum, Leprosy Museum, Gamle Bergen, and Edvard Grieg's Home.

Internet Access: The **TI** offers free, fast Wi-Fi (look for the password posted on the wall), but no terminals. **Kanel** in the

BERGEN

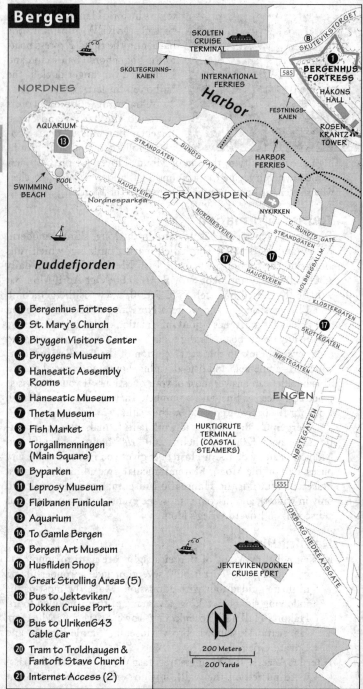

Bergen

SKOLTEN CRUISE TERMINAL

SKOLTEGRUNNS-KAIEN

INTERNATIONAL FERRIES

Harbor

SKUTEVIKSTORGET

B

1 BERGENHUS FORTRESS

HÅKONS HALL

FESTNINGS-KAIEN

ROSEN-KRANTZ TOWER

NORDNES

AQUARIUM

13

STRANDGATEN

C. SUNDTS GATE

HARBOR FERRIES

SWIMMING BEACH

POOL

HAUGEVEIEN

Nordnesparken

STRANDSIDEN

NYKIRKEN

NORDNESVEIEN

C. SUNDTS GATE

STRANDGATEN

Puddefjorden

17

17

HAUGEVEIEN

HOLBERGSALLM.

KLOSTERGATEN

17

SKOTTEGATEN

NØSTEGATEN

ENGEN

HURTIGRUTE TERMINAL (COASTAL STEAMERS)

NØSTEGATEN

555

TORBORG NEDREAASGATE

JEKTEVIKEN/DOKKEN CRUISE PORT

1. Bergenhus Fortress
2. St. Mary's Church
3. Bryggen Visitors Center
4. Bryggens Museum
5. Hanseatic Assembly Rooms
6. Hanseatic Museum
7. Theta Museum
8. Fish Market
9. Torgallmenningen (Main Square)
10. Byparken
11. Leprosy Museum
12. Fløibanen Funicular
13. Aquarium
14. To Gamle Bergen
15. Bergen Art Museum
16. Husfliden Shop
17. Great Strolling Areas (5)
18. Bus to Jekteviken/ Dokken Cruise Port
19. Bus to Ulriken643 Cable Car
20. Tram to Troldhaugen & Fantoft Stave Church
21. Internet Access (2)

N

200 Meters
200 Yards

BERGEN

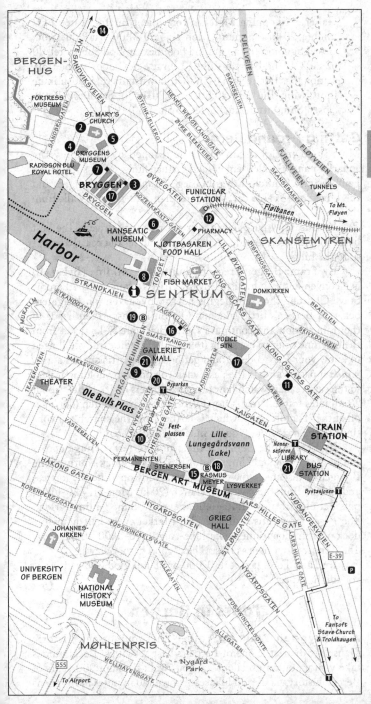

Galleriet Shopping Mall is a convenient Internet café (2 kr/minute, 20-kr minimum, Mon-Fri 7:30-21:00, Sat 9:00-18:00, closed Sun, located on ground floor next to Body Shop, tel. 40 62 22 27). The **Bergen Public Library,** next door to the train station, has free terminals in their downstairs café (30-minute limit, Mon-Thu 8:30-20:00, Fri 8:30-16:30, Sat 10:00-16:00, closed Sun, Strømgaten 6, tel. 55 56 85 60).

Getting Around Bergen

Most in-town sights can easily be reached by foot; only the aquarium and Gamle Bergen (and farther-flung sights such as the Fantoft Stave Church, Edvard Grieg's Home at Troldhaugen, and the Ulriken643 cable car) are more than a 10-minute walk from the TI.

By Bus: City buses cost 27 kr per ride (pay driver). The best buses for a Bergen joyride are #20 (north along the coast) and #11 (into the hills).

By Tram: Bergen's recently built light-rail line (Bybanen) is a convenient way to visit Edvard Grieg's Home or the Fantoft Stave Church. The tram begins next to Byparken (on Kaigaten, between Bergen's little lake and Ole Bulls Plass), then heads to the train station and continues south. Buy your 27-kr ticket from the machine prior to boarding (to use a US credit card, you'll need to know your PIN code). You'll get both a paper ticket and a gray *minikort* pass. Validate the pass when you board by holding it next to the card reader (watch how other passengers do it). Ride it about 20 minutes to the Paradis stop for Fantoft Stave Church (don't get off at the "Fantoft" stop, which is farther from the church); or continue to the next stop, Hop, to hike to Troldhaugen.

By Ferry: The *Beffen,* a little orange ferry, chugs across the harbor every half-hour, from the dock a block south of the Bryggens Museum to the dock that's directly opposite the fortress and a block from the Nykirken church (20 kr, Mon-Fri 7:30-16:00, plus Sat only in July 11:00-16:00, never on Sun, 3-minute ride). The *Vågen* ferry runs from the Fish Market every half-hour to a dock near the aquarium (45 kr, June-Aug 10:00-18:00, 10 minutes). These short "poor man's cruises" have good harbor views.

By Taxi: For a taxi, call 07000 or 08000 (not as expensive as you might expect).

Tours in Bergen

▲▲▲**Bryggen Walking Tour**—This tour of the historic Hanseatic district is one of Bergen's best activities. Local guides take visitors on an excellent 1.5-hour walk through 900 years of Bergen history via the old Hanseatic town (20 minutes in Bryggens

Museum, 20-minute visit to the medieval Hanseatic Assembly Rooms, 20-
minute walk through Bryggen, and
20 minutes in Hanseatic Museum).
Tours leave from the Bryggens
Museum (next to the Radisson Blu
Royal Hotel). When you consider
that the price includes entry tickets
to all three sights, the tour more than
pays for itself (120 kr, June-Aug daily
at 11:00 and 12:00, none Sept-May,
tel. 55 58 80 10, bryggens.museum
@bymuseet.no). While the museum

visits are a bit rushed, your tour ticket allows you to re-enter the
museums for the rest of the day. The 11:00 tour can sell out, especially in July; to be safe, you can call, email, or drop by ahead to
reserve.

Local Guides—**Sue Lindelid** and **Jim Paton** are British expats
who have spent more than 25 years showing visitors around Bergen
(600 kr for 1.5-hour group tour, 700 kr for 2 hours, mobile 90 78 59
52, suelin@hotmail.no).

▲Bus Tours—The TI sells tickets for various bus tours, includ-
ing a three-hour tour that goes to Edvard Grieg's Home at
Troldhaugen—a handy way to reach that distant sight (350 kr,
May-Sept daily at 10:00, departs from curb across from Fish
Market). Buses are comfy, with big views and a fine recorded com-
mentary. There are also several full-day tour options from Bergen,
including bus/boat tours to nearby Hardanger and Sogne fjords.
The TI is packed with brochures describing all the excursions.

Hop-On, Hop-Off Bus—City Sightseeing's hop-on, hop-off bus
links most of Bergen's major sights and also stops at the Skolten
cruise port. Buy tickets on board or at the TI (155 kr/24 hours,
late May-Aug 9:00-16:30, 2/hour, also stops right in front of Fish
Market, mobile 97 78 18 88, www.citysightseeing-bergen.net).

▲Harbor Tours—The *White Lady* leaves from the Fish Market
daily in summer at 14:30 for a 50-minute cruise. The ride is both
scenic and informative, with a relaxing sun deck and good—if
scant—recorded narration (130 kr, mid-May-Aug). A four-hour
fjord trip is also available (480 kr, May-mid-Sept daily at 10:00,
July-late Aug also daily at 15:30, tel. 55 25 90 00, www.white
lady.no).

Tourist Train—The tacky little "Bergen Express" train departs
from in front of the Hanseatic Museum for a 55-minute loop
around town (150 kr, 2/hour in peak season, otherwise hourly;
runs daily May 10:00-16:00, June-Aug 10:00-19:00, Sept 10:00-
15:00; headphone English commentary).

Self-Guided Walk in Bergen

Welcome to Bergen

For a quick orientation stroll through Bergen, follow this walk from the city's fortress, through its old wooden Hanseatic Quarter and smelly Fish Market, to the modern center of town. This walk is also a handy sightseeing spine, passing most of Bergen's best museums; ideally, you'll get sidetracked and take advantage of their excellent tours (included with admission). I've pointed out the museums you'll pass en route—all of them are described in greater detail later, under "Sights in Bergen."

• *Begin where Bergen did, at the historic fortress. From the harborfront road, enter the sprawling complex, then walk up into the courtyard at the heart of the place (through the gate marked 1728).*

Bergenhus Fortress: In the 13th century, Bergen became the Kingdom of Norway's first capital. (Prior to the 13th century, kings would circulate, staying on royal farms.) This fortress—built in the 1240s—was a garrison, with a tower for the king's residence (**Rosenkrantz Tower**) and a large hall for his banquets (**Håkon's Hall,** the stepped-gabled building facing the port). Today the fortress grounds are used for big events (Bruce Springsteen filled it in 2009). Visitors can go inside the tower and the hall; while they feel empty and a bit dull on your own, the guided tour (included in admission) brings them to life.

• *Head back out to the main road and continue with the harbor on your right. After a block, history buffs could follow* Bergenhus *signs (up the street to the left, Sandbrogaten) to reach the* **Fortress Museum**—*though its collection of Norwegian military history (focusing on World War II) isn't worth the detour for most.*

Proceed one more block along the harbor until you reach the open, parklike space on your left. Standing at the top of this area is...

St. Mary's Church (Mariakirken): Dating from the 12th century, this is Bergen's oldest building. It's closed through 2015 while a 100-million-kroner renovation is underway. This stately church of the Hanseatic merchants has a dour stone interior, enlivened by a colorful, highly decorated pulpit.

• *In front of the church, the boxy, modern building houses the excellent* **Bryggens Museum,** *which provides helpful historical context for the Hanseatic Quarter we're about to visit. The museum's outstanding* **Bryggen Walking Tour** *is your best bet for seeing this area (see "Tours in Bergen," earlier).*

*Behind the church is the back wall of the Hanseatic Quarter and the entrance to the communal **Hanseatic Assembly Rooms** (Schøtstuene)— not worth visiting on your own, but well explained by the Bryggen Walking Tour. The red house straight ahead marks the corner of the...*

Bergen Hanseatic Quarter (Bryggen): Bergen's fragile wooden old town is its iconic front door. The long "tenements" (rows of warehouses) hide atmospheric lanes that creak and groan with history.

BERGEN

• *To get your bearings, first read the "Bryggen's History" sidebar; if it's nice out, stand in the people zone in front of all the colorful buildings, or cross the street to the wharf and look back for a fine overview of this area. But let me guess—it's raining, right? In that case, huddle under an awning.*

Remember that while we think of Bergen as "Norwegian," Bryggen was German—the territory of *Deutsch*-speaking merchants and traders. From the front of Bryggen, look down at the Rosenkrantz Tower. The little red holes at its top mark where cannons were once pointed at the German quarter by Norwegian royalty. The threat was never taken seriously, however, because everyone knew that without German grain, the Norwegians would starve.

Now enter the woody guts of Bryggen. You can't get inside the lanes in the first stretch of houses, so proceed to the second stretch and explore some alleys. Strolling through Bryggen, you feel swallowed up by history. Long rows of planky buildings (medieval-style double tenements) lean haphazardly across narrow alleys. The last Hanseatic merchant moved out centuries ago, but this is still a place of (touristy) commerce. You'll find artists' galleries, massage parlors, T-shirt boutiques, leather workshops, atmospheric but overpriced restaurants, fishing tackle shops, and sweaters, sweaters, sweaters...plus trolls.

The area is flanked by two worthwhile museums within a five-minute walk of each other (the Bryggens Museum and Hanseatic Museum). Right in the middle of Bryggen is the tiny, often-closed **Theta Museum,** which gives a glimpse into the WWII resistance movement.

Up Bellgården (at the far-right end as you face wooden Bryggen—it's the lane under the golden deer head) is the little **"visitors center,"** which is more of a gift shop in disguise. Here you'll find a video and a few photos illustrating how they are trying to rebuild the tenement houses using the original methods and materials (good 80-kr Bryggen guidebook, daily June-Aug

Bryggen's History

Pretty as Bryggen is today, it has a rough-and-tumble history. A horrific plague decimated the population and economy of Norway in 1350, killing about half of its people. A decade later, German merchants arrived and established a Hanseatic trading post, bringing order to that rustic society. For the next four centuries, the port of Bergen was German territory.

Bergen's old German trading center was called "the German wharf" until World War II (and is now just called "the wharf," or "Bryggen"). From 1370 to 1754, German merchants controlled Bergen's trade. In 1550, it was a Germanic city of 1,000 workaholic merchants—surrounded and supported by some 5,000 Norwegians.

The German merchants were very strict and lived in a harsh, all-male world (except for Norwegian prostitutes). This wasn't a military occupation, but a mutually beneficial economic partnership. The Norwegian cod fishermen of the far north shipped their dried cod to Bergen, where the Hanseatic merchants marketed it to Europe. Norwegian cod provided much of Europe with food (a source of easy-to-preserve protein) and cod oil (which lit the lamps until about 1850).

While the city dates from 1070, little survives from before the last big fire in 1702. In its earlier heyday, Bergen was one of the largest wooden cities in Europe. Congested wooden buildings, combined with lots of small fires (to provide heat and light in this cold and dark corner of Europe), spelled disaster for Bergen. Over the centuries, the city suffered countless fires, including 10 devastating blazes. Each time the warehouses burned, the merchants would toss the refuse into the bay and rebuild. Gradually, the land crept out, and so did the buildings. (Looking at the Hanseatic Quarter from the harborfront, you can see how the buildings have settled. The foundations, composed of debris from the many fires, settle as they rot.)

9:00-17:00, May and Sept 10:00-16:00, closed Oct-April).

The visitors center faces a wooden tenement that is currently undergoing restoration. If this preservation work is still going on during your visit, it's a fascinating chance to see modern people wrestling with old technology in the name of history.

Just past the visitors center, you'll pop out into a small square with a wishing well and a giant, grotesque wooden sculpture of a **dried cod**—the unlikely resource that put this town on the map. As you may have noticed, around Bergen, cod is as revered as, well, God.

• *When you're done exploring the bowels of Bryggen, head back out to the main road and continue strolling with the harbor on your right.*

Half of Bryggen (the brick-and-stone stretch between the old

After 1702, the city rebuilt using more stone and brick, and suffered fewer fires. But this one small wooden quarter was built after the fire, in the early 1700s. To prevent future blazes, the Germans forbade all fires and candles for light or warmth except in isolated and carefully guarded communal houses behind each tenement. It was in these communal houses that apprentices studied, people dried out their soggy clothes, hot food was cooked, and the men drank and partied. One of these medieval Hanseatic Assembly Rooms is preserved and open to the public (the Schøtstuene—separate entrance behind St. Mary's Church, included in Bryggen Walking Tour, difficult to appreciate without a guide).

Flash forward to the 20th century. One of the biggest explosions of World War II occurred in Bergen's harbor on April 20, 1944. An ammunition ship loaded with 120 tons of dynamite blew up just in front of the fortress. The blast killed 160 people, leveled entire neighborhoods on either side of the harbor (notice the ugly 1950s construction opposite the fortress) and did serious damage to Håkon's Hall and Rosenkrantz Tower. How big was the blast? There's a hut called "the anchor cabin" a couple of miles away in the mountains. That's where the ship's anchor landed. The blast is considered to be accidental, despite the fact that April 20 happened to be Hitler's birthday and the ship blew up about 100 yards away from the Nazi commander's headquarters (in the fortress).

After World War II, Bryggen was again slated for destruction. Most of the locals wanted it gone—it reminded them of the Germans who had occupied Norway for several miserable years. Then excavators discovered rune stones indicating that the area predated the Germans. This boosted Bryggen's approval rating, and the quarter was saved. Today this picturesque and historic zone is the undisputed tourist highlight of Bergen.

wooden facades and the head of the bay) was torn down around 1900. Today these stately buildings—far less atmospheric than Bryggen's original wooden core—are filled with tacky trinket shops and touristy splurge restaurants.

Head to the lone wooden red house at the end of the row, which today houses the **Hanseatic Museum.** The man who owned this building recognized the value of the city's heritage and kept his house as it was. Considered a nutcase back then, today he's celebrated as a visionary, as his decision has left visitors with a fine example of an old merchant house that they can tour. This highly recommended museum is your best chance to get a peek inside one of those old wooden tenements.

• *Directly across the street from the Hanseatic Museum—past the Narvesen kiosk—is the...*

Fish Market (Fisketorget): A fish market has thrived here since the 1500s, when fishermen rowed in with their catch and haggled with hungry residents.

While it's now become a food circus of eateries selling fishy treats to tourists—no local would come here to actually buy fish—this famous market still offers lots of smelly photo fun and free morsels to taste. Many stands sell pre-made smoked-salmon *(laks)* sandwiches, fish soup, and other snacks ideal for a light lunch (confirm prices before ordering—it can get pricey). To try Norwegian jerky, pick up a bag of dried cod snacks *(torsk)*. The red meat is minke whale, caught off the coast of northern Norway. You'll also find local fruit in season and hand-knit sweaters (June-Aug daily 7:00-19:00, less lively on Sun; Sept-May Mon-Sat 7:00-16:00, closed Sun). Watch your wallet: If you're going to get pickpocketed in Bergen, it'll likely be here.

• *When you're done exploring, stand with your back to the market and harbor to get oriented.*

*The streets heading straight away from the market are worth exploring; within a few blocks, you'll find the **Leprosy Museum** and Bergen's **cathedral**.*

*Two short blocks up the street to the left (Vetrlidsallmenningen, past the red-brick market hall with frilly white trim) is the bottom station of the **Fløibanen funicular**, which zips you up to fine views from Mount Fløyen.*

But to continue our walk into the modern part of town, turn right and walk one block up to the wide square. Pause at the blocky monument.

Seafarers' Monument: Nicknamed "the cube of goat cheese"

for its shape, this monument dates from about 1950. It celebrates Bergen's contact with the sea and remembers those who worked on it and died in it. Study the faces: All classes are represented. The statues relate to the scenes depicted in the reliefs above. Each side represents a century (start with the Vikings and work clockwise): 10th century—Vikings, with a totem pole in the panel above recalling the pre-Columbian Norwegian discovery of America; 18th century—equipping Europe's ships; 19th century—whaling; 20th century—shipping and war. For the 21st century, see the real people—a cross-section of today's Norway—sitting at the statue's base. Major department stores (Galleriet, Xhibition, and Telegrafen) are all nearby.

• *The monument marks the start of Bergen's main square...*

Torgallmenningen: Allmenningen means "for all the people." Torg means "square." And, while this is the city's main gathering place, it was actually created as a fire break. The residents of this wood-built city knew fires were inevitable. The street plan was designed with breaks, or open spaces like this square, to help contain the destruction. In 1916, it succeeded in stopping a fire, which is why it has a more modern feel today.

• *Walk along the square to the angled slab. This "blue stone," a popular meeting point at the far end of the square, marks the center of a park-like swath known as...*

Ole Bulls Plass: This drag leads from the National Theater (above on right) to a little lake (below on left).

Detour a few steps up for a better look at the **National Theater,** built in Art Nouveau style in 1909. Founded by violinist Ole Bull in 1850, this was the first theater to host plays in the Norwegian language. After 450 years of Danish and Swedish rule, 19th-century Norway enjoyed a cultural awakening, and Bergen became an artistic power. Ole Bull (a pop idol and heartthrob in his day—women fainted when they heard him play his violin) collaborated with the playwright Henrik Ibsen. Ibsen commissioned Edvard Grieg to write the music for his *Peer Gynt.* These three lions of Norwegian culture all lived and worked right here in Bergen.

The park that spills downhill from the theater has a pleasantly bustling urban ambience. It leads past a popular fountain of Ole Bull (under the trees) to a cast-iron pavilion given to the city by Germans in 1889, and on to the little manmade lake (Lille Lungegårdsvann), which is circled by an enjoyable path. This green zone is considered a park and is cared for by the local parks department.

• *If you're up for a lakeside stroll, now's your chance. Also notice that alongside the lake (to the right as you face it from here) is a row of buildings housing the enjoyable **Bergen Art Museum.** And to the left of the lake are some fine residential streets (including the picturesque, cobbled Marken); within a few minutes' walk are the **Leprosy Museum** and the cathedral.*

The Hanseatic League, Blessed by Cod

Middlemen in trade, the clever German merchants of the Hanseatic League ruled the waves of northern Europe for 500 years (c. 1250-1750). These sea-traders first banded together in a *Hanse*, or merchant guild, to defend themselves against pirates. As they spread out from Germany, they established trading posts in foreign lands, cut deals with local leaders for trading rights, built boats and wharves, and organized armies to protect ships and ports.

By the 15th century, these merchants had organized more than a hundred cities into the Hanseatic League, a free-trade zone that stretched from London to Russia. The League ran a profitable triangle of trade: Fish from Scandinavia was exchanged for grain from the eastern Baltic and luxury goods from England and Flanders. Everyone benefited, and the German merchants—the middlemen—reaped the profits.

At its peak in the 15th century, the Hanseatic League was the dominant force—economic, military, and political—in northern Europe. This was an age when much of Europe was fragmented into petty kingdoms and dukedoms. Revenue-hungry kings and robber-baron lords levied chaotic and extortionist tolls and duties. Pirates plagued shipments. It was the Hanseatic League, rather than national governments, that brought the stability that allowed trade to flourish.

Bergen's place in this Baltic economy was all about cod—a form of protein that could be dried, preserved, and shipped anywhere. Though cursed by a lack of natural resources, the city

Sights in Bergen

Central Bergen

Several museums listed here—including the Bryggens Museum, Håkon's Hall, Rosenkrantz Tower, Leprosy Museum, and Gamle Bergen—are part of the Bergen City Museum (Bymuseet) organization. If you buy a ticket to any of them, you can pay half-price at any of the others simply by showing your ticket.

▲**Bergenhus Fortress: Håkon's Hall and Rosenkrantz Tower**—The tower and hall, sitting boldly out of place on the harbor just beyond Bryggen, are reminders of Bergen's importance as the first permanent capital of Norway. Both sights feel vacant and don't really speak for themselves; the included guided tours, which provide a serious introduction to Bergen's history, are essential for grasping their significance.

Cost and Hours: Hall and tower—60 kr each, includes guided tour; mid-May-Aug—both open daily 10:00-16:00; Sept-mid-May—hall open daily 12:00-15:00, Thu until 18:00, tower

was blessed with a good harbor conveniently located between the rich fishing spots of northern Norway and the markets of Europe. Bergen's port shipped dried cod and fish oil southward and imported grain, cloth, beer, wine, and ceramics.

Bryggen was one of four principal Hanseatic trading posts (*Kontors*), along with London, Bruges, and Novgorod. It was the last *Kontor* opened (c. 1360), the least profitable, and the final one to close. Bryggen had warehouses, offices, and living quarters. Ships docked here were unloaded by counterpoise cranes. At its peak, as many as a thousand merchants, journeymen, and apprentices lived and worked here.

Bryggen was a self-contained German enclave within the city. The merchants came from Germany, worked a few years here, and retired back in the home country. They spoke German, wore German clothes, and attended their own churches. By law, they were forbidden to intermarry or fraternize with the Bergeners, except on business.

The Hanseatic League peaked around 1500, then slowly declined. Rising nation-states were jealous of the Germans' power and wealth. The Reformation tore apart old alliances. Dutch and English traders broke the Hanseatic monopoly. Cities withdrew from the League and *Kontors* closed. In 1754, Bergen's *Kontor* was taken over by the Norwegians. When it closed its doors on December 31, 1899, a sea-trading era was over, but the city of Bergen had become rich...by the grace of cod.

open Sun only 12:00-15:00; tel. 55 31 60 67.

Visiting the Hall and Tower: While each sight is covered by a separate ticket and tour, it's best to consider them as one and start at Håkon's Hall (mid-May-Aug tours leave daily at the top of the hour; Sept-mid-May full tour runs on Sat, Sun Håkon's Hall tour only, no tours Mon-Fri). Stick with your guide, as the Rosenkrantz Tower is part two of the tour.

Håkon's Hall, dating from the 13th century, is the largest secular medieval building in Norway. It's essentially a giant, grand reception hall (used today for banquets) under a ceiling that feels

like an upturned Viking boat. While recently rebuilt, the ceiling's design is modeled after grand wooden roofs of that era. Beneath the hall is a whitewashed cellar. Banquets were a men-only affair. The raised seats gave royal, church, and military dignitaries the appropriate elevation.

Rosenkrantz Tower, the keep of a 13th-century castle, has a jumbled design, thanks to a Renaissance addition. The tour brings it to life. There's a good history exhibit on the top floors and a fine view from the rooftop.

Fortress Museum (Bergenhus Festningmuseum)—This humble museum, set back a couple of blocks from the fortress, may interest historians with its thoughtful exhibits about military history, especially Bergen's WWII experience. You'll learn about the resistance movement in Bergen (including its underground newspapers), the role of women in the Norwegian military, and Norwegian troops who have served with UN forces in overseas conflicts. Some exhibits are in English, while others are in Norwegian only.

Cost and Hours: Free, Tue-Sun 11:00-17:00, closed Mon, just behind Thon Hotel Bergen Brygge at Koengen, tel. 55 54 63 87.

▲▲**Bryggens Museum**—This modern museum explains the 1950s archaeological dig to uncover the earliest bits of Bergen (1050-1500). Brief English explanations are posted. From September through May, when there is no tour, consider buying the good museum guidebook (25 kr).

Cost and Hours: 60 kr; in summer, entry included with Bryggen Walking Tour described earlier; mid-May-Aug daily 10:00-16:00; Sept-mid-May Mon-Fri 11:00-15:00, Sat 12:00-15:00, Sun 12:00-16:00; inexpensive cafeteria with soup-and-bread specials; in big, modern building just beyond the end of Bryggen and the Radisson Blu Royal Hotel, tel. 55 58 80 10, www.bymuseet.no.

Visiting the Museum: The manageable, well-presented permanent exhibit occupies the ground floor. First up are the foundations from original wooden tenements dating back to the 12th century (displayed right where they were excavated) and a giant chunk of the hull of a 100-foot-long, 13th-century ship that was found here. Next, an exhibit (roughly shaped like the long, wooden double-tenements outside) shows off artifacts and explains lifestyles from medieval Bryggen. Behind that is a display of items you might have bought at the medieval market. You'll finish with exhibits about the church in Bergen, the town's role as a royal capital, and its status as a cultural capital. Upstairs are two floors of temporary exhibits.

▲▲**Hanseatic Museum (Hanseatiske Museum)**—This little museum was founded in the late 1900s to preserve a tenement interior. Today it offers the best possible look inside the wooden houses that are Bergen's trademark. Its creaky old rooms—with

hundred-year-old cod hanging from the ceiling—offer a time-tunnel experience back to Bryggen's glory days. It's located in an atmospheric old merchant house furnished with dried fish, antique ropes, an old oxtail (used for wringing spilled cod-liver oil back into the bucket), sagging steps, and cupboard beds from the early 1700s—one with a medieval pinup girl. You'll explore two upstairs levels, fully furnished and with funhouse floors. The place still feels eerily lived-in; neatly sorted desks with tidy ledgers seem to be waiting for the next workday to begin.

Cost and Hours: 60 kr; in summer, entry included with Bryggen Walking Tour; daily mid-May-mid-Sept 9:00-17:00; mid-Sept-mid-May Tue-Sat 11:00-14:00, Sun 11:00-16:00, closed Mon; Finnegården 7a, tel. 55 54 46 96, www.museumvest.no.

Tours: There are English explanations, but it's much better if you take the good, included 45-minute guided tour (3/day in English, mid-May-mid-Sept only, times displayed just inside door). Even if you tour the museum with the Bryggen Walking Tour, you're welcome to revisit (using the same ticket) and take this longer tour.

Theta Museum—This small museum highlights Norway's resistance movement (specifically, a 10-person local group called Theta) during the Nazi occupation in World War II. It's housed in Theta's former headquarters—a small room in a wooden Bryggen building.

Cost and Hours: 30 kr, June-Aug Tue and Sat-Sun 14:00-16:00, closed Mon, Wed-Fri, and off-season, Enhjørningsgården, tel. 55 31 53 93.

▲▲Fløibanen Funicular—Bergen's popular funicular climbs 1,000 feet in seven minutes to the top of Mount Fløyen for the best view of the town, surrounding islands, and fjords all the way to the west coast. The top is a popular picnic or pizza-to-go spot (a Peppe's Pizza is tucked behind the Hanseatic Museum, a block away from the base of the lift). The recommended Fløien Folkerestaurant, at the top of the funicular, offers affordable self-service food all day (both restaurant and cafeteria open daily in summer;

off-season only the cafeteria is open and only on weekends). The top is also the starting point for many peaceful hikes (ask for the *Fløyen Hiking Map* at the Fløibanen ticket window at the base). It's a pleasant but steep walk back down into Bergen. To save your knees, get off at the Promsgate stop halfway down and then wander through the delightful cobbled and shiplap lanes (note that only the :00 and :30 departures stop at Promsgate). This funicular is regularly used by locals commuting into and out of downtown.

Cost and Hours: 80 kr round-trip, Mon-Fri 7:30-23:00, Sat-Sun 8:00-23:00, departures generally 4/hour—on the quarter-hour most of the day, runs continuously if busy, tel. 55 33 68 00, www.floibanen.no.

Cathedral (Domkirke)—Bergen's main church, dedicated to St. Olav (the patron saint of Norway), dates from 1301. As it's just a

couple of blocks off the harbor, if you're nearby (for example, on way to the Leprosy Museum), drop in to enjoy its stoic, plain interior with stuccoed stone walls and giant wooden pulpit. Like so many old Norwegian structures, its roof makes you feel like you're huddled under an overturned Viking ship. The church is oddly lopsided, with just one side aisle. Before leaving, look up to see the gorgeous wood-carved organ over the main entrance. In the entryway, you'll see portraits of each bishop dating all the way back to the Reformation.

Cost and Hours: Free but donations appreciated; mid-June-mid-Aug Mon-Fri 10:00-16:00, Sun 9:30-13:00, closed Sat; off-season Tue-Fri 11:00-12:30, closed Sun-Mon except for worship; tel. 55 59 32 70, www.bergendomkirke.no.

Leprosy Museum (Lepramuseet)—Leprosy is also known as "Hansen's Disease" because in the 1870s a Bergen man named Armauer Hansen did groundbreaking work in understanding the ailment. This unique museum is in St. Jørgens Hospital, a leprosarium that dates back to about 1700. Up until the 19th century,

as much as 3 percent of Norway's population had leprosy. This hospital—once called "a graveyard for the living" (its last patient died in 1946)—has a meager exhibit in a thought-provoking shell attached to a 300-year-old church. It's really only worth your time and money if you stick around for one of the free tours, which generally leave at the top of the hour or by request.

Cost and Hours: 50 kr, mid-May-Aug daily 11:00-15:00, closed Sept-mid-May, between train station and Bryggen at Kong Oscars Gate 59, tel. 55 96 11 55, www.bymuseet.no.

▲**Bergen Art Museum (Bergen Kunstmuseum)**—If you need to get out of the rain (and you enjoyed the National Gallery in Oslo), check out this collection of collections in four neighboring buildings facing the lake along Rasmus Meyers Allé. The Lysverket building has an eclectic cross section of both international and Norwegian artists. The Rasmus Meyer branch specializes in Norwegian artists (with an especially good Munch exhibit). The Stenersen building has installations of contemporary art (and a recommended café), while the Permanenten building has decorative arts. Small description sheets in English are in each room.

Cost and Hours: 100 kr, daily 11:00-17:00, closed Mon mid-Sept-mid-May, Rasmus Meyers Allé 3, tel. 55 56 80 00, www.kunstmuseene.no.

Visiting the Museum: Many visitors focus on the **Lysverket** ("Lighthouse"), featuring an easily digestible collection. Here are some of its highlights: The ground floor includes an extensive collection of works by Nikolai Astrup (1880-1928), who depicts Norway's fjords with bright colors and Expressionistic flair. Up on the first floor is a great collection of J.C. Dahl and his students, who captured the majesty of Norway's natural wonders (look for Adelsteen Normann's impressive, photorealistic view of Romsdalfjord). "Norwegian Art 1840-1900" includes works by Christian Krohg, as well as some portraits by Harriet Backer. Also on this floor are icons and various European Old Masters.

Up on the second floor, things get modern. The Tower Hall (Tårnsalen) features Norwegian modernism and an extensive exhibit of Bergen's avant-garde art (1966-1985), kicked off by "Group 66." The International Modernism section has four stars: Pablo Picasso (sketches, etchings, collages, and a few Cubist paintings), Paul Klee (the Swiss childlike painter), and the dynamic Norwegian duo of Edvard Munch and Ludvig Karisten. Rounding it out are a smattering of Surrealist, Abstract Expressionist, and Op Art pieces.

▲**Aquarium (Akvariet)**—Small but fun, this aquarium claims to be the second-most-visited sight in Bergen. It's wonderfully laid out and explained in English. Check out the informative exhibit downstairs on Norway's fish-farming industry.

Cost and Hours: 200 kr, kids-150 kr, cheaper off-season, daily May-Aug 9:00-19:00, Sept-April 10:00-18:00, feeding times at the top of most hours in summer, cheery cafeteria with light sandwiches, Nordnesbakken 4, tel. 55 55 71 71, www.akvariet.no.

Getting There: It's at the tip of the peninsula on the south end of the harbor—about a 20-minute walk or short ride on bus #11 from the city center. Or hop on the handy little *Vågen* "Akvariet" ferry that sails from the Fish Market to near the aquarium (45 kr one-way, 70 kr round-trip, 2/hour, daily May-Aug 10:00-18:00).

Nearby: The lovely park behind the aquarium has views of the sea and a popular swimming beach (described later, under "Activities in Bergen"). The totem pole erected here was a gift from Bergen's sister city in the US—Seattle.

▲**Gamle Bergen (Old Bergen)**—This Disney-cute gathering of 50-some 18th- and 19th-century shops was founded in 1934 to save old buildings from destruction as Bergen modernized. Each of the houses was moved from elsewhere in Bergen and reconstructed here. Together, they create a virtual town that offers a cobbled look at the old life. It's free to wander through the town and park to enjoy the facades of the historic buildings, but to get into the 20 or so museum buildings, you'll have to join a tour (departing on the hour 10:00-16:00).

Cost and Hours: Free entry, 70-kr tour (in English) required for access to buildings, mid-May-early Sept Mon-Sat 11:00-15:00, Sun 10:00-16:00, closed off-season, tel. 55 39 43 04, www.gamle bergen.museum.no.

Getting There: Take any bus heading west from Bryggen (such as #20, direction: Lonborg) to Gamle Bergen (first stop after the tunnel). You'll get off at a freeway pullout and walk 200 yards, following signs to the museum. Any bus heading back into town takes you to the center (buses come by every few minutes). With the easy bus connection, there's no reason to taxi.

▲**Strolling**—Bergen is a great town for wandering. The harborfront is a fine place to kick back and watch the pigeons mate. Other good areas to explore are over the hill past Klostergaten, Knosesmauet, and Ytre Markevei; near Marken; and the area behind Bryggen.

Swimming—Bergen has two seaside public swimming areas: one at the aquarium and the other in Gamle Bergen. Each is a great local scene on a hot sunny day. **Nordnes Sjøbad,** near the aquarium, offers swimmers an outdoor heated pool and a protected area of the sea (40 kr, kids-20 kr, mid-May-Aug Mon-Fri 7:00-19:00, Sat 7:00-14:00, Sun 10:00-14:00, Sat-Sun until 19:00 in good weather, closed off-season, Nordnesparken 30, tel. 55 90 21 70). **Sandviken Sjobad,** at Gamle Bergen, is free. It comes with changing rooms, a roped-off bit of the bay (no pool), a high dive, and lots of sunbathing space.

Near Bergen

▲**Ulriken643 Cable Car**—It's amazingly quick and easy to zip to the 643-meter-high (that's 2,110 feet) summit of Ulriken, the

tallest mountain near Bergen. Stepping out of the cable car, you enter a different world, with views stretching to the ocean. A chart clearly shows the many well-marked and easy hikes that fan out over the vast rocky and grassy plateau above the tree line (circular walks of various lengths,

a 40-minute hike down, and a 4-hour hike to the top of the Fløibanen funicular). For less exercise, you can simply sunbathe, crack open a picnic, or enjoy the Ulriken restaurant.

Getting There: To get from downtown Bergen to the cable car, you can take a blue Bergen Sightseeing hop-on, hop-off bus (245 kr includes cable-car ride, ticket valid 24 hours, May-Sept daily 10:00-17:30, 2/hour, departs Fish Market and Bryggen, also stops at aquarium, buy ticket on board or at TI). The cable-car ride takes five minutes (prices without bus ride: 145 kr round-trip, 80 kr one-way, 8/hour, daily 9:00-21:00, off-season until 17:00, tel. 53 64 36 43, www.ulriken643.no).

▲▲**Edvard Grieg's Home, Troldhaugen**—Norway's greatest composer spent his last 22 summers here (1885-1907), soaking up

inspirational fjord beauty and composing many of his greatest works. Grieg fused simple Norwegian folk tunes with the bombast of Europe's Romantic style. In a dreamy Victorian setting, Grieg's "Hill of the Trolls" is pleasant for anyone and essential for Grieg fans. You can visit his house on your own, but it's more enjoyable if you take the

included 20-minute tour. The house and adjacent museum are full of memories and artifacts, including the composer's Steinway. The walls are festooned with photos of the musical and literary superstars of his generation. When the hugely popular Grieg died in 1907, 40,000 mourners attended his funeral. His little studio hut near the water makes you want to sit down and modulate.

Cost and Hours: 80 kr, includes guided tour in English, daily

May-Sept 9:00-18:00, Oct-April 10:00-16:00, tel. 55 92 29 92, www.troldhaugen.com.

Concerts: Delightful 30-minute lunch piano concerts in the concert hall at Grieg's home—a gorgeous venue with the fjord stretching out behind the big, black grand piano—are offered daily at 13:00 in peak season (20 kr plus entry ticket, daily June-Aug, Mon-Sat in Sept).

Getting to Troldhaugen: Bergen's slick **tram** drops you a long 20-minute walk from Troldhaugen. Catch the tram in the city center at its terminus near Byparken (between the lake and Ole Bulls Plass), ride it for about 25 minutes, and get off at the stop called Hop. Walk in the direction of Bergen (about 25 yards), cross at the crosswalk, and follow signs to Troldhaugen. Part of the way is on a pedestrian/bike path; you're halfway there when the path crosses over a busy highway. If you want to make the 13:00 lunchtime concert, leave Bergen at 12:00.

To avoid the long walk from the tram stop, consider the three-hour city bus tour promoted by the TI, which comes with informative recorded narration, gets you to within a five-minute walk of Troldhaugen, and includes a brief tour of the house (300 kr, May-Sept daily at 11:00).

Fantoft Stave Church—This huge, preserved-in-tar stave church burned down in 1992. It was rebuilt and reopened in 1997,

but it will never be the same. Situated in a quiet forest next to a mysterious stone cross, this replica of a 12th-century wooden church is bigger, though no better, than others in Norway. But if you're in the neighborhood, it's worth a look for its atmospheric setting.

Cost and Hours: 44 kr, mid-May-mid-Sept daily 10:30-18:00, interior closed off-season, no English information, tel. 55 28 07 10, www.fantoftstav kirke.com.

Getting There: The church is located three miles south of Bergen on E-39 in Paradis. Take the tram (from Byparken, between the lake and Ole Bulls Plass) or bus #83 (from Torget, by the Fish Market) to the Paradis stop (not the "Fantoft" stop). From Paradis, walk uphill to the parking lot on the left, and find the steep footpath to the church.

Shopping in Bergen

Most shops, including Husfliden (described below), are open Mon-Fri 9:00-17:00, Thu until 19:00, Sat 9:00-15:00, and closed Sunday. Many of the tourist shops at the harborfront strip along Bryggen are open daily—even during holidays—until 20:00 or 21:00.

Bryggen is bursting with sweaters, pewter, and trolls. The **Husfliden** shop is popular for its handmade Norwegian sweaters and goodies (fine variety and quality but expensive, just off Torget, the market square, at Vågsallmenninge 3, tel. 55 54 47 40).

The **Galleriet** shopping center on Torgallmenningen has six floors of shops, cafés, and restaurants. You'll find a pharmacy, photo shops, clothing, sporting goods, bookstores, mobile-phone shops, an Internet café, and a basement grocery store (Mon-Fri 9:00-20:00, Sat 9:00-18:00, closed Sun).

Eating in Bergen

Bergen has numerous choices: restaurants with rustic, woody atmosphere, candlelight, and steep prices (main dishes around 300 kr); trendy pubs and cafés that offer good-value meals (100-190 kr); cafeterias, chain restaurants, and ethnic eateries with less ambience where you can get quality food at lower prices (100-150 kr); and take-away sandwich shops, bakeries, and cafés for a light bite (50-100 kr).

You can always get a glass or pitcher of water at no charge, and fancy places give you free seconds on potatoes—just ask. Remember, if you get your food to go, it's taxed at a lower rate and you'll save 12 percent.

For information on Norwegian cuisine, see page 684.

Splurge in Bryggen

You'll pay a premium to eat here, but you'll have a memorable meal in a pleasant setting. If it's beyond your budget, remember that you can fill up on potatoes and drink tap water to dine for exactly the price of the plate.

Bryggeloftet & Stuene Restaurant, in a brick building just before the wooden stretch of Bryggen, is a vast eatery serving seafood, vegetarian, and traditional meals. Upstairs feels more elegant and less touristy than the main floor—if there's a line downstairs, just head on up (145-165-kr lunches,

BERGEN

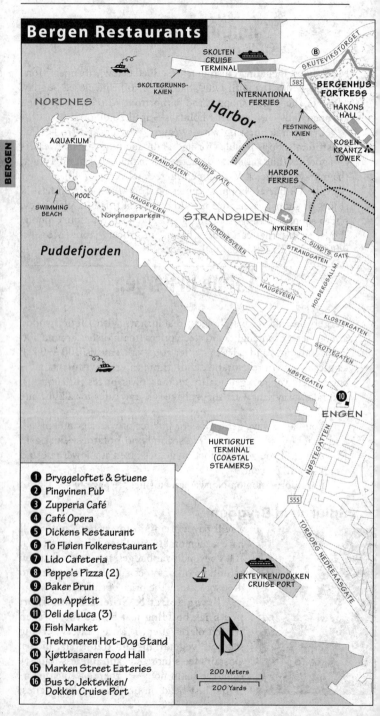

Bergen Restaurants

SKOLTEN CRUISE TERMINAL

SKOLTEGRUNNS-KAIEN

INTERNATIONAL FERRIES

SKUTEVIKSTORGET

585

BERGENHUS FORTRESS

HÅKONS HALL

ROSEN-KRANTZ TOWER

FESTNINGS-KAIEN

Harbor

NORDNES

AQUARIUM

STRANDGATEN

C. SUNDTS GATE

HARBOR FERRIES

POOL

HAUGEVEIEN

SWIMMING BEACH

Nordnesparken

STRANDSIDEN

NYKIRKEN

C. SUNDTS GATE

Puddefjorden

NORDNESVEIEN

STRANDGATEN

HAUGEVEIEN

HOLBERGSALLM.

KLOSTERGATEN

SKOTTEGATEN

NØSTEGATEN

🔟

ENGEN

HURTIGRUTE TERMINAL (COASTAL STEAMERS)

555

NØSTEGATTEN

TORBORG NEDREAASGATE

JEKTEVIKEN/DOKKEN CRUISE PORT

N

1. Bryggeloftet & Stuene
2. Pingvinen Pub
3. Zupperia Café
4. Café Opera
5. Dickens Restaurant
6. To Fløien Folkerestaurant
7. Lido Cafeteria
8. Peppe's Pizza (2)
9. Baker Brun
10. Bon Appétit
11. Deli de Luca (3)
12. Fish Market
13. Trekroneren Hot-Dog Stand
14. Kjøttbasaren Food Hall
15. Marken Street Eateries
16. Bus to Jekteviken/ Dokken Cruise Port

200 Meters
200 Yards

BERGEN

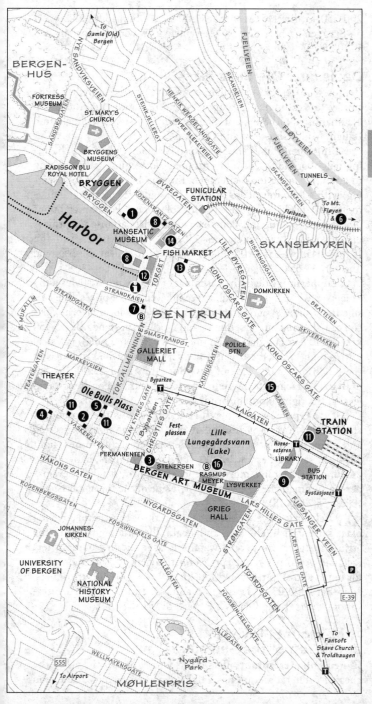

200-350-kr dinners, Mon-Sat 11:00-23:30, Sun 13:00-23:30, #11 on Bryggen harborfront, try reserving a view window upstairs, tel. 55 30 20 70).

Deals near Ole Bulls Plass

Bergen's "in" cafés are stylish, cozy, and small—a great opportunity to experience its yuppie scene. Around the cinema on Neumannsgate, there are numerous ethnic restaurants, including Italian, Middle Eastern, and Chinese.

Pingvinen Pub ("The Penguin") is a homey place in a charming neighborhood, serving traditional Norwegian home cooking to an enthusiastic local clientele. The pub has only indoor seating, with a long row of stools at the bar and five charming, living-room-cozy tables—a great setup for solo diners. For unpretentious Norwegian cooking in a completely untouristy atmosphere, this is one of your best budget choices (140-190-kr main dishes, Sun-Thu 14:00-12:45, Fri-Sat 12:00-20:45, Vaskerelven 14 near the National Theater, tel. 55 60 46 46).

Zupperia, a café in the basement of the Bergen Art Museum's Stenersen wing, has cool ambience and even cooler prices. The cuisine has a slight Asian twist (the Thai soup is a local favorite), but you can also find burgers, salads, and Norwegian standards (75-150 kr). The 109-kr lasagna special (includes bread and salad) is a steal in this high-price city. If you're not very hungry, you can order off the lunch menu any time of day (Sun-Thu 12:00-22:00, Fri-Sat until 22:30; facing the museum, go to the entrance on the ground level at the right, Nordahl Bruns Gate 9, tel. 55 55 81 14).

Café Opera, with a playful-slacker vibe, is the hip budget choice for its loyal, youthful following. With two floors of seating and tables out front across from the theater, it's a winner (light 30-40-kr sandwiches until 16:00, 100-150-kr dinners, daily 10:00-24:00, occasional live music, live locals nightly, English newspapers in summer, chess, around the left side of the theater at Engen 18, tel. 55 23 03 15).

Dickens is a lively, checkerboard, turn-of-the-century-feeling place serving fish, chicken, and steak. The window tables in the atrium are great for people-watching, as is the fine outdoor terrace, but you'll pay higher prices for the view. To save money, go for lunch and skip the view (150-kr lunches, 250-300-kr dinners, Mon-Sat 11:00-23:00, later on Fri and Sat, Sun 13:00-23:00, reservations smart, Kong Olav V's Plass 4, tel. 55 36 31 30).

Atop Mount Fløyen, at the Top of the Funicular

Fløien Folkerestaurant offers meals with a panoramic view. The cheaper cafeteria section has a light menu, with coffee, cake, and sandwiches for around 60 kr and a 139-kr soup buffet (May-Aug daily 10:00-22:00, Sept-April Sat-Sun only 12:00-17:00).

Cafeteria Overlooking the Fish Market

Lido offers basic, affordable food with great harbor and market views, better ambience than most self-serve places, and a museum's worth of old town photos on the walls. For cold items (such as open-face sandwiches and desserts, 50-80 kr), grab what you want, pay the cashier, and find a table. For hot dishes (120-170-kr Norwegian standards, including one daily special discounted to 109 kr), grab a table, order and pay at the cashier, and they'll bring your food to you (June-Aug Mon-Fri 10:00-22:00, Sat-Sun 13:00-22:00; Sept-May Mon-Sat 10:00-19:00, Sun 13:00-19:00; second floor at Torgallmenningen 1a, tel. 55 32 59 12).

Good Chain Restaurants

You'll find these tasty chain restaurants in Bergen and throughout Norway. All of these are open long hours daily (shorter off-season). In good weather, enjoy a take-out meal with sun-worshipping locals in Bergen's parks.

Peppe's Pizza has cold beer and good pizzas (medium size for 1-2 people-175-200 kr, large for 2-3 people-200-250 kr, take-out possible; consider the Moby Dick, with curried shrimp, leeks, and bell peppers). There are six Peppe's in Bergen, including one behind the Hanseatic Museum near the Fløibanen funicular station and another inside the Zachariasbryggen harborfront complex, next to the Fish Market (with views over the harbor).

Baker Brun makes 50-70-kr sandwiches, including wonderful shrimp baguettes and pastries such as *skillingsbolle*—cinnamon rolls—warm out of the oven (open from 9:00, seating inside or take-away; several locations, including Bryggen and the Storsenter shopping mall next to the bus station).

Bon Appétit sells 60-kr baguette sandwiches and wraps, plus ice cream (locations include Baneveien 15 and Bryggen). Restaurant desserts run 100 kr; strolling with an ice-cream cone can save plenty.

Deli de Luca is a cut above other take-away joints, adding sushi and calzones to the normal lineup of sandwiches. While a bit more expensive than the others, the variety and quality are appealing (open 24/7; branches in train station and near Ole Bulls Plass at Torggaten 5, branch with indoor seating on corner of Engen and Vaskerelven, tel. 55 23 11 47).

Budget Bets

The **Fish Market** has lots of stalls bursting with salmon sandwiches, fresh shrimp, fish-and-chips, and fish cakes. For a tasty,

What If I Miss My Boat?

Remember that you can get help from the cruise line's port agent (listed on the destination information sheet distributed on the ship) and the local TI (see page 715). If the port agent suggests a costly solution (such as a private car with a driver), you may want to consider public transit.

You can catch the boat to **Stavanger** (tel. 55 23 87 00 or 05505, www.tide.no). There's also an express boat to **Flåm** (tel. 51 86 87 00, www.norled.no).

Trains work well for other Norwegian destinations. Take the main east-west rail line to **Oslo;** partway along, you can take a bus or train down to the fjord at **Flåm.** For any points **outside Norway,** you're probably best connecting through Oslo. To research train schedules, see www.bahn.com.

If you need to catch a **plane** to your next destination, Bergen's Flesland Airport (tel. 67 03 15 55, www.avinor.no /bergen) is 12 miles south of the city center, connected by airport bus.

Local **travel agents** in Bergen can help you. For more advice on what to do if you miss the boat, see page 144.

memorable, and inexpensive Bergen meal, assemble a seafood picnic here (ask for prices first; June-Aug daily 7:00-19:00, less lively on Sun; Sept-May Mon-Sat 7:00-16:00, closed Sun).

Trekroneren, your classic hot-dog stand, sells a wide variety of sausages (various sizes and flavors—including reindeer). The well-described English menu makes it easy to order your choice of artery-clogging guilty pleasures (20-kr tiny weenie, 50-kr medium-size weenie, 75-kr jumbo, open daily 11:00-5:00 in the morning, you'll see the little hot-dog shack a block up Kong Oscar Gate from the harbor, Kenneht is the boss).

Kjøttbasaren, the restored meat market of 1887, is a genteel-feeling food hall with stalls selling groceries such as meat, cheese, bread, and olives—a great opportunity to assemble a bang-up picnic (Mon-Fri 10:00-17:00, Thu until 18:00, Sat 9:00-16:00, closed Sun).

Marken Pedestrian Street Eateries

This cobbled lane, leading from the train station to the harbor, is lined with creative little restaurants and trendy cafés. Strolling along here, you can choose among cheap chicken and burgers, the elegant **Bambus Marken** for Vietnamese (daily 14:00-23:00, seating indoors and out, Marken 33, tel. 55 56 00 60), the **Taste of Indian** (69-kr daily special, daily 13:00-24:00, Marken 12, tel. 55 31 11 55), and the **Aura Café** for classy sandwiches and salads (Mon-Sat until 22:00, Sun until 19:00, indoors and out, Marken 9).

NORWEGIAN FJORDS

Norway Practicalities

Norway (Norge) is stacked with superlatives—it's the most mountainous, most scenic, and most prosperous of all the Scandinavian countries. Perhaps above all, Norway is a land of intense natural beauty, its famously steep mountains and deep fjords carved out and shaped by an ancient ice age. Norway (148,900 square miles—just larger than Montana) is on the western side of the Scandinavian Peninsula, with most of the country sharing a border with Sweden to the east. Rich in resources like timber, oil, and fish, Norway has rejected joining the European Union, mainly to protect its fishing rights. Where the country extends north of the Arctic Circle, the sun never sets at the height of summer and never comes up in the deep of winter. The majority of Norway's 5 million people consider themselves Lutheran.

Money: 6 Norwegian kroner (kr, officially NOK) = about $1. An ATM is called a *minibank*. The local VAT (value-added sales tax) rate is 25 percent; the minimum purchase eligible for a VAT refund is 315 kr (for details on refunds, see page 139).

Language: The native language is Norwegian (the two official forms are Bokmål and Nynorsk). For useful phrases, see page 691.

Emergencies: Dial 112 for police, medical, or other emergencies. In case of theft or loss, see page 131.

Time Zone: Norway is on Central European Time (the same as most of the Continent, one hour ahead of Great Britain, and six/nine hours ahead of the East/West Coasts of the US).

Embassies in Oslo: The **US embassy** is at Henrik Ibsens Gate 48 (tel. 21 30 85 58, emergency tel. 21 30 85 40, http://norway.usembassy.gov). The **Canadian embassy** is at Wergelandsveien 7 (tel. 22 99 53 00, www.norway.gc.ca). Call ahead for passport services.

Phoning: Norway's country code is 47; to call from another country to Norway, dial the international access code (011 from the US/Canada, 00 from Europe, or + from a mobile phone), then 47, followed by the local number. For local calls within Norway, just dial the number as it appears in this book— whether you're calling from across the street or across the country. To place an international call from Norway, dial 00, the code of the country you're calling (1 for US and Canada), and the phone number. For more tips, see page 1110.

Tipping: As service is included at sit-down meals, you don't need to tip further, though for great service it's nice to round up your bill about 5-10 percent. Tip a taxi driver by rounding up the fare (pay 90 kr on an 85-kr fare). For more tips on tipping, see page 143.

Tourist Information: www.goscandinavia.com

NORWEGIAN FJORDS

Flåm, the Sognefjord, and Norway in a Nutshell
• Geirangerfjord

While Oslo and Bergen are fine cities, Norway is first and foremost a place of unforgettable natural beauty—and its greatest claims to scenic fame are its deep, lush fjords. Three million years ago, an ice age made this land as inhabitable as the center of Greenland. As the glaciers advanced and cut their way to the sea, they gouged out long grooves—today's fjords. The entire west coast of the country is slashed by stunning fjords.

Various Norwegian cruise ports offer a taste of fjord scenery (Oslo, Bergen, and Stavanger are all situated on or near fjords), but many cruises also head for two particularly scenic and accessible fjords unencumbered by big cities: the Sognefjord (at the village of Flåm) and the Geirangerfjord. Flåm is the hub for a well-coordinated web of train, boat, and bus connections—appropriately nicknamed the "Norway in a Nutshell" route—that let you see some of Norway's best scenery efficiently on your own. Geirangerfjord, more remote, works best by excursion. I've covered each of these fjords separately in this chapter.

Flåm, the Sognefjord, and Norway in a Nutshell

Among the fjords, the Sognefjord—Norway's longest (120 miles) and deepest (1 mile)—is tops. The seductive Sognefjord has tiny but tough ferries, towering canyons, and isolated farms and villages marinated in the mist of countless waterfalls.

While the port town of Flåm itself has modest charms, a series of well-organized and spectacular bus, train, and ferry connections—together called "Norway in a Nutshell"—lays Norway's beautiful fjord country before you on a scenic platter. With the Nutshell, you'll delve into two offshoots of the Sognefjord, which make an upside-down "U" route: the Aurlandsfjord and the Nærøyfjord. This trip brings you right back to where you started 6.5 hours earlier—after cruising Norway's narrowest fjord, riding a bus along an impossibly twisty and waterfall-lined road, taking the train across the mountainous spine of the country, then dropping back down to sea level on yet another super-scenic train. All connections are designed for tourists, explained in English, convenient, and described thoroughly in this chapter.

This region enjoys mild weather for its latitude, thanks to the warm Gulf Stream. (When it rains in Bergen, it just drizzles here.) But if the weather is bad, don't fret. I've often arrived to gloomy weather, only to enjoy sporadic splashes of brilliant sunshine all day long.

Recently the popularity of the Nutshell route has skyrocketed among both cruise ships and land-based travelers. July and August come with a crush of crowds, dampening some of the area's magic. Unfortunately, many tourists are overcome by Nutshell tunnel-vision, and spend so much energy scurrying between boats, trains, and buses that they forget to simply enjoy the fjords. Relax—you're on vacation.

Planning Your Time

There's very little to do in Flåm itself. If you're here for a full day, splurge and do the Nutshell loop (unless you're on a tight budget or your cruise schedule doesn't allow it, in which case you can still do one or two of the segments). Here are your options:

• **Norway in a Nutshell Round-Trip:** Outlined step-by-step in this chapter, this ultimate boat, bus, and train journey takes 6.5 hours.

• **"Poor Man's Nutshell":** If your schedule doesn't allow the full Nutshell, you could cobble together its two best parts (connected by a 20-25-minute bus ride): the two-hour Nærøyfjord cruise and the 2.5-hour round-trip on the Flåmsbana. This one-two punch lets you see the best of the Nutshell.

• **Flåmsbana Mountain Train Only:** From Flåm, you can take a round-trip on the Flåmsbana train steeply into the mountains, then back down into the valley. Allow an hour each way on the train, plus time at the top station, Myrdal (not much to see—basically killing time before the return train). Warning: Morning trains sell out quickly, particularly when multiple cruises are in town; to book a morning ticket, get off your ship as quickly as possible and make a beeline to the train ticket office.

• **Nærøyfjord Cruise Only:** While the first half of the Flåm-Gudvangen cruise is redundant with your cruise ship's sail-away, the second half takes you to a fjord too skinny for big ships: the Nærøyfjord. From Gudvangen, you can zip back to Flåm on the bus (20-25 minutes), or cruise all the way back (2.25 hours). Allow about three hours round-trip if returning by bus, or about five hours round-trip if cruising both ways.

• **Flåm:** If you choose one of the shorter options above, and have time to kill in Flåm, you'll find there's little to do other than shopping or dipping into the Railway Museum. Consider renting a boat for a ride on the fjord, taking one of the high-speed boat tours with FjordSafari, or going for a hike in the local area (the TI hands out a map suggesting local walks).

• **Borgund Stave Church:** One of Norway's finest stave churches sits 35 miles from Flåm. While visiting the church itself takes an hour or so, the whole excursion by public bus from Flåm takes four and a half hours round-trip (and there's only one possible connection per day—see page 752). That's a long way to go just to see a church—but it's one of the best examples anywhere of this uniquely Norwegian church architecture (and includes a museum).

• **Outlying Sights:** Several intriguing sights lie outside of Flåm, not easily reachable by public transportation. These include the Stegastein viewpoint, Otternes farm, and other fjordside villages (such as Undredal). While it's possible to reach these by taxi, a better option is likely the package tours offered by Sognefjorden Sightseeing & Tours (described on page 750).

In this destination (even more than others), it really pays to do some homework and decide what you want to do before you step off the ship. Line up early to be one of the first ashore (especially if tendering)—you won't regret it, as those few extra minutes might help you beat the crowds to the TI and train ticket office. Both offices open at 8:15 (though the line forms earlier); the first Flåmsbana train departs at 8:35; the first fjord cruise leaves at 9:00. That leaves you a fairly narrow window to make your plans.

In general, be completely clear on your entire day's plan. Double-
and triple-check connections with posted schedules, the TI, the
train station ticket-sellers, and so on. The connections are generally coordinated to work efficiently together, and the people you'll
meet along the way are typically patient about explaining things to
nervous tourists.

Arrival at the Port of Flåm

Arrival at a Glance: It's simple: From your ship or tender, it's
a very short stroll to the train station and boat dock. The key is
doing your homework and getting an early start.

Port Overview

Little Flåm has space for one big cruise ship to **dock** at its pier;
stepping off your ship, you'll turn left, go through the port gate,
and walk between the water and a row of shops to reach the train
station area.

Entering the train station through the door facing the pier,
you'll find the TI on your right and the train ticket office on your
left. If you're doing the whole Nutshell, go to the TI first and
buy their package. If you're doing only the Flåmsbana train—or
want to piece together your own Nutshell route—go to the train
ticket office to get your Flåmsbana ticket (and, while you're at
it, reserve a seat on the Voss-Myrdal train trip). The electronic
board above the ticket office notes which, if any, of today's Flåm-
Myrdal train departures are sold out. Farther into the station are
the Sognefjorden Sightseeing & Tours office, a gift shop, and a
cafeteria.

If multiple ships are in town, some will anchor in the harbor
and **tender** passengers to the pier right in front of the train station.

Tourist Information: Flåm's TI is inside its train station—
just look for the green-and-white *i* sign (see opposite page).

Strategies: Remember, time is of the essence here. If you
want to venture beyond Flåm, disembark as quickly as possible
and head for the TI to sort through your options and buy tickets.

Returning to Your Ship

It's easy—you can see your ship from anywhere in Flåm. But just
in case, see page 763 for help if you miss your boat.

Excursions from Flåm

Cruise lines push their own version of the **Norway in a Nutshell** loop, sometimes billed as "Best of Flåm"; you'll likely take some of the same boats, buses, and trains that are available to the public (though some legs may be chartered). If you're willing and able to figure out the Nutshell on your own (using this chapter's step-by-step tips), you'll save money. But if you'd just prefer to let someone else do the planning, an excursion can be worthwhile.

Other excursion options from Flåm include various individual legs of the Nutshell, such as the **Flåmsbana** mountain train up to Myrdal and back, or a cruise on the **Nærøyfjord.** You may also be offered a **kayak trip** on the Aurlandsfjord (near Flåm). All of these are easy to book on your own. However, a few farther-flung options are more challenging to reach by public transit, and worth considering by excursion: a bus trip to a **mountain farm** (Otternes) or a visit to **Borgund Stave Church** (doable but time-consuming by public bus).

In general, with various options possible on your own, I'd consider an excursion from Flåm only if you want to visit an out-of-the-way destination, or if you simply don't want to hassle with booking your own trip.

Orientation to Flåm

Flåm (sometimes spelled Flaam, pronounced "flome")—at the head of the Aurlandsfjord—feels more like a transit junction than a village. But its striking setting, easy transportation connections, and touristy bustle make it a popular springboard for exploring the nearby area.

The train station has most of the town services (see sidebar). The boat dock for fjord cruises is just beyond the end of the tracks. Surrounding the station are a Co-op grocery and a smattering of hotels, travel agencies, and touristy restaurants. Aside from a few scattered farmhouses and some homes lining the road, there's not much of a town here. (The extremely sleepy old town center—where tourists rarely venture, and which you'll pass on the Flåmsbana train—is a few miles up the river, in the valley.)

Tourist Information

At the TI inside the train station, you can purchase your boat tickets—or the entire Nutshell package—and load up on handy brochures (daily May and late Sept 8:15-16:00, June-mid-Sept 8:15-20:00, closed Oct-April, tel. 57 63 21 06, www.visitflam.com or www.alr.no, very helpful Vladimir). The TI hands out a variety

Services near the Port

Though it's a small town, Flåm has much of what you need. Most of Flåm's services are inside the train station, including the TI, train ticket desk, pay Wi-Fi, public WC, cafeteria, and souvenir shops hawking overpriced reindeer pelts (cheaper in Bergen).

ATMs: You'll find one at the bank in the yellow building just toward the water from the train station.

Internet Access: Vouchers sold at the TI give you access to Wi-Fi around the station area (20 kr/1 hour, 40 kr/3 hours, 50 kr/day).

Grocery Store: The Co-op grocery, near the cruise dock, has a basic pharmacy and post office inside (Mon-Fri 9:00-20:00, Sat 9:00-18:00, shorter hours off-season, closed Sun year-round).

Pharmacy: There's no real pharmacy in Flåm, but you will find some basics in the **Co-op** grocery store (noted above). The nearest pharmacy is in **Lærdal** (just east, through the world's longest tunnel); if you're doing the Nutshell route, note that there's a pharmacy in **Voss** (Vitus Apotek, a 5-minute walk into town from the train station and a few doors down from the TI, facing the town church at Vangsgatan 22D, Mon-Fri 8:30-17:00, Sat 9:00-15:00, closed Sun).

Car Rental: There's only one rental car in Flåm, and you'll find it at Heimly Pensjonat just around the harbor (tel. 57 63 23 00, www.heimly.no, post@heimly.no).

of useful items: an excellent flyer with a good map and up-to-date schedules for public transit options; a diagram of the train-station area, identifying services available in each building; and a map of Flåm and the surrounding area, marked with suggested walks and hikes. Answers to most of your questions can be found posted on the walls and from staff at the counter. Bus schedules, boat and train timetables, maps, and more are photocopied and available for your convenience. The TI also sells Wi-Fi vouchers (see sidebar).

Sights in and near Flåm

Along the Waterfront

All of the activities in Flåm village are along or near the pier.

The **Flåm Railway Museum** (Flåmsbana Museet), sprawling through the long old train station alongside the tracks, has surprisingly good exhibits about the history of the train that connects Flåm to the main line up above. You'll find good English explanations, artifacts, re-creations of historic interiors (such as the humble schoolhouse up at Myrdal), and an actual train car. It's the only real museum in town and a good place to kill time while waiting for your boat or train (free, daily 9:00-17:00).

The Torget Café is attached to a **fjord "panorama" movie** (55 kr, 23 minutes).

I'd skip the pointless and overpriced **tourist train** that does a 45-minute loop around Flåm (95 kr).

The pleasantly woody Ægir Bryggeri, a microbrewery designed to resemble an old Viking longhouse, offers tastes of its five beers (125 kr; also pub grub in the evening).

The TI hands out a map suggesting several **walks and hikes** in the area, starting from right in town.

If you want to linger, consider renting a **boat** to go out on the usually calm, peaceful waters of the fjord. You can paddle near the walls of the fjord and really get a sense of the immensity of these mountains. You can rent rowboats, motorboats, and paddleboats at the little marina across the harbor. If you'd rather have a kayak, Njord does kayak tours, but won't rent you one unless you're certified (tel. 91 32 66 28, www.njord.as).

But the main reason people come to Flåm is to leave it—see some options below.

Outside of Flåm

With a day in the port of Flåm, any of the following is possible— and reachable, to an extent, by public transit. But, as many options are time-consuming, you'll need to be selective.

▲▲Flåmsbana Mountain Railway

This historic rail line picturesquely links fjordside Flåm with mountaintop Myrdal. It can be done either round-trip, or one-way as part of the Norway in a Nutshell trip. Note: Because this is such an easy and fast way to reach grand views from Flåm, many of your fellow passengers head straight for the Flåmsbana mountain train. If you can wait to do it later in the day, you'll enjoy fewer crowds. But you should still buy your tickets as early as possible, as even the later trains can sell out on busy days. For details on the train, see page 762.

▲▲▲Cruising Nærøyfjord

The most scenic fjord I've seen anywhere in Norway is about an hour from Flåm (basically the last half of the two-hour Flåm-Gudvangen trip). Your cruise ship passes the mouth of the Nærøyfjord, but for a closer look, there are several ways to cruise it: You can take the state-run ferry as part of the Norway in a Nutshell trip (4.5-hour round-trips departing Flåm in peak season at 9:00, 11:00, and 13:20, 390 kr; it's faster to return from Gudvangen to

Flåm by 20-25-minute bus; for details on both options, see page 759). Or you can consider two other Flåm-based options:

Sognefjorden Sightseeing & Tours—This private company runs trips from Flåm to Gudvangen and back to Flåm, using their own boats and buses (rather than the public ones on the "official" Nutshell route). If the Nutshell departures don't work for you, consider these trips as an alternative. Their main offering, the World Heritage Cruise, is a boat trip up the Nærøyfjord with a return by bus (335 kr, 2.5-3 hours, multiple departures daily mid-May-mid-Sept). They also do a variation on this trip with a 45-minute stop in the village of Undredal for lunch and a goat-cheese tasting (630 kr, June-Aug only); a bus trip up to the Stalheim Hotel for the view (290 kr, or combined with return from Gudvangen by boat for 510 kr); a bus ride up to the thrilling Stegastein viewpoint (otherwise impossible to reach without a car, 190 kr, mid-May-mid-Sept); and more. For details, drop by their office inside the Flåm train station, call 57 66 00 55, or visit www.visitflam.com/sognefjorden.

▲▲**FjordSafari to Nærøyfjord**—FjordSafari takes little groups out onto the fjord in small, open Zodiac-type boats with an English-speaking guide. Participants wear full-body weather suits, furry hats, and spacey goggles (making everyone on the boat look like crash-test dummies). As the boat rockets across the water, you'll be thankful for the gear, no matter what the weather. You'll get the same scant information and stops as on the slow ferry, except that Safari boats stop right under a towering rock cliff—a magnificent experience. Their two-hour Flåm-Gudvangen-Flåm tour focuses on the Nærøyfjord, and gets you all the fjord magnificence you can imagine (590 kr). Their three-hour tour (700 kr) is the same as the two-hour tour, except that it includes a stop in Undredal, where you can see goat cheese being made, taste the finished product, and wander that sleepy village. They run several departures daily from June through August (fewer off-season, kids get discounts, tel. 99 09 08 60, www.fjordsafari.no, Maylene). They also offer a 1.5-hour "mini" tour that costs 490 kr and just barely touches on the Nærøyfjord...so what's the point?

▲Flåm Valley Bike Ride or Hike

For the best single-day, non-fjord activity from Flåm, take the Flåmsbana train to Myrdal, then hike or mountain-bike along the road (part gravel but mostly paved) back down to Flåm (2-3 hours by bike, gorgeous waterfalls, great mountain scenery, and a cute church with an evocative graveyard, but no fjord views). The Flåm TI rents mountain bikes (50 kr/hour, 250 kr/day) as does the local youth hostel. It costs 90 kr to take a bike to Myrdal on the train. Also, you can hike just the best two hours from Myrdal to

Berekvam, where you can catch the train into the valley. Pick up the helpful map with this and other hiking options (easy to strenuous) at the Flåm TI.

▲▲Otternes Farms

This humble but magical cluster of four centuries-old farms, realistically accessible only to drivers, is perched high on a ridge, up

a twisty gravel road midway between Flåm and the tiny town of Aurland. Laila Kvellestad runs this low-key sight, valiantly working to save and share traditional life as it was back when butter was the farmers' gold. (That was before emigration decimated the workforce, coinage

replaced barter, and industrialized margarine became more popular than butter, leaving farmers to eke out a living relying only on their goats and the cheese they produced.) Until 1919 the only road between Aurland and Flåm passed between this huddle of 27 buildings, high above the fjord. First settled in 1522, farmers lived here until the 1990s. Laila gives 45-minute English tours through several time-warp houses and barns at 10:00, 12:00, 14:00, and 16:00 (50-kr entry plus 30 kr for guided tour, June-mid-Sept daily 10:00-17:00, tel. 48 12 51 38). It's wise to call first to confirm tour times and that it's open. For an additional 65 kr, Laila serves a traditional snack with your tour (pancakes with coffee or tea), but you must book in advance.

Over (or Under) the Mountains, to Lærdal and Borgund

To reach these sights, you'll first head along the fjord to Aurland. Of the sights below, the Lærdal Tunnel, Stegastein viewpoint, and Aurlandsvegen "Snow Road" are best by taxi or excursion. The Borgund Stave Church can be reached by public bus from Flåm.

Lærdal Tunnel—Drivers find that this tunnel makes connecting Flåm and Lærdal a snap. It's the world's longest road-vehicle tunnel, stretching 15 miles between Aurland and Lærdal as part of the E-16 highway. It also makes the wonderful Borgund Stave Church (described below) less than an hour's drive from Aurland. The downside to the tunnel is that it goes beneath my favorite scenic drive in Norway (the Aurlandsvegen "Snow Road," described next). But with about two hours, you can drive through the tunnel to Lærdal and then return via the "Snow Road," with the Stegastein viewpoint as a finale, before dropping back into Aurland.

NORWEGIAN FJORDS

▲▲Stegastein Viewpoint and Aurlandsvegen "Snow Road"—With a car (or a taxi) and clear weather, consider twisting up the mountain behind Aurland on route 243 for about 20 minutes for a fine view over the Aurlandsfjord. A new viewpoint called Stegastein—which looks like a giant, wooden, inverted number "7"—provides a platform from which you can enjoy stunning views across the fjords.

Immediately beyond the viewpoint, you leave the fjord views and enter the mountaintop world of the Aurlandsvegen "Snow Road." When you finally hit civilization on the other side, you're a mile from the Lærdal tunnel entrance and about 30 minutes from the fine Borgund Stave Church.

▲▲Borgund Stave Church—About 16 miles east of Lærdal, in the village of Borgund, is Norway's most-visited and one of its best-preserved stave churches.

Borgund's church comes with one of the country's best stave-church history museums, which beautifully explains these icons of medieval Norway. Dating from around 1180, the interior features only a few later additions, including a 16th-century pulpit, 17th-century stone altar, painted decorations, and crossbeam reinforcements.

The oldest and most authentic item in the church is the stone baptismal font. In medieval times, priests conducting baptisms would go outside to shoo away the evil spirits from an infant before bringing it inside the church for the ritual. (If infants died before being baptized, they couldn't be buried in the churchyard, so parents would put their bodies in little coffins and hide them under the church's floorboards to get them as close as possible to God.)

Explore the dimly lit interior, illuminated only by the original, small, circular windows up high. Notice the X-shaped crosses of St. Andrew (the church's patron), carvings of dragons, and medieval runes.

Cost and Hours: 75 kr, buy tickets in museum across street, daily mid-June-mid-Aug 8:00-20:00, May-mid-June and mid-Aug-Sept 10:00-17:00, closed Oct-April. The museum has a shop and a fine little cafeteria serving filling and tasty lunches (70-kr soup with bread, tel. 57 66 81 09, www.stavechurch.com).

Getting There: It's about a 30-minute drive east of Lærdal, on E-16. A **bus** departs Flåm and Aurland around midday (direction: Lillehammer) and heads for the church, with a return bus departing Borgund in mid-afternoon (240-kr round-trip, get ticket from driver, about 1 hour each way with about 1 hour at the church, bus runs daily May-Sept, tell driver you want to get off at the church).

Eating in Flåm

Dining options are expensive and touristy. Don't aim for high cuisine here—go practical. Almost all eateries are clustered near the train station complex. Hours can be unpredictable, flexing with the season, but you can expect these to be open daily in high season.

The **Flåmsbrygga** complex, sprawling through a long building toward the fjord from the station, includes a hotel, the affordable **Furukroa Café** (cafeteria with 50-65-kr cold sandwiches, 100-150-kr fast-food meals, and 200-225-kr pizzas), and the pricey **Flåmstova Restaurant** (235-kr lunch buffet, 325-kr dinner buffet, plus other menu options at dinner). Next door is their fun, Viking-longhouse-shaped brewpub, Ægir Bryggeri (145-165-kr pub grub after 16:00). **Torget Café,** with seating in old train cars, is under new management that prides itself on using as many locally sourced and organic ingredients as possible (65-75-kr sandwiches, 160-195-kr main dishes).

Norway in a Nutshell

The most exciting single-day trip you could make from Flåm is this circular train/boat/bus/train jaunt through fjord country. Everybody does this famous trip...and if you're looking for a delicious slice of Norway's scenic grandeur, so should you.

Orientation to the Nutshell

From Flåm, the basic idea is this: Begin with a cruise on two arms of the Sognefjord, ride a bus up from the fjord to join Norway's main train line, and ride that train to catch a different train that goes steeply back down to Flåm and the fjord. Each of these steps is explained in the self-guided tour, later. Transportation along the Nutshell route is carefully coordinated. If any segment of the journey is delayed, your transportation for the next segment will wait (because everyone on board is catching the same connection).

Information: Local TIs (including the one at Flåm's train station) are well-informed about your options, and sell tickets for

NORWEGIAN FJORDS

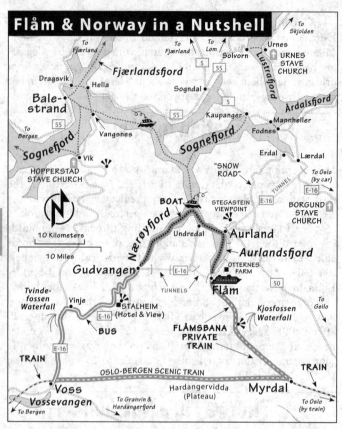

Flåm & Norway in a Nutshell

To Skjolden
To Fjærland
To Fjærland
To Lom
Urnes
Solvorn
URNES
STAVE
CHURCH
Dragsvik
Hella
Sogndal
Lustrafjord
Fjærlandsfjord
Bale-
strand
Kaupanger
Årdalsfjord
Mannheller
To Bergen
Vangsnes
Fodnes
Sognefjord
Erdal
Lærdal
Sognefjord
Vik
To Oslo
(by car)
HOPPERSTAD
STAVE CHURCH
"SNOW
ROAD"
E-16
TUNNEL
BORGUND
STAVE
CHURCH
10 Kilometers
BOAT
STEGASTEIN
VIEWPOINT
10 Miles
Undredal
Aurland
Gudvangen
E-16
Aurlandsfjord
OTTERNES
FARM
Tvinde-
fossen
Waterfall
TUNNELS
Flåm
50
Vinje
STALHEIM
(Hotel & View)
Kjosfossen
Waterfall
To
Geilo
E-16
BUS
FLÅMSBANA
PRIVATE
TRAIN
TRAIN
E-16
OSLO-BERGEN SCENIC TRAIN
TRAIN
Voss
Hardangervidda
(Plateau)
Myrdal
Vossevangen
To Granvin &
Hardangerfjord
To Oslo
(by train)
To Bergen
Nærøyfjord

various segments of the trip. At TIs, train stations, and hotels, look for souvenir-worthy brochures with photos, descriptions, and exact times. However, the suggested "day plan" schedules the TI hands out do not necessarily include *all* options. (For example, on my last visit, their suggested Nutshell day would have made me spend nearly 2 hours in dull Voss; I figured out a connection cutting that layover in half, and getting me back to Flåm with two hours to spare before my ship's departure.)

Timing: In the peak of summer (late June-late Aug), the connections are most convenient, the weather is most likely to be good...and the route is at its most crowded. Outside of this time, sights close and schedules become more challenging. It's easy to confirm schedules, connections, and prices locally or online (latest info posted each May on www.ruteinfo.net).

Eating: Options along the route aren't great—on the Nutshell I'd consider food just as a source of nutrition and forget about fine dining. You can buy some food on the fjord cruises (50-75-kr hot dogs, burgers, and pizza) and the express train line (50-100-kr hot meals, 150-kr daily specials). Depending on the timing of your layovers, Myrdal, Voss, or Flåm are your best lunch-stop options (the Myrdal and Flåm train stations have decent cafeterias, and other eateries surround the Flåm and Voss stations)—although you won't have a lot of time there if you're making the journey all in one day. Plan ahead and buy picnic fixings at a grocery store to bring along. Or consider discreetly raiding your cruise ship's breakfast buffet. (As this is frowned upon, don't tell them I suggested it.)

With a Package Deal or On Your Own? You can either buy the Nutshell loop as a package deal, or you can buy the tickets for each leg individually. As the cost is nearly the same, the main reason to buy the tickets on your own is if you're a student or a senior (and therefore eligible for discounts), or if you happen to have a railpass (which covers or discounts certain legs). Or, if the suggested route doesn't work for you, you can consider mixing and matching schedules to come up with a better plan.

Package Deal: To do the Nutshell as a round-trip loop from Flåm, you'll pay 740 kr. Sold by Fjord Tours (tel. 81 56 82 22, www.fjordtours.no), the Nutshell package can be purchased at the TI in Flåm. If your cruise is visiting Bergen or Oslo before landing in Flåm, you can also prebook the package at the train station in either town (not a bad plan—prebooking allows you to avoid the crowds waiting for the TI to open the morning of your arrival in Flåm). The package comes with all the tickets and reservations you need.

Buying Individual Tickets: If you're booking tickets individually, be aware that certain legs can sell out during busy times. The Flåmsbana ticket can only be purchased on-site, at the train station in Flåm—get there immediately when you get off your ship. In summer, it's smart to reserve the Voss-Myrdal segment in advance, but only if you're on an express train. (For tips on booking both of these trains, see the next section.) You can purchase your fjord-cruise ticket on the boat or from the TI in Flåm (or reserve a day ahead in peak season; see below); and buy the tickets for the Gudvangen bus on board from the driver. Remember, if you're a student or senior, always ask about discounts.

Reservations: Three segments of the Nutshell are prone to selling out, and should be reserved ahead of time: the fjord cruise, the Voss-Myrdal train, and the Myrdal-Flåm mountain train.

The **Voss-Myrdal train** is one segment of Norway's busiest train line, stretching from Bergen to Oslo. Express trains that go this entire distance often sell out, especially at the busiest part of peak season (July-Aug). However, the schedule I recommend uses a local train *(lokaltog)* that doesn't continue all the way to Oslo—

and, therefore, rarely sells out. First determine whether you're taking an intercity train (*fjerntog*, all the way from Bergen to Oslo) or a local train (*lokaltog*, runs only in this region). Then, if you are on an intercity train, reserve the Voss-Myrdal segment in advance, as soon as your itinerary is set—ideally at least a week ahead: Dial 81 50 08 88 or 23 15 15 15 (from the US, call 011-47-81-50-08-88 or 011-47-23-15-15-15), and press 9 for English. It can be difficult to get through to this number in peak season—keep trying. Once connected, you can make a seat reservation (works for railpass holders, too). After booking your seat, you'll be given a reservation number to use to pick up and pay for your ticket at the train station in Norway. It's also possible to obtain a seat reservation by sending an email to help@nsb.no with specifics about the ticket you need. Unfortunately, at this time, tickets cannot be purchased online from the US. Be sure to ask about cancellation policies before you book.

The **Flåmsbana train** is tricky: If several big cruise liners come into Flåm, a few departures of this train can sell out. You can only buy Flåmsbana tickets for a specific departure at one of the Flåmsbana train stations (in Flåm or Myrdal). The only exception is for those buying the Nutshell package, which includes a Flåmsbana ticket for the departure you'll need. (For details, see page 762.)

In busy times, it's smart to reserve ahead for the **Flåm-Gudvangen fjord boat trip**; sellouts are relatively rare, but it can happen (see page 759). You don't need a reservation for the **Gudvangen-Voss bus.**

Last Resort: If one or more of the needed segments are booked up, hope is not lost. If you buy your Nutshell package from the TI, they may have access to segments that are already sold out for those booking individually. And, in a pinch, the Sognefjorden Sightseeing & Tours company has trips that don't use the official Nutshell vehicles. In some cases you can ride their private boat one-way for the same price as the official Nutshell boat—potentially even at a time more convenient to your schedule than the official options. Carefully quiz the TI about this as you're sorting through your options.

A Cruiser's Guide to Doing the Nutshell on Your Own

While your cruise line may push overpriced package deals for doing the Nutshell loop, a savvy cruiser can do exactly the same thing on their own for a fraction of the price. However, to do it smoothly, you'll need to do a little homework (plan out your day ahead of time), get an early start, and stay organized. Once under way, you'll have a blast.

Whether you can do the entire Norway in a Nutshell route if

The Facts on Fjords

The process that created the majestic Sognefjord began during an ice age about three million years ago. A glacier up to 6,500 feet thick slid downhill at an inch an hour, following a former river valley on its way to the sea. Rocks embedded in the glacier gouged out a steep, U-shaped valley, displacing enough rock material to form a mountain 13 miles high. When the climate warmed up, the ice age came to an end. The melting glaciers retreated and the sea level rose nearly 300 feet, flooding the valley now known as the Sognefjord. The fjord is more than a mile deep, flanked by 3,000-foot mountains—for a total relief of 9,300 feet. Waterfalls spill down the cliffs, fed by runoff from today's glaciers. Powdery sediment tinges the fjords a cloudy green, the distinct color of glacier melt.

Why are there fjords on the west coast of Norway, but not, for instance, on the east coast of Sweden? The creation of a fjord requires a setting of coastal mountains, a good source of moisture, and a climate cold enough for glaciers to form and advance. Due to the earth's rotation, the prevailing winds in higher latitudes blow from west to east, so chances of glaciation are ideal where there is an ocean to the west of land with coastal mountains. When the winds blow east over the water, they pick up a lot of moisture, then bump up against the coastal mountain range, and dump their moisture in the form of snow—which feeds the glaciers that carve valleys down to the sea.

You can find fjords along the northwest coast of Europe—including western Norway and Sweden, Denmark's Faroe Islands, Scotland's Shetland Islands, Iceland, and Greenland; the northwest coast of North America (from Puget Sound in Washington state north to Alaska); the southwest coast of South America (Chile); the west coast of New Zealand's South Island; and on the continent of Antarctica.

As you travel through Scandinavia, bear in mind that, while we English-speakers use the word "fjord" to mean only glacier-cut inlets, Scandinavians often use it in a more general sense to include bays, lakes, and lagoons that weren't formed by glacial action.

NORWEGIAN FJORDS

arriving by cruise ship depends on what time your ship arrives and departs. Also, be aware that if more than one ship comes to Flåm in a day, some passengers will have to tender ashore—potentially pushing back your landfall substantially.

Here's a suggested schedule for a cruise arriving at 8:00 (or earlier) and departing at 17:00 (or later). These times are based on 2013 peak-season schedules; it's crucial to reconfirm that this plan will work for your schedule.

Counterclockwise Route (Recommended)

Stepping off your ship or tender, head directly to the TI (inside the train station—see directions on page 746, opens at 8:15) to confirm your plans and buy your Nutshell package, before any of the segments sell out. If all goes well, you may even have a few minutes to kill in Flåm before you hop on your fjord cruise boat.

Nutshell Leg	Depart	Arrive
Boat from Flåm to Gudvangen	9:00	11:10
Bus from Gudvangen up to Voss	11:40	12:55
Train from Voss to Myrdal	13:10	14:00
Flåmsbana train from Myrdal back down to Flåm	14:43	15:40

Clockwise Route

Going the other way—starting with the train from Flåm up to Myrdal, and ending with the fjord cruise back to Flåm—is impractical. Flaws with this plan include: it gets you back to Flåm late in the day (17:50—likely later than your ship's "all aboard" time); the morning Flåmsbana train departures are more likely to sell out; and this plan leaves you with more time in Voss and/or Gudvangen than most would want. But in case it works for you, here's a possible plan for an 8:00 cruise arrival:

Nutshell Leg	Depart	Arrive
Flåmsbana train from Flåm to Myrdal	8:35	9:27
Train from Myrdal to Voss	11:06	11:58
Bus from Voss to Gudvangen	13:00	13:50
Boat from Gudvangen to Flåm	15:45	17:50

Self-Guided Tour of the Nutshell Loop

If you're doing the full loop on your own, here are step-by-step instructions. While 2013 schedules made the counterclockwise loop best for cruisers, you may be able to do it in reverse, depending on your cruise schedule—but you'll have to hold the book upside down.

Nutshell Worksheet

Here's a worksheet for making the most of your time in port. Fill in the times based on schedules for the current year; even if the TI and train ticket office are closed when you arrive (both open at 8:15), use the schedules posted outside to sort this out, so you know what to ask for once you get in:

Nutshell Leg	Depart	Arrive
Your ship arrives in Flåm	N/A	_____
Boat from Flåm to Gudvangen	_____	_____
Bus from Gudvangen to Voss	_____	_____
Train from Voss to Myrdal	_____	_____
Flåmsbana train from Myrdal to Flåm	_____	_____
All aboard in Flåm	_____	N/A

▲▲▲Flåm-Gudvangen Fjord Cruise

From Flåm, scenic sightseeing boats ply the fjord's waters around the corner to Gudvangen. With minimal English narration, the boat takes you close to the goats, sheep, waterfalls, and awesome cliffs.

You'll cruise out the lovely **Aurlandsfjord,** motor by the town of **Aurland,** pass **Undredal,** and then hang a left at the stunning **Nærøyfjord** ("Narrow Fjord"). The cruise ends at the apex of the Nærøyfjord, in **Gudvangen.**

The trip is breathtaking in any weather. For the last hour, as

you sail down the Nærøyfjord, camera-clicking tourists scurry around the drool-stained deck like nervous roosters, scratching fitfully for a photo that will catch the magic. Waterfalls turn the black cliffs into bridal veils, and you can nearly reach out and touch the cliffs of the

Nærøyfjord. It's the world's narrowest fjord: six miles long and as little as 820 feet wide and 40 feet deep. On a sunny day, the ride is one of those fine times—like when you're high on the tip of an Alp—when a warm camaraderie spontaneously combusts between the strangers who've come together for the experience.

Cost: For the whole route (Flåm-Gudvangen), you'll pay 285 kr one-way (143 kr for students with ISIC cards; 390 kr round-trip).

Schedule: In summer (May-Sept), boats run four to five times each day in both directions. Specific departure times can vary, but generally boats leave Flåm at 9:00, 13:20, 15:10, and 18:00 (with an additional 11:00 departure from late June to late Aug); and leave Gudvangen at 10:30, 11:45, 15:45, and 17:40 (with an additional 13:30 departure from late June to late Aug). Frequency drops off-season. The trip takes about two hours and 15 minutes.

Reservations: If your itinerary hinges on a specific departure, it's smart to reserve the boat trip in advance: You can email booking @fjord1.no, book online at www.fjord1.no, or call 55 90 70 70 by 14:00 one business day before.

Other Ways to Cruise Nærøyfjord: While most visitors thunder onto the state-run ferry described above, consider taking a trip on a Sognefjorden Sightseeing & Tours ship, or a thrilling ride on little inflatable FjordSafari speedboats (both described on page 750).

Returning from Gudvangen to Flåm: To head from Gudvangen directly back to Flåm, you can ride a bus that cuts through a tunnel to get there in substantially less time than the two-hour return boat (about 20-25 minutes, 50-65 kr). Some buses depart from right in front of the boat dock, with others leaving from a stop out on the main E-16 highway (an easy 5-minute walk from the boat—just walk straight ahead off the boat and up the town's lone road, past its few houses, until you reach the big cross street; the bus stop is just across this road). While the specific schedule is often in flux, a bus always leaves soon after each boat arrives from Flåm—just ask around for where to catch it.

▲Gudvangen-Voss Bus

Nutshellers get off the boat at Gudvangen and take the bus to Voss. Gudvangen is little more than a boat dock and giant tourist kiosk. If you want, you can browse through the grass-roofed souvenir stores and walk onto a wooden footbridge—then catch your bus. Buses meet each ferry, or will show up soon. While some buses—designed for commuters rather than sightseers—take the direct route to Voss, buses tied to the Nutshell schedule take a super-scenic detour via Stalheim (described below). If you're a waterfall junkie, sit on the left.

First the bus takes you up the **Nærøydal** and plunges you

into a couple of long tunnels. Then you'll take a turnoff to drive past the landmark **Stalheim Hotel** for the first of many spectacular views back into fjord country. While some buses stop at the hotel for a photo op, others drive right past. Though the hotel dates from 1885, there's been an inn here since about 1700, where the royal mailmen would change horses. The hotel is geared for tour groups (genuine trolls sew the pewter buttons on the sweaters), but the priceless view

from the backyard is free. If your bus pauses here, snap your classic photo, then stop in the living room to survey the art showing this perch in the 19th century.

Leaving the hotel, the bus wends its way down a road called **Stalheimskleiva,** with a corkscrew series of switchbacks flanked by a pair of dramatic waterfalls. With its 18 percent grade, it's the steepest road in Norway.

After winding your way down into the valley, you're back on the same highway. The bus goes through those same tunnels again, then continues straight on the main road through pastoral countryside to Voss. You'll pass a huge lake, then follow a crystal-clear, surging river. Just before Voss, look to the right for the wide **Tvindefossen waterfall,** tumbling down its terraced cliff.

Cost: 98 kr, pay on board, no railpass discounts.

Reservations: Not necessary.

Voss

The Nutshell bus from Gudvangen drops you at the Voss train station, which is on the Oslo-Bergen train line. Nutshellers should

catch the next train out. A plain town in a lovely lake-and-mountain setting, Voss lacks the striking fjordside scenery of Flåm, Aurland, or Undredal, and is basically a home base for summer or winter sports (Norway's Winter Olympics teams often practice here). Voss surrounds its fine, 13th-century church with workaday streets—busy with both local shops and souvenir stores—stretching in several directions. Fans of American football may want to see the humble monument to player and coach Knute Rockne, who was born in Voss in 1888; look for the metal memorial plaque on a rock near the train station.

Voss' helpful **TI** is a five-minute walk from the train station—just head toward the church (June-Aug Mon-Fri 8:00-19:00, Sat 9:00-19:00, Sun 12:00-19:00; Sept-May Mon-Fri 8:30-17:00, Sat 9:00-15:00, closed Sun; facing the church in the center of town at Vangsgatan 20, mobile 40 61 77 00, www.visitvoss.no).

▲Voss-Myrdal Train

Although this train line stretches super-scenically all the way from Oslo to Bergen, you'll only do a brief, 40-minute segment right in the middle. Even on this short stretch, you'll see deep woods and lakes as well as barren, windswept heaths and glaciers. The tracks were begun in 1894 to link Stockholm and Bergen, but Norway won its independence from Sweden in 1905, so the line served to link the two main cities in the new country—Oslo and Bergen. The entire railway, an amazing engineering feat completed in 1909, is 300 miles long; peaks at 4,266 feet, which, at this Alaskan latitude, is far above the tree line; goes under 18 miles of snow sheds; trundles over 300 bridges; and passes through 200 tunnels in just under seven hours.

For the best views, sit on the right-hand side of the train. After passing above sprawling Voss, the train goes through two long tunnels and above canyons. You'll enjoy raging-river-and-waterfalls views, then pass over a lake that's very close to the tree line—vegetation clears out and the landscape looks nearly lunar.

Arriving at Myrdal, hop out of the train and simply cross the platform for your awaiting Flåm-bound train. (If it's not there, it will be shortly.)

Cost: The Voss-Myrdal segment costs 113 kr. It's cheaper to book in advance at www.nsb.no. Remember, second-class railpassholders pay just 50 kr to reserve, and first-class passholders pay nothing.

Schedule: The Oslo-Bergen intercity train *(fjerntog)* runs three to five times per day (overnight possible daily except Sat). In addition to this, a local train *(lokaltog)* runs the Voss-Myrdal leg (the one you're interested in). The local train costs the same and takes about 10 minutes longer (for a total travel time of 50 minutes) than the intercity train.

Reservations: In peak season, get reservations for the intercity train at least a week in advance (see page 755); local trains are less likely to fill up, and you can't prebook them online, but it can't hurt to reserve ahead when you buy your Flåmsbana ticket in the morning.

▲▲Myrdal-Flåm Train (Flåmsbana)

The little 12-mile spur line leaves the Oslo-Bergen line at Myrdal (2,800 feet), which is nothing but a scenic high-altitude train junc-

What If I Miss My Boat?

Remember that you can get help from the cruise line's port agent (listed on the destination information sheet distributed on the ship) and the local TI (see page 747). If the port agent suggests a costly solution (such as a private car with a driver), you may want to consider public transit.

If you get left behind, don't panic: You're right in the heart of the well-trafficked Norway in a Nutshell route. Use this chapter's tips to connect up to the main **Oslo-Bergen** train line to reach either of those cities. For **Stavanger,** head for Bergen to catch the boat (likely faster) or to Oslo to catch the train. Flåm is also connected to Bergen by express boat (tel. 51 86 87 00, www.norled.no).

If you need to catch a **plane** to your next destination, you'll probably be best off heading to the airports in Oslo (Gardermoen Airport, tel. 91 50 64 00, www.osl.no) or Bergen (Flesland Airport, tel. 67 03 15 55, www.avinor.no/bergen).

Local **travel agents** in Flåm can help you.

For more advice on what to do if you miss the boat, see page 144.

tion with a decent cafeteria. From Myrdal, the train winds down to Flåm (sea level) through 20 tunnels (more than three miles' worth) in 55 thrilling minutes. It's party time on board, and the engineer even stops the train for photos at the best waterfall, Kjosfossen. According to a Norwegian legend, a temptress lives behind these falls and tries to lure men to the rocks with her singing...look out for her.

The train line is an even more impressive feat of engineering when you realize it's not a cogwheel train—it's held to the tracks only by steel wheels, though it does have five separate braking systems. Before boarding, pick up the free, multilingual souvenir pamphlet with lots of info on the trip (or see www.flaamsbana.no). Video screens onboard and sporadic English commentary on the loudspeakers explain points of interest, but there's not much to say—it's all about the scenery.

While the grass is always greener on the other side of the train, if you're choosing seats, you'll enjoy slightly more scenery if you sit on the west-facing side of the train (on the left going down, on the right going up).

Cost: 280 kr one-way (railpass holders pay 195 kr), 380 kr round-trip. You can buy tickets only at the Flåmsbana stations in Myrdal or Flåm (not at other train ticket offices in Norway—though if you book the whole package in Oslo or Bergen, you can reserve a specific train). If you're in a rush to make a tight connection, you can try to buy them on board (but if the train is sold out, the ticket-takers may send you back to the ticket office).

Schedule: The train departs in each direction nearly hourly.

Reservations: This train can get jammed with travelers, particularly when multiple cruise ships are in Flåm. On trains going from Myrdal down to Flåm, you can always squeeze in, even if it's standing-room only. However, trains ascending from Flåm to Myrdal can sell out, particularly in the morning. You can buy advance tickets for a particular train (though not reserve a specific seat) at the Flåmsbana ticket office in either Flåm or Myrdal, or—if you're booking the full Nutshell—at the train stations in Oslo or Bergen. In practice, this is a concern only for those wanting to go from Flåm to Myrdal in the morning; get to the ticket office early (it opens at 8:15).

Geirangerfjord

The nine-mile-long, 2,000-foot-deep Geirangerfjord (geh-RAHN-gher-fyord), an offshoot of the long Storfjord, snakes like an S-shaped serpent between the cut-glass peaks of western Norway. Tucked amid cliffs one observer termed "the most preposterous mountains on the entire west coast," the Geirangerfjord is simply stunning. Cruising in—and back out again—you'll drift past steep cliffs and cover-girl waterfalls, such as the famous "Seven Sisters" cascades that tumble 800 feet down a long, craggy swath of gray granite. Facing them is a waterfall dubbed "The Suitor," which sputters endlessly in a futile attempt to impress the seven maidens across the way. (Supposedly the waterfall forms a bottle shape, because perennial rejection has driven the would-be suitor to drink.) And, while any Norwegian fjord waterfall looks like a bridal veil to me, Geirangerfjord actually has one named "The Bridal Veil."

All of this beauty makes Geirangerfjord a magnet for cruise ships, about 180 of which (carrying some 300,000 passengers) call at the town of Geiranger during their relatively short season. When even just one big ship is in town, the population of this village of about 250 hardy Norwegians can increase more than tenfold...things get very crowded.

While the town tries hard to entertain all those visitors, there's only so much to do in this sleepy corner of the fjord. And,

Excursions at Geirangerfjord

Of all the ports of call described in this book, Geirangerfjord may be the one where excursions are most worth considering. This is both because of the unique "technical call" arrangement many ships have at Hellesylt (which means paying for an excursion buys you an extra hour or two on land); and because there's relatively little to see in Geiranger town itself, while there's fantastic scenery from up above that's difficult to reach affordably on your own, but easy to reach on an excursion. While Geiranger-based tour operators can get you to many of the worthwhile outlying sights, others—including the fantastic Trollstigen mountain road—are easily accessible only by excursion.

Itineraries starting from **Geiranger town** may include a stop at the Geiranger Fjord Center, the Flydalsjuvet and Dalsnibba viewpoints, and a variety of waterfalls and mountain farms. Some excursions include a guided hike (after a bus ride to the trailhead) up to Storsæter Waterfall, which you can actually walk behind. Other trips head up the Ørnevegen ("Eagle Road") for more views, and some longer trips continue all the way to Trollstigen. You may also be offered kayak tours, RIB (rigid inflatable boat) tours, or mountain-bike trips, all of which can also be booked directly through local agencies (details in this chapter).

If your cruise includes a "technical call" at **Hellesylt,** you'll have the option to pay for an excursion that boards a bus there and drives (gradually) across the mountains to meet your ship in Geiranger, at the far end of the fjord. En route, the tour stops off at Hornindal Lake (Europe's deepest at more than 1,600 feet), the Nordfjord (at the town of Stryn), villages, waterfalls, and more; the final stretch takes you past the Dalsnibba and Flydalsjuvet viewpoints on the way back to your ship. Because it's a one-way journey, this option gives you the maximum Norwegian scenery for your time in this region—but note that it leaves you with very little time back in Geiranger before "all aboard."

compared with Flåm, Geiranger doesn't have the public-transit connections that provide an easy and scenic loop trip without your own wheels. No trains or lifts bring you up into the mountains. Instead, to gain some altitude and reach the famous views—which I highly recommend—you'll have to book a tour (either through your cruise line or a local company), hike steeply up, or pay for a steeply priced taxi.

About half of the cruises that visit the Geirangerfjord make two stops: First comes a "technical call" in the village of Hellesylt, partway along the fjord; second, an hour or two later, there's a call at the village of Geiranger, at the fjord's endpoint. The "technical

Services near the Port of Geiranger

Many of these services are either at the TI (right next to the tender dock) or at the Joker grocery store (marked *Dagligvarer/Grocerie/Lebensmittel*, facing the marina on a lonesome jetty a quick walk around the harbor to the right as you get off your tender).

ATMs: Geiranger's **ATM** (Minibank) is outside the front door of the Joker grocery store.

Internet Access: You can get online at the TI, as well as at Café Olé, Laizas Café, and Hotel Union.

Pharmacy: The Joker grocery stocks basic pharmacy items; there's no full-service pharmacy in Geiranger town or nearby (the nearest—Storfjord Apotek—is in Stranda, halfway out the fjord; tel. 70 26 08 11).

call" in Hellesylt means that only passengers who have paid the cruise line for an excursion are allowed off the ship at this point. (While adventurous travelers may be tempted to get off here to poke around, then make their way by public ferry up the fjord to Geiranger, this is typically not permitted.)

Planning Your Time

For many cruisers, the best part about the Geirangerfjord is the sail-in and sail-away. If you expect good weather in the morning, it's worth getting up early just to experience your ship plying the fjord's glassy waters when it's relatively quiet (the beauty crescendos about an hour before your call time in Geiranger). If you prefer to sleep in, you'll see the same scenery on the way out—but, as weather here can change on a dime, I'd take advantage of any clearing that you get.

To make the most of your Geiranger visit, consider your options before you arrive. Assuming you don't want to purchase a cruise-line excursion but still want to see some of the area (such as mountain farms and high-altitude viewpoints), your best bet is to book a tour through a local company. As these can fill up quickly, decide on your priorities and head straight for the ticket office when you get off your tender (better yet, book in advance).

If you just stick around the town of Geiranger, you'll quickly exhaust all of its sightseeing options. The Geiranger Fjord Center, which can be seen in about an hour, is a 30-minute uphill hike from the port (including a few minutes to dip into the church and enjoy the views). After that, it's just strolling, shopping, hiking, or renting a kayak or bike.

If you're fit and adventurous, and have plenty of time, you could ride a sightseeing boat to the fjord below the remote farm called Skageflå. It takes about an hour to hike up, up, up to the farm, after which you can either hike three to four hours all the way back to Geiranger, or walk back down to the fjord and catch a boat to town (be sure to arrange a pickup time in advance with your tour boat company).

Arrival at the Port of Geiranger

Arrival at a Glance: You'll step off the tender in the heart of town.

Port Overview

It's very simple. Cruise ships tender passengers in to a dock in the harborfront core of town. Stepping off your tender, look right to spot the TI (look for the green-and-white *i* sign). Nearby are the town bus stop, the boat dock for local ferries, souvenir shops, and eateries. Partway along the harbor to the right is the Joker grocery store, with various services (ATM, post office, and more—see the sidebar).

Taxis

If you need a taxi, ask at the TI or call Geiranger Taxi (tel. 40 00 37 41, www.geirangertaxi.no). Here are some sample round-trip fares (for up to 4 people) for trips into the surrounding countryside:

Flydalsjuvet or Ørnesvingen ("Eagle Bend") viewpoint (45 minutes): 700 kr

Flydalsjuvet and Dalsnibba viewpoints combined (2 hours): 1,600 kr

Trollstigen scenic road (4 hours): 3,500 kr

Orientation to Geiranger

Geiranger is basically a one-street town. That street passes the harbor (with the cruise tender dock), then twists up a hill alongside a waterfall, passing the town church, the big Hotel Union, and the Geiranger Fjord Center. Along the waterfront you'll find more hotels, the Joker grocery store, and a campground.

Tourist Information

Geiranger's TI is right along the harborfront (open long hours daily in summer, Internet access, WCs, tel. 70 26 30 99, www.visitalesund-geiranger.com). The TI also has a desk for Geiranger Fjordservice (described in the next section).

NORWEGIAN FJORDS

Tours in Geiranger

As public transportation isn't practical for reaching the country-side splendor near the Geirangerfjord, locally based tour operators may be your most cost-effective way to enjoy maximum fjord beauty in your limited time in port. As the various options tend to sell out when big ships are in port, it's smart either to pre-book (best choice), or to head from your tender straight to the ticket office.

Geiranger Fjordservice, the dominant operation (with a convenient office right inside the Geiranger town TI), offers various tours and excursions out on the fjord and up into the hills (www.geirangerfjord.no). They do sightseeing boat trips (with the option of hopping off for a steep hike up to a mountain farm), speedy RIB tours (ride on a rigid inflatable boat for 40 minutes, 445 kr, hourly departures), a humorously narrated "Viking ship" journey (240 kr, 4/day), panoramic bus rides (described next), fishing trips, helicopter rides, bike tours, and more. Their **scenic bus tour** to the mountain viewpoints at Dalsnibba and Flydalsjuvet helps you efficiently reach the famous Geiranger views (250 kr, 2 hours; mid-June-Aug daily at 9:40, 12:30, and 14:40; sporadically off-season). Their **"Fjord Country Highlights"** tour takes you in the opposite direction, up the "Eagle Road" to Ørnesvingen, tranquil lakes, and a remote cabin (250 kr, 2.75 hours, runs sporadically—check schedule online). For a more flexible alternative, their **hop-on, hop-off bus** loops you around to a variety of famous panoramic viewpoints—including Ørnesvingen and Flydalsjuvet—giving you a few minutes at each one (200 kr, 1.5-hour loop, 5/day). For any tour they offer, you can book ahead online, then bring your voucher to their desk in the TI to pick up your boarding pass.

Coastal Odyssey runs all-day kayak tours up and down the Geirangerfjord (800 kr, departs daily in season at 11:00, be clear on return time, tel. 95 11 80 62, www.coastalodyssey.com). They also offer stand-up paddleboarding lessons and rent kayaks.

Sights on and near Geirangerfjord

In Geiranger
Geiranger Town—This functional little burg, with a waterfall tumbling through its middle, is magnificently set, if not quite "charming." With time to kill in Geiranger, stroll around the harbor, consider a hike into the surrounding hills, and maybe rent a kayak at the campground. To stretch your legs and see the two real "sights" in town, huff steeply up the main street to dip into the small, octagonal town church (with great views from its front

yard) and to visit the Geiranger Fjord Center.

Geiranger Fjord Center (Norsk Fjordsenter)—Overlooking Geiranger's rushing waterfall at the top of town, this modern facility has interactive exhibits that illuminate both the geology and the hardscrabble lifestyles of Norway's fjords. You'll see replicas of typical fjordland homes, and learn about the traditional steamships that tied fjordside communities together when nothing else did.

Cost and Hours: 100 kr, May-Aug daily 10:00-18:00, until 15:00 off-season, a 30-minute walk out of town up the main road, across the road and waterfall from the big Hotel Union, tel. 70 26 38 10, www.dalsnibba.no.

Kayaking—Slicing through still fjord waters on a sea kayak can be an indelible Norwegian memory (and one that's worth booking ahead). You can rent kayaks at **Coastal Odyssey,** based at Geiranger Camping right along the waterfront (single kayak-150 kr/hr, double kayak-300 kr/hour, long hours daily in season, just around the harbor past Joker grocery, tel. 95 11 80 62, www.coastalodyssey.com). They also offer stand-up paddleboarding and lead kayak-plus-hiking tours. **Geiranger Fjordservice's** kayaks are inconveniently located at Grande Camping (on a little lip of land three miles out the fjord from Geiranger)—they can come pick you up in town for an additional fee (rental rates: single kayak-200 kr/up to 3 hours, double kayak-300 kr/up to 3 hours; company details and contact info under "Tours in Geiranger," earlier).

Mountain Biking—**Geiranger Adventure** drops you off at a high mountain road so you can coast back down to the fjord (4/day in summer, tel. 47 37 97 71, www.geiranger-adventure.com). They also rent bikes and cars.

Hiking—Ask the TI for advice about various hikes into the countryside around Geiranger (they sell "Rambling Maps" for 10 kr). Given the village's precarious position—bullied onto a narrow lip of land surrounded by vertical cliffs—expect a steep walk.

Near Geiranger

Most of these sights are best seen either with a cruise-ship excursion or on a tour run by a local company (for options, see earlier). While a public ferry does connect Geiranger to Hellesylt in about an hour (departs about every 1.5 hours, www.fjord1.no), it's unlikely you'll have time to take it on your short port visit—and it's redundant with your ship's sail-away anyway.

Hellesylt—The best way to see this village, which sits at the opposite end of the Geirangerfjord from Geiranger town—is if you pay for a cruise-line excursion that disembarks here. But even if you don't make it, you're not missing much; aside from the huge waterfall thundering furiously through its middle, Hellesylt is a

What If I Miss My Boat?

Remember that you can get help from the cruise line's port agent (listed on the destination information sheet distributed on the ship) and the local TI (see page 767). If the port agent suggests a costly solution (such as a private car with a driver), you may want to consider public transit.

If you're stuck in the town of Geiranger, you can ride a direct bus to **Oslo** (8.5 hours, summer only). To reach **Bergen,** first take the public ferry to Hellesylt (1 hour), where you can hop on the main bus line to Bergen (7.5 hours).

The closest airport to Geiranger is about a three-hour bus ride away, in the city of Ålesund; from here, you can fly to **Oslo, Bergen,** and other Norwegian towns (www.avinor.no /en/airport/alesund).

Local **travel agents** in Geiranger can help you. For more advice on what to do if you miss the boat, see page 144.

sleepy village used primarily as a springboard for the grand scenery that stretches to its east.

Viewpoints and Mountain Drives—From Geiranger, highway 63 twists northward up out of the fjord toward Eidsdal. Corkscrewing up 11 switchbacks, this so-called Ørnevegen ("Eagle Road") was built in 1955 to connect remote little Geiranger to the rest of Norway through the frigid winter months. At the highest hairpin (around 2,000 feet), the viewpoint called Ørnesvingen ("Eagle Bend") offers breathtaking Geirangerfjord panoramas. As the road isn't practical by public transit, you're best off reaching it with a tour, an excursion, or a taxi.

To the south, highway 63 scrambles up out of the Geirangerfjord to two other fantastic viewpoints, offering *the* quintessential Geiranger panoramas. The road first passes **Flydalsjuvet** (a modern viewpoint platform, just a few miles out of Geiranger, that stares straight down a 260-foot-deep gorge to the fjord) before summiting at **Dalsnibba** (high above the tree line at nearly 5,000 feet, more distant views of the fjord, accessible only on the three-mile Nibbevegen toll road off of highway 63, www .dalsnibba.no). Various bus tour itineraries combine these two grand viewpoints efficiently.

Yet another popular scenic road, **Trollstigen,** is farther from Geiranger proper but often included in cruise-line excursions. Connecting the fjord to the town of Åndalsnes, to the north, this famous "Troll's Ladder" (highway 63 past the Ørnevegen) traverses 11 switchbacks and provides perhaps the most spectacular scenery in this land of oh-so-spectacular scenery.

Shelf Farms—Because the cliffs rise directly from the deep—leaving precious few patches for fjordside settlements—any relatively flat surface high on the mountain wall seems occupied by a tidy, lonesome, and aptly named "shelf farm." Most of these, next to impossible to cultivate amid short summers, brutally cold winters, and a constant threat of rockslides, were active well into the 20th century but are now abandoned. A few have been turned into open-air museums that teach visitors about intrepid Norwegian fjord lifestyles. Two popular farms, both perched about 800 feet above the fjord waters, are **Knivsflå** (next to the Seven Sisters falls) and **Skageflå** (directly across the fjord). While visiting these on your own is impractical with a short day in port, various local tour companies offer boat rides from Geiranger to the fjord wall, where you get off and hike up to the farms (figure about an hour if you're in shape). When booking your boat ride, be sure to arrange a pickup time for your return to Geiranger. Alternatively, you can hike (about 3-4 hours) from Skageflå back to Geiranger. Guided visits of the farms are sometimes available—check with your tour company.

NORWEGIAN FJORDS

AMSTERDAM
The Netherlands

Netherlands Practicalities

The Netherlands (Nederland)—sometimes referred to by its nickname, "Holland"—is Europe's most densely populated and also one of its wealthiest and best-organized countries. Occupying a delta near the mouth of three large rivers, for centuries the Netherlands has battled the sea, reclaiming low-lying lands and converting marshy estuaries into fertile farmland. The Netherlands has 16.7 million people: 80 percent are Dutch, and half have no religious affiliation. Despite its small size (16,000 square miles—about twice the size of New Jersey), the Netherlands boasts the planet's 23rd largest economy. It also has one of Europe's lowest unemployment rates, relying heavily on foreign trade through its port at Rotterdam (Europe's largest).

Money: 1 euro (€) = about $1.30. An ATM is called a *geldautomaat*. The local VAT (value-added sales tax) rate is 19 percent; the minimum purchase eligible for a VAT refund is €50 (for details on refunds, see page 139).

Language: The native language is Dutch. For useful phrases, see page 831.

Emergencies: Dial 112 for police, medical, or other emergencies. In case of theft or loss, see page 131.

Time Zone: The Netherlands is on Central European Time (the same as most of the Continent—one hour ahead of Great Britain, and six/nine hours ahead of the East/West Coasts of the US).

Embassies in The Netherlands: The **US consulate** in Amsterdam is at Museumplein 19 (tel. 020/575-5309, after-hours emergency tel. 070/310-2209, http://amsterdam.usconsulate.gov). In The Hague, the **US embassy** is at Lange Voorhout 102 (tel. 070/310-2209, http://netherlands.usembassy.gov), and the **Canadian embassy** is at Sophialaan 7 (tel. 070/311-1600, www.canada.nl). Call ahead for passport services.

Phoning: The Netherland's country code is 31; to call from another country to the Netherlands, dial the international access code (011 from the US/Canada, 00 from Europe, or + from a mobile phone), then 31, followed by the area code (without initial zero) and the local number. For calls within the Netherlands, dial just the number if you are calling locally, and add the area code if calling long distance. To place an international call from the Netherlands, dial 00, the code of the country you're calling (1 for US and Canada), and the phone number. For more tips, see page 1110.

Tipping: As service is included at sit-down meals, you don't need to tip further, though it's nice to round up your bill about 5-10 percent for good service. Round up taxi fares a bit (pay €3 on a €2.85 fare). For more tips on tipping, see page 143.

Tourist Information: www.holland.com

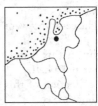

AMSTERDAM

Amsterdam still looks much like it did in the 1600s—the Dutch Golden Age—when it was the world's richest city, an international sea-trading port, and the cradle of capitalism. Wealthy, democratic burghers built a city upon millions of pilings, creating a wonderland of canals lined with trees and townhouses topped with fancy gables. Immigrants, Jews, outcasts, and political rebels were drawn here by its tolerant atmosphere, while painters such as young Rembrandt captured that atmosphere on canvas.

Today's Amsterdam is a progressive place of 820,000 people and almost as many bikes. It's a city of good living, cozy cafés, great art, street-corner jazz, stately history, and a spirit of live and let live. In 2013, Amsterdam celebrated the 400th birthday of its canal system with a series of art festivals, concerts, and special exhibits.

Amsterdam also offers the Netherlands' best people-watching. The Dutch are unique, and observing them is a sightseeing experience all in itself. They're a handsome and healthy people, and among the world's tallest. They're also open and honest—I think of them as refreshingly blunt—and they like to laugh. As connoisseurs of world culture, they appreciate Rembrandt paintings, Indonesian food, and the latest French film—but with an un-snooty, blue-jeans attitude.

Be warned: Amsterdam, a bold experiment in freedom, may box your Puritan ears. For centuries, the city has taken a tolerant approach to things other places try to forbid. Traditionally, the city attracted sailors and businessmen away from home, so it was profitable to allow them to have a little fun. In the 1960s,

Amsterdam became a magnet for Europe's hippies. Since then, it's become a world capital of alternative lifestyles. Stroll through any neighborhood and see things that are commonplace here but rarely found elsewhere. Prostitution is allowed in the Red Light District, while "smartshops" sell psychedelic drugs, and marijuana is openly sold and smoked. (The Dutch aren't necessarily more tolerant or decadent than the rest of us—just pragmatic and looking for smart solutions.)

Approach Amsterdam as an ethnologist observing a strange culture. It's a place where carillons chime quaintly from spires towering above coffeeshops where yuppies go to smoke pot. Take it all in, then pause to watch the clouds blow past stately old gables—and see the Golden Age reflected in a quiet canal.

Planning Your Time

Although Amsterdam does have a few must-see museums, its best attraction is its own carefree ambience. The city's a joy on foot—and a breezier and faster delight by bike. For sightseers who want to do more than relax, these are the top choices:

• **Rijksmuseum:** You can see the highlights of this world-class collection of Dutch Masters in about an hour and a half.

• **Van Gogh Museum:** The planet's best collection of this beloved Dutch artist's work demands at least an hour to see.

• **Anne Frank House:** This evocative sight, in the actual home where Jewish refugees were hidden from the Nazis, is worth an hour.

• **Other Museums:** Depending on your interests, consider the **Stedelijk Museum** (art since 1945), **Amsterdam Museum** (city history), **Amstelkring Museum** ("Our Lord in the Attic" hidden church), and **Dutch Resistance Museum** (ingenuity of anti-Nazi agitators). Each of these merits an hour.

• **Canal Cruise:** A one-hour boat trip offers a fine orientation to the city.

• **Explore Neighborhoods:** Of Amsterdam's many colorful and characteristic neighborhoods, the most popular to explore are the **Jordaan** (an upscale-hipster residential zone at the western edge of downtown) and the **Red Light District** (a fascinating, in-your-face look at legalized prostitution, southeast of Central Station). Allow an hour of strolling apiece.

The two great art museums (Rijks and Van Gogh) cluster near the south end of the town center, so you can tackle things in a geographically logical order: From Central Station, zip to the museums by tram. Then work your way back toward the station (and the cruise terminal), detouring to the Anne Frank House and other sights that interest you as time allows.

Reservations: Amsterdam's top sights—Rijksmuseum, Van

Excursions from Amsterdam

It's easy to do everything in **Amsterdam** on your own, thanks to the Dutch public transportation system and the fact that everyone here speaks English—even the tram drivers. But for those who want more help, you'll find various excursions advertised by your cruise line: bus tours; town walking tours; canal cruises; guided visits to the Van Gogh Museum, Anne Frank House, and Hermitage Amsterdam; diamond-themed tours (including a visit to Gassan Diamonds); and Jewish heritage tours (including a visit to the Jewish Historical Museum and important neighborhoods). All of these sights are easily visited on your own—and in many cases far cheaper for independent travelers. For example, a brief bus tour with a canal cruise offered through a cruise line might cost $50-60, while going with a local company offering an essentially identical cruise costs less than $20.

While Amsterdam is both grand and accessible, big cities aren't for everyone. Various cruise excursions focus on small-town and countryside sights. If you're here during the flower festival at **Keukenhof** (mid-March-mid-May), it's worth touring the remarkable flower gardens there—and a bit tricky by public transportation. Similarly, the beautiful Dutch countryside and villages are challenging to link on your own with limited time; excursion itineraries generally include some combination of the idyllic **Waterland** towns of Edam, Volendam, Marken, and/or Broek; the open-air museum (with great windmills) of **Zaanse Schans;** and the reclaimed land of **Beemster Polder.** And in this little country, you can even do a "Grand Tour of Holland" in one short day, with brief stops in the charming town of **Delft** and the bustling city of **The Hague.** If you'd like to see a lot of the Netherlands in a little time, these excursions are worth doing for the efficiency they provide. But most people find plenty in Amsterdam to keep them entertained.

Gogh Museum, Anne Frank House—suffer from long lines. It's essential to book your tickets for these ahead of time (easiest online; for details, see "Advance Tickets for Major Sights" on page 783). When booking your appointment times, use these guidelines:

• Rijksmuseum: About one hour after your scheduled disembarkation.

• Van Gogh Museum: About two hours after your Rijksmuseum appointment (assuming you'll see the Rijksmuseum very quickly).

• Anne Frank House: About three hours after your Van Gogh appointment (allowing time for lunch, exploring, and strolling to the Anne Frank House).

So, if your ship arrives at 8:00, book the Rijksmuseum for 9:00, Van Gogh for 11:00, and Anne Frank for 14:00. (If you'd prefer more time to savor the Rijksmuseum, push back your Van Gogh and Anne Frank reservations.)

Alternatively, you can spring for a sightseeing pass (described on page 783); for example, the €50 Museumkaart lets you skip lines at both the Rijks and the Van Gogh museums. This won't save you money on a short visit, but it will save you time (and avoid the hassle and tight timetable of reserving individual entrances).

Arrival at the Port of Amsterdam

Arrival at a Glance: Amsterdam's cruise terminal is a three-minute tram ride or 15-minute walk to the central train station, with connections by tram, bus, or boat to anywhere in the city.

Port Overview

Passenger Terminal Amsterdam (PTA)—an ultra-modern facility with a roof that looks like a glass whale—is just minutes away from the center of Amsterdam. Inside the terminal, you'll find an information desk, lockers, an ATM, and shops.

Tourist Information: When ships arrive, the Port of Amsterdam staffs an information desk on the ground floor of the terminal—ask for their map for cruisers. The main Amsterdam TI is right in front of nearby Central Station (for details, see page 781).

Getting into Town

A fleet of taxis wait right outside the terminal, but they're expensive; meanwhile, trams are easy, cheap, and fast. If you're ready to pretend you're an Amsterdammer, there's even a bike rental facility a few steps away.

From the Cruise Terminal to Central Station

It's easy to reach Central Station, either by tram or by foot.

By Tram: Amsterdam's public transit system waits just outside the cruise terminal door. Exiting the terminal, follow the *Town Center* sign and use the crosswalk to cross the busy portside street. You'll see a tram stop with an electric sign reading *Centraal Station* and displaying the arrival time for the next tram. Take tram #26 just one stop to the end of the line, Central Station (runs every 4-8 minutes, trip takes 3 minutes). A one-hour tram ticket costs €2.80; if you'll be taking more than two transit journeys on your visit, buy a €7.50 one-day transit pass, good for all trams and buses (for either ticket, pay the conductor in cash).

By Foot: From the cruise terminal, it's just 15 minutes by **foot** to Amsterdam's Central Station: As you leave the terminal, follow the *Town Center* sign, turn right at the busy road, and walk past the shops, hotel, and concert hall (Bimhuis). Continue walking with the water on your right—you'll see the glass-and-steel arch of the station's roof. You'll end up walking between the station and the water; when you come to a major crosswalk (on your left), follow the crowds crossing the street to enter the lower level of Central Station.

From Central Station to Other Parts of Town

The portal connecting Amsterdam to the world is the aptly named Central Station (Amsterdam Centraal). The station is packed with shops, eateries (including handy Albert Heijn "to go" supermarkets), ATMs, Internet access, and a pharmacy (see "Services near the Port of Amsterdam" on page 780). Through at least 2014, expect the station and the plaza in front of it to be a construction zone and in a state of some flux.

If you arrive by tram, you'll get off at the Centraal Station stop, in front of the station. If you walk here from the cruise terminal, you'll enter the station through its "back door"—just take the main corridor all the way through (crossing under all the platforms) and follow *Centrum* signs to pop out in front.

The plaza at the station's front is a local transit hub. Orient yourself, standing with your back to the station: Straight ahead, just past the canal, is Damrak street, leading to Dam Square (10-minute walk). To your left are the TI and GVB public-transit offices. Farther to your left are two bike rental places: MacBike (in the station building) and Star Bikes (a 5-minute walk past the station), both listed on page 788.

Just beyond the taxis are platforms for the city's blue **trams,** which come along frequently, ready to take you anywhere your feet won't (buy ticket or pass from conductor; if you bought a tram ticket for the ride from the cruise terminal, it's good for an hour and can be used for a connecting tram ride to wherever you're headed). The following trams are most useful for your sightseeing and depart from the west side of Stationsplein (with the station behind you, they're to your right): Trams #2 (marked *Nieuw Sloten*) and #5 (marked *A'veen Binnenhof*) head south from here to Dam Square, then Leidseplein, then Museumplein—with the **Van Gogh** and **Rijks museums;** tram #1 (marked *Osdorp*) also goes to Leidseplein.

To reach the **Anne Frank House,** it's about a 20-minute walk, or you can ride tram #13, #14, or #17 to the Westermarkt stop, about a block south of the museum's entrance.

Services near the Port of Amsterdam

ATMs: The Travelex ATM by the revolving door as you leave the cruise terminal may not have the best rates; ideally, wait to use the banks of ATMs inside Central Station.

Internet Access: It's easy at cafés all over town, but the best place for serious surfing and email is the towering **Central Library,** which has hundreds of fast terminals and Wi-Fi (€1/30 minutes, Openbare Bibliotheek Amsterdam, daily 10:00-22:00). It's very close to the cruise terminal: Turn right when you leave the terminal, walk with the water on your right, turn left at the first bike/pedestrian path that goes under the train tracks, and follow that path to a modern building facing the inner harbor. The library also has a great view and a comfy cafeteria. The **café** across the street from Central Station (in the white building next to the TI) has pay Internet access and Wi-Fi. **"Coffeeshops,"** which sell marijuana, usually also offer Internet access—letting you surf with a special bravado.

Pharmacy: For over-the-counter remedies, try **Hema** on the main floor of Central Station. For prescriptions, head for **BENU Apotheek** on Dam Square (Mon-Fri 8:30-17:30, Sat 10:00-17:00, Sun 12:00-17:00, Damstraat 2, tel. 020/624-4331). Farther afield, the shop named **DA** (Dienstdoende Apotheek) has all the basics—shampoo and toothpaste—as well as a pharmacy counter hidden in the back (Mon-Sat 9:00-22:00, Sun 11:00-22:00, Leidsestraat 74-76 near where it meets Keizersgracht, tel. 020/627-5351).

Other Services: There are **lockers** on the cruise terminal's first floor (€4-6/24 hours, coins only). AmsterBike **bike rentals** is in the parking garage under the Mövenpick Hotel next door; they offer electric bikes and bike tours as well as regular rentals (daily 9:00-18:00 except closed Wed in winter, tel. 020/419-9063, www.amsterbike.eu; more bike rental options are near Central Station—see page 788). There are also cafés, souvenir shops, and even a Segway rental office next to the terminal.

A variety of **canal boat tours** depart from in front of the station (for details, see page 789).

Other Options from the Cruise Terminal

A taxi ride to the Rijksmuseum or Van Gogh Museum costs about €16. For more on taxis, see page 789.

The blue line of Amsterdam's hop-on, hop-off **Canal Bus** stops at the cruise terminal on its way through scenic canals to the Rijksmuseum and Van Gogh Museum, Leidseplein, and back to Central Station. As you exit the terminal, you'll see the *Canal Bus* sign and dock at the end of the narrow inlet between the buildings and the highway (€24/24-hour pass, ticket also good on green and red lines, about 2/hour in summer, less frequent off-season, tel. 020/656-5574, www.canal.nl). Other canal boat options (including cheaper one-hour orientation tours) depart from in front of Central Station. For more on all of the options, see page 789.

By Tour

For information on local tour options in Amsterdam—including local guides for hire, walking tours, and bus or boat tours—see "Tours in Amsterdam" on page 790.

Returning to Your Ship

From Central Station, take tram #26 one stop to Muziekgebouw Bimhuis. As you face the station's main entrance, the tram stop is on the right—it will be marked *IJburg*.

If you have some extra time before heading back, check out the public library for its view, cheap Internet access, and cafeteria (near the cruise terminal and described in the "Services near the Port of Amsterdam" sidebar).

See page 824 for help if you miss your boat.

Orientation to Amsterdam

Amsterdam's Central Station (Amsterdam Centraal), on the north edge of the city, is your starting point, with the TI, bike rental, and trams branching out in all directions. Damrak is the main north-south axis, connecting Central Station with Dam Square (people-watching and hangout center) and its Royal Palace. From this main street, the city spreads out like a fan, with 90 islands, hundreds of bridges, and a series of concentric canals—named Herengracht (Gentleman's Canal), Keizersgracht (Emperor's Canal), and Prinsengracht (Prince's Canal)—that were laid out in the 17th century, Holland's Golden Age. Amsterdam's major sights are all within walking distance of Dam Square.

To the east of Damrak is the oldest part of the city (today's Red Light District), and to the west is the newer part, where you'll find the Anne Frank House and the peaceful Jordaan neighborhood. Museums and bustling Leidseplein are at the southern edge of the city center.

Tourist Information

"VVV" (pronounced "fay fay fay") is Dutch for "TI," a tourist information office. Amsterdam's tourist offices are crowded and inefficient—avoid them if you can. You can save yourself a trip by

AMSTERDAM

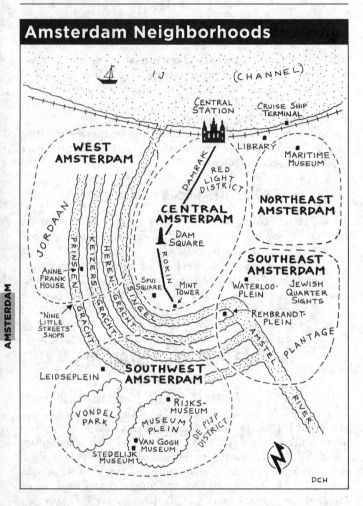

Amsterdam Neighborhoods

calling the TI at 020/201-8800 (Mon-Fri 8:00-18:00) or trying 0900-400-4040 (Mon-Fri 9:00-17:00).

The main TI at Central Station is busy but convenient (July-Aug Mon-Sat 9:00-19:00, Sun 10:00-17:00; Sept-June Mon-Sat 9:00-18:00, Sun 10:00-17:00). An affiliated office is in the AUB/Last Minute Ticket Shop on Leidseplein, tucked into the side of the giant Stadsschouwburg Theater (Mon-Fri 10:00-19:00, Sat 10:00-18:00, Sun 12:00-18:00).

Tickets: Although Amsterdam's main TI sells tickets to the Anne Frank House (€1 extra per ticket, same-day tickets available) and the Van Gogh and Stedelijk museums (no fee), it's quicker to get tickets in advance online (see next page).

Maps and Brochures: Given the city's maze of streets

and canals, I'd definitely get a good city map (€2.50 at Central Station TI, same map given away free at the TI in the AUB/Last Minute Ticket Shop—go figure). Also consider picking up any of the walking-tour brochures (€3 each, including tours covering city center, former Jewish Quarter, Jordaan, and funky De Pijp neighborhood).

Currency Exchange: At Central Station, **GWK Currency Exchange** offices have hotel reservation windows where clerks sell international phone cards and mobile-phone SIM cards, and answer basic tourist questions, with shorter lines than the TI (Mon-Sat 8:00-22:00, Sun 9:00-22:00, near front of station in both the east and west corridors, tel. 020/627-2731).

Resources for Gay Travelers: A short walk from Central Station down Damrak is **GAYtic,** a TI specifically oriented to the needs of gay travelers. The office stocks maps, magazines, and brochures, and dispenses advice on nightlife and general sightseeing (daily 11:00-20:00, Spuistraat 44, tel. 020/330-1461, www.gaytic.nl). **Pink Point,** in a kiosk outside Westerkerk, next to the Homomonument, is less of a resource, but has advice about nightlife (usually daily 10:00-18:00).

Advance Tickets and Sightseeing Cards

During high season (late March-Oct), you can avoid long ticket lines at the **Rijksmuseum, Van Gogh Museum,** and **Stedelijk** modern-art museum by booking tickets online or by getting a Museumkaart sightseeing pass. At the **Anne Frank House,** the only line-skipping option is booking tickets ahead (or, if you have a Museumkaart, reserving an entry time). The I amsterdam Card, also described below, lets you skip the line only at the Van Gogh Museum.

Advance Tickets for Major Sights: It's easy to buy tickets online through each museum's website: www.annefrank.org (€0.50 surcharge per ticket, but worth it), www.rijksmuseum.nl, www.vangoghmuseum.com, and www.stedelijk.nl (no extra fee for Rijks, Van Gogh, or Stedelijk). Print out your ticket and bring it to the ticket-holder's line for a quick entry.

You can also buy tickets for these sights in advance at the TIs (main TI only for Anne Frank House), but TI lines seem almost as long as the ones you're trying to avoid at the sights.

Sightseeing Cards: Two cards merit consideration for heavy-duty sightseers: The Museumkaart and the I amsterdam Card. Both cards allow you free entry to most sights in Amsterdam (including the Van Gogh Museum), but neither card covers the Heineken Brewery, Westerkerk tower, or any sights dealing with sex or marijuana. The Anne Frank House and Rijksmuseum are covered by the Museumkaart but not by the I amsterdam Card.

The Museumkaart is a better option for avoiding crowds (it lets you skip ticket-buying lines everywhere except the Anne Frank House; the I amsterdam Card lets you skip only at the Van Gogh). Note: Even if you skip the ticket line, you have to go through security (like everyone else). You'll also see ads for the Holland Pass, but it's not worth it.

The **Museumkaart** costs €50 and is valid for a year throughout the Netherlands, but it doesn't include public transit. It pays for itself if you visit six museums. While that's unlikely on your short port visit, the ability to skip lines at most sights (except the Anne Frank House) might still be worth the hefty price. The Museumkaart is sold at all participating museums (buy it at a less-crowded one to avoid lines).

The **I amsterdam Card** is probably not worth the cost on a brief port visit. This pass doesn't cover the Rijksmuseum or the Anne Frank House. It does, however, include most other Amsterdam sights (including the Van Gogh Museum), one free canal boat tour (otherwise about €13), and unlimited use of trams, buses, and metro (except for the canal tour, all of these public-transit options are also covered by a normal transit pass—see "Getting Around Amsterdam," later). This card's line-skipping perks are limited to the Van Gogh Museum. It's sold at major museums, TIs, and with shorter lines at the GVB public-transit office across from Central Station, next to the TI (€40/24 hours, €50/48 hours, or €60/72 hours; www.iamsterdamcard.com).

Which Pass to Buy?: On a brief cruise visit, I'd skip all the passes (and make individual reservations at the sights instead), or splurge on the Museumkaart solely for the ability to skip lines.

Helpful Hints

Theft Alert: Tourists are considered green and rich, and the city has more than its share of hungry thieves—especially in the train station, on trams, in and near crowded museums, at places of drunkenness, and at the many hostels. Wear your money belt.

Emergency Telephone Number: Throughout the Netherlands, dial 112.

Street Smarts: Beware of silent transportation—trams, electric mopeds, and bicycles—when walking around town. Don't walk on tram tracks or pink/maroon bicycle paths. Before you step off any sidewalk, do a double- or triple-check in both directions to make sure all's clear.

Sightseeing Strategies: To beat the lines at Amsterdam's most popular sights, plan ahead—either buy a sightseeing pass or advance online tickets (details in previous section). If you're staying in Amsterdam before or after your cruise, Friday night is a great time to visit the Van Gogh Museum, when it's open until 22:00 (with far smaller crowds). On Saturday nights in summer, the Anne Frank House stays open until 22:00.

Shop Hours: Most shops are open Tuesday through Saturday 10:00-18:00, and Sunday and Monday 12:00-18:00. Some shops stay open later (21:00) on Thursdays. Supermarkets are generally open Monday through Saturday 8:00-20:00 and have shorter hours or are closed on Sundays.

Busy Weekends: Every year, **King's Day** (Koningsdag, April 27 most years, but April 26 in 2014) and **Gay Pride** (Aug 1-3 in 2014) bring big crowds.

Cash Only: Thrifty Dutch merchants, who hate paying the unusually high fees charged by credit-card companies here, rarely take US credit cards; expect to pay cash in unexpected places, including grocery stores, cafés, train-station machines and windows, and at some museums.

English Bookstores: For fiction and guidebooks, try the **American Book Center** at Spui 12, right on the square (generally daily 10:00-20:00, tel. 020/535-2575). The huge and helpful **Selexyz Scheltema** is at Koningsplein 20 near the Leidsestraat (generally daily 9:30-18:00; lots of English novels, guidebooks, and maps; tel. 020/523-1411). **Waterstone's Booksellers,** a UK chain, also sells British newspapers (near Spui at 152 Kalverstraat, generally daily 10:00-18:30, tel. 020/638-3821). Expect shorter hours on Monday and Sunday.

Language Barrier: This is one of the easiest places in the non-English-speaking world for an English speaker. Nearly all signs and services are offered in two languages: Dutch and "non-Dutch" (i.e., English).

Maps: The free tourist maps can be confusing, except for *Amsterdam Museums: Guide to 37 Museums* (includes tram info and stops, ask for it at the big museums, such as the Van Gogh). If you want a top-notch map, buy one (about €2.50). I like the *Carto Studio Centrumkaart Amsterdam*. Amsterdam Anything's virtual "Go Where the Locals Go" city map is worth checking out, especially if you have mobile Internet access (www.amsterdamanything.nl).

Laundry: Try **Clean Brothers Wasserij** in the Jordaan (daily 8:00-20:00 for €7 self-service, €9 drop-off—ready in an hour—Mon-Fri 9:00-17:00, Sat 9:00-18:00, no drop-off Sun, Westerstraat 26, one block from Prinsengracht, tel. 020/627-9888) or **Powders,** near Leidseplein (daily 8:00-22:00, €6.50 self-service, €12 drop-off available Mon-Wed and Fri 8:00-17:00, Sat-Sun 9:00-15:00, no drop-off Thu, Kerkstraat 56, one block south of Leidsestraat, mobile 06-2630-6057).

Best Views: Although sea-level Amsterdam is notoriously horizontal, there are a few high points where you can get the big picture. The best city views are from the **Central Library** (Openbare Bibliotheek Amsterdam; see page 805). The **Westerkerk**—described on page 801 and convenient for anyone visiting the Anne Frank House—has a climbable tower with fine views. The tower of the **Old Church** (Oude Kerk), the top floor of the **Kalvertoren** shopping complex, and the rooftop terrace at the **NEMO science museum** also provide good views.

Updates to this Book: Check www.ricksteves.com/update for any significant changes that have occurred since this book was printed.

Getting Around Amsterdam

Amsterdam is big, and you'll find the trams handy. The longest walk a tourist would make is an hour from Central Station to the Rijksmuseum. When you're on foot, be extremely vigilant for silent but potentially painful bikes, trams, and crotch-high bollards.

By Tram, Bus, and Metro

Amsterdam's public transit system includes trams, buses, and an underground metro; of these, trams are most useful for the majority of tourists.

The helpful **GVB public-transit information office** in front of Central Station can answer questions (next to TI, Mon-Fri 7:00-21:00, Sat-Sun 10:00-18:00). Its free, multilingual *Public Transport Amsterdam Tourist Guide* includes a transit map and explains ticket options and tram connections to all the sights. For more public transit information, visit www.gvb.nl.

Tickets: The entire country's public transit network operates on a single ticket system called the OV-Chipkaart (for "Openbaar Vervoer"—public transit). However, this system works best for locals and isn't practical for visitors (it requires a non-refundable €7.50 deposit and can only be reloaded at train stations)—on a brief cruise visit, don't bother. Instead, most travelers rely on either single tickets or multiday passes. (While officially classified as "OV-Chipkaarten," these tickets and passes with electronic chips are nothing like the reloadable, valid-nationwide, plastic cards locals use.)

Within Amsterdam, a single transit ticket costs €2.80 and is good for one hour on the tram, bus, and metro, including transfers. Passes good for unlimited transportation are available for 24 hours (€7.50), 48 hours (€12), 72 hours (€16.50), and 96 hours (€21). (The I amsterdam sightseeing card, described on page 783, includes a transit pass.) Given how expensive single tickets are, consider buying a pass before you buy that first ticket. (A rental bike—described later—costs about the same as a transit pass...but is way more fun.)

The easiest way to buy a ticket or transit pass is to simply board a tram or bus and pay the conductor (no extra fee). Tickets and passes are also available at metro-station vending machines (which take cash but not US credit cards), at GVB public-transit offices, and at TIs.

Trams: Board the tram at any entrance not marked with a red/white "do not enter" sticker. If you need a ticket or pass, pay the

conductor (in a booth at the back); if there's no conductor, pay the driver in front. You must always "check in" as you board by scanning your ticket or pass at the pink-and-gray scanner, and "check out" by scanning it again when you get off. The scanner will beep and flash a green light after a successful scan. Be careful not to accidentally scan your ticket or pass twice while boarding, or it becomes

invalid. Checking in and out is very important, as controllers do pass through and fine violators. To open the door when you reach your stop, press a green button on one of the poles near an exit.

Trams #2 *(Nieuw Sloten)* and #5 *(A'veen Binnenhof)* travel the north-south axis, from Central Station to Dam Square to Leidseplein to Museumplein (Van Gogh and Rijks museums). Tram #1 *(Osdorp)* also runs to Leidseplein. At Central Station, these three trams depart from the west side of Stationsplein (with the station behind you, they're to your right).

Tram #14, which doesn't connect to Central Station, goes east-west (Westerkerk-Dam Square-Muntplein-Waterlooplein-Plantage). If you get lost in Amsterdam, don't sweat it—10 of the city's 17 trams take you back to Central Station.

Buses and Metro: Tickets and passes work on buses and the metro just as they do on the trams—scan your ticket or pass to "check in" as you enter and again to "check out" when you leave. The metro system is scant—used mostly for commuting to the suburbs—but it does connect Central Station with some sights east of Damrak (Nieuwmarkt-Waterlooplein-Weesperplein). The glacial speed of the metro-expansion project is a running joke among cynical Amsterdammers.

By Bike

Everyone—bank managers, students, pizza delivery boys, and police—uses this mode of transport. It's by far the smartest way to travel in a city where 40 percent of all traffic rolls on two wheels. You'll get around town by bike faster than you can by taxi. One-speed bikes, with *"brrrringing"* bells, rent for about €10 per day at any number of places.

Rental Shops: Star Bikes Rental has cheap rates, long hours, and inconspicuous black bikes (€5/3 hours, €7/day, €9/24 hours, €12/2 days, €17/3 days, daily 9:00-19:00, requires ID but no monetary deposit, 5-minute walk from east end of Central Station—walk underneath tracks near Doubletree Hotel and then turn right, De Ruyterkade 127, tel. 020/620-3215, www.starbikesrental.com).

MacBike, with thousands of bikes, is the city's bike-rental powerhouse—you'll see their bright-red bikes all over town (they do stick out a bit). It has a huge and efficient outlet at Central Station (€7/3 hours, €9.50/24 hours, €14/48 hours, €19/72 hours, more for 3 gears, 25 percent discount with I amsterdam Card; either leave €50 deposit plus a copy of your passport, or leave a credit-card imprint; free helmets, daily 9:00-17:45; at east end of station—on the left as you're leaving; tel. 020/620-0985, www.macbike.nl). They have two smaller satellite stations at Leidseplein (Weteringschans 2) and Waterlooplein (Nieuwe Uilenburgerstraat 116). Return your bike to the station where you rented it. MacBike sells several pamphlets (for €1-2) outlining bike tours with a variety of themes in and around Amsterdam.

Frederic Rent-a-Bike, a 10-minute walk from Central Station, has quality bikes and a helpful staff (€8/3 hours, €15/24 hours—€10 if returned by 17:30, €25/48 hours, €50/week, 10 percent discount with this book, daily 9:00-17:30, no after-hours drop-off, Brouwersgracht 78, tel. 020/624-5509, www.frederic.nl, Frederic and son Marne).

Lock Your Bike: Bike thieves are bold and brazen in Amsterdam. Bikes come with two locks and stern instructions to use both. The wimpy ones go through the spokes, whereas the industrial-strength chains are meant to be wrapped around the actual body of the bike and through the front wheel, and connected to something stronger than any human. (Note the steel bike-hitching racks sticking up all around town, called "staples.") Follow your rental agency's locking directions diligently. Once, I used both locks, but my chain wasn't around the main bar of my bike's body. In the morning, I found only my front tire (still safely chained to the metal fence). If you're sloppy, it's an expensive mistake and one that any "included" theft insurance won't cover.

More Tips: As the Dutch believe in fashion over safety, no one here wears a helmet. They do, however, ride cautiously, and so should you: Use arm signals, follow the bike-only traffic signals, stay in the obvious and omnipresent bike lanes, and yield to traffic on the right. Fear oncoming trams and tram tracks. Carefully cross tram tracks at a perpendicular angle to avoid catching your tire in the rut. Warning: Police ticket cyclists just as they do drivers. Obey all traffic signals, and walk your bike through pedestrian zones. Fines for biking through pedestrian zones are reportedly €30-50. A handy bicycle route-planner can be found at www.routecraft.com (select "bikeplanner," then click British flag for English).

For information on **bike tours,** see page 791.

By Boat

While the city is great on foot, bike, or tram, you can also get around Amsterdam by boat. **Rederij Lovers** boats shuttle tourists on a variety of routes covering different combinations of the city's top sights. Their Museum Line, for example, costs €16 and stops near the Hermitage, Rijksmuseum/Van Gogh Museum, and Central Station (at least every 45 minutes, 4 stops, 1.5 hours). Sales booths in front of Central Station (and the boats) offer free brochures listing museum hours and admission prices. Most routes come with recorded narration and run daily 10:00-17:30 (tel. 020/530-1090, www.lovers.nl).

The similar **Canal Bus** is actually a boat, offering 17 stops—including one at the cruise terminal—on three different boat routes (€24/24-hour pass, departures daily 9:30-18:30, until 19:00 April-Oct, leaves near Central Station and Rederij Lovers dock, tel. 020/623-9886, www.canal.nl).

If you're simply looking for a floating, nonstop tour, the regular canal tour boats (without the stops) give more information, cover more ground, and cost less (see "Tours in Amsterdam," next page).

For do-it-yourself canal tours and lots of exercise, Canal Bus also rents "canal bikes" (a.k.a. paddleboats) at several locations: near the Anne Frank House, near the Rijksmuseum, near Leidseplein, and where Leidsestraat meets Keizersgracht (€8/hour per person, daily July-Aug 10:00-22:00, Sept-June 10:00-18:00).

By Taxi

For short rides, Amsterdam is a bad town for taxis. Given the good tram system and ease of biking, I use taxis less in Amsterdam than in just about any other city in Europe. The city's taxis have a high drop charge (€7.50) for the first two kilometers (e.g., from Central Station to the Mint Tower), after which it's €2.30 per kilometer (no extra fee for luggage; it's worth trying to bargain a lower rate, as competition among cabbies is fierce). You can wave them down, find a rare taxi stand, or call one (tel. 020/677-7777). You'll also see **bike taxis,** particularly near Dam Square and Leidseplein. Negotiate a rate for the trip before you board (no meter), and they'll wheel you wherever you want to go (€1/3 minutes, no surcharge for baggage or extra weight, sample fare from Leidseplein to Anne Frank House: about €6).

Tours in Amsterdam

To sightsee on your own, download my series of **free audio tours** that illuminate some of Amsterdam's top neighborhoods: my Amsterdam City Walk, Red Light District Walk, and Jordaan Walk (see sidebar on page 52 for details).

By Boat

▲▲Canal Boat Tours—These long, low, tourist-laden boats leave continually from several docks around town for a relaxing, if unin-

spiring, one-hour introduction to the city (with recorded headphone commentary). Select a boat tour based on convenience of its starting point, or whether it's included with your I amsterdam Card (which covers Blue Boat Company and Holland International boats). Tip: Boats leave only when full, so jump on a full boat to avoid waiting at the dock. No fishing allowed—but bring your camera.

Choose from one of these three companies:

Rederij P. Kooij is cheapest (€9, 3/hour in summer 10:00-22:00, 2/hour in winter 10:00-17:00, at corner of Spui and Rokin streets, about 10 minutes from Dam Square, tel. 020/623-3810, www.rederijkooij.nl).

Blue Boat Company's boats depart from near Leidseplein (€14; every half-hour April-Sept 10:00-18:00, also at 19:00; hourly Oct-March 10:00-17:00; 1.25 hours, Stadhouderskade 30, tel. 020/679-1370, www.blueboat.nl).

Holland International offers a standard one-hour trip and a variety of longer tours from the docks opposite Central Station (€14, 1-hour "100 Highlights" tour with recorded commentary, 4/hour daily 9:00-18:00, 2/hour 18:00-22:00; Prins Hendrikkade 33a, tel. 020/625-3035, www.hir.nl).

Electric-Powered Canal Boats—Small, 12-person electric Canal Hopper boats leave every 20-30 minutes with live commentary on two different hop-on, hop-off routes (€24 day pass,

€17 round-trip ticket, July-Aug daily 10:00-17:00, Sept-June Fri-Sun only, "yellow" west route runs 2/hour and stops near Anne Frank House and Rijksmuseum, "orange" east route runs 3/hour and stops near Red Light District and Damrak, tel. 020/626-5574, www.canal.nl).

By Foot

Free City Walk—New Europe Tours "employs" native English-speaking students to give irreverent and entertaining three-hour walks (using the same "free tour, ask for tips, sell their other tours" formula popular in so many great European cities). While most guides lack a local's deep understanding of Dutch culture, not to mention professional training, they're certainly high-energy. This long walk covers a lot of the city with an enthusiasm for the contemporary pot-and-prostitution scene (free but tips expected, daily at 11:15 and 13:15, www.neweuropetours.eu). They also offer paid tours (Red Light District—€12, daily at 19:00; coffeeshop scene—€12, daily at 16:00; city by bike—€19, includes bike, daily at 14:00). Their walking tours leave from the National Monument on Dam Square; the bike tour leaves from Central Station.

Adam's Apple Tours—Frank Sanders' walking tour offers a two-hour, English-only look at the historic roots and development of Amsterdam. You'll have a small group of generally 5-6 people and a caring guide, starting off at Central Station and ending up at Dam Square (€25; May-Sept daily at 10:00, 12:30, and 15:00 based on demand; call 020/616-7867 to confirm times and book).

Private Guide—Albert Walet is a likeable, hardworking, and knowledgeable local guide who enjoys personalizing tours for Americans interested in knowing his city. Al specializes in history, architecture, and water management, and exudes a passion for Amsterdam (€70/2 hours, €120/4 hours, up to 4 people, on foot or by bike, mobile 06-2069-7882, abwalet@yahoo.com).

By Bike

Yellow Bike Guided Tours offers city bike tours of either two hours (€19.50, daily at 10:30) or three hours (€23.50, daily at 13:30), which both include a 20-minute break. They also offer a four-hour, 15-mile tour of the dikes and green pastures of the countryside (€29.50, lunch extra, includes 45-minute break, April-Oct daily at 10:30). All tours leave from Nieuwezijds Kolk 29, three blocks from Central Station (reservations smart, tel. 020/620-6940, www.yellowbike.nl). If you'd prefer a private guide, see Albert Walet, above.

Joy Ride Bike Tours is a creative little company run by English-speaking Sean and Allison Cody. Their most popular tours start just behind the Rijksmuseum (city by bike—€26, 2.5-3

Amsterdam at a Glance

▲▲▲**Rijksmuseum** Best collection anywhere of the Dutch Masters—Rembrandt, Hals, Vermeer, and Steen—in a spectacular setting. **Hours:** Daily 9:00-17:00. See page 794.

▲▲▲**Van Gogh Museum** 200 paintings by the angst-ridden artist. **Hours:** Daily 9:00-17:00, Fri until 22:00. See page 796.

▲▲▲**Anne Frank House** Young Anne's hideaway during the Nazi occupation. **Hours:** March 15-Sept 14 daily 9:00-21:00, Sat and July-Aug until 22:00; Sept 15-March 14 daily 9:00-19:00, Sat until 21:00. See page 800.

▲▲**Stedelijk Museum** The Netherlands' top modern-art museum, recently and extensively renovated. **Hours:** Tue-Wed 11:00-17:00, Thu 11:00- 22:00, Fri-Sun 10:00-18:00, closed Mon. See page 797.

▲▲**Vondelpark** City park and concert venue. **Hours:** Always open. See page 798.

▲▲**Amsterdam Museum** City's growth from fishing village to trading capital to today, including some Rembrandts and a playable carillon. **Hours:** Mon-Fri 10:00-17:00, Sat-Sun 11:00-17:00. See page 803.

▲▲**Amstelkring Museum** Catholic church hidden in the attic of a 17th-century merchant's house. **Hours:** Mon-Sat 10:00-17:00, Sun and holidays 13:00-17:00. See page 804.

▲▲**Red Light District Walk** Women of the world's oldest profession on the job. **Hours:** Best from noon into the evening; avoid late at night. See page 804.

▲▲**Netherlands Maritime Museum** Rich seafaring story of the Netherlands, told with vivid artifacts. **Hours:** Daily 9:00-17:00. See page 806.

▲▲**Hermitage Amsterdam** Russia's Tsarist treasures, on loan from St. Petersburg. **Hours:** Daily 10:00-17:00, Wed until 20:00. See page 809.

▲▲**Dutch Resistance Museum** History of the Dutch struggle against the Nazis. **Hours:** Tue-Fri 10:00-17:00, Sat-Mon 11:00-17:00. See page 811.

▲**Museumplein** Square with art museums, street musicians, crafts, and nearby diamond demos. **Hours:** Always open. See page 797.

▲**Leidseplein** Lively square with cafés and street musicians. **Hours:** Always open, best on sunny afternoons. See page 798.

▲**Royal Palace** Lavish City Hall that takes you back to the Golden Age of the 17th century. **Hours:** Daily 11:00-17:00 when not closed for official ceremonies. See page 801.

▲**Begijnhof** Quiet courtyard lined with picturesque houses. **Hours:** Always open. See page 803.

▲**Hash, Marijuana, and Hemp Museum** All the dope, from history and science to memorabilia. **Hours:** Daily 10:00-23:00. See page 805.

▲**EYE Film Institute Netherlands** Film museum and cinema complex housed in a futuristic new building. **Hours:** Exhibits open daily 11:00-18:00, cinemas open roughly 10:00-24:00. See page 807.

▲**Rembrandt's House** The master's reconstructed house, displaying his etchings. **Hours:** Daily 10:00-17:00. See page 808.

▲**Diamond Tours** Offered at shops throughout the city. **Hours:** Generally daily 9:00-17:00. See page 808.

▲**Willet-Holthuysen Museum** Elegant 17th-century house. **Hours:** Mon-Fri 10:00-17:00, Sat-Sun 11:00-17:00. See page 809.

▲**Jewish Historical Museum** The Great Synagogue and exhibits on Judaism and culture, with Portuguese Synagogue across the street. **Hours:** Daily 11:00-17:00. See page 810.

▲**Dutch Theater** Moving memorial in former Jewish detention center. **Hours:** Daily 11:00-16:00. See page 811.

▲**Tropical Museum** Re-creations of tropical-life scenes. **Hours:** Tue-Sun 10:00-17:00, closed Mon. See page 812.

hours, May-Sept departs Fri-Mon at 16:00, none Tue-Thu, no kids under 13; countryside by bike—€30, 4-4.5 hours, May-Sept departs Thu-Mon at 10:30, none Tue-Wed, no kids under 10; no tours off-season). Both tours are limited to 10-15 people, so it's smart to book ahead (save €3 by booking online, €7 cheaper with your own bike—must email or call ahead, tours meet 15 minutes before departure time, helmets and rain gear available, mobile 06-4361-1798, www.joyridetours.nl). Their four-hour "bespoke" tours, offered year-round, are tailored to match your interests (Jewish history, Amsterdam for kids, WWII history, or cannabis; €125/3 people).

Sights in Amsterdam

One of Amsterdam's delights is that it has perhaps more small specialty museums than any other city its size. From marijuana to Old Masters, you can find a museum to suit your interests.

For tips on how to save time otherwise spent in the long ticket-buying lines of the big three museums—the Anne Frank House, Van Gogh Museum, and Rijksmuseum—see "Advance Tickets and Sightseeing Cards" on page 783.

Most museums require baggage check (usually free, often in coin-op lockers where you get your coin back).

The following sights are arranged by neighborhood for handy sightseeing.

Southwest Amsterdam

▲▲▲Rijksmuseum—At the Rijksmuseum ("Rijks" rhymes with "bikes"), Holland's Golden Age shines with the best collection anywhere of the Dutch Masters—from Vermeer's quiet domestic scenes, to Steen's raucous family meals, to Hals' snapshot portraits, to Rembrandt's moody brilliance. Recently much improved after a long renovation, this delightful museum offers one of the most exciting and enjoyable art experiences in Europe.

The 17th century saw the Netherlands at the pinnacle of its power. The Dutch had won their independence from Spain, trade and shipping boomed, wealth poured in, the people were understandably proud, and the arts flourished. This era was later dubbed the Dutch Golden Age. With no church bigwigs or royalty around to commission big canvases in the Protestant Dutch republic, artists had to find different patrons—and they discovered the upper-middle-class businessmen who fueled Holland's capitalist economy. Artists painted their portraits and decorated their homes with pretty still lifes and nonpreachy, slice-of-life art.

Amsterdam

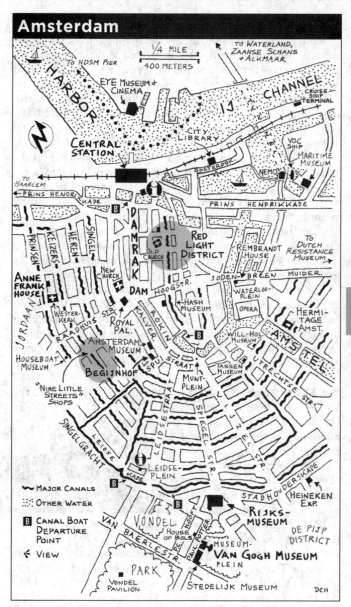

1/4 MILE
400 METERS

TO WATERLAND,
ZAANSE SCHANS
& ALKMAAR

TO NDSM PIER

HARBOR

IJ CHANNEL

CRUISE
SHIP
TERMINAL

EYE MUSEUM &
CINEMA

CITY
LIBRARY

VOC
SHIP

MARITIME
MUSEUM

CENTRAL
STATION

OOSTERDOK

NEMO

TO
HAARLEM

PRINS HENDRIKKADE

PRINS HENDRIKKADE

KADE

DAMRAK

RED
LIGHT
DISTRICT

REMBRANDT
HOUSE

TO
DUTCH
RESISTANCE
MUSEUM

PRINSEN

KEIZERS

HEREN

SINGEL

OLD
CHURCH

NEW
CHURCH

JODEN-BREEN MUIDER.

ANNE
FRANK
HOUSE

WESTER-
KERK

DAM

HOOGSTR.

HASH
MUSEUM

WATERLOO-
PLEIN

OPERA

HERMI-
TAGE
AMST.

JORDAAN

RAADHUIS STR.

ROYAL
PAL.

KALVER.

ROKIN

WILL-HOL
MUSEUM

AMSTEL

HOUSEBOAT
MUSEUM

AMSTERDAM
MUSEUM

SPUISTRAAT

TASSEN
MUSEUM

UTRECHTSE STR.

BEGIJNHOF

MUNT-
PLEIN

"NINE LITTLE
STREETS"
SHOPS

SINGELGRACHT

LEIDSE

LEIDSESTRAAT

SPIEGEL STR.

LIJN-...-STR.

LEIDSE-
PLEIN

KADE

STADHOUDERSKADE

HEINEKEN
EXP.

MAJOR CANALS

OTHER WATER

B CANAL BOAT
DEPARTURE
POINT

VIEW

VAN

VONDEL

BAERLESTR.

P.C. HOOFT

HOUSE
of BOLS

PAUL POTTER.

RIJKS-
MUSEUM

MUSEUM-

DE PIJP
DISTRICT

VAN GOGH MUSEUM
PLEIN

PARK

VONDEL
PAVILION

STEDELIJK MUSEUM

DCH

Dutch art is meant to be enjoyed, not studied. It's straight-forward, meat-and-potatoes art for the common man. The Dutch love the beauty of everyday things painted realistically and with exquisite detail. Set your cerebral cortex on "low" and let this art pass straight from the eyes to the heart, with minimal detours.

Cost and Hours: €15, not covered by I amsterdam Card, audioguide-€5, videoguide also available, daily 9:00-17:00, last entry 30 minutes before closing, tram #2 or #5 from Central Station to Hobbemastraat, info tel. 020/674-7047 or switchboard tel. 020/674-7000, www.rijksmuseum.nl. The entrance is off the passageway that tunnels right through the center of the building.

Avoiding Crowds: The museum is most crowded from April to September (especially April-June), on weekends, and during morning hours. You can avoid crowds by coming later in the day (it's least crowded after 16:00—but most visitors will want more than an hour here). Avoid waits in the ticket-buying line by buying your ticket or pass in advance. No one can completely avoid the security line.

You can buy and print your ticket in advance online at www.rijksmuseum.nl. The ticket is good any time (no entry time specified). Buying online has the added advantage of letting you enter through the "direct entry" doorway, scooting you to the front of the security line. If you're staying overnight in Amsterdam before or after a cruise, you may be able to buy your ticket through your hotel.

▲▲▲**Van Gogh Museum**—Near the Rijksmuseum, the Van Gogh Museum (we say "van GO," the Dutch say "van HHHOCK") is a cultural high even for those not into art. This remarkable museum features works by the troubled Dutch artist whose art seemed to mirror his life. Vincent, who killed himself

in 1890 at age 37, is best known for sunny, Impressionist canvases that vibrate and pulse with vitality. The museum's 200 paintings—which offer a virtual stroll through the artist's work and life—were owned by Theo, Vincent's younger, art-dealer brother. If you like brightly colored landscapes in the Impressionist style, you'll like this museum. If you enjoy finding deeper meaning in works of art, you'll really love it. The mix of Van Gogh's creative genius, his tumultuous life, and the traveler's determination to connect to it makes this museum as much a walk with Vincent as with his art.

The main collection of Van Gogh paintings on the first floor is arranged chronologically, taking you through the changes in Vincent van Gogh's life and styles. The paintings are divided into five periods of Vincent's life—the Netherlands, Paris, Arles, St. Rémy, and Auvers-sur-Oise—proceeding clockwise around the floor. Highlights include *Sunflowers, The Bedroom, The Potato Eaters,* and many brooding self-portraits.

The third floor shows works that influenced Vincent, from Monet and Pissarro to Gauguin, Cézanne, and Toulouse-Lautrec. The worthwhile audioguide includes insightful commentaries and quotes from Vincent himself. Temporary exhibits fill the new wing, down the escalator from the ground-floor lobby.

Cost and Hours: €15, more for special exhibits, audioguide-€5, kids' audioguide-€2.50, daily 9:00-17:00, Fri until 22:00—with no crowds in evening, Paulus Potterstraat 7, tram #2 or #5 from Central Station to Van Baerlestraat stop, tel. 020/570-5200, www.vangoghmuseum.com.

Avoiding Lines: Skip the 15-30-minute wait in the ticket-buying line by getting your ticket in advance, or by getting a Museumkaart or I amsterdam Card. You can buy and print tickets online (at www.vangoghmuseum.com) or at the TI.

▲▲**Stedelijk Museum**—The Netherlands' top modern-art museum is filled with a fun, far-out, and refreshing collection that

includes post-1945 experimental and conceptual art as well as works by Picasso, Chagall, Cézanne, Kandinsky, and Mondrian. The Stedelijk (STAYD-eh-lik), like the Rijksmuseum, also boasts a newly spiffed-up building, which now flaunts an architecturally daring entry facing Museumplein (near the Van Gogh Museum).

Cost and Hours: €15, Tue-Wed 11:00-17:00, Thu 11:00-22:00, Fri-Sun 10:00-18:00, closed Mon, café with outdoor seating, top-notch shop, Paulus Potterstraat 13/Museumplein 10, tel. 020/573-2911, www.stedelijk.nl.

▲**Museumplein**—Bordered by the Rijks, Van Gogh, and Stedelijk museums, and the Concertgebouw (classical music hall), this park-like square is interesting even to art-haters. Amsterdam's best acoustics are found underneath the Rijksmuseum, where street musicians perform everything from chamber music to Mongolian throat singing. Mimes, human statues, and crafts booths dot the square. Skateboarders careen across a concrete tube, while locals enjoy a park bench or a coffee at the Cobra Café.

Nearby is **Coster Diamonds,** a handy place to see a diamond-cutting and polishing demo (free, frequent, and interesting 30-minute tours followed by sales pitch, popular for decades with tour groups, prices marked up to include tour guide

kickbacks, daily 9:00-17:00, Paulus Potterstraat 2, tel. 020/305-5555, www.costerdiamonds.com). The end of the tour leads you straight into their Diamond Museum, which is worthwhile only for those who have a Museumkaart (which covers entry) or feel the need to see even more diamonds (€7.50, daily 9:00-17:00, tel. 020/305-5300, www.diamantmuseumamsterdam.nl). The tour at **Gassan Diamonds** is free and better (see page 808), but Coster is convenient to the Museumplein scene.

Heineken Experience—This famous brewery, having moved its operations to the suburbs, has converted its original headquarters into a slick, Disneyesque beerfest—complete with a beer-making simulation ride. The "experience" also includes do-it-yourself music videos, photo ops that put you inside Heineken logos and labels, and no small amount of hype about the Heineken family and the quality of their beer. It's a fun trip, if you can ignore the fact that you're essentially paying for an hour of advertising (overpriced at €17, includes two drinks, daily 11:00-19:00, last entry at 17:30; tram #16, #24, or #25 to Heinekenplein; an easy walk from Rijksmuseum, tel. 020/523-9222, www.heinekenexperience.com).

De Pijp District—This former working-class industrial and residential zone (behind the Heineken Experience, near the Rijksmuseum) is emerging as a colorful, vibrant district. Its spine is Albert Cuypstraat, a street taken over by a long, sprawling produce market packed with interesting people. The centerpiece is **Restaurant Bazar** (marked by a roof-capping golden angel), a church turned into a Middle Eastern food circus (see listing on page 819).

▲**Leidseplein**—Brimming with cafés, this people-watching mecca is an impromptu stage for street artists, accordionists, jugglers, and unicyclists. It's particularly bustling on sunny afternoons. The Boom Chicago theater—Europe's answer to Second City—fronts this square. Stroll nearby Lange Leidsedwarsstraat (one block north) for a taste-bud tour of ethnic eateries, from Greek to Indonesian.

▲▲**Vondelpark**—This huge, lively city park is popular with the Dutch—families with little kids, romantic couples, strolling seniors, and hippies sharing

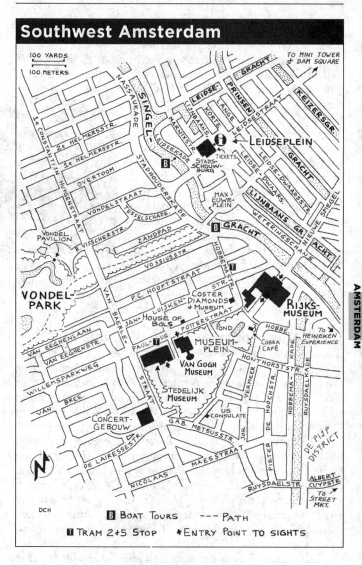

Southwest Amsterdam

100 YARDS
100 METERS

TO MINT TOWER
& DAM SQUARE

LEIDSEPLEIN

Tickets

STADS-SCHOUWBURG

MAX EUWE-PLEIN

GRACHT

VONDEL PAVILION

ZANDPAD

VOSSIUSSTR.

P.C. HOOFTSTRAAT

COSTER DIAMONDS + MUSEUM

VONDEL-PARK

House of BOLS

POTTERSTRAAT

RIJKS-MUSEUM

Pond

MUSEUM-PLEIN

COBRA CAFÉ

To HEINEKEN EXPERIENCE

VAN EEGHENLAAN

VAN EEGHENSTR.

Van Gogh Museum

US CONSULATE

WILLEMSPARKWEG

STEDELIJK Museum

DE PIJP DISTRICT

CONCERT-GEBOUW

GAB. METSUSSTR.

DE LAIRESSESTR.

MAESSTRAAT

NICOLAAS

RUYSDAELSTR.

ALBERT CUYPSTR.

To STREET MKT.

DCH

B BOAT TOURS   - - - PATH
T TRAM 2 & 5 STOP   ↟ ENTRY POINT TO SIGHTS

AMSTERDAM

blankets and beers. It's a favored venue for free summer concerts. On a sunny afternoon, it's a hedonistic scene that seems to say, "Parents...relax."

Rembrandtplein and Tuschinski Theater—One of the city's premier nightlife spots is the leafy Rembrandtplein (the artist's statue stands here, along with a jaunty group of statues giving us *The Night Watch* in 3-D) and the adjoining Thorbeckeplein. Several late-night dance clubs keep the area lively into the wee hours. Utrechtsestraat is lined with upscale shops and restaurants. Nearby

Reguliersdwarsstraat (a street one block south of Rembrandtplein) is a center for gay and lesbian nightclubs.

The **Tuschinski Theater,** a movie palace from the 1920s (a half-block from Rembrandtplein down Reguliersbreestraat),
glitters inside and out. Still a working theater, it's a delightful old place to see first-run movies (always in their original language—usually English—with Dutch subtitles). The exterior is an interesting hybrid of styles, forcing the round peg of Art Nouveau into the square hole of Art Deco. The stone-and-tile facade features stripped-down, functional Art Deco squares and rectangles, but is ornamented with Art Nouveau elements—Tiffany-style windows, garlands, curvy iron lamps,

Egyptian pharaohs, and exotic gold lettering over the door. Inside (lobby is free), the sumptuous decor features fancy carpets, slinky fixtures, and semi-abstract designs. Grab a seat in the lobby and watch the ceiling morph (Reguliersbreestraat 26-28).

West Amsterdam

▲▲▲**Anne Frank House**—A pilgrimage for many, this house offers a fascinating look at the hideaway of young Anne during the Nazi occupation of the Netherlands. Anne, her parents, an older sister, and four others spent a little more than two years in a "Secret Annex" behind her father's business. While in hiding, 13-year-old Anne kept a diary chronicling her extraordinary experience. Acting on a tip, the Nazis arrested the group in August of 1944 and sent them to concentration camps in Poland and Germany. Anne and her sister died of typhus in March of 1945, only weeks before their camp was liberated. Of the eight inhabitants of the Secret Annex, only Anne's father, Otto Frank, survived. He returned to Amsterdam and arranged for his daughter's diary to be published in 1947. It was followed by many translations, a play, and a movie.

The thoughtfully designed exhibit offers thorough coverage of the Frank family, the diary, the stories of others who hid, and the Holocaust. The Franks' story was that of Holland's Jews. The seven who died were among the more than 100,000 Dutch Jews killed during the war years. (Before the war, 135,000 Jews lived in the Netherlands.) Of Anne's school class of 87 Jews, only 20 survived. When her father returned to Amsterdam, he fought to preserve this house, wanting it to become, in his words, "more than a museum." It was his dream that visitors come away from the Anne Frank House with an indelible impression—and a better ability to apply the lessons of the Holocaust to our contemporary challenges.

Cost and Hours: €9, not covered by I amsterdam Card; March 15-Sept 14 daily 9:00-21:00, Sat and July-Aug until 22:00; Sept 15-March 14 daily 9:00-19:00, Sat until 21:00; last entry 30 minutes before closing, often less crowded right when it opens or after 18:00, no baggage check, no large bags allowed inside, Prinsengracht 267, near Westerkerk, tel. 020/556-7100, www .annefrank.org.

Avoiding Lines: Skip the long ticket-buying line (which is especially bad in the daytime during summer) by purchasing your ticket and reserving an entry time online at www.annefrank.org (€0.50/person fee). Museumkaart holders can purchase an online reservation without buying a separate Anne Frank House ticket. Book as soon as you're sure of your itinerary.

You must present a print-out of your ticket and/or reservation; if you don't have access to a printer, try going to an Internet café and asking them to print it—or bring your confirmation number to the museum and explain the situation. With your ticket (or Museumkaart plus reservation) in hand, you can skip the line and ring the buzzer at the low-profile door marked *Entrance: Reservations Only*. Without a reservation, try arriving when the museum opens (at 9:00) or after 18:00.

Westerkerk—Located near the Anne Frank House, this landmark church has a barren interior, Rembrandt's body buried somewhere under the pews, and Amsterdam's tallest steeple.

The tower is open only for tours and offers a grand city view. The tour guide, who speaks English and Dutch, tells of the church and its carillon. Only six people are allowed at a time (it's first-come, first-served), so lines can be long.

Cost and Hours: Church—free, generally April-Sept Mon-Sat 11:00-15:00, closed Sun and Oct-March. Tower—€7 for 30-minute tour—departures on the half hour April-Sept Mon-Sat 10:00-18:00, July-Aug until 20:00; Oct Mon-Sat 11:00-16:00; closed Sun year-round, last tour departs 30 minutes before closing, Nov-March tourable only by appointment—call 020/689-2565 or email anna@westertorenamsterdam.nl.

Central Amsterdam, near Dam Square

▲**Royal Palace (Koninklijk Huis)**—This palace was built as a lavish City Hall (1648-1655), when Holland was a proud new republic and Amsterdam was the richest city on the planet—awash in profit from trade. The building became a "Royal Palace" when Napoleon installed his brother Louis as king (1806). After Napoleon's fall, it continued as a residence for the Dutch royal family, the House of Orange. Today, it's one of King Willem-Alexander's official residences, with a single impressive floor open

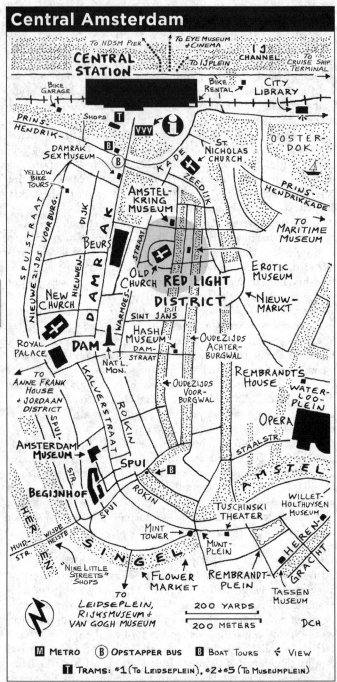

Central Amsterdam

AMSTERDAM

M METRO Ⓑ OPSTAPPER BUS 🅱 BOAT TOURS ⌐ VIEW

🔳 TRAMS: #1 (TO LEIDSEPLEIN), #2 & #5 (TO MUSEUMPLEIN)

to the public. Visitors can gawk at a grand hall and stroll about 20 rooms branching off from it, all of them lavishly decorated with chandeliers, paintings, statues, and furniture that reflect Amsterdam's former status as the center of global trade.

Cost and Hours: €7.50, includes audioguide, daily 11:00-17:00 but often closed for official business, tel. 020/620-4060, www.paleisamsterdam.nl.

▲**Begijnhof**—Stepping into this tiny, idyllic courtyard in the city center, you escape into the charm of old Amsterdam. (Please be considerate of the people who live around the courtyard, and don't photograph the residents or their homes.) Notice house #34, a 500-year-old wooden structure (rare, since repeated fires taught city fathers a trick called brick). Peek into the hidden Catholic church, dating from the time when post-Reformation Dutch Catholics couldn't worship in public. It's opposite the English Reformed church, where the Pilgrims worshipped while waiting for their voyage to the New World—marked by a plaque near the door.

Cost and Hours: Free and always open (though the churches have sporadic hours), on Begijnensteeg lane, just off Kalverstraat between #130 and #132, pick up flier at office near entrance, www.ercadam.nl.

▲▲**Amsterdam Museum**—Housed in a 500-year-old former orphanage, this creative museum tries hard to make the city's history engaging and fun (almost too hard—it recently dropped "history" from its name for fear of putting people off). But the story of Amsterdam is indeed engaging and fun, and this is the only museum in town designed to tell it. Your visit starts with a section called "DNA—City on Pilings to City of Freedom," which gives a quick overview. Then, with plenty of interactivity and fancy museum tricks, you'll follow the city's growth from fishing village to world trade center to hippie haven. On the way you'll enjoy Rembrandt paintings, good English descriptions, and a particularly interesting section on challenges of the 20th and 21st centuries (life during World War I, the gay scene in the 1920s, squatter riots, drug policy, immigration issues, prostitution, and so on). The museum's free pedestrian corridor—lined with old-time group portraits—is a powerful teaser.

Cost and Hours: €10, good audioguide-€4.50, Mon-Fri 10:00-17:00, Sat-Sun 11:00-17:00, pleasant restaurant, next to Begijnhof at Kalverstraat 92, tel. 020/523-1822, www.ahm.nl. This museum is a fine place to buy the Museumkaart, which you can then use to skip long lines at various museums (for details, see page 783).

Red Light District

▲▲**Amstelkring Museum (Our Lord in the Attic/Museum Ons' Lieve Heer op Solder)**—Although Amsterdam has long been known for its tolerant attitudes, 16th-century politics forced Dutch Catholics to worship discreetly. At this museum near Central Station, you'll find a fascinating, hidden Catholic church filling the attic of three 17th-century merchants' houses.

For two centuries (1578-1795), Catholicism in Amsterdam was illegal but tolerated (like pot in the 1970s). When hardline Protestants took power in 1578, Catholic churches were vandalized and shut down, priests and monks rounded up and kicked out of town, and Catholic kids razzed on their way to school. The city's Catholics were forbidden to worship openly, so they gathered secretly to say Mass in homes and offices. In 1663, a wealthy merchant built Our Lord in the Attic (Museum Ons' Lieve Heer op Solder), one of a handful of places in Amsterdam that served as a secret parish church until Catholics were once again allowed to worship in public.

This unique church—embedded within a townhouse in the middle of the Red Light District—comes with a little bonus: a rare glimpse inside a historic Amsterdam home straight out of a Vermeer painting. Don't miss the silver collection and other exhibits of daily life from 300 years ago.

Cost and Hours: €8, includes audioguide, Mon-Sat 10:00-17:00, Sun and holidays 13:00-17:00, no photos, Oudezijds Voorburgwal 40, tel. 020/624-6604, www.opsolder.nl.

▲▲**Red Light District Walk**—Europe's most popular ladies of the night tease and tempt here, as they have for centuries, in several hundred display-case windows around Oudezijds Achterburgwal and Oudezijds Voorburgwal, surrounding the Old Church (Oude Kerk, described later). If you're in town only for the day, the area still offers a fascinating stroll. If you're spending the night in Amsterdam before or after your cruise, this neighborhood is a fascinating walk in the early evening—but drunks and druggies make the streets uncomfortable late at night after the gawking tour groups leave (about 22:30).

The neighborhood, one of Amsterdam's oldest, has hosted prostitutes since 1200. Prostitution is entirely legal here, and the prostitutes are generally entrepreneurs, renting space and running their own businesses, as well as filling out tax returns and even paying union dues. Popular prostitutes net about €500 a day (for what's called "S&F" in its abbreviated, printable form, charging €30-50 per customer).

Sex Museums—Amsterdam has two sex museums: one in the Red Light District and another one a block in front of Central Station on Damrak street. While visiting one can be called sightseeing, visiting both is harder to explain. The one on Damrak is cheaper and more interesting. Here's a comparison:

The **Erotic Museum** in the Red Light District is five floors of uninspired paintings, videos, old photos, and sculpture (€7, not covered by Museumkaart, daily 11:00-1:00 in the morning, along the canal at Oudezijds Achterburgwal 54, tel. 020/624-7303).

The **Damrak Sex Museum** tells the story of pornography from Roman times through 1960. Every sexual deviation is revealed in various displays. The museum includes early French pornographic photos; memorabilia from Europe, India, and Asia; a Marilyn Monroe tribute; and some S&M displays (€4, not covered by Museumkaart, daily 9:30-23:00, Damrak 18, a block in front of Central Station, tel. 020/622-8376).

Old Church (Oude Kerk)—This 14th-century landmark—the needle around which the Red Light District spins—has served as a reassuring welcome-home symbol to sailors, a refuge to the downtrodden, an ideological battlefield of the Counter-Reformation, and, today, a tourist sight with a dull interior.

Cost and Hours: €5, more for temporary exhibits, Mon-Sat 11:00-17:00, Sun 13:00-17:00, tel. 020/625-8284, www.oudekerk .nl. It's 167 steps to the top of the church tower (€7, April-Sept Thu-Sat 13:00-17:00, closed Sun-Wed and Oct-March).

Marijuana Sights in the Red Light District—Three related establishments cluster together along a canal in the Red Light District. The **Hash, Marijuana, and Hemp Museum,** worth ▲, is the most worthwhile of the three; it shares a ticket with the less substantial **Hemp Gallery.** Right nearby is **Cannabis College,** a free nonprofit center that's "dedicated to ending the global war against the cannabis plant through public education." For more information, see "Smoking in Amsterdam" on page 821.

Cost and Hours: Museum and gallery—€9, daily 10:00-23:00, Oudezijds Achterburgwal 148, tel. 020/624-8926, www .hashmuseum.com. College—free, daily 11:00-19:00, Oudezijds Achterburgwal 124, tel. 020/423-4420, www.cannabiscollege.com.

Northeast Amsterdam

Central Library (Openbare Bibliotheek Amsterdam)—This huge, striking, multistory building holds almost 1,400 seats—many with wraparound views of the city—and lots of Internet terminals, not to mention Wi-Fi (€1/30 minutes, sign up at the desk). It's a classy place to check email. The library, which opened in 2007, demonstrates the Dutch people's dedication to a freely educated populace (the right to information, they point out, is enshrined in the UN's Universal Declaration of Human Rights). Everything's relaxed and inviting, from the fun kids' zone and international magazine and newspaper section on the ground floor to the cafeteria, with its dramatic view-terrace dining on the top (La Place, €10 meals, salad bar, daily 10:00-21:00). The library is a 10-minute walk from the east end of Central Station.

Cost and Hours: Free, daily 10:00-22:00, tel. 020/523-0900, www.oba.nl.

NEMO (National Center for Science and Technology)—

This kid-friendly science museum is a city landmark. Its distinctive copper-green building, jutting up from the water like a sinking ship, has prompted critics to nickname it the *Titanic*. Designed by Italian architect Renzo Piano (known for Paris' Pompidou Center and Berlin's Sony Center complex on Potsdamer Platz), the building's shape reflects its nautical surroundings as well as the curve of

the underwater tunnel it straddles. Several floors feature permanent and rotating exhibits that allow kids (and adults) to explore topics such as light, sound, and gravity, and play with bubbles, topple giant dominoes, and draw with lasers. The museum's motto: "It's forbidden NOT to touch!" Whirring, room-size pinball machines reputedly teach kids about physics. English explanations are available. Up top is a restaurant with a great city view, as well as a sloping terrace that becomes a popular "beach" in summer, complete with lounge chairs, a sandbox, and a lively bar. On the bottom floor is a cafeteria offering €5 sandwiches.

Cost and Hours: €13.50, June-Aug daily 10:00-17:00, Sept-May generally closed Mon, tel. 020/531-3233, www.e-nemo.nl. The roof terrace—open until 19:00 in the summer—is generally free.

Getting There: It's above the entrance to the IJ tunnel at Oosterdok 2. From Central Station, you can walk there in 15 minutes, or take bus #22, #42, or #43 to the Kadijksplein stop.

▲▲Netherlands Maritime Museum (Nederlands Scheepvaartmuseum)—

This huge, kid-friendly collection of model ships, maps, and sea-battle paintings fills the 300-year-old Dutch Navy Arsenal (cleverly located a little ways from the city center, as this was where they stored the gunpowder). The museum's core collection, on the east side of the courtyard, includes globes, an exhibit on the city's busy shipping port, original navigational tools, displays of ship ornamentation, and a beautifully lit gallery of maritime paintings, depicting dramatic 17th-century naval battles against British and Romantic seascapes from the 19th century. On the west side of the courtyard are exhibits on whaling and seafaring in the Dutch Golden Age. Just outside the museum is a replica of the *Amsterdam*, an 18th-century cargo ship. Given the Dutch seafaring heritage, this is an appropriately important and impressive place.

Cost and Hours: €15 covers both museum and ship, both open daily 9:00-17:00, bus #22 or #48 from Central Station to Kattenburgerplein 1, tel. 020/523-2222, www.scheepvaartmuseum .nl.

▲**EYE Film Institute Netherlands**—The newest and most striking feature of the Amsterdam skyline is EYE, a film museum and cinema housed in an übersleek modern building immediately across the water from Central Station. Heralding the coming gentrification of the north side of the IJ, EYE (a play on "IJ") is a complex of museum spaces and four theaters playing mostly art films (shown in their original language, with selections organized around various themes). Its many other offerings include a monthly program of silent films with live musical accompaniment, special exhibits on film-related themes, a free permanent exhibit in the basement, a shop, and a trendy terrace café with great waterside seating. Helpful attendants at the reception desk can get you oriented.

Cost and Hours: General entry is free, films cost €10, and exhibits cost around €10 (no cash accepted, but standard US credit cards OK), exhibits open 11:00-18:00, cinemas open daily at 10:00 until last screening (ticket office usually closes at 22:00 or 23:00), tel. 020/589-1400, eyefilm.nl.

Getting There: From the docks behind Central Station, catch the free ferry (labeled *Buiksloterweg*) across the river and walk left to IJpromenade 1.

Southeast Amsterdam

To reach the following sights from the train station, take tram #9 or #14. All of these sights (except the Tropical Museum) are close to one another and can easily be connected into an interesting walk—or, better yet, a bike ride. Several of the sights in southeast Amsterdam cluster near the large square, Waterlooplein, dominated by the modern opera house.

Waterlooplein Flea Market—For more than a hundred years, the Jewish Quarter flea market has raged daily except Sunday (at the Waterlooplein metro station, behind Rembrandt's House). The long, narrow park is filled with stalls selling cheap clothes, hippie stuff, old records, tourist knickknacks, and garage-sale junk.

AMSTERDAM

Southeast Amsterdam

TO NIEUWEMARKT + Red Light District

TO NEMO, MARITIME MUSEUM + IJ TUNNEL

REMBRANDT'S HOUSE

GASSAN DIAMONDS

UILENBURGERGRACHT

ST. ANT

FLEA MARKET

JODENBREE

MOSES + AARON CHURCH

VALKENBURGERSTRAAT

ENTRE. POTDOX

WATERLOO-PLEIN

MR. VISSER-PLEIN

PORTUGUESE SYNAGOGUE

HERENGRACHT

WERT-HEIM PARK

RESISTANCE MUSEUM

VERKLAAN

OPERA

MUIDER

JEWISH HISTORICAL MUSEUM

DOCK WORKER STATUE

NIEUWE PLANTAGE-MIDDEN

PLANTAGE

ARTIS ZOO

A.M.

WEESPER

HORTUS BOTANICAL GARDEN

DUTCH THEATER MEMORIAL

DRAW-BRIDGE

BLAUWBRUG

TO REMBRANDT-PLEIN

HERMITAGE AMSTERDAM

STRAAT

NIEUWE KEIZERSGR

PLANTAGE LAAN

TO TROPICAL MUSEUM

TO MAGERE (SKINNY) BRIDGE

DCH

200 YARDS
200 METERS

Ⓜ METRO   Ⓑ STOP/GO BUS
✦ ENTRY POINT TO SIGHTS

❶ Restaurant Plancius   ❷ Café Koosje

▲**Rembrandt's House (Museum Het Rembrandthuis)**—A middle-aged Rembrandt lived here from 1639 to 1658 after his wife's death, as his popularity and wealth dwindled down to obscurity and bankruptcy. As you enter, ask when the next etching demonstration is scheduled and pick up the excellent audioguide.

Tour the place this way: Explore Rembrandt's reconstructed house (filled with exactly what his bankruptcy inventory of 1656 said he owned); imagine him at work in his reconstructed studio; marvel at his personal collection of exotic objects, many of which he included in paintings; attend the etching demonstration and ask the printer to explain the etching process (drawing in soft wax on a metal plate that's then dipped in acid, inked up, and printed); and then, for the finale, enjoy several rooms of original Rembrandt etchings. You're not likely to see a single painting, but the master's etchings are marvelous and well-described. I came away wanting to know more about the man and his art.

Cost and Hours: €10, includes audioguide, daily 10:00-17:00, etching demonstrations almost hourly, Jodenbreestraat 4, tel. 020/520-0400, www.rembrandthuis.nl.

▲**Diamonds**—Many shops in this "city of diamonds" offer tours. These tours come with two parts: a chance to see experts behind magnifying glasses polishing the facets of precious diamonds, followed by a visit to an intimate sales room to see (and perhaps buy) a mighty shiny yet very tiny souvenir.

The handy and professional **Gassan Diamonds** facility fills a huge warehouse one block from Rembrandt's House. A visit

here plops you in the big-tour-group fray (notice how each tour group has a color-coded sticker so they know which guide gets the commission on what they buy). You'll get a sticker, join a free 15-minute tour to see a polisher at work, and hear a general explanation of the process. Then you'll have an opportunity to sit down and have color and clarity described and illustrated with diamonds ranging in value from $100 to $30,000. Before or after, you can have a free cup of coffee in the waiting room across the parking lot (daily 9:00-17:00, Nieuwe Uilenburgerstraat 173, tel. 020/622-5333, www.gassan.com, handy WC). Another company, **Coster,** also offers diamond demos. They're not as good as Gassan's, but convenient if you're near the Rijksmuseum (described on page 797).

▲Willet-Holthuysen Museum (a.k.a. Herengracht Canal Mansion)—This 1687 townhouse is a must for devotees of Hummel-topped sugar bowls and Louis XVI-style wainscoting. For others, it's a pleasant look inside a typical (rich) home with much of the original furniture and decor. Forget the history and just browse through a dozen rooms of beautiful saccharine objects from the 19th century.

Cost and Hours: €8, audio-guide-€3, Mon-Fri 10:00-17:00, Sat-Sun 11:00-17:00; take tram #4, #9, or #14 to Rembrandtplein—it's a 2-minute walk southeast to Herengracht 605, tel. 020/523-1822, www.willetholthuysen.nl. The museum also hands out a free brochure that covers the house's history.

▲▲Hermitage Amsterdam—The famous Hermitage Museum in St. Petersburg, Russia (described on page 386), loans art to Amsterdam for a series of rotating, and often exquisitely beautiful, special exhibits in the Amstelhof, a 17th-century former nursing home that takes up a whole city block along the Amstel River.

Why is there Russian-owned art in Amsterdam? The

Hermitage collection in St. Petersburg is so vast that they can only show about 5 percent of it at any one time. Therefore, the Hermitage is establishing satellite collections around the world. The one here in Amsterdam is the biggest, filling the large Amstelhof. By law, the great Russian collection can only be out of the country for six months at a time, so the collection is always changing (check the museum's website to see what's on during your visit). Curators in Amsterdam make a point to display art that complements—rather than just repeats—what the city's other museums show so well. The one small, permanent "History Hermitage" exhibit explains the historic connection between the Dutch (Orange) and Russian (Romanov) royal families.

Cost and Hours: Generally €15, but price varies with exhibit; audioguide-€4, daily 10:00-17:00, Wed until 20:00; if possible, come later in the day to avoid crowds; mandatory free bag check, café, Nieuwe Herengracht 14, tram #9 from the train station or #14 from Dam Square to Waterlooplein, recorded info tel. 020/530-7488, www.hermitage.nl.

▲**Jewish Historical Museum (Joods Historisch Museum)**— This interesting museum tells the story of the Netherlands' Jews

through three centuries, serving as a good introduction to Judaism and Jewish customs and religious traditions. Originally opened in 1932, the museum was forced to close during the Nazi years. Recent renovations have brought it into the 21st century. Its current location comprises four historic former synagogues that have been joined by steel and glass to make one modern complex.

The centerpiece of the museum is the Great Synagogue. First see its ground floor (for an overview of Jewish culture), then go upstairs to the women's gallery (for history from 1600 to 1900). From there, follow the sky bridge to the New Synagogue (for the 20th century story), and poke into the Aanbouw Annex (contemporary exhibits). Then, with the same ticket, finish your visit by crossing the street to the Portuguese Synagogue, with its treasury.

Cost and Hours: €12, includes Portuguese Synagogue, more for special exhibits, ticket also covers Dutch Theater—see next listing; museum daily 11:00-17:00, Portuguese Synagogue daily 10:00-16:00, last entry 30 minutes before closing; free audioguide, displays have English explanations, children's museum, Jonas Daniel Meijerplein 2, tel. 020/531-0310, www.jhm.nl. The museum has a modern, minimalist, kosher café.

▲**Dutch Theater (Hollandsche Schouwburg)**—Once a lively theater in the Jewish neighborhood, and today a moving memo-

rial, this building was used as an assembly hall for local Jews destined for Nazi concentration camps. On the wall, 6,700 family names pay tribute to the 104,000 Jews deported and killed by the Nazis. Some 70,000 victims spent time here, awaiting transfer to concentration camps. Upstairs is a small history exhibit with a model of the ghetto, plus photos and memorabilia (such as shoes and letters) of some victims, putting a human face on the staggering numbers. Television monitors show actual footage of the Nazis rounding up Amsterdam's Jews. You can also see a few costumes from the days when the building was a theater. While the exhibit is small, it offers plenty to think about. Back in the ground-floor courtyard, notice the hopeful messages that visiting school groups attach to the wooden tulips.

Cost and Hours: Covered by €12 Jewish Historical Museum ticket, daily 11:00-16:00, Plantage Middenlaan 24, tel. 020/531-0340, www.hollandscheschouwburg.nl.

▲▲**Dutch Resistance Museum (Verzetsmuseum)**—This is an impressive look at how the Dutch resisted (or collaborated with) their Nazi occupiers from 1940 to 1945. You'll see propaganda movie clips, study forged ID cards under a magnifying glass, and read about ingenious and courageous efforts—big and small—to hide local Jews from the Germans and undermine the Nazi regime.

The museum does a good job of presenting the Dutch people's struggle with a timeless moral dilemma: Is it better to collaborate with a wicked system to effect small-scale change—or to resist outright, even if your efforts are doomed to fail? You'll learn why some parts of Dutch society opted for the former, and others for the latter. While proudly describing acts of extraordinary courage, it doesn't shy away from the less heroic side of the story (for example, the fact that most of the population, though troubled by the persecution of their Jewish countrymen, only became actively anti-Nazi after gentile Dutch men were deported to forced-labor camps). The exhibit is interspersed with riveting first-person accounts of what it was like to go underground, strike, starve, or return from the

AMSTERDAM

camps—with every tragic detail translated into English.

Cost and Hours: €8 includes audioguide; Tue-Fri 10:00-17:00, Sat-Mon 11:00-17:00, English descriptions, no flash photos, mandatory and free bag check, tram #9 from station or #14 from Dam Square, Plantage Kerklaan 61. Tel. 020/620-2535, www.verzetsmuseum.org.

Nearby: Two recommended eateries—Restaurant Plancius and Café Koosje—are on the same block as the museum (see listings on page 821), and Amsterdam's famous zoo is just across the street.

▲**Tropical Museum (Tropenmuseum)**—As close to the Third World as you'll get without lots of vaccinations, this imaginative museum offers wonderful re-creations of tropical life and explanations of Third World problems (largely created by Dutch colonialism and the slave trade). Ride the elevator to the top floor, and circle your way down through this immense collection, opened in 1926 to give the Dutch people a peek at their vast colonial holdings. Don't miss the display case where you can see and hear the world's most exotic musical instruments. The Ekeko cafeteria serves tropical food.

Cost and Hours: €10, Tue-Sun 10:00-17:00, closed Mon, tram #9 to Linnaeusstraat 2, tel. 020/568-8200, www.tropenmuseum.nl.

Eating in Amsterdam

Of Amsterdam's thousand-plus restaurants, no one knows which are best. I'd pick an area and wander. The rowdy food ghetto thrives around Leidseplein; if you don't mind eating in a touristy area, wander along "Restaurant Row" (on Leidsedwarsstraat). The area around Spui Square and that end of Spuistraat is also trendy, and not as noisy. For fewer crowds and more charm, find something in the Jordaan district. I've listed some handy places to consider.

To dine cheaply yet memorably alongside the big spenders, grab a meal to go, then find a bench on a lively neighborhood square or along a canal. Sandwiches *(broodjes)* of delicious cheese on fresh bread are cheap at snack bars, delis, and *broodjes* restaurants. Ethnic restaurants serve cheap, splittable carryout meals. Ethnic fast-food stands abound, offering a variety of meats wrapped in pita bread. Easy to buy at grocery stores, yogurt in the Netherlands (and throughout northern Europe) is delicious and often drinkable right out of its plastic container.

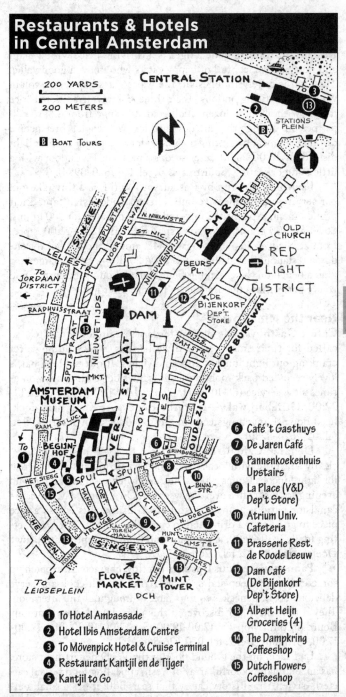

Restaurants & Hotels in Central Amsterdam

200 YARDS
200 METERS

B Boat Tours

CENTRAL STATION →

TO
3
13

2
STATIONS-PLEIN
B

N

OLD
CHURCH

RED

LIGHT

DISTRICT

SINGEL
SPUISTRAAT
N. NIEUWSTR.
ST. NIC.
VOORBURGWAL

LELIESTR.

To
JORDAAN
District

RAADHUISSTRAAT

NIEUWENDIJK
BEURS-PL.

DAM

11

12
DE
BIJENKORF
DEP'T
Store

NIEUWEZIJDS

SPUISTRAAT
13

PIJLS.
DAM STR.

OUDEZIJDS VOORBURGWAL

AMSTERDAM
MUSEUM

KALVER-STRAAT

ROKIN
NES

RAAM
ST. LUC.

To

BEGIJN-HOF
1
4

5
B
6
L. BRUG. GRIMBURGWAL
8

SPUI
SPUI

10
BINN.-STR.

HET STEEG

HEREN
KONING

15

14
HAND.
VOET.

HELLIGE
ROKIN

KALVER-TOREN-MALL

9

13

SINGEL
VIJZEL
N. DOELEN.

MUNT-PL.
AMSTEL

7

REGULIERS.

TO
LEIDSEPLEIN

FLOWER
MARKET
DCH

MINT
TOWER

1 To Hotel Ambassade
2 Hotel Ibis Amsterdam Centre
3 To Mövenpick Hotel & Cruise Terminal
4 Restaurant Kantjil en de Tijger
5 Kantjil to Go

6 Café 't Gasthuys
7 De Jaren Café
8 Pannenkoekenhuis Upstairs
9 La Place (V&D Dep't Store)
10 Atrium Univ. Cafeteria
11 Brasserie Rest. de Roode Leeuw
12 Dam Café (De Bijenkorf Dep't Store)
13 Albert Heijn Groceries (4)
14 The Dampkring Coffeeshop
15 Dutch Flowers Coffeeshop

AMSTERDAM

Central Amsterdam

On and near Spui

Restaurant Kantjil en de Tijger is a thriving place with a plain and noisy ambience, full of happy eaters who know a good value. The food is purely Indonesian; the waiters are happy to explain your many enticing options. Their three *rijsttafels* (traditional "rice tables" with about a dozen small courses) range from €24 to €30 per person. Though they are designed for two people, three people can make a meal by getting a *rijsttafel* for two plus a soup or light dish (daily 12:00-23:00, reservations smart, mostly indoor with a little outdoor seating, Spuistraat 291, tel. 020/620-0994).

Kantjil to Go, run by Restaurant Kantjil, is a tiny take-out bar serving up inexpensive but delicious Indonesian fare. Their printed menu explains the mix-and-match plan (€5 for 300 grams, €6.50 for 600 grams, vegetarian specials, daily 12:00-21:00, store-front at Nieuwezijds Voorburgwal 342, around the back of the sit-down restaurant listed above, tel. 020/620-3074). Split a large box, grab a bench on the charming Spui Square around the corner, and you've got perhaps the best cheap, hot meal in town.

Near the Mint Tower

Café 't Gasthuys, one of Amsterdam's many brown cafés (so called for their smoke-stained walls), has a busy dumbwaiter cranking out light lunches and sandwiches. It offers a long bar, a lovely secluded back room, peaceful canalside seating, and some-times slow service (€6-10 lunch plates, daily 11:00-16:30 & 17:30-22:00, Grimburgwal 7—from the Rondvaart Kooij boat dock, head down Langebrugsteeg, and it's one block down on the left; tel. 020/624-8230).

De Jaren Café ("The Years") is a chic yet inviting place—clearly a favorite with locals. The modern café (downstairs) is great for light lunches (soups, salads, and sandwiches served all day and evening) or just coffee over a newspaper. On a sunny day, the café's canalside patio is a fine spot to nurse a drink; this is also a nice place to go just for a drink and to enjoy the spacious Art Deco set-ting (daily 9:30-23:00, a long block up from Muntplein at Nieuwe Doelenstraat 20-22, tel. 020/625-5771).

Pannenkoekenhuis Upstairs is a tiny, characteristic perch up some extremely steep stairs, where Arno and Ali cook and serve delicious €6-12 pancakes to four tables throughout the afternoon. They'll tell you that I discovered this place long before Anthony Bourdain did (Mon-Fri 12:00-19:00, Sat 12:00-18:00, Sun 12:00-17:00, Grimburgwal 2, tel. 020/626-5603).

La Place, on the ground floor of the V&D department store, has an abundant, colorful array of fresh, appealing food served caf-eteria-style. A multistory eatery that seats 300, it has a small outdoor terrace upstairs. Explore before you make your choice. This bustling spot has a lively market feel, with everything from made-on-the-spot beef stir-fry, to fresh juice, to veggie soups (€4 pizza and €5 sandwiches, Sun-Mon 11:00-19:00, Tue-Wed 10:00-19:30, Thu-Sat 10:00-21:00, at the end of Kalverstraat near Mint Tower, tel. 020/622-0171). For fast and healthy take-out food (sandwiches, yogurt, fruit cups, and more), try the bakery on the department store's ground floor. (They run another branch, which has the city's ultimate view terrace, on the top floor of the **Central Library**—Openbare Bibliotheek Amsterdam—between Central Station and the cruise terminal.)

Atrium University Cafeteria, a three-minute walk from Mint Tower, feeds travelers and students from Amsterdam University for great prices, but only on weekdays (€7 meals, Mon-Fri 11:00-15:00 & 17:00-19:30; from Spui, walk west down Landebrug Steeg past canalside Café 't Gasthuys three blocks to Oudezijds Achterburgwal 237, then go through arched doorway on the right; tel. 020/525-3999).

Between Central Station and Dam Square

Brasserie Restaurant de Roode Leeuw ("Red Lion") offers a peaceful respite from the crush of Damrak. While this old standby is somewhat overpriced these days, you can still get a menu filled with traditional Dutch food, good service, and the company of plenty of tourists. The *stamppot* (pickled pork loin with bacon and mashed potatoes) is an adventure in Dutch comfort food. Call ahead to reserve a window seat (€17-25 entrées, €33 three-course fixed-price meal with traditional Dutch choices; daily 12:00-22:00, Damrak 93-94, tel. 020/555-0666).

Dam Café, on the first floor of the De Bijenkorf department store on Dam Square, has a small lineup of tasty salads, sandwiches, and desserts. Enjoying views of busy Damrak, comfortable (but limited) seating, and an upscale café vibe, you'll feel miles above the chaotic streets below (€8-11 salads; Sun-Mon 11:00-20:00; Tue-Sat 10:00-20:00, Thu-Fri until 21:00; Dam 1, tel. 088-245-9080). For a much wider range of dishes and lots of seating—but no Dam views—head up to **Kitchen,** the store's swanky fifth-floor self-service restaurant (similar prices and hours as café).

Munching Cheap

Traditional fish stands sell €4 herring sandwiches and other salty treats, usually from easy photo menus. **Stubbe's Haring,** where the Stubbe family has been selling herring for 100 years, is handy and well-established, a few blocks from Central Station (Tue-Fri 10:00-18:00, Sat 10:00-17:00, closed Sun-Mon, at the locks on

Restaurants & Hotels in

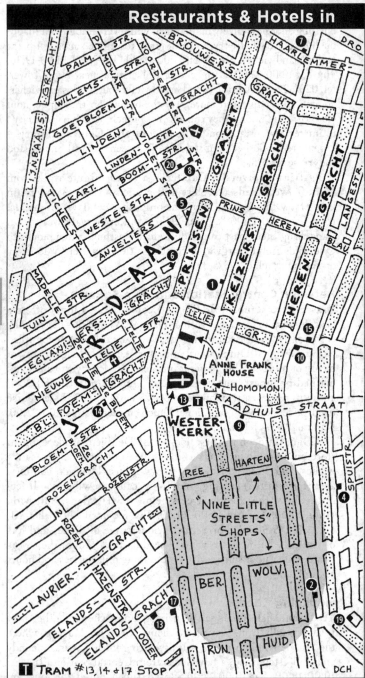

AMSTERDAM

T TRAM #13, 14 & 17 STOP

DCH

West Amsterdam

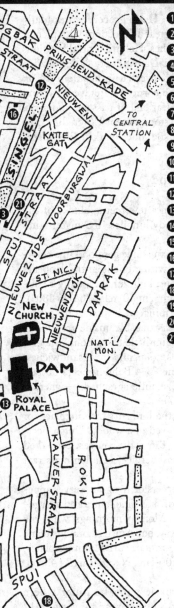

1. The Toren
2. Hotel Ambassade
3. Hotel Brouwer
4. Hotel Hoksbergen
5. De Bolhoed Restaurant
6. Café 't Smalle
7. Toscana Italian Restaurant
8. Winkel Café
9. Sara's Pancake House
10. Villa Zeesicht
11. Café 't Papeneiland
12. Stubbe's Haring (Fish Stand)
13. Albert Heijn Grocery (3)
14. Paradox Coffeeshop
15. The Grey Area Coffeeshop
16. Siberië Coffeeshop
17. La Tertulia Coffeeshop
18. The Dampkring Coffeeshop
19. Dutch Flowers Coffeeshop
20. Launderette
21. GAYtic (LGBT Tourist Info)

AMSTERDAM

Singel canal, near the train station, see map on page 817). Grab a sandwich and have a canalside picnic.

Supermarkets: You'll see **Albert Heijn** grocery stores (daily 8:00-22:00) all over town. They have great deli sections with picnic-perfect take-away salads and sandwiches. Helpful central locations include behind the Royal Palace on Dam Square (Nieuwezijds Voorburgwal 226), near the Mint Tower (Koningsplein 4), on Leidsestraat (at Konigsplein, on the corner of Leidsestraat and Singel), and inside Central Station (far end of passage under the tracks). Be aware that none of their stores accept US credit cards: Bring cash, and don't get in the checkout lines marked *PIN alleen*.

West Amsterdam
Near the Anne Frank House and in the Jordaan District

Nearly all of these places are within a few scenic blocks of the Anne Frank House, providing handy lunches in Amsterdam's most charming neighborhood.

De Bolhoed has serious vegetarian and vegan food in a colorful setting that Buddha would dig, with a clientele that appears to dig Buddha (big, splittable portions, light lunches, daily 12:00-22:00, dinner starts at 17:00, Prinsengracht 60, tel. 020/626-1803).

Café 't Smalle is extremely charming, with three zones where you can enjoy a light lunch or a drink: canalside, inside around the bar, and up some steep stairs in a quaint little back room. The café is open late, and simple meals (salads, soup, and fresh sandwiches) are served 11:00-17:30 (plenty of fine €3-4 Belgian beers on tap, interesting wines by the glass, at Egelantiersgracht 12—where it hits Prinsengracht, tel. 020/623-9617).

Toscana Italian Restaurant is the Jordaan's favorite place for good, inexpensive Italian cuisine, served in a woody, Dutch-beer-hall setting (€6-9 pizza and pastas, €16 main courses, Sun-Wed 16:00-23:30, Thu-Sat 12:00-23:30, fast service, Haarlemmerstraat 130, tel. 020/622-0353).

Winkel, the North Jordaan's cornerside hangout, serves appetizing Euro-Dutch meals at its plentiful outside tables and easygoing interior. It really gets hopping on Monday mornings, when the Noordermarkt flea market is underway, but Amsterdammers come from across town all week for the *appeltaart* (€11-14 dinner plates, €5 snacks served after 16:00, daily 8:00-late, Noordermarkt 43, tel. 020/623-0223).

Sara's Pancake House is a basic pancake diner where extremely hardworking Sara cranks out sweet and savory €8-12 flapjacks made from fresh, organic ingredients (daily until 22:30, later on weekends, breakfast served until noon, Raadhuisstraat 45, tel. 020/320-0662).

Villa Zeesicht has all the romantic feel of a classic European café. The cozy interior is crammed with tiny tables topped by tall candlesticks, and wicker chairs outside gather under a wisteria-covered awning. The menu is uninventive—come here instead for the famous *appeltaart* and for the great people-watching on Torensluis bridge (€11-16 plates, daily 9:00-21:30, Torensteeg 7, tel. 020/626-7433).

Drinks Only: **Café 't Papeneiland** is a classic brown café with Delft tiles, an evocative old stove, and a stay-awhile perch overlooking a canal with welcoming benches. It's been the neighborhood hangout since the 17th century (drinks but no food, overlooking northwest end of Prinsengracht at #2, tel. 020/624-1989). It feels a little exclusive; patrons who come here to drink and chat aren't eager to see it overrun by tourists. The café's name means "Papists' Island," since this was once a refuge for Catholics; there used to be an escape tunnel here for priests on the run.

Southwest Amsterdam
Near Leidseplein
Stroll through the colorful cancan of eateries on Lange Leidsedwarsstraat, the "Restaurant Row" just off Leidseplein, and choose your favorite (but don't expect intimacy or good value). Nearby, busy Leidsestraat offers plenty of starving-student options (between Prinsengracht and Herengracht) offering fast and fun food for around €5 a meal.

To escape the crowds without too long a walk from Leidseplein, wander a few blocks away from the hubbub to Lijnbaansgracht (via Kleine Gartmanplantsoen, the street to the right of The Bulldog Café).

Beyond the Rijksmuseum
Restaurant Bazar offers one of the most memorable and fun budget eating experiences in town. Converted from a church, it has spacious seating and mod belly-dance music, and is filled with young locals enjoying good, cheap Middle Eastern and North African cuisine (fill up with the €8.50 daily plate, delicious €13 couscous, or €16 main dishes; Mon-Fri 11:00-late, Sat-Sun 9:00-late, Albert Cuypstraat 182, tel. 020/675-0544). Restaurant Bazar marks the center of the thriving Albert Cuyp market.

In Vondelpark
Café Vertigo offers a fun selection of excellent soups, salads, and sandwiches, plus main courses such as steak, fish, and *satays*. It's a surprisingly large complex of outdoor tables, an indoor pub, and an elegant, candlelit back-room restaurant beneath the grand, Italian Renaissance Vondel Pavilion. Inside, try to guess the names of

Restaurants & Hotels in Southwest Amsterdam

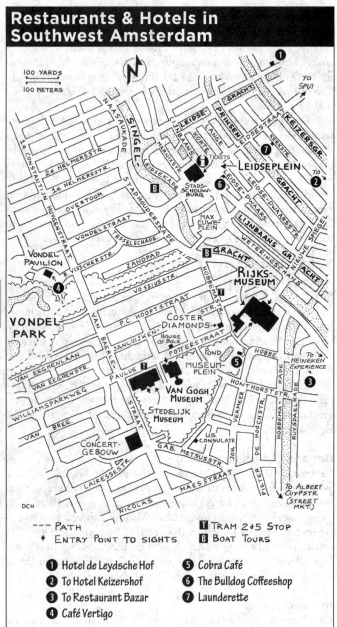

AMSTERDAM

100 YARDS
100 METERS

TO SPUI

LEIDSEPLEIN

TICKETS

STADS-
SCHOUWBURG

MAX
EUWE-
PLEIN

VONDEL
PAVILION

RIJKS-
MUSEUM

VONDEL
PARK

P.C. HOOFTSTRAAT

COSTER
DIAMONDS

House
of Bols

POTTERSTRAAT

TO
HEINEKEN
EXPERIENCE

MUSEUM-
PLEIN

VAN GOGH
MUSEUM

STEDELIJK
MUSEUM

U.S.
CONSULATE

CONCERT-
GEBOUW

TO ALBERT
CUYPSTR.
(STREET
MKT.)

DCH

- - - PATH
✦ ENTRY POINT TO SIGHTS

T TRAM 2 & 5 STOP
B BOAT TOURS

1 Hotel de Leydsche Hof
2 To Hotel Keizershof
3 To Restaurant Bazar
4 Café Vertigo

5 Cobra Café
6 The Bulldog Coffeeshop
7 Launderette

the Hollywood icons on the walls. The service can be slow, but if you grab an outdoor table, you can watch the world spin by (daily 10:00-24:00 except opens at 11:00 on off-season weekdays, Vondelpark 3, tel. 020/612-3021).

Southeast Amsterdam
Near the Dutch Resistance Museum
For locations of the following eateries, see the map on page 808.

Restaurant Plancius, adjacent to the Dutch Resistance Museum, is a handy, modern spot for lunch. Its good indoor and outdoor seating make it popular with the museum staff and broadcasters from the nearby local TV studios (creative breakfasts, hearty fresh sandwiches, light €6-9 lunches and €16-19 dinners, daily 10:00-22:00, Plantage Kerklaan 61a, tel. 020/330-9469).

Café Koosje, located halfway between the Dutch Resistance Museum and the Dutch Theater, is a corner lunchtime pub/bar ringed with outdoor seating. Inside, casual wooden tables and benches huddle under chandeliers, and the hip, young waitstaff serve beer and salads that are big enough for two (€5 sandwiches, €11 salads, €14-17 dinners, food served daily 9:00-22:00, on the corner of Plantage Kerklaan at Plantage Middenlaan 37, tel. 020/320-0817).

Smoking in Amsterdam

Marijuana (a.k.a. Cannabis)
For tourists from lands where you can do hard time for lighting up, the open use of marijuana here can feel either somewhat disturbing, or exhilaratingly liberating...or maybe just refreshingly sane. Several decades after being legalized in the Netherlands, marijuana causes about as much excitement here as a bottle of beer. When tourists call an ambulance after smoking too much pot, medics just say, "Drink something sweet and walk it off."

Marijuana Laws and "Coffeeshops"
Throughout the Netherlands, you'll see "coffeeshops"—cafés selling marijuana, with display cases showing various joints or baggies for sale.

Rules and Regulations: The retail sale of marijuana is strictly regulated, and proceeds are taxed. The minimum age for

purchase is 18, and coffeeshops can sell up to five grams of marijuana per person per day. It's also illegal for these shops (or anyone) to advertise marijuana. In fact, in many places, the prospective customer has to take the initiative, and ask to see the menu. In some coffeeshops, you actually have to push and hold down a button to see an illuminated menu—the contents of which look like the inventory of a drug bust.

Shops sell marijuana and hashish both in pre-rolled joints and in little baggies. Joints are generally sold individually (€3-5, depending on the strain you choose), though some places sell only small packs of three or four joints. Baggies usually cost €10-15. Some shops charge per gram. The better pot, though costlier, is actually a better value, as it takes less to get high—and it's a better high.

Each coffeeshop is allowed to keep an inventory of about a pound of pot in stock: The tax authorities don't want to see more than this on the books at the end of each accounting cycle, and a shop can lose its license if it exceeds this amount. A popular shop—whose supply must be replenished five or six times a day—simply has to put up with the hassle of constantly taking small deliveries. A shop can sell a ton of pot with no legal problems, as long as it maintains that tiny stock and just refills it as needed. The reason? Authorities want shops to stay small and not become export bases.

In recent years, various Dutch politicians have proposed new laws that would forbid sales of marijuana to nonresidents. Their big worry is European drug dealers who drive over the Dutch border, buy up large quantities of pot, and return home to sell it illegally. This law would be devastating for these Dutch businesses, who depend on out-of-towners to stay in business. The current mayor of Amsterdam is adamant that the city's coffeeshops will remain open—for the sake of the businesses, and because the city believes that the law would just drive business back into a black market, and cause an increase in street crime.

Smoking Tips: The Dutch (like most Europeans) are accustomed to mixing tobacco with marijuana—but any place that caters to Americans will have joints without tobacco; you just have to ask specifically for a "pure" joint. Shops have loaner bongs and inhalers, and dispense rolling papers like toothpicks. As long as you're a paying customer (e.g., you buy a cup of coffee), you can pop into any coffeeshop and light up, even if you didn't buy your pot there.

Tourists who haven't smoked pot since their college days are famous for overindulging in Amsterdam. Coffeeshop baristas nickname tourists about to pass out "Whitey"—the color their faces turn just before they hit the floor. They warn Americans (who aren't used to the strength of the local stuff) to try a lighter leaf. If you do overdo it, the key is to eat or drink something sweet to avoid getting sick. Cola is a good fast fix, and coffeeshops keep sugar tablets handy.

Don't ever buy pot on the street in Amsterdam. Well-established coffeeshops are considered much safer, and coffeeshop owners have an interest in keeping their trade safe and healthy. They're also generally very patient in explaining the varieties available.

Coffeeshops

Most of downtown Amsterdam's coffeeshops feel grungy and fore-boding to American travelers who aren't part of the youth-hostel crowd. The neighborhood places are much more inviting to people without piercings, tattoos, and favorite techno artists. I've listed a few places with a more pub-like ambience for Americans wanting to go local, but within reason. For locations, see the maps in the "Eating in Amsterdam" section.

Paradox is the most *gezellig* (cozy) coffeeshop I found—a mellow, graceful place. The managers, Ludo and Wiljan, and their

staff are patient with descriptions and happy to walk you through all your options. This is a rare coffeeshop that serves light meals. The juice is fresh, the music is easy, and the neighborhood is charming (single tobacco-free joints-€3, loaner bongs, games, free Wi-Fi, daily 10:00-20:00, two blocks from Anne Frank House at Eerste Bloemdwarsstraat 2, tel. 020/623-5639, www.paradoxcoffeeshop .com).

The Grey Area—a hole-in-the-wall spot with three tiny tables—is a cool, welcoming, and smoky place appreciated among local aficionados as a perennial winner of Amsterdam's Cannabis Cup awards. Judging by the autographed photos on the wall, many famous Americans have dropped in (say hi to Willie Nelson). You're welcome to just nurse a bottomless cup of coffee. It's run by friendly American Jon, with helpful Adam and Stevan. They even have a vaporizer if you want to try "smoking" without smoking (daily 12:00-20:00, they close relatively early out of consideration

What If I Miss My Boat?

Remember that you can get help from the cruise line's port agent (listed on the destination information sheet distributed on the ship) and the local TI (see page 781). If the port agent suggests a costly solution (such as a private car with a driver), you may want to consider public transit.

Amsterdam is well-connected by train to a variety of cruise ports, including **Zeebrugge** (via Brussels), **Le Havre** (via Paris), **Southampton** and **Dover** (Eurostar via Brussels/London, then train onward to either port), **Copenhagen, Warnemünde** (via Berlin), and beyond.

If you need to catch a **plane** to your next destination, it's an easy train ride from downtown Amsterdam to Schiphol Airport. For more information, see the next section.

Local **travel agents** in Amsterdam can help you. For more advice on what to do if you miss the boat, see page 144.

for their neighbors, between Dam Square and Anne Frank House at Oude Leliestraat 2, tel. 020/420-4301, www.greyarea.nl).

Siberië Coffeeshop is a short walk from Central Station, but feels cozy, with a friendly canalside ambience. Clean, big, and bright, this place has the vibe of a mellow Starbucks (daily 11:00-23:00, Fri-Sat until 24:00, free Wi-Fi for customers, helpful staff, English menu, Brouwersgracht 11, tel. 020/623-5909, www.coffeeshopsiberie.nl).

La Tertulia is a sweet little mother-and-daughter-run place with pastel decor and a cheery terrarium atmosphere (Tue-Sat 11:00-19:00, closed Sun-Mon, sandwiches, brownies, games, Prinsengracht 312).

The Bulldog Café is the high-profile, leading touristy chain of coffeeshops. These establishments are young but welcoming, with reliable selections. They're pretty comfortable for green tourists wanting to just hang out for a while. The flagship branch, in a former police station right on Leidseplein, is very handy, offering alcohol upstairs, pot downstairs, and fun outdoor seating. It's the rare place where you can have a beer while you smoke and watch the world skateboard by (daily 10:00-1:00 in the morning, Fri-Sat

until 3:00, Leidseplein 17, tel. 020/625-6278, www.thebulldog.com).

The Dampkring is a rough-and-ready constant party. It's

a high-profile, busy place, filled with a young clientele and loud music, but the owners still take the time to explain what they offer. Scenes from the movie *Ocean's Twelve* were filmed here (daily 10:00-1:00 in the morning, close to Spui at Handboogstraat 29, tel. 020/638-0705, www.dampkring.nl).

Dutch Flowers, conveniently located near Spui square on Singel canal, has a very casual "brown café" ambience, with a mature set of regulars. A couple of tables overlooking the canal are perfect for enjoying the late-afternoon sunshine (daily 10:00-23:00, until later Fri-Sat, on the corner of Heisteeg and Singel at Singel 387, tel. 020/624-7624).

Starting or Ending Your Cruise in Amsterdam

If your cruise begins and/or ends in Amsterdam, you'll want some extra time here; for most travelers, one extra day (beyond your cruise departure day) is a minimum to see the highlights of this grand city. For a longer visit here, pick up my *Rick Steves' Amsterdam, Bruges & Brussels* guidebook.

Airport Connections

Amsterdam's Schiphol Airport

Schiphol (SKIP-pol) Airport is located about 10 miles southwest of Amsterdam's city center (airport code: AMS, toll tel. 0900-0141, from other countries dial +31-20-794-0800, www.schiphol.nl). Schiphol has four terminals. Inside the airport, the terminal waiting areas are called lounges; an inviting shopping and eating zone called Holland Boulevard runs between Lounges 2 and 3. Baggage-claim areas for all terminals empty into the same arrival zone, called Schiphol Plaza—with ATMs, shops, eateries, a busy TI (near Terminal 2, daily 7:00-22:00), a train station, and bus stops for getting into the city.

To get train information or buy a ticket, take advantage of the fantastic "Train Tickets and Services" counter (Schiphol Plaza ground level, just past Burger King). They have an easy info desk and almost no lines (much quicker than the ticket desk at Amsterdam's Central Station), take US credit cards (unlike most Dutch train stations), and issue tickets for a fee (€0.50 for domestic tickets).

Getting from Schiphol Airport to Downtown

The cruise terminal is an easy tram ride (just one stop) from

Central Station, so your options are the same whether you're going straight from the airport to your cruise ship, or heading into the city to spend the night before your cruise.

Direct **trains** to Amsterdam's Central Station run frequently (4-6/hour, 15 minutes, €4.30).

The Connexxion **shuttle bus** takes you to your hotel neighborhood, or to the cruise terminal (which is right next to the Mövenpick Hotel Amsterdam City Centre); there are three different routes, so ask the attendant which one works best for your destination (2/hour, 20 minutes, €16 one-way, €26 round-trip, some routes may cost a couple euros more, departs from lane A7 in front of airport, reserve at least 2 hours ahead for shuttles to airport, tel. 088-339-4741, www.airporthotelshuttle.nl).

Allow about €60-70 for a **taxi** to the cruise terminal or downtown Amsterdam.

Bus #197 is handy only for those sleeping in the Leidseplein district (€4, buy ticket from driver, departs from lane B9 in front of airport).

Getting from Central Station to the Cruise Port

In front of Central Station, look for the tram stop marked *IJburg* (on the right, as you face the station). From here, catch tram #26 and ride it one stop to Muziekgebouw Bimhuis, which is right in front of the terminal.

Getting from the Cruise Terminal to the Airport

If your cruise ends in Amsterdam and you're flying out of Schiphol Airport, it's an easy connection (I'd skip the taxi, which charges a hefty €60-70 to the airport). First, ride tram #26 from in front of the cruise terminal one stop, to Central Station (for details, see page 778). Then head inside the train station and take a train to Schiphol Airport (4-6/hour, 15 minutes, €4.30).

Hotels in Amsterdam

If you need a hotel in Amsterdam before or after your cruise, here are a few to consider (for locations, see maps in the "Eating in Amsterdam" section). Amsterdam is a tough city for budget accommodations, and any hotel room under €140 (or B&B room under €100) will have rough edges. Still, you can sleep well and safely in a great location for €100 per double.

Some national holidays merit your making reservations far in advance. Amsterdam is jammed during tulip season (late March-mid-May), conventions, festivals, and on summer weekends. During peak season, some hoteliers won't take weekend bookings for those staying fewer than two or three nights.

Canalside rooms can come with great views—and early-morning construction-crew noise. If you're a light sleeper, ask the hotelier for a quiet room in the back. Smoking is illegal in hotel rooms throughout the Netherlands. Canal houses were built tight. They have steep stairs with narrow treads; almost none have elevators. If steep stairs are potentially problematic, book a hotel with an elevator.

Nightlife in Amsterdam: On summer evenings, people flock to the main squares for drinks at outdoor tables. Leidseplein is the liveliest square, surrounded by theaters, restaurants, and nightclubs. The slightly quieter Rembrandtplein (with adjoining Thorbeckeplein and nearby Reguliersdwarsstraat) is the center of gay clubs and nightlife. Spui features a full city block of bars. And Nieuwmarkt, on the east edge of the Red Light District, is a bit rough, but is probably the least touristy. The Red Light District (particularly Oudezijds Achterburgwal) is less sleazy in the early evening, and almost carnival-like as the neon lights come on and the streets fill with tour groups. But it starts to feel scuzzy after about 22:30. For entertainment and nightlife information, newsstands sell *Time Out Amsterdam* and Dutch newspapers (Thu editions generally list events). The free, irreverent *Boom!* has the basics on the youth and nightlife scene, and is packed with practical tips and countercultural insights (includes €5 discount on Boom Chicago comedy theater act, www.boomchicago.nl; available at TIs and many bars). Several **museums**—including the Anne Frank House, Van Gogh Museum, Hermitage Amsterdam, and Stedelijk—stay open late on certain days (see hours in "Amsterdam at a Glance" on page 792).

Stately Canalside Hotels in West Amsterdam

Both of these hotels, a half-mile apart, face historic canals. They come with lovely lobbies (some more ornate than others) and rooms that can feel like they're from another century. This area oozes elegance and class, and it is fairly quiet at night.

$$$ The Toren is a chandeliered, historic mansion with a pleasant, canalside setting and a peaceful garden out back for guests. Run by Eric and Petra Toren, this smartly renovated, super-romantic hotel is classy yet friendly, with 38 rooms in a great location on a quiet street two blocks northeast of the Anne Frank House. The capable staff is a great source of local advice. The gilt-frame, velvet-curtained rooms are an opulent splurge (tiny Sb-€115, Db-€200, deluxe Db-€250, third person-€40, prices bump way up during conferences and decrease in winter, rates do not include 6 percent tax, breakfast buffet-€14, air-con, elevator, Internet access and Wi-Fi, Keizersgracht 164, tel. 020/622-6033, fax 020/626-9705, www.thetoren.nl, info@thetoren.nl). To get the best prices, check their website for their "daily rate," book direct, and in the "remarks" field, ask for the 10 percent Rick Steves cash discount.

$$$ Hotel Ambassade, lacing together 59 rooms in a maze of connected houses, is elegant and fresh, sitting aristocratically on Herengracht. The staff is top-notch, and the public areas (including a library and a breakfast room) are palatial, with antique furnishings and modern art (Sb-€210, Db-€265, more expensive deluxe canal-view doubles and suites, Tb-€245-295, extra bed-€40, ask for Rick Steves discount when booking, see website for specials, rates do not include 6 percent tax, breakfast-€18, air-con, elevator, free Internet access and Wi-Fi, Herengracht 341, tel. 020/555-0222, www.ambassade-hotel.nl, info@ambassade-hotel .nl, Roos—pronounced "Rose").

Simpler Canalside Hotels

These places have basic rooms—some downright spare, none plush. Both of them, however, offer a decent night's sleep in a lovely area of town.

$$ Hotel Brouwer is a woody and homey old-time place. It's situated in a tranquil yet central location on the Singel canal and rents eight rooms with canal views, old furniture, and soulful throw rugs. It's so popular that it's often booked four or five months in advance—reserve as soon as possible (Sb-€60, Db-€95, Tb-€120, rates don't include 6 percent tax, cash only, breakfast-€7, small elevator, free Internet access and Wi-Fi, located between Central Station and Dam Square, near Lijnbaanssteeg at Singel 83, tel. 020/624-6358, www.hotelbrouwer.nl, akita@hotel brouwer.nl).

$$ Hotel Hoksbergen is a welcoming, well-run canalside place in a peaceful location where helpful, hands-on owners Tony and Bert rent 14 rooms with newly remodeled bathrooms (Db-€98, Tb-€143, five Qb apartments-€165-198, fans, free Wi-Fi, Singel 301, tel. 020/626-6043, www.hotelhoksbergen.com, info @hotelhoksbergen.nl).

Charming B&Bs near Leidseplein

The area around Amsterdam's rip-roaring nightlife center (Leidseplein) is colorful, comfortable, and convenient. These canalside mom-and-pop places are within a five-minute walk of rowdy Leidseplein, but generally are in quiet and typically Dutch settings. Within walking distance of the major museums, and steps off the tram line, this neighborhood offers a perfect mix of charm and location.

$$ Hotel de Leydsche Hof, a hidden gem located on a canal, doesn't charge extra for its views. Its four large rooms are a sym-

AMSTERDAM

phony in white, some overlooking a tree-filled backyard, others a canal. Frits and Loes give their big, elegant, old building a stylish air, but be prepared for lots of stairs. Breakfast is served in the grand canal-front room (Db-€120, cash only, 2-night minimum, free Internet access and Wi-Fi, Leidsegracht 14, tel. 020/638-2327, mobile 06-5125-8588, www.freewebs.com/leydschehof, loespiller@planet.nl).

$$ Hotel Keizershof is wonderfully Dutch, with six bright, airy rooms—some with canal views—in a 17th-century canal house with a lush garden and a fine living room. A very steep spiral staircase leads to rooms named after old-time Hollywood stars. The enthusiastic hospitality of Mrs. de Vries and her daughter, Hanneke, give this place a friendly, almost small-town charm (S-€70, D-€95, Ds-€110, Db-€115, 2-night minimum, reserve with credit card but pay with cash, free Internet access and Wi-Fi; tram #16, #24, or #25 from Central Station; Keizersgracht 618, where Keizersgracht crosses Nieuwe Spiegelstraat; tel. 020/622-2855, www.hotelkeizershof.nl, info@hotelkeizershof.nl).

Near the Train Station and Cruise Terminal

$$$ Hotel Ibis Amsterdam Centre, located next door to the Central Station, is a modern, efficient, 363-room place. It offers a central location, comfort, and good value—without a hint of charm (Db-€140-160 Nov-Aug, Db-€200 Sept-Oct, breakfast-€16, check website for deals, book long in advance—especially for Sept-Oct, air-con, elevators, free Wi-Fi, pay Internet access; facing Central Station, go left toward the multistory bicycle garage to Stationsplein 49; tel. 020/522-2899, fax 020/522-2889, www .ibishotel.com, h1556@accor.com).

To sleep right next door to the cruise terminal, consider the **$$$ Mövenpick Hotel Amsterdam City Centre** (www.moeven pick-hotels.com)—but keep in mind that this location is less practical for getting to anywhere other than your ship.

Dutch Survival Phrases

You won't need to learn Dutch, but knowing a few phrases can help if you're traveling off the beaten path. Taking a few moments to learn the pleasantries (such as please and thank you) will improve your connections with locals even in the bigger cities. In northern Belgium, they also speak Dutch, but with a Flemish accent.

To pronounce the difficult Dutch "g" (indicated in phonetics by hhh) make a hard, guttural, clear-your-throat sound, similar to the "ch" in the Scottish word "loch."

English	Dutch	Pronunciation
Hello.	Hallo.	hol-**loh**
Good day.	Dag.	dahhh
Good morning.	Goeiemorgen.	hhhoy-ah **mor**-hhhen
Good afternoon.	Goeiemiddag.	hhhoy-ah **mit**-tahk
Ma'am	Mevrouw	meh-frow
Sir	Meneer	men-ear
Yes	Ja	yah
No	Nee	nay
Please	Alstublieft	**ahl**-stoo-bleeft
Thank you.	Dank u wel.	dahnk yoo vehl
You're welcome.	Graag gedaan.	hhhrahhk hhkeh-dahn
Excuse me.	Pardon.	par-**dohn**
Do you speak English?	Spreekt u Engels?	spraykt oo **eng**-els
Okay.	Oké.	"okay"
Goodbye.	Tot ziens.	toht zeens
one / two	een / twee	ayn / t'vay
three / four	drie / vier	dree / feer
five / six	vijf / zes	fife / ses
seven / eight	zeven / acht	say-fen / ahkht
nine / ten	negen / tien	nay-hhhen / teen
What does it cost?	Wat kost?	vaht kost
I would like...	Ik wil graag…	ik vil hhhrahhhk
...a room.	…een kamer.	un kah-mer
...a ticket.	…een kaart.	un kart
...a bike.	…een fiets.	un feets
Where is...?	Waar is…?	vahr is
...the station	...het station	het sta-tsee-on
...the tourist info office	...de VVV	duh vay vay vay
left / right	links / rechts	links / rechts
open / closed	open / gesloten	"open" / hhhe-sloh-ten

AMSTERDAM

In the Restaurant

Dutch speakers have an all-purpose word, alstublieft (AHL-stoo-bleeft), that means: "Please," or "Here you are," (if handing you something), or "Thanks," (if taking payment from you), or "You're welcome" (when handing you change). Here are other words that might come in handy at restaurants, particularly if you're day-tripping to small towns:

English	Dutch	Pronunciation
I would like...	Ik wil graag...	ik vil hhhrahhk
...a cup of coffee.	...kopje koffie.	kop-yeh "coffee"
menu	menu	muh-**noo**
non-smoking	niet-roken	neet roh-ken
smoking	roken	roh-ken
with / without	met / buiten	met / bow-ten
and / or	en / of	en / of
bread	brood	broht
salad	sla	slah
cheese	kaas	kahs
meat	vlees	flays
chicken	kip	kip
fish	vis	fis
egg	ei	eye
fruit	vrucht	frucht
pastries	gebak	hhhe-bak
water	water	**wah**-tuhr
beer	bier	beer
wine	wijn	wayn
coffee	koffie	"coffee"
tea	thee	tay
I am vegetarian.	Ik ben vegetarish.	ik ben vay-hhhe-tah-rish
Tasty.	Lekker.	lek-ker
Enjoy!	Smakelijk!	smak-kuh-luk
Cheers!	Proost!	prohst
The bill, please.	De rekening, alstublieft.	duh Ray-kun-ing **ahl**-stoo-bleeft

BRUGES & BRUSSELS

Belgium

Belgium Practicalities

Travelers are often pleasantly surprised by Belgium (Belgie, Belgique, Belgien)—a pleasant, welcoming, and underrated land that produces some of Europe's best beer, creamiest chocolates, most beloved comic strips, and tastiest french fries. Squeezed between Germany, France, and the Netherlands, Belgium has 10.5 million people packed into nearly 12,000 square miles (similar to Maryland)—making it the second most densely populated country in Europe (after the Netherlands). About three-quarters of the population is Catholic. Belgium is a culturally, linguistically, and politically divided country, with 60 percent of the population speaking Dutch...but an economy dominated by French speakers. The capital city of Brussels is also important internationally as the capital of the European Union—more than 25 percent of the people living there are foreigners.

Money: €1 (euro) = about $1.30. The local VAT (value-added sales tax) rate is 21 percent; the minimum purchase eligible for a VAT refund is €125.01 (for details on refunds, see page 140).

Language: The official languages are Dutch, French, and German. For useful phrases, see pages 893, 1107, and 625.

Emergencies: Dial 112 for police, medical, or other emergencies. In case of theft or loss, see page 131.

Time Zone: Belgium is on Central European Time (the same as most of the Continent, one hour ahead of Great Britain, and six/nine hours ahead of the East/ West Coasts of the US).

Embassies in Brussels: The **US embassy** is at Boulevard du Régent 27 (tel. 02-811-4300, after-hours emergency tel. 02-811-4000, http://belgium.usembassy.gov). The **US consulate** is next door to the embassy at Boulevard du Régent 25. The **Canadian embassy** is at Avenue de Tervueren 2 (tel. 02-741-0611, www.ambassade-canada.be). Call ahead for passport services.

Phoning: Belgium's country code is 32; to call from another country to Belgium, dial the international access code (011 from the US/Canada, 00 from Europe, or + from a mobile phone), then 32, followed by the local number (drop the initial zero). For local calls within Belgium, just dial the number as it appears in this book—whether you're calling from across the street or across the country. To place an international call from Belgium, dial 00, the code of the country you're calling (1 for US and Canada), and the phone number. For more tips, see page 1110.

Tipping: The bill for sit-down meals already includes a tip, though for good service it's nice to round up about 5-10 percent. Round up taxi fares a bit (pay €3 on an €2.85 fare). For more tips on tipping, see page 143.

Tourist Information: www.visitbelgium.com

BRUGES, BRUSSELS,
and the PORT of ZEEBRUGGE

Zeebrugge • Bruges • Brussels • Ghent

Belgium's port of Zeebrugge is the gateway to this entire (small) country: With a few hours in port, you could visit literally any point within its borders. Most cruisers, however, set their sights on two places in particular: the charming, quintessentially medieval burg of Bruges (very close to Zeebrugge) and—farther out—the bustling capital of Belgium, and of Europe, Brussels.

With pointy, gilded architecture, stay-a-while cafés, vivid time-tunnel art, and dreamy canals dotted with swans, **Bruges** (pronounced "broozh") is a heavyweight sightseeing destination, as well as a joy. Where else can you ride a bike along a canal, munch mussels and wash them down with the world's best beer, savor heavenly chocolate, and see Flemish Primitives and a Michelangelo, all within 300 yards of a bell tower that jingles every 15 minutes? And do it all without worrying about a language barrier?

Six hundred years ago, **Brussels** was just a nice place to stop and buy a waffle on the way to Bruges. With no strategic importance, it was allowed to grow as a free trading town. Today it's a city of one million people, the capital of Belgium, the headquarters of NATO, and the seat of the European Union.

If neither of these options fits the bill, consider the mid-size city of **Ghent,** which lies halfway between Brussels and Bruges—both geographically and in spirit. A charming university city with historic, art-packed churches and cutting-edge museums, Ghent is about 50 minutes by train from Zeebrugge.

Cruise lines often advertise their Zeebrugge stop as "Brussels," but I recommend setting your sights on Bruges instead. Bruges is not only much closer and easier to reach from your ship, but—

thanks to its user-friendliness and overall charm—it's all-around the more preferable destination.

To sort through all the options from Zeebrugge, see the next section.

Planning Your Time

From Zeebrugge, it's a breeze (short walk, 10- to 15-minute tram ride to Blankenberge, then 15-minute train ride) to zip into **Bruges**—Belgium's most pleasant town, and a perfect place to spend a day. If you prefer a bigger city, you can continue on the same train to **Ghent** (50 minutes each way by train) or **Brussels** (1.5 hours). And for WWI history buffs, the famous **Flanders Fields** are also nearby. With one day in port, you'll need to choose just one of these; for tips on each, see below.

Note: On Mondays, most museums—including major ones in both Bruges (Groeninge, Memling) and Brussels (Royal Museums, BELvue, Musical Instruments, Comic Strip)—are closed.

In Bruges

With a day in Bruges, I'd do the following (ranked here by importance, and in a smart chronological order):

• **Bruges City Walk:** Stroll through town visiting the Markt (Market Square), the Basilica of the Holy Blood, the City Hall's Gothic Room, the Church of Our Lady, and the Begijnhof (allow 2 hours total); if your energy holds up, climb the bell tower on the Markt (add 30-45 minutes).

• **Groeninge Museum:** This fine collection of 15th-century Flemish art takes about an hour to see.

• **Memling Museum:** With a quirky collection of medieval medical trades, plus some paintings by Hans Memling, this deserves an hour.

• **Canal Cruise:** This relaxing and scenic trip takes 30 minutes.

• **De Halve Maan Brewery Tour:** If you have an hour to spare (see schedule on page 853), this tour offers a good taste of Belgian beer.

In Brussels

As a much bigger city, Brussels simply takes more time to get around. But several key sights are in the downtown core. Riding the train to the Central Station, you're within walking distance of these options:

• **Grand Place:** My self-guided tour of Brussels' spectacular main square includes a peek at the famous *Manneken-Pis* statue. Allow two hours.

• **Royal Museums:** For an excellent art collection, head to the Upper Town for the Ancient Art, Fin de Siècle, and René Magritte Museums (allow an hour to quickly see the highlights of the Ancient/Fin de Siècle collections, plus another hour for Magritte).

• **BELvue Museum:** This concise overview of Belgian history, next to the Royal Museums, is worth an hour.

• **Other Museums:** If the options noted above aren't appealing, consider Brussels' good Musical Instruments Museum or Comic Strip Center (allow an hour apiece).

In Ghent

From Ghent's Sint-Pieters Station, it's a 15-minute tram ride into the heart of town. On a short visit, I'd stroll the historic center, tour the Cathedral of St. Bavo (with its grand Van Eyck altarpiece; allow about an hour), and—depending on your interests—visit the castle or Design Museum (each deserves about an hour).

In Flanders Fields

This spread-out area is best seen on an excursion or with a hired driver/guide (for Bruges-based recommendations, see page 845). If you'd like to try it on your own, consider this: Take the coastal tram to Ostende, rent a car, and tour the WWI battlefields and museums near Ypres. Figure 50 minutes by coastal tram from Zeebrugge to Ostend, then an hour each way to drive between Ostend and Ypres.

Arrival at the Port of Zeebrugge

Arrival at a Glance: From your ship, you'll ride a shuttle bus to the port gate, walk (10 minutes) to a tram stop, then ride the tram 10-15 minutes to the Blankenberge train station. From there, hourly trains zip to Bruges (15 minutes), Ghent (50 minutes), and Brussels (1.5 hours).

Port Overview

Zeebrugge (ZAY-brew-gah), 10 miles north from the town of Bruges, is a little village with a gigantic port (Europe's ninth busiest). While the 21st-century industrial port has few amenities for cruisers, access to 15th-century Bruges is easy (and Brussels and Ghent are also reachable).

The sprawling port zone has two cruise berths, each one sandwiched between docks for container ships and other vessels. Larger cruise ships use **Swedish Quay** (Zweedse Kaai), which pokes straight up into the main harbor. Smaller cruise ships use

Excursions from Zeebrugge

Just about anything you'd want to see is doable on your own from Zeebrugge using public transportation—with the notable exception of Flanders Fields.

The most popular excursion options are tours to either charming, manageable **Bruges** or big, bustling **Brussels.** The Bruges excursion usually includes a walking tour around the Old Town. The Brussels excursion generally includes a tour that's part by bus and part on foot. Given the size and relative ease of reaching Bruges, seeing that city on your own is a no-brainer; for Brussels, less adventurous travelers may want to consider an excursion.

Other popular choices include the pleasant university town of **Ghent** (halfway between Bruges and Brussels); the big, fashion-oriented port city of **Antwerp** (including a visit to the Cathedral of Our Lady, decorated with several works by native son Peter Paul Rubens); or a trip to the town of **Ypres** and the surrounding World War I battlefields known as **Flanders Fields.** For something lower-impact, some cruise lines offer a relaxing canalside bike ride between Bruges and the neighboring hamlet of Damme.

Any of these tours may include a few Belgian clichés: canal boat ride, chocolate workshop, sampling a Belgian waffle, or beer tasting. Yes, these things are touristy—but they're also undeniably fun and tasty. Enjoy them.

Maritime Station (Zeestation), across the harbor along Leopold II-Dam. From these berths, a free shuttle bus brings you to either the port gate or a local tram stop. There is no terminal building.

Tourist Information: Zeebrugge has no TI. The most convenient TI is in the city of Blankenberge, near the train station (April-Sept daily 9:00-17:00 except July-Aug until 19:00; Oct-March Mon-Sat 9:00-17:00, Sun 10:00-13:00; Koning Leopold III Plein, tel. 050-412-227, www.blankenberge.be).

Getting into Town

Because the port authority doesn't want cruisers wandering around their cargo facility, a free shuttle bus takes you from your ship to the port gate or a tram stop. While a few taxis are generally standing by to hustle passengers to Bruges, public transit is nearby.

By Public Transportation

Belgium's coastal tram takes you from the port into the town of Blankenberge, with a TI, shops, a pharmacy, and (most importantly) frequent, direct trains to Bruges, Ghent, and Brussels.

Note: Although Zeebrugge does have its own train stations, they are inconvenient for cruisers and offer only milk-run connections to Bruges. Zeebrugge is also linked by bus to Bruges, but the schedule is infrequent. It's smartest to take the coastal tram all the way to Blankenberge's well-connected station.

By Tram from the Port Gate to Blankenberge Train Station

The coastal tram (Kusttram) runs every 20-30 minutes and is covered by a €2 ticket (good for up to one hour)—pay the driver, then validate your ticket in the yellow machine. If you'll also be taking public transit in Bruges, it's smart to buy a day pass for €7 (validate it each time you board, day pass not valid in Brussels; tram info: toll tel. 070-220-200, www.delijn.be).

Which tram stop you use depends on whether you arrive at Swedish Quay or Maritime Station.

From **Swedish Quay,** turn right as you leave the port gate and walk 10 minutes along the highway into the village of Zeebrugge. The Zeebrugge Kerk stop for the coastal tram is right in front of the church. Take any tram going in direction: Oostende or De Panne—use the closest platform (don't cross the tracks).

From **Maritime Station,** your shuttle bus drops you off very near the tram's Zeebrugge Strandwijk stop. Just board the tram going in direction: Oostende or De Panne.

Ride the tram to **Blankenberge Station** (about 14 minutes), an obvious stop in the middle of the first major city. (A video screen inside the tram displays the next stop.) The Blankenberge TI is right behind the tram stop in a building facing a large square (Koning Leopold III Plein). From the tram, cross the street to reach the train station.

By Train from Blankenberge Train Station to Bruges and Brussels

Every train leaving Blankenberge goes through Bruges—just take the next train. Most trains leave at :11 past the hour, arriving in **Bruges** in 15 minutes (€2.90 one-way), then continuing on to **Ghent** (€8.10 one-way, 50 minutes total, get off at Gent-Sint-Pieters station), then **Brussels** (€15.40 one-way, 1.5 hours total, get off at Brussel-Centraal/Bruxelles-Central station). Only local debit cards work in the Belgian railroad's ticket machines, so you'll need to use the station's ticket office, which takes US credit cards.

By Cruise-Line Shuttle Bus

Some cruise lines provide a shuttle bus from the dock all the way to Blankenberge's train station (generally for a fee), where there are services and frequent trains to Bruges and Brussels.

BRUGES & BRUSSELS

Services near the Port of Zeebrugge and in Blankenberge

ATMs: Two ATMs are a short distance from the Zeebrugge Kerk stop for the coastal tram, about a 15-minute walk from the port gate: Leaving the port area from Swedish Quay, turn right and walk along the coastal road. Once in town, pass the church and tram stop and continue along the tram tracks. At the next major intersection, there's a KBC bank on the left and a BNP Paribas bank on the right. If you're taking the tram to **Blankenberge,** you'll find ATMs at the train station there.

Internet Access: The Blankenberge library has free Wi-Fi and Internet access (Mon-Fri 14:00-18:00, Sat 10:00-13:00, closed Sun, near the train station at Onderwijsstraat 17, tel. 050-415-978, http://bibliotheek.blankenberge.be).

Pharmacy: The most convenient pharmacy is in Blankenberge. Ride the tram to Blankenberge's train station, cross the large square, and turn right up the pedestrian shopping street called Kerkstraat. You'll see a neon green cross about 100 feet up the street for **Apotheek Spaens** (Mon-Tue and Thu-Sat 9:00-12:00 & 14:00-18:30, closed Wed and Sun, staff speaks English, Kerkstraat 83, tel. 050-411-141). In Zeebrugge, **Apotheek Havendam,** near the beach, is open only on weekdays (Mon-Fri 9:00-13:30 & 14:00-18:45, closed Sat-Sun, Brusselstraat 34, tel. 050-545-514).

Grocery: If you want to buy a picnic or stock up on snacks, you'll find a Spar grocery store on the main street by the Zeebrugge Kerk tram stop.

By Taxi

Taxis queue up just outside the port gate. Fares are expensive—most cabs charge at least €50 one-way for a trip to Bruges. It's best to arrange for a taxi in advance; try Taxi Snel, which has a standard rate of €50 between Zeebrugge and Bruges (tel. 050-363-649, mobile 0478-353-535, www.taxisnel.be). A taxi from the port to the train station in Blankenberge—with trains to Bruges and Brussels—costs about €20, but it's much cheaper to use the tram (described earlier).

Here are some likely fares for one-way journeys to farther destinations:

Brussels: €225

Ghent: €140

Ypres (Flanders Fields): €180

Again, as taxis here are pricey, I'd be more inclined to consider the efficient and cheap public transit.

By Tour

For information on local tour options in Bruges—including local guides for hire, walking tours, and bus tours—see "Tours in Bruges" on page 845. For Brussels, see page 865.

Sights in Zeebrugge

Beach—Zeebrugge is a beach town as well as a North Sea port. If you'd rather just soak up some sun, grab your towel and a swimsuit and head for the Zeebrugge Strandwijk tram stop. (If you arrive at Maritime Station, your shuttle bus drops you right there; from Swedish Quay, walk to the Zeebrugge Kerk tram stop—directions given earlier—and then ride two stops). From the Zeebrugge Strandwijk stop, go toward the white church, and walk past it along an arbor-covered walkway. At the next street, turn left. At the next intersection, turn right and head for the sand. A small building has showers, WCs, and a summer-only TI that loans bikes (in summer Mon-Fri 9:00-12:30 & 14:00-18:45). Beach cafés and restaurants are nearby.

Returning to Your Ship

Coming by train from Bruges, Ghent, or Brussels, simply ride the train back to Blankenberge (you can't miss it—it's the end of the line). Once you arrive in Blankenberge, leave the station, cross the street, and take the tram in the direction of Knokke (if you need a ticket, get one at the ticket office at the tram stop, or buy from driver). If your ship is at **Maritime Station,** jump off at the Zeebrugge Strandwijk stop to catch the cruise-line shuttle bus. If your ship is at **Swedish Quay,** stay on the tram until the Zeebrugge Kerk stop (with a large brick church right next to the platform). From here, it's a 10-minute walk back to the cruise port gate and your shuttle bus. If you're in a hurry, you can spring for a cab (€20) from the Blankenberge train station to the dock.

See page 892 for help if you miss your boat.

Bruges

Right from the start, Bruges was a trading center. In the 11th century, the city grew wealthy on the cloth trade. By the 14th century, Bruges' population was 35,000, as large as London's. As the middleman in the sea trade between northern and southern Europe, it was one of the biggest cities in the world and an economic powerhouse. In addition, Bruges had become the most important cloth market in northern Europe.

In the 15th century, while England and France were slugging it out in the Hundred Years' War, Bruges was the favored residence of the powerful Dukes of Burgundy—and at peace. Commerce and the arts boomed. The artists Jan van Eyck and Hans Memling had studios here.

But by the 16th century, the harbor had silted up and the economy had collapsed. The Burgundian court left, Belgium became a minor Habsburg possession, and Bruges' Golden Age abruptly ended. For generations, Bruges was known as a mysterious and dead city. In the 19th century, a new port, Zeebrugge, brought renewed vitality to the area. And in the 20th century, tourists discovered the town.

Today, Bruges prospers because of tourism: It's a uniquely well-preserved Gothic city and a handy gateway to Europe. It's no secret, but even with the crowds, it's the kind of place where you don't mind being a tourist. Bruges' ultimate sight is the town itself, and the best way to enjoy it is to get lost on the back streets, away from the lace shops and ice-cream stands.

BRUGES & BRUSSELS

Orientation to Bruges

The town is Brugge (BROO-ghah) in Dutch, and Bruges (broozh) in French and English. Its name comes from the Viking word for wharf. The tourist's Bruges—and you'll be sharing it—is less than one square mile, contained within a canal (the former moat). Nearly everything of interest and importance is within a convenient cobbled swath between the train station and the Markt (Market Square; a 20-minute walk).

Tourist Information

The main TI, called **In&Uit** ("In and Out"), is in the big, red concert hall on the square called 't Zand (daily 10:00-18:00, take a number from the touch-screen machines and wait, 't Zand 34, tel. 050-444-646, www.brugge.be). They have three terminals with free Internet access and printers. The other TI is at the train station (Mon-Fri 10:00-17:00, Sat-Sun 10:00-14:00).

The TIs sell the €2.50 *Love Bruges Visitors' Guide*, which comes with a map (costs €0.50 if bought separately), a few well-described self-guided walking tours, and listings of all the sights and services (free with Brugge City Card). You can also pick up a free monthly English-language program called *events@brugge*, and information on train schedules and tours (see "Tours in Bruges," later). The TI also has a free "Use-It" map available for young-at-heart travelers—filled with tips for backpackers and well worth asking for.

Arrival at Bruges' Train Station

By train from Blankenberge (see details on page 839), you'll get off at Bruges' train station, in a clean, park-like setting, where travelers step out the door and are greeted by a taxi stand and a roundabout with center-bound buses circulating through every couple minutes. Coming in, you'll see the bell tower that marks the main square (Markt, the center of town). Upon arrival, stop by the train station TI, described above. The station has ATMs and lockers (€3-4).

The best way to get to the town center is by **bus.** Buses #1, #3, #4, #6, #11, #13, #14, and #16 go to the Markt (all marked *Centrum*). Simply hop on, pay €2 (€1.20 if you buy in advance at Lijnwinkel shop just outside the train station), and you're there in four minutes (get off at third stop—either Markt or Wollestraat). A **taxi** from the train station to downtown costs about €8.

It's a 20-minute **walk** from the station to the Markt: Cross the busy street and canal in front of the station, head up Oostmeers, and turn right on Zwidzandstraat. You can rent a **bike** at the station, but other bike-rental shops are closer to the center (see "Helpful Hints," next).

Helpful Hints

Blue Monday: In Bruges, many museums are open Tuesday through Sunday year-round from 9:30 to 17:00 and are closed on Monday. If you're in Bruges on a Monday, the following attractions are open: bell-tower climb on the Markt, Begijnhof, De Halve Maan Brewery Tour, Basilica of the Holy Blood, City Hall's Gothic Room, chocolate shops and museum, and Church of Our Lady. You can also join a boat, bus, or walking tour, or rent a bike and pedal into the countryside.

Museum Passes: The 't Zand TI and city museums sell a "Museumpas" **combo-ticket** (any five museums for €20, valid for 3 days). Because the Groeninge and Memling museums cost €8 each, art lovers who squeeze in at least three sights will save money with this pass. The **Brugge City Card** is a more extensive pass covering entry to 26 museums, including all the major sights, plus other discounts (€35/48 hours, €40/72 hours, sold at TIs). On a short day in port, you're unlikely to get your money's worth with this card.

Market Days: Bruges hosts markets on Wednesday morning (on the Markt) and Saturday morning ('t Zand). On good-weather Saturdays, Sundays, and public holidays, a flea market hops along Dijver in front of the Groeninge Museum. The Fish Market sells souvenirs daily and seafood Wednesday through Saturday mornings until 13:00.

Shopping: Shops are generally open from 10:00 to 18:00 and closed Sunday. Grocery stores usually are closed on Sunday. The main shopping street, Steenstraat, stretches from the Markt to 't Zand Square. The **Hema** department store is at Steenstraat 73. **FNAC,** the electronics/department store for all your needs, is on the Markt. There's a good travel bookstore (which carries my guidebooks) at #12 on the Markt.

Internet Access: There are three free terminals at the **TI** on 't Zand. **Call Shop,** just a block off the Markt, is the most central of the city's many "telephone shops" offering Internet access (€1.50/30 minutes, €2.50/hour, daily 9:00-20:00, Philipstockstraat 4). **Bean Around the World** is a cozy coffeehouse with imported Yankee snacks and free Wi-Fi for customers (€1/15 minutes on their computers, Thu-Mon 10:00-19:00, Wed 11:30-19:00, closed Tue, Genthof 5, tel. 050-703-572, run by American expat Olene).

Post Office: It's on the Markt near the bell tower (Mon-Fri 9:00-18:00, Sat 9:30-15:00, closed Sun, tel. 050-331-411).

Bike Rental: Bruges Bike Rental is central and cheap, with friendly service and long hours (€3.50/hour, €5/2 hours, €7/4 hours, €10/day, show this book to get student rate—€8/day, no deposit required—just ID, daily 10:00-22:00, free city maps and child seats, behind the far-out iron facade at Niklaas Desparsstraat 17, tel. 050-616-108, Bilal). **Fietsen Popelier Bike Rental** is also good (€4/hour, €8/4 hours, €12/day, no deposit required, daily 10:00-19:00, sometimes open later in summer, free Damme map, Mariastraat 26, tel. 050-343-262). **Koffieboontje Bike Rental** is just under the bell tower on the Markt (€4/hour, €9/day, €20/day for tandem, these prices for Rick Steves readers, daily 9:00-22:00, free city maps and child seats, Hallestraat 4, tel. 050-338-027). **De Ketting** is less central, but cheap (€6/day, Mon-Fri 9:00-12:15 & 13:30-18:30 except Mon opens at 10:00, Sat 9:30-12:15, closed Sun, Gentpoortstraat 23, tel. 050-344-196, www.deketting.be). **Fietspunt Brugge** is a huge outfit at the train station (7-speed bikes, €12/24-hours, €7/4 hours, free maps, Mon-Fri 7:00-19:30, Sat-Sun 9:00-21:30, just outside the station and to the right as you exit, tel. 050-396-826).

Best Town View: The bell tower overlooking the Markt rewards those who climb it with the ultimate town view.

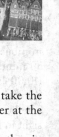

Updates to this Book: Check www.ricksteves.com/update for any significant changes that have occurred since this book was printed.

Getting Around Bruges

Most of the city is easily walkable, but you may want to take the bus or a taxi between the train station and the city center at the Markt.

By Bus: A bus ticket is good for an hour (€1.20 if you buy in advance at Lijnwinkel shop just outside the train station, or €2 on the bus). And though you can buy various day passes, there's really no need to buy one for your visit. Nearly all city buses go directly from the train station to the Markt and fan out from there; they then return to the Markt and go back to the train station. Note that buses returning to the train station from the Markt also leave from the library bus stop, a block off the square on nearby Kuiperstraat (every 5 minutes). Your key: Use buses that say either *Station* or *Centrum*.

By Taxi: You'll find taxi stands at the station and on the Markt (€8/first 2 km; to get a cab in the center, call 050-334-444 or 050-333-881).

Tours in Bruges

Bruges by Boat—The most relaxing and scenic (though not informative) way to see this city of canals is by boat, with the captain narrating. The city carefully controls this standard tourist activity, so the many companies all offer essentially the same thing: a 30-minute route (roughly 4/hour, daily 10:00-17:00), a price of €7.60 (cash only), and narration in three or four languages. Qualitative differences are because of individual guides, not companies. Always let them know you speak English to ensure you'll understand the spiel. Two companies give the group-rate discount to individuals with this book: **Boten Stael** (just over the canal from Memling Museum at Katelijnestraat 4, tel. 050-332-771) and **Gruuthuse** (Nieuwstraat 11, opposite Groeninge Museum, tel. 050-333-393).

Bruges by Bike—QuasiMundo Bike Tours leads daily five-mile English-language bike tours around the city (€25, €3 discount with this book, 2.5 hours, departs March-Oct at 10:00, in Nov only with good weather, no tours Dec-Feb). For more details and contact info, see their listing under "Near Bruges," later.

City Minibus Tour—City Tour Bruges gives a rolling overview of the town in an 18-seat, two-skylight minibus with dial-a-language headsets and video support (€16, 50 minutes, pay driver). The tour leaves hourly from the Markt (10:00-19:00, until 18:00 in fall, less in winter, tel. 050-355-024, www.citytour.be). The narration, though clear, is slow-moving and a bit boring. But the tour is a lazy way to cruise past virtually every sight in Bruges.

Walking Tour—Local guides walk small groups through the core of town (€9, 2 hours, daily July-Aug, Sat-Sun only mid-April-June and Sept-Oct, depart from TI on 't Zand Square at 14:30—just drop in a few minutes early and buy tickets at the TI desk). Though earnest, the tours are heavy on history and given in two languages, so they may be less than peppy. Still, to propel you beyond the pretty gables and canal swans of Bruges, they're good medicine.

Local Guide—A private two-hour guided tour costs €70 (reserve at least one week in advance through TI, tel. 050-448-686). Or contact **Christian Scharlé** and **Daniëlle Janssens**, who give two-hour walks for €80, three-hour walks for €120, and full-day tours of Bruges and Brussels for €210 (Christian's mobile 0475-659-507, Daniëlle's mobile 0476-493-203, www.tourmanagementbelgium .be, tmb@skynet.be).

Horse-and-Buggy Tour—The buggies around town can take you on a clip-clop tour (€36, 35 minutes; price is per carriage, not per person; buggies gather in Minnewater, near entrance to Begijnhof, and on the Markt). When divided among four or five people, this can be a good value.

Near Bruges

Popular tour destinations from Bruges are Flanders Fields (famous WWI sites about 40 miles to the southwest) and the picturesque town of Damme (4 easy-to-bike miles to the northeast). Note: Squeezing one of these trips into your day in the port of

Zeebrugge doesn't always work; it depends on your ship's departure and arrival times.

Quasimodo Countryside Tours—This company offers those with extra time two entertaining, all-day, English-only bus tours through the rarely visited Flemish countryside. The "Flanders Fields" tour concentrates on WWI battlefields, trenches, memorials, and poppy-splattered fields (Tue-Sun at 9:15, no tours Mon or in Jan, 8 hours, visit to In Flanders Fields Museum not included). The other tour, "Triple Treat," focuses on Flanders' medieval past and rich culture, with tastes of chocolate, waffles, and beer (departs Mon, Wed, and Fri at 9:15, 8 hours). Be ready for lots of walking.

Tours cost €63, or €53 if you're under 26 (cash preferred, €10 discount on second tour if you've taken the other, includes sandwich lunch, 9- or 30-seat bus depending on demand, non-smoking, reservations required—call 050-370-470, www.quasimodo.be). After making a few big-hotel pickups, the buses leave town from the Park Hotel on 't Zand Square (arrange for pickup when you reserve).

If you reserve well in advance and can fill a minibus, Quasimodo may be able to arrange a private tour that meets you at the ship (contact them for details).

Bike Tours—**QuasiMundo Bike Tours,** which runs bike tours around Bruges (listed earlier), also offers a daily "Border by Bike"

tour through the nearby countryside to Damme (€25, €3 discount with this book, March-Oct, departs at 13:00, 15 miles, 4 hours, tel. 050-330-775, www.quasimundo.com). Both their city and border tours include bike rental, a light raincoat (if necessary), water, and a drink in a local café. Meet at the metal "car wash" fountain on Burg Square 10 minutes before departure. If you already have a bike, you're welcome to join either tour for €15. Jos, who leads most departures, is a high-energy and entertaining guide.

Charming Mieke of **Pink Bear Bike Tours** takes small groups on an easy and delightful 3.5-hour guided pedal along a canal to the historic town of Damme and back, finishing with a brief tour of Bruges. English tours go daily through peak season and nearly daily the rest of the year (€23, €2 discount with

Bruges

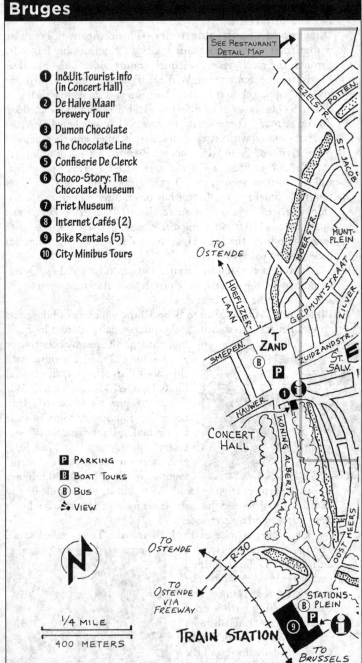

1. In&Uit Tourist Info (in Concert Hall)
2. De Halve Maan Brewery Tour
3. Dumon Chocolate
4. The Chocolate Line
5. Confiserie De Clerck
6. Choco-Story: The Chocolate Museum
7. Friet Museum
8. Internet Cafés (2)
9. Bike Rentals (5)
10. City Minibus Tours

P PARKING
B BOAT TOURS
Ⓑ BUS
⇴ VIEW

SEE RESTAURANT DETAIL MAP

TO OSTENDE

'T ZAND

MUNT-PLEIN

ST. SALV.

CONCERT HALL

TO OSTENDE

TO OSTENDE VIA FREEWAY

TO BRUSSELS

R-30

STATIONS-PLEIN

TRAIN STATION

N

¼ MILE

400 METERS

BRUGES & BRUSSELS

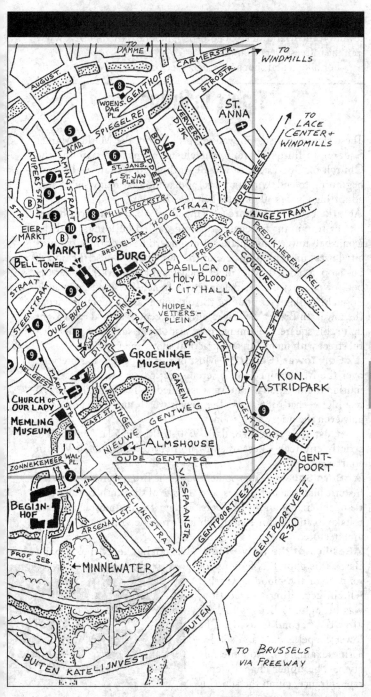

this book, €16 if you already have a bike, meet at 10:25 under bell tower on the Markt, tel. 050-616-686, mobile 0476-744-525, www.pinkbear.freeservers.com).

For bike rental shops in Bruges, see page 844.

Sights in Bruges

These sights are listed in walking order, from the Markt (Market Square), to Burg Square, to the cluster of museums around the Church of Our Lady, to the Begijnhof (10-minute walk from beginning to end, without stops). Be aware that many sights stop admitting visitors 30 minutes before closing.

▲**Markt (Market Square)**—Ringed by a bank, the post office, lots of restaurant terraces, great old gabled buildings, and the iconic bell tower, this square is the modern heart of the city (most city buses run from near here to the train station—use the library bus stop, a block down Kuiperstraat from the Markt). Under the bell tower are two great Belgian-style french-fry stands, a quadrilingual Braille description of the old town, and a metal model of the tower. In Bruges' heyday as a trading center, a canal came right up to this square. Geldmuntstraat, just off the square, is a delightful street with many fun and practical shops and eateries.

▲▲**Bell Tower (Belfort)**—Most of this bell tower has presided over the Markt since 1300, serenading passersby with carillon music. The octagonal lantern was added in 1486, making it 290 feet high—that's 366 steps. The view is worth the climb and probably even the pricey admission.

Cost and Hours: €8, daily 9:30-17:00, 16:15 last-entry time strictly enforced—best to show up before 16:00, €0.30 WC in courtyard.

▲▲**Burg Square**—This opulent square is Bruges' civic center, the historic birthplace of Bruges, and the site of the ninth-century castle of the first count of Flanders. Today, it's an atmospheric place to take in an outdoor concert while surrounded by six centuries of architecture.

▲**Basilica of the Holy Blood**—Originally the Chapel of Saint Basil, this church is famous for its relic of the blood of Christ, which, according to tradition, was brought to Bruges in 1150 after the Second Crusade. The lower chapel is dark and solid—a fine example of Romanesque style. The upper chapel (separate entrance, climb the stairs) is

decorated Gothic. An interesting treasury museum is next to the upper chapel.

Cost and Hours: April-Sept daily 9:30-12:00 & 14:00-18:00; Oct-March daily 10:00-12:00 & 14:00-16:00 except closed Wed afternoon; Burg Square, tel. 050-336-792, www.holyblood.com.

▲**City Hall**—This complex houses several interesting sights. Your €2 ticket includes an audioguide; access to a room full of old town maps and paintings; the grand, beautifully restored **Gothic Room** from 1400, starring a painted and carved wooden ceiling adorned with hanging arches (daily 9:30-17:00, last entry 30 minutes before closing, Burg 12); and the less impressive **Renaissance Hall** (Brugse Vrije), basically just one ornate room with a Renaissance chimney (same hours, separate entrance—in corner of square at Burg 11a).

▲▲**Groeninge Museum**—This museum has one of the world's best collections of the art produced in the city and surrounding area, from Memling to Magritte. In the 1400s, Bruges was northern Europe's richest, most cosmopolitan, and most cultured city. New ideas, fads, and painting techniques were imported and exported with each shipload. Beautiful paintings were soon an affordable luxury, like fancy clothes or furniture. Internationally known artists set up studios in Bruges, producing portraits and altarpieces for wealthy merchants from all over Europe.

While there's plenty of worthwhile modern art, the Groeninge's highlights are the vivid and pristine Flemish Primitives. ("Primitive" here means "before the Renaissance.") This early Flemish style, though less appreciated and understood today than the Italian Renaissance art produced a century later, is subtle, technically advanced, and beautiful. Flemish art is shaped by its love of detail, its merchant patrons' egos, and the power of the Church. Lose yourself in the halls of Groeninge: Gaze across 15th-century canals, into the eyes of reassuring Marys, and through town squares littered with leotards, lace, and lopped-off heads.

Cost and Hours: €8, Tue-Sun 9:30-17:00, closed Mon, Dijver 12, tel. 050-448-743, www.brugge.be.

▲▲**Church of Our Lady (Onze-Lieve-Vrouwekerk)**—The church stands as a memorial to the power and wealth of Bruges in its heyday. A delicate *Madonna and Child* by Michelangelo is near the apse (to the right if you're facing the altar). It's said to be the only Michelangelo statue to leave Italy in his lifetime (thanks to the wealth generated by Bruges' cloth trade). If

BRUGES & BRUSSELS

you like tombs and church art, pay to wander through the apse.

Cost and Hours: The rear of the church is free to the public. To get into the main section costs €4; church open Mon-Sat 9:30-17:00, Sun 13:30-17:00, Mariastraat, www.brugge.be.

▲▲Memling Museum/St. John's Hospital (Sint Jans-hospitaal)—The former monastery/hospital complex has a fine museum in what was once the monks' church. The museum offers a glimpse into medieval medicine, displaying surgical instruments, documents, and visual aids as you work your way to the museum's climax: several of Hans Memling's glowing masterpieces. Memling's art was the culmination of Bruges' Flemish Primitive style. His serene, soft-focus, motionless scenes capture a medieval piety that was quickly fading. The popular style made Memling (c. 1430-1494) one of Bruges' wealthiest citizens, and his work was gobbled up by visiting Italian merchants, who took it home with them, cross-pollinating European art. His *Mystical Wedding of St. Catherine* triptych is a highlight, as is the miniature, gilded-oak shrine to St. Ursula.

Cost and Hours: €8, includes good audioguide, Tue-Sun 9:30-17:00, closed Mon, last entry 30 minutes before closing, across the street from the Church of Our Lady, Mariastraat 38, Bruges museums tel. 050-448-713, www .brugge.be.

▲▲Begijnhof—Inhabited by Benedictine nuns, the Begijnhof courtyard (free, daily 6:30-18:30) almost makes you want to don a habit and fold your hands as you walk under its wispy trees and whisper past its frugal little homes. For a good slice of Begijnhof life, walk through the simple Beguine's House museum.

Cost and Hours: €2, Mon-Sat 10:00-17:00, Sun 14:30-17:00, shorter hours off-season, English explanations, museum is left of entry gate.

Minnewater—Just south of the Begijnhof is Minnewater, an idyllic world of flower boxes, canals, and swans.

Almshouses—As you walk from the Begijnhof back to the town center, you might detour along Nieuwe Gentweg to visit one of about 20 almshouses in the city. At #8, go through the door marked *Godshuis de Meulenaere 1613* into the peaceful courtyard (free). This was a medieval form of housing for the poor. The rich would pay for someone's tiny room here in return for lots of prayers.

Bruges Experiences

▲▲**De Halve Maan Brewery Tour**—Belgians are Europe's beer connoisseurs, and this handy tour is a great way to pay your respects. The brewery makes the only beers brewed in Bruges: Brugse Zot ("Fool from Bruges") and Straffe Hendrik ("Strong Henry"). The happy gang at this working-family brewery gives entertaining and informative 45-minute tours in two languages. Avoid crowds by visiting at 11:00.

Cost and Hours: €6.50 includes a beer, lots of very steep steps, great rooftop panorama; tours run April-Oct daily on the hour 11:00-16:00,
Sat until 18:00; Nov-March Mon-Fri 11:00 and 15:00 only, Sat-Sun on the hour 11:00-17:00; Walplein 26, tel. 050-444-223, www.halvemaan.be.

▲**Chocolate Shops**—Bruggians are connoisseurs of fine chocolate. You'll be tempted by chocolate-filled display windows all over town. While Godiva is the best big-factory/high-price/high-quality brand, there are plenty of smaller family-run places in Bruges that offer exquisite handmade chocolates. All three of the following chocolatiers are proud of their creative varieties, generous with their samples, and welcome you to assemble a 100-gram assortment of five or six chocolates.

Dumon: Perhaps Bruges' smoothest, creamiest chocolates are at Dumon, just off the Markt (a selection of 5 or 6 chocolates are a deal at €2.30/100 grams). Natale

Dumon runs the store, with Madame Dumon still dropping by to help make their top-notch chocolate daily and sell it fresh (Wed-Mon 10:00-18:00, closed Tue, old chocolate molds on display in basement, Eiermarkt 6, tel. 050-346-282). The Dumons don't provide English labels because
they believe it's best to describe their chocolates in person—and they do it with an evangelical fervor. Try a small mix-and-match box to sample a few out-of-this-world flavors, and come back for more of your favorites.

The Chocolate Line: Locals and tourists alike flock to The Chocolate Line (pricey at €5.60/100 grams) to taste the *gastronomique* varieties concocted by Dominique Person—the mad scientist of chocolate. His unique creations mix chocolate with various, mostly savory, flavors. Even those that sound gross can be surprisingly good (be adventurous). Options include Havana cigar (marinated in rum, cognac, and Cuban tobacco leaves—so, therefore, technically illegal in the US), lemongrass, lavender, ginger (shaped like a Buddha), saffron curry, spicy chili, Moroccan mint, Pop Rocks/cola chocolate, wine vinegar, fried onions, bay leaf, sake, lime/vodka/passion fruit, wasabi, and tomatoes/olives/basil. The kitchen—busy whipping up 80 varieties—is on display in the back. Enjoy the window display, refreshed monthly (daily 9:30-18:00 except Sun-Mon opens at 10:30, between Church of Our Lady and the Markt at Simon Stevinplein 19, tel. 050-341-090).

Confiserie De Clerck: Third-generation chocolate maker Jan sells his handmade chocolates for just €1.20/100 grams, making this one of the best deals in town. Some locals claim his chocolate's just as good as at pricier places—taste it and decide for yourself. The time-warp candy shop itself is so delightfully old-school, you'll want to visit no matter what (Mon-Wed and Fri-Sat 10:00-19:00, closed Sun and Thu, Academiestraat 19, tel. 050-345-338).

▲**Choco-Story: The Chocolate Museum**—The Chocolate Fairy leads you through 2,600 years of chocolate history—explaining why, in the ancient Mexican world of the Mayas and the Aztecs, chocolate was considered the drink of the gods, and cocoa beans were used as a means of payment. With lots of artifacts well-described in English, this kid-friendly museum fills you in on the production of truffles, bonbons, hollow figures, and solid bars of chocolate. You'll view a delicious little video (8 minutes long, runs continuously, English subtitles). Your finale is in the "demonstration room," where—after a 10-minute cooking demo—you get a taste.

Cost and Hours: €7, €11 combo-ticket includes nearby Friet Museum, daily 10:00-17:00; where Wijnzakstraat meets Sint Jansstraat at Sint Jansplein, 3-minute walk from the Markt; tel. 050-612-237, www.choco-story.be.

Nearby: The Chocolate Museum owner's wife got tired of his ancient lamp collection...so he opened a **Lamp Museum** next door (€11 combo-ticket with Chocolate Museum). While obscure, it's an impressive and well-described collection showing lamps through the ages.

Friet Museum—While this fun-loving and kid-friendly place tries hard to elevate the story of the potato, this is—for most—one museum too many. Still, it's the only place in the world that enthusiastically tells the story of french fries, which, of course, aren't even French—they're Belgian.

Cost and Hours: €6, €11 combo-ticket includes Chocolate Museum, daily 10:00-17:00, Vlamingstraat 33, tel. 050-340-150, www.frietmuseum.be.

Windmills and Lace by the Moat—A 15-minute walk from the center to the northeast end of town (faster by bike) brings you to four windmills strung along a pleasant grassy setting on the "big moat" canal. The St. Janshuys **windmill** is open to visitors (€2; May-Aug Tue-Sun 9:30-12:30 & 13:30-17:00, closed Mon, last entry at 16:30; Sept same hours but open Sat-Sun only; closed Oct-April; go to the end of Carmersstraat and hang a right).

The **Folklore Museum,** in the same neighborhood, is cute but

forgettable (€2, Tue-Sun 9:30-17:00, last entry at 16:30, closed Mon, Balstraat 43, tel. 050-448-764). To find it, ask for the Jerusalem Church. On the same street is a lace shop with a good reputation, 't Apostelientje (Tue 13:00-17:00, Wed-Sat 9:30-12:15 & 13:15-17:00, Sun 10:00-13:00, closed Mon, Balstraat 11, tel. 050-337-860, mobile 0495-562-420).

▲▲Biking—The Dutch word for bike is *fiets* (pronounced "feets"). And though Bruges' sights are close enough for easy walking, the town is a treat for bikers, and a bike quickly gets you into dreamy back lanes without a hint of tourism. Take a peaceful ride through the town's nooks and crannies and around the outer canal. Along the canal that circles the town is a park with a delightful bike lane. Rental shops have maps and ideas (see "Bike Rental" on page 844).

Eating in Bruges

Bruges' specialties include mussels cooked a variety of ways (one order can feed two), fish dishes, grilled meats, and french fries. The town's two indigenous beers are the prizewinning Brugse Zot, a golden ale, and Straffe Hendrik, a potent, bitter triple ale.

You'll find plenty of affordable, touristy restaurants on picturesque squares and along dreamy canals. Bruges feeds 3.5 million tourists a year, and most are seduced by a high-profile location. These can be great experiences

Bruges Restaurants

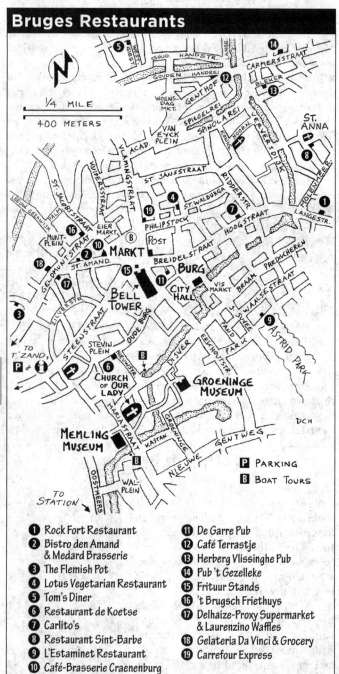

BRUGES & BRUSSELS

① Rock Fort Restaurant
② Bistro den Amand
   & Medard Brasserie
③ The Flemish Pot
④ Lotus Vegetarian Restaurant
⑤ Tom's Diner
⑥ Restaurant de Koetse
⑦ Carlito's
⑧ Restaurant Sint-Barbe
⑨ L'Estaminet Restaurant
⑩ Café-Brasserie Craenenburg

⑪ De Garre Pub
⑫ Café Terrastje
⑬ Herberg Vlissinghe Pub
⑭ Pub 't Gezelleke
⑮ Frituur Stands
⑯ 't Brugsch Friethuys
⑰ Delhaize-Proxy Supermarket
   & Laurenzino Waffles
⑱ Gelateria Da Vinci & Grocery
⑲ Carrefour Express

for the magical setting and views, but the quality of food and service will likely be mediocre. I wouldn't blame you for eating at one of these places, but I won't recommend any. I prefer the candle-cool bistros that flicker on back streets.

Restaurants

Rock Fort is a chic spot with a modern, fresh coziness and a high-powered respect for good food. Two young chefs, Peter Laloo and Hermes Vanliefde, give their French cuisine a creative, gourmet twist. At the bar they serve a separate tapas menu. Reservations recommended. This place is a winner (€6-12 tapas, great pastas and salads, €15 lunch special, open Mon-Fri 12:00-14:30 & 18:30-23:00, closed Sat-Sun, Langestraat 15, tel. 050-334-113).

Bistro den Amand, with a plain interior and a few outdoor tables, exudes unpretentious quality the moment you step in. In this mussels-free zone, Chef An is enthusiastic about stir-fry and vegetables, as her busy wok and fun salads prove. Portions are splittable and there are always good vegetarian options. The creative dishes—some with a hint of Asian influence—are a welcome departure from Bruges' mostly predictable traditional restaurants. It's on a bustling pedestrian lane a half-block off the Markt (€35 three-course meal, €20-25 plates; Mon-Tue and Thu-Sat 12:00-14:00 & 18:00-21:00, closed Wed and Sun; Sint-Amandstraat 4, tel. 050-340-122, An Vissers and Arnout Beyaert).

The Flemish Pot is a busy eatery where enthusiastic chefs Mario and Rik cook up a traditional menu of vintage Flemish specialties—from beef and rabbit stew to eel—served in little iron pots and skillets. Seating is tight and cluttered, and service can be spotty. But you'll enjoy huge portions, refills from the hovering "fries angel," and a good selection of local beers (€26-30 three-course meals, €16-24 plates, daily 12:00-22:00, reservations smart, family-friendly, just off Geldmuntstraat at Helmstraat 3, tel. 050-340-086).

Lotus Vegetarian Restaurant serves serious lunch plates (€10 *plat du jour* offered daily), salads, and homemade chocolate cake in a pleasantly small, bustling, and upscale setting. To keep carnivorous companions happy, they also serve several very good organic meat dishes (Mon-Fri from 11:45, last orders at 14:00, closed Sat-Sun, just north of Burg Square at Wapenmakersstraat 5, tel. 050-331-078).

Tom's Diner is a trendy, cozy little candlelit bistro in a quiet, cobbled residential area a 10-minute walk from the center. Young chef Tom gives traditional dishes a delightful modern twist, such as his signature Flemish meat loaf with rhubarb sauce. If you want to flee the tourists and experience a popular neighborhood joint, this is it—the locals love it (€15-20 plates, Tue-Sat 12:00-14:00 & 18:00-23:00, closed Sun-Mon, north of the Markt near Sint-Gilliskerk at West-Gistelhof 23, tel. 050-333-382).

Restaurant de Koetse is handy for central, good-quality, local-style food. The feeling is traditional, a bit formal (stuffy even) and dressy, yet accessible. The cuisine is Belgian and French, with an emphasis on grilled meat, seafood, and mussels (€30 three-course meals, €20-30 plates include vegetables and a salad, Fri-Wed 12:00-14:30 & 18:00-22:00, closed Thu, non-smoking section, Oude Burg 31, tel. 050-337-680, Piet).

Carlito's is a good choice for basic Italian fare. Their informal space, with whitewashed walls and tea-light candles, is two blocks from Burg Square (€8-13 pizzas and pastas, daily 12:00-14:00 & 18:00-22:30, patio seating in back, Hoogstraat 21, tel. 050-490-075).

Restaurant Sint-Barbe, on the eastern edge of town, is a homey little neighborhood place where Evi serves classy Flemish dishes made from local ingredients in a fresh, modern space on two floors (€12 soup-and-main lunch, €14-25 main courses, Thu-Mon 11:30-14:30 & 18:00-22:00, closed Tue-Wed, food served until 21:00, St. Annaplein 29, tel. 050-330-999).

L'Estaminet is a youthful, jazz-filled eatery, similar to one of Amsterdam's brown cafés. Don't be intimidated by its lack of tourists. Local students flock here for the Tolkien-chic ambience, hearty €9 spaghetti, and big meal-size salads. This is Belgium—it serves more beer than wine. For outdoor dining under an all-weather canopy, enjoy the relaxed patio facing peaceful Astrid Park (Fri-Wed 11:30-24:00, Thu 16:00-24:00, Park 5, tel. 050-330-916).

Restaurants on the Markt: Most tourists seem to be eating on the Markt with the bell tower high overhead and horse carriages clip-clopping by. The square is ringed by tourist traps with aggressive waiters expert at getting you to consume more than you intended. Still, if you order smartly, you can have a memorable meal or drink here on one of the finest squares in Europe at a reasonable price. Consider **Café-Brasserie Craenenburg,** with a straightforward menu, where you can get pasta and beer for €15 and spend all the time you want ogling the magic of Bruges (daily 7:30-23:00, Markt 16, tel. 050-333-402). While it's overpriced for dining, it can be a fine place to savor a before- or after-meal drink with the view.

Cheap Eats: **Medard Brasserie,** just a block off the Markt, serves the cheapest hot meal in town—hearty meat spaghetti (big plate-€3, huge plate-€5.50, sit inside or out, Fri-Wed 11:00-20:30, closed Thu, Sint Amandstraat 18, tel. 050-348-684).

Bars Offering Light Meals, Beer, and Ambience

My best budget-eating tip for Bruges: Stop into one of the city's bars for a simple meal and a couple of world-class beers with great Bruges ambience. The last three pubs listed are in the wonderfully *gezellig* (cozy) quarter, northeast of the Markt. Just walking out here is a treat as it gets you away from the tourists.

De Garre (deh-HHHHAHR-rah) is a good place to gain an appreciation of the Belgian beer culture. Rather than a noisy pub scene, it has a dressy, sit-down-and-focus-on-your-friend-and-the-fine-beer vibe. It's mature and cozy, with tables, light meals (cold cuts, pâtés, and toasted sandwiches), and a huge selection of beers, with heavy beers being the forte (Tue-Sun 12:00-24:00, closed Mon, additional seating up tiny staircase, off Breidelstraat between Burg and the Markt, on tiny Garre alley, tel. 050-341-029).

Café Terrastje is a cozy pub serving light meals. Enjoy the subdued ambience inside, or relax on the front terrace overlooking the canal and heart of the *gezellig* district (€6-8 sandwiches, €10-18 dishes; food served Fri-Mon 12:00-21:00, open until 23:30; Tue 12:00-18:00; closed Wed-Thu; corner of Genthof and Langerei, tel. 050-330-919, Ian and Patricia).

Herberg Vlissinghe is the oldest pub in town (1515). Bruno keeps things basic and laid-back, serving simple plates (lasagna, grilled cheese sandwiches, and famous €8 angel-hair spaghetti) and great beer in the best old-time tavern atmosphere in town. This must have been the Dutch Masters' rec room. The garden outside comes with a *boules* court—free for guests to watch or play (Wed-Sat 11:00-24:00, Sun 11:00-19:00, closed Mon-Tue, Blekersstraat 2, tel. 050-343-737).

Pub 't Gezelleke lacks the mystique of the Vlissinghe, but it's a true neighborhood pub offering spaghetti and a few basic plates and a good chance to drink with locals (if you sit at the bar). Its name is an appropriate play on the word for *cozy* and the name of a great local poet (daily 11:00-24:00, but closed Sun and Wed, Carmersstraat 15, tel. 050-338-381, Jean de Bruges). Don't come here to eat outdoors.

Fries, Fast Food, and Picnics

Local french fries *(friets)* are a treat. Proud and traditional *frituur*s serve tubs of fries and various local-style shish kebabs. Belgians dip their *friets* in mayonnaise, but ketchup is there for the Yankees (along with spicier sauces). For a quick, cheap, hot, and scenic snack, hit a *frituur* and sit on the steps or benches overlooking the Markt (convenient benches are about 50 yards past the post office).

Markt *Frituur***s:** Twin take-away fry carts are on the Markt at the base of the bell tower (daily 10:00-24:00). Skip the ketchup and have a sauce adventure. I find the cart on the left more user-friendly.

't Brugsch Friethuys, a block off the Markt, is handy for fries you can sit down and enjoy. Its forte is greasy, deep-fried Flemish fast food. The €12 "Big Hunger menu" comes with all the traditional gut bombs: shrimp, *frikandel* minced-meat sausage, and "gypsy stick" sausage (daily 11:00-late, at the corner of Geldmuntstraat and Sint Jakobstraat, Luc will explain your options).

Delhaize-Proxy Supermarket is ideal for picnics. Its push-button produce pricer lets you buy as little as one mushroom (Mon-Sat 9:00-19:00, closed Sun, 3 blocks off the Markt on Geldmuntstraat). You'll also find Indian-run corner grocery stores scattered around town.

Carrefour Express is handy for picnics. It's just off the Markt on Vlamingstraat (daily 8:00-19:00).

Belgian Waffles and Ice Cream

You'll see waffles sold at restaurants and take-away stands. **Laurenzino** is particularly good, and a favorite with Bruges' teens when they get the waffle munchies. Their classic waffle with chocolate costs €3 (daily in summer 10:00-22:00, until 23:00 Fri-Sat; winter 10:00-20:00, until 22:00 Fri-Sat; across from Gelateria Da Vinci at Noordzandstraat 1, tel. 050-333-213).

Gelateria Da Vinci, the local favorite for homemade ice cream, has creative flavors and a lively atmosphere. As you approach, you'll see a line of happy lickers. Before ordering, ask to sample the Ferrero Rocher (chocolate, nuts, and crunchy cookie) and plain yogurt (daily 11:00-23:00, later in summer, Geldmuntstraat 34, run by Sylvia from Austria).

Brussels

Brussels—which takes more effort to reach from Zeebrugge (1.5 hours each way by train)—is an urban and urbane alternative to sleepy and quaint Bruges. The Bruxelloise are cultured and genteel—even a bit snobby compared to their more earthy Flemish cousins. And yet you may notice an impish sparkle and *joie de vivre,* as evidenced by their love of comic strips (giant comic-strip panels are painted on buildings all over town) and their civic symbol: a statue of a little boy peeing.

About 500,000 people who call Brussels home, however,

aren't Bruxelloise, or even Belgian. As the unofficial capital of Europe, Brussels is multicultural, hosting politicians and businesspeople (not to mention immigrants) from around the globe, and featuring a world of ethnic restaurants. The city hosts 400 embassies (the US has three here, one each to the EU, NATO, and Belgium). Every sizable corporation has a lobbyist in Brussels.

While the city spoke mostly Dutch until 1900 and is entirely contained within the Dutch-speaking region of Flanders, today 65 percent of Bruxelloise speak French as their first language, and only 5 percent speak Dutch. Bone up on *bonjour* and *s'il vous plait* (see the French survival phrases on page 1107). The remaining third are non-natives who speak their own languages, including Brussels' businesspeople, diplomats, and politicians who use English as their common language. Many predict that in 20 years, English will be the city's first language. But language aside, the whole feel of the town is urban French, not rural Flemish.

Brussels enjoyed a Golden Age of peace and prosperity (1400-1550) while England and France were duking it out in the Hundred Years' War. It was then that many of the fine structures that distinguish the city today were built. In the late 1800s, Brussels had another growth spurt, fueled by industrialization, wealth taken from the Belgian Congo, and the exhilaration of the country's recent independence (1830). City expansion peaked at the end of the 19th century, when the "Builder King" Leopold II erected grand monuments and palaces.

Although the city is often overshadowed by Amsterdam, Bruges, and Paris, Brussels' rich, chocolaty mix of food and culture pleasantly surprises those who visit.

Orientation to Brussels

Central Brussels is surrounded by a ring of roads (which replaced the old city wall) called the Pentagon. (Romantics think it looks more like a heart.) All the sights I mention are within this ring. The epicenter holds the main square (the Grand Place), the TI, and Central Station (all within three blocks of one another).

What isn't so apparent from maps is that Brussels is a city divided by altitude. A ridgeline that runs north-south splits the town into the Upper Town (east half, elevation 200 feet) and Lower Town (west, at sea level), with Central

BRUGES & BRUSSELS

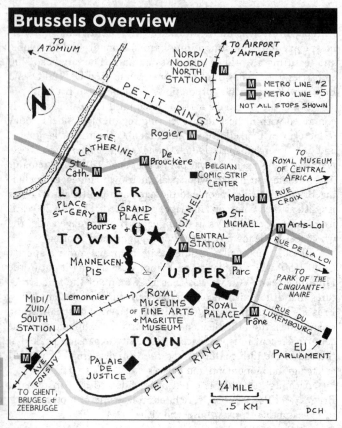

Brussels Overview

TO ATOMIUM

TO AIRPORT & ANTWERP

NORD/ NOORD/ NORTH STATION

PETIT RING

M METRO LINE #2
M METRO LINE #5
NOT ALL STOPS SHOWN

Rogier M

STE. CATHERINE

De Brouckère M

BELGIAN COMIC STRIP CENTER

TO ROYAL MUSEUM OF CENTRAL AFRICA

Ste. Cath. M

Madou M

RUE CROIX

L O W E R

PLACE ST-GÉRY M

GRAND PLACE

Bourse M

ST. MICHAEL

Arts-Loi M

T O W N

MANNEKEN-PIS

TUNNEL

CENTRAL STATION M

RUE DE LA LOI

U P P E R

Parc M

TO PARK OF THE CINQUANTE-NAIRE

MIDI/ ZUID/ SOUTH STATION

Lemonnier M

ROYAL MUSEUMS OF FINE ARTS & MAGRITTE MUSEUM

ROYAL PALACE

RUE DU LUXEMBOURG M

Trône M

T O W N

EU PARLIAMENT

M

AVE. FONSNY

PALAIS DE JUSTICE

PETIT RING

TO GHENT, BRUGES & ZEEBRUGGE

¼ MILE
.5 KM

DCH

BRUGES & BRUSSELS

Station in between. The Upper Town, traditionally the home of nobility and the rich, has big marble palaces, broad boulevards, and major museums.

The Lower Town, with the Grand Place (grahn plahs; in Dutch: Grote Markt, HHHROH-teh markt), narrow streets, old buildings, modern shops, colorful eateries, and the famous *Manneken-Pis* peeing-boy statue, has more character. Running along the western edge of the touristic center is a bustling boulevard (Boulevard Anspach/Anspachlaan) that runs over the city's forgotten river. Just beyond that—past a block or two of high-rise ugliness—is the lively market square called Place St-Géry/Sint-Goriksplein and a charming village-within-a-city huddled around the old fish market, the Ste. Catherine neighborhood.

Because the city is officially bilingual, most of Brussels' street signs and maps are in both French and Dutch; I've tried to follow suit in this text, but due to space constraints, on my maps I've generally given only the French name. Because the languages are so different (French is a Romance language, Dutch is Germanic), many places have two names that barely resemble each other (for example, Marché-aux-Herbes/Grasmarkt, or Place Royale/Koningsplein). This can make navigating the city confusing. Use one of the good local maps (such as the TI's €0.50 map), which list both languages, so you'll know both street names to look for.

Tourist Information

Brussels has two competing TIs (indicative of Belgium's latent Walloon-Flemish tension). The TI at Rue du Marché-aux-Herbes/Grasmarkt 63 covers **Brussels and Flanders** (July-Aug daily 9:00-18:00; April-June and Sept Mon-Sat 9:00-18:00, Sun 10:00-17:00; Oct-March Mon-Sat 9:00-17:00, Sun 10:00-16:00; three blocks downhill from Central Station, tel. 02-504-0390, www.visit flanders.com, fun Europe store nearby). They offer free Wi-Fi and several Internet terminals where you can get online free for up to 15 minutes.

The other TI, which focuses on just the **city of Brussels**, is inside the Town Hall on the Grand Place (April-Nov daily 9:00-18:00, shorter hours off-season; tel. 02-513-8940, www.visit brussels.be).

Both TIs have countless fliers. Day-trippers should pick up a free public transit map. The city map costs €0.50. The €3 *Brussels Guide* booklet is an overview of the city, including a more complete explanation of the city's many museums, and a series of neighborhood walks (including ones focusing on Art Nouveau, comic strips, and shopping).

Sightseeing Deals: The **Brussels Card,** sold at the TIs, provides unlimited public transportation and free entrance to nearly all the major museums (€24/24 hours, €34/48 hours, €40/72 hours, also sold at museums, public transportation offices, and some hotels, www.brusselscard.be). If you're in town for less than a day, it's unlikely this pass will pay for itself. The TIs also offer a deal called **Must of Brussels**—you pay €19 for 10 vouchers that you can mix and match for discounted entries into top sights. Though complicated to figure out, it could save you a few euros (www.must ofbrussels.com).

Alternative Tourist Information: The excellent, welcoming **USE-IT** information office, which is geared toward youthful backpackers, offers free Internet access and Wi-Fi, free coffee and tea, and in-the-know advice (Mon-Sat 10:00-13:00 & 14:00-18:00, closed Sun, Quai à la Houille/Steenkoolkaai 9B, Metro: Ste. Catherine/Sint-Katelijne, www.use-it.be). They also publish free user-friendly maps of Brussels, packed with homegrown insight.

Arrival at Brussels' Central Train Station

Brussels has three train stations; if you're coming by train from Blankenberge (see details on page 839), get off at the Brussel-Centraal/Bruxelles-Central station (pay close attention and ask your conductor for help to ensure you get off at the right stop). This station, nearest to the sights, has handy services: a small grocery store, fast food, waiting rooms, and luggage lockers (€3-4, between tracks 3 and 4). Walking from Central Station to the Grand Place takes about five minutes: Exit the station from the top floor (to the left of the ticket windows), where you'll see Le Meridien Hôtel across the square. Pass through the arch of Le Meridien Hôtel, turn right, and walk one block downhill on l'Infante Isabelle street to a small square with a fountain (officially "Herb Market"—Rue du Marché-aux-Herbes/Grasmarkt—but nicknamed "Agora"). For the Grand Place, turn left at the far end of the little square. Or, to head directly to one of the TIs, exit the small square at the far end and continue straight for one block, then look left.

Competitive hop-on, hop-off tourist buses depart from Central Station (you may meet ticket hustlers as you leave). You could hop on one of these buses upon arrival to orient yourself from the top deck (see "Tours in Brussels," later).

Helpful Hints

Theft Alert: Though the tourist zone—the area within the pentagon-shaped ring road—is basically safe at any hour of day or night, muggings do occur in some rough-and-tumble areas farther afield.

Sightseeing Schedules: Brussels' most important museums are closed on Monday. Of course, the city's single best sight—the Grand Place—is always open. You can also enjoy a bus tour any day of the week.

Internet Access: The **USE-IT** information office (listed earlier) has four free Internet terminals and free Wi-Fi; the **Brussels and Flanders TI** on Rue du Marché-aux-Herbes/Grasmarkt has one Internet terminal and offers 15 minutes free (plus unlimited free Wi-Fi). There's also an **Internet café** in a dreary urban area between the Grand Place and Ste. Catherine (€1.50/hour, also cheap calls and printing, calling cabins downstairs, computer terminals upstairs, daily 9:30-23:15, 18 Rue Marché aux Poulets/Kiekenmarkt).

Travel Bookstore: Anticyclone des Açores has a wide selection of maps and travel books, including many in English (Mon-Sat 11:00-18:00, closed Sun, Rue Fossé aux Loups/Wolvengracht 34, tel. 02-217-5246, www.anticyclonedesacores.be).

Getting Around Brussels

Most of central Brussels' sights can be reached on foot. But public transport is handy for climbing to the Upper Town (bus #95 from Rue du Lombard near the Grand Place).

By Métro, Bus, Tram, and Train: A single €2 ticket is good for one hour on all public transportation—Métro, buses, trams, and even trains shuttling between Brussels' three train stations. Buy individual tickets at newsstands, in Métro stations (vending machines accept credit cards or coins), or (for €0.50 extra) from the bus driver. Validate your ticket when you enter, feeding it into one of the breadbox-size orange machines. Notice the time when you first stamp it (you have an hour). Transit info: tel. 02-515-2000, www.mivb.be.

By Taxi: Cabbies charge a €2.40 drop fee, as well as €1.70 per additional kilometer. You'll pay about €10 to ride from the center to the European Parliament. Convenient taxi stands are at the Bourse (near the Grand Place), at the "Agora" square near the Grand Place (Rue du Marché-aux-Herbes/Grasmarkt), and at Place du Grand Sablon (in the Upper Town). To call a cab, try **Taxi Bleu** (tel. 02-268-0000) or **Autolux** (tel. 02-512-3123).

Tours in Brussels

Hop-On, Hop-Off Bus Tours—Various companies offer nearly identical introductory city tours: **City Tours** (tel. 02-513-7744, www.brussels-city-tours.com), **CitySightseeing/Open Tours** (tel. 02-466-1111, www.citysightseeingbrussel.be), and **Golden Tours** (mobile 0486-053-981, www.goldentours.be). The 1.5-hour loop and recorded narration give you a once-over-lightly of the city from the top deck (open on sunny days) of a double-decker bus. You can hop on and off for 24 hours with one ticket, but schedules are sparse (figure €20-22 for each company, about 2/hour, times listed on each flier; all companies run roughly April-Oct daily 10:00-16:00, Sat until 17:00; Nov-March daily 10:00-15:00, Sat until 16:00). Except for the trip out to the European Parliament and Cinquantenaire Park (which hosts the military and auto museums), I'd just stay on to enjoy the views and the minimal commentary. The fiercely competitive companies often have hustlers at Central Station trying to get you on board (offering "student" discounts to customers of all ages). The handiest starting points are Central Station and the Bourse.

Bus Tours—City Tours also offers a typical three-hour guided (in up to five languages) bus tour, providing you an easy way to get the grand perspective on Brussels. You start with a walk around the Grand Place, then jump on a tour bus (€26, year-round daily at 10:00, depart from their office a block off Grand Place at Rue du

Marché-aux-Herbes/Grasmarkt 82, you can buy tickets there or at the TI, tel. 02-513-7744, www.brussels-city-tours.com). You'll get off the bus at the Atomium for a quick photo stop.

Local Guides—You can hire a private guide through **Visit Brussels** (€117/3 hours, €216/full day, tel. 02-548-0448, guides @visitbrussles.be; I enjoyed the guiding of Didier Rochette). **Claude and Dominique Janssens** are a father-and-son team who lead tours both in Brussels and to other Belgian cities, including Bruges, Ghent, and Antwerp (€120/3 hours, €240/full day plus €25 for lunch, Claude's mobile 0485-025-423, Dominique's mobile 0486-451-155, www.discover-b.be, claude@discover-b .be). **Christian Scharlé** and **Daniëlle Janssens,** who are based in Bruges, offer a three-hour tour of Brussels for €120 (for contact info, see "Local Guide" on page 846).

Self-Guided Walk in Brussels

Grand Place and Nearby

This walk takes in Brussels' delightful old center, starting at its spectacular main square. After exploring the Grand Place, we'll loop a couple blocks north, see the Bourse, and then end south of the Grand Place at the *Manneken-Pis*. Allow about two hours for this walk.

• *Begin this walk standing on Brussels' very grand main square, the...*

Grand Place

This colorful cobblestone square is the heart—historically and geographically—of heart-shaped Brussels. As the town's market square for 1,000 years, this was where farmers and merchants sold their wares in open-air stalls, enticing travelers from the main east-west highway across Belgium, which ran a block north of the square. Today, shops and cafés sell chocolates, *gaufres* (waffles), beer, mussels, fries, *dentelles* (lace), and flowers.

Pan the square to get oriented. Face the Town Hall, with your back to the King's House. The TI is one block behind you, and "restaurant row" is another block beyond that. To your right, a block away (downhill), catch a glimpse of the Bourse building. The Upper Town is to your left, rising up the hill beyond the Central Station. Over your left shoulder a few blocks away is St. Michael's Cathedral. And most important? The *Manneken-Pis*

BRUGES & BRUSSELS

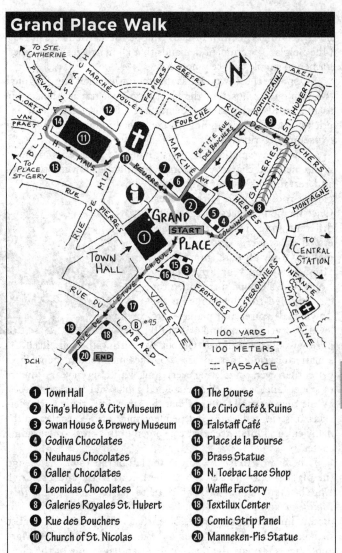

Grand Place Walk

1 Town Hall
2 King's House & City Museum
3 Swan House & Brewery Museum
4 Godiva Chocolates
5 Neuhaus Chocolates
6 Galler Chocolates
7 Leonidas Chocolates
8 Galeries Royales St. Hubert
9 Rue des Bouchers
10 Church of St. Nicolas

11 The Bourse
12 Le Cirio Café & Ruins
13 Falstaff Café
14 Place de la Bourse
15 Brass Statue
16 N. Toebac Lace Shop
17 Waffle Factory
18 Textilux Center
19 Comic Strip Panel
20 Manneken-Pis Statue

BRUGES & BRUSSELS

is three blocks ahead, down the street that runs along the left side of the Town Hall.

The **Town Hall** (Hôtel de Ville) dominates the square with its 300-foot-tall tower, topped by a golden statue of St. Michael slaying a devil (open only by tour; €3, Tue-Wed at 15:15, Sun at 10:45 and 12:15 except no Sun tours Oct-March). This was where the city council met to rule this free trading town. Brussels proudly maintained its self-governing independence while dukes, kings, and clergymen ruled much of Europe. These days, the Town Hall hosts weddings—Crown Prince Philippe got married here in 1999. (The Belgian government demands that all marriages first be performed in simple civil ceremonies.)

Opposite the Town Hall is the impressive, gray **King's House** (Maison du Roi), used by the Habsburg kings not as a house, but as an administrative center. Rebuilt in the 1890s, it's a stately and prickly Neo-Gothic building. Inside is the mildly interesting **City Museum** (described later).

The fancy smaller buildings giving the square its uniquely grand medieval character are former **guildhalls** (now mostly shops and restaurants), their impressive gabled roofs topped with statues. Once the home offices for the town's different professions (brewers, bakers, and *Manneken-Pis*-corkscrewmakers), they all date from shortly after 1695—the year French king Louis XIV's troops surrounded the city, sighted their cannons on the Town Hall spire, and managed to level everything around it (4,000

mostly wooden buildings) without ever hitting the spire itself. As a matter of pride, these Brussels businessmen rebuilt their offices better than ever, completing everything within seven years. They're in stone, taller, and with ornamented gables and classical statues. While they were all built at about the same time, the many differences in styles reflect the independent spirit of the people and the many cultural influences that converged in this crossroads trading center.

The **Swan House** (#9, just to the left of the Town Hall—find the plaque) once housed a bar where Karl Marx and Friedrich Engels met in February of 1848 to write their *Communist Manifesto*, and where the first German Workers' Association (the proto-communist party) met. Later that year, when their treatise sparked socialist revolution around Europe, Brussels exiled Marx and Engels. Today, the once-proletarian bar is one of the city's most expensive restaurants. Next door (#10) was and still is the brewers' guild, now housing the **Brewery Museum** (€5 includes an unnamed local beer, daily 10:00-17:00 except Dec-March Sat-Sun opens at 12:00, Grand Place 10, tel. 02-511-4987, www.beer paradise.be).

• *Inside the King's House (Maison du Roi)—across the Grand Place from the Town Hall—is the only museum of any importance on the square, the...*

City Museum

This museum has three stories of exhibits: The top floor displays

a chronological history of the city and an enjoyable room full of costumes dampened by the *Manneken-Pis* statue; the middle floor has a 20-minute film on city history and maps and models of 13th- and 17th-century Brussels; and the ground floor features tapestries and paintings. Borrow the English descriptions in each room.

Most visitors aim straight for the *Manneken-Pis* **outfits**, upstairs. It's a longstanding tradition for the statue to be outfitted in clothing—the little guy goes through several costume changes each week. Many of the costumes you'll see here were donated by other countries—you'll see everything from a Civil War Union soldier to an El Salvadorian farmer, from a Polish hussar to a Japanese samurai, from an Indian maharajah to a Spanish bullfighter, from a Russian cosmonaut to a Fiji islander...and much more. Once up here, sit down and enjoy the video showing visitors' reactions to the ridiculous little statue.

Cost and Hours: €4, borrow English descriptions in each room, Tue-Sun 10:00-17:00, Thu until 20:00, closed Mon, Grand Place, tel. 02-279-4350.

Tasty Treats on the Grand Place

Cafés: Mussels in Brussels, Belgian-style french fries, yeasty local beers, waffles...if all you do here is plop down at a café on the square, try some of these specialties, and watch the world go by— hey, that's a great afternoon in Brussels.

The outdoor cafés are casual and come with fair prices (a good Belgian beer costs €4.50—with no cover or service charge). Have a seat, and a waiter will serve you. The half-dozen or so cafés on the downhill side of the square are all roughly equal in price and quality for simple food and drink—check the posted menus. As they are generally owned by breweries, you won't have a big selection of beers.

Choco-Crawl: The best chocolate shops all lie along the north (uphill) side of the square, starting with Godiva at the high end (higher in both altitude and price). The cost goes down slightly as you descend to the other shops. Each shop has a mouthwatering display case of 20 or so chocolates and sells mixes of 100 grams—your choice of 8 pieces—for about €5, or individual pieces for about €1. Americans use the word "chocolates" indiscriminately to describe the different varieties you'd find in a box of chocolates, but the Belgians call them either "truffles" (soft, crumbly chocolate shells filled with buttercream) or "pralines" (made of a hard chocolate shell with a wide range of fillings—uniquely Belgian and totally different from the sugar-and-nuts French praline). Chocolate shops are generally open Monday to Saturday from 9:00 to 22:00 and Sunday from 10:00 to 22:00.

Godiva, with the top reputation internationally, is synonymous with fine Belgian chocolate. Now owned by a Turkish company, Godiva still has its management and the original factory (built in 1926) in Belgium. This store, at Grand Place 22, was Godiva's first (est. 1937). The almond and honey goes way beyond almond roca.

Neuhaus, a few doors down at #27, has been encouraging local chocoholics since 1857. Their main store is in the Galeries St. Hubert (described later). Neuhaus publishes a good little pamphlet explaining its products. The "caprice" (toffee with vanilla crème) tastes like Easter. Neuhaus claims to be the inventor of the praline.

Galler, just off the square at Rue au Beurre 44, is homier and less famous because it doesn't export. Still family-run (and the royal favorite), it proudly serves less sugary chocolate—dark. The new top-end choice, 85 percent pure chocolate, is called simply "Black 85"—and worth a sample if you like chocolate without the sweetness. Galler's products are well-described in English.

Leonidas, four doors down at Rue au Beurre 34, is where cost-conscious Bruxelloise get their fix, sacrificing 10 percent in quality to nearly triple their take (machine-made, only €2.20/100 grams). White chocolate is their specialty.

If all the chocolate has made you thirsty, wash it down with **250 Beers,** next to Leonidas.

• *Exit the Grand Place next to Godiva (from the northeast, or uphill, corner of the square), and go north one block on Rue de la Colline (passing a popular Tintin shop at #9) to Rue du Marché-aux-Herbes/ Grasmarkt, which was once the main east-west highway through Belgium. The little park-like square just to your right—a modest gathering place with market stalls—is nicknamed "Agora" (after the market-places of ancient Greece).*

Looking to the right, notice that it's all uphill from here to the Upper Town, another four blocks (and 200-foot elevation gain) beyond. Straight ahead, you enter the arcaded shopping mall called...

Galeries Royales St. Hubert

Built in 1847, Europe's oldest still-operating shopping mall served as the glass-covered model that inspired many other shopping galleries in Paris, London, and beyond. It celebrated the town's new modern attitude (having recently gained its independence from the Netherlands). Built in an age of expansion and industrial-

ization, the mall demonstrated efficient modern living, with elegant apartments upstairs above trendy shops, theaters, and cafés. Originally, you had to pay to get in to see its fancy shops, and that elite sensibility survives today. Even today, people live in the upstairs apartments.

Looking down the arcade, you'll notice that it bends halfway down, designed to lure shoppers farther. Its iron-and-glass look is still popular, but the decorative columns, cameos, and pastel colors evoke a more elegant time. It's Neo-Renaissance, like a pastel Florentine palace.

• *Midway down the mall, where the two sections bend, turn left and exit the mall onto...*

Rue des Bouchers

Yikes! During meal times, this street is absolutely crawling with tourists browsing through wall-to-wall, midlevel-quality restau-

rants. Brussels is known worldwide for its food, serving all kinds of cuisine, but specializing in seafood (particularly mussels). You'll have plenty to choose from along this table-clogged "restaurant row." To get an idea of prices, compare their posted *menùs*—the fixed-price, several-course meal offered by most restaurants. But don't count on getting a good value—better restaurants are just a few steps away (for specifics, see page 881).

The first intersection, with Petite Rue des Bouchers, is the heart of the restaurant quarter, which sprawls for several blocks around. The street names reveal what sorts of shops used to stand here—butchers *(bouchers)*, herbs, chickens, and cheese.

• *At this intersection, turn left onto Petite Rue des Bouchers and walk straight back to the Grand Place. (You'll see the Town Hall tower ahead.) At the Grand Place, turn right (west) on Rue du Beurre. Comparison-shop a little more at the Galler and Leonidas chocolate stores and pass by the little "Is it raining?" fountain. At the intersection with Rue du Midi is the...*

Church of St. Nicolas

Since the 12th century, there's been a church here. Inside, along the left aisle, see rough stones in some of the arches from the early church. Outside, notice the barnacle-like shops, such as De Witte Jewelers, built right into the church. The church was rebuilt 300 years ago with money provided by the town's jewelers. As thanks, they were given these shops with apartments upstairs. Close to God, this was prime real estate. And jewelers are still here.

• *Just beyond the church, you run into the back entrance of a big Neoclassical building.*

Bourse (Stock Exchange) and Art Nouveau Cafés

The stock exchange was built in the 1870s in the Historicist style— a mix-and-match, Neo-everything architectural movement. Plans are in the works for the former stock exchange to host a big beer museum. The **ruins** under glass on the right side of the Bourse are from a 13th-century convent; there's a small museum inside.

Several **historic cafés** huddle around the Bourse. To the right (next to the covered ruins) is the woody **Le Cirio,** with its delightful circa-1900 interior. Around the left side of the Bourse is the **Falstaff Café,** which is worth a peek inside. Some Brussels cafés, like the Falstaff, are still decorated in the early 20th-century style called Art Nouveau. Ironwork columns twist and bend like flower stems, and lots of Tiffany-style stained glass and mirrors make them light and spacious. Slender, elegant, willowy Gibson Girls decorate the wallpaper, while waiters in bowties glide by.

• *Circle around to the front of the Bourse, toward the busy Boulevard Anspach.*

Place de la Bourse and Boulevard Anspach

Brussels is the political nerve center of Europe (with as many lobbyists as Washington, DC), and the city sees several hundred demonstrations a year. When the local team wins a soccer match or some political group wants to make a statement, this is where people flock to wave flags and honk horns.

It's also where the old town meets the new. To the right along Boulevard Anspach are two shopping malls and several first-run movie theaters. Rue Neuve, which parallels Anspach, is a bustling pedestrian-only shopping street.

• *Now return to the Grand Place.*

From the Grand Place to the *Manneken-Pis*

• *Leave the square kitty-corner, heading south down the street running along the left side of the Town Hall, Rue Charles Buls (which soon changes its name to Stoofstraat). Just five yards off the square, under the arch, are two interesting monuments honoring illustrious Brussels mayors:*

The first monument features a beautiful young man—an Art Nouveau allegory of knowledge and science (which brings illumination, as indicated by the Roman oil lamp)—designed by Victor Horta. It honors **Charles Buls,** mayor from 1888 to 1899. If you enjoyed the Grand Place, thank him for saving it. He stopped

King Leopold II from blasting a grand esplanade from Grand Place up the hill to the palace.

A few steps farther you'll see tourists and locals rubbing a brass statue of a reclining man. This was **Mayor Evrard 't Serclaes,** who in 1356 bravely refused to surrender the keys of the city to invaders, and so was tortured and killed. Touch him, and his misfortune becomes your good luck. Judging by the reverence with which locals treat this ritual, I figure there must be something to it.

A half-block farther (on the left), the **N. Toebac Lace Shop** shows off some fine lace. Brussels is perhaps the best-known city for traditional lacemaking, and this shop still sells handmade pieces in the old style: lace clothing, doilies, tablecloths, and ornamental pieces. The shop gives travelers with this book a 15 percent discount. For more on lace, the **Costume and Lace Museum** is a block away and just around the corner (closed Wed).

A block farther down the street on the left (at the little yellow window before the busy street) is the always-popular **Waffle Factory,** where €2 gets you a freshly made take-away "Belgian" (Liège-style) waffle (up to €7 more if you opt for any of the fun toppings).

Across the busy street, step into the **Textilux Center** (Rue Lombard 41, on the left) for a good look at Belgian tapestries—both traditional wall-hangings and modern goods, such as tapestry purses and luggage in traditional designs.

High on the wall to the right, notice the delightful **comic strip panel** depicting that favorite of Belgian comic heroes, Tintin,

Brussels at a Glance

▲▲▲**Grand Place** Main square and spirited heart of the Lower Town, surrounded by mediocre museums and delectable chocolate shops. **Hours:** Always open. See page 866.

▲▲▲**Royal Museums of Fine Arts of Belgium** Museums displaying ancient art (14th-18th centuries) and turn-of-the-century art (19th-20th centuries). **Hours:** Tue-Sun 10:00-17:00, closed Mon. See page 878.

▲▲**Manneken-Pis** World-famous statue of a leaky little boy. **Hours:** Always peeing. See page 874.

▲▲**Magritte Museum** Biographical collection of works by the prominent Belgian Surrealist painter René Magritte. **Hours:** Tue-Sun 10:00-17:00, Wed until 20:00, closed Mon. See page 879.

▲▲**BELvue Museum** Interesting Belgian history museum with a focus on the popular royal family. **Hours:** Tue-Fri 10:00-17:00, Sat-Sun 10:00-18:00, closed Mon. See page 879.

▲**City Museum** Costumes worn by the Manneken-Pis statue and models of Brussels' history. **Hours:** Tue-Sun 10:00-17:00, Thu until 20:00, closed Mon. See page 869.

▲**Chocolate on Grand Place** Choco-crawl through Godiva, Neuhaus, Galler, and Leonidas. **Hours:** Generally Mon-Sat 9:00-

climbing a fire escape. (For those unfamiliar with this character—beloved by virtually all Europeans—his dog is named Snowy, Captain Haddock keeps an eye out for him, and the trio are always getting into misadventures.) Dozens of these building-sized comic-strip panels decorate Brussels (marked on the TI's €0.50 map), celebrating the Belgians' favorite medium. Just as Ireland has its writers, Italy its painters, and France its chefs, Belgium has a knack for turning out world-class comic artists.

• *Follow the crowds, noticing the excitement build, because in another block you reach the...*

Manneken-Pis

Even with low expectations, this bronze statue is smaller than you'd think—the little squirt's under two feet tall, practically the size of a newborn. Still, the little peeing boy is an appropriately low-key symbol for the unpretentious Bruxelloise. The statue was made in 1619 to provide drinking water for the neighborhood. Notice that the baby, sculpted in Renaissance style, actually has

22:00, Sun 10:00-22:00. See page 869.

▲**Costume and Lace Museum** World-famous Brussels lace, as well as outfits, embroidery, and accessories from the 17th-20th centuries. **Hours:** Thu-Tue 10:00-17:00, closed Wed. See page 873.

▲**St. Michael's Cathedral** White-stone Gothic church where Belgian royals are married and buried. **Hours:** Mon-Fri 7:00-18:00, Sat-Sun 8:30-18:00. See page 876.

▲**Belgian Comic Strip Center** Homage to hometown heroes including the Smurfs, Tintin, and Lucky Luke. **Hours:** Tue-Sun 10:00-18:00, closed Mon. See page 876.

▲**Musical Instruments Museum** Exhibits with more than 1,500 instruments, complete with audio. **Hours:** Tue-Fri 9:30-16:45, Sat-Sun 10:00-16:45, closed Mon. See page 879.

Town Hall Focal point of the Grand Place, with arresting spire but boring interior. **Hours:** Tours depart Tue-Wed at 15:15, Sun at 10:45 and 12:15, no Sun tours Oct-March. See page 867.

Ste. Catherine Neighborhood and Place St-Géry Pleasant areas with fun eateries west of the Grand Place. Hours: Always buzzing. See page 862.

the musculature of a man instead of the pudgy limbs of a child. The statue was knighted by the occupying King Louis XV—so

French soldiers had to salute the eternally pissing lad when they passed.

As it's tradition for visiting VIPs to bring the statue an outfit, and he also dresses up for special occasions, you can often see the *Manneken* peeing through a colorful costume. A sign on the fence lists the month's festival days and how he'll be dressed. For example, on January 8, Elvis Presley's birthday, he's an Elvis impersonator; on Prostate Awareness Day, his flow is down to a slow drip. He can also be hooked up to a keg to pee wine or beer.

There are several different legends about the story behind *Manneken*—take your pick: He was a naughty boy who peed inside a witch's house, so she froze him. A rich man lost his son and declared, "Find my son, and we'll make a statue of him doing what he did when found." Or—the locals' favorite version—the little tyke loved his beer, which came in handy when a fire threatened the wooden city: He bravely put it out. Want the truth? The city commissioned *the Manneken* to show the freedom and joie de vivre of living in Brussels—where happy people eat, drink...and drink... and then pee.

The gathering crowds make the scene more interesting. Hang out for a while and watch the commotion this little guy makes as tour groups come and go. When I was there, a Russian man marveled at the statue, shook his head, and said, "He never stop!"

Sights in Brussels

The Grand Place (described in the self-guided walk earlier) may be Brussels' top sight, but the city offers a variety of museums, big and small, to fill your time here. I've divided the sights between the Lower Town and the Upper Town.

North of Central Station

▲**St. Michael's Cathedral**—One of Europe's classic Gothic churches, built between roughly 1200 and 1500, Brussels' cathedral is made from white stone and topped by twin towers. For nearly 1,000 years, it's been the most important church in this largely Catholic country. (Whereas the Netherlands went in a Protestant direction in the 1500s, Belgium remains 80 percent Catholic—although only about 20 percent attend Mass.)

Cost and Hours: Free, but small fees to visit the underwhelming crypt and treasury, Mon-Fri 7:00-18:00, Sat-Sun 8:30-18:00.

▲**Belgian Comic Strip Center (Centre Belge de la Bande Dessinée)**—Belgians are as proud of their comics as they are of their beer, lace, and chocolates. Something about the comic medium resonates with the wry and artistic-yet-unpretentious Belgian sensibility. Belgium has produced some of the world's most popular comic characters, including the Smurfs, Tintin, and

Brussels

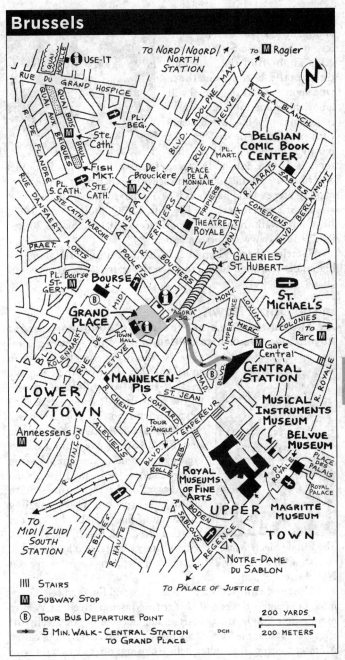

Lucky Luke. You'll find these, and many less famous local comics, at the Comic Strip Center. Kids might find the museum, like, totally boring, but those who appreciate art in general will enjoy this sometimes humorous, sometimes probing, often beautiful medium. The displays are mostly in French and Dutch, but

there is some English. The free, essential English guidebooklet describes the comics-making process (comparing it to the film-making process) and has short bios of famous cartoonists.

Cost and Hours: €8, Tue-Sun 10:00-18:00, closed Mon, 10-minute walk from the Grand Place to Rue des Sables 20, tel. 02-219-1980, www.comicscenter.net.

Getting There: From Central Station, walk north along the big boulevard, then turn left down the stairs at the giant comic character.

In the Upper Town

▲▲▲Royal Museums of Fine Arts of Belgium (Musées Royaux des Beaux-Arts de Belgique)

—This sprawling complex is worth visiting for its twin museums that show off the country's best all-around art collection (as well as the Magritte Museum—described next—which is in the same complex). The **Museum of Ancient Art** and the new **Fin de Siècle Museum** are covered by the same ticket. The Museum of Ancient Art—featuring Flemish and Belgian art of the 14th through 18th centuries—is packed with a dazzling collection of masterpieces by Van der Weyden, Brueghel, Bosch, and Rubens. The Fin de Siècle Museum gives visitors a contextual look at art of the late 19th and early 20th centuries, including an extensive Art Nouveau collection.

Cost and Hours: €9 for Ancient Art and Fin de Siècle museums, €13 combo-ticket adds Magritte Museum, free first Wed of month after 13:00; Ancient Art audioguide-€4, Fin de Siècle videoguide-€5, tour booklet-€2.50; open Tue-Sun 10:00-17:00, closed Mon, last entry 30 minutes before closing; pricey cafeteria with salad bar, Rue de la Régence 3, recorded info tel. 02-508-3211, www.fine-arts-museum.be.

▲▲**Magritte Museum (Musée Magritte)**—This exhibit, examining Surrealist painter René Magritte, is in the same museum complex as the Royal Museums of Fine Arts (above), and contains more than 200 works housed on three floors of a Neoclassical building. Although you won't see many of Magritte's most famous pieces, this lovingly presented museum offers an unusually intimate look at the life and work of one of Belgium's top artists.

Cost and Hours: €8, €13 combo-ticket with Royal Museums of Fine Arts, free first Wed of month after 13:00, audioguide-€4; open Tue-Sun 10:00-17:00, Wed until 20:00, closed Mon, last entry 30 minutes before closing; tel. 02-508-3333, www.musee-magritte-museum.be.

▲**Musical Instruments Museum (Musée des Instruments de Musique)**—One of Europe's best music museums (nicknamed

"MIM") is housed in one of Brussels' most impressive Art Nouveau buildings, the beautifully renovated Old England department store. This museum has more than 1,500 instruments—from Egyptian harps, to medieval lutes, to groundbreaking harpsichords, to the saxophone (invented in Brussels by Adolphe Sax). The included audioguide begins playing a recording of each instrument as you approach it.

Cost and Hours: €5, Tue-Fri 9:30-16:45, Sat-Sun 10:00-16:45, closed Mon, last entry 45 minutes before closing, mandatory free coat and bag check, Rue Montagne de la Cour 2, just downhill and toward Grand Place from the Magritte wing of the Royal Museums of Fine Arts, tel. 02-545-0130, www.mim.be.

▲▲**BELvue Museum**—This remarkable museum makes Belgian history fascinating. The exhibit—which fills two palatial floors with lots of real historical artifacts—illustrates the short sweep

of this nation's story, from its 1830 inception to today. To make the most of your visit, follow along with the wonderful and extensive flier translating all of the descriptions. The €2.50 audioguide simply repeats the information on the flier.

Cost and Hours: €5, €8 combo-ticket includes Coudenberg Palace, Tue-Fri 10:00-17:00, Sat-Sun 10:00-18:00, closed Mon, to the right of the palace at place des Palais 7, tel. 070-220-492, www.belvue.be.

Eating in Brussels

For many, the obvious eating tip in Brussels is simply to enjoy the very touristy but undeniably magnificent Grand Place. My vote for northern Europe's grandest medieval square is lined with hardworking eateries that serve predictable dishes to tourist crowds. Of course, you won't get the best quality or prices—but, after all, it's the Grand Place. Locals advise eating well elsewhere and enjoying a Grand Place perch for dessert or a drink. While many tourists congregate at the Rue des Bouchers, "Restaurant Row," consider a wander through the new, emerging eating zone—gay, ethnic, and trendy—past the Bourse near Place St. Géry/Sint-Goriksplein. Compare the ambience, check posted menus, and choose your favorite.

Brussels is known for both its high-quality, French-style cuisine and for multicultural variety. Seafood—fish, eel, shrimp, and oysters—is especially well-prepared here. As in France, if you ask for the *menù* (muh-noo) at a restaurant, you won't get a list of dishes; you'll get a fixed-price meal. *Menùs*, which include three or four courses, are generally a good value if you're hungry. Ask for *la carte* (lah kart) if you want to see a printed menu and order à la carte, like the locals do. To read local restaurant reviews, check out www.resto.be.

Mussels in Brussels

Mussels *(moules)* are available all over town. Mostly harvested from aquafarms along the North Sea, they are considered in-season from mid-July to about Easter, but are available all year. The classic Belgian method is *à la marinière,* cooked in white wine, shallots, parsley, and butter. Or, instead of wine, cooks use light Belgian beer for the stock. For a high-calorie version, try *moules à la crème,* where the stock is thickened with heavy cream.

You order by the kilo (just more than 2 pounds), which is a pretty big bucket. While restaurants don't promote these as split-table, they certainly are. Your mussels come with Belgian fries, which you probably think of as "french fries"—dip them in mayo. To accompany your mussels, try a French white wine such as Muscadet or Chablis, or a Belgian blonde ale such as Duvel or La Chouffe. When eating mussels, you can feel a little more local by nonchalantly using an empty mussel shell as a pincer to pull the meat out of other shells. It actually works quite nicely.

Dining on the Grand Place

For an atmospheric cellar or a table right on the Grand Place, **La Rose Blanche** and **L'Estaminet du Kelderke** each have the same formula, with tables outside overlooking the action. L'Estaminet du Kelderke—with its one steamy vault under the square packed with both natives and tourists—is a real Brussels fixture. It serves local specialties, including mussels (a splittable kilo bucket for €22-25; daily 12:00-24:00, no reservations taken, Grand Place 15, tel. 02-513-7344). **Brasserie L'Ommegang,** with a fancier restaurant upstairs, offers perhaps the classiest seating—and best food—on the square.

Rue des Bouchers ("Restaurant Row")

Brussels' restaurant streets, two blocks north of the Grand Place, are touristy and notorious for touts who aggressively suck you in and predatory servers who greedily rip you off. It's a little hard to justify eating here when far better options sit just a block or two away (see later listings). But the area is an exhilarating spectacle and is fun for at least a walk. If you are seduced into a meal here, order carefully, understand the prices thoroughly, and watch your wallet.

Restaurant Chez Léon is a touristy mussels factory that has been slamming out piles of good, cheap buckets since 1893. It's the original flagship branch of a chain that's now spreading throughout France. It's big and welcoming, with busy green-aproned waiters offering a "Formula Leon" for €12.90—a light meal consisting of a small bucket of mussels, fries, and a beer. They also offer a €31.30 fixed-price meal that comes with a starter, a large bucket of mussels, fries, and beer (daily 12:00-23:00, kids under 12 eat free, Rue des Bouchers/Beenhouwers 18, tel. 02-511-1415). In the family portrait of Léon's brother Honoré (hanging in the corner), the wife actually looks like a mussel.

Aux Armes de Bruxelles is a venerable restaurant that has been serving reliably good food to locals in a dressy setting for generations. This is another food factory, with white-suited waiters serving an older clientele impressed by the restaurant's reputation. You'll pay a bit more for the formality (€8-18 starters, €16-32 main dishes, €20 fixed-price lunch, daily 12:00-23:00, indoor seating only, Rue des Bouchers/Beenhouwers 13, tel. 02-511-5550).

Restaurant Vincent has you enter through the kitchen to enjoy their 1905-era ambience. This place is better for meat dishes than for seafood and better for wine than beer. Enjoy the engaging old tile murals of the seaside and countryside (€15-20 starters, €20-32 main dishes, daily 12:00-14:30 & 18:30-23:30, Rue des Dominicains/Predikherenstraat 8-10, tel. 02-511-2607, Michel and Jacques).

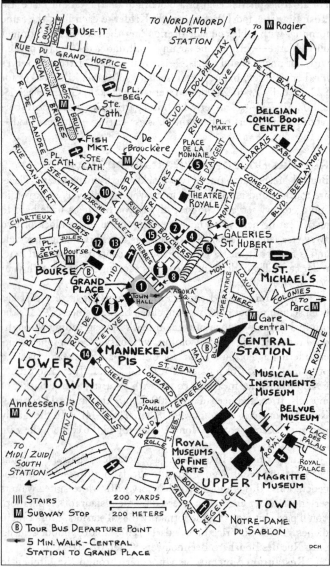

Brussels Restaurants

BRUGES & BRUSSELS

Brussels Restaurants Key

1. Grand Place Dining
2. Rest. Chez Leon, Rest. Vincent & Delirium Tap House
3. Aux Armes de Bruxelles
4. Restaurant de l'Ogenblik
5. Belga Queen Brasserie
6. Arcadi Café & Le Mokafé
7. La Maison des Crêpes
8. Osteria a l'Ombra
9. AD Delhaize Grocery
10. Super GB Grocery
11. A la Mort Subite Bar
12. Le Cirio Café
13. A la Bécasse Café
14. Poechenellekelder Estaminet
15. A l'Imaige Nostre-Dame & Au Bon Vieux Temps

Finer Dining near Rue des Bouchers

These options, though just steps away from those listed above, are more authentic and a better value.

Restaurant de l'Ogenblik, a remarkably peaceful eddy just off the raging restaurant row, fills an early 20th-century space in the corner of an arcade. The waiters serve well-presented, near-gourmet French cuisine. This mussels-free zone has a great, split-table rack of lamb with 10 vegetables. Their sea bass with risotto and truffle oil, at €26, is a hit with return eaters. Reservations are smart (€20 first courses, €30 plates, Mon-Sat 12:00-14:30 & 19:00-24:00, closed Sun, across from Restaurant Vincent—listed above—at Galerie des Princes 1, tel. 02-511-6151, Yves).

Belga Queen Brasserie, a huge, trendy, dressy brasserie filling a palatial former bank building, is *the* spot for Brussels' beautiful people and visiting European diplomats. Although a little more expensive than the alternatives, their "creative Belgian cuisine" is excellent, the service is sharp, and the experience is memorable—from the fries served in silver cones, to the double-decker platters of iced shellfish (€65/person for the Belga Queen platter), to the transparent toilet stalls (which become opaque only after you nervously lock the door). The high-powered trendiness can make you feel a little gawky, but if you've got the money, this is a great splurge. Consider their €50 four-course, fixed-price meal with matching beers (€15-25 starters, €20-30 main dishes, €30-47 fixed-price meals, daily 12:00-14:30 & 19:00-24:00, call to reserve, bar open all day, Rue Fosse-aux-Loups/Wolvengracht 32, tel. 02-217-2187). The vault downstairs is a plush cigar and cocktail lounge. For just a drink or a quicker bite, you can grab a stool at the white-marble oyster bar.

More Eateries near the Grand Place

Arcadi Café is a delightful little eatery serving daily plates (€10-15), salads, and a selection of quiche-like tortes (€7.50/slice). The interior comes with a fun, circa-1900 ambience; grab a table there, on the street, or at the end of Galeries St. Hubert (daily 7:30-23:30, 1 Rue d'Arenberg/Arenbergstraat, tel. 02-511-3343).

Le Mokafé is inexpensive but feels splurgy. They dish up light café fare at the quiet end of the elegant Galeries St. Hubert, with great people-watching outdoor tables (€3-6 sandwiches, €7-11 salads, €8-10 pastas, €9-12 main dishes, daily 8:00-24:00, Galerie du Roi 9, tel. 02-511-7870).

La Maison des Crêpes, a little eatery a half-block south of the Bourse, looks underwhelming but serves delicious €8-10 crêpes (both savory and sweet varieties) and salads. It has a brown-café ambience, and even though it's just a few steps away from the tourist bustle, it feels laid-back and local (good beers, fresh mint tea, sidewalk seating, daily 12:00-23:00, Rue du Midi/Zuidstraat 13, mobile 0475-957-368).

Osteria a l'Ombra, a true Italian joint, is good for a quality bowl of pasta with a glass of fine Italian wine. A block off the Grand Place, it's pricey, but the woody bistro ambience and tasty food make it a good value. If you choose a main dish (€15-18), your choice of pasta or salad is included in the price (otherwise €10-15 pasta meals). The ground-floor seating on high stools is fine, but also consider sitting upstairs (Mon-Sat 12:00-15:00 & 18:30-23:30, closed Sun, Rue des Harengs/Haringstraat 2, tel. 02-511-6710).

Cheap Eats near the Grand Place: The super-central square dubbed the "Agora" (officially Marché-aux-Herbes/Grasmarkt, just between the Grand Place and Central Station) is lined with low-end eateries, and is especially fun on sunny days.

Groceries: Two supermarkets are located about a block from the Bourse and a few blocks from the Grand Place. **AD Delhaize** is at the intersection of Anspach and Marché-aux-Poulets/Kiekenmarkt (Mon-Sat 9:00-20:00, Fri until 21:00, Sun 9:00-18:00), and **Super GB** is half a block away at Halles and Marché-aux-Poulets/Kiekenmarkt (Mon-Sat 9:00-20:00, Fri until 21:00, closed Sun). Mini-markets dot the city.

Sampling Belgian Beer with Food and Ambience

Looking for a good spot to enjoy that famous Belgian beer? Brussels is full of atmospheric cafés to savor the local brew. The eateries lining the Grand Place are touristy, but the setting—plush old medieval guildhalls fronting all that cobbled wonder—is hard to beat. I've listed several places a few minutes' walk off the square, all with a magical, old-time feel. If you'd like something to wash down with your beer, you can generally get a cold-meat plate, an open-face sandwich, or a salad.

All varieties of Belgian beer are available, but Brussels' most distinctive beers are *lambic*-based. Look for *lambic doux, lambic blanche, gueuze* (pronounced "kurrs"), and *faro,* as well as fruit-flavored *lambics,* such as *kriek* (cherry) and *framboise* (raspberry—*frambozen* in Dutch). These beers look and taste more like a dry, somewhat bitter cider. The brewer doesn't add yeast—the beer ferments naturally from yeast found floating only in the marshy air around Brussels.

A la Mort Subite, a few steps above the top end of the Galeries St. Hubert, is a classic old bar that has retained its 1928 decor... and its loyal customers seem to go back just about as far (daily 11:00-24:00, Rue Montagne-aux-Herbes Potagères/Warmoesberg 7, tel. 02-513-1318). Named after the "sudden death" playoff that workingmen used to end their lunchtime dice games, it still has an unpretentious, working-class feel. The decor is simple, with wood tables, grimy yellow wallpaper, and some-other-era garland trim. Tiny metal plates on the walls mark spots where gas-powered flames once flickered—used by patrons to light their cigars. A typical lunch or snack here is an omelet with a salad or a *tartine* (open-face sandwich, €5) spread with *fromage blanc* (cream cheese) or pressed meat. Eat it with one of the home-brewed, *lambic*-based beers. This is a good place to try the *kriek* (cherry-flavored) beer. While their beer list is limited, they do have Chimay on tap.

At **Le Cirio,** across from the Bourse, the dark tables bear the skid marks of over a century's worth of beer steins (daily 10:00-1:00 in the morning, Rue de la Bourse/Beursstraat 18-20, tel. 02-512-1395).

A la Bécasse is lower profile than Le Cirio, with a simple wood-panel and wood-table decor that appeals to both poor students and lunching businessmen. The *lambic doux* has been served in clay jars since 1825. This place is just around the corner from Le Cirio, toward the Grand Place, hidden away at the end of a courtyard (€3-5 *tartine* sandwiches, €5-9 light meals, daily 11:00-24:00, Tabora street 11, tel. 02-511-0006).

Poechenellekelder Estaminet is a great bar with lots of real character located conveniently, if oddly, right across the street from the *Manneken-Pis.* As the word *estaminet* (tavern) indicates, it's not brewery-owned, so it has a great selection of beers. Inside tables are immersed in *Pis* kitsch and puppets. Outside tables offer some fine people-watching (Rue du Chêne/Eikstraat 5, tel. 02-511-9262).

Two tiny and extremely characteristic bars are tucked away down long entry corridors just off Rue du Marché-aux-Herbes/Grasmarkt. **A l'Imaige Nostre-Dame** (closed Sun, at #8) and **Au Bon Vieux Temps** (at #12) each treat fine beer with great reverence and seem to have extremely local clientele, whom you're bound to meet if you grab a stool.

Delirium Tap House is a sloppy frat party with no ambience, a noisy young crowd, beer-soaked wooden floors, rock 'n' roll, and a famous variety of great Belgian beers on tap (deep in the restaurant zone not far from Chez Léon at Impasse de la Fidélité/Getrouwheidsgang 4).

Near Bruges: Ghent

At Zeebrugge, most cruisers choose between Bruges and Brussels, but another wonderful Belgian town sits directly between them: Ghent, a 50-minute train ride from your ship.

Made terrifically wealthy by the textile trade, medieval Ghent was a powerhouse—for a time, it was one of the biggest cities in Europe. It erected grand churches and ornate guild houses to celebrate its resident industry. But, like its rival Bruges, eventually Ghent's fortunes fell, leaving it with a well-preserved historic nucleus surrounded by a fairly drab modern shell.

Ghent doesn't ooze with cobbles and charm, as Bruges does; this is a living, thriving city—home to Belgium's biggest university. In contrast to the manicured-but-empty back lanes of Bruges, Ghent enjoys more urban grittiness and a thriving restaurant and nightlife scene. It's also a browser's delight, with a wide range of fun and characteristic little shops and boutiques that aren't aimed squarely at the tourist crowds. Simply put, Ghent feels more real than idyllic. Visitors enjoy exploring its historic quarter, ogling the breathtaking Van Eyck altarpiece in its massive cathedral, touring its impressive art and design museums, strolling its picturesque embankments, basking in its finely decorated historic gables, and prowling its newly revitalized Patershol restaurant quarter.

Orientation to Ghent

Although it's a mid-sized city (pop. 240,000), the tourist's Ghent is appealingly compact—you can walk from one end of the central zone to the other in about 15 minutes. Its Flemish residents call it Gent (gutturally: hhhent), while its French name is Gand (sounds like "gone").

Tourist Information

Ghent's TI is in the Fish Market (Vismijn) building next to the Castle of the Counts (daily mid-March-mid-Oct 9:30-18:30, off-season 9:30-16:30, tel. 09-266-5232, www.visitgent.be). Pick up a free town map and a pile of brochures (including a good self-guided walk).

Arrival at Ghent's Main Train Station

As you approach on the train from Blankenberge (explained on page 839), get off at Ghent's main train station, called **Gent-Sint-Pieters**. The station is about a mile and a half south of the city center. As the station is undergoing an extensive renovation (through 2020), you might find things different from what's described here. It's a dull 30-minute **walk** to the city center. Instead, take the **tram:** Buy a ticket from the Relay shop just inside the train station exit or at the ticket machines outside, then find the stop for tram #1 (out the front door and to the left, on the far side of the tram tracks). Board tram #1 in direction: Wondelgem/Evergem (departs about every 10 minutes, ride into town takes 15 minutes, €1.20 if you buy the ticket in advance at a shop or automated machine, €2 from the driver; you can also get a shareable 10-ride ticket for €9). Get off at the Korenmarkt stop; continue one block straight ahead to Korenmarkt, from where you can see most of the city's landmark towers. Figure €10 for a **taxi** into town (€8.50 drop good for about 2 miles).

Sights in Ghent

Ghent is a rewarding town to simply wander and explore. Most visitors focus on the city's historic core, along a gentle bend in the river. You could have an enjoyable day simply strolling the riverbank, crisscrossing the bridges, and lingering in the city's many fine squares (the best are described below). While the city has several fine museums, churches, and other sights, I've listed only those that most warrant your limited time.

▲▲**Squares**—Of Ghent's many inviting squares, be sure to at least pass through these:

Korenmarkt: The historic "Corn Market" square, next to St. Michael's Bridge (one of the town's best viewpoints), is squeezed between the palatial former post office and St. Nicholas' Church. This square flows directly into two others: **Emil-Braunplein** (watched over by a Neo-Gothic belfry) and **St. Bavo's Square** (in front of the namesake cathedral, described next).

Vegetable Market (Groentenmarkt): This tidy and atmospheric square, right on the river, is tucked alongside the old-fashioned Meat Hall (now housing artisanal local foods).

Friday Market Square (Vrijdagmarkt): Watched over by a statue of local hero Jakob van Artevelde, this fine square is ringed by skinny burghers' mansions and the "House of the People" (Ons Huis), the ornately decorated headquarters for the region's socialist movement.

▲▲Cathedral of St. Bavo (Sint-Baafskathedraal)—The main church of Ghent, this also houses three of the city's art treasures:

the exquisite Van Eyck *Adoration of the Mystic Lamb* altarpiece; an elaborately carved pulpit; and an altar painting by Rubens depicting the town's patron saint (and the church's namesake).

The highlight of the church (and, for art lovers, of all Ghent) is Jan and Hubert van Eyck's *Adoration of the Mystic Lamb* altarpiece. Hubert van Eyck (c. 1385-1426) began the painting, but after his death, his better-known younger brother, Jan (1395-1441), picked up the brush and completed Hubert's vision. Finished in 1432, this altarpiece represents a monumental stride in northern European art from medieval stiffness to Renaissance humanism, with a closely observed attention to detail. The first work signed by Jan van Eyck, it's also considered one of the first works of the Flemish Primitives (characterized by a precise dedication to detail, if an imperfect mastery of perspective). The audioguide gives you 50 wonderful minutes of narration, if you want the full experience. Over the next few years, restoration will make sections of the altarpiece unviewable. But most of this amazing painting will always be on display.

Cost and Hours: Free to enter, €4 to see original altarpiece—includes excellent audioguide, Mon-Sat 9:30-16:45, Sun 13:00-16:30, later in summer. During busy times, volunteer guides can show you around.

▲Castle of the Counts (Gravensteen)—Built in 1180 by Philip of Alsace, this fortress was designed not to protect the people of Ghent, but to intimidate the city's independence-minded citizens. Erected outside the city walls, it's morphed over the centuries, and was partly destroyed by an accidental explosion (when it served as a textile factory), then restored. It's impressive from the outside, but explanations and

exhibits inside are pretty modest. Still, it's a fun opportunity to twist through towers and ramble over ramparts.

Cost and Hours: €8, dry €1.50 guidebook tells the history of the place, daily May-Sept 10:00-18:00, Oct-April 10:00-17:00, last entry one hour before closing, tel. 09-225-9306.

▲**Design Museum**—Worth ▲▲▲ for those interested in decorative arts and design, and enjoyable to anybody, this collection celebrates the Belgian knack for design. It combines a classic old building with a creaky wood interior, with a bright-white, spacious, and glassy new hall in the center. Just explore: Everything is clearly explained in English and easy to appreciate.

Cost and Hours: €5, Tue-Sun 10:00-18:00, closed Mon, Jan Breydelstraat 5, tel. 09-267-9999, www.designmuseumgent.be.

Eating in Ghent

Fast and Cheap

These centrally located options are suitable for a quick lunch.

Souplounge is basic, but cheap and good. They offer four daily soups, along with salads; a bowl of soup, two rolls, and a piece of fruit runs just €4. Eat in the mod interior, or at the outdoor tables overlooking one of Ghent's most scenic stretches of canal (also €5 salads, daily 10:00-19:00, Zuivelbrugstraat 6, tel. 09-223-6203).

Tasty World serves up decent €5 veggie burgers with various toppings, plus a wide range of fresh fruit juices and salads (Mon-Sat 11:00-20:00, closed Sun, Hoogpoort 1, tel. 09-225-7407).

Damass is a popular ice cream place where you can hang out and enjoy people-watching or get a cone to stroll with (at the north end of Korenmarkt, #2-C).

In Patershol

For decades this former sailors' quarter was a derelict and dangerous no-man's land, where only fools and thieves dared to tread. But a generation ago, restaurateurs began to reclaim the area, and today it's one of Ghent's most inviting and happening neighborhoods for dining. Stroll the streets and simply drop in on any place that looks good. Continue north beyond the end of Oudburg to find Sleepstraat, which is lined with cheap Turkish eateries (locals recommend Gok Palace).

It's hard to go wrong in Patershol, but here are some particularly well-regarded favorites:

Bij den Wijzen en den Zot ("By the Wise One and the Crazy One") was the first restaurant that opened in Patershol, back when people figured you were either a genius or a madman to open up shop in such a sketchy area. Their prize-winning, €23 fish *waterzooi*—a creamy soup containing a variety of fish along with

BRUGES & BRUSSELS

Ghent Restaurants

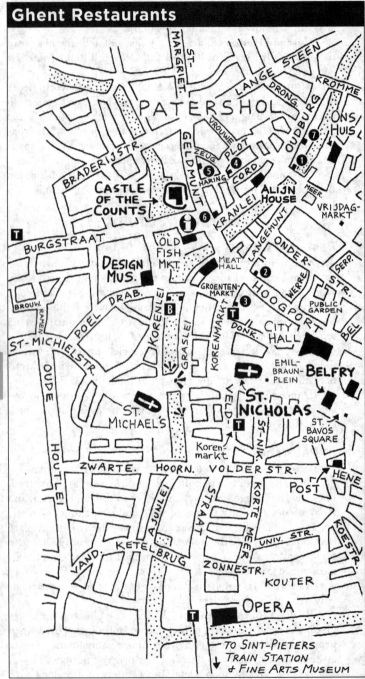

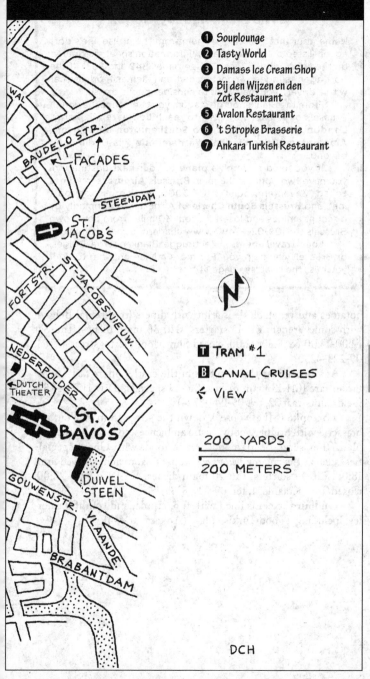

1 Souplounge
2 Tasty World
3 Damass Ice Cream Shop
4 Bij den Wijzen en den Zot Restaurant
5 Avalon Restaurant
6 't Stropke Brasserie
7 Ankara Turkish Restaurant

WAL

BAUDELO STR.

FACADES

STEENDAM

ST. JACOB'S

FORT STR.

ST-JACOBSNIEUW.

NEDERPOLDER

DUTCH THEATER

ST. BAVO'S

GOUWENSTR.

DUIVEL STEEN

VLAANDE.

BRABANTDAM

T TRAM #1
B CANAL CRUISES
VIEW

200 YARDS

200 METERS

DCH

BRUGES & BRUSSELS

What If I Miss My Boat?

Remember that you can get help from the cruise line's port agent (listed on the destination information sheet distributed on the ship) and the local TI (see pages 842 and 863). If the port agent suggests a costly solution (such as a private car with a driver), you may want to consider public transit.

From the Blankenberge station, you can connect through Brussels or Antwerp by train to reach **Le Havre** (via Paris), **London** (with connections to **Southampton** and **Dover**), **Amsterdam, Copenhagen, Warnemünde** (via Berlin), and beyond.

If you need to catch a **plane** to your next destination, you have two options: the main **Brussels Airport** (sometimes called "Zaventem," tel. 0900-70000, www.brusselsairport .be), and **Brussels South Charleroi** Airport, used primarily by discount airlines and located about 30 miles from downtown Brussels (tel. 09-020-2490, www.charleroi-airport.com).

Local **travel agents** in Zeebrugge, Blankenberge, Bruges, or Brussels can help you. For more advice on what to do if you miss the boat, see page 144.

---

potatoes and vegetables—is a hit with diners (traditional Belgian with some French, €11-15 starters, €20-30 main dishes, Tue-Sat 12:00-14:00 & 18:30-22:00, closed Sun-Mon, Hertogstraat 42, tel. 09-223-4230).

Avalon, across the street from the castle, offers tasty vegetarian fare (€11-13 main dishes, €16-19 specials, daily 11:30-14:30, Geldmuntstraat 32, tel. 09-244-3724).

't Stropke ("The Noose"), down the street from Avalon, is a brasserie with bright, woody, rustic ambience and a treehouse floor plan. They serve Belgian and French food, with Ghent specialties, such as the creamy *waterzooi* soup (€8 sandwiches served until 18:00, €10-14 starters, €16-20 main dishes, Fri-Wed 9:00-22:00, closed Thu, Kraanlei 1, tel. 09-329-8335).

Oudburg street is lined with fun, ethnic, and youthful eateries, including a good Turkish place (Ankara, at #44).

Dutch Survival Phrases

You won't need to learn Dutch, but knowing a few phrases can help if you're traveling off the beaten path. Taking a few moments to learn the pleasantries (such as please and thank you) will improve your connections with locals even in the bigger cities. In northern Belgium, they also speak Dutch, but with a Flemish accent.

To pronounce the difficult Dutch "g" (indicated in phonetics by hhh) make a hard, guttural, clear-your-throat sound, similar to the "ch" in the Scottish word "loch."

English	Dutch	Pronunciation
Hello.	*Hallo.*	hol-**loh**
Good day.	*Dag.*	dahhh
Good morning.	*Goeiemorgen.*	hhhoy-ah **mor**-hhhen
Good afternoon.	*Goeiemiddag.*	hhhoy-ah **mit**-tahk
Ma'am	*Mevrouw*	meh-frow
Sir	*Meneer*	men-ear
Yes	*Ja*	yah
No	*Nee*	nay
Please	*Alstublieft*	**ahl**-stoo-bleeft
Thank you.	*Dank u wel.*	dahnk yoo vehl
You're welcome.	*Graag gedaan.*	hhhrahhk hhkeh-dahn
Excuse me.	*Pardon.*	par-**dohn**
Do you speak English?	*Spreekt u Engels?*	spraykt oo **eng**-els
Okay.	*Oké.*	"okay"
Goodbye.	*Tot ziens.*	toht zeens
one / two	*een / twee*	ayn / t'vay
three / four	*drie / vier*	dree / feer
five / six	*vijf / zes*	fife / ses
seven / eight	*zeven / acht*	say-fen / ahkht
nine / ten	*negen / tien*	nay-hhhen / teen
What does it cost?	*Wat kost?*	vaht kost
I would like...	*Ik wil graag...*	ik vil hhhrahhhk
...a room.	*...een kamer.*	un kah-mer
...a ticket.	*...een kaart.*	un kart
...a bike.	*...een fiets.*	un feets
Where is...?	*Waar is...?*	vahr is
...the station	*...het station*	het sta-tsee-on
...the tourist info office	*...de VVV*	duh vay vay vay
left / right	*links / rechts*	links / rechts
open / closed	*open / gesloten*	"open" / hhhe-sloh-ten

In the Restaurant

Dutch speakers have an all-purpose word, alstublieft (AHL-stoo-bleeft), that means: "Please," or "Here you are," (if handing you something), or "Thanks," (if taking payment from you), or "You're welcome" (when handing you change). Here are other words that might come in handy at restaurants, particularly if you're day-tripping to small towns:

English	Dutch	Pronunciation
I would like...	Ik wil graag...	ik vil hhhrahhk
...a cup of coffee.	...kopje koffie.	kop-yeh "coffee"
menu	menu	muh-**noo**
non-smoking	niet-roken	neet roh-ken
smoking	roken	roh-ken
with / without	met / buiten	met / bow-ten
and / or	en / of	en / of
bread	brood	broht
salad	sla	slah
cheese	kaas	kahs
meat	vlees	flays
chicken	kip	kip
fish	vis	fis
egg	ei	eye
fruit	vrucht	frucht
pastries	gebak	hhhe-bak
water	water	**wah**-tuhr
beer	bier	beer
wine	wijn	wayn
coffee	koffie	"coffee"
tea	thee	tay
I am vegetarian.	Ik ben vegetarish.	ik ben vay-hhhe-tah-rish
Tasty.	Lekker.	lek-ker
Enjoy!	Smakelijk!	smak-kuh-luk
Cheers!	Proost!	prohst
The bill, please.	De rekening, alstublieft.	duh Ray-kun-ing **ahl**-stoo-bleeft

LONDON
Great Britain

Great Britain Practicalities

The island of Great Britain contains the countries of England, Wales, and Scotland. Hilly England—which contains all of the places in this chapter—occupies the lower two-thirds of the isle. The size of Louisiana (about 50,000 square miles), England's population is just over 52 million. England's ethnic diversity sets it apart from its fellow UK countries: Nearly one in three citizens is not associated with the Christian faith. The cradle of the Industrial Revolution, today's Britain has little heavy industry—its economic drivers are banking, insurance, and business services, plus energy production and agriculture. For the tourist, England offers a little of everything associated with Britain: castles, cathedrals, royalty, theater, and tea.

Money: 1 British pound (£1) = about $1.60. An ATM is called a cashpoint. The local VAT (value-added sales tax) rate is 20 percent; the minimum purchase eligible for a VAT refund is £30 (for details on refunds, see page 139).

Language: The native language is English.

Emergencies: Dial 999 for police, medical, or other emergencies. In case of theft or loss, see page 131.

Time Zone: Great Britain is one hour earlier than most of continental Europe, and five/eight hours ahead of the East/West Coasts of the US.

Embassies in London: The **US embassy** is at 24 Grosvenor Square (tel. 020/7499-9000, www.usembassy.org.uk). The **Canadian embassy** is at 1 Grosvenor Square (tel. 020/7258-6600, www.unitedkingdom.gc.ca). Call ahead for passport services.

Phoning: Britain's country code is 44; to call from another country to Britain, dial the international access code (011 from the US/Canada, 00 from Europe, or + from a mobile phone), then 44, followed by the area code (without initial zero) and the local number. For calls within Britain, dial just the number if you are calling locally, and add the area code if calling long distance. To place an international call from Britain, dial 00, the code of the country you're calling (1 for US and Canada), and the phone number. For more tips, see page 1110.

Tipping: Tipping in Britain isn't as automatic as it is in the US; always check your menu or bill to see if gratuity is included. If not, tip about 10 percent. To tip a cabbie, round up a bit (if the fare is £4.50, give £5). For more tips on tipping, see page 143.

Tourist Information: www.visitbritain.com

LONDON and the PORTS of SOUTHAMPTON and DOVER

Southampton • Portsmouth • Dover • Canterbury • London

Many cruises begin, end, or call at one of several English ports offering easy access to London. While this island nation has dozens of ports, cruise lines favor two in particular: Southampton, 80 miles southwest of London; and Dover, 80 miles southeast of London (each one within about a 1.5-hour drive or train ride into the city).

From Southampton and Dover, most people choose to head into **London**—and for good reason. London is more than its museums and landmarks. It's the L.A., D.C., and N.Y.C. of Britain—a living, breathing, thriving organism...a coral reef of humanity. London is a city of nearly eight million separate dreams, inhabiting a place that tolerates and encourages them. Those beginning or ending their cruise in one of these ports will want to allocate ample extra time to experience London. But if your cruise only stops here for the day—even if it's a long day—you'll be very limited in what you can see in London. For this reason, some people choose to skip the trip into the big city and visit towns closer to their port, which offer an enticing taste of English culture.

In **Southampton,** you could stick around town, but there's little to see there beyond its fine SeaCity Museum. However, it's a short train ride to **Portsmouth,** a gentrified city with a wide array of maritime and nautical-themed sights.

Dover has a castle that's well worth touring, famous White Cliffs (visible from the cruise dock)...and not much else. But it's a quick train trip to **Canterbury,** an exceptionally pleasant town with one of England's biggest and best cathedrals.

All of these destinations—Southampton, Portsmouth, Dover,

Canterbury, and, of course, London—are covered individually in this chapter, with "Planning Your Time" suggestions for each one.

The Port of Southampton

An important English port city for centuries, Southampton is best known for three ships that set sail from here and gained fame for very different reasons: the *Mayflower* in 1620, the *Titanic* in 1912, and in 1936, the *Queen Mary*—the luxurious great-grandma of the ship you arrived on. Like many port cities, Southampton was badly damaged by WWII bombs, obliterating whatever cobbled charm it once had. Today Southampton has one excellent museum (the state-of-the-art SeaCity Museum), but otherwise disappoints sightseers with a gloomy urban core, a few fragments of old city walls and towers, and an "Old Town" halfheartedly rebuilt to vaguely resemble a long-gone salty sailor's town.

These days, if Southampton is known for anything, it's for cruising. In 2012, 1.4 million cruise passengers passed through here. And, as the acres of waterfront parking lots and countless boxy hotels attest, Southampton is in the business of accommodating Brits who enjoy using the city as a launch pad for a holiday at sea.

If your cruise begins or ends in Southampton, you'll find it's an easy 1.25-hour train ride from downtown London and well organized for cruisers. If you're just here for the day, I'd resist the temptation to stay put; head for the station and get out of town—if not to London, then to nearby Portsmouth. For those staying in Southampton with time to kill, the new SeaCity Museum offers an excellent exhibit about the infamous ship whose fateful maiden voyage departed from right here—the *Titanic*.

Planning Your Time

Upon arrival in Southampton, most people will want to get out. London is a 1.25-hour train ride away, and Portsmouth (with a variety of great maritime exhibits) is just 50 minutes away. However, for those who want to stay in Southampton, there are a few ways to occupy yourself.

• **SeaCity Museum:** This well-presented museum thoughtfully tells the story of Southampton and the *Titanic*. It could occupy an attentive sightseer for two hours or longer.

• **Tudor House and Gardens:** Worth about 30 minutes, this modest museum peels back the layers of history of an old house in the town center.

There's little else to do in Southampton. The town center is

Excursions from Southampton and Dover

Cruise-line excursions from both ports feature visits to London, as well as local destinations.

Excursions to London: There are plenty of ways to skin this cat, but most begin with an orientation **bus tour** around town; you'll zip by (and possibly have a photo-op stop) at such landmarks as the Houses of Parliament (Big Ben), Westminster Abbey, Buckingham Palace, London Eye, and the Tower of London. Some also feature a guided sightseeing visit; popular options include the **Tower of London** and a guided tour of the interior of **Buckingham Palace. Shopping tours** ("West End shopping" at Harrods and other famous department stores) are also offered. A **London On Your Own** excursion—a round-trip bus ride to Piccadilly Circus and free time in the city with no guide—runs about $100 (compared to about $65 round-trip by train from Southampton, or about $55 from Dover).

If you're not up for the journey into London, consider some of these alternatives:

Other Excursions from Southampton: A side-trip to **Stonehenge and Salisbury** is perhaps the best choice, as it shows you Britain's iconic, mysterious, and ancient stone circle as well as a lovely mid-size market town with a grand cathedral. A tour of **Windsor Castle,** the primary residence of the royal family, is another good choice. Rounding out your options are a scenic drive through the **Dorset County Countryside** (often with a stop at the dramatic ruins of **Corfe Castle**); the stately **Palace of Beaulieu,** with its nearby National Motor Museum (displaying more than 250 historic automobiles); and a shopping-oriented visit to the town of **Winchester,** with yet another giant cathedral.

Other Excursions from Dover: The nearby town of **Canterbury** combines charm, history, and one of England's most important cathedrals—making it the best choice here. (Canterbury is also easy to do on your own, using the information in this chapter.) Other options include a boat trip for a closer look at Dover's famous **White Cliffs** and the South Foreland Lighthouse; the adorable village of **Rye** and a scenic drive through the Kent countryside; the stout, ninth-century **Leeds Castle;** the 15th-century, timber-framed **Great Dixter** house and its delightful gardens; Henry VIII's heavily fortified **Walmer Castle,** generally combined with the enchanting village of **Sandwich;** and the village of **Chilham** (a popular filming location).

While any of these offers a pleasant look at England's inimitable charm, none of these sights can challenge the greatness of London.

LONDON

nondescript, and the so-called "Old Town" near the Tudor House and Gardens is tiny and disappointing.

Arrival at the Port of Southampton

Arrival at a Glance: From the Ocean Cruise Terminal or City Cruise Terminal, you can walk into town or hop a free bus to the train station; from the others (QEII Cruise Terminal and Mayflower Cruise Terminal), spring for a taxi. Trains go to London (1.25 hours, 2/hour) and Portsmouth (50 minutes, hourly).

Port Overview

With 240,000 people, Southampton is a sprawling port town with a relatively compact downtown core. Everything is, to a point, walkable—though some of the cruise terminals are distant, and there's not much of interest to see en route, making it tempting to shave some time off your commute with taxis or the free Citylink bus.

Within Southampton's sprawling port, cruises use two different dock areas, each with two different terminals.

• The **Eastern Docks** consist of long piers jabbing straight out from Southampton, with two cruise terminals: **Ocean Cruise Terminal** at the near end (Berth 46), and **QEII Cruise Terminal** at the tip (Berth 38/39). You'll access this area through Dock Gate 4.

• The **Western Docks** hug Southampton's coastline west of downtown. Shuffled between the endless parking lots and container shipping berths are two cruise terminals: **City Cruise Terminal,** close to the town center (Berth 101); and **Mayflower Cruise Terminal,** farther out (Berth 106). You'll access this area through Dock Gate 8 (at the downtown end of the docks, close to City Cruise Terminal) or through Dock Gate 10 (farther from downtown but just south of the train station).

For details, see www.cruisesouthampton.com.

Terminal Services: Each of the four terminal buildings has similar services (or lack thereof). You'll typically find WCs, a rack of tourist brochures and maps, a basic café, and a taxi stand out front. There may be Wi-Fi available—ask for the password, or look around to see if it's posted. It's unlikely you'll find an ATM, and frustratingly, there's no convenient public transportation from your ship to the port gate. This means you'll have to either use a taxi (most take credit cards) or walk—either to the nearest public bus stop (5-25 minutes, depending on where you arrive) or all the way into town or the train station.

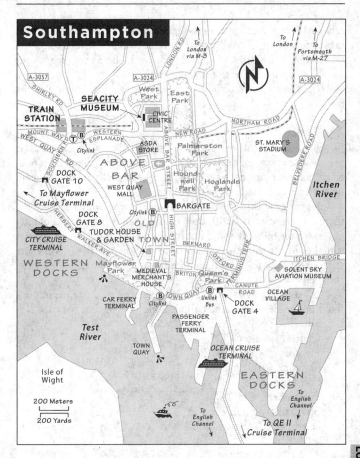

Tourist Information: None of the terminals has a TI, and the TI in town recently closed. Your best bet for visitor information is www.discoversouthampton.co.uk.

Getting into Town and to the Train Station

The train station—with convenient connections to London, Portsmouth, and more—sits northwest of the port zone; it's walkable, but far enough away that a taxi or bus is worth considering. Roughly between the port and the train station is the downtown core, including the underwhelming "Old Town," and above that, the street called Above Bar (because it's north of Bargate) and the Civic Centre (with the SeaCity Museum).

Depending on where you arrive, I'd consider the simplicity of a taxi. The free Citylink bus, which connects the port area to the train station, is also handy—though it doesn't go all the way to the cruise terminals, so you'll need to walk to reach it. Or, for those who feel like walking, it's possible to walk all the way from your ship to the museum or to the train station.

Details for each of these options are explained below, port by port.

By Taxi

Given the lack of direct public transportation to the ports, taxis are the main way for cruisers to get around town. Since it's a relatively compact city, cabs are affordable—especially if you can team up with other cruisers to split the cost.

For rides within the city limits, drivers are required to use the meter. Taxis start at £2.40, then charge about £1.80 per kilometer (£1 extra on Sun). It should cost around £5 from any cruise terminal either to the train station or to the town center (never more than £7-8). Ask for an estimate up front, then make sure they use the meter.

If leaving the city, you can either use the meter or negotiate a fixed price. Here are some ballpark one-way figures for trips farther afield:

Central London: £125
Heathrow Airport: £98
Gatwick Airport: £130
Salisbury: £40
Portsmouth: £35
Southampton Airport: £15

If you need to call a taxi, try West Quay Cars (tel. 023/8099-9999).

By Citylink Bus

If your cruise line offers an affordable **shuttle bus** to downtown or the train station, consider taking it.

Southampton's handy **Citylink bus** is a free service designed to help those arriving at the public ferry dock (called Town Quay) to reach the town center and train station. It runs through the city every 15 minutes, and is generally jam-packed with grungy backpackers fresh off the ferry. Unfortunately, it does not go to the cruise terminals themselves, so you'll have to walk to reach it. This is simple from the Ocean Cruise Terminal (at the Eastern Docks, a 10-minute walk from the bus stop) or the City Cruise Terminal (at the Western Docks, a 15-minute walk from the bus stop). If arriving at QEII Cruise Terminal, it's a long walk to the bus stop, making a taxi worth considering. And if arriving at Mayflower Cruise Terminal, it's faster to walk directly to the train station than to the bus stop. (For walking directions from each port, see the next section.)

The Citylink bus stop is at Town Quay, at the base of the passenger pier that sticks out into the bay from the end of Southampton's High Street. Board the bus at the stop in front of the Red Funnel ticket office. From the quay, the bus heads up into town, stopping at West Quay shopping center near the "Old Town" and Bargate, then continuing to the train station in about 10-15 minutes. If you want to visit the SeaCity Museum, ask if the driver will let you off at the Asda supermarket (between West Quay and the train station, a short walk from the Civic Centre).

Getting into Town from Each Port

The distance and specific directions for walking into town (or to the Citylink bus stop or the train station) vary dramatically from each of the four cruise terminals. Read over your options below, then decide whether it's worth the walk...or if you should spring for a cab.

From the Eastern Docks (Dock Gate 4)

On this very long pier, it's a short five-minute walk from **Ocean Cruise Terminal,** or a long 15-minute walk from the **QEII Cruise Terminal,** to reach Dock Gate 4. In both cases, just follow the main road to the exit.

Exiting Dock Gate 4, turn left onto the busy road. You'll see a stop for the Unilink bus (£2 to downtown or the train station), but keep on going—it's just five minutes more to the stop for the **free Citylink bus** (described earlier). Continue along the road with a park on your right and parking lots on your left. At the fork, continue straight, bearing left slightly and passing the old stone tower. When you reach the Town Quay pier, you could cross the street to reach the Citylink bus stop (in front of the Red Funnel ticket office).

Or, if you feel like **walking,** turn right when you reach Town Quay and head up High Street, which leads in about 15 minutes up through the town center to the Civic Centre area. This shop-lined drag isn't too inviting, but it does give you a sense of workaday England; a few blocks to your left is the unimpressive "Old Town." Halfway up the main drag, you reach Bargate, one of the original town wall's towers. Beyond that, the street becomes "Above Bar." After a few short blocks you'll see a big, stately building with a lighthouse tower on your left—this is the

LONDON

Services in Southampton

Unfortunately, there aren't many services available at the cruise terminals. For most, you'll need to head into town (or wait for London).

ATMs: As Southampton's cruise ports are more oriented to British travelers, you likely won't find an ATM in your terminal. Your best bet is either to find one in downtown Southampton (several banks with ATMs line High Street, the main drag) or in London (Waterloo Station, where you'll arrive, has several). Most taxi drivers take credit cards (ask before you hop in), the Citylink bus is free, and you can buy train tickets with credit cards—so it's relatively easy to get into London cash-free.

Internet Access: There may be Wi-Fi at some terminals—look for a posted password, or ask around. You'll find both Internet terminals and Wi-Fi free at the library (located in the Civic Centre). Otherwise, look for one of the many ubiquitous Costa Coffee shops (including one on High Street), which offer free Wi-Fi with a purchase.

Pharmacy: The biggest and handiest is Boots, on Above Bar just outside Bargate (Mon-Sat 8:00-19:00, Thu until 19:30, Sun 10:30-16:30).

Civic Centre, with the SeaCity Museum next door. To reach the train station, turn left from Above Bar onto Civic Centre Road (just before the Civic Centre itself), which takes you in about 10 minutes to the station.

From the Western Docks (Dock Gate 8 or 10)

The best plan here depends on which terminal you arrive at. **City Cruise Terminal** is within an easy walk of the free Citylink bus stop, while **Mayflower Cruise Terminal** is much farther out, requiring a dull slog through industrial ports to reach anything (from Mayflower, I'd spring for a taxi).

City Cruise Terminal: This terminal is conveniently situated at the near end of the Western Docks. To get into town, exit the terminal to the right, then continue straight until you pop out at Dock Gate 8. From here, continue straight along the street (keeping the port on your right) until you reach Town Quay—about 10 minutes' walk from your ship. At Town Quay, find the **Citylink bus** stop in front of the Red Funnel ticket office, and ride it for free (bus stops in Southampton's "Old Town" and train station). It's a dreary 20-minute **walk** to the train station (turn left out of the terminal, hike through the port area to Dock Gate 10—at the roundabout, turn right to exit through the gate, continue straight up Southern Road, then turn right after the second cross-street, cutting through the park to the station).

Mayflower Cruise Terminal: The most distant of any Southampton cruise terminal, Mayflower virtually requires a **taxi** (the taxi stand is to the left as you exit the terminal).

But if you're up for a **walk,** plan on a dreary 15-minute march to Dock Gate 10, followed by a 10-minute walk to the train station. (There's no point in trying to catch the free Citylink bus at Town Quay, because that bus stop is farther from Mayflower than the train station itself.) To reach Dock Gate 10, exit straight ahead out of the terminal, crossing the train tracks and proceeding one long block up Imperial Way. At the T-intersection, turn right (following signs for *City Centre / Exit 10 Gate*) and hike straight through endless parking lots and stacks of cargo containers to reach the big roundabout, where you'll see the big Dock Gate 10 on your left. Go through the gate and keep going straight up Southern Road, crossing two very busy cross-streets. After the second one, just before the overpass, turn right, following signs through the park to *Central Station*.

To reach the SeaCity Museum, carry on straight past the station and walk another 10 minutes; after cresting the hill, look left to spot the lighthouse tower marking the Civic Centre.

Taking the Train to London (or Elsewhere)

For tips on reaching the train station from various cruise ports, see the earlier sections.

Southampton Central Station is small and manageable, with ticket windows and automated ticket machines just inside the door. You can enter or exit the station from either side, but most people come and go from the southern entrance; this entrance faces the Western Docks (for those walking in) and is also the location of the Citylink bus stop to Town Quay. A walkway over the tracks connects this entrance to tracks 1 and 2, used by London-bound trains.

Trains depart every 30 minutes from Southampton to **London's Waterloo Station** (1.25 hours; additional departures require a change in Basingstoke and take 1.5 hours; slower trains go to London's Victoria Station in 2.5 hours). A "day return" (same-day round-trip) ticket to London costs £39; a "single"/one-way ticket costs £34.10. For details on arriving in London, see page 940.

For a closer and more manageable side-trip, consider **Portsmouth**. Trains leave Southampton about hourly (typically at :05 past the hour) and head directly to Portsmouth Harbour Station, within easy walking distance of the sights (50 minutes; £9.60 "single"/one-way, £10.40 "day return"/same-day round-trip). There are additional connections, with a change in Fareham or

Havant, but these take longer (60-70 minutes).

When returning to Southampton, be sure to get off at **Southampton Central Station;** the stop called Southampton Airport Parkway is much farther from the port.

By Shuttle Bus to London

Remember, many cruise lines offer a "London On Your Own" excursion, providing an unguided, round-trip bus transfer to Piccadilly Circus in London. Most lines charge about $100 for this trip—significantly more than the round-trip train ticket, but very convenient.

By Tour

Southampton doesn't have any tour options worth considering. For information on local tour options in London—including bus, walking, and bike tours—see "Tours in London" on page 947.

Returning to Your Ship

First take the train from London's Waterloo Station (or Portsmouth Harbour Station) to **Southampton Central Station** (don't get off at Southampton Airport Parkway). Exiting the station, you'll see a **taxi** stand (figure around £5 to your ship), and a stop for the **free Citylink bus.** If you're feeling thrifty and have plenty of time, consider the bus—but remember that it won't take you directly to your ship (you'll get off at Town Quay along the waterfront—a short walk from City or Ocean cruise terminals, and a much longer walk from Mayflower or QEII terminals). Here are the details: The Citylink bus comes by every 15 minutes and gets you to the port in about 10-15 minutes. Get off at the Town Quay stop, at the base of the passenger pier, across the street from the Red Funnel ticket office. Once off the bus, stand with your back to the port. City Cruise Terminal (at the Western Docks) is to your left—just walk along the portside road, then head through Dock Gate 8 just after the roundabout, and proceed straight to the terminal (about 10 minutes from the bus stop; Mayflower Cruise Terminal is another 15-20 minutes beyond this terminal, deeper into the port). Ocean Cruise Terminal is to your right—walk along the portside road until you see Port Gate 4 on your right (after passing the old stone tower and long park on your left). Go through the gate and proceed out to your ship—about 10 minutes total from the bus stop (QEII terminal is out at the tip of this pier, about 10-15 minutes longer walk).

See page 990 for help if you miss your boat.

Sights in Southampton

Southampton has little to offer sightseers, with the notable exception of the excellent SeaCity Museum (and its fine *Titanic* exhibit). With more time to kill, drop by the Tudor House and Gardens. An £11.50 combo-ticket covers both the museum and the house/gardens.

▲▲**SeaCity Museum**—This state-of-the-art facility, designed to consolidate and update various crusty old museums, features one of the best exhibits anywhere on the *Titanic*. It also has a good local history collection and well-presented temporary exhibits.

Cost and Hours: £8.50, daily 10:00-17:00, last entry at 15:00, Havelock Road, tel. 023/8083-3007, www.seacitymuseum.co.uk.

Visiting the Museum: From the ground-floor entrance level (with a gift shop, cafeteria, and temporary exhibits), head upstairs to the Grand Hall. From here, you can enter the two permanent collections.

The highlight, called **Southampton's *Titanic* Story,** explores every facet of the ill-fated ocean liner that set sail from here on April 10, 1912, and sank in the North Atlantic a few days later. Three-quarters of the *Titanic*'s 897 crew members lived in Southampton—making the global disaster a very local matter. With a smart multimedia approach, this outstanding exhibit invites you to linger over each detail. The introduction sets the stage with everyday life in Southampton, circa 1912. As you progress, you'll periodically zoom in on six specific crew members representing all levels of authority—from a lowly coal trimmer to a lookout, and from a steward to Captain Edward John Smith—both to personalize the event and to illustrate various aspects of life on board. Giant cutaway diagrams let you peek below decks, with touchscreens playing grainy footage of life on board ships of that age—emphasizing the stark contrast between the luxurious top decks and the hardscrabble peasants in the bowels of the ship. There's lots to read, a few replicas of rooms on board, some fun interactive exhibits (a simulator lets you steer the *Titanic* out of port, while another lets you shovel coal to keep the engines churning), and a few actual artifacts (including Captain Smith's ceremonial sword, as well as the pocket watch—found on the body of a steward—that stopped 30 minutes before the ship went under). You'll learn how, just before midnight on April 14, 1912, the ship struck an iceberg and gradually sank over three hours—killing 1,500 passengers and crew. You'll hear eyewitness reports from survivors, see a map of Southampton with a red dot marking the residence of each victim (driving home just how devastating the disaster was here—of the 715 Southamptoners who set sail, only

LONDON

175 returned), and use touchscreens to virtually view newspaper headlines. A chilling telegram from one of the few survivors reads simply: "safe coming home." A mock courtroom presents five three-minute films with dramatized testimony from the inquiry into how the supposedly "unsinkable" ship managed to sink. And, for cruisers who are left feeling a little wary about returning to their ship, the final exhibit examines how later ocean liners were redesigned to drastically reduce the odds of future such disasters (or, at least, to provide enough lifeboats).

Across the Grand Hall is the other permanent exhibit, **Southampton: Gateway to the World,** which traces the history of this shipping settlement from prehistoric and Anglo Saxon times until today. A giant interactive touchscreen map lets you delve into various eras of the town's history, while a film illustrates the lives of soldiers from Henry V's Battle of Agincourt in 1415 through modern times. Another exhibit focuses on how this gateway city was shaped by "transmigrants"—people passing through en route to new opportunities, some of whom stayed. Profiles of various immigrant groups—Indians, Poles, Pakistanis, Chinese, Ugandans—illustrate how people from everywhere have flocked to and through Southampton in search of a better life. The museum's prized possession is its 23-foot-long model of the *Queen Mary,* which made its maiden voyage from Southampton in 1936.

Tudor House and Gardens—A rare surviving 520-year-old home tucked in Southampton's underwhelming and mostly recon-

structed Old Town, this house offers a step back in time. Your visit begins with a 10-minute, semi-hokey audiovisual show of "ghosts" telling the building's history. Then you'll explore the various rooms, with exhibits and videos explaining how restorers have peeled back the historical layers of the place: Tudor, Georgian, Victorian, and even a WWII-era bunker. The experience is worthwhile for those with an interest in historical architecture (or anyone wanting to kill some time). But anyone can enjoy the pleasant garden and fine café (free to enter).

Cost and Hours: £4.75, includes audioguide, daily 10:00-18:00, Bugle Street, tel. 023/8083-4242, www.tudorhouseand garden.com.

Near Southampton: Portsmouth

Portsmouth, the age-old home of the Royal Navy and Britain's second-busiest ferry port after Dover, is best known for its Historic Dockyard and many nautical sights. For centuries, Britain, a maritime superpower, relied on the fleets in Portsmouth to expand and maintain its vast empire and guard against invaders. When sea power was needed, British leaders—from

Henry VIII to Winston Churchill to Tony Blair—called upon Portsmouth to ready the ships. Today, the large city of Portsmouth (with about 200,000 inhabitants) has a revitalized urban core and old nautical sights that are as impressive as ever. Visiting landlubbers can tour the HMS *Victory*, which played a key role in Britain's battles with Napoleon's navy, and see what's left of the *Mary Rose*, a 16th-century warship.

Planning Your Time

On a day in port from nearby Southampton, Portsmouth can easily fill a day. Focus your time on the Historic Dockyards (allow 2-3 hours to tour all of the museums and ships). With more time, explore Old Portsmouth or ascend Spinnaker Tower.

Orientation to Portsmouth

Tourist Information: The TI is inconveniently located inside the D-Day Museum in Southsea, about two miles east of the Portsmouth Harbour train station (daily April-Sept 10:00-17:30, Oct-March 10:00-17:00, tel. 023/9282-6722, www.visitportsmouth .co.uk, vis@portsmouthcc.gov.uk).

Arrival by Train in Portsmouth: Trains from Southampton are described on page 905. Portsmouth has two train stations. Stay on the train until the final stop at the Portsmouth Harbour Station, conveniently located one long block from the entrance to the Historic Dockyard.

Sights in Portsmouth

▲▲Historic Dockyard

When Britannia ruled the waves, it did so from Portsmouth's Historic Dockyard. Britain's great warships, known as the

Portsmouth

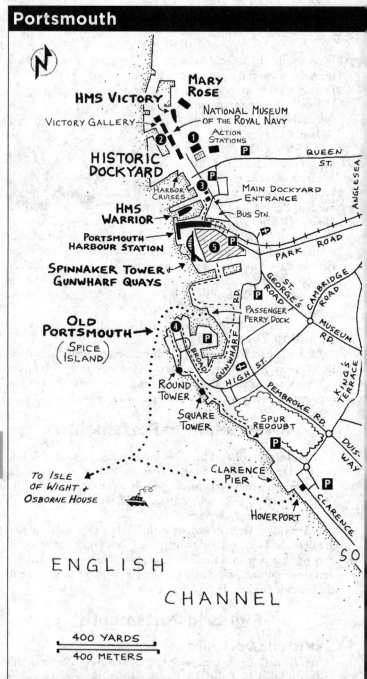

MARY ROSE

HMS VICTORY

Victory Gallery

NATIONAL MUSEUM OF THE ROYAL NAVY

Action Stations

QUEEN ST.

HISTORIC DOCKYARD

Harbor Cruises

Main Dockyard Entrance

Bus Stn.

ANGLESEA

HMS WARRIOR

Portsmouth Harbour Station

PARK ROAD

SPINNAKER TOWER
GUNWHARF QUAYS

ST. GEORGE'S ROAD

CAMBRIDGE ROAD

Passenger Ferry Dock

MUSEUM RD.

OLD PORTSMOUTH
(SPICE ISLAND)

BROAD

GUNWHARF RD.

HIGH ST.

KING'S TERRACE

ROUND TOWER

Square Tower

PEMBROKE RD.

SPUR REDOUBT

DUIS-WAY

CLARENCE PIER

TO ISLE OF WIGHT +
OSBORNE HOUSE

HOVERPORT

CLARENCE

SO

ENGLISH

CHANNEL

400 YARDS
400 METERS

LONDON

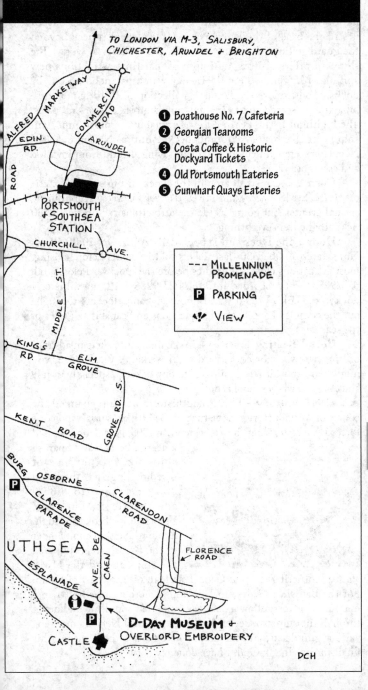

To London via M-3, Salisbury, Chichester, Arundel & Brighton

1 Boathouse No. 7 Cafeteria
2 Georgian Tearooms
3 Costa Coffee & Historic Dockyard Tickets
4 Old Portsmouth Eateries
5 Gunwharf Quays Eateries

MARKETWAY
ALFRED ROAD
EDIN. RD.
COMMERCIAL ROAD
ARUNDEL
ROAD

PORTSMOUTH & SOUTHSEA STATION

CHURCHILL AVE.

MIDDLE ST.

--- MILLENNIUM PROMENADE
P PARKING
✿ VIEW

KING'S RD.
ELM GROVE
GROVE RD. S.

KENT ROAD

LONDON

BURG OSBORNE
P
CLARENCE PARADE
CLARENDON ROAD

UTHSEA
AVE. DE CAEN
FLORENCE ROAD

ESPLANADE

P
CASTLE

D-DAY MUSEUM & OVERLORD EMBROIDERY

DCH

"Wooden Walls of England," were all that lay between the island nation and invaders from the Continent. Today, this harbor is still the base of the Royal Navy. (If you sneak a peek beyond the guard stations, you can see the British military at work.) The shipyard offers visitors a glimpse of maritime attractions new and old. Marvel at the modern-day warships anchored on the docks, then explore the fantastic collection of historic memorabilia and preserved ships. The museum complex has several parts. The highlight is the HMS *Victory*, arguably the most important ship in British history. From its deck, Admiral Nelson defeated Napoleon's French fleet at Trafalgar, saving Britain from invasion and escargot.

Cost: You can stroll around the Dockyard to see the exteriors of the HMS *Victory* and HMS *Warrior* for free (except during special events), but going inside the attractions requires a £23.50 ticket that covers everything.

Hours: The Dockyard is open daily April-Oct 10:00-18:00, Nov-March 10:00-17:30 (last tickets sold 1.5 hours before closing, most attractions close 30 minutes before the Dockyard closes, tel. 023/9283-9766, recorded info tel. 023/9286-1512, www.historic dockyard.co.uk). Friendly and knowledgeable docents throughout the complex happily answer questions and capably tell tales of the sea.

Crowd-Beating Tips: To skip the line, buy tickets in advance online (www.historicdockyard.co.uk/tickets). Otherwise, you might have to wait 20-45 minutes to buy tickets, especially in July and August, when school is out.

▲▲▲**HMS *Victory***—This grand historic warship changed the course of world history. At the turn of the 19th century, Napoleon's forces were terrorizing the Continent. In 1805, Napoleon amassed

a fleet of French and Spanish ships for the purpose of invading England. The Royal Navy managed to blockade the fleets, but some French ships broke through. Admiral Nelson, commander of the British fleet, pursued the ships aboard the HMS *Victory*, cornering them at Cape Trafalgar, off the coast of Spain. For the British, this dry-docked ship is more a cathedral than a museum. Visitors follow a one-way route that spirals up and down through the ship's six decks. You'll see Admiral Nelson's quarters, various gun decks, and the place where Nelson died, gasping his final words: "Thank God, I have done my duty."

▲**Mary Rose**—Next to the *Victory* is the home of the *Mary Rose*, which sank in 1545 and was raised in 1982. The £35 million museum, shaped like an oval jewel box, reunites the preserved hull with thousands of its previously unseen contents. All sorts of Tudor-era items were found inside the wreck, such as clothes, dishes, weapons, and even a backgammon board and an oboe-like instrument. It's a fascinating look at everyday shipboard life from almost 500 years ago.

HMS *Warrior*—This ship, while impressive, never saw a day of battle...which explains why it's in such good condition. The *Warrior* was the first ironclad warship, a huge technological advance. Compare this ship, built in 1860, with the *Victory*, which was similar to the warships common at the time. The *Warrior* was unbeatable, and the enemy knew it. Its very existence was sufficient to keep the peace. The late 19th century didn't see many sea battles, however, and by the time warships were needed again, the *Warrior* was obsolete.

Other Sights at the Dockyards—With more time, dip into the **National Museum of the Royal Navy**, tour the "**Action Stations**" exhibit (thinly veiled propaganda for the military), and consider a 45-minute **harbor cruise** (departs about hourly during the summer starting at 11:00).

Other Sights in Portsmouth

Spinnaker Tower—Out at the far end of the Gunwharf Quays shopping zone is this futuristic-looking 557-foot-tall tower, evocative of the billowing ships' sails that have played such a key role in the history of this city and country. You can ride to the 330-foot-high view deck for a panorama of the port and sea beyond, or court acrophobia with a stroll across "Europe's biggest glass floor."

Cost and Hours: £8.25, daily 10:00-18:00, last entry 30 minutes before closing; since it can be crowded at midday July-Aug, it's smart to book ahead—and doing so online gets you a 15 percent discount; info tel. 023/9285-7520, booking tel. 023/9285-7521, www.spinnakertower.co.uk.

Old Portsmouth—Portsmouth's historic district—once known as "Spice Island" after the ships' precious cargo—is surprisingly quiet. For a long time, the old sea village was dilapidated and virtually empty. But successful revitalization efforts have brought a few inviting pubs and B&Bs. It's a pleasant place to stroll around and imagine how different this district was in the old days, when it was filled with salty fishermen and sailors who told tall tales and sang sea shanties in rough-and-tumble pubs.

▲**D-Day Museum and Overlord Embroidery**—This small museum features the remarkable 272-foot long Overlord

LONDON

Embroidery. Its 34 appliquéd panels—stitched together over five years by a team of seamstresses—chronologically trace the years from 1940 to 1944, from the first British men receiving their call-up papers in the mail to the successful implementation of D-Day. It celebrates everyone from famous WWII figures to unsung heroes of the home front. A worthwhile audioguide narrates the whole thing, panel by panel (rent when you buy your ticket).

Cost and Hours: £6.50, audioguide-£2, daily April-Sept 10:00-17:30, Oct-March 10:00-17:00, last entry 30 minutes before closing. A café is on site (open April-Sept). The museum is on the waterfront about two miles south of the Spinnaker Tower (Clarence Esplanade, Southsea, tel. 023/9282-7261, www.dday museum.co.uk). From Portsmouth's Hard Interchange bus station, take First Bus Company's buses #5/5A or #16 or Stagecoach bus #700.

Eating in Portsmouth

At the Historic Dockyard

The Historic Dockyard has an acceptable **cafeteria,** called **Boathouse No. 7,** with a play area that kids enjoy (£4-8 meals, daily 10:00-15:00). The **Georgian Tearooms** are across the pedestrian street in Storehouse #9, with good sandwich and cake offerings (daily 10:00-17:00). The **Costa Coffee** inside the entrance building offers surprisingly good grilled sandwiches, and coffee drinks to go (daily 10:00-17:00).

In Old Portsmouth

The Still & West Country House pub has dining in two appealing zones. Eat from the simpler and cheaper menu on the main floor, or outside on the picnic benches with fantastic views of the harbor (£7 baguette sandwiches and £8 fish-and-chips). Or head upstairs to the dining room, with higher prices (£9-17 main dishes) but a gorgeous glassed-in conservatory that offers sea views—especially enticing in cold weather (dining room open Mon-Sat 12:00-15:00 & 18:00-21:00, Sun 12:00-19:00, longer hours in the bar, 2 Bath Square, tel. 023/9282-1567).

The Spice Island Inn, at the tip of the Old Portsmouth peninsula, has terrific outdoor seating, a family-friendly dining room upstairs, and many vegetarian offerings, although service can be slow (£5-9 lunches, £7-12 dinners, food served daily 11:00-21:30, bar open longer, 1 Bath Square, tel. 023/9287-0543).

Tearoom: If you could do with a proper afternoon tea, visit the **Sallyport Tea Rooms,** named for a gateway in a fortification—specifically, the one in Portsmouth's ramparts that Nelson passed through on his final departure (£4-5 sandwiches, £7 afternoon tea—order in advance, daily 10:00-17:00, 35 Broad Street, tel. 023/9281-6265).

Returning to Southampton

Most of Portsmouth's sights (Historic Dockyards, Spinnaker Tower, Old Portsmouth) are within walking distance of the Portsmouth Harbour Station. From here, direct trains depart about hourly for the 45-minute trip to **Southampton Central Station** (more connections possible with changes).

The Port of Dover

Dover—like much of southern England—sits on a foundation of chalk. Miles of cliffs stand at attention above the beaches; the most famous are the White Cliffs of Dover. Sitting above those cliffs is the impressive Dover Castle, England's primary defensive stronghold from Roman through modern times. From the nearby port, ferries, hydrofoils, and hovercrafts shuttle people and goods back and forth across the English Channel. France is only 23 miles away—on a sunny day, you can see it off in the distance.

Dover's run-down town center isn't worth a second look. Focus instead on Dover's looming castle, standing guard as it has for almost a thousand years. Or take a train ride to nearby and far more charming Canterbury (described on page 930).

Planning Your Time

London is the main attraction from here (a 1.25-hour train ride away), but those preferring to stay closer to the ship could fill the better part of a day in Dover if you linger at the castle or cliffs. Better yet, for a busy but satisfying day, make a quick trip up to Dover Castle, then ride the train just 20-30 minutes to pleasant Canterbury for the afternoon.

• **Dover Castle:** If you do both of the guided tours at the Secret Wartime Tunnels, as well as touring the Great Tower and hiking around the battlements, this could easily take 4-5 hours; if you're in a rush, do only the Operation Dynamo tour and sprint through the tower (allow 2 hours).

LONDON

Dover

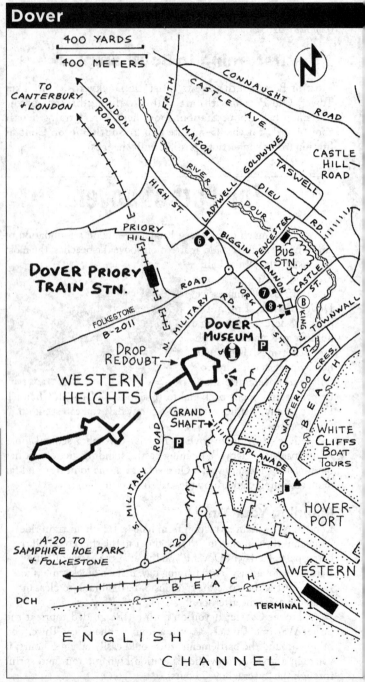

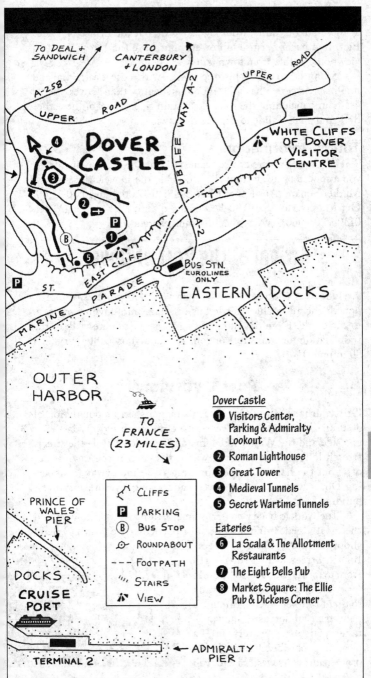

TO DEAL & SANDWICH

TO CANTERBURY + LONDON

A-258

UPPER ROAD

UPPER ROAD

JUBILEE WAY A-2

A-2

DOVER CASTLE

WHITE CLIFFS OF DOVER VISITOR CENTRE

BUS STN. EUROLINES ONLY

EASTERN DOCKS

EAST CLIFF

MARINE PARADE

ST.

OUTER HARBOR

TO FRANCE (23 MILES)

PRINCE OF WALES PIER

DOCKS

CRUISE PORT

TERMINAL 2

ADMIRALTY PIER

Dover Castle

1 Visitors Center, Parking & Admiralty Lookout
2 Roman Lighthouse
3 Great Tower
4 Medieval Tunnels
5 Secret Wartime Tunnels

Eateries

6 La Scala & The Allotment Restaurants
7 The Eight Bells Pub
8 Market Square: The Ellie Pub & Dickens Corner

Map Legend

- Cliffs
- P Parking
- B Bus Stop
- Roundabout
- --- Footpath
- Stairs
- View

LONDON

• **White Cliffs:** There are a number of ways to get a good look at these famous cliffs, from an easy walk out the Prince of Wales Pier, to a harbor cruise (allow an hour for either), to a trip to a viewpoint farther from town (allow 2-3 hours).

• **Canterbury:** This historic town—with a great cathedral and fine historic core—has a lot more personality than Dover. Allow 4-5 hours, including the round-trip train ride, a tour of the cathedral, and a bit of time to explore the town.

Tourist Information

There's no TI at the cruise terminal, but the shuttle bus drops you a few steps away from the TI inside the Dover Museum, on Market Square (April-Sept Mon-Sat 9:30-17:00, Sun 10:00-15:00; Oct-March Mon-Sat 9:30-17:00, closed Sun; Market Square, tel. 01304/201-066, www.whitecliffscountry.org.uk).

Arrival at the Port of Dover

Arrival at a Glance: As it's a long walk (30 minutes or more), opt for the affordable shuttle bus or a taxi into downtown or up to the castle. From downtown, it's an easy 15-minute walk to the train station for trains to London (1.25 hours) or Canterbury (20-30 minutes).

Port Overview

Gritty, urban-feeling Dover seems bigger than its population of 30,000. The town lies between two cliffs, with Dover Castle on one side and the Western Heights on the other. While the streets stretch longingly toward the water, the core of the town is cut off from the harbor by the rumbling A-20 motorway (connecting Dover with cities to the west) and a long, eyesore apartment building.

The workaday city center is anchored by Market Square and the mostly pedestrianized (but not particularly charming) main shopping drag, Cannon Street/ Biggin Street, which runs north from Market Square to the old town jail. A short five-minute walk south of Market Square, through a pedestrian underpass ("subway"), takes you to the waterfront—a pleasant pebbly beach lined with a promenade; at its western end, you

Services in Dover

There aren't many services at the port itself. But if you make your way to Market Square (by shuttle bus or taxi), you'll find the following:

ATMs: Several ATMs are on or near Market Square and Cannon Street/Biggin Street.

Internet Access: The library, called the Dover Discovery Centre—next to the Dover Museum/TI, just off Market Square—has terminals with free Internet access (Mon-Fri 9:00-18:00, Wed until 20:00, Sat 9:00-17:00, closed Sun). Three eateries along Cannon Street/Biggin Street, up from the TI, have free Wi-Fi for customers: Heading up this street, after one short block, you'll first reach The Eight Bells pub (on the left); one long block farther, on the right, you'll pass Costa Coffee; and just beyond that, on the left, is McDonald's.

Pharmacy: The most convenient is Boots, next door to Costa Coffee, two blocks up Cannon Street/Biggin Street from Market Square (Mon-Sat 9:00-17:30, Sun 10:00-16:00).

can enjoy fine views of the castle and White Cliffs. But this is only worth it on a gorgeous day—views of the White Cliffs are better from out of town, and the beach is pretty tame even by British standards.

Little Dover has a huge port, and cruises put in at its far western edge—at the **Western Docks,** along the extremely long Admiralty Pier. Near the port gate at the base of the pier, Terminal 1 is a converted old railway station; farther out at the tip, Terminal 2 is a modern facility. For more info, see www.whitecliffscountry.org.uk.

Tourist Information: There's no TI at the cruise terminal, but the shuttle bus drops you near one that is inside the Dover Museum (described earlier).

Getting into Town

Walking into town is possible, but grueling and dull. Spring for the reasonably priced shuttle bus or a taxi into town or to the castle. To reach the train station, you'll either take the shuttle downtown, then walk 15 minutes; or take a taxi straight there.

By Taxi

In this small town, taxis are reasonable. For two or more people traveling together within town, taxis are the cheapest way to go. Most taxis take credit cards, as well as British pounds and US dollars. Taxis are standing by, or you can call 01304/204-040, 01304/204-420, or 01304/228-882.

Expect to pay around £7-8 for a ride from either terminal to downtown (Market Square), to the train station, or to the castle. The hourly rate is about £30. Licensed taxis are not allowed to charge more than the following rates (one-way); the numbers in parentheses indicate what most companies actually charge:

To Dover Castle or the train station: £8

To downtown London or Heathrow Airport: £180 (usually £140-155)

To Gatwick Airport: £150 (usually £110-115)

To Canterbury: This rate is not regulated—figure on a one-way fare of around £27-30.

By Shuttle Bus

When cruise ships are in port, Classic Omnibus runs a bright-blue shuttle bus into town from the terminals (10-minute trip). There are two stops: first at Market Square (in the heart of town, next to the TI and a 15-minute walk from the train station); and then up at the castle. If you don't have British pounds, you can pay in dollars or euros (£3/€4/$5 one-way into town; add £1/€1/$1 to continue up to the castle; www.opentopbus.co.uk). For more than two people, it's cheaper to take a taxi.

Arriving at Market Square

If you're getting off the bus at Market Square, here's what you'll find: From the bus stop, walk straight ahead a few steps and curl around to the left into the square. The TI and Dover Museum are just to your left; down the street beyond that is the Discovery Centre/library (with Internet access). The main drag, Cannon Street—which becomes Biggin Street—begins across the square from the TI. Head up this street to find some eateries with free Wi-Fi, and eventually the train station. There are ATMs all around Market Square and along Cannon/Biggin Street.

Walking to the Train Station: Figure about 15 minutes from Market Square to the station (a bit less if you hustle). First, head up Cannon Street (directly across the square from the TI), and follow it for three blocks. Just after passing Costa Coffee and Boots pharmacy, and just before the street ahead of you becomes cobbled and traffic-free, turn left onto Priory Street. After a short block, you'll come to a big roundabout; circle around the right and use the crosswalks to go more or less straight through it. On the far side of the roundabout, continue slightly uphill on Folkestone Road; a half-block after the gas station, watch for *Dover Priory* signs on the right marking the station.

By Foot

You can walk from your cruise terminal into town, but it's a very long hike, mostly through dull industrial territory. From Terminal 1, plan on about 30 minutes; from Terminal 2, it's roughly 40 minutes.

First, walk along the pier road from the terminal to the port gate. Passing through it, veer left with the road, then jog right again, and continue up and over the tall overpass. Reaching the end of the overpass and hitting the mainland, turn right at the round-about and continue straight along this very busy street (highway A-20) into town. After about a half-mile, at the big roundabout, turn left on York Street (following road signs for *Town Centre/ North*); from here, you can turn right to get to Market Square and the TI (you can cut through the Dover Discovery Centre on the right), or turn left at the next roundabout to reach Folkestone Road and the train station.

To London or Canterbury by Train

Once you reach the train station (all options explained above) you can continue on to London or Canterbury.

To **London,** you can choose between the faster "Javelin" train (hourly, 1.25 hours to St. Pancras Station; £38.10 "single"/ one-way, £40.60 same-day "day return"/round-trip, £71.20 anytime return) and the slower train (hourly to Victoria Station or hourly to Charing Cross Station, each 2 hours; £31.20 "single"/ one-way, £31.40 same-day "day return"/round-trip). When choosing which train to take, consider this: St. Pancras and Victoria Stations are both well-connected to any point in the city by Tube (subway) or bus (and St. Pancras is right next to the British Library); but Charing Cross Station is particularly handy, as it's within easy walking distance of the sights many first-timers want to see (Trafalgar Square, National Gallery, West End, Whitehall, Houses of Parliament)—so the extra time spent on that train could save you some time commuting to your sightseeing later in London. For details on arriving by train in London, see page 940.

Trains depart for **Canterbury** twice hourly; some are direct (16 minutes), while others make a few stops en route (27 minutes; for either train, fares are £7.50 "single"/one-way, £7.60 "day return"/same-day round trip). These trains stop at the Canterbury East Station (for arrival tips in Canterbury, see page 932).

Returning to Your Ship

Arriving at the Dover Priory train station, there's no direct public-transit option to the ship. You can either take a taxi directly there (about £7-8 without luggage), or walk 15 minutes to Market

Square, then take the cruise shuttle bus from there (£3/€4/$5, described earlier). If you stick around Dover for the day, you can use this same bus, from either Market Square or the castle.

See page 990 for help if you miss your boat.

Sights in Dover

▲▲Dover Castle

Strategically located Dover Castle—considered "the key to England" by would-be invaders—perches grandly atop the White Cliffs of Dover. English troops were garrisoned within the castle's medieval walls for almost 900 years, protecting the coast from European invaders (a record of military service rivaled only by Windsor Castle and the Tower of London). With a medieval Great Tower as its cen-  terpiece and battlements that survey 360 degrees of windswept coast, Dover Castle has undeniable majesty. Today, the biggest invading menaces are the throngs of school kids on field trips, so it's best to arrive early. While the historic parts of the castle are unexceptional, the exhibits in the WWII-era Secret Wartime Tunnels are unique and engaging—particularly the new, power- ful, well-presented tour that tells the story of Operation Dynamo, a harrowing WWII rescue operation across the English Channel.

Cost and Hours: £16.50, £43 family ticket; April-Sept daily 10:00-18:00, from 9:30 in Aug; Oct daily 10:00-17:00; Nov-March Sat-Sun 10:00-16:00, closed Mon-Fri; last entry one hour before closing, keep yard may close in high winds, tel. 01304/211-067, www.english-heritage.org.uk/dovercastle. The easiest way to get here is by taxi or shuttle bus from the cruise port (both options explained earlier).

Information: Ticket kiosks at either entrance distribute helpful maps of the castle grounds. In the middle of the complex, just below the Great Tower, a handy visitors center also dispenses information.

Avoiding Lines: Arrive early for the fewest crowds (busiest on summer bank holidays and weekends; worst around 11:30). While crowds can impede your progress throughout the site, the biggest potential headaches are lines for the two tours of the Secret Wartime Tunnels: The line for the Operation Dynamo exhibit can be quite long (up to two hours at the worst), while the Underground Hospital line is usually shorter. When you buy your

---

Dover Castle and Operation Dynamo

It was during World War II that Dover Castle lived its most dramatic moments, most notably as the headquarters for the inspiring Operation Dynamo—a story you'll hear retold again and again on your visit here.

In the spring of 1940, in the early days of the war, a joint French-British-Dutch-Belgian attack on the Nazis was met by a shockingly aggressive German counteroffensive. While Allied forces were distracted with their eastern front, the Nazis flanked them to the west, pinning them into an ever-narrowing corner of northern France (around the port cities of Calais and Dunkerque, which Brits call Dunkirk). As the Nazis closed in, it became clear that hundreds of thousands of British and other Allied troops being squeezed against the English Channel would soon be captured—or worse. From the tunnels below Dover Castle, Admiral Sir Bertram Ramsay oversaw Operation Dynamo. In 10 days, using a variety of military and civilian ships, Ramsay staged a dramatic evacuation of 338,000 Allied soldiers from the beaches of Dunkirk (several thousand troops, both British and French, were captured).

Because so many survived the desperate circumstances, the operation has been called a "victory in defeat." And although the Allies were forced to leave northern France to Hitler, Operation Dynamo saved an untold number of lives and bolstered morale in a country just beginning the most devastating war it would ever face. This unlikely evacuation is often called the "Miracle at Dunkirk."

---

ticket, ask about wait times and organize your visit accordingly (see "Planning Your Time," later).

Entrances: Two entry gates have kiosks where you'll pause to buy your ticket before entering the grounds. The Cannon Gate is closer to the Secret Wartime Tunnels, at the lower end of the castle, while the Constable's Gate is near the Great Tower, at the top of the castle. Buses (including shuttles from Dover's cruise port) drop off near Constable's Gate; walkers or those arriving by taxi can choose either gate. Note that from either gate, you still have to hike uphill quite a ways to reach the main points of interest.

Planning Your Time: The key is planning your day around the Secret Wartime Tunnels tours—especially the excellent Operation Dynamo tour. Each tour allows 30 people to enter at a time, with departures every 10-15 minutes. Your decision depends on two things: Which entrance you use (see above), and how long the lines are.

If arriving at **Cannon Gate,** you're a short walk from the starting point for the tours. Survey the line and ask the attendants how long the wait is. If it'll be a while, consider hiking up to the Great Tower, then returning here later, in the hope that the lines will die down. But if the wait isn't too long, consider taking the tour now.

If arriving at **Constable's Gate,** ask at the ticket kiosk about wait times for the Operation Dynamo tour. If lines are relatively short, do the tour first, then backtrack to the Great Tower. But if the wait is long, see the Great Tower first, and hope lines for the tour get shorter later on.

Note: The lines for the two Secret Wartime Tunnels tours (Operation Dynamo and Underground Hospital) are next to each other. If possible, do the Operation Dynamo tour (often with a longer wait) first.

Getting Around the Castle: The sporadic and free "land train" does a constant loop around the castle's grounds, shuttling visitors between the Secret Wartime Tunnels, the entrance to the Great Tower, and the Medieval Tunnels (at the top end of the castle). Though handy for avoiding the ups and downs, the train doesn't run every day. Nothing at the castle is more than a 10-minute walk from anything else—so you'll likely spend more time waiting for the train than you would walking.

Background: Armies have kept a watchful eye on this strategic lump of land since Roman times (as evidenced by the partly standing ancient lighthouse). A linchpin for English defense starting in the Middle Ages, Dover Castle was heavily used in the time of Henry VIII and Elizabeth I. After a period of decline, the castle was reinvigorated during the Napoleonic Wars, and became a central command in World War II (when naval headquarters were buried deep in the cliffside). Parts of the tunnels were also used as a hospital and triage station for injured troops. After the war, in the 1960s, the tunnels were converted into a dramatic Cold War bunker—one of 12 designated sites in the UK that would house government officials and a BBC studio in the event of nuclear war. When it became clear that even the stout cliffs of Dover couldn't be guaranteed to stand up to a nuclear attack, Dover Castle was retired from active duty in 1984.

◐ Self-Guided Tour: The sights at Dover Castle basically cluster into two areas: The Secret Wartime Tunnels (with two very different tunnel tours and a modest exhibit) and the Great Tower and surrounding historical castle features (such as the old Roman lighthouse and the Medieval Tunnels). The order you see these sights depends on where you enter and the crowds—see "Planning Your Time," earlier, for tips.

Secret Wartime Tunnels

In the 1790s, with the threat of Napoleon looming, the castle's

fortifications were beefed up again. So many troops were stationed here that they needed to tunnel into the chalk to provide sleeping areas for up to 2,000 men. These tunnels were vastly expanded during World War II, when operations for the war effort moved into a bomb-proofed, underground air-raid shelter safe from Hitler's feared Luftwaffe planes. Winston Churchill watched air battles from here, while Allied commanders looked out over a battle zone nicknamed "Hellfire Corner." There are three layers of tunnels: Annexe at the top, Casemates in the middle, and Dumpy at the lowest point. Two different tours take you into the tunnels: Operation Dynamo (Casemates tunnels) and Underground Hospital (Annexe tunnels). A small exhibit near the Operation Dynamo exit tells the whole story of the tunnels.

Operation Dynamo: From these tunnels in May of 1940, Admiral Sir Bertram Ramsay oversaw the rescue mission wherein the British managed, in just 10 days, to evacuate some 338,000 Allied soldiers from the beaches of Dunkirk, in Nazi-occupied France. In this 45-minute tour, you're led from room to room, where a series of exceptionally well-produced audiovisual shows narrate, step-by-step, the lead-up to World War II and the exact conditions that led to the need for Operation Dynamo. You'll hear fateful radio addresses from Winston Churchill and King George VI (immortalized in the 2010 movie, *The King's Speech*) announcing the declaration of war, and watch newsreel footage of Britain preparing its war effort. Imagine learning about war in this somber way (in the days before bombastic 24-hour cable news). Sitting around an animated map, you'll learn how the Allied troops advanced toward Germany and how the strategic tables turned, pinning the Allies down against the English Channel. Then you'll walk slowly down a long tunnel, as footage projected on the wall tells the stirring tale of the evacuation.

At the end of the guided portion, you're set free to explore several rooms still outfitted as they were back in World War II—such as the mapping room, repeater station, and telephone exchange. An unusually clever combination of state-of-the-art technology and good old-fashioned history, the exhibit is one of the best on World War II in this country so full of museums and memorials to that defining struggle.

You'll exit the Operation Dynamo exhibit into the gift shop and café area, where a smaller exhibit, **Wartime Tunnels Uncovered,** uses diaries, uniforms, archival films, and other artifacts to chart the development of the tunnels from the Napoleonic era to the Cold War.

Underground Hospital: Immediately next to the Operation Dynamo tour is the entrance to this shorter, lower-tech, 20-minute tour of the topmost Annexe levels of the tunnels, which were used during World War II as a hospital, then as a triage-type dressing station for wounded troops. Your guide leads you through the various parts of a re-created 1941 operating room and a narrow hospital ward, as you listen to the story of an injured Mosquito (fighter-bomber) pilot—with occasional smells and lighting effects to enhance the tale. Finally, you'll climb a 78-step double-helix staircase and pop out next to the Admiralty Lookout (described next). Although the Underground Hospital lacks the excellent storytelling of the (much newer) Operation Dynamo tour, they complement each other well (though if you're triaging, choose Dynamo).

Great Tower and Nearby

• *If you take the Underground Hospital tour, you'll surface right next to the Admiralty Lookout; otherwise, hike up toward the visitors center and follow signs to find it. The lookout is near the grassy slope on the seaward side of the officers' barracks.*

Admiralty Lookout: The White Cliffs of Dover are directly beneath you. Take in the superb view across the Channel. Can you see France from here? The statue is of British Admiral Sir Bertram Ramsay, who heroically orchestrated Operation Dynamo (see sidebar).

• *Backtrack past the visitors center (if you're starting at the lookout, climb up the hill and bear right past the big barracks building to reach the visitors center on the hill above), and hike up the path (following signs to the Great Tower) through the stubby guard tower. Emerging on the other side of the guard tower, you'll be facing the Great Tower. But before going there, look up the hill to your right. The round tower behind the flagpole is the oldest structure at the castle, the...*

Roman Lighthouse: The lighthouse *(pharos)* was built during the first century A.D., when Julius Caesar's Roman fleet for the colony of Britannia was based in the harbor below. To guide the boats, they burned wet wood by day (for maximum smoke), and dry wood by night (for maximum light). When the Romans finally left England 400 years later, the *pharos* is said to have burst into flames as the last ship departed. Adjacent to the lighthouse is the unimpressive St. Mary-in-the-

Castle Church, built to guard against invading Saxons in the sixth century.

• *Back at the guard tower, go past the parking lot and head through the archway to enter the courtyard of...*

Henry II's Great Tower: The heart of this frontier fortress first beat in 1066, when a castle was built here after the Battle of Hastings. In the 12th century, King Henry II added heavy castle fortifications. For centuries, Dover Castle was the most secure fortress in all of England, and an important symbol of royal might on the coast.

Examine the Tower of London-like central building, which was the original tower (also called a "keep"). The walls are up to 20 feet thick. King Henry II slept on the top floor, surrounded by his best protection against an invading army. Imagine the attempt: As the thundering enemy cavalry makes its advance, the king's defenders throw caltrops (four-starred metal spikes meant to cut through the horses' hooves). His knights unsheathe their swords, and trained crossbow archers ring the tower, sending arrows into foreign armor. Later kings added buildings near the tower (along the inner bailey, which lines the keep yard) to garrison troops during wartime, to provide extra rooms for royal courtiers during peacetime, and to be filled centuries later with museum exhibits and a gift shop. On summer weekends, and for most of August, costumed actors wandering the grounds add to the fun.

Before going in the tower itself, check out some of the exhibits in the surrounding garrison buildings. To the right as you enter the courtyard, you'll first see the **Great Tower Story** exhibit, which uses colorful displays and animated films to bring meaning to the place. You'll learn how Henry II established the mighty empire of Aquitaine (encompassing much of today's England and France), how his heirs squandered it, and how it evolved into the Plantagenet dynasty that ruled England for some 400 years (including many of the famous Henrys and Richards).

Next door, the **Princess of Wales's Royal Regiment and Queen's Regiment Museum** collects military memorabilia and tells the story of these military units, which have fought in foreign conflicts for centuries—you'll see gritty helmet-cam footage from their recent participation in Afghanistan. (Sorry, no Princess Diana items.)

Now enter the **Great Tower** itself. While fun to poke around, it's somewhat empty-feeling, decorated with brightly colored

furnishings from the period—a dining hall, a throne room, a kitchen, a bedroom, and so on. While there's no real exhibit, docents are standing by to answer questions, and the kid-friendly furnishings give a sense of what the castle was like in King Henry VIII's time. Find the well, which helped make the tower even more
siege-resistant. Fans of Thomas Becket can look for his chapel, a tiny sacristy called the "upper chapel" (it's hiding down a forgotten hallway high in the building—ask a docent for directions). If you're feeling energetic, climb all the way to the top of the tower's spiral staircase for a sweeping view of the town and sea beyond. The basement holds the medieval kitchen and royal armory.

• *Exit the keep yard at the far end through the King's Gate. Cross a stone bridge and then descend a wooden staircase. Under these stairs is the entrance to the...*

Medieval Tunnels: This system of steep tunnels was originally built in case of a siege. While enjoyable for a kid-in-a-castle experience, there's actually little to see. From here, you can catch the tourist train (if it's running) or do the Battlements Walk. Much of Dover's success as a defendable castle came from these unique concentric walls—the battlements—which protected the inner keep.

• *Our tour of the castle is finished. For a fast return to town, pop out the Constable's Gate near the Medieval Tunnels and follow the path steeply down.*

Other Sights in Dover

Dover Museum—This museum, right off the tiny main square, houses a large, impressive, and well-preserved 3,600-year-old

Bronze Age boat unearthed near Dover's shoreline. The boat is displayed on the top floor along with other finds from the site, an exhibit on boat construction techniques, and a 12-minute film. Nearby, an endearing exhibit fills one big room (the Dover History Gallery) with the story of how this small but strategically located town has shaped history—from Tudor times to the Napoleonic era to World War II. The ground floor has exhibits covering the Roman and Anglo-Saxon periods.

Cost and Hours: £3.50; Mon-Sat 10:00-17:00, also Sun 10:00-15:00 April-Sept; tel. 01304/201-066, www.dovermuseum .co.uk.

Prince of Wales Pier—If it's a sunny day and you want a nice view of the White Cliffs and castle without heading out of town, stroll to the western end of the beachfront promenade (to the right as you face the water), then hike out along the Prince of Wales Pier for perfect panoramas back toward the city.

Cost and Hours: Free, daily June-Aug 8:00-21:00, Sept-May 8:00-19:00.

Eating in Dover

If you're touring the **castle,** consider having lunch at one of its two cafés. Other dining options in town include:

La Scala is tiny, but in a romantic way, and serves a good variety of Italian dishes (£9-11 pastas, £13-17 meat and fish dishes, Mon-Sat 12:00-14:30 & 18:00-22:30, closed Sun, 19 High Street, tel. 01304/208-044).

The Allotment is trying to bring class to this small town, with an emphasis on locally sourced ingredients (in Brit-speak, an "allotment" is like a community garden). The rustic-chic interior feels a bit like an upscale deli (£3-6 breakfast dishes, £5-6 starters, £8-16 main dishes, Tue-Sat 8:30-23:00, closed Sun-Mon, 9 High Street, tel. 01304/214-467).

The Eight Bells, lively and wood-paneled, is a huge Wetherspoon chain pub that feels like a Vegas lounge (£4-7 "pub classics," bigger £6-10 meals, £8 lunch specials, daily 8:00-24:00, kids OK before 20:00, facing the small church at 19 Cannon Street, tel. 01304/205-030).

Lunch Eateries on Market Square: Dover's main shopping square is surrounded by places for a quick lunch. **The Ellie,** a generic, modern pub at a convenient location (right next door to the Dover Museum), spills out onto Market Square (£4 sandwiches, £6 main dishes, open daily 10:00-24:00, food served April-Sept 11:00-15:00 only, inviting outdoor seating on the square, tel. 01304/215-685). Across the square is the more genteel **Dickens Corner,** a comfy diner with a tearoom upstairs (£3-5 "jacket potatoes," sandwiches, and soups; Mon-Sat 8:30-16:30, closed Sun, 7 Market Square, tel. 01304/206-692).

LONDON

Near Dover: Canterbury

Canterbury—an easy train ride from Dover (less than 30 minutes away)—is one of England's most important religious destinations. For centuries, it has welcomed hordes of pilgrims to its grand cathedral. Pleasant, walkable Canterbury, like many cities in southern England, was originally founded by the pagan Romans. Later, as Christianity became more established in England, Canterbury became its center, and the Archbishop of Canterbury emerged as one of the country's most powerful men. The famous pilgrimages to Canterbury began in the 12th century, after the assassination of Archbishop Thomas Becket by followers of King Henry II (with whom Becket had been in a long feud). Becket was canonized as a martyr, rumors of miracles at the cathedral spread, and flocks of pilgrims showed up at its doorstep. Today, much of the medieval city—heavily bombed during World War II—exists only in fragments. Miraculously, the cathedral and surrounding streets are fairly well-preserved. Thanks to its huge student population and thriving pedestrian-and-shopper-friendly zone in the center, Canterbury is an exceptionally livable and fun-to-visit town.

Planning Your Time

On a quick visit to Canterbury, head straight for the cathedral, then spend the rest of your time strolling the town's pleasant pedestrian core.

Orientation to Canterbury

With about 45,000 people, Canterbury is big enough to be lively but small enough to be manageable. The center of town is enclosed by the old city walls, a ring road, and the Stour River to the west. High Street (also known as St. Peter's Street at one end and St. George's Street at the other) bisects the town center. The center is walkable—it's only about 20 minutes on foot from one end to the other.

Tourist Information: The TI, housed in the atrium of the "Beaney Institute" library, assists modern-day pilgrims. Pick up the free Visitors Guide with a map (Mon-Sat 9:00-17:00, Sun 10:00-17:00, on High Street, just past Best Lane, tel. 01227/378-100, www.canterbury.co.uk).

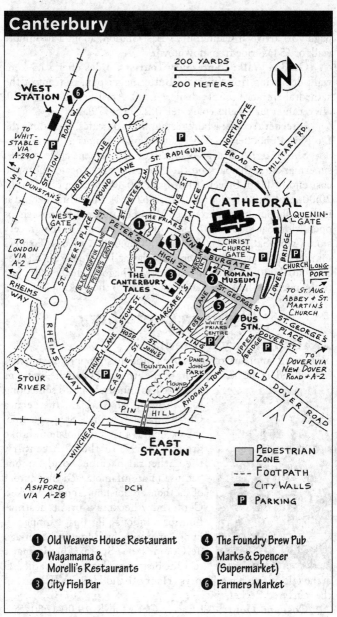

Canterbury

200 YARDS
200 METERS

WEST STATION
TO WHITSTABLE VIA A-290
STATION ROAD W.
ROAD W.
NORTH LANE
POUND LANE
ST. PETER'S LN.
ST. RADIGUND
NORTHGATE
BROAD ST.
MILITARY RD.
ST. DUNSTAN'S
WEST GATE
ST. PETER'S
ST. PETER'S PLACE
BLACK GRIFFIN LANE
ST. PETER'S GROVE
HIGH ST.
THE FRIARS
SUN
KING ST.
PALACE ST.
CATHEDRAL
QUENINGATE
CHRIST CHURCH GATE
BURGATE
MERCERY LANE
ROMAN MUSEUM
CHURCH ST.
LOWER BRIDGE
LONGPORT
TO LONDON VIA A-2
RHEIMS WAY
TO ST. AUG. ABBEY & ST. MARTIN'S CHURCH
THE CANTERBURY TALES
ST. MARGARET'S
WATLING
ROSE LANE
ST. GEORGE'S
BUS STN.
WHITE FRIARS CENTRE
ST. GEORGE'S PLACE
DOVER ST.
TO DOVER VIA NEW DOVER ROAD & A-2
STOUR ST.
HOSP.
ST. JOHN'S
CASTLE ST.
CHURCH LANE
RHEIMS WAY
STOUR RIVER
FOUNTAIN
DANE JOHN PARK
MOUND
RHODAUS TOWN
UPPER BRIDGE
PIN HILL
WINCHEAP
EAST STATION
TO ASHFORD VIA A-28
OLD DOVER ROAD
DCH

PEDESTRIAN ZONE
--- FOOTPATH
— CITY WALLS
P PARKING

❶ Old Weavers House Restaurant
❷ Wagamama & Morelli's Restaurants
❸ City Fish Bar
❹ The Foundry Brew Pub
❺ Marks & Spencer (Supermarket)
❻ Farmers Market

LONDON

Arrival in Canterbury: Trains from Dover (see details on page 921) arrive at Canterbury's East Station, about a 10-minute walk or £5 taxi ride from downtown.

Guided Walk: Canterbury Tourist Guides offer a 1.5-hour walk departing from The Old Buttermaker pub, in front of the cathedral entrance (£6.50, daily at 11:00, April-Sept also at 14:00, www.canterbury-walks.co.uk, tel. 01227/459-779).

Internet Access: Many restaurants and cafés, including the **Dolphin Pub,** offer free Wi-Fi for paying customers.

Shopping: A **Marks & Spencer** department store, with a supermarket at the back on the ground floor, is located near the east end of High Street (Mon-Sat 8:00-19:00 except Thu until 20:00, Sun 11:00-17:00, tel. 01227/462-281). Sprawling behind it is a vast shopping complex called **Whitefriars Centre** (most shops open Mon-Sat 9:00-18:00, Sun 11:00-17:00) and a **Tesco** grocery store (Mon-Sat 7:00-23:00, Sun 11:00-17:00). A modest **farmers market** is held every day except Monday at The Goods Shed (Tue-Sat 9:00-18:00, Sun 10:00-16:00, www.thegoodsshed.co.uk), just to the north of the West Station, adjacent to the parking lot.

Sights in Canterbury

▲▲▲Canterbury Cathedral

This grand landmark of piety, one of the most important churches in England, is the headquarters of the Anglican Church—in terms

of church administration, it's something like the English Vatican. It's been a Christian site ever since St. Augustine, the cathedral's first archbishop, broke ground in 597. In the 12th century, the cathedral became world-famous because of an infamous act: the murder of its then-archbishop, Thomas Becket. Canterbury became a prime destination for religious pilgrims, trumped in importance only by Rome and Santiago de Compostela, Spain. The dramatic real-life history of Canterbury Cathedral is the tale of two King Henrys (Henry II and Henry VIII), and of the martyred Becket.

Cost and Hours: £8; Easter-Oct Mon-Sat 9:00-17:30, Sun 12:30-14:00; slightly shorter hours Nov-Easter; last entry 30 minutes before closing, tel. 01227/762-862, www.canterbury-cathedral.org.

Tours: Guides wearing golden sashes are posted throughout the cathedral to answer your questions. Guided £5 tours are

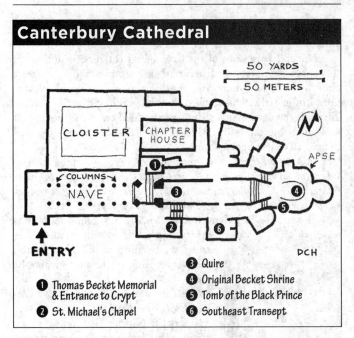

Canterbury Cathedral

50 YARDS
50 METERS

CLOISTER

CHAPTER HOUSE

APSE

① COLUMNS
NAVE

③

④

⑤

②

⑥

ENTRY

DCH

① Thomas Becket Memorial & Entrance to Crypt
② St. Michael's Chapel
③ Quire
④ Original Becket Shrine
⑤ Tomb of the Black Prince
⑥ Southeast Transept

offered Mon-Fri at 10:30, 12:00, and 14:30 (14:00 in winter); and Sat at 10:30, 12:00, and 13:30 (no tours Sun). At the shop inside the cathedral, you can rent a dry but informative £4 audioguide.

◗ Self-Guided Tour: Although guided tours and audioguides are available, it's simple just to wander through on your own.

• *Begin your tour in the pedestrian shopping zone just outside the cathedral grounds. Before going through the passageway, take a moment to appreciate the...*

Christ Church Gate: This highly decorated gate is the cathedral yard's main entrance. Find the royal seals and symbols on the gate, including the Tudor rose. This rose was the symbol of Henry VIII, who—shortly after the Christ Church Gate was built—divorced both his wife and the Vatican, establishing the Anglican Church.

• *Go through the gate (where you'll buy your ticket) and walk into the courtyard that surrounds this massive, impressive church. Examine the...*

Cathedral Exterior: Notice the cathedral's length, and how each section is distinctive. The church was already considered large in pre-pilgrim days, but in the 15th century, builders began another 100 years of construction (resulting in a patchwork effect that you'll notice in the interior).

• *Enter the church through the side door—the front doors of English cathedrals tend to be used only for special occasions—and pick up a map at the desk before you take a seat in the...*

Nave: The interior of the nave shows the inner workings of this sprawling, eclectic structure. Look around, and you'll see a church that's had many incarnations. Archaeological excavations in the early 1990s showed that the building's core is Roman. Through the ages, new sections were added on, with the biggest growth during the 1400s, when the cathedral had to be expanded to hold all of its pilgrims.

• *From here, we'll follow the route laid out by the map you picked up when you entered. Head up the left aisle. When you get to the quire (marked by a beautifully carved stone portal in the center of the nave), go down the stairs to your left. Immediately to your right is the...*

Thomas Becket Memorial: This is where Thomas Becket was

martyred. You'll see a humble plaque and a wall sculpture of lightning-rod arrows pointing to the place where he died.

• *Continue down the stairs next to the memorial and enter the...*

Crypt: Notice the heavy stone arches. This lower section was started by the Normans, who probably built on top of St. Augustine's original church. Work your way to the other (right) side of the crypt. The small chapel marked Église *Protestante Française* celebrates a Mass in French every Sunday at 15:00. This chapel has been used for hundreds of years by French (Huguenot) and Belgian (Walloon) Protestant communities, who fled persecution in their home countries for the more welcoming atmosphere in Protestant England.

• *Facing this chapel, turn right, walk to the end of the crypt, and climb up the stairs. At the landing, turn left to find...*

St. Michael's Chapel: Also known as the Warrior's Chapel, this was built by Lady Margaret Holland (d. 1439) to house family tombs. The chapel, which may be undergoing restoration when you visit, is also associated with the Royal East Kent Regiment ("The Buffs").

• *Head up the stairs across from the tomb, and go through the ornate stone portal we passed earlier. This will bring you into the **quire**, where the choir sings evensong. Walk toward the high altar, then turn left through the gate and walk with the quire on your right to the far end of the church (the apse). Behind the quire, you'll see a candle in the center of the floor. This was the site of the...*

Thomas Becket and Canterbury Cathedral

In the 12th century, Canterbury Cathedral had already been a Christian church for more than 500 years. The king at the time was Henry II (who rebuilt and expanded nearby Dover Castle). Henry was looking for a new archbishop, someone who would act as a yes-man and allow him to gain control of the Church (and its followers). He found a candidate in his drinking buddy and royal chancellor: Thomas Becket (also called Thomas à Becket). In 1162, the king's friend was consecrated as archbishop.

But Becket surprised the king, and maybe even himself. Inspired by his new position—and wanting to be a true religious leader to his mighty flock—he cleaned up his act, became dedicated to the religious tenets of the Church (dressing as a monk), and refused to bow to the king's wishes. As tensions grew, Henry wondered aloud, "Will no one rid me of this turbulent priest?" Four knights took his words seriously, and assassinated Becket during vespers in the cathedral. The act shocked the medieval world. King Henry later submitted to walking barefoot through town while being flogged by priests as an act of pious penitence.

Not long after Becket's death in 1170, word spread that miracles were occurring in the cathedral, prompting the pope to canonize Becket. Soon the pilgrims came, hoping some of Becket's steadfast goodness would rub off (perhaps they also wanted to see the world—just like travelers today).

Original Becket Shrine: Beginning in the 12th century, hundreds of thousands of pilgrims came to this site to leave offerings. Imagine this site in the Dark Ages. You're surrounded by humble, devout pilgrims who've trudged miles upon miles to reach this spot. (Try to ignore the B.O.) Now that they've finally arrived, they're hoping to soak up just a bit of the miraculous power that's supposed to reside here.

Then came King Henry VIII, who broke away from the pope so he could marry on his own terms. In 1538, he destroyed the original altar (and lots more, including the original abbey on the edge of town). Dictatorial Henry VIII—no fan of a priest who would stand up to a king—had Thomas Becket's body removed from the cathedral. Legend says that Henry had Becket's body burned and the ashes scattered, as part of his plan to drive religious pilgrims away from the site.

• *Follow the curve of the apse to the...*

Tomb of the Black Prince: This is the final resting place of the Black Prince, Edward of Woodstock (d. 1376). The Prince of Wales and the eldest son of Edward III, the Black Prince was famous for his cunning in battle and his chivalry—the original "knight in shining armor."

• *Head downstairs and make your way to the southeast transept (on your left).*

Southeast Transept: The bell standing to the left may be moved back to St. Michael's Chapel after restoration work is done there. This bell once rang from the HMS *Canterbury,* a ship that waged war against those disobedient colonists during the American Revolution. Each day at 11:00, the bell is rung and a prayer is said here to honor those who have lost their lives in battle.

The stained-glass windows in the transept are actually modern, relatively speaking, created by Hungarian-born artist and refugee Ervin Bossányi, who was commissioned by the Dean of Canterbury to replace earlier windows damaged by WWII bombs.

Our tour is finished. As you leave the cathedral, consider this: Even with all their power, wealth, and influence, two English kings were unable to successfully eradicate Thomas Becket's influence (if they had, the line to get into the cathedral would be shorter). A man of conscience—who once stood up to the most powerful ruler in England—continues to inspire visitors, nearly a thousand years after his death.

Eating in Canterbury

As a student town, Canterbury is packed with eateries—especially along the pedestrianized shopping zone.

Old Weavers House serves solid English food in a pleasant, historic building along the river. Sit inside beneath sunny walls and creaky beams, or outside on their riverside garden patio. This is the most atmospheric of my listings (£6-7 lunch specials, daily 12:00-23:00, 1 St. Peter's Street, tel. 01227/464-660).

Wagamama, part of the wildly popular British chain known for slinging tasty pan-Asian fare, has a convenient location just off the main shopping street (£8-12 main dishes, daily 12:00-22:00, 7-11 Longmarket Street, tel. 01227/454-307).

Morelli's Restaurant serves typical soups, sandwiches, and "jacket potatoes" with take-away options. You'll find it above the recommended Wagamama on Longmarket Street, with glassy indoor seating and a fine outdoor terrace (£5-7 light lunches, daily 8:00-17:00, tel. 01227/454-307).

City Fish Bar is your quintessential British "chippie," serving several kinds of fried fish. Get yours for take-away or grab a sidewalk table on this charming pedestrian street (£5-8 fish-and-chips, Mon-Sat 10:00-19:00, Sun 11:00-16:00, 30 St. Margaret's Street, tel. 01227/760-873).

The Foundry Brew Pub offers about 20 homebrews on tap and beer-inspired dishes like steak-and-ale pie and BBQ beer ribs. Bartenders happily pour generous samples for curious customers (with the intent of selling you a pint) and explain the inspiration behind the name of their signature draft, Torpedo (£4-7 starters and salads, £9-10 meat pies, £8-14 main dishes, food served daily 12:00-18:00, pub open until 23:00, White Horse Lane, tel. 01227/455-899).

Returning to Dover

Canterbury has two train stations, East and West. Dover-bound trains depart from **Canterbury East** about twice hourly, making the speedy trip in just 20-30 minutes. Get off at the station called **Dover Priory.**

London

London, which has long attracted tourists, seems perpetually at your service, with an impressive slate of sights, entertainment, and eateries, all linked by a great transit system. With just a few hours here, you'll get no more than a quick splash in this teeming human tidal pool. But with a good orientation, you'll find London manageable and fun.

Blow through the city on a double-decker bus, or take a pinch-me-I'm-in-London walk through the West End. Gawk at the crown jewels at the Tower of London, hear the chimes of Big Ben, or see the Houses of Parliament in action. Cruise the Thames River, or take a spin on the London Eye. Hobnob with poets' tombstones in Westminster Abbey, or visit with Leonardo, Botticelli, and Rembrandt in the National Gallery. Whisper across the dome of St. Paul's Cathedral, or rummage through our civilization's attic at the British Museum. Sip your tea with pinky raised and clotted cream dribbling down your scone.

Planning Your Time

The sights of London alone could easily fill a trip to Great Britain. But you only have a few hours...so you'll need to be very selective. I've clustered sights geographically and listed them roughly in the order of priority for a first-time visitor who just wants a taste.

• **Westminster:** For the best single-day visit to London, focus on the big, famous sights on and near Whitehall. Begin by ogling the Houses of Parliament, then consider dipping into **Westminster Abbey** (allow an hour). Follow my self-guided **Westminster Walk** up Whitehall for about 30 minutes—possibly poking into the **Churchill War Rooms** (history buffs will want at least an hour)—to reach Trafalgar Square. Here you can pop into the **National Gallery** and/or the **National Portrait Gallery** (allow an hour each). Or, to get a look at non-museum London, stroll behind the National Gallery to explore **Leicester Square, Piccadilly Circus, Chinatown, Soho, Covent Garden,** and other bits of London's famously trendy and lively "West End" (allow an hour or more just to wander here). With time to spare, you could also hook around to see **Buckingham Palace** (from the outside; little to see inside). All told, the options noted here will more than eat up your London time (pick and choose museum and church visits carefully). But if you'd rather focus on other parts of the city, see the next few options.

• **London Eye:** While famous and relatively close to the Westminster sights mentioned above, this gigantic observation wheel is very expensive and—due to long lines—can be time-consuming (allow 30 minutes for the ride itself, but likely much more time waiting in lines).

• **British Museum:** One of the world's best collections of antiquities (from Egyptian mummies to the Rosetta Stone to the Parthenon Frieze)—but inconveniently located relative to other places on this list—this museum is worth at least two hours.

• **British Library:** This succinct collection of great works of literature can be seen in an hour, and is conveniently located next door to St. Pancras Station (with trains to Dover).

• **St. Paul's Cathedral:** It takes about an hour to tour London's biggest church and Christopher Wren's masterpiece (add another hour to climb the dome).

• **Tower of London:** London's original fortress takes about two hours to see (including an entertaining Beefeater tour).

With limited time, it may be folly to focus too tightly on any particular sight. Consider instead a **hop-on, hop-off bus tour** to get your bearings in this grand and sprawling metropolis. For suggested companies, see page 947.

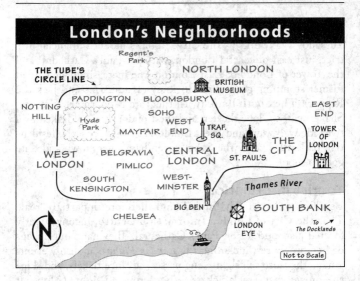

London's Neighborhoods

Regent's Park

THE TUBE'S CIRCLE LINE

NORTH LONDON

BRITISH MUSEUM

NOTTING HILL

PADDINGTON

BLOOMSBURY

EAST END

Hyde Park

SOHO

WEST END

TRAF. SQ.

TOWER OF LONDON

MAYFAIR

THE CITY

WEST LONDON

BELGRAVIA

CENTRAL LONDON

ST. PAUL'S

PIMLICO

SOUTH KENSINGTON

WESTMINSTER

Thames River

BIG BEN

SOUTH BANK

LONDON EYE

To The Docklands

CHELSEA

Not to Scale

Orientation to London

London is more than 600 square miles of urban jungle—a world in itself and a barrage on all the senses. On my first visit, I felt extremely small. To grasp London more comfortably, see it as the old town in the city center without the modern, congested sprawl. (Even from that perspective, it's still huge.)

The Thames River (pronounced "tems") runs roughly west to east through the city, with most of the visitor's sights on the North Bank. On a brief visit, focus on **Central London.** This area contains Westminster and what Londoners call the West End. The Westminster district includes Big Ben, Parliament, Westminster Abbey,

and Buckingham Palace—the grand government buildings from which Britain is ruled. Trafalgar Square, London's gathering place, has many major museums. The West End is the center of London's cultural life, with bustling squares: Piccadilly Circus and Leicester Square host cinemas, tourist traps, and nighttime glitz. Soho and Covent Garden are thriving people-zones with theaters, restaurants, pubs, and boutiques. And Regent and Oxford streets are the city's main shopping zones.

Other neighborhoods include **North London** (with the

British Museum, British Library, and overhyped Madame Tussauds Waxworks); **"The City"** (today's modern financial district, just east of central London, with St. Paul's Cathedral and the Tower of London); **East London** (the increasingly gentrified former stomping ground of Cockney ragamuffins and Jack the Ripper); **The South Bank** (with the Tate Modern art museum, Shakespeare's Globe theater, and the London Eye, all linked by a riverside walkway); and **West London** (a mostly upscale, residential, park-filled zone where the Queen hangs her crown and Kate goes to shop).

Tourist Information

London's only publicly funded (and therefore impartial) "real" TI is the **City of London Information Centre,** inconveniently located just south of St. Paul's Cathedral. They hand out dozens of free brochures, including the *London Planner* monthly events guide. They also sell sightseeing passes, advance tickets, and skip-the-queue Fast Track tickets to big, crowded sights (Mon-Sat 9:30-17:30, Sun 10:00-16:00, across the busy street from St. Paul's Cathedral—around the right side as you face the main staircase, Tube: St. Paul's, www.visitthecity.co.uk). For phone inquiries, contact the more commercial **Visit London TI** (toll tel. 0870-156-6366, www.visitbritain.com, www.visitlondon.com).

You'll see "Tourist Information" offices elsewhere around town, but most of them are either private agencies pushing tours and tickets for big profits or are primarily focused on providing public-transit advice.

London Pass: This pricey pass, which covers many big sights and lets you skip some lines, is worthwhile only if you'll be cramming in lots of sightseeing (£46/1 day, sold at TI and major train stations, tel. 0870-242-9988, www.londonpass.com).

Arrival in London

By Train from Southampton: You'll ride to London's **Waterloo Station** (for details, see page 905). The Jubilee Promenade along the South Bank and London Eye are both a short walk from the station. Or you can hop on the Tube to get anywhere in town: As you exit the train, with the tracks to your back, the stop for the Jubilee line is to the right, and the stop for the Northern/Waterloo and Bakerloo lines are to the left.

By Train from Dover: Remember that you have the option of riding the train to three of London's stations: St. Pancras (fastest connection), Charing Cross, or Victoria (see details on page 921). All three are right in the thick of London's transit system. If arriving at **St. Pancras Station,** head down the escalator and go toward the big, glass, modern entryway nearby; you'll find an

Underground (Tube) station just inside the door. Alternatively, if you want to reach the British Library or buses, first follow signs for Euston Station, then turn left and head all the way down the long main hall, and follow signs for Way Out and Euston Road. You'll pop out the station's front door along busy Euston Road. The public bus stops are on the road in front of you, and the British Library is a block to your right. If arriving at **Charing Cross Station,** you can simply exit the station, turn left along the busy street called The Strand, and you're a short walk from Trafalgar Square—right in the heart of town. From **Victoria Station,** you'll want to hop on the Tube; the Circle or District line zips you in two stops to Westminster, where you can exit the Tube station and peer up at Big Ben.

By Shuttle Bus: If you're taking an "On Your Own" shuttle bus excursion into London from your ship, it will likely drop you off at Piccadilly Circus, in the center of London's bustling West End. From this point, it's an easy 10-minute walk to Trafalgar Square, with the National Gallery and National Portrait Gallery. You can also hop on the Tube; the Piccadilly Circus Tube stop serves the Bakerloo line and the Piccadilly line.

Helpful Hints

Theft Alert: Wear your money belt. The Artful Dodger is alive and well in London. Be on guard, particularly on public transportation and in places crowded with tourists, who, considered naive and rich, are targeted. The Changing of the Guard scene is a favorite for thieves. And more than 7,500 purses are stolen annually at Covent Garden alone.

Pedestrian Safety: Cars drive on the left side of the road—which can be as confusing for foreign pedestrians as for foreign drivers. Before crossing a street, I always look right, look left, then look right again just to be sure. Most crosswalks are even painted with instructions, reminding foreign guests to "Look right" or "Look left."

Travel Bookstores: Located between Covent Garden and Leicester Square, the very good **Stanfords Travel Bookstore** stocks current editions of many of my books (Mon-Fri 9:00-20:00, Sat 10:00-20:00, Sun 12:00-18:00, 12-14 Long Acre, second entrance on Floral Street, Tube: Leicester Square, tel. 020/7836-1321, www.stanfords.co.uk).

Two impressive **Waterstone's** bookstores have the biggest collection of travel guides in town: on Piccadilly (Mon-Sat 9:00-22:00, Sun 12:00-18:00, Costa Café, great views from top-floor bar, 203 Piccadilly, tel. 020/7851-2400) and on Trafalgar Square (Mon-Sat 9:00-21:00, Sun 11:30-18:00, Costa Café on second floor, tel. 020/7839-4411).

LONDON

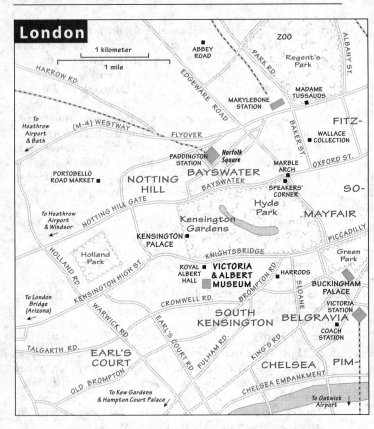

Updates to this Book: Check www.ricksteves.com/update for any significant changes that have occurred since this book was printed.

Getting Around London

In London, you're never more than a 10-minute walk from a stop on the Underground (the Tube). Buses are also convenient, and taxis are everywhere. For public transit info, see www.tfl.gov.uk.

Buying Tickets and Public-Transit Passes

A single ticket to ride the Tube costs a whopping £4.30, and buses are £2.30. But the options explained below are much cheaper, and cover both the Tube and the bus system.

Oyster Card: This pay-as-you-go plastic debit card lets you travel at about half the price per ride of single Tube or bus tickets (£2 or £2.70 per Tube ride—depending on time of day, £1.35 per bus ride). You must pay a £5 (refundable) deposit when you buy the card, then load it up with as much credit as you want. When your

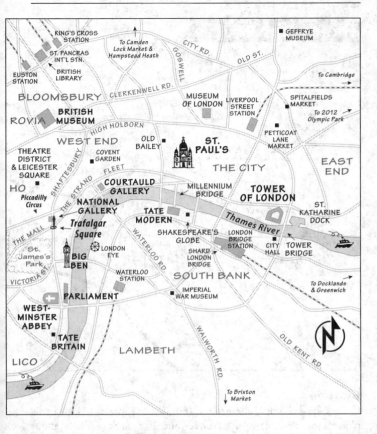

balance gets low, you simply add credit—or "top up"—at a ticket window or machine. To use it, you simply touch the card to the turnstile/reader when you enter the Tube system or board the bus. The cost of the ride is automatically deducted from your account. No matter how much you travel in a 24-hour period, you never pay more than £8.40.

One-Day Travelcard: This pass gives unlimited travel on the Tube and buses for a day for £8.40. (The £7 off-peak version is good for travel after 9:30 on weekdays and anytime on weekends.) To use it, feed the Travelcard into the Tube turnstile like a paper ticket (and retrieve it), or show it to the bus driver. There's also a seven-day version (issued on an Oyster card) for £29.20.

Buy Oyster cards and Travelcards at any Tube station, from a ticket window or vending machine. For more detailed info on tickets, passes, and prices, see www.tfl.gov.uk.

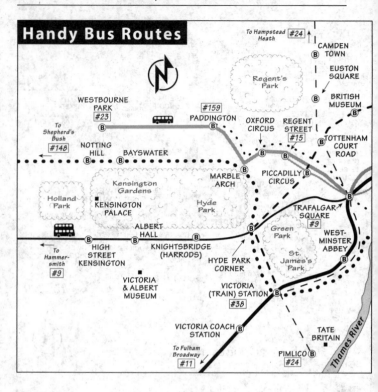

Handy Bus Routes

To Hampstead Heath #24

CAMDEN TOWN Ⓑ

EUSTON SQUARE

Regent's Park

BRITISH MUSEUM Ⓑ

WESTBOURNE PARK #23

#159 PADDINGTON Ⓑ

OXFORD CIRCUS

REGENT STREET #15

TOTTENHAM COURT ROAD Ⓑ

To Shepherd's Bush #148

NOTTING HILL

BAYSWATER

MARBLE ARCH

PICCADILLY CIRCUS Ⓑ

Kensington Gardens

Holland Park

KENSINGTON PALACE

Hyde Park

TRAFALGAR SQUARE #9

ALBERT HALL

Green Park

WEST-MINSTER ABBEY

To Hammer-smith #9

HIGH STREET KENSINGTON

KNIGHTSBRIDGE (HARRODS)

HYDE PARK CORNER

St. James's Park

VICTORIA & ALBERT MUSEUM

VICTORIA (TRAIN) STATION #38

VICTORIA COACH STATION Ⓑ

To Fulham Broadway #11

PIMLICO Ⓑ #24

TATE BRITAIN

Thames River

By Tube

Called the Tube or Underground (but never "subway"), one of this planet's great people-movers runs Monday through Saturday about 5:00–24:00, Sunday about 7:00–23:00.

Begin by studying a Tube map (available locally and posted in stations). Each line has a name (such as Circle, Northern, or Bakerloo) and two directions (indicated by the end-of-the-line stops). Find the line that will take you to your destination, and figure out roughly which direction (north, south, east, or west) you'll need to go to get there.

In the Tube station, use your Oyster card, Travelcard, or ticket to pass through the turnstile. Find your train by following signs to your line and the direction it's headed (such as "Central Line: east"). Since some tracks are shared by several lines, read signs on the platform to confirm that the approaching train is going to your specific destination. Transfers to another train are free (but transferring to a bus requires a new ticket). You'll need your Oyster

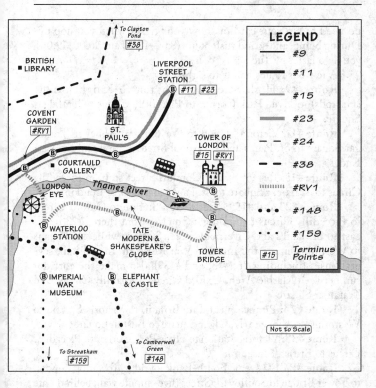

LEGEND

———	#9
▬▬▬	#11
———	#15
▬▬▬	#23
– – –	#24
- - -	#38
⋯⋯⋯	#RV1
●●●	#148
•••	#159
#15	Terminus Points

BRITISH LIBRARY

To Clapton Pond #38

LIVERPOOL STREET STATION
Ⓑ #11 #23

COVENT GARDEN #RV1

ST. PAUL'S

TOWER OF LONDON #15 #RV1

Ⓑ COURTAULD GALLERY

Thames River

LONDON EYE

Ⓑ WATERLOO STATION

TATE MODERN & SHAKESPEARE'S GLOBE

TOWER BRIDGE

Ⓑ IMPERIAL WAR MUSEUM

Ⓑ ELEPHANT & CASTLE

Not to Scale

To Streatham #159

To Camberwell Green #148

---

card, Travelcard, or ticket to pass through the exit turnstile. Save walking time by choosing the best street exit—check the maps on the walls or ask any station personnel.

Rush hours (8:00–10:00 and 16:00–19:00) can be packed and sweaty. Be prepared to walk significant distances within Tube stations and ride long escalators (stand on the right to let others pass). Delays are common; bring something to pass the time. Be wary of thieves, especially amid the jostle of boarding and leaving crowded trains. For more info on the Tube, see www.tfl.gov.uk.

By Bus

London's excellent bus system works like buses anywhere. Every bus stop has a name, and every bus is headed to one end-of-the-line stop or the other. Buses are covered by Travelcards and Oyster cards. Or you can buy single-trip tickets (£2.30) from a machine at bus stops.

As you board, show your ticket or Travelcard to the driver, or touch your Oyster card to the card reader. There's

no need to tap your card or show your ticket when you hop off. During bump-and-grind rush hours (8:00–10:00 and 16:00–19:00), you'll go faster by Tube.

A few bus routes handy to sights are:

Route #9: High Street Kensington to Knightsbridge (Harrods) to Hyde Park Corner to Piccadilly Circus to Trafalgar Square.

Route #11: Victoria Station to Westminster Abbey to Trafalgar Square to St. Paul's and Liverpool Street Station and the East End.

Route #15: Regent Street (Conduit Street stop) to Piccadilly Circus to Trafalgar Square to St. Paul's to Tower of London.

Routes #23 and #159: Paddington Station to Oxford Circus to Piccadilly Circus to Trafalgar Square; from there, #23 heads east to St. Paul's and Liverpool Street Station, while #159 heads to Westminster and the Imperial War Museum. In addition, several buses (including #6, #13, and #139) also make the corridor run between Marble Arch, Oxford Circus, Piccadilly Circus, and Trafalgar Square.

Route #24: Pimlico (near Tate Britain) to Victoria Station to Westminster Abbey to Trafalgar Square to Euston Square.

Route #38: Victoria Station to Hyde Park Corner to Piccadilly Circus to British Museum.

Route #RV1 (a scenic South-Bank joyride): Tower of London to Tower Bridge to Southwark Street (five-minute walk behind Tate Modern/Shakespeare's Globe) to London Eye/Waterloo Station, then over Waterloo Bridge to Aldwych and Covent Garden.

Route #148: Westminster Abbey to Victoria Station to Notting Hill and Bayswater (by way of the east end of Hyde Park and Marble Arch).

By Taxi

London is the best taxi town in Europe. Big, black cabs are everywhere, and there's no meter-cheating. They know every nook and cranny in town. I've never met a crabby London cabbie.

If a cab's top light is on, just wave it down—even if it's going the opposite way—or find the nearest taxi stand. Telephoning a cab will get you one in minutes, but costs about £2–3 more (tel. 0871-871-8710).

Rides start at £2.20. All extra charges are explained in writing on the cab wall. Tip a cabbie by rounding up (maximum 10 percent).

A typical daytime trip—from Trafalgar Square to St. Paul's—costs about £8. All cabs can carry five passengers, and some take six, for the same cost as a single traveler. So for a short ride, three adults in a cab travel at close to Tube prices. Avoid cabs when traffic is bad—they're slow and expensive, because the meter keeps running even at a standstill.

Tours in London

To sightsee on your own, download my series of free audio tours that illuminate some of London's top sights and neighborhoods: Westminster Walk, British Museum, British Library, St. Paul's Cathedral, and City of London Walk (see sidebar on page 52 for details).

▲▲▲**Hop-On, Hop-Off Double-Decker Bus Tours**—For a grand and efficient intro to London, ride through the city on an open-air bus past the main sights, while you listen to commentary. Hop on at any of the 30 stops along the two-hour loop, pay as you board, ride awhile, hop off to sightsee, then catch the next bus (10-20 minutes later) to carry on. Some routes have good live guides, while others have mediocre recorded commentary.

Several similar companies offer several different routes. Pick up their brochures or check online for the various options, extras, and discounts. **Big Bus London Tours** tend to have more dynamic guides and more frequent buses (£27, tel. 020/7233-9533, www .bigbustours.com). **Original London Sightseeing Bus Tour** is cheaper and nearly as good (£26, £4 Rick Steves discount for up to two people with this book—raise bloody hell if they won't honor it, tel. 020/8877-1722, www.theoriginaltour.com).

▲▲**Walking Tours**—Top-notch, highly entertaining local guides lead groups on two-hour tours through specific slices of London's past. Choose from the world of Charles Dickens, Harry Potter, the Plague, Shakespeare, Legal London, the Beatles, the ever-popular Jack the Ripper, plus many others. To see what's available, look for brochures, check *Time Out* magazine, or contact the various companies directly. To take a walking tour, you simply show up at the announced location and pay the guide (usually cash only).

London Walks has a wide and fascinating repertoire of tours led by professional guides and actors (£9, tel. 020/7624-3978, recorded info 020/7624-9255, www.walks.com). **The Essential London Walk** offers a low-budget, high-quality highlights tour of the historic core (£6 for my readers, 365 days a year, just show up at 10:00 at the Eros statue on Piccadilly Circus, www.guidelondon .org.uk).

Private Guides—If you'd like your own personal tour guide, standard rates for registered Blue Badge guides are about £135-160 for four hours, and £210-230 or more for nine hours (tel. 020/7611-2545, www.touristguides.org.uk or www.britainsbestguides.org). For a personal guide who can also drive you around London (£450/day) try www.driverguidetours.com or http://seeitinstyle.syntha site.com.

Bike Tours—Though London traffic is pretty intense to navigate on your own, consider pedaling through London's pleasant parks or taking a guided bike tour. **London Bicycle Tour Company** rents to individuals (£3.50/hour, £20/day) and leads tours (£19, includes bike) on three different routes (located at 1a Gabriel's Wharf on the South Bank, Tube: Waterloo, tel. 020/7928-6838, www.londonbicycle.com). **Fat Tire Bike Tours** offers two differ-ent itineraries (£20–30, £2 discount with this book, mobile 078-8233-8779, www.fattirebiketourslondon.com).

▲▲Thames Cruises—Several boat companies ply the Thames, useful for either a relaxing guided cruise or for point-A-to-B travel around London. The handiest boats leave from Westminster Pier (near Big Ben) and Waterloo Pier (near the London Eye). Some helpful stops for sightseers are: Bankside (Shakespeare's Globe), Blackfriars (St. Paul's), London Bridge, and Tower of London.

From **Westminster Pier**, City Cruises is handy to the Tower of London (£9 one-way, £15.50 all-day pass, tel. 020/7740-0400, www.citycruises.com), as is the similar Thames River Services (tel. 020/7930-4097, www.thamesriverservices.co.uk). Crown River Services has a hop-on, hop-off "Circular Cruise" route (£3 to go one stop, £11 round-trip, tel. 020/7936-2033,).

From **Waterloo Pier**, Thames Clippers is more like an express commuter bus than a tour cruise, traveling fast and making all the stops along the way (£6 single trip, £13.60 all-day, tel. 020/7001-2222, www.thamesclippers.com).

Buy tickets at the docks. Some companies give discounts for the Tube's TravelCard and Oyster card, and for children and seniors—it's worth asking.

London Duck Tours takes 30 tourists on goofy-but-fun tours on amphibious vehicles. You drive past Big Ben and other sights before splashing into the Thames for a cruise (£21, departs from near London Eye, tel. 020/7928-3132, www.londonducktours.co.uk).

Self-Guided Walk in London

Westminster Walk

Just about every visitor to London strolls along historic Whitehall from Big Ben to Trafalgar Square. This walk gives meaning to that touristy ramble (most of the sights you'll see are described in more detail later). Under London's modern traffic and big-city bustle

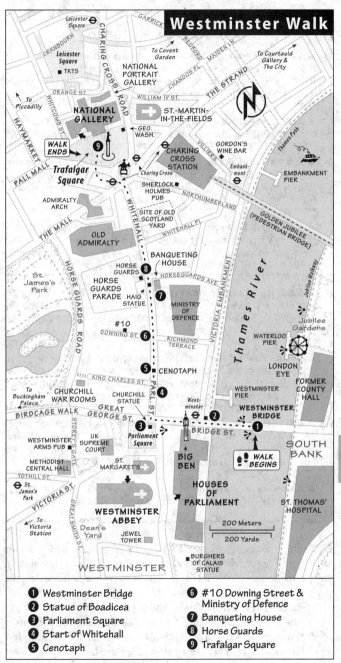

Westminster Walk

1 Westminster Bridge
2 Statue of Boadicea
3 Parliament Square
4 Start of Whitehall
5 Cenotaph
6 #10 Downing Street & Ministry of Defence
7 Banqueting House
8 Horse Guards
9 Trafalgar Square

LONDON

London at a Glance

▲▲▲**Westminster Abbey** Britain's finest church and the site of royal coronations and burials since 1066. **Hours:** Mon-Fri 9:30-16:30, Wed until 19:00, Sat 9:30-14:30, closed Sun to sightseers except for worship. See page 952.

▲▲▲**Churchill War Rooms** Underground WWII headquarters of Churchill's war effort. **Hours:** Daily 9:30-18:00. See page 957.

▲▲▲**National Gallery** Remarkable collection of European paintings (1250-1900), including Leonardo, Botticelli, Velázquez, Rembrandt, Turner, Van Gogh, and the Impressionists. **Hours:** Daily 10:00-18:00, Fri until 21:00. See page 958.

▲▲▲**British Museum** The world's greatest collection of artifacts of Western civilization, including the Rosetta Stone and the Parthenon's Elgin Marbles. **Hours:** Daily 10:00-17:30, Fri until 20:30 (selected galleries only). See page 966.

▲▲▲**British Library** Impressive collection of the most important literary treasures of the Western world. **Hours:** Mon-Fri 9:30-18:00, Tue until 20:00, Sat 9:30-17:00, Sun 11:00-17:00. See page 970.

▲▲▲**St. Paul's Cathedral** The main cathedral of the Anglican Church, designed by Christopher Wren, with a climbable dome and daily evensong services. **Hours:** Mon-Sat 8:30-16:30, closed Sun except for worship. See page 971.

▲▲▲**Tower of London** Historic castle, palace, and prison housing the crown jewels and a witty band of Beefeaters. **Hours:** March-Oct Tue-Sat 9:00-17:30, Sun-Mon 10:00-17:30; Nov-Feb Tue-Sat 9:00-16:30, Sun-Mon 10:00-16:30. See page 975.

▲▲**Houses of Parliament** London's Neo-Gothic landmark, famous for Big Ben and occupied by the Houses of Lords and

LONDON

lie 2,000 fascinating years of history. You'll get a whirlwind tour as well as a practical orientation to London. (You can download a free, extended audio version of this walk to your mobile device; see page 52.)

Start halfway across ❶ **Westminster Bridge** for that "Wow, I'm really in London!" feeling. Get a close-up view of the **Houses of Parliament** and **Big Ben.** Downstream you'll see the **London Eye.** Down the stairs to Westminster Pier are boats to the Tower of London and Greenwich (downstream) or Kew Gardens (upstream).

Commons. **Hours:** Always viewable from the outside; interior not worth touring on a short visit. See page 956.

▲▲**Trafalgar Square** The heart of London, where Westminster, The City, and the West End meet. **Hours:** Always open. See page 957.

▲▲**National Portrait Gallery** A *Who's Who* of British history, featuring portraits of this nation's most important historical figures. **Hours:** Daily 10:00-18:00, Thu-Fri until 21:00, first and second floors open Mon at 11:00. See page 962.

▲▲**Covent Garden** Vibrant people-watching zone with shops, cafés, street musicians, and an iron-and-glass arcade that once hosted a produce market. **Hours:** Always open. See page 964.

▲▲**Changing of the Guard at Buckingham Palace** Hour-long spectacle at Britain's royal residence. **Hours:** Generally May-July daily at 11:30, Aug-April every other day. See page 964.

▲▲**London Eye** Enormous observation wheel, dominating—and offering commanding views over—London's skyline. **Hours:** Daily July-Aug 10:00-21:30, April-June 10:00-21:00, Sept-March 10:00-20:00. See page 978.

▲▲**Tate Modern** Works by Monet, Matisse, Dalí, Picasso, and Warhol displayed in a converted powerhouse. **Hours:** Daily 10:00-18:00, Fri-Sat until 22:00. See page 979.

▲▲**Shakespeare's Globe** Timbered, thatched-roofed reconstruction of the Bard's original wooden "O." **Hours:** Theater complex, museum, and actor-led tours generally daily 9:00-17:00; in summer, morning theater tours only. Plays are also held here. See page 980.

LONDON

En route to Parliament Square, you'll pass a ❷ **statue of Boadicea,** the Celtic queen defeated by Roman invaders in A.D. 60.

For fun, call home from near Big Ben at about three minutes before the hour to let your loved one hear the bell ring. You'll find four red phone booths lining the north side of ❸ **Parliament Square** along Great George Street—also great for a phone-box-and-Big-Ben photo op.

Wave hello to Winston Churchill and Nelson Mandela in Parliament Square. To Churchill's right is **Westminster Abbey,** with its two stubby, elegant towers. The white building (flying the Union Jack) at the far end of the square houses Britain's new **Supreme Court.**

Head north up Parliament Street, which turns into ❹ **Whitehall,** and walk toward Trafalgar Square. You'll see the thought-provoking ❺ **Cenotaph** in the middle of the boulevard, reminding passersby of the many Brits who died in the last century's world wars. To visit the **Churchill War Rooms,** take a left before the Cenotaph, on King Charles Street.

Continuing on Whitehall, stop at the barricaded and guarded ❻ **#10 Downing Street** to see the British "White House," home of the prime minister. Break the bobby's boredom and ask him a question. The huge building across Whitehall from Downing Street is the **Ministry of Defence** (MOD), the "British Pentagon."

Nearing Trafalgar Square, look for the 17th-century ❼ **Banqueting House** across the street and the ❽ **Horse Guards** behind the gated fence.

The column topped by Lord Nelson marks ❾ **Trafalgar Square.** The stately domed building on the far side of the square is the **National Gallery,** which has a classy café in the Sainsbury wing. To the right of the National Gallery is **St. Martin-in-the-Fields Church** and its Café in the Crypt.

To get to Piccadilly from Trafalgar Square, walk up Cockspur Street to Haymarket, then take a short left on Coventry Street to colorful **Piccadilly Circus** (see map on page 963).

Near Piccadilly, you'll find a number of theaters. **Leicester Square** thrives just a few blocks away. Walk through seedy **Soho** (north of Shaftesbury Avenue) for its fun pubs. From Piccadilly or Oxford Circus, you can take a taxi, bus, or the Tube to wherever you're going next.

Sights in London

I've grouped these sights by neighborhood. With limited time, focus on just one area.

Central London
Westminster

These sights are listed in roughly geographical order from Westminster Abbey to Trafalgar Square, and are linked by my self-guided Westminster Walk, above.

▲▲▲**Westminster Abbey**—The greatest church in the English-speaking world, Westminster Abbey is where the nation's royalty has been wedded, crowned, and buried since 1066. Indeed, the histories of Westminster Abbey and England are almost the same. A thousand years of English history—3,000 tombs, the remains

of 29 kings and queens, and hundreds of memorials to poets, politicians, scientists, and warriors—lie within its stained-glass splendor and under its stone slabs.

Cost and Hours: £16, £32 family ticket (covers 2 adults and 1 child), cash or credit cards accepted (line up in the correct queue to pay), ticket includes audioguide and entry to cloisters and Abbey Museum; abbey—Mon-Fri 9:30-16:30, Wed until 19:00 (main church only), Sat 9:30-14:30, last entry one hour before closing, closed Sun to sightseers but open for services; museum—daily 10:30-16:00; cloisters—daily 8:00-18:00; no photos, café in solarium, Tube: Westminster or St. James's Park, tel. 020/7654-4834, www.westminster-abbey .org. It's free to enter just the cloisters and Abbey Museum (through Dean's Yard, around the right side as you face the main entrance), but if it's too crowded inside, the marshal at the cloister entrance may not let you in.

When to Go: The place is most crowded every day at mid-morning and on Saturdays and Mondays. Try to visit early, during lunch, or late to avoid tourist hordes. Weekdays after 14:30 are less congested. The main entrance, on the Parliament Square side, often has a sizable line. Of the two queues (cash or credit) at the admissions desk, the cash line is probably moving faster.

Music and Services: Mon-Fri at 7:30 (prayer), 8:00 (communion), 12:30 (communion), 17:00 evensong (except on Wed, when the evening service is generally spoken—not sung); Sat at 8:00 (communion), 9:00 (prayer), 15:00 (evensong; June-Sept it's at 17:00); Sun services generally come with more music: at 8:00 (communion), 10:00 (sung Matins), 11:15 (sung Eucharist), 15:00 (evensong), 18:30 (evening service). Services are free to anyone, though visitors who haven't paid church admission aren't allowed to linger afterward.

❷ Self-Guided Tour: You'll have no choice but to follow the steady flow of tourists circling clockwise through the church. My tour covers the Abbey's top stops.

• *Walk straight in, through the north transept and into the center of the church.*

North Transept and View of Nave: The "high" (main) altar (which usually has a cross and candlesticks atop it) sits on the platform up the five stairs. This is the culminating point of the long, high-ceilinged nave. In the opposite direction, nestled in the nave, is the elaborately carved wooden seating of the choir (a.k.a. "quire" in British churchspeak), where monks once chanted their services and where, today, the Abbey boys' choir sings the evensong. The

Abbey's 10-story nave is the tallest in England. The north transept is nicknamed "Statesmen's Corner" and specializes in tombs and memorials of famous prime ministers.

• *Turn left and follow the crowd. Stop at the wooden staircase on your right.*

Tomb of Edward the Confessor: Step back and peek over the dark coffin of Edward I to see the tippy-top of the green-and-gold wedding-cake tomb of King Edward the Confessor—the man who built Westminster Abbey. God had told pious Edward to visit St. Peter's Basilica in Rome. But with the Normans thinking conquest, it was too dangerous for him to leave England. Instead, he built this grand church and dedicated it to St. Peter. It was finished just in time to bury Edward and to crown his foreign successor, William the Conqueror, in 1066. After Edward's death, people prayed at his tomb, and, after getting good results, Pope Alexander III canonized him. This elevated, central tomb—which lost some of its luster when Henry VIII melted down the gold coffin-case—is surrounded by the tombs of eight kings and queens.

• *At the top of the stone staircase, veer left into the private burial chapel of Queen Elizabeth I.*

Tomb of Queen Elizabeth I and Mary I: Although there's only one effigy on the tomb (Elizabeth's), there are actually two queens buried beneath it, both daughters of Henry VIII (by different mothers). Bloody Mary—meek, pious, sickly, and Catholic—enforced Catholicism during her short reign (1553-1558) by burning "heretics" at the stake.

Elizabeth—strong, clever, and Protestant—steered England on an Anglican course. She holds a royal orb, symbolizing that she's queen of the whole globe. When 26-year-old Elizabeth was crowned in the Abbey, her right to rule was questioned (especially by her Catholic subjects) because she was the bastard seed of Henry VIII's unsanctioned marriage to Anne Boleyn. But Elizabeth's long reign (1559-1603) was one of the greatest in English history, a time when England ruled the seas and Shakespeare explored human emotions. When she died, thousands turned out for her funeral in the Abbey. Elizabeth's face on the tomb, modeled after her death mask, is considered a very accurate take on this hook-nosed, imperious "Virgin Queen."

• *Continue into the ornate, flag-draped room up a few more stairs, directly behind the main altar.*

Chapel of King Henry VII (a.k.a. the Lady Chapel): The light from the stained-glass windows; the colorful banners overhead; and the elaborate tracery in stone, wood, and glass give this room the festive air of a medieval tournament. The prestigious Knights of the Bath meet here, under the magnificent ceiling studded with gold pendants. The ceiling—of carved stone, not plaster (1519)—is the finest English Perpendicular Gothic and fan vaulting you'll see (unless you're going to King's College Chapel in Cambridge). The ceiling was sculpted on the floor in pieces, then jigsaw-puzzled into place. It capped the Gothic period and signaled the vitality of the coming Renaissance.

• *Go to the far end of the chapel and stand at the banister in front of the modern set of stained-glass windows.*

Royal Air Force Chapel: Saints in robes and halos mingle with pilots in parachutes and bomber jackets. This tribute to WWII flyers is for those who earned their angel wings in the Battle of Britain (July-Oct 1940). A bit of bomb damage has been preserved—look for the little glassed-over hole in the wall below the windows in the lower left-hand corner.

• *Exit the Chapel of Henry VII. Turn left into the side chapel with the tomb (the central one of three in the chapel).*

Tomb of Mary, Queen of Scots: The beautiful, French-educated queen was held under house arrest for 19 years by Queen Elizabeth I, who considered her a threat to her sovereignty. Elizabeth got wind of an assassination plot, suspected Mary was behind it, and had her first cousin (once removed) beheaded. When Elizabeth—who was called the "Virgin Queen"—died heirless, Mary's son, James VI, King of Scots, also became King James I of England and Ireland. James buried his mum here (with her head sewn back on) in the Abbey's most sumptuous tomb.

• *Exit Mary's chapel. Ahead of you, at the foot of the stairs, is the...*

Coronation Chair: The gold-painted oak chair waits here—with its back to the high altar—for the next coronation. For every English coronation since 1308 (except two), it's been moved to its spot before the high altar to receive the royal buttocks. The chair's legs rest on lions, England's symbol.

• *Turn left into the south transept. You're in...*

Poets' Corner: England's greatest artistic contributions are in the written word. Here the masters of arguably the world's

most complex and expressive language are remembered—Geoffrey Chaucer *(Canterbury Tales)*, Lord Byron, Dylan Thomas, W. H. Auden, Lewis Carroll *(Alice's Adventures in Wonderland)*, T. S. Eliot *(The Waste Land)*, Alfred, Lord Tennyson, Robert Browning, and Charles Dickens. Many writers are honored with plaques and monuments; relatively few are actually buried here. Shakespeare is commemorated by a fine statue that stands near the end of the transept, overlooking the others.

• *Return to the center of the church in front of the high altar. (You may have to peek over a row of chairs.)*

The Coronation Spot: The area immediately before the high altar is where every English coronation since 1066 has taken place. Royals are also given funerals here. Princess Diana's coffin was carried to this spot for her funeral service in 1997. The "Queen Mum" (mother of Elizabeth II) had her funeral here in 2002. This is also where most of the last century's royal weddings have taken place, including the unions of Queen Elizabeth II and Prince Philip (1947), Prince Andrew and Sarah Ferguson (1986), and Prince William and Kate Middleton (2011).

• *Exit the church (temporarily) at the south door, which leads to the...*

Cloisters and Abbey Museum: The buildings that adjoin the church housed the monks. Cloistered courtyards gave them

a place to meditate on God's creations. The small Abbey Museum, formerly the monks' lounge, is worth a peek for its fascinating and well-described exhibits. Look into the impressively realistic eyes of Elizabeth I, Charles II, Admiral Nelson, and a dozen others, part of a compelling series of wax-and-wood statues that, for three centuries, graced coffins during funeral processions. The once-exquisite, now-fragmented Westminster Retable, which decorated the high altar in 1270, is the oldest surviving altarpiece in England.

• *Go back into the church and stand in the...*

Nave: On the floor near the west entrance of the Abbey is the flower-lined **Tomb of the Unknown Warrior,** one ordinary WWI soldier buried in soil from France with lettering made from melted-down weapons from that war. Think about that million-man army from the empire and commonwealth, and all those who gave their lives. Their memory is so revered that, when Kate Middleton walked up the aisle on her wedding day, by tradition she had to step around the tomb (and her wedding bouquet was later placed atop this tomb, also in accordance with tradition).

Other Sights in Westminster

▲▲Houses of Parliament (Palace of Westminster)—This Neo-Gothic icon of London, the royal residence from 1042 to 1547, is now the meeting place of the legislative branch of government. The Houses of Parliament are located in what was once the Palace of Westminster—long the palace of England's medieval kings—

until it was largely destroyed by fire in 1834. The palace was rebuilt in the Victorian Gothic style (a move away from Neoclassicism back to England's Christian and medieval heritage, true to the Romantic Age) and completed in 1860. While it's possible to visit the interior, on a quick visit to London, the views from outside are most worthwhile.

▲▲▲**Churchill War Rooms**—This excellent sight offers a fascinating walk through the underground headquarters of the British

government's fight against the Nazis in the darkest days of the Battle for Britain. It has two parts: the war rooms themselves, and a top-notch museum dedicated to the man who steered the war from here, Winston Churchill. For details on all the blood, sweat, toil, and tears, pick up the excellent, essential, and included audioguide at the entry, and dive in.

Cost and Hours: £16.50 (includes 10 percent optional donation), £5 guidebook, daily 9:30-18:00, last entry one hour before closing; on King Charles Street, 200 yards off Whitehall, follow the signs, Tube: Westminster, tel. 020/7930-6961, www.iwm.org.uk/churchill. The museum's gift shop is great for anyone nostalgic for the 1940s.

▲▲**Trafalgar Square**

London's central square—at the intersection of Westminster, The City, and the West End—is the climax of most marches and demonstrations, and a thrilling place to simply hang out. A recent remodeling of the square has rerouted car traffic, helping reclaim

the area for London's citizens. At the top of Trafalgar Square (north) sits the domed National Gallery with its grand staircase, and to the right, the steeple of St. Martin-in-the-Fields, built in 1722, inspiring the steeple-over-the-entrance style of many town churches in New England. The pedestal called the Fourth

LONDON

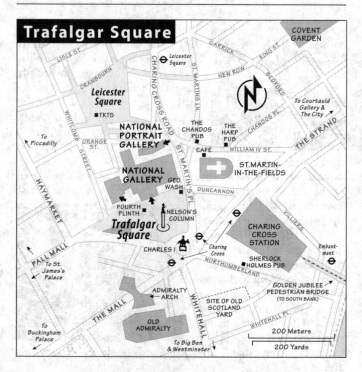

Trafalgar Square

(Map labels:) COVENT GARDEN, GARRICK, LISLE ST., CRANBOURN, Leicester Square, NEW ROW, KING ST., BEDFORD, WHITCOMB ST., Leicester Square, CHARING CROSS ROAD, ST. MARTIN'S LN., CHANDOS PL., To Courtauld Gallery & The City, ■TKTS, THE CHANDOS PUB, THE HARP PUB, THE STRAND, To Piccadilly, ORANGE ST., NATIONAL PORTRAIT GALLERY, CAFÉ, WILLIAM IV ST., NATIONAL GALLERY, GEO. WASH., ST. MARTIN-IN-THE-FIELDS, HAYMARKET, FOURTH PLINTH, NELSON'S COLUMN, DUNCANNON, VILLIERS, Trafalgar Square, CHARING CROSS STATION, Embankment, CHARLES I, Charing Cross, PALL MALL, To St. James's Palace, NORTHUMBERLAND, SHERLOCK HOLMES PUB, ADMIRALTY ARCH, SITE OF OLD SCOTLAND YARD, GOLDEN JUBILEE PEDESTRIAN BRIDGE (TO SOUTH BANK), THE MALL, WHITEHALL, WHITEHALL PL., To Buckingham Palace, OLD ADMIRALTY, To Big Ben & Westminster, 200 Meters, 200 Yards

LONDON

Plinth is often topped with a temporary work of art. In the center of the square, Lord Horatio Nelson stands atop his 185-foot-tall fluted granite column, gazing out toward Trafalgar, where he lost his life but defeated the French fleet. Part of this 1842 memorial is made from his victims' melted-down cannons. He's surrounded by spraying fountains, giant lions, hordes of people, and—until 2005—even more pigeons. A former London mayor decided that London's "flying rats" were a public nuisance and evicted Trafalgar Square's venerable seed salesmen (Tube: Charing Cross).

▲▲▲**National Gallery**—Displaying Britain's top collection of European paintings from 1250 to 1900—including works by Leonardo, Botticelli, Velázquez, Rembrandt, Turner, Van Gogh, and the Impressionists—this is one of Europe's great galleries. You'll peruse 700 years of art—from gold-backed Madonnas to Cubist bathers.

Cost and Hours: Free, but suggested donation of £2, temporary (optional) exhibits extra, floor plan-£1; daily 10:00-18:00, Fri until 21:00, last entry to special

exhibits 45 minutes before closing; no photos, on Trafalgar Square, Tube: Charing Cross or Leicester Square.

Information: Helpful £1 floor plan available from information desk; free one-hour overview tours leave from Sainsbury Wing info desk daily at 11:30 and 14:30, plus Fri at 19:00; excellent £3.50 audioguides—choose from one-hour highlights tour, several theme tours, or tour option that lets you dial up info on any painting in the museum; info tel. 020/7747-2885, switchboard tel. 020/7839-3321, www.nationalgallery.org.uk.

Eating: Consider splitting afternoon tea at the excellent-but-pricey National Dining Rooms, on the first floor of the Sainsbury Wing. The National Café, located near the Getty Entrance, also has afternoon tea.

○ Self-Guided Tour: Go in through the Sainsbury Entrance (in the smaller building to the left of the main entrance), and approach the collection chronologically.

Medieval and Early Renaissance: In the first rooms, you see shiny paintings of saints, angels, Madonnas, and crucifixions floating in an ethereal gold never-never land.

After leaving this gold-leaf peace, you'll stumble into Uccello's *Battle of San Romano* and Van Eyck's *The Arnolfini Portrait,* called by some "The Shotgun Wedding." This painting—a masterpiece of down-to-earth details—was once thought to depict a wedding ceremony forced by the lady's swelling belly. Today it's understood as a portrait of a solemn, well-dressed, well-heeled couple, the Arnolfinis of Bruges, Belgium (she likely was not pregnant—the fashion of the day was to gather up the folds of one's extremely full-skirted dress).

Renaissance: In painting, the Renaissance meant realism. Artists rediscovered the beauty of nature and the human body, expressing the optimism and confidence of this new age. Look for Botticelli's *Venus and Mars,* Michelangelo's *The Entombment,* Raphael's *Pope Julius II,* and Leonardo's *The Virgin of the Rocks.*

Hans Holbein the Younger's *The Ambassadors* depicts two well-dressed, suave men flanking a shelf full of books, globes, navigational tools, and musical instruments—objects that symbolize the secular knowledge of the Renaissance. So what's with the gray, slanting blob at the bottom? If you view the blob from the right-hand edge of the painting (get real close, right up to the frame), the blob suddenly becomes...a skull, a reminder that—despite the fine clothes, proud poses, and worldly knowledge—we will all die.

LONDON

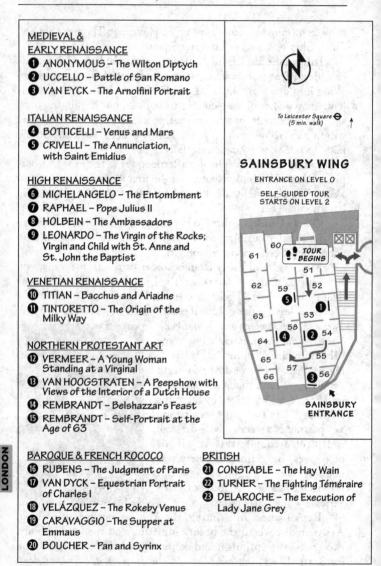

MEDIEVAL &
EARLY RENAISSANCE
1 ANONYMOUS – The Wilton Diptych
2 UCCELLO – Battle of San Romano
3 VAN EYCK – The Arnolfini Portrait

ITALIAN RENAISSANCE
4 BOTTICELLI – Venus and Mars
5 CRIVELLI – The Annunciation, with Saint Emidius

HIGH RENAISSANCE
6 MICHELANGELO – The Entombment
7 RAPHAEL – Pope Julius II
8 HOLBEIN – The Ambassadors
9 LEONARDO – The Virgin of the Rocks; Virgin and Child with St. Anne and St. John the Baptist

VENETIAN RENAISSANCE
10 TITIAN – Bacchus and Ariadne
11 TINTORETTO – The Origin of the Milky Way

NORTHERN PROTESTANT ART
12 VERMEER – A Young Woman Standing at a Virginal
13 VAN HOOGSTRATEN – A Peepshow with Views of the Interior of a Dutch House
14 REMBRANDT – Belshazzar's Feast
15 REMBRANDT – Self-Portrait at the Age of 63

To Leicester Square (5 min. walk)

SAINSBURY WING
ENTRANCE ON LEVEL 0
SELF-GUIDED TOUR STARTS ON LEVEL 2

TOUR BEGINS

SAINSBURY ENTRANCE

BAROQUE & FRENCH ROCOCO
16 RUBENS – The Judgment of Paris
17 VAN DYCK – Equestrian Portrait of Charles I
18 VELÁZQUEZ – The Rokeby Venus
19 CARAVAGGIO –The Supper at Emmaus
20 BOUCHER – Pan and Syrinx

BRITISH
21 CONSTABLE – The Hay Wain
22 TURNER – The Fighting Téméraire
23 DELAROCHE – The Execution of Lady Jane Grey

In *The Origin of the Milky Way* by Venetian Renaissance painter Tintoretto, the god Jupiter places his illegitimate son, baby Hercules, at his wife's breast. Juno says, "Wait a minute. That's not my baby!" Her milk spurts upward, becoming the Milky Way.

Northern Protestant: Greek gods and Virgin Marys are out, and hometown folks and hometown places are in. Highlights include Vermeer's *A Young Woman Standing at a Virginal* and Rembrandt's *Belshazzar's Feast*.

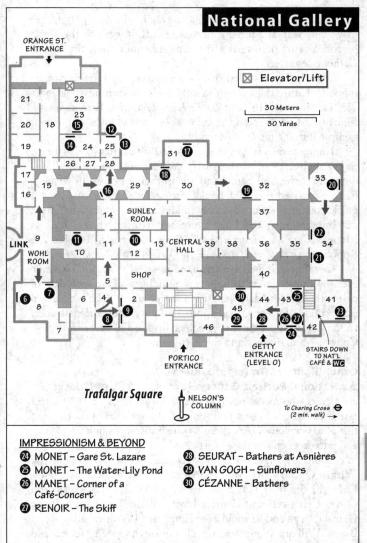

National Gallery

⊠ Elevator/Lift

ORANGE ST. ENTRANCE

30 Meters
30 Yards

21 22
23
20 18 ⑮
19   ⑫
14 24 25 ⑬
26 27 28 31 ⑰
17 15   29 30 ⑱ 32 33 ⑳
16   ⑯
14 SUNLEY ROOM 37
9 ⑪ 11 ⑩ 13 CENTRAL HALL 39 38 36 35 34 ㉒ ㉑
LINK WOHL ROOM 10 12
5 SHOP 40
⑥ ⑦ 6 4 2 ㉚ 44 43 ㉕ 41 ㉓
8 ⑧ ⑨ 45 ㉙ ㉘ ㉖ ㉗ 42 ㉔
7 46

PORTICO ENTRANCE

GETTY ENTRANCE (LEVEL 0)

STAIRS DOWN TO NAT'L CAFÉ & **WC**

Trafalgar Square NELSON'S COLUMN

To Charing Cross ⊖ (2 min. walk) →

IMPRESSIONISM & BEYOND

㉔ MONET – *Gare St. Lazare*
㉕ MONET – *The Water-Lily Pond*
㉖ MANET – *Corner of a Café-Concert*
㉗ RENOIR – *The Skiff*

㉘ SEURAT – *Bathers at Asnières*
㉙ VAN GOGH – *Sunflowers*
㉚ CÉZANNE – *Bathers*

Rembrandt painted his *Self-Portrait at the Age of 63* in the year he would die. He was bankrupt, his mistress had just passed away, and he had also buried several of his children. We see a disillusioned, well-worn, but proud old genius.

Baroque: The museum's outstanding Baroque collection includes Van Dyck's *Equestrian Portrait of Charles I* and Caravaggio's *The Supper at Emmaus*. In Velázquez's *The Rokeby Venus*, Venus lounges diagonally across the canvas, admiring herself, with flaring red, white, and gray fabrics to highlight her rosy white skin and inflame our passion. This work by the king's personal court painter is a rare Spanish nude from that ultra-Catholic country.

British: The reserved British were more comfortable cavorting with nature than with the lofty gods, as seen in Constable's *The Hay Wain* and Turner's *The Fighting Téméraire*. Turner's messy, colorful style influenced the Impressionists and gives us our first glimpse into the modern art world.

Impressionism: At the end of the 19th century, a new breed of artists burst out of the stuffy confines of the studio. They donned scarves and berets and set up their canvases in farmers' fields or carried their notebooks into crowded cafés, dashing off quick sketches in order to catch a momentary...impression. Check out Impressionist and Post-Impressionist masterpieces such as Monet's *Gare St. Lazare* and *The Water-Lily Pond*, Renoir's *The Skiff*, Seurat's *Bathers at Asnières*, and Van Gogh's *Sunflowers*.

Cézanne's *Bathers* are arranged in strict triangles. Cézanne uses the Impressionist technique of building a figure with dabs of paint (though his "dabs" are often larger-sized "cube" shapes) to make solid, 3-D geometrical figures in the style of the Renaissance. In the process, his cube shapes helped inspire a radical new style—Cubism—bringing art into the 20th century.

Other Sights on Trafalgar Square

▲▲National Portrait Gallery—Put off by halls of 19th-century characters who meant nothing to me, I used to call this "as interesting as someone else's yearbook." But a selective walk through this 500-year-long *Who's Who* of British history is quick and free, and puts faces on the story of England.

Some highlights: Henry VIII and wives; portraits of the "Virgin Queen" Elizabeth I, Sir Francis Drake, and Sir Walter Raleigh; the only real-life portrait of William Shakespeare; Oliver Cromwell and Charles I with his head on; portraits by Gainsborough and Reynolds; the Romantics (William Blake, Lord Byron, William Wordsworth, and company); Queen Victoria and her era; and the present royal family, including the late Princess Diana.

The collection is well-described, not huge, and in historical sequence, from the 16th century on the second floor to today's royal family on the ground floor.

Cost and Hours: Free, but suggested donation of £5, temporary (optional) exhibits extra, audioguide-£3, floor plan-£1; daily 10:00-18:00, Thu-Fri until 21:00, first and second floors open Mon at 11:00, last entry to special exhibits 45 minutes before closing, no photos, basement café and top-floor view restaurant; entry

100 yards off Trafalgar Square (around the corner from National Gallery, opposite Church of St. Martin-in-the-Fields), Tube: Charing Cross or Leicester Square, tel. 020/7306-0055, recorded info tel. 020/7312-2463, www.npg.org.uk.

▲**St. Martin-in-the-Fields**—The church, built in the 1720s with a Gothic spire atop a Greek-type temple, is an oasis of peace on wild and noisy Trafalgar Square.

St. Martin cared for the poor. "In the fields" was where the first church stood on this spot (in the 13th century), between Westminster and The City. Stepping inside, you still feel a compassion for the needs of the people in this neighborhood—the church serves the homeless and houses a Chinese community center. The modern east window—with grillwork bent into the shape of a warped cross—was installed in 2008 to replace one damaged in World War II.

A freestanding glass pavilion to the left of the church serves as the entrance to the church's underground areas. There you'll find the concert ticket office, a gift shop, brass-rubbing center, and the recommended support-the-church Café in the Crypt.

Cost and Hours: Free, but donations welcome, £3.50 audio-guide at shop downstairs; hours vary but generally Mon-Fri 8:30-13:00 & 14:00-18:00, Sat 9:30-13:00 & 14:00-18:00, Sun 15:30-17:00; Tube: Charing Cross, tel. 020/7766-1100, www.smitf .org.

Music: The church is famous for its free lunchtime concerts (suggested £3 donation; Mon, Tue, and Fri at 13:00).

The West End and Nearby
▲**Piccadilly Circus**—Although this square is slathered with neon billboards and tacky attractions (think of it as the Times Square of London), the surrounding streets are packed with great shopping opportunities and swimming with youth on the rampage.

Nearby Shaftesbury Avenue and Leicester Square teem with fun-seekers, theaters, Chinese restaurants, and street singers. To the northeast is London's Chinatown and, beyond that, the funky Soho neighborhood (described next). And curling to the northwest from Piccadilly Circus is genteel Regent Street, lined with the city's most exclusive shops.

▲**Soho**—North of Piccadilly, seedy Soho has become trendy—with many recommended restaurants (see page 987)—and is well worth a gawk. It's the epicenter of London's thriving, colorful youth scene, a fun and funky *Sesame Street* of urban diversity.

Although gentrifying, Soho is also London's red light district (especially near Brewer and Berwick Streets), and a center of its gay community.

▲▲**Covent Garden**—This large square teems with people and street performers—jugglers, sword swallowers, and guitar players. London's buskers (including those in the Tube) are auditioned, licensed, and assigned times and places where they are allowed to perform. The square's centerpiece is a covered marketplace whose venerable arcades have been converted to boutiques, cafés, and antiques shops.

Buckingham Palace

While it's possible to enter various sights related to the palace, on a brief visit I'd just take a quick look at its famous facade. The Changing of the Guard (described below) might entice you, but planning your day around it leaves little time for other options; because you'll need to fight the crowds to secure a suitable vantage point, this is more time-consuming than it sounds.

▲▲**Changing of the Guard at Buckingham Palace**—This is the spectacle every visitor to London wants to see: stone-faced, red-coated, bearskin-hatted guards changing posts with much

fanfare, in an hour-long ceremony accompanied by a brass band.

It's 11:00 at Buckingham Palace, and the on-duty guards (the "Queen's Guard") are ready to finish their shift. Nearby at St. James's Palace (a half-mile northwest), a second set of guards is also ready for a break. Meanwhile, fresh replacement guards (the "New Guard") gather for a review and inspection at Wellington Barracks, 500 yards east of the palace (on Birdcage Walk).

LONDON

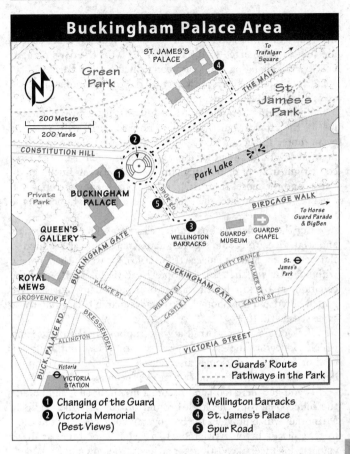

Buckingham Palace Area

St. James's Palace

Green Park

To Trafalgar Square

THE MALL

St. James's Park

200 Meters
200 Yards

CONSTITUTION HILL

Park Lake

BUCKINGHAM PALACE

Private Park

SPUR RD.

BIRDCAGE WALK

To Horse Guard Parade & Big Ben

QUEEN'S GALLERY

WELLINGTON BARRACKS

GUARDS' MUSEUM

GUARDS' CHAPEL

St. James's Park

BUCKINGHAM GATE

ROYAL MEWS

PALACE ST.

GROSVENOR PL.

WILFRED ST.

CASTLE LN.

BUCKINGHAM GATE

PETTY FRANCE

PALMER ST.

CAXTON ST.

BRESSENDEN

ALLINGTON

BUCK. PALACE RD.

VICTORIA STREET

Victoria

VICTORIA STATION

..... Guards' Route
--- Pathways in the Park

❶ Changing of the Guard
❷ Victoria Memorial (Best Views)
❸ Wellington Barracks
❹ St. James's Palace
❺ Spur Road

LONDON

At 11:15, the tired St. James's guards head out to the Mall, and then take a right turn for Buckingham Palace. At 11:30, the replacement troops, led by the band, also head for Buckingham Palace. Meanwhile, a fourth group—the Horse Guard—passes by along the Mall on its way back to Hyde Park Corner from its own changing-of-the-guard ceremony on Whitehall (which just took place at Horse Guards Parade at 11:00, or 10:00 on Sun).

At 11:45, the tired and fresh guards converge on Buckingham Palace in a perfect storm of Red Coat pageantry. Everyone parades around, the guard changes (passing the regimental flag, or "colour") with much shouting, the band plays a happy little concert, and then they march out. At noon, two bands escort two detachments of guards away: the tired guards to Wellington Barracks and the fresh guards to St. James's Palace. As the fresh guards set up at St. James's Palace and the tired ones dress down at the barracks, the tourists disperse.

Cost and Hours: Free, daily May-July at 11:30, every other day Aug-April, no ceremony in very wet weather; exact schedule subject to change—call 020/7766-7300 for the day's plan, or check www.changing-the-guard.com; Buckingham Palace, Tube: Victoria, St. James's Park, or Green Park. Or hop into a big black taxi and say, "Buck House, please."

Sightseeing Strategies: Most tourists just show up and get lost in the crowds, but those who know the drill will enjoy the event more. The action takes place in stages over the course of an hour, at several different locations. The main event is in the forecourt right in front of Buckingham Palace (between Buckingham Palace and the fence) from 11:30 to 12:00. To see it close up, you'll need to get here no later than 10:30 to get a place right next to the fence.

But there's plenty of pageantry elsewhere. Get out your map and strategize. You could see the guards mobilizing at Wellington Barracks or St. James's Palace (11:00-11:15). Or watch them parade with bands down The Mall and Spur Road (11:15-11:30). After the ceremony at Buckingham Palace is over (and many tourists have gotten bored and gone home), the parades march back along those same streets (12:10).

Pick one event and find a good, unobstructed place from which to view it. The key is to get either right up front along the road or fence, or find some raised elevation to stand or sit on—a balustrade or a curb—so you can see over people's heads.

If you get there too late to score a premium spot right along the fence, head for the high ground on the circular Victoria Memorial, which provides the best overall view (come before 11:00 to get a place). If you arrive too late to get any good spot at all, or you just don't feel like jostling for a view, stroll down to St. James's Palace and wait near the corner for a great photo-op. At about 12:15, the parade marches up The Mall to the palace and performs a smaller changing ceremony—with almost no crowds. Afterward, stroll through nearby St. James's Park.

North London
▲▲▲British Museum

Simply put, this is the greatest chronicle of civilization...anywhere. A visit here is like taking a long hike through *Encyclopedia Britannica* National Park. While the vast British Museum wraps around its Great Court (the huge entrance hall), the most popular sections of the museum fill

the ground floor: Egyptian, Assyrian, and ancient Greek, with the famous frieze sculptures from the Parthenon in Athens. The museum's stately Reading Room—famous as the place where Karl Marx hung out while formulating his ideas on communism and writing *Das Kapital*—sometimes hosts special exhibits.

Cost and Hours: Free, but £5/$7/€6 donation requested; temporary exhibits usually extra (and with timed ticket); daily 10:00-17:30, Fri until 20:30 (selected galleries only), least crowded weekday late afternoons; Great Russell Street, Tube: Tottenham Court Road.

Information: Information desks offer a standard museum map (£1 suggested donation) and a £2 version that highlights important pieces; the *Visitor's Guide* (£3.50) offers 15 different tours and skimpy text. Free 30-minute **eyeOpener tours** are led by volunteers, who focus on select rooms (daily 11:00-15:45, generally every 15 minutes). Free 45-minute **gallery talks** on specific subjects are offered Tue-Sat at 13:15. The £5 **multimedia guide** offers dial-up audio commentary and video on 200 objects, as well as several theme tours (must leave photo ID). There's also a fun children's audioguide (£3.50). And finally, you can download a free Rick Steves **audio tour** of the museum (see page 52). General info tel. 020/7323-8299, ticket desk tel. 020/7323-8181, collection questions tel. 020/7323-8838, www.britishmuseum.org.

Visiting the Museum: From the Great Court, doorways lead to all wings. To the left are the exhibits on Egypt, Assyria, and Greece—the highlights of your visit.

Egypt: Start with the Egyptian section. Egypt was one of the world's first "civilizations"—a group of people with a government, religion, art, free time, and a written language. The Egypt we think of—pyramids, mummies, pharaohs, and guys who walk funny—lasted from 3000 to 1000 B.C. with hardly any change in the government, religion, or arts. Imagine two millennia of Eisenhower.

The first thing you'll see in the Egypt section is the **Rosetta Stone.** When this rock was unearthed in the Egyptian desert in 1799, it was a sensation in Europe. This black slab caused a quantum leap in the study of ancient history; finally, Egyptian writing could be decoded. It contains a single inscription repeated in three languages. The bottom third is plain old Greek, while the middle is medieval Egyptian. By comparing the two known languages with the one they didn't know, translators figured out the hieroglyphics.

Next, wander past the many **statues,** including a seven-ton Ramesses, with the traditional features of a pharaoh (goatee, cloth headdress, and cobra diadem on his forehead). When Moses told the king of Egypt, "Let my people go!" this was the stony-faced

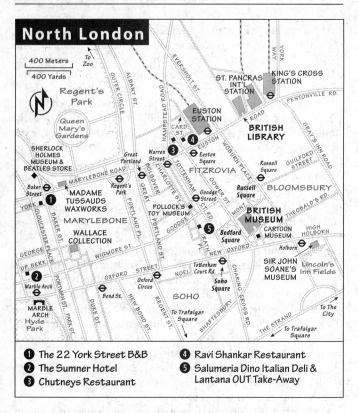

North London

400 Meters
400 Yards

To Zoo

Regent's Park

Queen Mary's Gardens

SHERLOCK HOLMES MUSEUM & BEATLES STORE

Baker Street

❶ MADAME TUSSAUDS WAXWORKS

WALLACE COLLECTION

MARYLEBONE

ST. PANCRAS INT'L STATION

KING'S CROSS STATION

EUSTON STATION

BRITISH LIBRARY

❹
❸ Warren Street   Euston Square

FITZROVIA

Great Portland   Regent's Park

Goodge Street

Russell Square

BLOOMSBURY

Russell Square

BRITISH MUSEUM

POLLOCK'S TOY MUSEUM

❺ Bedford Square

CARTOON MUSEUM

HIGH HOLBORN

GEORGE ST.   WIGMORE ST.

Holborn

SIR JOHN SOANE'S MUSEUM

Lincoln's Inn Fields

UP. BERK. ST.

❷ Marble Arch

MARBLE ARCH Hyde Park

Bond St.

OXFORD   STREET

Oxford Circus

NOEL

SOHO

Tottenham Court Rd.

Soho Square

To Trafalgar Square

SHAFTESBURY

To The City

THE STRAND

To Trafalgar Square

❶ The 22 York Street B&B
❷ The Sumner Hotel
❸ Chutneys Restaurant
❹ Ravi Shankar Restaurant
❺ Salumeria Dino Italian Deli & Lantana OUT Take-Away

look he got. You'll also see the Egyptian gods as animals—these include Amun, king of the gods, as a ram, and Horus, the god of the living, as a falcon.

At the end of the hall, climb the stairs to **mummy** land (use the elevator if it's running). To mummify a body, disembowel it (but leave the heart inside), pack the cavities with pitch, and dry it with natron, a natural form of sodium carbonate (and, I believe, the active ingredient in Twinkies). Then carefully bandage it head to toe with hundreds of yards of linen strips. Let it sit 2,000 years, and...*voilà!* The mummy was placed in a wooden coffin, which was put in a stone coffin, which was placed in a tomb. The result is that we now have Egyptian bodies that are as well-preserved as Joan Rivers. Many of the mummies here are from the time of the Roman occupation, when they painted a fine portrait in wax on the wrapping. X-ray photos in the display cases tell us more about these people. Don't miss the animal mummies. Cats were popular pets. They were also considered incarnations of the goddess Bastet. Worshiped in life as the sun god's allies, preserved in death, and memorialized with statues, cats were given the adulation they've come to expect ever since.

Assyria: Long before Saddam Hussein, Iraq was home to other palace-building, iron-fisted rulers—the Assyrians, who conquered their southern neighbors and dominated the Middle East for 300 years (c. 900-600 B.C.). Their strength came from a superb army (chariots, mounted cavalry, and siege engines), a policy of terrorism against enemies ("I tied their heads to tree trunks all around the city," reads a royal inscription), ethnic cleansing and mass deportations of the vanquished, and efficient administration (roads and express postal service). They have been called "The Romans of the East."

Standing guard over the Assyrian exhibit halls are two human-headed **winged lions.** These lions guarded an Assyrian palace. Carved into the stone between the bearded lions' loins, you can see one of civilization's most impressive achievements— writing. This wedge-shaped **(cuneiform)** script is the world's first written language, invented 5,000 years ago by the Sumerians (of southern Iraq) and passed down to their less-civilized descendants, the Assyrians.

The **Nimrud Gallery** is a mini version of the throne room of King Ashurnasirpal II's palace at Nimrud. It's filled with royal propaganda reliefs, 30-ton marble bulls, and panels depicting wounded lions (lion-hunting was Assyria's sport of kings).

Greece: During their civilization's Golden Age (500-430 B.C.), the ancient Greeks set the tone for all of Western civilization to follow. Democracy, theater, literature, mathematics, philosophy, science, gyros, art, and architecture, as we know them, were virtually all invented by a single generation of Greeks in a small town of maybe 80,000 citizens.

Your walk through Greek art history starts with **pottery,** usually painted red and black and a popular export product for the sea-trading Greeks. The earliest featured geometric patterns (eighth century B.C.), then a painted black silhouette on the natural orange clay, then a red figure on a black background. Later, painted vases show a culture really into partying.

The highlight is the **Parthenon Sculptures,** taken from the Parthenon—the temple dedicated to Athena, goddess of wisdom and the patroness of Athens, which was the crowning glory of an enormous urban-renewal plan during Greece's Golden Age. These are the so-called Elgin Marbles, named for the shrewd British ambassador who had his men hammer, chisel, and saw them off the Parthenon in the early 1800s. Though the Greek government complains about losing its marbles, the Brits feel they rescued and preserved the sculptures. These much-wrangled-over bits of the Parthenon (from about 450 B.C.) are indeed impressive. The marble panels you see lining the walls of this large hall are part of the frieze that originally ran around the exterior of the Parthenon (under the eaves). The statues at either end of the hall once filled the Parthenon's triangular-shaped pediments and showed the birth of Athena. The relief panels known as metopes tell the story of the struggle between the forces of human civilization and animal-like barbarism.

The Rest of the Museum: Be sure to venture upstairs to see artifacts from **Roman Britain** that surpass anything you'll see at Hadrian's Wall or elsewhere in the country. Also look for the Sutton Hoo Ship Burial artifacts from a seventh-century royal burial on the east coast of England (room 41). A rare Michelangelo cartoon (preliminary sketch) is in room 90 (level 4).

Other Sights in North London

▲▲▲**British Library**—The British Empire built its greatest monuments out of paper; it's through literature that England has made her lasting contribution to history and the arts. Here, in just two rooms, are the literary treasures of Western civilization, from early Bibles, to the Magna Carta, to Shakespeare's *Hamlet*, to Lewis Carroll's *Alice's Adventures in Wonderland*.

You'll see the Lindisfarne Gospels transcribed on an illuminated manuscript, as well as Beatles lyrics scrawled on the back of a greeting card. Pages from Leonardo da Vinci's notebook show his powerful curiosity, his genius for invention, and his famous backward and inside-out handwriting, which makes sense only if you know Italian and have a mirror. A *Beowulf* manuscript from A.D. 1000, *The Canterbury Tales*, and Shakespeare's First Folio also reside here. (If the First Folio is not out, the library should have other Shakespeare items on display.)

Exhibits change often, and many of the museum's old, fragile manuscripts need to "rest" periodically in order to stay well-preserved. If your heart's set on seeing that one particular rare Dickens book or letter penned by Gandhi, call ahead to make sure it's on display.

Cost and Hours: Free, but £2 suggested donation, admission charged for some (optional) temporary exhibits, Mon-Fri 9:30-18:00, Tue until 20:00, Sat 9:30-17:00, Sun 11:00-17:00, 96 Euston Road, Tube: King's Cross St. Pancras or Euston, tel. 019/3754-6060 or 020/7412-7676, www.bl.uk.

Tours: While the British Library doesn't offer an audioguide or guided tours, you can download a free Rick Steves **audio tour** that describes its highlights (see page 52).

The City

When Londoners say "The City," they mean the one-square-mile business center in East London that 2,000 years ago was Roman

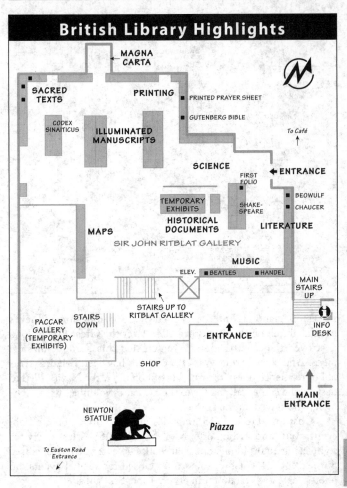

British Library Highlights

- MAGNA CARTA
- SACRED TEXTS
- PRINTING
- PRINTED PRAYER SHEET
- CODEX SINAITICUS
- ILLUMINATED MANUSCRIPTS
- GUTENBERG BIBLE
- To Café
- SCIENCE
- ENTRANCE
- FIRST FOLIO
- BEOWULF
- TEMPORARY EXHIBITS
- SHAKE-SPEARE
- CHAUCER
- HISTORICAL DOCUMENTS
- LITERATURE
- MAPS
- SIR JOHN RITBLAT GALLERY
- MUSIC
- ELEV.
- BEATLES
- HANDEL
- MAIN STAIRS UP
- STAIRS UP TO RITBLAT GALLERY
- PACCAR GALLERY (TEMPORARY EXHIBITS)
- STAIRS DOWN
- INFO DESK
- ENTRANCE
- SHOP
- MAIN ENTRANCE
- NEWTON STATUE
- Piazza
- To Euston Road Entrance

Londinium. The outline of the Roman city walls can still be seen in the arc of roads from Blackfriars Bridge to Tower Bridge. Within The City are 23 churches designed by Sir Christopher Wren, mostly just ornamentation around St. Paul's Cathedral. Today, while home to only 7,000 residents, The City thrives with nearly 300,000 office workers coming and going daily. It's a fascinating district to wander on weekdays, but since almost nobody actually lives there, it's dull after hours and on weekends.

For a walking tour, you can download a free Rick Steves **audio tour** of The City, which peels back the many layers of history in this oldest part of London (see page 52).

▲▲▲St. Paul's Cathedral

Sir Christopher Wren's most famous church is the great St.

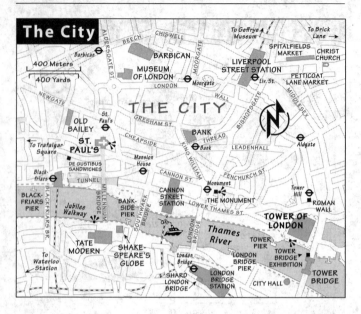

Paul's, its elaborate interior capped by a 365-foot dome. There's been a church on this spot since 604. After the Great Fire of 1666 destroyed the old cathedral, Wren created this Baroque masterpiece. And since World War II, St. Paul's has been Britain's symbol of resilience. Despite 57 nights of bombing, the Nazis failed to destroy the cathedral, thanks to the St. Paul's volunteer fire watchmen, who stayed on the dome.

Cost and Hours: £15, includes church entry, dome climb, crypt, tour, and audioguide; Mon-Sat 8:30-16:30, last entry for sightseeing 16:00 (dome opens at 9:30, last entry at 16:15), closed Sun except for worship, sometimes closed for special events, no photos, café and restaurant in crypt, Tube: St. Paul's.

Music and Services: Communion is Mon-Sat at 8:00 and 12:30. Sunday services are held at 8:00, 10:15 (Matins), 11:30 (sung Eucharist), 15:15 (evensong), and 18:00.

Information: Admission includes an **audioguide** as well as a 1.5-hour guided tour (Mon-Sat at 10:45, 11:15, 13:30, and 14:00; confirm schedule at church or call 020/7246-8357). Free 15-minute talks are offered throughout the day, and a stand-up, wrap-around **film** program titled *Oculus: An Eye into St. Paul's* gives some historical background and shows the view from atop the dome (find it near Nelson's tomb). You can also download a free Rick Steves **audio tour** of St. Paul's (see page 52). Recorded info tel. 020/7236-4128, reception tel. 020/7246-8350, www.stpauls.co.uk.

Visiting the Cathedral: Even now, as skyscrapers encroach, the 365-foot-high dome of St. Paul's rises majestically above the

St. Paul's Cathedral

ENTER

STAIRS

To St. Paul's ⊖

DOME

NAVE

CHOIR

HIGH ALTAR

BISHOP'S CHAIR

30 Meters
30 Yards

To Millennium Bridge

1 Nave
2 Wellington Monument
3 Dome
4 Choir & High Altar
5 HUNT–The Light of the World
6 MOORE–Mother and Child
7 American Memorial Chapel
8 John Donne Statue
9 Nelson & Cornwallis Monuments
10 Climb the Dome (2 Entrances)
11 Crypt Entrance

rooftops of the neighborhood. The tall dome is set on classical

columns, capped with a lantern, topped by a six-foot ball, and iced with a cross. As the first Anglican cathedral built in London after the Reformation, it is Baroque: St. Peter's in Rome filtered through clear-eyed English reason. Often the site of historic funerals (Queen Victoria and Winston Churchill), St. Paul's most famous ceremony was a wedding—when Prince Charles married Lady Diana Spencer in 1981.

Inside, this big church feels big. At 515 feet long and 250 feet wide, it's Europe's fourth largest, after Rome (St. Peter's), Sevilla, and Milan. The spaciousness is accentuated by the relative lack of decoration. The simple, cream-colored ceiling and the clear glass in the windows light everything evenly. Wren wanted this: a simple, open church with nothing to hide. Unfortunately, only this entrance area keeps his original vision—the rest was encrusted with 19th-century Victorian ornamentation.

The **dome** you see, painted with scenes from the life of St.

Paul, is only the innermost of three. From the painted interior of the first dome, look up through the opening to see the light-filled lantern of the second dome. Finally, the whole thing is covered on the outside by the third and final dome, the shell of lead-covered wood that you see from the street. Wren's ingenious three-in-one design was psychological as well as functional—he wanted a low, shallow inner dome so worshippers wouldn't feel diminished.

Do a quick clockwise spin around the church. In the north transept (to your left as you face the altar), find the big painting *The Light of the World* (1904), by the Pre-Raphaelite William Holman Hunt. Inspired by Hunt's own experience of finding Christ during a moment of spiritual crisis, the crowd-pleasing work was criticized by art highbrows for being "syrupy" and "simple"—even as it became the most famous painting in Victorian England.

Along the left side of the choir is the modern statue *Mother and Child*, by the great modern sculptor Henry Moore. Typical of Moore's work, this Mary and Baby Jesus—inspired by the sight of British moms nursing babies in WWII bomb shelters—renders a traditional subject in an abstract, minimalist way.

The area behind the altar, with three bright and modern stained-glass windows, is the **American Memorial Chapel**—honoring the Americans who sacrificed their lives to save Britain in World War II. In colored panes that arch around the big windows, spot the American eagle (center window, to the left of Christ), George Washington (right window, upper-right corner), and symbols of all 50 states (find your state seal). In the carved wood beneath the windows, you'll see birds and foliage native to the US. The Roll of Honor (a 500-page book under glass, immediately behind the altar) lists the names of 28,000 US servicemen and women based in Britain who gave their lives during the war.

Around the other side of the choir is a shrouded statue honoring **John Donne** (1621-1631), a passionate preacher in old St. Paul's, as well as a great poet ("never wonder for whom the bell tolls—it tolls for thee").

In the south transept are monuments to military greats **Horatio Nelson,** who fought Napoleon, and **Charles Cornwallis,** who was finished off by George Washington at Yorktown.

Climbing the Dome: During your visit, you can climb 528 steps to reach the dome and great city views. Along the way, have some fun in the Whispering Gallery (257 steps up). Whisper sweet nothings into the wall, and your partner (and anyone else) standing far away can hear you. For best effects, try whispering (not talking) with your mouth close to the wall, while your partner stands a few dozen yards away with his or her ear to the wall.

Visiting the Crypt: The crypt is a world of historic bones and interesting cathedral models. Many legends are buried here—Horatio Nelson, who wore down Napoleon; the Duke of Wellington, who finished Napoleon off; and even Wren himself. Wren's actual tomb is marked by a simple black slab with no statue, though he considered the church itself to be his legacy. Back up in the nave, on the floor directly under the dome, is Christopher Wren's name and epitaph (written in Latin): "Reader, if you seek his monument, look around you."

▲▲▲Tower of London

The Tower has served as a castle in wartime, a king's residence in peacetime, and, most notoriously, as the prison and execution site

of rebels. You can see the crown jewels, take a witty Beefeater tour, and ponder the executioner's block that dispensed with Anne Boleyn, Sir Thomas More, and troublesome heirs to the throne.

Cost and Hours: £21, family-£55 (both prices include a 10 percent optional donation), entry fee includes Beefeater tour (described later), skip the £4 audioguide and the £5 guidebook; March-Oct Tue-Sat 9:00-17:30, Sun-Mon 10:00-17:30; Nov-Feb Tue-Sat 9:00-16:30, Sun-Mon 10:00-16:30; last entry 30 minutes before closing; cafeteria, Tube: Tower Hill, switchboard tel. 0844-482-7777, www.hrp.org.uk.

Advance Tickets: To avoid the long ticket-buying lines at the Tower, buy your ticket at the Trader's Gate gift shop, located down the steps from the Tower Hill Tube stop (tickets here are generally slightly cheaper than at the gate; similar, discounted "Fast Track" tickets are sold at various locations throughout London). You can also buy tickets, with credit card only, at the Tower Welcome Centre to the left of the normal ticket lines—though on busy days, it can be crowded here as well. It's easy to book online (www.hrp.org.uk, £1 discount, no fee) or by phone (tel. 0844-482-7799 within UK or tel. 011-44-20-3166-6000 from the US; £2 fee), then pick up your tickets at the Tower.

More Crowd-Beating Tips: It's most crowded in summer, on weekends (especially Sundays), and during school holidays. Any time of year, the line for the crown jewels—the best on earth—can be just as long as the line for tickets. For fewer crowds, try to arrive before 10:00 and go straight for the jewels, then tour the rest of the Tower. Crowds die down after 16:30.

Yeoman Warder (Beefeater) Tours: Today, while the Tower's military purpose is history, it's still home to the Beefeaters—the 35 Yeoman Warders and their families. (The original duty of the

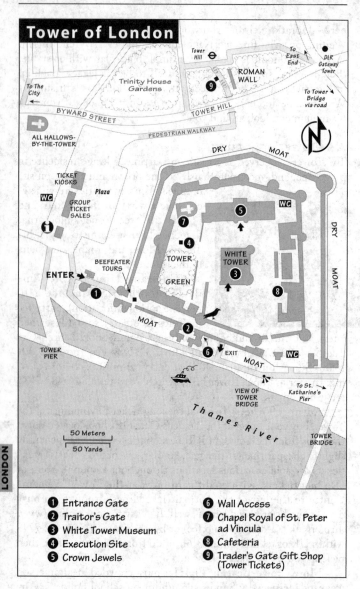

Tower of London

- **1** Entrance Gate
- **2** Traitor's Gate
- **3** White Tower Museum
- **4** Execution Site
- **5** Crown Jewels
- **6** Wall Access
- **7** Chapel Royal of St. Peter ad Vincula
- **8** Cafeteria
- **9** Trader's Gate Gift Shop (Tower Tickets)

Yeoman Warders was to guard the Tower, its prisoners, and the jewels.) The free, worthwhile, 1-hour Beefeater tours leave every 30 minutes from inside the gate (first tour at 10:00, last one at 15:30—or 14:30 in Nov-Feb). The boisterous Beefeaters are great entertainers, and their talks include lots of bloody anecdotes about the Tower and its history. They relish telling corny jokes.

Visiting the Tower: William I, still getting used to his new title of "the Conqueror," built the stone "White Tower" (1077-1097) to keep the Londoners in line. Standing high above the rest of old London, the White Tower provided a gleaming reminder of the monarch's absolute power over his subjects. If you made the wrong move here, you could be feasting on roast boar in the banqueting hall one night and chained to the walls of the prison the next. The Tower also served as an effective lookout for seeing invaders coming up the Thames.

This square, 90-foot-tall tower was the original structure that gave this castle complex of 20 towers its name. William's successors enlarged the complex to its present 18-acre size. Because of the security it provided, the Tower of London served over the centuries as a royal residence, the Royal Mint, the Royal Jewel House, and, most famously, as the prison and execution site of those who dared oppose the Crown.

You'll find more bloody history per square inch in this original tower of power than anywhere else in Britain. Inside the White Tower is a museum with exhibits re-creating medieval life and chronicling the torture and executions that took place here. In the Royal Armory, you'll see some suits of armor of Henry VIII—slender in his youth (c. 1515), heavy-set by 1540—with his bigger-is-better codpiece. On the top floor, see the Tower's actual execution ax and chopping block.

The actual **execution site,** however, in the middle of the Tower Green, looks just like a lawn. It was here that enemies of the crown would kneel before the king for the final time. With their hands tied behind their backs, they would say a final prayer, then lay their heads on a block, and—*shlit*—the blade would slice through their necks, their heads tumbling to the ground. Tower Green was the most prestigious execution site at the Tower. Henry VIII axed a couple of his ex-wives here (divorced readers can insert their own joke), including Anne Boleyn and his fifth wife, teenage Catherine Howard.

The Tower's hard stone and glittering **crown jewels** represent the ultimate power of the monarch. The Sovereign's Scepter is encrusted with the world's largest cut diamond—the 530-carat Star of Africa, beefy as a quarter-pounder. The Crown of the Queen Mother (Elizabeth II's famous mum, who died in 2002) has the 106-carat Koh-I-Noor diamond glittering on the front (considered unlucky for male rulers, it only adorns the crown of the king's wife). The Imperial State Crown is what the Queen wears for official functions such as the State Opening of Parliament. Among its 3,733 jewels are Queen Elizabeth I's former earrings (the hanging pearls, top center), a stunning 13th-century ruby look-alike in the center, and Edward the Confessor's ring (the blue sapphire on top, in the center of the Maltese cross of diamonds).

The Tower was defended by state-of-the-art **walls** and fortifications in the 13th century. Walking along them offers a good look at the walls, along with a fine view of the famous Tower Bridge, with its twin towers and blue spans.

Nearby: The iconic **Tower Bridge** (often mistakenly called London Bridge) was recently painted and restored. The hydraulically powered drawbridge was built in 1894 to accommodate the growing East End. While fully modern, its design was a retro Neo-Gothic look.

The South Bank

The South Bank of the Thames is a thriving arts and cultural center, tied together by the riverfront Jubilee Walkway.

▲▲**London Eye**—This giant Ferris wheel, towering above London opposite Big Ben, is the world's highest observation wheel and London's answer to the Eiffel Tower. Riding it is a memorable experience, even though London doesn't have much of a skyline, and the price is borderline outrageous. Whether you ride or not, the wheel is a sight to behold.

The experience starts with a brief (four-minute) and engaging show combining a 3-D movie with wind and water effects. Then it's time to spin around the Eye. Designed like a giant bicycle wheel, it's a pan-European undertaking: British steel and Dutch engineering, with Czech, German, French, and Italian mechanical parts. It's also very "green," running extremely efficiently and virtually silently. Twenty-five people ride in each of its 32 air-conditioned capsules for the 30-minute rotation (you go around only once). Each capsule has a bench, but most people stand. From the top of this 443-foot-high wheel even Big Ben looks small.

Cost: £19, or pay roughly twice as much for a combo-ticket with Madame Tussauds Waxworks (sold cheaper online), other packages are available. Buy tickets at the box office (in the corner of the County Hall building nearest the Eye), in advance by calling 0870-500-0600 or save 10 percent by booking online at www.londoneye.com.

Hours: Daily July-Aug 10:00-21:30, April-June 10:00-21:00,

LONDON

Sept-March 10:00-20:00, these are last-ascent times, closed Dec 25 and a few days in Jan for annual maintenance; Tube: Waterloo or Westminster. Thames boats come and go from Waterloo Pier at the foot of the wheel.

Crowd-Beating Tips: The London Eye is busiest between 11:00 and 17:00, especially on weekends year-round and every day in July and August. When it's crowded, you might have to wait up to 30 minutes to buy your ticket, then another 30-45 minutes to board your capsule. If you plan to visit during a busy time, call ahead or go online to pre-book your ticket, then punch your confirmation code into the automated machine in the ticket office (otherwise, you can pick up your ticket in the short "Groups and Ticket Collection" line at desk #5; if you pre-reserve, there's rarely a wait to pick up your ticket, but you'll still wait to board the wheel). You can pay an extra £10 for a Fast Track ticket that lets you jump the queue, but the time you save is probably not worth the expense.

By the Eye: The area next to the London Eye has developed a cotton-candy ambience of kitschy, kid-friendly attractions. There's an aquarium, game arcade, and London Film Museum dedicated to movies filmed in London, from *Harry Potter* to *Star Wars* (not to be confused with the far-superior British Film Institute, a.k.a. the BFI Southbank, just to the east).

▲▲**Tate Modern**—Dedicated in the spring of 2000, the striking museum across the river from St. Paul's opened the new cen-

tury with art from the previous one. Its powerhouse collection of Monet, Matisse, Dalí, Picasso, Warhol, and much more is displayed in a converted powerhouse.

The permanent collection is on the third and fifth floors. Paintings are arranged according to theme, not chronologically or by artist. Paintings by Picasso, for example, are scattered all over the building. Don't just come to see the Old Masters of modernism. Push your mental envelope with more recent works by Pollock, Miró, Bacon, Picabia, Beuys, Twombly, and others.

Of equal interest are the many temporary exhibits featuring cutting-edge art. Each year, the main hall features a different monumental installation by a prominent artist—always one of the highlights of the art world. The Tate is constructing a new wing to the south, which will double its exhibition space. While the performance halls should be open in 2013, the rest of the complex is set to open in 2014.

Cost and Hours: Free, but £4 donation appreciated, fee for special exhibitions, audioguide-£4, daily 10:00-18:00, Fri-Sat until 22:00, last entry to temporary exhibits 45 minutes before closing, especially crowded on weekend days, free 45-minute **guided tours** are offered about four times daily (ask for schedule at info desk), no photos beyond entrance hall, several cafés, tel. 020/7887-8888, www.tate.org.uk.

Getting There: Cross the Millennium Bridge from St. Paul's; or take the Tube to Southwark, London Bridge, or Mansion House and walk 10-15 minutes.

▲▲**Shakespeare's Globe**—This replica of the original Globe Theatre was built, half-timbered and thatched, to appear as it did in Shakespeare's time. (This is the first thatched roof constructed in London since they were outlawed after the Great Fire of 1666.) The Globe originally accommodated 2,200 people seated and another 1,000 standing. Today, slightly smaller and leaving space for reasonable aisles, the theater

holds 800 seated and 600 groundlings. Its promoters brag that the theater melds "the three A's"—actors, audience, and architecture—with each contributing to the play. The working theater hosts authentic performances of Shakespeare's plays with actors in period costumes, modern interpretations of his works, and some works by other playwrights.

The complex has three parts: the theater itself, the box office, and a museum. The Globe Exhibition ticket includes both a tour of the theater and the museum.

Cost and Hours: £13.50 includes museum and 40-minute tour, £10 when only the Rose Theatre is available for touring, tickets good all day; complex open daily 9:00-17:00; exhibition and tours: May-Sept—Globe tours offered mornings only with Rose Theatre tours in afternoon; Oct-April—Globe tours run all day, tours start every 15-30 minutes; on the South Bank directly across Thames over Southwark Bridge from St. Paul's, Tube: Mansion House or London Bridge plus a 10-minute walk; tel. 020/7902-1400 or 020/7902-1500, www.shakespearesglobe.com.

Eating: The Swan at the Globe café offers a sit-down restaurant (reservations recommended, tel. 020/7928-9444), a drinks-and-plates bar, and a sandwich-and-coffee cart (daily 9:00-closing, depending on performance times).

Shopping in London

London is great for shoppers—and thanks to the high prices, perhaps even better for window-shoppers. In the 1960s, London set the tone for Mod clothing, and it's been a major fashion capital ever since.

British clothing sizes are different from those in the US. For example, a woman's size 10 dress (US) is a UK size 14, and a size 8 woman's shoe (US) is a UK size 5½.

Most stores are open Monday through Saturday from roughly 10:00 to 18:00, and many close Sundays. Large department stores stay open until 20:00 or 21:00. For one-stop shopping for essential items, try large chain stores such as Marks & Spencer (www.marksandspencer.com).

West End High Fashion—You'll find big-name fashion stores along Regent Street (between Oxford Circus and Piccadilly), old-fashioned gentlemen's stores on Jermyn Street, bookstores along Charing Cross Road, and more boutiques around Covent Garden.

Harrods and "Harvey Nick's"—Near Hyde Park, you'll find London's most famous and touristy department store, **Harrods.** With more than four acres of retail space covering seven floors, it has everything from elephants to toothbrushes, from artisan cheese to a £10,000 toy car. (Mon-Sat 10:00-20:00, Sun 11:30-18:00, on Brompton Road, Tube: Knightsbridge, tel. 020/7730-1234, www.harrods.com).

A few blocks away is **Harvey Nichols.** Once Princess Diana's favorite (and now serving Kate Middleton), "Harvey Nick's" remains the department store du jour (Mon–Sat 10:00–20:00, Sun 12:00–18:00, near Harrods, 109–125 Knightsbridge, Tube: Knightsbridge, tel. 020/7235-5000, www.harveynichols.com).

Street Markets—London's weekend flea markets are legendary. **Covent Garden's** daily market is handy to other sightseeing (open daily 10:00–18:30, tel. 020-7836-9136, www.coventgardenlife.com). **Portobello Road Market** is the classic London street market. On Saturdays, this funky-yet-quaint Notting Hill street of pastel-painted houses and offbeat antiques shops is enlivened even more with 2,000 additional stalls (market is Sat 5:30–17:00, on Sundays everything is closed, Tube: Notting Hill Gate, tel. 020/7229-8354, www.portobelloroad.co.uk). **Camden Lock Market** in north London is a huge, trendy, youth-oriented arts-and-crafts festival. It runs daily 10:00–18:00, but is busiest on weekends (Tube: Camden Town, 020/7485-7963, www.camdenlockmarket.com).

London Chain Restaurants

I know—you're going to Britain to enjoy characteristic little hole-in-the-wall pubs, so mass-produced food is the farthest thing from your mind. But several good chains can be a nice break from pub grub. Each of these places has multiple branches throughout London—keep an eye out for the ones that sound good to you.

Carry-Out Chains

While the following places might have some seating, they're an easy place to grab some prepackaged food on the go.

Major supermarket chains have smaller, offshoot branches that specialize in sandwiches, salads, and other prepared foods "to go." These can be a picnicker's dream come true. Some shops are stand-alone, while others are located inside a larger store. The most prevalent—and best—is **M&S Simply Food** (part of the Marks & Spencer department-store chain; no seating but plasticware is provided). **Sainsbury's Local** grocery stores also offer some decent prepared food; **Tesco Express** and **Tesco Metro** are a distant third.

Other "cheap and cheery" chains, such as **Pret à Manger** and **Eat,** provide office workers with good, healthful sandwiches, salads, and pastries to go.

West Cornwall Pasty Company sells a variety of these traditional savory pies for around £3—as do many smaller, independent bakeries.

Sit-Down Chains

Busaba Eathai offers tasty £7-12 Thai dishes at mostly shared, square tables with boisterous atmosphere. (The Soho location is listed on page 987.)

LONDON

Eating in London

With "modern English" cuisine on the rise, London's sheer variety of foods—from every corner of its former empire and beyond—is astonishing. You'll be amazed at the number of hopping, happening new restaurants of all kinds. I've listed places by neighborhood—handy to your sightseeing. Pub grub (at one of London's 7,000 pubs) and ethnic restaurants (especially Indian and Chinese) are good low-cost options. Of course, picnicking is the fastest and cheapest way to go. Good grocery stores and sandwich shops, fine park

Wagamama Noodle Bar, serving up pan-Asian cuisine (udon noodles, fried rice, and curry dishes), is stylish, youthful, and popular. There's one in almost every midsize city in the UK, usually located in sprawling, loud halls filled with long shared tables and busy servers who scrawl your order on the placemat (£8-11 main dishes big enough for light eaters to share, good veggie options).

Masala Zone is a predictably good alternative to the many one-off, hole-in-the-wall Indian joints around town.

At **Yo! Sushi,** freshly prepared sushi dishes trundle past on a conveyor belt. Color-coded plates tell you how much each dish costs (£1.70-5), and a picture-filled menu explains what you're eating. Just help yourself.

Côte offers contemporary ambience and £9-14 French classics in a bistro setting.

Gourmet Burger Kitchen (GBK) assembles burgers that are, if not quite gourmet, very good. Choices range from a simple cheeseburger to more elaborate options, such as Jamaican (£7-8 burgers). Choose a table and order at the counter—they'll bring the food to you. **Byron** takes things up a notch, adding a pound or two to the price but offering more interesting interiors in exchange.

Loch Fyne Fish Restaurant, a Scottish chain, serves up fish, oysters, and mussels in a lively, upscale-but-unpretentious setting (£10-17 main dishes, early-bird deals).

Ask and **Pizza Express** serve quality pasta and pizza in a pleasant, sit-down atmosphere that's family-friendly. **Jamie's Italian** (from celebrity chef Jamie Oliver) is hipper and pricier, and feels more upmarket.

LONDON

benches, and polite pigeons abound in Britain's most expensive city.

I've clustered the following restaurants by neighborhood, to be handy to your sightseeing. You'll also find advice on eateries in the **National Gallery** on page 959, and on the **South Bank** near Shakespeare's Globe on page 980.

Near Trafalgar Square

The first three places, all of which provide a more "jolly olde" experience than high cuisine, are within about 100 yards of Trafalgar Square.

St. Martin-in-the-Fields Café in the Crypt is just right for a tasty meal on a monk's budget—maybe even on a monk's tomb. You'll dine sitting on somebody's gravestone in an ancient crypt. Their enticing buffet line is kept stocked all day, serving

Central London Eateries

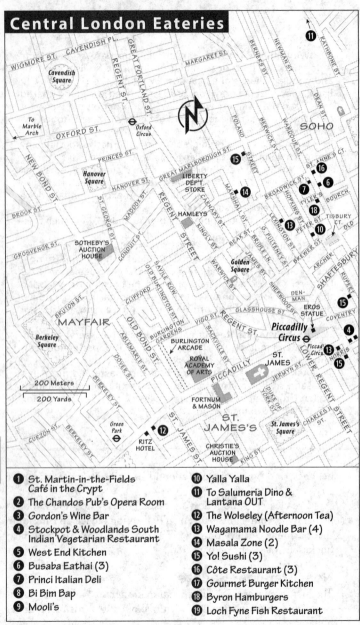

1. St. Martin-in-the-Fields Café in the Crypt
2. The Chandos Pub's Opera Room
3. Gordon's Wine Bar
4. Stockpot & Woodlands South Indian Vegetarian Restaurant
5. West End Kitchen
6. Busaba Eathai (3)
7. Princi Italian Deli
8. Bi Bim Bap
9. Mooli's
10. Yalla Yalla
11. To Salumeria Dino & Lantana OUT
12. The Wolseley (Afternoon Tea)
13. Wagamama Noodle Bar (4)
14. Masala Zone (2)
15. Yo! Sushi (3)
16. Côte Restaurant (3)
17. Gourmet Burger Kitchen
18. Byron Hamburgers
19. Loch Fyne Fish Restaurant

LONDON

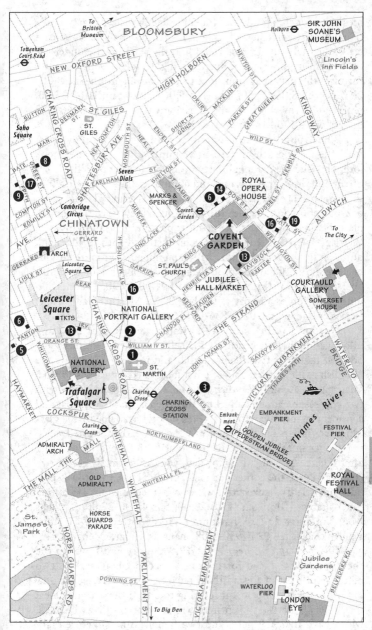

breakfast, lunch, and dinner (£6-10 cafeteria plates, hearty traditional desserts, free jugs of water). They also serve a restful cream tea (£6, daily 14:00-18:00). You'll find the café directly under the St. Martin-in-the-Fields Church, facing Trafalgar Square—enter through the glass pavilion next to the church (Mon-Tue 8:00-20:00, Wed 8:00-22:30, Thu-Sat 8:00-21:00, Sun 11:00-18:00, profits go to the church, Tube: Charing Cross, tel. 020/7766-1158 or 020/7766-1100).

The Chandos Pub's Opera Room floats amazingly apart from the tacky crush of tourism around Trafalgar Square. Look for it opposite the National Portrait Gallery (corner of William IV Street and St. Martin's Lane) and climb the stairs (to the right of the pub entrance) to the Opera Room. This is a fine Trafalgar rendezvous point and wonderfully local pub. They serve traditional, plain-tasting £5-8 pub meals—meat pies and fish-and-chips are their specialty. The ground-floor pub is stuffed with regulars and offers snugs (private booths), the same menu, and more serious beer drinking. Chandos proudly serves the local Samuel Smith beer at £4 a pint (kitchen open daily 11:00-19:00, Fri and Sun until 18:00, order and pay at the bar, 29 St. Martin's Lane, Tube: Leicester Square, tel. 020/7836-1401).

Gordon's Wine Bar, with a simple, steep staircase leading into a candlelit 15th-century wine cellar, is filled with dusty old bottles, faded British memorabilia, and nine-to-fivers. At the "English rustic" buffet, choose a hot meal or cold meat dish with a salad (figure around £7-8/dish); the £8.20 cheese plate comes with two cheeses, bread, and a pickle. Then step up to the wine bar and consider the many varieties of wine and port available by the glass (this place is passionate about port). The low, carbon-crusted vaulting deeper in the back seems to intensify the Hogarth-painting atmosphere. Although it's crowded, you can normally corral two chairs and grab the corner of a table. On hot days, the crowd spills out onto a leafy back patio, where a barbecue cooks for a long line of tables (Mon-Sat 11:00-23:00, Sun 12:00-22:00, 2 blocks from Trafalgar Square, bottom of Villiers Street at #47, Tube: Embankment, tel. 020/7930-1408, manager Gerard Menan).

Cheaper Options near Piccadilly: Hungry and broke in the theater district? Head for Panton Street (off Haymarket, two blocks southeast of Piccadilly Circus), where several hardworking little places compete, all seeming to offer a three-course meal for about £9. Peruse the entire block (vegetarian, Pizza Express, Moroccan, Thai, Chinese, and two famous diners) before making your choice. **Stockpot** is a meat, potatoes, gravy, and mushy-peas kind of place, famous and rightly popular for its edible, cheap English meals (£6-11, Mon-Sat 7:00-23:00, Sun 7:00-22:00, cash only, 38-40 Panton Street, tel. 020/7839-5142). The **West End**

Kitchen (across the street at #5, same hours and menu) is a direct competitor that's also well-known and just as good (£5-10 meals). Vegetarians may prefer the **Woodlands South Indian Vegetarian Restaurant,** which serves an impressive £19 *thali* (otherwise £7-9 main courses, 37 Panton Street).

In Soho

London has a trendy scene that most Beefeater-seekers miss entirely. Foodies who want to eat well skip the more staid and touristy zones near Piccadilly and Trafalgar Square, and head to Soho instead. The following options are on or near Wardour Street—ground zero for creative restaurateurs hoping to break into the big leagues. Strolling up this street—particularly from Brewer Street northward—you can take your pick from a world of options: Thai, Indonesian, Vietnamese, Italian, French...and English.

The **Busaba Eathai** Thai restaurant is a hit with locals for its snappy (sometimes rushed) service, casual-yet-high-energy ambience, and good, inexpensive Thai cuisine. Be prepared to be wedged communally around big, square 16-person hardwood tables or in two-person tables by the window—with everyone in the queue staring at your noodles (£7-12 meals, Mon-Thu 12:00-23:00, Fri-Sat 12:00-23:30, Sun 12:00-22:30, 106 Wardour Street, tel. 020/7255-8686).

Princi is a vast, bright, efficient, wildly popular Italian deli/bakery with Milanese flair. Along one wall is a long counter with display cases offering a tempting array of pizza rustica, panini sandwiches, focaccia, a few pasta dishes, and desserts (look in the window from the street to see their wood-fired oven in action). Order your food at the counter, then find a space at a long shared table; or get it "to go" for an affordable and fast meal (£3-5 light meals, £7-8 pastas, Mon-Sat 8:00-24:00, Sun 8:30-22:00, 135 Wardour Street, tel. 020/7478-8888).

Bi Bim Bap is named for what it sells: *bibimbap* (literally "mixed rice"), a scalding stone bowl filled with rice, thinly sliced veggies, and topped with a fried egg. Mix it all up with your spoon, flavor it to taste with the two sauces, then dig in with your chopsticks. While purists go with the straightforward rice bowl, you can pay a few pounds extra to add other toppings—including chicken, *bulgogi* (marinated beef strips), and mushrooms. Though the food is traditional Korean, the stylish, colorful interior lets you know you're in Soho (£7-10 meals, Mon-Fri 12:00-15:00 & 18:00-23:00, Sat 12:00-23:00, closed Sun, 11 Greek Street, tel. 020/7287-3434).

Mooli's is made-to-order for a quick, affordable, flavorful jolt of Indian street food. Their £5-6 *mooli* wraps, sort of like an Indian burrito, are filled with pork, chicken, beef, *paneer* (cheese),

LONDON

chickpea, or spicy goat. Top it with your choice of chutneys and Indian salsas. Eat in or grab one to go; their "mini" version makes a good £3 snack (Mon-Sat 10:00-23:30, closed Sun, 50 Frith Street, tel. 020/7494-9075).

Yalla Yalla is a hole-in-the-wall serving up high-quality Beirut street food—hummus, baba ghanoush, tabbouleh, and *shawarmas*. Stylish as you'd expect for Soho, it's tucked down a seedy alley between a sex shop and a tattoo parlor. Eat in the cramped and cozy interior or one of the few outdoor tables, or get your food to go (£3-4 sandwiches, £4-6 *mezes,* £7 *mezes* platter available until 17:00, £10-12 bigger dishes, daily 10:00-22:00, 1 Green's Court—just north of Brewer Street, tel. 020/7287-7663).

Near the British Museum

Salumeria Dino serves up hearty sandwiches, pasta, and Italian coffee. Dino, a native of Naples, has run his little shop for more than 30 years and has managed to create a classic Italian deli that's so authentic, you'll walk out singing "O Sole Mio" (£3-5 sandwiches, £1 take-away cappuccinos, Mon-Fri 9:00-17:00, closed Sat-Sun, 15 Charlotte Place, tel. 020/7580-3938).

Lantana OUT, next door to Salumeria Dino, is an Australian coffee shop that sells modern soups, sandwiches, and salads at their take-away window. Their changing menu features a soup-salad-sweet combo deal for £5.50 (£3-7 meals, pricier sit-down café next door, Mon-Fri 7:30-15:00, café open Sat-Sun 9:00-17:00, 13 Charlotte Place, tel. 020/7637-3347).

Near St. Paul's Cathedral

De Gustibus Sandwiches is where an artisan bakery meets the public, offering fresh, you-design-it sandwiches, salads, and soups. Communication can be difficult, but it's worth the effort. Just one block below St. Paul's, it has simple seating or take-out picnic sacks for lugging to one of the great nearby parks (£4-8 sandwiches, £6 hot dishes, Mon-Fri 7:00-17:00, closed Sat-Sun, from church steps follow signs to youth hostel a block downhill, 53-55 Carter Lane, tel. 020/7236-0056; another outlet is inside the Borough Market in Southwark).

Near the British Library

Drummond Street (running just west of Euston Station—see map on page 968) is famous for cheap and good Indian vegetarian food (£5-10 dishes, £7 lunch buffets). Consider **Chutneys** (124 Drummond, tel. 020/7388-0604) and **Ravi Shankar** (133-135 Drummond, tel. 020/7388-6458) for a good *thali* (both open long hours daily).

Taking Tea in London

Tea Terms

The cheapest "tea" on the menu is generally a "cream tea"; the most expensive is the "champagne tea." **Cream tea** is simply a pot of tea and a homemade scone or two with jam and thick clotted cream. (For maximum pinkie-waving taste per calorie, slice your scone thin like a miniature loaf of bread.) **Afternoon tea**—what Americans usually call "high tea"—generally is a cream tea plus a tier of three plates holding small finger foods (such as cucumber sandwiches) and an assortment of small pastries. **Champagne tea** includes all of the goodies, plus a glass of champagne. **High tea** to the British generally means a more substantial late-afternoon or early-evening meal, often served with meat or eggs.

Tearooms, which often also serve appealing light meals, are usually open for lunch and close about 17:00. At all the places listed below, it's perfectly acceptable for two people to order one afternoon tea and one cream tea (at about £5) and share the afternoon tea's goodies. Fancier places still require a jacket and tie (and a bigger bank account), but most listed here (except, perhaps, The Wolseley and Fortnum & Mason) happily welcome tourists in jeans and sneakers.

Places to Sip Tea

The Wolseley serves a good afternoon tea in between their meal service. Split one with your companion and enjoy two light meals at a great price in classic elegance (£10 cream tea, £22 afternoon tea—can be split between two people, served Mon-Fri 15:00-18:30, Sat 15:30-17:30, Sun 15:30-18:30).

The **Fortnum & Mason** department store offers tea at several different restaurants within its walls; the easiest choice is "Take Tea in the Parlour" for £18 (Mon-Sat 10:00-18:45, Sun 12:00-16:45), or try the all-out "Gallery Tea" for £26 (daily 15:00-17:00; 181 Piccadilly, tel. 0845-602-5694, www.fortnumandmason.com).

Other Places Serving Good Tea: **The National Dining Rooms,** within the National Gallery on Trafalgar Square, offers a £17 afternoon tea (served 15:00-17:00, in Sainsbury Wing of National Gallery, Tube: Charing Cross or Leicester Square, tel. 020/7747-2525, www.peytonandbyrne.co.uk). **The National Café,** at the other end of the building, is a bit cheaper (£15 afternoon tea served 15:00-17:30).

Cheaper Options: If you want the teatime experience but are put off by the price, most department stores on Oxford Street (including those between Oxford Circus and Bond Street Tube stations) offer an afternoon tea. **John Lewis'** mod third-floor

What If I Miss My Boat?

Remember that you can get help from the cruise line's port agent (listed on the destination information sheet distributed on the ship) and the local TI (see page 940). If the port agent suggests a costly solution (such as a private car with a driver), you may want to consider public transit.

You'll very likely find that your best option is to **fly.** London has several airports, and many low-cost, no-frills carriers are based here, offering frequent and cheap (sometimes even last-minute) flights to just about anywhere. Check www.skyscanner.com for options. For information on London's airports, see "Airport Connections," later.

Overland, it could be more complicated to reach your next destination. The fast option is to head back to London and hop the speedy Eurostar ("Chunnel") train under the English Channel to Paris (then 2 hours by train to **Le Havre**) or Brussels (1.5 hours by train from **Zeebrugge,** 3.5 hours by train from **Amsterdam**). For points west or north (such as **Copenhagen** or **Berlin/Warnemünde**), you'll probably find it's best to Chunnel to Brussels and connect from there.

To reach **Le Havre,** you could consider some of the ferry connections across the English Channel from South England, such as LD Lines' route from Portsmouth to Le Havre (www.ldline.co.uk) or Brittany Ferries' route from Portsmouth to Ouistreham (9 miles north of Caen, www.brittany-ferries.co.uk).

Local **travel agents** in London, Southampton, or Dover can help you. For more advice on what to do if you miss the boat, see page 144.

brasserie serves a nice afternoon tea platter from 15:00 (£10, on Oxford Street one block west of the Bond Street Tube station, tel. 020/3073-0626, www.johnlewis.com). Many museums and bookstores have cafés serving afternoon tea goodies à la carte, where you can put together a spread for less than £10—**Waterstone's** fifth-floor café is one of the best.

Returning to Southampton or Dover

To make it back to your ship, follow the instructions under "Getting from Central London to the Cruise Ports," on page 993.

Starting or Ending Your Cruise in London

If your cruise begins and/or ends in London, you'll want plenty of extra time here; for most travelers, two days is a bare minimum. For a longer visit here, pick up my *Rick Steves' London* guidebook; for other destinations in the country, see *Rick Steves' England* or *Rick Steves' Great Britain*.

Airport Connections

London has six airports. Most tourists arrive at **Heathrow** or **Gatwick** airport, although flights from elsewhere in Europe may land at **Stansted, Luton, Southend,** or **London City** airport.

To get from any airport to your cruise port (or vice versa), you'll have to connect through London. I've given specific directions for each airport below, followed by tips for continuing on to Southampton or Dover. For a list of hotels in London, see the end of this chapter.

Some cruise lines offer convenient **shuttle bus service** directly from the airport to the cruise port; check with your cruise line for details.

Heathrow Airport
One of the world's busiest airports, Heathrow has five terminals, T-1 through T-5. Each terminal has all the necessary travelers' services (info desks, ATMs, shops, eateries, etc.). T-1, T-2, and T-3 are connected and walkable, while T-4 and T-5 are separate and farther away. You can travel between terminals on free trains and buses, but it can be time-consuming—plan ahead if you'll need to change terminals. For airport and flight information, call 0844-335-1801 or visit www.heathrowairport.com (airport code: LHR).

Getting from Heathrow to London
To get between Heathrow and London (14 miles away), you have several options:

Taxi: The one-hour trip costs £45–70 to west and central London, for up to four people. Just get in the queue outside the terminal.

Tube: For £4.50, the Tube takes you from any Heathrow terminal to downtown London in 50–60 minutes on the Piccadilly Line (6/hour). Follow signs in the terminal to the Tube station. Before buying a Heathrow-to-London ticket, consider buying an Oyster card or Travelcard covering Zone 1-2 (central London) and

Public Transportation near London

To North England & Scotland

To York & Scotland

King's Lynn • Norwich

Coventry • ENGLAND

Long Buckby • Bedford • Hunt. • Ely

Stratford-upon-Avon • Warwick • Leam. Spa • Cambridge

Worcester • Moreton • Banbury • Luton

Cheltenham • Stow • Oxford • Stansted

COTSWOLDS • Blenheim • Didcot • To Hoek van Holland

To Cardiff • Swindon • Reading • Slough • Harwich

Avebury • Windsor • London • London City • Southend

Bristol • Bath • Bedwyn • Heathrow • Greenwich • To Ostende

Wells • Stonehenge • EUROSTAR • Ramsgate • Canterbury • Dover

Glaston-bury • Salisbury • South-ampton • Gatwick • Ashford • Rye • (CHUNNEL) • Calais

To Cornwall • Poole • Brighton • East-bourne • Hastings • Calais-Fréthun

Weymouth • Bourne-mouth • Isle of Wight • English Channel • To Paris

Note: Bus Lines Follow Most Rail Lines

⋯⋯ Rail
--- Bus
⋯⋯ Boat

30 Kilometers

30 Miles (approx. scale)

FRANCE

paying a small supplement for the Heathrow-to-London portion.

Train: From terminals T-1/T-2/T-3, the **Heathrow Connect** train goes to Paddington Station (£9.10 one-way, 2/hour, 30 minutes, tel. 0845-678-6975, www.heathrowconnect.com). From T-1/T-2/T-3 and T-5, the **Heathrow Express** goes to Paddington (£19, 4/hour, 15–20 minutes, tel. 0845-600-1515, www.heathrowexpress.co.uk).

Bus: There's a central bus station outside terminals T-1/T-2/T-3. National Express buses go to Victoria Coach Station near the Victoria train and Tube station (£5, 1–2/hour, 45–60 minutes, tel. 0871-781-8181, www.nationalexpress.com).

Heathrow Shuttle: These share-the-ride shuttle vans work like those at home, carrying passengers directly to or from their hotel (£15/person, book at least 24 hours in advance, tel. 0845-257-8068, www.heathrowshuttle.com).

From London to Heathrow: To get to Heathrow from central London, your transportation options are the same as above. Here are a few tips: Confirm with your airline in advance which terminal your flight will use, to avoid having to transfer between terminals. If arriving by Tube, note that not every Piccadilly Line train stops at every terminal. Before boarding, make sure your train is going to the terminal you want. A taxi arranged through

LONDON

your hotel can often be cheaper (£30–40) than from Heathrow to London. Bold negotiators may do even better by flagging a cab down on the street and asking for their best "off-meter" rate.

Gatwick and London's Other Airports

Of London's five airports, **Gatwick** is second-biggest (tel. 0844-335-1802, www.gatwickairport.com). To get from Gatwick into London, **Gatwick Express trains** shuttle conveniently to Victoria Station (£19 one-way, 4/hour, 30 minutes, tel. 0845-850-1530, www.gatwickexpress.com).

London's other, lesser airports are **Stansted Airport** (tel. 0870-0000-303, www.stanstedairport.com), **Luton Airport** (tel. 01582/405-100, www.london-luton.co.uk), **London City Airport** (tel. 020/7646-0088, www.londoncityairport.com), and **Southend Airport** (tel. 01702/608-100, www.southendairport.com).

Getting from Central London to the Cruise Ports

Even if you're coming directly from any of London's airports, you'll need to transfer through London to reach either Southampton or Dover (unless your cruise line offers **shuttle service** from the airport to your ship). For either port, also ask your cruise line whether they're offering a shuttle from the train station in Southampton or Dover to your ship. Compare it to the taxi cost to decide if it's right for you.

To Southampton

To reach Southampton's cruise ports, bus, Tube, or taxi to London Waterloo train station, where trains depart twice hourly to Southampton Central (£34.10 "single"/one-way, 1.25 hours; a few more options with a change in Basingstoke; a few slow trains go from London Victoria in 2.5 hours). Don't get off at "Southampton Airport Parkway"—stay on until "Southampton Central."

Exiting the station in Southampton, you'll find a row of **taxis** ready to take you to your ship. Figure around £5, but it shouldn't be more than £7-8 (£1 extra on Sun)—ask for an estimate first, then insist on the meter.

If you're packing light and feeling thrifty and energetic, you could take advantage of the **free Citylink bus** that departs from the curb just outside the station; however, note that it does not take you all the way to your ship—you'll still have to walk between 10 and 25 minutes, depending on where your ship is. The bus makes more sense for City Cruise Terminal or Ocean Cruise Terminal; for Mayflower or QEII terminals, take a taxi. For details on the Citylink bus, see page 903.

LONDON

To Dover

Trains head to Dover from various London stations. The fastest connection is on the "Javelin" train from St. Pancras Station (£38.10 "single"/one-way hourly, 1.25 hours). Slower trains to Dover leave from Victoria or Charing Cross Stations (for either one: £31.20 "single"/one-way, hourly, 2 hours).

If you're staying near Victoria or Charing Cross Stations, you might as well take the train from there; but all other things being equal, I'd take the faster connection from St. Pancras Station. First, ride the Tube or bus to St. Pancras. Entering the station at the front, walk all the way down the very long main hall (passing the Eurostar terminal) to the back end, then jog right to find the National Rail ticket offices and machines. Ride the escalator up to tracks 11-13, where trains depart for Dover.

Arriving at Dover Priory Station, your best bet is to pay £7-8 for a **taxi** to your ship. While it's possible to walk 15 minutes to Market Square to catch a **shuttle bus** to your ship, two people can take a taxi for about the same price. There's no public bus from the station to the cruise port, and walking the entire way is dull and inadvisable with luggage.

Departing from London

If your cruise finishes at Southampton or Dover, first head into London using the instructions at the beginning of this chapter. From there, you can make your way to your departure airport, using the tips under "Airport Connections," earlier.

Hotels in London

If you need a hotel in London before or after your cruise, here are a few to consider. London is an expensive city for lodging. Cheaper rooms are relatively dumpy. Don't expect £130 cheeriness in an £80 room. For £70, you'll get a double with breakfast in a safe, cramped, and dreary place with minimal service and the bathroom down the hall. For £90, you'll get a basic, clean, reasonably cheery double with a private bath in a usually cramped, cracked-plaster building, or a soulless but comfortable room without breakfast in a huge Motel 6-type place. My London splurges, at £160-290, are spacious, thoughtfully appointed places good for entertaining or romancing.

Looking for Hotel Deals Online: Given London's high hotel prices, using the Internet can help you score a deal. Various websites list rooms in high-rise, three- and four-star business hotels. You'll give up the charm and warmth of a family-run establishment, and breakfast probably won't be included, but you might find that the price is right. Start by browsing the websites of several chains to get a sense of typical rates and online deals. Midrange chains to consider include Premier Inn (www.premierinn.com), Travelodge (www.travelodge.co.uk), Ibis (www.ibishotel.com), Jurys Inn (www.jurysinns.com), and the stripped-down easyHotel (www.easyhotel.com). Pricier London hotel chains include Millennium/Copthorne (www.millenniumhotels.com), Thistle (www.thistle.com), Intercontinental/Holiday Inn (www.ichotels group.com), Radisson (www.radisson.com), Hilton (www.hilton .com), and Red Carnation (www.redcarnationhotels.com).

Nightlife: London bubbles with top-notch entertainment seven days a week: plays, movie premieres, concerts, Gilbert and Sullivan, tango lessons, stand-up comedy, Baha'i meetings, walking tours, shopping, museums open late, and the endlessly entertaining pub scene. Perhaps your best entertainment is just to take the Tube to Leicester Square on a pleasant evening, and explore the bustling West End. The two best sources for what's on are *Time Out* magazine (£3, sold everywhere, www.timeout.com) and the TI's free monthly *London Planner*.

Theater (a.k.a. "Theatre"): London's theater scene rivals Broadway's in quality and usually beats it in price. Choose from 200 offerings—Shakespeare, glitzy musicals, sex farces, serious chamber drama, cutting-edge fringe, revivals starring movie celebs, and more. London does it all well. To see what's showing, pick up the Official London Theatre Guide or (free at hotels and box offices) or check www.officiallondontheatre.co.uk. Tickets range from about £15 to £60. Buy in person from the theater box office (no booking fee), or order by phone (some charge a booking fee) or online from the theater's website (£2-3 booking fee). Other easy online sites (which charge similar booking fees) are www .ticketmaster.co.uk and www.seetickets.com. The famous half-price "tkts" booth at Leicester Square sells discounted tickets for top-price seats to shows on the push list (Mon-Sat 10:00–19:00, Sun 11:00–16:00, check the day's list of available shows at www .tkts.co.uk). Other ticket agencies, located in offices around London, can be convenient but generally charge a 25 percent fee above the face value. Most theaters are found in the West End, between Piccadilly and Covent Garden, especially along Shaftesbury Avenue. **Shakespeare's Globe** (on the South Bank) presents a full repertoire May through September in a thatched, open-air replica of the Bard's original theater. The £5 "groundling" tickets—standing-room at the foot of the stage—are most fun (tel. 020/7401-9919, www.shakespeareglobe.com).

Victoria Station Neighborhood

The streets behind Victoria Station teem with little, moderately priced-for-London B&Bs. It's a safe, surprisingly tidy, and decent area without a hint of the trashy, touristy glitz of the streets in front of the station.

$$$ Lime Tree Hotel, enthusiastically run by Charlotte and Matt, comes with 25 spacious, stylish, comfortable, thoughtfully decorated rooms and a fun-loving breakfast room (Sb-£99, Db-£150, larger superior Db-£175, Tb-£195, family room-£210, usually cheaper Jan-Feb, free Internet access and Wi-Fi, small lounge opens onto quiet garden, 135 Ebury Street, tel. 020/7730-8191, www .limetreehotel.co.uk, info@limetreehotel.co .uk, Ariane manages the office, trusty Alan covers the night shift).

$$ Luna Simone Hotel rents 36 fresh, spacious, nicely remodeled rooms with modern bathrooms. It's a smartly managed place, run for more than 40 years by twins Peter and Bernard—and Bernard's son Mark—and they still seem to enjoy their work (Sb-£75, Db-£110, Tb-£135, Qb-£165, these prices with cash and this book in 2013, free Internet access and Wi-Fi, near the corner of Charlwood Street and Belgrave Road at 47 Belgrave Road, handy bus #24 to Victoria Station and Trafalgar Square stops out front, tel. 020/7834-5897, www.lunasimonehotel.com, stay@luna simonehotel.com).

$ Cherry Court Hotel, run by the friendly and industrious Patel family, rents 12 very small but bright and well-designed rooms in a central location. Considering London's sky-high prices, this is a fine budget choice (Sb-£55, Db-£65, Tb-£105, Qb-£120, Quint/b-£130, these prices with this book in 2013, 5 percent fee to pay with credit card, fruit-basket breakfast in room, air-con, free Internet access and Wi-Fi, laundry, peaceful garden patio, 23 Hugh Street, tel. 020/7828-2840, fax 020/7828-0393, www.cherry courthotel.co.uk, info@cherrycourthotel.co.uk).

South Kensington

To stay on a quiet street so classy it doesn't allow hotel signs, surrounded by trendy shops and colorful restaurants, call "South Ken" your London home. Shoppers like being a short walk from Harrods and the designer shops of King's Road and Chelsea. When I splurge, I splurge here.

$$$ Aster House, well-run by friendly and accommodating Simon and Leonie Tan, has a cheerful lobby, lounge, and breakfast room. Its 13 rooms are comfy and quiet, with TV, phone, and air-conditioning. Enjoy breakfast or just lounging in the whisperelegant Orangery, a glassy greenhouse. Simon and Leonie offer free loaner mobile phones to their guests (Sb-£125, Db-£190, bigger Db-£235 or £270, does not include 20 percent VAT; significant discount offered to readers of this book in 2013—up to 20 percent discount if you book three or more nights, up to 25 percent discount for five or more nights; additional 5 percent off with cash, check website for specials, pay Internet access, free Wi-Fi, 3 Sumner Place, tel. 020/7581-5888, fax 020/7584-4925, www.aster house.com, asterhouse@btinternet.com).

$$$ Number Sixteen, for well-heeled travelers, packs over-the-top formality and class into its 41 rooms, plush lounges, and tranquil garden. It's in a labyrinthine building, with boldly modern decor—perfect for an urban honeymoon (Sb-from £140, Db-from £225—but prices are soft, ask for discounted "seasonal rates," especially on weekends and in Aug—subject to availability, does not include 20 percent VAT, breakfast buffet in the garden-£18 continental or £19 full English, elevator, free Internet access, pay Wi-Fi, 16 Sumner Place, tel. 020/7589-5232, fax 020/7584-8615, US tel. 800-553-6674, www.firmdalehotels.com, sixteen@firm dale.com).

Marble Arch Neighborhood

This neighborhood is located north of Hyde Park and near Oxford Street, a busy shopping destination. There's a convenient Marks & Spencer department store within walking distance.

$$$ The 22 York Street B&B offers a casual alternative in the city center, renting 10 traditional, hardwood, comfortable rooms, each named for a notable London landmark (Sb-£95, Db-£129, free Internet access and Wi-Fi, inviting lounge; from Baker Street Tube station, walk 2 blocks down Baker Street and take a right to 22 York Street—since there's no sign, just look for #22; tel. 020/7224-2990, www.22yorkstreet.co.uk, mc@22yorkstreet.co.uk, energetically run by Liz and Michael Callis).

$$$ The Sumner Hotel rents 19 rooms in a 19th-century Georgian townhouse. Decorated with fancy modern Italian furniture, this swanky place packs in all the extras (Db-£170-220 depending on size, 20 percent discount with this book, cheaper off-season, extra bed-£60, air-con, elevator, free Wi-Fi, 54 Upper Berkeley Street, a block and a half off Edgware Road, Tube: Marble Arch, tel. 020/7723-2244, fax 0870-705-8767, www.the sumner.com, hotel@thesumner.com).

LONDON

PARIS
France

France Practicalities

 France is Europe's most diverse, tasty, and, in many ways, most exciting country to explore. It's a complex cultural bouillabaisse—and a day in port at Le Havre lets you get an enticing taste. France is a big country by European standards, but it's only about the size of Texas. Bordering eight countries, France has three impressive mountain ranges (the Alps, Pyrenees, and Massif Central), two very different coastlines (Atlantic and Mediterranean), cosmopolitan cities (including Paris), charming villages (such as Honfleur), and romantic castles. The majority of its population of 65 million people is Roman Catholic, and virtually everyone speaks French.

Money: 1 euro (€) = about \$1.30. An ATM is called a *distributeur*. The local VAT (value-added sales tax) rate is 19.6 percent; the minimum purchase eligible for a VAT refund is €175 (for details on refunds, see page 139).

Language: The native language is French. For useful phrases, see page 1107.

Emergencies: In case of any emergency, dial 112; to summon an ambulance, dial 15. In case of theft or loss, see page 131.

Time Zone: France is on Central European Time (the same as most of the Continent, one hour ahead of Great Britain, and six/nine hours ahead of the East/West Coasts of the US).

Embassies in Paris: The **US embassy** is at 4 Avenue Gabriel (tel. 01 43 12 22 22, http://france.usembassy.gov). The **Canadian embassy** is at 35 Avenue Montaigne (tel. 01 44 43 29 00, www.amb-canada.fr). Call ahead for passport services.

Phoning: France's country code is 33; to call from another country to France, dial the international access code (011 from the US/Canada, 00 from Europe, or + from a mobile phone), then 33, followed by the local number (drop the initial zero). For local calls within France, just dial the number as it appears in this book—whether you're calling from across the street or across the country. To place an international call from France, dial 00, the code of the country you're calling (1 for US and Canada), and the phone number. For more tips, see page 1110.

Tipping: Restaurant prices already include a tip, and most French people never leave anything extra, but for special service, it's kind to tip up to 5 percent. To tip a cabbie, round up a bit (if the fare is €13, pay €14). For more tips on tipping, see page 143.

Tourist Information: www.us.franceguide.com

PARIS
and the PORT of LE HAVRE

Le Havre • Paris • Honfleur • D-Day Beaches • Rouen

Paris—the City of Light—offers sweeping boulevards, chatty crêpe stands, chic boutiques, and world-class art galleries. Sip decaf with deconstructionists at a sidewalk café, then step into an Impressionist painting in a tree-lined park. Climb Notre-Dame and rub shoulders with the gargoyles. Cruise the Seine, zip to the top of the Eiffel Tower, or saunter down Avenue des Champs-Elysées. Master the Louvre and Orsay museums.

To reach Paris from the port city of Le Havre, you'll ride a train for just over two hours each way. If you'd rather stick closer to your ship, consider these alternatives (also covered in this chapter): the harbor town of Honfleur (30 minutes by bus); the historic D-Day beaches (an hour or so to the west); and the pleasant small city of Rouen (one hour by train).

Planning Your Time

Most visitors arriving at Le Havre will zip into Paris. While the round-trip is time-consuming (about 2.25 hours each way by train), if this is your one chance to experience the City of Light, it's hard to resist. On the other hand, several good, easier-to-visit options sit much closer to Le Havre—worth considering for those who've already been to Paris (or want to save it for a longer visit).

Here are your basic options:

• **Paris:** With just a few hours in Paris, you'll need to be selective—but if that's all the time you have, you can still see a lot. For details, see page 1014.

• **Honfleur:** An easy (though relatively infrequent) bus ride from Le Havre, this sleepy, colorful port town that inspired the Impressionists can fill a lazy day.

Excursions from Le Havre

Most cruisers can't resist Paris' allure. Yes, it takes a while to reach, but even a few hours there leaves you with some powerful memories. If you're heading into Paris, consider skipping the excursions and doing it on your own, by train (using the advice in this chapter). On the other hand, if you've already been to Paris—or want to save it for a longer trip—there's no shortage of fascinating destinations near Le Havre. Because the destinations in Normandy (especially the D-Day beaches) are challenging to efficiently link using public transportation, a guided excursion (or a privately arranged guide) can be a smart choice here.

In and near Paris: The basic excursion option is a bus-and-riverboat tour of the city, with fleeting glimpses of the Arc de Triomphe, Champs-Elysées, Opéra Garnier, Louvre, Isle de la Cité with Notre-Dame Cathedral, Latin Quarter, and Hôtel des Invalides. Some tours include a guided tour of the **Louvre;** on others, you'll get about three hours of free time to see what you'd like on your own. For even more independence, the cruise lines' **Paris On Your Own** excursion—a round-trip bus ride with no guiding—is pricier than a round-trip train ticket ($110-130 for the excursion, compared to about $85 for the train), but saves you the hassle and stress of getting there and back.

Just outside Paris, the sumptuous **Palace of Versailles** (with its sprawling gardens and famously opulent Hall of Mirrors) is another popular excursion. As the public-transit connection from Le Havre to Versailles is a hassle, the palace is best seen by excursion.

Between Paris and Normandy: The city of **Rouen** has a charming old town, a church honoring Joan of Arc (who was burned here), and a cathedral that was famously painted 30 different times by Claude Monet as a way to study how light clings to surfaces. Note that Rouen is easy to reach by train from Le

---

- **D-Day Beaches:** The historic beaches of the WWII Allied invasion, west of Le Havre, are best visited with a guide.
- **Rouen:** About halfway to Paris on the train line, this city (with a cobbled old town and historic ties to Joan of Arc) is worth a day.
- **More Normandy:** With a driver or on an excursion, you can reach other points in Normandy—such as **Caen** (top-notch D-Day Museum), **Bayeux** (historic tapestry), and the evocative pilgrim town of **Mont St-Michel.** Another popular choice for art- and garden-lovers is **Giverny,** whose water lily ponds inspired Monet. (For details on all of these, see the "Excursions from Le Havre" sidebar.) I wouldn't recommend any of these by public transit.

Havre, and covered in detail in this chapter. Excursions to Rouen may include the enchanting lily-pad gardens at **Giverny,** built by Monet to be his muse.

In Normandy: The region of Normandy, perhaps best known to Americans as the site of the World War II D-Day landing, bursts with sights both related and unrelated to that famous military action. **Le Havre** itself may be offered as a tour, though if you're opting for a lazy day around town, you might as well see it on your own using the tips in this chapter. Adorable **Honfleur,** with its colorful harbor and historic ties to Impressionist painters like Boudin and Monet, is the nearest attraction to Le Havre (just a 30-minute drive; also doable by public bus and covered in this chapter). Trips to the so-called **Alabaster Coast** north of Le Havre (including the chalky cliffs at Etrétat, which were a muse for many Impressionists, and the salty fishing harbor of Fécamp) are pretty but lack the impact of other options.

The historic and sobering **D-Day beaches,** where the Allies came ashore on June 6, 1944, are farther away but well worth touring for history buffs. Excursions often include some beaches, the **American Cemetery, Arromanches** (the tiny seafront town that became the staging area for the invasion), and the **Longues-sur-Mer** gun battery. The city of **Caen** has the definitive museum about Operation Overlord.

A couple more sights are even farther afield, and only occasionally offered as an excursion. While enticing, they'll eat up lots of transit time. Bayeux, just beyond the D-Day beaches, houses the famous **Bayeux Tapestry,** a remarkable, intricately woven medieval masterwork detailing another invasion—the Battle of Hastings in 1066. The famous castaway abbey at **Mont St-Michel,** connected to the mainland only by a tenuous causeway, is understandably touristy.

The Port of Le Havre

A city of 180,000, Le Havre is France's second-biggest port (after Marseille), and the primary French port on the Atlantic. Its name (pronounced "luh ahv") means, simply, "The Port." Situated at the mouth of the Seine River (which also flows through Paris), Le Havre faces the English Channel and the British Isles. Its sprawling port area—harboring industrial, leisure, and cruise ships—stretches along the northern bank of the Seine.

Le Havre is proud of its connection to the Impressionist painters who found inspiration in this part of France, and nine panels scattered around town show Impressionist depictions of real-world locations (ask the TI for a pamphlet identifying these).

Fittingly, the city's best sight is the fine Impressionist collection at the Malraux Museum. Le Havre was bombed to bits in World War II, and rebuilt (by local hero Auguste Perret) in an old-meets-modern style that lacks charm. But the city is a useful springboard for northern France and Paris.

Planning Your Time

A full day in port is more than you need to fully experience Le Havre, and allows you to see it at a relaxed pace. If you decide to stick around, visit the Malraux Museum, dip into your choice of other museums, visit St. Joseph Church, browse the market, consider a stroll through the Hanging Gardens, or relax at the beach. Any of these activities can take as little or as long as you like.

Tourist Information

The full-service **main TI** is at the western edge of town, between the marina and the beach (daily July-Aug 9:00-19:00, Sept-June 9:30-12:30 & 14:00-18:30; Wi-Fi and Internet access—free for up to 20 minutes, get code from desk; 186 Boulevard Clemenceau, tel. 02 32 74 04 04, www.le-havre-tourism.com). Another TI is **downtown,** a block straight ahead from the City Hall park at 181 Rue de Paris (tel. 02 35 22 31 22). There's also a TI at the port (see below).

Arrival at the Port of Le Havre

Arrival at a Glance: Ride a cruise-line shuttle bus or walk about 35 minutes from the port to the train/bus station; from there, connect to Paris (2.25 hours by train), Rouen (one hour by train), or Honfleur (30 minutes by bus).

Port Overview

Le Havre's cruise port is located at Pointe de Floride, which is flanked by two piers: Roger Meunier Pier and Pierre Callet Pier. Both feed into a spacious, modern terminal building with Internet access, car rental, bike rental, a gift shop, and WCs. Port information: www.cruiselehavre.com.

Tourist Information: There's a TI right at the **cruise terminal** (daily from 7:00 until the last ship departure). Pick up a map of the city, info on local and regional sights, and current train and bus schedules. You can also rent bicycles here (€6/5 hours, €10/day, requires ID or €200 credit-card deposit). The main TI, described earlier, rents bikes for half these prices.

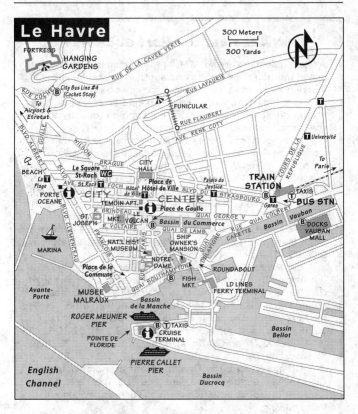

Getting into Le Havre and to the Train/Bus Station

Le Havre's cruise port is about a mile and a half from the train station (to the northeast) or downtown (due north). While you can walk through industrial port areas into town (figure about 35 minutes), most cruise lines offer a shuttle bus. (Shuttle bus drop-off points vary by company.) Taxis are also readily available at the port (charging €8 to most points in town). Once in Le Havre, you can hop a train to Paris or Rouen, or a bus to Honfleur.

Step 1: From the Cruise Port to Downtown Le Havre

To make the short trip from your ship to downtown Le Havre, you can either take the shuttle bus, walk, or pay for a taxi. The first two options are outlined in detail below.

By Cruise-Line Shuttle Bus

Most cruise ships provide a shuttle bus (sometimes free, sometimes

Services near the Port of Le Havre

ATMs: While there are no ATMs at the terminal, you'll find one inside the train/bus station and another across the street. If you're walking from the port into the city center, the nearest ATM is at the post office on the left-hand side of Rue de Paris, just up the street from Quai de Southampton (directly across the harbor from the cruise terminal).

Internet Access: You can get online at the Internet stations in the terminal building (pay for access code at souvenir shop); there's no Wi-Fi at the terminal.

Pharmacy: The nearest pharmacy to the port is on Rue du Général Faidherbe, one block up from the first roundabout as you leave the port area (toward downtown). Several more are downtown (including one on Rue de Paris, across from Notre-Dame Cathedral). French pharmacies are generally open Monday-Friday 9:00-12:30 and 14:30-19:30, Saturday 9:00-12:30, and closed Sunday.

Car Rental: The terminal's **Rent-A-Car** agency often runs out of cars by mid-morning, making it smart to book ahead (tel. 02 35 41 76 76, www.rentacar.fr, le_havre@rentacar.fr). Other options line the nearby Quai de Southampton, across the harbor from the cruise terminal: **Europcar** (at #51, tel. 02 35 25 21 95, www.europcar.fr), **Avis** (at #87, tel. 02 35 53 17 20, www.avis.fr), and **National/Citer** (at #91, tel. 02 35 21 30 81, www.citer.fr).

Other Services: The TIs at the terminal and on Boulevard Clemenceau rent **bikes** (see details earlier). The TIs also have information about **aquatic activities** such as kayaking, fishing, or sailing.

Tramway: Le Havre's sleek new **tram** zips silently through the city center (from the train station west to City Hall, the inviting Square St-Roch, and Porte Océane near the TI and beach). While it's not useful for getting into town from the port, the tram can be handy for sightseers who stick around Le Havre. For details, ask at the TI.

for a fee) that takes you into different stops in Le Havre. As you may arrive at one or more of the following, I've listed tips for each one. For the train/bus station, get off either at the station itself or at Les Docks; for in-town sightseeing, consider Quai de Southampton or Place Général de Gaulle.

Train/Bus Station: Ideally, your shuttle bus will drop you here—with easy connections to Paris, Rouen, Honfleur, and elsewhere (for details, see later).

Les Docks: This giant complex houses performance space, the Docks Vauban shopping mall, a movie theater, restaurants, and a supermarket. The train/bus station is an easy five-minute walk from here, across the harbor canal to the north: Cross the water on the skinny Passerelle Hubert Raoul Duval footbridge, continue straight through a few crosswalks, and you'll arrive on the bus station side of the train/bus station.

Quai de Southampton: This embankment hemming in the northern edge of the port area is a convenient stop if you are heading to the **Malraux Museum** (a fine Impressionist museum). Other nearby sights include the Baroque-style **Cathédrale de Notre Dame du Havre,** the **Ship Owner's Mansion,** and the **Natural History Museum** (housed in the former Palace of Justice). Also nearby are the post office (with ATM) and the rental-car offices noted under "Services near the Port of Le Havre," earlier.

Place Général de Gaulle: This square—right in the heart of town—is graced by a proud, yet solemn, Monument Aux Morts (erected in 1924 to honor WWI casualties). Across the street, you'll see Le Volcan, dubbed *le pot de yaourt* ("the yogurt pot") by locals. It's the city's *maison de la culture*—a cultural center for music, theater, dance, and cinema. Most sightseeing is south and west of here; the **market** is just one block west on Rue Voltaire.

By Foot

Walking into town takes about 35 minutes (25 minutes to the roundabout at the edge of the port, another 10 minutes to the town center or train/bus station): Turn right out of the terminal, look left for the *centre-ville* sign, and follow it—green pedestrian-area stripes guide you along the length of the pier. After the second bridge, turn left, continuing to follow signs for *centre-ville* (and passing the LD Lines ferry terminal on your right). Eventually, you'll come to a roundabout; from here, important places around town are well-marked. To get to the **city center,** bear left through the roundabout. To get to the **train/bus station,** bear right through the roundabout onto Quai Casimir Delavigne, staying on the right side of the street (along the water). Turn right onto Rue André Carette, which becomes Quai Colbert (follow signs for *gares*). Finally, turn left on the wide Cours de la République; after a block, the train station is on your right (the ugly concrete box marked *Gare du Havre/SNCF*), with the bus station just behind it.

PARIS

Step 2: From Le Havre's Train/Bus Station to Paris, Rouen, Honfleur, or Other Points

Once you've reached the train/bus station, you can make your way to anywhere in northern France. The train station *(gare)* and bus station *(gare routière)* are conveniently located side by side. (Facing the front entrance of the train station, the bus station is directly to the right of and behind the train station.)

Train Connections: There are two ways to buy train tickets at the station: For regional trips (to Rouen or Caen, for example),

Buses Between Le Havre and Honfleur/Caen

These times are based on the 2012/2013 schedules; confirm locally.

Bus #	Depart Le Havre	Arrive Honfleur	Arrive Caen	Days
39	7:10	7:34	8:33	M-F
20	7:49	8:19	—	M-F
20	8:40	9:19	—	M-Sat
39	10:45	11:09	12:08	Sun
50	12:42	13:15	—	M-Sat
20	14:00	14:30	—	Sun
39	14:20	14:44	15:43	M,W,F,Sat
20	14:32	15:02	—	M-Sat

Bus #	Depart Caen	Depart Honfleur	Arrive Le Havre	Days
50	N/A	11:47	12:20	M-Sat
50	N/A	13:07	13:40	Sun
20	N/A	13:22	13:51	M-Sat
39	12:30	13:34	13:59	Sat
39	12:30	13:42	14:07	M,W,F
20	N/A	16:12	16:37	M-Sat
20	N/A	17:12	17:41	Sun
20	N/A	17:40	18:18	M-Sat
39	18:20	19:27	19:52	M-Sat
39	19:00	19:59	20:24	Sun

the yellow automated machines accept American credit cards. To buy a ticket to destinations farther afield—such as Paris—or if you simply prefer speaking with a human or paying cash, you can buy tickets at the *guichets* (ticket windows). Before boarding the train, be sure to validate your ticket at the slender yellow ticket puncher near the doors leading to the train tracks. If you're tight on time, you can hop on the train and buy a ticket from the conductor on board—but find him before he finds you (or you could be charged a hefty fine).

Trains leave nearly hourly for **Paris** (St. Lazare station, 2.25 hours, €32.80 one-way); all of these also stop in **Rouen** (station called "Rouen-Rive-Droite," one hour, €14.90 one-way). A few Paris connections require a change in Rouen. In 2012, Paris-bound trains departed Le Havre at 7:59, 9:03 (requires change in

Rouen), 9:59, and 12:00. If you're going only as far as Rouen, there are additional trains at 7:25, 7:54 (this fast TGV train requires a reservation), and 12:45. Be aware that on weekends there are fewer trains, which may run at slightly different times. For return train times, see page 1010.

For tips on what to do when you arrive in Paris, see page 1014; for Rouen, see page 1095.

Bus Connections: From Le Havre's bus station, buses #20, #39, and #50 go over the Normandy Bridge to **Honfleur** (see sidebar for schedule, 25-30 minutes, €4.50 one-way, www.busverts.fr). Bus #39 continues on to **Caen** (1.5 hours total; otherwise you can reach Caen by a slower train connection via Rouen). For tips on Honfleur, see page 1082.

Other Options

In addition to the options explained above, consider these ways to reach downtown Le Havre, Paris, or elsewhere.

By Taxi

Taxis wait to the right as you exit the cruise terminal. A ride to anywhere in the Le Havre city center (including to the train/bus station) costs about €8. Taxis waiting at the cruise port or train station offer "discovery tours," with some commentary en route, for the following round-trip rates (these prices are for up to 4 people):

Around Le Havre (1.5 hours): €60
Etrétat (3 hours): €125
Honfleur (3 hours): €125
Rouen (6 hours): €280
Giverny (6 hours): €340
Normandy (8 hours): €320
Versailles (8 hours): €395
D-Day Beaches (8 hours): €450
Mont St-Michel (10 hours): €460
Paris (10 hours): €460

While most cabbies speak a bit of English, some are more fluent than others; if you're paying for a tour, feel free to chat with several drivers to assess their language abilities before choosing. Note: These cabbies may provide information, but they're not trained guides. Most drivers belong to **Radio Taxi Le Havre** (tel. 02 35 25 81 00, www.radiotaxi-lehavre.com).

By Cruise-Line Shuttle Bus to Paris

Most cruise lines offer a "Paris On Your Own" excursion, which consists of an un-narrated bus ride to a designated point in Paris (generally near Place de la Concorde, between the Champs-Elysées and the Louvre), then back again at an appointed time.

PARIS

While the price is hefty compared to public transit (typically $110-130, compared to $85 for the round-trip train), some cruisers appreciate the efficiency and the lack of stress about making it back to the ship on time. For tips on arriving via shuttle bus in Paris, see page 1017.

By Tour

The Le Havre TI can help you arrange a private guide in town. **Normandy Sightseeing Tours** can pick you up at the ship, and offers a wide variety of tours in the region, including Paris, Bayeux/Caen, Mont St-Michel, various D-Day itineraries (described on page 1089), Monet-themed tours, and more. Of their many guides, the best-regarded are David, Olivier, and Karinne (all-day tour: €720/up to 4 people, €740/up to 6 people, €760/up to 8 people, does not include lunch or entry fees; tel. 02 31 51 70 52, www.normandy-sightseeing-tours.com, fredericguerin@wanadoo.fr). For other tour options for the D-Day beaches, see "Getting Around the D-Day Beaches," on page 1089.

For information on local tour options in Paris itself—including local guides for hire, walking tours, and bus tours on the Seine—see "Tours in Paris" on page 1028.

Returning to Your Ship

If you're returning from **Paris** to Le Havre, be sure to leave plenty of time for the 2.25-hour train ride (plus the time it takes to get back to your ship from the Le Havre train station). Confirm and double-check the departure time of your return train before you head out. In 2012, trains left Paris for Le Havre at 12:50 (arriving 14:57), 14:50 (arriving 16:57), 15:50 (arriving 17:57), 16:50 (arriving 18:57), 17:25 (arriving 19:30), 17:50 (arriving 19:57), 18:50 (arriving 20:59), 19:50 (arriving 21:57), and 20:50 (arriving 23:22).

Returning from **Honfleur**, carefully confirm the bus schedule (see times on page 1008).

Back at the **Le Havre** train/bus station, the easiest choice is to spring for a **taxi** (€8; you'll find them at the bus station end of the complex), or ride your cruise line's **shuttle bus** back to your ship (catch the bus where you got off earlier).

If you prefer to **walk**, allow about 35 minutes: Leaving the train station, turn left and head toward the water on Cours de la République. Go straight across to the water side of Quai Colbert, turn right, and follow the street (with the water on your left) as it becomes Rue André Carette. Turn left at Quai Casimir Delavigne; at the roundabout, bear left to continue toward the port (passing the LD Lines Ferry terminal). After crossing the bridge, turn right and look for green stripes on the ground—these mark the pedestrian route back to the terminal.

If you have some time to kill before heading back, see the options described under "Sights in Le Havre," earlier.

See page 1105 for help if you miss your boat.

Sights in Le Havre

Pooped cruisers who skip the trip to Paris find that Le Havre has several worthwhile sights of its own. While none of these can match the thrills of Paris, if you're in the mood to stick around town, here are some ideas to fill your day.

▲**Malraux Museum (a.k.a. "MuMa")**—Named for the former Minister of Culture, André Malraux, this delightfully airy and modern space is home to a superb collection of works by Impressionist biggies who lived and worked in Normandy: Monet, Renoir, Degas, Manet, Courbet, Cézanne, Camille Corot, and others. It also boasts the world's largest collection of works by Eugène Boudin, Monet's mentor. While it may not quite live up to its billing as the "finest Impressionist collection in France outside Paris," it's certainly worthwhile for art lovers. It lacks the wall-to-wall crowds of Paris' Musée d'Orsay, creating a wonderful opportunity to get up close and personal with quality examples of late 19th- and early 20th-century artwork. Beyond the Impressionists, the collection spans five centuries, from the 16th century up to modern works by Matisse and Pierre Bonnard. Take a break and enjoy sea views in their restaurant or tea room.

Cost and Hours: €5, Wed-Mon 11:00-18:00, Sat-Sun until 19:00, closed Tue, 2 Boulevard Clemenceau, tel. 02 35 19 62 62, www.muma-lehavre.fr.

St. Joseph Church—Built in the 1950s, this church serves as a memorial to the 5,000 Le Havre civilians who died during World War II. Its 350-foot-tall octagonal tower (which resembles a Chicago skyscraper more than a steeple) is *the* dominant structure on Le Havre's skyline. The stark, somber, Neo-Gothic interior is worth a quick visit only to appreciate its Greek-cross floor plan and to peer up inside the tower. On a sunny day, the whimsical play of light through its 13,000 panels of stained glass is delightful.

Cost and Hours: Free, daily 10:00-18:00 except during services, at the corner of Boulevard François I and Rue Louis Brindeau.

Ship Owner's Mansion (La Maison de l'Armateur)—This historic building offers a glimpse into the 18th-century lifestyle of a wealthy Le Havre citizen. Five stories of furnishings, artwork, and collectibles evoke life in this port city from 1750-1870. The rooms

PARIS

Le Havre Experiences for Cruisers

To experience the city like a local, stop by **Les Halles Centrales** indoor market, featuring stalls selling fresh produce, fresh-made deli foods, baked goods, regional specialties, and more (one block west of Le Volcan on Rue Voltaire, Mon-Fri 9:00-12:30 & 14:30-18:00, Sat 9:00-12:30 & 14:30-16:30, closed Sun). On Sundays, Les Halles Centrales' parking lot hosts a farmers market (9:00-13:00).

Bring your freshly purchased picnic on a 10-minute walk north to **Le Square St-Roch** (at the corner of Avenue Foch and Rue Raoul Dufy)—a serene oasis in the middle of the city—where you can park yourself on a bench or a patch of grass, enjoy your lunch, and watch as families, businessmen on break, wise grandmothers, and couples in love go by. This park is dappled with wistful willows that tickle a petite pond, flamboyant flowers, humble statues, and play areas for children. WCs are available on the east end, not far from the entrance.

For a more competitive experience, try your hand at *pétanque*, the French cousin to American horseshoes and Italian *bocce*. The best place is at the small, gravelly square called **Place de la Commune** (near the Malraux Museum, on the corner of Boulevard François I and Rue Jeanne d'Arc). In the afternoons, you'll often find crusty old fishermen and their not-yet-crusty descendants playing this traditional French game. Don't be shy—ask if you can join in for a round or two.

---

are arranged around an octagonal, vertical space reminiscent of the St. Joseph Church tower.

Cost and Hours: €5, includes obligatory guided tour in French (English pamphlet provided), Thu-Mon 11:00-12:30 & 13:30-18:00, Wed 14:00-18:00, closed Tue, 3 Quai de l'Ile, tel. 02 35 19 09 85.

Témoin Apartment (L'Appartement Témoin Perret)—At the 1947 World's Fair, architect and urban planner André Perret presented a "show flat" to illustrate his vision for how Le Havre could be rebuilt after having been pummeled by WWII bombs. Today, this replica of that apartment is still smartly decorated with period furniture, appliances, knickknacks, and products. It's cute but skippable—particularly since the required guided tours are only in French.

Cost and Hours: €3 includes obligatory tour in French; daily at 14:00, 15:00, 16:00, and 17:00; additional tour departures mid-June-mid-Sept, 181 Rue de Paris, tel. 02 35 22 31 22.

▲Hanging Gardens (Les Jardins Suspendus)—For nature enthusiasts who need a break from shipboard life, this fine park—

about two miles north of the port—is the place. The grass-topped walls of a former fortress enclose a massive complex, with splendid city and beach views that invite you to wander and explore. Inside the fort are more gardens, along with extensive greenhouses that feature plants from five continents. The gardens are popular with picnickers and often host special events.

Cost and Hours: Free, €1 to enter greenhouses, daily April-Sept 10:30-20:00, Oct and March 10:30-18:00, Nov-Feb 10:30-17:00, Rue du Fort, tel. 02 35 19 45 45.

Getting There: It's easiest by taxi (€8 each way from the port), but prearrange a pickup to avoid getting stranded. You can also take bus #4 (to Cochet or Copieux) or #6 (to Eglise de Sanvic).

Beach—On a sunny day, relax at Le Havre's pebbly beach (at the western edge of town, just north of the main TI). Bring your flip-flops (better than going barefoot on pebbles) and find your own patch of beach (the tempting cabanas are usually rented monthly or yearly). While working on your tan, enjoy the view of dozens of sailboats gliding across the water. The boardwalk offers all types of tasty treats, plus activities and services including bike rentals, water equipment rentals, volleyball, *pétanque*, WCs, and showers (most open April-Sept). You can get there by taxi, bus #4 (get off at the Plage-Le Havre stop), or tram.

Near Le Havre

▲**Normandy Bridge (Pont de Normandie)**—The 1.25-mile-long Normandy Bridge, just upriver from Le Havre's port, is the longest cable-stayed bridge in the Western world. This is a key piece of a super-expressway that links the Atlantic ports from Belgium to Spain. The Seine finishes its winding 500-mile journey here, dropping only 1,500 feet from its source. The river flows so slowly that, in certain places, a stiff breeze can send it flowing upstream.

▲**Etrétat**—France's answer to the White Cliffs of Dover, these chalky cliffs soar high above a calm, crescent beach. Walking trails lead hikers from the small seaside resort of Etrétat along a vertiginous route with sensational views (and crowds in summers and on weekends). You'll recognize these cliffs—and the arches and stone spire that decorate them—from countless Impressionist paintings, including several by Eugène Boudin. The small, Coney Island-like town holds plenty of cafés and a **TI** (Place Maurice Guillard, tel. 02 35 27 05 21, www.etretat.net).

Getting There: Etrétat is north of Le Havre; while reachable by bus, the connection is infrequent (5/day, 1 hour, www.cars-perier.com)—it's safer to visit by taxi or on an excursion.

PARIS

Paris

Paris has been a beacon of culture for centuries. As a world capital of art, fashion, food, literature, and ideas, it stands as a symbol of all the fine things human civilization can offer. Come prepared to celebrate this, rather than judge our cultural differences, and you'll capture the romance and *joie de vivre* this city exudes.

Planning Your Time

Of course, "seeing" Paris in just a few hours is in-Seine. But if that's all the time you have, here are your most likely choices:

• **Historic Paris Walk:** My self-guided stroll orients you to the city's core (Ile de la Cité, Notre-Dame, Latin Quarter, Sainte-Chapelle) in about four hours.

• **Louvre:** While art lovers could spend all day at one of the world's great museums, a targeted visit can take two hours. You can tack on a visit to the nearby **Orangerie** (a misty world of Monet's water lilies) in about an hour.

• **Orsay:** This sumptuous collection of Impressionist art can be seen succinctly in two hours.

• **Eiffel Tower:** If you reserve ahead to avoid the long line (see page 1058), you can zip to the top of Paris' most iconic structure, and back down, in two hours; to save time, do only the first level.

• **Arc de Triomphe and Champs-Elysées:** On a quick visit, you can stroll down Paris' finest boulevard in about an hour (or even less, if you only do the more interesting upper half, to Rond Pont). Add an hour to ascend to the top of the Arc de Triomphe.

• **Other Museums and Sights:** With a special interest, consider some of Paris' other excellent museums, including Rodin, Army Museum/Napoleon's Tomb, Marmottan Museum, Cluny Museum, and more. Any of these can take an hour or two (at least). The Montmartre neighborhood (surrounding Sacré-Cœur basilica) and the Luxembourg Garden are also fine places to explore, but either one will take an hour or two.

As you'll never be able to fit all of the above into a brief visit, you'll need to be very selective. Choose just two or three, and take geography and public-transit connections into account to be as efficient as possible. The best first-time visit plan may be the Historic Paris Walk, followed by a visit to the Louvre or Orsay.

PARIS

Orientation to Paris

Paris (population of city center: 2,234,000) is split in half by the Seine River, divided into 20 arrondissements (proud and independent governmental jurisdictions), circled by a ring-road freeway (the *périphérique*), and speckled with Métro stations. You'll find Paris easier to navigate if you know which side of the river you're on, which arrondissement you're in, and which Métro stop you're closest to. If you're north of the river (the top half of any city map), you're on the Right Bank (Rive Droite). If you're south of it, you're on the Left Bank (Rive Gauche). The bull's-eye of your Paris map is Notre-Dame, which sits on an island in the middle of the Seine. Most of your sightseeing will take place within five blocks of the river.

Arrondissements are numbered, starting at the Louvre and moving in a clockwise spiral out to the ring road. The last two digits in a Parisian zip code indicate the arrondissement number. The abbreviation for "Métro stop" is "Mo." In Parisian jargon, the Eiffel Tower is on *la Rive Gauche* (the Left Bank) in the *7ème* (7th arrondissement), zip code 75007, Mo: Trocadéro.

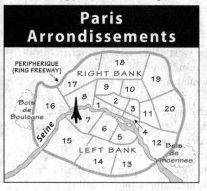

Paris Métro stops are used as a standard aid in giving directions, even for those not taking the Métro. As you're tracking down addresses, these words and pronunciations will help: Métro (may-troh), *place* (plahs; square), *rue* (roo; road), *avenue* (ah-vuh-noo), *boulevard* (boo-luh-var), and *pont* (pohn; bridge).

PARIS

Tourist Information

Paris TIs can provide useful information but may have long lines. Pick up the free *Paris for You!* booklet. If you're looking for a map, they may charge you for it (all you really need are the freebie maps available on racks around town, or the one in the front of this book). TIs also sell individual tickets to sights (see "Avoiding Lines with Advance Tickets" on page 1019), as well as Paris Museum Passes (described later).

Paris has several TI locations, including **Pyramides** (daily May-Oct 9:00-19:00, Nov-April 10:00-19:00, at Pyramides Métro stop between the Louvre and Opéra), **Gare du Nord** (daily 8:00-18:00), and two in **Montmartre,** both with a focus on their neighborhood (one on Place du Tertre, daily 10:00-18:00, tel. 01 42 62 21 21, and the other above the Anvers Métro stop, daily 10:00-18:00). In summer, TI kiosks may pop up in the squares in front of Notre-Dame and Hôtel de Ville. The official website for Paris' TIs is www.parisinfo.com.

The weekly €0.40 *Pariscope* magazine (or one of its clones, available at any newsstand) lists museum hours, art exhibits, concerts, festivals, plays, movies, and nightclubs. Smart sightseers rely on this for the latest listings. These **websites** come highly recommended for local information and events: www.gogoparis.com, www.secretsofparis.com, and www.bonjourparis.com.

Paris Museum Pass: This sightseeing pass admits you to many of Paris' most popular sights (€39 for a 2-day pass, no 1-day version). The pass covers most of the sights listed in this chapter, except the Eiffel Tower, Marmottan Museum, Notre-Dame Treasury, and Sacré-Cœur's dome. Most importantly, the pass lets you skip ticket-buying lines at most sights. If you're in town for just a few hours, you'll have to sightsee like crazy to get your money's worth. Still, it might be worth the price of purchase just to skip long lines (but keep in mind you can also pre-buy line-skipping tickets for a few individual sights—see page 1019). Add up the costs of the sights you'll realistically have time to visit during your day in town, compare that with the cost of the pass, weigh the likelihood that you'll waste time standing in ticket lines, and decide. The pass is sold at participating sights, FNAC department stores, and TIs. Avoid buying the pass at a major museum (such as the Louvre), where supply can be spotty and lines long. For more info, visit www.parismuseumpass.com or call 01 44 61 96 60.

To use your pass at sights, boldly walk to the front of the ticket line (after going through security if necessary), hold up your pass, and ask the ticket-taker: *"Entrez, pass?"* (ahn-tray pahs). You'll either be allowed to enter at that point, or you'll be directed to a special entrance. Don't be shy—some places (Sainte-Chapelle and

PARIS

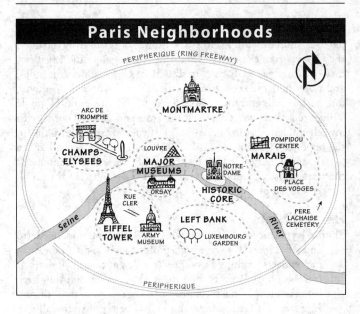

Paris Neighborhoods

PERIPHERIQUE (RING FREEWAY)

MONTMARTRE

ARC DE TRIOMPHE

CHAMPS-ELYSEES

LOUVRE

MAJOR MUSEUMS

ORSAY

POMPIDOU CENTER

MARAIS

NOTRE-DAME

PLACE DES VOSGES

HISTORIC CORE

RUE CLER

Seine

EIFFEL TOWER

ARMY MUSEUM

LEFT BANK

LUXEMBOURG GARDEN

River

PERE LACHAISE CEMETERY

PERIPHERIQUE

the Arc de Triomphe, in particular) have long lines where timid passholders wait needlessly.

Arrival in Paris

By Train at St. Lazare Station (Gare St. Lazare): All trains from Le Havre (described on page 1004) arrive and depart at this compact station, about a mile north of the river. Trains are one floor above street level. Trains to and from Le Havre use tracks 23-27; from here, it's a long, well-signed walk from the tracks to the Métro. The ticket office is near track 27; train information offices *(accueil)* are scattered about the station. St. Lazare Station also has a three-floor shopping mall with food, clothing, and more, including an ATM on each level.

Assuming you'd like to head straight to Notre-Dame Cathedral to begin my self-guided walk of historic Paris, your best bet is to either take the Métro (faster, but it's a longer walk to Notre-Dame) or the bus (which drops you closer to the cathedral). Take the **Métro** line 14 (purple) south, in direction: Olympiades, and ride three stops to Châtelet; this stop is three short blocks north of the river and Ile de la Cité. **Bus #24** departs from in front of the station and goes to Place de la Concorde, Orsay Museum, the Louvre, St. Michel, Notre-Dame, and beyond.

By Shuttle Bus, on or near Place de la Concorde: If you arrive in Paris via an "On Your Own" shuttle-bus excursion, the bus will likely drop you off on or near the square called Place de la Concorde, which is wedged between the Louvre and the bottom of the grand Champs-Elysées boulevard. From here, it's an easy 15- to 20-minute **walk** to either the Louvre or (just across the river) the Orsay. From the nearby Concorde **Métro** stop, line 1 (yellow) makes things easier: Ride it in direction: Château de Vincennes, and hop off at the second stop, Palais Royal-Musée du Louvre, for the Louvre's entrance; two later stops, Châtelet and Hôtel de Ville, are a short walk north of the river and Notre-Dame (with my self-guided Historic Paris Walk). If you ride this Métro line in the opposite direction, toward La Défense, you can get off at the fourth stop, Charles de Gaulle-Etoile, for the Arc de Triomphe at the start of the Champs-Elysées. **Bus #24,** described in the previous section, stops at Place de la Concorde.

Helpful Hints

Theft Alert: Thieves thrive near famous monuments and on Métro and RER lines that serve high-profile tourist sights. Beware of pickpockets working busy lines (such as at ticket windows at train stations). Pay attention when it's your turn and your back is to the crowd—keep your bag firmly gripped in front of you. In general, it's smart to wear a money belt, put your wallet in your front pocket, loop your day bag over your shoulders, and keep a tight grip on your purse or shopping bag. Muggings are rare, but they do occur. If you're out late, avoid the dark riverfront embankments and any place where the lighting is dim and pedestrian activity is minimal.

Paris is taking action to combat crime by stationing police at monuments, on streets, and on the Métro, as well as using security cameras at key sights. You'll go through quick and reassuring airport-like security checks at many major attractions.

Tourist Scams: Be aware of the latest scams, including these current favorites. The "found ring" scam involves an innocent-looking person who picks up a ring off the ground and asks if you dropped it. When you say no, the person examines the ring more closely, then shows you a mark "proving" that it's pure gold. He offers to sell it to you for a good price—several times more than he paid for it before dropping it on the sidewalk.

In the "friendship bracelet" scam, a vendor approaches you and asks if you'll help him with a demonstration. He proceeds to make a friendship bracelet right on your arm. When finished, he asks you to pay for the bracelet he created just for you. And since you can't easily take it off on the spot, he counts on your feeling obliged to pay up.

Distractions by a stranger—often a "salesman," someone asking you to sign a petition, or someone posing as a deaf person to show you a small note to read—can all be tricks that function as a smokescreen for theft. As you try to wriggle away from the pushy stranger, an accomplice picks your pocket.

In popular tourist spots (such as in front of Notre-Dame) young ladies ask if you speak English, then pretend to beg for money while actually angling to get your wallet.

To all these scammers, simply say "no" firmly, don't apologize, don't smile, and step away purposefully.

Pedestrian Safety: Parisian drivers are notorious for ignoring pedestrians. Look both ways (many streets are one-way) and be careful of seemingly quiet bus/taxi lanes. Don't assume you have the right of way, even in a crosswalk. When crossing a street, keep your pace constant and don't stop suddenly. By law, drivers are allowed to miss pedestrians by up to just one meter—a little more than three feet (1.5 meters in the countryside). Drivers calculate your speed so they won't hit you, provided you don't alter your route or pace.

Watch out for bicyclists. This popular and silent transportation may come at you from unexpected places and directions—cyclists ride in specially marked bike lanes on wide sidewalks and also have a right to use lanes reserved for buses and taxis. Bikes commonly go against traffic, as many bike paths are on one-way streets. Again, always look both ways.

Busy Parisian sidewalks are much like freeways, so conduct yourself as if you were a foot-fueled-car: Stick to your lane, look to the left before passing a slow-moving pedestrian, and if you need to stop, look for a safe place to pull over.

Medical Help: The American Hospital, established by a group of expat doctors, provides medical attention from English-speaking staff (63 Boulevard Victor Hugo, in Neuilly suburb, Mo: Porte Maillot, then bus #82, tel. 01 46 41 25 25, www.american-hospital.org).

Avoiding Lines with Advance Tickets: If a Museum Pass (described on page 1016) doesn't fit your needs, you do have other line-skipping options. TIs and FNAC stores sell individual fast-track *"coupe-file"* tickets, letting you use the Museum Pass entrance at sights. TIs sell these tickets for no extra fee, but FNACs add a surcharge of 10-20 percent—often worth it, as these stores are everywhere, even on the Champs-Elysées (ask around for the nearest one). For sights that can otherwise have long waits (such as the Arc de Triomphe), these tickets are a good idea.

For some sights, you can book tickets online and print a receipt that serves as your entry pass. This works great at the Eiffel Tower (though you must choose an entry time).

Bookstores: Paris has many English-language bookstores, where you can pick up guidebooks (at nearly double their American prices). Most carry my guidebooks. My favorites include:

• **Red Wheelbarrow Bookstore** (in the Marais neighborhood, for sale and may be gone in 2013; if open, generally Mon 10:00-18:00, Tue-Sat 10:00-19:00, Sun 14:00-18:00; 22 Rue St. Paul, Mo: St. Paul, tel. 01 48 04 75 08).

• **Shakespeare and Company** (some used travel books, Mon-Fri 10:00-23:00, Sat-Sun 11:00-23:00, 37 Rue de la Bûcherie, across the river from Notre-Dame, Mo: St. Michel, tel. 01 43 25 40 93).

• **W. H. Smith** (Mon-Sat 9:00-19:00, Sun 12:30-19:00, 248 Rue de Rivoli, Mo: Concorde, tel. 01 44 77 88 99).

• **San Francisco Book Company** (Mon-Sat 11:00-21:00, Sun 14:00-19:30, 17 Rue Monsieur le Prince, Mo: Odéon, tel. 01 43 29 15 70).

Public WCs: Most public toilets are free. If it's a pay toilet, the price will be clearly indicated. If the toilet is free but there's an attendant, it's polite (but not necessary) to leave a tip of €0.20-0.50. Booth-like pay toilets on the sidewalks provide both relief and a memory (don't leave small children inside unattended). The restrooms in museums are free and the best you'll find. Or walk into any sidewalk café like you own the place, and find the toilet in the back. If you have to buy something, your cheapest option is to order a shot of espresso (*un café*) standing at the bar. Keep toilet paper or tissues with you, as some WCs are poorly stocked.

Tobacco Stands (*Tabacs*): These little kiosks—usually just a counter inside a café—are handy and very local. They sell public-transit tickets, cards for parking meters, postage stamps (though not all sell international postage—to mail something home, use two domestic stamps, or go to a post office), pre-paid phone cards, and...oh yeah, cigarettes. To find one of these kiosks, just look for a *Tabac* sign and the red cylinder-shaped symbol above certain cafés. A *tabac* can be a godsend for avoiding long ticket lines at the Métro, especially at the end of the month when ticket booths get crowded with locals buying next month's pass.

Updates to this Book: For news about changes to this book's coverage since it was published, see www.ricksteves.com/update.

Getting Around Paris

Paris is easy to navigate. Your basic choices are Métro (in-city subway), RER (suburban rail tied into the Métro system), public bus, and taxi. (Also consider the hop-on, hop-off bus and boat tours, described under "Tours in Paris," later.)

You can buy tickets and passes at Métro stations and at many *tabacs*. Staffed ticket windows in stations are gradually being phased out in favor of ticket machines, so expect some stations to have machines only—be sure to carry coins or small bills of €20 or less (not all machines take bills, and none takes American credit cards). If a ticket machine is out of order or if you're out of change, buy tickets at a *tabac*.

Public-Transit Tickets: The Métro, RER, and buses all work on the same tickets. You can make as many transfers as you need on a single ticket, except when transferring between the Métro/RER system and the bus system, which requires using an additional ticket. A **single ticket** costs €1.70. A shareable *carnet* (kar-nay) of 10 tickets is sold for €12.70 (cheaper for ages 4-10)—buy this only if you'll be riding enough to use up all (or most) of the 10 tickets.

Other Passes: A handy one-day bus/Métro pass (called **Mobilis**) is available for €6.40. The overpriced **Paris Visite** passes are poorly designed for tourists and offer minor discounts at minor sights (1 day/€9.75, 2 days/€15.85, 3 days/€21.60, 5 days/€31.15). The **Passe Navigo** card allows for cheaper rides, but requires a €5 starter fee and a small photo of yourself—too much hassle for a brief day in Paris.

By Métro

In Paris, you're never more than a 10-minute walk from a Métro station. Europe's best subway system allows you to hop from sight to sight quickly and cheaply (runs daily 5:30-24:30, Fri-Sat until 2:00 in the morning, www.ratp.fr). Learn to use it. Begin by studying a Métro map (free at Métro stations and included on various freebie Paris maps around town).

Using the Métro System: To get to your destination, determine the closest "Mo" stop and which line or lines will get you there. The lines are color-coded and numbered, and you can tell their direction by their end-of-the-line stops. For example, the La Défense/Château de Vincennes line, also known as line 1 (yellow), runs between La Défense, on its west end, and Vincennes on its east end. Once in the Métro station, you'll see the color-coded line numbers and/or blue-and-white signs directing you to the train going in your direction (e.g., *direction: La Défense*). Insert your ticket in the automatic turnstile, reclaim your ticket, pass through, and keep it until you exit the system (some stations require you to pass your ticket through a turnstile to exit). The smallest stations are unstaffed and have ticket machines (coins are essential). Be warned that fare inspectors regularly check for cheaters and accept absolutely no excuses—keep that ticket or pay a minimum fine of €25.

PARIS

Métro Basics

- The same tickets are good on the Métro, RER (within the city), and city buses (but not to transfer between Métro/ RER and bus).
- Beware of pickpockets, and don't buy tickets from men roaming the stations.
- Find your train by its end-of-the-line stops.
- Insert your ticket into the turnstile, retrieve it, and keep it until the end of your journey.
- Transfers (correspondances) within the Métro and RER system are free.

Key Words for the Métro and RER

French	Pronounced	English
direction	dee-rek-see-ohn	direction
ligne	leen-yuh	line
correspondance	kor-res-pohn-dahns	connection/transfer
sortie	sor-tee	exit
carnet	kar-nay	discounted set of 10 tickets
Pardon, madame/ monsieur.	par-dohn, mah-dahm/ mes-yur	Excuse me, ma'am/ sir.
Je descends.	juh day-sahn	I'm getting off.
Donnez-moi mon porte-monnaie!	duh-nay-mwah mohn port-moh-nay	Give me back my wallet!

Be prepared to walk significant distances within Métro stations (especially when you transfer). Transfers are free and can be made wherever lines cross, provided you do so within 1.5 hours. When you transfer, follow the appropriately colored line number for your next train, or find orange correspondance (connection) signs that lead to your next line.

When you reach your destination, look for the blue-and-white sortie signs pointing you to the exit. Before leaving the station, check the helpful plan du quartier (map of the neighborhood) to get your bearings. At stops with several sorties, you can save time by choosing the best exit.

After you exit the system, toss or tear your used ticket so you don't confuse it with unused tickets—they look almost identical.

Beware of Pickpockets: Thieves dig the Métro and RER.

Etiquette

- When your train arrives, board only after everyone leaving the car has made it out the door.
- Avoid using the hinged seats near the doors of some trains when the car is crowded; they take up valuable standing space.

- Always offer your seat to the elderly, those with disabilities, and pregnant women.
- Talk softly in cars. Listen to how quietly Parisians communicate (if at all) and follow their lead.
- If you find yourself blocking the door at a stop, step out of the car to let others off, then get back on.
- When you're getting off at a stop, the door may open automatically. If it doesn't, open the door by either pushing a square button (green or black) or lifting a metal latch.
- Métro doors close automatically. Don't try to hold open the door for late-boarding passengers.
- Dispose of used tickets after you complete your ride and leave the station (not before) to avoid confusing them with fresh ones.
- On escalators, stand on the right and pass on the left.
- When leaving a station, hold the door for the person behind you.

Be on guard. If your pocket is picked as you pass through a turnstile, you end up stuck on the wrong side (after the turnstile bar has closed behind you) while the thief gets away. Stand away from Métro doors to avoid being a target for a theft-and-run just before the doors close. Any jostling or commotion—especially when boarding or leaving trains—is likely the sign of a thief or a team of thieves in action. Keep your bag close. Make any fare inspector show proof of identity (ask locals for help if you're not certain). Never show anyone your wallet.

PARIS

By RER

The RER (Réseau Express Régionale; air-ay-air) is the suburban arm of the Métro, serving outlying destinations such as Versailles, Disneyland Paris,

Scenic Buses for Tourists

Of Paris' many bus routes, these are some of the most scenic. They provide a great, cheap, and convenient introduction to the city.

Bus #69 crosses the city east-west, running between the Eiffel Tower and Père Lachaise Cemetery, and passing these great sights and neighborhoods: Eiffel Tower, Rue Cler, Les Invalides (Army Museum and Napoleon's Tomb), Louvre Museum, Ile de la Cité, Ile St. Louis, Hôtel de Ville, Pompidou Center, Marais, Bastille, and Père Lachaise.

Bus #87 also links the Marais and Rue Cler areas, but stays mostly on the Left Bank, connecting the Eiffel Tower, St. Sulpice Church, Luxembourg Garden, St. Germain-des-Prés, the Latin Quarter, the Bastille, and Gare de Lyon.

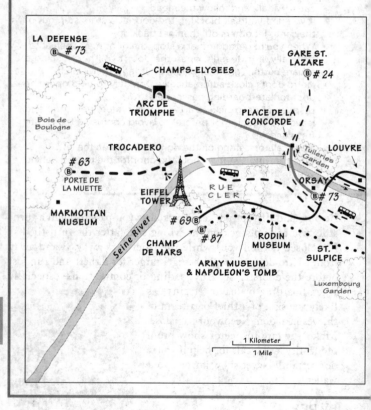

Bus #24 runs east-west along the Seine riverbank from Gare St. Lazare to Madeleine, Place de la Concorde, Orsay Museum, the Louvre, St. Michel, Notre-Dame, and Jardin des Plantes, all the way to Bercy Village (cafés and shops).

Bus #63 is another good east-west route, connecting the Marmottan Museum, Trocadéro (Eiffel Tower), Pont de l'Alma, Orsay Museum, St. Sulpice Church, Luxembourg Garden, Latin Quarter/Panthéon, and Gare de Lyon.

Bus #73 is one of Paris' most scenic lines, starting at the Orsay Museum and running westbound around Place de la Concorde, then up the Champs-Elysées, around the Arc de Triomphe, and down Avenue Charles de Gaulle to La Défense.

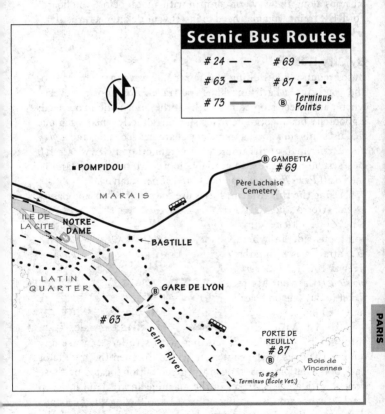

and the airports. These routes are indicated by thick lines on your subway map and identified by the letters A, B, C, and so on.

On a short visit from Le Havre, you're unlikely to use the RER for distant locations, but you may use it to zip between points in town. Within the city center, the RER works like the Métro and can be speedier if it serves your destination directly, because it makes fewer stops. Métro tickets are good on the RER when traveling in the city center. You can transfer between the Métro and RER systems with the same ticket. (To travel outside the city—to Versailles, for example—you'd need a separate, more expensive ticket.) Unlike the Métro, not every train stops at every station along the way; check the sign or screen over the platform to see if your destination is listed as a stop (*"toutes les gares"* means it makes all stops along the way), or confirm with a local before you board. For RER trains, you may need to insert your ticket in a turnstile to exit the system.

By City Bus

Buses require less walking and fewer stairways than the Métro, and you can see Paris unfold as you travel. Bus stops are everywhere, and every stop comes with all the information you need: a good city bus map, route maps showing exactly where each bus that uses this stop goes, a frequency chart and schedule, and a *plan du quartier* map of the immediate neighborhood (www.ratp.fr). Bus-system maps are also available in any Métro station (and in the €6.50 *Paris Pratique* map book sold at newsstands).

Using the Bus System: Buses use the same tickets and passes as the Métro and RER. One Zone 1 ticket buys you a bus ride anywhere in central Paris within the freeway ring road *(le périphérique).* Use your Métro ticket or buy one on board for €0.20 more.

Board your bus through the front door. (Families with strollers can use any doors—the ones in the center are wider. To open the middle or back doors on long buses, push the green button located by those doors.) Validate your ticket in the machine and reclaim it. Keep track of what stop is coming up next by following the on-board diagram or listening to recorded announcements. When you're ready to get off, push the red button to signal you want a stop, then exit through the central or rear door. Even if you're not certain you've figured out the system, do some joyriding.

More Bus Tips: Avoid rush hour (Mon-Fri 8:00-9:30 & 17:30-19:30), when buses are jammed and traffic doesn't move. Not all city buses are air-conditioned, so they can become rolling greenhouses on summer days. You can transfer from one bus to another on the same ticket (within 1.5 hours, revalidate your ticket on the next bus), but you can't do a round-trip or hop on and off on the same line. You also can't transfer between the bus and the Métro/RER systems using the same ticket, or between buses with a ticket bought on board (go figure).

For a list of Paris' most scenic and convenient routes, see the sidebar.

By Taxi

Parisian taxis are reasonable, especially for couples and families. The meters are tamper-proof. Fares and supplements (described in English on the rear windows) are straightforward and tightly regulated.

A taxi can fit three people comfortably. Cabbies are legally required to accept four passengers, though they don't always like it. If you have five in your group, you can book a larger taxi in advance, or try your luck at a taxi stand. Beyond three passengers, expect to pay €3 extra per person.

Rates: All Parisian taxis start with €2.40 on the meter and have a minimum charge of €6.40. A 20-minute ride (such as from Bastille to the Eiffel Tower) costs about €20 (versus €1.27/person to get anywhere in town using a *carnet* ticket on the Métro or bus). Drivers charge higher rates at rush hour, at night, all day Sunday, and for extra passengers (see above). Each piece of luggage you put in the trunk is €1 extra (though it won't appear on the meter, it is a legitimate charge). To tip, round up to the next euro (at least €0.50).

How to Catch *un Taxi:* You can try waving down a taxi, but it's often easier to ask someone for the nearest taxi stand (*"Où est une station de taxi?"*; oo ay ewn stah-see-ohn duh "taxi"). Taxi stands are indicated by a circled "T" on good city maps, and on many maps in this chapter. To order a taxi in English, call 01 41 27 66 99. When you summon a taxi by phone, the meter starts running as soon as the call is received, often adding €6 or more to the bill. Taxis are tough to find during rush hour and when it's raining.

PARIS

Tours in Paris

To sightsee on your own, download my series of free audio tours that illuminate some of Paris' top sights and neighborhoods, including my Historic Paris Walk, the Louvre, the Orsay, and Versailles Palace (see page 52 for details).

By Bus

Bus Tours—Paris Vision (also called Cityrama) offers bus tours of Paris (advertised around town). But you'll get a better value and more versatility by taking a hop-on, hop-off bus tour or Batobus boat, which provide transportation between sights (both described in this section).

Hop-On, Hop-Off Bus Tours—Double-decker buses connect Paris' main sights, allowing you to hop on and off along the way. You get a disposable set of earbuds to listen to a basic running commentary (dial English for the so-so narration). You can get off at any stop, tour a sight, then catch a later bus. These are best in good weather, when you can sit up top. There are two companies: L'Open Tours and Les Cars Rouges (pick up their brochures showing routes and stops from any TI or on their buses). You can start either tour at just about any of the major sights, such as the Eiffel Tower.

L'Open Tours uses bright yellow buses and provides more extensive coverage (and slightly better commentary) on four different routes, rolling by most of the important sights in Paris. Their Paris Grand Tour (the green route) offers the best introduction. The same ticket gets you on any of their routes within the validity period. Buy your tickets from the driver (1 day-€31, 2 days-€34, kids 4-11 pay €15 for 1 or 2 days, allow 2 hours per tour). Two to four buses depart hourly from about 10:00 to 18:00; expect to wait 10-15 minutes at each stop (stops can be tricky to find—look for yellow signs; tel. 01 42 66 56 56, www.parislopentour.com). A combo-ticket includes the Batobus boats, too (2 days-€43, 3 days-€46, kids 4-11 pay €20 for 2 or 3 days; described later).

Les Cars Rouges' bright red buses offer one route with just nine stops and recorded narration, but for a little less (adult-€29, kids 4-12 pay €15, good for 2 days, 10 percent cheaper if you book online, tel. 01 53 95 39 53, www.carsrouges.com).

By Boat

Seine Cruises—Several companies run one-hour boat cruises on the Seine. While best at night, these can also be enjoyable during the daytime. Some offer discounts for early online bookings.

Bateaux-Mouches, the oldest boat company in Paris, departs from Pont de l'Alma's right bank and has the biggest

open-top, double-decker boats (higher up means better views). But this company caters to tour groups, making their boats jammed and noisy (€11.50, kids 4-12 pay €5.50, tel. 01 42 25 96 10, www.bateaux-mouches.fr).

Bateaux Parisiens has smaller covered boats with handheld audioguides, fewer crowds, and only one deck. It leaves from right in front of the Eiffel Tower. From April to October, they usually have a second departure point on the Quai de Montebello near Notre-Dame (€12, kids 3-12 pay €5, tel. 01 76 64 14 45, www.bateauxparisiens.com).

Vedettes du Pont Neuf offers essentially the same one-hour tour as the other companies, but starts and ends at Pont Neuf. The boats feature a live guide whose delivery (in English and French) is as stiff as a recorded narration—and as hard to understand, given the quality of their sound system (€13, €11 if you book direct with this book in 2013, online booking costs just €9, kids 4-12 pay €7, tip requested, nearly 2/hour, daily 10:30-22:30, tel. 01 46 33 98 38, www.vedettesdupontneuf.com).

Hop-On, Hop-Off Boat Tour—Batobus allows you to get on and off as often as you like at any of eight popular stops along the Seine. The boats, which make a continuous circuit, stop in this order: Eiffel Tower, Orsay Museum, St. Germain-des-Prés, Notre-Dame, Jardin des Plantes, Hôtel de Ville, the Louvre, and Pont Alexandre III, near the Champs-Elysées (1 day-€15, 2 days-€18, 5 days-€21, April-Aug boats run every 20 minutes 10:00-21:30, Sept-March every 25 minutes 10:00-19:00, 45 minutes one-way, 1.5-hour round-trip, worthless narration, www.batobus.com). If you use this for getting around—sort of a scenic, floating alternative to the Métro—it can be worthwhile. But if you just want a guided boat tour, the Seine cruises (described above) are a better choice.

By Foot

Paris Walks—This company offers a variety of two-hour walks, led by British and American guides. Tours are thoughtfully prepared and entertaining. Don't hesitate to stand close to the guide to hear (€12-15, generally 2/day—morning and afternoon, private tours available, family guides and Louvre tours a specialty, call 01 48 09 21 40 for schedule in English or check printable online schedule at www.paris-walks.com). Tours focus on the Marais (4/week), Montmartre (3/week), medieval Latin Quarter (Mon), Ile de la Cité/Notre-Dame (Mon), the "Two Islands" (Ile de la Cité and Ile St. Louis, Wed), the Revolution (Tue), and Hemingway's Paris (Fri). They also run less-regular tours of Paris' Puces St. Ouen flea market and of the Catacombs, plus a themed walk on the Occupation and Resistance in Paris during the 1940s. Call a day or two ahead to hear the current schedule and starting point. Most tours don't require reservations, but specialty tours—such as the Louvre, fashion, or chocolate tours—require advance reservations and prepayment with credit card (deposits aren't refundable).

Context Paris—These "intellectual by design" walking tours, geared for serious learners, are led by docents (historians, architects, and academics). They cover both museums and specific neighborhoods, and range from traditional topics such as French art history in the Louvre and the Gothic architecture of Notre-Dame to more thematic explorations like immigration and the changing face of Paris, jazz in the Latin Quarter, and the history of the baguette. It's best to book in advance—groups are limited to six participants and can fill up fast (€40-90/person, admission to sights extra, generally 3 hours, tel. 01 72 81 36 35, US tel. 800-691-6036, www.contextparis.com).

Classic Walks—The antithesis of Context Paris' walks, these lowbrow, lighter-on-information but high-on-fun walking tours are run by Fat Tire Bike Tours. Their 3.5-hour Classic Walk covers most major sights (€20, departs May-Sept daily at 10:00; Mon, Wed, Fri and Sun only March-April and Oct; meet at their office at 24 Rue Edgar Faure, Mo: Dupleix, tel. 01 56 58 10 54, www.classicwalksparis.com). They also offer neighborhood walks of Montmartre, the Marais, and Latin Quarter, as well as themed walks on the French Revolution and World War II (€20, tours leave several times a week—see website for details). Their Easy Pass tours are designed to allow you to skip the lines at major sights. They run tours of the Louvre, Catacombs, Eiffel Tower, Pompidou, Orsay, and Versailles (€45-85/person, includes entry and guided tour, www.easypasstours.com). Also ask about their skip-the-line tickets to key sights. The company promises a €2 discount on all walks with this book.

Local Guides—For many, Paris merits hiring a Parisian as a personal guide. **Arnaud Servignat** is an excellent licensed guide (€190/half-day, also does car tours of the countryside around Paris for a little more, mobile 06 68 80 29 05, www.french-guide.com, arnotour@me.com). **Thierry Gauduchon** is a terrific guide well worth his fee (€200/half-day, €400/day, tel. 01 56 98 10 82, mobile 06 19 07 30 77, tgauduchon@aol.com). **Elisabeth Van Hest** is another likable and capable guide (€190/half-day, tel. 01 43 41 47 31, elisa.guide@gmail.com).

Food Tours—Friendly Canadian **Rosa Jackson** designs personalized "Edible Paris" itineraries based on your interests and three-hour "food-guru" tours of Paris led by her or one of her two colleagues (unguided itineraries from €125, €300 guided tours for up to 3, mobile 06 81 67 41 22, www.edible-paris.com, rosa@rosa jackson.com).

By Bike, Segway, or Pedicab

A bike tour is a fun way to see Paris. Two companies—Bike About Tours and Fat Tire Bike Tours—offer tours, sell bottled water and bike maps of Paris, and give advice on cycling routes in the city. Their tour routes cover different areas of the city, so avid cyclists could do both without much repetition.

Bike About Tours—Run by Christian (American) and Paul (New Zealander), this company offers easygoing tours with a focus on the eastern half of the city. Their four-hour tours run daily year-round at 10:00 (also at 15:00 June-Sept). You'll meet at the statue of Charlemagne in front of Notre-Dame, then walk to the nearby rental office to get bikes. The tour includes a good back-street visit of the Marais, Rive Gauche outdoor sculpture park, Ile de la Cité, heart of the Latin Quarter (with a lunch break), Louvre, Les Halles, and Pompidou Center. Group tours have a 12-person maximum—reserve online to guarantee a spot, or show up and take your chances (€30, €5 discount with this book, maximum 2 discounts per book, 15 percent discount for families, includes helmets upon request, private tours available, www.bikeabouttours.com).

Fat Tire Bike Tours—A hardworking gang of young Anglophone expats runs an extensive program of bike, Segway, and walking tours (see Classic Walks listing, earlier). Their high-energy guides run four-hour bike tours of Paris (adults-€30, kids-€28, show this book to get a €4 discount per person, maximum 2 discounts per book, reservations not necessary—just show up). Kid-sized bikes are available, as are nifty tandem attachments that hook on to a parent's bike.

On the day tour, you'll pedal with a pack of 10-20 riders, mostly in parks and along bike lanes, with a lunch stop in the Tuileries Garden (tours leave daily rain or shine at 11:00, April-Oct at 15:00 as well, no minimum number of participants required). Tours meet at the south pillar of the Eiffel Tower, where you'll get a short history lesson, then walk six minutes to the Fat Tire office to pick up bikes (helmets available upon request at no extra charge, tel. 01 56 58 10 54, www.fattirebiketoursparis.com).

TripUp Pedicab Tours—You'll see these space-age pedicabs *(cyclopolitains)* everywhere in central Paris. The hard-pedaling, free-spirited drivers (who get some electrical assistance) are happy to either transport you from point A to B or give you a tour at a snail's pace—which is a lovely way to experience Paris (€40-50/hour, www.tripup.fr).

Self-Guided Walk in Paris

Historic Paris

(This information is distilled from the Historic Paris Walk chapter in *Rick Steves' Paris*, by Rick Steves, Steve Smith, and Gene Openshaw. You can download a free audio version of this walk to your mobile device; see page 52.)

Allow four hours to do justice to this three-mile walk; just follow the dotted line on the "Historic Paris Walk" map. Start where the city did—on the Ile de la Cité, the island in the Seine River and the physical and historic bull's-eye of your Paris map. The closest Métro stops are Cité, Hôtel de Ville, and St. Michel, each a short walk away.

For suggestions on eateries near this part of Paris, see page 1073.

• *On the square in front of Notre-Dame Cathedral, view the facade from the bronze plaque on the ground marked "Point Zero" (30 yards from the central doorway). You're standing at the center of the country, the point from which all distances in France are measured. Find the circular window in the center of the cathedral's facade.*

▲▲▲Notre-Dame Cathedral

This 700-year-old cathedral is packed with history and tourists. Study its sculpture and windows, take in a Mass, eavesdrop on guides, and walk all around the outside.

Cost and Hours: Cathedral—free, Mon-Fri 8:00-18:45, Sat-Sun 8:00-19:15; Treasury—€4, not covered by Museum Pass, Mon-Fri 9:30-17:40, Sat-Sun 9:30-18:10; audioguide-€5, free English tours—normally Wed-Thu at 14:15, Sat-Sun at 14:30. The cathedral hosts several Masses every morning, plus Vespers at 17:45. The international Mass is held Sun at 11:30, with an organ concert at 16:30. Call or check the website for a full schedule. On Good Friday and the first Friday of the month at 15:00, the (visually underwhelming) relic known as Jesus' Crown of Thorns goes on display (Mo: Cité, Hôtel de Ville, or St. Michel; tel. 01 42 34 56 10, www.notredamedeparis.fr).

Tower Climb: The entrance for Notre-Dame's towers is outside the cathedral, along the left side. It's 400 steps up, but it's worth it for the gargoyle's-eye view of the cathedral, Seine, and city (€8.50, covered by Museum Pass but no bypass line for pass-

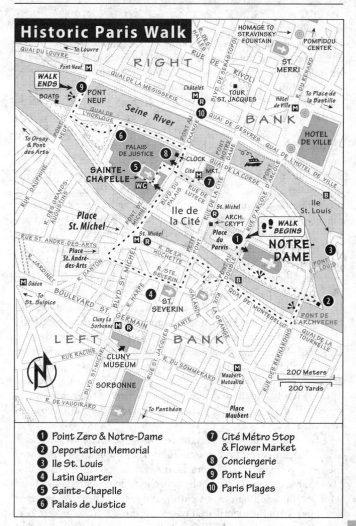

Historic Paris Walk

1. Point Zero & Notre-Dame
2. Deportation Memorial
3. Ile St. Louis
4. Latin Quarter
5. Sainte-Chapelle
6. Palais de Justice
7. Cité Métro Stop & Flower Market
8. Conciergerie
9. Pont Neuf
10. Paris Plages

holders; daily April-Sept 10:00-18:30, Sat-Sun until 23:00 in July-Aug, Oct-March 10:00-17:30, last entry 45 minutes before closing; tel. 01 53 10 07 00, www.notre-dame-de-paris.monuments -nationaux.fr).

● **Self-Guided Tour:** The **cathedral facade** is worth a close look. The church is dedicated to "Our Lady" *(Notre Dame)*. Mary is center stage—cradling God, right in the heart of the facade, surrounded by the halo of the rose window. Adam is on the left and Eve is on the right.

Below Mary and above the arches is a row of 28 statues known as the Kings of Judah. During the French Revolution, these biblical kings were mistaken for the hated French kings, and Notre-Dame represented the oppressive Catholic hierarchy. The citizens stormed the church, crying, "Off with their heads!" All were decapitated, but have since been recapitated.

Speaking of decapitation, look at the carving to the left of the doorway on the left. The man with his head in his hands is St. Denis. Back when there was a Roman temple on this spot, Christianity began making converts. The fourth-century bishop of Roman Paris, Denis was beheaded as a warning to those forsaking the Roman gods. But those early Christians were hard to keep down. The man who would become St. Denis got up, tucked his head under his arm, headed north, paused at a fountain to wash it off, and continued until he found just the right place to meet his maker: Montmartre. (Although the name "Montmartre" comes from the Roman "Mount of Mars," later generations—thinking of their beheaded patron, St. Denis—preferred a less pagan version, "Mount of Martyrs.") The Parisians were convinced by this miracle, Christianity gained ground, and a church soon replaced the pagan temple.

Medieval art was OK if it embellished the house of God and told biblical stories. For a fine example, move to the base of the central column (at the foot of Mary, about where the head of St. Denis could spit if he were really good). Working around from the left, find God telling a barely created Eve, "Have fun, but no apples." Next, the sexiest serpent I've ever seen makes apples à la mode. Finally, Adam and Eve, now ashamed of their nakedness, are expelled by an angel. This is a tiny example in a church covered with meaning.

Enter the church at the right doorway (the line moves quickly). You'll be routed around the ambulatory, in much the same way medieval pilgrims were. Notre-Dame has the typical basilica floor plan shared by so many Catholic churches: a long central nave lined with columns and flanked by side aisles. It's designed in the shape of a cross, with the altar placed where the crossbeam intersects. The church can hold up to 10,000 faithful, and it's probably buzzing with visitors now, just as it was 600 years ago. The quiet, deserted churches we see elsewhere are in stark contrast to the busy, center-of-life places they were in the Middle Ages.

Don't miss the **rose windows** that fill each of the transepts. Just past the altar is the **choir,** enclosed with carved-wood walls, where more intimate services can be held in this spacious building. Circle the choir—the back side of the choir walls features **scenes of the resurrected Jesus** (c. 1350). Just ahead on the right is the **Treasury.** It contains lavish robes, golden reliquaries, and the humble tunic of King (and St.) Louis IX, but it probably isn't worth the entry fee.

Back outside, walk around the church through the park on the riverside for a close look at the **flying buttresses.** The Neo-Gothic 300-foot **spire** is a product of the 1860 reconstruction of the dilapidated old church. Around its base (visible as you approach the back end of the church) are apostles and evangelists (the green men) as well as Eugène-Emmanuel Viollet-le-Duc, the architect in charge of the work. The apostles look outward, blessing the city, while the architect (at top) looks up the spire, marveling at his fine work.

Nearby: The **archaeological crypt** is a worthwhile 15-minute stop if you have a Paris Museum Pass (€4 without Museum Pass, Tue-Sun 10:00-18:00, closed Mon, last entry 30 minutes before closing, enter 100 yards in front of the cathedral, tel. 01 55 42 50 10). You'll see remains of the many structures that have stood on this spot in the center of Paris: Roman buildings that surrounded a temple of Jupiter; a wall that didn't keep the Franks out; the main medieval road that once led grandly up the square to Notre-Dame; and even (wow) a 19th-century sewer.

• *Behind Notre-Dame, cross the street and enter through the iron gate into the park at the tip of the island. Look for the stairs and head down to reach the...*

▲Deportation Memorial (Mémorial de la Déportation)

This memorial to the 200,000 French victims of the Nazi concentration camps (1940-1945) draws you into their experience. France was quickly overrun by Nazi Germany, and Paris spent the war years under Nazi occupation. Jews and dissidents were rounded up and deported—many never returned.

As you descend the steps, the city around you disappears. Surrounded by walls, you have become a prisoner. Your only freedom is your view of the sky and the tiny glimpse of the river below. Enter the dark, single-file chamber up ahead. Inside, the circular plaque in the floor reads, "They went to the end of the earth and did not return."

The hallway stretching in front of you is lined with 200,000 lighted crystals, one for each French citizen who died. Flickering at the far end is the eternal flame of hope. The tomb of the unknown deportee lies at your feet. Above, the inscription reads, "Dedicated to the living memory of the 200,000 French deportees shrouded by the night and the fog, exterminated in the Nazi concentration camps." The side rooms are filled with triangles—reminiscent of the identification patches inmates were forced to wear—each bearing the name of a concentration camp. Above the exit as you leave is the message you'll find at many other Holocaust sites: "Forgive, but never forget."

Cost and Hours: Free, April-Sept Tue-Sun 10:00-19:00, Oct-March Tue-Sun 10:00-18:00, closed Mon year-round, may randomly close at other times; at the east tip of the island named Ile de la Cité, behind Notre-Dame and near Ile St. Louis (Mo: Cité); tel. 06 14 67 54 98.

• *Back on street level, look across the river (north) to the island called...*

Ile St. Louis

If Ile de la Cité is a tugboat laden with the history of Paris, it's towing this classy little residential dinghy, laden only with high-rent apartments, boutiques, characteristic restaurants, a great picnic spot (see page 1073), and famous ice cream shops.

Ile St. Louis wasn't developed until much later than Ile de la Cité (17th century). What was a swampy mess is now harmonious Parisian architecture and one of Paris' most exclusive neighborhoods. Consider taking a brief detour across the pedestrian bridge, Pont St. Louis. It connects the two islands, leading right to Rue St. Louis-en-l'Ile. This spine of the island is lined with appealing shops and reasonably priced restaurants. A short stroll takes you to the famous Berthillon ice cream parlor at #31. Gelato lovers head instead to Amorino Gelati at 47 Rue St. Louis-en-l'Ile. When you're finished exploring, loop back to the pedestrian bridge along the park-like quays (walk north to the river and turn left). This walk is about as peaceful and romantic as Paris gets.

• *From the Deportation Memorial, cross the bridge to the Left Bank. All those* **padlocks** *adorning the railing are akin to lighting candles in a church. Locals and tourists alike honor loved ones by writing a brief message on the lock and attaching it to the railing. You can buy a lock (called* cadenas, *€5) at a nearby bookseller's stall along the river.*

Turn right after crossing the bridge and walk along the river, toward the front end of Notre-Dame. Stairs detour down to the riverbank if you need a place to picnic. This side view of the church from across the river is one of Europe's great sights and is best from river level. For the best view and the sweetest crêpes you've ever had, look for the old river barge Daphné *and see if* Valeria *is open (€2.50-3.50). If the sun is out, he should be there.*

After passing the Pont au Double (the bridge leading to the facade of Notre-Dame), watch on your left for **Shakespeare and Company,** *an atmospheric reincarnation of the original 1920s bookshop and a good spot to page through books (37 Rue de la Bûcherie; see page 1020). Before returning to the island, walk a block behind Shakespeare and Company, and take a spin through the...*

▲Latin Quarter

This area's touristy fame relates to its intriguing, artsy, bohemian character. This was perhaps Europe's leading university district in the Middle Ages, when Latin was the language of higher education.

The neighborhood's main boulevards (St. Michel and St. Germain) are lined with cafés—once the haunts of great poets and philosophers, now the hangouts of tired tourists. Though still youthful and artsy, much of this area has become a tourist ghetto filled with cheap North African eateries. Exploring a few blocks up- or downriver from here gives you a better chance of feeling the pulse of what survives of Paris' classic Left Bank. For colorful wandering and café-sitting, afternoons are best.

Walking along Rue St. Séverin, you can still see the shadow of the medieval sewer system. The street slopes into a central channel of bricks. In the days before plumbing and toilets, when people still went to the river or neighborhood wells for their water, flushing meant throwing it out the window. At certain times of day, maids on the fourth floor would holler, *"Garde de l'eau!"* ("Watch out for the water!") and heave it into the streets, where it would eventually wash down into the Seine.

Consider a visit to the **Cluny Museum** for its medieval art and unicorn tapestries (see page 1063). The **Sorbonne**—the University of Paris' humanities department—is also nearby; visitors can ogle the famous dome, but they are not allowed to enter the building (two blocks south of the river on Boulevard St. Michel).

Be sure to see **Place St. Michel.** This square (facing the Pont St. Michel) is the traditional core of the Left Bank's artsy, liberal, hippie, bohemian district of poets, philosophers, and winos. In less commercial times, Place St. Michel was a gathering point for the city's malcontents and misfits. In 1830, 1848, and again in 1871, the citizens took the streets from the government troops, set up barricades *Les Miz*-style, and fought against royalist oppression. During World War II, the locals rose up against their Nazi oppressors (read the plaques under the dragons at the foot of the St. Michel fountain). Even today, whenever there's a student demonstration, it starts here.

• *From Place St. Michel, look across the river and find the prickly steeple of the Sainte-Chapelle church. Head toward it. Cross the river on Pont St. Michel and continue north along the Boulevard du Palais. On your left, you'll see the doorway to Sainte-Chapelle (usually with a line of people).*

You'll need to pass through a strict security checkpoint to get into the Sainte-Chapelle complex (this is more than a tourist attraction: France's Supreme Court meets to the right of Sainte-Chapelle in the Palais de Justice). Expect a long wait. (The Annexe Café across the street sells €1 coffee to-go—perfect for sipping while you wait in line.) First comes the security line (all sharp objects are confiscated). No one can skip this line. Security lines are shortest on weekday mornings and on weekends (when the courts are closed). Once past security, you'll enter the courtyard outside Sainte-Chapelle, where you'll find WCs. You'll also encounter another line to buy tickets to go into the church. Those with combo-tickets or Museum Passes can skip the ticket-buying line.

▲▲▲Sainte-Chapelle

This triumph of Gothic church architecture is a cathedral of glass like no other. It was speedily built between 1242 and 1248 for King

Louis IX—the only French king who is now a saint—to house the supposed Crown of Thorns. Its architectural harmony is due to the fact that it was completed under the direction of one architect and in only six years—unheard of in Gothic times. In contrast, Notre-Dame took over 200 years.

Cost and Hours: €8.50, €12.50 combo-ticket with Conciergerie, under 18 free, covered by Museum Pass, audioguide-€4.50; daily March-Oct 9:30-18:00, Wed until 21:30 mid-May-mid-Sept, Nov-Feb 9:00-17:00; last entry 30 minutes before closing, be prepared for long lines, 4 Boulevard du Palais, Mo: Cité, tel. 01 53 40 60 80, www.sainte-chapelle.monuments-nationaux.fr.

Visiting the Church: Though the inside is beautiful, the exterior is basically functional. The muscular buttresses hold up the stone roof, so the walls are essentially there to display stained glass. The lacy spire is Neo-Gothic—added in the 19th century.

Inside, the layout clearly shows an *ancien régime* approach to worship. The low-ceilinged basement was for staff and other common folks—worshipping under a sky filled with painted fleurs-de-lis, a symbol of the king. Royal Christians worshipped upstairs. The paint job, a 19th-century restoration, helps you imagine how grand this small, painted, jeweled chapel was. (Imagine Notre-Dame painted like this...) Each capital is playfully carved with a different plant's leaves.

Climb the spiral staircase to the **Chapelle Haute.** Fill the place with choral music, crank up the sunshine, face the top of the altar, and really believe that the Crown of Thorns is there, and this becomes one awesome space.

Fiat lux. "Let there be light." From the first page of the Bible, it's clear: Light is divine. Light shines through stained glass like God's grace shining down to earth. Gothic architects used their new technology to turn dark stone buildings into lanterns of light. The glory of Gothic shines brighter here than in any other church.

There are 15 separate panels of **stained glass** (6,500 square

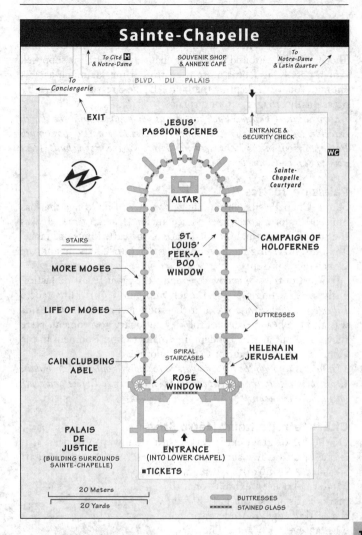

Sainte-Chapelle

To Cité Ⓜ & Notre-Dame

SOUVENIR SHOP & ANNEXE CAFÉ

To Notre-Dame & Latin Quarter

To Conciergerie

BLVD. DU PALAIS

EXIT

JESUS' PASSION SCENES

ENTRANCE & SECURITY CHECK

WC

Sainte-Chapelle Courtyard

ALTAR

STAIRS

ST. LOUIS' PEEK-A-BOO WINDOW

CAMPAIGN OF HOLOFERNES

MORE MOSES

LIFE OF MOSES

BUTTRESSES

CAIN CLUBBING ABEL

SPIRAL STAIRCASES

HELENA IN JERUSALEM

ROSE WINDOW

PALAIS DE JUSTICE (BUILDING SURROUNDS SAINTE-CHAPELLE)

ENTRANCE (INTO LOWER CHAPEL)

▪TICKETS

20 Meters

20 Yards

BUTTRESSES

STAINED GLASS

feet—two thirds of it 13th-century original), with more than 1,100 different scenes, mostly from the Bible. These cover the entire

Christian history of the world, from the Creation in Genesis (first window on the left, as you face the altar), to the coming of Christ (over the altar), to the end of the world (the round "rose"-shaped window at the rear of the church). Each individual scene is interesting, and the whole effect

is overwhelming.

The **altar** was raised up high to better display the Crown of Thorns, the relic around which this chapel was built. The supposed crown cost King Louis more than three times as much as this church. Today it is kept by the Notre-Dame Treasury (though it's occasionally brought out for display).

• *Exit Sainte-Chapelle. Back outside, as you walk around the church exterior, look down to see the foundation and take note of how much Paris has risen in the 750 years since Sainte-Chapelle was built. Next door to Sainte-Chapelle is the...*

Palais de Justice

Sainte-Chapelle sits within a huge complex of buildings that has housed the local government since ancient Roman times. It was the site of the original Gothic palace of the early kings of France. The only surviving medieval parts are Sainte-Chapelle and the Conciergerie prison.

Most of the site is now covered by the giant Palais de Justice, built in 1776, home of the French Supreme Court. The motto *Liberté, Egalité, Fraternité* over the doors is a reminder that this was also the headquarters of the Revolutionary government. Here they doled out justice, condemning many to imprisonment in the Conciergerie downstairs or to the guillotine.

• *Now pass through the big iron gate to the noisy Boulevard du Palais. Cross the street to the wide, pedestrian-only Rue de Lutèce and walk about halfway down.*

Cité "Metropolitain" Métro Stop

Of the 141 original early-20th-century subway entrances, this is one of only a few survivors—now preserved as a national art treasure. (New York's Museum of  Modern Art even exhibits one.) It marks Paris at its peak in 1900—on the cutting edge of Modernism, but with an eye for beauty. The curvy, plantlike ironwork is a textbook example of Art Nouveau, the style that rebelled against the erector-set squareness of the Industrial Age. Other similar Métro stations in Paris are Abbesses and Porte Dauphine.

The flower and plant market on Place Louis Lépine is a pleasant detour. On Sundays this square flutters with a busy bird market. And across the way is the Préfecture de Police, where Inspector Clouseau of *Pink Panther* fame used to work, and where the local resistance fighters took the first building from the Nazis

in August of 1944, leading to the Allied liberation of Paris a week later.
• *Pause here to admire the view. Sainte-Chapelle is a pearl in an ugly architectural oyster. Double back to the Palais de Justice, turn right onto Boulevard du Palais, and enter the...*

▲Conciergerie

Though pretty barren inside, this former prison echoes with history (and is free with the Museum Pass—remember that pass-

holders can skip the ticket-buying line). Positioned next to the courthouse, the Conciergerie was the gloomy prison famous as the last stop for 2,780 victims of the guillotine, including France's last *ancien régime* queen, Marie-Antoinette. Before then, kings had used the building to torture and execute failed assassins. (One of its towers along the river was called "The Babbler," named for the pain-induced sounds that leaked from it.) When the Revolution (1789) toppled the king, the building kept its same function, but without torture. The progressive Revolutionaries proudly unveiled a modern and more humane way to execute people—the guillotine.

Inside, pick up a free map and breeze through the one-way circuit. It's well-described in English. See the spacious, low-ceilinged Hall of Men-at-Arms (room 1), used as the guards' dining room, with four large fireplaces (look up the chimneys). This big room gives a feel for the grandeur of the Great Hall (upstairs, not open to visitors), where the Revolutionary tribunals grilled scared prisoners on their political correctness.

You'll also see a re-creation of Marie-Antoinette's cell, which houses a collection of her mementos. In another room, a list of those made "a foot shorter at the top" by the "national razor" includes ex-King Louis XVI, Charlotte Corday (who murdered the Revolutionary writer Jean-Paul Marat in his bathtub), and—oh, the irony—Maximilien de Robespierre, the head of the Revolution, the man who sent so many to the guillotine.

Cost and Hours: €8.50, €12.50 combo-ticket with Sainte-Chapelle, covered by Museum Pass, daily March-Oct 9:30-18:00, Nov-Feb 9:00-17:00, last entry 30 minutes before closing, 2 Boulevard du Palais, Mo: Cité, tel. 01 53 40 60 80, www.conciergerie.monuments-nationaux.fr.
• *Back outside, turn left on Boulevard du Palais and head north. On the corner is the city's oldest public clock. The mechanism of the present clock is from 1334, and even though the case is Baroque, it keeps on ticking.*

PARIS

Paris at a Glance

▲▲▲**Notre-Dame Cathedral** Paris' most beloved church, with towers and gargoyles. **Hours:** Cathedral Mon-Fri 8:00-18:45, Sat-Sun 8:00-19:15; tower daily April-Sept 10:00-18:30, Sat-Sun until 23:00 in July-Aug, Oct-March 10:00-17:30; Treasury Mon-Fri 9:30-17:40, Sat-Sun 9:30-18:10. See page 1032.

▲▲▲**Sainte-Chapelle** Gothic cathedral with peerless stained glass. **Hours:** Daily March-Oct 9:30-18:00, Wed until 21:30 mid-May-mid-Sept, Nov-Feb 9:00-17:00. See page 1038.

▲▲▲**Louvre** Europe's oldest and greatest museum, starring *Mona Lisa* and *Venus de Milo*. **Hours:** Wed-Mon 9:00-18:00, Wed and Fri until 21:45, closed Tue. See page 1044.

▲▲▲**Orsay Museum** Nineteenth-century art, including Europe's greatest Impressionist collection. **Hours:** Tue-Sun 9:30-18:00, Thu until 21:45, closed Mon. See page 1052.

▲▲▲**Eiffel Tower** Paris' soaring exclamation point. **Hours:** Daily mid-June-Aug 9:00-24:00, Sept-mid-June 9:30-23:00. See page 1058.

▲▲▲**Champs-Elysées** Paris' grand boulevard. **Hours:** Always open. See page 1064.

▲▲▲**Versailles** The ultimate royal palace (Château), with a Hall of Mirrors, vast gardens, a grand canal, plus a queen's playground (Trianon Palaces and Domaine de Marie-Antoinette). As this is challenging to reach on a brief day in the port of Le Havre, I haven't covered it in depth. **Hours:** Château April-Oct Tue-Sun 9:00-18:30, Nov-March Tue-Sun 9:00-17:30, closed Mon year-round. Trianon/Domaine April-Oct Tue-Sun 12:00-18:30, Nov-March Tue-Sun 12:00-17:30, closed Mon year-round; in winter only the two Trianon Palaces are open. Gardens generally open

PARIS

Turn left onto Quai de l'Horloge and walk west along the river, past "The Babbler" tower. The bridge up ahead is the Pont Neuf, where we'll end this walk. At the first corner, veer left into a sleepy triangular square called Place Dauphine. Marvel at how such coziness could be lodged in the midst of such greatness. At the equestrian statue of Henry IV (at the other end of Place Dauphine), turn right onto the old bridge and take refuge in one of the nooks halfway across, on the Eiffel Tower side.

Pont Neuf

This "new bridge" is now Paris' oldest. Built during Henry IV's reign (about 1600), its arches span the widest part of the river.

April-Oct daily 9:00-20:30, Nov-March Tue-Sun 8:00-18:00, closed Mon. See page 1070.

▲▲**Orangerie Museum** Monet's water lilies, plus works by Utrillo, Cézanne, Renoir, Matisse, and Picasso, in a lovely setting. **Hours:** Wed-Mon 9:00-18:00, closed Tue. See page 1052.

▲▲**Army Museum and Napoleon's Tomb** The emperor's imposing tomb, flanked by museums of France's wars. **Hours:** Museum—daily April-Sept 10:00-18:00, may be open Tue until 21:00, Oct-March 10:00-17:00, closed first Mon of month year-round. Tomb—daily April-June and Sept 10:00-18:00, may be open Tue until 21:00; July-Aug 10:00-19:00, may be open Tue until 21:00; Oct-March 10:00-17:00, closed first Mon of month Sept-May. See page 1061.

▲▲**Rodin Museum** Works by the greatest sculptor since Michelangelo, with many statues in a peaceful garden. **Hours:** Tue-Sun 10:00-17:45, Wed until 20:45, closed Mon. See page 1062.

▲▲**Marmottan Museum** Untouristy art museum focusing on Monet. **Hours:** Tue-Sun 10:00-18:00, Thu until 20:00, closed Mon. See page 1062.

▲▲**Cluny Museum** Medieval art with unicorn tapestries. **Hours:** Wed-Mon 9:15-17:45, closed Tue. See page 1063.

▲▲**Arc de Triomphe** Triumphal arch with viewpoint, marking start of Champs-Elysées. **Hours:** Interior—daily April-Sept 10:00-23:00, Oct-March 10:00-22:30. See page 1066.

▲▲**Sacré-Cœur and Montmartre** White basilica atop Montmartre with super views. **Hours:** Daily 6:00-22:30; dome climb daily May-Sept 9:00-19:00, Oct-April 9:00-17:00. See page 1067.

PARIS

Unlike other bridges, this one never had houses or buildings growing on it. The turrets were originally for vendors and street entertainers. In the days of Henry IV, who promised his peasants "a chicken in every pot every Sunday," this would have been a lively scene. From the bridge, look downstream (west) to see the next bridge, the pedestrian-only Pont des Arts. Ahead on the Right

Bank is the long Louvre Museum. Beyond that, on the Left Bank, is the Orsay. And what's that tall black tower in the distance?

• *Our walk is finished. From here, you can tour the Seine by boat (the departure point for Seine river cruises offered by Vedettes du Pont Neuf is through the park at the end of the island—see page 1028), continue to the Louvre, or (if it's summer) head to the...*

▲Paris *Plages* (Paris Beaches)

The Riviera it's not, but this string of fanciful faux beaches—assembled in summer along a one-mile stretch of the Right Bank of the Seine—is a fun place to stroll, play, and people-watch on a sunny day. Each summer, the Paris city government closes the embankment's highway and trucks in potted palm trees, hammocks, lounge chairs, and 2,000 tons of sand to create colorful urban beaches. You'll also find "beach cafés," climbing walls, prefab pools, trampolines, *boules*, a library, beach volleyball, badminton, and Frisbee areas.

Cost and Hours: Free, mid-July-mid-Aug daily 8:00-24:00, no beach off-season; on Right Bank of Seine, just north of Ile de la Cité, between Pont des Arts and Pont de Sully; for information, go to www.paris.fr, click on "English," then "Visit," then "Highlights."

Sights in Paris

Paris has some of Europe's—arguably the world's—best sightseeing, with Notre-Dame Cathedral and the city's historic core (covered by the self-guided walk, earlier), blockbuster museums (the Louvre and Orsay are just the start), one of the planet's most famous boulevards (the Champs-Elysées), a sights-studded hilltop (Montmartre), a certain famous erector-set tower, and plenty more. Cruisers in town for just a few hours are spoiled for choice: You'll need to be picky and quick to hit a few highlights from the many options listed here.

Major Museums Neighborhood

Paris' grandest park, the Tuileries Garden, was once the private property of kings and queens. Today it links the Louvre, Orangerie, and Orsay museums.

▲▲▲Louvre (Musée du Louvre)

This is Europe's oldest, biggest, greatest, and second-most-crowded museum (after the Vatican). Housed in a U-shaped, 16th-century palace (accentuated by a 20th-century glass pyramid), the Louvre is Paris' top museum and one of its key landmarks. It's

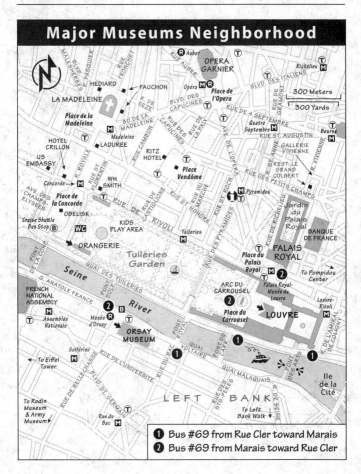

Major Museums Neighborhood

1 Bus #69 from Rue Cler toward Marais
2 Bus #69 from Marais toward Rue Cler

home to *Mona Lisa*, *Venus de Milo*, and hall after hall of Greek and Roman masterpieces, medieval jewels, Michelangelo statues, and paintings by the greatest artists from the Renaissance to the Romantics (mid-1800s).

Touring the Louvre can be overwhelming, so be selective. Focus on the Denon wing (south, along the river), with Greek sculptures, Italian paintings (by Raphael and Leonardo da Vinci), and—of course—French paintings (Neoclassical and Romantic), and the adjoining Sully wing, with Egyptian artifacts and more French paintings. For extra credit, tackle the Richelieu wing (north, away from the river), displaying works from ancient Mesopotamia (today's Iraq), as well as French,

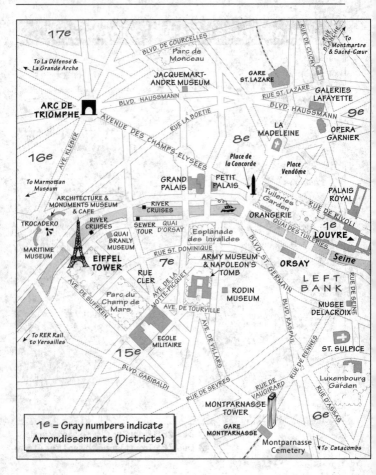

Dutch, and Northern art.

Expect changes—the sprawling Louvre is constantly shuffling its collection. Rooms are periodically closed for renovation, and pieces are removed from display if they're being restored or loaned to other museums. The new Islamic art space—with its glass roof modeled on a head scarf (visible in the Cour de Visconti courtyard of the Denon wing) may be open by the time you visit. If you don't find the artwork you're looking for, ask the nearest guard for its new location.

Cost and Hours: €11, free on first Sun of month, covered by Museum Pass, tickets good all day, reentry allowed; Wed-Mon 9:00-18:00, Wed and Fri until 21:45 (except on holidays), closed Tue, galleries start shutting 30 minutes before closing, last entry 45 minutes before closing; crowds worst in the morning and all day Sun, Mon, and Wed; several cafés, tel. 01 40 20 53 17, recorded

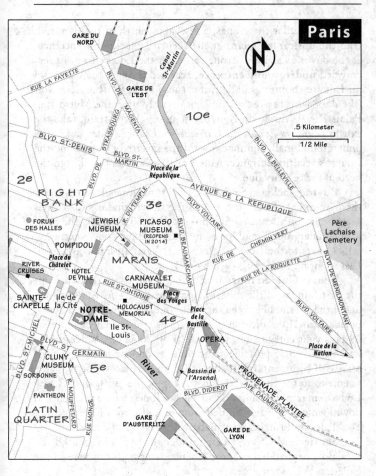

Paris

GARE DU NORD

Canal St-Martin

RUE LA FAYETTE

BLVD. DE

GARE DE L'EST

MAGENTA

STRASBOURG

10e

BLVD. DE BELLEVILLE

.5 Kilometer

1/2 Mile

BLVD. ST-DENIS

BLVD. DE

BLVD. ST-MARTIN

Place de la République

2e

AVENUE DE LA REPUBLIQUE

RIGHT BANK

RUE DU TEMPLE

3e

BLVD. VOLTAIRE

Père Lachaise Cemetery

FORUM DES HALLES

JEWISH MUSEUM

PICASSO MUSEUM (REOPENS IN 2014)

BLVD. BEAUMARCHAIS

POMPIDOU

MARAIS

CHEMIN VERT

Place du Châtelet

RIVER CRUISES

HOTEL DE VILLE

CARNAVALET MUSEUM

RUE DE

RUE DE LA ROQUETTE

BLVD. DE MENILMONTANT

SAINTE-CHAPELLE

Ile de la Cité

RUE ST-ANTOINE

Place des Vosges

NOTRE-DAME

HOLOCAUST MEMORIAL

Place de la Bastille

4e

BLVD. VOLTAIRE

Ile St-Louis

OPERA

Place de la Nation

BLVD. ST-MICHEL

BLVD. ST-GERMAIN

River

CLUNY MUSEUM

5e

Bassin de l'Arsenal

PROMENADE PLANTEE

AVE. DAUMESNIL

SORBONNE

R. MOUFFETARD

PANTHEON

BLVD. DIDEROT

LATIN QUARTER

RUE MONGE

GARE D'AUSTERLITZ

GARE DE LYON

info tel. 01 40 20 51 51, www.louvre.fr.

Getting There: It's at the Palais Royal-Musée du Louvre Métro stop. (The old Louvre Métro stop, called Louvre-Rivoli, is farther from the entrance.) Buses #69 and #24 also run past the Louvre.

Getting In: There is no grander entry than through the main entrance at the **pyramid** in the central court-yard, but metal detectors (not ticket-buyers) can create a long line. Museum Pass holders can use the **group entrance** in the pedestrian pas-sageway (labeled *Pavilion Richelieu*) between the pyramid and Rue de

PARIS

Rivoli. It's under the arches, a few steps north of the pyramid; find the uniformed guard at the security checkpoint entrance, at the down escalator. Anyone can enter the Louvre from its less crowded **underground entrance,** accessed through the Carrousel du Louvre shopping mall. Enter the mall at 99 Rue de Rivoli (the door with the red awning) or directly from the Métro stop Palais Royal-Musée du Louvre (stepping off the train, take the exit to *Musée du Louvre-Le Carrousel du Louvre*). Once inside the underground mall, continue toward the inverted pyramid and the Louvre's security entrance. Museum Pass holders can skip to the head of the security line.

Buying Tickets: Self-serve ticket machines located under the pyramid are faster to use than the ticket windows (machines accept euro bills, coins, and chip-and-PIN Visa cards). The *tabac* in the underground mall (near the Carrousel du Louvre entrance) sells tickets to the Louvre, Orsay, and Versailles, plus Museum Passes, for no extra charge (cash only).

Tours: Guided tours in English leave twice daily (except the first Sunday of the month) from the *Accueil des Groupes* area, under the pyramid between the Sully and Denon wings (1.5 hours; normally at 11:00 and 14:00, sometimes more often in summer; €9 plus your entry ticket, tour tel. 01 40 20 52 63). **Videoguides** on Nintendo 3DS portable game consoles provide tech-savvy visitors with commentary on about 700 masterpieces (€5, available at entries to the three wings, at the top of the escalators). A free Louvre **smartphone app** is available at iTunes, where you can also download my free self-guided Louvre **audio tour** (see page 52). You'll also find English explanations throughout the museum.

Services: WCs are located under the pyramid, behind the escalators to the Denon and Richelieu wings. Once you're in the galleries, WCs are scarce.

Eating near the Louvre: The Louvre has several cafés, including **Café Mollien,** located near the end of our tour (€12 for sandwich or salad and drink on terrace overlooking pyramid, closes at 18:00). A reasonably priced self-service lunch **cafeteria** is up the escalator from the pyramid in the Richelieu wing. **Le Grand Louvre Café** under the pyramid is a pricier option. Your best bet is in the underground shopping mall, the **Carrousel du Louvre** (daily 8:30-23:00), which has an assortment of decent-value, multiethnic fast-food eateries, including—*quelle horreur*—a McDonald's (near the inverted pyramid). For a fine, elegant lunch near the Louvre, head to the venerable **Café le Nemours** (good €10-12 *croque monsieur* and salads, open daily; leaving the Louvre, cross Rue de Rivoli and veer left to 2 Place Colette, adjacent to Comédie Française) or the classy **Le Fumoir** (€19 lunch *menu*, open daily, 6 Rue de l'Amiral de Coligny, near

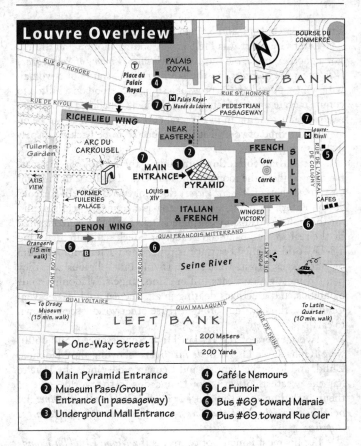

Louvre Overview

BOURSE DU COMMERCE

RUE ST. HONORE

Place du Palais Royal

PALAIS ROYAL

RIGHT BANK

RUE ST. HONORE

Palais Royal-Musée du Louvre

PEDESTRIAN PASSAGEWAY

Louvre-Rivoli

RUE DE RIVOLI

RICHELIEU WING

NEAR EASTERN

FRENCH

RUE DE L'AMIRAL DE COLIGNY

Tuileries Garden

ARC DU CARROUSEL

MAIN ENTRANCE

PYRAMID

Cour Carrée

SULLY

AXIS VIEW

FORMER TUILERIES PALACE

LOUIS XIV

GREEK

ITALIAN & FRENCH

WINGED VICTORY

CAFES

DENON WING

QUAI FRANÇOIS MITTERRAND

To Orangerie (15 min walk)

PONT ROYAL

PONT CARROUSEL

Seine River

PONT DES ARTS

QUAI VOLTAIRE

To Orsay Museum (15 min. walk)

QUAI MALAQUAIS

LEFT BANK

RUE DE SEINE

To Latin Quarter (10 min. walk)

➡ One-Way Street

200 Meters
200 Yards

❶ Main Pyramid Entrance
❷ Museum Pass/Group Entrance (in passageway)
❸ Underground Mall Entrance
❹ Café le Nemours
❺ Le Fumoir
❻ Bus #69 toward Marais
❼ Bus #69 toward Rue Cler

Louvre-Rivoli Métro stop).

◑ Self-Guided Tour: Start in the Denon Wing and visit the highlights, in the following order (thanks to Gene Openshaw for his help writing this tour).

Look for the famous *Venus de Milo (Aphrodite)* statue (pictured here). This goddess of love (c. 100 B.C., from the Greek island of Melos) created a sensation when she was discovered in 1820. Most "Greek" statues are actually later Roman copies, but *Venus* is a rare Greek original. She, like Golden Age Greeks, epitomizes stability, beauty, and balance.

After viewing *Venus*, wander through the **ancient Greek and Roman works** to room 6 to see the Parthenon frieze (stone fragments that once decorated the exterior of the greatest Athenian temple), mosaics from the ancient city of Antioch,

PARIS

Etruscan sarcophagi, and Roman portrait busts.

Later Greek art was Hellenistic, adding motion and drama. For a good example, see the exciting *Winged Victory of Samothrace* (*Victoire de Samothrace*, on the landing). This statue of a woman with wings, poised on the prow of a ship, once stood on a hilltop to commemorate a naval victory. The statue is scheduled to undergo restoration beginning in in September of 2013, and may not be on view at the time of your visit. It is expected to be back on display by the spring of 2014.

The **Italian collection**—including the *Mona Lisa*—is scattered throughout the rooms of the long Grand Gallery, to the right (as you face her) of *Winged Victory* (look for **two Botticelli frescoes** as you enter). In painting, the Renaissance meant realism, and for the Italians, realism was spelled "3-D." Painters were inspired by the realism and balanced beauty of Greek sculpture. Painting a 3-D world on a 2-D surface is tough, and after a millennium of Dark Ages, artists were rusty. Living in a religious age, they painted mostly altarpieces full of saints, angels, Madonnas-and-bambinos, and crucifixes floating in an ethereal gold-leaf heaven. Gradually, though, they brought these otherworldly scenes down to earth.

Two masters of the Italian High Renaissance (1500-1600) were Raphael (see his *La Belle Jardinière*, showing the Madonna, Child, and John the Baptist) and Leonardo da Vinci. The Louvre has the greatest collection of Leonardos in the world—five of them, including the exquisite *Virgin and Child with St. Anne;* the neighboring *Virgin of the Rocks;* and the androgynous *John the Baptist.*

But his most famous, of course, is the *Mona Lisa* (*La Joconde* in French), located in the Salle des Etats, midway down the Grand Gallery, on the right. After several years and a €5 million renovation, Mona is alone behind glass on her own false wall. Leonardo was already an old man when François I invited him to France. Determined to pack light, he took only a few paintings with him. One was a portrait of Lisa del Giocondo, the wife of a wealthy Florentine merchant. When Leonardo arrived, François immediately fell in love with the painting, making it the centerpiece of the small collection of Italian masterpieces that would, in three centuries, become the Louvre museum. He called it *La*
Gioconda (*La Joconde* in French)—a play on both her last name and the Italian word for "happiness." We know it as the *Mona Lisa*—a contraction of the Italian for "my lady Lisa." Warning: François

was impressed, but *Mona* may disappoint you. She's smaller than you'd expect, darker, engulfed in a huge room, and hidden behind a glaring pane of glass.

The huge canvas opposite *Mona* is Paolo Veronese's ***The Marriage at Cana,*** showing the Renaissance love of beautiful things gone hog-wild. Venetian artists like Veronese painted the good life of rich, happy-go-lucky Venetian merchants.

Now for something **Neoclassical.** Exit behind *Mona Lisa* and turn right into the Salle Daru to find ***The Coronation of Emperor Napoleon*** by Jacques-Louis David. Neoclassicism, once the rage in France (1780-1850), usually features Greek subjects, patriotic sentiment, and a clean, simple style. After Napoleon quickly conquered most of Europe, he insisted on being made emperor (not merely king) of this "New Rome." He staged an elaborate coronation ceremony in Paris, and rather than let the pope crown him, he crowned himself. The setting was Notre-Dame Cathedral, with Greek columns and Roman arches thrown in for effect. Napoleon's mom was also added, since she couldn't make it to the ceremony. A key on the frame describes who's who in the picture.

The **Romantic** collection, in an adjacent room (Salle Mollien), has works by Théodore Géricault (***The Raft of the Medusa***—one

of my favorites) and Eugène Delacroix ***(Liberty Leading the People).*** Romanticism, with an emphasis on motion and emotion, is the flip side of cool, balanced Neoclassicism, though they both flourished in the early 1800s. Delacroix's *Liberty,* commemorating the stirrings of democracy in France, is also an appropriate tribute to the Louvre, the first museum ever opened to the common rabble of humanity. The good things in life don't belong only to a small, wealthy part of society, but to everyone. The motto of France is *Liberté, Egalité, Fraternité*—liberty, equality, and the brotherhood of all.

Exit the room at the far end (past Café Mollien) and go downstairs, where you'll bump into the bum of a large, twisting male nude looking like he's just waking up after a thousand-year nap. The two ***Slaves*** (1513-1515) by Michelangelo are a fitting end to this museum—works that bridge the ancient and modern worlds. Michelangelo, like his fellow Renaissance artists, learned from the Greeks. The perfect anatomy, twisting poses, and idealized faces appear as if they could have been created 2,000 years earlier. Michelangelo said that his purpose was to carve away the marble to reveal the figures God put inside. The *Rebellious Slave,* fighting against his bondage, shows the agony of that process and the ecstasy of the result.

Although this makes for a good first tour, there's so much more. After a break (or on a second visit), consider a stroll through a few rooms of the Richelieu wing, which contain some of the Louvre's most ancient pieces. Bible students, amateur archaeologists, and Iraq War vets may find the collection especially interesting.

▲▲Orangerie Museum (Musée de l'Orangerie)

Step out of the tree-lined, sun-dappled Impressionist painting that is the Tuileries Garden, and into the Orangerie (oh-rahn-zheh-

ree), a little bijou of select works by Claude Monet and his contemporaries. Start with the museum's claim to fame: Monet's water lilies. These eight mammoth-scale paintings are displayed exactly as Monet intended

them—surrounding you in oval-shaped rooms—so you feel as though you're immersed in his garden at Giverny.

Working from his home there, Monet built a special studio with skylights and wheeled easels to accommodate the canvases—1,950 square feet in all. Each canvas features a different part of the pond, painted from varying angles at distinct times of day—but the true subject of these works is the play of reflected light off the surface of the pond. The Monet rooms are considered the first art installation, and the blurry canvases signaled the abstract art to come.

Downstairs you'll see artists that bridge the Impressionist and Modernist worlds—Renoir, Cézanne, Utrillo, Matisse, and Picasso. Together they provide a snapshot of what was hot in the world of art collecting, circa 1920.

Cost and Hours: €7.50, €5 after 17:00, under 18 free, €14 combo-ticket with Orsay Museum (valid for four days, one visit per sight), covered by Museum Pass; Wed-Mon 9:00-18:00, closed Tue, galleries shut down 15 minutes before closing time; audioguide-€5, €6 English tours usually offered Mon and Thu at 14:30; located in Tuileries Garden near Place de la Concorde (Mo: Concorde), 15-minute stroll from the Orsay, tel. 01 44 77 80 07, www.musee-orangerie.fr.

▲▲▲Orsay Museum (Musée d'Orsay)

The Musée d'Orsay (mew-zay dor-say) houses French art of the 1800s and early 1900s (specifically, 1848-1914), picking up where the Louvre's art collection leaves off. For us, that means

Impressionism, the art of sun-dappled fields, bright colors, and crowded Parisian cafés. The Orsay houses the best general collection anywhere of Manet, Monet, Renoir, Degas, Van Gogh, Cézanne, and Gauguin.

Cost: €9, €6.50 Fri-Wed after 16:15 and Thu after 18:00, free on first Sun of month and right when the ticket booth stops selling tickets (Tue-Wed and Fri-Sun at 17:00, Thu at 21:00; they won't let you in much after that), covered by Museum Pass, €14 combo-ticket with Orangerie Museum (valid for four days, one visit per sight).

Hours: Tue-Sun 9:30-18:00, Thu until 21:45, closed Mon, Impressionist galleries start shutting 45 minutes before closing, last entry one hour before closing (45 minutes before on Thu); crowded on Tue, when Louvre is closed; cafés and restaurant, tel. 01 40 49 48 14, www.musee-orsay.fr.

Getting There: The museum, at 1 Rue de la Légion d'Honneur, sits above the RER-C stop called Musée d'Orsay; the nearest Métro stop is Solférino, three blocks southeast of the Orsay. Buses #69 and #24 also stop at the Orsay. From the Louvre, it's a lovely 15-minute walk through the Tuileries Garden and across the pedestrian bridge to the Orsay.

Getting In: As you face the museum from Rue de la Légion d'Honneur (with the river on your left), passholders and ticket-holders enter on the right (Entrance C). Ticket purchasers enter closer to the river (Entrance A).

Tours: Audioguides cost €5. English guided tours usually run daily at 11:30 (€7.50/1.5 hours, none on Sun, may run at other times—inquire when you arrive). Or you can download my free self-guided Orsay **audio tour** (see page 52).

Eating at the Orsay: The snazzy Le Restaurant is on the second floor, with affordable tea and coffee served 15:00-17:30 (daily except Thu). Cafés with fair prices are on the main floor near the entry and on the fifth-floor beyond the Impressionist galleries. Outside, behind the museum, a number of classy eateries line Rue du Bac.

Background: The Impressionist painters rejected camera-like detail for a quick style more suited to capturing the passing moment. Feeling stifled by the rigid rules and stuffy atmosphere of the Academy (the state-funded art school), the Impressionists took as their motto, "Out of the studio, into the open air." They grabbed their berets and scarves and went on excursions to the country, where they set up their easels (and newly invented tubes

PARIS

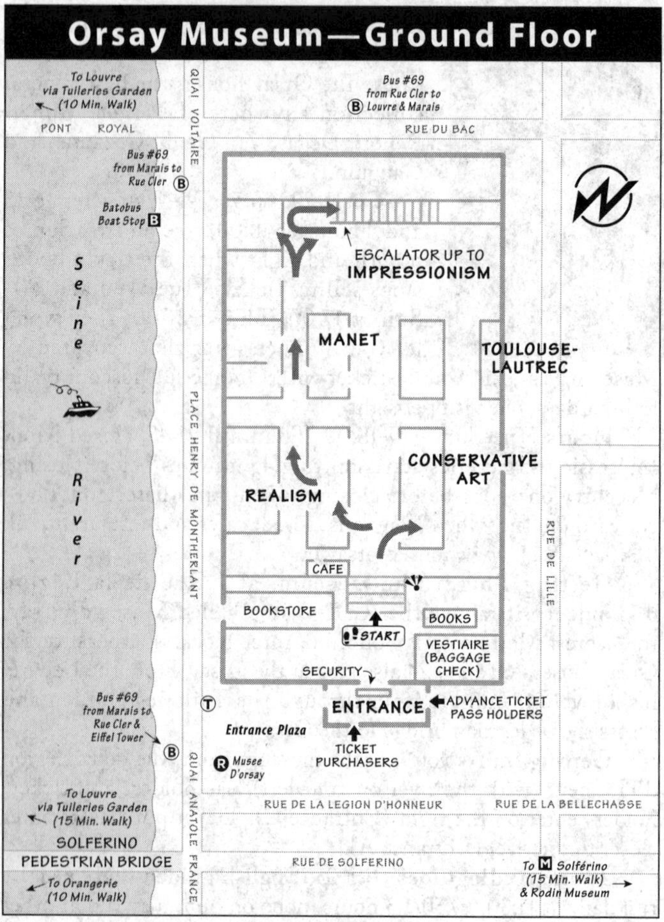

Orsay Museum—Ground Floor
To Louvre via Tuileries Garden (10 Min. Walk)
QUAI VOLTAIRE
Bus #69 from Rue Cler to Louvre & Marais
PONT ROYAL
RUE DU BAC
Bus #69 from Marais to Rue Cler
Batobus Boat Stop
Seine River
ESCALATOR UP TO IMPRESSIONISM
MANET
TOULOUSE-LAUTREC
CONSERVATIVE ART
REALISM
PLACE HENRY DE MONTHERLANT
RUE DE LILLE
CAFE
BOOKSTORE
BOOKS
START
VESTIAIRE (BAGGAGE CHECK)
SECURITY
ENTRANCE
ADVANCE TICKET PASS HOLDERS
Bus #69 from Marais to Rue Cler & Eiffel Tower
Entrance Plaza
TICKET PURCHASERS
Musee D'orsay
To Louvre via Tuileries Garden (15 Min. Walk)
QUAI ANATOLE FRANCE
RUE DE LA LEGION D'HONNEUR
RUE DE LA BELLECHASSE
SOLFERINO PEDESTRIAN BRIDGE
RUE DE SOLFERINO
To Orangerie (10 Min. Walk)
To Solférino (15 Min. Walk) & Rodin Museum

PARIS

of premixed paint) on riverbanks and hillsides, or they sketched in cafés and dance halls. Gods, goddesses, nymphs, and fantasy scenes were out; common people and rural landscapes were in.

The quick style and everyday subjects were ridiculed and called childish by the "experts." Rejected by the Salon (where works were exhibited to the buying public), the Impressionists staged their own exhibition in 1874. They brashly took their name from an insult thrown at them by a critic who laughed at one of Monet's "impressions" of a sunrise. During the next decade, they exhibited their own work independently. The public, opposed at first, was slowly won over by the simplicity, the color, and the vibrancy of Impressionist art.

➲ **Self-Guided Tour:** This former train station, or *gare*, barely escaped the wrecking ball in the 1970s, when the French realized it'd be a great place to exhibit the enormous collections of 19th-century art scattered throughout the city. The ground floor (level 0) houses early 19th-century art, mainly conservative art of the Academy and Salon, plus Realism. On the top floor is the core of the collection—the Impressionist rooms. If you're pressed for time, go directly there. Keep in mind that the collection is always on the move—paintings on loan, in restoration, or displayed in different rooms. The museum updates its website daily with the latest layout (www.musee-orsay.fr).

Conservative Art to Realism: In the Orsay's first few rooms, you're surrounded by visions of idealized beauty—nude women in languid poses, Greek mythological figures, and anatomically perfect statues. This was the art adored by French academics and the middle-class *(bourgeois)* public.

Farther along on the ground floor, you'll witness the shift to Realism. **Jean-François Millet's** *The Gleaners* (*Les Glaneuses,* 1867) depicts the poor women who pick up the meager leftovers after a field has already been harvested by the wealthy. This is "Realism" in two senses. It's painted "realistically," not prettified. And it's the "real" world—not the fantasy world of Greek myth, but the harsh life of the working poor.

Alexandre Cabanel's *The Birth of Venus* (*La Naissance de Vénus,* 1863) and **Edouard Manet's** *Olympia* (1863) offer two opposing visions of Venus. Cabanel's Venus is a perfect fantasy, an orgasm of beauty. Manet's nude is a Realist's take on the traditional Venus. Manet doesn't gloss over anything. The pose is classic, but the sharp outlines and harsh, contrasting colors are new and shocking. Manet replaced soft-core porn with hard-core art.

Impressionism: The Impressionist collection is scattered somewhat randomly through rooms 29-36 of the top floor. You'll see Monet hanging next to Renoir, Manet sprinkled among Pissarro, and a few Degas here and a few Cézannes there. Shadows dance and the displays mingle. Where they're hung is a lot like their brushwork...delightfully sloppy.

In **Manet's** *Luncheon on the Grass* (*Le Déjeuner sur l'Herbe,* 1863), a new revolutionary movement is starting to bud— Impressionism. Notice the background: the messy brushwork of trees and leaves, the play of light on the pond, and the light that filters through the trees onto the woman who stoops in the haze. Also note the strong contrast of colors (white skin, black clothes, green grass). This is a true out-of-doors painting, not a studio production.

Edgar Degas blended classical lines with Impressionist color, spontaneity, and everyday subjects from urban Paris. He loved the unposed "snapshot" effect, catching his models off guard. In *The Dance Class* (*La Classe de Danse,* c. 1873-1875), bored, tired dancers scratch their backs restlessly at the end of a long rehearsal. *In a Café*, or *Absinthe* (*Au Café, dit L'Absinthe*, 1876) captures a weary lady of the evening meeting morning with a last, lonely, nail-in-the-coffin drink in the glaring light of a four-in-the-morning café. Degas approaches his dance students, women at work, and café scenes from odd angles that aren't always ideal, but that make the scenes seem more real.

To paint common Parisians living and loving in the afternoon sun, **Pierre-Auguste Renoir** headed for the fields on Butte Montmartre (near the Sacré-Cœur basilica) on Sunday afternoons, when working-class folk would dress up and dance, drink, and eat little crêpes (galettes) till dark. In *Dance at the Moulin de la Galette* (*Bal du Moulin de la Galette*, 1876), the sunlight filtering through the trees creates a kaleidoscope of colors—the 19th-century equivalent of a mirror ball throwing darts of light onto the dancers. Like a photographer who uses a slow shutter speed to show motion, Renoir paints a waltzing blur.

Next, it's the father of Impressionism, **Claude Monet.** Look for paintings from his garden at Giverny and *The Cathedral of Rouen* (*La Cathédrale de Rouen*, 1893), "a series of differing impressions" of the cathedral facade at various times of day and year. In all, he did 30 paintings of the cathedral, and each is unique. The time-lapse series shows the sun passing slowly across the sky, creating different-colored light and shadows.

Post-Impressionism: It was **Paul Cézanne** who brought Impressionism into the 20th century. Compared with the color of Monet, the warmth of Renoir, and Van Gogh's passion, Cézanne's rather impersonal canvases can be difficult to appreciate. Bowls of fruit, landscapes, and a few portraits were Cézanne's passion. Because of his style (not his content), he is often called the first modern painter.

Find his paintings in room 36. In *Landscape* (*Rochers près des Grottes au-dessus de Château-Noir*, 1904), Cézanne uses chunks of green, tan, and blue paint as building blocks to construct this rocky brown cliff. These chunks are like little "cubes" (a style that later influenced the...Cubists). The subjects of Cézanne's *The Card Players* (*Les Joueurs de Cartes*, c. 1890-1895) aren't people—they're studies in color and pattern. The subject matter—two guys playing cards—is less important than the pleasingly balanced pattern they make on the canvas, two sloping forms framing a cylinder (a bottle) in the center. Later, abstract artists would focus solely on shapes and colors.

Like Michelangelo, Beethoven, Rembrandt, Wayne Newton, and a select handful of others, **Vincent van Gogh** put so much of himself into his work that art and life became one. In the Orsay's collection of Van Goghs (level 2), you'll see both the artist's paint-

PARIS

ing style and his life unfold.

Encouraged by his art-dealer brother, Van Gogh moved to Paris, and *voilà!* The color! He met Monet, drank with Paul Gauguin and Henri de Toulouse-Lautrec, and soaked up the Impressionist style. In his *Self-Portrait, Paris* (*Portrait de l'Artiste,* 1887), you can see how he built a bristling brown beard with thick, side-by-side strokes of red, yellow, and green.

The social life of Paris became too much for the solitary Van Gogh, and he moved to southern France. At first, in the glow of the bright spring sunshine, he had a period of incredible creativity and happiness, as he was overwhelmed by the bright colors, landscape vistas, and common people—an Impressionist's dream. But being alone in a strange country began to wear on him. An ugly man, he found it hard to get a date. The close-up perspective of *Van Gogh's Room at Arles* (*La Chambre de van Gogh* à *Arles,* 1889) makes his tiny rented room look even more cramped.

Van Gogh wavered between happiness and madness, even mutilating his own ear at one point. He despaired of ever being sane enough to continue painting. His *Self-Portrait, St. Rémy* (1889) shows a man engulfed in a confused background of brush-strokes that swirl and rave, setting in motion the waves of the jacket. But in the midst of this rippling sea of mystery floats a still, detached island of a face with probing, questioning, yet wise eyes. Do his troubled eyes know that only a few months on, he will take a pistol and put a bullet through his chest? Vincent van Gone.

Nearby are the paintings of **Paul Gauguin,** who got the travel bug early in childhood and grew up wanting to be a sailor. He traveled to the South Seas in search of the exotic, finally settling on Tahiti. There he found his Garden of Eden. *Arearea,* or *Joyousness* (*Joyeusetés,* 1892) shows native women and a dog. In the "distance" (there's no attempt at traditional 3-D here), a procession goes by with a large pagan idol.

Pointillism, as illustrated by many paintings in the next rooms, brings Impressionism to its logical conclusion. Little dabs of pure colors are placed side by side to blend in the viewer's eye. In works such as *The Circus* (*Le Cirque,* 1891), **Georges Seurat** (1859-1891) used only red, yellow, blue, and green points of paint to create a mosaic of colors that shimmers at a distance, capturing the wonder of the dawn of electric light.

The Rest of the Orsay: The open-air mezzanine of level 2 is lined with statues. Stroll the mezzanine, enjoying the works of great French sculptors, including **Auguste Rodin,** who combined classical solidity with Impressionist surfaces. Look for *The Walking Man* (*L'Homme Qui Marche,* c. 1900) by room 71. Like this statue, Rodin had one foot in the past, while the other was stepping into the future. With no mouth or hands, the subject speaks with his

PARIS

body. The rough, "unfinished" surface reflects light in the same way the rough Impressionist brushwork does, making the statue come alive, never quite at rest in the viewer's eye. Rodin's powerful, haunting works are a good place to end this tour. With a stable base of 19th-century stone, he launched art into the 20th century.

▲▲▲Eiffel Tower (La Tour Eiffel)

It's crowded, expensive, and there are probably better views in Paris, but visiting this 1,000-foot-tall ornament is worth the trou-

ble. Visitors to Paris may find *Mona Lisa* to be less than expected, but the Eiffel Tower rarely disappoints, even in an era of skyscrapers.

Cost: €14 for an elevator ride all the way to the top, €8.50 if you're only going up to the two lower levels, not covered by Museum Pass; save some time in line by climbing the stairs to the first and second levels for €5 (€3.50 if you're under 25); once inside the tower, you can buy your way to the top with no penalty—ticket booths and machines on the first and second levels sell supplements for €5.50.

Hours: Daily mid-June-Aug 9:00-24:00, Sept-mid-June 9:30-23:00.

Reservations: Frankly, you'd be crazy to show up without a reservation. At www.tour-eiffel.fr, you can book an entry time and skip the initial line (the longest)—at no extra cost. Book well in advance, as soon as you know when you'll be in Paris. Just pay online with a credit card and print your own ticket. When buying tickets online, make sure you select "Lift entrance ticket with access to the summit" in order to go all the way to the top. For "Type of ticket," it doesn't really matter whether you pick "Group" or "Individual"; a "Group" ticket just gives you one piece of paper covering everyone in your party. You must enter a mobile phone number for identification purposes, so if you don't have one, make one up—and jot it down so you won't forget it (French mobile phone numbers begin with 06 or 07 and have 10 digits). Arrive at the tower 10 minutes before your entry time and look for either of the two entrances marked *Visiteurs avec Reservation (Visitors with Reservation)*, where attendants scan your ticket and put you on the first available elevator. Alternatively, Classic Walks may have tickets with reservations (see page 1030).

Avoiding Lines: Crowds overwhelm this place much of the year, with one- to two-hour waits to get in (unless it's rainy, when lines can evaporate). Weekends and holidays are worst, but prepare

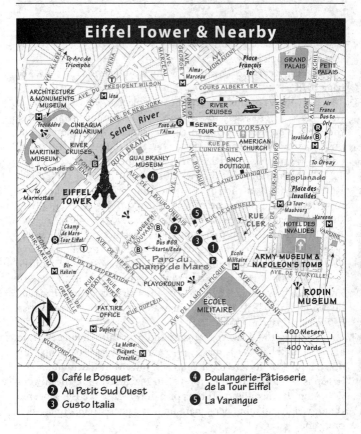

Eiffel Tower & Nearby

① Café le Bosquet
② Au Petit Sud Ouest
③ Gusto Italia
④ Boulangerie-Pâtisserie de la Tour Eiffel
⑤ La Varangue

for ridiculous crowds almost any time. The best solution is to make an online reservation (see above) and to take the stairs down (from first or second levels). When you buy tickets, all members of your party must be with you. You can bypass some (but not all) lines if you have a reservation at either of the tower's view restaurants or hike the stairs.

Getting There: The tower is about a 10-minute walk from the Métro (Bir-Hakeim or Trocadéro stops) or train (Champ de Mars-Tour Eiffel RER stop). The Ecole Militaire Métro stop in the Rue Cler area is 20 minutes away. Buses #69 and #87 stop nearby on Avenue Joseph Bouvard in the Champ de Mars park.

Pickpockets: Beware. Street thieves plunder awestruck visitors gawking below the tower. And tourists in crowded elevators are like fish in a barrel for predatory pickpockets. *En garde.* There's a police station at the Jules Verne pillar.

Security Check: Bags larger than 19" × 8" × 12" are not allowed, but there is no baggage check. All bags are subject to a security search. No knives, glass bottles, or cans are permitted.

Services: Free WCs are at the base of the tower, behind the east pillar. Inside the tower itself, WCs are on all levels, but they're small, with long lines.

Eating near the Tower: For lunch suggestions nearby, see page 1078.

Best Views of the Tower: The best place to view the tower is from Place du Trocadéro to the north. It's a 10-minute walk across the river. Consider arriving at the Trocadéro Métro stop for the view, then walking toward the tower. Another delightful viewpoint is from the Champ de Mars park to the south.

Background: Built on the 100th anniversary of the French Revolution (and in the spirit of the Industrial Revolution), the tower was the centerpiece of a World Expo designed simply to show off what people could build in 1889. Bridge-builder Gustave Eiffel (1832-1923) won the contest to construct the fair's centerpiece by beating out rival proposals such as a giant guillotine. To a generation hooked on technology, the tower was the marvel of the age, a symbol of progress and human ingenuity. Not all were so impressed, however; many found it a monstrosity. The writer Guy de Maupassant (1850-1893) routinely ate lunch in the tower just so he wouldn't have to look at it.

Visiting the Tower: Delicate and graceful when seen from afar, the Eiffel Tower is massive—even a bit scary—close up. You don't appreciate its size until you walk toward it; like a mountain, it seems so close but takes forever to reach. Despite the tower's 7,300 tons of metal and 60 tons of paint, it is so well-engineered that it weighs no more per square inch at its base than a linebacker on tiptoes.

There are three observation platforms, at roughly 200, 400, and 900 feet. To get to the top, you'll wait in line to ride an elevator to the second level. A separate elevator—with another line—shuttles between the second level and the top. (Note: Whether you have a ticket for the top or just for the second level, elevators going up do not stop at the first level. You can see the first level on the way back down, but not all elevators descending from the second level stop at the first level—ask before boarding.) Although being on the windy top of the Eiffel Tower is a thrill you'll never forget, the view is better from the second level, where you can actually see Paris' monuments.

The stairs—yes, you can walk up to the first and second levels—are next to the entrance to the pricey Jules Verne restaurant. As you ascend through the metal beams, imagine being a worker, perched high above nothing, riveting this thing together.

The **top level,** called *le sommet,* is tiny. (It can close temporarily without warning when it reaches capacity or in windy conditions.) All you'll find here are wind and grand, sweeping views.

PARIS

The city lies before you (pick out sights with the help of the panoramic maps). On a good day, you can see for 40 miles.

The **second level** has the best views because you're closer to the sights, and the monuments are more recognizable. (While the best views are up the short stairway, on the platform without the wire-cage barriers, at busy times much of that zone is taken up by people waiting for the elevator to the top.) This level has souvenir shops, public telephones to call home, and a small stand-up café. While you'll save no money, consider taking the elevator up and the stairs down (5 minutes from second level to first, 5 minutes more to ground) for good exercise and views.

The **first level** has more great views, all well-described by the tower's panoramic displays. There are a number of photo exhibits on the tower's history, WCs, a conference hall (closed to tourists), an ATM, and souvenirs. A small café sells pizza and sandwiches (outdoor tables in summer). This level also has two fine restaurants run by famous French chef Alain Ducasse: 58 Tour Eiffel (€20 lunch *menu*, daily 11:30-16:00, no reservations possible) has more accessible prices than the Jules Verne Restaurant (€90 weekday lunch *menu*, €170-220 weekend lunch *menus*, reserve 2-3 months in advance, tel. 01 45 55 61 44, www.lejulesverne-paris.com). Climb the stairs to Cineiffel for a small gallery and theater. A tired eight-minute video that shows continuously features clips of the tower's construction, its paint job, its place in pop culture, and the millennium fireworks.

Near the Eiffel Tower

▲▲Army Museum and Napoleon's Tomb (Musée de l'Armée)—The Hôtel des Invalides, a former veterans' hospital topped by a golden dome, houses Napoleon's

over-the-top-ornate tomb, as well as Europe's greatest military museum. Visiting the Army Museum's different sections, you can watch the art of war unfold from stone axes to Axis powers. At the center of the complex, Napoleon Bonaparte lies majestically dead inside several coffins under a grand dome—a goose-bumping pilgrimage for historians. Your visit continues through an impressive range of museums filled with medieval armor, cannons and muskets, Louis XIV-era uniforms and weapons, and Napoleon's horse—stuffed and mounted. The best section is dedicated to the two World Wars.

Cost and Hours: €9, €7 after 17:00, free for military personnel in uniform, free for kids but they must wait in line for ticket, covered by Museum Pass, audioguide—€6; museum—daily April-Sept 10:00-18:00, may be open Tue until 21:00, Oct-March 10:00-17:00, closed first Mon of month year-round; tomb—daily April-June and Sept 10:00-18:00, may be open Tue until 21:00; July-Aug 10:00-19:00, may be open Tue until 21:00; Oct-March 10:00-17:00, closed first Mon of month Sept-May, last tickets sold 30 minutes before closing, cafeteria, tel. 01 44 42 38 77 or 08 10 11 33 99, www.invalides.org.

Getting There: The Hôtel des Invalides is at 129 Rue de Grenelle; Mo: La Tour Maubourg, Varenne, or Invalides. Bus #69 from the Marais and Rue Cler area also takes you there, or it's a 10-minute walk from Rue Cler.

▲▲Rodin Museum (Musée Rodin)—This user-friendly museum is filled with passionate works by the greatest sculptor since Michelangelo. Note that the museum is undergoing a major renovation until 2014. Expect some statues to be moved around and some rooms to be closed altogether. The gardens remain open. To compensate for the closures, the museum has added a few rarely displayed pieces to its exhibits.

Auguste Rodin (1840-1917) sculpted human figures on an epic scale, revealing through their bodies his deepest thoughts and feelings. Like many of Michelangelo's unfinished works, Rodin's statues rise from the raw stone around them, driven by the life force. With missing limbs and scarred skin, these are prefab classics, making ugliness noble. Rodin's people are always moving restlessly. Even the famous *Thinker* is moving. While he's plopped down solidly, his mind is a million miles away.

Cost and Hours: €6, under 18 free, free on first Sun of the month, €1 for garden only (possibly Paris' best deal, as many works are on display there), both museum and garden covered by Museum Pass, audioguide—€4; Tue-Sun 10:00-17:45, Wed until 20:45, closed Mon; gardens close at 18:00, Oct-March at 17:00; last entry 30 minutes before closing, mandatory baggage check, self-service café in garden, near the Army Museum and Napoleon's Tomb at 79 Rue de Varenne, Mo: Varenne, tel. 01 44 18 61 10, www.musee-rodin.fr.

▲▲Marmottan Museum (Musée Marmottan Monet)—This intimate, less-touristed mansion on the southwest fringe of urban Paris has the best collection of works by the father of Impressionism, Claude Monet (1840-1926). Fiercely independent and dedicated to his craft, Monet gave courage to the other Impressionists in the face of harsh criticism.

Cost and Hours: €10, not covered by Museum Pass, audio-guide-€3, Tue-Sun 10:00-18:00, Thu until 20:00, closed Mon, last entry 30 minutes before closing, 2 Rue Louis-Boilly, Mo: La Muette, tel. 01 44 96 50 33, www.marmottan.com.

Left Bank

Opposite Notre-Dame, on the left bank of the Seine, is the Latin Quarter. (For more information on this neighborhood, see my self-guided walk of historic Paris, earlier.)

▲▲**Cluny Museum (Musée National du Moyen Age)**—This treasure trove of Middle Ages (Moyen Age) art fills old Roman

baths, offering close-up looks at stained glass, Notre-Dame carvings, fine gold-smithing and jewelry, and rooms of tapestries. The highlights are several original stained-glass windows from Sainte-Chapelle and the exquisite Lady and the Unicorn series of six tapestries: A delicate, as-medieval-as-can-be noble lady introduces a delighted unicorn to the senses of taste, hearing, sight, smell, and touch. This museum helps put the Middle Ages in perspective, reflecting a time when Europe was awakening from a thousand-year slumber and Paris was emerging on the world stage. Trade was booming, people actually owned chairs, and the Renaissance was moving in like a warm front from Italy.

Cost and Hours: €8, free on first Sun of month, covered by Museum Pass, ticket includes audioguide though passholders must pay €1; Wed-Mon 9:15-17:45, closed Tue, ticket office closes at 17:15; near corner of Boulevards St. Michel and St. Germain at 6 Place Paul Painlevé; Mo: Cluny-La Sorbonne, St. Michel, or Odéon; tel. 01 53 73 78 16, www.musee-moyenage.fr.

▲**Luxembourg Garden (Jardin du Luxembourg)**—Paris' most beautiful, interesting, and enjoyable garden/park/recreational area, le Jardin du Luxembourg is a great place to watch Parisians

at rest and play. This 60-acre garden, dotted with fountains and statues, is the property of the French Senate, which meets here in the Luxembourg Palace.

Luxembourg Garden has special rules governing its use (for example, where cards can be played, where dogs can be walked, where joggers can run, and when and where music can be played). The brilliant flower beds are changed three times a year, and the boxed trees are brought out of the *orangerie* in May. Children enjoy the rentable toy sailboats. The park hosts marionette shows several times weekly (Les Guignols, Wed 15:30, Sat-Sun 11:00 and 15:30). Pony rides are available from April through October. (Meanwhile, the French CIA plots espionage in their underground offices beneath the park.)

Challenge the card and chess players to a game (near the tennis courts), or find a free chair near the main pond and take a well-deserved break.

Cost and Hours: Free, daily dawn until dusk, Mo: Odéon, RER: Luxembourg.

Nearby: The grand Neoclassical-domed Panthéon, now a mausoleum housing the tombs of great French notables, is three blocks away.

Champs-Elysées and Nearby

▲▲▲**Champs-Elysées**—This famous boulevard is Paris' backbone, with its greatest concentration of traffic. From the Arc

de Triomphe down Avenue des Champs-Elysées, all of France seems to converge on Place de la Concorde, the city's largest square. And though the Champs-Elysées has become as international as it is Parisian, a walk here is still a must.

Background: In 1667, Louis XIV opened the first section of the street as a short extension of the Tuileries Garden. This year is considered the birth of Paris as a grand city. The Champs-Elysées soon

became *the* place to cruise in your carriage. (It still is today; traffic can be gridlocked even at midnight.) One hundred years later, the café scene arrived. From the 1920s until the 1960s, this boulevard was pure elegance; Parisians actually dressed up to come here. It was mainly residences, rich hotels, and cafés. Then, in 1963, the government pumped up the neighborhood's commercial metabolism by bringing in the RER (commuter train). Suburbanites had easy access, and *pfft*—there went the neighborhood.

The *nouveau* Champs-Elysées, revitalized in 1994, has newer benches and lamps, broader sidewalks, all-underground parking, and a fleet of green-suited workers who drive motorized street cleaners. Blink away the modern elements, and it's not hard to imagine the boulevard pre-1963, with only the finest structures lining both sides all the way to the palace gardens.

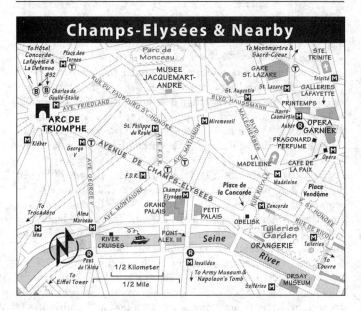

Champs-Elysées & Nearby

● **Self-Guided Walk:** To reach the top of the Champs-Elysées, take the Métro to the Arc de Triomphe (Mo: Charles de Gaulle-Etoile), then saunter down the grand boulevard (Métro stops every few blocks, including George V and Franklin D. Roosevelt). If you plan to tour the Arc de Triomphe (see next listing), do it before starting this walk.

Fancy car dealerships include **Peugeot,** at #136 (showing off its futuristic concept cars, often alongside the classic models), and **Mercedes-Benz,** a block down at #118, where you can pick up a Mercedes watch and cufflinks to go with your new car. In the 19th century this was an area for horse stables; today, it's the district of garages, limo companies, and car dealerships. If you're serious about selling cars in France, you must have a showroom on the Champs-Elysées.

Next to Mercedes is the famous **Lido,** Paris' largest cabaret (and a multiplex cinema). You can walk all the way into the lobby. Paris still offers the kind of burlesque-type spectacles that have been performed here since the 19th century, combining music, comedy, and scantily clad women. Movie-going on the Champs-Elysées provides another kind of fun, with theaters showing the very latest releases. Check to see if there are films you recognize, then look for the showings *(séances).* A "v.o." *(version originale)* next to the time indicates the film will be shown in its original language; a "v.f." stands for *version française.*

The flagship store of leather-bag maker **Louis Vuitton** may be the largest single-brand luxury store in the world. Step inside.

The store insists on providing enough salespeople to treat each customer royally—if there's a line, it means shoppers have overwhelmed the place.

Fouquet's café-restaurant (#99), under the red awning, is a popular spot among French celebrities, serving the most expensive shot of espresso I've found in downtown Paris (€8). Opened in 1899 as a coachman's bistro, Fouquet's gained fame as the hangout of France's WWI biplane fighter pilots—those who weren't shot down by Germany's infamous "Red Baron." It also served as James Joyce's dining room.

Since the early 1900s, Fouquet's has been a favorite of French actors and actresses. The golden plaques at the entrance honor winners of France's Oscar-like film awards, the Césars (one is cut into the ground at the end of the carpet). There are plaques for Gérard Depardieu, Catherine Deneuve, Roman Polanski, Juliette Binoche, and several famous Americans (but not Jerry Lewis). More recent winners are shown on the floor just inside.

Ladurée (two blocks downhill at #75) is a classic 19th-century tea salon/restaurant/*pâtisserie*. Non-patrons can discreetly wander around the place, though photos are not allowed. A coffee here is *très* élégant (only €3.50).

From posh cafés to stylish shops, monumental sidewalks to glimmering showrooms, the Champs-Elysées is Paris at its most Parisian.

▲▲▲**Arc de Triomphe**—Napoleon had the magnificent Arc de Triomphe commissioned to commemorate his victory at the battle of Austerlitz. There's no triumphal arch bigger (165 feet high, 130 feet wide). And, with 12 converging boulevards, there's no traffic circle more thrilling to experience—either from behind the wheel or on foot (take the underpass).

The foot of the arch is a stage on which the last two centuries of Parisian history have played out—from the funeral of Napoleon to the goose-stepping arrival of the Nazis to the triumphant return of Charles de Gaulle after the Allied liberation. Examine the carvings on the pillars, featuring a mighty Napoleon and excitable Lady Liberty. Pay your respects at the Tomb of the Unknown Soldier. Then climb the 284 steps to the observation deck up top, with sweeping skyline panoramas and a mesmerizing view down onto the traffic that swirls around the arch.

Cost and Hours: Outside and at the base—free, always viewable; steps to rooftop—€9.50, under 18 free, free on first Sun of month Oct-March, covered by Museum Pass; daily April-Sept 10:00-23:00, Oct-March 10:00-22:30, last entry 30 minutes before closing; Place Charles de Gaulle, use underpass to reach arch, Mo: Charles de Gaulle-Etoile, tel. 01 55 37 73 77, www.arc-de-triomphe.monuments-nationaux.fr.

Avoiding Lines: Bypass the slooow ticket line with a Museum Pass (though if you have kids, you'll need to line up to get the free tickets for children). There may be another line (that you can't skip) at the entrance to the stairway up the arch.

Montmartre

Stroll along Paris' highest hilltop (420 feet) for a different perspective on the City of Light. Walk in the footsteps of the people who've lived here—monks stomping grapes (1200s), farmers grinding grain in windmills (1600s), dust-coated gypsum miners (1700s), Parisian liberals (1800s), Modernist painters (1900s), and all the struggling artists, poets, dreamers, and drunkards who came here for cheap rent, untaxed booze, rustic landscapes, and cabaret nightlife. With vineyards, wheat fields, windmills, animals, and a village tempo of life, it was the perfect escape from grimy Paris.

▲▲**Sacré-Cœur**—The Sacré-Cœur (Sacred Heart) Basilica's exterior, with its onion domes and bleached-bone pallor, looks

ancient, but was finished only a century ago by Parisians humiliated by German invaders. Otto von Bismarck's Prussian army laid siege to Paris for more than four months in 1870. Things got so bad for residents that urban hunting for dinner (to cook up dogs, cats, and finally rats) became accepted behavior. Convinced they were being punished for the country's liberal sins, France's Catholics raised money to build the church as a "praise the Lord anyway" gesture.

Cost and Hours: Church—free, daily 6:00-22:30, last entry at 22:15; dome—€6, not covered by Museum Pass, daily May-Sept 9:00-19:00, Oct-April 9:00-17:00; tel. 01 53 41 89 00, www.sacre-coeur-montmartre.com.

Getting There: You have several options. You can take the Métro to the Anvers stop (to avoid the stairs up to Sacré-Cœur, buy one more Métro ticket and ride the funicular, though it's sometimes closed for maintenance). The Abbesses stop is closer but less scenic. Or you can go to Place Pigalle, then take the tiny electric Montmartrobus, which drops you right by Place du Tertre, near Sacré-Cœur (costs one Métro ticket, 4/hour). A taxi to the

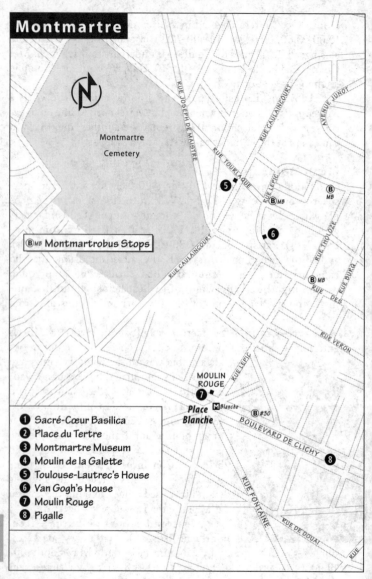

Montmartre

Montmartre Cemetery

Ⓑᴹᴮ Montmartrobus Stops

MOULIN
ROUGE

Place Blanche

❶ Sacré-Cœur Basilica
❷ Place du Tertre
❸ Montmartre Museum
❹ Moulin de la Galette
❺ Toulouse-Lautrec's House
❻ Van Gogh's House
❼ Moulin Rouge
❽ Pigalle

PARIS

top of the hill saves time and avoids sweat (about €13).

The Heart of Montmartre—Montmartre's main square **(Place du Tertre),** one block from the church, was once the haunt of Henri de Toulouse-Lautrec and the original bohemians. Today, it's mobbed with tourists and unoriginal bohemians, but it's still fun (to beat the crowds, go on a weekday or early on weekend mornings). From here, head up Rue des Saules to find Paris' lone vine-

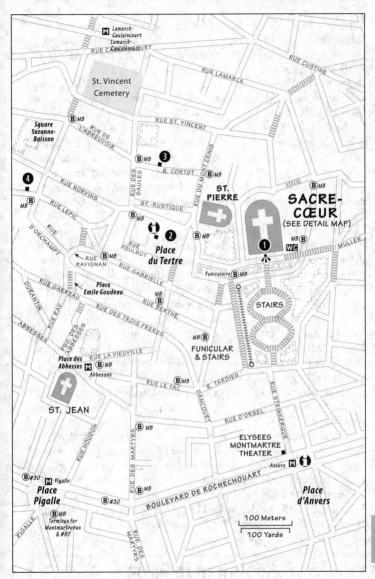

yard and the **Montmartre Museum** (open daily). Return uphill, then follow Rue Lepic down to the old windmill, **Moulin de la Galette,** which once pressed monks' grapes and farmers' grain, and crushed gypsum rocks into powdery plaster of Paris (there were once 30 windmills on Montmartre). When the gypsum mines closed (c. 1850) and the vineyards sprouted apartments, this windmill turned into the ceremonial centerpiece of a popular outdoor dance hall. Farther down Rue Lepic, you'll pass near the former homes of **Toulouse-Lautrec** (at Rue Tourlaque—look for the brick-framed art-studio windows under the heavy mansard roof) and **Vincent van Gogh** (54 Rue Lepic).

Pigalle—Paris' red light district, the infamous "Pig Alley," is at the foot of Butte Montmartre. *Ooh la la.* It's more racy than dangerous. Walk from Place Pigalle to Place Blanche, teasing desperate barkers and fast-talking temptresses. In bars, a €150 bottle of cheap champagne comes with a friend. Stick to the bigger streets, hang on to your wallet, and exercise good judgment. Cancan can cost a fortune, as can con artists in topless bars. After dark, tour guides make big bucks by bringing their groups to touristy nightclubs like the famous **Moulin Rouge** (Mo: Pigalle or Abbesses).

Near Paris: Versailles

Every king's dream, Versailles (vehr-"sigh") was the residence of French monarchs and the cultural heartbeat of Europe for about 100 years—until the Revolution of 1789 changed all that. The Sun King (Louis XIV) created Versailles, spending freely from the public treasury to turn his dad's hunting lodge into a palace fit for the gods (among whom he counted himself). Louis XV and Louis XVI spent much of the 18th century gilding Louis XIV's lily. In 1837, about 50 years after the royal family was evicted by citizen-protesters, King Louis-Philippe opened the palace as a museum. Today you can visit parts of the huge palace and wander through acres of manicured gardens sprinkled with fountains and studded with statues. Europe's next-best palaces are just Versailles wannabes.

While well worth a visit for those home-basing in Paris, if you're coming from Le Havre, the public-transportation connection to Versailles is too complicated to attempt (train from Le Havre to Paris' St. Lazare train station, then use the Métro to connect to the RER suburban rail line, which you'll ride out to Versailles). With one day in Le Havre, Paris is easier to reach and appreciate. If you're determined to see Versailles, it can be done, but is best seen with an excursion.

Shopping in Paris

Even staunch anti-shoppers may be tempted to indulge in chic Paris. Wandering among elegant and outrageous boutiques provides a break from the heavy halls of the Louvre and, if you approach it right, a little cultural enlightenment. Even if you don't intend to buy anything, budget some time for window-shopping. The expression for "window-shopping" in French is *faire du lèche-*

French Shopping Etiquette

Before you enter a Parisian store, remember the following points:

- In small stores, always say, "*Bonjour, Madame* or *Mademoiselle* or *Monsieur*" when entering. And remember to say "*Au revoir, Madame* or *Mademoiselle* or *Monsieur*" when leaving.
- The customer is not always right. In fact, figure the clerk is doing you a favor by waiting on you.
- Except in department stores, it's not normal for the customer to handle clothing. Ask first before you pick up an item: "*Je peux?*" (zhuh puh), meaning, "Can I?"
- For clothing size comparisons between the US and Europe, see page 139.
- Forget returns (and don't count on exchanges).
- Saturday afternoons are *très* busy and not for the faint of heart.
- Observe French shoppers. Then imitate.
- Stores are generally closed on Sunday, except at the Carrousel du Louvre (underground shopping mall at the Louvre) and some shops near Sèvres-Babylone, along the Champs-Elysées, and in the Marais.
- Some small stores don't open until 14:00 on Mondays.
- Don't feel obliged to buy. If a shopkeeper offers assistance, just say, "*Je regarde, merci.*"

vitrines—"window-licking." Here are a few of your options for picking up gifts, souvenirs, and something special for yourself.

Souvenir Shops—Avoid souvenir carts in front of famous monuments. You can find cheaper gifts around the Pompidou Center, on the streets of Montmartre, and in some department stores. The riverfront stalls near Notre-Dame sell a variety of used books, old posters and postcards, magazines, refrigerator magnets, and other tourist paraphernalia in the most romantic setting. You'll find better deals at the souvenir shops that line Rue d'Arcole between Notre-Dame and Hôtel de Ville and on Rue de Rivoli, alongside the Louvre.

Department Stores (Les Grands Magasins)—Like cafés, department stores were invented here (surprisingly, not in America). Parisian department stores begin with their showy perfume sections, almost always central on the ground floor and worth a visit to see how much space is devoted to pricey, smelly water. Helpful information desks are usually located at the main entrances near the perfume section (with floor plans in English). Stores generally have affordable restaurants (some with view terraces) and a good selection of fairly priced souvenirs and toys.

PARIS

Shop at these great Parisian department stores: Galeries Lafayette (Mo: Chaussée d'Antin-La Fayette, Havre-Caumartin, or Opéra), Printemps (next door to Galeries Lafayette), and Bon Marché (Mo: Sèvres-Babylone). Opening hours are customarily Monday through Saturday from 10:00 to 19:00. Some are open later on Thursdays, and all are jammed on Saturdays and closed on Sundays (except in December).

Market Streets—Several traffic-free street markets overflow with flowers, produce, fish vendors, and butchers, illustrating how most Parisians shopped before there were supermarkets and department stores. **Rue Cler** is like a refined street market, serving an upscale neighborhood near the Eiffel Tower (Mo: Ecole Militaire). **Rue Montorgueil** (Mo: Etienne Marcel), a thriving and less touristy market street, is famous as the last vestige of the once-massive Les Halles market; gather a picnic here and take it to the park at Les Halles. **Rue Mouffetard,** hiding several blocks behind the Panthéon (Mo: Censier Daubenton), has an upper stretch that is pedestrian and touristic and a bottom stretch that is purely Parisian. Shops are open daily except Sunday afternoons, Monday, and lunchtime throughout the week (13:00-15:00).

Eating in Paris

With just a few hours to spend in Paris, you likely won't be able to spare the time for a long lunch. Therefore, although Paris is famous for its cuisine, I've focused my recommendations on eateries convenient to your sightseeing, listed by neighborhood. These places are (mostly) authentically local, but—for the most part—fast and functional rather than haute cuisine. Below you'll find suggestions near **Notre-Dame and the historic core of Paris,** as well as options near the **Eiffel Tower.** For eateries near the **Louvre,** see page 1048; for choices at and near the **Orsay,** see page 1053.

To save piles of euros, go to a bakery for takeout, or stop at a café for lunch. Cafés and brasseries are happy to serve a *plat du jour,* or *plat* (garnished plate of the day, about €12-18), or a chef-like salad (about €10-13). To save even more, consider picnics (tasty take-out dishes are available at charcuteries).

If you have more time to eat, most restaurants I've listed have set-price *menus.* The few extra euros you pay are well-spent, and

Good Picnic Spots

Paris is picnic-friendly. Almost any park will do. Many have benches or grassy areas, though some lawns are off-limits—obey the signs. Parks generally close at dusk, so plan your sunset picnics carefully. Here are some especially scenic areas located near major sights:

Palais Royal: Escape to a peaceful courtyard full of relaxing locals across from the Louvre (Mo: Palais Royale). The nearby Louvre courtyard surrounding the pyramid is less tranquil, but very handy.

Place des Vosges: Relax in an exquisite grassy courtyard in the Marais, surrounded by royal buildings (Mo: Bastille).

Square du Vert-Galant: For great river views, try this little triangular park on the west tip of Ile de la Cité. It's next to the statue of King Henry IV (Mo: Pont Neuf).

Pont des Arts: Munch from a perch on this pedestrian bridge over the Seine (near the Louvre)—it's equipped with benches (Mo: Pont Neuf).

Along the Seine: A grassy parkway runs along the left bank of the Seine between Les Invalides and Pont de l'Alma (Mo: Invalides, near Rue Cler).

Tuileries Garden: Have an Impressionist "Luncheon on the Grass" nestled between the Orsay and Orangerie museums (Mo: Tuileries).

Luxembourg Garden: The classic Paris picnic spot is this expansive Left Bank park (Mo: Odéon).

Les Invalides: Take a break from the Army Museum and Napoleon's Tomb in the gardens behind the complex (Mo: Varenne).

Champ de Mars: The long grassy strip below the Eiffel Tower has breathtaking views of this Paris icon. However, you must eat along the sides of the park, as the central lawn is off-limits (Mo: Ecole Militaire).

Pompidou Center: There's no grass, but the people-watching is unbeatable; try the area by the *Homage to Stravinsky* fountains (Mo: Rambuteau or Hôtel de Ville).

open up a variety of better choices. A service charge is included in the prices (so little or no tipping is expected). Before choosing a seat outside, remember that smokers love outdoor tables.

Near the Ile de la Cité and Historic Paris
In the Marais Neighborhood

The lively, colorful Marais district is a short stroll north of the river, just northeast of Notre-Dame, where you can follow my self-guided Historic Paris Walk (see page 1032). I've focused on two parts of this neighborhood: near Hôtel de Ville, and a bit farther northeast, in the heart of the Marais. Another option is to head

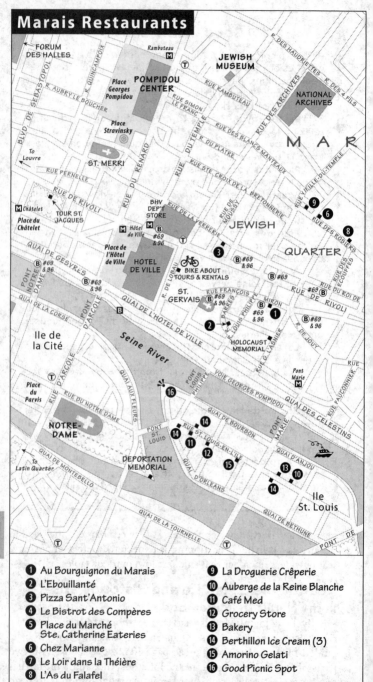

Marais Restaurants

1. Au Bourguignon du Marais
2. L'Ebouillanté
3. Pizza Sant'Antonio
4. Le Bistrot des Compères
5. Place du Marché
   Ste. Catherine Eateries
6. Chez Marianne
7. Le Loir dans la Théière
8. L'As du Falafel
9. La Droguerie Crêperie
10. Auberge de la Reine Blanche
11. Café Med
12. Grocery Store
13. Bakery
14. Berthillon Ice Cream (3)
15. Amorino Gelati
16. Good Picnic Spot

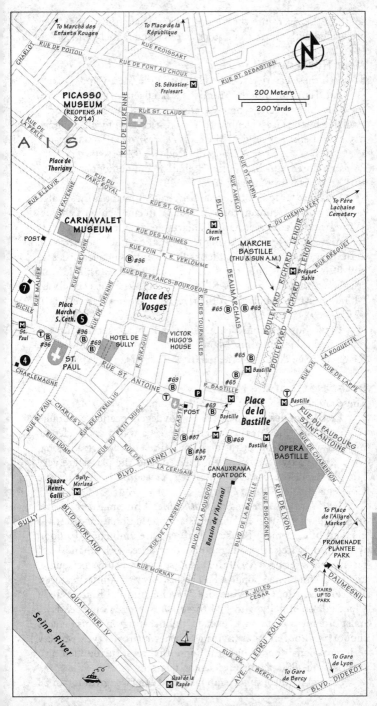

south of the river, into the Latin Quarter, where the dense streets are loaded with touristy but quick *crêperies* and falafel joints.

Near Hôtel de Ville

To reach these eateries, use the Hôtel de Ville Métro stop.

Au Bourguignon du Marais is a handsome wine bar/bistro for Burgundy lovers, where excellent wines (Burgundian only, available by the glass) blend with a good selection of well-designed dishes and efficient service. The œufs *en meurette* are mouthwatering, and the *bœuf bourguignon* could feed two (€10-14 starters, €20-26 *plats*, closed Sun-Mon, pleasing indoor and outdoor seating, 52 Rue François Miron, tel. 01 48 87 15 40).

L'Ebouillanté is a breezy *crêperie*-café, romantically situated near the river on a broad, cobbled pedestrian lane behind a church. With great outdoor seating and an artsy, cozy interior, it's perfect for an inexpensive and relaxing tea, snack, or lunch. Their *Brick*, a Tunisian-inspired dish that looks like a stuffed omelet, has several filling options and comes with a small salad (€15); it left me stuffed (*plats* and big salads-€13, daily 12:00-21:30 except closed Mon Nov-March, a block off the river at 6 Rue des Barres, tel. 01 42 71 09 69).

Pizza Sant'Antonio is bustling and cheap, serving up €11 pizzas and salads on a fun Marais square (daily, barely off Rue de Rivoli at 1 Rue de la Verrerie, tel. 01 42 77 78 47).

In the Heart of the Marais

These are closest to the St. Paul Métro stop.

Le Bistrot des Compères has a privileged location on a quiet corner in the thick of the Marais; there's a warm and welcoming feel whether you sit inside or out. The cuisine is traditional with creative twists, the staff is relaxed, and the prices are very fair (€7 starters, €15 *plats*, €7 desserts, closed Sun-Mon, 16 Rue Charlemagne, tel. 01 42 72 14 16).

On Place du Marché Ste. Catherine: This small, romantic square, just off Rue St. Antoine, is an international food festival cloaked in extremely Parisian, leafy-square ambience. In good weather, this is clearly a neighborhood favorite, with a handful of restaurants offering €20-30 three-course meals. Study the square, and you'll find three popular French bistros with similar features: **La Terrasse Ste. Catherine, Le Marché,** and **Au Bistrot de la Place** (all open daily with €24 three-course *menus* on weekdays, must order à la carte on weekends, tight seating on flimsy chairs indoors and out). Other inviting eateries nearby serve a variety of international food. You'll eat under the trees, surrounded by a futuristic-in-1800 planned residential quarter.

Several hardworking **Asian fast-food eateries,** great for an €8

PARIS

meal, line Rue St. Antoine.

On Rue des Rosiers in the Jewish Quarter: These places line up along the same street in the heart of the Jewish Quarter.

Chez Marianne is a neighborhood fixture that blends delicious Jewish cuisine with Parisian élan and wonderful atmosphere. Choose from several indoor zones with a cluttered wine shop/deli feeling, or sit outside. You'll select from two dozen *Zakouski* elements to assemble your €12-16 *plat*. Vegetarians will find great options (€8 falafel sandwich—only €6 if you order it to go, long hours daily, corner of Rue des Rosiers and Rue des Hospitalières-St.-Gervais, tel. 01 42 72 18 86). For takeout, pay inside first and get a ticket before you order outside.

Le Loir dans la Théière ("The Dormouse in the Teapot") is a cozy, mellow teahouse offering a welcoming ambience for tired travelers. It's ideal for lunch and popular for weekend brunch. They offer a daily assortment of creatively filled quiches, and bake up an impressive array of homemade desserts that are proudly displayed in the dining room. Try the mile-high lemon meringue "pie" or the oversized *mille-feuille* (Mon-Fri 12:00-19:00, Sat-Sun 10:00-19:00, 3 Rue des Rosiers, tel. 01 42 72 90 61).

L'As du Falafel rules the falafel scene in the Jewish quarter. Monsieur Isaac, the "Ace of Falafel" here since 1979, brags, "I've got the biggest pita on the street...and I fill it up." (Apparently it's Lenny Kravitz's favorite, too.) Your inexpensive meal comes on plastic plates, in a bustling setting that seems to prove he's earned his success. The €7 "special falafel" is the big hit (€6 to go), but many Americans enjoy his lighter chicken version *(poulet grillé)* or the tasty and massive *assiette de falafel* (€9). Wash it down with a cold Maccabee beer. Their take-out service draws a constant crowd (long hours daily except closed Fri evening and all day Sat, air-con, 34 Rue des Rosiers, tel. 01 48 87 63 60).

La Droguerie, an outdoor crêpe stand a few blocks farther down Rue des Rosiers, is an option if falafels don't work for you, but cheap does (€5 crêpes, closed Mon, 56 Rue des Rosiers).

On Ile St. Louis

This romantic and peaceful neighborhood, just a few minutes behind Notre-Dame (across the bridge), is filled with promising and surprisingly inexpensive possibilities. Cruise the island's main street for a variety of options, from cozy *crêperies* to Italian eateries to Alsatian brasseries and romantic bistros. After your meal, sample Paris' best ice cream and stroll across to Ile de la Cité to see Notre-Dame. These recommended spots line the island's main drag, Rue St. Louis-en-l'Ile (see map on page 1074; to get here use the Pont Marie Métro stop).

Auberge de la Reine Blanche welcomes diners willing to rub elbows with their neighbors under heaving beams. Earnest owner Michel serves traditional cuisine at reasonable prices. The giant goat-cheese salad is a beefy meal in itself (€20 two-course *menu*, €25 three-course *menu*, daily, 30 Rue St. Louis-en-l'Ile, tel. 01 46 33 07 87).

Café Med, near the pedestrian bridge to Notre-Dame, is a tiny, cheery *crêperie* with good-value salads, crêpes, and €11 *plats* (€14 and €20 *menus*, daily, limited wine list, 77 Rue St. Louis-en-l'Ile, tel. 01 43 29 73 17). Two similar *crêperies* are just across the street.

Riverside Picnic for Impoverished Romantics on Ile St. Louis: During sunny lunchtimes, the *quai* on the Left Bank side of Ile St. Louis is lined with locals who have more class than money, spreading out tablecloths and even lighting candles for elegant picnics. And tourists can enjoy the same budget meal. A handy grocery store at #67 on Ile St. Louis' main drag (open until 22:00, closed Tue) has tabouli and other simple, cheap take-away dishes for your picnicking pleasure. The bakery a few blocks down at #40 serves quiche and pizza (open until 20:00, closed Sun-Mon).

Ice-Cream Dessert: Half the people strolling Ile St. Louis are licking an ice-cream cone, because this is the home of *les glaces Berthillon* (now sold throughout Paris). The original **Berthillon** shop, at 31 Rue St. Louis-en-l'Ile, is marked by the line of salivating customers (closed Mon-Tue). For a less famous but at least as satisfying treat, the homemade Italian gelato a block away at **Amorino Gelati** is giving Berthillon competition (no line, bigger portions, easier to see what you want, and they offer little tastes—Berthillon doesn't need to, 47 Rue St. Louis-en-l'Ile, tel. 01 44 07 48 08). Having some of each is not a bad thing.

Near the Eiffel Tower

Café le Bosquet is a modern Parisian brasserie with dressy waiters. Dine in their snappy interior or at tables on a broad sidewalk. Come here for standard café fare—salad, French onion soup, steak, or a *plat du jour* for about €14-19. The escargots are tasty, and the house red wine is plenty good (continental breakfast for €6, free Wi-Fi, closed Sun, reservations smart Fri-Sat, corner of Rue du Champ de Mars and Avenue Bosquet, 46 Avenue Bosquet, tel. 01 45 51 38 13).

La Varangue is an entertaining one-man show featuring English-speaking Philippe, who once ran a catering business in Pennsylvania. He now lives upstairs and has found his niche serving a mostly American clientele. The food is cheap and basic, and the tables are few. Norman Rockwell would dig his minuscule dining room—with the traditional kitchen sizzling just over the counter. Try his snails and chocolate cake—but not together (€12 *plats,* €18 *menu,* always a vegetarian option, closed Sun, 27 Rue Augereau, tel. 01 47 05 51 22).

Au Petit Sud Ouest has stone walls and wood beams, making it a cozy place to sample fine cuisine from southwestern France. Duck, goose, foie gras, *cassoulet,* and truffles are among its specialties. Tables come with toasters to heat your bread—it enhances the flavors of the foie gras (closed Sun-Mon, 46 Avenue de la Bourdonnais, tel. 01 45 55 59 59).

Gusto Italia serves up tasty, good-value Italian cuisine in a shoebox-size place with a few tables outside. Arrive early or plan to wait (€12 salads, €14 pasta, daily, 199 Rue de Grenelle, tel. 01 45 55 00 43).

Boulangerie-Pâtisserie de la Tour Eiffel delivers inexpensive salads, quiches, and sandwiches. Enjoy the views of the Eiffel Tower (daily, outdoor and indoor seating, one block southeast of the tower at 21 Avenue de la Bourdonnais, tel. 01 47 05 59 81).

Returning to Le Havre

Remember, **trains** to Le Havre leave nearly hourly from Paris' **St. Lazare Station** (for schedule and price details, and how to get back to your ship once in Le Havre, see page 1010). To get to this station from central Paris, your best bet is to hop a taxi, ride the Métro (line 14/purple stops near Notre-Dame, but many other lines also reach the station), or take bus #24 (which stops at Notre-Dame, the Orsay, and Place de la Concorde); either way, get off at the stop called "Gare Saint-Lazare."

"On Your Own" **shuttle-bus excursions** from your cruise line will tell you when and where to meet them for the trip back; most use Place de la Concorde.

Other Destinations near Le Havre

While Paris is the big draw for most cruisers, several other options lie closer to Le Havre. The most likely choices are the charming seafront town of Honfleur (a quick 30-minute bus ride from Le Havre), the historic WWII D-Day beaches of Normandy (best seen with a local guide or on an excursion), and—about halfway to Paris—the fine cathedral at Rouen (an hour from Le Havre by train). I've covered the basics for each of these below.

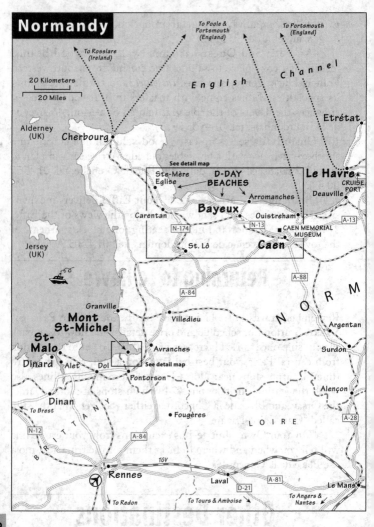

Normandy

To Rosslare (Ireland)
To Poole & Portsmouth (England)
To Portsmouth (England)

English Channel

20 Kilometers
20 Miles

Alderney (UK)

Cherbourg

Etrétat

Le Havre
CRUISE PORT

See detail map

Ste-Mère Eglise   D-DAY BEACHES
Arromanches
Deauville

Carentan   Bayeux   Ouistreham

Jersey (UK)

N-174   N-13   A-13
St. Lô   CAEN MEMORIAL MUSEUM
Caen

A-88

N O R M

Granville
Villedieu   Argentan

Mont St-Michel

St-Malo   Avranches   Surdon

Dinard   Alet   Dol
Pontorson   See detail map
Alençon

Dinan
To Brest   Fougères

A-84   L O I R E

B R I T T A N Y

N-12   A-84   TGV
A-28

Rennes   Laval   Le Mans
A-81
To Redon   To Tours & Amboise   D-21
To Angers & Nantes

Honfleur

Gazing at its cozy harbor lined with skinny, soaring houses, it's easy to overlook the historic importance of this port. For more than a thousand years, sailors have enjoyed Honfleur's (ohn-flur) ideal location, where the Seine River greets the English Channel. The town was also a favorite of 19th-century Impressionists who were captivated by Honfleur's unusual light—the result of its river-meets-sea setting. Eugène Boudin (boo-dahn) lived and painted in Honfleur, drawing Monet and other creative types from Paris.

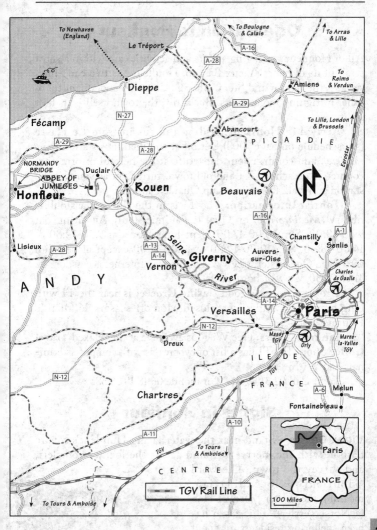

In some ways, modern art was born in the fine light of idyllic little Honfleur.

Unlike Le Havre, Honfleur escaped the bombs of World War II—and today offers a romantic port enclosed on three sides by sprawling outdoor cafés. Long eclipsed by the gargantuan port of Le Havre just across the Seine, Honfleur happily uses its past as a bar stool...and sits on it.

Orientation to Honfleur

All of Honfleur's engaging streets and activities are within a short stroll of its old port (Vieux Bassin). Honfleur has two can't-miss sights—the harbor and Ste. Catherine Church—and a handful of other intriguing monuments. But really, the town itself is its best sight.

Arrival in Honfleur: Riding the bus in from Le Havre (see schedule on page 1008), get off at the small bus station *(gare routière)*, and confirm your departure at the helpful information counter. To reach the TI and old town, turn right as you exit the station and walk five minutes up Quai le Paulmier.

Tourist Information: The TI is in the flashy glass public library *(Mediathèque)* on Quai le Paulmier (July-Aug Mon-Sat 9:30-19:00, Sun 10:00-17:00; Sept-June Mon-Sat 9:30-12:30 & 14:00-18:00, Sun 10:00-12:30 & 14:00-17:00 except closed Sun afternoon Oct-Easter; free WCs inside, pay Internet access, tel. 02 31 89 23 30, www.ot-honfleur.fr).

Grocery Store: A good **Casino Grocery** is near the TI with long hours (daily July-Aug, closed Mon off-season, 16 Quai le Paulmier).

Internet Access: Free Wi-Fi is available at the relaxed **Travel Coffee Shop.** The TI has a list of cybercafés with computer terminals and Wi-Fi.

Taxi: Call 02 31 89 81 22 or mobile 06 18 18 38 38.

Sights in Honfleur

Vieux Bassin—Stand near the water facing Honfleur's square harbor, with the merry-go-round across the lock to your left, and survey the town. The word "Honfleur" is Scandinavian, meaning the shelter *(fleur)* of Hon (a Norse settler). This town has been sheltering residents for about a thousand years. During the Hundred Years' War (14th century), the harbor was fortified by a big wall with twin gatehouses (the one surviving gatehouse, *La Lieutenance*, is on your right) and a narrow boat passage protected by a chain.

Those skinny houses on the right side were designed at a time when buildings were taxed based on their width, not height (and when knee replacements were unheard of). How about a room on the top floor, with no elevator? Imagine moving a piano into one of these units today. The spire halfway up the left side of the port belongs to Honfleur's oldest church and is now home to the Marine Museum. The port, once crammed with fishing boats, now harbors sleek sailboats. Walk toward the *La Lieutenance* gatehouse. In front of the barrel-vaulted arch (once the entry to the town), you can see a bronze bust of Samuel de Champlain—the explorer who sailed with an Honfleur crew 400 years ago to make his discoveries in Canada.

Turn around to see various tour and fishing boats and the high-flying Normandy Bridge in the distance. Fisherfolk catch flatfish, scallops, and tiny shrimp daily and bring them here. On the left you may see fishermen's wives selling *crevettes* (shrimp). You can buy them *cuites* (cooked) or *vivantes* (alive and wiggly). They are happy to let you sample one (rip off the cute little head and tail, and pop the middle into your mouth—*délicieuse!*), or buy a cupful to go for a few euros (daily in season).

You'll probably see artists sitting at easels around the harbor, as Boudin and Monet did. Many consider Honfleur the birthplace of 19th-century Impressionism. This was a time when people began to revere, not fear, the out-of-doors, and started to climb mountains "because they were there." Pretty towns like Honfleur and the nearby coast were ideal subjects to paint—and still are—thanks to what locals called the "unusual luminosity" of the region. And with the advent of trains in the late 1800s, artists could travel to the best light like never before. Artists would set up easels along the harbor to catch the light playing on the line of buildings, slates, timbers, geraniums, clouds, and reflections in the water. Monet came here to visit the artist Boudin, a hometown boy, and the battle cry of the Impressionists—"Out of the studio and into the light!"—was born.

▲▲**Ste. Catherine Church (Eglise Ste. Catherine)**—The unusual wood-shingled exterior suggests that this church has a different story to tell than most. Walk inside. You'd swear that if it were turned over, it would float—the legacy of a community of sailors and fishermen, with plenty of boat-builders and no cathedral architects. The church's bell tower is equally unusual, as it was built not adjacent to the church but across the square. That's so it wouldn't overburden the wooden church's roof, and to help minimize fire hazards. In the tiny museum, with a few church artifacts, a useful 15-minute video (in English) describes the tower's history.

Cost and Hours: Church—free, daily July-Aug 9:00-18:30, Sept-June 9:00-17:15; museum—not worth the entry fee but free with ticket to the Eugène Boudin Museum, April-Sept Wed-Mon 10:00-12:00 & 14:00-18:00, Oct-March Wed-Mon 14:00-18:00 only, closed Tue year-round.

Boat Excursions—Boat trips in and around Honfleur depart near Hôtel le Cheval Blanc (Easter-Nov usually about 11:00-17:00). The

Honfleur

R. ALPHONESE ALLAIS

R. BAUDELAIRE

RUE DU TROUILLIARD

RUE HAUTE

D-513

BLVD CHARLES V

Jardin

MAISONS SATIE

CHARRIERE DE GRACE

R. L DELARUE-MARDRUS

RUE VARIN

RUE DE L'HOMME DE BOIS

❸

RUE ALBERT

EUGENE BOUDIN MUSEUM

200 Meters
200 Yards

RUE CAPUCINS

RUE BUCAILLE

RUE JEAN DOUBLET

RUE DES CAPUCINS

RUE BOULANGER

RUE BARBEL

RUE DES LINGOTS

❹

RUE DU PUITS

To Côte de Grâce

❺

Place du Puits

CHARRIERE DE LA CROIX ROUGE

RUE EUGENE BOUDIN

RUE BRÛLEE

RUE DE LA FOULERIE

RUE DES PRES

RUE DE LA BAVOLE

RUE DE LA REPUBLIQUE

VOIE COMMUNALE LE BOUTOIR

Leaving Honfleur

Ⓑ Ⓑ
To Honfleur Center

D-579A

To Free Parking
Ecole Maternelle

❶ Le Bouilland Normand Restaurant
❷ Côté Resto
❸ L'Homme de Bois Rest.
❹ La Commanderie Rest.
❺ Travel Coffee Shop
❻ Café de l'Hôtel de Ville
❼ Waterfront Crêpe Stand
❽ Casino Grocery
❾ Art Gallery Row
❿ Calypso Boat Tours

PARIS

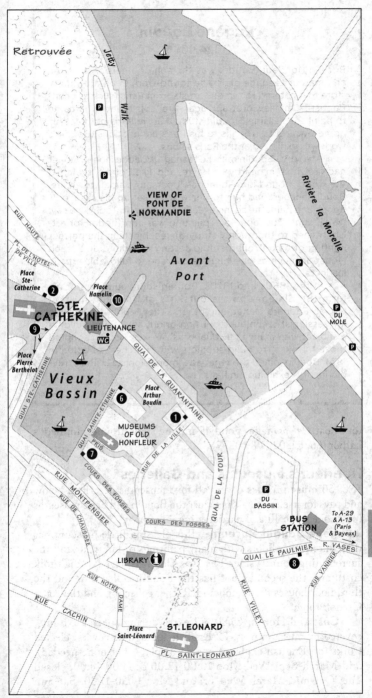

Eugène Boudin
(1824-1898)

Born in Honfleur, Boudin was the son of a harbor pilot. As an amateur teenage artist, he found work in an art-supply store that catered to famous artists from Paris (such as Jean-Baptiste-Camille Corot and Jean-François Millet) who came to paint the seaside. Boudin studied art in Paris but kept his hometown roots. Thanks to his Paris connections, Boudin's work was exhibited at the Paris salons.

At age 30 Boudin met the teenaged Claude Monet. Monet had grown up in nearby Le Havre, and, like Boudin, sketched the world around him—beaches, boats, and small-town life. Boudin encouraged him to don a scarf, set up his easel outdoors, and paint the scene exactly as he saw it. Today, we say: "Well, duh!" But "open-air" painting was unorthodox for artists trained to thoroughly study their subjects in the perfect lighting of a controlled studio setting. Boudin didn't teach Monet as much as give him the courage to follow his artistic instincts.

In the 1860s and 1870s, Boudin spent summers at his farm (St. Siméon) on the outskirts of Honfleur, hosting Monet, Edouard Manet, and others. They taught Boudin the Impressionist techniques of using bright colors and building a subject with many individual brushstrokes. Boudin adapted those "strokes" to build subjects with "patches" of color. In 1874, Boudin joined the renegade Impressionists at their "revolutionary" exhibition in Paris.

tour boat *Calypso* takes good 45-minute spins around Honfleur's harbor (€6, tel. 02 31 89 07 77).

Honfleur's Museums and Galleries

A €9.50 **museum pass** covers all four museums described below and pays for itself with visits to just the Boudin and Satie museums (pass sold at the TI and participating museums).

▲**Eugène Boudin Museum**—This pleasing little museum has three interesting floors with many paintings of Honfleur and the surrounding countryside. The first floor displays Norman folk costumes, the second floor has the Boudin collection, and the third floor houses the Hambourg/Rachet collection and the Katia Granoff room.

Cost and Hours: €5.80, €2 extra during special exhibits, covered by museum pass, €2 English audioguide covers selected works (no English explanations on display—but none needed); mid-March-Sept Wed-Mon 10:00-12:00 & 14:00-18:00, closed Tue; Oct-mid-March Wed-Fri and Mon 14:30-17:30, Sat-Sun

10:00-12:00 & 14:30-17:30, closed Tue; elevator, no photos, Rue de l'Homme de Bois, tel. 02 31 89 54 00.

▲**Maisons Satie**—This peaceful museum, housed in composer Erik Satie's birthplace, presents his music in a creative and enjoyable way. As you wander from room to room with your included audioguide, infrared signals transmit bits of Satie's music, along with a first-person story (in English).

Cost and Hours: €5.80, includes audioguide, covered by museum pass; May-Sept Wed-Mon 10:00-19:00, closed Tue; Oct-Dec and mid-Feb-April Wed-Mon 11:00-18:00, closed Tue; closed Jan-mid-Feb; last entry one hour before closing, 5-minute walk from harbor at 67 Boulevard Charles V, tel. 02 31 89 11 11.

Museums of Old Honfleur—Two side-by-side folk museums combine to paint a picture of daily life in Honfleur during the time when its ships were king and the city had global significance: The **Museum of the Navy** (Musée de la Marine) faces the port and fills Honfleur's oldest church (15th century) with a cool collection of ship models, marine paraphernalia, and paintings. The **Museum of Ethnography and Norman Popular Art** (Musée d'Ethnographie et d'Art Populaire), located in the old prison and courthouse, re-creates typical rooms from various eras and crams them with objects of daily life (€3.70 each or €5 for both, covered by museum pass; both museums open April-Sept Tue-Sun 10:00-12:00 & 14:00-18:30, closed Mon; March and Oct-mid-Nov Tue-Fri 10:00-12:00 & 14:30-17:30, Sat-Sun 10:00-12:00 & 14:00-17:30, closed Mon; closed mid-Nov-Feb).

Eating in Honfleur

Eat seafood or cream sauces here. It's a tough choice between the irresistible waterfront tables of the many look-alike places lining the harbor and the eateries with more solid reputations elsewhere in town. Trust my suggestions below.

Le Bouilland Normand hides a block off the port on a pleasing square and offers a true Norman experience at reasonable prices. Annette and daughter Claire provide quality *Normand* cuisine and enjoy helping travelers (€18-26 *menus,* closed Wed-Thu, dine inside or out, 7 Rue de la Ville, tel. 02 31 89 02 41).

Côté Resto saddles up on the left side of Ste. Catherine Church and serves a top selection of seafood (including seafood *choucroute* and real cheesecake—not served together) in a classy setting. The value is excellent for those in search of a special meal (€22 two-course *menu*, €28 three-course *menu*, great selection, closed Thu, 8 Place Ste. Catherine, tel. 02 31 89 31 33).

L'Homme de Bois combines great ambience with authentic Norman cuisine and decent prices (€19 three-course *menu* with

PARIS

few choices, €23 *menu* gives more choices, daily, a few outside tables, 30 Rue de l'Homme de Bois, tel. 02 31 89 75 27).

La Commanderie, specializing in pizza and crêpes (€10-12), is cozy and welcoming (daily July-Aug, closed Mon-Tue off-season, across from Le Corsaire restaurant on Place Ste. Catherine, tel. 02 31 89 14 92).

Travel Coffee Shop is an ideal breakfast or lunch option for travelers wanting conversation (in either English or French) and good food at very fair prices (Thu-Tue 8:00-19:00, closed Wed, 74 Rue du Puits).

Of the harbor-front options, **Café de l'Hôtel de Ville** owns the best afternoon sun exposure (and charges for it) and looks across to Honfleur's soaring homes (open daily July-Aug, closed Tue off-season, Place de l'Hôtel de Ville, tel. 02 31 89 07 29).

Dessert: Honfleur is ice-cream crazy, with gelato and traditional ice cream shops on every corner. If you need a Ben & Jerry's ice cream fix or a scrumptious dessert crêpe, find the **waterfront stand** at the southeast corner of Vieux Bassin.

Returning to Le Havre

Buses run sporadically to Le Havre; for the full schedule, see page 1008—but, as this service is relatively infrequent, be sure to double-check your connection locally.

D-Day Beaches

The 75 miles of Atlantic coast stretching from Ste-Marie-du-Mont to Ouistreham (about 40 miles west of Le Havre) are littered with WWII museums, monuments, cemeteries, and battle remains left in tribute to the courage of the British, Canadian, and American armies that successfully carried out the largest military operation in history: D-Day. (It's called *Jour J* in French.) It was on these serene beaches, at the crack of dawn on June 6, 1944, that the Allies finally gained a foothold in France, and Nazi Europe was doomed to crumble.

The most famous D-Day sights lie significantly west of Le Havre; for example, Omaha Beach is about a 1.5-hour drive from your cruise port (in good traffic). Other sights are closer—Caen, with its exceptional museum, is about an hour from Le Havre—but still far enough to make it challenging and rushed to see in a short day in port. Many of the best D-Day guides are based closer to the beaches, making it a long journey for them to come meet your ship, then take you back later. All of this makes visiting the D-Day beaches more expensive and less efficient than it could be (ideally, save it for another trip when you can really give it some time). However, if this is your one chance to see this historic sliver of French coastline, and you don't mind splurging on a guide or an excursion to do it efficiently, a D-Day side-trip is worth considering.

Getting Around the D-Day Beaches

By Fully-Guided Minivan Tour: An army of small companies offers all-day excursions to the D-Day beaches. Most are based in or near Bayeux, about 75 miles west of Le Havre, and prefer not to do tours from Le Havre's cruise port. However, the companies listed below are willing to make the trip...for a price. Because they pick up and drop off in Le Havre, they are popular with cruisers (and other day-trippers). Book your tour as far in advance as possible (three months is best), or pray for a last-minute cancellation.

Request extra time at the American Cemetery to see the excellent visitors center. Don't be afraid to take charge of your tour if you have other specific interests (some guides can get lost in the minutiae of battles that you don't have time for). Keep in mind that it's a long return trip to Le Havre, your guide is hustling to get you back in time, and it's impossible to see everything in a short day. In addition to the guides listed here, many others are happy to do a D-Day tour for you...*if* you can get yourself to Bayeux (most likely by taxi) to meet them.

Mathias Leclere brings a thoughtful, French perspective to his tour. Born four miles from Juno Beach to a family with three centuries of roots in Normandy, he is part of its soil. Mathias is a self-taught historian who leads tours in his minivan (€650/up to 4 passengers, €750/up to 6 passengers, 6-person maximum, does not include lunch or entrance fees, www.ddayguidedtours.com).

Normandy Sightseeing Tours delivers a French perspective through the voices of its small fleet of licensed guides. They offer a variety of tours from Le Havre, including D-Day tours focused on either the US, British, or Canadian sectors (as well as other itineraries). Because there are many guides, the quality of their teaching is less consistent—guides David, Olivier, and Karinne get the best reviews (€720/up to 4 people, €740/up to 6 people, €760/up to 8 people, does not include lunch or entrance fees; tel. 02 31 51 70 52, www.normandy-sightseeing-tours.com, fredericguerin@wanadoo.fr).

On Your Own: Though the minivan excursions listed above teach important history lessons, **renting a car** can be a good and less expensive way to visit the beaches, particularly for three or more people (for rental suggestions in Le Havre, see page 1006). Park in monitored locations at the sites, since break-ins are a problem—particularly at the American Cemetery—and consider hiring a guide to join you (see "Private Tours," later). Of course, be

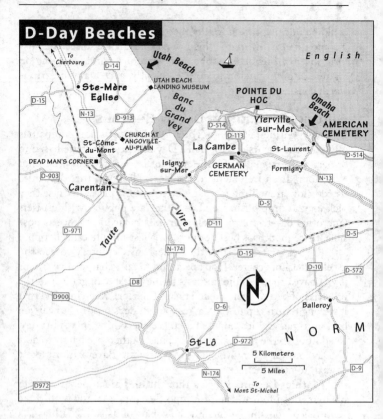

D-Day Beaches

To Cherbourg
D-14
Utah Beach
English

D-15

Ste-Mère Eglise

UTAH BEACH LANDING MUSEUM

N-13

D-913

Banc du Grand Vey

POINTE DU HOC

Omaha Beach

Vierville-sur-Mer

AMERICAN CEMETERY

D-514

CHURCH AT ANGOVILLE-AU-PLAIN

La Cambe

St-Laurent

D-514

St-Côme-du-Mont

D-113

DEAD MAN'S CORNER

Isigny-sur-Mer

GERMAN CEMETERY

Formigny

N-13

D-903

Carentan

D-971

Taute

Vire

D-11

D-5

D-5

N-174

D-15

D-10

D-572

D8

D-6

Balleroy

D900

N

O R M

St-Lô

D-972

5 Kilometers

N-174

5 Miles

D-9

D972

To Mont St-Michel

---

sure to leave yourself plenty of time to make it back to Le Havre to drop off your car and get back to your ship.

For small groups, hiring a **taxi for the day** is cheaper than taking a minivan tour (see rates on page 1009), but you don't get the full history lesson.

D-Day Sights

With one day from Le Havre, you'll only have time to visit a few of the many D-Day locations. Most Americans prefer to focus on the American sector (west of Arromanches), rather than the British and Canadian sectors (east of Arromanches), which have been overbuilt with resorts, making it harder to envision the events of June 1944. Unfortunately, the American sector is even farther

from Le Havre, making your day even more rushed. Here are quick descriptions of some of the top sights:

• **Arromanches:** This small town was ground zero for the D-Day invasion. Almost overnight, it sprouted the immense Port Winston, which gave the Allies a foothold in Normandy, allowing them to begin their victorious push to Berlin and end World War II. You'll find a view over the site of that gigantic makeshift harbor, a good museum, an evocative beach and bluff (with an interesting film), and a touristy-but-fun little town that offers a pleasant cocktail of war memories, cotton candy, and beachfront trinket shops.

• **Longues-sur-Mer Gun Battery:** Four German casemates (three with guns intact)—built to guard against seaborne attacks—hunker down at the end of a country road. This battery—with the only original coastal artillery guns remaining in place in the D-Day region—was a critical link in Hitler's Atlantic Wall defense, which consisted of more than 15,000 structures stretching from Norway to the Pyrenees. Today visitors can see the bunkers at this strategic site.

Countdown to D-Day

1939 On September 1, Adolf Hitler invades the Free City of Danzig (today's Gdańsk, Poland), sparking World War II.

1940 Germany's "Blitzkrieg" ("lightning war") quickly overwhelms France, Nazis goose-step down the Avenue des Champs-Elysées, and the country is divided into Occupied France (the north) and Vichy France (the south, ruled by right-wing French). Just like that, nearly the entire Continent is fascist.

1941 The Allies (Britain, the Soviet Union, and others) peck away at the fringes of "fortress Europe." The Soviets repel Hitler's invasion at Moscow, while the Brits (with American aid) battle German U-boats for control of the seas. On December 7, Japan bombs the US naval base at Pearl Harbor, Hawaii. The US enters the war against Japan and its ally, Germany.

1942 Three crucial battles—at Stalingrad, El-Alamein, and Guadalcanal—weaken the German forces and their ally Japan. The victorious tank battle at El-Alamein in the deserts of North Africa soon gives the Allies a jumping-off point (Tunis) for the first assault on the Continent.

1943 More than 150,000 Americans and Brits, under the command of George Patton and Bernard ("Monty") Montgomery, land in Sicily and begin working their way north through Italy. Meanwhile, Germany has to fend off tenacious Soviets on their eastern front.

1944 On June 6, 1944, the Allies launch "Operation Overlord," better known as D-Day. The Allies amass three million soldiers and six million tons of *matériel* in England in preparation for the biggest fleet-led invasion in history—across the English Channel to France, then

• **WWII Normandy American Cemetery and Memorial:** Crowning a bluff just above Omaha Beach (described next) and the eye of the D-Day storm, 9,387 brilliant white-marble crosses and Stars of David glow in memory of Americans who gave their lives to free Europe on the beaches below.

• **Vierville-sur-Mer and Omaha Beach:** Omaha Beach witnessed by far the most intense battles of any along the D-Day beaches. The hills above were heavily fortified, and a single German machine gun could fire 1,200 rounds a minute. The highest casualty rates in Normandy occurred at Omaha Beach, nicknamed "Bloody Omaha." Here you'll find a museum and a chance to walk on the beach where anywhere from 2,500 to 4,800

eastward toward Berlin. The Germans, hunkered down in northern France, know an invasion is imminent, but the Allies keep the details top secret. On the night of June 5, 150,000 soldiers board ships and planes, not knowing where they are headed until they're under way. Each one carries a note from General Dwight D. Eisenhower: "The tide has turned. The free men of the world are marching together to victory."

At 6:30 on June 6, 1944, Americans spill out of troop transports into the cold waters off a beach in Normandy, code-named Omaha. The weather is bad, seas are rough, and the prep bombing has failed. The soldiers, many seeing their first action, are dazed, confused, and weighed down by heavy packs. Nazi machine guns pin them against the sea. Slowly, they crawl up the beach on their stomachs. More than a thousand die. They hold on until the next wave of transports arrives.

All day long, Allied confusion does battle with German indecision—the Nazis never really counterattack, thinking D-Day is just a ruse, not the main invasion. By day's end, the Allies take several beaches along the Normandy coast and begin building artificial harbors, providing a tiny port-of-entry for the reconquest of Europe. The stage is set for a quick and easy end to the war. Right.

1945 Having liberated Paris (August 26, 1944), the Allied march on Berlin from the west bogs down, hit by poor supply lines, bad weather, and the surprising German counterpunch at the Battle of the Bulge. Finally, in the spring, the Americans and Brits cross the Rhine, Soviet soldiers close in on Berlin, Hitler shoots himself, and—after nearly six long years of war—Europe is free.

Americans were killed and wounded, making way for some 34,000 to land on the beach by day's end.

• **Pointe du Hoc:** The intense bombing of the beaches by Allied forces is best experienced here, where US Army Rangers scaled impossibly steep cliffs to disable a German gun battery. Pointe du Hoc's bomb-cratered, lunar-like landscape and remaining bunkers make it one of the most evocative of the D-Day sites.

• **German Military Cemetery:** To ponder German losses, visit this somber, thought-provoking resting place of 21,000 German soldiers. Compared with the American Cemetery, which symbolizes hope and victory, this one is a clear symbol of defeat and despair. A small visitors center gives more information on this

PARIS

and other German war cemeteries.

• **Utah Beach Landing Museum:** This thorough yet manageable museum pieces together the many parts of the Allied invasion: Paratroopers had to be dropped inland, the French Resistance had to disable bridges and cut communications, bombers had to deliver payloads on target and on time, the infantry had to land safely on the beaches, and supplies had to follow the infantry closely.

• **Church at Angoville-au-Plain:** At this simple Romanesque church, two American medics (Kenneth Moore and Robert Wright) treated German and American wounded while battles raged only steps away.

• **Dead Man's Corner Museum:** In 1944, the Germans used this French home as a regional headquarters. Today, a tiny museum recounts the terrible battles that took place around the town of Carentan from June 6 to 11.

• **Ste-Mère Eglise:** Made famous by the film *The Longest Day*, this was the first village to be liberated by the Americans. The area around Ste-Mère Eglise was the center of action for American paratroopers, whose objective was to land behind enemy lines in support of the American landing at Utah Beach. It was around this village that many paratroopers, facing terrible weather and heavy anti-aircraft fire, landed off-target—including one who dangled from the town's church steeple for two hours. Today, the village greets travelers with flag-draped streets, that famous church, and a museum honoring paratroopers.

• **Juno Beach Centre:** Located on the beachfront in the Canadian sector, this facility is dedicated to teaching travelers about the vital role Canadian forces played in the invasion.

• **Canadian Cemetery:** This small, touching cemetery makes a modest statement when compared with other, more grandiose cemeteries in this area. To me, it captures the understated nature of Canadians perfectly.

• **Caen Memorial Museum:** Caen, the modern capital of lower Normandy, has the most thorough WWII museum in France. Located at the site of an important German headquarters during World War II, its official name is "The Caen Memorial: Center for the History for Peace" *(Le Mémorial de Caen: La Cité de l'Histoire pour la Paix)*. With two video presentations and numerous exhibits on the lead-up to World War II, the actual Battle of Normandy, the Cold War, and more, it effectively puts the Battle of Normandy into a broader context.

For more information on visiting the D-Day beaches, www
.normandiememoire.com is a useful resource.

Rouen

This 2,000-year-old city mixes Gothic architecture, half-timbered
houses, and contemporary bustle like no other place in France.

Busy Rouen (roo-ahn) is
France's fifth-largest port and
Europe's biggest food exporter
(mostly wheat and grain).
Rouen is nothing new. It was a
regional capital during Roman
times, and France's second-
largest city in medieval times
(with 40,000 residents—only
Paris had more). In the ninth century, the Normans made the
town their capital. William the Conqueror called it home before
moving to England. Rouen walked a political tightrope between
England and France for centuries, and was an English base during
the Hundred Years' War. Joan of Arc was burned here (in 1431).
Rouen's historic wealth was based on its wool industry and trade—
for centuries, it was the last bridge across the Seine River before
the Atlantic. In April of 1944, as America and Britain weakened
German control of Normandy prior to the D-Day landings, Allied
bombers destroyed 50 percent of Rouen. And though the industrial suburbs were devastated, most of the historic core survived,
keeping Rouen a pedestrian haven.

Rouen is right along the main Paris-bound train line, just an
hour from Le Havre. If you've been to Paris before (or prefer to
save it for another trip), and want a dose of a smaller—yet lively—
French city, Rouen is your best bet.

Orientation to Rouen

PARIS

Although Paris embraces the Seine, Rouen ignores it. The area
we're most interested in is bounded by the river to the south, the
Museum of Fine Arts (Esplanade Marcel Duchamp) to the north,
Rue de la République to the east, and Place du Vieux Marché to
the west. It's a 20-minute walk from the train station to the Notre-
Dame Cathedral or TI. Everything else of interest is within a
10-minute walk of the cathedral or TI.

Tourist Information: Pick up the map with information on
Rouen's museums at the TI, which faces the cathedral. The TI
also has €5 audioguide tours covering the cathedral and Rouen's

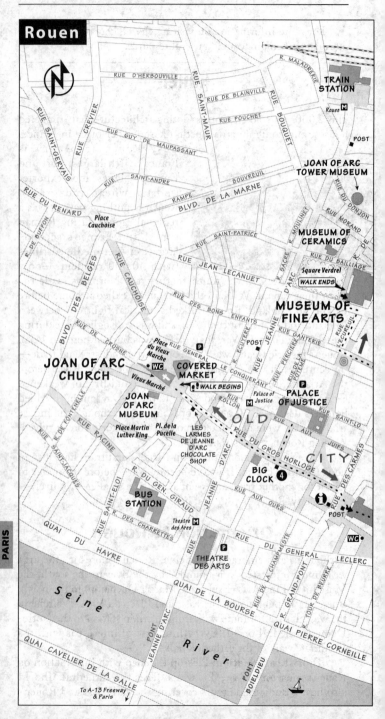

Rouen

N

RUE D'HERBOUVILLE
RUE SAINT-MAUR
RUE DE BLAINVILLE
RUE POUCHET
R. MALADRERIE

TRAIN STATION
Rouen M

POST

RUE SAINT-GERVAIS
RUE CREVIER
RUE GUY DE MAUPASSANT
RUE SAINT-ANDRE
KAMPE
BOUVREUIL
BLVD. DE LA MARNE

JOAN OF ARC TOWER MUSEUM

RUE DU DONJON
RUE MORAND

RUE DU RENARD
R. DE BUFFON
Place Cauchoise

RUE SAINT-PATRICE

MUSEUM OF CERAMICS
R. SACRE
RUE DU BAILLIAGE

BLVD. DES BELGES
RUE CAUCHOISE
RUE JEAN LECANUET
RUE DES BONS ENFANTS

Square Verdrel
WALK ENDS

MUSEUM OF FINE ARTS

RUE DE CROSNE
RUE GENERAL
RUE DE LA POTERIE
RUE PERCIERE
RUE GANTERIE
RUE JEANNE
RUE ECUYERE

Place du Vieux Marche
WC
COVERED MARKET

JOAN OF ARC CHURCH
Vieux Marché
WALK BEGINS
LE CONQUERANT
POST

JOAN OF ARC MUSEUM
Place Martin Luther King
Pl. de la Pucelle
LES LARMES DE JEANNE D'ARC CHOCOLATE SHOP
RUE ROLLON

Palace of Justice
M
PALACE OF JUSTICE
P

OLD
RUE DU GROS HORLOGE

CITY
RUE AUX
RUE SAINT-LO

RUE DE FONTENELLE
RUE RACINE
RUE SAINT-JACQUES
RUE SAINT-ELOI

R. DU GEN. GIRAUD
RUE JEANNE D'ARC

BIG CLOCK

RUE DES CARMES
JUIFS

BUS STATION
R. DES CHARRETTES
Théâtre des Arts
M

RUE AUX OURS

i
RUE DES CARMES
POST

QUAI DU HAVRE

THEATRE DES ARTS
P

RUE DE LA CHAMPMESLE
RUE DU GENERAL LECLERC
WC

PONT JEANNE D'ARC
QUAI DE LA BOURSE
RUE GRAND-PONT
R. TOUR DE BEURRE
QUAI PIERRE CORNEILLE

Seine River

QUAI CAVELIER DE LA SALLE

To A-13 Freeway & Paris

PONT BOIELDIEU

PARIS

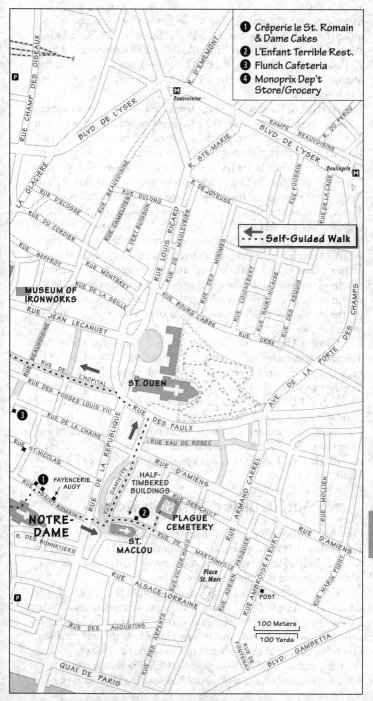

1. Crêperie le St. Romain & Dame Cakes
2. L'Enfant Terrible Rest.
3. Flunch Cafeteria
4. Monoprix Dep't Store/Grocery

Self-Guided Walk

PARIS

historic center, though this book's self-guided walk is enough for most (May-Sept Mon-Sat 9:00-19:00, Sun 9:30-12:30 & 14:00-18:00; Oct-April Mon-Sat 9:30-12:30 & 13:30-18:00, closed Sun; 25 Place de la Cathédrale, tel. 02 32 08 32 40, www.rouentourisme .com). A small office in the TI changes money (closed during lunch year-round).

Arrival in Rouen (by Train from Le Havre): Train connections are explained on page 1007. Remember, get off at the station called "Rouen-Rive-Droite." Rue Jeanne d'Arc cuts down from Rouen's train station through the town center to the Seine River. Day-trippers should **walk** from the station down Rue Jeanne d'Arc toward Rue du Gros Horloge—a busy pedestrian mall in the medieval center. This cobblestone street connects Place du Vieux Marché and Joan of Arc Church (to your right, the starting point of my self-guided walk) with Notre-Dame Cathedral (to your left). For a faster alternative, Rouen's **subway** (Métrobus) whisks travelers from under the train station to the Palais de Justice in one stop (€1.80; descend and buy tickets from machines one level underground, then validate ticket on subway two levels down; subway direction: Technopôle or Georges Braque). **Taxis** (to the right as you exit station) will take you to various points in town for about €8.

Closed Days: Most of Rouen's museums are closed on Tuesday, and many sights also close midday (12:00-14:00). The cathedral is closed Monday morning and during Mass (usually Tue-Sat at 10:00, July-Aug at 18:00; Sun and holidays at 8:30, 10:00, and 12:00). The Joan of Arc Church is closed Friday and Sunday mornings, and during Mass.

Supermarket: It's inside the **Monoprix,** at the back of the store (Mon-Sat 8:30-21:00, closed Sun, on Rue du Gros Horloge).

Taxi: Call **Les Taxi Blancs** at 02 35 61 20 50 or 02 35 88 50 50.

Self-Guided Walk in Rouen

On this 1.5-hour walk, you'll see the essential Rouen sights. Remember that many sights are closed midday (12:00-14:00). This walk is designed for day-trippers coming by train (who will start with a 10-minute downhill walk from the station).

From Place du Vieux Marché, you'll walk the length of Rue du Gros Horloge to Notre-Dame Cathedral. From there, walk four blocks west to the plague cemetery (Aître St. Maclou), loop up to the church of St. Ouen, and return along rues de l'Hôpital and Ganterie, ending at the Museum of Fine Arts (a 5-minute walk to the train station). The map on page 1096 highlights our route.

• *From the train station, walk down Rue Jeanne d'Arc and turn right on Rue du Guillaume le Conquérant (notice the Gothic Palais de Justice building across Rue Jeanne d'Arc—we'll get to that later). This takes you to our starting point...*

Place du Vieux Marché

• *Stand near the entrance of the striking Joan of Arc Church.*

Surrounded by half-timbered buildings, this old market square has a covered produce market, a park commemorating Joan of Arc's burning, and a modern church named after her. A tall aluminum cross, planted in a flowery garden near the church entry, marks the spot where Rouen publicly punished and executed people. The pillories stood here, and during the Revolution, the town's guillotine made 800 people "a foot shorter at the top." In 1431, Joan of Arc—only 19 years old—was burned at this site. Find her flaming statue facing the cross. As the flames engulfed her, an English soldier said, "Oh my God, we've killed a saint." (Nearly 500 years later, Joan was canonized, and the soldier was proved right.)

▲▲Joan of Arc Church (Eglise Jeanne d'Arc)

This modern church is a tribute to the young woman who was canonized in 1920 and later became the patron saint of France. The church, completed in 1979, feels Scandinavian inside and out—another reminder of Normandy's Nordic roots. Sumptuous 16th-century windows, salvaged from a church lost during World War II, were worked into the soft architectural lines (the €0.50 English pamphlet provides some background and describes the stained-glass scenes). Similar to modern churches designed by the 20th-century architect Le Corbusier, this is an uplifting place to be, with a ship's-hull vaulting and sweeping wood ceiling that sail over curved pews and a wall of glass below. Make time to savor this unusual place.

Cost and Hours: Free; April-Oct Mon-Thu and Sat 10:00-12:00 & 14:00-18:00, Fri and Sun 14:00-17:30; Nov-March daily 14:00-18:00; closed during Mass. A public WC is 30 yards straight ahead from the church doors.

• *Turn left out of the church and step over ruins of a 15th-century church that once stood on this spot (destroyed during the French Revolution). Straight ahead is the waxy...*

Joan of Arc Museum

Enter through a souvenir shop sandwiched between big restaurants. This museum tells the story of this inspirational teenager of supreme faith who, after hearing voices for several years, won the confidence of her countrymen, was given an army, and rallied the French against their English invaders. Those touched by her story will enjoy this little museum, with excellent English information

PARIS

Joan of Arc
(1412-1431)

The cross-dressing teenager who rallied French soldiers to drive out English invaders was the illiterate daughter of a humble farmer. One summer day, in her dad's garden, 13-year-old Joan heard a heavenly voice accompanied by bright light. It was the first of several saints (including Michael, Margaret, and Catherine) to talk to her during her short life.

In 1429, the young girl was instructed by the voices to save France from the English. Dressed in men's clothing, she traveled to see the king and predicted that the French armies would be defeated near Orléans—as they were. King Charles VII equipped her with an ancient sword and a banner that read "Jesus, Maria," and sent her to rally the troops.

Soon "the Maid" *(la Pucelle)* was bivouacking amid rough soldiers, riding with them into battle, and suffering an arrow wound to the chest—all while liberating the town of Orléans. On July 17, 1429, she held her banner high in the cathedral of Reims as Charles was officially proclaimed king of a resurgent France.

Joan and company next tried to retake Paris (1429), but the English held out. She suffered a crossbow wound through the thigh, and her reputation of invincibility was tarnished. During a battle at Compiègne (1430), she was captured and turned over to the English for £10,000. The English took her to Rouen where she was chained by the neck inside an iron cage, while the local French authorities (allied with the English) plotted against her. The Inquisition—insisting that Joan's voices were "false and diabolical"—tried and sentenced her to death for being a witch and heretic.

On May 30, 1431, Joan of Arc was tied to a stake on Rouen's old market square (Place du Vieux Marché). She yelled, "Rouen! Rouen! Must I die here?" Then they lit the fire; she fixed her eyes on a crucifix and died chanting, "Jesus, Jesus, Jesus."

After her death, Joan's place in history was slowly rehabilitated. French authorities proclaimed her trial illegal (1455), prominent writers and artists were inspired by her, and the Catholic Church finally beatified (1909) and canonized her (1920) as St. Joan of Arc.

PARIS

and nifty models throughout.

Cost and Hours: €5, daily mid-April-Sept 9:30-18:00, Oct-mid-April 10:00-12:00 & 14:00-17:30, tel. 02 35 88 02 70, www.jeanne-darc.com.

• *Leave the square and join the busy pedestrian street, Rue du Gros Horloge—the town's main shopping street since Roman times. A block up on your right (at #163) is Rouen's most famous chocolate shop...*

Les Larmes de Jeanne d'Arc

The chocolate-makers of Les Larmes de Jeanne d'Arc would love to tempt you with their chocolate-covered almond "tears *(larmes)* of Joan of Arc." Although you must resist touching the chocolate fountain, you are welcome to taste a tear. The first one is free; a small bag costs about €8 (Mon-Sat 9:00-19:00, closed Sun).

• *Your route continues past a medieval McDonald's and across busy Rue Jeanne d'Arc to the...*

▲Big Clock (Gros Horloge)

This impressive, circa-1528 Renaissance clock, le Gros Horloge (groh oar-lohzh), decorates the former city hall. Is something missing? Not really. In the 16th century, an hour hand offered sufficient precision; minute hands became necessary only in a later, faster-paced age. The lamb at the end of the hour hand is a reminder that wool rules—it was the source of Rouen's wealth. The town medallion features a sacrificial lamb, which has both religious and commercial significance (center, below the clock). The black-and-silver orb above the clock makes one revolution in 29 days. The clock's artistic highlight fills the underside of the arch (walk underneath and stretch your back), with the "Good Shepherd" and lots of sheep.

To see the inner workings and an extraordinary panorama over Rouen (including a memorable view of the cathedral), climb the clock tower's 100 steps. You'll tour several rooms with the help of an audioguide that suffers from a Goldilocks-and-the-Three-Bears narration. The big bells ring on the hour—a deafening experience if you're in the tower.

Cost and Hours: €6, includes audioguide; April-Oct Tue-Sun 10:00-12:00 & 13:00-18:00; Nov-March Tue-Sun 14:00-18:00; closed Mon year-round.

• *Walk under le Gros Horloge, then take a one-block detour left on Rue Thouret to see the...*

Palace of Justice (Palais de Justice)

Years of cleaning have removed the grime that once covered this fabulously flamboyantly Gothic building, the former home of Normandy's *parlement*. The result is striking; think of this as you visit Rouen's other Gothic structures; many are awaiting baths of their own. Pockmarks on the side of the building that faces Rue Jeanne d'Arc are leftovers from bombings during the Normandy invasion. Look for the English-language plaques on the iron fence—they provide some history, and describe the damage and tedious repair process.

• *Double back and continue up Rue du Gros Horloge. In a block you'll see a plaque dedicated to Cavelier de la Salle (high on the left), who explored the mouth of the Mississippi River, claimed the state of Louisiana for France, and was assassinated in Texas in 1687. Soon you'll reach...*

▲▲Notre-Dame Cathedral (Cathédrale Notre-Dame)

This cathedral is a landmark of art history. You're seeing essentially what Claude Monet saw as he painted 30 different studies of this

frilly Gothic facade at various times of the day. Using the physical building only as a rack upon which to hang light, mist, dusk, and shadows, Monet was capturing "impressions." One of the results is in Rouen's Museum of Fine Arts; four others are at the Orsay Museum in Paris. Find the plaque showing two of these paintings (in the corner of the square, about 30 paces to your right if you were exiting the TI). Look up at the soaring facade and find the cleaned sections, with bright statues on either side of the central portal. The interior has chapels in a range of architectural styles, and stone tombs dating from when Rouen was the Norman capital (including one that holds the heart of Richard the Lionhearted).

Cost and Hours: Tue-Sun 8:00-19:00, Mon 14:00-19:00; closed during Mass Tue-Sat at 10:00, July-Aug also at 18:00, Sun at 8:30, 10:30, and 12:00; also closed Nov-March daily 12:00-14:00.

• *From this courtyard, a gate deposits you on a traffic-free street. Turn right and walk along...*

Rue St. Romain

This street has half-timbered buildings and lanes worth a look. In a short distance, you can look through an arch, back at the cathedral's spire. Made of cast iron in the late 1800s—about the same time Gustave Eiffel was building his tower in Paris—the spire is, at 490 feet, the tallest in France. You can also see the former location of the missing smaller (green) spire—downed during a catastrophic windstorm in December of 1999.

• *Farther down the street, find a shop that shows off a traditional art form in action.*

At **Fayencerie Augy** (at #26), Monsieur Augy welcomes shoppers to browse his studio/gallery/shop and see Rouen's clay "china" being made the traditional way. First, the clay is molded and fired. Then it's dipped in white enamel, dried, lovingly hand-painted, and fired a second time. Rouen was the first city in France to make faience, earthenware with colored glazes. In the 1700s, the town

PARIS

had 18 factories churning out the popular product (Tue-Sat 9:00-19:00, closed Sun, 26 Rue St. Romain, VAT tax refunds nearly pay for the shipping, www.fayencerie-augy.com).

• *Continue along Rue St. Romain, which (after crossing Rue de la République) leads to the fancy...*

St. Maclou Church

This church's unique, bowed facade is textbook Flamboyant Gothic (sadly, its doorways are blackened by pollution—visualize what a world without pollution would be like). Notice the flame-like tracery decorating its gable. Because this was built at the very end of the Gothic age—and construction took many years—the doors are from the next age: the Renaissance (c. 1550). The bright and airy interior is worth a quick peek.

Cost and Hours: Free, Fri-Mon 10:00-12:00 & 14:00-17:30, closed Tue-Thu.

• *Leaving the church, turn right, and then take another right (giving the little boys on the corner wall a wide berth). Wander past a fine wall of half-timbered buildings fronting Rue Martainville, to the end of St. Maclou Church.*

Half-Timbered Buildings

Because the local stone—a chalky limestone from the cliffs of the Seine River—was of poor quality (your thumbnail is stronger), and because local oak was plentiful, half-timbered buildings became a Rouen specialty from the 14th through 19th centuries. Cantilevered floors were standard until the early 1500s. These top-heavy designs made sense: City land was limited, property taxes were based on ground-floor square footage, and the cantilevering minimized unsupported spans on upper floors. The oak beams provided the structural skeleton of the building, which was then filled in with a mix of clay, straw, pebbles...or whatever was available.

• *A block farther down on the left, at 186 Rue Martainville, a covered lane leads to the...*

Plague Cemetery (Aître St. Maclou)

During the great plagues of the Middle Ages, as many as two-thirds of the people in this parish died. For the decimated community, dealing with the corpses was an overwhelming task. This half-timbered courtyard (c. 1520) was a mass grave, an ossuary where the bodies were "processed." Bodies would be dumped into the grave (where the well is now) and drenched in liquid lime to help speed decomposition. Later, the bones would be stacked in alcoves above the colonnades that line this courtyard. Notice the ghoulish carvings (c. 1560s) of gravediggers' tools, skulls, crossbones, and characters doing the "dance of death." In this *danse macabre*, Death, the great equalizer, grabs people of all social classes. The place is now an art school. Peek in on the young artists. As you leave, spy the dried black cat (died c. 1520, in tiny glass case to the left of the door). To overcome evil, it was buried during the building's construction.

Cost and Hours: Free, daily mid-March-Oct 8:00-20:00, Nov-mid-March 8:00-19:00.

Nearby: Farther down Rue Martainville, at Place St. Marc, a colorful market blooms Sunday until about 12:30 and all day Tuesday, Friday, and Saturday. If it's not market day, you can double back to the cathedral and Rue du Gros Horloge, or continue with me to explore more of Rouen and find the Museum of Fine Arts (back toward the train station).

• *To reach the museum, turn right upon leaving the boneyard, then right again at the little boys (onto Rue Damiette), and hike up antique row to the vertical St. Ouen Church (a seventh-century abbey turned church in the 15th century, fine park behind). Turn left at the church on Rue des Faulx (an English-language bookstore, ABC Books, is a block to the right), and cross the busy street. (The horseman you see to the right is a short yet majestic Napoleon Bonaparte, who welcomes visitors to Rouen's city hall.) Continue down Rue de l'Hôpital's traffic-free lane, which becomes Rue Ganterie. A right at the modern square on Rue l'Ecrueil leads you to the **Museum of Fine Arts** and the **Museum of Ironworks** (both described next, under "Sights in Rouen"). This is the end of our tour. The tower where Joan of Arc was imprisoned (also explained later) is a few blocks uphill, on the way back to the train station.*

Sights in Rouen

The first three museums are within a block of one another, closed on Tuesdays, never crowded, and can all be visited with the same €8 combo-ticket (www.rouen-musees.com).

▲**Museum of Fine Arts (Musée des Beaux-Arts)**—Paintings from many periods are beautifully displayed in this overlooked two-floor museum, including works by Caravaggio, Peter Paul Rubens, Paolo Veronese, Jan Steen, Théodore Géricault, Jean-Auguste-Dominique Ingres, Eugène Delacroix, and several Impressionists. With its reasonable entry fee and calm interior, this museum is worth a short visit for the Impressionists and a surgical hit of a few other key artists. The museum café is good for a peaceful break from the action outside.

Cost and Hours: €5, occasional temporary exhibitions cost extra, €8 combo-ticket includes ironworks and ceramics museums; open Wed-Mon 10:00-18:00, 15th-17th-century rooms closed

What If I Miss My Boat?

Remember that you can get help from the cruise line's port agent (listed on the destination information sheet distributed on the ship) and the local TI (see page 1016). If the port agent suggests a costly solution (such as a private car with a driver), you may want to consider public transit.

For destinations on the Continent, your best bet is to ride the 2.25-hour train to Paris, where you can connect to **Zeebrugge** (via Brussels), **Amsterdam, Warnemünde** (via Berlin), **Copenhagen,** and beyond.

To reach the ports for **London** (Southampton or Dover), consider a cheap flight. But it may be easier to hop an overnight ferry, several of which leave from Normandy. From Le Havre, LD Lines runs each evening to Portsmouth (£25, departs at 17:00, arrives at 21:30, tel. 08 25 30 43 04, www.ldline.co.uk). From Caen, Brittany Ferries also runs to Portsmouth (£25, up to 3/day, including an overnight option departing at 23:00 and arriving at 06:45, goes from Ouistreham—9 miles north of Caen, tel. 02 31 36 36 36, www .brittany-ferries.co.uk). And from Dieppe, LD Lines goes to Newhaven twice daily (£20, 5:30-8:30 and 18:00-21:00, see contact info above).

If you need to catch a **plane** to your next destination, your best bet is to head to one of Paris' two main airports (allow at least 3-4 hours by train, with a connection in Paris): Charles de Gaulle or Orly (these share a website: www.adp .fr). Slightly closer to Le Havre, at the northern edge of Paris, is Beauvais Airport, used predominantly by budget carriers (www.aeroportbeauvais.com).

Local **travel agents** in Le Havre or Paris can help you. For more advice on what to do if you miss the boat, see page 144.

13:00-14:00, closed Tue; a few blocks below train station at 26 bis Rue Jean Lecanuet, tel. 02 35 71 28 40.

Museum of Ironworks (Musée le Secq des Tournelles, a.k.a. Musée de la Ferronnerie)—This deconsecrated church houses iron objects, many of them more than 1,500 years old. Locks, chests, keys, tools, thimbles, coffee grinders, corkscrews, and flatware from centuries ago—virtually anything made of iron is on display. You can duck into the entry area for a glimpse of a medieval iron scene without passing through the turnstile.

Cost and Hours: €3, €8 combo-ticket includes fine arts and ceramics museums, no English explanations—bring a French/English dictionary, Wed-Mon 10:00-13:00 & 14:00-18:00, closed Tue, behind Museum of Fine Arts, 2 Rue Jacques Villon, tel. 02 35 88 42 92.

PARIS

Eating in Rouen

You can eat well in Rouen at fair prices. Because you're in Normandy, *crêperies* abound. For a simple meal inside or out, prowl the places between the St. Maclou and St. Ouen churches (along rues Martainville and Damiette), or the ever-so-hip Rue de l'Eau de Robec. Otherwise, try the recommendations below.

Near the Cathedral

Crêperie le St. Romain, between the cathedral and St. Maclou Church, is an excellent budget option. It's run by gentle Mr. Pegis, who serves filling €9 crêpes with small salads in a warm setting (lunch Tue-Sat, closed Sun-Mon, 52 Rue St. Romain, tel. 02 35 88 90 36).

Dame Cakes is ideal if it's lunchtime or teatime and you need a Jane Austen fix. The decor is from another, more precious era, and the baked goods are out of this world (€12-15 salads and *plats,* garden terrace in back, Mon-Sat 11:00-18:00, closed Sun, 70 Rue St. Romain, tel. 02 35 07 49 31).

L'Enfant Terrible is a sharp, wine-loving place serving well-prepared dishes at reasonable prices. There's plenty of contemporary music and lots of yellow (€18 two-course *menu,* €23 three-course *menu,* closed Sun-Mon, 234 Rue Martainville, tel. 02 35 89 50 02).

At **Flunch** you'll find family-friendly, cheap, point-and-shoot, cafeteria-style meals in a fast-food setting (*menus* under €10 include salad bar, main course, and drink; good kids' *menu,* open daily until 22:00, a block from cathedral at 66 Rue des Carmes, tel. 02 35 71 81 81).

Returning to Le Havre

From downtown, just reverse the walk to the station—from Rue du Gros Horloge, a block west of the big clock, head up Rue Jeanne d'Arc. For a quicker return, take the subway in direction: Boulingrin and get off at Gare-Rue Verte. Trains head back to Le Havre about hourly and take less than an hour.

French Survival Phrases

When using the phonetics, try to nasalize the n sound.

English	French	Pronunciation
Good day.	Bonjour.	bohn-zhoor
Mrs. / Mr.	Madame / Monsieur	mah-dahm / muhs-yur
Do you speak English?	Parlez-vous anglais?	par-lay-voo ahn-glay
Yes. / No.	Oui. / Non.	wee / nohn
I understand.	Je comprends.	zhuh kohn-prahn
I don't understand.	Je ne comprends pas.	zhuh nuh kohn-prahn pah
Please.	S'il vous plaît.	see voo play
Thank you.	Merci.	mehr-see
I'm sorry.	Désolé.	day-zoh-lay
Excuse me.	Pardon.	par-dohn
(No) problem.	(Pas de) problème.	(pah duh) proh-blehm
It's good.	C'est bon.	say bohn
Goodbye.	Au revoir.	oh vwahr
one / two	un / deux	uhn / duh
three / four	trois / quatre	twah / kah-truh
five / six	cinq / six	sank / sees
seven / eight	sept / huit	seht / weet
nine / ten	neuf / dix	nuhf / dees
How much is it?	Combien?	kohn-bee-an
Write it?	Ecrivez?	ay-kree-vay
Is it free?	C'est gratuit?	say grah-twee
Included?	Inclus?	an-klew
Where can I buy / find...?	Où puis-je acheter / trouver...?	oo pwee-zhuh ah-shuh-tay / troo-vay
I'd like / We'd like...	Je voudrais / Nous voudrions...	zhuh voo-dray / noo voo-dree-ohn
...a room.	...une chambre.	ewn shahn-bruh
...a ticket to ___.	...un billet pour ___.	uhn bee-yay poor
Is it possible?	C'est possible?	say poh-see-bluh
Where is...?	Où est...?	oo ay
...the train station	...la gare	lah gar
...the bus station	...la gare routière	lah gar root-yehr
...tourist information	...l'office du tourisme	loh-fees dew too-reez-muh
Where are the toilets?	Où sont les toilettes?	oo sohn lay twah-leht
men	hommes	ohm
women	dames	dahm
left / right	à gauche / à droite	ah gohsh / ah dwaht
straight	tout droit	too dwah
When does this open / close?	Ça ouvre / ferme à quelle heure?	sah oo-vruh / fehrm ah kehl ur
At what time?	À quelle heure?	ah kehl ur
Just a moment.	Un moment.	uhn moh-mahn
now / soon / later	maintenant / bientôt / plus tard	man-tuh-nahn / bee-an-toh / plew tar
today / tomorrow	aujourd'hui / demain	oh-zhoor-dwee / duh-man

In a French-Speaking Restaurant

English	French	Pronunciation
I'd like / We'd like...	Je voudrais / Nous voudrions...	zhuh voo-dray / noo voo-dree-oh<u>n</u>
...to reserve...	...réserver...	ray-zehr-vay
...a table for one / two.	...une table pour un / deux.	ewn tah-bluh poor uh<u>n</u> / duh
Non-smoking.	Non fumeur.	noh<u>n</u> few-mur
Is this seat free?	C'est libre?	say lee-bruh
The menu (in English), please.	La carte (en anglais), s'il vous plaît.	lah kart (ah<u>n</u> ah<u>n</u>-glay) see voo play
service (not) included	service (non) compris	sehr-vees (noh<u>n</u>) koh<u>n</u>-pree
to go	à emporter	ah ah<u>n</u>-por-tay
with / without	avec / sans	ah-vehk / sah<u>n</u>
and / or	et / ou	ay / oo
special of the day	plat du jour	plah dew zhoor
specialty of the house	spécialité de la maison	spay-see-ah-lee-tay duh lah may-zoh<u>n</u>
appetizers	hors-d'oeuvre	or-duh-vruh
first course (soup, salad)	entrée	ah<u>n</u>-tray
main course (meat, fish)	plat principal	plah pra<u>n</u>-see-pahl
bread	pain	pa<u>n</u>
cheese	fromage	froh-mahzh
sandwich	sandwich	sah<u>n</u>d-weech
soup	soupe	soop
salad	salade	sah-lahd
meat	viande	vee-ah<u>n</u>d
chicken	poulet	poo-lay
fish	poisson	pwah-soh<u>n</u>
seafood	fruits de mer	frwee duh mehr
fruit	fruit	frwee
vegetables	légumes	lay-gewm
dessert	dessert	duh-sehr
mineral water	eau minérale	oh mee-nay-rahl
tap water	l'eau du robinet	loh dew roh-bee-nay
milk	lait	lay
(orange) juice	jus (d'orange)	zhew (doh-rah<u>n</u>zh)
coffee	café	kah-fay
tea	thé	tay
wine	vin	va<u>n</u>
red / white	rouge / blanc	roozh / blah<u>n</u>
glass / bottle	verre / bouteille	vehr / boo-teh-ee
beer	bière	bee-ehr
Cheers!	Santé!	sah<u>n</u>-tay
More. / Another.	Plus. / Un autre.	plew / uh<u>n</u> oh-truh
The same.	La même chose.	lah mehm shohz
The bill, please.	L'addition, s'il vous plaît.	lah-dee-see-oh<u>n</u> see voo play
tip	pourboire	poor-bwar
Delicious!	Délicieux!	day-lee-see-uh

For more user-friendly French phrases, check out *Rick Steves' French Phrase Book and Dictionary* or *Rick Steves' French, Italian & German Phrase Book*.

APPENDIX

Contents

Tourist Information

Tourist Information Offices

Before your trip, scan the websites of national tourist offices for the countries you'll be visiting, or contact them to briefly describe your trip and request information. Some will mail you a general-interest brochure, and you can often download other brochures free of charge.

General Scandinavia: www.goscandinavia.com
Denmark: www.visitdenmark.com
Sweden: www.visitsweden.com
Finland: www.visitfinland.com
Norway: www.visitnorway.com
Estonia: www.visitestonia.com
Latvia: www.latvia.travel
Poland: www.poland.travel
France: www.franceguide.com
Russia: www.russia-travel.com
Germany: www.germany.travel
The Netherlands: www.holland.com
Belgium: www.visitbelgium.com

Great Britain: www.visitbritain.com

In Europe, a good first stop in a new town is the official tourist information office (abbreviated **TI** in this book). TIs are usually good places to get a city map and information on public transit (including bus and train schedules), walking tours, and special events. But be wary of the travel agencies or special information services that masquerade as TIs but serve fancy hotels and tour companies. They're in the business of selling things you don't need.

Travel Advisories

For up-to-date information on health and security abroad, check these helpful resources before leaving on your cruise.

US Department of State: Tel. 888-407-4747, from outside US tel. 1-202-501-4444, www.travel.state.gov

Canadian Department of Foreign Affairs: Canadian tel. 800-267-8376, from outside Canada tel. 1-613-996-8885, www .voyage.gc.ca

US Centers for Disease Control and Prevention: Tel. 800-CDC-INFO (800-232-4636), www.cdc.gov/travel

Telephoning

Smart travelers use the telephone to get tourist information, reserve restaurants, confirm tour times, and phone home. For details on your options for making calls—both from a cruise ship and from mobile phones—see page 91. For more in-depth information, see www.ricksteves.com/phoning.

For emergency telephone numbers, see the country-overview chapters earlier in this book.

How to Dial

Calling from the US to Europe, or vice versa, is simple—once you break the code. The European calling chart on page 1112 will walk you through it.

No matter where you're calling from, to dial internationally you must first dial the international access code of the place you're calling from (to "get out" of the domestic phone system), and then the country code of the place you're trying to reach.

The US and Canada have the same international access code: 011. Most European countries use the same international access code: 00. The exceptions are Russia (where you dial 8 to get an international line) and Finland (where you dial 999 or another 900 number, depending on the phone service you're using). You might see a + in front of a European number; that's a reminder to dial the access code of the place you're calling from. If you're calling from a mobile phone, you can simply insert a "+" before the number—no additional access code required.

Each country has its own country code; you'll see those listed in the European calling chart. Specific dialing instructions for each country are also included in each country-overview chapter in this book.

Transportation

While in port, you're likely to use public transportation to get around (and, in some cases, to get to) the cities you're here to see.

Taxis

Taxis are underrated, scenic time-savers that zip you effortlessly from the cruise terminal to any sight in town, or between sights. Especially for couples and small groups who value their time, a taxi ride can be a good investment. Unfortunately, many predatory taxi drivers prey on cruisers who are in town just for the day by charging them inflated fares for short rides. Prepare yourself by reading the "Taxi Tips" on page 126.

City Transit

Shrink and tame big cities by mastering their subway, bus, and tram systems. Europe's public-transit systems are so good that many Europeans go through life never learning to drive. With a map, anyone can decipher the code to cheap and easy urban transportation.

Subway Basics

Most of Europe's big cities are blessed with an excellent subway system, often linked effortlessly with suburban trains. Learning a city's network of underground trains is a key to efficient sightseeing. European subways go by many names, but "Metro" is the most common term. In Scandinavia, these systems often start with "T" (*T-bane* in Oslo and *T-bana* in Stockholm, for example). In some cities—such as Copenhagen and Berlin—the network also includes suburban trains, often marked with "S."

Plan your route. Figure out your route before you enter the station so you can march confidently to the correct train. Get a good subway map (often included on free city maps, or ask for one at the station) and consult it often. In the stations, maps are usually posted prominently. A typical subway map is a spaghetti-like tangle of intersecting, colorful lines. Individual lines are color-coded, numbered, and/or lettered; their end points are also indicated. These end points—while probably places you will never go—are

European Calling Chart

Just smile and dial, using this key:
AC = Area Code, LN = Local Number.

European Country	Calling long distance within ...	Calling from the US or Canada to ...	Calling from a European country to ...
Austria	AC + LN	011 + 43 + AC (without initial zero) + LN	00 + 43 + AC (without initial zero) + LN
Belgium	LN	011 + 32 + LN (without initial zero)	00 + 32 + LN (without initial zero)
Bosnia-Herzegovina	AC + LN	011 + 387 + AC (without initial zero) + LN	00 + 387 + AC (without initial zero) + LN
Britain	AC + LN	011 + 44 + AC (without initial zero) + LN	00 + 44 + AC (without initial zero) + LN
Croatia	AC + LN	011 + 385 + AC (without initial zero) + LN	00 + 385 + AC (without initial zero) + LN
Czech Republic	LN	011 + 420 + LN	00 + 420 + LN
Denmark	LN	011 + 45 + LN	00 + 45 + LN
Estonia	LN	011 + 372 + LN	00 + 372 + LN
Finland	AC + LN	011 + 358 + AC (without initial zero) + LN	999 (or other 900 number) + 358 + AC (without initial zero) + LN
France	LN	011 + 33 + LN (without initial zero)	00 + 33 + LN (without initial zero)
Germany	AC + LN	011 + 49 + AC (without initial zero) + LN	00 + 49 + AC (without initial zero) + LN
Gibraltar	LN	011 + 350 + LN	00 + 350 + LN
Greece	LN	011 + 30 + LN	00 + 30 + LN
Hungary	06 + AC + LN	011 + 36 + AC + LN	00 + 36 + AC + LN
Ireland	AC + LN	011 + 353 + AC (without initial zero) + LN	00 + 353 + AC (without initial zero) + LN
Italy	LN	011 + 39 + LN	00 + 39 + LN

European Country	Calling long distance within ...	Calling from the US or Canada to ...	Calling from a European country to ...
Latvia	LN	011 + 371 + LN	00 + 371 + LN
Montenegro	AC + LN	011 + 382 + AC (without initial zero) + LN	00 + 382 + AC (without initial zero) + LN
Morocco	LN	011 + 212 + LN (without initial zero)	00 + 212 + LN (without initial zero)
Netherlands	AC + LN	011 + 31 + AC (without initial zero) + LN	00 + 31 + AC (without initial zero) + LN
Norway	LN	011 + 47 + LN	00 + 47 + LN
Poland	LN	011 + 48 + LN	00 + 48 + LN
Portugal	LN	011 + 351 + LN	00 + 351 + LN
Russia	8 + AC + LN	011 + 7 + AC + LN	00 + 7 + AC + LN
Slovakia	AC + LN	011 + 421 + AC (without initial zero) + LN	00 + 421 + AC (without initial zero) + LN
Slovenia	AC + LN	011 + 386 + AC (without initial zero) + LN	00 + 386 + AC (without initial zero) + LN
Spain	LN	011 + 34 + LN	00 + 34 + LN
Sweden	AC + LN	011 + 46 + AC (without initial zero) + LN	00 + 46 + AC (without initial zero) + LN
Switzerland	LN	011 + 41 + LN (without initial zero)	00 + 41 + LN (without initial zero)
Turkey	AC (if there's no initial zero, add one) + LN	011 + 90 + AC (without initial zero) + LN	00 + 90 + AC (without initial zero) + LN

- The instructions above apply whether you're calling to or from a European landline or mobile phone.

- If calling from any mobile phone, you can replace the international access code with "+" (press and hold 0 to insert it).

- The international access code is 011 if you're calling from the US or Canada.

- To call the US or Canada from Europe, dial 00, then 1 (country code for US and Canada), then the area code and number. In short, 00 + 1 + AC + LN = Hi, Mom!

important, since they tell you which direction the train is moving and appear (usually) as the name listed on the front of the train. Figure out the line you need, the end point of the direction you want to go, and (if necessary) where to transfer to another line.

Validate your ticket. You may need to insert your ticket into a slot in the turnstile (then retrieve it) in order to validate it. If you have an all-day or multi-day ticket, you may only need to validate it the first time you use it, or not at all (ask when you buy it).

Get off at the right place. Once on the train, follow along with each stop on your map (some people count stops). Sometimes the driver or an automated voice announces the upcoming stop—but don't count on this cue, as a foreign name spoken by a native speaker over a crackly loudspeaker can be difficult to understand. As you pull into each station, its name will be posted prominently on the platform or along the wall.

Transfer. Changing from one subway line to another can be as easy as walking a few steps away to an adjacent platform—or a bewildering wander via a labyrinth of stairs and long passageways. Fortunately, most subway systems are clearly signed—just follow along (or ask a local for help).

Exit the station. When you arrive at your destination station, follow exit signs up to the main ticketing area, where you'll usually find a posted map of the surrounding neighborhood to help you get your bearings. Individual exits are signposted by street name or nearby landmarks. Bigger stations have multiple exits. Choosing the right exit will help you avoid extra walking and having to cross busy streets.

Bus and Tram Basics

Getting around town on the city bus or tram system has some advantages over subways. Buses or trams are often a better bet for shorter distances. Some buses go where the subway can't. Since you're not underground, it's easier to stay oriented and get the lay of the land. The obvious disadvantage of buses and trams is that they're affected by traffic, so avoid them during rush hour.

Plan your route. Tourist maps often indicate bus and tram lines and stops. If yours doesn't, ask for a specific bus map at the TI. Many bus and tram stops have timetables and route maps posted.

Validate your ticket. Tickets are checked on European buses and trams in a variety of ways. Usually you enter at the front of the bus or tram and show your ticket to the driver, or validate it by sticking it in an automated box. In some cases, you buy your ticket directly from the driver; other times, you'll buy your ticket at a kiosk or automated machine near the stop.

Trains

If you venture beyond your port city, European trains generally go where you need them to go and are fast, frequent, and affordable. "Point-to-point" or buy-as-you-go tickets can be your best bet for short travel distances anywhere. (If you're doing a substantial amount of pre- or post-cruise travel on your own, a railpass can be a good value.) You can buy train tickets either from home, or once you get to Europe. If your travel plans are set, and you don't want to risk a specific train journey selling out, it can be smart to get your tickets before your trip. For details on buying tickets on European websites and complete railpass information, see www.ricksteves.com/rail. To study ahead on the Web, check www.bahn.com (Germany's excellent Europe-wide timetable).

If you want to be more flexible, you can keep your options open by buying tickets in Europe. Nearly every station has old-fashioned ticket windows staffed by human beings, usually marked by long lines. Bridge any communication gap by writing out your plan: destination city, date (European-style: day/month/year), time (if you want to reserve a specific train), number of people, and first or second class.

To get tickets faster, savvy travelers figure out how to use automated ticket machines: Choose English, follow the step-by-step instructions, and swipe your credit card (though you may need to know your PIN, and some machines don't accept American cards—see page 136). Some machines accept cash. It's often possible to buy tickets on board the train, but expect to pay an additional fee for the convenience.

Seat reservations guarantee you a place to sit on the train, and can be optional or required depending on the route and train. Reservations are required for any train marked with an "R" in the schedule. Note that seat reservations are already included with many tickets, especially for the fastest trains (such as France's TGV). But for many trains (local, regional, interregional, and many EuroCity and InterCity trains), reservations are not necessary and not worth the trouble and expense unless you're traveling during a busy holiday period.

Be aware that many cities have more than one train station. Ask for help and pay attention. Making your way through stations and onto trains is largely a matter of asking questions, letting people help you, and assuming things are logical. I always ask someone on the platform if the train is going where I think it is (point to the train or track and ask, *"Pah-ree?"*).

Buses

In most countries, trains are faster, more comfortable, and have more extensive schedules than buses. Bus trips are usually less expensive than trains—especially in the British Isles—but often take longer. Use buses mainly to pick up where Europe's great train system leaves off.

Resources

Resources from Rick Steves

Rick Steves' Northern European Cruise Ports is one of many books in my series on European travel, which includes country guide-

books, city guidebooks (including Paris, London, Amsterdam, and more), Snapshot Guides (excerpted chapters from my country guides), Pocket Guides (full-color little books on big cities), and my budget-travel skills handbook, *Rick Steves' Europe Through the Back Door.* Most of my titles are available as ebooks. My phrase books—for French, Spanish, German, Italian, and Portuguese—are practical and budget-oriented. My other books include *Europe 101* (a crash course on art and history) and *Travel as a Political Act* (a travelogue sprinkled with tips for bringing home a global perspective). A more complete list of my titles appears near the end of this book.

Video: My public television series, *Rick Steves' Europe,* covers European destinations in 100 shows. To watch episodes online, visit www.hulu.com; for scripts and local airtimes, see www.ricksteves.com/tv.

Audio: My weekly public radio show, *Travel with Rick Steves,* features interviews with travel experts from around the world. I've also produced free, self-guided audio tours of the top sights in Paris, London, and Amsterdam—and other great cities. All of this audio content is available for free at Rick Steves Audio Europe, an extensive online library organized by destination. Choose whatever interests you, and download it for free via the Rick Steves Audio Europe smartphone app, www.ricksteves.com/audioeurope, iTunes, or Google Play.

Maps

The black-and-white maps in this book are concise and simple, designed to help you locate recommended places and get to local TIs, where you can pick up more in-depth maps of cities and

Begin Your Trip at www.ricksteves.com

At our travel website, you'll find a wealth of free information on European destinations, including fresh monthly news and helpful tips from thousands of fellow travelers. You'll also find my latest guidebook updates (www.ricksteves.com/update), a monthly travel e-newsletter (easy and free to sign up), my personal travel blog, and my free Rick Steves Audio Europe smartphone app (if you don't have a smartphone, you can access the same content via podcasts). You can even follow me on Facebook and Twitter.

Our online Travel Store offers travel bags and accessories that I've designed specifically to help you travel smarter and lighter. These include my popular carry-on bags (roll-aboard and rucksack versions), money belts, totes, toiletries kits, adapters, other accessories, and a wide selection of guidebooks, planning maps, and DVDs.

Want to travel with greater efficiency and less stress? We organize free-spirited, small-group tours to dozens of Europe's top destinations. Many of our tours begin or end at the major ports of embarkation (Copenhagen, Stockholm, Amsterdam, and London). Tours such as Scandinavia in 14 Days, Heart of Belgium and Holland in 11 Days, or England in 14 Days are great ways to extend your European adventure before or after a cruise. For all the details, and to get our Tour Catalog and a free Rick Steves Tour Experience DVD (filmed on location during an actual tour), visit www.ricksteves.com or call us at 425/608-4217.

regions (usually free). Better maps are sold at newsstands and bookstores, though you likely won't need them for a brief port visit. Before you buy a map, look at it to be sure it has the level of detail you want.

Other Resources

If you're like most travelers, this book is all you need. But if you're heading beyond my recommended destinations, $40 for extra maps and books can be money well-spent. There's a staggering array of websites, guidebooks, and other useful resources for people interested in cruising. Every avid cruiser has their favorite go-to site for tips and information, but my list below will help you get started with some of the best.

Books

For reviews of various cruise lines and ships, refer to my list on page 18. For more destination-specific information, the following books are worthwhile, though are not updated annually; check the publication date before you buy. The Rough Guide and Lonely Planet series, which individually cover various countries and cities included in this book, are both quite good. If choosing between these two titles, I'd buy the one that was published most recently. Lonely Planet's far-ranging *Scandinavia* overview book gives you little to go on for each destination, but their country- and city-specific guides are more thorough.

The colorful Eyewitness series, which focuses mainly on sights, is fun for their great graphics and photos, but relatively skimpy on content, and they weigh a ton. You can buy them in Europe (no more expensive than in the US), or simply borrow a book for a minute from other travelers at certain sights to make sure you're aware of that place's highlights. The tall, green Michelin guides include great maps and lots of solid, encyclopedic coverage of sights, customs, and culture (sold in English in some parts of Europe). The Cadogan guides offer a thoughtful look at the rich and confusing local culture, as does the Culture Shock series.

Beyond the guidebook format, look for the well-written history of the cruise industry, *Devils on the Deep Blue Sea* (by Kristoffer Garin). There's also a variety of tell-all type books offering behind-the-scenes intrigue from a life working on cruise ships. More titillating than well-written, these are good vacation reads to enjoy poolside. They include *Cruise Confidential* (by Brian David Bruns) and *The Truth about Cruise Ships* (by Jay Herring).

APPENDIX

Holidays and Festivals

Europe celebrates many holidays, which close sights and bring crowds.

Note that the following list isn't complete. Your best source for general information is the TI in each town. Before your trip, you can check with the national tourist offices of the countries you'll be visiting, listed at the beginning of this appendix. It's worth a quick look at websites of your must-see sights to turn up possible holiday closures.

Jan 1	New Year's Day
Jan 6	Epiphany
April 18, 2014	Good Friday
April 20-21, 2014	Easter Sunday and Monday
May 1	Labor Day
May 29, 2014	Ascension
June 8, 2014	Pentecost
June 9, 2014	Whitmonday
June 19, 2014	Corpus Christi
Aug 15	Assumption
Nov 1	All Saint's Day
Nov 11	Armistice Day/St. Martin's Day
Dec 25	Christmas Day
Dec 31	New Year's Eve

Note that many of the above holidays are Catholic and Protestant dates; in Orthodox countries (such as Russia and certain communities in Estonia, Latvia, and Finland), the dates for these holidays can differ.

Conversions and Climate

Numbers and Stumblers

- Europeans write a few of their numbers differently than we do. 1 = 1, 4 = 4, 7 = 7.
- In Europe, dates appear as day/month/year, so Christmas is 25/12/14.
- Commas are decimal points and decimals commas. A dollar and a half is $1,50, one thousand is 1.000, and there are 5.280 feet in a mile.
- When counting with fingers, start with your thumb. If you hold up your first finger to request one item, you'll probably get two.
- What Americans call the second floor of a building is the first floor in Europe.
- On escalators and moving sidewalks, Europeans keep the left "lane" open for passing. Keep to the right.

Metric Conversions (approximate)

A kilogram is 2.2 pounds, and 1 liter is about a quart, or almost four to a gallon. A kilometer is six-tenths of a mile. I figure kilometers to miles by cutting them in half and adding back 10 percent of the original (120 km: 60 + 12 = 72 miles, 300 km: 150 + 30 = 180 miles).

1 foot = 0.3 meter	1 square yard = 0.8 square meter
1 yard = 0.9 meter	1 square mile = 2.6 square kilometers
1 mile = 1.6 kilometers	1 ounce = 28 grams
1 centimeter = 0.4 inch	1 quart = 0.95 liter
1 meter = 39.4 inches	1 kilogram = 2.2 pounds
1 kilometer = 0.62 mile	32°F = 0°C

Imperial Weights and Measures

Britain hasn't completely gone metric. Driving distances and speed limits are measured in miles. Beer is sold as pints (though milk can be measured in pints or liters), and a person's weight is measured in stone (a 168-pound person weighs 12 stone).

1 stone = 14 pounds
1 British pint = 1.2 US pints
1 imperial gallon = 1.2 US gallons or about 4.5 liters

Clothing Sizes

For US-to-European clothing size conversions, see page 139.

Climate

First line, average daily high; second line, average daily low; third line, average days without rain. For more detailed weather statistics for European destinations (as well as the rest of the world), check www.worldclimate.com.

	J	F	M	A	M	J	J	A	S	O	N	D
DENMARK												
Copenhagen												
	37°	37°	42°	51°	60°	66°	70°	69°	64°	55°	46°	41°
	29°	28°	31°	37°	45°	51°	56°	56°	51°	44°	38°	33°
	14	15	19	18	20	18	17	16	14	14	11	12
SWEDEN												
Stockholm												
	30°	30°	37°	47°	58°	67°	71°	68°	60°	49°	40°	35°
	26°	25°	29°	37°	45°	53°	57°	56°	50°	43°	37°	32°
	15	14	21	19	20	17	18	17	16	16	14	14

	J	F	M	A	M	J	J	A	S	O	N	D

FINLAND
Helsinki

	J	F	M	A	M	J	J	A	S	O	N	D
	26°	25°	32°	44°	56°	66°	71°	68°	59°	47°	37°	31°
	17°	15°	20°	30°	40°	49°	55°	53°	46°	37°	30°	23°
	11	10	17	17	19	17	17	16	16	13	11	11

RUSSIA
St. Petersburg

	J	F	M	A	M	J	J	A	S	O	N	D
	29°	28°	37°	50°	60°	69°	74°	71°	60°	48°	35°	30°
	18°	15°	22°	32°	40°	49°	55°	52°	44°	36°	26°	20°
	10	11	15	15	16	13	15	15	14	09	10	11

ESTONIA
Tallinn

	J	F	M	A	M	J	J	A	S	O	N	D
	25°	25°	32°	45°	57°	66°	68°	66°	59°	50°	37°	30°
	14°	12°	19°	32°	41°	50°	54°	52°	48°	39°	30°	19°
	12	12	18	19	19	20	18	16	14	14	12	12

LATVIA
Rīga

	J	F	M	A	M	J	J	A	S	O	N	D
	33°	33°	40°	53°	62°	69°	74°	72°	62°	51°	39°	33°
	26°	24°	28°	36°	44°	51°	56°	56°	47°	40°	32°	26°
	12	12	15	16	17	15	16	15	15	12	11	12

POLAND
Gdańsk

	J	F	M	A	M	J	J	A	S	O	N	D
	35°	36°	42°	52°	62°	67°	71°	71°	62°	53°	41°	35°
	27°	27°	30°	35°	43°	49°	54°	54°	47°	41°	33°	28°
	30	27	30	29	30	30	30	30	29	29	29	29

GERMANY
Berlin

	J	F	M	A	M	J	J	A	S	O	N	D
	35°	37°	46°	56°	66°	72°	75°	74°	68°	56°	45°	38°
	26°	26°	31°	39°	47°	53°	57°	56°	50°	42°	36°	29°
	14	13	19	17	19	17	17	17	18	17	14	16

NORWAY
Oslo

	J	F	M	A	M	J	J	A	S	O	N	D
	28°	30°	39°	50°	61°	68°	72°	70°	60°	48°	38°	32°
	19°	19°	25°	34°	43°	50°	55°	53°	46°	38°	31°	25°
	16	16	22	19	21	17	16	17	16	17	14	14

THE NETHERLANDS
Amsterdam

	J	F	M	A	M	J	J	A	S	O	N	D
	41°	42°	49°	55°	64°	70°	72°	71°	66°	56°	48°	41°
	30°	31°	35°	40°	45°	52°	55°	55°	51°	43°	37°	33°
	8	9	16	14	16	16	14	12	11	11	10	9

BELGIUM
Brussels

	J	F	M	A	M	J	J	A	S	O	N	D
	41°	44°	51°	58°	65°	71°	73°	72°	69°	60°	48°	42°
	30°	32°	34°	40°	45°	53°	55°	55°	52°	45°	38°	32°
	9	11	14	12	15	15	13	12	15	13	10	11

	J	F	M	A	M	J	J	A	S	O	N	D

GREAT BRITAIN
London

	43°	44°	50°	56°	62°	69°	71°	71°	65°	58°	50°	45°
	36°	36°	38°	42°	47°	53°	56°	56°	52°	46°	42°	38°
	16	15	20	18	19	19	19	20	17	18	15	16

FRANCE
Paris

	43°	45°	54°	60°	68°	73°	76°	75°	70°	60°	50°	44°
	34°	34°	39°	43°	49°	55°	58°	58°	53°	46°	40°	36°
	14	14	19	17	19	18	19	18	17	18	15	15

Temperature Conversion: Fahrenheit and Celsius

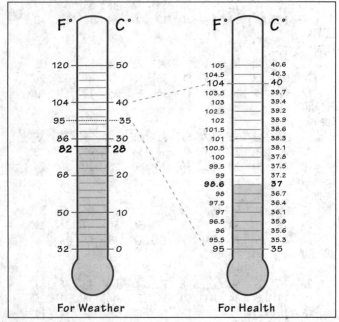

Europe takes its temperature using the Celsius scale, while we opt for Fahrenheit. For a rough conversion from Celsius to Fahrenheit, double the number and add 30. For weather, remember that 28°C is 82°F— perfect. For health, 37°C is just right.

APPENDIX

INDEX

INDEX

INDEX

MAP INDEX

Rick's Free Travel App

Free information and great gear to

▸ Plan Your Trip

Browse thousands of articles and a wealth of money-saving tips for planning your dream trip. You'll find up-to-date information on Europe's best destinations, packing smart, getting around, finding rooms, staying healthy, avoiding scams and more.

▸ Travel News

Subscribe to our free Travel News e-newsletter, and get monthly updates from Rick on what's happening in Europe!

▸ Graffiti Wall & Travelers Helpline

Learn, ask, share—our online community of savvy travelers is a great resource for first-time travelers to Europe, as well as seasoned pros.

turn your travel dreams into affordable reality

▶ Rick's Free Audio Europe™ App

The Rick Steves Audio Europe™ app brings history and art to life. Enjoy Rick's audio tours of Europe's top museums, sights and neighborhood walks—plus 200 tracks of travel tips and cultural insights from Rick's radio show—all organized into geographic playlists. Learn more at ricksteves.com.

▶ Great Gear from Rick's Travel Store

Pack light and right—on a budget—with Rick's custom-designed carry-on bags, wheeled bags, day packs, travel accessories, guidebooks, journals, maps and DVDs of his TV shows.

130 Fourth Avenue North, PO Box 2009 • Edmonds, WA 98020 USA
Phone: (425) 771-8303 • Fax: (425) 771-0833 • ricksteves.com

Rick Steves guidebooks are published by Avalon Travel,
a member of the Perseus Books Group.

NOW AVAILABLE:
eBOOKS, DVD & BLU-RAY

TRAVEL CULTURE

Europe 101
European Christmas
Postcards from Europe
Travel as a Political Act

eBOOKS

Nearly all Rick Steves guides are available as eBooks. Check with your favorite bookseller.

RICK STEVES' EUROPE DVDs

11 New Shows 2013–2014
Austria & the Alps
Eastern Europe
England & Wales
European Christmas
European Travel Skills & Specials
France
Germany, BeNeLux & More
Greece, Turkey & Portugal
Iran
Ireland & Scotland
Italy's Cities
Italy's Countryside
Scandinavia
Spain
Travel Extras

BLU-RAY

Celtic Charms
Eastern Europe Favorites
European Christmas
Italy Through the Back Door
Mediterranean Mosaic
Surprising Cities of Europe

PHRASE BOOKS & DICTIONARIES

French
French, Italian & German
German
Italian
Portuguese
Spanish

JOURNALS

Rick Steves Pocket Travel Journal
Rick Steves Travel Journal

PLANNING MAPS

Britain, Ireland & London
Europe
France & Paris
Germany, Austria & Switzerland
Ireland
Italy
Spain & Portugal

RickSteves.com 📘 🐦 **@RickSteves**

Rick Steves books and DVDs are available at bookstores and through online booksellers.

Photo © Patricia Feaster.

Credits

Contributors

Ian Watson

Ian has worked with Rick's guidebooks since 1993, after starting out with Let's Go and Frommer's guides. Originally from upstate New York, Ian speaks several European languages, including German, and makes his home in Reykjavík, Iceland.

Steve Smith

Steve manages tour planning for Rick Steves' Europe Through the Back Door and co-authors the France guidebooks with Rick (as well as this book's coverage of that country). Fluent in French, he's lived in France on several occasions starting when he was seven, and has traveled there annually since 1986.

Gene Openshaw

Gene is a writer, composer, and lecturer on art and history. Specializing in writing walking tours of Europe's cultural sights (including many featured in this book), Gene has co-authored 10 of Rick's books. Gene lives near Seattle with his daughter, and roots for the Mariners in good times and bad.

Acknowledgments

This book would not have been possible without the help of our cruising friends. Special thanks to Todd and Carla Hoover, cruisers extraordinaire, and to Sheri Smith at Elizabeth Holmes Travel (www.elizabethholmes.com). Applause for Vanessa Bloy at Windstar Cruises, Paul Allen and John Primeau at Holland America Line, Courtney Recht at Norwegian Cruise Line, and Melissa Rubin at Oceania Cruises. And high fives for Ben Curtis, Sheryl Harris, Paul and Bev Hoerlein, Jenn Schutte, Lisa Friend, and Noelle Kenney.

Images

Location	Photographer
Introduction: Flåm Port, Norway	Cameron Hewitt
PART I	
Full-page Image: Toulon, French Riviera	Cameron Hewitt
Choosing a Cruise: Istanbul	Cameron Hewitt
Booking a Cruise: Oslo, Norway	Cameron Hewitt

PART II

Full-page Image: Aboard Ship	Cameron Hewitt
Before Your Cruise: Civitavecchia	Cameron Hewitt
On the Ship: View from the Ship	Cameron Hewitt
In Port: Sognefjord	Cameron Hewitt

PART III

Full-page Image: Copenhagen Port	Cameron Hewitt
Stockholm Port	Cameron Hewitt
Northern European Cruise Ports:	
Full-page Image:	
Copenhagen's Nøjbroplads	Rick Steves
Nyhavn, Copenhagen	Cameron Hewitt
Full-page Image:	
Stockholm City Overview	Cameron Hewitt
Drottningholm Palace, Stockholm	Rick Steves
Full-page Image:	
Helsinki's Lutheran Cathedral	Cameron Hewitt
Helsinki Harbor	Cameron Hewitt
Full-page Image: Church on	
Spilled Blood, St. Petersburg	Cameron Hewitt
Peter and Paul Fortress	Cameron Hewitt
Full-page Image: Tallinn	Cameron Hewitt
Old Town Square, Tallinn	Cameron Hewitt
Full-page Image: Rīga's Old Town	Cameron Hewitt
Rīga's Skyline	Cameron Hewitt
Full-page Image: Gdansk's Ulica Długa	Cameron Hewitt
Artus Court on Ulica Długa	Cameron Hewitt
Full-page Image:	
French Cathedral, Berlin	Cameron Hewitt
Gendarmenmarkt, Berlin	Cameron Hewitt
Full-page Image: Frogner Park, Oslo	Rick Steves
Vigeland Sculpture Garden, Oslo	Rick Steves
Full-page Image:	
Stavanger's Main Walking Street	Cameron Hewitt
South Norway Port Town	Rick Steves
Full-page Image: Bryggen, Bergen	Cameron Hewitt
Bryggen, Bergen	Cameron Hewitt
Full-page Image: Sognefjord	Rick Steves
Aurlandsfjord	Cameron Hewitt
Full-page Image: Amsterdam	Cameron Hewitt
Amsterdam Canal	Rick Steves
Full-page Image: Bruges Canal View	Dominic Bonuccelli
Bruges Canal	Dominic Bonuccelli
Full-page Image: Thames River, London	Cameron Hewitt
Houses of Parliament	Rick Steves
Full-page Image:	
Notre Dame Cathedral, Paris	Cameron Hewitt
Louvre	Rick Steves

Avalon Travel
a member of the Perseus Books Group
1700 Fourth Street
Berkeley, CA 94710

Printed in Canada by Friesens.
Second printing October 2014

ISBN 978-1-61238-589-1
ISSN 2328-0190

For the latest on Rick's lectures, guidebooks, tours, public radio show, and public television
series, contact Europe Through the Back Door, Box 2009, Edmonds, WA 98020, tel.
425/771-8303, fax 425/771-0833, www.ricksteves.com, rick@ricksteves.com.

Europe Through the Back Door
Managing Editor: Risa Laib
Editors: Jennifer Madison Davis, Glenn Eriksen, Tom Griffin, Cameron Hewitt, Suzanne
Kotz, Cathy Lu, John Pierce, Gretchen Strauch
Editorial Intern: Caitlin Fjelsted, Andrés Garza
Writing and Research: Cameron Hewitt, Ian Watson
Graphic Content Director: Laura VanDeventer
Maps & Graphics: David C. Hoerlein, Twozdai Hulse, Lauren Mills, Dawn Tessman
Visser

Avalon Travel
Senior Editor and Series Manager: Madhu Prasher
Editor: Jamie Andrade
Associate Editor: Nikki Ioakimedes
Copy Editor: Patrick Collins
Proofreader: Rebecca Freed
Indexer: Stephen Callahan
Production & Typesetting: McGuire Barber Design
Cover Design: Kimberly Glyder Design
Maps & Graphics: Kat Bennett, Mike Morgenfeld

Front Matter Color Photos: Oslo Port, Norway © Cameron Hewitt
Front Cover Photo: Geiranger, Norway © Cunard Line
Additional Photography: Dominic Bonuccelli, Rich Earl, Barb Geisler, Tom Griffin, Sonja
Groset, Jennifer Hauseman, Cameron Hewitt, David C. Hoerlein, Lauren Mills, Sarah
Murdoch, Gene Openshaw, Sarah Slauson, Steve Smith, Rick Steves, Rob Unck, Laura
VanDeventer, Ian Watson, Wikimedia Commons

ABOUT THE AUTHOR

RICK STEVES

Since 1973, Rick Steves has spent 100 days every year exploring Europe. Along with writing and researching a bestselling series of guidebooks, Rick produces a public television series *(Rick Steves' Europe)*, a public radio show *(Travel with Rick Steves)*, and an app and podcast *(Rick Steves Audio Europe)*; writes a nationally syndicated newspaper column; organizes guided tours that take over 10,000 travelers to Europe annually; and offers an information-packed website (www.ricksteves.com). With the help of his hardworking staff of 80 at Europe Through the Back Door—in Edmonds, Washington, just north of Seattle—Rick's mission is to make European travel fun, affordable, and culturally enlightening for Americans.

Connect with Rick:

 facebook.com/RickSteves   twitter: @RickSteves

Writer and Researcher
CAMERON HEWITT

Cameron Hewitt is a writer and editor for Rick Steves' guidebooks. His favorite area is Central and Eastern Europe, where he co-authors Rick's books on Eastern Europe, Croatia & Slovenia, and Budapest. For this book, Cameron cruised the Baltic Sea and North Sea to research and write the port arrival instructions and new destination coverage on several ports. While on board, he climbed the rock wall, played a round of bingo, aced the "name that TV theme song" contest in the piano lounge, battled the dreaded cruise-ship virus, and went back for thirds at the midnight buffet... but refused to join the conga line. When he's not traveling, Cameron lives in Seattle with his wife, Shawna.